DEVIANCE
Studies in Definition, Management, and Treatment

Second Edition

302.5
D585d

SIMON DINITZ
RUSSELL R. DYNES
ALFRED C. CLARKE

NEW YORK · OXFORD UNIVERSITY PRESS · LONDON 1975 TORONTO

Second printing, 1977

Copyright © 1969, 1975 by Oxford University Press, Inc.
Library of Congress Catalogue Card Number: 74-21819
Printed in the United States of America

To our Parents
who knew little about these matters

To our Children
who perhaps know too much

Preface

In some circles, it is currently popular to condemn collections of readings as nonbooks. We feel that bringing together interesting and significant articles on a particular topic serves a legitimate purpose, not only as an instructional device but also as a medium for the dissemination of a broader understanding. What follows here is not a random collection of articles, but a selection that was guided by our particular view of the concept of deviance. In Part I we have attempted to outline this view. The readings included were chosen for their relevance to this view of deviance, and for their ability to illuminate it. Since the selected articles touch on every major aspect of deviance, the book can be used alone as an integrated set of readings, or it can be used as a supplement to other text treatments.

The over-all objective of the selections is to place deviance in the social context, rather than outside it—to see deviance as human, not inhuman, behavior. Since deviance seems to hold intrinsic interest for many people, it is unfortunate that most accessible information about the subject emphasizes melodrama, not knowledge; eccentricity, not commonness; peculiarity, not universality. By our selections we hope to encourage the reader to do some unconventional thinking about the conventional wisdom of deviance. Too often, people seek simple answers rather than increased understanding. Many forms of simplistic answers are widespread. There have been many pat genetic explanations—poor genes, "bad seed," inherited tendencies. There have been even more pat psychological explanations—weak super-egos, possessive mothers, sexual frustrations. While genes, mothers, and sex are interesting topics of conversation, they provide little understanding of deviance. As sociologists we feel the kind of understanding most meaningful, but as yet less prevalent in the conventional wisdom, is sociological. Since we have chosen readings that are primarily sociological in nature, we have departed from, and thus challenged, much of the conventional wisdom of deviance.

We had another major criterion of selection: we wished to emphasize critical issues of deviance as they appeared to us in the middle of the 1970's. While we have included some historical materials, the major emphasis is on current issues. For those who are familiar with the first edition, we have included, by contrast, proportionately more materials on the management and control of deviance. We have done this because we feel that these are issues which will be particularly important in the years to come. A number of new technologies, still unfamiliar to most, have emerged in recent years. They have emerged in large part because of the failure of traditional, punitive, rehabilitative, preventive and control programs. Since they involve the application of new techniques to the end of "behavior control," they raise serious moral, ethical, and legal problems. Such issues will have to be confronted. They can no longer be avoided or ignored. Even though now most courses in deviance give intrusive methods of behavior control little attention, we have given these issues special emphasis in the management section of this reader.

Beside this new emphasis, we used several other criteria in the final process of choosing from the hundreds of articles we considered. In general, we have included articles dealing with broad conceptual issues. We wanted to raise questions, not to reinforce answers. Consequently, we have excluded a number of valuable studies on specific and delimited topics. For example, we have chosen to deal with the *concept* of mental illness rather than include delimited studies on particular clinical symptoms.

We have also used summaries that provide inventories of current knowledge. In this connection we have drawn heavily on the President's Commission on Law Enforcement and the Administration of Justice. The reports of this Commission are the collective products of persons who are both concerned and knowledgeable about their topics. In addition to these summaries, we have selected a few articles on the basis of their interest and the vividness of their content and style. Some journalists are adept at writing on social science subjects, and some social scientists do not always provide models of clarity in their exposition. While interest and style rather than professional identification were occasionally emphasized, this does not mean that we sought the lowest common denominator in style. Simplicity can reflect lack of understanding, and style should never be confused with cleverness. Complex ideas often require complex exposition. The reader, then, will find various levels of difficulty.

After the selection process, each article was carefully edited. Material not central to the main thrust of the topic was eliminated. Footnotes were also eliminated. The functions of footnotes—to acknowledge intellectual ancestry, to add supporting evidence, and to suggest further enquiry—are not crucial to a volume of this kind. Each writer has many intellectual ancestors, only some of whom become footnoted. We can offer here as a substitute our general footnote of appreciation to those, past and present, acknowledged and unacknowledged, who have attempted to understand human behavior. Even with the absence of footnotes, we hope the readings will encourage those who read this book to seek out other sources to extend their knowledge. We have included a bibliography to assist the reader in this process.

We wish to thank the many authors for their willingness to have their work included, even with our editing. We wish to thank our own students and the many others who used the first edition for their comments. Their suggestions have guided our decisions in this revision. Finally, we should thank each other for the charity shown to the absurd ideas of the other two. This charity has sustained a relationship of over twenty years as colleagues and, more importantly, as friends. In these days, such an accomplishment should not go unnoticed.

Columbus, Ohio   S.D.
                                                                                                                         R.R.D.
                                                                                                                         A.C.C.

Contents

I *THE CONCEPT OF DEVIATION*

1. Approaches and Issues in the Study of Deviation   3
   QUESTIONS FOR DISCUSSION   19
   BIBLIOGRAPHY   20

II *CRIMINAL DEVIATION*

2. Crime: A National Overview   23
   THE CHALLENGE OF CRIME IN A FREE SOCIETY
   The President's Commission on Law Enforcement and Administration of Justice   24
   AMERICA'S SYSTEM OF CRIMINAL JUSTICE
   The President's Commission on Law Enforcement and Administration of Justice   30
   QUESTIONS FOR DISCUSSION   38
   BIBLIOGRAPHY   39

3. Street Crimes and Delinquency   40
   VIOLENT CRIME: HOMICIDE, ASSAULT, RAPE, ROBBERY
   The National Commission on the Causes and Prevention of Violence   43
   FORCIBLE RAPE   *Menachem Amir*   53
   THE CRIME OF ROBBERY IN THE UNITED STATES
   National Institute of Law Enforcement and Criminal Justice   59
   THE MAKING OF A BURGLAR: FIVE LIFE HISTORIES   65
   Pedro R. David
   LARCENY-THEFT   *Uniform Crime Reports*   73
   AUTO THEFT   *Uniform Crime Reports*   74
   THE BEHAVIOR OF THE SYSTEMATIC CHECK FORGER   75
   Edwin M. Lemert
   PROPERTY NORMS AND LOOTING: THEIR PATTERNS IN COMMUNITY CRISES   81
   E. L. Quarantelli and Russell R. Dynes
   LOWER CLASS CULTURE AS A GENERATING MILIEU OF GANG DELINQUENCY   91
   Walter B. Miller
   THE BEYOND CONTROL GIRL   101
   Nancy B. Greene and T. C. Esselstyn

QUESTIONS FOR DISCUSSION   107
BIBLIOGRAPHY   108

4. Economic and Occupational Crimes   110
THE NUMBERS MAN   Julian B. Roebuck   112
MASTERS SWINDLERS   Kenneth Slocum   117
ORGANIZED CRIME   123
The President's Commission on Law Enforcement and Administration of Justice
COMBATING ORGANIZED CRIME IN AMERICA   Stuart L. Hills   129
THE NATURE, IMPACT AND PROSECUTION OF WHITE COLLAR CRIME   135
Herbert Edelhertz
CRIMINAL TAX FRAUD   151
The President's Commission of Law Enforcement and Administration of Justice
QUESTIONS FOR DISCUSSION   154
BIBLIOGRAPHY   154

III DEVIANT STATUSES

5. Alcohol and Drug Abuse   159
THE ALCOHOLIC OFFENDER   162
Daniel Glaser and Vincent O'Leary
DRUNKENNESS OFFENSES   167
The President's Commission on Law Enforcement and Administration of Justice
THE PUBLIC DRINKING HOUSE AND SOCIETY   172
Marshall B. Clinard
THE AFTER-HOURS CLUB: NOTES ON A DEVIANT ORGANIZATION   181
Julian Roebuck and D. Wood Harper, Jr.
MIND-ALTERING DRUGS AND DANGEROUS BEHAVIOR   188
Richard H. Blum
DRUG ABUSE PROBLEMS: CAUSES AND RESPONSES   197
The Strategy Council
QUESTIONS FOR DISCUSSION   212
BIBLIOGRAPHY   212

6. Homosexuality and Transsexuality   214
COMING OUT IN THE GAY WORLD   Barry M. Dank   216
HOMOSEXUALITY: THE FORMULATION OF A SOCIOLOGICAL PERSPECTIVE   230
William Simon and John A. Gagnon
THE FEMALE HOMOSEXUAL: SOCIAL AND ATTITUDINAL DIMENSIONS   235
Jack H. Hedblom
THE TRANSSEXUAL IN SOCIETY   Michele S. Matto   248
QUESTIONS FOR DISCUSSION   259
BIBLIOGRAPHY   260

7. Mental Illness   262
THE MYTH OF MENTAL ILLNESS   Thomas S. Szasz   265
THE ROLE OF THE MENTALLY ILL AND THE DYNAMICS OF MENTAL DISORDER: A
RESEARCH FRAMEWORK   271
Thomas J. Scheff
ON BEING SANE IN INSANE PLACES   D. L. Rosenhan   279

THE WEAPONS OF INSANITY   291
Arnold M. Ludwig and Frank Farrelly
QUESTIONS FOR DISCUSSION   299
BIBLIOGRAPHY   300

IV   *WILLING VICTIMS AND VICTIMLESS ACTS*

8.   Abortion   303
CRIME WITHOUT VICTIMS: ABORTION   *Edwin M. Schur*   305
CRIMINAL ABORTION   *Gilbert Geis*   313
QUESTIONS FOR DISCUSSION   323
BIBLIOGRAPHY   324

9.   Prostitution   325
THE SOCIOLOGY OF PROSTITUION   *Kingsley Davis*   326
PROSTITUTION   *Gilbert Geis*   331
QUESTIONS FOR DISCUSSION   348
BIBLIOGRAPHY   348

10.   Pornography   350
THE VOLUME OF TRAFFIC AND PATTERNS OF DISTRIBUTION OF SEXUALLY ORIENTED MATERIALS   351
Commission on Obscenity and Pornography
THE EFFECTS OF EXPLICIT SEXUAL MATERIAL   363
Commission on Obscenity and Pornography
QUESTIONS FOR DISCUSSION   367
BIBLIOGRAPHY   367

11.   Suicide   369
CLASSIFICATIONS OF SUICIDAL PHENOMENA   370
Edwin S. Shneidman
STUDIES OF ADOLESCENT SUICIDAL BEHAVIOR   378
Richard H. Seiden
QUESTIONS FOR DISCUSSION   404
BIBLIOGRAPHY   404

V   *INNOVATIONS IN MANAGEMENT, CONTROL, AND TREATMENT*

12.   The Rise and Fall of Total Institutions   407
CHARACTERISTICS OF TOTAL INSTITUTIONS   409
Erving Goffman
STATE OF PRISONS IN THE UNITED STATES: 1870–1970   419
Negley K. Teeters
CORRECTIONS AND SIMPLE JUSTICE   425
John P. Conrad
JUVENILE JUSTICE: A LOVE-HATE STORY   436
David L. Bazelon
QUESTIONS FOR DISCUSSION   442
BIBLIOGRAPHY   442

13. The Medicalization of Management   444

WILL THE XYY SYNDROME ABOLISH GUILT?   446
Nicholas N. Kittrie

DRUG TREATMENT OF THE SOCIOPATHIC OFFENDER: THE "JUICE MODEL"
APPROACH   453
Simon Dinitz, Harold Goldman, Lewis Lindner, Harry Allen, and Thomas Foster

AN ALTERNATIVE FOR THE DRUNKENNESS OFFENDER: THE MANHATTAN
BOWERY PROJECT   458
Vera Institute

METHADONE MAINTENANCE FOR THE MANAGEMENT OF PERSONS WITH DRUG
DEPENDENCE OF THE MORPHINE TYPE   467
Nathan B. Eddy

THE DIVERSION AND ABUSE OF METHADONE USED TO TREAT DRUG
ADDICTS   471
Report of Committee of Judiciary, United States Senate

HEROIN MAINTENANCE FOR HEROIN ADDICTS: ISSUES AND EVIDENCE   477
Lorrin M. Koran

QUESTIONS FOR DISCUSSION   484

BIBLIOGRAPHY   485

14. Behavior Modification as Management and Control   487

BEHAVIOR MODIFICATION PROGRAMS   488
Ralph K. Schwitzgebel

THE USE OF ELECTRONICS IN THE OBSERVATION AND CONTROL OF HUMAN
BEHAVIOR AND ITS POSSIBLE USE IN REHABILITATION AND PAROLE   502
Barton L. Ingraham and Gerald W. Smith

QUESTIONS FOR DISCUSSION   510

BIBLIOGRAPHY   511

15. The Rise of Voluntary Associations   512

VOLUNTARY ASSOCIATIONS AMONG SOCIAL DEVIANTS   513
Edward Sagarin

DWARFS: LITTLE PEOPLE WITH BIG PROBLEMS   522
Edward Sagarin

SYNANON: THE LEARNING ENVIRONMENT   528
Guy Endore

QUESTIONS FOR DISCUSSION   531

BIBLIOGRAPHY   531

16. Environmental Design for Prevention, Management, and Control   533

DEFENSIBLE SPACE AS A CRIME PREVENTIVE MEASURE   534
Oscar Newman

CURBSIDE DETERRENCE?   547
John F. Decker

QUESTIONS FOR DISCUSSION   552

BIBLIOGRAPHY   533

17. Community Based Treatment Programs as Alternatives to Institutionalization   554

THE PREVENTION OF HOSPITALIZATION IN SCHIZOPHRENIA   556
Anne E. Davis, Simon Dinitz, and Benjamin Pasamanick

THE HALFWAY HOUSE   565
Diane Vaughan

WORK RELEASE—A STUDY OF CORRECTIONAL REFORM   573
Elmer H. Johnson

INTRODUCTION TO THE OFFENDERS AS A CORRECTIONAL MANPOWER RE-
SOURCE   579
Keith A. Stubblefield and Larry L. Dye

BACKGROUND AND DEVELOPMENT OF THE USE OF EX-OFFENDERS IN
OHIO   582
Joseph E. Scott and Pamela A. Bennett

QUESTIONS FOR DISCUSSION   588

BIBLIOGRAPHY   588

18. Rights of Victims and Rights of Deviants   590

MAKING THE VICTIM WHOLE   592
Donal E. J. MacNamara and John J. Sullivan

LEGAL RIGHTS OF THE DISABLED AND DISADVANTAGED   599
Richard C. Allen

UNIONIZATION BEHIND THE WALLS   606
C. Ronald Huff

QUESTIONS FOR DISCUSSION   614

BIBLIOGRAPHY   614

Appendix   617

I.   GLOSSARY OF LEGAL PHRASES AND DEFINITIONS   619

II. CLASSIFICATION OF MENTAL DISORDERS   626

III. CLASSIFICATION OF WHITE COLLAR CRIMES   639

I

THE CONCEPT
OF DEVIATION

The nonconformist—whether he be foreigner or "odd ball," intellectual or idiot, genius or jester, individualist or hobo, physically or mentally abnormal—pays a penalty for "being different," unless his peculiarity is considered acceptable for his particular group, or unless he lives in a place or period of particularly high tolerance or enlightenment. The socially visible characteristic ... is that he becomes a stranger among his own people.

Action for Mental Health

It is not difficult to be unconventional in the eyes of the world when your unconventionality is but the convention of your set.

W. Somerset Maugham

If men would consider not so much wherein they differ as wherein they agree, they would be far less of uncharitableness and angry feeling in the world.

Addison

Approaches and Issues in the Study of Deviance

Human deviance is just as characteristic of society as is conformity. Every human group, no matter how cohesive, stable, and well integrated, must somehow respond to such problems as mental illness, violence, theft, and sexual misconduct, as well as to other similarly difficult behaviors. Problems of deviance inevitably are defined as being a real or perceived threat to the basic and core values of the society. For whatever reasons, some persons act, at times at least, in so bizarre, eccentric, outlandish, abhorrent, dangerous, or merely unique and annoying a manner that they cannot readily be tolerated. Thus, every society must somehow deal with its saints and sinners, its kooks and clowns, and its politically and economically challenging, dependent, disruptive, inadequate, and aberrant members. Understanding deviance involves, at a basic minimum, at least three dimensions. First, it is apparent that every society defines behaviors that are to be labeled as deviant and proscribed as undesirable. Second, since deviance may be "commonplace," and even widespread, some explanations or theories must be offered for the existence and persistence of such deviant behavior in the face of negative social sanctions. Third, there would be little reason to define, sanction, and explain deviance without also doing something to, for, or with the deviant in order to correct, deter, prevent,

and/or punish him. Every society, then, defines, explains, and acts with regard to deviance.

DEVIANCE AND NORMS

It is necessary to initiate our discussion of deviance by giving attention to norms. Without reference to norms, it is impossible to talk about deviation, since norms provide the baseline, the standard, the unit against which deviation is defined, measured, and sanctioned. Sumner, the early American sociologist, was the originator of the widely quoted phrase, "the mores can make anything right." It is also true that the mores (norms) can make anything wrong and deviant. Group norms can establish almost any form of behavior, from the most innocent to the most harmful, as deviant. By the same token, norms can even "purify" and legitimize destructive behavior, such as waging war, gouging the public, and engaging in economic depredations, as not only acceptable but even highly honorific. Because of such normative definitions, variations in norms over time and across societies make it impossible to speak of deviance in universal or absolute terms. What is sinful or criminal to one era and to one society may well be revered at another time or in another society. Nevertheless, regardless of the specific content of behavior, the essential nature of deviance lies in the departure of certain types of behavior from the norms of a particular society at a particular time. Deviance is always and irrevocably normative.

Norms are the *should's* and *should not's* in society. They evolve out of the experience of people interacting within society. In turn, they guide, channel, and limit future relationships. So integral a part of human life are norms that many are unaware of their pervasiveness. Most persons are oblivious to the importance of norms in giving substance and meaning to human life. The reason for this lack of awareness is that norms become so internalized as a part of personality that people take them for granted. Norms are seldom consciously thought about unless they are challenged by contact with persons conforming to another normative order—perhaps "foreigners," "hillbillies," or "outsiders." This "unconscious" quality of norms arises from the fact that persons are rewarded for behaving in certain ways and punished for behaving in other ways until behavior according to the norms becomes almost automatic.

Within every society, norms tend to cluster around the major, recurrent activities in which its members are involved. Such norms are often called social institutions. For example, what is called "the family" is in actuality a complex set of norms that regulates relations between the sexes, legitimizes children, prescribes methods for their socialization, determines the boundaries of the family unit, regulates sexual behavior, provides for a division of labor, and guides the complexities of day-to-day activities. While each specific family unit may be unique in certain ways, depending on the individuality of its members and their interaction, there is an element of commonness among all families within a society. These commonalities stem from the normative proscriptions. In the same context, we can also talk of economic, legal, religious, educational, and political institutions as each being a cluster of norms.

The way norms function can best be

understood, however, in contrasting societal contexts. It is useful to contrast the nature of the normative order of modern industrial societies with that of the more traditional societies of the past. Such a contrast will suggest that the nature of deviation would be somewhat different in the two types of societies.

In traditional folk societies, the norms are generally simple. There is a limited range of possibilities for human action, so the rules necessary are also limited. Too, the norms tend to be tied together in a "neater" package. Family life, educational life, and economic life are so closely related that they are difficult to separate. The norms that govern a father and son working in a field are, at the same time, familially, educationally, and economically important. Were the son to violate a norm, the negative sanctions, that is, punishments, for this violation would be immediate and certain. The specific deviant act by the son, however, would be considered in terms of his "whole" personality, his total actions, past and present. His behavior would be seen as "bad," but the son would not likely be considered a deviant *person* because of such isolated action.

Traditional Folk Societies	Modern Industrial Societies
simple set of norms	complex set of norms
internalized norms	imposed norms
integrated norms	lack of integrated norms
immediate and certain sanctions	uncertain and delayed sanctions
deviant behavior seen as one part of total behavior	deviant behavior seen as characteristic of total person

The situation is quite different in modern societies. The normative order becomes more and more complex since there is greater diversity within the society itself. Social life becomes more segmentalized. Family behavior is separated from educational and economic behavior, and the norms regulating these several areas often become inconsistent and lack integration. Since the society is more impersonal, the sanctions for the deviant act are neither certain nor immediate. Since the society is segmentalized, deviant acts in one segment very often stigmatize the *person* in others. The norms and sanctions in modern industrial societies, then, are quite different from those of the more traditional societies.

It is useful to indicate briefly some of the forces which have created such normative differences between traditional and modern societies. While many factors have combined to create these results, one way to summarize them is in terms of the "silent" revolutions as they have affected American society.[1] Among these we mention revolutions in industry, mobility, science, and organization. These social forces have transformed the physical and material existence of mankind, and have altered, disrupted, and changed the earlier normative order. One might suggest that, just as traditional societies had a type of social organization that minimized deviance, modern societies have developed a normative order and a social organization that facilitate deviance. For example, the Industrial Revolution has changed man's relationship to the world of work. Earlier systems of norms, based on a state of perpetual scarcity of goods and need for manpower, no longer fit in a world of complex technology and relative affluence. The traditional yoke of hard physical labor has been lifted—first by the introduction of the machine, then by the factory, later by mass production techniques, and in more recent years by the development of servomechanisms and automation, which allow workerless factories. To a world used to physical labor, these changes have had tremendous impact on traditional norms of work. Those who dreamed of leisure in the future have found the future already here.

The mobility revolution has shaken the historic normative patterns in several respects. First, the tremendous geographic mobility in this century has been without parallel. This age may yet be designated by future historians as the century of the "refugee"—voluntary and involuntary. Vast floods of refugees fleeing from war, persecutions, and economic catastrophes—as well as immigrants searching for greater opportunity—have moved across the world. Too, there have been continual internal migrations. There has been a shifting of populations from East to West, to the point that in California a "native" is defined as one who has lived there for five years. In addition to this shift westward, rural to urban migration has altered the United States, changing it from an overwhelmingly rural society to a metropolitan society. There has also been the continuous shift of the Negro out of the South and into Northern and, lately, Western urban areas. Many of the largest cities in these areas are already predominately black—a phenomenon beyond imagination a quarter-century ago. The movement of Mexican braceros and "wetbacks," the Appalachian (hillbilly) migrations, and the Puerto Rican and Cuban group settlements in metropolitan New York and Florida, respectively, continue to alter the population mosaic. Another less visible aspect of the mobility revolution is taking place: millions of families move and resettle every year in different cities, counties, and states. Whereas most people formerly lived and died within a fifty-mile radius of their birthplace, now the typical American often feels underprivileged unless he has traveled widely or moved frequently from place to place.

All of this geographical mobility has had its normative consequences. Internal migrations have shattered the continuity of life in the small community, and traditional norms, which arise from intimate face-to-face interaction with the same persons over many years, cannot be sustained under such conditions. This decline of the small stable community raises the interesting question of how to maintain expected—normative—behavior when the "expecters," that is, the

1. For a more extensive treatment see Russell R. Dynes, Alfred C. Clarke, Simon Dinitz, and Iwao Ishino, *Social Problems, Dissensus and Deviation in an Industrial Society* (New York: Oxford University Press, 1964), Chapter 2, "The Development of an Industrial Society."

community, and the expectations are changing. The primary problems of today are urban ones—congestion, slums, pollution, the emergence of the "black core and the white ring," the confrontation of the rich and the poor, the inability of local governments to cope with a mobile population, and so forth.

The mobility revolution can also be seen as movement in "social space," that is, social mobility. In stable social settings, people "fit in" on the basis of status ascribed to them—according to their age, sex, and/or family position. In the past, men were often faced with permanent inequalities that came from such ascription. For example, the black in America has had—and still has—the problem of overcoming such placement because of his race. In industrial societies, however, achievement replaces ascription as a norm and as a value. Fitting in now involves notions such as "climbing and achieving," although less so since the urban and student revolts of the late 1960's. Norms which were functional to the older ascribed system do not fit in social structures geared to achievement. In societies that emphasize achievement, however, there are new psychological and social costs, particularly for those who do not or cannot achieve—the "failures." For example, in more traditional societies, the older person was often given high status by virtue of his age; but in societies in which achievement is a principal value around which status and prestige are organized, the older person often cannot achieve and therefore is assigned low status. Indeed, all who are nonproductive and economically dependent, whether aged or not, tend to be viewed with disdain. When nonachievement is considered to be willful and purposeful, as is sometimes imputed to the unemployed, the school dropout, or the other cop-outs, the lack of achievement is considered to border on the deviant. The point here is that in a society geared to achievement, those who cannot or do not wish to achieve have difficulty in finding a place.

Although the scientific revolution did not specifically alter interaction among people,

it undermined traditional concepts of knowledge and truth. Man's understanding of his world and his approach to knowledge have become so radically different that previous dogmas, taboos, beliefs, and norms have lost their immediacy. Science as a way of life, as a secular religion, as a mode of thought, as a system for obtaining and systematizing information, has superseded previous approaches. The possibilities of understanding, prediction, and control of the physical, biological, and social worlds continue to stir the imagination. Science is a method of achieving and a system for integrating knowledge; yet the knowledge science has already achieved has created problems which we cannot overcome using our existing norms.

The scientific mode of thought spawned the "hardware" revolution, which is directed toward man's unquenchable desire for gadgets and products. The scientific "genie" in its various applications has transformed everything from man's conception of the universe to woman's role as co-equals in the marital partnership. No aspects of life have remained untouched. Everything from ultimate destruction to ultimate destiny has been affected by this revolution.

Of the various other silent revolutions, perhaps only the organizational revolution warrants comment here. The growth of mass society is characterized by the phenomenal development of large-scale and complex organizations. Man still has illusions about his uniqueness, individuality, and captaincy of his fate. But, like the interchangeable components in the industrial machine, he has become specialized, bureaucratized, and expendable. Having so laboriously developed norms more applicable to an earlier setting of face-to-face relationships, his problem now is how to adapt to a world of mass organization. This point is far from academic. Complex organization gives rise to some very vexing issues for deviance. For example, whereas an individual might be quite reluctant to steal from a parent, or a friend, or a neighbor, what is to keep him from "helping himself" to the property of a large impersonal organization? Where are the controls in such impersonal situations? Even more to the point, criminologists and many others are now concerned with a wholly different kind of criminality—white-collar crime on a massive scale. In a landmark conspiracy case of the early 1960's, large electrical companies were involved in rigging, bidding, and dividing the "profits" on a percentage basis. Who was guilty of such unlawful acts? Can a corporation be guilty? Or are the executives, the board of directors, the department heads guilty? How far down among personnel in organizations does criminal responsibility extend? The norms governing responsibility and liability of individuals have been considerably distorted by the organizational revolution.

TYPES OF NORMATIVE CHANGE

The foregoing discussion points to only some of the consequences of the silent revolutions that have transformed modern society and have changed the nature of the normative order. The types of change in the normative order that have particular significance for deviance need to be further discussed. Seven types of normative problems will be specified here: (1) norm breakdown; (2) norm conflict; (3) unreachable goal norms; (4) discontinuous norms; (5) impotent and sanctionless norms; (6) evasive norms; and (7) stressful norms.

Norm Breakdown

Most, or all, of today's most pressing social issues, including those pertaining to deviant behavior, are attributed in some measure to norm breakdown. The clarity, precision, and holding power of historic and traditional norms are no more; new norms are always in the emergent state. As a result, deviant behavior becomes a plausible and common occurrence. Norm breakdown can be illustrated in many ways. The most meaningful, perhaps, is to note that the traditional status role of the adolescent has been shattered. That is, the cluster of norms that guides adolescent behavior no longer possesses clarity. Adolescence is no longer another stage in the life process with clearly defined duties, privileges, and obligations. Today the adolescent is "freed" from traditional family, neighborhood, and community ties. He is also more affluent than ever before and represents a potent economic market. As such, adolescents are style and fashion setters, and a "teenage subculture" has developed and is being perpetuated, a subculture responsive to their particular conditions of life. Teenage argot (language) with its references and allusions now serves as a focus of self-identification for the adolescent, emphasizing his distinctiveness vis-à-vis other age groups. Such distinctiveness is enhanced because the world of work does not need the adolescents' labor; present educational institutions are inappropriate for some; religious institutions can speak to only a few; and the family has lost much of its hold. The norms that once provided the adolescent a context in which he was a responsible and economically productive person, norms characterized by rigid parental discipline, filial piety, and stern sexual morality, with work and thrift as ultimate values, now seem "ancient" to contemporary adolescents. Under such circumstances of norm breakdown and the lack of clarity, delinquency and various other problems are hardly unexpected.

Norm Conflict

Only in well-integrated societies are the various levels of culture, society, and personality so well meshed that norm conflict is minor. In complex societies, norm conflict becomes inevitable. The demands and expectations are at times antithetical in the different roles people must play. The norms governing conduct in the marketplace, for example, often conflict with those that cover role behavior in the family. It is in terms of this conflict of norms that much deviance, particularly criminal deviance, is to be explained.

Norm conflict is most frequent when different social categories (age, race, religion, sex, occupation, education, area of residence) become the basis of subcultures. In

these subcultures, norms develop that frequently clash with those of the larger society. As previously noted, this was one consequence of the breakdown of the older norms
that guided adolescent behavior. When the
norms of peer group, family, and neighborhood are in conflict with those of other
groups and of the larger society, the holding
power of each set of norms is weakened.

In dynamic societies, norm conflict is
"built into" the system. In such societies,
deviant subcultures develop and are maintained. The effect is to support and to perpetuate certain deviance, particularly the
criminal types. Too, cases of acute norm
conflict provide one basis of explanation for
the emergence of such types of deviation as
mental illness.

Unreachable Goal Norms

One consequence of a stable, integrated society is that the goals held out to individuals
are reasonable and reachable. By following
the prescribed pathways, most members can
reach the goals they set. Industrial societies,
however, present a far different picture.
Some of the widespread values are attainable
by only a minority of the population. Relatively few can be successful, wealthy, carefree, of high status, or "jet setters." Yet such
goals are often accepted as "ideal" norms
and as the measure of success. Since lack of
attainment (relative failure) is actually the
rule rather than the exception, emotional
disturbance and social disaffection come to
be built into the social order.

Responses to such unreachable goals are
varied. Some may reject the goals entirely,
for example, the drifter. Some may strike
out in frustration and grief, as reflected in
the slogan, "burn, baby, burn" in the
ghettos during the riots. Others may retreat
from life as being too complicated to master
or even understand, for example, the drug
addict, the alcoholic. While there are also
other reactions, aggressive, escapist, criminal,
and rebellious types are potential deviants in
a society that makes unreachable goals the
goals for everyone.

Discontinuous Norms

There are few things so continuous as the
life cycle, the unfolding and maturation of
the person from birth to death. In traditional societies the norms regulating this
cycle were continuous. There was a more or
less gradual transition facilitated by various
rites of passage from one status to another.
In industrial societies, by contrast, these
transitions go by fits and starts, rather than
making a smooth progression from stage to
stage. For example, there are two periods in
the life cycle which are difficult by definition. The first, adolescence, has already been
mentioned. The second, aging, is even more
difficult, if only because there is nothing else
to grow *into,* as the adolescent grows into
early adulthood. One need only observe the
treatment of the aged in the mass media to
recognize the low estate into which they
have fallen. Grandmother strives valiantly to
be like granddaughter in everything—from
physical appearance (dress, manner) to
"cool" conversation. There is no easy shifting of status in the process of physical maturation; there is discontinuity and much
tragedy here. Throughout the life cycle there
is discontinuity. The demands made on the
traditional woman in her roles of housewife
and mother are quite different from the demands made on her later, when her children
leave home. She has spent her life learning to
be a good mother; suddenly she has no one
on whom to practice her art. Adequate preparation for the earlier roles may leave her
totally unprepared for the roles that she
must play in the future. There is some suggestion that at such critical points in the life
cycle mental illness may be a common response.

Impotent and Sanctionless Norms

Some norms, even historically important
ones, lose their vigor long before they are
replaced by emergent norms. They survive as
relics of a world that was. It is interesting
that these survivals continue to define normative behavior without being able to control
it.

There are many illustrations of impotent and sanctionless norms. While most persons in an industrial society continue to profess some sort of religious identity and commitment, the hold of religious norms on conduct is frequently minimal. The potent norms are more likely to be those from the occupational and economic realms. Religious norms, which were once translated into blue laws, often remain on the books as part of the structure of modern society. Enforcing such norms, however, is quite another matter. While leading citizens make speeches praising the official norms of the society—honesty and other virtues—those very speakers will admit privately that they themselves often do not follow the norms they uphold. Cheating, for example, is deviant; yet it characterizes many areas of society, not merely the classroom. Many believe that, in order to succeed in a tough, competitive world—and success is perhaps our most potent norm—one *must* cheat; hence, cheating is built into the structure itself, just as much as the norm of honesty is. The point in all of this is that deviance frequently occurs in the context of norms that are accepted as binding but, because of the realities they contradict, are violated almost as often as they are observed. The existence of sanctionless norms is yet another facet of the problems of the normative order and deviant conduct.

Evasive Norms

More self-defeating and at the same time more comprehensible than the sanctionless norms are the evasive norms. By definition, evasive norms are those that permit, encourage, and reward behaviors defined by other norms as being illegal or immoral. These are the so-called loopholes in the norms, which are common in industrial societies. Thus, bribes are reprehensible, but gifts, "flower funds," and a variety of kickbacks are sanctified by the norms of evasion. Gambling is usually illegal, but bingo and lotteries are not. Extramarital sexual relationships are unacceptable, but swinging exists *sub rosa*. In one sense, these norms of evasion provide

safety valve action, but they also replace positive norms, with the result that deviant conduct, such as prostitution and gambling, becomes institutionalized even if never quite wholly acceptable.

Stressful Norms

Except possibly in the most isolated and simple of societies, some norms are inevitably more stressful than others. In industrial societies in which status must be achieved, and in which one's "place" is rarely secure, stressful norms are perhaps the rule more than the exception. For example, industrial societies require highly trained specialists. Increasingly greater ability and training are demanded if one is to compete effectively in the system and to run complex and technologically sophisticated devices. Such expectations become normative, so that there is constant pressure for ever more training and proficiency. Such normative expectations may be reasonable for those who can fit in without undue stress and strain. For many others, such expectations are deleterious and may possibly be correlated with a variety of personality disturbances.

Norms that emphasize pecuniary standards as the measure of man and as the basis of position in the status hierarchy are also a continuing source of frustration. The success-failure orientation is perhaps the central theme in American society. Its stressful potential may be seen in the high incidence of neurosis, alcoholism, coronary heart disease, and psychosomatic impairments. The consequences may be seen in certain types of crime and in the proliferation of evasive norms.

Thus, deviance is defined normatively—always. The normative order defines and creates the limits of acceptable and unacceptable (deviant) conduct. Just as it is impossible to grasp the concept of deviance except in relation to the social definition of what behavior should or ought to be, so the explanation of much of deviant behavior lies, directly or indirectly, in the normative realm. Norm breakdown, conflict, discontinuity, impotence, and stressfulness create the conditions that eventuate in large-scale deviancy.

CHARACTERISTICS OF DEVIATION

We have already discussed the nature of norms. In addition to norms which proscribe behavior, deviance involves a numerical minority of persons within a society who have some uniquely different and, when made visible, readily identifiable attribute(s). Thus, deviance reflects a type of difference which is defined normatively as being undesirable. These undesirable attributes evoke disapproval in the form of legal, extra-legal, quasi-legal sanctions on the part of the various social control agencies within the society. As a consequence of these attributes and sanctions, deviants are accorded low status within the society and are forced into less desirable occupational, social, and economic roles.

In certain respects, each category of deviants can be considered as a minority group within the society. But there is one critical difference between traditional minority groups and deviants. A racial, ethnic, or religious minority possess attributes which their members did not choose. Deviants have attributes which are considered by the larger society to be subject to individual control and choice. While one does not choose to be black, one "chooses" to be criminal. While one does not choose to be Italian, one "chooses" to be homosexual. In deviance, then, the element of personal control and choice are seen as the determining factor in the "setting apart" and for the apparent minority status.

The processes whereby the deviant is set apart have certain consequences, both for the individual and for the society. Deviants must accept a definition conferred by others which, in effect, devalues them. This devaluation in turn leads to alienation, despair, low self-esteem, rage, and frustration. In the attempt to deal with such devaluation, deviants often develop sets of rationalizations and fantasies about the normality and even the "moral" superiority of their behavior. They tell themselves and others that those who engage in such behavior openly are thus morally superior.

As a result of this devaluation, their "spoiled identity" makes it difficult to engage in normal social relationships since such relationships become increasingly painful and threatening. Withdrawing from these painful relationships often leads to the emergence of deviant organizations and collectivities. Organizations develop which center around those who have similar problems. Within the community, separate subcultures develop around deviant minorities. A unique life style may develop. Various institutionalized mechanisms may develop to allow the deviant minority to accommodate and exist within the very society which devalues them.

Again these characteristics have certain similarities to minority group adaptation and survival. However, there is still a critical difference. In pluralistic and democratic societies, minority groups have a cause on which to base their complaints of discrimination and devaluation but deviant minorities have no "cause," nor claim that can be made on the larger society. Blacks have been able to make a plea for equity and equality in the name of justice. Women have been able to attack inequities in employment and pay in the name of equality and fairness. Deviants have a more difficult case to make. This difference, however, has become less distinct in recent years. Deviant minorities have learned from other minorities and have begun to utilize social movement techniques to plead their case in the larger society. For example, beginning with the Mattachine Foundation, homosexuals began to organize. In the mid-sixties, a national organization, the North American Conference of Homophile Organization, was formed. Within specific communities, homosexuals have picketed stores and agencies which "discriminated" against them. Gay Liberation Days were designated with marches marked by signs proclaiming "Gay Power" and "Gay is Good." In many other ways, these homosexual groups imitated the tactics which the black movement had used earlier. The results have been different since the deviant groups lack the same legitimacy for their cause.

The characteristics of deviation, then, involve the following elements:

1. Norms within a society which proscribe certain attributes and behavior.

2. Individuals within the society who visibly exhibit the proscribed attributes and behavior.

3. Effective societal disapproval for those exhibiting the attributes and behavior.

4. The development of negative self-definitions by those disapproved.

5. The gradual withdrawal from "normal" patterns of social interaction.

6. The increasing social isolation leads toward the development of a deviant collectivity.

All of these characteristics will be illustrated in the subsequent chapters.

A TYPOLOGY OF DEVIATION

It is obvious that societies differ in their definitions of what is deviant. In addition, definitions of deviation, like styles and fashions, may differ over time within any society. Yesterday's sinners, rebels, misfits, malcontents, outsiders, and even criminals

may well become the cultural heros and heroines at some later point in history. On the other hand, there is a degree of uniformity and consistency among societies and over time as to the form of the undesirable attributes and behavior. Such attributes can be viewed from the vantage point of normative orders which are present in all societies (see Figure 1-1). Based on these normative orders, five major types emerge: (1) the deviant as freak; (2) the deviant as "sinful"; (3) the deviant as criminal; (4) the deviant as "sick"; and (5) the deviant as alienated. Each of these views presents a different yet related view of deviation.

The Deviant as Freak

There are those who insist that deviation be used in a precise and literal sense—as variation from the average or norm. In this view, most behavior is distributed more or less along a normal curve. This definition of deviance focuses on the exception, on the "freak" in a statistical sense. The deviant is one who is some distance from the mean, at the extreme ends of the distribution.

Such a definition adds little, however, to understanding of the etiology of deviance or its treatment. It has two basic difficulties. First, it assumes that attitudes, values, and

Figure 1-1. A typology of deviance

Type of Deviant	Example of Deviation	Nature of Normative Order	Nature of Deviation
Freak	Midget, Dwarf, or Giant; Ugly, fat, or disfigured person; Mentally retarded person	Physical, physiological, and intellectual ideals	Aberrant in being
Sinful	Sinner, Apostate, Heretic, Traitor	Religious or secular ideologies	Rejects orthodoxy
Criminal	Murderer, Burglar, Embezzler, Addict	Legal codes	Unlawful in action
Sick	Psychotic, Psychoneurotic, Character disorder	Cultural definitions of mental health	Aberrant in action
Alienated	Bum, Tramp, Suicide, Hippie, Bohemian	Cultural ends and/ or means	Rejects dominant cultural values

behavior are distributed in a population in the same way as attributes such as height, weight, strength, appearance, and intellect. The terminology used for physical attributes, as tall and taller, cannot be used to describe deviance, as criminal and more criminal. In many areas significant to deviancy, behavior is more likely to be dichotomous rather than continuous. For example, behavior is seen as being either criminal or law-abiding, loyal or disloyal, hallucinatory or rational. The second basic difficulty is that, even if behavior were distributed in a continuous fashion, there is no assurance that the extreme ends—the "freaks"—would necessarily be defined as undesirable. For example, in dealing with physical attributes, there are certain persons at the extremes who are defined as unfortunate—the severely retarded, the midget, the female Amazon, the obese person, etc. Others, who are also at the extremes, such as the genius, the seven-foot-tall basketball player, the 300-pound football tackle, and the overendowed female, may be positively valued. Or, again, a physical attribute such as skin color, on one end of a distribution may be positively valued, while on the other end it may be negatively valued. Both ends may be equidistant from the average, or norm. This underscores the point that it is not the extreme, the variation, or the freakishness in itself that defines social deviation; the extreme has to be evaluated by the society in a negative fashion.

The Deviant as "Sinful"

The religious-ideological definition of deviance (and of social problems) has traditionally centered on the concepts originally derived from religious terminology: sinner, heretic, and apostate. In the religious context, a sinner is one who violates the central proscriptions and ritually proper ways of thinking, being, acting. Whether this is called sinfulness, or the secular equivalent, immorality, the meaning is clear. Commandments, codes, texts, and other types of prescribed norms are the standards against which behav-

ior is judged. The presumption is that the sinner, or the immoral person, *accepts* the doctrines and norms that he *violates.*

The heretic, unlike the sinner, is considered a deviant precisely because he *rejects* some, or all, of the dogma or prescriptions. It is not the heretic's failure to live up to the prescriptions, but rather his conscious and willful rejection of them as binding norms or standards, that causes concern. The sinner does not reject the Word; the heretic does. Thus, the heretic is invariably considered a far more serious threat to group welfare than the sinner. This suggests that rejection of values and ideological principles is inherently more threatening to the maintenance of social solidarity than is the negative behavior of a person who accepts the norms.

The most devastating form of deviance from this point of view is apostasy, or "ideological treason." This type of deviance involves not only the rejection of the dogma and faith, but also the acceptance of another, "alien" set of principles, norms, and traditions. Every group strives tenaciously to prevent apostasy. To do otherwise courts group destruction. Seen in this light, it is little wonder that various religious groups, particularly in the past, have viewed religious intermarriage as threatening. In the past religious apostasy was subject to the same negative definitions and sanctions as the more familiar forms of secular "treason." In this sense, the ex-communist, the ex-John Bircher, and the defector can be considered deviant since they now reject norms they previously accepted. Thus, the sinner, the heretic, and the apostate, as defined in sacred and theocratic societies, now have secular equivalents in the immoralist and the traitor.

The Deviant as Criminal

The legal approach to a definition of deviant behavior is embodied in the criminal law. In the legal framework, deviance worthy of concern is a violation of one or more criminal statutes and therefore a crime. Theoretically, at least, all criminal laws prohibit behaviors that are socially harmful, disruptive, or dangerous. Unfortunately, some laws may outlaw acts that are not especially detrimental to society, leading thereby to the development of disrespect for law and legal processes.

Basically there are four types of criminal acts proscribed by law. The first class, *mala in se,* involves acts thought to be intrinsically bad and with little redeeming virtue. There is widespread consensus in the society that such acts are socially intolerable. *Mala in se* crimes include all the major felony offenses from murder to theft, and from incest to treason. Offenses against a person, or theft of or damage to his property, constitute the essence of *mala in se* acts by present legal standards. Legally, the commission of any such acts, whether for the first or tenth time, stamp one as a deviant who must be deterred, punished, and, if possible, reformed.

If the legal definition were wholly restricted to *mala in se* acts, the problem of defining criminal deviance would be simple. That definition is not restricted, however. The second category of illegal acts, *mala prohibita,* is a source of confusion both to the law and to any rational understanding of deviation. *Mala prohibita* acts are not necessarily immoral, abnormal, harmful, unique, or unusual, but they are still illegal. Their illegality stems from the fact that contemporary social life requires a degree of conformity to "rules of the game." Without a degree of such conformity, chaos and anarchy might follow. The law, then, enshrines rules, demands conformity to them, and imposes penalties on those who transgress. Such offenses, usually called misdemeanors, include traffic and parking violations, the breaking of curfew restrictions, petty violations of all types, and other so-called folk crimes. Neither the law nor tradition nor the current social definition of such rules stamps violators of these rules as being necessarily deviant.

In addition to *mala in se* and *mala prohibita* offenses, a third category exists, which can be called *status offenses.* Criminal law is sometimes used as a means of enforcing specific religious and moral conceptions and values; breaking such a law is a status offence. By such laws we create the paradox of having *crimes without victims.* Among the status offences are drug addiction and homosexuality. In status offenses, the *condition* of the person constitutes deviance. Neither necessary harm to others nor willfulness or maliciousness is involved. Nevertheless, the status of homosexual, vagrant, drunk, and drug addict is defined and treated as being criminal.

Equally perplexing is a fourth type of criminal offense. This type might best be viewed as constituting *crimes with willing victims.* In these offenses, the victim may actively seek the criminal service. Examples of crimes with willing victims include abortion, prostitution, and illegal gambling. Status offenses and offenses with willing victims occur in situations in which the values and styles of life of the larger society are superimposed on segments of the society that do not accept them. Such segments, however, may be large enough to constitute subsocieties and subcultures within the larger society.

Compared with those of most other societies, the legal codes in the United States are most unusual. On the one hand, the United States is characterized by a strong tradition of lawlessness and a general disrespect for legal institutions, in part as a carry-over from the frontier tradition and as a historic reaction against autocratic institutions. On the other hand, and not wholly unrelated, various states have attempted to incorporate into criminal law specific conceptions of vice and sin. Thus, such issues as gambling, pornography, lewdness, and abortion recurrently become critical concerns and divisive questions. The definition of pornography, for example, has been the subject of several recent Supreme Court decisions. Criminal law, in becoming involved with what are essentially moral issues, often becomes identified with maintaining a "narrow" moral viewpoint. *Without* agreement on this viewpoint, laws are difficult to enforce. *With* agreement throughout the society, such laws would be unnecessary. In many countries, the relation between morality and criminality is not as troublesome, and legal sanctions need not be used as the means to achieve morally acceptable behavior.

The Deviant as "Sick"

Whereas in the legal framework a deviant is defined as the willful violator of various specific criminal laws, in the pathological ("sick") framework the deviant is seen as not being responsible for his conduct. Deviant behavior in this context is viewed as being partly or wholly irrational. In ordinary language, the behavior is "sick" and the deviant is more patient than perpetrator, and more confused than willful. In public usage, the words "deviant" and "crazy" have almost become synonymous.

This approach is based on a disease model of deviance. In this view, just as various human organs may become infected, diseased, or give pathological evidence of impaired functioning and capacity, so also psychic and social behavior may be unhealthy or impaired. Some conditions, such as psychoses, are considered to be intrinsically abnormal and comparable to disease. And sometimes persistent and excessive anxiety, hostility, dependency, aggression, submissiveness, gregariousness, personal isolation, low self-esteem, guilt, remorse, shame, escapism, withdrawal, phantasy life, and many other psychic states and attributes are also labeled pathological and deviant. The central focus in this view is always on internal, intrapsychic symptoms as constituting and reflecting deviance.

The view of deviance as being abnormal, or pathological, has been extremely significant in changing societal reaction from a punitive to a treatment orientation. Thus, before the alcoholic was considered "sick," when he was still defined as a "drunken bum," the idea that alcoholics could be successfully treated made little or no sense. Once the element of willfulness and personal responsibility was removed as a focal concern, the approach to treatment changed. Similarly, this pathological-medical frame-

work has helped alter public attitudes on mental "illness," nonviolent but legally criminal sexual activity, suicide, and a wide range of modes of deviance previously considered criminal.

Despite its utility in reducing some of the stigma of the deviant inherent in public attitudes, the pathological or disease framework does not solve all problems of definition. A number of its assumptions, such as the universal pathology of some intrapsychic symptoms—for example, dissociational states—cannot be proven cross-culturally. In other words, in other societies such dissociational states are "normal." Other assumptions also seem unreasonable. For example, while many physical symptoms can be traced back to specific diseases or disabilities, much deviant conduct has no organic locus at all. While the notion of pathology may be comforting, it is also confusing. As a result, emphasis is now shifting in this view to a definition of "sickness" as unsuccessful and faulty coping behavior rather than symptomatic and pathological conduct.

The Deviant as Alienated

Almost diametrically opposed to the conception of deviance as an individual pathological state is the view that members of modern industrial societies have become "alienated" from the normative order. The classic views of alienation have emphasized certain recurrent themes. In large part, these views have been based on certain Marxian notions about the results of industrialization. In this view the emergence of the modern world has had certain consequences for those individuals who live in it. One consequence is a sense of powerlessness. Modern man feels powerless to determine those events around him as well as powerless to determine his own fate. He is trapped and impotent. As the limits of the "world" increase, decisions are made increasingly at levels more and more remote from him. Another consequence for the individual is that personal meaning is often lost. As traditional belief systems break down, predictability and certainty can no longer be expected in everyday life. Too, the segmentation of modern life makes man alien to himself. Since people have to play different roles in society, seldom can they be "whole" in their activities. They must constantly wear false fronts, but seldom have the opportunity to express themselves as "real" persons. Like puppets, they move as the situation requires, but they cannot anticipate their future actions because the strings are controlled by someone else, someone they do not know. In this view, people become isolated from the values and norms of the society in which they live. And gradually they become alienated.

Even without alienation, there would still be deviants, but the alienated can also be seen in a deviant context since they are estranged from the society in which they live. They are *in* the society but not *of* the society since they do not accept most of the norms the larger society uses as standards.

The theme of alienation is frequently offered as an explanation for suicide, which involves the loss of individual meaning; as a reason for the persistence of certain groupings of persons, the Bohemians, beats, religious "freaks," cults, and hippies; and as a reason for the growth and continued attraction of certain mass movements, which some segments of the population hope may give new meaning to their lives.

While this initial discussion of the definition of deviation is useful as an orientation, the issue of definition is not solved and, in fact, will be one of the continuing discussions in this book. Too, in the articles which follow, we have concentrated primarily on three aspects of deviation—the criminal, the sick, and the alienated. As a further orientation to these articles, it is useful to suggest that there are three different approaches to the study of deviance and that there are certain persistent issues which cut through all discussions of deviance.

APPROACHES TO THE STUDY OF DEVIANCE

It is possible to distinguish three different approaches to the study of deviance. These different approaches will be reflected in the following articles. Each of the approaches represents a somewhat different focus of understanding and explanation. Consequently, each approach has its own emphasis, its favorite topics and its primary explanatory scheme. These three approaches can be described as follows: (1) deviance as the manifestation of aberrant behavior, (2) deviance as the outcome of stigmatization, and (3) deviance as the outcome of political process.

Deviance as Aberrant Behavior

A considerable portion of the literature on deviance is concerned with descriptions of the behavior which is defined as deviant. In doing this, it focuses on the individual and his internal, psychological processes. These internal psychological processes are often phrased in terms of theories which suggest that such individuals have been unable to resolve the tensions which arise as a consequence of social life. In the course of everyday social life, certain individuals fail to mobilize the necessary resources needed to perform usual social roles and that deviant behavior is often a reflection of this failure. The focus in this approach, thus, is on the behavior of the individual and the "internal" psychological processes which attempt to explain this behavior.

The emphasis on the descriptions of deviant behavior in this approach has another important value. Such descriptions are necessary since deviance is neither "usual" nor "common" and thus is not a part of one's everyday experience. Since such knowledge is not familiar to the casual observer or since such knowledge is mediated through the more sensationalized accounts of the mass media, descriptions in the framework of aberrant behavior serve the function of providing some familiarity with that which is often shielded from view.

In addition, an approach which focuses on the individual and his aberrant behavior also tends to consider attempts to treat and manage deviant behavior in more individualistic terms. If the "causes" of deviation are "internal" tensions, then the "correct" therapeutic approach would have to deal with these tensions on an individual level. Hence, the emphasis on rehabilitation and reformation.

The other two approaches to the study of deviance focus much more on the "external" social processes which impinge on the individual.

Deviance as the Outcome of Stigmatization

A second approach to the study of deviance emphasizes the processes whereby the norm violator becomes separated out and comes to be defined by others as deviant. This approach takes as its starting point the fact that from the viewpoint of the larger society, deviance and deviants are seen as threats to continuity of the normative structure. Society responds to this threat in a number of ways. One reaction is fear, anxiety, disgust, and sometimes revulsion. Another response is to evoke various types of social control mechanisms to compel conformity on the part of the deviant and to deter others from pursuing similar modes of conduct. These social control devices range from mild and informal techniques, such as pleading and counseling, to highly formal ones, such as imprisonment and execution.

The major consequence of all such control techniques is to stigmatize and isolate the deviant. Stigmatization is inherent in committing a person to a mental hospital, sending a drunk to the workhouse, labeling an individual a homosexual, convicting a criminal, or bringing a teenager into the juvenile court. Stigmatization shifts the focus of deviation from the act itself to the actor. Although it is the *act* of stealing, or the use of heroin, that is illegal, it is the *person* who is the thief or the drug addict. The process of stigmatization publicly defines the person as being unacceptable and reprehensible. This act of labeling is therefore critical. Once an individual has been officially stigmatized—as mentally ill, a sexual offender, a psychopath, a traitor, a mental retardate, a delinquent—the consequences are hard to undo. The "tainted" find it difficult, often impossible, to alter their conception of

themselves as being unacceptable. Others find it difficult to accept those once defined as deviant. Although the stigma attached to some forms of psychiatric disorder, alcoholism, and illegitimacy may have lessened in recent years, American society still remains highly intolerant toward these and other forms of deviance.

This approach also tends to focus on understanding the social circles which support deviance but also tend to perpetuate it. Stigmatization tends to force individuals into association with others with similar problems and perspectives. The Bohemian retreats to a particular section of a large community; the addict moves to the world of "needle park"; the homosexual lives in a "gay" world; the criminal has his underworld. Instead of reintegrating such deviants, which is one intent of social control methods, the stigmatization and subsequent isolation tend to reinforce and confirm deviants as "outsiders." Thus, the paradoxical result is that formal control methods, designed to prevent and reform, often lead to the opposite effect. This may be the reason deviancy continues to flourish despite stern attempts at control. It may also account for the greater effectiveness of treatment and rehabilitation that occurs when persons define themselves as deviants, e.g. members of Alcoholics Anonymous or Synanon, than when they are stigmatized through the usual institutional channels and compelled to be "reformed."

In contrast to the approach which sees deviance as primarily aberrant behavior and thus focuses on the modification of an individual's behavior, the approach which emphasizes stigmatization focuses on the various elements in the larger social system which impinge on the individual and label the person as a result of this behavior. As a result of this labeling, individual psychological processes are affected. In particular, this approach tends to emphasize how deviants develop and alter conceptions of self. Considerable attention is given to how persons learn deviant roles and to the various steps which lead to the development of "deviant" careers. In addition, attention is given to deviant subcultures which socialize, maintain, and sustain deviant identity. Many of the articles which follow deal with aspects of this approach.

The third approach is less concerned with individual behavior or with the deviant as a stigmatized person than with the processes by which norms are determined.

Deviance as the Outcome of Political Process

The first two approaches have focused on the behavior of individuals and on the societal reaction which turns primary into secondary or subcultural deviance through the process of labeling. The third approach focuses on the norms which define the deviant behavior. The essence of this approach might be simplified in this fashion: no behavior is inherently deviant; it becomes deviant when norms are established and enforced; thus the understanding of deviance necessitates the understanding of how norms come about and how they are enforced. Thus, the approach is broadly political in the sense that the focus is on the definers and enforcers and the economic and political motives which condition their thinking and conduct.

As we suggested earlier, in traditional folk societies, norms tend to be simple, integrated, and internalized. The sanctions which are applied for violation are certain and immediate. In general, there tended to be consensus on the normative structure in such societies. In modern industrial societies, however, the normative structure becomes much more complex and segmentalized. As a result of rapid change, the constant adaptation required in modern societies results in the continual development of new norms. New norms enhance the powers of certain segments of the societies and impose sanctions on the behavior of others in other segments. Given this, then, to understand deviance, the focus of attention is on the processes whereby norms are established and announced. Attention should be given to the enforcement of norms and the use of coer-

cion in their enforcement. Such issues are basically political, but cannot be seen as narrowly partisan, since they deal with issues of power and they deal with the establishment of norms even in "nonpolitical" institutions, for example, educational, economic, religious. With this approach, statistics which are reported on crime rates are less an indication of rates of "deviant" behavior than they are an indication of social concern about certain types of behavior. The important question, from this vantage point, is to understand how this concern came about and how this concern was implemented in the legal structure and the various social mechanisms for enforcement. Such an approach leads directly to understanding the processes of conflict within a complex society.

ISSUES IN THE STUDY OF DEVIATION

Regardless of the approach used for the study of deviation, there are certain persistent themes which are found in the literature on deviance. These themes center around three major issues. The first issue is a *definitional* one and can be phrased as "What constitutes deviation?" The second one is concerned with the *management* of deviation and is oriented toward "What should be done?" The third issue centers on *treatment* in dealing with "How should deviation be treated?" These three issues are the focus of much of the discussion and controversy within the study of deviation. Some further explanations of these three issues are presented below.

Definition

We have already indicated that the definition of deviation is problematic. While earlier in the chapter, we presented a typology of deviation which we find useful as an initial orientation, this exercise in classification does not solve the definitional problem. The issue is exceedingly complex. To restate: behavior is not deviant until it is defined normatively. This leaves much to discussion and interpretation. The continuing arguments over homosexuality, drug use, pornographic literature, vagrancy, and similar conduct, illustrate the problem of defining deviance. Various expert commission reports have argued that none of these acts should be defined as deviant. Thus, in late 1973, the City Council of New York City rejected a bill which would have prohibited discrimination against homosexuals in housing, employment, and public accommodations. The same conclusion occurred in the Columbus, Ohio, City Council in 1974. In addition to the legality of homosexuality, is such behavior a manifestation of some underlying pathology? In late 1973, the Board of Trustees of the American Psychiatric Association approved a change in its official manual of psychiatric disorders suggesting that homosexuality per se should no longer be considered a "psychiatric disorder" but should instead be defined as a "sexual orientation disturbance, only if it were troublesome to the person." As one psychiatrist said at the time "The central issue is: Is homosexuality a normal sexual variant, that develops like left-handedness does in some people or does it represent some kind of disturbance in sexual development?" Certain groups, usually labeled "gay activists," are engaged in various forms of challenge to existing legal and psychiatric definitions of homosexual behavior. Similar continuing controversies can and will be illustrated in many of the other areas we mentioned earlier. All of them center around the question of what constitutes deviation and requires negative social sanction?

Management

Another major issue in the study of deviation centers around the problem of management. This issue is of paramount importance for those who have responsibility for the punishment and rehabilitation as well as the prevention and control of deviance. Obviously of critical concern for police departments is how to prevent and control crime. Like many other maladies, there is no shortage of folk wisdom concerning the management of deviance. Playgrounds, street lights,

summer camps, more patrol cars, and more education are common proposals to "manage" criminal deviation. Advances in technology, however, provide new techniques which are interesting but still only barely tested. For example, in late 1973, concern for the high crime rate in New York's Times Square prompted merchants, theater owners and *The New York Times* to put up money for a number of TV's to monitor the Times Square area. Operated and monitored from a trailer in the middle of the Square, the police claimed some limited success with the new electronic surveillance system. They claimed that adding color cameras and zoom lenses would help even more and suggested that the use of video tape might be used as evidence in court. Television monitoring is, of course, routine in many banks, stores, and high rise apartment buildings. Whatever their effectiveness, the use of such and even more sophisticated devices have raised the issue of a possible infringement of civil liberties. Discussions concerning the feasibility of such emerging techniques, their effectiveness and their legitimacy are all subsumed under what we call the "management" of deviance.

Treatment

The third issue in the study of deviation centers around treatment. Beyond the problems associated with the prevention and control of deviation, there is the question of treatment. Perhaps this is more easily seen in reference to the mentally ill. Should the mentally ill be institutionalized? Should only certain types of mentally ill be institutionalized? How many patients can be effectively treated in the community? Can types of home care drug therapy be provided so that people can maintain their "normal" lives? Is psychotherapy necessary? What types of help are needed when persons move back into "normal" social relationships? Are individual or group therapies more effective?

While the issues of definition, management and control, and treatment are presented as separable here, they are obviously interrelated. Conceptions of treatment generally emerge from the ways in which devia-

Figure 1–2. Approaches and issues in the study of deviation

Approaches	Definition	Issues Management and Control	Treatment
Aberrent Behavior	Deviance resides in inability of individuals to conform to norms	Emphasis is given to the detection and isolation of deviant to protect society and deter others	Emphasis is on changing individual behavior through punishment, therapy, isolation, and the eventual reintegration of deviant
Stigmatization	Deviance resides in status which is stigmatized and labeled by various social systems	Emphasis is on the modification of the formal and informal processes which stigmatize	Emphasis is on reduction of stigmatization and the reintegration and modification of community processes
Political Process	Deviance is the outcome of political processes whereby authorities establish norms which sanction behavior	Emphasis is on political change-reducing arbitrary power of norm definers and increasing power of deviant	Emphasis is on both legalization and decriminalization of behavior

tion is defined. Notions of control are related to conceptions of definition and of treatment. Thus, there is some consistency in the "answers" to these various issues which stem from the approaches mentioned earlier. For example, if the "problem" resides in the behavior of the individual, then the treatment process would logically focus on the individual. If the "problem" resides in the way in which the social system defines the norms, then the treatment process would likely involve some element of social and especially legal rather than individual change. Figure 1–2 suggests some of the continuities among the three approaches to the three issues. In the articles which follow, such continuity will not be as explicit as it is here. We have included articles which illustrate all three of the approaches and all of the three issues. In reference to the approaches, more of the articles are concerned with what we have called stigmatization. In reference to the three issues, the last section is primarily concerned with issues of management and treatment.

The readings which follow were selected to serve as an introduction to the topic of deviancy. Because of the scope of the materials available the readings are intended to introduce a range of problems rather than to provide an intensive view of any specific type of deviance. After an overview on the nature of crime, we will look more closely at certain types of street crime and economic crime. We will then move to a consideration of delinquency. We then discuss alcohol and drug abuse before moving on to analyze homosexuality. The next part is focused on victimless acts—such as abortion, prostitution, pornography—and suicide. After discussing mental illness in the context of pathology as deviation, the last part of the book is concerned with various approaches to management, control, and treatment.

QUESTIONS FOR DISCUSSION

1. Define deviant behavior. How does it differ from abnormal, immoral, eccentric, unethical, illegal, sacrilegious, or related activities?

2. Why is it that deviant behavior, instead of defining only the undesirable conduct, comes to define the entire person? Thus, a person who uses alcohol to excess becomes an alcoholic, one who steals is a criminal, etc.

3. What are the critical elements of characteristics of deviance?

4. Deviant behavior is a boundary maintenance mechanism. It is not only uni-

versal but necessary for society. Is this proposition valid? Discuss.

5. How is deviance related to the normative structure of a society? If there were no agreed upon norms, as in a state of *anomie,* would there still be deviance?
6. In terms of norms, what is meant by dissensus?
7. What is societal reaction theory?
8. What are the principal types of deviance? Discuss each type in relation to the norm it violates.
9. There is considerable conflict in the field concerning what might be called the rage, low self-esteem, and terrible frustration of the deviant? Are these problems inherent in being a deviant? Is it possible to have great self-esteem, for example, and still be defined by others as an "outsider"?
10. Discuss the various types of normative change.
11. Does tolerance of deviance increase or decrease with anonymity and impersonality as in urban society?
12. Does deviance involve an act, an actor, a role?
13. Why is ugliness responded to as a most repugnant form of deviance?
14. Is deviance merely a convenient social tool for ostracizing those who promote social, political, or economic change?
15. The radical tradition in criminology and deviance argues that the major deviance establishments—mental health, criminal justice, welfare—are simply our way of preventing changes in the status quo. What do you think?
16. What are the differences between the deviant and other minorities?

BIBLIOGRAPHY

Becker, Howard S. *Outsiders: Studies in the Sociology of Deviance.* New York: The Free Press, 1963.

Becker, Howard S., ed. *The Other Side: Perspectives on Deviance.* New York: The Free Press, 1964.

Bell, Robert. *Social Deviance.* Homewood, Illinois: Dorsey Press, 1971.

Cohen, Albert K. *Deviance and Control.* Englewood Cliffs, N.J.: Prentice-Hall, 1966.

Connor, Walter D. *Deviance in Soviet Society.* New York: Columbia University Press, 1972.

Denisoff, Serge R., and McCaghy, Charles H. *Deviance, Conflict and Criminality.* Chicago: Rand McNally, 1973.

Douglas, Jack D., ed. *Observations of Deviance.* New York: Random House, 1970.

Douglas, Jack D., ed. *Deviance and Respectability.* New York: Basic Books, 1970.

Erikson, Kai T. *Wayward Puritans: A Study in the Sociology of Deviance.* New York: John Wiley and Sons, 1966.

Glaser, Daniel. *Social Deviance.* Chicago: Markham Publishing Co., 1971.

Goffman, Erving. *The Presentation of Self in Everyday Life.* Glencoe, Illinois: Free Press, 1959.

Goffman, Erving. *Stigma.* Englewood Cliffs, N.J.: Prentice-Hall, 1963.

Lemert, Edwin M. *Human Deviance: Social Problems and Social Control.* Englewood Cliffs, N.J.: Prentice-Hall, 1967.

Lofland, John. *Deviance and Identity.* Englewood Cliffs, N.J.: Prentice-Hall, 1969.

Matza, David. *Becoming Deviant.* Englewood Cliffs, N.J.: Prentice-Hall, 1969.

Menninger, Karl. *The Crime of Punishment.* New York: Viking, 1968.

Rubington, Earl, and Weinberg, Martin S., eds. *Deviance: The Interactionist Perspective.* New York: Macmillan, 1968.

Rushing, William A., ed. *Deviant Behavior and Social Process.* Chicago: Rand McNally, 1969.

Schur, Edwin M. "Reactions to Deviance: A Critical Assessment." *American Journal of Sociology* 75 (November 1969): 309–22.

Shoham, Shlomo. *The Mark of Cain.* Dobbs Ferry, New York: Oceana Publications, 1970.

Simmons, J. L. "Public Stereotypes of Deviants." *Social Problems* 13 (1965): 223–32.

Weihofen, Henry. *The Urge to Punish.* New York: Farrar, Straus, and Cudahy, 1956.

Wilkins, Leslie. *Social Deviance: Social Policy, Action and Research.* Englewood Cliffs, N.J.: Prentice-Hall, 1965.

CRIMINAL DEVIATION

...America's system of criminal justice is overcrowded and over-worked, undermanned, underfinanced and very often misunderstood.

The President's Commission

Crime is only the retail department of what, in the wholesale, we call penal law.

George Bernard Shaw

Organized crime can be viewed essentially as an adjunct to our private profit economy.

Stuart Hills

. . . perhaps we should marvel that there is not more violent crime in the cities of our nation.

National Commission on the Causes
and Prevention of Violence

It is better that ten guilty persons escape than one innocent suffer.

Blackstone

Crime and society's response to it resemble a gigantic disassembled jigsaw puzzle . . .

The President's Commission

Get money by fair means if you can; if not, get money.

Horace, 1st Century B.C.

If once a man indulges himself in murder, very soon he comes to think little of robbing; and from robbing he next comes to drinking and Sabbath-breaking, and from that to incivility and procrastination.

Thomas De Quincy

. . . the only significant deterrent to bank robbers examined appeared to be the closeness of a police station to the bank.

George Camp

Fear follows crime and is its punishment.

Voltaire

Society prepares the crime; the criminal commits it.

Alfieri

2

Crime: A National Overview

The selections in this chapter deal with two major concerns: first, the nature and extent of criminal deviation in the United States; and, second, the operation of the criminal justice system.

Any stock-taking enterprise of the nature and extent of crime within a society tends to be rather overwhelming. Compiling events which happen each day in thousands of communities adds up to impressive and depressing results. Newspaper headlines usually report "increases" in crimes. Politicians suggest that law and order is a major problem. Citizens' polls usually show crime to be the number one concern.

The first selection, drawn from the President's Commission on Law Enforcement and Administration of Justice, provides some suggestion of the scope of crime in the United States—about those who commit crime and those who are its victims. One of the points which is made and which will be apparent in other sections is that crime covers a wide variety of acts. Crime is not just the tough teenager snatching a lady's purse. It is a professional thief stealing a car on order. It is a loan shark taking over a legitimate business for organized crime. It is a corporation executive conspiring with competitors to keep the price high. No one explanation can cover the vast range of behavior called crime. This selection concentrates

on providing a stock taking of the American experience.

One of the important contributions of the President's Commission was its insistence on looking not only at the problems of law enforcement but at the processes involved in administration of justice. The second selection concentrates on a description of America's adversary system of criminal justice, which includes as subsystems the police, the courts, and the correctional systems. The emphasis in this selection is on how the various parts fit together and suggests that changes in one part of the system—for example, the activities of the police—will affect the tasks of the courts and the success of correctional programs. This system is very convoluted—some of it planned, parts of it the by-products of different traditions, some of common law and practices going back hundreds of years in England, and all of it compounded by conflicts of jurisdiction and responsibility: federal, state, county, municipal. The selection provides a useful summary of a very complex network of social relationships.

The intent here is to provide an initial overview of criminal deviation and to describe the social subsystems of police, courts, and corrections which emerged to administer justice. Since we have drawn heavily on the President's Commission, it may be important to indicate here certain objectives of the Commission which it felt would result in a significant reduction in crime. While the objectives are stated here in general terms, the Commission did provide over 200 very specific recommendations which related to these more general objectives. The Commission suggested the following objectives:

First, society must seek to prevent crime before it happens by assuring all Americans a stake in the benefits and responsibilities of American life, by strengthening law enforcement, and by reducing criminal opportunities.

Second, society's aim of reducing crime would be better served if the system of criminal justice developed a far broader range of techniques with which to deal with individual offenders.

Third, the system of criminal justice must eliminate existing injustices if it is to achieve its ideals and win the respect and coopera-

tion of all citizens.

Fourth, the system of criminal justice must attract more people and better people—police, prosecutors, judges, defense attorneys, probation and parole officers, and corrections officials with more knowledge, expertise, initiative, and integrity.

Fifth, there must be much more operational and basic research into the problems of crime and criminal administration, by those both within and without the system of criminal justice.

Sixth, the police, courts, and correctional agencies must be given substantially greater amounts of money if they are to improve their ability to control crime.

Seventh, individual citizens, civic and business organizations, religious institutions, and all levels of government must take responsibility for planning and implementing the changes that must be made in the criminal justice system if crime is to be reduced.

THE CHALLENGE OF CRIME IN A FREE SOCIETY

The President's Commission on Law Enforcement and Administration of Justice

There is much crime in America, more than ever is reported, far more than ever is solved, far too much for the health of the Nation. Every American knows that. Every American is, in a sense, a victim of crime. Violence and theft have not only injured, often irreparably, hundreds of thousands of citizens, but have directly affected everyone. Some people have been impelled to uproot themselves and find new homes. Some have been made afraid to use public streets and parks. Some have come to doubt the worth of a society in which so many people behave so badly. Some have become distrustful of the Government's ability, or even desire, to protect them. Some have lapsed into the attitude that criminal behavior is normal human

From *The Challenge of Crime in a Free Society*, Washington, U.S. Government Printing Office, 1967, pp. 1–6.

behavior and consequently have become indifferent to it, or have adopted it as a good way to get ahead in life. Some have become suspicious of those they conceive to be responsible for crime: adolescents or Negroes or drug addicts or college students or demonstrators; policemen who fail to solve crimes; judges who pass lenient sentences or write decisions restricting the activities of the police; parole boards that release prisoners who resume their criminal activities.

The most understandable mood into which many Americans have been plunged by crime is one of frustration and bewilderment. For "crime" is not a single simple phenomenon that can be examined, analyzed and described in one piece. It occurs in every part of the country and in every stratum of society. Its practitioners and its victims are people of all ages, incomes and backgrounds. Its trends are difficult to ascertain. Its causes are legion. Its cures are speculative and controversial. An exmaination of any single kind of crime, let alone of "crime in America," raises a myriad of issues of the utmost complexity.

The underlying problems are ones that the criminal justice system can do little about. The unruliness of young people, widespread drug addiction, the existence of much poverty in a wealthy society, the pursuit of the dollar by any available means are phenomena the police, the courts, and the correctional apparatus, which must deal with crimes and criminals one by one, cannot confront directly. They are strands that can be disentangled from the fabric of American life only by the concerted action of all of society. They concern the Commission deeply, for unless society does take concerted action to change the general conditions and attitudes that are associated with crime, no improvement in law enforcement and administration of justice, the subjects this Commission was specifically asked to study, will be of much avail.

Of the everyday problems of the criminal justice system itself, certainly the most delicate and probably the most difficult concern the proper ways of dealing individually with individuals. Arrest and prosecution are likely to have quite different effects on delinquent boys and on hardened professional criminals. Sentencing occasional robbers and habitual robbers by the same standards is clearly inappropriate. Rehabilitating a drug addict is a procedure that has little in common with rehabilitating a holdup man. In short, there are no general prescriptions for dealing with "robbers." There are no general prescriptions for dealing with "robbery" either. Keeping streets and parks safe is not the same problem as keeping banks secure. Investigating a mugging and tracking down a band of prudent and well-organized bank robbers are two entirely distinct police procedures. The kind of police patrol that will deter boys from street robberies is not likely to deter men with guns from holding up storekeepers.

Robbery is only one of 28 crimes on which the Federal Bureau of Investigation reports in its annual Uniform Crime Reports. In terms of frequency of occurrence, it ranks fifth among the UCR's "Index Crimes," the seven serious crimes that the FBI considers to be indicative of the general crime trends in the Nation. (The others are willful homocide, forcible rape, aggravated assault, burglary, theft of $50 or over, and motor vehicle theft.) The Index Crimes accounted for fewer than 1 million of the almost 5 million arrests that the UCR reports for 1965. Almost half of those arrests were for crimes that have no real victims (prostitution, gambling, narcotics use, vagrancy, juvenile curfew violations and the like) or for breaches of the public peace (drunkenness, disorderly conduct). Other crimes for which more than 50,000 people were arrested were such widely different kinds of behavior as vandalism, fraud, sex offenses other than rape or prostitution, driving while intoxicated, carrying weapons, and offenses against family or children. Each of the 28 categories of crime confronts the community and the criminal justice system, to a greater or a lesser degree, with unique social, legal, correctional, and law enforcement problems. Taken together, they raise a multitude of questions about how the police, the courts, and corrections should be organized; how their personnel should be selected, trained and paid; what modern technology can do to help their work; what kinds of knowledge they need; what procedures they should use; what resources they should be given; what the relations between the community and the various parts of the criminal justice system should be.

And so, when the President asked the Commission to "deepen our understanding of the causes of crime and of how society should respond to the challenge of the present levels of crime," he gave it a formidable assignment.

Crime and society's response to it resemble a gigantic disassembled jigsaw puzzle whose pieces the Commission was asked to assemble into as complete and accurate a picture as it could. It was charged with discovering whether the popular picture of crime in America is how it really looks and, if not, what the differences are; with determining how poverty, discrimination and other social ills relate to crime; with ascertaining whether America's system of criminal justice really works the way the public thinks it does and the books say it should and, if it does not, where, when, how, and why it does not.

TOWARD UNDERSTANDING AND PREVENTING CRIME

A skid-row drunk lying in a gutter is crime. So is the killing of an unfaithful wife. A Cosa Nostra conspiracy to bribe public officials is crime. So is a strong-arm robbery by a 15-year-old boy. The embezzlement of a corporation's funds by an executive is crime. So is the possession of marijuana cigarettes by a student. These crimes can no more be lumped together for purposes of analysis than can measles and schizophrenia, or lung cancer and a broken ankle. As with disease, so with crime: if causes are to be understood, if risks are to be evaluated, and if preventive or remedial actions are to be taken, each kind must be looked at separately. Thinking of "crime" as a whole is futile.

In any case it is impossible to answer with precision questions about the volume or trends of crime as a whole, or even of any particular kind of crime. Techniques for measuring crime are, and probably always will be imperfect. Successful crime, after all, is secret crime. The best, in fact almost the only, source of statistical information about crime volumes is the Uniform Crime Reports of the FBI. The UCR is the product of a nationwide system of crime reporting that the FBI has painstakingly developed over the years. Under this system local police agencies report the offenses they know of to the FBI; the UCR is a compilation of these reports. This compilation can be no better than the underlying information that local

agencies supply to the FBI. And because the FBI has induced local agencies to improve their reporting methods year by year, it is important to distinguish better reporting from more crime.

What the UCR shows is a rise in the number of individual crimes over the years at a rate faster than the rise in America's population. It shows an especially rapid rise in crimes against property. Furthermore, Commission surveys of the experience of the public as victims of crime show that there is several times as much crime against both property and persons as is reported to the police. Even in the areas having the highest rates of crime in our large cities, the surveys suggested that citizens are victimized several times as often as official records indicate. As might be expected, crimes the public regards as most serious, particularly those involving violence, are generally better reported than less serious crimes. . . .

Obviously the most serious crimes are the ones that consist of or employ physical aggression: willful homicide, rape, robbery, and serious assault. The injuries such crimes inflict are grievous and irreparable. There is no way to undo the damage done to a child whose father is murdered or to a woman who has been forcibly violated. And though medicine may heal the wounds of a victim of a mugging, and law enforcement may recover his stolen property, they cannot restore to him the feeling of personal security that has been violently wrested from him. . . .

The most damaging of the effects of violent crime is fear, and that fear must not be belittled. Suddenly becoming the object of a stranger's violent hostility is as frightening as any class of experience. A citizen who hears rapid footsteps behind him as he walks down a dark and otherwise deserted street cannot be expected to calculate that the chance of those footsteps having a sinister meaning is only one in a hundred or in a thousand or, if he does make such a calculation, to be calmed by its results. Any chance at all is frightening. . . .

Controlling violent crime presents a number of distinct problems. To the extent that these crimes occur on private premises, as most murders and rapes and many assaults do, they are little susceptible to deterrence by police patrol. To the extent that they are the passionate culmination of quarrels between acquaintances or relatives—as again many murders and assaults are—there is little that can be done to increase the deterrent effect of the threat of punishment. More than nine-tenths of all murders are cleared by arrest, and a high proportion of those arrested are convicted. Yet people continue to commit murders at about the same rate year after year. Almost a third of all robberies are committed by juveniles and are, therefore, one aspect of the enormously complicated phenomenon of juvenile delinquency. Some robberies are committed by drug addicts, and a certain number of rapes are committed by sexually pathological men (or boys). Effective treatment for these diseases, in the community or in the criminal justice system, has not yet been found. Finally, more than one-half of all willful homicides and armed robberies, and almost one-fifth of all aggravated assaults, involve the use of firearms. As long as there is no effective gun-control legislation, violent crimes and the injuries they inflict will be harder to reduce than they might otherwise be.

Only 13 percent of the total number of Index Crimes in the UCR for 1965 were crimes of violence. The remaining 87 percent were thefts: thefts of $50 or over in money or goods, automobile thefts, and burglaries (thefts that involve breaking into or otherwise unlawfully entering private premises). Of these three kinds of stealing, burglary was the most frequent; 1,173,201 burglaries were reported to the FBI in 1965, approximately one-half of them involving homes and one-half commercial establishments. Burglary is expensive; the FBI calculates that the worth of the property stolen by burglars in 1965 was some $284 million. Burglary is frightening; having one's home broken into and ransacked is an experience that unnerves almost anyone. Finally, burglars are seldom caught; only 25 percent of the burglaries known to the police in 1965 were solved, and many burglaries were not reported to the police.

Because burglary is so frequent, so costly, so upsetting and so difficult to control, it makes great demands on the criminal justice system. Preventing burglary demands imaginative methods of police patrol, and solving burglaries calls for great investigative patience and resourcefulness. Dealing with individual burglars appropriately is a difficult problem for prosecutors and judges; for while burglary is a serious crime that carries heavy penalties and many of its practitioners are habitual or professional criminals, many more are youthful or marginal offenders to whom criminal sanctions in their most drastic form might do more harm than good. Burglars are probably the most numerous class of serious offenders in the correctional system. It is a plausible assumption that the prevalence of the two crimes of burglary and robbery is a significant, if not a major, reason for America's alarm about crime, and that finding effective ways of protecting the community from those two crimes would do much to make "crime" as a whole less frightening and to bring it within manageable bounds.

Larceny—stealing that does not involve either force or illegal entry—is by far the most frequent kind of stealing in America. It is less frightening than burglary because to a large, perhaps even to a preponderant extent, it is a crime of opportunity, a matter of making off with whatever happens to be lying around loose: Christmas presents in an unlocked car, merchandise on a store counter, a bicycle in a front yard, and so forth. Insofar as this is so, it is a crime that might be sharply reduced by the adoption of precautionary measures by citizens themselves. The reverse side of this is that it is an extremely difficult crime for the police to deal with; there are seldom physical clues to go on, as there are more likely to be in cases of breaking and entering, and the likelihood of the victim identifying the criminal is far less than in the case of a face-to-face crime like robbery. Only 20 percent of reported major larcenies are solved, and the solution rate for minor ones is considerably lower.

A unique feature of the crime of automobile theft is that, although only a quarter of all automobile thefts . . . are solved, some 87 percent of all stolen automobiles are recovered and returned to their owners. The overwhelming majority of automobile thefts are for the purpose of securing temporary transportation, often for "joyriding." . . .

These three major crimes against property do not tell the whole story about stealing. In fact, the whole story cannot be told. There is no knowing how much embezzlement, fraud, loan sharking, and other forms of thievery from individuals or commercial institutions there is, or how much price-rigging, tax evasion, bribery, graft, and other forms of thievery from the public at large there is. The Commission's studies indicate that the economic losses those crimes cause are far greater than those caused by the three index crimes against property. Many crimes in this category are never discovered; they get lost in the complications and convolutions of business procedures. Many others are never reported to law enforcement agencies. Most people pay little heed to crimes of this sort when they worry about "crime in America," because those crimes do not, as a rule, offer an immediate, recognizable threat to personal safety.

However, it is possible to argue that, in one sense, those crimes are the most threatening of all—not just because they are so expensive, but because of their corrosive effect on the moral standards by which American business is conducted. Businessmen who defraud consumers promote cynicism towards society and disrespect for law. The Mafia or Cosa Nostra or the Syndicate, as it has variously been called, is deeply involved in business crime, and protects its position there by bribery and graft and, all too often, assault and murder. White-collar crime and organized crime are subjects about which the criminal justice system, and the community

as a whole, have little knowledge. Acquiring such knowledge in a systematic way is an extremely high-priority obligation of those entrusted with protecting society from crime.

"Crimes without victims," crimes whose essence is providing people with goods or services that, though illegal, are in demand, are peculiarly vexatious to the criminal justice system. Gambling, narcotics, and prostitution offenses, and their like, are not only numerous, but they present policemen, prosecutors, judges, and correctional officials with problems they are ill-equipped to solve. Since such crimes have no direct victims, or at any rate no victims with complaints, investigating them obliges policemen to employ practices like relying on informants who may turn out to be accomplices, or walking the streets hoping to be solicited by prostitutes. These practices may be legal, but they are surely distasteful and they can lead, in addition, to discriminatory enforcement or out-and-out corruption.

When offenders of this sort are arrested, corrections or punishment seldom has much effect on them; they resume their activities as soon as they return to the street. Yet offenses of this sort cannot be ignored. Gambling is an activity that is controlled by organized criminals and is a major source of their wealth and power. The growing use of drugs, especially by young people, is a matter of profound concern to almost every parent in America and, of course, the distribution of narcotics is also an important part of the activities of organized crime. Often the statutes that deal with these offenses are obsolete or ambiguous. Treatment programs are still in an experimental stage. The connection between these offenses and social conditions is little understood. Finding ways of dealing with crimes without victims is not only a task for the criminal justice system but for legislators, doctors, sociologists, and social workers.

Finally, there are "petty offenses" and "breaches of the peace" like public drunkenness and public quarreling, which are the most numerous of all crimes. Most Americans have never actually seen a serious crime committed, but every American has seen a petty offense. Such offenses are undoubted public nuisances against which the public has every right to protect itself. Yet a curious thing about them is that usually the only person who suffers real damage from one of these crimes is the offender himself. Breaches of the peace are the most exasperating everyday problem of the criminal justice system. Petty offenders, many of whom, like chronic alcoholics, are repeated and incurable lawbreakers, occupy much of the time of policemen, clog the lower courts and crowd city and county jails. . . .

Two striking facts that the UCR and every other examination of American crime disclose are that most crimes, wherever they are committed, are committed by boys and young men, and that most crimes, by whomever they are committed, are committed in cities. . . . In short, crime is evidently associated with two powerful social trends: the increasing urbanization of America and the increasing numerousness, restlessness, and restiveness of American youth. The two trends are not separate and distinct, of course. They are entangled with each other in many ways, and both are entangled with another trend, increasing affluence, that also appears to be intimately associated with crime. An abundance of material goods provides an abundance of motives and opportunities for stealing, and stealing is the fastest growing kind of crime. . . .

What appears to be happening throughout the country, in the cities and in the suburbs, among the poor and among the well-to-do, is that parental, and especially paternal, authority over young people is becoming weaker. The community is accustomed to rely upon this force as one guarantee that children will learn to fit themselves into society in an orderly and peaceable manner, that the natural and valuable rebelliousness of young people will not express itself in the form of warring violently on society or any of its members. The programs and activities of almost every kind of social institution with which children come in contact—

schools, churches, social-service agencies, youth organizations—are predicated on the assumption that children acquire their fundamental attitudes toward life, their moral standards, in their homes. The social institutions provide children with many opportunities: to learn, to worship, to play, to socialize, to secure expert help in solving a variety of problems. However, offering opportunities is not the same thing as providing moral standards. The community's social institutions have so far not found ways to give young people the motivation to live moral lives; some of them have not even recognized their duty to seek for such ways. Young people who have not received strong and loving parental guidance, or whose experience leads them to believe that all of society is callous at best, or a racket at worst, tend to be unmotivated people, and therefore people with whom the community is most unprepared to cope. Much more to the point, they are people who are unprepared to cope with the many ambiguities and lacks that they find in the community. Boredom corrodes ambition and cynicism corrupts those with ethical sensitivity.

That there are all too many ambiguities and lacks in the community scarcely needs prolonged demonstration. Poverty and racial discrimination, bad housing and commercial exploitation, the enormous gap between American ideals and American achievements, and the many distressing consequences and implications of these conditions are national failings that are widely recognized. Their effects on young people have been greatly aggravated by the technological revolution of the last two decades, which has greatly reduced the market for unskilled labor. A job, earning one's own living, is probably the most important factor in making a person independent and making him responsible. Today education is a prerequisite for all but the most menial jobs; a great deal of education is a prerequisite for really promising ones.

And so there are two continually growing groups of discontented young people: those whose capacity or desire for becoming educated has not been developed by their homes or schools (or both), and who therefore are unemployed or even unemployable; and those whose entry into the adult working world has been delayed by the necessity of continuing their studies long past the point at which they have become physically and psychologically adult. Young people today are sorely discontented in the suburbs and on the campuses as well as in the slums.

However, there is no doubt that they more often express this discontent criminally in the slums. So do older people. It is not hard to understand why. The conditions of life there, economic and social, conspire to make crime not only easy to engage in but easy to invent justifications for. A man who lives in the country or in a small town is likely to be conspicuous, under surveillance by his community so to speak, and therefore under its control. A city man is often almost invisible, socially isolated from his neighborhood and therefore incapable of being controlled by it. He has more opportunities for crime. At the same time in a city, much more than in a small community, he rubs constantly, abrasively, and impersonally against other people; he is likely to live his life unnoticed and unrespected, his hopes unfulfilled. He can fall easily into resentment against his neighbors and against society, into a feeling that he is in a jungle where force and cunning are the only means of survival. There have always been slums in the cities, and they have always been places where there was the most crime. What has made this condition even more menacing in recent years is that the slums, with all their squalor and turbulence, have more and more become ghettos, neighborhoods in which

racial minorities are sequestered with little chance of escape. People who, though declared by the law to be equal, are prevented by society from improving their circumstances, even when they have the ability and the desire to do so, are people with extraordinary strains on their respect for the law and society.

It is with the young people and the slum dwellers who have been embittered by these painful social and economic pressures that the criminal justice system preponderantly deals. Society insists that individuals are responsible for their actions, and the criminal process operates on that assumption. However, society has not devised ways for ensuring that all its members have the ability to assume responsibility. It has let too many of them grow up untaught, unmotivated, unwanted. The criminal justice system has a great potential for dealing with individual instances of crime, but it was not designed to eliminate the conditions in which most crime breeds. It needs help. Warring on poverty, inadequate housing and unemployment, is warring on crime. A civil rights law is a law against crime. Money for schools is money against crime. Medical, psychiatric, and family-counseling services are services against crime. A community's most enduring protection against crime is to right the wrongs and cure the illnesses that tempt men to harm their neighbors.

Finally, no system, however well staffed or organized, no level of material well-being for all, will rid a society of crime if there is not a widespread ethical motivation, and a widespread belief that by and large the government and the social order deserve credence, respect and loyalty.

AMERICA'S SYSTEM OF CRIMINAL JUSTICE

The President's Commission on Law Enforcement and Administration of Justice

The system of criminal justice America uses to deal with those crimes it cannot prevent

From *The Challenge of Crime in a Free Society,* Washington, U.S. Government Printing Office, 1967, pp. 7–12.

and those criminals it cannot deter is not a monolithic, or even a consistent, system. It was not designed or built in one piece at one time. Its philosophic core is that a person may be punished by the Government if, and only if, it has been proved by an impartial and deliberate process that he has violated a specific law. Around that core layer upon layer of institutions and procedures, some carefully constructed and some improvised, some inspired by principle and some by expediency, have accumulated. Parts of the system—magistrates' courts, trial by jury, bail—are of great antiquity. Other parts—juvenile courts, probation and parole, professional policemen—are relatively new. The entire system represents an adaptation of the English common law to America's peculiar structure of government, which allows each local community to construct institutions that fill its special needs. Every village, town, county, city, and State has its own criminal justice system, and there is a Federal one as well. All of them operate somewhat alike. No two of them operate precisely alike.

Any criminal justice system is an apparatus society uses to enforce the standards of conduct necessary to protect individuals and the community. It operates by apprehending, prosecuting, convicting, and sentencing those members of the community who violate the basic rules of group existence. The action taken against lawbreakers is designed to serve three purposes beyond the immediately punitive one. It removes dangerous people from the community; it deters others from criminal behavior; and it gives society an opportunity to attempt to transform lawbreakers into law-abiding citizens. What most significantly distinguishes the system of one country from that of another is the extent and the form of the protections it offers individuals in the process of determining guilt and imposing punishment. Our system of justice deliberately sacrifices much in efficiency and even in effectiveness in order to preserve local autonomy and to protect the individual. Sometimes it may seem to sacrifice too much. For example, the American system was not designed with Cosa Nostra-type criminal organizations in mind, and it has been notably unsuccessful to date in preventing such organizations from preying on society.

The criminal justice system has three separately organized parts—the police, the courts, and corrections—and each has distinct tasks. However, these parts are by no means independent of each other. What each one does and how it does it has a direct effect on the work of the others. The courts must deal, and can only deal, with those whom the police arrest; the business of corrections is with those delivered to it by the courts. How successfully corrections reforms convicts determines whether they will once again become police business and influences the sentences the judges pass; police activities are subject to court scrutiny and are often determined by court decisions. And so reforming or reorganizing any part or procedure of the system changes other parts or procedures. Furthermore, the criminal process, the method by which the system deals with individual cases, is not a hodge-podge of random actions. It is rather a continuum—an orderly progression of events—some of which, like arrest and trial, are highly visible and some of which, though of great importance, occur out of public view. A study of the system must begin by examining it as a whole. . . .

The chart (which follows) sets forth in simplified form the process of criminal administration and shows the many decision points along its course. Since felonies, misdemeanors, petty offenses, and juvenile cases generally follow quite different paths, they are shown separately.

The popular, or even the lawbook, theory of everyday criminal process oversimplifies in some respects and overcomplicates in others what usually happens. That theory is that when an infraction of the law occurs, a policeman finds, if he can, the probable offender, arrests him and brings him promptly before a magistrate. If the offense is minor, the magistrate disposes of it forthwith; if it is serious, he holds the defendant for further action and admits him to bail. The case then is turned over to a prosecuting attorney who charges the defendant with a specific statutory crime. This charge is subject to review by a judge at a preliminary hearing of the evidence and in many places if the offense charged is a felony, by a grand jury that can dismiss the charge, or affirm it by delivering

FIGURE 2.1

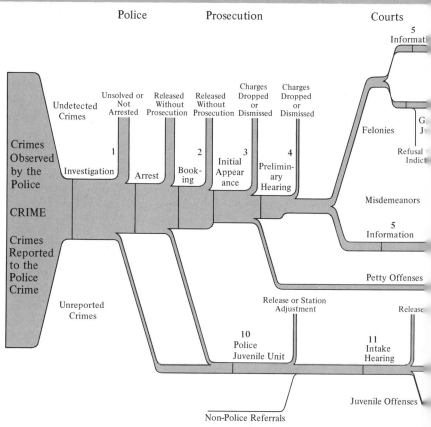

A general view of The Criminal Justice System

This chart seeks to present a simple yet comprehensive view of the movement of cases through the criminal justice system. Procedures in individual jurisdictions may vary from the pattern shown here. The differing weights of line indicate the relative volumes of cases disposed of at various points in the system, but this is only suggestive since no nationwide data of this sort exists.

1   May continue until trial.

2   Administrative record of arrest. First step at which temporary release on bail may be available.

3   Before magistrate, commissioner, or justice of peace. Formal notice of charge, advice of rights. Bail set. Summary trials for petty offenses usually conducted here without further processing.

4   Preliminary testing of evidence against defendant. Charge may be reduced. No separate preliminary hearing for misdemeanor in some systems.

5   Charge filed by prosecutor on basis of information submitted by police or citizens. Alternative to grand jury indictment; often used in felonies, almost always in misdemean

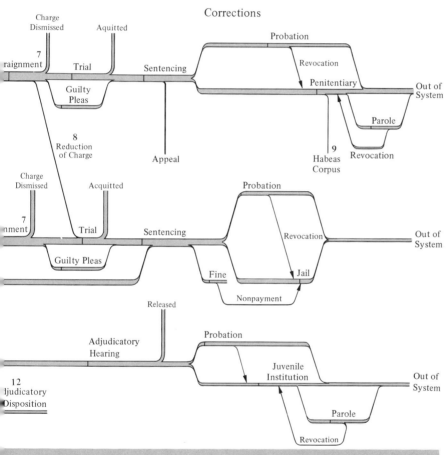

Corrections

Reviews whether Government evidence
sufficient to justify trial. Some States have no
grand jury system; others seldom use it.
Appearance for plea; defendant elects trial by
judge or jury (if available); counsel for indigent
usually appointed here in felonies. Often not
at all in other cases.
Charge may be reduced at any time prior to
trial in return for plea of guilty or for other
reasons.

9   Challenge on constitutional grounds to legality
    of detention. May be sought at any point in
    process.
10 Police often hold informal hearings, dismiss or
    adjust many cases without further processing.
11 Probation officer decides desirability of further
    court action.
12 Welfare agency, social services, counselling,
    medical care, etc., for cases where adjudicatory
    handling not needed.

it to a judge in the form of an indictment. If the defendant pleads "not guilty" to the charge he comes to trial; the facts of his case are marshaled by prosecuting and defense attorneys and presented, under the supervision of a judge, through witnesses, to a jury. If the jury finds the defendant guilty, he is sentenced by the judge to a term in prison, where a systematic attempt to convert him into a law-abiding citizen is made, or to a term of probation, under which he is permitted to live in the community as long as he behaves himself.

Some cases do proceed much like that, especially those involving offenses that are generally considered "major": serious acts of violence or thefts of large amounts of property. However, not all major cases follow this course, and, in any event, the bulk of the daily business of the criminal justice system consists of offenses that are not major—of breaches of the peace, crimes of vice, petty thefts, assaults arising from domestic or street-corner or barroom disputes. These and most other cases are disposed of in much less formal and much less deliberate ways.

The theory of the juvenile court is that it is a "helping" social agency, designed to prescribe carefully individualized treatment to young people in trouble, and that its procedures are therefore nonadversary. Here again there is, in most places, a considerable difference between theory and practice. Many juvenile proceedings are no more individualized and no more therapeutic than adult ones.

What has evidently happened is that the transformation of America from a relatively relaxed rural society into a tumultuous urban one has presented the criminal justice system in the cities with a volume of cases too large to handle by traditional methods. One result of heavy caseloads is highly visible in city courts, which process many cases with excessive haste and many others with excessive slowness. In the interest both of effectiveness and of fairness to individuals, justice should be swift and certain; too often

in city courts today it is, instead, hasty or faltering. Possibly, the pressure of numbers has effected a series of adventitious changes in the criminal process. Informal shortcuts have been used. The decision making process has often become routinized. Throughout the system the importance of individual judgment and discretion, as distinguished from stated rules and procedures, has increased. In effect, much decision making is being done on an administrative rather than on a judicial basis. Thus, an examination of how the criminal justice system works and a consideration of the changes needed to make it more effective and fair must focus on the extent to which invisible, administrative procedures depart from visible, traditional ones, and on the desirability of that departure.

THE POLICE

At the very beginning of the process—or, more properly, before the process begins at all—something happens that is scarcely discussed in lawbooks and is seldom recognized by the public: law enforcement policy is made by the policeman. For policemen cannot and do not arrest all the offenders they encounter. It is doubtful that they arrest most of them. A criminal code, in practice, is not a set of specific instructions to policemen but a more or less rough map of the territory in which policemen work. How an individual policeman moves around that territory depends largely on his personal discretion.

That a policeman's duties compel him to exercise personal discretion many times every day is evident. Crime does not look the same on the street as it does in a legislative chamber. How much noise or profanity makes conduct "disorderly" within the meaning of the law? When must a quarrel be treated as a criminal assault: at the first threat or at the first shove or at the first blow, or after blood is drawn, or when a serious injury is inflicted? How suspicious must conduct be before there is "probable cause," the constitutional basis for an arrest?

Every policeman, however complete or sketchy his education, is an interpreter of the law.

Every policeman, too, is an arbiter of social values, for he meets situation after situation in which invoking criminal sanctions is a questionable line of action. It is obvious that a boy throwing rocks at a school's windows is committing the statutory offense of vandalism, but it is often not at all obvious whether a policeman will better serve the interests of the community and of the boy by taking the boy home to his parents or by arresting him. Who are the boy's parents? Can they control him? Is he a frequent offender who has responded badly to leniency? Is vandalism so epidemic in the neighborhood that he should be made a cautionary example? With juveniles especially, the police exercise great discretion.

Finally, the manner in which a policeman works is influenced by practical matters: the legal strength of the available evidence, the willingness of victims to press charges and of witnesses to testify, the temper of the community, the time and information at the policeman's disposal. Much is at stake in how the policeman exercises this discretion. If he judges conduct not suspicious enough to justify intervention, the chance to prevent a robbery, rape, or murder may be lost. If he overestimates the seriousness of a situation or his actions are controlled by panic or prejudice, he may hurt or kill someone unnecessarily. His actions may even touch off a riot.

THE MAGISTRATE

In direct contrast to the policeman, the magistrate before whom a suspect is first brought usually exercises less discretion than the law allows him. He is entitled to inquire into the facts of the case, into whether there are grounds for holding the accused. He seldom does. He seldom can. The more promptly an arrested suspect is brought into magistrate's court, the less likelihood there is that much information about the arrest other than the arresting officer's statement will be available to the magistrate. Moreover many magistrates, especially in big cities, have such congested calendars that it is almost impossible for them to subject any case but an extraordinary one to prolonged scrutiny.

In practice the most important things, by far, that a magistrate does are to set the amount of a defendant's bail and in some jurisdictions to appoint counsel. Too seldom does either action get the careful attention it deserves. In many cases the magistrate accepts a waiver of counsel without insuring that the suspect knows the significance of legal representation.

Bail is a device to free an untried defendant and at the same time make sure he appears for trial. That is the sole stated legal purpose in America. The Eighth Amendment to the Constitution declares that it must not be "excessive." Appellate courts have declared that not just the seriousness of the charge against the defendant, but the suspect's personal, family, and employment situation, as they bear on the likelihood of his appearance, must be weighed before the amount of his bail is fixed. Yet more magistrates than not set bail according to standard rates: so and so many dollars for such and such an offense.

The persistence of money bail can best be explained not by its stated purpose but by the belief of police, prosecutors, and courts that the best way to keep a defendant from committing more crimes before trial is to set bail so high that he cannot obtain his release.

THE PROSECUTOR

The key administrative officer in the processing of cases is the prosecutor. Theoretically the examination of the evidence against a defendant by a judge at a preliminary hearing, and its reexamination by a grand jury, are important parts of the process. Practically they seldom are because a prosecutor seldom has any difficulty in making a prima facie case against a defendant. In fact most defendants waive their rights to preliminary hearings and much more often than not grand juries indict precisely as prosecutors ask them to. The prosecutor wields almost undisputed sway over the pretrial progress of most cases. He decides whether to press a case or drop it. He determines the specific charge against a defendant. When the charge is reduced, as it is in as many as two-thirds of all cases in some cities, the prosecutor is usually the official who reduces it.

In the informal, noncriminal, nonadversary juvenile justice system there are no "magistrates" or "prosecutors" or "charges," or, in most instances, defense counsel. An arrested youth is brought before an intake officer who is likely to be a social worker or, in smaller communities, before a judge. On the basis of an informal inquiry into the facts and circumstances that led to the arrest, and of an interview with the youth himself, the intake officer or the judge decides whether or not a case should be the subject of formal court proceedings. If he decides it should be, he draws up a petition, describing the case. In very few places is bail a part of the juvenile system; a youth whose case is referred to court is either sent home with orders to reappear on a certain date, or remanded to custody. This decision, too, is made by the screening official. Thus, though these officials work in a quite different environment and according to quite different procedures from magistrates and prosecutors, they in fact exercise the same kind of discretionary control over what happens before the facts of a case are adjudicated.

THE PLEA AND THE SENTENCE

When a prosecutor reduces a charge it is ordinarily because there has been "plea bargaining" between him and a defense attorney. The issue at stake is how much the prosecutor will reduce his original charge or how lenient a sentence he will recommend, in return for a plea of guilty. There is no way of judging how many bargains reflect the prosecutor's belief that a lesser charge or

sentence is justified and how many result from the fact that there may be in the system at any one time ten times as many cases as there are prosecutors or judges or courtrooms to handle them, should every one come to trial. In form, a plea bargain can be anything from a series of careful conferences to a hurried consultation in a courthouse corridor. In content it can be anything from a conscientious exploration of the facts and dispositional alternatives available and appropriate to a defendant, to a perfunctory deal. If the interests of a defendant are to be properly protected while his fate is being thus invisibly determined, he obviously needs just as good legal representation as the kind he needs at a public trial. Whether or not plea bargaining is a fair and effective method of disposing of criminal cases depends heavily on whether or not defendants are provided early with competent and conscientious counsel.

Plea bargaining is not only an invisible procedure but, in some jurisdictions, a theoretically unsanctioned one. In order to satisfy the court record, a defendant, his attorney, and the prosecutor will at the time of sentencing often ritually state to a judge that no bargain has been made. Plea bargaining may be a useful procedure, especially in congested urban jurisdictions, but neither the dignity of the law, nor the quality of justice, nor the protection of society from dangerous criminals is enhanced by its being conducted covertly.

In the juvenile system there is, of course, no plea bargaining in the sense described above. However, the entire juvenile process can involve extra-judicial negotiations about disposition. Furthermore, the entire juvenile process is by design invisible. Though intended to be helpful, the authority exercised often is coercive; juveniles, no less than adults, may need representation by counsel.

An enormously consequential kind of decision is the sentencing decision of a judge. The law recognizes the importance of fitting sentences to individual defendants by giving judges, in most instances, considerable latitude. For example the recently adopted New

York Penal Code, which will go into effect in autumn of 1967, empowers a judge to impose upon a man convicted of armed robbery any sentence between a 5-year term of probation and a 25-year term in prison. Even when a judge has presided over a trial during which the facts of a case have been carefully set forth and has been given a probation report that carefully discusses a defendant's character, background, and problems, he cannot find it easy to choose a sentence. In perhaps nine-tenths of all cases there is no trial; the defendants are self-confessedly guilty.

In the lower or misdemeanor courts, the courts that process most criminal cases, probation reports are a rarity. Under such circumstances judges have little to go on and many sentences are bound to be based on conjecture or intuition. When a sentence is part of a plea bargain, which an overworked judge ratifies perfunctorily, it may not even be his conjecture or intuition on which the sentence is based, but a prosecutor's or a defense counsel's. But perhaps the greatest lack judges suffer from when they pass sentence is not time or information, but correctional alternatives. Some lower courts do not have any probation officers, and in almost every court the caseloads of probation officers are so heavy that a sentence of probation means, in fact, releasing an offender into the community with almost no supervision. Few States have a sufficient variety of correctional institutions or treatment programs to inspire judges with the confidence that sentences will lead to rehabilitation.

CORRECTIONS

The correctional apparatus to which guilty defendants are delivered is in every respect the most isolated part of the criminal justice system. Much of it is physically isolated; its institutions usually have thick walls and locked doors, and often they are situated in rural areas, remote from the courts where the institutions' inmates were tried and from the communities where they lived. The correctional apparatus is isolated in the sense that its officials do not have everyday working relationships with officials from the system's other branches, like those that commonly exist between policemen and prosecutors, or prosecutors and judges. It is isolated in the sense that what it does with, to, or for the people under its supervision is seldom governed by any but the most broadly written statutes, and is almost never scrutinized by appellate courts. Finally, it is isolated from the public partly by its invisibility and physical remoteness; partly by the inherent lack of drama in most of its activities, but perhaps most importantly by the fact that the correctional apparatus is often used—or misused—by both the criminal justice system and the public as a rug under which disturbing problems and people can be swept.

The most striking fact about the correctional apparatus today is that, although the rehabilitation of criminals is presumably its major purpose, the custody of criminals is actually its major task. On any given day there are well over a million people being "corrected" in America, two-thirds of them on probation or parole and one-third of them in prisons or jails. However, prisons and jails are where four-fifths of correctional money is spent and where nine-tenths of correctional employees work. Furthermore, fewer than one-fifth of the people who work in State prisons and local jails have jobs that are not essentially either custodial or administrative in character. Many jails have nothing but custodial and administrative personnel. Of course many jails are crowded with defendants who have not been able to furnish bail and who are not considered by the law to be appropriate objects of rehabilitation because it has not yet been determined that they are criminals who need it.

What this emphasis on custody means in practice is that the enormous potential of the correctional apparatus for making creative decisions about its treatment of convicts is largely unfulfilled. This is true not only of offenders in custody but of offenders on probation and parole. Most authorities agree that while probationers and parolees need varying degrees and kinds of supervision, an average of no more than 35 cases per officer is necessary for effective attention; 97 percent of all officers handling adults have larger caseloads than that. In the juvenile correctional system the situation is somewhat better. Juvenile institutions, which typically are training schools, have a higher proportion of treatment personnel and juvenile probation and parole officers generally have lighter caseloads. However, these comparatively rich resources are very far from being sufficiently rich.

Except for sentencing, no decision in the criminal process has more impact on the convicted offender than the parole decision, which determines how much of his maximum sentence a prisoner must serve. This again is an invisible administrative decision that is seldom open to attack or subject to review. It is made by parole board members who are often political appointees. Many are skilled and conscientious, but they generally are able to spend no more than a few minutes on a case. Parole decisions that are made in haste and on the basis of insufficient information, in the absence of parole machinery that can provide good supervision, are necessarily imperfect decisions. And since there is virtually no appeal from them, they can be made arbitrarily or discriminatorily. Just as carefully formulated and clearly stated law enforcement policies would help policemen, charge policies would help prosecutors and sentencing policies would help judges, so parole policies would help parole boards perform their delicate and important duties.

In sum, America's system of criminal justice is overcrowded and overworked, undermanned, underfinanced, and very often misunderstood. It needs more information and more knowledge. It needs more technical resources. It needs more coordination among its many parts. It needs more public support. It needs the help of community programs and institutions in dealing with offenders and potential offenders. It needs, above all, the willingness to reexamine old ways of doing things, to reform itself, to experiment, to run risks, to dare. It needs vision.

QUESTIONS FOR DISCUSSION

1. What are the various stages in the criminal justice process? Trace each step indicating all possible alternatives.
2. American criminal justice is based on the *adversary* system. What does an adversary system involve? Is this similar to the procedures and logic in Europe and in the eastern or Soviet bloc?
3. Discretion is at the heart of the functioning of our criminal justice system. What is discretion and how does it work in the case of the police, the prosecutor, the courts, corrections?
4. How much crime do we have in the U.S.? How do we know how much crime we have? What is wrong with our present reporting and recording system, if anything? What alternatives to the current reporting system have been urged? Which have been tried? How have those which have been tried work in practice?
5. How does the U.S. crime problem compare with the problem in England? In the U.S. 25 years ago? Was there always a crime problem?
6. What are the ten most important characteristics of crime in America? How do these compare with other countries?
7. Check the Legal Definitions Appendix and see whether it is possible to operate in these terms and categories.
8. What is meant by the American tendency to overcriminalize conduct?
9. Why is it so hard to recruit minorities for police, prosecutor, and corrections work?
10. Why are most offenders male, young, black, poor, and criminal repeaters? Is it something in them that we must alter or is the problem simply a function of the nature of our society?
11. Criminologists contend that it is not the severity of punishment but the certainty of detection that deters potential offenders. What do you think?
12. Why has the severity of punished lessened through the last two centuries? Are we simply more civilized? What then?
13. Should capital punishment be reinstituted for such heinous crimes as hijacking, terrorist activities, and kidnapping as well as for aggravated murder?

BIBLIOGRAPHY

Blumberg, Abraham S., ed. *The Scales of Justice.* Trans-Action Books, Aldine, 1970.

Casper, Jonathan D. *American Criminal Justice: The Defendant's Perspective.* Englewood Cliffs, N.J.: Prentice-Hall, 1972.

Chambliss, William J. *Crime and the Legal Process.* New York: McGraw-Hall, 1968.

Clinard, Marshall, and Abbott, D. J. *Crime in Developing Countries.* New York: Wiley-Interscience, 1973.

Duster, Troy. *The Legislation of Morality.* New York: The Free Press, 1970.

Jacob, Herbert, ed. *Problems in the Criminal Justice System: Police, Prosecution and the Courts.* Beverly Hills, California: Sage Publications, 1974.

Nagel, Stuart. *The Legal Process From a Behavioral Perspective.* Homewood, Illinois: The Dorsey Press, 1969.

Nagel, Stuart S. *The Rights of the Accused: In Law and Action.* Beverly Hills, California: Sage Publications, 1972.

Nettler, Gwynn. *Explaining Crime.* New York: Mc Graw-Hill, 1974.

Packer, Herbert L. *The Limits of the Criminal Sanction.* Stanford, California: Stanford University Press, 1969.

Quinney, Richard. *The Social Reality of Crime.* Boston: Little, Brown and Company, 1970.

Ruchelman, Leonard, ed. *Who Rules the Police.* New York: New York University Press, 1973.

Shover, Neil. "The Civil Justice Process as Societal Reactions." *Social Forces* 52 (December 1973), 253–258.

Skolnick, Jermoe. *Justice Without Trial.* New York: Wiley, 1966.

Taylor, Ian, Walton, P., and Young, J. *The New Criminology for a Social Theory of Deviance.* London: Routledge and Kegan Paul, 1973.

Turk, A. T. "Conflict and Criminality." *American Sociological Review* 31 (June 1966), 338–352.

Turk, Austin T. *Criminality and Legal Order.* Chicago: Rand McNally, 1969.

Wilson, James Q. *Varieties of Police Behavior: The Management of Law and Order in Eight Communities.* New York: Atheneum, 1973.

Zimring, Franklin P., and Hawkins, Gordon J., *Deterrence: The Legal Threat in Crime Control.* Chicago: University of Chicago Press, 1973.

3

Street Crimes and Delinquency

Since crimes include many personal as well as property violations, in addition to acts which have been "overcriminalized," there are a number of typologies of crimes. We start with the so-called "street" crimes. These include most of the offenses which are conventionally designated as major felony crimes. The first selection concentrates on crimes of violence—homicide, rape, robbery, and assault. While such crimes constitute only about 13 to 16 per cent of all reported Part I crimes, as designated by the Uniform Crime Reports of the FBI, the nature of these offenses is so fraught with danger and humiliation that they have come to dominate lay thinking of crime. In the late 1960's, the concern about increasing conventional rates of violence as well as assassinations, ghetto disturbances, hijackings, kidnappings, and politically motivated violence led to the establishment of a National Commission on the Causes and Prevention of Violence. This Commission had a broad mandate and studied the broad spectrum of violence, and the first selection provides an overview and profile of conventional violent crimes in the United States. Noting the high incidence of violent crime in large cities and especially among youth of the inner-city, the article also explores some of the causal factors of violent crime. Looking at various factors which influence inner-city males, the

article points out the importance of a sub-culture which creates a climate conducive to and supportive of violence. It should be noted in reading this article that the data and conclusions are based on reported or known crimes. The results would be even more conclusive if the nonreported events were included.

Until the promising research by Professor Amir of the Hebrew University in Jerusalem, Israel, very little was known about forcible rape as a serious felony offense. The article, "Forcible Rape," is based on an analysis of 646 cases occurring in Philadelphia in a two-year period. The data disprove many misconceptions about forcible rape. The article discusses this problem in terms of the characteristics of offenders and victims, the location of the offense, its planning, degree of violence, victim resistance, victim precipitation of the event, and multiple rapes. As a specific order of violent crime, forcible rape is highly complex, involving far more than a guileless victim and a sadistic, aggressive offender. Instead, an understanding of the dynamics of forcible rape demands an interactional perspective. The event itself is a culmination of a complicated series of inter-relationships and signals between the offender(s) and victim in a specific setting.

The third selection provides a more intensive look at robbery. It points out that the term "robbery" covers a variety of specific actions, ranging from a street stick-up of an individual to a bank robbery. The article raises the question of the close association usually made between robbery and the use of violence. It also provides information on the characteristics of the offender as well as the validity of certain standard deterrents to robbery. The fourth selection provides a description of the cycle of events which are involved in the events surrounding the "making of a burglar." Both these articles on robbery and burglary are attempts to present these common street crimes in a broad perspective. Burglary, it should be noted is the most common Part I offense with over 2,000,000 such crimes reported annually to the police and in turn to the Uniform Crime Reports. Because it most often occurs at night and involves inhabitated dwellings (residences), burglary is a fearsome event to its victims. In neither burglary nor robbery are victims likely to recover their stolen property. The present fad of labeling and numbering each valuable item for later identification and recovery has, as yet, had only a negligible deterrent effect—about the same deterrent value as the automobile serial numbers in preventing auto thefts.

In "The Making of a Burglar: Five Life Histories," Professor Pedro David analyzes the developmental patterns, usually starting with juvenile delinquency, resulting in a career as a burglar. From their case histories, and despite their protestations, it appears that burglary is so ingrained a pattern of life that the criminal justice system is unequal to the task of redirecting their energies. Impulsive, shrewd, hooked on drugs, relating to fences and others on the margin of society, there seems to be no significant countervailing forces in their lives.

Next to burglary, two of the most frequent crimes are larceny and auto theft. Short summaries of these types of offenses are drawn from the Uniform Crime Reports. These offenses are quite different from those types of offenses which involve elements of violence or potential violence as in robbery or burglary.

While the Uniform Crime Reports do not include forgery as a part of larceny-theft, the next article explores this offense and more importantly a particular type of offender. Professional thievery is usually characterized by a high degree of skill—an unnecessary attribute in homicide or rape. To the professional, theft is an occupation and the principal, if not the sole, source of income. Professional thieves share their deviant norms, codes of conduct, and argot. In "The Behavior of the Systematic Check Forger," Professor Lemert uses these characteristics of professional theft as a backdrop against which he describes the former and future life styles of seventy-two systematic check forgers—all but three of whom were serving time in prison when interviewed. While there are certain similarities in occupational habits between the systematic check forgers and more traditional professionals such as con men and pickpockets, the check forger builds his criminal style around a solitary life largely devoid of criminal group contacts. Of relatively high socioeconomic status, well-educated, and without other criminal antecedents or associations, the professioal bad-check passer seems to be a most unusual type of criminal deviant.

The various offense categories covered in the previous articles are seldom subject to discussion as to whether they involve deviant acts. "It goes without saying" that they are crimes. As we mentioned in the initial chapter, one of the issues in deviance is definition. The article in this section, "Property Norms and Looting," deals directly with this issue. From 1964 to 1969, there were at least 325 civil disturbances in American cities which involved mass activities by black people in the streets and the deployment of extra police forces within the community. Vandalism, looting, arson, and sniping occurred in most of the disturbances, and according to American legal codes, these are all criminal offenses. Quarantelli and Dynes argue that, rather than thinking of these acts in conventional individualistic fashion, it is more appropriate to see them as aspects of massive social protest. Looting was one manifestation of this protest which suggested a direct attack on property rights— an attack which was selective and symbolic but one which had widespread support within the ghetto. Essentially, the authors' point is that the looting, which legally is a criminal offense, could not be explained in the deviant motivations of individuals; the looting was actually conforming behavior to new norms which developed in the ghettos. Rather than being meaningless or irrational behavior, the outbreak of looting in the ghetto disturbances in the late 1960's carried a message of protest. The decline of ghetto disturbances in the early part of the 1970's suggests that the message was heard as a manifestation of protest by a sufficient number of people to initiate change.

In this connection, looting as described by Dynes and Quarantelli as part of the ghetto uprisings, is merely a special case of what is surely the most distinctive American crime—vandalism. Only in affluent societies can individuals or groups maliciously destroy property. Such destruction would be inconceivable in Third World nations or in the consumption starved socialist bloc.

Much of the behavior described in this chapter—including rape and other violent crimes, all the conventional property offenses, and even involvement in civil disturbances—involves juveniles in excessive proportions. Consequently, street crime and juvenile delinquency, except legally, are closely linked not only in the United States but in most of the rest of the world as well.

Juvenile delinquency is so much of a world-wide problem that nearly every language has a word or phrase—always negative—to describe and stereotype young people who violate the law. Compared with the terms used to designate the delinquents in other countries, our term, "juvenile delinquent," is neutral and benign. There are "mods" and "rockers" in England, *taiyozuku* in Japan, *Halbstarken* in Germany, and *stiliagyi* in Russia.

Allowing for cultural differences, juvenile delinquency most frequently involves theft, vandalism and physical damage to property, sex offenses (mostly girls), truancy, running away from home, incorrigibility, gambling, drinking, and vagrancy. By law, delinquency includes all those deviant acts which, if committed by adults, would be criminal. Delinquency also includes a variety of other acts which are exclusive to the minor, such as running away from home, violations of curfew, disrespect for parents, incorrigibility, use of alcohol, and school truancy.

The delinquency problem is serious. Absurd as it may seem, the largest number of arrests in the United States are of boys aged 15, 16, and 17. Arrests for the major felony crimes such as auto theft and burglary are predominantly of juveniles. Finally and tragically, current estimates indicate that one boy in five, and 8 per cent of all girls, will have become involved with the police and courts by age 18. In a child-oriented society like ours, delinquency rates of this order point to failures in the socialization process, to a social structure which provides no meaningful status or roles for the young, to laws and concepts that are inadequate and archaic, and to the existence of a delinquency subculture.

The readings included here only touch on very selected aspects of the field. Professor Walter Miller in "Lower Class Culture as a Generating Milieu of Gang Delinquency" focuses principally on the law-violating behavior of lower-class "street corner" boys, although there is reason to believe that his analysis can be generalized to other types of delinquents as well. The theme of the article is that the "focal concerns" in lower-class culture promote delinquency, which becomes an integral part of the cultural style in slum areas. In simple terms, adhering to the cultural practices of lower-class life automatically involves the violation of legal codes and norms.

In this brilliant analysis, Professor Miller persuasively states one of the two major theories of the development of the lower-class gang. The other thesis is that lower-class boys become gang members because the gang represents a solution to their status problems. Unable to achieve socially acceptable goals, many lower-class boys find an answer to their frustrations in the special values of the delinquent group. These values are the deliberate and exact opposite of those accepted in middle-class life.

Almost all sociological studies have focused on the behavior of lower-class youth. For one thing, very few middle-class adolescents ever get to the juvenile court. Hidden behind a mask of respectability, middle-class deviants are usually funneled into private schools and psychiatric treatment and, if necessary, are sent out of the country to "study." They are shielded from public approbation in all possible ways, with the result that little is known of how they function in their normal environments.

Nearly everything written about delinquency involves adolescent males. It would appear, from the various prevention, control, and treatment programs, no less than from police and court statistics, that the adolescent girl is somehow relatively immune from delinquent involvement. Such is far from

being the case, especially in regard to running away from home, truanting from school, and that all-embracing misdeed called incorrigibility. At one time, parenthetically, there was an even quainter phrase applied when all other legal categories failed: minors in need of supervision (MINS being the acronym). In any case, the wandering, street people, runaway phenomenon, neither a new nor unusual deviation, received enormous attention in the wake of the student and urban ghetto disturbances. This popular attention revealed what the experts had long known: girls run away with almost as great a frequency as adolescent boys and are nearly as often brought into court for incorrigibility. In "The Beyond Control Girl," Greene and Esselstyn examine the problem of female incorrigibility and pay special attention to the various types of runaway girls. They reach four conclusions about female incorrigibility which cast serious doubt about the efficiency of present practices of management and control.

VIOLENT CRIME: HOMICIDE, ASSAULT, RAPE, ROBBERY

The National Commission on the Causes and Prevention of Violence

When citizens express concern about high levels of violence in the United States, they have in mind a number of different types of events: homicides and assaults, rioting and looting, clashes between demonstrators and police, student seizures of university buildings, violence in the entertainment media, assassinations of national leaders. Foremost in their minds, no doubt, is what appears to be a rising tide of individual acts of violent crime, especially "crime in the streets."

Only a fraction of all crime is violent, of course. Major crimes of violence—homicide, rape, robbery, and assault—represent only 13 percent (or 588,000) of the Federal Bureau of Investigation's Index of reported serious

From *To Establish Justice, To Insure Domestic Tranquility* (Final Report), Washington, December 1969, pp. 17–37.

crimes (about 4.5 million in 1968). Moreover, deaths and personal injuries from violent crime cause only a small part of the pain and suffering which we experience: one is five times more likely to die in an auto accident than to be criminally slain, and one hundred times more likely to be injured in a home accident than in a serious assault.

But to suffer deliberate violence is different from experiencing an accident, illness or other misfortune. In violent crime man becomes a wolf to man, threatening or destroying the personal safety of his victim in a terrifying act. Violent crime (particularly street crime) engenders fear—the deep-seated fear of the hunted in the presence of the hunter. Today this fear is gnawing at the vitals of urban America.

In a recent national survey, half of the

women and one-fifth of the men said they were afraid to walk outdoors at night, even near their homes. One-third of American householders keep guns in the hope that they will provide protection against intruders. In some urban neighborhoods, nearly one-third of the residents wish to move because of high rates of crime, and very large numbers have moved for that reason. In fear of crime, bus drivers in many cities do not carry change, cab drivers in some areas are in scarce supply, and some merchants are closing their businesses. Vigilante-like groups have sprung up in some areas.

Fear of crime is destroying some of the basic human freedoms which any society is supposed to safeguard—freedom of movement, freedom from harm, freedom from fear itself. Is there a basis for this fear? Is there an unprecedented increase in violent crime in this country? Who and where are most of the violent criminals and what makes them violent? What can we do to eliminate the causes of that violence?

PROFILE OF VIOLENT CRIME

Between 1960 and 1968, the national rate of criminal homicide per 100,000 population increased 36 percent, the rate of forcible rape 65 percent, of aggravated assault 67 percent, and of robbery 119 percent. These figures are from the *Uniform Crime Reports* published by the Federal Bureau of Investigation.* These Reports are the only national indicators we have of crime in America. But, as the FBI recognizes, they must be used with caution.

There is a large gap between the reported rates and the true rates. In 1967 the President's Commission on Law Enforcement and Administration of Justice stated that the true rate of total major violent crime was roughly twice as high as the reported rate. This ratio has probably been a changing one. Decreasing public tolerance of crime is seemingly causing more crimes to be reported.

*Editors note: These crimes continue to increase. The 1974 picture was no brighter than in 1968.

Changes in police practices, such as better recording procedures and more intensive patrolling, are causing police statistics to dip deeper into the large well of unreported crime. Hence, some part of the increase in reported rates of violent crime is no doubt due to a fuller disclosure of the violent crimes actually committed.

Moreover, while current rates compare unfavorably, even alarmingly, with those of the 1950s, fragmentary information available indicates that at the beginning of this century there was an upsurge in violent crime which probably equaled today's levels. In 1916, the city of Memphis reported a homicide rate more than seven times its present rate. Studies in Boston, Chicago and New York during the years of the First World War and the 1920s showed violent crime rates considerably higher than those evident in the first published national crime statistics in 1933.

Despite all these factors, it is still clear that significant and disturbing increases in the true rates of homicide and, especially, of assault and robbery have occurred over the last decade.

While the reported incidence of forcible rape has also increased, reporting difficulties associated with this crime are too great to permit any firm conclusion on the true rate of increase.

Violent crimes are not evenly distributed throughout the nation. Using new data from a Victim-Offender Survey conducted by our staff Task Force on Individual Acts of Violence, standard data from the FBI, and facts from other recent studies, we can sketch a more accurate profile of violent crime in the United States than has hitherto been possible. We note, however, that our information about crime is still unsatisfactory and that many critical details in the profile of violent crime remain obscure. Moreover, we strongly urge all who study this profile to keep two facts constantly in mind. First, violent crime is to be found in all regions of the country, and among all groups of the population—not just in the areas and groups of greatest concentration to which we draw attention. Second, despite heavy concentrations of crime in certain groups, the overwhelming majority of individuals in these groups are law-abiding citizens.

1. *Violent crime in the United States is primarily a phenomenon of large cities. This is a fact of central importance.*

The 26 cities with 500,000 or more residents and containing about 17 percent of our total population contribute about 45 percent of the total reported major violent crimes. Six cities with one million or more residents and having ten percent of our total population contribute 30 percent of the total reported major violent crimes.

Large cities uniformly have the highest reported violent crime levels per unit of population. Smaller cities, suburbs and rural areas have lower levels. The average rate of major violent offences in cities of over 500,000 inhabitants is eleven times greater than in rural areas, eight times greater than in suburban areas, and five and one-half times greater than in cities with 50,000 to 100,000 inhabitants.

For cities of all sizes, as well as for suburbs and rural areas, there has been a recent upward trend in violent crime; the increase in the city rate has been much more dramatic than that for the other areas and subdivisions.

The result in our larger cities is a growing risk of victimization: in Baltimore, the nation's leader in violent crime,* the risk of being the victim of a reported violent crime is one in 49 per year. Thus, in the context of major violent crimes, the popular phrase "urban crisis" is pregnant with meaning.

2. *Violent crime in the city is overwhelmingly committed by males.*

Judgments about overall trends and levels of violent crime, and about variations in violent crime according to city size, can be based upon reported offense data. But conclusions about the sex, age, race and socioeconomic status of violent offenders can be based only on arrest data. Besides the gap

*Editors note: In 1972 and 1973 Detroit had this distinction.

previously mentioned between true offense rates and reported offense rates, we must now deal also with the even larger gap between *offenses reported* and *arrests made*. Accordingly, conclusions in these areas must be drawn with extreme care, especially since arrests, as distinguished from convictions, are made by policemen whose decisions in apprehending suspects thus determine the nature of arrest statistics.

In spite of the possibly wide margins of error, however, one fact is clearly indisputable: violent crimes in urban areas are disportionately caused by male offenders. To the extent that females are involved, they are more likely to commit the more "intimate" violent crimes like homicide than the "street crimes" like robbery. Thus, the 1968 reported male homicide rate was five times higher than the female rate; the robbery rate twenty times higher.

3. *Violent crime in the city is concentrated especially among youths between the ages of fifteen and twenty-four.*

Urban arrest rates for homicide are much higher among the 18–24 age group than among any other; for rape, robbery and aggravated assault, arrests in the 15–24 age group far outstrip those of any other group. Moreover, it is in these age groups that the greatest increases in all arrest rates have occurred. Surprisingly, however, there have also been dramatic and distrubing increases in arrest rates of the 10–14 age group for two categories—a 300 percent increase in assault between 1958 and 1967, and 200 percent in robbery in the same period.

4. *Violent crime in the city is committed primarily by individuals at the lower end of the occupational scale.*

Although there are no regularly collected national data on the socioeconomic status of violent offenders, local studies indicate that poor and uneducated individuals with few employment skills are much more likely to commit serious violence than persons higher on the socioeconomic ladder. A University of Pennsylvania study of youthful male offenders in Philadelphia, for example, shows that boys from lower income areas in the city have delinquency rates for assaultive crimes nearly five times the rates of boys from higher income areas; delinquency rates for robbery are six times higher.[1] Other studies have found higher involvement in violence by persons at the lower end of the occupational scale. A succession of studies at the University of Pennsylvania, using Philadelphia police data, show that persons ranging from skilled laborers to the unemployed constitute about 90–95 percent of the criminal homicide offenders, 90 percent of the rape offenders and 92–97 percent of the robbery offenders. A St. Louis study of aggravated assault found that blue collar workers predominate as offenders. The District of Columbia Crime Commission found more than 40 percent of the major violent crime offenders to be unemployed.

5. *Violent crime in the cities stems disproportionately from the ghetto slum where most Negroes live.*

Reported national urban arrest rates are much higher for Negroes than for whites in all four major violent crime categories, ranging from ten or eleven times higher for assault and rape to sixteen or seventeen times higher for robbery and homicide. As we shall show, these differences in urban violent crime rates are not, in fact, racial; they are primarily a result of conditions of life in the ghetto slum. The gap between Negro and white crime rates can be expected to close as the opportunity gap between Negro and white also closes—a development which has not yet occurred.

The large national urban differentials between Negroes and whites are also found in the more intensive Philadelphia study previously cited. Of 10,000 boys born in 1945, some 50 percent of the three thousand non-whites had had at least one police contact by age 18, compared with 20 percent of the seven thousand whites. (A police contact means that the subject was taken into custody for an offense other than a traffic viola-

tion and a report recording his alleged offense was prepared and retained in police files.) The differences were most pronounced for the major violent offenses: of fourteen juveniles who had police contacts for homicide, all were non-whites; of 44 who had police contacts for rape, 86 percent were non-whites and fourteen percent whites; of 193 who had police contacts for robbery, 90 percent were non-whites and ten percent whites; and of 220 who had police contacts for aggravated assault, 82 percent were non-whites and eighteen percent whites. When the three sets of figures for rape, robbery and assault are related to the number of non-whites and whites, respectively, in the total group studied (3,000 vs. 7,000), the differences between the resulting ratios closely reflect the differentials in the national urban arrest rates of non-whites and whites in the 10–17 age group.

6. *The victims of assaultive violence in the cities generally have the same characteristics as the offenders: victimization rates are generally highest for males, youths, poor persons, and blacks. Robbery victims, however, are very often older whites.*

There is a widespread public misconception that most violent crime is committed by black offenders against white victims. This is not true. Our Task Force Victim-Offender Survey covering seventeen cities has confirmed other evidence that serious assaultive violence in the city—homicide, aggravated assault and rape—is predominantly between white offenders and white victims and black offenders and black victims. The majority of these crimes involves blacks attacking blacks, while most of the remainder involve whites victimizing whites. Indeed, our Survey found that 90 percent of urban homicide, aggravated assaults and rapes involve victims and offenders of the same race.

In two-thirds of homicides and aggravated assaults in the city, and in three-fifths of the rapes, the victim is a Negro. Rape victims tend strongly to be younger women; the victims of homicide and aggravated assault are usually young males but include a higher proportion of older persons. Nearly four-

[1] This study is the Wolfgang, Figlio, Sellin study cited in the bibliography titled *Delinquency in a Birth Cohort.*

fifths of homicide victims and two-thirds of the assault victims are male. Generalizing from these data, we may say that the typical victim of a violent assaultive crime is a young Negro male, or in the case of rape, a young Negro woman.

Robbery, on the other hand, is the one major violent crime in the city with a high inter-racial component: although about 38 percent of robberies in the Survey involve Negro offenders and victims, 45 percent involve Negroes robbing whites—very often young black males robbing somewhat older white males. In three-fifths of all robberies the victim is white and nearly two-thirds of the time he or she is age 26 or over. Four-fifths of the time the victim is a man.

Data collected by the Crime Commission indicate that victimization rates for violent crimes are much higher in the lower-income groups. This is clearly true for robbery and rape, where persons with incomes under $6,000 were found to be victimized three to five times more often than persons with incomes over $6,000. The same relation held, but less strongly, for aggravated assault, while homicide victimization rates by income could not be computed under the investigative techniques used.

7. *Unlike robbery, the other violent crimes of homicide, assault and rape tend to be acts of passion among intimates and acquaintances.*

The Victim-Offender Survey shows that homicide and assault usually occur between relatives, friends or acquaintances (about two-thirds to three-fourths of the cases in which the relationship is known). They occur in the home or other indoor locations about 50–60 percent of the time. Rape is more likely to be perpetrated by a stranger (slightly over half of the cases), usually in the home or other indoor location (about two-thirds of the time). By contrast, robbery is usually committed outside (two-thirds of the cases) by a stranger (more than 80 percent of the cases).

The victim, the offender, or both are likely to have been drinking prior to homicide, assault, and rape, and the victim often provokes or otherwise helps precipitate the crime. The ostensible motives in homicide and assault are often relatively trivial, usually involving spontaneous altercations, family quarrels, jealous rages, and the like. The two crimes are similar; there is often no reason to believe that the person guilty of homicide sets out with any more intention to harm than the one who commits an aggravated assault. Except for the seriousness of the final outcomes, the major distinction is that homicides most often involve handguns while knives are most common in assault.

8. *By far the greatest proportion of all serious violence is committed by repeaters.*

While the number of hard-core repeaters is small compared to the number of one-time offenders, the former group has a much higher rate of violence and inflicts considerably more serious injury. In the Philadelphia study, 627 of the 10,000 boys were chronic offenders, having five or more police contacts. Though they represented only six percent of the boys in the study, they accounted for 53 percent of the police contacts for personal attacks—homicide, rape and assault—and 71 percent of the contacts for robberies.

Offenders arrested for major criminal violence generally have long criminal histories, but these careers are mainly filled with offenses other than the final serious acts. Generally, though there are many exceptions, the more serious the crime committed, the less chance it will be repeated.

9. *American's generally are no strangers to violent crime.*

Although it is impossible to determine accurately how many Americans commit violent crimes each year, the robbing whites—very often young black males robbing somewhat older white males. In three-fifths of all robberies the victim is white and violent crimes each year, the data that are available suggest that the number is substantial, ranging from perhaps 600,000 to 1,000,000—or somewhere between one in every 300 and one in every 150 persons. Undoubtedly, a far greater number commit a serious violent crime at some time in their lives. The Philadelphia study found that of about 10,000 boys 35 percent (3475) were taken into police custody for delinquency, and of the delinquents ten percent (363) were apprehended once or more for a major crime of violence before age eighteen.

A comparison of reported violent crime rates in this country with those in other modern, stable nations shows the United States to be the clear leader. Our homicide rate is more than twice that of our closest competitior, Finland, and from four to twelve times higher than the rates in a dozen other advanced countries including Japan, Canada, England and Norway. Similar patterns are found in the rates of other violent crimes: averages computed for the years 1963–1967 show the United States rape rate to be twelve times that of England and Wales and three times that of Canada; our robbery rate is nine times that of England and Wales and double that of Canada; our aggravated assault rate is double that of England and Wales and eighteen times that of Canada.

CAUSES OF VIOLENT CRIME

Violent crime occurs in many places and among all races, but we have just shown that it is heavily concentrated in large cities and especially among poor black young men in the ghettos. We must therefore focus on the conditions of life for the youth of the inner-city to find the root causes of a high percentage of violent crime.

Much has been written about inner-city slums where crime and delinquency are bred. Social scientists have analyzed slum conditions and their causal link to crime and violence, writers and artists have dramatized the sordidness and the frustrations of life in the inner cities, and a number of Commissions prior to this one have produced comprehensive reports on this subject. In its 1967 Report the Crime Commission described the linkage between violent crime and slum conditions in large cities as "one of the most fully documented facts about crime." Referring to numerous studies conducted over a period of years, the Commission found that

violent crime, its offenders and its victims are found most often in urban areas characterized by:

low income
physical deterioration
dependency
racial and ethnic concentrations
broken homes
working mothers
low levels of education and vocational
   skills
high unemployment
high proportions of single males
overcrowded and substandard housing
low rates of home ownership or single
   family dwellings
mixed land use
high population density.

A series of studies by Clifford Shaw and Henry McKay remains the classic investigation of these ecological patterns. Extensive data on the distribution of delinquency among neighborhoods were collected in a number of large American cities, and the results for Chicago have recently been updated to cover the period from 1900 through 1965. Finding uniformly high correlations between delinquency and areas having the characteristics listed above, Shaw and McKay focused on the process of change in the communities studied.

Neighborhoods disrupted by population movements and social change contained high proportions of delinquents. Although the same central core areas tended to experience social change and high delinquent rates over time, high or low delinquent rates were not permanently associated with any particular ethnic or racial group. The newest immigrant or migrant groups tended to settle initially in the core areas and be responsible for the highest delinquency rates in each city; yet the rates for these groups went down as the groups either moved outward to better areas or achieved a more stable community structure. In Chicago, first the Germans and Irish, then the Poles and Italians, and finally southern Negroes and Spanish-speaking peoples replaced one another as the newest groups settling in the inner-city and producing the highest delinquency rates. Consistent with these findings has been a regular decline in delinquency rates from the innermost to the outermost areas around the centers of each city examined. Crime and delinquency are thus seen as associated with the disorganization and deprivation experienced by new immigrant or migrant groups as they strive to gain a foothold in the economic and social life of the city.

Negroes, however, have not been able, even when they have improved their economic condition, to move freely from the central cities. Therefore, movement of Negroes with higher income has tended merely to extend the ghetto periphery. The southern Negro migrants who have now been concentrated in the cities for two generations—as well as Negroes who have been living under conditions of urban segregation even longer—have experienced the same disorganizing forces as the earlier European settlers, but there are a number of reasons why the impact of these forces has been more destructive in the case of the Negro. Discrimination by race in housing, employment and education has been harder to overcome than discrimination based on language or ethnic background. With changes in the economy, there has been less demand for the Negro's unskilled labor than for that of the earlier immigrants. The urban political machines which furthered the political and economic interests of earlier immigrants had declined in power by the time the Negroes arrived in large numbers. The cultural experience which Negroes brought with them from the segregation and discrimination of the rural South was of less utility in the process of adaptation to urban life than was the cultural experience of many of the European immigrants. The net effect of these differences is that urban slums have tended to become *ghetto* slums from which escape has been increasingly difficult.

The National Commission on Urban Problems observed in its Report that "one has to see and touch and smell a slum before one appreciates the real urgency of the problem." Some of the urgency comes through, however, even in a simple verbal description of the facts and figures of slum life. Before presenting this description (much of which is drawn from the Reports of the Crime Commission and the Kerner Commission), we emphasize again that many slum residents manage to live peaceful and decent lives despite the conditions that surround them, and that the characterizations which follow are typical only of the ghetto core and those who fall into delinquency. They do not describe all neighborhoods or all residents of the inner city.

The Home

If the slums in the United States were defined strictly on the basis of dilapidated housing, inadequate sanitary facilities, and overcrowding, more than five million families could be classified as slum inhabitants. To the inner-city child, home is often characterized by a set of rooms shared by a shifting group of relatives and acquaintances, furniture shabby and sparse, many children in one bed, plumbing in disrepair, plaster falling, roaches and sometimes rats, hallways dark or dimly lighted, stairways littered, air dank and foul.

In such circumstances, home has little holding power for a child, adolescent or young adult. Physically unpleasant and unattractive, it is not a place to bring friends; it is not even very much the reassuring gathering place of one's own family. Indeed, the absence of parental supervision early in the slum child's life is not unusual, a fact partly due to the condition of the home.

The Family

Inner-city families are often large. Many are fatherless, permanently or intermittently; others involve a conflict-ridden marital relationship; in either instance the parents may communicate to their offspring little sense of permanence and few precepts essential to an orderly, peaceful life.

Loosely organized, often with a female focus, many inner-city families bestow upon their children what has been termed "premature autonomy." Their children do not experience adults as being genuinely interested or caring persons. These children may, rather, experience adults as more interested in their own satisfactions than those of their children. Consequent resentment of authority figures, such as policemen and teachers, is not surprising. With a lack of consistent, genuine concern for children who are a burden to them, the parents may vacillate from being unduly permissive to becoming overly stern. Child rearing problems are exacerbated where the father is sometimes or frequently absent, intoxicated, or replaced by another man; where coping with everyday life with too little money for the size of the family leaves little time or energy for discipline; or where children have arrived so early and unbidden that parents are too immature to put their child's needs above their personal pleasure.

The seeds of delinquency in young boys are sown, studies suggest, in families where there is an absence of consistent affection from both parents and where consistent parental direction is lacking. Identification of the boy with a stable positive male image is difficult when the father is frequently absent, erratic in his behavior, often unemployed, unfair in his discipline, or treated without respect by others. Conversely, studies indicate that a stable integrated family life can do much to counteract powerful external influences that pull young men toward delinquency. If the inner-city family, particularly the ghetto black family, were stronger and more secure, with good family relationships, more of its offspring could avoid criminal behavior. However, even where there is a stable family which wishes to avoid the problems of slum-ghetto life, continuing racial discrimination makes it difficult for them to remove themselves and their children from the pernicious influences of the slums.

The Neighborhood

In many center city alleys are broken bottles and snoring "winos"—homeless, broken men, drunk constantly on cheap wine. Yards, if any, are littered and dirty. Fighting and drunkenness are everyday occurrences. Drug addiction and prostitution are rampant. Living is crowded, often anonymous. Predominantly white store ownership and white police patrols in predominantly black neighborhoods are frequently resented, reviled, and attacked, verbally and physically. Municipal services such as garbage collection, street repairs and utilities maintenance and the like are inadequate and, at times, all but nonexistent.

Many ghetto slum children spend much of their time—when they are not watching television—on the streets of this violent, poverty-stricken world. Frequently, their image of success is not the solid citizen, the responsible, hard-working husband and father. Rather, the "successful" man is the cynical hustler who promotes his own interests by exploiting others—through dope selling, numbers, robbery and other crimes. Exploitation and hustling become a way of life.

The School

The low-income ghetto child lives in a home in which books and other artifacts of intellectual interest are rare. His parents usually are themselves too poorly schooled to give him the help and encouragement he needs. They have not had the time—even had they the knowledge—to teach him basic skills that are routinely acquired by most middle-class youngsters: telling time, counting, learning the alphabet and colors, using crayons and paper and paint. He is unaccustomed to verbalizing concepts or ideas. Written communication is probably rare in his experience.

The educational system in the slums is generally poorly equipped. Most schools in the slums have outdated and dilapidated buildings, few text and library books, the least qualified teachers and substitute teachers, the most overcrowded classrooms, and the least developed counseling and guidance services. These deficiencies are so acute that the school cannot hold the slum child's interests. To him it is boring, dull, and apparently useless, to be endured for awhile and then abandoned.

The school experience often represents the last opportunity to counteract the forces in a child's life that are influencing him toward crime and violence. The public school program has always been viewed as a major force for the transmission of legitimate values and goals, and some studies have identified a good school experience as a key factor in the development of "good boys out of bad environments." The link between school failure and delinquency is not completely known, but there is evidence that youth who fail in school contribute disporportionately to delinquency. One estimate is that the incidence of delinquency among dropouts is ten times higher than among youths who stay in school.

The Job

Getting a good job is harder than it used to be for those without preparation, for an increasing proportion of all positions require an even higher level of education and training. To be a Negro, an 18-year-old, a school dropout, a resident of the slums of a large city, is to have many times more chances of being unemployed than a white 18-year-old high school graduate living a few blocks away. Seventy-one percent of all Negro workers are concentrated in the lowest paying and lowest skilled occupations. They are the last to be hired. Union practices, particularly in the building trades, have always been unduly restrictive toward new apprentices (except those related to union members), and this exclusionary policy has a major impact on young blacks. The unemployment rate, generally down in the last few years, remains twice as high for non-whites as for whites; and for black teenagers in central cities in 1968 the unemployment rate was 30 percent, up a third over 1960.

Success in job hunting is dependent on information about available positions. Family and friends in middle-class communities are good sources for obtaining information about employment. In the ghetto, however, information about job openings is limited by restricted contact with the job market. The slum resident is largely confined to his own neighborhood, where there are few new plants and business offices, and unfortunately State Employment Services have been generally ineffective even when used.

Most undereducated youngsters do not choose a job. Rather, they drift into one. Since such jobs rarely meet applicants' aspirations, frustration typically results. Some find their way back to school or into a job training program. Some drift fortuitously among low paying jobs. Others try crime and, if successful, make it their regular livelihood; others lack aptitude and become failures in the illegal as well as the legal world—habitues of our jails and prisons. And there are those who give up, retreat from conventional society, and search for a better world in the private fantasies induced by drink and drugs.

The realities of the employment problem faced by ghetto Negroes are reflected in the data on family income. Negro family income in the cities is only sixty-eight percent of the median white family income. One-third of Negro families in cities live on $4,000 a year or less, while only sixteen percent of the whites do so. [1968]

When poverty, dilapidated housing, high unemployment, poor education, overpopulation, and broken homes are combined, an inter-related complex of powerful criminogenic forces is produced by the ghetto environment. These social forces for crime are intensified by the inferiority-inducing attitudes of the larger American society—attitudes that today view ghetto blacks as being suspended between slavery and the full rights and dignity of free men.

The competitive road to success is accorded great emphasis in American life. Achievement often tends to be measured largely in material terms. Our consumer-oriented culture pressures us to desire goods and services and to feel successful if one obtains them, unsuccessful if one does not. The network of mass communications spreads a culture of consumer desires over a vast audience. Happiness, we are endlessly reminded, is obtaining and having things.

Most Americans operate on the premise that in the race to material success all men have an equal chance at the starting line, and that anyone who falls behind has only himself to blame. Yet not all can be at the front of the pack, especially not those who started far behind in the first place. And the race has different rules for different participants.

There are many ways of coping with the frustration of failure. Some take solace in the fact that others are even further behind. Some withdraw entirely from the race: alcohol, drugs, mental illness and even suicide are avenues of escape. Others, especially college youth whose parents have succeeded in the race, experiment with "alternative life-styles" such as those associated with the hippie phenomenon. In the inner city, where the chances of success are less, many adopt illegal means in the effort to achieve their goals of securing more money and higher status among their peers.

To be a young, poor male; to be under-educated and without means of escape from an oppressive urban environment; to want what the society claims is available (but mostly to others); to see around oneself il-legitimate and often violent methods being used to achieve material success; and to ob-serve others using these means with impu-nity—all this is to be burdened with an enor-mous set of influences that pull many toward crime and delinquency. To be also a Negro, Mexican or Puerto Rican American and subject to discrimination and segrega-tion adds considerably to the pull of these other criminogenic forces.

Believing they have no stake in the sys-tem, the ghetto young men see little to gain by playing according to society's rules and little to lose by not. They believe the odds against their success by legitimate means are greater than the odds against success by crime. The step to violence is not great, for in an effort to obtain material goods and services beyond those available by legitimate means, lower-class persons without work skills and education resort to crimes for which force or threat of force has a func-tional utility, especially robbery, the princi-pal street crime.

But the slum ghetto does more than gen-erate frustration that expresses itself in vio-lent acquisitive crime. It also produces a "subculture" within the dominant American middle-class culture in which aggressive vio-lence tends to be accepted as normal in everyday life, not necessarily illicit. In the contemporary American city we find the necessary conditions not only for the birth but also for the accelerated development of violent subcultures, and it is in these settings that most violent aggressive crimes in fact occur.

From the perspective of dominant middle-class standards, the motives in most criminal homicides and other assaults—altercations, family quarrels, jealousy—are cheap issues for which people give their lives or suffer serious injury. Similarly, the transi-ent gratifications to be obtained from the rape or the robbery do not seem to warrant the risk of punishment or the burden of guilt that is presumably involved. Yet these events are much more reasonable to those in the ghetto slum subculture of violence, where a wide range of situations is perceived as justi-fying violent responses. An altercation with overtones threatening a young man's mascu-linity, a misunderstanding between husband and wife, competition for a sexual partner, the need to get hold of a few dollars—these "trivial" events can readily elicit a violent response in an environment that accepts vio-lence as a norm, allows easy access to wea-pons, is physically and culturally isolated from the rest of the wider American com-munity, and has limited social controls—including inadequate law enforcement.

Violence is actually often used to enable a young man to become a successful member of ghetto society. In the subculture of vio-lence, proving masculinity may require fre-quent rehearsal of the toughness, the exploi-tation of women, and the quick aggressive responses that are characteristic of the lower-class adult male. Those who engage in subcultural violence are often not burdened by conscious guilt, because their victims are likely to belong to the same subculture or to a group they believe has exploited them. Thus, when victims see their assaulters as agents of the same kind of aggression they themselves represent, violent retaliation is readily legitimized.

Moreover, if the poor, young, black male is conditioned in the ways of violence by his immediate subculture, he is also under the influence of many forces from the general, dominant culture. As we have said in another statement, violence is a pervasive theme in the mass media. The frequency of violent themes in myriad forms in the media tends to foster permissive attitudes toward violence. Much the same can be said about guns in American society. The highest gun-to-population ratio in the world, the glorification of guns in our culture, and the television and movie displays of guns by heroes surely contribute to the scope and extent of urban violence.

Taking all the foregoing facts and circumstances into account, perhaps we should marvel that there is not more violent crime in the cities of our nation.

FORCIBLE RAPE

Menachem Amir

The term "rape" arouses hostile and aggressive feelings in many societies and in many countries. In a number of jurisdictions it is punishable by death. There is sympathy for the victim and hostility toward the offender. Since the crime of rape includes many elements other than sex, judicial decisions relating to punishment and treatment are difficult to render.

This article is based on an empirical study which was designed to explore and disclose the patterns of forcible rape among 646 cases occurring in Philadelphia, Pennsylvania, from January 1 to December 31, 1958, and from January 1 to December 31, 1960. The cases were those in the files of the Morals Squad of the Philadelphia Police Department where all complaints about rapes are recorded and centrally filed.

The emphasis in this study has not been on the psychological dynamics underlying the behavior of the individual offender and his victim but rather on their social charac-

teristics, social relationships, and on the act itself, that is, the *modus operandi* of the crime and the situations in which rape is likely to occur.

The patterns which emerged were derived from a study of 646 victims and 1,292 offenders who were involved in single and multiple rape. Patterns were sought regarding race, marital status, and employment differences, as well as seasonal and other temporal patterns, spatial patterns, the relationships between forcible rape and the presence of alcohol, and the previous arrest record of victims and offenders.

Further questions were raised relating to rape during the commission of another felony, the relationship between the victim and offender, victim-precipitated rape, and unsolved cases of rape. Finally, all of these aspects were related to group rape and to leadership functions in such situations.

SOME MISCONCEPTIONS ABOUT RAPE

Following are some misconceptions about rape disclosed in this study:

1. Negroes are more likely to attack white

From *Federal Probation*, XXI, No. 1 (March 1967) 51–58. Reprinted by permission. Dr. Amir is at the Institute of Criminology, The Hebrew University, Jerusalem, Israel.

women than Negro women. Rape, we found, is an intraracial act, especially between Negro men and women.

2. Rape reflects a demographic strain due to sex-marital status imbalance in the community. This theory was refuted, along with the derivative assumption about age-sex imbalance which might exist within the general population.

3. Rape is predominantly a hot-season crime. The "thermic law of delinquency" was not confirmed by the present study.

4. Rape usually occurs between total strangers. This assumption was challenged by the analysis of several variables.

5. Rape is associated with drinking. In two-thirds of our cases alcohol was absent from the rape situation.

6. Rape victims are innocent persons. One-fifth of the victims had a police record, especially for sexual misconduct. Another 20 percent had "bad" reputations.

7. Rape is predominantly an explosive act. In almost three-quarters of the cases rape was found to be a planned event.

8. Rape is mainly a dead-end street or dark alley event. Rape was found to occur in places where the victim and offender initially met each other (especially when the meeting was in the residence of one of the participants).

9. Rape is a violent crime in which brutality is inflicted upon the victim. In a large number of cases (87 percent) only temptation and verbal coercion were used initially to subdue the victim.

10. Victims generally do not resist their attackers. As it is commonly believed that almost no woman wants to be deprived of her sexual self-determination, it was surprising to find that over 50 percent of the victims failed to resist their attackers in any way.

11. Victims are responsible for their victimization either consciously or by default. The proportion of rape precipitated by the victim and the characteristics of such acts refute this claim.

FINDINGS OF THIS STUDY

In the following pages are discussed the major significant patterns emerging from the study:

Race

A significant association was found between forcible rape and the race of both victims and offenders. Negroes exceed whites both among victims and offenders in absolute numbers as well as in terms of their proportion in the general population. Negroes have four times their expected number of victims, and the proportion of Negro offenders was four times greater than their proportion in the general population of Philadelphia.

When specific rates by age and sex were calculated on the basis of the "potential" population of each race, it was found that the rates for the Negro victims (on the basis of total Negro female population) is almost 12 times higher than that of the white women who were victims (on the basis of total white female population).

Age

A statistical association existed between age and forcible rape, the age group 15–19 years having the highest rates among offenders and among victims.... For victims there is a wider range of "critical" age groups, with the Negro victim rate exceeding that of the white victims in all age groups.

Marital status

After examination of the marital status of both offenders and victims, it was found that both generally were unmarried. The highest rates for victims were in the "dependent" category (below marriageable age and still unmarried).

Occupational status

Examination of the occupational status of the offenders indicated that 90 percent of the offenders of both races belonged to the lower part of the occupational scale. The rate of Negro offenders in the unemployed category was twice as high as the rate of unemployed Negroes in Philadelphia at that time, and five times as high as that of white offenders.

Season

Although the number of forcible rapes tended to increase during the hot summer months, there was no significant association either with the season or with the month of the year.... Summer was also found to be the season when multiple rapes were most likely to occur.

Days of the week

Forcible rape was found to be significantly associated with days of the week. We found the highest concentration of rapes (53 percent) to be on weekends, with Saturday being the peak day.

Time of day

A study of the distribution of forcible rapes by hours of the day found the top "risk" hours to be between 8:00 P.M. and 2:00 A.M. Almost half of all the rape events occurred during these hours.

Ecological patterns

The analysis of the ecology of forcible rape reveals that in various areas of Philadelphia there was a correspondence between high rates of crime against the person and the rates of forcible rape. Moreover, those police districts where Negroes are concentrated were also the areas where the rates of forcible rape were highest.

A check was made to determine whether the offenders lived in the vicinity of the victims or the offense. In the majority of cases (82 percent) offenders and victims lived in the same area, while in 68 percent a "neighborhood triangle" was observed, i.e., offenders lived in the vicinity of victim and

offense. Also observed was the pattern of "residence mobility triangle," i.e., instances in which the site of the crime was in the area of the residence of the offender but not that of the victim. . . .

Drinking

Unlike previous studies the present one examined the consumption of alcohol by the offender and the victim separately and together. Alcohol was found only in one-third of all the rape events. In 63 percent of the 217 cases in which alcohol was present, it was present in both the victim and the offender.

Alcohol is a factor found to be strongly related to violence used in the rape situation, especially when present in the offender only. In terms of race, it was drinking Negro victims or the offenders who were involved most frequently in violent rapes. Also, alcohol was found to be significantly associated with sexual humiliation forced upon a drinking victim.

Finally, weekend rapes were found to be associated with the presence of alcohol in either the victim, the offender, or both. As an explanation, we offered the fact that Friday is a payday with greater purchase of alcohol and the more intense social and leisure activities.

Previous Arrest Records of Offenders and Victims

A relatively high proportion of rapists in Philadelphia (50 percent) had previous arrest records. Contrary to past impressions, it was found that there are slight differences between the races, for offenders or victims, in terms of police or arrest record, although Negro offenders had a statistically significant higher proportion of two or more offenses in their past than white offenders.

When cases of persistence in violating the law were examined, it was found that over 50 percent of those who had an arrest record as adults also had a record as juveniles.

Analysis of the type of previous offenses

committed by the offenders revealed that only 20 percent of those who had a past arrest record had previously committed a crime against the person. . . . Among offenders with criminal records, 9 percent had committed rape in the past, and 4 percent had been arrested before for sexual offenses other than rape. . . .

The analysis of the victims' criminal records revealed that 19 percent had an arrest record, the highest proportion of these arrests being for sexual misconduct (56 percent).

The victims' "bad" reputation was explored. It was found that 128, or 20 percent, of the 646 victims had such reputations, with significantly higher proportion of Negro victims having such a reputation. The assumption was made, and later confirmed, that a "bad" reputation, together with other factors such as ecological proximity, was a factor in what was termed "victim-precipitated" forcible rape.

Modus Operandi

The analysis of the *modus operandi* was made in terms of processes and characteristics of the rape situation, i.e., sequences and conjunctions of events which enter into the perpetration of the offense. Five phases were distinguished according to offender's behavior, victim's reaction, and situational factors which finally set the stage for the rape event.

In phase one we were concerned with the initial interaction between victim and offender, and the relevant problems such as the meeting place and the degree of planning of the offense. It was found that the most dangerous meeting places were the street, and the residence of the victims or offenders. In one-third of the cases, the offender met the victim at and committed the offense in the victim's home or place where she stayed. . . .

Planning of the act

On the basis of the description of the event by the victim and offender, three degrees of

planning were distinguished. Contrary to past impression, the analysis revealed that 71 percent of the rapes were planned. Most planned events were intraracial events when the meeting place was the residence of one of the participants or when the rape was a group affair. Explosive rapes were characterized as being single interracial rapes, with the street as the meeting place.

Location of the Event

Phase two concerned itself with the location of the offense and was found to be associated with the place of initial meeting. Thus, when the meeting place was outside the participant's residence, the offense also took place there. Movement of the crime scene was mainly from outdoors to inside. The automobile was revealed to be the location of the offense in only 15 percent of the cases. A significant association was also found between the location of the rape in the participant's place and use of violence in the commission of the offense, as well as the subjection of the victim to sexually humiliating practices.

Degrees of Violence

In phase three we examined various aspects in the actual commission of the offense: Nonphysical methods used to manipulate the victim into submission, the degrees of violence used against her, and sexual humiliating practices which she was forced to endure.

Besides temptation, three forms of nonphysical methods were distinguished: Verbal coercion, intimidation by physical gestures, and intimidation with a weapon or other physical object to force the victim into submission. Combined with verbal coercion, nonphysical aggression was used in the majority of cases (87 percent). . . .

Degrees of violence were classified into three main groups: roughness, beatings (brutal and nonbrutal), and choking. In 15 percent of the 646 rapes, no force was used. Of the cases in which force was used, 29 percent took the form of roughness, one-quarter were nonbrutal beatings, one-fifth were brutal beatings, and 12 percent involved choking the victim. Violence, especially in its extreme forms, was found to be significantly associated with Negro intraracial events and with cases in which the offender was Negro and the victim white. Also, a significant association was found between multiple rape and the use of force in the rape situation and between the latter and the outside as the place of rape.

Sexual Humiliation

It was not merely to forced intercourse that the female was subjected in rape, but also to various forms of sexual practices usually defined as sexual deviations. It was found that sexual humiliation existed in 27 percent of all rape cases. . . .

Victim Behavior

The behavior of the victim—that is, whether she "consented" or resisted the offender—was, and still is, the basis in determining in the court whether the offender is guilty of forcible rape. This problematic dimension was, therefore, analyzed in the present work.

The varieties of victim behavior have been divided into three groups—submission, resistance, and fight. The analysis revealed that in over half of the rapes the victims displayed only submissive behavior; in 173, or 27 percent, victims resisted the offender; and in 116, or 18 percent, the victims put up a strong fight against their attackers. . . .

Multiple Rape

Multiple rape situations were divided into "pair rapes," in which two offenders rape one victim, and "group rapes," in which three or more males rape one victim. Of the 646 cases of forcible rape, 276 cases, or 43 percent, were multiple rapes. Of these cases, 105 were pair rapes and 171 were group rapes. Of 1,292 offenders, 210, or 16 percent, were involved in pair rapes and 712, or 55 percent, participated in group rapes. . . .

Group rape shows a tendency to occur more on weekends and to occur in the evening as well as late at night.

In group rapes, alcohol was more likely to be present, especially in the victim only, while in pair rapes it was more often present only in the offender who was the leader.

A significant proportion of participants in multiple rapes, compared with single-rape offenders, had a previous arrest record either for offenses against the person, for sex offenses other than rape, or for forcible rape. This was true for pair-rape leaders, as compared to their partners, but not for group-rape leaders vis-à-vis their followers.

Turning to the *modus operandi* aspect in multiple-rape situations, it was observed that multiple-rape offenders are most likely to attack victims who live in their area (neighborhood or delinquency triangles). The initial interaction between victims and offenders usually occurred in the street, where the rape also took place. There was little "mobility of crime scene" in multiple-rape situations.

Multiple rapes, especially group rapes, were found to be planned events. Compared to group rapes, pair rapes showed a high proportion of cases of explosiveness or partial planning.

Turning to the problems of intimidation and coercion, it was found that multiple-rape situations, especially group rapes, are characterized by temptation and coercion, with intimidation more used in pair-rape events. The leader was found to be the initiator of the manipulating acts, i.e., he was the first to tempt or to intimidate the victim into submission.

A significant association existed between violence and multiple rapes, especially group rapes. Multiple rapes also are characterized by the greater use of nonbrutal beatings. Extreme violence and brutality characterize the single-rape events, since the lone offender must constantly subdue the victim alone. The leader in pair and group rapes was more violent than his followers, and he was also the one to initiate the beatings.

Group rapes were also found to be characterized by tormenting the victim with perverted sexual practices.

The futility of resistance and fight by the group-rape victim is revealed by the fact that in group-rape situations the victim was more submissive or lightly resisted the offender but was less inclined to put up a strong fight. Pair-rape victims showed no definite pattern in this respect.

For many variables pair rapes and group rapes show some variations from the cluster of patterns which distinguished the multiple-rape situations. We found that in many instances pair rape resembled single rape more than group rape. Thus, it may be better to see pair rapes not as a form of group event but rather as a form of criminal "partnership."

Felony Rape

In 76 cases, or 4 percent, of the 646 rape situations, a felony in the form of burglary or robbery was committed in addition to the rape. These cases were mainly single rapes, and especially Negro intraracial rapes. A special trait of felony rape is the age disparity between victim and offender. In more than half of these cases the offender was at least 10 years younger than the victim, especially when the offender was Negro and the victim white. . . .

Victim-Offender Relationships

Almost half (48 percent) of the identified victim-offender relationships conformed to our definition of "primary" relationships. When the types of primary contacts were further divided into "acquaintanceship" and more "intimate" contacts, the former constituted 34 percent and the latter contributed 14 percent of all types of victim-offender relationships.

A detailed analysis of victim-offender relationships revealed that when primary relationships existed, a relatively large proportion of cases involved Negro victims whose assailants were their close neighbors, or victims who were drinking acquaintances of their white assaulters.

As expected, Negro intraracial events involved mainly close neighbors. White intraracial events occurred mainly between acquaintances who established their relations just before the offense. Again, as expected, acquaintanceships were formed mainly between victims and offenders who were at the same level.

Neighbors met initially in the residence of one of the participants and the rape also took place there. The automobile was the place of rape for those who were intimate.

Although nonphysical means of coercion in its light forms were used between acquaintances, the closer the relationship was between victim and offender the greater was the use of physical force against the victim, and neighbors and acquaintances were found to be the most dangerous people so far as brutal rape was concerned.

As hypothesized, a greater proportion of multiple than single rape was found to take place between strangers. In general, the analysis of the interpersonal relations between victim and offender lent support to those who reject the myth of the offender who attacks victims unknown to him. But equally rejected is the notion that rape is generally an affair between, or a result of intimate relations between, victims and offenders.

Victim-Precipitated Rape

The term "victim-precipitated," initiated by Wolfgang in his study of homicide, was introduced to refer to those rape cases in which the victims actually—or so it was interpreted by the offender—agreed to sexual relations but retracted before the actual act or did not resist strongly enough when the suggestion was made by the offenders. The term applies also to cases in which the victim enters vulnerable situations charged with sexuality, especially when she uses what could be interpreted as indecent language and gestures or makes what could be taken as an invitation to sexual relations.

Philadelphia data revealed . . . 122 victim-precipitated rapes, which comprised 19 percent of all forcible rape studies. . . .

Solved and Unsolved Rape

We distinguished two types of "unsolved" cases: the "undetected"—those cases in which the police could not attribute the recorded offense to any identifiable offender(s), and the "vanished"—those cases about which the police had some informa-tion on suspected, identified, or alleged offenders but which suspects were still at large. In 124, or 19 percent, of the rape events the offenders were classified as "undetected" and in 24, or 4 percent, as "vanished." Of 1,292 offenders, 405, or 33 percent, were classified as undetected.

THE CRIME OF ROBBERY IN THE UNITED STATES

National Institute of Law Enforcement and Criminal Justice

GENERAL DISCUSSION

Robbery, as the FBI Uniform Crime Reports indicate, is essentially a large-city problem. The 57 large core cities—so identified by the FBI and with populations over 250,000—experience 75% of all the robberies that take place in the United States each year. Yet despite the fact that this particular crime constitutes one of the most urgent problems confronting our law enforcement and criminal justice systems, very little has been done to produce the information needed to so identify and describe the problem as to facilitate development of appropriate counter-measures to control and reduce it. . . .

Indeed, not only is information about the offense and those who commit it quickly dated, but its validity and value are often limited by geography. Available studies and data indicate that the problems of robbery vary greatly not only from city to city, but also from neighborhood to neighborhood. For example, the FBI reports that nationally 58% of all robberies in 1968 occurred on the street. A study by Andre Normandeau of robberies that took place in Philadelphia between 1960 and 1967 showed this percentage to be nearer 47%, while another recent study, of the high-crime Second District in Chicago, found that street robberies accounted for 65% of all of the robberies in that district.

From U.S. Department of Justice, Law Enforcement Assistance Administration, January 1971.

The discrepancy and problem described above is dramatized by studies in New York City involving two different precincts. In the Fiftieth Precinct, a white, middle-class area, street robberies accounted for 75% of the robberies. Yet in that same city in the Forty-fourth Precinct, which is a changing neighborhood, data collected at the same time showed only 34% of the robberies occurred on the street. Sixty-six percent of all robberies in this precinct took place inside buildings—that is, hallways, lobbies and elevators of apartment buildings, which accounted for a large part of the housing of this area.

What this points up is that it is very difficult to make generalizations about robberies, even within one city.

Unfortunately, it seems evident that most police departments lack data on robberies in the amount and detail needed to make any kind of statistical analysis for rpedictive purposes. Consequently, they are greatly handicapped in assigning and employing their manpower on a purposeful and effective basis. In the absence of good predictive data and analysis or of reliable intelligence, they are forced to patrol and conduct preventive measures on a very rudimentary, hit-or-miss basis.

As a result, the general practice today is essentially what it has been in the past: when confronted with an increase in crime, the Chief of Police merely diverts more manpower or makes more hours of manpower available to increase the number of police personnel available on the street to control and reduce the offenses on an emergency basis. Unfortunately, the traditional kinds of tactics employed, such as stake-outs, decoys, and preventive patrols must in turn rely on the same inadequate information. The results are bound to prove less effectual and efficient than they should be. . . .

The Uniform Crime Reports break down robbery into seven broad classifications: "Highway" (street), "Commercial House," "Gas or Service Station," "Chain Store," "Residence," "Bank," and "Miscellaneous." These very general categories do not provide any information or knowledge relative to various specific types of robberies involved, i.e., purse snatchings, taxicab, bus or delivery truck robberies, hold-ups of laundry-dry cleaning shops, clothing, liquor, grocery, drug stores, or of restaurants and pedestrians. . . .

While the UCR in its summary of robberies presents other data, including the percentage of armed robbery and the type of weapons employed, clearances, persons arrested and charged, these are not broken down according to sub-classification, either. Thus, in the UCR report covering the year 1968, the FBI reported that approximately 58% of all robberies committed occurred in the street. As noted above, this category includes a wide variety of types and degrees of robberies, ranging from strong-arm robberies of newsboys and ladies' purse-snatchings, to armed hold-ups of taxis, buses and armed trucks.

Information on armed or unarmed robberies, which is also very limited, indicates that sixty percent of the robberies involve armed offenders, with the remaining 40% strong-arm. Of the armed robberies, 63% were committed with firearms, 24% with a knife or other cutting instrument, and the remaining 13% with a blunt object, such as a club. Here, too, these figures are very general and are not broken down by even the broad UCR robbery classifications—i.e., "Highway," "Commercial House," "Chain Store," etc.

With respect to the ages of the offenders, the information available from the UCR is again sparse and quite general. In essence, we learn that seventy-five percent of all persons arrested for robbery were under 25 years of age, 56% were under 21, and 33% were under 18; that adult offenders were involved in about 80% of the robberies cleared by arrest, while juveniles arrested accounted for 12% of the armed and 34% of the strong-arm type robberies which were cleared; that this "greater proportion of young-age arrests, compared to solutions," is due in part to the fact that the youths tend to act in groups; that 39% of those processed for robbery offenses were juveniles (whose cases were referred to juvenile court); that juvenile arrests for robbery showed a 22% increase in 1968 over 1967; and that in the suburban areas, young persons comprised 26% of robbery arrests and in rural areas, 15%. . . .

Contrary to the commonly held belief that a robbery usually involves the actual employment of violence and that a large proportion of the victims suffer injuries, a number of the studies reviewed disclose that the percentage and degree of violence used in actual practice by robbers proved to be relatively small.

Armed robberies in particular tend to result in little injury. In large measure, this appears to be attributable to the fact that the overwhelming nature of the threat of the weapons discourages and minimizes resistance. Most injuries that are suffered occur in strong-arm robberies where the victim is more likely to resist and where the offender tends to be youthful and more prone to readily employ physical force.

The Bronx, New York study, for example, found that less than 10% of robbery victims suffered any injury. In his study of 722 cases of robberies in Philadelphia between 1960 and 1966, Normandeau found that 44% of all the robberies resulted in no injuries. Of the remaining 56% involving injuries, 26% were minor, 25% were discharged after treatment, and only 5% required hospitalization. Normandeau reported that most of the injuries resulted from strong-arm robberies, which usually involved the employment of the physical force by younger offenders. Similarly, a survey of robbery cases in 17 cities conducted in 1967 for the Violence Commission Task Force on Individual Acts of Violence found that injuries occurred in only 14% of the armed robberies and in 28% of the strong-arm robberies. By way of comparison, injuries resulted in 21% of the rape cases and in 80% of the aggravated assault cases. . . .

"Robbers," Normandeau holds, "are not a special class, but are primarily thieves who occasionally, though rather rarely, use force to achieve their object. The display of violence in this context is on the whole an isolated episode. It is general persistence in crime, not a widespread specialization in crimes of violence, which is the main characteristic of robbers." Therefore, he states, the term "violent offender class" could not be applied to robbers without distorting the factual data to fit preconceived ideas. On the basis of his data, Normandeau concluded that robbery should be termed "a subculture of theft, rather than violence." Violence, he maintained, was used only as a tool by the robbery offender who kept it largely under control.

This conclusion receives support from research studies undertaken in California. As a result of the work and recommendations of John P. Conrad, [the then] Chief of the Research Division of the California Department of Corrections in 1963, the California Department of Corrections undertook to classify all inmates according to an aggressive history profile (AHP). Violent offenders were classified according to seven categories: culturally violent, criminally violent and pathologically violent, situationally violent, accidentally violent, institutionally violent, and nonviolent. All persons sentenced on charges of robbery were classified as "criminally violent." The definition for "criminally violent" was those who "will commit violence if necessary to gain some end, as in robbery." The criteria for such offenders was: (1) violence was used as a tool in carrying out some criminal act, typically robbery;

(2) the offender carried a concealed weapon and is not classifiable as culturally, pathologically, or situationally violent.

According to Conrad's theory, the criminally violent offender regards violence as a tool of his trade. He uses it not for personal satisfaction as does the culturally violent, but to gain other ends. Thus the robber, through planning and the judicious use of violence, hopes to gain a certain mastery over his circumstances and reap quick rewards. He does not use violence to inflict deliberate injury. If he can achieve his goal with only a threat of injury to his victim, so much the better.

In a follow-up study of the criminal career occupational history and demographic characteristics of offenders classified in the AHP, Dr. Carol Spencer's findings corroborate Conrad's conclusions that the "criminally violent" type rarely uses actual violence. Spencer reported that 83% of those classified as criminally violent—which would cover the robbers—had no conviction for actual violence at any time in their criminal careers.

"Rarely causing physical injury to their victims when committing their felonies, they were not much given to assaultive behavior at other times. They differ sharply from the other groups where approximately 90% had convictions for actual violence." Spencer also found that fewer of the robbers she studied had a police record before the age of 18 than did other offenders; that juvenile violent offenses were relatively rare.

In a summary of findings on the Criminally Violent group, Dr. Spencer reported: "The relative lack of assaultive behavior, greater consistency of motivation, fewer conflicts with law enforcement and more cautious driving record all suggest better control. The criminally violent channel their aggressions into profitable avenues of robbery rather than into impulsive assaults."

The above findings as to the high degree of control exercised by robbers over the violence at their employ and the very low record of any violence or injuries that result from robberies would seem to suggest that more attention needs to be given to this factor of violence and its reality in the crime of robbery. To the extent that a typical robber is not a violence-prone person and is unlikely to employ violence unless he is provoked or encounters resistance has important meaning and consequences for those who are victims of robberies, as well as for those responsible for preventing and controlling such offenses.

It is far from certain, however, that the relatively small number of injuries experienced in robberies which occurred in past years presents a reliable picture of what is currently happening. As in the drug problem, the non-violent nature of robberies and those who commit them may be changing. . . .

Another important consideration is the intolerable nature of the violence and danger inherent in a crime where serious bodily harm is threatened. This very point was made by [the late] J. Edgar Hoover in discussing bank robberies where the number of physical injuries suffered by victims has been relatively minimal. Referring to "the potential for violence and death inherent" in such robberies, Hoover pointed out that the threat to human life cannot be ignored. Thus the public sense of personal as well as property security requires that the potential, horrendous threat of deadly force and serious bodily harm inherent in a robbery must be taken into full account in assessing the seriousness of the crime, even though the frequency or level of violence actually employed is relatively small. . . .

THE OFFENDER

On the basis of available studies to date, it is apparent that more up-to-date information and far greater research is required in order to obtain a fuller picture of who is responsible today for committing the various types of robbery and how he operates.

Such information as exists tends to be very fragmentary and sketchy, with insufficient detail and often obsolete.

More studies and related data have been

conducted on bank robberies than on possibly any other type of robbery. Yet, after analyzing reports on 238 bank robberies which took place during a three-month period in 1964, the FBI concluded: "There is no such thing as a typical bank robber . . . There is no typical method of operation used by bank robbers."

A training pamphlet on robbery published in 1966 by the International Association of Chiefs of Police describes a number of different types of robberies and tries to provide some guidance with respect to the commission of these crimes and the offenders. It notes that whereas bank robbery used to be committed by highly skilled professional criminals, in recent years a new type of bank robber has emerged who is essentially an amateur and "may strike at any time, sometimes almost compulsively." Store and shop robberies are seen committed by "criminals ranging from the skilled and ruthless gunman to drug addicts." Gasoline stations, particularly the all-night service station, located in outlying areas of a city or on the fringes of the metropolitan community are called "highly vulnerable" targets which attract robbers in the late evening and early morning hours. According to the IACP, the offender who robs residences usually possesses information as to the amount of valuables or currency he may obtain. This home invader is characterized as "one of the most vicious of all robbers," who frequently operates as a member of a gang.

However, too little is known about whether or not a person who is robbing banks or residences is the same or different person who robs chain stores, gas stations, taxicabs, liquor and small retail stores or holds up pedestrians on the street. Nor do we know enough about the motivations or *modus operandi* of such robbers, including which type of offender is apt to be armed and with what kind of weapon or what measures and tactics to employ which will most effectively control and deter him.

Too little is known also about the economic factors involved. In two studies by the Pennsylvania Board of Parole of convicted robbers, it was found that 57% of those involved in the 1950 study and 74% in the 1965 study were unemployed at the time the robbery was committed. This led the Pennsylvania Parole Board to conclude that "a positive relationship exists between the crime of robbery and unemployment." This would tend to corroborate other studies which have emphasized the essentially monetary gain motivation of the robber as the primary factor in this offense. Here again, however, there is inadequate information available on which to draw any useful conclusion and research efforts should be directed towards this need.

The Youthful Nature of the Robber

Studies of robberies by the FBI on a national basis disclosed that young offenders are responsible for a very large proportion of robberies that occur in the United States. The last available figures, covering the year 1968 for example, showed that 75% of all persons arrested for robbery were under the age of 25. Fifty-six percent were under 21 and 33% were juveniles. The FBI noted that youths tend to operate in groups, particularly in strong-arm robberies and most of the juveniles involved in robberies were arrested on charges of strong-arm robberies.

The Chicago study of robberies in the Second District found that sixty-seven percent of robbery offenders were between 14 and 25 years of age. The strong-arm robbers tended to be youthful, 69% being 19 or under. Juveniles between the ages of 14 and 16 accounted for the highest number of strong-arm robberies. The Chicago study also disclosed that 92% of the strong-arm robberies took place on the street. No strong-arm robberies were found to have taken place in any business establishment. A large number of victims were newsboys between the ages of 8 and 15 who were robbed by one, two or three unarmed boys a few years older than themselves. Where there was no resistance, there were usually no injuries.

In a study of crimes of violence involving youth groups or gangs in 17 cities in 1967,

the Task Force on Individual Acts of Violence found that youth groups and gangs were involved in a "significant percentage of all robberies . . ." An analysis of major crimes cleared by arrests showed that 9.5% of youth groups or gangs were involved in armed robbery and 6.8% in unarmed robbery. With respect to groups or gangs where the majority of offenders were juveniles, the percentage involved in armed robbery was 14.1% and in unarmed robberies, 18.6%. However, no youth group or gang was involved in 76% of the armed robberies or in 74% of the unarmed robberies.

In view of the apparent contradictions between the above findings and those reported by the FBI Uniform Crime Reports and in other statistical analyses of robberies, more research is needed to clarify this aspect of robberies.

The Lone Offender

Unlike the study of bank robberies by the FBI, which found that the bank robber worked alone in 72% of the cases, the Pennsylvania Board of Parole study showed that 32% of all robberies studied were committed by a lone robber. More than two-thirds had accomplices. This led the Board of Parole to conclude that another characteristic of robbers is that a large majority do not operate alone, but are assisted by accomplices. (The Pennsylvania study was not limited to bank robberies, however.)

Dr. Donald Newman also found in his study of robbery offenders that the majority had partners in their crimes. These accomplices were not friends as much as someone with whom the robber could share responsibility and guilt for his offense. He also stated that there was little sense of guilt among the offenders studied. Rather, they tended to picture themselves more victimized than their victims. Dr. Newman also concluded that some of the robbers committed the crime deliberately in order to be returned to prison because of their need for a structured environment.

A study conducted by Gerald Wolcott in

March 1967 of 81 convicted robbers incarcerated at the California Conservation Center in Susanville found that 79% of all the robbers (none of whom appeared to have been bank robbers), had accomplices. The study also showed that 40% of all the robberies were committed against lone individuals; and that 65% of these were crimes of opportunity that were committed on the spur of the moment. Such situational spur-of-the moment robberies were likely to be committed by lone robbers and involve a lone victim. . . .

A COMMENT ON DETERRENTS

The studies conducted on robbery raise some serious questions about the validity of accepted deterrents to the crime or robbery. In a study of bank robberies, for example, Dr. Franklin Huddle of the Legislative Reference Service of the Library of Congress noted that the law enforcement profession has long believed and relied on the premise that "crime will be inversely proportional to probability and severity of punishment." Pointing out that these presumed deterrents depend (1) on the perceptions of the robber as to the likelihood and severity of punishment, as well as (2) the rationality of the criminal in acting in accordance with his perceptions, Dr. Huddle questioned whether bank robbers do indeed perceive clearly the risks and penalties that society is prepared to impose and whether such offenders do in fact act rationally on the basis of this perception. For despite the fact that bank robberies have an extremely high rate of apprehension and usually result in very severe sentences for those convicted, these "deterrents" do not in fact stop persons from continuing to rob banks.

A study by the Bureau of Social Science Research on the deterrent value of crime prevention measures as perceived by criminal offenders indicated that insofar as traditional police "deterrents" (such as maximizing police presence and employing aggressive patrol) are concerned, they were not very effective. The report concluded that those

committing serious crime do not tend to be highly rational; either they do not fear the consequences or else they block out the fear during the commission of the crime.

In another study involving convicted robbers, Dr. George Camp, Assistant Warden of the Federal Penitentiary at Marion, Illinois, found that the only significant deterrent to bank robbers examined appeared to be the closeness of a police station to the bank. Neither police patrols nor the capability of police response was found to be considered a deterrent by those engaged in bank robberies. The large amount of cash available, the ease of access and of getting away from the crime scene seemed to outweigh other considerations.

In examining robberies, the attractiveness of the prize and the ease of taking the money from the victim or custodian by the use of the threat of force, appears to make this crime so inviting that large numbers of offenders fail to be deterred by presumed deterrents. The availability of how effective current robbery deterrents are—primarily the risk of detection, apprehension and punishment—therefore needs to be reexamined. This is especially true with respect to the young and nonprofessional offenders who are responsible for such a large proportion of serious crimes like robbery. Factors that might deter older persons do not appear to carry the same weight with these young offenders. So long as the financial reward appears as attractive and easy to obtain as perceived by the offender, all available information indicates that robberies will continue to increase.

Robbery Control and Tactical Measures

The results of inquiries to major police departments across the country pointed to the need for a practical method of developing and exchanging information between cities with common problems on common needs. By way of illustration, a number of communities are currently seeking to develop or improve their robbery response and apprehension capabilities by cordoning off escape routes and assigning police manpower according to predetermined apprehension plans. Philadelphia has developed a relatively successful system which it calls "Operation FIND," while the Kansas City system is tagged "Operation Barrier." Other cities have equally well-developed criminal apprehension systems.

Taxicab hold-ups have been a source of concern to major cities for some time and many police departments have found some sort of signal system atop the taxicab was a valuable aid in alerting passersby and police and serving as a deterrent.

Other examples involve developments to reduce or eliminate the opportunity factor in robberies, such as the exact change and scrip systems to minimize the monetary gain for a would-be robber; the use of inexpensive vaults in commercial establishments, delivery trucks, and other vulnerable targets of the robber.

Law enforcement agencies could profit from the experience and planning that have gone into the design, testing and experience of these and many other measures to control and deter robberies. In this connection, it is recommended that the Institute fund a series of small studies which would assemble, assess and circularize among law enforcement agencies effective control and prevention meausres and tactics designed to deal with specific robbery problems and which would be of application and value to sister agencies. . . .

THE MAKING OF A BURGLAR: Five Life Histories

Pedro R. David

DESCRIPTION OF THE STUDY

The objective of this research project was to explore the criminal justice system from the point of view of the offender, to focus on problems of the criminal justice system and of community life that tend to motivate a potential offender to pursue a life of crime, and to investigate the "deterrent" or "rehabilitative" role of law enforcement agencies, courts, and corrections agencies from the offender's point of view.

These are five life histories as they were told to us in taped interviews by five ex-convicts, four of whom were native New Mexicans. The five were carefully selected after a detailed study of relevant criminal cases in the area. They represent types of criminal patterns highly important in the criminological milieu of Albuquerque and Bernalillo County: burglars and robbers,

From an unpublished paper. Materials based on *The Making of a Burglar,* Albuquerque: University of New Mexico Press, 1973. Pedro David is Professor of Sociology at the University of New Mexico.

most of them involved in the drug spectrum as either addicts or pushers. At the time of the interviews, they were all between 20 and 35 years of age, with the median age of 26.

Since Albuquerque is a heterogeneous community, both from a cultural and ethnic point of view, we selected three Mexican-Americans (one female and two males), one black male, and one Anglo male for the study. We followed a structured interview guide, but subjects were allowed to comment freely on any topic they wished. All interviews were recorded, transcribed, and published with the subjects' permission. Sessions lasted from two to four hours. The study began in February 1972 and was completed in October 1972. . . .

We believe, as Albert Morris said on criminals' views of themselves: "Even when they are lacking in penetration or sincerity, the verbalizations of criminals may have a diagnostic value as great as other overt behavior."

These accounts represent life-styles expressed in the criminals' own words, language patterns, and idiomatic expressions; they were not subjected to any modifications or changes, except as necessary to alter individual names, places, and educational references to ensure anonymity of the subjects. . . .

CRIMINOLOGICAL IMPLICATIONS

It seems plausible to infer from these interviews that property crime and drug addiction in Albuquerque are part of an established system of criminal behavior, if we take into account fencing activities and drug pushers. The presence of "fences" operating in the social scene and acting as providers of the opportunity to dispose of stolen goods provided the essential catalyst for property crime.

It also seems plausible to believe that from early childhood there were few options open to children from broken homes who lived in deprived neighborhoods with little parental supervision and with intensive associations with deviant peer groups (environments in which there is a basic breakdown of norms and values) other than criminal life patterns. The cases described here show intense lack of stable and organized families. All the subjects came from less-advantaged or less-privileged sections of society. As part of their socialization process, they were involved in deviant acts from early life. They were later involved in the escalation of deviance into more severely punished crimes and, finally, were easy prey of the interrelations among drug addiction, burglaries, and other crimes, such as armed robberies. The subjects were involved in what could be called "careers in crime." For example, Jack, the Anglo subject, said: "I started out stealing groceries and shoplifting and from there . . . I was sentenced to fifty years."

The psychology of the burglar—his "intuition" for the right circumstance, time, and place; his profound knowledge of the prevailing mores and folkways that help provide anonymity for his wrongdoing; his relationships with the keystone of property crime, the "fence"; the interrelations between

drugs and crime—all of these were vividly exposed in the interviews. Even the rationalizations of burglars about the effects crime may have on their victims were present, as when Ralph, the black subject, said: "I didn't mind too much about them. I figured all they have to do is call up the insurance man to get his money. Insurance will take care of it."

They count, of course, on impunity, since only a small fraction of their crimes were ever detected. Jack could say that he probably pulled 100 to 150 armed robberies before being caught; and Ralph, in the year he was in Albuquerque, "ripped off about two or three hundred houses."

The subjects agreed that probation and court proceedings had little, if any, deterrent effect. Soledad says: "Each time I went to court, I was sick; but I gave 'em a good story." Jack summarizes all their feelings about the courts when he declares: "At that time, I more or less thought it was a big joke. I'd say, 'Well, they'll give me a chance this time.' I'd know I could do it and get away with it because if they catch me, so what."

Finally, the prison is portrayed by Jack: "It's a jungle, that's what it is." Each of them gave detailed profiles of their experiences in the Santa Fe Penitentiary. When they were on parole, after serving their period, most of them viewed themselves as Jack did: "Well, the first weeks I was out, I had the, you might call it a schizophrenia complex—people staring at me, you know, they all know I was in the penitentiary."

Did they reform? We may answer in Soledad's words: "I feel that the penitentiary did me a whole lot of good . . . just the time . . . the time for you to find yourself. . . . It was a long road, you know, but I've finally come to the end of it. . . ." We may interject that within only a few months after the interviews were taped, Soledad was back in prison.

At this point, it seems important to remark that modern psychotherapy has vigorously stated the importance of an orientation toward the future as a basic step toward spiritual and mental recovery. But orientation toward the future was largely absent in the subjects' lives. All those interviewed were rigidly crystallized into the present. A rational calculation of the risks involved in further criminal behavior appeared in varying degrees of intensity in all the cases interviewed. In the past, they settled the issue in favor of the commission of criminal acts, minimizing the actual probability of being detected and prosecuted. Of course, they considered the intrinsic possibility that some day they would be discovered. But they regarded such an outcome as part of the balance between positive and negative sanctions upon which every human decision rests. Incentives for their criminal involvement existed in direct proportion to the probability that they could "beat the system," even to the degree of rationalizing the potential for harm to their victims. Almost everybody, they said, is "insured" in today's society.

COMMON PATTERNS

Broken Homes and Deviant Environments

Broken homes, criminal or deviant associations from early years, and in some cases even delinquent behavior at home, characterized the childhoods of all of the subjects interviewed.

Soledad del Valle saw her mother become an alcoholic and then commit suicide by taking rat poison, after being divorced by her father.

Ralph was raised by his grandmother in what he calls a "highly criminal environment," and describes the illicit gambling operation conducted in her home.

Jack remarks that his mother was divorced when he was three years old and that: "Sometimes we didn't have the rent or the food, see? ... If we wanted to eat, we had to go out and steal it. ... She [his mother] might not have liked it but she'd never get down to where she'd give you a hard time about it. ... My mother never

knew where I was going or what I was doing or what I was going to do."

Modesto was raised by his godfather (padrino). He never lived with his mother, and he doesn't remember when she married his stepfather. Francisco described his father's excessive alcoholism and how he was eventually found dead in a downtown Albuquerque parking lot after a drinking bout.

They were all left by themselves with no supervision or control. Schools seem to have played no significant role in the formation of their character or moral values. Jack, talking of his teachers and of school asserted that: "The job was a teacher and when the bell rang at the end of the day, they went their way, and you went yours." Modesto, on the contrary, claims that he had good teachers in grade school. His troubles started when he was in junior high.

Their peers generally displayed a similar lack of parental control. Jack was associated with similar types of kids in his neighborhood—"little supervision through their homes or their families, parents didn't care where they were." Jack was sent to the detention home in Boston when he was 12. Like most of those interviewed, he did not take it seriously nor did it have any deterrent effect.

You go to the detention home for 30 days and come out and 30 days isn't really too long. You laugh at it, and say "Well, big deal." They didn't teach you nothin'. They told you to behave yourself and don't do it again.

The court put you on probation, you report to your probation officer once a week or once a month and he asks you, "How are you doing?" "O.K." "Are you staying out of trouble?" "Yeah." Most of the guys would just tell a lie. They aren't staying out of trouble. And you'd be right back on the corner that night.

But like I say, anybody that's been in crime all their life started from the time they were juveniles. You can never say a guy starts crime in his twenties. You might get one guy out of two or three thousand who's never had crime previously and he really did it because he got depressed or he's tight for money or something. Overall, it goes back to the time the kid is eight or nine years old.

Early Involvement with Deviant Behavior

All of the subjects began their deviant behavior (including delinquent acts and in some cases drug use) early in life, some before they were teenagers.

Modesto's friends introduced him to marijuana. He "graduated" to heroin at the age of 17. Asked about his options at the time, he said: "You can't blame no one but yourself. I mean, of course, like having friends that are in the same boat that you are has something to do with it to a certain extent."

Modesto started shoplifting when he was 13. He was placed in the detention home many times and finally spent an extended stretch in a reformatory in Colorado. The first day out, he started smoking marijuana.

Jack also started shoplifting at an early age, although he was never drawn into the drug scene. The reaction of his friends to his first encounter with the juvenile court (at age 12) was: "Well, they ain't gonna do nothin' noway and if they do they give you two weeks, thirty days. No big deal. I never gave it much thought."

Jack was concerned about the lack of effective rehabilitation for juvenile offenders. He advised the interviewers:

Keep institutions but have the correct staff. In other words, don't just bring a persons up off the streets and say, "Well, your qualifications are good. You've never been in trouble, you've got a Ph.D. in this and a master's degree in that" because all these degrees don't really mean nothing unless they can get down and circulate and be part of the group that they're trying to straighten out. . . . Now, if you're understaffed, you're just wasting your time. . . . You put 50 kids on the street and three men can't go out and circulate with them.

In describing his first major delinquent act (grand larceny at the age of seven) Ralph states: "I went downtown and this bank deposit box was wide open and I was curious and I reached in there and pulled out these two big money bags. Like I didn't have a sense of value of money so there I go and so after then . . . I started shoplifting."

Of his reactions to being placed in jail at the age of nine, he said: "I guess that's why I continued to get in trouble because I never feared the police and I've seen a lot of guys that shake just at the mere sight of them. To me, it was just . . . it was funny."

Springer, the correctional institution for boys, was for him "a vacation, a resting period. Soledad went to live with her father and stepmother after her mother's suicide, but she never overcame her bitterness toward them. Her rebelliousness finally led her to try heroin at the age of 15:

I finally ran away from home. . . . On top of that I had a boyfriend that I though would take care of me and he was only 15, a little kid. . . . He was a pusher. He dealt a lot in drugs, you know. . . . He was an addict. When I saw this, I became curious, you know. I was very curious. That's what got me started using drugs. . . . Anyway, that's the first time I ever fixed with heroin.

Early deviance, as a factor of peer involvement, was perhaps most graphic with Francisco. He described it as a learning process:

The way it started out with me, I used to hang around with some older fellows than me, you know. . . . So these two guys that I was getting older. . . . I was learning a little more, you know, just a little more.

Social Psychology of the Burglar

The successful burglar is an up-to-date urban social psychologist. He knows very well when and how to strike. All of the subjects stole regularly, some of them committing an average of 300 burglaries a year. Jack and Ralph, the two nonaddicts, described their craft with an aura of detached professionalism. Jack says:

Usually on the weekends you don't get a burglar . . . just during the week because the man of the family is working. The kids are gone to school, of course. That leaves the house for you. The average housewife is not gonna pay no attention to what's going on next door or across the street unless it's a personal friend.

And, Ralph added:

Maybe I'd walk past this certain house. Maybe I'd walk past it three times in a couple of hours or sometimes I would pretend like I was looking for someone and, if they didn't answer the door, I'd just go around back and break on in. . . . Nine times out of ten I was successful with it.

Jack described his *modus operandi* for commercial burglaries:

Stealing is, well I guess you might say, it's the element of surprise. You know what you're doing but the other person doesn't. Now you're robbing a place or burglarizing a place or whatever you're gonna do. . . . You're only gonna be there three, five minutes. What are the odds of (a policeman) coming in that store during that five minute period? Very slim odds that you're gonna get caught. . . .
You might look at [a place of business] for a week, two weeks, couple of days, see what their routine is, how many people are in the store or place of business at a certain time of the day, maybe 5:00 at night when they're getting ready to close, and there might be only three people there, where at four o'clock there are twenty people there. You watch the place for a period of time, a few days and you can more or less tell the routine every day. But people, especially in this country, are basically in a routine. They have the same routine every day. They go to bed at a certain hour of the night, they get up at a certain hour, they work a certain hour, they open the place of business and they close at a certain time. There's usually a slow period during the day and there's a busy period. . . . And, you pick your weakest point or your weakest hour of the day, which might be the slowest time of the day, that's when he'll rob you. . . . The average burglar in this city right now strikes probably from eleven to one in the mornin.

For a residential burglary, his technique is far more bold:

Well, if I was going to go back into burglarizing right now, I would probably rob a place, if there's nobody there, in the daytime, in broad daylight because the neighbors are not going to suspect anybody coming up there with a truck, in overalls that say ABC Furniture Company, coming in through the front door and moving the furniture out. They're not gonna pay no attention. They may even want to come over and help. A police car comes up, you're blocking the traffic. He may get out and direct the traffic around your truck. He's not gonna think nothing of it.

Francisco, also, had a detailed methodology for selecting houses to burglarize: "If you catch 'em there and like I said, you're pretty well, you know perceptive, you see 'em the way they're dressed . . . and you can tell . . . if they're housewives or . . . they're there all the time."

All of the subjects reported strikingly high and relatively stable incomes from crime—far higher than they could expect to earn in the normal job market. Ralph, for example, said he averaged $500 to $550 a week. Prior to their last conviction, Soledad and her husband, both addicts, stole $400 to $500 a day to support their habit. Their levels of "success" in their chosen "professions," then, were far greater than any of them could hope to achieve in "straight" society.

Interrelations Between Drug Addiction and Crime

There is once more, through the data collected, ample evidence of the direct reciprocal relationship between drug addiction and crime. Three of the subjects (Modesto, Soledad, and Francisco) were heroin addicts and relied on burglary and shoplifting to support their habits. Ralph admitted to popping pills, mainly amphetamines ("as many as 2000 milligrams a day"). Only Jack, who regarded himself as a professional thief, remained drug free.

Soledad del Valle elaborated:

Every day we would have to steal. We'd have to steal at least $300 worth of merchandise a day to support the habit we had. At first it started out to be about five dollars you know.... Days that we would have good luck ... and get a whole lot of money, you know, like people would think it would last us for a week but an addict isn't that way. The more money he has, the more he shoots, you know.

Modesto and Francisco were very frank about their criminal activity in support of their heroin habits. Modesto, an addict since the age of 17, described how heroin caused him to lose his job and freely admits that when he needed money: "I'd go steal or go shoplift or things of that nature."

Francisco, talking about his involvement with heroin, explained:

Before, even before I went to Springer I was already messing with it but very, very slightly, you know, and after I got out I got more involved and I finally got hooked.... I had a habit of about oh ... 14, 12 caps a day ... about $75 to $100 more or less a day.... What I used to do to get the money? Well, like I used to ... sneak thief.... I would go up to the Heights or anywhere and pull, you know, some burglaries....

Relationships with Fences

The burglar's reliance on the fence is well-documented in all of these accounts. Each of the subjects described the integral relationship of fencing activity with burglary. Their dependence on the fence for quick conversion of stolen goods into money and for fast disposal of "hot" property to avoid arrest was a necessary component of their "success" and indicates that no city can sustain a consistently high burglary rate without well-established, sophisticated fencing operations.

The intervention of fences was well explained by Ralph:

Well, most fences, you know, they'll come to you. They'll look through the records and say, like they'll go around town and check your record.... Like they'll go down to the police department and ask them to check this guy's record, let them have the informa-

tion. And, if he feels like you're a pretty safe dude, he'll stop you one day and he might tell you, say "Well, I need a typewriter, and adding machines, stereo console" or something like that.

He's the businessman type dude, you know.... He has a certain air about him, you know.... You can detect it right away, you know.... He may run a bar, grocery store, shoeshine parlor. Just something to put up a front, you know, so he won't get busted.

Jack was certain that:

In any large city there's always a fence system. If you were raised in a city, just through the grapevine or being associated with different thieves, you're gonna meet the fences.... Like I say, if I had a load of supplies right now, I know where to get rid of them. Or, if I wanted to buy something that was hot for a cheap price, I'd know where to go right now....

Soledad said:

Everyday we'd go to about eight stores. What we'd do is we'd get orders for people you know.... They'd give us an order— "clothes for our daughter and clothes for us." They'd give us the size and how many they wanted, ... what price range and we'd go out and we'd get these things for them and we'd bring them back and sell it to them half price.... Any addict will give things away.... Something worth $100 and an addict would let it go for $25, you know, because it's hot or stolen. There's been times that we were so sick, then we'd have something that was worth maybe $50, $60 and we'd say, "Here, just give me $5," enough for a cap you know.

Ralph, who sold his stolen goods at 75 percent of their price most of the time, said he always got almost full value. On the other hand, Modesto "never did get a good price" even though he was selling to individuals and not to fences. Fences, for him, were a last resort: "It was like ... say I got a $50 record player or a $50 radio. You were lucky if you got $20, $25."

Francisco, talking about his relationship with fences, said:

As a matter of fact, I used to borrow money from them all the time. I used to borrow $200, $300 and I used to pay it about a week later. . . . Well, let's say you would lend me $100 at that time. Let's say, you know, like you would lend me $100 and maybe two, three, four days later I stole a big old color T.V. and I say, "Well I owe you $100—here. I'll see you." And, you're paid . . . and that's the way it went. See, but these people they can afford to, even if they get a little bust on them, they can afford it, because they got the money, you know. See they could get some of the best lawyers in town. I say if they can do that and get away with it, what they call little is buying hot stock from somebody. . . . They get away with it because they got the money, right? . . . They'll pay that cash, you know. Like if you go to a store you pay about $900 for something like that. But they'll pay about $200 or $300 for it.

Impact of Police, Courts, and Correctional Institutions

The deterrent and rehabilitative impact of police, courts, and correctional institutions was generally described by the subjects as minimal, especially during the juvenile years, characterized by light treatment and short sentences. All of the subjects seemed to feel that inequality in the system was more a factor of the income level of the offender rather than his ethnic background—that society meted out harsher punishment to the poor. Their accounts seemed to indicate that any deterrent effects of the system were more a function of the offender's desire to avoid future contact rather than the counseling, vocational training, and other "rehabilitative" programs offered by the system.

About the police, Jack said: "Well, they're after one thing. If you did something wrong, they want to catch you and prosecute you. . . . Most of them will try to use force to scare you."

Modesto, talking about county detention and courts, said:

The Juvenile Home didn't do nothing to me in the way of straightening me out or it was too easy for me compared to the county jail. . . . It's not fair. . . . I could be caught with a T.V. in my hands and I couldn't get myself a lawyer or anything like that. I'd probably get sent up to Santa Fe. The next guy could be caught with the same T.V. in his hands but with money in his pocket or his family with money in their pocket. He wouldn't go to Santa Fe. So it just depends on who you are, who your family is."

Of prison, he said:

If you were an Anglo, a Chicano, or a black . . . if you were an informer, you would have it made. . . . They have no understanding whatsoever. . . . Well, you know, that you're supposed to get up . . . and be ready for work. Now, they don't have to go around picking up your bunk and throwing it down or going in the dormitory and hollering like wild Indians. . . . They can show you all types of paper where it says "We have this program and this program and this program." It looks beautiful in writing man, but in reality it's not what it says on that piece of paper. They do have a plumbing shop, electrical shop, all the vocational things but what good if you go over there at 8:00 in the morning and sit with a magazine?

Jack talks of ethnic segregation in the Santa Fe Penitentiary: "You have your black cliques, you have your Chicano cliques, then you have your gray cliques (whites). . . . Everybody up there has a weapon."

To the question, how do inmates get drugs, he replied:

Well, most of it comes through the guards. . . . Probably the other half comes in through the visiting room. . . . I'd say, in a week up there, you'd probably get 50 caps of heroin, maybe a pound of marijuana, maybe 1,000 pills, quite a bit. The only way you can buy narcotics up there is with green money. . . . There's no secrets in the penitentiary. No matter what you do or what you are, what are your causes for being there, they always know. . . . The strong survive, the weak don't.

He described at length the homosexual problem:

72

You got a population of 700 and there are probably about 150 homosexuals up there—free world homosexuals and penitentiary homosexuals.... You're there by yourself with all the rest of the guys.... You know, no guard there.... You go up there on a tour, you see everything looks real dandy.... But, when you live there with the guys you see things that you don't normally see on a tour.

Frequently, Jack pointed to the need for more adequate staffing and supervision:

I've noticed in this state along with other states, this is a very poor state because the legislature, your city and state government won't give you the funds to hire the staff you need. You're understaffed in every institution I've seen in this state that deals with juveniles or adults and unless you have the right amount of people on your staff with the right qualifications and enough offered you can't do a good job anywhere.

THE CONVERSION PROCESS

Once in prison, most of the subjects reported a gradual attitudinal transformation, beginning with great hostility and bitterness toward the "system" and its "perpetrators" (lawyers, judges, and, especially, prison officials and guards), gradual acceptance of prison life, and finally something that might be described as a "conversion" process or the desire to "go straight." In most cases, the onset of the conversion process seemed to be a direct function of the subject's ability to foresee the possibility of parole (i.e., having passed the midpoint of that portion of his sentence which must be served before he is eligible for parole). It was at that point that most of the subjects began to more heavily blame themselves rather than the system for their plight and began to take an active interest in various rehabilitative programs that might enhance their chances for parole.

Jack described the process for us: "I finally sat down and thought, 'What in the hell am I doing? If I want to get out of here, I'd better straighten up and try to do something that will benefit myself instead of the other guy.' "

Modesto expressed the same views:

My main thought was that, as I looked around me, I said to myself that, "For what purpose was I put on this earth?" Being locked up behind bars was not it. That was my constant thought. Cause I feel that being locked up is not for me, and by going back to the same thing that I was doing is going to lead to that.... To myself, I mean for my own benefit, it did me a lot of good because I don't know ... my outlook changed from what it was.

Ralph claimed that when he was committed, he was already reformed, although he still had difficulty in adjusting:

Because I finally realized that they were taking away my freedom you know, which was what meant so much to me and I finally knew what freedom meant. So really they didn't have to send me up because I was already reformed just by fear alone.... It took a little while for me to get adjusted. Like I got into quite a few fights, arguments. I couldn't get along with a lot of the guards that worked up there.

It is difficult to assess the longevity of the "conversion" process. Probably it varies considerably from individual to individual—ranging perhaps from months (or even weeks) to a lifetime. Soledad del Valle stayed out of prison only a few months, and Francisco, by his own admission after the taping sessions, appeared headed in a similar direction.

Perhaps Ralph stated the problem most eloquently:

Like I've seen quite a few losers that won't ever come out and I've seen a lot of them return and I've tried to figure out why. I guess they say they get institutionalized, you know. Like they stay there so long that's all they know. When they're free, they can't face reality out here. It's supposed to be a cold dark world.

LARCENY-THEFT

Uniform Crime Reports

Larceny-theft is the unlawful taking or stealing of property or articles of value without the use of force, violence, or fraud. It includes crimes such as shoplifting, pocket-picking, purse-snatching, thefts from autos, thefts of auto parts and accessories, bicycle thefts, etc. In the Uniform Crime Reporting Program this crime category does not include embezzlement, "con" games, forgery, and worthless checks. Auto theft, of course, is excluded from this category for crime reporting purposes inasmuch as it is a separate Crime Index offense.

VOLUME

In 1972 there were 1,837,800 offenses of larceny $50 and over, which was a decrease from 1,875,200 such crimes in 1971. This offense makes up 31 percent of the Crime Index total. From a seasonal standpoint, the volume of larceny was highest during the summer months of 1972.

When considering all larceny, $50 and over in value and under $50, the number of offenses for 1972 was 4,101,900. The total larceny offenses for 1971 was 4,371,700. The 1972 total larceny figure decreased 6 percent from 1971.

Geographically, the volume of larceny $50 and over was highest in the Southern States which reported 27 percent of the total number, followed by the Western States with 26 percent, the North Central States with 25 percent, and the Northeastern States with 21 percent.

LARCENY RATE

During 1972, the larceny crime rate was 883 offenses per 100,000 inhabitants, a decrease of 3 percent from the 1971 rate. The rate has increased 66 percent since 1967. In

From *Crime in the United States 1972,* Washington: Superintendent of Documents, 1973, pp. 21–25.

1972, the large core cities registered a larceny rate of 1,105 per 100,000 inhabitants. The suburban larceny rate was 890 and the rural rate was 364. Viewed geographically, the Western States reported the highest larceny rate with 1,350 offenses per 100,000 inhabitants which was 1 percent below 1971. The Northeastern States had a rate of 775 down 10 percent; the North Central States 808 down 1 percent, and the Southern States 771 reported a decrease of 2 percent in the rate.

NATURE OF LARCENY-THEFT

The average value of property stolen in each larceny in 1972 was $111, up from $95 in 1967, and $74 in 1960. This average value includes losses from the large number of thefts under $50 in value. When average value is applied to the estimated crimes in this category, the dollar loss to victims was in excess of $475 million. It is true that a portion of the goods stolen was recovered and returned to victims, but the relatively low percentage of these crimes cleared by arrest, and the lack of specific identification characteristics on such property indicates these recoveries did not materially reduce the overall loss. In addition, many offenses in this category, particularly where the value of the stolen goods is small, never come to police attention.

In 1972, the average value of goods and property reported stolen from victims of pickpockets was $98, by purse-snatchers $53, by shoplifters $25, by thefts from autos $149, and by miscellaneous thefts from buildings $187.

From year to year, the distribution of larceny as to type of theft remains relatively constant. As in prior years, a major portion of these thefts, 35 percent, represented thefts of auto parts and accessories and other thefts from automobiles. Other major types of thefts which contributed to the

Table 3–1. Larceny Analysis, 1972
(Percent distribution)

Classification	Area			
	Total United States	Cities Over 250,000	Suburban	Rural
Pocket-picking	1.0	2.0	0.4	0.3
Purse-snatching	2.2	4.3	0.7	0.4
Shoplifting	10.8	10.5	9.4	4.0
From autos (except accessories)	17.3	18.8	15.7	14.7
Auto accessories	17.5	20.1	18.1	13.6
Bicycles	16.5	12.1	17.5	4.9
From buildings	17.0	18.6	14.9	16.5
From coin-operated machines	1.4	1.1	1.3	1.5
All others	16.3	12.5	22.0	44.1
Total	100.0	100.0	100.0	100.0

large number of these crimes were thefts from buildings and stolen bicycles with 17 percent each. Miscellaneous types of larcenies, not falling into any of the specific categories for which data were collected, made up 16 percent of the total. The remainder was distributed among pocket-picking, purse-snatching, shoplifting, and thefts from coin-operated machines.

CLEARANCES

The nature of larceny, a crime of opportunity, sneak thievery, and petty unobserved thefts, makes it an extremely difficult offense for law enforcement officers to solve.

A lack of witnesses and the tremendous volume of these crimes work in the offender's favor. In 1972, 20 percent of all larceny offenses brought to police attention were solved. Involvement of the young age group is demonstrated by the fact that 40 percent of these crimes which were cleared in the Nation's cities were solved by arrest of persons under 18 years of age. Juvenile clearance figures for suburban areas and rural areas were 42 percent and 27 percent respectively.

The larceny clearance percentage for the cities over 250,000 inhabitants was 21 percent. The suburbs reported a 16 percent clearance rate and the rural areas an 18 percent rate.

AUTO THEFT

Uniform Crime Reports

In Uniform Crime Reporting, auto theft is defined as the unlawful taking or stealing of a motor vehicle, including attempts. This definition excludes taking for temporary use by those persons having lawful access to the vehicle.

From Crime in the United States 1972, Washington: Superintendent of Documents, 1973, pp. 25–28.

VOLUME

In 1972, 881,000 motor vehicles were reported stolen. This is a 6 percent decrease compared to 1971 when 941,600 motor vehicles were reported stolen. Geographically, the volume of auto theft in 1972 was highest in the Northeastern States which reported 31 percent of the total number followed by the North Central States with 25 percent. The Western States reported 23 percent and the Southern States reported the remainder. This crime made up 15 percent of the total Crime Index offense volume. Seasonal variations during 1972 disclosed the volume of auto theft was highest during the month of September.

AUTO THEFT RATE

The 1972 auto theft rate of 423 offenses per 100,000 inhabitants is 7 percent lower than in 1971. Since 1967, the auto theft rate has risen 28 percent. People in cities with over one million population were deprived more often of their motor vehicles in 1972 than in any other population group, with 10 thefts per 1,000 inhabitants.

Nationally, the auto theft rate in large core cities with 250,000 or more inhabitants was 967 which was a decrease of 12 percent as compared to the rate in 1971. The suburban areas had a decrease of 6 percent in the auto theft rate which was 288 per 100,000 inhabitants in 1972. The rural areas had an auto theft rate of 70, which was the same as in 1971.

Regionally the Western States had the highest auto theft rate in 1972. This rate was 555, a decrease of 4 percent from 1971. The Northeastern States had a rate of 541 per 100,000 inhabitants which was a decrease of 10 percent. The North Central States had a rate of 383 which was 6 percent lower than the prior year and the Southern States reported a decrease of 7 percent in the auto theft rate to 295 auto thefts per 100,000 inhabitants.

Across the Nation in 1972, one of every 109 registered automobiles was stolen. Re-gionally, this rate was the highest in the Northeastern States where 13 cars per 1,000 registered vehicles were stolen. In the other three regions the figures were 11 in the Western States, 8 in the North Central States, and 6 in the Southern States.

NATURE OF AUTO THEFT

Auto theft rates again clearly indicate that this crime is primarily a large city problem, since the highest rates appear in the most heavily populated sections of the Nation. In 1972, the average value of stolen automobiles was $936 at the time of theft.

CLEARANCES

Law enforcement agencies were successful in solving 17 percent of the auto thefts by arrest of the offender.

In the Nation's largest cities 17 percent of auto thefts were cleared during 1972. Police in the suburban areas were somewhat less successful, clearing 16 percent. Throughout the Nation auto theft clearance percentages ranged from 12 percent in the Middle Atlantic States to over 20 percent in the South Atlantic States.

In all geographic divisions and population groups the participation of the young age group population is indicated by the high proportion of these clearances which were through the arrest of persons under 18 years of age. In the large core cities, 37 percent of the auto thefts cleared were cleared by arrests in this age group while juveniles accounted for 39 percent of the solutions in the suburbs and 34 percent in the rural areas.

THE BEHAVIOR OF THE SYSTEMATIC CHECK FORGER
Edwin M. Lemert

. . . The five elements of the behavior system of the thief are as follows: (1) stealing is

From *Social Problems*, 6, No. 2 (Fall 1958), 141–48. Reprinted by permission. Lemert is Professor of Sociology at University of California, Davis.

made a regular business; (2) every act is carefully planned, including the use of the "fix"; (3) technical skills are used, chiefly those of manipulating people; this differentiates the thief from other professional criminals; (4) the thief is migratory but uses a specific city as a headquarters; and (5) the thief has criminal associations involving acquaintances, congeniality, sympathy, understandings, rules, codes of behavior, and a special language.

Altogether 72 persons currently serving sentences for check forgery and writing checks with insufficient funds were studied. Three additional check offenders were contacted and interviewed outside of prison. The sample included eight women and 67 men, all of whom served time in California correctional institutions.

Thirty of the 75 check criminals could be classified as systematic in the sense that they (1) thought of themselves as check men; (2) had worked out or regularly employed a special technique of passing checks; and (3) had more or less organized their lives around the exigencies or imperatives of living by means of fraudulent checks. The remaining 45 cases represented a wide variety of contexts in which bogus check passing was interspersed with periods of stable employment and family life, or was simply an aspect of alcoholism, gambling, or one of a series of criminal offenses having little or no consistency.

FINDINGS

... The behavior of the persons falling into the systematic check forgery category qualified only in a very general way as professional crime. In other words, although it is possible to describe these forgeries as *systematic*, it is questionable whether more than a small portion of them can be subsumed as *professional* under the more general classification of professional theft. A point-by-point comparison will serve to bring out the numerous significant differences between systematic forgery and professional theft.

Forgery as a "Regular Business"

It is questionable whether check men look upon their crimes as a "regular business" in the same way as do members of "other occupational groups" who "wish to make money in safety." In virtually all cases the motiva-

tion proved to be exceedingly complex. This fact was self-consciously recognized and expressed in different ways but all informants revealed an essential perplexity or conflict about their criminal behavior. The following statement may be taken as illustrative:

Nine out of ten check men are lone wolves. Those men who work in gangs are not real check men. They do it for money; we do it for something else. It gives us something we need. Maybe we're crazy....

The conflicts expressed involved not merely the rightness or wrongness of behavior; they also disclosed a confusion and uncertainty as to the possibility of living successfully or safely by issuing false checks. All of the cases, even the few who had a history of professional thieving, admitted that arrest and imprisonment are inevitable. None knew of exceptions to this, although one case speculated that "It might be done by an otherwise respected business man who made one big spread and then quit and retired."

The case records of the systematic check forgers gave clear testimony of this. Generally they had but shortlived periods of freedom, ranging from a few months to a year or two at the most, followed by imprisonment. Many of the cases since beginning their forgery careers had spent less total time outside prisons than within, a fact corroborated by the various law-enforcement officers queried on the point.

Many of the check men depicted their periods of check writing as continuous sprees during which they lived "fast" and luxuriously. Many spoke of experiencing considerable tension during these periods, and two cases developed stomach ulcers which caused them to "lay off at resorts." A number gambled and drank heavily, assertedly to escape their internal stress and sense of inevitable arrest. A number spoke of gradual build-up of strain and a critical point just before their arrest at which they became demoralized and after which they "just didn't care any more" or "got tired of running." The arrests of several men having a very long experience with checks resulted from blunders in technique of which they were aware at the time they made them. Some of the men gave themselves up to detectives or FBI agents at this point.

In general the picture of the cool, calculating professional with prosaic, matter-of-fact attitudes toward his crimes as a trade or occupation supported by rationalizations of a subculture was not valid for the cases in question.

Planning as an Aspect of Forgery

In regard to the second element of professional theft—planning—the behavior of check forgers is again divergent. Actually the present techniques of check passing either preclude precise planning or make it unnecessary. Although systematic check passers undeniably pay careful attention to such things as banking hours, the places at which checks are presented, and the kinds of "fronts" they employ, these considerations serve only as generalized guides for their crimes. Most informants held that situations have to be *exploited as they arise,* with variation and flexibility being the key to success. What stands out in the behavior of systematic check forgers is the rapid tempo—almost impulsiveness—with which they work.

The cases seemed to agree that check forgers seldom attempt to use the "fix" in order to escape the consequences of their crimes. The reason for this is that although one or a small number of checks might be made good, the systematic forger has too many bad checks outstanding and too many victims to mollify by offering restitution. Although the forger may be prosecuted on the basis of only one or two checks, ordinarily the prosecuting attorney will have a choice of a large number of complaints upon which to act. About the best the check forger can hope for through fixing activities is a short sentence or a sentence to jail rather than to prison.

Technical Skills

Although the systematic check man relies upon technical skills—those of manipulating

others—these are usually not of a high order, nor do they require a long learning period to master. From the standpoint of the appearance of the check or the behavior involved at the time of its passing, there need, of course, be no great difference between passing a bad check and passing a good check. This is particularly true of personal checks, which are at least as favored as payroll checks by check men.

When check men impersonate others or when they assume fictitious roles, acting ability is required. To the extent that elaborate impersonations are relied upon by the forger, his check passing takes on qualities of a confidence game. Most of the check men showed strong preference, however, for simple, fast-moving techniques. A number expressed definite dislike for staged arrangements, such as that of the "out of town real estate buyer" or for setting up a fictitious business in a community, then waiting several weeks or a month before making a "spread" of checks. As they put it, they "dislike the slow build-up involved."

Mobility

Like the thief, the systematic forger is migratory. Only one check man interviewed spoke of identifying himself with one community, and even he was reluctant to call it a headquarters. Generally check men are migratory within regions.

Associations

The sharpest and most categorical difference between professional theft and systematic forgery lies in the realm of associations. In contrast to pickpockets, shoplifters, and con men, whose criminal techniques are implicitly cooperative, most check men with highly developed systems work alone, carefully avoiding contacts and interaction with other criminals. Moreover, their preference for solitude and their secretiveness gives every appearance of a highly generalized reaction; they avoid not only cooperative crime but also any other kinds of association with criminals. They are equally selective and cautious in their contacts and associations with the non-criminal population, preferring not to become involved in any enduring personal relationships.

A descriptive breakdown of the 30 check forgers classified as systematic bears out this point. Only four of the 30 had worked in check passing gangs. Two of these had acted as "fences" who organized the operations. . . .

Three other systematic check forgers did not work directly with other criminals but had criminal associations of a *contractual* nature. One oldtime forger familiar with the now little-used methods for forging signatures and raising checks usually sold checks to passers but never had uttered [passed] any of his forgeries. Two men were passers who purchased either payroll checks from a "hot printer" or stolen checks from burglars. Apart from the minimal contacts necessary to sell or obtain a supply of checks, all three men were lone operators and very seclusive in their behavior.

Six of the 30 systematic forgers worked exclusively with one other person, usually a girl or "broad." The check men seemed to agree that working with a girl was equivalent to working alone. These pairs ordinarily consisted of the check man and some girl not ordinarily of criminal background with whom he had struck up a living arrangement and for whom he felt genuine affection. The girl was used either to make out the checks or to pass them. In some cases she was simply used as a front to distract attention. Some men picked up girls in bars or hotels and employed them as fronts without their knowledge.

The remaining 17 of the 30 systematic check forgers operated on a solitary basis. The majority of these argued that contact with others is unnecessary to obtain and pass a supply of checks. Most of them uttered personal checks. However, even where they made use of payroll or corporation checks they contrived to manufacture or obtain them without resorting to interaction with criminal associates or intermediaries. For example, one Nisei check man arranged with a printer to make up checks for a fraternal organization of which he represented himself as secretary-treasurer. Another man frequented business offices at noon time, and when the clerk left the office, helped himself to a supply of company checks, in one instance stealing a check-writing machine for his purposes.

It was difficult to find evidence of anything more than rudimentary congeniality, sympathy, understandings, and shared rules of behavior among the check forgers, including those who had worked in gangs. Rather the opposite seemed true, suspicion and distrust marking their relationships with one another. One organizer of a gang, for example, kept careful account of all the checks he issued to his passers and made them return torn off corners of checks in case they were in danger of arrest and had to get rid of them. Only two of the thirty forgers indicated that they had at times engaged in recreational activities with other criminals. Both of these men were lone wolves in their work. . .

The two men who had organized gangs of check passers worked with a set of rules, but they were largely improvised and laid down by the fence rather than voluntarily recognized and obeyed by the passers. The other check men with varying degrees of explicitness recognized rules for passing checks—rules learned almost entirely on an individual trial-and-error basis. The informants insisted that "you learn as you go" and that one of the rules was "never use another man's stunt."

Such special morality as was recognized proved to be largely functional in derivation. Thus attitudes toward drinking and toward picking up women for sexual purposes were pretty much the result of individual perceptions of what was likely to facilitate or hamper the passing or checks or lead to arrest. Many of the men stated that since they were dealing primarily with business, professional, and clerical persons, their appearance and behavior had to be acceptable to these people. "Middle class" is probably the best term to describe their morality in most areas.

Careful inquiries were made to discover the extent to which the check men were familiar with and spoke an argot. Findings proved meager. Many of the men had a superficial acquaintance with general prison slang, but only four men could measurably identify and reproduce the argot of check forgery or that of that of thieves. . . .

INTERPRETATION

. . . In the past forgery was a much more complex procedure in which a variety of false instruments such as bank notes, drafts, bills of exchange, letters of credit, registered bonds, and post office money orders as well as checks were manufactured or altered and foisted off. A knowledge of chemicals, papers, inks, engraving, etching, lithography, and penmanship as well as detailed knowledge of bank operations were prime requisites for success. The amounts of money sought were comparatively large, and often they had to be obtained through complex monetary transactions. The technological characteristics of this kind of forgery made planning, timing, specialization, differentiation of roles, morale, and organization imperative. Capital was necessary for living expenses during the period when preparations for the forgeries were being made. Intermediates between the skilled forger and the passers were necessary so that the latter could swear that the handwriting on the false negotiable instruments was not theirs and so that the forger himself was not exposed to arrest. A "shadow" was often used for protection against the passer's temptation to abscond with the money and in order to alert the others of trouble at the bank. "Fall" money was accumulated and supplied to assist the passer when arrested. Inasmuch as forgery gangs worked together for a considerable length of time, understandings, congeniality, and rules of behavior, especially with regard to the division of money, could and did develop. In short, professional forgery was based upon the technology of the period.

Although precise dating is difficult, the heyday of professional forgery in this country probably began after the Civil War and lasted through the 1920's. It seems to have corresponded with the early phases of industrialization and commercial development before business and law-enforcement agencies developed methods and organization for preventing forgery and apprehending the offenders. Gradually technological developments in inks, papers, protectographs, and check-writing machines made the forging of signatures and the manufacture of false negotiable instruments more difficult. . . . The establishment of a protective committee by the American Bankers Association in 1894, related merchants' protective agencies, and improvements in police methods have made the risks of organized professional forgery exceedingly great.

Check gangs have always been vulnerable to arrest but this vulnerability has been multiplied many times by the large amounts of evidence left behind them in the form of countless payroll checks. Vulnerability is also heightened by the swiftness of communication today. If one person of a check-passing gang is arrested and identifies his associates, it becomes a relatively simple matter for police to secure their arrest. A sexually exploited and angered female companion may easily do the same to the check man. This goes far to explain the extreme seclusiveness of systematic check forgers and their almost abnormal fear of stool pigeons or of being "fingered." The type of persons who can be engaged as passers—unattached women, bar waitresses, drug addicts, alcoholics, petty thieves, and transient unemployed persons—also magnifies the probabilities that mistakes will be made and precludes the growth of a morale which might prevent informing to the police. These conditions also explain the fact that when the forger does work with someone it is likely to be one other person upon whom he feels he can rely with implicit confidence. Hence the man-woman teams in which the woman is in love with the man, or the case of two homosexual girls, or of two brothers check-passing teams.

Further evidence that organized forgery is a hazardous type of crime, difficult to professionalize under modern conditions, is indicated by the fact that the organizer or fence is apt to be an older criminal with a long record, whose handwriting methods are so well known that he has no choice other than to work through passers. Even then he does it with recognition that arrest is inevitable.

A factor of equal importance in explaining the decline of professional organized forgery has been the increasingly widespread use of business and payroll checks as well as personal checks. Whereas in the past the use of checks was confined to certain kinds of business transactions, mostly involving banks, today it is ubiquitous. Attitudes of business people and their clerical employees have undergone great change, and only the most perfunctory identification is necessary to cash many kinds of checks. Check men recognize this in frequent unsolicited comments that passing checks is "easy." Some argue that the form of the check is now relatively unimportant to passing it, that "you can pass a candy bar wrapper nowadays with the right front and story." It is for this reason that the systematic check man does not have to resort to criminal associates or employ the more complex professional procedures used in decades past.

These facts may also account for the presence among lone-wolf check forgers of occasional persons with the identification, orientation, skills, codes, and argot of the thief. Case histories as well as the observations of informants show that older professional criminals in recent decades have turned to check passing because they face long sentences for additional crimes or sentencing under habitual criminal legislation. They regard checks as an "easy racket" because in many states conviction makes them subject to jail sentences rather than imprisonment. Check passing may be a last resort for the older criminal.

The presence of the occasional older professional thief in the ranks of check forgers also may token a general decline and slow disappearance of professional thieving. One professional thief turned check passer had this to say:

I'm a thief—a burglar—but I turned to checks because it's getting too hard to operate. Police are a lot smarter now, and they have better methods. People are different nowadays too; they report things more. It's hard to trust anyone now. Once you could trust cab drivers: now you can't. We live in a different world today.

THE CHECK FORGER AS AN ISOLATE

The preference of many systematic check forgers for solitary lives and their avoidance of primary-group associations among criminals may also be explicable in terms of their educational characteristics and class origins. The history of forgery reveals that in medieval times it was considered to be the special crime of the clerical class, as indeed it had to be inasmuch as the members of this class monopolized writing skills. It also seems to be true from the later history of the crime that it has held a special attraction for more highly educated persons, for those of higher socio-economic status and those of "refined" or artistic tastes. The basic method of organized forgery is stated to have been invented and perfected in England, not by criminals but by a practicing barrister of established reputation in 1840. . . .

All of this is not to say that less-educated persons do not frequently pass bad checks but rather that the persons who persist in the behavior and develop behavior systems of forgery seem much more likely than other criminals to be drawn from a segment of the population distinguished by a higher socio-economic status. Generally this was true of the systematic forgers in this study. Eight of the 30 had completed two or more years of college. Fourteen of the 30 had fathers who were or had been in the professions and business, including a juvenile court judge, a minister, a postmaster of a large city, and three very wealthy ranch owners. One woman came from a nationally famous family of farm implement manufacturers. Four others had siblings well established in business and the professions, one of whom was an attorney general in another state. Two of the men had been successful businessmen themselves before becoming check men.

The most important implication of these data is that systematic check forgers do not seem to have had criminal antecedents or early criminal associations. For this reason, as well as for technical reasons, they are not likely to seek out or to be comfortable in informal associations with other criminals who have been products of early and lengthy socialization and learning in a criminal sub-culture. It also follows that their morality and values remain essentially "middle" or "upper" class and that they seldom integrate these with the morality of the professional criminal. This is reflected in self-attitudes in which many refer to themselves as "black sheep" or as a kind of Dr. Jekyll—Mr. Hyde person. Further support for this interpretation comes from their status in prison where, according to observations of themselves and others, they are marginal so far as participation in the primary groups of the prison is concerned. . . .

PROPERTY NORMS AND LOOTING: THEIR PATTERNS IN COMMUNITY CRISES

E. L. Quarantelli and Russell R. Dynes

Massive civil disturbances are not new in American society. And since the turn of the century at least, blacks as well as white citizens have participated on a large scale in intermittent street disorders that peaked in 1919 in the famous Chicago riot, and again in 1943 in the equally well known Detroit racial clash. However, starting [about 1964] a somewhat new pattern involving the conflict of blacks and community law enforcement agencies appeared.

From 1964 through September 1969 these disturbances have numbered in the high hundreds. At least 189 of them can be considered major incidents. At a very minimum, looting occurred in 122 of these events. Looters have perhaps struck 10,000 different stores, buildings and other places in both the major and minor incidents. The dollar cost of the loot taken—difficult to estimate because it is impossible to distinguish from losses stemming from vandalism and burning, has probably been over $55 million. Just by late spring of 1968, about 60,000 persons had been arrested for looting and directly related activities.

Scholarly, ideological, political and other explanations of the civil disturbances as a whole abound in the literature. There have been somewhat fewer systematic attempts to account for looting behavior, which is not only recognized as a major feature of such events but also as a basic change from patterns in pre-1960 disturbances. The explanations advanced tend to be predominately variations upon one theme. Looters are viewed as manifesting personal desocialization under stress. Looting is seen as deviant behavior of individuals and is interpreted as primarily being expressive in function. Our position is that a rather different perception of this phenomena in civil disturbances is required than is currently held by many social scientists as well as most laymen.

We develop this point of view in what follows by: (1) contrasting two different perspectives on massive looting behavior; (2) noting differences in patterns of looting in dissensus and in consensus situations (i.e., between civil disturbances and natural disasters); (3) advancing an explanation of loot-

From *Phylon*, 31 (Summer 1970), pp. 168–82 E.L. Quarantelli and Russell R. Dynes are Professors of Sociology at The Ohio State University and Co-Directors of the Disaster Research Center.

ing in terms of the emergence of new group norms, particularly those pertaining to property, at times of major crises; (4) suggesting that massive looting has become a semi-institutionalized response pattern even though a less prominent feature of civil disturbances since mid-1968; and, (5) indicating what accounts for the failure of contemporary social scientists to see looting as normative behavior.

THE INDIVIDUAL PERSPECTIVE ON LOOTING

Most people, governmental and other organizational officials who have to deal with the problem as well as many academicians essentially have an invalid overall perspective about the looting behavior seen in recent ghetto disturbances in American cities. They seek the explanation for looting in the psychological makeup or characteristics of the individual. We believe that the evidence at hand does not support such a view.

Although the basic theme is the same, this perspective on looting takes variant forms depending upon the sophistication of the explainer. At the simpler end of a continuum are explanations that rest on the assumption that behind the civilized facade of man lurks a savage animal that will surface especially under stress circumstances. Looting, from this viewpoint, represents a breakdown of the thin "cultural veneer" that overlays human behavior. Although the imagery can be traced back to Le Bon, this model of man is still used today as can be noted in a current social psychology text in its discussion of different kinds of community emergencies.

Under unusual conditions, the socialization process may be more or less reversed, so that individuals are "disassimilated" from the social system. For example, under conditions of catastrophe, war, or natural disasters ... the effects of socialization and social control appear to be generally undone ... Frequently, in times of natural disaster such as fires, floods, or hurricanes, mobs of plunderers raid the broken shopwindows, scooping up displayed goods.

In a later passing reference to the disturbances in Watts, California, these same authors note "that many ordinarily law-abiding citizens took part because of their inability to resist the seductive pressures of mob action" and relate this to "the temporary suspension of organized social controls that normally inhibit impulsive eruptions of hostile feelings." In short, the baser part of man will come to the fore given the opportunity.

In non-scholarly circles, this conception of course also fits in well with widely held racial notions about Negroes. Less diplomatic police officials have been known to talk of "animals in the zoo" in connection with civil disorders. Some of the earlier mass media accounts of looting likewise have tended to imply a breaking loose of "mad dogs" in such situations.

A somewhat more complex but related explanation of looting behavior is one popularly used several decades ago to explain war between nations as well as individual violence, i.e., the frustration-aggression thesis. More recent versions of this formulation have discarded some of the simpler notions in the earlier statements, but the basic model remains the same. Insofar as looting is concerned, it is seen as an expression of object focused aggression that surfaces as a result of long lasting frustrations among ghetto dwellers. The looter deviates from the norms because he has reached the limits of his endurance and in giving vent to his normally suppressed rage strikes out indiscriminately.

Since the frustration-aggression notion has slowly permeated much popular thinking, it is not surprising to see it applied to this aspect of current civil disturbances. However, unlike the previous explanation which seems to be most popular among lawmen, this explanation of looting appears to be more prevalent among community officials and political figures. Furthermore, instead of talking in academic terms of "grievance banks" or "relative deprivation" the layman is more likely to say that the looting was a way of "blowing off steam," that the tension built up had to be released in some way.

The most sophisticated of the versions of the individual approach to looting behavior tend to use two closely related notions frequently associated with mass societies, i.e., alienation and anomie. Thus, one very recent study concretely applied the concept of alienation in analyzing the behavior of participants in civil disturbances. It is treated as perceived isolation from the larger society giving such persons a feeling of being unable to control events in their world, and consequently increasing their readiness to engage in extreme behavior. If this is valid, presumably looting would most likely be undertaken by the most alienated of the ghetto dwellers. Other writers talk of the social isolation of the ghetto inhabitant instead of his alienation or anomie neighborhoods, but the logic appears to be the same.

At a more lay level, particularly in the early days of the disturbances, recent urban migrants were frequently seen as being the core of the participants. Implicitly at least the more deviant actions in disturbances, such as looting, were thought more likely to be undertaken by those without local social ties. For example, such a view is implied in part in the McCone Commission report on the Watts disturbance.

All of the preceding explanations of looting rest basically on the notion of shallow, incomplete or faulty socialization. Given the opportunity, the animal in man comes forth. Given enough stress, the frustrated creature strikes out. Given a feeling of isolation and powerlessness, extreme violent actions are undertaken. In this logic, looters of course are seen as deviating from accepted patterns, not behaving as fully socialized human beings.

This is one general perspective on looting. It is quite congenial to the individualistic and nominalistic view of social reality that prevails in American society. It also fits in well with the idea that no major structural changes are necessary if deviants can be taught to change their outward behavior. Whether it is police chiefs, politicians or social scientists who are talking, in this approach the "evil" of looting is seen as rooted in man and not in his social conditions. Of course it can be noted that Tolstoy in his *To The Working People* declared that nothing does more harm to man than attributing misery to circumstances rather than to man himself, so this general point of view is neither particularly new or specially American.

Conceptions of looting primarily as a form of regressive or desocialized behavior, lend themselves to functional interpretations in expressive terms. That is, the behavior is viewed as an overt manifestation or symptom of some underlying psychological state. Since the expressed behavior however is illegal and thus publically deviant, the problem then essentially is thought of as one of formal social control. Such ideas are more implied than stated and appear more in popular thought than academic discussions, but nevertheless are part of tthe individual perspective on looting behavior.

Occasionally this interpretation is set forth in very explicit terms. For example, Wilson very recently stated:

The Negro riots are in fact *expressive* acts— that is, actions which are either intrinsically satisfying ("play") or satisfying because they give expression to a state of mind.

Some public officials and police use rather different language, but frequently the general idea is roughly equivalent. They see looting as an expression of criminal tendencies, as opportunistic stealing by individuals already inclined in such directions and who use civil strife as a cover for their everyday deviant personal proclivities.

The general public recognizes that the police generally have no expertise in dealing with psychic states, but still feel that law enforcement agencies have the responsibility for preventing at least this outward manifestation of deviancy. Thus, the Campbell and Schuman survey found that about one-third of the white population sampled thought the racial civil disturbances as criminal in character and felt that tougher police measures were the prime answer to the problem (another third of the sample believed that perhaps some real grievances were involved, but still supported repressive police measures). In essence, the matter is defined as one of law enforcement. In general, this means the application of formal control measures of a repressive nature. Looting is to be treated in such a way so that prone individuals will hesitate to give overt expression to their attitudes and tendencies. If the police cannot do anything about the *covert* psychic states responsible, it is assumed that they can at least suppress the *overt* symptom.

Popular as the individual approach to looting behavior may be, it does not square with a number of empirical observations and studies. Thus, the Jekyll and Hyde image of man implied in some of the previous discussion, is not supported. For example, it is true that natural disaster contexts also present extensive "opportunities" for widespread looting. However, as we shall detail later, almost all of the potentials for much deviant behavior of this kind are never realized in such emergency situations. To assert that looting is wide-spread in disasters and then to attempt in part to account for similar behavior in civil disturbance on the same basis as Obserschall did recently, for example, is to make an incorrect assumption.

Similarly, frustration-aggression formulations with regard to disturbances and looting within them, also have to ignore certain observations. For example, study after study has shown it is not the most downtrodden, the Marxian *lumpen-proletariat,* the "down and outer" who participates and who loots in civil disturbances. In fact, if arrest records can be taken seriously, the vast majority of looters are regularly employed. Some studies that have attempted to work with more sophisticated versions of frustration such as "relative deprivation" have likewise produced disappointing results. Thus, one study of civil disturbances concluded that the relationship with regard to "relative deprivation and participation [was] less than expected and in many cases [there was] no consistent pattern of relationship between activity and either level of aspiration or extent of discontent." Another study of 14 cities found that "the relative deprivation explanation as tested in this paper is apparently in need of amplification if we are to be able to explain and predict ghetto riots." Furthermore, few persons would claim that blacks as a whole are less frustrated today than say four years ago, yet there are far fewer massive street disorders.

With regard to social isolation as the explanatory factor the picture is somewhat the same. Looters do not see themselves as particularly isolated, and objectively have many social ties in that arrestees are typically employed, married and long time residents of their cities. Warren, in an intensive study of Detroit, found that "in neighborhoods with a high degree of withdrawal from the riot, informal social ties and both attitudinal and behavioral linkage to the larger white and black communities were lacking." Geschwender, although believing the social isolation conception is of some value perhaps best expresses the major criticism of this view in his statement that "this model is too simplistic. It ignores the effect of emergent norms in attracting individuals other than social isolates with severe grievances into the riot."

We do not believe looting behavior can be understood as simply a failure of persons to incorporate or maintain surrounding societal values or that it can be interpreted primarily as expressive behavior. The evidence does not seem to support such an approach. Looting has to be seen in more than individual psychological terms or as primarily a problem in social control.

THE GROUP PERSPECTIVE ON LOOTING

Another perspective on massive looting is possible. It is to think of looting in urban areas as normative behavior of a particular segment of American society, i.e., as a subcultural pattern that becomes manifest under certain appropriate stress circumstances and no different in this respect from other normative behavior. Thus, looting in this formulation is viewed as a characteristic of a group, not actions of individuals. It can consequently be thought of as conforming rather than deviant behavior, and as a problem in social change rather than in social control.

We will document this not only by looking at civil disorders but also at the pattern that looting behavior assumes in another kind of major community stress, i.e., natural disasters. The most parsimonious common explanation for the looting behavior in these emergency situations is that the usual group norms which govern property in both instances change. Because one of these community crises is a consensus type and the other is a dissensus type situation, the resulting pattern of looting behavior is different, but nevertheless the major explanatory factor is to be found in emergent norms of groups not in expressions of individual characteristics.

TWO PATTERNS OF LOOTING

There are two major types of community crises, some reflecting consensus, others mirroring dissensus. The best example of these two are natural disasters in the former instance, and civil disturbances in the latter case. Contrary to the image presented in most news accounts as well as fictional stories of emergencies, there is not total social chaos and anarchy in such situations. Behavior in both kinds of crises shows definite patterns being neither random nor idiosyncratic for each specific case. Furthermore, while there is a pattern to the behavior, it differs in the two kinds of crises. This is as true of looting behavior as it is of many other emergency behaviors.

There are at least three major differences in the looting that occurs in civil disorders and in natural disasters.

1. In civil disorders looting is very widespread whereas in natural disasters actual looting incidents are quite rare. The behavior is widespread in at least three senses. One, it occurs in almost all major disorders and many of the less serious ones. Two, looters come from all segments of the population, females as well as males, oldsters as well as

youngsters, middle class as well as lower class persons, and so on. Looting is not the behavior solely of a delimited or distinctive part of black communities. Third, if we extrapolate figures from some studies made by other researchers, in at least the major disturbances it seems possible that as many as a fifth of the total ghetto residents may participate in the activity. This contrasts sharply with natural disaster situations. In those, looting often does not occur at all, and in the infrequent cases where it does take place, is apparently undertaken by a handful of individuals in the general population.

Furthermore, looting in civil disorders is almost always if not exclusively engaged in by local residents, whereas in natural disasters it is undertaken by "outsiders." It is the local ghetto dweller who participates in urban civil disturbances. Arrest records for all offenses show that those involved overwhelmingly reside in the city experiencing the disorder. There is in fact reason to suspect, when the high percentage of women who engage in massive looting is taken into account, that the great majority of looters are from the local neighborhoods around the places looted. In natural disasters instead, such looting as there is, in general, is done by non-local persons who venture into the impacted community. Sometimes they are part of the very security forces often sent in from outside the area to prevent such behavior (as was recently reported to be the case regarding some National Guardsmen dispatched to the Gulf coast of Mississippi after Hurricane Camille).

2. One of the most striking aspects about looting in civil disturbances is its collective character. This is dramatically depicted in many television and movie films of such incidents. Looters often work together in pairs, as family units or small groups. This is a marked contrast to natural disasters where such looting as occurs is carried out by solitary individuals. In the civil disturbances, the collective nature of the act sometimes reaches the point where the availability of potential loot is called to the attention of bystanders, or in extreme instances where

spectators are handed goods by looters coming out of stores.

The collective nature of massive looting is also manifest in its selective nature in civil disorders compared with its situational nature in disasters. Press reports to the contrary, ghetto dwellers have been far from indiscriminate in their looting. Grocery, furniture, apparel and liquor stores have been the prime object of attack. In Newark they made up 49 percent of those attacked; in Watts they made up a majority. Many other kinds of establishments such as plants, offices, schools and private residences have been generally ignored. Furthermore, within the general category of stores and places selected for attack, there has been even finer discrimination. One chain store in Washington, D.C., had 19 of its 50 stores looted while supermarkets of other companies located in the same neighborhoods were left untouched. Obviously, such massive action is not a matter of individual but of collective definition of "good" and "bad" stores from the viewpoint of ghetto dwellers. In contrast to this focus in civil disorders on commercial enterprises, in natural disasters such early looting as there is, often seems to center on personal effects and goods. It likewise appears to depend on the opportunity presented by the availability of discarded clothing of victims, open doors into residences, spilled items on sidewalks from storefronts and the like. In other words, the looting in natural disasters is highly influenced by situational factors that present themselves to looters rather than any conscious selection and choice of places to loot as is the case in civil disturbances. (However, even in natural disasters, there are far more situational opportunities for looting that could be taken advantage of, but which are not.)

3. The public nature of the looting behavior in civil disorders is also striking. It is not a private act as it is in natural disasters. Goods are taken openly and in full view of others, bystanders as well as co-participants, and often even policemen. In natural disasters, such looting as occurs is very covert and secret with care being taken not to be observed by others. The open dashing into stores or the carrying of stolen goods through the streets in broad daylight as is common in the urban disturbances, just does not occur in the wake of such catastrophes as hurricanes and earthquakes.

Furthermore, in natural disaster, acts which are defined as looting are condemned very severely. In civil disturbances instead, both during and after the event there is little local community sanction for such behavior. In fact, while the disturbances are going on, and looting is at its peak, there is actually strong local social support for the activity. The so-called "carnival spirit" observed in the major civil disturbances, rather than being a manifestation of anarchy is actually an indication of the open collective support of a local nature for looting. Even after the disturbances are over, as different studies and surveys show, the disorders are justified by most blacks and judged as helpful in bringing about change. In contrast, looting is considered a very serious crime in natural disasters, spoken of in highly condemnatory tones by residents of the area, and is never seen as justifiable behavior.

To summarize: looting in civil disorders is widespread, collective and public, being undertaken by local people who are selective in their activity and who receive community support for their actions. In contrast, looting in natural disasters is very limited, individual and private being engaged in by outsiders to the community taking advantage of certain situations they find themselves in but who are strongly condemned for their actions.

EMERGENT PROPERTY NORMS

In order to explain the looting patterns in the two kinds of community crises just considered, it is necessary to examine the nature of property. In this we may be misled by the term looting. In the military context from which it is derived, looting implies the taking of goods and possessions.

However, property has reference not to any concrete thing or material object, but to a right. "Property consists of the *rights* held by an individual ... to certain valuable things, whether material or immaterial." But if we talk of rights we are talking of shared expectations about what can or cannot be done with respect to something. Property can therefore be viewed as a set of cultural norms that regulate the relation of persons to items with economic value. In effect, property is a shared understanding about who can do what with the valued resources within a community.

Normally, these understandings or expectations are widely shared and accepted. There are all kinds of norms, the legal ones in particular, which specify the legitimate forms of use, control, and disposal of economically valued resources within a community. It is these expectations which change in both kinds of community crises we are talking about.

In natural disasters, in American society at least, there quickly develops a consensus that all private property rights are temporarily suspended for the common good. In one way, all goods become "community property" and can be used as needed for the general welfare. Thus, warehouses can be broken into without the owner's permission to obtain generators necessary to keep hospitals functioning, and the act is seen as legitimate if undertaken for this purpose even though the participants might agree that it was technically an act of burglary. However, the parties involved, the local legal authorities and the general public in the area at the time of the crisis do not define such actions as looting and would react very negatively to attempts to impose such a definition.

On the other hand, there is very powerful social pressure against the use of goods for purely personal use while major community emergency needs exist. In a way, the individual who uses anything for himself alone is seen as taking from the common store. The new norm as to property is that the affected group, as long as it has emergency needs, has priority.

It is this community expectation or consensus that develops which explains the char-

acteristic pattern of looting in natural disasters outlined earlier. Thus, it is understandable why such looting as occurs is typically undertaken by someone from outside the impacted area. Such persons not having undergone the experience are not part of the new although temporary community consensus regarding property. They can act as individuals toward strangers, pursuing highly personal goals and appropriating whatever resources opportunities provide them.

In civil disturbances, there is also a redefinition of property rights. The looting undertaken is likewise a temporary manifestation of a new group norm. The "current" right to use of available resources becomes problematical. If property is thought of as the shared understanding of who can do what with the valued resources within a community, in civil disorders we see a breakdown in that understanding. What was previously taken for granted and widely shared, becomes a matter of dispute among certain segments of the general population.

Viewed in this way much of the pattern of looting in civil disturbances discussed earlier also makes sense. At the height of such situations, plundering becomes the normative, the socially accepted thing to do. Far from being deviant, it becomes the conforming behavior in the situation. As in natural disasters, the legal right does not change, but there is local group consensus on the massive use and appropriation of certain public and private goods, be these police cars or items on grocery store shelves. In many ways, a new property norm has emerged.

As most sociologists have argued, social behavior is always guided by norms, traditional or emergent. Looting does not constitute actions in the absence of norms. Even situations of civil disorder are not that unstructured. The observed cases of looters continuing to pay attention to traffic lights should be seen as more than humorous anecdotes; they are simple indications of the continuous operations of traditional norms even in situations that seem highly confused. The parties involved in massive looting are simply acting on the basis of new, emergent norms in the ghetto group with regard to some categories of property. They are not behaving in a situation devoid of social structuring.

Of course, there is differential distribution of the frequency of looting in different civil disorders, and even where there is maximization of the behavior, not everyone loots. Civil disturbances are not of one kind as the various typologies of them that have been developed, clearly indicate. Looting, for example, is more likely in a disorder that is explicitly focused on protest than one not involving such a kind of focus. Furthermore, black ghettoes are not of one piece and neither are the neighborhoods within them as both Warren, and Hill and Larson have documented. The former, in his studies for example, has shown that degree of participation in disorders (and therefore presumably looting) is related to the kind of prevailing social organization in the local neighborhood area.

SEMI-INSTITUTIONALIZATION OF LOOTING BEHAVIOR

Looting may not be engaged in by everyone and there is no doubt an illusion of greater unanimity regarding public support of the behavior among the actual participants than is the case. Nevertheless, it seems fairly clear that in the period from 1964 through 1968, this kind of response on the part of ghetto dwellers became partly institutionalized, i.e., it seems to be the immediate behavioral response if a disorder grows beyond a very minimal point. Massive looting can start almost immediately in a community as it did in many ghettos in the very widespread disturbances that occurred after the King assassination. There are also other indirect signs of the probable institutionalization of the behavior. After the disorders are over, there seems to be far less returning or turning in of looted goods by repentant looters than was the case several years ago. Furthermore, in the more recent ghetto disturbances there are no reports of looters destroying the goods they have taken. Yet, in the earlier

disorders, for example, in Plainfield, New Jersey in 1964 and even in Watts in 1965, some of the liquor taken was destroyed rather than consumed.

The semi-institutionalization of looting behavior as a group response pattern under certain circumstances has been facilitated by a number of factors. For one, the police have generally been unable, and perhaps even unwilling for a variety of complex factors that can not be discussed here, to stop attempts at massive looting. This of course contributes to recidivism. Probably, however, the mass communication system has been more important in this respect by providing role models and even a degree of legitimation. As Janowitz and Mattick have noted, television in particular, has inadvertently taught ghetto dwellers all around the country, the details of the disturbances, how people participate in them, and the tactics to be used and gratifications to be obtained in looting goods. The overall definition of the situation and its general acceptance has also been reinforced by some radio and television stations, who at the height of disturbances, repeatedly point out that the police are standing by while looting is pursued with impunity.

Since early 1968 the number of large scale civil disturbances has dropped considerably compared with the prior four years. As such, massive looting behavior on the Newark scale occurs less frequently. In this sense the behavior is less prominent. Noticeable, however, is the fact that when disturbances do occur currently, even on a small scale, looting almost inevitably takes place, usually developing quickly and without any build up. This argues for the present semi-institutionalized nature of the action—it is the expected and accepted normative action and almost automatically appears in certain stress situations.

If looting is seen as a form of normative group behavior, it lends itself quite readily to interpretations in instrumental terms. It can be visualized as communicating a message from the ghetto areas to the larger society. In other words, massive looting can be defined as a form of group protest about certain aspects of interracial relationships in American society. The looters themselves may or may not be conscious of such a message, but the motives of actors need not necessarily correspond to the functions of their actions. Looting can have a communication function and in a way serve as a kind of primitive political protest mechanism.

This would not be a new pattern in history. Subordinate groups in the past have developed subcultural traditions of violent protest with regard to property. This has been well-documented by European historians who have analyzed many instances where groups of workers and shopkeepers—incidentally, not the unemployed or criminal elements—in the 18th and 19th centuries in different communities protested in the streets to communicate discontent about their economic positions in their societies.

As Hobsbawm has noted of the "pre-industrial city mob," its actions were partly guided by the expectation of achieving something by its disruptive actions. Groups who undertake such activities are not necessarily incorrect in this assumption. Instructive in this respect was the behavior of the Luddites, the so-called "machine breakers" who as recent historical analysis shows, were far from indiscriminate in their destructive acts than is generally supposed. Perhaps more important, it has been said of their behavior that "collective bargaining by rioting was at least as effective as any other means of bringing trade union pressure, and probably *more* effective than any other means available before the era of national trade unions." In other words, the recurrent violent behavior of the Luddites and similar groups was instrumental in bringing about a change in their relative socio-economic position in the society.

Could anything similar be said of the looting behavior that seems to have established itself in American ghettos over the last few years? Certainly there has been increasing recognition that the civil disturbances as a whole are more than a matter of breakdown of law and order. One of the last

studies sponsored by the National Advisory Commission on Civil Disorders took the position that the ghetto disorders are a form of social protest engaged in by non-criminal elements and justified as such by a majority of black people. In fact, the Campbell and Schuman survey showed that a consistent majority of from 51 to 60 percent of all Negro respondents, varying somewhat with age, interpreted the urban disturbances as protest activities.

Many scholars are also beginning to interpret the civil disorders in similar terms. Paige observes that "rioting can profitably be considered a form of disorganized political protest engaged in by those who have become highly distrustful of existing political institutions." Boesel has said that "when violence erupts in the ghetto, it ordinarily constitutes a violent protest without ideology which focuses on certain key institutional points of contact between the ghetto and white society—such as the police and the stores—without developing a comprehensive collective rationality." This is similar to our more delimited theme. Massive looting can be interpreted as a form of violent group protest, and not merely individualistic expressive acts. The protest is focused on existing property rights in American society.

Furthermore, if looting is seen not as expressive reactions on the part of individuals but as instrumental behavior by a group, it suggests thinking of it not as absolute *deviation* from existing norms, but as relative *conformity* to new norms or expectations. If that is the case, social control by the larger society can only be achieved by creating new institutional patterns that will be the functional equivalent in the group of the existing pattern of looting. In other words, instead of thinking about the repression of unsocialized or aggressive impulses of individuals, it is necessary to think of the institutionalization of new social structures. The problem viewed in this way thus becomes one of bringing about social change rather than suppressing deviant behavior. The issue therefore is one that goes far beyond law enforcement, although the actions of the police are not irrelevant to what will occur in certain kinds of community emergencies.

RESISTANCE TO THE NORMATIVE VIEW OF LOOTING

Many persons, scholars, political figures and otherwise, have failed to note or to accept the view of looting as normative behavior and its interpretation in instrumental terms. Illustrative of the more general societal reaction is that taken by the Mayor's Special Task Force in Pittsburgh in its examination of the disorders in the city after the King assassination. It very correctly notes, for example, that the looting was highly selective, but attributes this to advance planning and preparation. The conspiracy theory of history is of course an ancient one, and is a particular favorite of public authorities. It is certainly not peculiar to American society. Jones and Molnar in a wide ranging examination of civil disorders in a variety of places and at different historical times note:

Those in power have usually assumed that the rioters had no worthwhile aspirations and could be motivated to activity only by the promise of reward from outside agitators or conspirators. Until the deeper aspirations of the poor began to be investigated their periodic rebellions and riots were often attributed to the manipulation of a political opponent or a "hidden hand." This attitude has been so popular in history that it has been shared by all authority, regardless of whether the governing elite was aristocratic, middle class, conservative, liberal, or revolutionary.

Along with playing up the conspiracy theory, there is also a tendency to downplay the massive nature of the disturbances or their acceptability among ghetto dwellers. Thus, the mistaken position is taken that only a tiny fraction of black people participate. As earlier indicated also, another general reaction is to attribute the disorders to malcontents or individuals without ties to the social system. There seems to be an unwillingness to face up to the fact that looters, for example, are not persons without jobs. In particular there is a great reluctance to believe that if there is a protest involved, it is by a group with any sense of power or hope of achievement through street tactics. Yet the evidence is that there is a "genuine protest temper" among the participants in disturbances. Rimilinger discussing the development of European trade unionism notes that this temper demands that those involved "be convinced of the righteousness not only of their demands but also of the novel means proposed to enforce them." Substantial numbers of black people in American urban areas seem convinced about both aspects. . . .

CONCLUSION

In what preceded, we have not attempted to analyze or to account for all phases of the civil disturbances that have wracked urban American society from 1964 through 1969. On the contrary, if we have learned anything from our studies of these situations, it is that the behaviors and participants involved are far more heterogeneous than is implied in a statement that "violence" broke out in this ghetto or that the Negroes in a particular community "rioted." Sniping and looting, arson and vandalism and other behaviors are not the same kinds of acts; different participants take part in these activities, the action takes place at different locations and at different time periods of the disturbances. To treat such varying activities separated in time and space and undertaken by different persons and groups as only one kind of phenomena is to blur vital empirical as well as analytical distinctions, and to make homogeneous that which is not. Our focus in this paper was almost exclusively on massive looting behavior. We have not pretended to explain outbreaks, when and where they occur, but mostly have focused on attempting to identify the nature of and to account for one of their most prominent features, i.e., massive looting.

LOWER CLASS CULTURE AS A GENERATING MILIEU OF GANG DELINQUENCY

Walter B. Miller

The etiology of delinquency has long been a controversial issue and is particularly so at present. As new frames of reference for explaining human behavior have been added to traditional theories, some authors have adopted the practice of citing the major postulates of each school of thought as they pertain to delinquency, and of going on to state that causality must be conceived in terms of the dynamic interaction of a complex combination of variables on many levels. The major sets of etiological factors currently adduced to explain delinquency are, in simplified terms, the physiological (delinquency results from organic pathology), the psychodynamic (delinquency is a "behavioral disorder" resulting primarily from emotional disturbance generated by a defective mother-child relationship), and the environmental (delinquency is the product of disruptive forces, "disorganization," in the actor's physical or social environment).

This paper selects one particular kind of "delinquency"—law-violating acts committed by members of adolescent street corner groups in lower class communities—and attempts to show that the dominant component of motivation underlying these acts consists in a directed attempt by the actor to adhere to forms of behavior, and to achieve standards of value, as they are defined within that community. It takes as a premise that the motivation of behavior in this situation can be approached most productively by attempting to understand the nature of cultural forces impinging on the acting individuals as they are perceived *by the actor himself*—although by no means only that segment of these forces of which the actor is consciously aware—rather than as they are

perceived and evaluated from the reference position of another cultural system. In the case of "gang" delinquency, the cultural system which exerts the most direct influence on behavior is that of the lower class community itself—a long-established, distinctively patterned tradition with an integrity of its own—rather than a so-called "delinquent subculture" which has arisen through conflict with middle class culture and is oriented to the deliberate violation of middle class norms.

The bulk of the substantive data on which the following material is based was collected in connection with a service-research project in the control of gang delinquency. During the service aspect of the project, which lasted for three years, seven trained social workers maintained contact with twenty-one corner group units in a "slum" district of a large eastern city for periods of time ranging from ten to thirty months. Groups were Negro and white, male and female, and in early, middle, and late adolescence. Over eight thousand pages of direct observational data on behavior patterns of group members and other community residents were collected; almost daily contact was maintained for a total time period of about thirteen worker years. Data include workers contact reports, participant observation reports by the writer—a cultural anthropologist—and direct tape recordings of group activities and discussions.

FOCAL CONCERNS OF LOWER CLASS CULTURE

There is a substantial segment of present-day American society whose way of life, values, and characteristic patterns of behavior are the product of a distinctive cultural system which may be termed "lower class." Evi-

From *The Journal of Social Issues,* 14, No. 3 (1958), 5–19. Reprinted by permission. Professor Miller is in the Harvard Law School.

dence indicates that this cultural system is becoming increasingly distinctive, and that the size of the group which shares this tradition is increasing. The lower class way of life, in common with that of all distinctive cultural groups, is characterized by a set of focal concerns—areas or issues which command widespread and persistent attention and a high degree of emotional involvement. The specific concerns cited here, while by no means confined to the American lower classes, constitute a distinctive *patterning* of concerns which differs significantly, both in rank order and weighting, from that of American middle class culture. Chart 1 presents a highly schematic and simplified listing of six of the major concerns of lower class culture. Each is conceived as a "dimension" within which a fairly wide and varied range of alternative behavior patterns may be followed by different individuals under different situations. They are listed roughly in order of the degree of *explicit* attention accorded each and, in this sense, represent a weighted ranking of concerns. The "perceived alternatives" represent polar positions which define certain parameters within each dimension. As will be explained in more detail, it is necessary in relating the

influence of these "concerns" to the motivation of delinquent behavior to specify *which* of its aspects is oriented to, whether orientation is *overt* or *covert, positive* (conforming to or seeking the aspect) or *negative* (rejecting or seeking to avoid the aspect).

The concept "focal concern" is used here in preference to the concept "value" for several interrelated reasons: (1) It is more readily derivable from direct field observation. (2) It is descriptively neutral—permitting independent consideration of positive and negative valences as varying under different conditions, whereas "value" carries a built-in positive valence. (3) It makes possible more refined analysis of subcultural differences, since it reflects actual behavior, whereas "value" tends to wash out intracultural differences since it is colored by notions of the "official" ideal.

Trouble

Concern over "trouble" is a dominant feature of lower class culture. The concept has various shades of meaning; "trouble" in one of its aspects represents a situation or a kind of behavior which results in unwelcome or complicating involvement with official au-

Table 3–2. Focal Concerns of Lower Class Culture

Area	Perceived alternatives (state, quality, condition)	
1. Trouble:	law-abiding behavior	law-violating behavior
2. Toughness:	physical prowess, skill; "masculinity"; fearlessness, bravery, daring	weakness, ineptitude; effeminacy; timidity, cowardice, caution
3. Smartness:	ability to outsmart, dupe, "con"; gaining money by "wits"; shrewdness, adroitness in repartee	gullibility, "con-ability"; gaining money by hard work; slowness, dull-wittedness, verbal maladroitness
4. Excitement:	thrill; risk, danger; change, activity	boredom; "deadness," safeness; sameness, passivity
5. Fate:	favored by fortune, being "lucky"	ill-omened, being "unlucky"
6. Autonomy:	freedom from external constraint; freedom from superordinate authority; independence	presence of external constraint; presence of strong authority; dependency, being "cared for"

thorities or agencies of middle class society. "Getting into trouble" and "staying out of trouble" represent major issues for male and female, adults and children. For men, "trouble" frequently involves fighting or sexual adventures while drinking; for women, sexual involvement with disadvantageous consequences. Expressed desire to avoid behavior which violates moral or legal norms is often based less on an explicit commitment to "official" moral or legal standards than on a desire to avoid "getting into trouble," e.g., the complicating consequences of the action.

The dominant concern over "trouble" involves a distinction of critical importance for the lower class community—that between "law-abiding" and "non-law-abiding" behavior. There is a high degree of sensitivity as to where each person stands in relation to these two classes of activity. Whereas in the middle class community a major dimension for evaluating a person's status is "achievement" and its external symbols, in the lower class personal status is very frequently gauged along the law-abiding—non-law-abiding dimension. A mother will evaluate the suitability of her daughter's boyfriend less on the basis of his achievement potential than on the basis of his innate "trouble" potential. This sensitive awareness of the opposition of "trouble-producing" and "non-trouble-producing" behavior represents both a major basis for deriving status distinctions and an internalized conflict potential for the individual.

As in the case of other focal concerns, which of two perceived alternatives—"law-abiding" or "non-law-abiding"—is valued varies according to the individual and the circumstances; in many instances there is an overt commitment to the "law-abiding" alternative, but a covert commitment to the "non-law-abiding." In certain situations, "getting into trouble" is overtly recognized as prestige-conferring; for example, membership in certain adult and adolescent primary groupings ("gangs") is contingent on having demonstrated an explicit commitment to the law-violating alternative. It is most impor-

tant to note that the choice between "law-abiding" and "non-law-abiding" behavior is still a choice *within* lower class culture; the distinction between the policeman and the criminal, the outlaw and the sheriff, involves primarily this one dimension; in other respects they have a high community of interests. Not infrequently brothers raised in an identical cultural milieu will become police and criminals respectively.

For a substantial segment of the lower class population "getting into trouble" is not in itself overtly defined as prestige-conferring, but is implicitly recognized as a means to other valued ends, e.g., the covertly valued desire to be "cared for" and subject to external constraint, or the overtly valued state of excitement or risk. Very frequently "getting into trouble" is multi-functional and achieves several sets of valued ends.

Toughness

The concept of "toughness" in lower class culture represents a compound combination of qualities or states. Among its most important components are physical prowess, evidenced both by demonstrated possession of strength and endurance and by athletic skill; "masculinity," symbolized by a distinctive complex of acts and avoidances (bodily tatooing, absence of sentimentality, non-concern with "art," "literature," conceptualization of women as conquest objects, etc.); and bravery in the face of physical threat. The model for the "tough guy"— hard, fearless, undemonstrative, skilled in physical combat—is represented by the movie gangster of the thirties, the "private eye," and the movie cowboy.

The genesis of the intense concern over "toughness" in lower class culture is probably related to the fact that a significant proportion of lower class males are reared in a predominantly female household and lack a consistently present male figure with whom to identify and from whom to learn essential components of a "male" role. Since women serve as a primary object of identification during pre-adolescent years, the almost obsessive lower class concern with "masculinity" probably resembles a type of compulsive reaction-formation. A concern over homosexuality runs like a persistent thread through lower class culture. This is manifested by the institutionalized practice of baiting "queers," often accompanied by violent physical attacks, an expressed contempt for "softness" or frills, and the use of the local term for "homosexual" as a generalized pejorative epithet (e.g., higher class individuals or upwardly mobile peers are frequently characterized as "fags" or "queers"). The distinction between "overt" and "covert" orientation to aspects of an area of concern is especially important in regard to "toughness." A positive overt evaluation of behavior defined as "effeminate" would be out of the question for a lower class male; however, built into lower class culture is a range of devices which permit men to adopt behaviors and concerns which in other cultural milieux fall within the province of women, and at the same time to be defined as "tough" and manly. For example, lower class men can be professional short-order cooks in a diner and still be regarded as "tough." The highly intimate circumstances of the street corner gang involve the recurrent expression of strongly affectionate feelings towards other men. Such expressions, however, are disguised as their opposite, taking the form of ostensibly aggressive verbal and physical interaction (kidding, "ranking," rough-housing, etc.).

Smartness

"Smartness," as conceptualized in lower class culture, involves the capacity to outsmart, outfox, outwit, dupe, "take," "con" another or others and the concomitant capacity to avoid being outwitted, "taken," or duped oneself. In its essence, smartness involves the capacity to achieve a valued entity—material goods, personal status— through a maximum use of mental agility and a minimum use of physical effort. This capacity has an extremely long tradition in lower class culture and is highly valued.

Lower class culture can be characterized as "non-intellectual" only if intellectualism is defined specifically in terms of control over a particular body of formally learned knowledge involving "culture" (art, literature, "good" music, etc.), a generalized perspective on the past and present conditions of our own and other societies, and other areas of knowledge imparted by formal educational institutions. This particular type of mental attainment is, in general, overtly disvalued and frequently associated with effeminacy; "smartness" in the lower class sense, however, is highly valued.

The lower class child learns and practices the use of this skill in the street corner situation. Individuals continually practice duping and outwitting one another through recurrent card games and other forms of gambling, mutual exchanges of insults, and "testing" for mutual "conability." Those who demonstrate competence in this skill are accorded considerable prestige. Leadership roles in the corner group are frequently allocated according to demonstrated capacity in the two areas of "smartness" and "toughness"; the ideal leader combines both, but the "smart" leader is often accorded more prestige than the "tough" one—reflecting a general lower class respect for "brains" in the "smartness" sense.

The model of the "smart" person is represented in popular media by the card shark, the professional gambler, thc "con" artist, the promoter. A conceptual distinction is made between two kinds of people: "suckers," easy marks, "lushes," dupes, who work for their money and are legitimate targets of exploitation; and sharp operators, the "brainy" ones, who live by their wits and "getting" from the suckers by mental adroitness.

Involved in the syndrome of capacities related to "smartness" is a dominant emphasis in lower class culture on ingenious aggressive repartee. This skill, learned and practiced in the context of the corner group, ranges in form from the widely prevalent semi-ritualized teasing, kidding, razzing, "ranking," so characteristic of male peer group interaction, to the highly ritualized type of mutual insult interchange known as "the dirty dozens," "the dozens," "playing house," and other terms. This highly patterned cultural form is practiced on its most advanced level in adult male Negro society, but less polished variants are found throughout lower class culture—practiced, for example, by white children, male and female, as young as four or five. In essence, "doin' the dozens" involves two antagonists who vie with each other in the exchange of increasingly inflammatory insults, with incestuous and perverted sexual relations with the mother a dominant theme. In this form of insult interchange, as well as on other less ritualized occasions for joking, semi-serious, and serious mutual invective, a very high premium is placed on ingenuity, hair-trigger responsiveness, inventiveness, and the acute exercise of mental faculties.

Excitement

For many lower class individuals the rhythm of life fluctuates between periods of relatively routine or repetitive activity and sought situations of great emotional stimulation. Many of the most characteristic features of lower class life are related to the search for excitement or "thrill." Involved here are the highly prevalent use of alcohol by both sexes and the widespread use of gambling of all kinds—playing the numbers, betting on horse races, dice, cards. The quest for excitement finds what is perhaps its most vivid expression in the highly patterned practice of the recurrent "night on the town." This practice, designated by various terms in different areas ("honky-tonkin' "; "goin' out on the town"; "bar hoppin' "), involves a patterned set of activities in which alcohol, music, and sexual adventuring are major components. A group or individual sets out to "make the rounds" of various bars or night clubs. Drinking continues progressively throughout the evening. Men seek to "pick up" women, and women play the risky game of entertaining sexual advances. Fights between men involving women, gambling, and

claims of physical prowess, in various combinations, are frequent consequences of a night of making the rounds. The explosive potential of this type of adventuring with sex and aggression, frequently leading to "trouble," is semi-explicitly sought by the individual. Since there is always a good likelihood that being out on the town will eventuate in fights, etc., the practice involves elements of sought risk and desired danger.

Counterbalancing the "flirting with danger" aspect of the "excitement" concern is the prevalence in lower class culture of other well-established patterns of activity which involve long periods of relative inaction or passivity. The term "hanging out" in lower class culture refers to extended periods of standing around, often with peer mates, doing what is defined as "nothing," "shooting the breeze," etc. A definite periodicity exists in the pattern of activity relating to the two aspects of the "excitement" dimension. For many lower class individuals the venture into the high risk world of alcohol, sex, and fighting occurs regularly once a week, with interim periods devoted to accommodating to possible consequences of these periods, along with recurrent resolves not to become so involved again.

Fate

Related to the quest for excitement is the concern with fate, fortune, or luck. Here also a distinction is made between two states—being "lucky" or "in luck" and being unlucky or jinxed. Many lower class individuals feel that their lives are subject to a set of forces over which they have relatively little control. These are not directly equated with the supernatural forces of formally organized religion, but relate more to a concept of "destiny," or man as a pawn of magical powers. Not infrequently this often implicit world view is associated with a conception of the ultimate futility of directed effort towards a goal: if the cards are right, or the dice good to you, or if your lucky number comes up, things will go your way; if luck is against you, it's not worth trying.

The concept of performing semi-magical rituals so that one's "luck will change" is prevalent; one hopes as a result to move from the state of being "unlucky" to that of being "lucky." The element of fantasy plays an important part in this area. Related to and complementing the notion that "only suckers work" (Smartness) is the idea that once things start going your way, relatively independent of your own effort, all good things will come to you. Achieving great material rewards (big cars, big houses, a roll of cash to flash in a fancy night club), valued in lower class as well as in other parts of American culture, is a recurrent theme in lower class fantasy and folk lore; the cocaine dreams of Willie the Weeper or Minnie the Moocher present the components of this fantasy in vivid detail.

The prevalence in the lower class community of many forms of gambling mentioned in connection with the "excitement" dimension, is also relevant here. Through cards and pool which involve skill, and thus both "toughness" and "smartness"; or through race horse betting, involving "smartness"; or through playing the numbers, involving predominantly "luck," one may make a big killing with a minimum of directed and persistent effort within conventional occupational channels. Gambling in its many forms illustrates the fact that many of the persistent features of lower class culture are multi-functional—serving a range of desired ends at the same time. Describing some of the incentives behind gambling has involved mention of all of the focal concerns cited so far—Toughness, Smartness, and Excitement, in addition to Fate.

Autonomy

The extent and nature of control over the behavior of the individual—an important concern in most cultures—has a special significance and is distinctively patterned in lower class culture. The discrepancy between what is overtly valued and what is covertly sought is particularly striking in this area. On the overt level there is a strong and fre-

quently expressed resentment of the idea of external controls, restrictions on behavior, and unjust or coercive authority. "No one's gonna push *me* around," or "I'm gonna tell him he can take the job and shove it . . ." are commonly expressed sentiments. Similar explicit attitudes are maintained to systems of behavior-restricting rules, insofar as these are perceived as representing the injunctions and bearing the sanctions of superordinate authority. In addition, in lower class culture a close conceptual connection is made between "authority" and "nurturance." To be restrictively or firmly controlled is to be cared for. Thus the overtly negative evaluation of superordinate authority frequently extends as well to nurturance, care, or protection. The desire for personal independence is often expressed in such terms as "I don't need *nobody* to take care of me. I can take care of myself!" Actual patterns of behavior, however, reveal a marked discrepancy between expressed sentiment and what is covertly valued. Many lower class people appear to seek out highly restrictive social environments wherein stringent external controls are maintained over their behavior. Such institutions as the armed forces, the mental hospital, the disciplinary school, the prison or correctional institution, provide environments which incorporate a strict and detailed set of rules, defining and limiting behavior and enforced by an authority system which controls and applies coercive sanctions for deviance from these rules. While under the jurisdiction of such systems, the lower class person generally expresses to his peers continual resentment of the coercive, unjust, and arbitrary exercise of authority. Having been released, or having escaped from these milieux, however, he will often act in such a way as to insure recommitment, or choose recommitment voluntarily after a temporary period of "freedom."

Lower class patients in mental hospitals will exercise considerable ingenuity to insure continued commitment while voicing the desire to get out; delinquent boys will frequently "run" from a correctional institution to activate efforts to return them; to be caught and returned means that one is cared for. Since "being controlled" is equated with "being cared for," attempts are frequently made to "test" the severity or strictness of superordinate authority to see if it remains firm. If intended or executed rebellion produces swift and firm punitive sanctions, the individual is reassured, at the same time that he is complaining bitterly at the injustice of being caught and punished. Some environmental milieux, having been tested in this fashion for the "firmness" of their coercive sanctions, are rejected, ostensibly for being too strict, actually for not being strict enough. This is frequently so in the case of "problematic" behavior by lower class youngsters in the public schools, which generally cannot command the coercive controls implicitly sought by the individual. . . .

FOCAL CONCERNS OF THE LOWER CLASS ADOLESCENT STREET CORNER GROUP

The one-sex peer group is a highly prevalent and significant structural form in the lower class community. There is a strong probability that the prevalence and stability of this type of unit is directly related to the prevalence of a stabilized type of lower class child-rearing unit—the "female-based" household. This is a nuclear kin unit in which a male parent is either absent from the household, present only sporadically, or, when present, only minimally or inconsistently involved in the support and rearing of children. This unit usually consists of one or more females of child-bearing age and their offspring. The females are frequently related to one another by blood or marriage ties, and the unit often includes two or more generations of women, e.g., the mother and/or aunt of the principal child-bearing female.

The nature of social groupings in the lower class community may be clarified if we make the assumption that it is the *one-sex peer unit* rather than the two-parent family unit which represents the most significant relational unit for both sexes in lower class communities. Lower class society may be pictured as comprising a set of age-graded one-sex groups which constitute the major psychic focus and reference group for those over twelve or thirteen. Men and women of mating age leave these groups periodically to form temporary marital alliances, but these lack stability, and after varying periods of "trying out" the two-sex family arrangement, they gravitate back to the more "comfortable" one-sex grouping, whose members exert strong pressure on the individual *not* to disrupt the group by adopting a two-sex household pattern of life. Membership in a stable and solidary peer unit is vital to the lower class individual precisely to the extent to which a range of essential functions—psychological, educational, and others—are not provided by the "family" unit.

The adolescent street corner group represents the adolescent variant of this lower class structural form. What has been called the "delinquent gang" is one subtype of this form, defined on the basis of frequency of participation in law-violating activity; this subtype should not be considered a legitimate unit of study per se, but rather as one particular variant of the adolescent street corner group. The "hanging" peer group is a unit of particular importance for the adolescent male. In many cases it is the most stable and solidary primary group he has ever belonged to; for boys reared in female-based households the corner group provides the first real opportunity to learn essential aspects of the male role in the context of peers facing similar problems of sex-role identification.

The form and functions of the adolescent corner group operate as a selective mechanism in recruiting members. The activity patterns of the group require a high level of intragroup solidarity; individual members must possess a good capacity for subordinating individual desires to general group interests as well as the capacity for intimate and persisting interaction. Thus highly "disturbed" individuals, or those who cannot tolerate consistently imposed sanctions on "deviant" behavior cannot remain accepted members; the group itself will extrude those whose behavior exceeds limits defined as "normal." This selective process produces a type of group whose members possess to an unusually high degree both the *capacity* and *motivation* to conform to perceived cultural norms, so that the nature of the system of norms and values oriented to is a particularly influential component of motivation.

Focal concerns of the male adolescent corner group are those of the general cultural milieu in which it functions. As would be expected, the relative weighting and importance of these concerns pattern somewhat differently for adolescents than for adults. The nature of this patterning centers around two additional "concerns" of particular importance to this group—concern with "belonging," and with "status." These may be conceptualized as being on a higher level of abstraction than concerns previously cited, since "status" and "belonging" are achieved *via* cited concern areas of Toughness, etc.

Belonging

Since the corner group fulfills essential functions for the individual, being a member in good standing of the group is of vital importance for its members. A continuing concern over who is "in" and who is not involves the citation and detailed discussion of highly refined criteria for "in-group" membership. The phrase "he hangs with us" means "he is accepted as a member in good standing by current consensus"; conversely, "he don't hang with us" means he is not so accepted. One achieves "belonging" primarily by demonstrating knowledge of and determination to adhere to the system of standards and valued qualities defined by the group. One maintains membership by acting in conformity with valued aspects of Toughness, Smartness, Autonomy, etc. In those instances where conforming to norms of this reference group at the same time violates norms of other reference groups (e.g., middle class adults, institutional "officials"), immediate reference group norms are much more compelling since violation risks invok-

ing the group's most powerful sanction: exclusion.

Status

In common with most adolescents in American society, the lower class corner group manifests a dominant concern with "status." What differentiates this type of group from others, however, is the particular set of criteria and weighting thereof by which "status" is defined. In general, status is achieved and maintained by demonstrated possession of the valued qualities of lower class culture—Toughness, Smartness, expressed resistance to authority, daring, etc. It is important to stress once more that the individual orients to these concerns *as they are defined within lower class society;* e.g., the status-conferring potential of "smartness" in the sense of scholastic achievement generally ranges from negligible to negative.

The concern with "status" is manifested in a variety of ways. Intra-group status is a continued concern and is derived and tested constantly by means of a set of status-ranking activities; the intragroup "pecking order" is constantly at issue. One gains status within the group by demonstrated superiority in Toughness (physical prowess, bravery, skill in athletics and games such as pool and cards), Smartness (skill in repartee, capacity to "dupe" fellow group members), and the like. The term "ranking," used to refer to the pattern of intragroup aggressive repartee, indicates awareness of the fact that this is one device for establishing the intragroup status hierarchy.

The concern over status in the adolescent corner group involves in particular the component of "adultness," the intense desire to be seen as "grown up," and a corresponding aversion to "kid stuff." "Adult" status is defined less in terms of the assumption of "adult" responsibility than in terms of certain external symbols of adult status—a car, ready cash, and, in particular, a perceived "freedom" to drink, smoke, and gamble as one wishes and to come and go without external restrictions. The desire to be seen as "adult" is often a more significant component of much involvement in illegal drinking, gambling, and automobile driving than the explicit enjoyment of these acts as such.

The intensity of the corner group member's desire to be seen as "adult" is sufficiently great that he feels called upon to demonstrate qualities associated with adultness (Toughness, Smartness, Autonomy) to a much greater degree than a lower class adult. This means that he will seek out and utilize those avenues to these qualities which he perceives as available with greater intensity than an adult and less regard for their "legitimacy." In this sense the adolescent variant of lower class culture represents a maximization or an intensified manifestation of many of its most characteristic features.

Concern over status is also manifested in reference to other street corner groups. The term "rep" used in this regard is especially significant and has broad connotations. In its most frequent and explicit connotation, "rep" refers to the "toughness" of the corner group as a whole relative to that of other groups; a "pecking order" also exists among the several corner groups in a given interactional area, and there is a common perception that the safety or security of the group and all its members depends on maintaining a solid "rep" for toughness vis-a-vis other groups. This motive is most frequently advanced as a reason for involvement in gang fights: "We *can't* chicken out on this fight; our rep would be shot!"; this implies that the group would be relegated to the bottom of the status ladder and become a helpless and recurrent target of external attack.

On the other hand, there is implicit in the concept of "rep" the recognition that "rep" has or may have a dual basis—corresponding to the two aspects of the "trouble" dimension. It is recognized that group as well as individual status can be based on both "law-abiding" and "law-violating" behavior. The situational resolution of the persisting conflict between the "law-abiding" and "law-violating" bases of status comprises a vital set of dynamics in determining whether a "delinquent" mode of behavior will be adopted by a group, under what circumstances, and how persistently. The determinants of this choice are evidently highly complex and fluid, and rest on a range of factors including the presence and perceptual immediacy of different community reference-group loci (e.g., professional criminals, police, clergy, teachers, settlement house workers), the personality structures and "needs" of group members, the presence in the community of social work, recreation, or educational programs which can facilitate utilization of the "law-abiding" basis of status, and so on. . . .

LOWER CLASS CULTURE AND THE MOTIVATION OF DELINQUENT BEHAVIOR

The customary set of activities of the adolescent street corner group includes activities which are in violation of laws and ordinances of the legal code. Most of these center around assault and theft of various types (the gang fight; auto theft; assault on an individual; petty pilfering and shoplifting; "mugging"; pocketbook theft). Members of street corner gangs are well aware of the law-violating nature of these acts; they are not psychopaths, or physically or mentally "defective"; in fact, since the corner group supports and enforces a rigorous set of standards which demand a high degree of fitness and personal competence, it tends to recruit from the most "able" members of the community.

Why, then, is the commission of crimes a customary feature of gang activity? The most general answer is that the commission of crimes by members of adolescent street corner groups is motivated primarily by the attempt to achieve ends, states, or conditions which are valued and to avoid those that are disvalued within their most meaningful cultural milieu, through those culturally available avenues which appear as the most feasible means of attaining those ends.

The operation of these influences is well illustrated by the gang fight—a prevalent and characteristic type of corner group delinquency. This type of activity comprises a highly stylized and culturally patterned set of sequences. Although details vary under different circumstances, the following events are generally included. A member or several members of group A "trespass" on the claimed territory of group B. While there they commit an act or acts which group B defines as a violation of their rightful privileges, an affront to their honor, or a challenge to their "rep." Frequently this act involves advances to a girl associated with group B; it may occur at a dance or party; sometimes the mere act of "trespass" is seen as deliberate provocation. Members of group B then assault members of group A, if they are caught while still in B's territory. Assaulted members of group A return to their "home" territory and recount to members of their group details of the incident, stressing the insufficient nature of the provocation ("I just *looked* at her! Hardly even said anything!"), and the unfair circumstances of the assault ("About *twenty* guys jumped just the *two* of us!"). The highly colored account is acutely inflammatory; group A, perceiving its honor violated and its "rep" threatened, feels obligated to retaliate in force. Sessions of detailed planning now occur; allies are recruited if the size of group A and its potential allies appears to necessitate larger numbers; strategy is plotted, and messengers dispatched. Since the prospect of a gang fight is frightening to even the "toughest" group members, a constant rehearsal of the provocative incident or incidents and declamations of the essentially evil nature of the opponents accompany the planning process to bolster possibly weakening motivation to fight. The excursion into "enemy" territory sometimes results in a full scale fight; more often group B cannot be found, or the police appear and stop the fight, "tipped off" by an anonymous informant. When this occurs, group members express disgust and disappointment; secretly there is much relief; their honor has been avenged without incurring injury; often the anonymous tipster is a member of one of the involved groups. . . .

It would be possible to develop in considerable detail the processes by which the commission of a range of illegal acts is either explicitly supported by, implicitly demanded by, or not materially inhibited by factors relating to the focal concerns of lower class culture. In place of such a development, the following three statements condense in general terms the operation of these processes:

1. Following cultural practices which comprise essential elements of the total life pattern of lower class culture automatically violates certain legal norms.

2. In instances where alternate avenues to similar objectives are available, the non-law-abiding avenue frequently provides a relatively greater and more immediate return for a relatively smaller investment of energy.

3. The "demanded" response to certain situations recurrently engendered within lower class culture involves the commission of illegal acts.

The primary thesis of this paper is that the dominant component of the motivation of "delinquent" behavior engaged in by members of lower class corner groups involves a positive effort to achieve states, conditions, or qualities valued within the actor's most significant cultural milieu. If "conformity to immediate reference group values" is the major component of motivation of "delinquent" behavior by gang members, why is such behavior frequently referred to as negativistic, malicious, or rebellious? Albert Cohen, for example, in *Delinquent Boys* (Glencoe, Ill.: Free Press, 1955) describes behavior which violates school rules as comprising of "active spite and malice, contempt and ridicule, challenge and defiance." He ascribes to the gang "keen delight in terrorizing 'good' children, and in general making themselves obnoxious to the virtuous." A recent national conference on social work with "hard-to-reach" groups characterized lower class corner groups as "youth groups in conflict with the culture of their (sic) communities." Such characterizations are obviously the result of taking the middle class community and its institutions as an implicit point of reference.

A large body of systematically inter-related attitudes, practices, behaviors, and values characteristic of lower class culture are designed to support and maintain the basic features of the lower class way of life. In areas where these differ from features of middle class culture, action oriented to the achievement and maintenance of the lower class system may violate norms of middle class culture and be perceived as deliberately non-conforming or malicious by an observer strongly cathected to middle class norms. This does not mean, however, that violation

of the middle class norm is the dominant component of motivation; it is a by-product of action primarily oriented to the lower class system. The standards of lower class culture cannot be seen merely as a reverse function of middle class culture—as middle class standards "turned upside down"; lower class culture is a distinctive tradition many centuries old with an integrity of its own. . . .

THE BEYOND CONTROL GIRL

Nancy B. Greene and T. C. Esselstyn

INTRODUCTION

Statutes often allow the juvenile court to distinguish between two categories of delinquent girls. In one, there are those who have violated a law or ordinance in such a way as to constitute a felony or misdemeanor had the act been committed by an adult. In another, there are girls who are often described as ungovernable, unmanageable, incorrigible, wayward, or predelinquent. The following discussion concerns the second of these two groups. It omits reference to the first although it is recognized that a clear distinction cannot always be made between the two and that the category to which a girl is assigned may follow no logical system of classification.

There is another problem. Boys can be ungovernable, unmanageable, or incorrigible quite as readily as girls. To discuss these behaviors among girls seems to link them to girls only when actually they are found in boys too. Why, then, limit the discussion to girls?

There are two reasons. One is that relative to the abundant material on delinquent boys, comparatively little has been said

From *Juvenile Justice*, 23, No. 3 (November, 1972) 13–19. Nancy Greene is a probation supervisor in the Santa Clara County Probation Department, California. T. C. Esselstyn is a Sociologist at California State University, San Jose, California.

about delinquent girls. Any thoughtful report therefore helps fill a gap. The second reason is to call attention to one consequence of a developing trend. Nation-wide, legislators and local administrators are being encouraged to divert all juvenile offenders except law violators away from the juvenile justice apparatus and into non-court services. The discussion to follow will suggest that preponderantly, what that means is the diversion of girls without much comprehension of what this involves.

The term "beyond control" is employed below to suggest what is usually meant by ungovernable, unmanageable, incorrigible or similar expressions intended to describe the juvenile whose behavior is displeasing, baffling, defiant, threatening. There may be an overt violation of the law in behavior described as beyond control, for example, drunkenness, unauthorized use of a motor vehicle, theft and forgery of a check. Generally, however, a serious violation of the law is absent. When present, the feature that distinguishes the beyond control juvenile from the law violator is that the act is usually committed against the family group. In most other instances, "delinquent tendencies" rather than "delinquent acts" characterize the beyond control juvenile.

Much subjectivity enters into the decision as to whether the juvenile is beyond control or a law violator. Local procedures tend to apply the label in a somewhat uniform fashion, employing such guides as duration of the behavior, family concern, family resources, and the absence of a victim other than the child. There may be no practical difference between being judged beyond control instead of a law violator. Either may be placed on probation, either may be committed. There is the view that if the history of prior delinquency is reviewed later in life, it is judged to be less serious if it was labeled as beyond control than if the label read violation of the law. However, there is no clear proof that this is so.

VOLUME

With such an imprecise concept and with such variation in its use, it is difficult to say how large the phenomenon is and how it varies by sex. In California, which is probably typical of larger states, 44 percent of all juvenile arrests are for law violations, but 56 percent are for delinquent tendencies or beyond control behavior. In probation referrals, twice as many juveniles are referred for law violations as for beyond control behavior. Within the law violator group, there are about eight boys for every two girls. Within the beyond control group, there are 5.5 boys to 4.5 girls. How the foregoing compares with other jurisdictions is impossible to tell because of differences in terminology, procedures, reporting, and consequent non-comparability of data.

Without attempting to review beyond control behavior among both boys and girls, attention will now be focused on the beyond control girl for the reasons stated at the outset—the general paucity of information about delinquent girls and the possibility that the national trend toward diversion will affect her more than the boy. Additionally, insofar as figures provide any basis for estimates, it is here in the beyond control sphere that the girl makes her major contribution to the total volume of delinquency.

Beyond control conduct is often thought of as a synonym for sex precocity. While this may be true in part, the term includes much more. The principal areas of beyond control behavior among girls are those reviewed below.

SCHOOL

Although not an invariable outcome, it is fairly well established that when a girl is truant, this is often a prelude to serious delinquency and even adult crime. Truancy, insubordination, and disorderly conduct constitute behavior which provides the school system with the basis for a petition to the juvenile court for supportive action to help constrain the girl toward normative standards.

To meet her problems and demands, some school systems have launched imaginative programs for her. Teaching materials have been updated. Movies and television are employed along with older teaching media. Classes are sometimes scheduled on the quarter system to facilitate the achievement of short-term goals and thus reduce the delay in experiencing success. Some beyond control girls have been provided with hand-tailored curricula. Students have been allowed more choice in the selection of both courses and teachers, but there are obvious limits to this. Girls who are poor readers cannot productively elect a course in existentialism. Chronic class-cutters often absent themselves from the very classes and teachers whom they voted the most liked. Either the reasons for the popularity of the course and the teacher are spurious, or persistent truancy is part of the established life style for this kind of girl. Often the truant is not regarded as a problem when she is not present to cause difficulty. School authorities fail to notify the parents that the girl is absent. Parents sometimes fail to notify the school when they know of her absence. A reciprocal failure may therefore exist, and the girl gradually understands the mutually supportive roles played by her parents and the school. Ultimately the problem is one of improving school services so as to disclose the problems in the girls' environment for which her truancy is a clue. The following summary from a California report of investigation illustrates the interplay between child, parent, school, and probation department.

Mary, age 14, good pupil until seventh grade. Then began staying home. Mother and father separated, mother worked, no home phone. Mother ignored requests of school to come in and discuss Mary. Mary refused to open front door when school staff visited her, saying she was too sick. Matter referred to Probation Department. Upon investigation it was disclosed that Mary had forged school excuses for nine months. Was consuming variety of dangerous drugs without knowledge of mother or school. Mother said she had become used to Mary's seclusiveness, day-dreaming, sleeping long hours. Petition filed to have Mary declared beyond control of parents and school authorities.

Of a different stamp is a girl who strikes her peers and her teachers, the fighter, the angry child, one of the "children who hate." She may be retarded, homely, disturbed, abused, or all of these. She knows no response other than to hit her tormentors or lash out at whatever she defines as a frustration. She is certainly beyond control. Often the school responds by suspending her and refusing to readmit her until radical changes have been made in her home. This may involve the probation department in a beyond control action if resources to modify the girl's behavior cannot be found short of this.

UNWED PREGNANCY

The soft revolution has touched the girl whose beyond control behavior has resulted in unwed pregnancy. In many school systems she is dismissed at once or is allowed to continue her enrollment until she begins "to show." Other school systems go to great lengths to continue her education into confinement and beyond. One such system has expanded its regular curriculum for her to include child care, family life, health and education, crafts, sewing, cooking, and a variety of other family care skills which she has not acquired from parental example. It has a nursery for ten babies staffed by two

of the young mothers under the supervision of a special teacher who has been carefully selected for this assignment. Every effort is made to keep the girl in school beyond delivery and the first months of motherhood so that she completes high school and is awarded her diploma.

The guidance director of this program estimates that 80 percent of these pupils showed serious behavior difficulties or lack of attendance in prior schools and would probably never have completed high school if the specialized program had not been available. Measures like these indicate that the beyond control girl can and should be kept in school for as long a period as possible. Pregnancy should not exclude her from the system as it has in the past. Day care programs, nurseries, conventional curricula, and realistic vocational training can be marshalled to aid the young mother still attending school. Girls can be taught in school that they have choices in their lives, that they are not passive, hapless, and helpless, and that they can achieve. Such a persistent theme may not terminate beyond control behavior before it starts. But it will convert the beyond control girl into a young woman with an improved self-concept and an enhanced social potential.

SEX DELINQUENCY

It was said earlier that beyond control or incorrigible behavior was for years a synonym for sex misconduct. In these days, the term has been broadened to include much else. However it does not exclude what may be individually or communally defined as sex offenses. Sex offenses may also be law violations. It is not an easy thing for the girl or her partner or anyone outside the juvenile justice system to say when a sexual act will be called beyond control and when it will be treated as a law violation. As a rule of thumb, forcible rape, prostitution, solicitation, some instances of statutory rape where there is antagonism between the girl's parents and her lover, and some instances of incest, but by no means all, tend to be handled as law violations. All other forms of sex congress involving a girl are likely to be perceived as beyond control behavior.

Here, if ever, there is marked overlap in the application of labels. What difference there is in the disposition of the girl is almost impossible to see. There is the persuasion that the beyond control girl who misbehaves sexually is "treated." If her sexual behavior is such that she is judged to be a law violator, she may also be "treated" but tied to her treatment is an imputation of badness and a need to punish her.

Sexual delinquency in girls often reflects a breakdown of both parental authority and the minor's controls. It can reflect a serious disturbance in the parent-child relationship in which the real problem may be not only the young girl's seductive behavior but also her mother's immaturity. On occasion, rivalry between mother and daughter may be so severe that the girl or the mother will request the minor's placement outside of the home.

The beyond control girl who is sexually promiscuous is in fact emotionally abandoned. She has not necessarily disregarded prevailing sexual mores and values but seems to be a victim of her own anxiety-ridden world. Her self-concept is bound up in her effort to succeed in what she defines as the female role. If her role models have been faulty, then she is further deprived. If those closest to her have failed to protect, love, and provide, and if they have shattered her trust by their own deviance, then the girl loses her ability to cope with life around her. She becomes a device, as it were, for the portrayal of these disturbances and conflicts.

RUNAWAYS

There is a great need to distinguish between types of girls (and boys) who run away. Among the several that are encountered, the principal traits of only three will be summarized here.

The Rootless

Pleasure seeking, hedonistic, seeks immediate gratification. Cannot see consequences of her behavior. Guilt-free, narcissistic. Hence peer relations are impermanent and lack trust. Pseudo-intellectual, lacks self-discipline. She drops out of a series of schools and jobs. Likely to become sexually promiscuous and a drug user. As these increase, her mental and physical health suffer. A skilled manipulator, especially of her family. They long treated her as special, exceptional, and lavished praise upon her as a child. Gave her much freedom but never held her to account. She grew up feeling on the one hand she was infallible and on the other that her family did not lover her because they never controlled her. Her dependency needs were dismissed by her parents as incredible or they were met by effusive material indulgence. Feelings of depression are frequent and unresolved. Moves into middle and late adolescence emotionally a child and physically a woman. At this point the family becomes frightened and for the first time sets limits on her. Girl rebels, runs away, is soon taken into custody. Family rallies "to get her out of it". Girl dictates the terms, family is often ready to concede. The process then repeats itself as release from custody is followed by another of her whims, an ineffectual blocking of this, protest, rebellion, flight, and again custody. Unless a powerful regimen of conjoint family therapy is instituted, her prognosis, if she survives disease and drugs, is unwed pregnancy. She loves her baby as a toy but lacks the basic qualitites to nurture it for sustained periods. Eventually law enforcement steps in on complaint of neglect or abandonment. The infant is often placed with its grandparents—who renew the pattern of relationship they developed with their daughter. Thus the daughter, through her child, has acquired a new tool to use in her attempt to control her family.

The Anxious

Comes from a problem-loaded family. Has had to share adult responsibilities with her mother—household chores, rearing siblings, worry about finances, feeding, clothing. If father is present, she has had to worry about his excessive drinking, unemployment, and physical abuse of family members. Girl may feel ashamed of herself and her family. Knows she has problems and that parents do too. Wants help for herself and also for them. Often runs away for a few hours, overnight, or a few days. Spends this interval at a girl friend's home and enjoys talking to her friend's mother. Often asks for a probation officer so she can have someone to talk to and help her. Poor school performance, finds the work dull. Looks forward to marriage and children. Has no career goal or personal aspirations, says she would have no way of achieving them. Wants to talk with someone about boy-girl relations, sex, her own body, grooming, clothes, manners, but is reluctant to bring any of this up until firm trust is established. Fears and is confused by large bureaucratic impersonal agencies and services. Shows great feelings of powerlessness, anxiety, and depression. Runs away sporadically but is glad to return home, hopes this will lead to concrete help. May become pregnant out of wedlock. If so, she will need much careful support if she is not to repeat the cycle of her mother and grandmother.

The Terrified

Most frequently, but not always, this is the girl who runs away because of the threat of incest with her father or stepfather, and an awareness of its hurricane consequences. The mother feels she has been prevented from realizing her potential because of her marriage and children. She withdraws from her husband increasingly over the years. The father works well at his job but is ineffective or disinterested in the family. He gradually finds he talks more easily to his daughter than his wife. In time, daddy's little girl becomes daddy's big girl. He begins to have sexual fantasies about her and acts these out with touches, kisses, opening the door when she is bathing, or walking about the house where she will see him nude. The mother becomes aware of this and subtly encourages it since it displaces the husband's sexual demands from herself to her daughter. The girl,

on the other hand, resents her mother's lack of attention to her father as well as her father's increasingly insistent overtures to her. She tried to avoid being alone with him by pleading with her mother to stay home more often, inviting numerous peers to visit her, absenting herself as frequently as she can, or by running away. If the runaway is investigated and if she reveals her true motives, the mother reacts, first, by disbelief, but later by admitting she knew of it for a long while. Either as an incident to running away or to its subsequent investigation, the girl may attempt suicide. She has by this time probably developed a "bad me" concept, a severely and perhaps irreparably damaged self-image. She sees herself as the central agent of inevitable family collapse, that she caused it all, that somehow she could have prevented it but failed. Her sense of guilt is overwhelming.

There are other dynamics which produce the terrified girl. She may be victimized by the mental illness of either or both parents. She may be repeatedly beaten by alcoholic parents. She may be the object of severe parental hatred or neglect. She may have been compelled to act as a drug runner for her pusher father, brother, or uncle. Most frequently, however, she is the product of a web of incest. In all these eventualities, the girl is literally in fear for her life, especially if she is to be returned home. She has also learned not to trust adults including those in the helping professions for if she does the family unit may be shattered, someone may go to jail, her guilt will therefore be aggravated, and in the whole process she cannot conceive that anyone will accept her unconditionally. She is beyond control in the sense that she feels she is beyond help. Her running away is her symbolic expression of this deep conviction.

INCORRIGIBLE

Incorrigible children, so-called, frequently have parents whose pattern of discipline vacillates from harsh to none at all. Inconsistency is their life mode. One parent may hate the other and use the child as an outlet:

"I knew he (she) would turn out to be a bum (whore) just like his father (her mother)."

The incorrigible child may be playing a role which has been carefully structured for her by one or both of her parents. She may be cast as the family scapegoat or identified patient. The parent represses his or her own anti-social tendencies and encourages the child to act them out. This is done subtly and unconsciously. There is some evidence that the parent who adopts this mechanism is actually enraged with her own parents. The parent was not protected from danger or abuse by her own parents and she punishes them by exposing her daughter to the same situations. Consciously, she sees her daughter as incorrigible and beyond control. Unconsciously, she maneuvers her daughter to express impulses which she herself has sternly inhibited. Any improvement in the daughter is countered by the nudging of another member of the family into the role which the daughter has vacated, for the family cannot survive without an ugly duckling.

If incorrigibility has any meaning at all, it implies impulsivity, tempestuousness, wildness, an irrational or non-rational stance, defiance when there is no challenge, a goading of the helpless, a tormenting of others as well as one's self. These traits characterize either parent or child, sometimes both at the same time. The word historically carried a great deal of moral freight and perhaps still does. Hence the incorrigible girl has long been thought of as lewd and wanton. However accurate that may be, it tends to obscure the gaps in her parents' personalities. Hence, approaching the girl without also undertaking a long-term program of reconstruction with her parents is likely to be unprofitable. It may even be aggravating.

Omitted from the above discussion is the possibility that some beyond control behavior may have physiological determinants. It may be traceable to minimal brain damage, to unrecognized sequels of physical illness, possibly to dietary imbalance. Among girls, there is the age-old question as to whether some amount of beyond control behavior is associated biochemically rather than socially with menstruation. While not meaning to minimize these possibilities the focus of this paper has been on social rather than somatic influences. It is recognized that such an emphasis is selective and does not cover the entire range of causal factors.

CONCLUSION

The foregoing review leads to several conclusions. First, beyond control behavior is invariably a serious matter. Contrary to much popular belief, it is not a mere temper tantrum, not mere impatience on the part of an intolerant adult, not a mere innocuous aspect of youth culture. Beyond control behavior includes many deep-seated problems, many violations of the law, and much of this is repetitive.

Second, much beyond control behavior requires court action. In one jurisdiction, out of 2712 referrals for beyond control conduct in one year, about 30 percent required formal petitions, short term supervision, or out-of-home placement. The remaining 70 percent were settled at intake but this does not mean that nothing was done. Some help was provided ranging from immediate onsite counseling to detention of an anemic and infected runaway who refused to say what her name was or where she came from. Furthermore, "settled at intake" may not mean that the subject will never come up again. In many instances it will. Hence, settled at intake could more properly be viewed as one point on a continuum of court services for one client.

Third, the current appeal to divert beyond control cases away from the juvenile justice system is based on at least three assumptions. One is that their needs are not being met by the system or are met poorly. Another is that resources actually exist elsewhere or can be developed to which beyond control cases be diverted efficiently and humanely. Both of these assumptions are quite precarious. So far as now appears they are based on a few dramatic local examples. The matter is far more profound than this.

Another assumption is that if the child gets into the juvenile justice system, a bad situation will be made worse. He or she will be traumatized or stigmatized and confirmed as a career delinquent. While there are grounds to support this fear, the data have not been refined to the point where one can make a blanket statement about the resulting damage. Obviously, some *are* damaged. Not-so-obviously, many are actually helped. In the present state of the art, the time has not yet arrived when one whole category of juveniles can safely be eliminated from the court's purview.

A fourth general conclusion is that a program to divert beyond control cases away from the juvenile courts may actually mean the diversion of girls while increasing the court's intake of boys. The percentages shown earlier suggest why this is likely to be so. In Calfiornia and in other comparable jurisdictions, beyond control referrals, like the referrals of law violators, originate primarily from police arrests. In a community experimenting with diversion, one might predict that complaints about beyond control boys will be redrafted by police agencies so that they are referred as law violators in order to make sure that the authority of the court is invoked. Beyond control girls might be diverted provided community resources make this possible and good working ties are developed between them and the police. In view of the high proportion of girls involved and in view of the universal reluctance of the police to handle the female offender wherever this can be avoided, it might be anticipated that the net effect of a diversion policy will be to increase the volume of male law-violators and limit diversion almost exclusively to girls.

All of this probably argues in favor of rethinking what the term means. If it is to continue as a part of the philosophy and services of the juvenile court, there should be some substantive difference between what happens to the law violator and what happens to the juvenile who is described as beyond control. If beyond control behavior is to be eliminated from the juvenile court,

then policy decisions are needed in advance as to what is to be done in cases of serious unmanageability which have relied upon court authority in the past. How to stimulate the growth of non-court services and how to train court personnel to meet the needs of beyond control referrals more effectively are issues of community and staff development. These issues loom especially large when one considers the high proportion of females in the beyond control population and the scant systematic, empirical, or descriptive material about them.

QUESTIONS FOR DISCUSSION

1. What is meant by the subculture of violence?
2. Violence rates in the U.S. have increased steadily since 1960. Why? Nevertheless, the present murder rate is still lower than the murder rate at the time the Uniform Crime Reports (FBI) were initially published. Since the 1930 rates occurred long before the "crime in the streets" issue and before the student and ghetto rioting and problems, how is it that the 1930 rates were higher than those of our most difficult present?
3. Why has Congress and why have the states (with only a few exceptions) refused to outlaw the sale of handguns which are the weapons used in at least 60 percent of the murders in this country? How do you stand on gun legislation? How would you advise your representatives to vote on the "Saturday Night Special" issue?

    Survey your friends and acquaintances on this issue. Mount a poll to check opinions as a project for the class.
4. Assaults differ from murder in only one general respect other than the life or death of the victim. How do they differ? Why is assault so grossly underreported? What night of the week would you think the violence rate would be highest? Why?
5. Rape is the most underreported major crime. Why? Do you know of any programs to help the victims of rape? If not, what should a program attempt to

do? Research this subject to see what is, can, or has been done.

6. What "myths" exist concerning forcible rape based on the Amir research? Describe this study in detail indicating its methodology, findings, and weaknesses. Does this study truly represent the problem or only that part of the problem which victims are willing to report?

7. Legally, what is the difference between robbery, burglary, and larceny?

8. According to the Uniform Crime Reports the property offenses have a low rate of clearance by arrest. Why are so few crimes solved? How might the police be more effective in this property offense area?

9. Describe a typical robber (age, sex, race, record of crime, weapon, time of robbery, place of robbery, type of victim). Do the same for burglary and auto theft.

10. What kinds of robberies are there? Which is the most frequent type? What percentage involve the use of a weapon?

11. What are the characteristics of the systematic check forger? Do these characteristics affirm or refute Sutherland's theory of professional theft?

12. Quarantelli and Dynes suggest that looting and vandalism during rioting tend to occur because the usual norms become inapplicable under conditions of relative *anomie*. What justifications do they offer for this position? Do these arguments account for the phenomena of the late 1960's?

13. At least one-fourth of the juveniles who appear before the juvenile court have not committed offenses in adult criminal terms. They are brought to the court in large numbers for such things as running away from home, school truancy, incorrigibility, parental neglect, and being under the influence of an undesirable adult. What should be done with these minors in need of supervision (MINS)? Why should they be treated like juvenile offenders? What practical alternatives are there for this ever growing number of dependent, neglected, and unruly children?

14. How does a middle-class gang differ from a lower-class ghetto gang? Why are there so few middle-class gangs? Why have they been studied so little?

15. What would be the middle-class equivalent of the lower-class gang? Read W. F. Whyte's *Street Corner Society* and compare the Doc and Chick groups. Also read and report on *Tally's Corner* by Elliott Liebow. Finally, read the first book written in the U.S. on gangs, *The Gang* by F. Thrasher.

16. What does Walter Miller mean by lower-class "focal concerns"? How do these concerns differ from middle-class focal concerns?

17. Compare Albert Cohen's theory of delinquent gang formation with Miller's "focal concerns" theory.

18. Why is it that every developing nation soon begins to develop a delinquency problem? What is the relationship between modernization and delinquency? See Marshall Clinard's book *Crime in Developing Countries* which treats with this problem.

19. Study a house or refuge for runaway juveniles in your community. See if you can think of ways of resolving family crises so that running away can be minimized. Also, investigate the new family crisis intervention centers around the country.

BIBLIOGRAPHY

Ahlstrom, Winton M., and Havighurst, Robert J. *400 Losers*. San Francisco: Jossey-Bass, 1971.

Cameron, Mary O. *The Booster and the Snitch: Department Store Shoplifting*. Free Press, 1964.

Clinard, Marshall B. and Quinney, Richard. *Criminal Behavior Systems*. New York: Holt, Rinehart and Winston, 1967.

Cohen, Albert K. *Delinquent Boys*. Glencoe, Illinois: Free Press, 1955.

Conklin, John. *Robbery and the Criminal Justice System*. Philadelphia: J. B. Lippincott, 1972.

Cloward, Richard A., and Ohlin, Lloyd E. *Delinquency and Opportunity*. New York: The Free Press, 1960.

Dinitz, Simon, and Reckless, Walter C. *Critical Issues in the Study of Crime: A Book of Readings*. Boston: Little, Brown and Company, 1968.

Glueck, Sheldon, and Glueck, E. *Unraveling Juve-*

nile Delinquency. Cambridge, Mass.: Harvard University Press, 1951.

Glueck, Sheldon, and Glueck, E. (eds.). *Identification of Predelinquents.* New York: Intercontinental Medical Book Co., 1972.

Juvenile Delinquency. Task Force Report, President's Commission on Law Enforcement and the Administration of Justice, 1967.

Kirkham, George L. *The Female Offender,* San Jose, Calif.: The Spartan Book Store, San Jose College, 1966.

Moynihan, Daniel P. *Violent Crime: The Challenge to Our. Cities.* The Report of the National Commission on the Causes and Prevention of Violence. New York: Braziller, George, 1969.

Platt, A. M. *The Child Savers: The Invention of Delinquency.* Chicago, Ill.: University of Chicago Press, 1969.

Reckless, Walter C. *The Crime Problem.* New York: Appleton-Century-Crofts, 1973.

Reckless, Walter C. and Dinitz, Simon. *The Prevention of Juvenile Delinquency: An Experiment.* Columbus, Ohio: Ohio State University Press, 1972.

Sellin, T. and Wolfgang, M. *The Measurement of Delinquency.* New York: Wiley, 1964.

Short, James F., Jr., ed. *Gang Delinquency and Delinquent Subcultures.* New York: Harper and Row, 1968.

Shover, Neal. "The Social Organization of Bur-

glary." *Social Problems,* 20, No. 4 (Spring 1973), 499–514.

Sutherland, Edwin H. *The Professional Thief.* Chicago: University of Chicago Press, 1937.

Sykes, G. M., and Matza, D. "Techniques of Neutralization: A Theory of Delinquency." *American Sociological Review* 22 (December 1957), 664–670.

To Establish Justice, To Insure Domestic Tranquility: Final Report of the National Commission on the Causes and Prevention of Violence. Washington D.C.: U.S. Government Printing Office, 1969.

Winslow, Robert W. (ed.). *Crime in a Free Society.* California: Dickenson, 1973.

Wolfgang, Marvin E. *Patterns in Criminal Homicide.* Philadelphia: University of Pennsylvania Press, 1958.

Wolfgang, Marvin E., and Ferracuti, Franco. *The Subculture of Violence.* London: Tavistock, 1967.

Wolfgang, Marvin E., Savitz, Leonard and Johnston, Norman. *The Sociology of Crime and Delinquency* (2nd ed.). New York: Wiley and Sons, 1970.

Wolfgang, Marvin E., Figlio, Robert M. and Sellin, Thorsten. *Delinquency in a Birth Cohort.* Chicago: University of Chicago Press, 1972.

Yablonsky, Lewis. *The Violent Gang.* New York: Macmillan, 1962.

4

Economic and Occupational Crimes

The Uniform Crime Index of street crimes—murder, forcible rape, robbery, aggravated assault, burglary, larceny, and auto theft—create fear and dissension in America. Far more costly in every way, however, is the insidious influence of the economic and occupational crimes. One major activity—consumer fraud—takes more money and destroys more societal trust than the depredations of all inmates in all prisons, jails, and reformatories together. Another occupational activity, illegal gambling, may have a gross "handle" of as much as $50 billion and a net variously estimated from $7 billion up. Narcotics add greatly to the overall health and welfare of the syndicate, and tax fraud (from former Vice President Agnew up and down) is probably even costlier.

Economic and occupational crimes is a category which hardly seems to concern the public. Most of the operatives are generally colorless individuals whose personal lives are filled to overflowing with integrity and the other moral virtues we seem to cherish so much in the abstract. Even the syndicate types, or at least their college-educated children, have begun to seem more like upper-echelon business and professional men than the "gorillas" of the Godfather era.

There are, of course, some colorful semi-professionals left who live by their skill, wits, and "con" talents. They live on the margin of society and, with luck and connections, do quite well. While the organized syndicate remains firmly in Italian and Sicilian control, the numbers game represents one of the major inroads by blacks into syndicate operation. The "Numbers Man," as described by Roebuck, is a character who enjoys high status in the black ghetto. He has all the accoutrements of American style success—money, glamour, class. Along with the pimp, the numbers man was once the Horatio Alger of the ghetto. His status, while still high, is rapidly diminishing as blacks enter the mainstream of economic life in the urban community.

The aftermath of the greatest scandal in American history, the Watergate fiasco and its related and attendant immoralities and criminality, has detracted attention from the major criminal frauds and conspiracies in the last 20 years or so. Forgotten is the Equity Funding computer-assisted insurance confidence game of the early 1970's which, if the facts are ever ascertained, will run at least to $20 billion. Forgotten, too, are such interesting characters as Anthony De Angelis who in the 1960's cornered the soybean market and eventually swindled $100 million or more before getting a light prison sentence and parole. Our second selection concerns some equally classy Master Swindlers of an earlier era. Return with us then to the likes of an Ivar Kreuger ($500 million) or a Charles Ponzi ($15 million) and see the other side of the crime problem. Remember, too, that this kind of professional theft is very much alive in the United States and that the authorities remain unequal to the task of coping with it even now.

The third and fourth selections concern syndicate, or organized, crime—an economic activity both pernicious and fearsome. Although federal authorities estimated that three-fourths of the major·syndicate figures in the United States were either under indictment, in prison, or on parole in 1973, syndicate crime remains a threat to legal enterprise as well as a major criminal activity. Organized crime is based on supplying illegal goods and services—gambling, narcotics, vice—to eager and willing victims. More recently and surely more ominously, syndicate money has been invested in real estate, resorts, construction, and securities, to mention but a few, providing the syndicates or criminal families with legitimate front activities. The President's Commission article discusses not only these matters but details the internal structure and mode of operation of the 24 major syndicate families in this country. Although there are more popular journalistic accounts of the 500 or so organized criminals in America, this selection contains the most authoritative information now available.

Stuart Hills, in "Combating Organized Crime in America," examines—dispassionately and with both a fine historical and sociological perspective—the dilemma posed by syndicate activity. He asks, "How can we centralize, coordinate, and make more efficient our law enforcement machinery to combat the activities of organized crime, without inviting the abuses of political authoritarianism and the encroachment and ultimate loss of our civil liberties?"

Criminologists agree that white collar crime is by far the most damaging of all violations and deviations. Not only is it the most costly form of deviation, but it also undermines trust in our basic economic arrangements; none of us can adequately pro-

tect ourselves from it. White collar crime is a development of the entrepreneurial and corporate eras. It knows no political ideology as such, occurring in socialist, capitalist, and, in a somewhat different format, in developed and undeveloped nations. Traditional approaches to its special attributes included differential treatment under the law and the peculiar attitude of the public and the violators, neither of whom thought these economic depredations as being criminal.

One of the most important reports is the 1970 monograph by Herbert Edelhertz, "The Nature, Impact and Prosecution of White Collar Crime." In this selection, unfortunately largely abridged, Edelhertz broadens the term "white collar crime" to include many illegal activities—consumer fraud, credit card violations, corruption and bribery of all sorts, planned bankruptcies, fraudulent claims for welfare or social security benefits, and various ingenious schemes involving concealment or guile for self-enrichment. Edelhertz, a prominent lawyer and former prosecutor, approaches the problem in the hardheaded, pragmatic manner of his profession. He defines the crimes, talks about their impact on society, and discusses the detection, investigation, prosecution, and sentencing of offenders. At no point can one fail to understand that conventional criminal law concepts and procedures are inadequate in dealing with the issues raised by these economic depredations. Edelhertz's article and his research may well represent the conceptual basis for the muckraking of a modern Ralph Nader and other interest action groups trying to find ways of coping with impersonal organizations using illegal practices for self-aggrandizement.

The final selection in this chapter concerns criminal tax fraud—one of the most pervasive of the so-called folk crimes. The article "Criminal Tax Fraud" was prepared for the President's Commission by the Tax Division of the Department of Justice. It provides a low-keyed account of the problem of criminal tax fraud in terms of the offenders, the nature of the offense, the procedural steps in enforcement, and the outcome of prosecution. Since about 68 million people file federal tax returns, many

with fraudulent intent, the fact that a mere 593 defendants were convicted in 1966 suggests the problems of enforcement in this area of economic crime.

THE NUMBERS MAN

Julian B. Roebuck

Numbers game operators are usually defined as lottery law or policy violators. They are defined by themselves, the police, the underworld and the betting public as numbers men. . . . The numbers game, a variant form of policy, is a special type of *lottery* which constitutes a notorious form of gambling among Negroes in the large metropolitan areas of the Eastern Seaboard and the Midwest. Some have claimed that the numbers game has a certain integrative function for the Negro community, furnishing much of the content of casual conversation, imparting temporal structure to the day and offering a sense of participation in a community-wide institution. It has a widespread patronage among the lower-income and working classes, especially in Negro residential areas. Although only small amounts are generally involved in individual bets, many Negroes who play the game regularly can ill afford to lose. One survey shows that during 1960, almost three out of every eight persons who gambled in this country played the numbers. It is estimated that these 32,000,000 Americans, of whom 14,000,000 were women, wagered the sum of five billion dollars in an effort to hit a lucky number. The numbers game constitutes professional organized crime. It represents the only such area, at present, that Negroes have participated in in large numbers at the higher echelons of organization.

From *Criminal Typology; The Legalistic, Physical-Constitutional-Hereditary, Psychological-Psychiatric and Sociological Approaches,* Springfield, Ill.: Charles C Thomas, 1967. Chap. VIII, pp. 136–54. Reprinted by permission. Julian Roebuck is Professor of Sociology at Mississippi State University.

The numbers player bets one cent upward on a three digit number (any combination of numbers from 000 to 999) which he notes on a "slip" and turns over to a "numbers writer," a street numbers bookie (with his wager commonly from ten cents to a quarter), who in turn passes it on to a "pick-up man," and it finally reaches the counting office (the "bank" or "drop") of the numbers ring. At the drop, clerical workers check and tally each individual numbers slip and wager and sift out the slips bearing the winning combination, which is usually determined from pari-mutuel totals at a certain race track. The total payoff figures for the three, five and seven races may be used, or any combination of prices in any three designated races. The last dollar numeral before the decimal is used. The last three digits of the daily total amount bet may also be designated the winning combination. Odds, though varying from one city to another, are usually in excess of 1000 to 1 that any particular combination of three numbers will turn up. The operators pay a winner from 500 to 800 to 1.

THE NUMBERS MAN AS A CRIMINAL TYPE

. . . A qualitative examination of [16 Negro numbers men in the District of Columbia Reformatory at Lorton, Virginia] indicated a stable family background relatively free of emotional conflict, economic deprivation and physical violence. These remarks from one numbers man about his parental family were typical:

My father worked at the post office as a mail clerk. He retired a few years ago. My mother worked in the government at one time as a clerk. You know, she typed. When us children came along she quit and stayed home. There were times when things were tight but we managed. We didn't bother with no welfare. We had enough to eat and wear. We had to go to school and keep clean. Also Sunday School. We didn't run the streets either. We stayed at home when we were not at school or at the playground. The old man brought his check home at the end of each month and we all shared alike. He didn't drink it up or live it up with the chicks. He wore the pants in the family, but he wasn't rough. You know he didn't cuss and slap everybody around. He was good to my mother. All in all we had a happy home. If we got out of line they [parents] mostly talked to us and made us stay in the house for a day or two. I never got but two whippings.

In discussing their infrequent juvenile delinquent activities, not one mentioned housebreaking, strong-arm activities, robbery. Involvement in sporadic, unplanned pursuits such as petty thefts from grocery stores were mentioned. Their friends were free of police and juvenile court contact. Accounts of this kind were common:

I had no use for gang boys. Most of them were thugs who lived in the bottom. They never was my kind. I scuffled around with some of them at school. You know, I was no sissy, but I gave them plenty of traveling space and they just left me alone. Sure, I stole a few things as I went through life. I guess everybody does. You know, like a toy or something. I sure had no habit of stealing. My buddies were good boys. We didn't get in trouble with the teachers and we steered clear of cops. . . .

Though the numbers men grew up in non-slum areas, they claimed that their family members and neighborhood acquaintances were tolerant of the numbers game.

My folks were respectable, law-abiding people. None of them went to jail. They knew about the numbers. Man, everybody knows about the numbers. My mother and father use to play a number now and then.

My sister, who went to college, was married to a numbers man. Everybody in the neighborhood knew what the number was each day whether they played one or not. Everybody knew too when somebody hit [won]. Of course my folks didn't like no craps or poker playing. At home we used to joke about dreaming up a good number to play.

In reference to later community adjustment, all of these men had strong primary group ties. Eleven maintained strong ties with their first primary group, the parental family; thirteen experienced strong marital ties; the remaining three sustained stable relationships with a paramour.

Their difficulties as adults stemmed from gambling. Though professional gamblers with some understanding of odds and the laws of chance, these men spent much of their leisure time betting at the racetrack, prize fights, poker games and at various other major sports events throughout the Northeast. Betting on horses was their chief recreation. They earned their money from "marks" (numbers players), and at the same time they were "marks" themselves at the race track. Their reactions to this anomaly are illustrated by these comments:

Money that comes easy, goes easy. Money you win from gambling moves around like ice on top of a red-hot stove. But you know horse racing is the sport of kings. I got to have some fun, you know. Then too, I don't gamble all the money I make from the numbers away.

A sizable portion of their time was spent with attractive young women whom they euphemistically alluded to as "slick chicks," "fine broads," "foxes," and "party girls." They wined, dined and socialized with these women at two plush cocktail lounges situated in a Negro commercial section of Washington, D.C. They passed these girls around among themselves at what they termed "respectable time intervals" (3–6 months). Many of these "playmates" worked in a numbers ring as clerical workers. At times they were actually "kept women," who accepted their roles as companions and sex partners. These remarks were characteristic:

These chicks as a rule were for real. I mean they would never squeal. They knew we were in the life, and with us they knew they got the best of what there was to get like entertainment, clothes, perfume, booze. Everybody knew who was going with who. The fruit basket would turn over now and then and we would change partners in a nice way, but we didn't get upset and jealous. It was the life. You know we lived it up. We were gentlemen. No girl had to worry about us beating her up or pushing her around. You know many men do slap women around. They understood we were married. They never called us at home. In fact we were all good friends. Some of the chicks worked for us at clerical help.

Their leisure-time nexus of gambling and women seemed to constitute prescribed role playing:

Well, you know in my business you have to be a sport and a spender. You got to have front. You have to impress the public that you are a man in the know who knows how to live it up. You got to wear sharp clothes, hang out in the best places, set up the boys and girls at the bar with drinks. And you know, give the chicks a break. When these suckers see you swinging out now and then with a fine broad they know you have some money, and they figure they can play their numbers with you safely. This is a competitive business. Of course it's not too hard on me to play the game. My wife understands this. She's been with me now ten years. She isn't going anywhere. Of course she is not happy when I go out and blow a chunk (money) after a big run, but I have to do that. At that time I have to prove I can stand the run.

Their statements demonstrated that the numbers game was a regular, day-by-day occupation and that they were interested in upward mobility in an activity which called for differential responsibility and skills at various levels of performance. As one numbers man reported:

I've made my living by the numbers for years. I started out working for a "numbers writer" twenty years ago as a "runner." He died two years later. I had worked hard and had played him square. The big boy "num-

bers backer" knew I knew the territory and everybody in it. He also knew I was a pleasant, fast talker and a hard worker who could put on a front. I know to keep my mouth shut when necessary. I could shoot the breeze with the customers about most anything they wanted to talk about ... you know, sports, gambling, women, even politics. He knew I could also keep my hand out of his bag (steal the backer's take). Five years later he made me a "pick-up man." You see I had a head for figures. I could estimate the normal take in most areas of the city. It was hard for a "writer" to hold out on me cause I knew what the people bet in his area. A few years later the big boy's "head man" was 'busted' [arrested] at the drop and then I got my big break. He called me up to help supervise the drop. Three of us fought it out for "head man" for two years. The competition was keen. I had to be nice to everybody there though I knew some were gunning for me. I really had to be a politician and learn more about numbers too. You know, a little bookkeeping and percentages. I also had to get to know the strong and weak points of workers. I had to learn when to recommend hiring and firing certain people. It takes a certain kind of head for figures and a certain kind of personality for numbers. You got to be careful who you hire. You can't afford to hire a "willy" [country boy]. You got to pick a man with some class who knows what's happening, and who knows how to dress and talk right. You got to stay away from gorillas [strong armers] unless you are hiring a bouncer. Finally I made a "head man." After the big boy was finally busted I took over as a backer. Not everybody makes it. You can get froze at my level. I was lucky, and I guess I got more class than most people.

Though all these men made their living primarily from numbers, ten of them claimed that at one time or another they had invested money as "silent partners" in what they referred to as legitimate enterprises—bars, liquor stores, tourist homes, poolrooms and used car lots. Five said they owned rental property. The capital for these business ventures was invariably made from numbers. Their general attitude toward legitimate business, money, and the numbers game may be adduced from the following expressions of one numbers man:

What good is a lot of money less it's put to use? Stepping out into business was just like another gamble to me. Many Negro business-men in this town got their start from work-ing at numbers. Some retire, some don't. If it wasn't for numbers some people wouldn't have jobs and homes. I went into numbers for the same reason other people go into teaching or medicine or anything else. I no-ticed some outstanding successful people in the game. They attracted me so I went in.

None of them claimed any association with other aspects of the organized under-world, though they were quite familiar with the criminal argot. They asserted only a newspaper knowledge of other underworld activities and admitted to no more than a nodding acquaintance with offenders outside the gambling fraternity. Their criminal com-panions were usually other numbers men, though they admitted to some association with other types of gamblers, e.g., owners and operators of gambling houses, racetrack bookies, boxing, football and baseball bookies, and "house" card and dice dealers. . . .

The interview material suggested that fif-teen of these men were products of the Negro middle class. All were reared in non-slum neighborhoods by respectable parents; twelve graduated from high school; three attended college, ten stated that one or more of their siblings had attended college; twelve stated that their wives attended college; fourteen claimed that their parents had steady, non-laboring jobs; and all mentioned friends and family connections among pro-fessionals and semiprofessionals. . . . The men presented themselves as respectable, middle class people who were churchgoers, homeowners, and fathers.

Perhaps, though products of the Negro middle class, these men who lived in the noncriminal as well as the criminal world could best be described as middle and upper class "shadies." But no less a scholar than E. Franklin Frazier lends support to their claim of respectability. He contends that "playing

the numbers" has become respectable among members of the Negro middle class and that some members of Negro "society" derive their income from the numbers. He claims further that the Negro middle class is also being recruited from the successful under-world Negroes who have gained their money from numbers and that the sporting and criminal elements are acquiring a dominant position among Negroes.

Regardless of their class position in the Negro community, these men were criminals because they engaged in an illegal racket. They evinced in the interviews the "fast buck" philosophy of the "angel boy" and the professional criminal and expressed nega-tive feelings about all law enforcement ma-chinery, especially the police. Moreover they seemed to have rationalized away their spe-cific form of criminal activity. Gambling to them did not constitute "real" criminal be-havior. These assertions by one interviewee were typical:

Why don't the cops spend their time on these hoodlums and leave us numbers men alone. All we do is provide opportunity for people to gamble. You can't stop gambling. We provide a service for which we deserve some return. Hell, we pay 800 to 1 odds. Everybody has his angle. Take you, you got your racket. You probably will write a book. The police have theirs. They will take a red hot stove [accept bribes]. Trying to do away with crooked cops is as easy as dipping all the water out of the Atlantic Ocean with a saucer.

All claimed that the gambling ring for which they worked retained a criminal lawyer on a permanent basis. It is interesting to note that their court records revealed that only four different lawyers (three Negro and one white) were involved in the sixteen dif-ferent court cases.

Though, according to their reports, the various numbers rings in which they worked competed with each other for personnel and for betting customers, there was no evidence of syndicated numbers activity. On the con-trary, the data indicated that the leaders (numbers backers) were local products.

There appeared to be a feudal system (minus a king) including several rings, each maintaining its own organizational pattern and its own base of operations and each possessing an individual set of employees. . . .

The arrest histories of these men were comparatively brief (mean: 5.2 per man), and the overwhelming number of their arrests were for lottery law charges. There were a few disorderly conduct charges, usually connected with the presence of the offender in a house dice or card game or in a numbers-counting office and an occasional intoxication charge. Other types of charges were rare. Criminal progression was not in evidence; the arrest histories generally began and terminated with lottery law violation charges. . . .

The numbers men appeared to be in good health and made few somatic complaints. Medical examinations showed that twelve were organically sound, one had diabetes, one had a hyperthyroid condition, and two suffered from mild heart murmurs. They reacted to the interview situation in a friendly and cooperative manner. There were no obvious diagnostic signs of neurosis, psychopathy or psychosis. They appeared to be extroverted and outgoing personalities, who verbalized well at a highly literate level. Neither verbal aggression nor verbal passivity was noted. These men expressed strong emotional ties with friends and family members. Comparatively speaking, they appeared to be sophisticated in reference to the criminal as well as the noncriminal world. Though not regular church attenders, they expressed a strong religious orientation of an orthodox type. They were well poised, confident and self-satisfied. In short, they seemed to relate well and to have well-integrated personalities. . . .

What peculiar constellation of background and personality characteristics disposed them to this and not to other patterns of criminal behavior? The full answer to this question is not known. However, their developmental histories offer some hypothetical clues in this direction. They grew up in home and neighborhood situations which

were quite tolerant of the numbers game racket. Parents, friends and acquaintances played numbers. In fact, some of their neighbors and in-laws were numbers men. In a sense they were reared in a cultural milieu where the numbers game constituted a community institution which, though illegal, was not defined as "really criminal." In late adolescence they adopted an adult recreation pattern of drinking, gambling and dancing which they did not conceive of as reprehensible or illegal. Sexually precocious, they began dating early and engaging in promiscuous heterosexual relations. The role of the "sport," the "smoothie" and the "big spender" which was tied in with their early recreation pattern intrigued them. They became interested in "sharp clothes," expensive tastes and what they called "high living." They were surreptitious in these activities because of their desire to please "conventional parents." They avoided juvenile delinquents and juvenile delinquent gang activity. Fighting, stealing, and violence were defined as behavior outside of their life style. They were especially concerned with remaining clear of arrest and police contacts. In a sense they conceived of themselves as . . . "good boys." As young adults they admired the numbers men with whom they came in contact through family and neighborhood acquaintances. They considered some of these racketeers to be outstanding successes in their field. Material success and the way of life of the numbers man that went with this success appealed to them. Consequently they rationalized away the illegal aspects of the numbers game and entered it as a "business pursuit."

This rationalization was probably not too difficult. Perhaps the urban Negro middle class has in part accepted the numbers man. Perhaps he is acceptable because of his money. Material wealth is undoubtedly a great determinant of social status among members of a minority group who are at the bottom of the economic ladder, who have not been stratified into functional social classes until quite recently and who are discriminated against and segregated. In these circumstances the social class lines of urban Negroes are probably fluid. It must also be remembered that the Negro middle and upper classes are much smaller in base and less economically secure than are the white middle and upper classes.

Treatment prospects with such a group of offenders do not appear heartening. Perhaps when the urban Negro comes to be less spatially separated and socially isolated from the remainder of the community, and when his middle and upper class membership increases in size, economic base and security, the numbers man will come to be viewed for what he is, a racketeer. Perhaps then the moral indignation of the Negro community will fall upon him, and all supports for his claim to respectability will be removed. . . .

In prison, the numbers men were generally tractable, pleasant and courteous inmates who were usually liked by other inmates as well as by prison employees. They accepted their time philosophically, and they did not seek special favors. The prison term was viewed as an occupational hazard. In the prison setting they made themselves as unobtrusive as possible. As a rule they were not interested in status within the inmate subculture. Neither "peddler-connivers" nor prison toughs, they seemed to approximate in type the "real man" construct suggested by Gresham Sykes—the dignified, composed inmate who does not exploit others and who is able to endure the hardships of incarceration. Their short sentences (usually three years) and their strong primary group ties on the outside perhaps

militated against preoccupation with prison status. On the other hand, they subscribed to the principle that every man has his price, that all occupations are rackets. They saw little use for and they avoided such therapy programs as group counseling, group therapy, and individual therapy. The institution's religious and educational programs were of no interest to them. They appeared to have crystallized their social values and the attitudes which underpinned their specific form of criminal behavior—a behavior which appears to have strong support among their peer groups in "free" society. . . .

Generally, these professional gamblers are model prisoners. To the writer's knowledge, not one "numbers man" has been reported for a serious violation of prison regulations during his sentence at the D.C. Reformatory. They are tractable, pleasant and courteous inmates. They usually competently fill clerical positions as inmate clerks. They are generally liked by other inmates as well as by prison officials. Contrary to what would be expected of the professional criminal, they do not seek special favors. In short, they make "good" adjustments in prison, where they make themselves as unobtrusive as possible. As other professional criminals, they subscribe to the principle that "every man has his price," that all occupations are rackets. In short, they are what is generally referred to in prison slang as "angle boys." For these reasons they should be separated (housing and work details) from nonprofessional criminals in the prison setting.

MASTER SWINDLERS

Kenneth Slocum

Bible-quoting Billie Sol Estes, whatever his ambitions when he started building his now-

From *Wall Street Journal,* © Dow Jones & Company, Inc., May 23, 1962, pp. 12, 19. Reprinted by permission. Kenneth Slocum is a Staff Reporter for the *Wall Street Journal.*

shattered business empire, can at least be assured of one thing: At 37 years old, the Texas wheeler-dealer already seems destined to go down in history with some of the most noted swindlers of the past half century.

Republican Senators freely predict the

unraveling of Mr. Estes' tangled affairs will disclose a public scandal "bigger than Teapot Dome." Though it remains to be seen whether that forecast will be borne out, even Democratic Senator John L. McClellan, whose Senate Investigations subcommittee began hearings on Mr. Estes' activities this week, has called the case "the darnedest mess I've ever seen." Others have likened Billis Sol to a "modern day Ponzi" and a "Democratic Goldfine."

The case histories of some of the notable con men of the past indicate that Mr. Estes may have surpassed some of them in total dollar depradations but probably will not achieve top ranking. So far, the principal charge against him from a dollar point of view is that he allegedly duped finance companies into accepting fraudulent mortgages, estimated between $22 million and $24 million.

However, the annals of past corporate crimes include thefts as high as $500 million:

	Period	Funds involved
Ivar Kreuger	1917–1932	$500 million
Teapot Dome	1921–1929	$200 million
Charles Ponzi	1919–1920	$15 million
Lowell Birrell	1954–1959	$14 million
F. Donald Coster	1908–1938	$8 million

The methods by which these super-swindlers hoodwinked an unsuspecting public as well as supposedly sophisticated bankers and accountants included switches of funds from legitimate companies into ghost-like concerns that were little more than private savings accounts; schemes to whet the public's perennial appetite for quick-and-easy riches; and outright bribery of public officials to obtain illegal advantages over competitors.

Here are sketches of a few of the famous swindlers of the 20th Century:

IVAR KREUGER

For sheer size, geographical scope and complexity of operation, probably no swindle in history compares with the illicit financial maneuvers of Swedish-born Ivar Kreuger. And because of tough new laws, probably none ever will. From 1917 until he killed himself in 1932, the international financier, who at one point controlled three quarters of the world's match production, took in some $650 million, mostly from sales of securities. Although he left assets of $200 million, claims against his enterprises totaled $1,168,000,000. After 13 years of investigation, officials estimated that he probably bilked shareholders and moneylenders out of some $500 million.

A silent, self-reliant man, he founded a Swedish building concern, Kreuger & Toll, in 1908, and in three years expanded it into Sweden's biggest building company. In 1913, he combined 10 tiny match companies in Sweden and four years later, through expansion and merger, he controlled production in the nation.

While these operations seemed honest enough, there were certain departures from recognized bookkeeping procedures. Annual reports, for instance, often identified the source of two-thirds of the net income as "various transactions." As the world was to find out later, he also was switching assets and liabilities between companies to fit the occasion and was creating fictional assets when existing ones ran short.

Over the years, as he pyramided company upon company, funds flowed into his own pockets through the simple procedure of transferring them abroad. For instance in 1923, International Match Corp., a Delaware concern he founded, had an initial stock offering of $15 million. Mr. Kreuger, then the president, pocketed $13 million by charging it off to "A. B. Russia," a dummy company abroad that was little more than a personal savings account. Between 1923 and 1932, International Match sold $148 million in securities and Mr. Kreuger transferred $143 million of it to Europe.

In the late 1920's, the "Puritan of Finance" as newspapers called him, exuded prosperity from his empire of 250 match factories in 37 countries. Mr. Kreuger loaned money freely to poor European countries, receiving match monopolies in return. He was on friendly terms with international leaders, including President Hoover, and was generally conceded to be the world's top financier. While he worked 18 hours a day manipulating his empire, shareholders were kept happy with big dividends, paid mostly out of capital.

But while his stock held up relatively well in the early days of the great depression, the squeeze was on for more funds to cover up his thefts. With this in mind, he agreed in 1931 to a merger of one of his companies, L. M. Ericsson Telephone Co. of Sweden, with International Telephone & Telegraph Corp., New York, which paid a preliminary sum of $11 million.

A few months later ITT discovered that much of the information given on Ericsson was fabricated, tried to call off the merger and demanded its $11 million back. Mr. Kreuger already had spent the funds shoring up his other operations. In the final months before the crash of his empire, he lost an estimated $50 million in the stock market in an attempt to recover. He also personally forged $142 million in Italian government bonds and notes, which he planned to use for collateral to raise funds.

It was never determined what happened to many Kreuger millions, although much of it obviously went to pay huge shareholder dividends to attract more investment. Friends said also that he apparently paid many millions in blackmail, not only to cover up his thefts but to hide his decidedly unpuritanical private life. Mr. Kreuger, a bachelor, maintained a list of 30 women "friends" together with prices and graded rating scale, and he lived in constant fear of tarnishing his facade of respectability.

THE TEAPOT DOME

For high level government scandals, Teapot Dome up to the present has had no peer. It produced front page headlines for most of the 1920s and remains to this day as the synonym for graft and malfeasance in public office.

The scandal, which unfolded slowly in the summer of 1923, when Calvin Coolidge became President following the death of President Harding, resulted in the resignation of three cabinet members appointed by President Harding.

The central figures were Albert B. Fall, Interior Secretary, and two oilmen, Harry F. Sinclair and Edward L. Doheny. All three went to trial on criminal conspiracy charges in Government leasing of U.S.-owned oil reserves to companies controlled by the two oilmen. All were acquitted of charges of conspiracy. Mr. Sinclair served a brief jail term on charges of tampering with the jury—an act that resulted in a mistrial. In 1929, Mr. Fall got a year's prison sentence on a separate charge of accepting a bribe. It had been alleged that he accepted $100,000 from Mr. Doheny. It also had been alleged out of court that he got $300,000, plus other favors from Mr. Sinclair. Mr. Fall insisted these were loans. One key fact was that Mr. Fall previously had been deeply in debt. In return for the oil leases, estimated by the oil men to be worth $200 million, the U.S. Navy was to get some oil tanks at Pearl Harbor.

The first whiff of scandal came in the spring of 1922 when Senators and Congressmen began getting rumors that leases had been executed on two Navy oil reserves, the so-called Teapot Dome area of Wyoming and the Elk Hills reserve in California. An investigation resulted. The facts were that Interior Secretary Fall had, a short time earlier, secretly granted the leases—Elk Hills to the Doheny interests and Teapot Dome to Sinclair interests. A year earlier, less than two months after Mr. Harding took office, the President had ordered transfer of the reserves from the Navy to the Interior Department at the insistence of Mr. Fall. In 1929, the U.S. Supreme Court upheld a lower court decision revoking the leases.

F. DONALD COSTER

F. Donald Coster was a quiet, home-loving family man, who spent as many as 16 hours a day at his job and whose only hobby was raising chow dogs. But before he was through, he perpetrated a classic Wall Street swindle.

Mr. Coster, whose real name was Philip Musica, dribbled some $3 million into his personal kitty by conjuring a fake drug division to a very real company, McKesson & Robbins, Inc., of which he was president. Other illicit escapades brought his total illegal take to an estimated $8 million.

Prior to his big time thievery, Mr. Coster broadened his experience by such skullduggery as gyping Uncle Sam out of import duties on cheese and borrowing bank money on trumped up securities. In prohibition days, under the guise of a dandruff-remover business, he acquired denatured alcohol through bogus orders and peddled it to bootleggers.

Armed with $1 million, he bought control of McKesson & Robbins in 1926. The company, small with a good name, grew speedily, becoming the world's third largest drug producer in a few years. Most of the company's operations were delegated to lower executives, supposedly to give Mr. Coster full time to devote to the crude drug division, which he handled alone. McKesson & Robbins' speculative investments in crude drugs soared, on the books at least, to $21 million in little more than a decade. The profit the ghost division invariably showed on paper was "plowed back into more drugs."

But the Italian-born Mr. Coster, who was listed in *Who's Who* and was on the board of two banks, actually neither bought nor sold crude drugs. Through a bewildering array of figures on the ledgers, he merely gave the impression of dealing in crude drugs, while he siphoned into his own pockets funds slated for sales commissions and other expenses of the bogus division.

His plot involved fictitious names of wholesale concerns, to which he supposedly sold things, and an accomplice, a brother who utilized one secretary with seven typewriters to send letters to his non-existent division. For instance, when McKesson &

Robbins' auditors, the highly esteemed firm of Price Waterhouse & Co., wrote a fictitious warehouse concern asking for verification of inventories, the letter was forwarded to the hole-in-the-wall New York office of Mr. Coster's brother. There, it was promptly answered and sent to a Canadian contact, who mailed it to the auditors so it would have an appropriate postmark. The masquerade worked for ten years.

"I live for this company," Mr. Coster was fond of telling his McKesson & Robbins executives. "I'm not interested in money." His salary as president of the company was a modest $40,000 a year.

Mr. Coster met his downfall not because of auditors, suspicious employes or clever police work but because of hard times. In 1937, the hard-pressed board of McKesson & Robbins, which had grown to $150 million in annual sales, began casting about for more cash and ordered Mr. Coster to liquidate part of his nonexistent inventory of crude drugs. When he failed to act, directors stumbled onto the truth. In December, 1938, Mr. Coster killed himself.

The Coster experience brought massive changes in accounting practices. McKesson & Robbins, while hard hit by the thefts, survived.

CHARLES PONZI

One of the oldest swindles known to man is that of paying high dividends or interest to early investors with the money of late comers, and skipping other business operations completely. The effectiveness of this sham was demonstrated in the early 1920s by Charles "Get Rich Quick" Ponzi. Mr. Ponzi, a dapper little man who sported a cane and cocky smile, took in some $15 million in less than a year on the simple promise to make Boston folks rich. He wooed money-happy secretaries and workers with a slogan of "50% return in 45 days, double your money in 90."

While a $15-a-week stock boy at an export concern, the Italian-born Mr. Ponzi noted that a postal reply coupon bought in

Spain at one cent was redeemable in the U.S. for a nickel. Mr. Ponzi maintained that he could convert these coupons, designed to provide return postage when a letter-writer desired a reply, into cash. He solicited $250 from friends, returned them $375 in a few days and the swindle was on. The natural flow of such breathless investment possibilities was helped along by hired agents who spread the word.

By the spring of 1920, he was taking in $250,000 a day from eager investors. In less than a year, he collected an estimated $15 million and became the best known financial figure in the nation. The exact amount of his take was not known, since he kept no books.

Mr. Ponzi's dealing in postal coupons was only for a short time and the amount was not great. It was simpler to pay off early investors with the funds of later ones. In the span of a few months, he discarded the gear of a $16 week clerk for an estate, which he furnished at a cost of $500,000, a custom blue limousine and a cellar of fine wines. He also bought the brokerage firm that had employed him as a stock boy three years before.

The Boston Post lit a fuse under Mr. Ponzi when it confronted him and the public with the fact that the entire issue of postal reply coupons over the prior six years totaled only about $1 million; Mr. Ponzi supposedly had accumulated close to $15 million worth in a few months. In August, Montreal police identified him as an ex-convict sentenced on a forgery charge, and Federal agents seized him a short time later.

Indicted on 86 counts of larceny and mail fraud, he was convicted and served about 10 years. From his jail cell, he sent Christmas cards to his victims with the wish that the "recent miscarriage of your investment should not mar the spirit of the Christmas season." Among letters he received in return was money which people asked him to invest on their behalf. He was deported to Italy after his jail term. In 1949, partially blind and paralyzed, he died in a hospital charity ward.

LOWELL M. BIRRELL

Not all free-wheeling corporate looters have been forced to pay the penalty for their activities. A case in point is Lowell M. Birrell, very much alive and enjoying life in Brazil.

Mr. Birrell, a razor-witted attorney with a penchant for booze and pretty girls, allegedly made off with some $14 million of funds in various companies in the mid-1950s. A New York grand jury indicted him in 1959 on 69 counts of grand larceny. He has not faced his accusers, since the U.S. has no extradition agreement with Brazil.

The 200-pound, 55-year-old Mr. Birrell, whose high living currently makes him somewhat of a tourist attraction in Brazil, was unusually successful in one technique. In a typical operation, he acquired control of Swan-Finch Oil Corp., New York, in 1954, then began a widely balleyhooed program of expansion and diversification. He negotiated mergers that gave Swan-Finch, established to distribute sperm oil products, ownership in gas and uranium fields and grain storage facilities. He ran huge ads in New York papers announcing that "we're expanding from fish oil to fission." While he increased shares to 60 times the number outstanding when he took over, market price of the stock declined only to about half the original market price.

With the stock moving briskly, he then flicked a million shares into his own pocket, according to New York authorities. He had Swan-Finch issue 300,000 shares of stock, then worth $2 million at open market prices, to acquire a small loan company which he had picked up personally for $250,000. Similarly, in 1957, some 700,000 shares of Swan-Finch were issued to acquire a drilling company that Mr. Birrell had acquired at a sheriff's auction for a few hundred dollars. Most of his Swan-Finch shares were posted as collateral for $1.5 million in loans and were sold by lenders when he defaulted on payment.

Mr. Birrell, whose dislike for shareholders took such turns as turning off the air conditioning at annual meetings, also is accused of making off with several million dollars of stock of Doeskin Products, Inc., New York, a producer of facial tissues that he controlled.

Mr. Birrell ran into trouble in 1957, when, with his loans overdue, lenders began unloading on the market the Swan-Finch shares deposited as collateral. The sudden flow attracted Securities and Exchange Commission officials who halted sale of the stock. Mr. Birrell, handed a supboena as he alighted from a plane from Canada, climbed aboard an outbound aircraft the same day and skipped the country. Swan-Finch later filed bankruptcy proceedings.

Mr. Birrell, on arrival in Brazil, was jailed by the authorities there for entering the country on a false passport. However, he immediately launched through his attorneys a publicity campaign, spiced with numerous cocktail parties, to spread the word that he had come to Brazil to invest his $14 million. Brazilians also were told that his troubles back home involved mainly a matter of income tax, an item for which Brazilians traditionally have had little regard. New York authorities, who originally were confident of returning Mr. Birrell to this country, found relations with Brazilian authorities becoming cooler and cooler. There's no indication that Mr. Birrell ever will be ordered back to this country.

BERNARD GOLDFINE

The current Billie Sol Estes case is reminiscent in many ways of the recent rise and fall of Bernard Goldfine. The Boston industrialist went to prison ... for evading nearly $800,000 of income taxes. He's best known, though, for his gift-giving friendship with Sherman Adams, chief White House assistant to former President Eisenhower. Disclosure of gifts and favors forced Mr. Adams' resignation in September 1958.

Mr. Goldfine combined a seeming contempt for the law with assiduous courting of favor in high political places. He was friendly with Boston mayors, New England governors and legislators; and his political ties reached to the White House and Capitol Hill in Washington. He wooed newsmen, too. In balmier days, Mr. Goldfine had built up a public image in Boston as a Horatio Alger success, and a generous philanthropist.

Mr. Adams' critics maintained that Mr. Goldfine received preferential treatment in his legal troubles with Uncle Sam because of his gift-laden friendship with the Presidential assistant. For instance, testimony before Congress brought out that in one case, where one of Mr. Goldfine's companies was accused of fabric mislabeling by the Federal Trade Commission, Mr. Adams telephoned the FTC for information. As a result, and contrary to FTC rules, Mr. Goldfine received information as to the identification of the individuals who were making the complaint.

He found political pull not only useful, but satisfying to his ego. He delighted in introducing high political officials to his friends. Once he called a friend on a mobile phone in his limousine and said "how would you like to talk personally to a United States Senator?" With that, he put the Senator on the phone.

Mr. Goldfine's questionable dealings went much deeper than the tax charges that sent him to jail. In short, he milked a number of real estate and textile companies he controlled through fictitious loans and unvouchered expenses. But, ironically, he might have escaped unscathed if he had been willing 10 years ago to settle for $25,000 an obscure lawsuit he eventually had to terminate for nearly $700,000.

In 1952, he was sued by George Heddendorf, a minority stockholder in one of his real estate companies, East Boston Corp. Mr. Heddendorf wanted to look at the company's books, because he was dissatisfied with its showing. Later that year he offered to drop the case if he could sell back his stock for $25,000. The matter dragged on, without trial, until 1956, when other shareholders joined Mr. Heddendorf in a suit charging mismanagement.

In April, 1958, one of the plaintiffs' attorneys, John Fox, a former associate of Mr.

Goldfine, charged in court that Mr. Goldfine had embezzled nearly $6.7 million. Mr. Fox said he once asked Mr. Goldfine how he expected to get away with it and the industrialist stated that "as long as he had Sherman Adams in his pocket he could do it." Mr. Goldfine later denied under oath that he made the statement.

By coincidence, investigators of a U.S. House subcommittee were in Boston on another matter and read of the charges of Mr. Fox. Two months later, Mr. Adams was called before the subcommittee, and the investigation eventually led to the income tax charges against Mr. Goldfine. The Goldfine case became a political issue in the 1958 Congressional campaign, much as the Estes case is expected to this year [1962].

ORGANIZED CRIME

The President's Commission on Law Enforcement and Administration of Justice

Organized crime is a society that seeks to operate outside the control of the American people and their governments. It involves thousands of criminals, working within structures as complex as those of any large corporation, subject to laws more rigidly enforced than those of legitimate governments. Its actions are not impulsive but rather the result of intricate conspiracies, carried on over many years and aimed at gaining control over whole fields of activity in order to amass huge profits.

The core of organized crime activity is the supplying of illegal goods and services—gambling, loan sharking, narcotics, and other forms of vice—to countless numbers of citizen customers. But organized crime is also extensively and deeply involved in legitimate business and in labor unions. Here it employs illegitimate methods—monopolization, terrorism, extortion, tax evasion—to drive out or control lawful ownership and leadership and to exact illegal profits from the public. And to carry on its many activities secure from governmental interference, organized crime corrupts public officials....

... Organized crime affects the lives of millions of Americans, but because it desperately preserves its invisibility many, perhaps most, Americans are not aware how they are affected, or even that they are affected at

From The Task Force Report, *Organized Crime,* 1967, pp. 1–8.

all. The price of a loaf of bread may go up one cent as the result of an organized crime conspiracy, but a housewife has no way of knowing why she is paying more. If organized criminals paid income tax on every cent of their vast earnings everybody's tax bill would go down, but no one knows how much.

But to discuss the impact of organized crime in terms of whatever direct, personal, everyday effect it has on individuals is to miss most of the point. Most individuals are not affected, in this sense, very much. Much of the money organized crime accumulates comes from innumerable petty transactions: 50-cent bets, $3-a-month private garbage collection services, quarters dropped into racketeer-owned jukeboxes, or small price rises resulting from protection rackets....

Sometimes organized crime's activities do not directly affect individuals at all. Smuggled cigarettes in a vending machine cost consumers no more than tax-paid cigarettes, but they enrich the leaders of organized crime.... Even when organized crime engages in a large transaction, individuals may not be directly affected. A large sum of money may be diverted from a union pension fund to finance a business venture without immediate and direct effect upon the individual members of the union.

It is organized crime's accumulation of money ... that has a great and threatening impact on America.... Organized crime exists by virtue of the power it purchases with its money. The millions of dollars it can invest in narcotics or use for layoff money give it power over the lives of thousands of people and over the quality of life in whole neighborhoods. The millions of dollars it can throw into the legitimate economic system give it power to manipulate the price of shares on the stock market, to raise or lower the price of retail merchandise, to determine whether entire industries are union or non-union, to make it easier or harder for businessmen to continue in business.

The millions of dollars it can spend on corrupting public officials may give it power to maim or murder people inside or outside the organization with impunity; to extort money from businessmen; to conduct businesses in such fields as liquor, meat, or drugs without regard to administrative regulations; to avoid payment of income taxes or to secure public works contracts without competitive bidding.

The purpose of organized crime is not competition with visible, legal government but nullification of it. When organized crime places an official in public office, it nullifies the political process. When it bribes a police official, it nullifies law enforcement. . . .

THE TYPES OF ORGANIZED CRIMINAL ACTIVITIES

Catering to Public Demands

Organized criminal groups participate in any illegal activity that offers maximum profit at minimum risk of law enforcement interference. They offer goods and services that millions of Americans desire even though declared illegal by their legislatures.

Gambling

Law enforcement officials agree almost unanimously that gambling is the greatest source of revenue for organized crime. It ranges from lotteries, such as "numbers" or "bolita," to off-track horse betting, bets on

sporting events, large dice games and illegal casinos. In large cities where organized criminal groups exist, very few of the gambling operators are independent of a large organization. Anyone whose independent operation becomes successful is likely to receive a visit from an organization representative who convinces the independent, through fear or promise of greater profit, to share his revenue with the organization.

Most large-city gambling is established or controlled by organized crime members through elaborate hierarchies. Money is filtered from the small operator who takes the customer's bet, through persons who pick up money and slips, to second-echelon figures in charge of particular districts, and then into one of several main offices. The profits that eventually accrue to organization leaders move through channels so complex that even persons who work in the betting operation do not know or cannot prove the identity of the leader. Increasing use of the telephone for lottery and sports betting has facilitated systems in which the bookmaker may not know the identity of the second-echelon person to whom he calls in the day's bets. Organization not only creates greater efficiency and enlarges markets, it also provides a systematized method of corrupting the law enforcement process by centralizing procedures for the payment of graft.

Organization is also necessary to prevent severe losses. More money may be bet on one horse or one number with a small operator than he could pay off if that horse or that number should win. The operator will have to hedge by betting some money himself on that horse or that number. This so-called "layoff" betting is accomplished through a network of local, regional, and national layoff men, who take bets from gambling operations.

There is no accurate way of ascertaining organized crime's gross revenue from gambling in the United States. Estimates of the annual intake have varied from $7 to $50 billion. Legal betting at racetracks reaches a gross annual figure of almost $5 billion, and most enforcement officials believe that illegal wagering on horse races, lotteries, and sporting events totals at least $20 billion each year. While the Commission cannot judge the accuracy of these figures, even the most conservative estimates place substantial capital in the hands of organized crime leaders.

Loan-sharking

In the view of most law enforcement officials loan sharking, the lending of money at higher rates than the legally prescribed limit, is the second largest source of revenue for organized crime. Gambling profits provide the initial capital for loan-shark operations. . . .

Interest rates vary from 1 to 150 per cent a week, according to the relationship between the lender and borrower, the intended use of the money, the size of the loan, and the repayment potential. The classic "6-for-5" loan, 20 per cent a week, is common with small borrowers. Payments may be due by a certain hour on a certain day, and even a few minutes' default may result in a rise in interest rates. The lender is more interested in perpetuating interest payments than collecting principal; and force, or threats of force of the most brutal kind, are used to effect interest collection, eliminate protest when interest rates are raised, and prevent the beleaguered borrower from reporting the activity to enforcement officials. No reliable estimates exist of the gross revenue from organized loan sharking, but profit margins are higher than for gambling operations, and many officials classify the business in the multi-billion-dollar range.

Narcotics

The sale of narcotics is organized like a legitimate importing-wholesale-retailing business. The distribution of heroin, for example, requires movement of the drug through four or five levels between the importer and the street peddler. . . .

The large amounts of cash and the international connections necessary for large, long-term heroin supplies can be provided only by organized crime. Conservative estimates of the number of addicts in the nation and the average daily expenditure for heroin indicate that the gross heroin trade is $350 million annually, of which $21 million are probably profits to the importer and distributor. . . .

Other Goods and Services

Prostitution and bootlegging play a small and declining role in organized crime's operations. Production of illegal alcohol is a risky business. The destruction of stills and supplies by law enforcement officers during the initial stages means the loss of heavy initial investment capital. Prostitution is difficult to organize and discipline is hard to maintain. . . .

Business and Labor Interests

Infiltration of Legitimate Business

A legitimate business enables the racket executive to acquire respectability in the community and to establish a source of funds that appears legal and upon which just enough taxes may be paid to avoid income tax prosecution. Organized crime invests the profit it has made from illegal service activities in a variety of businesses throughout the country. To succeed in such ventures, it uses accountants, attorneys, and business consultants, who in some instances work exclusively on its affairs. Too often, because of the reciprocal benefits involved in organized crime's dealings with the business world, or because of fear, the legitimate sector of society helps the illegitimate sector. The Illinois Crime Commission, after investigating one service industry in Chicago, stated:

There is a disturbing lack of interest on the part of some legitimate business concerns regarding the identity of the persons with whom they deal. This lackadaisical attitude is conducive to the perpetration of frauds and the infiltration and subversion of legitimate businesses by the organized criminal element.

Because business ownership is so easily concealed, it is difficult to determine all the types of businesses that organized crime has penetrated. Of the 75 or so racket leaders who met at Apalachin, N.Y., in 1957, at least 9 were in the coin-operated machine industry, 16 were in the garment industry, 10 owned grocery stores, 17 owned bars or restaurants, 11 were in the olive oil and cheese business, and 9 were in the construction business. Others were involved in automobile agencies, coal companies, entertainment, funeral homes, ownership of horses and race tracks, linen and laundry enterprises, trucking, waterfront activities, and bakeries.

Today, the kinds of production and service industries and businesses that organized crime controls or has invested in range from accounting firms to yeast manufacturing. One criminal syndicate alone has real estate interests with an estimated value of $300 million. In a few instances, racketeers control nationwide manufacturing and service industries with known and respected brand names.

Control of business concerns has usually been acquired through one of four methods: (1) investing concealed profits acquired from gambling and other illegal activities; (2) accepting business interests in payment of the owner's gambling debts; (3) foreclosing on usurious loans; and (4) using various forms of extortion.

Acquisition of legitimate businesses is also accomplished in more sophisticated ways. One organized crime group offered to lend money to a business on condition that a racketeer be appointed to the company's board of directors and that a nominee for the lenders be given first option to purchase if there were any outside sale of the company's stock. Control of certain brokerage houses was secured through foreclosure of usurious loans, and the businesses then used

to promote the sale of fraudulent stock, involving losses of more than $2 million to the public. . . .

Too little is known about the effects on the economy of organized crime's entry into the business world, but the examples above indicate the harm done to the public and at least suggest how criminal cartels can undermine free competition. . . .

Strong-arm tactics are used to enforce unfair business policy and to obtain customers. A restaurant chain controlled by organized crime used the guise of "quality control" to insure that individual restaurant franchise holders bought products only from other syndicate-owned businesses. In one city, every business with a particular kind of waste product useful in another line of industry sold that product to a syndicate-controlled business at one-third the price offered by legitimate business.

The cumulative effect of the infiltration of legitimate business in America cannot be measured. Law enforcement officials agree that entry into legitimate business is continually increasing and that it has not decreased organized crime's control over gambling, usury and other profitable, low-risk criminal enterprises.

Labor Racketeering

Control of labor supply and infiltration of labor unions by organized crime prevent unionization of some industries, provide opportunities for stealing from union funds and extorting money by threats of possible labor strife, and provide funds from the enormous union pension and welfare systems for business ventures controlled by organized criminals. Union control also may enhance other illegal activities. Trucking, construction, and waterfront shipping entrepreneurs, in return for assurance that business operations will not be interrupted by labor discord, countenance gambling, loan sharking, and pilferage on company property. Organized criminals either direct these activities or grant "concessions" to others in return for a percentage of the profits.

MEMBERSHIP AND ORGANIZATION OF CRIMINAL CARTELS

National Scope of Organized Crime

In 1951 the Kefauver Committee declared that a nationwide crime syndicate known as the Mafia operated in many large cities and that the leaders of the Mafia usually controlled the most lucrative rackets in their cities.

In 1957, 20 of organized crime's top leaders were convicted (later reversed on appeal) of a criminal charge arising from a meeting at Apalachin, N.Y. At the sentencing the judge stated that they had sought to corrupt and infiltrate the political mainstreams of the country, that they had led double lives of crime and respectability, and that their probation reports read "like a tale of horrors."

Today the core of organized crime in the United States consists of 24 groups operating as criminal cartels in large cities across the nation. Their membership is exclusively men of Italian descent, they are in frequent communication with each other, and their smooth functioning is insured by a national body of overseers. To date, only the Federal Bureau of Investigation has been able to document fully the national scope of these groups, and FBI intelligence indicates that the organization as a whole has changed its name from the Mafia to La Cosa Nostra.

In 1966 J. Edgar Hoover told a House of Representatives Appropriations Subcommittee:

La Cosa Nostra is the largest organization of the criminal underworld in this country, very closely organized and strictly disciplined. They have committed almost every crime under the sun . . .

La Cosa Nostra is a criminal fraternity whose membership is Italian either by birth or national origin, and it has been found to control major racket activities in many of our larger metropolitan areas, often working in concert with criminals representing other ethnic backgrounds. It operates on a nationwide basis, with international implications, and until recent years it carried on its activities with almost complete secrecy. It functions as a criminal cartel, adhering to its own body of "law" and "justice" and, in so doing, thwarts and usurps the authority of legally constituted judicial bodies . . .

In individual cities, the local core group may also be known as the "outfit," the "syndicate," or the "mob." These 24 groups work with and control other racket groups, whose leaders are of various ethnic derivations. In addition, the thousands of employees who perform the street-level functions of organized crime's gambling, usury, and other illegal activities represent a cross section of the nation's population groups. . . . The wealthiest and most influential core groups operate in states including New York, New Jersey, Illinois, Florida, Louisiana, Nevada, Michigan, and Rhode Island. . . .

Internal Structure

Each of the 24 groups is known as a "family," with membership varying from as many as 700 men to as few as 20. Most cities with organized crime have only one family; New York City has five. Each family can participate in the full range of activities in which organized crime generally is known to engage. Family organization is rationally designed with an integrated set of positions geared to maximize profits. Like any large corporation, the organization functions regardless of personnel changes, and no individual—not even the leader—is indispensable. If he dies or goes to jail, business goes on.

The hierarchical structure of the families resembles that of the Mafia groups that have operated for almost a century on the island of Sicily. Each family is headed by one man, the "boss," whose primary functions are maintaining order and maximizing profits. Subject only to the possibility of being overruled by the national advisory group, which will be discussed below, his authority in all matters relating to his family is absolute.

Beneath each boss is an "underboss," the vice president or deputy director of the family. He collects information for the boss;

he relays messages to him and passes his instructions down to his own underlings. In the absence of the boss, the underboss acts for him.

On the same level as the underboss, but operating in a staff capacity, is the *consigliere,* who is a counselor, or adviser. Often an elder member of the family who has partially retired from a career in crime, he gives advice to family members, including the boss and underboss, and thereby enjoys considerable influence and power.

Below the level of the underboss are the *caporegime,* some of whom serve as buffers between the top members of the family and the lower-echelon personnel. To maintain their insulation from the police, the leaders of the hierarchy (particularly the boss) avoid direct communication with the workers. All commands, information, complaints, and money flow back and forth through a trusted go-between. A *caporegima* fulfilling this buffer capacity, however, unlike the underboss, does not make decisions or assume any of the authority of his boss.

Other *caporegime* serve as chiefs of operating units. The number of men supervised in each unit varies with the size and activities of particular families. Often the *caporegima* has one or two associates who work closely with him, carrying orders, information, and money to the men who belong to his unit. From a business standpoint, the *caporegima* is analogous to plant supervisor or sales manager.

The lowest level "members" of a family are the *soldati;* the soldiers or "button" men who report to the *caporegime.* A soldier may operate a particular illicit enterprise, *e.g.,* a loan-sharking operation, a dice game, a lottery, a bookmaking operation, a smuggling operation, on a commission basis, or he may "own" the enterprise and pay a portion of its profit to the organization, in return for the right to operate. Partnerships are common between two or more soldiers and between soldiers and men higher up in the hierarchy. Some soldiers and most upper-echelon family members have interests in more than one business.

Beneath the soldiers in the hierarchy are large numbers of employees and commission agents who are not members of the family and are not necessarily of Italian descent. These are the people who do most of the actual work in the various enterprises. They have no buffers or other insulation from law enforcement. They take bets, drive trucks, answer telephones, sell narcotics, tend the stills, work in the legitimate businesses. For example, in a major lottery business that operated in Negro neighborhoods in Chicago, the workers were Negroes; the bankers for the lottery were Japanese-Americans; but the game, including the banking operation, was licensed, for a fee, by a family member. . . .

There are at least two aspects of organized crime that characterize it as a unique form of criminal activity. The first is the element of corruption. The second is the element of enforcement, which is necessary for the maintenance of both internal discipline and the regularity of business transactions. In the hierarchy of organized crime there are positions for people fulfilling both of these functions. But neither is essential to the long-term operation of other types of criminal groups. The members of a pickpocket troupe or check-passing ring, for example, are likely to take punitive action against any member who holds out more than his share of the spoils, or betrays the group to the police; but they do not recruit or train for a well-established position of "enforcer."

Organized crime groups, on the other hand, are believed to contain one or more fixed positions for "enforcers," whose duty it is to maintain organizational integrity by arranging for the maiming and killing of recalcitrant members. And there is a position for a "corrupter," whose function is to establish relationships with those public officials and other influential persons whose assistance is necessary to achieve the organization's goals. By including these positions within its organization, each criminal cartel, or "family," becomes a government as well as a business.

The highest ruling body of the 24 families is the "commission." This body serves as a combination legislature, supreme court, board of directors, and arbitration board; its principal functions are judicial. Family members look to the commission as the ultimate authority on organizational and jurisdictional disputes. It is composed of the bosses of the nation's most powerful families but has authority over all 24. The composition of the commission varies from 9 to 12 men. According to current information, there are presently 9 families represented, 5 from New York City and 1 each from Philadelphia, Buffalo, Detroit, and Chicago.

The commission is not a representative legislative assembly or an elected judicial body. Members of this council do not regard each other as equals. Those with long tenure on the commission and those who head large families, or possess unusual wealth, exercise greater authority and receive utmost respect. The balance of power on this nationwide council rests with the leaders of New York's 5 families. They have always served on the commission and consider New York as at least the unofficial headquarters of the entire organization.

In recent years organized crime has become increasingly diversified and sophisticated. One consequence appears to be significant organizational restructuring. As in any organization, authority in organized crime may derive either from rank based on incumbency in a high position or from expertise based on possession of technical knowledge and skill. Traditionally, organized crime groups, like totalitarian governments, have maintained discipline through the unthinking acceptance of orders by underlings who have respected the rank of their superiors. However, since 1931, organized crime has gained power and respectability by moving out of bootlegging and prostitution and into gambling, usury, and control of legitimate business. Its need for expertise, based on technical knowledge and skill, has increased. Currently both the structure and operation of illicit enterprises reveal some indecision brought about by attempting to follow both patterns at the same time. Organized crime's "experts" are not fungible, or interchangeable, like the "soldiers" and street workers, and since experts are included within an organization, discipline and structure inevitably assume new forms. It may be awareness of these facts that is leading many family members to send their sons to universitites to learn business administration skills. . . .

COMBATING ORGANIZED CRIME IN AMERICA

Stuart L. Hills

This country is about to witness another spectacular battle against the forces of evil. With the findings of the President's Commission on Law Enforcement and Administration of Justice as an impetus, another crusade to combat organized crime is underway. Already there are reports in the mass media of the stepped-up "war" on the Cosa Nostra and its alleged 24 "families" in various cities of the country by the Department of Justice. These crusades undoubtedly are appreciated by the public, as were the investigations into organized crime over the last 20 years stemming from the McClellan and Kefauver Senate committee hearings. However, the difficulties in achieving any significant and lasting results from these well-intentioned efforts are not well understood by the American public.

In popular discussions on crime, relatively little attention has been directed to the recognition that organized crime is an *integral* and vital part of the American way of life.

From *Federal Probation*, XXXIII, No. 1, (March 1969) 23–27. Stuart Hills is Professor of Sociology at St. Lawrence University, Canton, N.Y.

The reasons for the existence and vitality of this pattern of syndicated, systematic criminal activity cannot be fully comprehended—much less adequately coped with—if we persist in viewing it as an essentially separate and detached social phenomenon—alien to our country's values and social institutions.

STEREOTYPES IN THE MASS MEDIA

In the mass media it is commonplace to depict organized crime as a foreign cancer that has invaded an otherwise healthy society. To root it out, therefore, one must use such major surgical instruments as increased severity of penalties, centralization or improved coordination of the presently fragmented and overlapping police agencies at the federal level that touch on aspects of organized crime, greater investigative freedom for grand juries, increased use of wiretapping and electronic bugging devices, and so forth. Although such an arsenal of legal and judicial weapons may be desirable and useful, such efforts will not suffice in themselves, and the dangers of abuse may outweigh the benefits.

Most sociologically oriented criminologists tend to see the scope and vitality of organized crime as interrelated with basic cultural values, behavior patterns, and social institutions in American life. Yet the utility of this perspective is obscured in popular treatments of the topic that attempt to explain it by reciting a long list of unsavory gangsters sworn to codes of silence in their Mafia organizations that have a stranglehold over the innocent citizenry of our large metropolitan cities. Perhaps such vivid images function to reassure us as we envision organized crime as essentially a foreign transplant—brought to this country by incompletely assimilated minority groups and, therefore, help to absolve Americans from any responsibility for the persistence and strength of organized crime in America. As Gus Tyler has noted through this scapegoating process the ". . . culture is not only relieved of sin but can indulge itself in an orgy of righteous indignation."

Information on organized crime generally

has been presented to the public in a lurid, sensational manner that prevents an understanding of the true nature and ramifications of the problem. As Donald Cressey has pointed out, newspapermen typically depict the participants as nothing but "gangsters," "muscle men," and "gorillas" who mainly prey on each other in their "gangland slayings" or victimize shady characters in such illicit activities as "the juice racket," "the scam racket," or "the fix":

For example, there are few newspaper accounts in which Mr. Lucchese is called "Mr. Lucchese" or Mr. Ricca is called "Mr. Ricca." The writer always displays his "inside knowledge" about how things *really* are by using the first name, parenthesis, corny "alias," parenthesis, last name. "Mr. Lucchese," when he was alive, could possibly have been someone who was corrupting my labor union, but "Three Finger Brown" could only have been a somewhat fictitious character in a "cops and robbers" story. Similarly, usury is almost always called "the juice racket," and this terminology lets the reader believe that the activity has nothing to do with him or the safety of his community. The criminals' terminology is similarly used when the word "scam" is used to describe bankruptcy fraud. Most of us can understand the seriousness of usury, bankruptcy fraud, and bribery, but we have a hard time realizing that our friends and neighbors are, in the long run, the victims of "the juice racket," "the scam racket," or "the fix."

In the discussion that follows, I shall attempt to articulate some of the diverse kinds of close relationships between organized crime and the American way of life—and some of the consequences. An awareness of the nature and strength of these linkages must be a starting point for any successful comprehension of the difficulties in effectively limiting the operations of organized crime.

PUBLIC DEMAND FOR ILLICIT GOODS AND SERVICES

First, organized crime can be viewed essentially as an adjunct to our private profit economy. It is a large-scale business that provides goods and services demanded by sizable segments of the American public—gambling, drugs, alcohol, prostitution, abortion, etc.—but not permitted under our legal codes. Many quite respectable citizens support the legal prohibition of such activities, yet may have little interest in seeing the laws enforced at their expense. Al Capone, the Chicago gangster, clearly perceived this hypocrisy when he was quoted as saying: "I call myself a business man. I make my money by supplying popular demand. If I break a law, my customers are as guilty as I am. When I sell liquor, it's bootlegging. When my patrons serve it on a silver tray on Lake Shore Drive, it's hospitality."

This attempt to curb the human appetite by passing laws reflects, in part, our puritanical value system which allows no compromise with "evil" but insists that the laws must express the highest ideals, even if unenforceable. In contrast, the European legal philosophy places a much greater emphasis on adapting laws to existing practices in order to avoid the undesirable consequences of driving underground such human "vices."

In few instances are American citizens forced to patronize the criminal syndicate. As Robert Woetzel has pointed out, it is the public's desire for entertainment after regular closing hours that supports the syndicate's illegal afterhour establishments. It is not the syndicate which provokes violations of the "bluelaws," but the demand of the American public. Similarly, no one coerces the victims of the $350 million-a-year loan-sharking business (the lending of money at usurious interest rates backed up by force) who, as G. Robert Blakey has noted, come from all segments of society—professionals, industrialists, contractors, stockbrokers, bar and restaurant owners, narcotics addicts, bettors, and laborers. All such persons have in common, however, an urgent need for ready cash and no recourse to regular channels of credit. Once deeply in debt, such victims may sometimes be pressured into criminal activities to pay off, such as embezzlement or acting as number writers.

KEEPING UP WITH CHANGING TIMES

As with any efficient entrepreneur, criminal businessmen must keep up with changing consumer habits and tastes or go out of business. For example, with the increasing permissiveness of sexual norms and behavior resulting in a reduced demand for commercial prostitution ("this amateur competition is ruining our business," one street walker recently complained) and the increasing legalization of alcohol, organized crime is moving into other areas to keep up with changing times.

Adapting to the urbanization and insutrialization of society and the increasing scale and scope of its operations, criminal syndicates tend to become bureaucratic in structure. They possess most of the characteristics of any large modern corporation: a hierarchy of authority, a complex division of labor (complete with secretaries and college-trained accountants, financial advisors, and lawyers), departmental specialization, impersonality, the profit motive, and a desire for continuity and survival. Such criminal businesses attempt to bring some control over their market and engage in "mergers" and "consolidations" to eliminate "cutthroat" competition, though without the normal restraints imposed by the courts, government agencies, and the laws.

RELATIONS WITH LEGITIMATE BUSINESSES

Today organized crime is moving into such legitimate enterprises as the coin-operated machine industry, night clubs, hotels, food products, the garment industry, banking and finance, oil, steel, trucking, meat-packing, and dozens of other business areas. According to the report of the President's Commission, one organized criminal syndicate alone has real estate interests with a value estimated at $300 million. Control of such businesses has been acquired by inconspicuous investments funded from the tremendous profits in gambling, narcotics, and other illegal operations. The infiltration of legitimate enterprise may also result from force and intimidation, from acceptance of business interests in payment of gambling debts, or from foreclosure of usurious loans. After obtaining control, the syndicate may operate the business in a variety of ways: as a front to conceal other illegal activities, liquidating the business through bankruptcy fraud or arson to collect the insurance, or using fear and strong-arm tactics to gain a monopoly on the product or service of the business.

The thin line that often exists between the operations of criminal syndicates and legitimate businesses is further breached through the purchase of stolen goods by some presumably respectable businessmen and by their hiring of labor-boss racketeers to strike competitors to gain a more favorable trade advantage. In addition, the infiltration of some labor unions by criminal elements has resulted in "sweetheart contracts" in collusion with management, while in others it has prevented the legitimate unionization of some industries. Such syndicate control has led to the theft of union funds, extortion through threat of economic pressure, and the manipulation of welfare and pension funds. Waterfront, trucking, and construction businessmen have been persuaded for the sake of labor tranquility to tolerate gambling, pilfering, loan sharking, and kickbacks.

A conservative estimate puts the annual total take of the operations of organized crime at one-tenth of our gross national product, or approximately $80 billion. The consequences of this expansion of organized crime into the legitimate business area are clear: reduction of product quality, increase in prices, loss of revenue to the state, creation of fear and anxiety, defrauding of workers and businessmen, and the malfunctioning of a free economy.

SOCIAL MOBILITY AND MINORITY GROUPS

Second, organized crime viewed from another perspective is a vehicle for upward social mobility for various disadvantaged, minority groups in the United States. Historically, organized crime, along with the political machine, has represented an important means to obtain wealth, power, and fame. Each major immigrant group has taken its turn successively in the upper echelons of syndicated crime. With the rags-to-riches paths preempted by earlier arrivals, opportunities in organized crime have provided short cuts to the great American dream of individual success. When the members of each group found increasing opportunities in more conventional forms of enterprise as discriminatory barriers declined, the group itself became less prominent in the world of gangs and rackets.

As Gus Tyler has pointed out, the roots of organized crime run deep in American history. The colonial period had its pirates and smugglers. The early 19th century produced the urban mobs of New York and San Francisco, reflecting the poverty, ethnic strife, and ruthless politics of the times. The Old West had its highwaymen, gamblers, and slave snatchers. New Orleans had its river and port pirates. The frontier lawlessness and social unrest of the last half of the 19th century produced the James, Dalton, and Younger gangs. By the end of the century, numerous frontier gangs, often consisting of mercenaries, struggled for control over land, cattle, grazing fields, mining and timber properties. The early part of the 20th century gave rise to great citywide gangs, often in alliance with the new wealth and political talent of the growing urban centers, as seen in the Irish gangs of New York. To the chagrin of the Jewish community in the mid-1920's, the "Jewish racketeer" emerged, only to be replaced by the Italian-Sicilians who gained dominance by the 1930's. This last great immigrant group consolidated and expanded the structure and scope of criminal operations in feudal-like confederations, and cooperated in loose alliances to delimit geographical and trade jurisdictions to minimize gang warfare.

The immigrant may have brought the kinship-based Mafia with him as part of his cultural baggage, but, as Blakey has emphasized, to have survived and prospered on the scale of its present operations, it must have found a fertile soil. Moreover, he notes, the present preoccupation with such groups as the Italian and Sicilian dominated Mafia or Cosa Nostra encourages the risk of assuming that as soon as the acculturation process has been completed, the whole problem will disappear—a dubious assumption; and it binds us to the considerable involvement of those of other ethnic backgrounds in organized crime.

Perhaps the American cultural tendency to emphasize the symbols of success and their display, rather than the means of obtainment, helps to account for the begrudging admiration and celebration of some of our notorious leaders of orgnaized crime and the ease with which some gain entree to the more polite circles of society. (It is reported that Al Capone received over one thousand fan letters a day and served on a welcoming committee in Chicago during a goodwill visit of an emissary from the Italian government. As their success increases with movement into legitimate business areas, such leaders may polish up their manners, change their taste in clothes, move into exclusive suburbs, contribute to popular charities, and send their children to our finest private schools and colleges.

One can perhaps sympathize with the chagrin felt by the families of such syndicate members residing in a prestigious suburb of Detroit when their neighborhood recently was invaded by television cameramen intent on a documentary exposé. As the taint of new money gained by questionable means subsides—along with some of the more déclassé traits of occupation and background— the great-grandchildren of these syndicate leaders may come to revere them, much as the inheritors of the great financial dynasties of this country honor the founders who were not always above using illicit and ruthless methods to obtain their wealth.

With the opportunity structure only gradually widening for our dark-skinned minorities, it is perhaps likely that we shall see a continuation of this route of upward mobility, with Puerto Ricans and Negroes moving into the higher levels of organized crime.

POLITICS, CORRUPTION, AND LAW ENFORCEMENT

Third, it is doubtful that organized crime could thrive so successfully in America without the cooperation and outright connivance of a portion of our political and law enforcement machinery. From the Prohibition era to the present, most of the various municipal, state, and federal committees investigating political corruption have consistently revealed an unholy alliance of syndicate members, politicians, public officials, and law enforcement agents. Well-intentioned political reforms, however, have been typically short-lived. The "new broom" philosophy designed to sweep out the rascals did not basically alter the structural and cultural conditions that facilitate and encourage political corruption. For example, running for political office in America tends to be costly, and most large financial contributors to political campaigns expect some favors in return—including simply being "left alone." A conservative estimate puts the level of all political contributions stemming from criminal sources at 15 percent.

The sordid story of bribes, delivery of votes, fixes, payoffs, and public officials beholden to the syndicate continues ad nauseum, allowing organized crime in many large and small cities to operate in comparative immunity. At various times, organized crime has been the dominant political force in Chicago, New York, Miami, and New Orleans, although few large metropolitan centers have been immune to such corrupting influences.

This interdependence of organized crime and the law enforcement process oeprates at various levels. For example, when a bookie "talked" in New York City a number of years ago, 450 policemen of all ranks either resigned, retired, or were dismissed. Numerous mayors and district attorneys in our large cities have been found to have friendly relations with criminal elements. Even judges have been indebted to the syndicate for their position. One of the best authenticated of many such cases is the famous telephone conversation in which a newly appointed judge thanked gangster Frank Costello for arranging his nomination as justice of the State Supreme Court of New York and pledged his undying loyalty.

Today, corruption by organized crime is far more threatening. According to the President's Crime Commission, such corruption is becoming less visible, more subtle, and thus more difficult to detect and evaluate than during the Prohibition era. The need to corrupt public officials at every level of government has grown as the scale of organized crime's activities has expanded.

It seems clear, then, that organized crime requires the active and conscious cooperation of diverse elements of respectable society. As former Chief Justice Earl Warren noted in a speech before the National Conference on Crime Control, the flamboyant funerals of leading syndicate leaders have been attended by leading citizens of the community and police chiefs eager to pay deference to the power of the syndicate. Communion breakfasts have brought together at the same table high-ranking members of the clergy and leading gangsters.

INDIVIDUALISTIC BIAS IN LAW ENFORCEMENT

A fourth major difficulty in combating organized crime in America reflects our cultural tendency to view criminality in terms of *individual* maladjustment, rather than as a consequence of an individual's participation in social systems. The failure to perceive and cope with the organizational nature of our crime problem is, in fact, generally inherent in our criminal codes. As Donald Cressey has stressed, our law enforcement process is largely designed for the control of individuals—not for the control of organizations. Police and investigative agencies, consequently, are more concerned with collecting evidence that will lead to prosecution of individuals than with securing evidence of the relationships between criminals or the structure and operations of illicit business organizations. This myopic view also affects the way we compile and publish data on crime, thereby allowing the public—and the police, too, if they so desire—to ignore organized crime because it does not show up in the statistics.

This individualistic bias creates various legal loopholes through which most of the higher-placed participants in these criminal organizations escape arrest, prosecution, and imprisonment. And, in general, this cultural astigmatism makes it difficult for most of the citizenry—as well as many social scientists—to view organized crime as a serious social problem. Many of the customers who place a friendly bet with that nice old man in the corner bar do not perceive, in fact, that this criminal bookmaker is a businessman—not an unorganized, individual gambler. He is typically linked to a far-reaching organization that channels and pools thousands of $5 bets that can finance a professional murder of a government agent, corrupt a judge or a district attorney, or fund the takeover of a legitimate business.

DISTRUST OF CENTRALIZED LAW ENFORCEMENT

Finally, the immense difficulties in coping effectively with large-scale organized crime can be directly traced to certain of our traditional political values embodied in our Constitution. Our deep-seated distrust of centralized government—especially the expansion of federal law enforcement activities with its possible use for political dictatorship—has resulted in a splintered system of decentralized and overlapping law enforcement agencies having separate jurisdictions. Over 40,000 different police agencies exist in America, each insistent on its local autonomy, thereby facilitating the operations of organized crime. Political investigation and court action are vested in separate agencies—the sheriff, district attorney, and judge, for example, all can operate independently of one another—and are further divided into federal, state, and local levels. The activities of organized crime, however, cut across political boundaries, spanning across entire regions and increasingly the whole nation.

Similarly, the resistance to the legal use of electronic surveillance to combat organized crime is related to the value we place on individual privacy and protection from the total scrutiny of centralized political authority. In part in response to this resistance, some federal police agencies tend to exaggerate, consciously or unconsciously, the degree of closure and control in organized crime in the United States. The conception of organized crime as a single national organization directing local crime operations across the country much as a board of directors runs a corporation—of questionable validity—is perhaps an attempt by such agencies to convince the American public of the necessity of removing the traditional restraints on the use of eavesdropping in the law enforcement process; conventional police methods, it is felt, are inadequate to confront this criminal leviathan.

Thus our dilemma: How can we centralize, coordinate, and make more efficient our law enforcement machinery to combat the activities of organized crime, without inviting the abuses of political authoritarianism and the encroachment and ultimate loss of our civil liberties?

PROSPECTS

If our analysis is essentially correct, any significant reduction in organized crime in the near future is unlikely. This assertion is not put forth as a counsel of despair, nor is it to imply that there are no concrete steps that might be taken to curb the operations of organized crime in America. Rather it is a plea for a recognition of the interrelatedness of these criminal activities with much of the American way of life and to try to assess more realistically the magnitude of the task in launching any "war" on organized crime.

As long as we attempt to blame organized crime on individually maladjusted "foreigners"; as long as we persist in equating "sinful" behavior with crime and thereby make illegal activity in which significant segments of the American public wish to indulge; as long as we accord a higher value to the rewards of individual success than to the means to their attainment, and invite all comers to compete for these rewards but restrict the opportunities for their realization from various segments of the population; as long as we insist on a fragmented, decentralized, and locally autonomous police system in the name of grassroots democracy—in short, as long as we cling to various myths and cherish certain cultural values and institutional practices, large-scale syndicated crime is likely to continue to flourish in America.

This is not to argue that the price we pay for these social and cultural patterns is not worth paying; rather that we cannot have our proverbial cake and eat it too. When we are willing to sacrifice and modify selected portions of the American way, only then will our attempts to cope with organized crime have any meaningful chance of success.

THE NATURE, IMPACT AND PROSECUTION OF WHITE COLLAR CRIME

Herbert Edelhertz

DEFINITION OF WHITE-COLLAR CRIME

The term "white-collar crime" is not subject to any one clear definition. Everyone believes he knows what the term means, but when definitions are compared there are usually sharp divergences as to whether one crime or another comes within the definition.

From National Institute of Law Enforcement and Criminal Justice, U.S. Department of Justice, Law Enforcement Assistance Administration, May 1970, pp. 3–11, 23–38, 54, 58–60, 63–69.

Herbert Edelhertz is Research Scientist, Law and Justice Center, Battelle Memorial Institute, Northwest, Seattle. He is former Chief, Fraud Section, Criminal Division, U.S.

For the purpose of this paper, the term will be defined as *an illegal act or series of illegal acts committed by nonphysical means and by concealment or guile, to obtain money or property, to avoid the payment or loss of money or property, or to obtain business or personal advantage.*

The definition, in that it hinges on the modifying words "an illegal act or series of illegal acts," does not go to the question whether particular activities should be the subject of criminal proscriptions.

It is a definition which differs markedly from that advanced by Edwin H. Sutherland, who said that ". . . white-collar crime may be defined approximately as a crime committed by a person of respectability and high social status in the course of his occupation." Sutherland introduced this definition with the comment that these white-collar crimes are violations of law by persons in the "upper socio-economic class."

Sutherland's definition is far too restrictive. His view provided a rational basis for the economic determinism which was the underlying theme of this analysis, but did not comprehend the many crimes committed outside one's occupation. Ready examples of crimes falling outside one's occupation would be personal and nonbusiness false income tax returns, fraudulent claims for social security benefits, concealing assets in a personal bankruptcy, and use of large-scale buying on credit with no intention or capability to ever pay for purchases. His definition does not take into account crime as a business, such as a planned bankruptcy, or an old fashioned "con game" operated in a business milieu. Though these crimes fall outside Sutherland's definition, they were considered and discussed by him.

Sutherland made a valuable contribution. He illuminated the double standard built into our law enforcement structure, and contrasted society's treatment of abusive acts by the well-to-do with law enforcement and penal provisions applicable to abusive acts by those less fortunate or well placed. He forcefully pointed out that our legislation had established a unique legal structure with a complex of administrative proceedings, injunctions, and cease and desist orders, to meet common law fraud if committed in a business context, thus largely preempting the field of enforcement and making criminal proceedings unlikely or seemingly inappropriate. He showed how fraudulent sales practices, or sale of drugs by misrepresentations, or patent abuses, can continue through years of administrative and judicial proceedings to a determination which is no more than a slap on the wrist, whereas the less sophisticated thief must face additional criminal charges if he commits further and similar acts in the course of his much briefer and less lucrative activity.

Sutherland was basically concerned with society's disparate approach to the crimes of the respectable and well-to-do on the one hand, and those of the poor and disadvantaged on the other. His definition of white-collar crime concentrated, therefore, on characterizing violators rather than violations. The definition on which this paper is based is, hopefully, a more inclusive one.

White-collar crime is democratic. It can be committed by a bank teller or the head of his institution. The offender can be a high government official with a conflict of interest. He can be the destitute beneficiary of a poverty program who is told to hire a work group and puts fictional workers on the payroll so that he can appropriate their wages. The character of white-collar crime must be found in its modi operandi and its objectives rather in the nature of the offenders.

It is important that in our definitions of crime we concentrate on the nature of the crime rather than on the personal characteristics or status of the criminal. The latter analysis may be relevant and even of primary utility in the design and implementation of specific law enforcement programs, or to rehabilitation of offenders. Confusion and discriminatory application if penal sanctions must necessarily flow, however, from personalizing our conceptions of the nature of any one crime or group of crimes.

The above definition is the cornerstone of the following conceptualizations of various aspects of white-collar crime. It is crucial to this discussion of deterrence, investigation, evaluation, prosecution, and sentencing.

THE IMPACT OF WHITE-COLLAR CRIME

Sutherland published his "White Collar Crime" in 1949, a year already in the buried past. The complexity of our society in the intervening fifth of a century has increased so rapidly that it is difficult to do more than recognize resemblances between the problem he described and that which we face today. He saw the problem as one of victimization and discrimination, valid today as then. More important now, however, is our expanded vulnerability to white-collar crime because of changes in our economic and social environment.

We should not fall into the trap of idealizing the past (as with Rousseau's noble savage) but we can recognize that progress has its harmful side effects. In the white-collar field the basic side effect is the weakening of certain safeguards which were built into the marketing and distribution patterns of an earlier age, and which retained much of their vitality only 20 years ago.

Most purchases were once made in stores which were managed and serviced by their individual owners. Owners either lived in the communities which they serviced, or had close ties to these communities. They were known to their customers and had to face them after a purchase as well as before. These proprietors competed on the basis of service and reliability and, even though products might be presold by advertising, they would bear the brunt of customer dissatisfaction. Today most consumer goods—food, drugs, appliances, are sold by chains or similar large organizations, and the mobility of their personnel is matched, in part at least, by the mobility of their customers. On the retail level there has developed an essentially faceless transactional environment.

Today transactions are executed or moved by nonpersonal or credit instrumentalities. Retail credit is no longer carried on the books of the retailer, to be financed by retailer bank loans, but is now the subject of highly sophisticated and costly credit transactions involving bank and non-bank credit cards, revolving credit, credit life insurance—all substituting the credit granting and administering entities for the retailer after the sale is made. .

The genesis of transactions between businesses, and within businesses, is less the subject of individual decisions and more the result of programed procedures. Thus we now have electronic links, managed by computers. A perpetual inventory system may trigger a purchase order which in turn galvanizes a series of computer-induced stages culminating in an automatically written and signed check to pay for the purchase.

Conflicting objectives internal to business operations multiply exposure to white-collar crimes. Thus manufacturing and sales departments within a company will seek to override the restraints imposed by a credit department with consequent vulnerability to bankruptcy fraud operations. Sales departments will deliberately court risks, as by mailing of unsolicited credit cards, relegating possible fraud losses to the status of costs of doing business as if mere rent or utility charges. This may be an acceptable price to pay for economic growth, but it does invite white-collar crime.

Business planning is more and more keyed to the creation of needs, rather than to discovering or satisfying needs. Thus we have patterns of built-in style obsolescence, in hard goods and soft, and products may also be manufactured with a limited useful life.

Our economy has passed the point where it is geared to meet only the basic and elemental needs of the greater part of our population. The number of "haves" is very high, and large numbers of "have-nots" possess items which generate the desire for similar items on the part of their neighbors. Television exposes even the poorest to an incessant barrage of incitation to consumption of nonnecessities and to the titillation of desires based on nothing more than the exploitation of longing for status, beauty, or virility. The juxtaposition of these desires with our credit economy intensifies the incentive and opportunity for fraud in the marketing of consumer goods and services.

Our social and economic organization exposes us to new species of white-collar crime, having different or mixed objectives. In an earlier age the unlawful or ethically questionable amassing of wealth was characteristically accomplished by bald plunder or seizure of the public domain. "Teapot Dome" was a classic case, as was the land-grant device which provided the capital for building much of this Nation's railroad grid. Today such blatant power and property grabs are avoided. The new avenues for creation of wealth often involve tax avoidance (or evasion, which is criminal) to facilitate the accumulation of capital on which further acquisitions of wealth may be based. Tax avoidance or evasion are advantages to be wielded as is the ability to obtain favored treatment by zoning commissions, or special favors in connection with public guarantees of real property loans, or to be free from regulation in the operation of quasi-public utilities. The boundaries of the permissible and the impermissible are not drawn with precision, and perhaps they should not be. But as a consequence substantial loopholes persist, permitting the commission of crimes or acts inconsistent with policy limits set by our society.

The affluence of our society heightens exposure to criminal abuses by fiduciaries, an exposure which was once confined to the wealthy and the upper middle classes. More of us are now beneficiaries of trusts and quasi-trusts managed by the growing fiduciary industry. New targets for crime are the increasing proportion of trusts and estates of middle-class decedents, interests in union and company pension, welfare, and profit-sharing funds, and the broad panoply of mutual funds, investment trusts, credit unions, and investment clubs. . . .

As individuals we are more exposed to abuse. We are more likely to deal with strangers than with those we know (whose blemishes we can assess), and we are more vulnerable than we used to be because we tend to rely more on one another or on protection by Government. Those who buy securities are better protected than ever before because of the work of the Securities and Exchange Commission and comparable State agencies, yet are more exposed to the stock fraud artist who deceives the regulatory agency or totally circumvents its supervision. The buyer of food relies on weights and measures marked on prepackaged merchandise, since there is no occasion to look for the thumb on the seller's scale. We find it hard to believe that Government food inspectors would permit most unesthetic portions of animals to be ground into our hamburgers or sausages, and are therefore most shocked when sporadic inquiries disclose what we are eating. The physician relies on the vigilance of the Food and Drug Administration, and therefore accepts his education as to prescribable drugs from detail men sent to his office by pharmaceutical manufacturers. The certificates of guarantee which accompany our purchases of appliances and automobiles give us a false sense of security, no matter how often we have been burned in the past. *Caveat emptor* loses meaning when we buy closed packages.

Technical developments increase our exposure to white-collar crime. A prime objective of computerization is the cutting of labor costs, which means substituting hardware and computer programs for expensive labor. Our experience has given us an extensive fund of knowledge (often imperfect) as to how we can control, audit, and monitor people, but we have only the most elementary knowledge of how to audit computers and those who have learned how to use them. Much thought is being given to methods of coping with computers from a management point of view, i.e., internal controls, but little to audit by outsiders such as regulatory or law enforcement agencies. The search for control procedures is complicated by the accelerating rate at which the computer art is developing, a rate which makes controls obsolete almost as quickly as they are developed. Existing control methodology is not adequate for internal control, or for investigation by investigating agencies, or for regulation by regulatory agencies.

White-collar crime is a low visibility, high impact factor in our society. Because of the changes in the nature of our economic organization, particularly new developments in marketing, distribution, and investment, it is a fair assumption that white-collar crime has increased at a rate which exceeds population growth. Its effects intersect with and interact with other problems of our society, such as poverty and discrimination. It also weighs heavily on the aged who are, in our society, divorced from the homes and community of their children in contrast to most prior human social organization.

The increasing complexity of our society heightens vulnerability because it increases the difficulty of obtaining redress for losses suffered. Legal services are costly, prosecutors and investigators are overburdened, and court calendars are clogged. A victim must measure the time it takes to obtain redress and wonder whether he will not be the major sufferer, rather than the target of his complaint.

The prevention, deterrence, investigation, and prosecution of white-collar crime must compete with other interests for allocation of law enforcement dollars, in an atmosphere in which every other national problem is made more serious and more costly of solution by the increasing complexities of our society.

No dollar amount can adequately identify the costs of white-collar crime, though many figures have been used in various studies. Invariably these are projections based on known cases yet even with highly publicized cases there is no way of truly determining costs to victims and to the public. . . .

White-collar crime, like common crime, can have a serious influence on the social fabric, and on the freedom of commercial and interpersonal transactions. Every stock market fraud lessens confidence in the securities market. Every commercial bribe or kickback debases the level of business competition, often forcing other suppliers to join

in the practice if they are to survive. The business which accumulates capital to finance expansion by tax evasion places at a disadvantage the competitor who pays his taxes and is compelled to turn to lenders (for operating and expansion capital). The pharmaceutical company which markets a new drug based on fraudulent test results undercuts its competitors who are still marketing the properly tested drugs, and may cause them to adopt similar methods. Competitors who join in a conspiracy to freeze out their competition, or to fix prices, may gravely influence the course of our economy, in addition to harming their competitors and customers. The tax evader adds to the ultimate burden of the man who pays his taxes.

We should take special note of the impact of white-collar crime on the elderly and the poor, especially ghetto residents. These groups are the victims of minor offenses, such as housing violations, and of what we conventionally refer to as "consumer frauds." The impact is self-evident, but there is little comprehension of the outward rippling from consumer frauds on the elderly and the poor.

The very poor, and particularly the destitute elderly, are not profitable targets for those engaged in white-collar criminal activities. They may "pay more", as some surveys have indicated, but they are relatively impervious to the general harassment of process servers and collection agents, whose success is the ultimate reliance and *raison d'etre* of every consumer fraud operation. If a mother on welfare is given a short weight when she buys food the impact on her family is clear, but the transaction itself is not a vehicle for continued oppression and victimization. . . .

The true and ultimate vulnerability is the possession of an asset which can be lost. Such an asset may be tangible, such as a house, or an intangible such as a job which can be lost or made less desirable if wages are garnisheed, or some relationship which can be exploited by the fraud operator. A surprisingly large number of people living in ghettoes do have something to lose, but unlike the established middle classes the asset in jeopardy is very often the only asset which stands between its owner and utter destitution.

In the case of a home improvement fraud the fraud operator will solicit a job such as installation of aluminum siding for a house, making misrepresentations as to cost, quality, and credit terms. The victims are often past their prime working years, with perhaps very small savings to piece out the submarginal existence afforded by social security payments. Such victims have just about worked out their life schemes to avoid becoming public charges in their old age. The monthly payments required are more or less manageable, but the victims do not realize that these installments are largely interest payments on the inflated cost and that the major part of the contract price will be payable immediately following the final monthly payment in what is called a "balloon." The victims also do not understand that their house has been mortgaged to secure the exorbitant cost of the repair or improvement and interest and fees in connection therewith. Nor do they understand that their promissory note and mortgage will be promptly negotiated to a so-called holder in due course who will demand payment even if the work is never done, or never properly done. When the balloon payment is due the victims must refinance and subject themselves to what often is a form of perpetual peonage to finance companies, inevitably resulting in a desperate economic situation with consequent loss of house, savings, and all payments made. The victims are then on welfare, or a burden on their children.

Merchandising frauds may have similar impact. The typical case would involve an overpriced television set or furniture, with heavy finance charges. This kind of credit is extended only to those with jobs (to be endangered if wages are garnisheed) or to those whose obligations can be guaranteed by relatives or parents who have jobs or other assets. When installment payments are missed the entire obligation becomes imme-diately due and payable, and the victims are faced with the choice of refinancing and assuming even greater obligations, or becoming subject to garnishment procedures which could cost them their jobs. . . .

The social and economic costs of tax violations, self-dealing by corporate employees and bank officials, adulteration or watering of foods and drugs, charity frauds, insurance frauds, price fixing, frauds arising out of government procurement, and abuses of trust are clearly enormous even though not easily measured. If substantial progress can be made in the prevention, deterrence, and successful prosecution of these crimes we may reasonably anticipate substantial benefits to the material and qualitative aspects of our national life. . . .

DETECTION OF WHITE-COLLAR CRIMES

There are three basic sources of detection. They are: (1) complaints by victims; (2) informants; and (3) affirmative searches for violations by law enforcement agencies.

Complaints by Victims

When a common crime is committed, the victim immediately knows that something has been done to him. He has been assaulted, or robbed, or injured in some clearly definable way. He then has the plain option to report the crime to law enforcement authorities, or to refrain from doing so. This is not necessarily the case with respect to white-collar crimes in which the victim may never learn he has been victimized, or the realization comes too late to do him any good, or too late to be of meaningful assistance to law enforcement authorities. In the case of a charity fraud, where the victim makes a small contribution, it is highly unlikely that he will even take the trouble to think about the possibility of a loss, since his consideration is of a nonmaterial nature without practical consequences except for the remote disallowance of a charity deduction claimed on an income tax return. In the case of a magazine-selling fraud, the salesman "working his way through college" will also falsely represent that the subscriptions offered are at a discount price. In fact the price may well be higher than that available by regular subscription—yet the victim may never know it. The victim is quite likely, especially where small amounts are involved, to attribute his disappointments to the factors other than criminality, and will simply decide to write off the entire episode as not worth further trouble.

In many instances white-collar crimes are based upon predictable delays in victims' awareness of the fact that they have been defrauded. Arid desert land was sold by mail for millions of dollars, in reliance that very few purchasers would quickly travel from the East to parched areas of Arizona or Nevada to see their expensive oases (which in fact are waterless patches of scrub and sand). Ponzi schemes rely on perpetual delay in victim realization, as do chain referral schemes, work-at-home schemes, fraudulent self-improvement schools, advance fee schemes, and credit card frauds.

There are frauds committed every day, where the victims never learn about the frauds and as a practical matter it is impossible for them to learn. A typical example would be a check kite by an otherwise legitimate businessman who cannot obtain a bank loan but needs operating capital to tide him over his busy season. To obtain $50,000 he may put millions of dollars of checks in circulation between several bank accounts and, if his season goes as planned, he settles up. The banks have, in fact, made a $50,000 loan without interest to one who might be an ineligible credit risk for this amount, and they have been exposed to loss without knowing it. In most cases, these check kites work out, and, although a mail fraud has been committed, law enforcement authorities will never have the violation brought to their attention.

Many white-collar crimes against governments are based on "playing the percentages" that the victim will never know and, if by chance it should find out, will easily be induced to settle. The false entertainment deduction, where the taxpayer expects his claim to be passed without examination, is a good example. Another example of this would be the padding of expenses on cost reimbursable contracts, or "accidental" shifting of costs from work on fixed-cost contracts to those which are cost reimbursable.

Once the victim knows, or suspects that he has been criminally wronged, he must make a decision as to whether he should complain to law enforcement authorities, and then, a second decision as to where he must go to lodge his complaint. This is a crucial stage from the law enforcement point of view for several reasons: (1) If the victim does not complain a crime will go unheeded, and others may similarly suffer; (2) the success of a white-collar criminal prosecution is dependent on a showing of criminal intent, inferable from the circumstances—which often means a showing of similar acts and transactions. The number of complaints will therefore play a key role in the prosecutive evaluation, and in the ultimate success of a prosecution; (3) if there are not clear lines for intake of complaints, victims who make the threshold determination to complain may very well cease their efforts after unsuccessful initial attempts to reach appropriate law enforcement officials.

At this point we should recognize that many white-collar crimes are technical and not worthy of serious prosecutive consideration. Our concern that complaints be made and properly received should not be carried so far as to cause us to seek ways to "drum up business." There are more than enough cases in every investigator's office and in every prosecutor's office.

If we assume that appropriate complaints by victims should be encouraged (without attempting to define which complaints are "appropriate") we should also appreciate that victims' confidence in law enforcement is a necessary precondition to the success of the enforcement effort. The law enforcement effort must have credibility. Victims are unlikely to complain if they believe nothing will be done as a result of their complaints. A negative view of the criminal process may stem from prior unsatisfactory personal experience with complaints, or from the community reputation of law enforcement agencies. In some way his relationship with the law enforcement authority must benefit a complainant, and certainly not hurt him. Consideration must also be given to the interpersonal relationship between the victim and the representative of the appropriate law enforcement agency.

Informants:

Informants are an established detection resource with respect to certain white-collar crimes, such as tax or customs violations where the reward or bounty system is employed. Informants play a role, though a lesser one, with respect to Securities Act violations, banking violations, and frauds against the Government, but are practically a nonexistent factor in consumer frauds and con games. Informants are valuable in the investigation of white-collar crimes but, except as indicated above, they are of minimal significance in bringing possible white-collar violations to the attention of investigating or prosecuting agencies in the first instance.

Affirmative Searches for Violations by Law Enforcement Personnel

Distinctions must be made between classes of white-collar crimes, and perpetrators of such crimes, in assessing the desirability and cost effectiveness of intensive affirmative searches for violations by law enforcement personnel.

If we use the classifications of white collar crimes advanced above it will be apparent that there is more likelihood of victim complaints in the cases of personal crimes, abuses of trust, or con games, than with respect to business crimes (crimes incidental to and in furtherance of business operations, but not the central purpose of such business operations).

Business crimes, as defined, are carefully contrived in private transactions to avoid total destructive impact on other parties, to only partially affect such transactions, or to appear to be only a matter of degree. In transactions with governmental bodies they are designed to shade liabilities or obtain only incremental profits or advantages, and are extremely surreptitious and sophisticated in implementation.

The most intensive pattern of affirmative searches is to be found in the area of such business crimes. The Antitrust Division of the Department of Justice and the Federal Trade Commission maintain oversight with respect to mergers, trade association activities, and pricing policies of dominant firms in important markets. The Internal Revenue Service and State tax authorities strive to more carefully audit larger returns. The Department of Agriculture and the Food and Drug Administration make qualitative and quantitative examinations of food and drug products. The Securities and Exchange Commission examines new stock issues and monitors over-the-counter and exchange trading. All of these activities have, of course, nonprosecutive objectives such as collecting tax revenues, civil injunctions, maintenance of qualitative standards of food and drugs on a preventive basis, and protection of the interests of the investing public. Yet, always in the background, is the ultimate sanction of criminal prosecution. Agencies operating in the area of business crimes cannot rely on others to give them the information necessary to meet their responsibilities. They must maintain a solid capability to mount and sustain affirmative searches for violations.

In the case of business crimes, the desirability of beefing up affirmative investigative capabilities is self-evident. In other areas, such as consumer frauds, increased investigatory capability is more likely to be utilized in the handling and investigation of complaints which are not being adequately and fully dealt with at the present time. This might be a correct decision, since there are more than enough complaints at the post office (for example) to produce a very good payoff in worthwhile consumer fraud cases if the staff of postal inspectors is increased. However, we should ask ourselves the hard question whether this would not result in better protection for certain classes of victims, such as those most prone to make complaints, while more silent sufferers (ghetto residents, or the elderly, or the unknowing victims of charity frauds) are an overlooked or minimized constituency. We must always be careful not to operate on the principle that "only the squeaky wheel gets the grease." However, since investigators of consumer fraud are generally an idealistic lot (though they might well balk at this adjective) it would take but little support and encouragement to make them look up from overloaded complaint desks to give greater attention to criminal abuses which are not the subject of complaints.

INVESTIGATIONS

The question how investigations can be conducted more efficiently and a listing of all possible investigatory problems are not within the scope of this paper. The varieties of techniques available are infinite, and so are the problems. We should, however, concentrate on a few specific problems of almost universal applicability, and on the special problem of ghetto or inner city investigations.

Jurisdiction

Most white-collar crimes are violations of laws in multiple jurisdictions, either vertically (State-Federal) or horizontally (between States, between jurisdictions in one State, or between jurisdictions in the Federal Government). This leads to problems of coordination of effort where more than one jurisdiction is fully on the case, or cooperation where one jurisdiction assumes or is ceded the laboring oar, or conflicts, or attempts to avoid responsibility by claiming another jurisdiction has primary responsibility. . . .

Facilitating Private Aid to Investigators

There is a tradition that governments should run their own investigations, separate and apart from any involvement with interested private parties. It is a good tradition. Any other course would open the door to use of the prosecutive mechanism of government to improper exploitation by private parties. Every prosecutor's office is haunted by the spectre of becoming a collection agency for private debts, and it would be unthinkable for public policy on investigative priorities to be determined by private interests willing to pick up the costs. The halls of law enforcement agencies should not be frequented by lobbyists or special pleaders.

Having said this, we should recognize that existing practices implicitly recognize the desirability, and even the necessity of private support for the investigative process. Thus a prosecution for fraud on a telephone company in connection with long distance tolls will inevitably be based on investigations by telephone company security departments. The security department of a credit card company will already have completed the major part of the necessary criminal investigation before the matter is turned over to local police or to federal investigators. A bank embezzlement case will necessarily exploit the work of the bank's own auditors. In a bankruptcy fraud, work by creditors' investigators and attorneys often represent the basic case ultimately prosecuted. . . .

Conflicting Interests of Victims and Private Parties

Since white-collar crimes more often than not deal with deprivations of money or property, the first concern of any victim is restitution rather than punishment. The complaint made by a victim is usually preceded by a failure to obtain such restitution, and is in fact triggered by it, but the desire for restitution (even at the cost of denying or minimizing cooperation with the Government whose aid has been invoked) continues unabated.

While it may have no legal significance, a civil settlement by a victim or victims during a criminal investigation or prosecution has an almost lethal effect on criminal enforcement. To start with, the dividing line between civil abuse and a criminal violation is often less than clear in the white-collar crime area, and therefore prosecutors and investigators will tend to accept the fact of a settlement as an indication that the civil aspect outweighed the criminal. The investigator (or prosecutor) also knows that the victim will no longer be a wholehearted witness for the prosecution, and that any defense counsel worth his salt will find some way to make the jury aware that the case was mooted by civil settlement, even though evidence of such settlement might be inadmissible. Civil settlement may also be pursued as a device to dispose of an issue of fact crucial to criminal prosecution; this is a particularly effective technique where the settlement requires judicial approval (and thus judicial imprimatur). . . .

Cooperation of Victims and Witnesses

An observer might conclude that victims and witnesses exist only insofar as they are useful to law enforcement authorities, rather than the other way around. This anomaly is not characteristic of the white-collar crime area alone, or even more of a problem in this area than in others. However, in light of greater difficulty of assembling white-collar prosecutions and the larger numbers of victims and witnesses usually involved in any one case, the impact of this problem is greater in the white-collar crime field. . . .

Benefits of Investigation

No private party or nonpublic body has available to it the evidence gathering powers of a law enforcement agency. Banks will often give information to an FBI agent, subject only to the condition that subpoena will be subsequently delivered if the data produced will be used in some public way. Indi-viduals will commonly talk to a Government investigator or prosecutor in situations where they would not talk to private litigants. Where cooperation with law enforcement agencies is not voluntary, there is available the administrative subpoena, the grand jury subpoena, or the trial subpoena—sometimes backed up by the power to grant immunity from prosecution and thus the ultimate compulsion which overrides even a plea against self-incrimination.

It is therefore completely understandable that victims of white-collar crimes, who are more likely to be pursuing related civil remedies than victims of common crimes, will seek to obtain the benefits of a public investigation. . . .

Investigative Techniques

White-collar crimes are investigated by all of the usual techniques, plus a few very special ones. The methods employed depend on the agencies, both state and federal, and on prosecutors who often supervise the latter stages of investigations. Underlying government action is, of course, private inquiry (formal or informal, amateurish or professional) which so often precedes the complaint triggering an official investigation.

With a complaint on his desk, the investigator must first determine whether the facts alleged, if supported by legal evidence, would constitute a crime and if so, what crime. He is usually not an attorney. If it would be a crime worthy of prosecution the investigator will interview witnesses and seek seek to examine pertinent records. If an agency has regulatory or special investigatory powers, it may compel answers or production of records by threat of suspension of business operations, or by subpoena, or both. If there is a refusal to cooperate with a regulatory agency there may be a grant of immunity. At some point there is a shift in the theater of action to the prosecutor's bailiwick, and an investigation may be continued by a grand jury.

The methods described work very well

with respect to the usual run of SEC cases, financial cases, procurement frauds, and similar crimes. In many instances of consumer fraud, or housing maintenance or health offenses on the local level, these methods may not be adequate. They are certainly inconvenient if large numbers of victims are to be interviewed in a consumer fraud case, or with respect to wage and hour violations. . . .

PROSECUTIVE EVALUATIONS

. . . If prosecutive evaluations are mishandled the consequences may be serious and far reaching, both to the subjects of evaluation and to the administration of justice:

1. A sense of injustice on the part of those who know they are singled out for prosecution whereas others escape the net after being apprehended.
2. Failure to effectively use prosecutions and investigations for maximum effect in prevention, deterrence, and detection.
3. Blurring of standards for measuring the effectiveness of law enforcement efforts.
4. Vulnerability to disparity in treatment of offenders based on influence or quality of defense counsel.
5. Imposition of the brand of criminality on those who should not have been prosecuted in the first instance, whether they are convicted or found not guilty.
6. Failure to adequately prosecute certain crimes, particularly some white-collar crimes which may have little publicity value or provide for minimal penalties, may discourage enforcement efforts by agencies and investigators. . . .

PLEAS AND PLEA BARGAINING

White-collar cases are generally characterized by the use of representative charges, in many counts, rather than charges which comprehend the entire range of criminal conduct which is the subject of the indictment. The exception would be the common use of the conspiracy charge, which is an effort to sweep together all the bits and pieces. The fact that white collar criminal charges are narrow in scope does not mean that a defendant's full range of conduct will not be comprehended on the trial, but it is a reflection of the structured framework of criminal enforcement.

Thus a bank robber will be charged with the bank robbery which resulted in his apprehension, while the white-collar defendant is usually being charged with specific acts which represent points on a line which is a continuum of conduct. A securities promotor may have made 5,000 sales of unregistered stock, but the indictment will charge in 15 counts that he mailed confirmations of purchases, or certificates, to 15 specific customers. There may also be a conspiracy charge if two or more persons were involved in the sale. . . .

Although the use of representative counts in white-collar cases only occasionally has the effect of restricting proof at the trial, it does establish the dimensions of the arena for plea bargaining. The bank robber or burglar has one act to answer for, and his counsel may direct his efforts to negotiating a plea to a lesser-included offense. The white-collar defendant usually must target in on the additional objective of pleading to a lesser number of counts.

The objectives of a plea are therefore several, in white-collar areas:

1. As in all plea bargaining, to restrict the punishment by pleading to lesser offenses or lesser-included offenses.
2. As in all plea bargaining, to restrict the punishment by pleading to the smallest possible number of counts.
3. By minimizing the number of counts to which guilty pleas are entered, to establish a basis for a defense argument on sentencing aimed at narrowing the scope of the overall conduct for which the judge is meting out punishment.
4. By minimizing the number of counts, to limit the extent to which the defendant may be civilly liable to the victims of his conduct.
5. By seeking permission to enter *nolo contendere* pleas, to eliminate civil consequences which might flow from guilty pleas.

6. By seeking permission to enter a *nolo contendere* plea to deter the court from imposing a severe sentence. While the traditional doctrine is that a *nolo* plea is the same as a guilty plea for sentencing purposes, it is plain that courts regard government acquiescence or nominal objection to the proffer of a *nolo* plea as a downgrading of the importance or true criminal impact of the acts charged in the indictment or information. If the prosecutor genuinely objects, overriding of such an objection by the court will generally be followed by a light or only nominal sentence. . . .

SENTENCING

There is a general impression that the more serious the white-collar crime, the less severe the sentence. This is part of the folk myth that if one steals it is better to steal big. Part of the rationale for this generalization is that the penalties are no greater, the chances of being caught are less, and operating on a large scale will ensure that money is available for hiring most able counsel.

While one should be wary of generalizations, they usually emerge because they are valid most of the time. They fail us when we do not realize that they may not be valid in all situations. This generalization, that it pays to steal big, can be the subject of innumerable illustrations, and also can be countered with a few dramatic opposites.

Assuming the validity of the generalization, the explanation may partially be that those who steal big can afford to hire the best counsel, but this can only be a partial explanation since white-collar crimes generally result in the lighter sentences than common crimes, whether the defendants be rich or poor.

Analyses of white-collar crimes and those who commit them may provide us with better explanations for disparities of treatment on sentencing than the simplistic division between the defense resources of the rich and those of the poor. Or, if there be some credit to be given to the rich versus poor explanation, we would probably find

that it is only one factor for consideration.

In the analysis of white-collar crimes, supra, four categories were outlined: (1) personal crimes; (2) abuses of trust; (3) business crimes; and (4) con games. Consideration of these categories would make it obvious that, except for the fourth category, con games, the vast majority of defendants would have no criminal records, and that the recidivism rate would be almost nonexistent. Sentencing judges would, therefore, have before them (in the first three categories) a defendant with no record, already severely punished by criminal charges because part of business and social milieus in which arrestees or people with records are almost unknown, and with little likelihood of recidivism. This narrows the judge's objectives to two, deterrence and punishment supplementary to that already suffered by the defendant. Under these circumstances it is not surprising that sentences in white-collar cases tend to be lighter in the first three categoreis, even though the judge's discretion to inflict severe punishment does not differ markedly from that available to him in most non-white-collar cases.

Notwithstanding this apparently rational explanation for presumed judicial leniency in sentencing white-collar criminal defendants guilty of crimes other than con games, two questions remain: (1) As to any specific white-collar crime, are there disparities in sentencing which are not attributable to idiosyncracies of individual judges, but to some more general cause or causes; and (2) do present levels of sentencing in white-collar cases adequately meet the deterrence and punishment objectives which should be considered by judges? This assumes that the problems of correction and rehabilitation are comparatively unimportant in these areas.

In the absence of hard data the first question can only be answered by reference to impressions gained from observations over a period of time. The impressions of the writer are that, as to embezzlement and misapplication violations by bank personnel, the bank teller is more likely to go to prison than the bank officer or director. With respect to most other violations the writer has no clear impressions as to disparities of sentencing within violation categories. The writer is of the view, however that within violation categories the wealthier or better placed subject has a substantially smaller likelihood of being charged or if charged tried, or if tried, convicted. There would thus be an unrepresentative sampling at the sentencing level even if the disparities at that level were found to be minor.

Deterrence and punitive considerations are not, in the writer's view, given sufficient weight in the sentencing of white-collar criminals. White-collar crimes are not reactive or spontaneous and in most cases they are not the result of irresistible impulses. Sentences will therefore have marked deterrent effect to the extent that they are known. This would be true even for suspended sentences, for the brand of felon is a heavy burden for most men to carry, and the higher the social scale the heavier and more disabling the burden. . . .

In discussing deterrence one's first inclination is to think of prison. In the white-collar crime area we often deal, however, with corporate defendants. Top management is highly sophisticated in its ability to insulate itself from exposure to prosecution for the crimes it generates and supervises, and the prosecutor is often relegated to charging only the corporation and lower level officials or employees. Punishment for the corporation can rarely be measured on any scale other than money. Such punishments could be quite meaningful, especially if nondeductible for tax purposes, yet the scale of such penalties bears no true relationship to the conduct on which the prosecution is grounded. The power of the Securities and Exchange Commission to suspend the activity of a broker-dealer for failure to properly supervise its employees provides more meaningful monetary penalties than any fines provided for in our penal codes. Unless such administrative penalty or parallel civil litigation is available, corporate fines are no more than a modest, though somewhat messy cost of doing business. Fines, at anything like

their present levels, constitute neither meaningful punishment for the corporation or wealthy defendant, nor deterrence to those tempted to commit similar transgressions.

If punishment is a valid consideration in sentencing, apart from deterrence and rehabilitation, it suffers in this area as compared to non-white-collar crimes. In the abuse of trust and business crimes categories, the crimes are only possible because the violators are given the opportunity to commit crimes, by society, because they have presumably shown themselves worthy. Under these circumstances white-collar violations may well be more reprehensible, and more deserving of punishment if punishment is the sole criterion, than common crimes such as burglary. . . .

LEGISLATION

There are many inconsistent and anomalous statutory provisions dealing with white-collar crimes, on Federal and State levels, which should be thoroughly reviewed. Many of them are being considered on the Federal level by the committee presently reviewing the Federal Criminal Code. Particular stress should be given to the feasibility of a number of proposals, the need for which is quite evident in all jurisdictions.

Criminal fines should be raised to levels which realistically punish and realistically deter, and not merely to levels reflecting decreases in the value of the dollar since enactment of the fines presently on our statute books. Fines of merely a few thousand dollars on each count for violations of securities acts, or broad scale consumer frauds, or procurement frauds which may have cost the public or the Government millions of dollars, are poor deterrence and little or no punishment. . . .

Basic inconsistencies in our statutory patterns should be eliminated. One example would be the existence of 18 U.S.C. 215 which makes it a Federal misdemeanor for a banker to accept a bribe for granting a loan, while it is not a criminal violation to offer or pay such a bribe. Is it rational to make it a specific Federal felony to procure a loan from a federally insured savings and loan association by submission of a false financial statement, but not to proscribe the same abuse of the loan processes of a federally insured or chartered commercial bank?

Legislation should be considered as a vehicle for using the criminal process to provide a basis for restitution to victims, whenever they are part of the class victimized by the scheme or pattern of acts charged in the indictment on information.

Consideration should be given to possibilities of injunctive relief, analogous to that which the Securities and Exchange Commission may apply for, either during investigations or between indictment and trial, to protect further victimization of the public. We are all familiar with receiverships and trusteeships to prevent looting of business or wastage of assets on a proper showing of danger, or involuntary bankruptcy proceedings. The public as a class of prospective victims should be entitled to the same protection, on a proper showing, where criminal processes, investigatory or prosecutorial, are pending or impending.

Consideration should be given to statutes of general application authorizing investigatory subpoenas, on State and Federal levels.

On the State and local level the problem is so diverse and amorphous that it is difficult to suggest any simple pattern of legislation. One possible avenue, which would have deterrence value and be punitive in a monetary sense, would be to adopt one of the various existing proposals to create Federal rights in consumer fraud cases, which could be the subject of private derivative actions or actions by law enforcement officers in State as well as Federal courts.

For criminal law to be an adequate deterrent and remedy in the white-collar criminal field, it must be employed flexibly and with imagination, for the varieties of culpable human behavior in the white-collar area are almost without limit. It would be impossible to create specific statutes to proscribe all such wrongful conduct. . . .

CONSIDERATION OF SPECIFIC AREAS OF CONCERN

Implications of the Cashless Society

We must make a start on consideration of the law enforcement implications of the creditless person in the looming cashless, credit card society. . . .

Cash is losing much of its utility as a medium of exchange. For a host of reasons, including crime, buses and possibly taxis within less than a decade will be charging fares by accepting credit cards pushed into a slot. Bank credit cards have expanded retailer credit from large sales outlets to the neighborhood specialty store, and supermarkets may soon be expected to succumb to this trend.

The expansion of our credit card environment will create broad scale opportunities for thefts of cards, for disavowals of use by fraudulent reports that cards were stolen, by misuse of restricted cards, and by retailer-facilitated misuse of credit cards.

There should be careful studies, now, of avenues for prevention, deterrence, investigation, and prosecution in the credit card area. Among the matters for consideration should be:

1. Should there not be some control over the distribution of unsolicited credit cards? Should they be permitted? If permitted, should their mailing by certified or registered mail be compulsory?

2. Should identification pictures on credit cards be made compulsory? Or should legislation make the requirement of such pictures a condition of holder liability whenever a lost or stolen credit card is used?

3. What are the technical possibilities in this area? Would it not be desirable to foster uniformity of shape and size of cards, so that service establishments could have a single processing machine for all cards which would be wired to computers which could instantly identify stolen cards or the attempted unauthorized use for prohibited classes of goods or services?

4. Credit cards add a new element to the problem of fraud by computers. Most people tend to accept their bills without checking, as they have a tendency to do with bank statements, merely adjusting for errors. More and more retailers and credit card companies are moving away from submission of duplicate invoices, and substituting coded listings referring to merchandise classifications. This opens the way to frauds by insiders in retail establishments, particularly in billing departments, who may be able to work out methods for thefts of merchandise under this system, and even for compensating if account holders catch the errors in their bills.

6. If we assume that credit cards may well be necessary for those on welfare, the question of control to prevent misuse should be a first priority. Prevention here would be a primary objective.

7. What will be the role of state and local law enforcement authorities in the credit card area? Is the problem itself so vast, with cards becoming more and more national in character, that it should be primarily a Federal problem? . . .

Civil Rights and White-Collar Crime

Under what circumstances should civil rights violations be considered white-collar crimes and punishable as such? This is not an academic question since the tools of white-collar enforcement are both available and applicable to problems of civil rights compliance. Under the Federal false statement statute, 18 U.S.C. 1001, it is a felony to make a false statement, or to conceal a fact which would be material to the making of an administrative decision or determination. Where statements of compliance with civil rights mandates are required, i.e. by government contractors, false statements would be prosecutable. Where they are not now required, to compel such filings would shift the arena from the regulatory to the criminal area and provide options for increased enforcement. . . .

Election Laws and Corrupt Practices

This is a complex area with limitless ramifications, criminal, social, and political. Such legislation as exists is still ill suited to achieving reporting and public disclosure on a level which serves to inform the public of the true costs of electing public officials and the equally crucial question of who is paying these costs. The first problem, therefore, is a legislative one, to amend existing statutes, Federal and State, to close many obvious loopholes. The second problem is the investigatory and prosecutive one of coordinating election problems with tax enforcement, since all those familiar with the field are quite convinced that many campaign costs such as printing and provision of office space are met by contributions in the form of picking up bills, and end up as deductions on business tax returns.

Environmental Problems

Enforcement in the environmental field, with respect to air and water pollution and disposition of waste, is necessary if we hope to maintain or improve the quality of life. While there are some petty substantive criminal violations, usually at the level of technical misdemeanors, available as enforcement tools, the primary thrust of enforcement efforts has been to induce compliance by persuasion, conferences, subsidies, and regulatory measures of various kinds.

The pollution of our atmosphere, water, and soil is obviously too great a problem for draconian criminal solutions. Major efforts must be non-criminal, as they are now. But the ultimate sanction, the penal sanction, may be every bit as important in achieving civil compliance in this area as it is in the securities and banking areas, where only a very small portion of entrepreneurial violations ever reach the level of criminal prosecution. The potential is, however, of the utmost importance in meeting the overall regulatory responsibilities of the agencies involved. . . .

Consumer Protection

Many proposals have been advanced to provide for improved consumer protection. Some provide for new consumer rights and remedies, some for organizational changes to make possible more effective government action. All are directed, at a minimum, to the conversion of technical rights into meaningful and realistic remedies.

Certain problems in this area call for particular attention:

1. Consumer protection is undermined by the "holder in due course" doctrine which strips a victim of his right to defend or to interpose a setoff, when he is sued for payment by one who purchased the right to collect installment payments. It is easy to recommend a statutory elimination of "holder in due course status" in connection with purchases of goods and services by ultimate consumers, but the existence of mechanisms for legally protected purchases of installment paper is necessary to the maintenance of credit installment sales. Developing new approaches to the "holder in due course" doctrine, new forms of debt instruments, and legislation to reconcile the need for credit generating mechanisms with consumer protection, should be priority objectives for legislators and researchers.

2. Concern for the consumer inspires the structuring of proposals for consumer relief through class actions, restraining orders, and the statutory right to rescind contracts. As such proposals are enacted they will be evaluated to determine their effectiveness. It is important, however, that there be continuous scrutiny to determine whether criminal sanctions are being used, where available, and whether such sanctions should not be provided for in any new proposed consumer protection legislation. Those who seek to abuse the consumer must be required to recognize that they may face penalties which cannot be mentally assessed as being no more than a supportable cost of doing business.

3. Special consideration should be given to the problem of preventing victimization of the public after an abuse has been brought to the attention of investigative agencies. This is a most difficult problem, since restraining orders and injunctions are not customarily available to law enforcement agencies. Methods must be devised to stop ongoing frauds during State and Federal criminal investigations without risking immunity baths, and also without risking irreparable injury to those who may be falsely accused.

Diversion of Cases to Non-Criminal Channels

Truly effective and intelligent prosecutive evaluation would serve to screen out many of the cases which currently clog our courts and prosecutors' offices. The development of effective evaluation procedures may well be hampered by the absence of procedures and standards which offer prosecutors a meaningful alternative when they consider a case which is prosecutable but not truly worthy of prosecution.

Alternative remedies, whether in the form of arbitration or priority civil or civil class actions, would provide many benefits. Victims could obtain faster relief. Perpetrators of fraud would be subject to restraint by the use of legal tools which would not be available if there was to be an impending prosecution. And, most important, our courts and prosecutors would be freed to deal with prosecutions which would provide a more meaningful return because more significant in character and more intensively pursued. . . .

CRIMINAL TAX FRAUD

The President's Commission on Law Enforcement and Administration of Justice

We demand compliance with tax laws for an intensely practical reason: Taxes support the Federal Government. In 1966, taxpayers filed more than 104 million tax returns and paid over $128 billion in taxes. Almost 94 cents of each budget dollar came from income, estate, gift, and excise taxes. The Federal income tax alone produced more than 80 percent of budget receipts.

To induce compliance, Congress has crafted a finely calibrated scale of sanctions, ranging from interest on unpaid tax liability, to statutory additions to tax, to civil and criminal penalties. The civil penalties can add from 5 to 100 per cent to the amount of unpaid taxes due. Criminal penalties include felonies and misdemeanors punishable by fine or imprisonment or both. More than 10 separate criminal statutes protect the income tax alone.

THE OFFENDER

Our system of self-assessment and the sheer number of taxpayers make criminal tax fraud a unique white-collar crime. Each taxpayer computes his tax on the basis of facts which he sets out in his return. Annually, some 68 million individuals have an opportunity to commit tax fraud, while few have, for example, the opportunity to embezzle money from a bank.

Criminal tax fraud is committed not mainly by the famous or even by the infamous. The popular impression that celebrities or gamblers and racketeers are the usual subjects of income tax prosecutions is a distortion of publicity. Gamblers and racketeers account for fewer than 10 per cent of such prosecutions, and celebrities are not a visible statistic. If there is a bright line of tax evasion, it divides the self-employed—whose

From The Task Force Report, *Crime and Its Impact—An Assessment,* 1967, Attachment B, pp. 113–15.

compensation is not subject to withholding and whose opportunity for under-reporting income is thereby increased—from the employee. In 1965, almost two-thirds of those prosecuted for income tax fraud were self-employed. Heading the list of prosecutions were the medical, legal, and accounting professions (20 per cent) followed by the real estate, building and construction trades (6 per cent) and farmers (4 per cent).

THE OFFENSE

The nature of tax fraud creates unusual difficulties of proof. The crime is usually committed in the privacy of the home or office, without eye-witnesses or physical traces. While many white-collar crimes of misrepresentation have victims who may provide evidence, e.g. competitors, consumers, investors, stockholders, tax fraud has none. The inferences required to prove a tax fraud case must commonly be drawn from events largely independent of the commission of the crime and within control of the offender (increased net worth and expenditures or bank deposits in excess of declared and available resources). In combination, these factors pose formidable obstacles not only to proof of the commission of the crime but also to knowledge of the existence of the crime.

SELECTION, INVESTIGATION AND PROSECUTION

The selection and investigation of criminal tax fraud cases is done within the 58 District Director's offices of the Internal Revenue Service throughout the United States. Within those offices, the Intelligence Division is responsible for conducting investigations, through its special agents, into possible criminal violations of most internal revenue laws.

Every criminal tax fraud case begins with a lead. Most leads, of course, are obtained from the audit of tax returns. But leads also come from the Internal Revenue Service's data processing centers, from other governmental units, from items appearing in the press, from informants, and from sources developed by Intelligence itself. The leads are evaluated by the chief of the Intelligence Division who determines if a preliminary investigation is warranted. After that investigation, he then decides whether the facts developed call for a full-scale fraud investigation.

The selection of leads to investigate is guided by the desire for uniform enforcement of compliance with the tax laws in all occupations, income groups, and geographic areas. The limited number of agents, however, prohibits strict uniformity. In the 4-year period 1963 through 1966, for example, the number of special agents ranged from 1,691 to 1,721. Preliminary investigations totaled less than 9,000 per year and full-scale investigations around 2,000. In that same period, the number of income tax returns filed increased from 73 million to 80 million, of which, in 1966, about 4 per cent or 3 million were audited. Because every possible case cannot be investigated, the Intelligence Division concentrates on the more aggravated individual cases and on categories of low-compliance taxpayers where prosecution would be most effective in deterring similar violations.

The decision to invoke the criminal process does not rest with the investigator. The odds are 16 to 1 that the case he investigates will not ultimately be prosecuted. Each case that he recommends for prosecution will be reviewed by at least 12 people as it passes through the district and regional levels of the Internal Revenue Service to the Department of Justice, Tax Division, in Washington, and then back to the local level for further review and prosecution by a United States Attorney.

At each of the four levels—district, regional, national, local—the standard of prosecution is the same; whether the evidence is sufficient to indicate guilt beyond a reasonable doubt and whether a reasonable proba-

bility of conviction exists. At each level, the taxpayer may obtain a conference. There, the taxpayer is informed of the nature and basis of the charge against him and has an opportunity to make any explanations or to present any evidence he thinks might affect the Government's decision to prosecute. Conferences are held for information rather than for settlement purposes. A criminal tax fraud case will not be settled in return for payment of taxes due, interest, and civil penalties. However, if prior to the investigation or threat of investigation of a criminal tax fraud case, the taxpayer makes a voluntary disclosure and seeks to correct the errors, that fact will be given some weight in deciding whether to prosecute.

THE SIFTING PROCESS

The 2,000 cases that enter the review process after full-scale investigation are sifted through each level with the result that about 600 to 700 emerge as cases commenced in the District Courts. After investigation, the special agent determines whether prosecution is warranted. His decision is reviewed by his group supervisor and by the chief of the Intelligence Division. The criminal aspects of the case are closed if the decision against prosecution is unanimous. Otherwise, the case is transferred from the District Director's office to the Regional Office for review by the Assistant Regional Commissioner for Intelligence. He may recommend further investigation, no prosecution or prosecution. If the latter, the case is forwarded to Regional Counsel and is reviewed by an attorney, a technical advisor and the Assistant Regional Counsel. If they recommend prosecution, the case is transferred to the Department of Justice, Tax Division.

The Justice attorney to whom the case is assigned may also request further investigation or recommend for or against prosecution. His decision is reviewed by the Assistant Section Chief and by the Chief of the Criminal Section, Tax Division. Depending upon the nature of the case and the recommendations of the staff attorneys, the case may also be reviewed by the Second Assistant and by the Assistant Attorney General for the Tax Division. If the Department recommends against prosecution, the case is transferred to Chief Counsel's office, Internal Revenue Service, which may refer the case to Regional Counsel for closing or to the Department of Justice for reconsideration. If the Department recommends prosecution, the case is transferred to the appropriate United States Attorney's office for prosecution. There, a final review is given the case by an attorney and by the United States Attorney or his representative. The United States Attorney's office may advise the Department of Justice that the case should not be prosecuted, but final authority for prosecution rests with the Department.

The extensive review process is largely attributable to the uncertainties surrounding the existence and commission of criminal tax fraud. But comprehensive review also assures taxpayers that indictments for criminal tax fraud, which may seriously affect one's reputation, are not obtained haphazardly. And it assures the Government of a higher percentage of successful prosecutions, thereby increasing their deterrent effect. In 1966, the conviction rate for criminal income tax offenses was 97 per cent. Most defendants plead guilty or *nolo contendere* (*nolo* pleas are accepted over the Justice Department's continuing objection). In cases actually tried, the conviction rate is about 64 per cent.

SENTENCING

Sentencing practices for defendants convicted of income tax evasion vary widely from district to district and from judge to judge. When 54 Federal judges were polled to determine what sentence they would impose on a hypothetical defendant convicted of income tax evasion, they divided almost evenly between incarceration, on the one hand, and probation or fine, on the other. An Internal Revenue Service study of sentencing for income tax fraud for the years

1946 through 1963 shows that the percentage of prison sentences to convictions ranged from zero in South Dakota and 3 percent in the Western District of Virginia to 83 percent in the Western District of Washington and 93 percent in the Western District of Tennessee. In all districts during that period, imprisonment was imposed in only 38 percent of the cases. And of the 593 defendants convicted of criminal income tax fraud in 1966, 40 percent received prison terms. Terms of less than one year were imposed on 80 percent of those imprisoned.

Some of the traditional purposes of sentencing—isolation, rehabilitation—have little application to the typical individual convicted of income tax evasion. Most offenders have no prior record of conviction and do not require isolation from society for its protection. Moreover, severe sentences are not required to rehabilitate the offender. Statistics of the Department of Justice suggest that there is a negligible amount of recidivism. Of the 1,186 persons convicted of criminal tax fraud in 1963 and 1964, only two persons were repeat offenders. The ignominy of indictment, prosecution and conviction rather than the particular type of sentence imposed discourages the ordinary defendant from repeating his crime.

The purpose of sentencing for income tax crimes is to deter others from committing the same offense. As a general matter, the principle of deterrence may be of doubtful validity, but it has been regarded as particularly effective for crimes, such as tax fraud, where rational considerations are predominant. The threat of jail has "a most benign effect on those who do not like to pay taxes." Accordingly, it is our policy to recommend jail sentences for defendants convicted of criminal tax fraud. We follow this policy in the hardest case—where the defendant is a community leader with an otherwise spotless record who has already suffered the disgrace of conviction for income tax evasion. As Judge Skelly Wright has remarked:

. . . no jail sentence can add to that punishment in any degree. So we say then, why send such a man to jail? And I say to you the answer is that the only real purpose of an income tax sentence is its deterrent value. Unless we use the income tax sentence as a deterrent, we are overlooking one of our responsibilities as Judges.

QUESTIONS FOR DISCUSSION

1. What is the numbers game, where and how did it originate? How does it work? What accounts for the special status of the numbers man?
2. With state lotteries gaining popularity all over the country, will the numbers game be likely to survive this competition? Why or why not?
3. Criminologists, and even lesser souls, have an adage that you cannot swindle an honest person. Do the cases of Ponzi, Birrell, Estes, and the entire rogues gallery of master swindlers tend to confirm this belief? Read the *Big Con* by David Maurer for additional insight into the psychology of being swindled as well as for some understanding of big and short con games.
4. Is organized crime for real, or is it more mythical and disorganized gang activity than it has been portrayed? Discuss the *Mafia* and *Cosa Nostra* in this connection. Read Joseph Albini's book on the Mafia and Donald Cressey's volume *Theft of a Nation* for different perceptions.
5. Discuss the history of organized crime in America.
6. What is a "criminal family" in organized crime? How many are there supposed to be in the U.S.? What is their typical structure? How many major league syndicate operations are there? Discuss the size, integration, operation, and structure of these syndicate groups.
7. What are the chief sources of revenue of syndicate crime groups. Why do these sources represent a threat to legitimate business?
8. Compare Edwin Sutherland's and Herb Edelhertz' definitions of white collar crime. How do they differ? How are they similar?
9. White collar crime always involves a vio-

lation of "trust" as well as a crime. What does this mean?
10. Why, as in criminal tax fraud, is white collar crime so infrequently prosecuted? So rarely results in incarcertaion? In more generic terms, why is white collar crime differentially implemented from conventional crimes?
11. Examine the Edelhertz classification of white collar crime in the Appendix. Choose one specific type and do some local research on it. For example, a TV repair racket, home improvement scheme, land development fraud, commercial bribery, misgrading of goods.
12. Study the Better Business Bureau in your area. What do such bureaus really do? How much of a deterrent are they to illegal practices?
13. Check with your police department. Try to determine the last time they were called and/or made an arrest in a white collar crime case.
14. Is white collar crime "real crime?" Contrast the arguments of Sutherland, Paul Tappan, Ernest Burgess, Vilhelm Aubert, and Frank Hartung.
15. Read Gilbert Geis' book on *White Collar Criminal;* Marshall Clinard's, *The Black Market;* and Normal Jaspan and Hillel Black's, *The Thief in the White Collar* and report to the class, orally or in writing, on the state of knowledge in the field.
16. Do a special investigation of the most celebrated (nonpolitical) white collar crime event—the elcctrical conspiracy case. Report your findings to the class.

BIBLIOGRAPHY

Bernard, Viola W. "Why People Become the Victims of Medical Quackery." *American Journal of Public Health* 55 (August 1965): 1142–47.
Clinard, Marshall B. *The Black Market: A Study of White Collar Crime.* New York: Holt, 1952.
Cressey, Donald R. *Other People's Money: A Study in the Social Psychology of Embezzlement.* Glencoe, Illinois: Free Press, 1953.
Cressey, Donald R. "The Respectable Criminal." In *Modern Criminals,* James F. Short, Jr., ed., Chicago: Aldine, 1970.
Fuller, John G. *The Gentlemen Conspirators: The*

Story of Price-Fixers in the Electrical Indus-try. New York: Grove-Press, 1962.

Geis, Gilbert, ed. *White Collar Criminal.* New York: Atherton, 1968.

Herling, John. *The Great Price Conspiracy: The Story of the Anti-Trust Violations in the Electrical Industry.* Washington, D.C.: Robert B. Luce, 1962.

Lane, Robert E. *The Regulation of Business: Social Conditions of Government Economic Control.* New Haven, Connecticut: Yale University Press, 1954.

Newman, Donald J. "Public Attitudes Toward a Form of White-Collar Crime." *Social Problems* 4 (1957): 228–32.

Newman, Donald J. "White-Collar Crime." *Law and Contemporary Problems* 23 (1958): 735–53.

Quinney, Richard. "Occupational Structure and Criminal Behavior: Prescription Violation by Retail Pharmacists." *Social Problems* 11 (Fall 1963): 179–85.

Smigel, Ervin O. "Public Attitudes Toward Stealing as Related to the Size of the Victim Organization." *American Sociological Review* 21 (June 1956): 320–27.

Smigel, Ervin O., and Ross, Laurence H. *Crimes Against Bureaucracy.* New York: Van Nostrand Reinhold, 1970.

Sutherland, Edwin H. *White Collar Crime.* New York: Dryden, 1949.

Walton, Clarence C., and Cleveland, Frederick W., Jr. *Corporations on Trial: The Electrical Cases.* Belmont, California: Wadsworth, 1964.

DEVIANT STATUSES

Drunkeness is nothing else but a voluntary madness.

Seneca

O God, that men should put an enemy in their mouths to steal away their brains.

Shakespeare, Othello

The increase in drug use and misuse can be viewed as a part of a rapidly developing biological revolution.

Oakley Ray

Two heads are better than one.

John Heywood, Proverbs

Coming out ... often signifies ... the end of a search for his identity.

Barry Dank

Breathes there a man with hide so tough
Who says two sexes aren't enough.

Samuel Hoffenstein

Show me a happy homosexual and I'll show you a gay corpse.

Line from *Boys in the Band*

Madness severs the strongest bonds that hold human beings together. It separates husband from wife, mother from child. It is death without death's finality and without death's dignity.

R. S. deRopp

That he is mad, 'tis true; 'tis true 'tis pity and pity 'tis 'tis true.

Shakespeare, Hamlet

Is there such a thing as mental illness?

Thomas Szasz

If sanity and insanity exist, how shall we know them?

D. L. Rosenhan

Who then is sane?

Horace

5

Alcohol and Drug Abuse

Both alcohol and drug abuse constitute *status offenses*. As we discussed in Chapter 1, a *status offense* is a form of deviation in which harm is not necessarily done to any victims; status offenses lack the essential criminal ingredient of willfulness, being involuntary in character. One is a deviant because he is an alcoholic and not necessarily because he has victimized or may victimize others. The deviation is inherent in the chronic state of intoxication.

Status deviations are now undergoing marked transformation in social and legal definition. As the United States Court of Appeals for the Fourth Circuit said, in part, with regard to alcoholism:

This addiction—chronic alcoholism—is now almost universally accepted medically as a disease. The symptoms, as already noted, may appear as a "disorder of behavior." Obviously, this includes appearances in public, as here, unwilled and ungovernable by the victim. When that is the conduct for which he is criminally accused, there can be no judgement of criminal conviction passed upon him. To do so would affront the Eighth Amendment, as cruel and unusual punishment in branding him a criminal, irrespective of consequent detention or fine.

Although his misdoing objectively comprises the physical elements of a crime, nevertheless no crime has been perpetrated because the conduct was neither activated by an evil intent nor accompanied with a consciousness of wrongdoing, indispensable ingredients of a crime. . . .

It may yet come to pass, then, that status offenses will assume the character of medical problems and thus fall outside the purview of law.

ALCOHOL ABUSE

This chapter is concerned initially with drunkenness and alcoholism and with the institution of drinking and the role of alcohol in complex society. The first two selections explore the relationship between alcohol and crime.

In the first article, Glaser and O'Leary discuss the nature of the alcohol offender and examine interrelationships among alcoholism, drunken behavior, and crime. Alcohol acts as a physiological depressant, impairing reasoning and inhibition powers before depressing abilities to act and to express emotion; however, if enough alcohol is consumed, the latter functions will become depressed also. Individuals not only vary greatly in their behavioral reactions to alcohol, but there are also systematic cultural differences associated with drinking patterns and forms of drunken behavior. For example, violent behavior occurs much more frequently in those countries where alcoholic beverages are not routinely used as a food. The concluding sections evaluate the influence of alcohol on crime.

"Drunkenness Offenses" is the summary statement of the President's Commission of Law Enforcement and the Administration of Justice. In this very brief review of the problem and of recommendations for action, the President's Commission discusses the extent of the problem of drunkenness, the existing laws on the subject, the characteristics of the offenders, and their handling and disposition in the criminal justice system. Some of the hard facts in these areas are startling. For example, one third of all United States arrests—two million in all each year—are made for the "crime" of public drunkenness. Some of those arrested are part of the "revolving door" problem—arrest, thirty-day sentence in a jail or workhouse, release, and re-arrest. The President's Commission makes four recommendations designed to improve the situation. Of these, one concerns the redefinition of the problem, two involve new treatment approaches, and the last deals with the need for research.

The next two articles deal with the organizational context of drinking—the public centered drinking institution—the tavern, pub, or bar. Professor Marshall Clinard's "The Public Drinking House and Society" is the most complete work on the subject. The article describes the characteristics of a public drinking house, the types of drinking establishments, and the various social functions of the tavern in addition to its function as a place to drink. The last part of the article is devoted to a discussion of the tavern as a problem institution—its relation to alcoholism and the extent of juvenile participation. There is the implication in this article that the tavern, or at least certain of its types, may well function as an agent of social control over drinking.

Roebuck and Harper provide a more detailed look at a particular after-hours club. While not directly related just to alcohol use

and abuse, such a club provides drinks (after legal closing time), food, entertainment, and a relaxed atmosphere not only to "straights," but to those involved in many different types of deviant behavior. A majority of the regular clients are night-people, swingers, criminals, prostitutes, and people associated with show-business. The authors describe this type of club as essentially a "tension-managing organization." It represents a way in which its patrons, who work in tension-providing occupations, can relax and enjoy themselves in an atmosphere free from the rule-makers and the possibility of being publicly processed as a deviant. The club is a public organization. Dues are not required for membership, but there is a prescribed set of ritualistic behaviors associated with admittance to the premises. The authors focus on the organizational matrix of the club and emphasize the fact that deviant organizations provide varied supports for behavior defined as both deviant and nondeviant.

DRUG ABUSE

It is one of those peculiar aspects of our culture that the more serious problems associated with alcohol—drunkenness, driving while intoxicated, vagrancy, "Blue Mondays," and alcoholism—evoke less concern than the numerically and medically less important problems of dangerous drug use. Public fascination with the use and abuse of narcotics and the hallucinogens is a phenomenon worthy of study in itself. The simplest explanation for this paradox is that alcohol "fits" better into complex society because of its tension reduction properties and facilitation of interpersonal relationships. Drugs, on the other hand, tend to turn the person inward—back on the self. In a competitive, impersonal, urban society, turning in on the self (retreatism) and privatizing one's life are incomprehensible to many. (Some of our fear of schizophrenics and other psychotics is based on the inability of such persons to communicate and relate.) In other parts of the world, given a different value-orientation and a greater emphasis on the contemplative life, it is drugs which are tried and used, while alcohol is the more feared.

Whereas the narcotic and hallucinogenic drugs are of paramount concern, other kinds of mind-altering drugs are used in many perfectly legally and socially acceptable ways. For example, amphetamines are widely prescribed by physicians for weight reduction, in controlling fatigue, and in overcoming "blues" and minor depressions. Students, truckers, and other night persons frequently resort to "pep" pills. Barbiturate usage is, if anything, even more acceptable than amphetamine use. Millions of insomniacs depend on the sedative effect of "goof balls." And who is unaware of the tremendous revolution occasioned by the tranquilizers? Thus, it is not the use and abuse of all psychotropic and psychoactive drugs which are deviant. Only the use of certain classes of dangerous drugs—the narcotics, hallucinogens, and marihuana—are considered deviant. Because such use is labeled deviant, criminal, and outside legitimate medical practice, users develop a life style quite far removed from that of straight society. The roles, statuses, functioning, and self-concepts of the users are derived from this subculture. Quite apart from the effects of the drugs, it is this involvement and participation in a deviant subculture which nullifies most treatment efforts and leads to the high rates of return to drug use after treatment.

The contribution by Richard H. Blum is a calm description by the President's Commission on Law Enforcement and the Administration of Justice of the state of current knowledge about marihuana and the hallucinogens. This summary examines the extent of the use of these substances in the United States and the characteristics of the users. The reported risks of such use are contrasted with the verified risks. The latter, naturally, are far less extreme. There is also a discussion of the effectiveness of legal controls, and some tentative recommendations are offered. There is one extremely interesting recommendation regarding marihuana. It is that marihuana acquisition and possession be reduced from a felony to a misdemeanor. Although very unlikely to occur, the implementation of this recommendation would certainly alter the status of the problem and reduce the "speakeasy" aspects of present use. The report also suggests that states which have or are in the process of making the possession of hallucinogens unlawful may be acting precipitously. The result of such laws may lead to the repetition of the problems presently encountered with heroin and other "hard" drugs.

The final selection focuses more directly on drug abuse. In the United States, the Drug Abuse Office and Treatment Act of 1972 attempted to develop a comprehensive, coordinated, long-term Federal strategy for all drug abuse prevention and drug traffic programs related to the Federal government. The Strategy Council was composed of the Secretaries of State, Treasury, Defense, and HEW; the Attorney General; the Administrator of the Veterans Administration; the Director of the Special Action Office for Drug Abuse Prevention; and the Director of the Office for Drug Abuse Law Enforcement. In their initial report, the Council took the position that they were dealing not with one problem but with many. The Council also took the position that "drug abuse" meant "the illegal use of a controlled substance or use of a drug in a manner or to a degree that leads to adverse personal and social consequences." In the selection chosen here, the emphasis is primarily on heroin addiction. The report also comments on various approaches to treatment, including nonvoluntary treatment. It also discusses the control of drug availability, an issue which moves into delicate problems of international relations. The report was intended as an initial statement which would be reviewed continuously and modified as new knowledge develops. The Council admitted that the problems are so diverse that any totally coordinated consistent response was an elusive goal.

THE ALCOHOLIC OFFENDER

Daniel Glaser and Vincent O'Leary

DRINKING AND DRUNKEN BEHAVIOR

The use of alcoholic beverages is as ancient as our oldest recorded history. Foodstuffs with starch or sugar content and moisture ferment if left standing at normal temperatures. The fermentation process gives them an alcoholic content. Numerous societies have learned to prepare beverages with such natural alcohol, and even to distill the natural fermentation products to derive beverages of higher alcohol content.

We shall use the phrase "drunken behavior" to designate changes in behavior that distinctly follow consumption of alcoholic beverages. Noticeable change in behavior may not always be associated with drinking. Also, drunken behavior may vary tremendously not just with the amount of alcohol consumed, but with the person, time, and place involved in the drinking.

The usual explanation for drunken behavior is that alcohol, which is a physiological depressant, impairs operation of the higher brain centers more rapidly than it affects the lower nervous system. Consequently, it impairs reasoning and inhibition powers before it depresses the ability to act and to express emotion. However, sufficient alcohol will depress the latter functions too.

The government of Finland operates the liquor sales stores in that country and invests a portion of this income in research on alcoholism. In one interesting experiment, careful observations were made through a one-way mirror to record the behavior of four groups of four men brought into a room and provided with alcoholic beverages. Each group went through two five-hour afternoon sessions, a few weeks apart, one session with

From *The Alcoholic Offender*, National Parole Institute, Washington: U.S. Department of Health, Education and Welfare, 1966, pp. 1–9, 15–16.
Daniel Glaser is Professor in the Department of Sociology, University of Southern California. Vincent O'Leary is in the Department of Criminal Justice, State University of New York, Albany.

beer and one with brandy. The men were all given the same lunch before the session; they were then given blood tests at approximately 90-minute intervals. They were also given a variety of psychological tests. In portions of the sessions the men were given topics on which to reach consensus by group discussion. Similar tests and procedures also were employed with men without alcohol, who formed control groups.

As might have been expected, these Finnish experiments showed that alcohol intake was followed, for most participants, by an increase in the frequency of hostile, deflating, and otherwise negative remarks in the group efforts to reach consensus when discussing assigned topics. Such changes were greater with brandy than with beer, even when the total alcohol absorbed into the bloodstream was the same with each beverage. This finding suggests that the social expectations associated with each of these beverages, rather than just the alcohol, affected behavior. They also found that individuals differed greatly in the extent of their behavior changes with each beverage, at any level of blood alcohol.

In general, the Finnish experiments showed that the most constructive participants in group discussion, and those most often preferred by members of the group as work associates, were least changed in behavior when they consumed brandy. The persons seldom chosen by the group as preferred work associates were most frequently chosen as preferred drinking companions, and they had the greatest increase in negative behavior when drinking brandy. These men also most often agreed that a person's deviant behavior should be forgiven when he is drunk. What seems to be suggested by these findings is that drunken behavior may result, in part, from the belief that deviant behavior is acceptable, and perhaps even socially expected, when a person has been drinking strong beverages. It also suggests that there is a strong contrast between persons who are popular in drinking activity and persons who are effective in getting a task done.

Certainly, a factor in the association of alcohol with crime is the social and cultural setting in which alcoholic beverages are consumed. Where intoxication connotes loud and aggressive behavior, less inhibition is expected of a person defined by others as somewhat "high." Thus, when a person thinks of himself as "drunk" he assumes—and is granted by others—some license to engage in deviant behavior without rebuke, regardless of whether or not the physiological effects of alcohol actually reduce his control over his behavior. One familiar indication of this is that many persons, when drinking in relatively formal and sedate social situations, behave with much more restraint, after the same consumption of alcohol, than at a more informal and convivial party.

No analysis of alcoholism should overlook the distinctive cultural variability in drunken behavior. On the whole, it appears that where alcoholic beverages are most widely consumed, in terms of the frequency with which they are imbibed and the proportion of the population taking them, disorderly drunken behavior as a problem seems minimal. The French, Italian, and other Mediterranean and Latin American countries characteristically use wine as a food on a daily basis and for all age groups. While alcoholism is by no means absent in these countries, problems of violent behavior associated with heavy drinking have been much more prominent in countries where alcoholic beverages are not routinely used as a food. Notable here are the Scandinavian countries and Ireland.

Within the United States, persons of certain ethnic ancestry, such as the Jews and the Chinese, have had notoriously low rates of alcoholism. Persons of Irish descent, Mexicans, and Negroes, have been disproportionately high among those arrested for alcoholism. In some parts of the country, notably the Northwest, drunkenness arrests are especially frequent among American Indians.

There is some evidence that violent drunken behavior on a repetitive basis is particularly characteristic of cultures in which there is a high level of insecurity. Two analyses of drinking among primitive peoples agreed that drunkenness was especially a problem in societies in which there was great insecurity in subsistence. The introduction of alcoholic beverages to American Indian tribes by white settlers was reported generally to have been most disturbing to tribes with a marginal existence dependent on hunting, as contrasted with tribes dependent on agricultural crops and domestic animals.

The purely physiological effects of alcohol are very much like those of fatigue. Individual personality and social and cultural influences apparently greatly determine how these effects are reflected in changed behavior as alcohol is consumed. Therefore, one can assert that alcohol alone does not "cause" drunken behavior; drunken behavior expresses personal character, cultural traditions, and social circumstances, as they influence a person's reactions to the physiological effects of alcohol on his body. For some people, and in some circumstances, these personal, cultural, and social factors may readily express themselves as criminal behavior. Before exploring further such relationships of drinking to crime, let us consider the ailment called "alcoholism."

ALCOHOLISM

"Alcoholism" has been broadly defined as "any use of alcoholic beverages that causes any damage to the individual or society or both." Somewhat more specific definitions add to this personal or social damage feature the idea that the persons with alcoholism undergo "loss of control when drinking has begun." Most other definitions provide little which augments these descriptions of symptoms identifying alcoholism, but add speculations as to its causes. A few definitions propose more specific criteria to distinguish varieties of alcoholism, but leave the overall concept vaguely defined. However, there is little consensus in prevailing distinctions between types of alcoholism.

It is clear from the foregoing that only a hazy borderline differentiates much heavy drinking from alcoholism. The Public Health Service describes the onset of alcoholism, as distinct from ordinary imbibing, as follows:

One of the more obvious early signs . . . is that the individual drinks more than is customary among his associates and makes excuses to drink more often. This is an indication that he is developing an insistent need—or a psychological dependence—on alcohol to help him escape from unpleasant worries or tensions.

As the condition progresses he begins to experience "blackouts." He does not "pass out" or become unconscious, but the morning after a drinking bout he cannot remember what happened after a certain point. If this happens repeatedly or after taking only a moderate amount of alcohol, it is a strong indication of developing alcoholism.

As his desire for alcohol becomes stronger, the alcoholic gulps, rather than drinks, his beverage. He senses that his drinking is getting out of hand, and he starts drinking surreptitiously so that others will not know how much is consuming.

Finally he loses control of his drinking. After one drink, he feels a physical demand for the drug so strong that he cannot stop short of intoxication. Suffering from remorse, but not wanting to show it, he strikes out unreasonably at others. As he realizes that he is losing the respect of his associates and hurting his loved ones, he tries to stop or drink moderately, but he can't. He becomes filled with discouragement and self-pity and tries to "drown his troubles" in more liquor. But his drinking has passed beyond the point where he can use it as a way of coping with his problems and he is faced with the disease of alcoholism.

In several studies, alcoholics were asked to date the onset of their various types of drinking experience. Jellinek's pioneer research suggested that there is a continuous and steady progression, and a standard sequence, for different features of alcoholism, such as experiencing blackouts, drinking first thing in the morning, drinking alone, having convulsions, and having tremors. More recent studies of this sort, by Trice and others, suggest that not all alcoholics have each of these experiences, and most have several almost simultaneously. However, convulsions, tremors, and feeling that they have reached their lowest point, generally characterize the last phases in becoming clearly an alcoholic.

Since alcoholism is dealt with as an individual problem, it is commonly presumed to be a defect of personality. Some have speculated that it could be a hereditary tendency, since alcoholic parents more frequently have alcoholic children than do nonalcoholic parents. However, the fact that children of alcoholics reared in foster homes do not have the high alcoholism rates of children reared with alcoholic parents suggests that social influences in the home, rather than biological inheritance, account for what tendency there is for alcoholism to run in families.

Efforts to distinguish alcoholics from others by personality tests have revealed no marked and consistent distinctions in terms of standard personality categories. Rorschach, Thematic Apperception Tests, intelligence tests, personality inventories, and electroencephalograms, showed no diagnostically useful differentiation of alcoholics from nonalcoholics. Apparently alcoholics are quite diverse in terms of the personality distinctions made by such tests.

In spite of these findings with traditional tests, there are several types of evidence that distinctive personality patterns characterize alcoholics. Connor gave a list of 75 adjectives to 347 alcoholics and 230 nonalcoholics, asking each to check those terms which best described them. The terms most frequent in the self-descriptions by alcoholics were "affectionate," "appreciative," "easy-going," and "soft-hearted." Nonalcoholics differed most from the alcoholics in describing themselves by such terms as "active," "ambitious," "cautious," "curious," "loyal," "honest," "reliable," and "sincere." This suggests that the alcoholic has a conception of himself as possessing the traits necessary for success in informal social relations, but lacking the traits needed for success in most occupations, or for a responsible position in any organization. Such a finding would be consistent with the cited Finnish evidence that people who change their behavior most while drinking are those most liked for drinking sociability, but least preferred as coworkers.

Peter Park analyzed responses of over a thousand college students to a long questionnaire which included inquiries on problem-drinking traits, and inquiries on the behavior they would adopt in a large variety of hypothetical situations involving action dilemmas. In general, problem drinking was associated with preferring to act in favor of a friend or relative rather than on the basis of principle, where a choice had to be made between these two types of action. Also, the problem drinkers were more likely than the nonproblem drinkers to take an action yielding immediate plasure rather than an action yielding greater advantages in the long run, but less immediate satisfaction. These responses again seem to characterize the alcoholics as sociable and agreeable, but not oriented to the impersonal job-centered mentality demanded in most responsible work positions.

It is notable that not only do alcoholics seem to be distinguished for their amiability in interpersonal relations like those of a family, but drinking characteristically occurs in a small group situation in which more familiarity between strangers is accepted than generally prevails elsewhere. One study distinguished a "social drinking," "excessive drinking," and an "alcoholic" phase in the careers of alcoholics. In comparing alcoholics in the social drinking phase with non-alcoholic tavern patrons, it concluded: "Nine out of ten alcoholics and an estimated three out of four regular patrons drink in the company of others. Some two-thirds of the alcoholics thought that the social contacts of the tavern were more important than the drinking at this stage."

The role of the bartender as confidante, and as promoter of amiable conversation between patrons, is noteworthy. From this standpoint, the tavern or other drinking place can be thought of as providing a "home away from home," a home for the homeless, and a home for those who do not feel "at home" in their own residences.

This social function of drinking may be evident in the first introduction to alcoholic beverages during adolescence and may explain early steps toward alcoholism. As Maddox has observed:

Teenage drinking ... appears to most adequately understood as a social act, as a mechanism of identification by which many teenagers attempt to relate themselves, however prematurely, to the adult world. Drinking is one of the available mechanisms by which the drinker may say to himself and others, "I am a man" or "I am one of the crowd." This is possible because a segment of the cultural tradition to which he is likely to be exposed has defined drinking in this way.

Alcoholism in our society often seems to characterize persons insecure in making a transition from adolescent to adult roles. They alternate between adult assertion of independence and the shelter-seeking dependence of the adolescent, even decades past their adolescent years. In much usage there is a reluctance to apply the term "alcoholic" to anyone younger than about 30 years of age; before that he is a "heavy drinker" who may or may not become an alcoholic. Nevertheless, interviews with 500 successive admissions to the Massachusetts Youth Service Board Reception Center, concluded that 10 percent were "addictive drinkers" who drank whenever they could. Their modal age was 16.

Two recent studies followed up as adults persons who, a few decades earlier, had been investigated by clinics and other agencies as presumed problem children. The records of these agencies permitted a comparison of the childhoods of those who became alcoholics with the childhoods of adults without alcoholism or other serious deviant behavior. Alcoholics had objectively less adequate parental care than nonalcoholics, to a significant extent; this was a difference in "the basic obligation of physical care, financial support, supervision, and provision of a socially acceptable model." As children, the later alcoholics differed from the nonalcoholics in more often being described as aggressive, sadistic, and hyperactive.

From such findings, it is theorized that the future alcoholic first tries to compensate for parental neglect by asserting his independence in childhood aggressiveness. Drinking later serves as a symbol of independence. However, it is inferred that the alcoholic's basic deprivation of parental attention in childhood makes him actually have great need to be dependent, that the display of masculinity and aggressiveness in male drinking is simply a facade which hides a great need for affection. Drinking serves both to facilitate this search for affection in the sociability of the drinking activity and to express masculine independence. A vicious circle in alcoholism, therefore, may be that heavy drinking actually impairs ability to achieve masculinity and to gain affection, so that as a result of drinking, the need to seek its presumed satisfactions remains at a high level.

There has been some theorizing that the chronic alcoholic is typically an individual who not only was abnormally dependent on his mother, but thereby filled the mother's need to dominate. The indulgent but rebuking mother or wife derives a sense of moral superiority over the alcoholic. The intense loyalty, often expressed in excessive indulgence, which such persons often show towards alcoholics, may be a factor in the persistence of the alcoholic's difficulty. According to this theory, these nonalcoholic persons, in a sense, aggressively keep the alcoholic dependent and morally subordinate. Many an alcoholic is in a cycle of being rebuked at home for his drinking, therefore longing for the moral equality or dominance he can enjoy with his associates in the drinking place. When the drinking spree is over, he finds solace and shelter with the indulgent family members. He then gains ascendancy over them by forcing them to care for him, and by embarrassing them, which may avenge the humiliation he receives from their rebukes.

Clinical descriptions of alcoholics by psychiatrists generally employ terms like those used to describe the narcotic addict. These include such adjectives as "immature," "passive," and "dependent." (Sometimes alcoholics and narcotics addicts are grouped together as "addiction prone" personalities.) In clinical diagnoses of alcoholics, the term "dependent" is particularly prominent. The alcoholic is described as an individual who never outgrew a close dependence on mother. In this connection, the fact that alcoholic beverages are taken through the mouth leads a number of psychoanalytically oriented clinicians to suggest that the alcoholic is an individual who remains at the oral stage of development. This implies that he remains fixed at, or has regressed to, the relationship characteristic of a nursing infant.

THE CHRONIC POLICE CASE INEBRIATE

The most frequent basis for arrest in the United States is on the charge of drunkenness, although it sometimes has a different designation, such as "public intoxication." A large proportion of other arrests, such as those for disorderly conduct and vagrancy, involve drunkenness. The individuals taken into custody on these charges are distinctly older than most felony arrestees. The median age of persons arrested for drunkenness in 1962 was 42, for disorderly conduct 30, and for vagrancy 37.

An analysis of the records of 187 men committed to sentences of 30 or more days in Rochester, New York, during 1953–54 indicated that the average arrestee had a record of 16.5 prior arrests, of which 12.8 were for public intoxication and the remainder for other offenses. The most frequent other offense was larceny, which comprised about a quarter of all nondrunkenness charges. These offenders, now mostly subsisting at a marginal economic level on Skid Row, usually had committed their serious felonies at an earlier age and had a greater frequency of purely drunkenness arrests when they became older. It has been suggested by Cloward and Ohlin that such men, like many drug addicts, are "double failures"; they have resorted to a "retreatist" approach to social demands, because they failed first at legitimate and then at illegitimate (criminal) means of achieving a conventional standard of living.

Characteristically, these Skid Row alcoholics were found to be homeless men, who left the parental home at an early age following the death of one or both parents, or conflict with parents. This departure contributed to their failure to complete their studies or to progress in a vocational career. They seem to have then moved continually from one protective environment to another, between drinking sprees, being either in a correctional institution or in a shelter for homeless men.

Interviews by Robert Straus with 203 men in the New Haven Salvation Army Center during 1946 concluded that they were of predominantly low education and experienced only at unskilled or casual labor. Straus inferred from his interviews that heavy drinking led to homelessness in two-thirds of the cases, and the homelessness led to heavy drinking in one-third of the cases. It should be stressed, incidentally, that being on Skid Row is not synonymous with being an alcoholic; data indicate that, for many nonalcoholic homeless men, subsistence is more feasible in Skid Row than elsewhere—when they suffer extreme poverty, lack of family, or physical or mental defects.

Older offenders who are homeless and chronically alcoholic have a difficult time completing a parole without committing persistent rule violations. Nevertheless, their rates of serious felony acts on parole seem to decline with age. However, their drinking makes them incapable of holding a regular job or of accumulating funds. It also is difficult to provide them with a home and employment at release from prison, except as residents in a "shelter program" such as supplied by the Salvation Army or other voluntary agencies.

DRUNKENNESS OFFENSES

The President's Commission on Law Enforcement and Administration of Justice

Two million arrests in 1965—one of every three arrests in America—were for the offense of public drunkenness. The great volume of these arrests places an extremely heavy load on the operations of the criminal justice system. It burdens police, clogs lower criminal courts, and crowds penal institutions throughout the United States. . . .

THE EXISTING SYSTEM

Drunkenness Laws

Drunkenness is punishable under a variety of laws, generally describing the offense as being "drunk in a public place," often with-

From The Task Force Report, *Drunkenness,* 1967, pp. 1—6.

out providing a precise definition of drunkenness itself. Some laws include as a condition that the offender is "unable to care for his own safety."

In some jurisdictions there are no laws prohibiting drunkenness, but any drunkenness that causes a breach of the peace is punishable. In Georgia and Alabama, for example, drunkenness that is manifested by boisterous or indecent conduct, or loud and profane discourse, is a crime. Other jurisdictions apply disorderly conduct statutes to those who are drunk in public. In Chicago, for example, the police, having no drunkenness law to enforce use a disorderly conduct statute to arrest nondisorderly inebriates. Some jurisdictions permit police to make public drunkenness arrests under both State laws and local ordinances.

The laws provide maximum jail sentences ranging from 5 days to 6 months; the most common maximum sentence is 30 days. In some States an offender convicted of "habitual drunkenness" may be punished by a 2-year sentence of imprisonment.

The Offenders

The 2 million arrests for drunkenness each year involve both sporadic and regular drinkers. Among the number are a wide variety of offenders—the rowdy college boy; the weekend inebriate; the homeless, often unemployed single man. How many offenders fall into these and other categories is not known. Neither is it known how many of the offenders are alcoholics in the medical sense of being dependent on alcohol. There is strong evidence, however, that a large number of those who are arrested have a lengthy history of prior drunkenness arrests, and that a disproportionate number involve poor persons who live in slums. In 1964 in the city of Los Angeles about one-fifth of all persons arrested for drunkenness accounted for two-thirds of the total number of arrests for that offense. Some of the repeaters were arrested as many as 18 times in that year. . . .

The great majority of repeaters live on "skid row"—a dilapidated area found in most large and medium-size cities in the United States. On skid row substandard hotels and roominghouses are intermingled with numerous taverns, pawn shops, cheap cafeterias; employment agencies that specialize in jobs for the unskilled, and religious missions that provide free meals after a service. Many of the residents—including the chronic drunkenness offenders—are homeless, penniless, and beset with acute personal problems.

The police do not arrest everyone who is under the influence of alcohol. Sometimes they will help an inebriate home. It is when he appears to have no home or family ties that he is most likely to be arrested and taken to the local jail.

One policeman assigned to a skid row precinct in a large eastern city recently described how he decided whom to arrest:

I see a guy who's been hanging around; a guy who's been picked up before or been making trouble. I stop him. Sometimes he can convince me he's got a job today or got something to do. He'll show me a slip showing he's supposed to go to the blood bank, or to work. I let him go. But if it seems to me that he's got nothing to do but drink, then I bring him in.

Drunkenness arrest practices vary from place to place. Some police departments strictly enforce drunkenness statutes, while other departments are known to be more tolerant. In fact, the number of arrests in a city may be related less to the amount of public drunkenness than to police policy. . . .

In some large and medium-size cities, police departments have "bum squads" that cruise skid rows and border areas to apprehend inebriates who appear unable to care for their own safety, or who are likely to annoy others. Such wholesale arrests sometimes include homeless people who are not intoxicated.

Operation of the Criminal System after Arrest

Following arrest, the drunk is usually placed in a barren cell called a "tank," where he is detained for at least a few hours. The tanks in some cities can hold as many as 200 people, while others hold only 1 or 2. One report described the conditions found in a tank in this way:

Although he may have been picked up for his own protection, the offender is placed in a cell, which may frequently hold as many as 40–50 men where there is no room to sit or lie down, where sanitary facilities and ventilation are inadequate and a stench of vomit and urine is prevalent.

The drunken behavior of some of the inmates is an added hazard. It is questionable whether greater safety is achieved for the individual who is arrested for his safe keeping.

The chronic alcoholic offender generally suffers from a variety of ailments and is often in danger of serious medical complications, but medical care is rarely provided in the tank; and it is difficult to detect or to diagnose serious illness since it often resembles intoxication. Occasionally, chronic offenders become ill during pretrial detention and die without having received adequate medical attention. . . .

If the offender can afford bail, he usually obtains release after he sobers up. In many jurisdictions an offender is permitted to forfeit bail routinely by not appearing in court. Thus, if the arrested person has the few dollars required, he can avoid prosecution; if he has no money, as is usually the case, he must appear in court.

Drunkenness offenders are generally brought before a judge the morning after their arrest, sometimes appearing in groups of 15 or 20. Rarely are the normal procedural or due process safeguards applied to these cases. Usually defendants are processed through the court system with haste and either released or sentenced to several days or weeks in jail. In some cities only those offenders who request it are jailed. In others chronic offenders, who are likely to be alcoholics, are generally sent to jail.

When a defendant serves a short sentence, he is fed, sheltered, and given access to available recreational facilities. In most institutions there is such a lack of facilities and financial resources that it is not possible to do more. Austin MacCormick, a former New York City commissioner of corrections, noted recently:

The appallingly poor quality of most of the county jails in the United States is so well known that it is probably not necessary to discuss this point at any great length. The fact that the majority of all convicted alcoholics go to these institutions, however, makes it imperative that the public, and particularly those thoughtful citizens who are interested in the treatment of alcoholics, never be allowed to forget that our county jails are a disgrace to the country . . . and that they have a destructive rather than a beneficial effect not only on alcoholics who are committed to them but also on those others who are convicted of the most petty offenses.

After serving a brief sentence, the chronic offender is released, more likely than not to return to his former haunts on skid row, with no money, no job, and no plans. Often he is rearrested within a matter of days or hours. . . .

EVALUATION OF THE EXISTING SYSTEM

Effect on the Offender

The criminal justice system appears ineffective to deter drunkenness or to meet the problems of the chronic alcoholic offender. What the system usually does accomplish is to remove the drunk from public view, detoxify him, and provide him with food, shelter, emergency medical service, and a brief period of forced sobriety. As presently constituted, the system is not in a position to meet his underlying medical and social problems.

Effect on the System of Criminal Justice

Including drunkenness within the system of criminal justice seriously burdens and distorts its operations. Because the police often do not arrest the intoxicated person who has a home, there is in arrest practices an inherent discrimination against the homeless and the poor. Due process safeguards are often considered unnecessary or futile. The defendant may not be warned of his rights or permitted to make a telephone call. And although coordination, breath, or blood tests to determine intoxication are common practice in "driving-while-intoxicated" cases, they are virtually nonexistent in common drunk cases. Yet, without the use of such chemical tests, it is often difficult to determine whether the individual is intoxicated or suffering from a serious illness that has symptoms similar to intoxication.

The handling of drunkenness cases in court hardly reflects the standards of fairness that are the basis of our system of criminal justice. One major reason is that counsel is rarely present. Drunkenness cases often involve complex factual and medical issues. Cross-examination could be conducted on "observations" of the arresting officer such as "bloodshot" and "glassy" eyes, "staggering gait," "odor" of alcohol on the defendant's breath. The testimony of an expert medical witness on behalf of the defendant could be elicited.

The extent of police time allotted to handling drunkenness offenders varies from city to city and from precinct to precinct. In most cities a great deal of time is spent. The inebriate must be taken into custody, transported to jail, booked, detained, clothed, fed, sheltered, and transported to court. In some jurisdictions, police officers must wait, often for hours, to testify in court.

There is a commensurate burden on the urban courts. Notwithstanding the fact that an overwhelming caseload often leads judges to dispose of scores of drunkenness cases in minutes, they represent a significant drain on court time which is needed for felony and serious misdemeanor cases. More subtly, drunkenness cases impair the dignity of the criminal process in lower courts, which are forced to handle defendants so casually and to apply criminal sanctions with so little apparent effect.

In correctional systems, too, resources are diverted from serious offenders. After court appearance, some offenders are sent to short-term penal institutions, many of which are already overcrowded. Correctional authorities estimate that one-half the entire misdemeanant population is comprised of drunkenness offenders. In one city it was reported that 95 percent of short-term prisoners were drunkenness offenders.

LINES FOR ACTION

The sheer size of the drunkenness problem in relation to the very limited knowledge about causes and treatment makes it impossible to speak in terms of "solutions." There are, however, some important and promising lines that the Commission believes should be explored.

Treating Drunkenness as Noncriminal

The Commission seriously doubts that drunkenness alone (as distinguished from disorderly conduct) should continue to be treated as a crime. Most of the experts with whom the Commission discussed this matter, including many in law enforcement, thought that it should not be a crime. The application of disorderly conduct statutes would be sufficient to protect the public against criminal behavior stemming from intoxication. This was the view of the President's Commission on Crime in the District of Columbia, which recommended that the District of Columbia drunkenness law "be amended to require specific kinds of offensive conduct in addition to drunkenness."

Perhaps the strongest barrier to making such a change is that there presently are no clear alternatives for taking into custody and treating those who are now arrested as drunks. The Commission believes that current efforts to find such alternatives to treatment within the criminal system should be expanded. For example, if adequate public health facilities for detoxification are developed, civil legislation could be enacted authorizing the police to pick up those drunks who refuse to or are unable to cooperate—if, indeed, such specific authorization is necessary. Such legislation could expressly sanction a period of detention and allow the individual to be released from a public health facility only when he is sober.

The Commission Recommends:

Drunkenness should not in itself be a criminal offense. Disorderly and other criminal conduct accompanied by drunkenness should remain punishable as separate crimes. The implementation of this recommendation requires the development of adequate civil detoxification procedures.

Among those seeking alternatives to processing drunkenness cases through the criminal system are the Vera Institute of Justice in New York City and the South End Center for Alcoholics and Unattached Persons in Boston. The Vera Institute has recently undertaken a project to explore the feasibility of using personnel other than the police to pick up drunks. Included in the study is an attempt to determine what percentage of drunks will come to a treatment facility voluntarily. The Vera program would circumvent the criminal process by establishing a system within a public health framework to care for the immediate and long-range needs of the skid row inebriate.

The Boston program, which has received funds from the Office of Economic Opportunity, provides an alternative to the police-correctional handling of the homeless alcoholic. Staff personnel of the Boston South End Center have approached homeless inebriates in skid row and offered them assistance. An official of the program estimates that 80 percent of the people approached in this way responded willingly. The center screens and evaluates the cases and refers homeless alcoholics to appropriate community facilities. In the past year it has handled the cases of over 900 homeless alcoholics. . . .

Detoxification Centers

An alternate approach to present methods of handling drunkenness offenders after arrest and a prerequisite to taking drunkenness out of the criminal system is the establishment of civil detoxification centers. The detoxification center would replace the police station as an initial detention unit for inebraites. Under the authority of civil legislation, the inebriate would be brought to this public health facility by the police and detained there until sober. Thereafter, the decision to continue treatment should be left to the individual. Experience in New York and Boston indicates that some alcoholics may be willing to accept treatment beyond the initial "sobering up" period. . . .

The Commission Recommends:

Communities should establish detoxification units as part of comprehensive treatment programs.

The Department of Justice has recently provided funds to establish detoxification centers as demonstration projects in St. Louis and Washington, D.C. The St. Louis center is already in full operation; plans for the Washington center are underway. Both units have sufficient facilities to house for a period of a few days those who are in need of "drying out." They also have "inpatient programs," in which patients are given high protein meals with vitamin and mineral supplements and appropriate medication to alleviate alcohol withdrawal symptoms. Bath and laundry facilities are available, as are basic clothing and limited recreational facilities. Regularly scheduled Alcoholics Anonymous meetings, film showings, work projects, group therapy, and lectures are part of the program. During their stay patients are counseled by social workers and other staff members.

The police might also bring to such a center intoxicated persons charged with a variety of petty offenses apart from drunkenness, with violations of administrative codes, and with such felony offenses as driving while intoxicated, assault, and larceny. If the police planned to prosecute the case, a summons could be left with the offender to appear in court at a later date. If an intoxicated defendant was charged with committing a felony, the police could make an individual determination as to the most appropriate detention facility. If he seemed likely to appear in court he might be taken to the detoxification facility. Otherwise, he would presumably be taken to the local jail, unless there were adequate detention facilities on the premises of the detoxification center.

Aftercare Programs

There is little reason to believe that the chronic offender will change a life pattern of drinking after a few days of sobriety and care at a public health unit. The detoxification unit should therefore be supplemented by a network of coordinated "aftercare" facilities. Such a program might well begin with the mobilization of existing community resources. Alcoholics Anonymous programs, locally based missions, hospitals, mental health agencies, outpatient centers, employment counseling, and other social service programs should be coordinated and used by the staff of the detoxification center for referral purposes. It is well recognized among authorities that homeless alcoholics cannot be treated without supportive residential housing, which can be used as a base from which to reintegrate them into society. Therefore, the network of aftercare facilities should be expanded to include halfway houses, community shelters, and other forms of public housing.

The Commission recommends:

Communities should coordinate and extend aftercare resources, including supportive residential housing.

The success of aftercare facilities will depend upon the ability of the detoxification unit to diagnose problems adequately and to make appropriate referrals. A diagnostic unit attached to, or used by, the detoxification unit could formulate treatment

plans by conducting a thorough medical and social evaluation of every patient. Diagnostic work should include assistance to the patient and his family in obtaining counseling for economic, marital, or employment problems. . . .

Research

With over 5 million alcoholics in the country, alcoholism is the Nation's fourth largest health problem. Research aimed at developing new methods and facilities for treating alcoholics should be given the priority called for by the scope of the need.

The Commission recommends:

Research by private and governmental agencies into alcoholism, the problems of alcoholics, and methods of treatment, should be expanded.

The application of funds for research purposes appears to be an appropriate supplement to the proposed detoxification and treatment units. Consideration should be given to providing further legislation on the Federal level for the promotion of the necessary coordinated treatment programs. Only through such a joint commitment will the burdens of the present system, which fall on both the criminal system and the drunkenness offender, be alleviated.

THE PUBLIC DRINKING HOUSE AND SOCIETY
Marshall B. Clinard

Since time immemorial, man has enjoyed the use of alcoholic beverages, and for centuries society has argued, fought, and sought to control its use and misuse. The conflict over the use of alcohol has been directed at not

From *Society, Culture and Drinking Patterns,* edited by David J. Pittman and Charles R. Snyder, New York: John Wiley & Sons, 1962, pp. 270–92. Reprinted by permission. Professor Clinard is in the Department of Sociology, University of Wisconsin.

only those who consume it but also those who dispense it. As the institutionalized public drinking house became the focal point of the drink, the drinker, and the dispenser, values and conflicts over this institution developed. . .,.

Although public drinking houses are known by a variety of names, such as taverns, bars, pubs, bistros, wine houses, and beer halls, we shall largely use the term "tavern." For purposes of definition, one might simply say that public drinking houses are establishments whose business consists mainly of selling and serving beer, wine, or other intoxicating liquors for consumption on the premises. Actually this definition is inadequate, for it does not emphasize several important institutional features of a public drinking house.

A more complete definition would include these characteristics: (1) The serving of alcoholic beverages is an indispensable feature and an important source of revenue even if food is served. Because they do not serve alcoholic beverages, such places as soda fountains or milk bars, coffee houses of Greece and the Middle East, or tea houses of the Orient are not public drinking houses as the term is used here. (2) As a drinking establishment it is commercial and public in the sense that theoretically the opportunity to purchase a drink is open to all, whereas the bar of a private club or fraternal organization is restricted to members and their guests. (3) The drinking of alcoholic beverages is *group drinking* in the sense that it is done in the company of others in a public place. (4) It must have a functionary—a tavernkeeper, bartender, or, as in Europe, a barmaid. This person, in addition to serving alcoholic beverages, also acts as a sort of receptionist. (5) Finally, it has a physical structure and a set of norms. Patrons are served at a bar, tables, or booths, in specially decorated surroundings, with entertainment or recreational facilities like cards, darts, and shuffleboard available, thus distinguishing it in some way from the customary activities of other similar establishments. Certain norms are also well established, including certain hours of drinking and appropriate drinking behavior. . . .

TYPES OF TAVERNS

The tavern is often stereotyped by persons not personally acquainted with it. These stereotyped attitudes appear to be based on a combination of "hearsay," half-truths, misinformation, ignorance, prejudice, propaganda, and biased on inadequate data. The stereotyped conception of the tavern is also based on stories of saloon days, newspaper reports, observations of the worst taverns, and the belief that the drinking of alcoholic beverages is its only function. Some people believe tavern patronage is one of the chief causes of alcoholism, broken homes, neglected children, highway accidents, juvenile delinquency, and even crime.

A significant factor in this stereotyped conception of a tavern is the general lack of familiarity with this institution. Actual investigations have shown that the majority of the taverns do not fit the stereotype but are of different types. Four criteria may be used in describing types of patronage and the functions it performs. A tentative classification is the Skid-Row tavern, the downtown bar and cocktail lounge, the drink and dine tavern, the night club, and the neighborhood tavern.

Skid-Row Taverns

These taverns are usually located in the deteriorated Skid-Row areas close to the central business district. Many establishments are simply "holes in the wall" with only a bar and stools, while others may have tables and poorly lighted booths. The patronage is largely single and homeless men, migrant laborers, and alcoholics. Although their primary function is to provide a place for cheap drinking, they are often the site of gambling and soliciting for prostitution. There are frequent violations of state and municipal laws relating to taverns, as well as drunk and disorderly conduct and gambling. In this type of tavern, violations of regulations which are strictly enforced in other places are often permitted; for example, closing hours are widely disobeyed, and many establishments virtually operate on a 24-hour basis. While taverns somewhat similar to this description may be found in nearly all cities, the most typical ones are found on New York's Bowery or Chicago's West Madison Street. The reputation of this type of tavern has contributed much toward the development of the stereotype of all taverns.

The Downtown Bar and Cocktail Lounge

These drinking places are located in business and shopping areas of cities. They usually have long bars, booths, and attractive decorations, and are predominantly patronized by men of the white-collar and business class. Besides drinking, visiting, and talking about business problems the patrons can often watch television or a professional performer, or listen to juke box music. Occasionally a sport like shuffleboard or bowling is available. The downtown cocktail lounge serves primarily mixed drinks and attracts some unaccompanied women. It is open for business chiefly in the early afternoon and caters to afternoon and late evening patrons. Most customers of the bars and cocktail lounges are transient. Because of the location and type of patrons there is much less emphasis on the social and recreational activities than in the neighborhood taverns.

Drink-and-Dine Taverns

These taverns are located either in business districts or near the city limits along main highways. The bar is not the center of attraction but is frequently part of a spacious, well-appointed dining room. Patrons are most frequently businessmen, but many women patronize this type of drinking establishment. While serving alcoholic beverages is an important source of income, the primary drawing card is the service of fine foods, and often there is music. Many business deals are transacted over cocktails and steaks. There is little interaction between patrons as they tend to come in small individual groups. Although the frequency of attendance is much less than at a downtown bar, the length of stay is generally longer.

Night Clubs and Roadhouses

Located generally in city amusement centers or along main highways outside of but near the city limits, the night club or roadhouse is usually large and impressive, with neon lights and illuminated billboards attracting the traveler's attention. The bar is usually located adjacent to the dining room whose seating arrangement centers around a stage and dance floor. Although the night club or roadhouse is situated out from the city center, its patronage is predominantly urban couples who come chiefly on weekends. While drinking is encouraged and there is some visiting, the primary functions are dancing, the enjoyment of fine foods, listening to the orchestra, and watching the floor show. Most persons who attend are spectators and there is little social interaction among the patrons.

Neighborhood Taverns

Of all taverns the most numerous and apparently the most important type functionally is the neighborhood tavern.... This type can be divided primarily by location and secondarily by patronage into four subtypes: rural, village, suburban, and city. Neighborhood taverns are more than places for people to drink, visit, exchange ideas, discuss politics and problems, joke, play cards or other games, watch television, and listen to their favorite records on the juke box. Generally speaking, these establishments tend to cater to a local clientele; the bulk of the patrons are "regulars" who are often on intimate speaking terms with one another and with the owner and bartenders. In addition, these taverns do most of their business in the evenings and on weekends and holidays.

Rural neighborhood taverns are located either in the open country along a highway, usually at a crossroad, or in some small unincorporated village. Besides the bar stools they usually have tables and booths, and on weekends may serve fish and chicken dinners. Practically all have juke boxes, many have radio or television, and some have pianos; playing cards are also available.... An important function is providing a meeting place for friends and neighbors where they may share like interests and problems, or relax and enjoy visiting together.

Village neighborhood taverns are located in an incorporated village usually at or near the center of the small business district. Structurally and functionally it is about the same as the rural neighborhood tavern. As is the case with all neighborhood taverns, one of the most important functions is to provide a meeting place and social center for patrons and friends.

The city neighborhood tavern is located in a more densely populated area often at or near street intersections, and the suburban neighborhood tavern is located near the city limits, often on highways leading to the city. Structurally they are similar, with a bar, tables, and chairs, although the suburban tavern is usually more modern in appearance with larger and more attractive signs to attract the attention of highway patrongae. . . .

Almost all neighborhood taverns have television, juke boxes, card games, and other games. As with the rural and village taverns, both suburban and city neighborhood taverns provide a meeting place for people to talk and relax from the monotony of work.

A British neighborhood pub often represents a combination of several types of taverns. Most English pubs have three rooms; the vault, the taproom and the lounge. The essential difference between them is in the relationship among the people themselves and with the people who run the tavern. The vault has a bar or counter where an exclusively male patronage drink standing. Most men come singly, and some are total strangers. In the taproom, drinking is a male group affair, and they are seated around plain wooden tables and benches. It is like a clubroom and strangers are not welcome. While games are played in both the vault and the taproom, most are in the latter. The lounge, or "best room," is well decorated and comfortably furnished with tables, chairs, and a piano; it attracts women and couples. There are no games, the demeanor is more homelike, and it attracts mostly middle-class patrons.

THE SOCIAL FUNCTIONS OF PUBLIC DRINKING HOUSES

Most taverns in the United States or the pubs of England are of the neighborhood type. While the consumption of alcohol plays a predominant but not exclusive part in taverns of the Skid-Row type, as well as in downtown bars and cocktail lounges, alcoholic drinking in neighborhood taverns or pubs plays a secondary role. People go to the tavern to drink, but they also go there for other reasons. In fact to "have a drink in a tavern" actually often means "let's talk" or "play a game or two," in much the same way that "let's play bridge" often means "let us get together and visit." The British pub has been characterized not only as a center of social activities but as the principal locale of the pub-goers' social life.

Worktown working people rarely meet in each other's homes for social activities in the way middle classes do. For some there is the social activity of politics, football or cricket clubs. But participators in these activities are a small minority. The place where most Worktowners meet their friends and acquaintances is the pub. Men can meet and talk of the way of their womenfolk.

A drink is the only price of admission into this society. And so, for the pubgoers, drink becomes inseparably connected with social activity, relaxation, and pleasure. And the picnic, the outing, the angling competition, the bowls match, the savings club, games of cards and darts, betting—all these forms of non-pub social activity become connected with the pub, and thus are "incomplete" without drink.

The forms taken by pub social activity bear on the conclusions that we have drawn from the behavior of drunks. Here, too, the social and the alcoholic motive cannot be disentangled. The alcoholic motive itself is primarily social, if it is given a long term definition; it is a motive that seeks the breaking down of barriers between men, the release from the strain of everyday life in the feeling of identification with a group. And the rituals of the Bulls and the clubs, the merging of groups in singing, all in different ways are part of this process.

Other than drinking there appear to be three chief functions of the tavern: (1) as a meeting place where social relationships with other persons can be established; (2) as a place for recreation such as games, and; (3) as a place to talk over personal problems with the tavernkeeper or others.

The Public Drinking House as a Meeting Place

The primary purpose of most taverns appears to be that of serving as a place where people can meet, become acquainted, and enjoy social relationships. In one survey a considerable proportion of more than five hundred Wisconsin regular tavern-goers said they felt the tavern played an important social role in their lives and those of others. About three-fourths felt that the tavern was a social club, two-thirds thought that the tavern provided a place for friends to meet, and one-half felt that meeting friends is an even more important function of the tavern than drinking. In fact, 43 percent felt that the tavern was as important as the church to many patrons. Persons attending a church, the theater, or various athletic events are usually spectators. Instead of being the audience, tavern patrons are participating actively; instead of having their thoughts and actions patterned for them, they are free to act and think and talk as they wish. To the extent that these needs are met, the tavern acts as an integrating force in the lives of its patrons.

The anonymous opinions of tavern-keepers, while possibly revealing some vested interests, may also be considered valid insomuch as tavern-keepers, both as observers and as tavern functionaries, participate daily in tavern life. Some 150 Wisconsin tavern-keepers indicated that an hour with friends is the most important reason for tavern patronage, followed in order by drinking, talking over problems, and recreation in the form of cards or other games. Over nine-tenths of all responding tavernkeepers said that their taverns were social centers. Over half of the tavernkeepers commented on their patrons' meeting and visiting together regularly; three-tenths made remarks about patrons discussing work, business, family, social, and political problems; about one-fifth mentioned playing either cards or other games; and about 15 percent gave as a reason enjoying drinks together. The common thread running through all of these responses is the word or the implication of the word "together."

Chandler has pointed out the importance of the tavern in the social organization of persons living in rooming-house areas. Taverns serve as meeting places for people who have no way of meeting other persons living in rooming-house areas. In the tavern the individual finds a sense of belonging and a place in the community. In the tavern group the individual seeks friendship and prestige, during his leisure hours. At night it becomes the working man's club. The social life of the rooming-house tavern-goer is confined either to a single tavern or to a type of tavern, and the average tavern has a remarkably stable and regular group of patrons. "The tavern-goer could be counted on to appear at a certain place at a certain time. When others wanted to seek him out they knew exactly where to find him. The tavern-goer met his friends at the bar in the same way that the corner boy met them on his corner. This regular patterned participation involved close interpersonal relations."

The extensive participation in British pubs also cannot be explained as merely the desire to consume ale, beer, and other alcoholic beverages. People seldom go to pubs exclusively to drink or get drunk; rather, they go primarily for sociability and recreation. One study has definitely stated:

No pub can simply be regarded as a drinking shop. It may be lacking in facilities for games and music, present no organized forms of social activity, and its actual accommodation be of the crudest; but none the less the activities of the drinkers are not confined to drinking. . . . The pub is a centre of social activities—for the ordinary pubgoer the main scene of social life.

Recreational Activities

Recreation in the form of games, music, and other activities is a leading function of the tavern. Most communities provide, except for bowling or billiards, few opportunities for the average person to play games or enjoy other recreational outlets in small groups outside of the home. Some of the games regularly played inside British pubs, for example, are darts, dominoes, cards, and raffles. There is also much singing. It is possible that these activities reduce the amount of actual drinking in a tavern or pub.

When asked why they went to taverns, a large number of Wisconsin patrons also replied that they went for various recreational activities. Consequently, as one might expect, a survey of 150 Wisconsin taverns indicated that among the recreational outlets offered, 44 percent provided card games, 41 percent shuffleboard, and others pinball machines and various mechanical games. Other forms of recreation included the 90 percent who had juke boxes for their patrons' enjoyment, while others had television, radio, dancing, singing, and bowling. Many provided not one but various forms of recreation. Some of the comments of the tavernkeepers were:

All know each other and gather to play cards for relaxation. Quite a few of them are retired and card games seem to be the only pleasure they have left at a low cost. [City neighborhood tavern, 250–300 patrons a day.]

I believe my tavern is a social center because most of my patrons are the type that enjoy an evening of friendly companionship. They enjoy visiting and singing, and where you have singing you never have arguing. I believe in keeping my customers happy and willing to come back again and enjoy themselves. [Village neighborhood tavern, 100–150 patrons per day.]

Talking over Problems

Neighborhood taverns often serve as places where one can talk over personal problems. This "talking over" may serve simply as a release for tensions while in other instances the person may actively be able to get "help" from the tavernkeeper or others. In one survey, responses from regular patrons indicated that the tavern had played an important role in offering a place for discussing personal problems.

When Wisconsin tavernkeepers were asked about why people went to one tavern rather than another and what they considered to be the important qualifications of a "good bartender," they obviously mentioned serving good drinks and keeping an orderly place, but they also mentioned, as more significant, being friendly, being attentive, understanding the patron's problems, keeping confidences, sharing the good fortunes and sympathizing with the misfortunes of the patrons, and giving advice to a patron in a "jam." Some of the patrons' difficulties may involve family problems and problems in personal adjustment and on the job. One bartender stated:

We try to be cheerful. Customers never want to hear your troubles, only to tell us theirs without fear of them being repeated. We are honest and try to show our appreciation of patronage. We try to show interest in their work, crops and family. We greet all by their names and interest ourselves in local things— ball games, legion affairs, etc. [Village neighborhood tavern.]

TAVERN DRINKING NORMS

Certain norms and values often develop in those taverns which have a large proportion of regular patrons. These norms and values control the behavior of the customer to a large extent. Customers are largely known to each other by first names and the bartender is familiar not only with the person's name but with his drinking and other habits as well. In fact one of the ways in which a "regular" tavern patron can be identified is by the degree of familiarity with the staff. In a British pub, for example, a whole system of social norms involve not only the various pub-goers but also the staff. Pub. regulars "tend to sit or stand in the same places every night; and this is particularly noticeable with regular groups who stand at the bar; they always retain the same relative positions to one another, and if the room is crowded or they find their usual space in front of the bar partly occupied, though the shape of the group will have to change, their positions relative to one another tend to remain the same."

Group drinking whether in a tavern or pub involves other social factors. The tavern-goer never sits without a drink, he adapts his drinking pace to the group, and the person must pay in his turn, and if he misses there is danger of social stigma. If a man knocks another man's glass over, it often means that he must buy him another drink. Often games are played for rounds of drinks.

Regular tavern patrons not only regulate the behavior of other regular patrons but can identify and often will reject the newcomer. Even the extent of drinking and drunkenness which is permitted is subject to social control in taverns where there is a good deal of close social interaction. In some taverns old timers may be allowed more freedom than others. On the other hand the customers of certain taverns may not permit any drunkenness or boisterousness and may ostracize offenders. One neighborhood bartender commented:

Every once in a while one of the fellows will overdo it ... too much drinking. ... The others don't go for it, and they tell him. ... We've got one guy that still comes in here ... used to be a pretty steady drinker. Then he started drinking heavy. ... The fellows liked him, and we all tried to get him to cut down. ... It was no use. ... After awhile the fellows started to complain so we asked the guy not to come. ... Well, he still comes in, but they've got nothing to do with him. ... I guess he's found a new place by now.

THE TAVERN AND ALCOHOLISM

... Since millions of drinkers go to taverns and do not become alcoholics, this would indicate that the tavern does not have a direct relationship to alcoholism. On the other hand patronage of taverns in many cases probably speeds up progression in alcoholism. This was the conclusion of a study of 197 members of Alcoholics Anonymous in Wisconsin where an attempt was made to determine the relation of the tavern to each of the three drinking phases of alcoholism,

namely the social, the excessive, and the alcoholic. As a control group estimates of the patronage of regular tavern patrons were secured from 106 tavernkeepers. The alcoholics most frequently cited social rather than drinking reasons for their visits in the social drinking phase, and on most of the variables examined the alcoholics could not be differentiated from regular tavern patrons as social drinkers. As they progressed from social drinkers to excessive drinkers, and finally to alcoholics, however, there was a statistically significant increase in their tavern participation as measured by chi-square tests and coefficients of contingency. In all phases, taverns were more important than package stores as sources of supply of alcoholic beverages.

The Social Drinking Phase

In the social drinking phase, the tavern was the principal source of alcoholic beverages, two-thirds procuring and consuming most of their intoxicating drinks in the tavern. For the alcoholic subjects and for the regular customers, however, the tavern did not necessarily serve as the place in which to get drunk. A minority of only about one-third did most of their "serious" drinking, that is, indulgence for the direct purpose of intoxication, in the tavern, and this was approximately the same figure given by tavern proprietors for their regular patrons.

The mean attendance of taverns by alcoholics at this stage was slightly over once a week. About one in eleven frequented the tavern at least five times a week, although about one in twenty did not patronize taverns at all. According to the estimates of tavernkeepers, regular patrons visit taverns on an average of four times weekly.

It is difficult to see how the tavern during this drinking phase would have significantly affected the drinking patterns of most of these subjects since only a limited amount of time was spent in taverns. About three-fourths of the alcoholics estimated that at this time they spent less than 10 percent of their leisure time in taverns, and about the same percent stated that an average visit was an hour or less in duration.

As social drinkers, alcoholics tended to frequent taverns at the same time of day or week as other patrons. The chief times of patronage for the alcoholics, like regular patrons, were weekends, evenings, holidays, and after work. In both groups, however, about 10 percent of the individuals patronized taverns in the mornings, during lunch hours, and during the working day. The chief places of patronage for the subjects were downtown bars, followed in order of preference by neighborhood taverns near their homes and places of work.

Nine out of ten alcoholics and an estimated three out of four regular patrons drank in the company of others. Some two-thirds of the alcoholics thought that the social contacts in the taverns were more important than the drinking at this stage. Slightly over one-half of the tavern proprietors felt that this was also true for their regular customers. Among the social reasons most often given by both the alcoholic and the regular group were the meeting of friends, the spending of free time, the lack of anything else to do, the playing of cards, and celebrating.

Excessive and Alcoholic Phases

Between the social and excessive drinking phases and between the excessive and alcoholic phases there was a statistically significant increase in the frequency of tavern patronage, the estimated percentage of leisure time spent in taverns, and the amount of time spent per average visit. Significantly more of them did their "serious" drinking in the tavern in the excessive phase.

The amount of morning and daytime patronage of taverns, as well as visitation at other times, significantly increased between the social and excessive and the excessive and alcoholic phases. On the other hand, there was a statistically significant shift of patronage from certain downtown bars and neighborhood taverns to the places nearest the subjects when they wanted a drink.

During the excessive and alcoholic phases, the reasons for patronizing the tavern changed significantly. For most of the subjects social factors became subsidiary, as they most often went to the tavern to drink, get drunk, and forget their problems. There was a decreasing interest in games and friends and a marked increased interest in drinking. This shift was also indicated by the fact that more of the subjects came alone to the tavern and fewer preferred the company of others while drinking, although even as alcoholics about half the subjects still were accompanied by other persons.

Tavern Practices and Alcoholism

Charges are often made that tavern patronage contributes to excessive drinking and alcoholism through encouraging excessive drinking, extension of credit, cashing pay checks, and gambling, and by serving persons already intoxicated. Slightly over half of the alcoholic subjects believed that they were encouraged, at least once, to continue drinking until they were drunk. On at least one occasion, one-third of the alcoholics drank more than they cared to because of friendship with the bartender. Though the extension of credit is generally illegal, 85 percent were able to buy drinks on credit on at least one occasion, but of those who received credit in taverns fewer than one in three found this to be a reason for drinking more. Only about one-third was able to procure liquor from package stores on credit. Approximately four out of five at some time in their drinking histories cashed their pay checks in taverns. Of those who did so, fewer than one out of three, howver, felt that this led to greater indulgence.

In general, gambling in taverns appears to have a negligible influence on excessive drinking. Almost two out of five alcoholics never gambled in taverns for drinks as social drinkers. An additional one-fourth gambled for the pleasure of doing so and were not concerned with winning drinks. Of those persons who had gambled for drinks, one-half did so less frequently after becoming excessive drinkers while the other half did so more often than before. Almost all the alcoholics were served drinks on at least one occasion in spite of the fact that they were intoxicated, as compared with about two-thirds who were able to procure liquor in package stores while intoxicated.

In summary, as the alcoholics progressed through the various phases in their drinking histories, their tavern patronage tended not only to increase quantitatively but to become subjectively more meaningful. The general social functions of the tavern became of subsidiary importance to the alcoholic, but the tavern did provide a comfortable environment for drinking and this seemed, in part, to account for the added tavern patronage.

TAVERN PARTICIPATION AND JUVENILE DELINQUENCY

It has been stated that often delinquent acts are committed under the influence of alcoholic beverages, largely obtained from taverns. Likewise, taverns and tavernkeepers are often regarded as a leading source of immoral influence for delinquency and crime among youth. There is little evidence to support such beliefs. In the first place, delinquent or criminal acts seldom appear to be committed under the influence of alcohol. When drunkenness does occur among juveniles it is an unwarranted assumption to maintain that the tavern was necessarily the source. Undoubtedly one major source of delinquency, however, is the arrest of those under 18 yeras of age for drinking.

In one of the few specific studies it was found that the tavern was not an important factor in producing delinquency. Taverns which sell to minors, however, are a source of trouble among teenagers. Two types of taverns are frequented by teenagers. One type makes an effort to prevent teenage drinking by checking ages, refusing to serve to known minors, and in general upholding the laws concerning minor drinking and tavern participation. This type, classified as the "good" tavern, is in the majority. The sec-

ond type caters to teenage trade, seldom checks ages, often provides lewd entertainment, and is even sometimes a source of drugs. This "bad" type was generally frequented by delinquents, whereas the control group frequented the "good" type.

The delinquents frequented taverns more often than non-delinquents, and those who did generally had a previous official record of antisocial acts, in high school and among neighbors. They used the tavern more frequently for admittedly antisocial acts, drunkenness, and for the prestige gained through illegal drinking. Their behavior in the tavern was more often loud and boisterous, and invited trouble such as fights and brawls. The delinquents tended to frequent taverns which catered to minors, and because such taverns are checked more frequently by the police, the delinquents' preference for this type of tavern increased their chances of being apprehended and committed to an institution.

In general, taverns did not play as important a part as often assumed among teenagers. There were many teenagers in both groups who did not go to taverns. The chief source of alcoholic beverages for teenagers was the home, and drunkenness tended to occur in the home of friends. Many illegal methods were used by teenagers in both groups to obtain alcoholic beverages, a common method involved adults buying them.

In spite of laws prohibiting a minor from entering taverns, many tavernkeepers are of the opinion that the illegal patronage of minors is their gravest problem. In a Wisconsin survey tavernkeepers generally approved of the Age Certificate Law which provides penalties for minors who misrepresent their age and permits the tavernkeeper to ask for proof of age, but there was noticeable lack of agreement as to its workability and effectiveness. About one-sixth of them were in favor of permitting minors 18 years of age or over to drink intoxicating liquor in taverns, while approximately half were in favor of raising the age limit to 21 for beer drinking. Some were of the opinion that both the law and a considerable proportion of the public consider teenage business detrimental to the best interests of society and that there exists a lack of cooperation on the part of some public leaders in working with tavernkeepers in attempting to solve the problem of minors drinking in taverns. About one-seventh indicated that minors should be punished more severely for entering taverns unlawfully, for falsifying their ages, and for drunken driving. . . .

THE AFTER-HOURS CLUB: NOTES ON A DEVIANT ORGANIZATION

Julian Roebuck and D. Wood Harper, Jr.

INTRODUCTION

In the words of Albert Reiss, the "action" is in "the organizational matrix that encompasses the deviant behavior of persons and the deviant behavior of organizations." Taking this lead, the present paper is a report of research that explores the assertion that "much individual deviance is intricately linked to organized systems and organizations that also are defined as deviant."

The after-hours club is such an organization insofar as it operates outside of the law and appears to cater to a clientele who represent a potpourri of deviant types. Popular opinion suggests that attendance at an after-hours club is a behavior pattern of people-of-the-night, criminals, swingers, show-people, prostitutes, and the hell-raising, thrill seeking marginals of the middle and upper classes.

After-hours clubs are found in most cities of over 250,000 and in small resort areas of the United States. It should be clarified that the after-hours club of the type reported in this research is a public organization that does not require membership, nominal or otherwise, to be admitted. . . . It does seem to require a sufficient number of regular clients who desire the services of such a place (e.g., drinks after normal closing time, food, entertainment, and a relaxed atmosphere).

It would seem that systematic research has not been accomplished on this type of

social organization for the following reasons: (1) the general assumption that the after-hours club caters exclusively to the pariahs of society (e.g., criminals and marginals) and is therefore unsafe; (2) the assumption that any organized club behavior found in the after-hours club setting is for strictly instrumental purposes; (3) difficulties involved in gaining study access to such an illegal establishment; (4) the reluctance of many sociologists to study "deviants in the open."

THEORETICAL FRAMEWORK

As Jack Douglas has so aptly observed, American society is a morally pluralistic society which contains many different and partially unrelated situational moralities. The existence of this pluralistic value system allows for, and in many instances demands, organizations of the type discussed in the present work. The after-hours club at first glance appears to be just another among many forms of patterned evasion found in the United States (e.g., tax evasion, gambling, voting dry and drinking wet, so-called racial inspired "private clubs").

Reiss has added a level of conceptual sophistication to the study of institutionalized or patterned deviance by drawing the distinction between (1) patterned evasion as the aggregative effect of individuals deviating from norms (their evasion carries relatively low risk of detection and at least moderate cultural support if not publicly processed) and (2) patterned evasion that possesses an organizational base or system that facilitates mass evasion.

Professor Roebuck and Professor Harper are in the Department of Sociology and Anthropology at Mississippi State University. This paper is published here for the first time.

The type of organization discussed in the present work seems to fit the second form of patterned evasion. What may be useful about the observations reported here is that, contrary to Reiss' thesis, there appears to be substantial evidence to support the proposition that *deviant organizations perform or provide a varied array of supports for behavior both deviant and nondeviant.*

Flowing from this assertion is the observation that it is conceivable, if not essential, that the nature of organizations, deviant or otherwise, requires a set of norms related to smooth, efficient operation in order to provide the supports and services that are the organizations' *raison d'etre.* Thus, one might expect the after-hours club to provide more than just an organizational facilitation for a type of patterned evasion. In order to function, such clubs must subscribe to essentially the same type of behavioral norms found in "straight" organizations. That is to say, the only characteristics not held in common with legitimate organizations are the services provided.

There appear to be three major types of support provided by the club organization. (1) In the traditional sense, the organization *facilitates mass evasion,* or an opportunity for covert violation of a publicly accepted norm without being publicly processed as a deviant. The types of individuals that seem to seek out the after-hours club for this purpose are hip squares, squares, night people, and some "hidden deviants." (2) *Tension management* is a support inasmuch as another category of people frequents the after-hours club for the purpose of relaxing and enjoying themselves without fear of having to interact with the rule makers and of being publicly processed as deviant. The types of individuals that seem to seek out the after-hours club for this purpose are individuals that work in high risk (of arrest) and tension provoking deviant and nondeviant occupations. Occupationally, these types range from night club entertainers, prostitutes, and organized criminals to pimps and strong arm men. (3) Additionally, the after-hours club appears to provide *a setting for behaving normally* for individuals whose life-

style for the most part, is the inversion of the normative. This microcosmic reflection of the "straight world" provides them this opportunity by constructing a rather strict and rigidly defined system of rules of behavior and interaction among the types of individuals in attendance. (As mentioned earlier, it appears that this strict normative structure is also essential for the organization to function as any other organization functions.

These types of support seem to correspond with three basic types of deviancy: (1) situational deviance, for example, behavior that is not usual for the individuals involved or behavior that the individual is involved in at many different times but which is not a part of the rest of his life. Nudists, for example, remain involved in nudism for long periods of time but they are not usually nudists at any other time except when they go to nudist's parks or nudist's camps. Nudists, moreover, are careful to isolate their involvement in nudism from the rest of their lives, so that it is relevant to them and to others only when they are taking part in it. (2) Styles of deviance which involve important parts of the lives of deviants but do not constitute their basic identity or way of life. For example, homosexuality in correctional institutions constitutes only a style of deviance, that is, few homosexuals in prison remain homosexuals when released. Homosexuality for prisoners then, is not an identity but a long-run situation involvement important to them at one time. (3) Deviance as a basic way of life characterizes deviants who have organized their primary life activities, identities, self-concepts, and aspirations in terms of their specific form of deviance. Professional criminals and organized criminals, for example, inside and out of prison view the pursuit of crime as fundamentally important to what they are, who they are, and what their life is all about.

METHODOLOGY AND SOURCES OF DATA

The after-hours club as an object of study presented the authors of this paper initially, with an opportunity to study and observe a varied collection of deviant types in their apparent natural habitat. This paper reports only a part of a larger research enterprise which includes the study of (1) employees who regularly engage in deviant and illegal behavior on a business-like basis and (2) patrons who frequent the club but who appear to have no career interest in the deviant setting of the club.

Certain personal and background information were obtained on both patrons and employees in an effort to determine who they were outside as well as inside the club setting. Research materials were collected in two ways. (1) There was systematic participant observation of the club activities through interaction as a regular "hip square" in the club setting (at least one night every two weeks) for a period of two years. The club where most of the observations reported were made is located in a northeastern city in the United States with a metropolitan population of two million. The club has been in operation for about fifteen years. The researchers knew, on an intimate social basis, employees and club patrons of various memberships over a two year period, though they did not really belong to any of the deviant groups involved nor were they considered to be deviant group members by any of the patrons. In short they had "fictitious memberships" among several groups of patrons. They accepted their researchers as harmless and acceptable "hip squares." Only those formally interviewed knew they were under sociological observation. (2) A former after-hours club owner-manager known to the senior author assisted in arranging extensive interviews (approximately one and one-half hours) with ten employees and twenty patrons outside of the club setting. Structured interview schedules of a topical nature were utilized. These interviews occurred after the respondents had been observed in the club for one year. Anonymity was assured by the club manager and the researchers. Additionally, the former owner-manager, who referred to the club under study as "a typical, high-class after-hours club," was utilized in the anthropological

sense as an informer of the culture of the club.

PHYSICAL SETTING

The club is situated in what was formerly a two-story brick detached residence within a lower-middle-class neighborhood. The area, two miles from the city's dominant business district, was at one time a middle-class residential neighborhood. Along with other residences it was previously a two-family dwelling unit. The neighborhood is presently changing from a residential to a mixed residential-commercial area.

An enlarged full basement is the chief center of operations. A heavy, peephole, speakeasy-type door opens from a front side entrance into a foyer leading to a waiting room furnished with sofas and stuffed leather chairs. A door at the rear of the waiting room opens into a lounge bar. To the left of the entrance, flush with the wall, are four six-seat high-back booths, to the right are seven, four-chair tables. A slightly raised dance floor occupies the center of the lounge. Beyond and to the left of the dance floor there is a horizontal twenty-stool bar. To the right of the bar on a dais, overlooking the dance floor, is a bandstand. To the far left of the bar there is a double door opening into a small restaurant which has a seating capacity of fifteen people at a diner-type bar.

The lounge is decorated with a "gay nineties" motif. Rich mahogony woodwork, simulated marbletopped tables, and leather upholstering are in evidence. Rich red wall-to-wall carpeting (excepting the dance floor), gas-light electrical fixtures, and several murals (depicting victorian women in various stages of dress and undress, some perched on large wheeled bicycles) set the style. A large dimly lit chandelier is suspended over the dance floor.

Patrons enter and leave the club only via the entrance way which opens into the lounge from the waiting room. One step forward from this door and a quick look from left to right gives one a panoramic view of the club's physical structure and activities. The patron may choose to go slightly leftward and across the floor to the bar that provides the least private seating arrangement and the maximum opportunity for social encounters with club patrons and employees. The patron may choose the high-back booths to his immediate left where he would find the maximum physical distance from others, or he may choose a table to his right readily available to the dance floor. The tables are intermediary in terms of the physical distance they interpose between the client and other people in the club.

The club opens at 1:00 p.m. and closes at 7:00 a.m. Mixed alcohol and drinks of all kinds are served. Live music is provided for listening and for dancing by a combo of from three to five musicians. Short-order dinners and breakfasts are served in the restaurant.

THE ORGANIZATION AS FACILITATOR

For all those who attend the after-hours club, drink, entertainment, food, and camaraderie are provided illegally. That is, after closing hours all clients engage in a covert violation of a publicly accepted norm without fear of being publicly processed.

Though the patrons fall within different social categories they engage in similar free-time activity in the club. This uniformity includes two dimensions: time of activity and type of activity. They obviously prefer to drink, dance, eat, socialize, and be entertained in a public organization beyond the closing time of legal establishments. These behaviors cluster together as part of a very pronounced heterosexual scene and require large blocks of leisure time. Moreover, participants in these unserious, "time out" activities must have available to them more irregular play time than that accorded to most people. They are probably more affluent than most bar customers. Drinks in the club cost from $1.25 up. Expected and customary tips exceed 15 percent. Food in the restaurant bar costs twice as much as that found in a regular restaurant.

The life style of club patrons is at least in part, akin. Club behavior is relatively free from outside instrumental constraints. Clients like to cavort at odd hours in a "good safe place." They have extended play time and a certain type of play for themselves more appropriate to a younger age level and more in keeping with people possessing less responsibility. One might apply the term "delayed adolescence" (i.e., in a social sense) to the male patrons. All of the club's patrons are willing if not eager to play dangerously in an exciting, diverse, and illegal milieu.

It is useful for illustrative purposes to focus on only those who typify the clients whose sole functional connection with the organization is the opportunity to be a recipient of its services. The *Middle-class swinger* typifies this group. Swingers are people who play conventional roles in the wider society but from time to time like to participate in or observe deviant behavior. Many come to gape at the sordid, and in their eyes dangerous but exciting pariahs of life. There is a standing joke among regulars that many squares come to the club to view various deviant types (e.g., freaks) and unknowingly gaze at each other and recognize each other as freaks.

The "hip squares" are quite knowledgeable about jazz music, cafe society, night club entertainment, and the gambling and sporting world. They constitute a heavy drinking, hell-raising, philandering group of playboys and playgirls who pride themselves on knowing "what's happening" in the city. They conceive of themselves as hedonists belonging to the "in crowd" that from time to time flirt and play in the light as well as the grey world. Many are acquainted with organized professional criminals within gambling and sporting contexts.

Male hip squres vary in age from 25 to 50 (median age 35). Educationally they vary from high school graduates to professional graduates (median education two years college). Most are currently married (60 percent) with 20 percent single and the remainder divorced. Occupationally, they range from clerical and sales personnel to management and professional status. Approximately 20 percent have no regular employment and live on inherited wealth or investment incomes. None have been adjudicated delinquents or criminals. All are heavy social drinkers but none appear to be alcoholic. A few have experimented with various types of drugs but none are on hard drugs. Most are avid gamblers engaging in table stakes poker, sports betting, and horse bets on and off the track establishments. As a group they express few negative attitudes toward the basic social institutions. Most feel that the prescriptions and proscriptions of the basic institutions do not apply to them, but that they do apply to others. They deplore squares from all classes and admire hipsters in all classes who are monetarily successful; they are all ideologically capitalists. They suffer no occupational status problems and appear to be satisfied with their present occupational status. They dress in a fashionable, casual, and expensive manner. They conceive of themselves as sophisticated playboys.

Female hip squares resemble their counterparts in many of their personal characteristics, attitudes, and self concepts. They are younger (age 21–38; median age 32). They differ in marital status in that 50 percent are single, 40 percent are divorced, and only 10 percent are currently married. Occupationally they vary from sales and clerical to professional; one-fifth live on their parents' inheritance or investment incomes. None have delinquent or criminal histories. All are heavy social drinkers, and though some have experimented with various drugs none are on hard narcotics. They conceive of themselves as exciting, sophisticated, happy go lucky pleasure seekers with vague aspirations to marry and settle down some time in the future. They, too, dress in a fashionable, chic, casual, and expensive manner. As a rule they are attractive. Their language is primarily conventional, but occasionally is mixed with hip expressions.

Squares usually attend the club in groups of two to four couples. Many like to impress their out-of-town guests with a trip to the after-hours club. Squares gain initial entrance to the club in the company of acquaintances who are regular "hip square" patrons. In short their initial visits are invariably in the company of some regular patron of the club. Square couples as a rule occupy tables or sit at the bar and interact with their own group membership, that is, other square couples. Other regulars remain aloof from them, and they do not receive good service despite the fact that they are big tippers (e.g., their infrequent request addressed to the musicians for certain musical numbers may be ignored or receive low priority). They are tolerated and treated by employees in a business-like manner. Their behavior is circumspect and they rarely enter into the various spontaneous behaviors engaged in by many other patrons. They express themselves verbally in the conventional language and in the argot of the hip square. Despite these constraints squares attend the bar frequently and rank third as a support base of attendance. At any one time there will be from ten to fifteen hip-squares in attendance. Few are regular patrons in the club, therefore, they do not seem to form a cohesive group.

Square men infrequently come stag. The square man with a female partner is more acceptable and considered less dangerous than a stag square. He is considered safer still if he comes with a woman known to be "in the life." Square stag men find it difficult to pick up a girl in the club unless they are well known. Square men (or square couples) are not permitted to table hop. They must use the cocktail waitresses or bar maids in their attempts to make social contacts with unknowns via the gift drink technique. Square men never directly approach escorted or unescorted females. Violations of these unwritten rules result in reprimands by the employees and/or patrons approached and may (certainly, if persistent) result in immediate expulsion from the club. Square men do not find the club to be a sexual market place. When they score it is generally with square females.

THE ORGANIZATION AS TENSION MANAGER

For others the after-hours club appears to serve the primary function of tension management. "Women in the life" or *call girls* typify those who seek out the after-hours club for this reason.

Call girls are very attractive, luxuriously dressed young women between the ages of 21 and 30 who usually work out of their own apartments and hotels with the aid of an answering service. They do not use the word prostitute in self-definition, but rather refer to themselves as "girls in the life" or call girls. They identify with the underworld though they work for themselves and are not members of any organized ring. They usually charge from $30 to $100 a trick. Call girls' educational achievements vary from 10th grade through 3 years in college (median grade completed 11). Class backgrounds are mixed with most coming from the lower-middle class. Most of them have been married at one time or another (80 percent); present marital status usually is divorced or separated. At the time they were interviewed, all were professional call girls and had no other means of support. All at one time or another have worked at legitimate enterprises (e.g., as waitresses, cocktail hostesses, typists, secretaries, models, beauticians, manicurists, sales clerks, factory workers, strippers). Most could qualify for white collar jobs. Approximately 20 percent were adjudicated juvenile delinquents. Approximately 25 percent have at one time or another been convicted for misdemeanors as adults. Call girls suffer with their occupational situation and they attempt to justify prostitution in terms of its institutionalized nature. On the other hand, they are also aware of their low social status and lack of respectability. Most call girls avoid contacts with all law abiding and respectable people insofar as possible. They feel much more at ease with hustlers of all types than with "straights"; and they speak in the criminal argot. They express vague aspirations in the direction of eventual marriage and family life. Paradoxically enough, they verbalize negative and hostile feelings toward marriage and the family.

All of this groups' membership drink heavily and most have experimented with types of drugs though none appear to be on hard narcotics. All at one time or another have had regular pimps—boyfriends not procurers—three-quarters at any one time have pimps. They evince a blasé attitude toward sex as a means of making a living. Companionship rather than sex appears to be the cement binding them to pimps. Approximately three-quarters of those interviewed admitted to intermittent homosexual relationships. Approximately 20 percent are actively bi-sexual. As a group they express negative attitudes toward the basic social institutions. They are particularly contemptuous of straights, especially johns, squares, and policemen. They admire monetarily successful hustlers and show people.

At times they attend the club as loners; at times they are escorted by their boyfriends (pimps); and at times they attend in the company of other call girls. When escorted by their pimps, they usually interact only with their pimps and with other call girls with or without their pimps. When attending the club alone or with other call girls they interact with professional criminals attending the club (i.e., those with whom they are intimately acquainted).

Call girls enjoy a high status at the club and receive excellent service. They are on intimate terms with club employees. They are regular customers with from four to ten in attendance at the club at any one time. They use the club as a home territory bar. They come for relaxation and recreation and not to work, and though they clown around in a coquetish way with various regular customers, time at the bar is time out behavior for them. The club offers them a haven and a place of refuge from the square world and squares after work hours (which generally terminate from 2 to 4 a.m.).

THE ORGANIZATION AS A NORMAL BEHAVIOR SETTING

In the tense, uncertain, inverted, and fast moving context of the entertainment world a chance to relax as a "normal" person in a normal behavior setting seems to be the goal of the *Night People.*

In this group we include people who are

employed at night in legitimate establishments to serve or entertain others: show
people and entertainers and owners, managers, and employees of bars, night clubs,
restaurants, hotels, motels, and theaters. Included in this group, among others, are
maitre d's, waitresses, strippers, dancers,
musicians, singers, stand-up comedians, actors, actresses, show girls of various types.
This somewhat amorphous group is the
largest numerical group frequenting the club.
Its membership ranges from 40–50 percent
(N=25+–) of patrons at any one time during
the club's operation.

Show people within this group come
from within and outside the city of the
club's operation. Out of town show people
who attend the club are usually employed at
various legitimate night spots in the city—
usually one week engagements. They find
out about the club from other show people.
They vary in occupational status from unknowns to nationally known celebrities. Occasionally, well-known and lesser movie
actors and actresses attend.

Though groups membership varies in age
(from 20 to 50; median age 30), sex (from
50–60 percent males), education (from
grade school to college graduates; median
grade completed 11), marital status (two-
thirds have been married at one time or
another, but only 10 percent are currently
stably married), occupationally (membership
from skillful artists to unskilled workers),
social class (from upper-lower to upper-
middle class; most products of the lower-
middle class), they have much in common.
They usually work when other people play
or sleep. They are primarily "children of the
night" who "work at and play at" exciting
night-life activities. The club offers them an
after-work haven. Most of these people are
quite knowledgable about various night
spots, jazz music, prostitution, and gambling
activities. Most of them come in contact
with hipsters, musicians, and criminals
during their legitimate work-time activities.

Though very few of this group's membership (less than 5 percent) have official juvenile or criminal histories, they speak in the
hip vernacular and criminal argot. They con-

ceive of themselves as being hip in a true
sense. Many of their friends and acquaintances are either members of the underworld
or have contacts in it. Many of these group
members buy "hot clothes" from criminal
fences. They are far from conventional in
their expressed thoughts, talk, or habits.
Much of their recreation revolves around
alcohol, sex, gambling, and night club entertaining; in short, they go on many "bus-
men's holidays." Most of them lead promiscuous sex lives. About three-fourths are
heavy social drinkers, the rest experiment
with various types of drugs, focusing primarily on the "speed drugs." Most are heterosexual. A few who are homosexual (less
than 10 percent) occasionally socialize with
other homosexuals at the bar though they
strongly prefer homosexuals in their own
group. The few homosexuals in this group
(primarily show people) have much higher
status in the club than other homosexual
patrons. This group membership is not hostile and bitter toward conventional society
and its institutions. Most express indifference, pity, or mild disdain for squares and
the eight-to-five man. Attitudes are ambivalent toward the basic social institutions.
They express negative attitudes toward marriage and the family. They admire winners
(materially successful people) in both the
upper and underworld. They appear to be a
contented present-oriented group of people
who do not suffer from occupational status
(or other) problems. They conceive of themselves as playboys and playgirls.

Though this group's membership is quite
democratic in terms of its contact with other
groups in the club, there is a tendency for its
group members to hang together in a loose
sense at the bar, at the tables, and in the
booths. They utilize the club as a convenience bar and a sexual marketplace. Most of
their club contacts (for example, the exchange of gift drinks) occur within their own
group and with professional criminals.

As with other groups, their behavior at
the club is time-out behavior (unserious).
Seldom do they discuss work or career problems or for that matter consequential events
outside the club's environs. According to

them they come to the club to play and relax in a normal setting. This is the most carefree and acting-out group in the club. Group members more frequently than other group-members mill to and fro from the booths, tables, and bar. Moreover, they more frequently move in and out of various group situations within the club than do others, and they unceremoniously break into and out of conversations in a spontaneous manner.

Members of this group are the heaviest drinkers in the club, and any inappropriate behavior on their part is more likely to be overlooked by the management than that of any other membership. They receive excellent service from all of the club's employees with whom most are acquainted. They are big spenders and good tippers though they do not tip as high as the professional criminal and call girls. They form the most important economic base for the club's activities. Group members are extremely flirtatious, and they engage in much heavy petting throughout the lounge. Many of their activities, including their amorous antics, appear to be of a clowning rather than of a serious nature. Some attend the club escorted, some unescorted; most come in mixed sexed groups of two to five. Frequently group members meet other group members at the club. Many females and males are definitely on the make though pick-ups are more frequent within the groups membership. Males occasionally pick up female squares.

SUMMARY AND CONCLUSIONS

It seems apparent that services provided by the after-hours club go much beyond simply providing food, drink, entertainment, and camaraderie after legal closing times. It is clear also, that certain support services are not the exclusive monopoly of any one type of patron, although certain occupational categories seem to be attracted to the club more often for one of the three social-psychological functions provided.

For all in attendance, the after-hours club is an *organized system of mass evasion* in which "time-out" behavior is in evidence. "Normal" people seem attracted to the organization primarily for this reason.

Unlike other drinking establishments reported by Cavan, the after-hours club has rather strict norms governing bar sociability. That is, roles of interaction among various social types in attendance is carefully proscribed and enforced by the staff and the regular patrons. This extremely structured interactional setting seems to be designed especially for those who operate in high tension-provoking occupations. The after-hours club is for them first and foremost a *tension-managing organization.* Finally, the nature of the organization and another service provided by it is a normative behavioral setting at an abnormal time of day. Taken together, the after-hours club provides multiple supports for both deviant and nondeviant behavior.

If the "action" in the study of deviant behavior is in the organizational matrix that encompasses the deviant behavior of persons and the deviant behavior of organizations, then it should be recognized that it does not necessarily follow that "deviant organizations" support only deviant behavior; they may instead support "nondeviant behavior" for those thought to be deviant and deviant behavior for those thought to be "straight."

MIND-ALTERING DRUGS AND DANGEROUS BEHAVIOR

Richard H. Blum

Mind-altering drug use is common to mankind. Such drugs have been employed for millennia in almost all cultures. In our own work we have been able to identify only a

From *Narcotics and Drug Abuse,* The Task Force Report, The President's Commission on Law Enforcement and the Administration of Justice, 1967, pp. 23–29.

few societies in the world today where no mind-altering drugs are used; these are small and isolated cultures. Our own society puts great stress on mind-altering drugs as desirable products which are used in many acceptable ways (under medical supervision, as part of family home remedies, in self-medication, in social use [alcohol, tea parties, coffee klatches, etc.] and in private use [cigarettes, etc.]). In terms of drug use the rarest or most abnormal form of behavior is not to take any mind-altering drugs at all. Most adult Americans are users of drugs, many are frequent users of a wide variety of them. If one is to use the term "drug user" it applies to nearly all of us. Given this fact, the frequently expressed concern about drug "use" might better be put in terms of drug "abuse." "Abuse" of course is also ill defined. Presumably judgments of abuse rest on such questions as (a) How much of the drug, or drug combinations, is taken and how is intake distributed? (b) Does the person take disapproved drugs? (for example, heroin instead of alcohol, marihuana instead of tranquilizers), (c) Does he take drugs in unapproved settings? (an adolescent drinking wine with a gang rather than at the family dinner table, an adult taking amphetamines without medical approval), (d) Does his behavior under drugs offer some real risk to himself or to others? (Our primary concern here: Crime, accidents, suicide, but also dependency, medical danger, etc.) There are, no doubt, other factors that would be revealed should one do a study of how people come to judge that drug "abuse" is occurring. The critical point for us is the realization that "use," "abuse," and "risk" are emotionally charged terms that may be based on hidden determinants or open assumptions that cannot be shown to have a factual basis.

To offer one conclusion at the outset, it is that current evaluations of drug use by the public, by the mass media, and by some officials, are often emotional. The programs, laws, and recommendations that arise from these emotional responses may well be inappropriate if the steps taken do not match drug use realities. What those "realities"

might be is most uncertain, for at the present time we know little about the extent of the use of any of the mind-altering drugs, about the characteristics of those using one or another "dangerous drug" (excluding alcohol and opiates), or about the kinds and frequencies of risks as a function of dosage, frequency, setting, and kinds of persons using any of these drugs. Consequently, we do not presently have enough knowledge at hand about persons, about conduct, about drugs per se, or about the effects of one or another programs of control or cure to make any recommendations for prevention, control, or cure where there can be certainty about the results even if those recommendations were to be fully implemented. . . .

MARIHUANA

Distribution

Nearly worldwide in both production and use.

Extent of Use in the United States

Only limited epidemiological data available. A few sociological studies of special using groups (musicians, professional people, slum Negroes, students.) Police statistics are an inadequate source of data because of apparent concentration of arrests in lower class groups and because marihuana arrests may be combined statistically with heroin and opium arrests. There is no current way of assessing the relationship of cases known to the authorities to actual prevalence of use in the population. Furthermore, fashions in drug use appear to be changing rapidly so that earlier data is likely to be inaccurate. One recent pilot study . . . in two west coast metropolitan communities, the sample size too small to allow any assumption of accuracy of estimate, reported 9 percent of the adult population had tried marihuana and 2 percent were using it either occasionally or regularly. In one west coast university, a university health officer . . . estimated 20 percent of the students were using marihuana; the police department . . . estimated only 1 percent use. Another unpublished student study . . . reported 11 percent experienced but none as regular users. . . . Great Britain . . . reports six-fold increase in hashish smuggling from 1963 to 1964 and other British reports suggest, as do impressionistic United States reports, a continuing increase in use.

Characteristics of Users

There are no epidemiological or "drug census" studies for the Nation as a whole. Descriptions made in the 1930's and 1940's found use was predominantly among minority group members and economically depressed urban youth, especially those judged as having inadequate personalities. Studies in Asia and Africa . . . suggest use is concentrated among the young, urban poor and is associated with dissatisfaction, deprivation, and mobility. In India upper class and "respectable" use occurs. . . . In the United States the impression, not supported by adequate studies, is that use ranges from young urban poor, including minorities, to disaffected "beatniks" through artistic and university communities to younger professional persons in metropolitan centers. Use appears to be concentrated in the 18 to 30 age group but reports of both downward . . . and upward (over 30) diffusion are appearing. The best estimate is that experimentation is far more common than regular use and that heavy use (as occurs in Africa and Asia) is quite rare.

Reported Risks

Some law enforcement officials and Federal Bureau of Narcotics personnel have held that marihuana leads to (a) criminal acts associated with impulsivity, recklessness, and violence, (b) distasteful behavior associated with disregard for cleanliness, unrestrained sexuality, rebelliousness, unpredictable relations with others, (c) risk of later heroin dependency because marihuana use creates interest in having drugs experiences which

marihuana cannot produce and because it is obtained through illicit channels which also provide opportunities for access to heroin (and cocaine). . . .

Verified Risks

Studies in India . . . and North Africa . . . show that cannabis psychoses occur in association with heavy use of potent forms of cannabis. Dependency is also described, as is apathy, reduced work, and social effectiveness, etc. These effects may be due, in some measure, to the vulnerability of the using population (already hopeless, sick, hungry, etc.). In the United States neither cannabis psychosis nor cannabis dependency has been described, although marihuana may be one of a variety of drugs used in the multihabituation . . . pattern, where a person takes many different drugs and appears dependent, but not on any one of them. Case history material suggests that many identified heroin users have had earlier experiences with marihuana, but their "natural history" is also likely to include even earlier illicit use of cigarettes and alcohol. The evidence from our college students . . . and news articles is clear that many persons not in heroin-risk neighborhoods who experiment with marihuana do not "progress" to "hard" narcotics.

With regard to crime, other than the violation of law occurring by virtue of acquiring and possessing marihuana, there is no reliable evidence that marihuana "causes" crime. One Brazilian study . . . observed 120 marihuana-using criminals and .concluded their criminal actions were not a result of their drug use. A Nigerian study . . . suggests that those who are at risk of hashish use are also at risk of criminality because of their primary social and psychological characteristics (being members of frustrated underprivileged groups living in urban areas with opportunities for committing crimes). In Nigerian hospitals with patients with histories of cannabis psychosis or use, there was no relationship of use to crime. In Indian studies . . . a negative relationship has been suggested, for with heavy cannabis use stupor occurs during which the commission of crimes is unlikely. Among populations of students, artists, and other more "privileged" pot smokers in the United States there is no recent evidence of associated criminality; similarly in the famous "La Guardia Report" . . . in New York City marihuana was not found to be either criminogenic nor associated with criminal subgroups. With regard to traffic accidents, data is lacking. One study . . . using a cannabis-like compound suggested that motor performance was not impaired but that the ability to shift attention was reduced. Effects are no doubt related to dosage but no studies on varied dosage using driving tasks have been done.

Legal Controls and Their Effectiveness

Except for very limited research purposes, marihuana is not legally available. Its acquisition and/or possession are punishable by law in the United States. Both felony and misdemeanor charges may be levelled; we are not aware of any studies of actual charges and dispositions. In spite of legal controls marihuana is said to be obtainable in most metropolitan centers in the United States. It is not, however, readily available in the sense that a naive person has an easy opportunity to obtain it. Acquisition is dependent upon being a member of, or having access to, some social group where it is used. The penalty has clearly not prevented all marihuana use nor the reported recent upsurge in use. To what extent controls on availability and the penalty risks have reduced use cannot be said. If one were to argue by analogy, taking alcohol which is available without penalty as a comparison, then one would suggest that legal controls have worked to suppress if not to prevent marihuana use. Some users interviewed recently argue that they have chosen to smoke "pot" because the laws are so patently inappropriate and they wish to signify their disapproval through direct disobedience. In California, a movement called LEMAR (legalize marihuana) is now collecting signatures for a referendum asking the voters to make the drug legally available. There is in addition sentiment among scholars and some liberal legislators not to legalize use but drastically to reduce the penalties now written in the law. . . .

Comment

We have suggested that educational and legal efforts should reflect a rational policy about marihuana. We have further suggested that policy itself should be based on the facts. The inadequate data available today indicate that risk of crime, accidents, and suicide (and of undesirable physiological side effects) are not likely to be greater than those associated with alcohol (and may be less). If the equivalence between alcohol and marihuana is to be accepted as an operating assumption until more facts are at hand—and we think that is a prudent position to take—it then follows that a public debate is in order with regard to the best regulation of marihuana.

It must be acknowledged that there are other "facts" besides those of risk which will enter into policymaking. Perhaps the most significant of these is the widespread law enforcement and public belief that marihuana is as dangerous as heroin in terms of dependency-producing potential and that its use is associated with criminality. These beliefs, even if incorrect, are facts to which policy must address itself. Since there is no strong evidence . . . of the medical value of marihuana, there cannot be said to be any urgent reason to make it available, except for research purposes. Similarly if there is a parallel in kinds of outcomes between it and alcohol, there is clearly a risk of unknown proportion that increased marihuana availability, as for example with its legalization, might lead to increased dependency and dangerous outcomes of the sort associated with alcohol itself, the latter unquestionably being a "dangerous" drug in the social rather than legal sense. The recent experience of Asian and African countries is compatible with such a fear.

In the meantime there appears to be good reason to encourage research on marihuana which in turn requires increased ease of obtaining it and permission to employ it on human subjects for bona fide experiments. There also appears to be good reason to moderate present punitive legislation so that penalties are more in keeping with what is now known about risks; that is, they are not great. A revision of penal codes so that marihuana acquisition and possession becomes a misdemeanor only would not seem inappropriate. In addition, since the significance of marihuana use may well be for some persons that of rebellion or disrespect for law or tentative explorations in criminality, or it may portend developing dependency proneness on drugs as such, it would appear worthwhile for apprehended persons to undergo social and psychological (psychiatric) evaluations. If destructive tendencies (toward self or others) are found the person can then become the subject of nonpunitive rehabilitative or preventive efforts by welfare, medical, probation, or community psychiatric agencies.

In point of fact we do not know if such preventive or therapeutic efforts are of value; the hope is that they will be. We may at least expect them not to be harmful.

Tentative Recommendation

In consultation with police, legal, and health personnel and with participation of research workers and interested citizen groups to formulate procedures (a) allowing for increased access to and human experimentation with marihuana by bona fide research workers, (b) to encourage funds for epidemiological research on drug use aimed at defining the characteristics of users and non-users, their interests, conduct, health, etc., (c) to revise present penal codes so that marihuana acquisition and possession becomes a misdemeanor rather than a felony, (d) to support research and practical experiments in education, in schools and among parents and peers, focusing on conveying information about drugs which encourages nondamaging

conduct, (e) to assume a policy stance of flexibility and objectivity which will not only allow for but anticipate that changes in legislative, health, and educational programs will occur as new facts about drug use arise and as new public problems or benefits become apparent.

In addition to the immediate steps set forth above, there are several areas in which long-term endeavors may be envisioned. We conceive of these to involve planning and consultative efforts with law enforcement agencies, with health and behavioral scientists, and with legislators. Work with the public both in terms of assessment of views on drug use and on the determinants of those views and educational efforts designed to alter incorrect opinions might also be appropriate. It is premature to set forth in this paper the details of these several efforts.

In general, the goal would be to provide a common base among informed and interested persons and institutions for planning—in concert—revisions in the law, in police procedures, and perhaps in public health and other medical-psychiatric practice so that marihuana and related drug use—and we must stress here that marihuana is frequently but one of a number of drugs being interchangeably used—can be handled with minimum cost to the taxpayer, minimum damage to the offender, with minimum strain on the police, and without creating anxiety among the public which in turn expresses itself as pressure on legislators for inappropriate laws. These goals, while sounding utopian, may very well be capable of at least partial achievement for of all the drugs considered in this report, marihuana is the one where there is the greatest discrepancy between public beliefs and probable drug effects, and between present versus reasonable legislation. The development of a moderate and consistent policy will much improve the present state of affairs.

HALLUCINOGENS

A group of drugs whose effects often include imagery and changes in felt sensory intensity—less often hallucinations as such—including lysergic acid diethylamide LSD-25, dimethyltriptamine DMT, mescaline, peyote, and others.

Distribution

Naturally occurring in many plants (mushrooms, cactus, tree barks, flower seeds, seaweed, etc.) and capable of being synthesized in laboratories, hallucinogens are widely distributed over the world.

Extent of Use

Hallucinogen use has been restricted to relatively isolated nonliterate societies. Certain South and North American Indian groups and Siberian tribes have employed the hallucinogen historically. Within the last century the use of peyote by American Indians has spread widely and within the last decade the use of LSD, DMT, mescaline, and other products has been adopted in metropolitan areas of the Western countries, primarily in the United States.

Use in the United States

No reliable epidemiological or "drug" census data exist. Use appears to be concentrated in young adults age 20 to 35 but there are signs of rather rapid diffusion to high school age levels and less rapidly to middle and older age adults. Employed in medical research, LSD has been given to small numbers of psychiatric patients, alcoholics, schizophrenic children and has been tested on terminal (dying) patients as a means of easing their distress. Employed in pharmacological and behavioral research, it has been given to volunteers, for the most part students. Employed by religious and philosophical seekers it has been given in institutions and centers, and other settings. These institutional uses account for only a fraction of current use; impressionistic but probably trustworthy reports indicate expanding social and private use of the drug derived from black market sources. Ease of transport and of synthesis make LSD distribution easy. The use of other hallucinogens, peyote for example . . . has been fairly well confined to traditional (Indian) groups, but their use, too, is expanding to young urban people.

As has been the history with many mind-altering drugs, the pattern of LSD diffusion has been over time from older prestigeful persons downward to younger less prestigeful ones, also from instutionalized medical and religious (or pseudoreligious) settings to more secular use. . . . With secular use, a drug becomes "social," use is subject to less constraint, and greater variability in outcomes can be expected as a greater variety of personalities, settings, and expectations are involved. At the present time, it would be unwise to venture any estimate of the number of Americans who have tried one or another hallucinogen; any numerical estimates must be suspect. one may presume that given a condition of continued easy availability of the drug plus wide publicity about its favorable effects, use would expand rapidly; historically the epidemic spread of tobacco smoking, opium use, and distilled alcoholic beverages provide illustrations. What effect current legislation to control manufacture, distribution, sale—and in some States, possession—will have on LSD use cannot be said at this time. It has generally been the case that interest in drugs can be channeled but not repressed; so it is that the choice of available drugs may be limited, but not the practice of using one or another drug. Historical examples showing shifts are those of opium to heroin, hashish to alcohol, and more generally from naturally occurring milder drugs to synthetic stronger ones.

Characteristics of Users

In the United States—as has been indicated—peyote use is concentrated among American Indians, but does not occur among all tribes. LSD, DMT, etc., were first confined to physicians and other research workers and then spread to their subjects, patients, families, and friends. Until a few years ago, LSD remained limited to an "elite" group of successful professionals, artists, and communications industry personnel, their families and friends. These same groups still appear to be using hallucinogens, but the concentration of use appears to have shifted to younger persons. Among teenagers, motorcycle club members, delinquents, urban poor and minorities, etc., there are reports ... of spreading interest, suggesting the expected diffusion down the socioeconomic scale. No common psychological or sociological features may be expected among the users of any secular and social drug; different people take drugs for different reasons. Within groups sharing common sociological characteristics it is sometimes possible to differentiate drug-interested persons, regular users, heavy users, etc., on the basis of psychological or background factors. For example, among graduate students one study reports that LSD-interested persons are more introverted and at the same time more excitement seeking than disinterested persons. .,. . Similar studies comparing psychological and background characteristics have identified certain differences among those trying (and not trying), continuing (and discontinuing) to use, and becoming dependent (and not becoming dependent upon) other drugs, for example, tobacco, heroin, alcohol. . . .

Reported Risks

Risks reported in popular articles include, especially for LSD, psychosis, suicide, continuing undesirable personality changes, release of sexual and aggressive impulses (leading to murder, rape, homosexual episodes, etc.), habitation, hallucinatory redintegration (return of the LSD state unasked and without taking the drug), development of interests in illicit drugs (marihuana, "goof balls," etc.), development of "cult" interests, and consequent warping of ordinary social outlooks, reduced work and social effectiveness, risk of divorce, increased accident risks when driving under drug influence, etc. Its exploitative use (control,

seduction, purposeful production of psychoses) has also been reported.

Verified Risks

Psychosis following LSD is verified. . . . there is no adequate estimate of the frequency of psychosis as a function of incidence of use. Mescaline psychoses are also verified. Some psychotic reactions are temporary, many are now "treated" at home by the subject's friends; counteracting tranquilizers (e.g., thorazine) are now sold on the black market as part of the LSD "trip" equipment. Other psychotic reactions require long-term hospitalization. The most recent study available to us ... studied 70 post-LSD psychiatric admissions during a 6-month period in a Los Angeles medical center, these patients representing 12 percent of all admissions during that period. One-third of the LSD patients were psychotic on admission; two-thirds of the patients required more than ·1 month of hospitalization. Recently reported in California ... is teenage use of jimsonweed (datura stramonium) a substance employed by Luiseno and Chumash Indians to achieve visions. Deaths among these Indians occurred following overdose ... and overdose among contemporary youth may also be expected to lead to illness or death. Suicide attempts are hard to distinguish from bizarre behavior occurring under LSD, for example jumping from windows because "I can fly," so it is that although suicidal feelings are reported and clinical workers describe attempts, there is no sound data on the probability of suicide attempts as a function of dosage, setting, personality, incidence of use, etc.

Crime associated with hallucinogen use appears to have been minimal. Police reports before a California legislative committee emphasized disturbances of the peace ... rather than felonies. Occasional accounts of homicide ... violence, resisting arrest, etc., have not been subject to followup case studies. It would appear that insofar as decent citizens take hallucinogens their behavior will remain lawful. We may expect that with the expansion of hallucinogen use to delinquent groups—and perhaps because it is now unlawful in some States, so that its use becomes criminal—a greater frequency of crime will be reported. A tangential remark is offered here. It is the person, not the drug, which is "responsible" for criminal acts. When an already delinquent youth takes LSD and commits yet another delinquent act, it may well be that the timing or expression of the delinquency is shaped by the drug-induced state of mind, but—as an example—aggression will not be a drug phenomenon. Generally speaking, one would expect (although the scientific evidence is far from adequate) that well-integrated people under heavy drug doses will not do things contrary to their ordinary conduct. Less mature, more neurotic or otherwise less well integrated persons would seem to be more vulnerable to the acting-out of impulses, the temporary expression of conflicts or of being persuaded by others to misbehave. Consequently, one's review of crimes reportedly committed under drug influence must attend to the prior criminal and sociopsychological history of the offender. It is also necessary to have regard for the role of clouded judgment or reduced muscular coordination in producing behavior (e.g., a traffic accident leading to manslaughter) that is criminal. There can also be long-run changes associated with drug use, as for example, the clouding of judgment associated with habituation and drug stupor or in psychotic personality change, where criminal acts may conceivably occur (e.g., smuggling marihuana, perjury, theft) as part of a poor judgment syndrome.

With regard to vehicle accidents and hallucinogens, there have been no studies and no verified reports in spite of some remarkable "I was there" accounts. Experimental work showing slowed responses and reduced information processing make it highly likely that accidents will occur when under hallucinogen influence. This expectation should be tested in laboratory studies.

With regard to the other claims about hallucinogens—dependency, social and work decrement, divorce, etc.—the scientific sources are reliable but samples are small and insufficient followup studies exist.

Comment

It is particularly difficult to assess either the significance or the social effects of the hallucinogens during the present period when there is such a widespread change in the pattern of use. The present LSD "epidemic" generates interest and alarm as well as social research; unfortunately, the research results take a while to be generated—by which time they may no longer be applicable. As a best estimate one may suggest that any powerful drug produces dangerous side effects and that any powerful mind-altering drug is likely to alter judgment and conduct, some of which alteration is likely to make trouble for someone. But the problem of trouble over frequency of drug use remains a critical one and until the facts are at hand any extreme programs—either for the use of the drug or for punishment of use—would appear precipitous. Indeed, the present spate of publicity, whether crying alarm or claiming untold delights, is likely to be highly undesirable in itself; creating interest in the use of potent substances among a number of young people or disturbed personalities who are clearly ill-equipped to handle an intense drug experience. Similarly, this same publicity creates fear in the public and generates pressures on legislators to pass premature punitive legislation. We agree with the present plans of the National Institutes of Health ... to conduct epidemiological research on expanding American drug use and to finance further research on the hallucinogens. We also agree with the present policy of the Food and Drug Administration setting up controls over the manufacture and distribution of LSD but not making possession a law violation.

Precipitously, several States (California and Nevada) have made possession unlawful.

Peace officers have pressed for such laws partly because of the difficulty they have in proving intent to sell in cases where persons possess drugs at the time of arrest, but where no long preparation of a case has taken place, so that a sale is witnessed by officers. The dilemma of the law enforcement people is genuine and arises out of pressures on them to "crack down" on sales alone, since the (mostly undercover) effort in such cases consumes an immense amount of time. The arrest and conviction of those possessing drugs is much easier. Since much police experience with narcotics suggests that those possessing and those selling will be one and the same (except at upper echelons of organization), the popular desire to "bear down heaviest" on drug sellers results in fact in bearing down on user-possessors. Whether or not the narcotics seller-user pattern will be repeated with LSD and the other "soft" drugs is not yet known. It remains likely that some of the best organized production and distribution will be by persons not users; whether or not they can be controlled by local police using ordinary procedures is a question beyond the scope of this report. In any event, it must be recognized that if the law does outlaw sale, but does not allow arrest for possession, whether this be for LSD, marihuana, or any other drug, the work of the police will be long and hard and the public must not expect large numbers of arrests. As a corollary it is quite possible that such a policy would, as many law enforcement persons might fear, result in less suppression of illicit drug traffic and subsequent greater use.

Should this prove to be the case—and an evaluative effort is most strongly recommended to find out—there are several alternatives. One is to accept some illicit use as a fact of modern life and to concentrate on its control through educational and social rather than legal means. Another is to retain the nonpunitive aspects of the law, but nevertheless to require mandatory examination of all illicit and dangerous drug user-possessors by health, psychiatric, and pos-

sibly welfare (or other socio-criminological) authorities. Any found to be ill, disturbed, or otherwise maladapted might be referred to outpatient clinics for care or, failing their appearance for treatment, be subject to hospitalization under public health rather than criminal codes. These suggestions are only tentative and can be seen to follow present developments in the treatment of alcoholics and narcotic users. They also introduce serious problems of civil rights in terms of deprivation of liberty by health officers without due process. . . .

Recommendations

It is recommended that Federal agencies be encouraged to support clinical and experimental research on the hallucinogens and epidemiological studies of population drug use. It is recommended that current FDA codes on hallucinogens be accepted as adequate, at least until more is known, and that individual States be discouraged from making hallucinogen possession a felony. It is recommended that the difficulty of the police task in controlling illicit drug traffic be acknowledged, especially when arrest for possession is not possible. In consultation with persons and staff groups interested in the prevention of drug dependency and in rehabilitation it is further recommended that various plans and programs for nonpunitive handling of the user of illicit drugs be evaluated. . . .

As a final recommendation we would request of the mass media an emphasis on less sensational reporting and feature writing in regard to LSD and other drugs, would invite the public to give their legislators a moratorium during which time knowledge can be evaluated and reasonable approaches proposed, and would generally suggest as a matter of school and public health education that an effort be made to admit to uncertainty and to restrain emotion in the consideration of drug effects and the changing pattern of drug use. . . .

DRUG ABUSE PROBLEMS: CAUSES AND RESPONSES
The Strategy Council

THEORIES ABOUT THE CAUSES OF DRUG USE AND ABUSE

The fundamental causes of drug use are likely to be found in human biology: humans use drugs because they like the effects that the drugs produce. Which drugs are used and under what circumstances are determined by other factors. We find it helpful to accept the view that the causes of initial drug use are not necessarily the same as those for continued drug use and that these, in turn, are different from the factors involved in addiction and relapse after a period of non-use. In addition, some theories attempt to account for individual cases of drug abuse while others deal with the causes of mass outbreaks.

A number of different factors appear to be causally related to drug use both on the individual and group level. Often the many theories seem to be mutually contradictory. At other times they can be viewed (with equal justification) as complementary rather than competitive.

Any candid analysis must accept the fact that our knowledge is such that no single explanatory theory is fully satisfactory. Under these circumstances multiple strategies are required, and all must be provisional, subject to revision on the basis of new insights or new information.

Availability

One fundamental factor that we will address from a number of perspectives is drug availability. Both in instances of individual drug use and in a number of outbreaks or "epidemics" of drug use the easy availability of the drugs themselves is found to have been

From *Federal Strategy for Drug Abuse and Drug Traffic.* Prepared for the President by The Strategy Council pursuant to The Drug Abuse Office and Treatment Act of 1972, pp. 6–66.

essential. Examples of major outbreaks are the amphetamine-use epidemics in Japan following World War II, and in Sweden in the mid-1960's, and the British heroin epidemic in the early to mid-1960's which involved the excessive prescribing practices of a few physicians. The Japanese experience is of particular interest because it developed among a people noted for a low rate of alcoholism and of other forms of excessive drug use.

Of the many factors that have been put forth as causally related to both isolated cases and large scale outbreaks, availability is the one factor over which society can exert the most direct control; and while many other factors (to be described below) may be equally important in the genesis of drug use and abuse, our capacity to modify these factors is still quite limited. Consequently, the effort to control availability will be a recurrent theme in the overall strategy.

The Individual Drug User

The initial use of any drug seems to be an outcome of numerous personal and social forces. The personal factors have much to do with the individual's need to explore or escape from various aspects of his environment, to take risks (if the use of the drug is believed to be risky), to find relief from some inner distress (if the substance is believed to have distress relieving effects), to have an unusual mental experience (if that is what a given substance is reputed to do) or to conform to the expectations of friends and associates.

The Epidemic of the 1960's

In retrospect, a number of factors, all of which have been postulated by one theory or another to be conducive to increased drug use, coincided in the 1960's. This historic coincidence of potential causes may help to explain the explosive increase in the use of a wide variety of drugs during that period.

Among the major factors were the demographic shifts in American society. Between 1960 and 1970 the population between the ages of 15 and 24 increased by about 11 million. Even had the rate of drug use remained constant, the absolute increase in population of young people would have brought about a dramatic increase in the number of people using drugs. Conversely, to have kept the number of narcotics addicts and other drug users at the same level would have required a major reduction in the rate of addiction and drug use among the most susceptible groups.

This great increase in the number of young people (a maturing of the post World War II "baby boom") coincided with a period of major social change. The mid-1960's was also a period where many young people felt a sense of alienation from the established institutions and values of society. All of these factors, as well as the sheer size of the youthful population, tended to weaken the influence of adult values on the values of young people and increased their dependence on each other as role models.

In addition, a number of criminal justice procedural changes became operative in the mid-1960's resulting in increased difficulty for law enforcement activities in the drug abuse area. The net effect of the changes was that for a given level of police effort, drug users and drug traffickers spent fewer years in jail and more time in contact with susceptible groups, resulting in an increased availability of a variety of drugs.

All of this coincided with a period of increased affluence, increased leisure, and, also, unfortunately, with the appearance of adults who actively proselytized the use of drugs as integral to efforts to remold society. These proselytizers glorified the tendency of young people to reject traditional values of American society and indeed their slogan was "turn on" (to drugs), "tune in" (focus on internal values rather than the challenges

of society), and "drop out" (of traditional social roles).

Other theorists point out that many young people who did not actually drop out still adopted the new dress styles modeled after the "hippies" who actually did drop out; many young people also emulated the experimentation with drugs that was another outstanding characteristic of the hippie movement. The entire tendency toward the drug using lifestyle was glorified in the mass media, the theatre and popular music so that, for a time, for some segments of society, the hippies were thought to be the nation's folk heroes.

Many of these explanations seem to be specific to contemporary American society, but facile theories that drug use is peculiarly American and is an outcome of either our present values, economics or social structure, do not hold up well under scrutiny. Drug use patterns similar to those we have experienced in the United States are being experienced by other countries such as Sweden and France, and alcoholism is a major problem in several Eastern European countries with very different economic and social systems.

Drug Use and the Family

In any analysis of causality we cannot overlook the fact that rejection of certain current adult values and identification with certain aspects of adult behavior are not mutually exclusive, but in many situations both occur. Thus, it is appropriate to ask about the effect of adult use of drugs—alcohol, tobacco, tranquilizers, and over-the-counter preparations on the drug taking of young people. In this context we must also ask about the role of advertising on the consumption of mood-changing prescriptions and over-the-counter drugs.

There have been only a few careful studies that shed any light at all on these complex interrelationships. In general, these studies lead to the conclusion that the use of mood-altering medications, or heavy use of alcohol and tobacco among parents, does increase the likelihood that the children will experiment with or use illicit drugs, particularly marihuana, and various pills found in the household. According to these studies, other factors being equal, drug use is lowest among children who have close relationships with parents and where parents report very low levels of use of mood-changing medications, alcohol and tobacco.

However, other studies indicate that, contrary to some popularly held views, America is not an overmedicated society and the people who are prescribed drugs by their physicians are more likely to take less than the amount prescribed than to take more than what is prescribed.

When an effort is made to examine the relative impact of drug use (particularly marihuana) by peers and the drug-using behavior of parents, the finding is that the drug-using behavior of the young person's best friends is a far more powerful determinant of that person's behavior than either the behavior of the parent or the relationship of the young person to the parents. Drug use by one's best friend may more than outweigh a close relationship with a non-drug-using parent; on the positive side, a non-drug-using best friend can overcome the effects of a poor relationship with parents or of a parent who uses more than average amounts of mood-changing medicines and over-the-counter medications.

Most of these studies were done on the relationships of various factors to marihuana use of young people, but with suitable caution can probably give some hint as to the relative importance of the factors that lead to other forms of drug use. These findings are supportive of other studies that emphasize the "communicable" aspects of drug use and addiction.

From Use and Abuse to Dependence and Addiction

The reasons for using a drug more than once include most of the factors related to initial use plus the interactions of the drug effect on the individual.

There is still much that is unknown about why individuals respond differently to the same drugs given under identical conditions. Most observers have tended to emphasize the personality of the user as determined by the individual's life experience, but recent work has pointed to what may be genetic determinants of the reaction to drugs and the tendency to develop excessive drug-use patterns. Included among the various factors that are conducive to continued or repetitive drug use are the alternatives available to the individual and this in turn depends on the individual, his family, and his environment.

When drug use began to spread among young people in the late 1960's there were few mechanisms or institutions that were adequately prepared to stop the spread. The two major mechanisms that usually acted as inhibiting factors could not stem the tide; law enforcement activity that reduced availability by arresting users and sellers of drugs was not prepared to act with vigor on otherwise non-deviant young people, and the tendency of young people to reject and ostracize those whose behavior was too deviant (e.g., drug users) was neutralized by the tendency of the media and of some adults to portray the drug users as cultural leaders.

Most of these factors were germane to the general problem of drug use. But, there are also considerations that stem from the different pharmacological effects of drugs on the user (e.g., the very different effect of heroin as compared to LSD) and the different responses of some segments of society to the use of various drugs (e.g., the deep and distressed concern about experimentation with heroin as contrasted with a disapproving, but often less distressed, view of the use of marihuana) that lead to different patterns of use as well as to different problems. For example, outbreaks of experimentation with heroin leave in their wake a varying percentage of chronic addicts; episodes of glue sniffing tend to pass leaving virtually none of the users chronically dependent on inhaling solvents.

These differences necessitate the development of distinct strategies for each of the problems. The tendency of some drugs, such as heroin, to produce the sought-after effects, and so that ceasing drug use causes distress, place such drugs in a very different category from substances which do not have these properties. Some of the theoretical consequences of these effects for perpetuating drug use are briefly described under the section on treatment approaches.

Having taken the position that different drug abuse problems may require somewhat different approaches in order to reduce the social cost to an irreducible minimum, we must consider several factors for each drug: the extent and pattern of its use; its social cost in terms of adverse consequences to the individual user and society; our understanding of the reasons for its use or abuse; our capacity to alter the causal factors or repair the consequences; and the alternative benefits that might be achieved by allocating Federal resources to reducing the social costs of a different drug abuse problem or indeed to another social problem entirely. . . .

HEROIN AND OTHER NARCOTIC DRUGS

Discussions of heroin and narcotic use in the United States are inevitably controversial. We cannot adequately summarize here all the materials examined or the divergent views that were considered. Thi section is, therefore, a summary of conclusions and the policy decisions flowing from these conclusions.

The use of narcotics in the United States began prior to the Civil War. By the turn of the century, misuse of narcotics had become an issue of some national concern, and after half a century of variable prominence, it emerged in the mid-1960's as a problem of major significance. The rise in public concern paralleled the rapid increase in the number of people addicted to narcotics—primarily heroin, and a correspondingly rapid increase in crime that changed the very fabric of life in most of our large urban areas. Although not all of this increase in crime was related to drugs, the two issues have become closely associated.

We have tried to focus on four major issues: 1) how widespread is the narcotics use problem (and is it growing); 2) how serious is it (in terms of producing crime, sickness, human misery); 3) how can we best treat those who have already become narcotics users or addicts; and, 4) how can we prevent the problem from developing among new generations of potential users in the future.

Extent and Costs of the Problem

In considering the size of the narcotics using population, we immediately confront issues that destroy some long held beliefs. Until very recently, many Americans, including those who were experts in the field, believed that experimentation with a narcotic drug such as heroin inevitably led, in most cases, to addiction (a state where the narcotics use becomes a compulsion). This was not a totally inaccurate view of those who began drug use in the late 1950's when the decision to experiment required the individual to seek out a deviant user group. In that situation, the seeking out was, itself, often a manifestation of some psychological problem and the experimenter did quite often become an addict. But with the glamorization of all drug use that swept across this country (and many others throughout the world) in the mid and late 1960's, many young people were caught up in the fashion of drug experimentation. While the wave of experimentation often began with marihuana and hallucinogens, it gradually began to include a tendency to experiment with amphetamines, barbiturates and heroin.

These new users often developed hepatitis, were sometimes arrested, occasionally died of overdoses, or sought treatment from the increasing number of treatment programs across the country; but we cannot yet conclude that the natural history of their drug use will be the same as it was for those who began in the late 1950's and early 1960's and who seemed to develop chronic relapsing patterns and a persistent identification with a criminal subculture. Some young people who began in the epidemic of the late 1960's did not inevitably adopt the values of a criminally oriented subculture. While they sometimes committed illegal acts, they often maintained contact with their families and retained many other normal social ties. For some of this latter group of addicts the eventual outcome may not be as dismal as the experiences with earlier groups of addicts would lead us to expect.

A very profound change in our previous perceptions about the natural history of opiate use was suggested by the experience of American military drug abusers in Vietnam. Some servicemen experimented with heroin and other drugs, a certain percentage used heavily and a substantial percentage of these became addicted. Yet, evidence is beginning to accumulate that relatively few of the servicemen who abused heroin in Vietnam remained or became heroin addicts after their return home. This conclusion is based on a follow-up study of 500 Army enlisted men randomly selected from among those who had positive urine tests for opiates prior to their departure from Vietnam in September of 1971. All of these men had been in Vietnam during what was believed to have been the peak of the heroin epidemic in late 1970 and early 1971, and at one time 96% of this group admitted to having experimented with heroin, and two-thirds had used narcotics (mainly heroin) regularly for more than 6 months of their year's tour in Vietnam. Yet, one year later, according to follow-up interviews and urine tests, only 7% of this group of men were still addicted to narcotics of any kind.

These findings suggest that where drug use patterns have not become deeply ingrained into the user's values and his way of relating to his friends, family and home community, and where they do not involve use of drugs by injection, there is room for optimism that a return to the mainstream of

society as a productive citizen is possible and even probable.

The net implication of these observations is that any estimate of the extent of the narcotics problem in the United States must recognize that not all who use narcotics are narcotic addicts. This need to differentiate among users creates major difficulties in estimating the size of "the problem."

There is no entirely satisfactory method for estimating the number of heroin addicts in the United States. After considering the results of several methods, our best estimate placed the number of addicts and users, in 1972, between 500,000 and 600,000. But we know the population also contains ex-addicts and many who are temporarily abstinent as well as addicts and active users. The difficulty is in knowing how many people fall into each category. At present we cannot provide precise estimates, although new methods are being developed. Nevertheless, the major expansion of treatment programs has permitted the development of new ways of estimating the rate at which the number of drug dependent individuals is increasing or decreasing.

It is now possible to obtain information about thousands of individuals admitted into treatment programs with respect to what drugs they have been using and what year this use first began. When the information about year of first narcotics use is analyzed it reveals a clear pattern. For the country as a whole, there was a rapid rise in the number of new heroin addicts starting in the early 1960's; each year through 1968 the number of new addicts increased. Since there is a lag or one or more years between the onset of drug use and the time that a person seeks treatment, it is difficult to estimate just how many people first began narcotics use in 1970 using information from people admitted to treatment in 1972. Yet, preliminary estimates based on these 1972 admissions at least suggest that by 1969–1970 the rising curve of more new addicts each year had flattened out. Should this pattern be confirmed by data available in 1973, it would mean a reversal of a 6-year pattern of more new addicts each year. It should be emphasized that any such trend would be for the United States as a whole. It would not mean that the epidemic had peaked in every community in the country. In some, the problem might still be worsening.

A decrease in the rate of growth also does not necessarily mean that the pool of narcotics addicts who need treatment is decreasing. Even a small number of new narcotics addicts each year will increase the total pool until the number of addicts moving out of the pool each year is larger than the number becoming addicted. We know that a certain number of addicts die each year and that others stop using narcotics entirely as a result of successful treatment, prolonged incarceration or spontaneous recovery. At any given time, more than 100,000 addicts and users may be incarcerated in the prisons, jails and reformatories of the nation, if we assume that roughly 20% of all people incarcerated were narcotics users.

At present, however, we do not know the precise size of the population needing care, whether it is still growing or actually shrinking. We do know, however, that if it is still growing, it is doing so much less rapidly. Some of the theories on why the number of narcotics users increased have already been mentioned.

In spite of this uncertainty about the precise numbers, we are, in most parts of the country, no longer in a situation where many want treatment but cannot get it. All over the country, treatment programs are being expanded or initiated on an unprecedented scale. Where drug users once waited for months or years to enter treatment programs, the waiting period has been reduced to a few days or weeks in more and more areas and is growing shorter each passing month. In a number of communities, treatment is now immediately available to all who want it. In some communities, programs have excess capacity. In some areas, the number of addicts seeking treatment may be on the decline.

Other indicators of social cost are also showing changes. The number of men seeking admission into the armed forces who are rejected because of positive urine tests for illicit drugs has shown a slight decline and the number of deaths due to narcotics use were less in 1972 than in 1971, a reversal of a trend of progressive increase that seems to have begun more than 4 years ago. These hopeful signs must not be a cause for slackening of effort. There are areas of the country where death rates are still rising, where there is no decline in admissions to programs and where narcotics abusers must still wait too long for treatment. Property crimes have shown an absolute drop in some cities, but they are rising in others.

We have no satisfactory units to measure the true social cost of narcotics use in the United States. It is a direct cause of death for more than 2,000 people each year. Most of these deaths appear to be due to accidental use of amounts of narcotic in excess of an individual's tolerance. Other deaths and illnesses are due to the unhygienic methods of injecting narcotics which result in a variety of infections—hepatitis and bacterial infections of the heart valves and skin. The social costs of narcotics use in terms of sickness, lost productivity, and crime have been estimated, but with great difficulty and even greater uncertainty. Only part of this uncertainty is due to our inability to measure the size of the active narcotic addict population.

An equally perplexing issue is in deciding whether a given cost would have occurred in the absence of the narcotics problem. For example, many addicts are chronically unemployed and many are repeatedly arrested for income-producing crimes. We cannot assume that they all would have been gainfully employed or law abiding but for their use of narcotics.

The more sophisticated analyses of social cost have tried to incorporate these uncertainties in their estimtes, by adjusting for the number of narcotics addicts who are not actively using drugs at any time, for those in treatment, for those incarcerated, for the number who would probably not be working even in the absence of drug use, and by assuming that a substantial percentage of users do not earn drug money by crimes against property and persons but by selling drugs to those who do. The best, but still crude, estimtes indicate that in urban areas about 35% of persons arrested for property crimes are narcotics users (this percentage varies widely from community to community across the country). However, the calculation of the real costs of narcotic addict-related crime must recognize that when robbery is included in the analysis, about 25% of addict crimes involve crimes against persons with undetermined costs in terms of injury to victims.

To these costs we must add all law enforcement costs at all levels of government, court costs, the costs of private protection efforts, the costs of all treatment, rehabilitation and prevention efforts as well as welfare payments to addicts and their families. . . .

There have been many attempts to estimate the cost of property crime related to heroin addiction. None of these estimtes put the annual costs below one billion dollars and several are many times higher. Some of the higher multi-billion dollar crime cost estimates are obtained by multiplying crude estimates of the number of addicts by estimates of the amount of money required for a heroin habit and the amount of property that needs to be stolen to yield this amount. These estimates may be inaccurate if they fail to take account of the number of addicts temporarily abstinent or incarcerated, the number in treatment and the number who do not commit property crimes to obtain drugs. The latter include pimps, prostitutes, those with legitimate jobs and those involved in selling drugs—a group that may be as large as 25% of the heroin addict population.

However, the policy implications of even the lowest of these estimates of the economic and human losses suggest that the costs of effective efforts to reduce the social costs of heroin addiction are well invested. Continued investment in the heroin problem is consistent with overall Federal strategy, and will continue to be consistent to the extent that the actions undertaken are, in fact, effective in reducing the social and economic costs of the problem to society. In heroin addiction we are faced not only with problems of overall cost in dollars, but also with the effect narcotics addiction has on the individual who becomes an addict, the effect on his or her family, and the impact that large numbers of addicts have on crime rates and on the quality of life in all of our metropolitan areas.

In addition to all of these societal costs of heroin addiction, a national strategy cannot overlook the human suffering that is not translatable into economic terms. In order to prevent continued spread of heroin addiction, we hope to make heroin increasingly difficult to obtain. Under these circumstances, life for an addicted individual will be one of constant physical and emotional distress; a primary obligation of those concerned with the treatment must be to alleviate that suffering.

Approaches to the Treatment of Narcotics Addiction: Overview

The treatment of heroin addiction and its complications is one of a number of approaches to reducing the social cost of heroin use in the United States. Making treatment available is a major goal of this national strategy, not only because treatment can produce positive effects for the individuals who are treated, but also because the very availability of treatment will change the attitude of the criminal justice system toward those drug users who commit crimes or sell drugs to others.

No discussion of treatment can avoid a consideration of two issues: 1) many heroin users and addicts do not seem interested in treatment; 2) even for those who do seek treatment, no one approach seems suited to all narcotics addicts, and there seems to be a substantial number for whom none of the available treatment methods seem to be effective.

There are a number of conceptually distinct approaches now in operation. They differ not only in the ways in which narcotics users are handled, but also in the premises upon which the treatment operations are based, and in the goals that treatment efforts are trying to reach. Any effort to compare these approaches to each other will be meaningful only if they are trying to reach the same goals. Most experts agree that treatment should be directed at helping drug users become law-abiding, productive, non-drug using members of the community, but there is still disagreement about which goals will be given emphasis if it becomes apparent that all goals cannot be reached. It is becoming clearer that these goals are not inextricably intertwined, and that different patterns of outcome for different types of patients participating in different treatment programs are the rule and not the exception.

There are at least eight conceptually and operationally distinct treatment approaches to the compulsive narcotics use syndrome.

These approaches, or models, include the *supervisory deterrent* approach which is based on the premise that whatever underlying social, biochemical, or psychological factors may make one person more susceptible to narcotics use than another, the individual who is not physically dependent still has a large degree of choice as to whether or not to use a narcotic. The fundamental operations in this model are withdrawal from narcotics, usually in an institutional setting, followed by supervision in the community. If there is evidence of a return to narcotics use, the individual may be required to return to the institutional setting for an additional period. This general approach has been used by both medically-oriented and correctional systems; it is the primary premise on which civil commitment and parole programs are operated.

Because of the special significance of this approach for those situations where individuals do not seek out treatment, this approach will be discussed more extensively.

The *psychotherapeutic* approach is based on the premise that personal and social problems cause people to use drugs and that until these problems are resolved the drug use will continue. The treatment process involves

withdrawal from the drug (detoxification) generally in a hospital under medical supervision, followed by some form of post-hospital care (aftercare) during which a variety of psychological approaches (e.g., individual or group therapy) may be used to try to resolve the problems that motivate the individual to use drugs.

The *maintenance* approach views compulsive narcotics use as a chronic relapsing syndrome. Medicine that can permit a narcotics user to become a productive citizen is viewed as an appropriate therapeutic agent. On this premise, oral methadone, a synthetic narcotic, is seen as a medicine that permits social function. Some proponents of the maintenance approach view the repeated return to narcotics as a manifestation of a specific "narcotics hunger" that is, in turn, due to metabolic changes produced by chronic use of high doses of narcotics.

Other treatment experts do not accept this view of a specific narcotics-induced defect and believe that patients can be successfully withdrawn from methadone after social stabilization has been achieved. The supporters of either approach agree that a significant number of compulsive heroin users can become reasonably productive citizens when provided with regular doses of oral methadone or other related substances, but will relapse to heroin use if they are simply detoxified. Because this approach is both widely used and controversial, it too is discussed at greater length below.

The *medical distributive* approach in its simplest form is based on the premise that compulsive narcotics use is a syndrome poorly understood, but probably due to multiple causes. A companion premise is that the syndrome is virtually impossible to treat and that society and the individual are best served when that individual is given access to the narcotic drug he wishes to use under medical supervision. This is essentially the system now employed in England, where specialized clinics are set up to supervise the prescribing of heroin to heroin users.

However, since narcotics are provided for intravenous self-administration, the complications of intravenous use are present. Furthermore, since patients are given quantities of heroin for self-administration at home, there is no way to prevent illicit diversion. The disadvantages of this approach are discussed below.

Faith and dedication is an approach that should not be overlooked even though it may not be possible for governmental agencies to contract for its development or expansion. Apparently for many drug users, the drug-using behavior is based as much on the way it structures life and gives it meaning, as it is on the pharmacological effects of the substance being used. From time to time such individuals find other values more meaningful than those of the drug-using subculture. Whether these be turning to new religious beliefs, returning to the religion of their forefathers, or dedicating themselves to secular political activity, the behavioral changes can be rapid and profound.

The *conditioning-antagonist* approach is based on the hypothesis that, in addition to any characterological problems that may have antedated narcotics use, individuals who become narcotics users acquire a complex set of conditioned reflexes. Thus, each injection of an opiate, by producing a positive reinforcement or alleviating distress, increases the tendency to make a similar drug-using response. With repeated use, physical dependence develops. The withdrawal syndrome then produces a regularly recurring distress, increasing the occasions for reinforcing drug-using behavior. Furthermore, withdrawal symptoms may become conditioned to the environment, so that long after withdrawal is completed, a return to the environment in which drug use occurred elicits conditioned withdrawal phenomena to which a former narcotics user responds by re-initiating the drug-use cycle.

Theoretically, to eliminate such behavior the narcotics user should be permitted to engage in drug-using behavior but get no reinforcement. Theoretically, such a situation can be brought about by administering a narcotic antagonist on a chronic basis. If the drug user elects to use a narcotic he will

feel no narcotic effect. Furthermore, even regular use will not lead to physical dependence, and to a considerable degree the likelihood of an overdose is reduced.

Thus far, it has been difficult to test this approach because the available narcotic antagonists were either too short-acting or had too many side effects. The development of more useful narcotic antagonists has been one of the research areas which has been given a high priority. The interest in antagonists is due not only to their potential use in the treatment of confirmed addicts, but because they may also have potential in approaches to prevention of addiction.

In the *character-restructuring, self-regulating therapeutic community,* drug use is viewed as a manifestation of immaturity and an incapacity to delay gratification. To correct this, the patient is required to undergo maturation and character change during a period of 12 to 18 months' residence in a community largely run by ex-addicts. In general, all these programs tend to be highly selective in terms of who is admitted to treatment. Prospective residents must demonstrate their motivation by expressing, among other things, a willingness to undergo abrupt withdrawal from narcotics. The dropout rate is quite high. The individual who remains for periods of a year or more appears to undergo significant changes in his outlook on life, but adequate follow-up studies on the adjustment of those who successfully complete treatment are still lacking. In spite of the limitations of this approach for hard-core narcotics users, it does have the advantage of being applicable to non-narcotics problems and is therefore important to an overall drug abuse strategy.

Multimodality is a term which was originally coined to describe a situation in which a number of very distinct treatment approaches were synthesized under a single administrative structure. The concept has undergone some evolution in the past several years, and it has come to refer to an eclecticism that views all approaches as having some relevance, but holds that different factors may weigh more heavily in the case of one patient than another, and that different approaches may be needed for the same patient at different stages of his or her life.

These different approaches vary widely in cost, in the kinds of individuals who volunteer for treatment, in the percentage of patients retained in treatment, and in the behavioral changes produced in those who are treated. . . .

On the basis of all the information now available, we must conclude that current voluntary treatment approaches, either singly or in combination, no matter how available they are, cannot affect all or even most of the narcotic addict population, since many will not volunteer and others do not benefit from any of the available voluntary approaches. Furthermore, even the present effectiveness of the available treatment approaches depends, in part, on the availability of heroin which is, in turn, dependent on public attitudes and the effectiveness of drug traffic prevention efforts.

Clearly, we should not have unrealistic expectations about the impact of treatment on the heroin addiction problem. Yet, the cost to society of the problem when it is untreated is so high that we have felt that an expansion of a variety of treatments was a high priority. As a matter of policy, we have set treatment availability for heroin addiction as a goal. Much progress has been made toward this goal. An obvious next step is to examine the kinds of treatments available and to re-program the resources into those programs which are most effective. . . .

At present we can make only approximate estimates of how large a treatment capacity will be needed for the country as a whole.

Since we have only approximate estimates of the narcotics-using population and of the proportion of narcotics users who would seek treatment if it were available, we have tentatively projected a need to be able to offer treatment to approximately 200,000 to 250,000 individuals annually.

Since an individual does not remain in treatment indefinitely, any treatment systems analysis must consider the turnover rate in estimating the number of individuals who will need services at any given time. Efforts to obtain more precise estimates of the total capacity that may be required are limited by the realization that: 1) effective law enforcement may lead to a decreased demand for treatment rather than the increase in demand that was previously anticipated; 2) with substantial improvements in treatment approaches, the relapse rate could decline; and 3) local programs for compulsory treatment or for linking the arrest process to the treatment system can substantially alter the demand for specific types of treatment. For example, a large proportion of narcotics addicts in many therapeutic communities are now referred by the courts, but self-referrals to such programs are progressively less common.

Over the past two years, the expansion of various treatment approaches has been guided by several principles.

First, we did not believe it was appropriate to focus solely on the heroin addict even though reducing the social cost and spread of heroin addiction is at present a high priority. Therefore, the expansion of programs using methadone maintenance or narcotics antagonists which are specific for narcotics programs had to be balanced by programs such as self-regulating communities, detoxification facilities, and drug-free programs that could be of value to non-narcotics users as well.

Second, we believed that no narcotics user should be forced into a maintenance program if he wishes to attempt to be entirely drug free.

Third, we have tried to make treatment available first to those who were seeking it voluntarily before considering the development of involuntary approaches. . . .

Non-Voluntary Treatment—Civil Commitment and Other Forms of External Pressure

Authorities in the field of drug abuse point out that many drug users accept treatment only when their life situation forces them to do so. The pressure for treatment may come from relatives, friends, employees, or because the problems of obtaining the drug are temporarily too great. Many will not enter treatment until serious adverse consequences to the user or society have already occurred. Thus any overall strategy must consider the use of those more formal methods by which a society pressures the individual drug user to enter treatment or to remain in treatment after entry.

Two basic approaches have been used: (1) Civil Commitment; and (2) Treatment in lieu of criminal prosecution or in lieu of sentence and incarceration.

Civil commitment involves a legal procedure that utilizes the civil authority of the state to require a person to enter treatment. It is not necessary for the individual to have committed a crime. Although there have been some objections to civil commitment for drug users, the Supreme Court has held that its use by the states is not unconstitutional.

Where civil commitment has been used most widely (at the Federal level, and in California and New York) it has been the practice to require a period of several months of institutional care followed by mandatory supervision for a period of several years after release from the institution. Depending on the progress in treatment, there is the possibility of returning to the institution.

The criminal justice system has also been used to exert pressure on drug users to enter and remain in treatment. Drug users may be required to participate in treatment programs following their release from prison as a condition of parole. In other cases a drug user who has either been charged with or convicted of a crime may be offered treatment in lieu of prosecution, sentencing or incarceration. In these situations, treatment is often viewed by the drug user as preferable to normal criminal justice procedures. The theoretical advantages of this variety of coercion are several. Drug users are diverted from

a system that does not generally alter their behavior and into one that may. This may benefit the user and it generally reduces the overcrowding in the criminal justice system (courts and jails) with attendent reductions in costs. Referral of drug users from the courts, particularly narcotics users, is now quite common throughout the United States and the patient load of some treatment programs consists primarily of individuals who are referred by the criminal justice system.

We cannot assume, however, that the community inevitably benefits if these referral and diversion procedures result in the release of individuals who continue criminal behavior injurious to others. Indeed, there are many unanswered questions about the effectiveness of using these types of external pressure on the long-term outcome of treatment both for the individual and the community. In considering these questions, it is necessary to distinguish between problems in practice and problems in principle.

Some programs that are sound in theory may fail because they have been inadequately funded, poorly administered or too narrow in scope. For example, narcotics addicts referred to an outpatient program by a court as a condition of probation may quickly drop out of treatment when they find that there is no follow-up by the probation officer, or that there is no interest in using the power of the court to retain the person in treatment.

Another reason for uncertainty is that in their early states of development, many of these programs used unrealistically high standards for judging progress. Some, for example, considered an individual to require long-term reinstitutionalization if he experimented with an illicit drug even on one or two occasions during a prolonged period of aftercare supervision. More recently, the criminal justice system has begun to use a wider range of treatment and supervision alternatives and to judge progress more realistically. Drug users have been referred to ex-addict operated therapeutic communities, psychiatric services, methadone maintenance programs, and programs using narcotics antagonists. Furthermore, new developments in techniques of urine testing have simplified the problems of monitoring drug-using behavior.

This willingness to combine the use of external pressure with a variety of approaches has blurred the distinction between voluntary and non-voluntary programs. In many parts of the country there are no separate programs. Instead, the same treatment or prevention program may offer services to individuals who entered the program under a variety of external pressures, including formal arrangements with the criminal justice system. All the clients are treated similarly, except that in the case of clients who enter under pressure by the criminal justice system, a third party (the criminal justice system) is kept informed of the client's status.

The major differences, then, between the voluntary and the non-voluntary client are to be found in the consequences of noncooperation with the program or in discontinuing treatment before it is completed.

Theoretically, this external pressure should result in a better outcome or at least a higher probability of retaining the client in treatment long enough to have some positive effect. Yet, at this time, we cannot say if this theoretical advantage is generally realized. . . .

Control of Drug Availability

Treatment is a response to a drug problem that has already developed. Given the difficulties of successful treatment, any practical approach that can reliably prevent the development of a problem will, under most circumstances, be given priority in the overall approach to drug abuse. It is within this framework that we consider the efforts to control the availability of drugs, for it appears to be self-evident that if a particular drug is not available, abuse of that substance cannot occur.

Much less self-evident, but apparently equally valid, is the observation that when all other factors are held constant, the abuse of a drug is directly related to its availability. When and whether an available drug becomes widely used is a separate question and appears dependent on accidental as well as social factors. Certainly the higher incidence of opiate addiction among medical and paramedical personnel in the United States as compared to the general population supports the view that the availability of a drug is directly related to the extent of its use. A similar relationship between availability and experimentation was observed when relatively pure heroin at low cost became available to U.S. servicemen serving in Southeast Asia in 1970–1971. Thus, efforts to reduce the availability of abusable drugs, particularly heroin, are essential to the success of the Federal drug control program.

The activities designed to control availability are varied. Ideally, cost-effectiveness analysis should be applied to each regulatory activity so that resources may be reallocated until the greatest effect will be achieved for a given social and financial cost. Unfortunately, an illicit production and distribution system does not yield the data that are required for precise analysis. Instead, we must base on other grounds several alternative strategies for reducing social cost, among them variations on the general theme of controlling availability.

The most extensive discussions of alternative approaches relate to the control of illicit opiates. One such proposition argues that the social cost of heroin addiction would be reduced most if heroin or a comparable substance for intravenous use were made available to addicts.

Certainly much of the present social cost of heroin addiction arises from associated property crime. It is, therefore, essential to consider the impact of proposed heroin distribution systems on the level of criminal activities.

First, a popular attitude toward heroin use must be corrected. It is not true that all heroin users commit crime only to buy heroin. Very many heroin users had established a pattern of property crimes prior to their first contact with drugs. It is reasonable to assume that providing them with cheap or free heroin would not initially affect this longstanding pattern.

There is, however, a substantial portion of drug users whose criminal activity is directly related to drug use. To this extent, then, there is validity to the view that providing a narcotic to those addicts who would otherwise commit crimes to obtain it, would reduce crime and demand for illicit narcotics. However, proposals for intravenous heroin maintenance should be compared to alternative treatment systems now available, and analyzed in light of the factors which have enlarged the spread of heroin addiction in the United States.

It is now generally accepted that the large-scale trafficker plays a minimal role in introducing new people to the use of narcotics. Most commonly, the first experience with illicit heroin occurs when one user offers to share his drug with a friend or acquaintance. There need be no financial motivation for this sharing. This process of heroin use passing from one peer to another has led to a comparison with the spread of contagious diseases. Without necessarily accepting this analogy, it is appropriate to note that heroin use does tend to spread within friendship groups and that it is often the experimenter rather than the hard-core addict who "turns on" his curious friends. Once occasional users become addicted, the friendship group tends to dissolve as each member becomes preoccupied with obtaining drugs and daily use of heroin.

Legalized distribution of heroin to confirmed users would not alter this process by which new addicts are created. We cannot even assume that all confirmed addicts would be willing to register at heroin clinics since it is likey that the drug would be administered under supervision and addicts may be required to attend at least once (and probably several times) each day. Furthermore, most addicts would probably demand an "euphoric" dose, and would not settle for a "maintenance" level. Intravenously, heroin is a relatively short-acting drug, with effects

lasting about 4 to 6 hours. Given this situation, unless all drugs were administered in clinics, there would be almost certain diversion to the illicit market that would still exist to serve those who are not yet confirmed addicts. Thus, an illicit narcotic market of some size would persist along with legal heroin distribution unless all citizens should lose interest in experimenting with narcotics or, alternatively, unless we are willing to dispense narcotics to any citizen who would like to experiment with them. Since we believe that the latter is not socially or morally acceptable, we must consider how we can best reduce the size of the illicit market, reduce heroin availability and thereby reduce the recruitment of new addicts.

Contrary to some assertions, adopting the British system would offer little help for problems in the United States. Although physicians working in the British clinic system can still prescribe intravenous heroin, relatively few of the addicts in treatment are actually receiving heroin. Most are actually receiving oral or intravenous methadone. In addition, most British physicians do not prescribe heroin for experimenters, but only for those who are addicted to narcotics. Recent admissions to the clinic system have become addicted to narcotics obtained illicitly.

The British recognize that some patients in the clinic system sell or give away their drugs to others, but because the total number in treatment is less than 2,000, the system tolerates this problem. It is hardly likely that we could tolerate the leakage from hundreds of clinics treating thousands of individuals.

By contrast, oral methadone, where most of the doses can be ingested under supervision, presents a much lower risk of diversion while retaining most of the advantages of the British medical approach.

Although difficult, there would seem to be no alternative to the enforcement of laws designed to control illicit traffic in narcotics. And having acknowledged the need to control local availability, we are forced to examine the entire chain of supply.

At present the most widely used illicit

narcotic is the opium derivative, heroin. Opium poppy farming is distributed among about a dozen countries around the world.

A major strategic issue is whether we should attempt to affect the entire chain of production and distribution or focus exclusively on what are postulated to be the more vulnerable links in the cahin. After considering a wide range of options from exclusive focus on border inspections and domestic control, to increased penalties on simple possession, to eradication of opium production, we have concluded that we must attempt to break the chain of supply in as many places as possible.

There are obvious limitations on efforts to limit the growth of the opium poppy. Only a small percentage of the world's output is required to supply the United States' illicit market; there is the possibility that synthetic narcotics would be introduced should the production of opium be totally eliminated; and there is the likelihood that as less and less opium is produced, the price for the residual production will rise making further reductions in production progressively more difficult. We are also concerned with the problem that elimination of opium production would create for legitimate medical needs. All of these considerations have been advanced by those arguing that efforts to reduce or eliminate opium production should be abandoned. Yet, this alternative appears to have even greater disadvantages as a long-term strategy.

Since opium can be cultivated in many areas around the world, if there were no effort to limit its production, the domestic control efforts of those countries where illicit heroin is a problem would be magnified many fold and quite possibly rendered impossible. Each country would have to be concerned with hundreds of sources of production and thousands of points of origin for the illicit traffic.

The issues, then, are what are the alternatives to the long-term goal of eliminating opium production and what benefits can we expect from this effort over the short run. Alternatives to total elimination with crop

substitution range from no effort at all, to various degrees of reduced production with the attendant difficulties in controlling illicit diversion from the residual production.

Over the short range, the effort to eliminate opium production in various countries will reduce the geographic areas which need to be monitored and thereby increase the probability of effective interdiction of illicit narcotics traffic. The willingness of several producer countries to eliminate their domestic production has been of considerable help to the United States, and those countries, particularly Turkey, merit our gratitude. The disruption of the usual illicit channels has made these channels more vulnerable to penetration and control. Since traffickers may seek out other more remote sources of supply (e.g., Afghanistan, India and Burma instead of Turkey), this period of disruption may be temporary and we must use it to advantage by increased efforts to reduce demand domestically and by developing sufficient systematic intelligence to prevent the continued functioning of the domestic distribution systems.

We will continue to work with producer countries to develop a system that motivates all countries that produce opium to eliminate such production and to exercise complete control of illicit production.

An alternative policy emphasizing controlled production with careful control of diversion could be considered only when the sources of illicit opium or heroin can be accurately pinpointed, and when methods to prevent diversion have been perfected.

The effort to restrict licit poppy cultivation and, particularly, to induce foreign governments to eliminate illicit growth should continue given our present knowledge and technological ability to prevent diversion into illicit channels. It must be supplemented by intensive efforts to reduce legitimate medical dependence on natural opium derivatives. A full exploration of the use of synthetic substances for codeine is particularly critical. In addition, alternative methods of harvesting should be developed, which, if instituted on a wide scale, could substantially reduce diversion from legitimate growth areas.

However, given the practical limitations to reducing availability by eliminating opium production, the major thrust of our control efforts in terms of manpower, dollars, and effort, must remain directed at interdicting the international trafficking in heroin and at disrupting the domestic wholesale and retail distribution systems. Even domestically produced synthetic narcotics must be distributed, so destruction of the retail distribution network would be just as effective in reducing availability of such synthetics as it is in controlling the availability of heroin. . . .

Summary of Approaches to Heroin Addiction

In the long run, we must avoid the dangers of oversimplification. Heroin addiction is neither a crime nor a disease in the usual sense of the words. It is a complex social problem with many facets, each of which has a number of policy implications. There are many social costs of narcotics addiction (human misery and disease, lost productivity, and crime) and many approaches to reducing them. These include efforts at prevention through reducing the availability of narcotic drugs, penalties to deter experimentation and use, and efforts to find and offer help to early users, thus simultaneously preventing progression to addiction and the spread of use patterns from one early user to another.

Other approaches attempt to bring those already addicted into a variety of treatment programs intended to help them become law abiding and productive citizens. Related to these programs are those activities to increase job skills and to create opportunities for employment. None of these approaches is entirely satisfactory and with some individuals our best efforts are only marginally effective. Research on better and more efficient approaches to both drug abuse treatment and drug traffic prevention have been given high priority.

But with respect to the crime related to narcotics use, we must be realistic in our analysis and in our expectations. We must understand that no manipulation of the supply of heroin—neither its total removal from our country or its free distribution through medical channels—would totally eliminate all the crime that is now committed by heroin users. Heroin users are a heterogeneous group. Many were involved in crime prior to their involvement with drugs, many continue to commit crime while in treatment programs, and others do so during periods of abstinence from drugs. Others were not involved in criminal activity prior to their first use of narcotics and might have been relatively law abiding, but for the complications of narcotics use and its associated life styles.

When a society provides few pathways for individuals to turn away from drug use and the criminal subculture, it is difficult to distinguish between these two groups and this inability to differentiate has had a profound impact on our criminal justice system. An understandable reluctance to be severe with individuals whose behavior was believed to be not entirely under their control led to situations where in some jurisdictions, heroin users were, in practice, not held fully accountable for their crimes. Often, the crime of selling narcotics was (and still is) included among the offenses for which the addict may be viewed more leniently than the non-addict on the assumption that the accused was forced to sell narcotics to cope with an addiction problem beyond his control. In some jurisdictions the effect of the inability to differentiate is that individuals who could have become law abiding citizens if treatment had been available are incarcerated for long periods. In other jurisdictions, individuals whose crime pattern would have shown little change even in the absence of narcotics use, are treated with great leniency in the belief that they should have an opportunity for treatment before being held fully accountable for their crimes.

We will, of course, continue to strive for effective non-punitive ways of preventing narcotics use and addiction, but until such approaches are available a major element in the national strategy will be increasing the availability of a variety of treatment approaches. Under these conditions, even those who become dependent on heroin will have ample opportunity to seek treatment prior to the time when their dependency motivates them to sell drugs or commit crimes to obtain money. We will soon reach the point all over the country where no one can claim that he committed a crime because he could not get treatment. Thus, the ambivalence of the criminal justice system about penalties should, and must, end.

It will be an additional element in the strategy to toughen Federal laws dealing with heroin traffickers and to bring this changed situation to the attention of prosecutors and the judiciary at all levels so that the efforts of the law enforcement officials who arrest criminals are not neutralized by a failure to prosecute or to provide appropriate sentences for those convicted.

In short, the impact of the vast expansion of our treatment efforts will not be limited solely to the positive changes in the lives of those who obtain treatment, but will have an equally significant impact on the operations of the criminal justice system and on the attitudes of the public toward those who continue to commit crimes even when treatment is readily available.

The state of addiction should no longer be viewed as a mitigating factor in the prosecution or sentencing of addicted drug-sellers. Indeed, while the narcotics user who sells narcotics to his acquaintances may not be the major profiteer of the illicit traffic, he is a major factor in the spread of addiction, and the penalties for this activity must be appropriate to the threat that the behavior poses to society. . . .

Thus, treatment and its supportive services are made more effective when the availability of illicit narcotics is reduced to a minimum by effective drug traffic prevention. Drug traffic prevention activities are made more efficient when the criminal justice system and the judiciary believe that narcotics users and addicts have had a reasonable set of alternatives to drug use, crime, and trafficking in illicit substances.

QUESTIONS FOR DISCUSSION

1. Which article gives you the greatest insight into the problem of alcoholism? Why? Succinctly state, in one or two statements, the most penetrating insight you have learned.
2. What is meant by the concept "pharmacological revolutions"? Discuss its implications.
3. Analyze the type of taverns in your community in terms of the categories discussed in the article by Clinard. Which type predominates? Why?
4. Interview someone who is willing to talk about a drug problem he or she has had. Which ideas contained in the preceding articles best describe the problem of this individual?
5. Read a novel or short story centering around the use of alcohol or drugs. How are the major issues portrayed? What are the points of conflict or agreement when you compare the analysis of the novelist with those of the authors in this chapter? If there are differences, what might account for them?
6. Is alcoholism a disease? Discuss the characteristics of obsessive-compulsive disorders such as excessive drinking.
7. Is the detoxification center a treatment center or another version of the traditional drunk tank?
8. Is it fair to generalize the proposition that cultures high in mood altering drug use are low in alcohol consumption and vice versa? If so, why?
9. Discuss the after hours drinking club as a subcultural phenomenon. What does it represent subculturally? Should the police enforce the laws regulatin such operations?
10. What is the relationship between alcohol, drugs, and crime?

BIBLIOGRAPHY

Anderson, Nels. *The Hobo: The Sociology of the Homeless Man.* Chicago: University of Chicago Press, 1923.

Bahr, Howard M. *Skid Row: An Introduction to Disaffiliation.* New York: Oxford University Press, 1973.

Ball, John C., and Chambers, Carl D. *The Epidemiology of Opiate Addiction in the United States.* Springfield, Ill.: Charles C Thomas, 1970.

Brill, Leon, and Harms, Ernest, eds. *The Yearbook of Drug Abuse.* New York: Behavioral Publications, 1973.

Cohen, Sidney. *The Drug Dilemma.* New York: McGraw Hill, 1969.

Evans, W., and Kline, N., eds. *Psychotopic Drugs in the Year 2000: Use by Normal Humans.* New York: McGraw-Hill, 1971.

Fort, J. *The Pleasure Seekers.* New York: Bobbs-Merrill, 1969.

Goode, Erich. *The Marijuana Smokers.* New York: Basic Books, 1970.

Grupp, Stanley E. *The Marihuana Muddle.* Lexington: D.C. Heath, 1972.

Inciardi, James A., and Chambers, Carl D. eds. *Drugs and the Criminal Justice System.* Beverly Hills, Calif.: Sage Publications, 1973.

Johnson, Bruce. *Marihuana Users and Drug Subcultures.* New York: John Wiley, 1973.

King, S. H. *Youth in Rebellion: An Historical Perspective.* Drug Dependence 2: 5–9, 1969.

Klerman, G. L. "Drugs and Social Values." *International Journal of Addictions* 5 No. 2 (1970), 313–21.

Lindesmith, Alfred R. *The Addict and the Law.* Bloomington: Indiana University Press, 1965.

Lingeman, Richard R. *Drugs from A to Z: A Dictionary.* New York: McGraw-Hill, 1969.

Robbins, L., Robbins, E. S., and Stern, M. *Psychological and Environmental Factors Associated with Drug Abuse.* Drug Dependence (National Institute for Mental Health) 5 (1970), 1–6.

Spradley, James P. *You Owe Yourself a Drunk: An Ethnography of Urban Nomads.* Boston: Little Brown, 1970.

Suchman, E. A. "The 'Hang-loose' Ethic and the Spirit of Drug Use." *Journal of Health and Social Behavior* 9 (1968), 146–55.

Wallace, Samuel E. *Skid Row as a Way of Life.* Totowa, N.J.: Bedminster Press, 1965.

Wilkinson, Rupert. *The Prevention of Drinking Problems: Alcohol Control and Cultural Influences.* New York: Oxford University Press, 1970.

Wiseman, Jacqueline P. *Stations of the Lost: The Treatment of Skid Row Alcoholics.* Englewood Cliffs, N.J.: Prentice-Hall, 1971.

Zinberg, Norman E., and Robertson, John A. *Drugs and the Public.* New York: Simon and Schuster, 1972.

6
Homosexuality and Transsexuality

Even more than drunkenness, alcoholism, and drug addition, homosexuality is a status rather than an offense. That is, the deviation lies in the stigmatization of the person by others and in the self-concept of the homosexual. It is also a *status offense* in that the participants are quite willing so that the relationship is voluntary in character rather than the type described by a victim-perpetrator model. Because of the willingness of the persons involved, law enforcement in this area is bound to be ineffective. Yet the disgust, fear, and ignorance that surround homosexuality have also prevented major alterations in public policy.

Precedent for the decriminalization of homosexuality was provided by the British Parliament in 1967. At that time, by an overwhelming majority, the Parliament repealed the ancient statute that made homosexuality a criminal offense. The logic for this reversal was provided by the Wolfenden Commission. The report of the Commission, depending on legal, medical, psychiatric, and other expert testimony as evidence, recommended that homosexual acts committed in private were beyond the proper sphere of the law's concern.

Bolstered by the actions taken in Britain, a number of newly organized groups have attempted to modify the status of homosexuals in the United States. While this has not led to significant change in the legal norms, homosexuals have maintained certain organizations which focus attention on types of discrimination. Such attention, they hope, will lead to a greater degree of consciousness of the "problems" of homosexuals.

No one really knows very much about the prevalence of this form of deviation. There are at least two important reasons for this. First, homosexuality is not very clearly defined. Should an occasional episode categorize an individual as a homosexual, or does homosexuality mean the chronic, if not exclusive, desire to express one's sexuality in response to members of one's own sex? If the former, then Kinsey has suggested that over one-third of the male population has probably experienced such encounters. If the latter, then the prevalence may be as low as 3 or 4 percent or as high as 15 percent.

Second, the homosexual experience, like the heterosexual one, is not a public matter. Because it is masked or hidden, there is no good way to estimate its prevalence. Most estimates are derived from an occasional research study, like Kinsey's pioneering effort, or from psychiatrists and other clinicians. There are obvious problems connected with each of these sources of data. Since homosexuality carries great stigma and opens the person to all manner of exploitation, homosexuals are not very likely to present themselves for evaluation in any situation in which their deviation is likely to become a matter of public record. Just how hidden homosexuality really is can be surmised from interview data on 550 "hard core" male homosexuals gathered by Kinsey. Over 75 percent had experienced no trouble with the police and were not officially known as homosexuals. An even higher percentage were free of trouble at work. Most surprising, of those who had been in the military, only 20 percent reported having had any difficulties. It is clear, then, that much of even chronic homosexuality is unreported and unrecorded.

Still, whether known officially or not, homosexuality, like all other forms of deviancy, is a socially devalued status. On the personal level, such social devaluation results in alienation, despair, and self-hatred. Fear of exposure and depreciation of the self force the homosexual into relationships with others equally devalued. Out of this push and pull—push from legitimate society and pull from those with similar status and problems—arises the subculture. Like all subcultures, the homosexual community provides the individual homosexual with a shared set of norms and practices and a feeling of belonging.

This chapter is concerned with the subcultural aspects of homosexuality. Our concern is only peripherally with the individual homosexual and centrally with his community. The homosexual "community," consists of persons tied together by friendships and sexual contacts. Along with a knowledge of one another, they share common interests, and the need to cooperate, if only to protect themselves from legal punishment and social condemnation.

The development of a homosexual identity is discussed by Professor Dank in the article, "Coming Out in the Gay World." The special focus of this paper is with the *transition* to a homosexual identity, not in the learning of homosexual behavior per se. Succinctly phrased, the article attempts to determine what conditions enable a person

to say "I am a homosexual." The fact that a person has homosexual feelings and engages in homosexual behavior does not mean that he views himself as a homosexual. In order for this to happen he must be placed in a new social context in which knowledge of homosexuality can be found. "Coming out" usually involves a transformation of the meaning of homosexuality for the individual—a transformation that permits him to preserve a favorable concept of self. Dank underlines the point that the function of viewing homosexuality as mental illness inhibits the development of a homosexual identity. Currently, the definition of homosexuality-as-mental-illness is in competition with the view of homosexuality-as-a-way-of-life.

In the next article, Professors Simon and Gagnon deal with what might be called the life cycle problems in homosexuality. Apart from the usual exigencies of everyday life, such as earning a living, which the homosexual shares with the heterosexual, there are special and unique problems that the homosexual alone faces. Among them is the problem that occurs when the homosexual first begins to think of himself as a deviant and to make contacts in the homosexual community—"coming out." A second critical life cycle crisis is that of aging. Tough as it is for the heterosexual male in a youth-oriented society to grow older, the problems of the homosexual may be even greater. Aging may not only increase the difficulty in finding suitable partners, but may raise questions about the self that are particularly troublesome. Nevertheless, most homosexuals, like most heterosexuals, weather these stages. The options and crises in the management of homosexual careers is the subject matter of "Homosexuality: The Formulation of a Sociological Perspective."

It is perhaps a comment on the definition of sex roles within a society that homosexuality is usually thought of in masculine terms. This is reflected in the greater volume of research on male homosexuality and a relative lack of research on female homosexuality. Hedblom's study on "The Female

Homosexual: Social and Attitudinal Dimensions" is one attempt to build a solid body of knowledge on lesbianism. He points out how the female homosexual maintains a front of heterosexuality for the straight community, but her network of friends and associates in the homosexual community allows her to support her definition of homosexuality as normal. The lesbian, in contrast to the male homosexual, is more likely to enter into long-term, stable relationships. Hedblom explores lesbianism in the context of three different approaches—the medical model, the family interaction model, and the subcultural model which emphasizes the supportive nature of the homosexual community in perpetuating the life style of the lesbian.

The final article by Michele S. Matto discusses "The Transsexual in Society." Transsexualism is much more complex than homosexuality and much more infrequent. Consequently, it tends to be more dramatic and evoke more attention. Matto looks at the transsexual as a deviant type and suggests some of the ways in which he or she is socially processed. In addition, the article emphasizes certain characteristic attempts on the part of the transsexual to deal with problems of identity. While sex change operations solve certain problems, they also create a whole series of new problems involved in the resocialization of the transsexual. Transsexualism also illustrates the interrelations between biological and social factors in deviation.

COMING OUT IN THE GAY WORLD
Barry M. Dank

There is almost no sociological literature on "becoming" homosexual. There is a vast literature on the etiology of homosexuality— that is, the family background of homosexuals—but little is known concerning how the actor learns that he is a homosexual, how he decides that he is a homosexual. In terms of identity and behavior, this paper is concerned with the transition to a homosexual identity, not in the learning of homosexual behavior per se, or the antecedent or situational conditions that may permit an actor to engage in a homosexual act. One may engage in a homosexual act and think of oneself as being homosexual, heterosexual, or bisexual. One may engage in a heterosexual act and think of oneself as being heterosexual, homosexual, or bisexual, or one may engage in no sexual acts and still have a sexual identity of heterosexual, homosexual, or bisexual. This study is directed toward

determining what conditions permit a person to say, "I am a homosexual."

RESEARCH METHOD

This report is part of a study that has been ongoing for over two years in a large metropolitan area in the United States. The analysis is based on data obtained from lengthy interviews with 55 self-admitted homosexuals, on observations of and conversations with hundreds of homosexuals, and on the results of a one-page questionnaire distributed to 300 self-admitted homosexuals attending a meeting of a homophile organization. The statistical data are based on the 182 questionnaires that were returned.

The 4- to 5-hour interviews with the 55 self-admitted homosexuals were generally conducted in the subject's home, and in the context of a "participant-observation" study in which the researcher as researcher became integrated into friendship networks of homosexuals. The researcher was introduced to this group by a homosexual student who

From *Psychiatry*, 34 (May 1971), 180–97. Barry Dank is in the Department of Sociology, Long Beach State.

presented him correctly as being a hetero-sexual who was interested in doing a study of homosexuals as they exist in the "outside world." He was able to gain the trust of the most prestigious person in the group, which enabled him, on the whole, to gain the trust of the rest of the group. The guidelines employed in the study were based on those outlined by Polsky for participant-observation studies.

There is no way of determining whether the sample groups studied here, or any similar sample, would be representative of the homosexual population. Thus it remains problematic whether the findings of this study can be applied to the homosexual population in general or to other samples of homosexuals. Since age is a critical variable in this study, the questionnaire sample was used in the hope that the replies to a questionnaire would represent a fairly wide age range. The age distribution of the questionnaire sample is shown on Table 1.

COMING OUT

The term "coming out" is frequently used by homosexuals to refer to the identity change to homosexual. Hooker states: "Very often, the debut, referred to by homosexuals as the coming out, of a person who believes himself to be homosexual but who has struggled against it will occur when he identifies himself publicly for the first time as a homosexual in the presence of other homosexuals by his appearance in a bar." Gagnon and Simon refer to coming out as that ". . . point in time when there is self-recognition by the individual of his identity as a homosexual and the first major exploration of the homosexual community."

In this study it was found that the meaning that the informant attached to this expression was usually directly related to his own experiences concerning how he met other gay people and how and when he decided he was homosexual. For purposes of this study the term "coming out" will mean identifying oneself as being homosexual. This self-identification as being homosexual may or may not occur in a social context in which other gay people are present. One of the tasks of this paper is to identify the social contexts in which the self-definition of homosexual occurs.

THE SOCIAL CONTEXTS OF COMING OUT

The child who is eventually to become homosexual in no sense goes through a period of anticipatory socialization; if he does go through such a period, it is in reference to heterosexuality, not homosexuality. It is sometimes said that the homosexual minority is just like any other minority group; but in the sense of early childhood socialization it is not, for the parents of a Negro can communicate to their child that he is a Negro and what it is like to be a Negro, but the parents of a person who is to become homosexual do not prepare their child to be homosexual—they are not homosexual themselves, and they do not communicate to him what it is like to be a homosexual.

The person who has sexual feelings or desires toward persons of the same sex has no vocabulary to explain to himself what these feelings mean. Subjects who had homosexual feelings during childhood were asked how they would have honestly responded to the question, "Are you a homosexual?," at the time just prior to their graduation from high school. Some typical responses follow:

Subject 1: I had guilt feelings about this being attracted to men. Because I couldn't understand why all the other boys were dating, and I didn't have any real desire to date.
Interviewer: Were you thinking of yourself as homosexual?
Subject 1: I think I did but I didn't know how to put it into words. I didn't know it existed. I guess I was like everybody else and thought I was the only one in the world. . . . I probably would have said I didn't know. I don't think I really knew what one was. I would have probably asked you to explain what one was.
Subject 2: I would have said, "No. I don't know what you are talking about." If you

Table 6–1. Age characteristics of sample

	Age distribution		Age of first sexual desire toward same sex		Age at which decision was made that respondent was a homosexual	
Age	N	(%)	N	(%)	N	(%)
0–4	0	(0)	1	(0.5)	0	(0)
5–9	0	(0)	28	(15)	1	(0.5)
10–14	0	(0)	83	(46)	27	(15)
15–19	13	(7)	54	(29)	79	(44)
20–24	36	(20)	14	(8)	52	(29)
25–29	39	(22)	1	(0.5)	11	(6)
30–34	28	(16)	1	(0.5)	4	(2)
35–39	21	(12)	0	(0)	3	(2)
40–44	18	(10)	0	(0)	1	(0.5)
45–49	6	(3)	0	(0)	0	(0)
50–59	11	(6)	0	(0)	0	(0)
60–69	8	(4)	0	(0)	1	(0.5)
Total	180	(100)	182	(99.5)	179	(99.5)

$\bar{X} = 32.5, S = 11.3$ $\bar{X} = 13.5, S = 4.3$ $\bar{X} = 19.3, S = 6.4$

had said "queer," I would have thought something about it; this was the slang term that was used, although I didn't know what the term meant.

Subject 3: I don't think I would have known then. I know now. Then I wasn't even thinking about the word. I wasn't reading up on it.

Table 6–2. Time interval between first homosexual desire and the decision that one is a homosexual.

Time Interval (years)	Distribution	
	N	%
0	29	(16)
1–4	66	(37)
5–9	49	(27)
10–14	21	(12)
15–19	7	(4)
20–29	5	(3)
30–39	1	(0.5)
40–49	0	(0)
50–59	1	(0.5)
Total	179	(100)

$\bar{X} = 5.7, S = 6.4$

Respondents were asked the age at which they first became aware of any desire or sexual feeling toward persons of the same sex; subsequently they were asked when they decided they were homosexual. Results are presented in Table 1. On the average, there was a six-year interval between time of first sexual feeling toward persons of the same sex and the decision that one was a homosexual. The distribution of the differing time intervals between a person's awareness of homosexual feelings and the decision that he is homosexual is presented in Table 2. As Table 2 indicates, there is considerable variation in this factor.

The fact that an actor continues to have homosexual feelings and to engage in homosexual behavior does not mean that he views himself as being homosexual. In order for a person to view himself as homosexual he must be placed in a new social context, in which knowledge of homosexuals and homosexuality can be found; in such a context he learns a new vocabulary of motives, a vocabulary that will allow him to identify himself as being a homosexual. This can occur in any number of social contexts—through meeting self-admitted homosexuals, by meeting knowledgeable straight persons, or by reading about homosexuals and homosexuality. Knowledge of homosexuals and homosexuality can be found in numerous types of physical settings: a bar, a park, a private home, a psychiatrist's office, a mental hospital, and so on (see Table 3). It is in contexts where such knowledge tends to be concentrated that the actor will be most likely to come out. It is therefore to be expected that an actor is likely to come out in a context in which other gay people are present; they are usually a ready and willing source of knowledge concerning homosexuals and homosexuality. In the questionnaire sample, 50 percent came out while associating with gay people.

It is also to be expected that a likely place for an actor to come out would in one-sex situations or institutions. Sexually

Table 6–3. Social contexts in which respondents came out

Social contexts	N	(%)
Frequenting gay bars	35	(10)
other gatherings	46	(26)
Frequenting parks	43	(24)
Frequenting men's rooms	37	(21)
Having a love affair with a homosexual man	54	(30)
Having a love affair with a heterosexual man	21	(12)
In the military	34	(19)
Living in a YMCA	2	(1)
Living in all-male quarters at a boarding school or college	12	(7)
In prison	2	(1)
Patient in a mental hospital	3	(2)
Seeing a psychiatrist or professional counselor	11	(6)
Read for the first time about homosexuals and/or homosexuality	27	(15)
Just fired from a job because of homosexual behavior	2	(1)
Just arrested on a charge involving homosexuality	7	(4)
Was not having any homosexual relations	36	(20)

*Total N of social contexts is greater than 180 (number of respondents) because there was overlap in contexts.

segregated environments provide convenient locales for knowledge of homosexuality and homosexual behavior. Examples of these one-sex environments are mental institutions, YMCAs, prisons, the military, men's rooms, gay bars, and school dormitories. The first six case histories below illustrate the influence of such milieux.

The first example of an actor coming out in the context of interacting with gay persons concerns a subject who came out in a mental hospital. The subject was committed to a mental hospital at age 20; his commitment did not involve homosexuality and the hospital authorities had no knowledge that the subject had a history of homosexual behavior. Prior to commitment he had a history of heterosexual and homosexual behavior, thought of himself as bisexual, had had no contact with self-admitted homosexuals, was engaged to marry, and was indulging in heavy petting with his fiancée. In the following interview excerpt the subject reports on his first reaction to meeting gay persons in the hospital:

Subject: I didn't know there were so many gay people, and I wasn't use to the actions of gay people or anything, and it was quite shocking walking down the halls, going up to the ward, and the whistles and flirting and everything else that went on with the new fish, as they called it.

And there was this one kid who was a patient escort and he asked me if I was interested in going to church, and I said yes ... and he started escorting me to church and then he pulled a little sneaky to see whether I'd be shocked at him being gay. There was this queen on the ward, and him and her, he was looking out the hall to see when I'd walk by the door and they kissed when I walked by the door and this was to check my reaction. And I didn't say a word. So he then escorted me to the show, and we were sitting there and about half-way through the movie he reaches over and started holding my hand, and when he saw I didn't jerk away, which I was kind of upset and wondering exactly what he had in mind, and then when we got back to the ward, he wrote me a long love letter and gave it to me; before we knew it we were going together, and went together for about six months.

[After 3 weeks] he had gotten me to the point where I'd gotten around the hospital, where I picked up things from the other queens and learned how to really swish and carry on and got to be one of the most popular queens in the whole place. [About that same time] I'd gotten to consider myself—I didn't consider myself a queen. I just considered myself a gay boy; we sat down, a bunch of us got together and made out the rules about what was what as far as the joint was concerned, drew definitions of every little thing ... if someone was completely feminine, wanted to take the female role all the time, then they were a "queen," if they were feminine but butchy, then they were a "nellie-butch," and I was considered a "gay boy" because I could take any role, I was versatile.

Interviewer: Before this bull session were you considering yourself gay?

Subject: Yes, I had definitely gotten to be by this time; after three months my folks came down to see me and I told them the whole thing point blank.

Interviewer: What would you say was the most important effect the hospital had on you?

Subject: It let me find out it wasn't so terrible. . . . I met a lot of gay people that I liked and I figured it can't be all wrong. If so and so's a good Joe, and he's still gay, he can't be all that bad. . . . I figured it couldn't be all wrong, and that's one of the things I learned. I learned to accept myself for what I am—homosexual.

This subject spent a year and a half in the mental hospital. After release he did not engage in heterosexual relations, and has been actively involved in the gay subculture for the past four years.

The above example clearly demonstrates how a one-sex environment can facilitate the development of a homosexual identity. Although some one-sex environments are created for homosexuals, such as gay bars, any one-sex environment can serve as a meeting and recruiting place for homosexuals, whether or not the environment was created with that purpose in mind.

The YMCA is a one-sex environment that inadvertently functions as a meeting place for homosexuals in most large urban areas in the United States. The following subject came out while living and working at a YMCA. He was 24 when he first visited a Y, never had had a homosexual experience, and had just been separated from his wife.

I became separated from my wife. I then decided to go to Eastern City. I had read of the Walter Jenkins case and the name of the YMCA happened to come up, but when I got to the city it was the only place I knew of to stay. I had just $15.00 in my pocket to stay at the Y, and I don't think I ever had the experience before of taking a group shower. So I went into the shower room, that was the first time I remember looking at a man's body and finding it sexually enticing. So I started wondering to myself—that guy is good-looking. I walked back to my room and left the door open and the guy came in, and I happened to fall in love with that guy.

After this first experience, the subject became homosexually active while living and working at the Y and became part of the gay subculture that existed within the Y.

. . . . I found that the kids who were working for me, some of them I had been to bed with and some of them I hadn't, had some horrible problems and trying to decide the right and wrong of homosexuality. . . . and they would feel blunt enough or that I had the experience enough to counsel them along the lines of homosexuality or anything else. . . . Part of this helped me realize that one of the greatest things that you can do is to accept what you are and if you want to change it, you can go ahead and do it. . . .

This subject spent six months living in this Y; by the end of three months he had accepted himself as being homosexual and has been exclusively homosexual for the last two years.

The prison is another one-sex environment in which homosexual behavior is concentrated. Although there have been studies of situational homosexuality in prison, and of how homosexual activities are structured in prison, there have been no studies that have looked at the possible change of the sexual identity of the prisoner. In the following case the subject was sentenced to prison on a charge of sodomy at the age of 32, and spent five years in prison. He had been homosexually active for 22 years, and before his arrest he had been engaging predominantly in homosexual behavior, but he had not defined himself as being a homosexual. He had had only peripheral contacts with the gay subculture before his arrest, largely because he was married and held a high socioeconomic position.

Interviewer: In prison did you meet homosexuals?

Subject: Yes.

Interviewer: I'm not talking about people who are just homosexual while in prison.

Subject: People who are homosexual, period. I became educated about the gay world, how you can meet people and not lay yourself open to censure, and how to keep from going to prison again. And still go on being homosexual. While in prison I definitely accepted myself as being homosexual.... I had frequent meetings with psychiatrists, various social workers. We were all pretty much in tacit agreement that the best thing to do would be to learn to live with yourself. Up until then, I rationalized and disillusioned myself about a lot of things. As I look back on it, I was probably homosexual from ten years on.

After his release from prison, this subject became involved in the gay subculture and has been exclusively homosexual for the last eight years.

The military is a one-sex environment that is a most conducive setting for homosexual behavior. In the military, a large number of young men live in close contact with one another and are deprived of heterosexual contacts for varying periods of time; it is not surprising that a homosexual subculture would arise. Given the young age of the military population, it should also be expected that a certain proportion of men would be entering military service with homosexual desires and/or a history of homosexual behavior, but without a clearly formulated homosexual identity. Approximately 19 percent of the sample came out

while in military service. The following subject had a history of homosexual desires and behavior previous to joining the Navy, but came out while in military service.

Interviewer: How did you happen to have homosexual relations while in the Navy?

Subject: We were out at sea and I had heard that one of the dental technicians was a homosexual, and he had made advances toward me, and I felt like masturbation really wouldn't solve the problem so I visited him one night. He started talking about sex and everything. I told him I had never kissed a boy before. And he asked me what would you do if a guy kissed you, and I said you mean like this and I began kissing him. Naturally he took over then.... There were other people on the ship that were homosexual and they talked about me. A yeoman aboard ship liked me quite a bit, was attracted to me; so he started making advances toward me, and I found him attractive, so we got together, and in a short period of time, we became lovers. He started to take me to the gay bars and explain what homosexuality was all about. He took me to gay bars when we were in port.

Interviewer: Did you start to meet other gay people aboard ship?

Subject: The first real contact with gay people was aboard ship....

Interviewer: Was it while you were in the Navy that you decided you were a homosexual?

Subject: Yes. Once I was introduced to gay life, I made the decision that I was a homosexual.

Public restrooms, another part of society which is sexually segregated, are known in the gay world as T-rooms, and some T-rooms become known as meeting places for gay persons and others who are looking for homosexual contacts. Sex in T-rooms tends to be anonymous, but since some nonsexual social interaction also occurs in this locale, some homosexuals do come out in T-rooms. In the sample studied here 21 percent came out while frequenting T-rooms for sexual purposes. The following subject came out in the context of going to T-rooms when he was 15. Previously he had been homosexually active, but had not thought of himself as being a homosexual.

I really didn't know what a homosexual was. In the back of my mind, my definition of a homosexual or queer was someone who wore girls' clothes and women's shoes, 'cause my brothers said this was so, and I knew I wasn't.

At the age of 15 this subject had a sexual relationship with a gay man.

And he took me out and introduced me to the gay world. I opened the door and I went out and it was a beautiful day and I accepted this whole world, and I've never had any guilt feelings or hang-ups or regrets.... I was young and fairly attractive and I had men chasing me all the time.... He didn't take me to bars. We went to restrooms, that was my outlet. He started taking me to all the places they refer to in the gay world as T-rooms, and I met other people and I went back there myself and so on.

After meeting other gay persons by going to T-rooms, this subject quickly discovered other segments of the gay world and has been exclusively homosexual for the last nine years.

Gay bars are probably the most widespread and well-known gay institutions. For many persons who become homosexual, gay bars are the first contact with organized gay society and therefore a likely place to come out. In this sample 19 percent came out while going to gay bars. Since gay bars apparently are widespread throughout the nation, this could be viewed as a surprisingly low percentage. However, it should be remembered that generally the legal age limit for entering bars is 21. If the age limit is enforced, this would reduce the percentage of persons coming out in gay bars. T-rooms and gay private parties and other gatherings perform the same function as gay bars, but are not hampered by any age limit. Thus, it is not really surprising that the percentages of persons who came out in several other ways are higher than the percentage coming out in gay bars.

The following subject came out in the context of going to gay bars. He had been predominantly homosexual for a number of years and was 23 at the time he came out.

Subject: I knew that there were homosexuals, queers and what not; I had read some books, and I was resigned to the fact that I was a foul, dirty person, but I wasn't actually calling myself a homosexual yet.... I went to this guy's house and there was nothing going on, and I asked him, "Where is some action?," and he said, "There is a bar down the way." And the time I really caught myself coming out is the time I walked into this bar and saw a whole crowd of groovy, groovy guys. And I said to myself, there was the realization, that not all gay men are dirty old men or idiots, silly queens, but there are some just normal-looking and acting people, as far as I could see. I saw gay society and I said, "Wow, I'm home."
Interviewer: This was the first time that you walked into this gay bar that you felt this way?
Subject: That's right. It was that night in the bar. I think it saved my sanity. I'm sure it saved my sanity.

This subject has been exclusively homosexually active for the last 13 years.

Even after an introduction to gay bars, labeling oneself as homosexual does not always occur as rapidly as it did in the previous example. Some persons can still, for varying periods of time, differentiate themselves from the people they are meeting in gay bars. The following subject came out when he was 22; he had been predominantly homosexual before coming out. He interacted with gay people in gay bars for several months before he decided he was a homosexual. He attempted to differentiate himself from the other homosexuals by saying to himself, "I am not really homosexual since I am not as feminine as they are."

Finally after hanging around there for so long, some guy came up to me and tried to take me for some money, and I knew it, and he said, "You know, you're very nellie." And I said I wasn't, and he said, "Yes, you are, and you might as well face facts and that's the way it is, and you're never going to change." And I said, "If that's the case, then that's the way it's going to be." So I finally capitulated.

This subject has been predominantly homosexually active for the last 21 years.

It should be made clear that such a change in sexual identity need not be accompanied by any change in sexual behavior or any participation in homosexual behavior. It is theoretically possible for someone to view himself as being homosexual but not engage in homosexual relations just as it is possible for someone to view himself as heterosexual but not engage in heterosexual relations. Approximately 20 percent of this sample came out while having no homosexual relations. The following subject is one of this group; he came out during his late twenties even though he had had his last homosexual experience at age 20.

I picked up a copy of this underground newspaper one day just for the fun of it. . . . and I saw an ad in there for this theatre, and after thinking about it I got up enough nerve to go over there. . . . I knew that they had pictures of boys and I had always liked boys, and I looked at the neighborhood and then I came home without going in. . . . I went back to the neighborhood again and this time I slunk, and I do mean slunk through the door. . . . and I was shocked to see what I saw on the screen, but I found it interesting and stimulating and so I went back several more times.

Eventually this subject bought a copy of a gay publication, and subsequently he went to the publication's office.

I visited with the fellows in the office and I had time on my hands and I volunteered to help and they were glad to have me. And I have been a member of the staff ever since and it was that way that I got my education of what gay life is like. . . . For the last ten years, I had been struggling against it. Back then if I knew what homosexuality was, if I had been exposed to the community . . . and seen the better parts, I probably would have admitted it then.

This subject has been very active socially but not sexually in the gay subculture for the last year.

In contrast to the previous examples, there are cases in which the subject has no direct contact with any gay persons, but yet comes out in that context. Fifteen percent (27) of the sample came out upon first reading about homosexuals or homosexuality in a book, pamphlet, etc.; ten of these (about 6 percent of the sample) were not associating with gay people at the time they came out. The following subject came out in this context. He was 14 at the time, had just ended a homosexual relationship with a person who considered himself to be straight, and had had no contact with gay society.

I had always heard like kids do about homosexuals and things, but that never really entered my mind, but when I read this article, when I was in the 8th grade, and it had everything in it about them sexually, not how they looked and acted and where they go. It was about me and that was what I was thinking. I just happen one day to see a picture of a guy, and thought he was kind of cute, so I'll read the article about him. But before that I didn't realize what was happening. I didn't even realize I wasn't right as far as heterosexuals were concerned. I didn't realize that what I was thinking wasn't kosher. . . . If people don't like it I'll keep my mouth shut. The article said people wouldn't like it, so I decided to keep my mouth shut. That's the way I was, so I accepted it.

This subject has been active sexually and socially in the gay subculture for the last five years.

Another context in which a subject can come out is that of having a homosexual relationship with a person who defines himself as being heterosexual; 12 percent (21) of the sample came out in such a context. Of these, 12 (about 7 percent of the sample) had never met any self-admitted homosexuals and had never read any material on homosexuality. The following case involves a subject who came out in such a context. At the age of 21 he was having an intense love affair with a serviceman who defined himself as straight. The subject also became involved in a triangular relationship with the serviceman's female lover.

This got very serious. I told him I loved him. . . . He wanted me for a sex release; I didn't admit it then, but now I see, through much heartbreak. He liked me as a person. . . . At the same time he was dating a married woman; he was dating her and having sex with her. . . . She couldn't admit to having a relationship with him 'cause she was married, but he told me and I was extremely jealous of her. [We worked together] and privately she was a very good friend of mine. So I started feeling hatred toward her because she was coming between he and I, competition. I was strong competition, 'cause I frankly dominated it, and she sensed this; so one day she said, "I bet he'd be very good in bed." So I said, "You know he is." She said, "What did you say?" and I said, "Oh, I guess he would be." And I wanted to tell her; so I finally acted like I just broke down and I told her everything in order to make her not like him. So she got on his tail and told him to stop seeing me or she wouldn't have anything to do with him. . . . I taped all their phone conversations and told her if she wouldn't leave him alone, I'd play them for her husband. She got furious, so she said if I tried to blackmail her she would go to the police with the whole thing . . . it all backfired on me and I really didn't want to hurt her, but my love for him was so strong; I'd hurt anybody to keep him, so I erased the tape. And later I bawled and bawled and cried about it to her because I was very sensitive at this time and I told her I was sorry, didn't want to hurt her, but I loved him so much. . . . After I fell in love with him I knew I was homosexual. I talked to my brother about it and he said I wasn't really in love. He said you're just doing it cause you want to; it's not right, boys don't fall in love with boys. He wasn't nasty about it . . . I really loved him; he was my first love; I even dream about him once in a while to this very day. . . . It was during this time that I came out, and I was extremely feminine, not masculine in any way. I wore male clothing, but dressed in a feminine way, in the way I carried myself, the way I spoke. . . . I realized that I was afraid of gay people; heard they did all kinds of weird things from straight people talking about them.

Before this relationship, the subject had engaged in both homosexual and heterosexual petting. Shortly after the relationship termi-

nated the subject became involved in the gay subculture and has been almost exclusively homosexual since that time.

COGNITIVE CHANGE

What is common to all the cases discussed is that the subject placed himself in a new cognitive category, the category of homosexual. In some cases, such placement can occur as soon as the person learns of the existence of the category; an example of this is the boy who placed himself in that category after reading about homosexuals in a magazine. However, probably most persons who eventually identify themselves as homosexuals require a change in the meaning of the cognitive category *homosexual* before they can place themselves in the category.

The meaning of the category must be changed because the subject has learned the negative stereotype of the homosexual held by most heterosexuals, and he knows that he is no queer, pervert, dirty old man, and so on. He differentiates himself from the homosexual image that straight society has presented to him. Direct or indirect contact with the gay subculture provides the subject with information about homosexuals that will challenge the "straight" image of the homosexual. The subject will quite often see himself in other homosexuals, homosexuals he finds to be socially acceptable. He now knows who and what he is because the meaning of the cognitive category has changed to include himself. As one subject said: "Wow, I'm home"; at times that is literally the case since the homosexual now feels that he knows where he really belongs.

A person's identification of himself as being homosexual is often accompanied by a sense of relief, of freedom from tension. In the words of one subject:

I had this feeling of relief; there was no more tension. I had this feeling of relief. I guess the fact that I had accepted myself as being homosexual had taken a lot of tensions off me.

Coming out, in essence, often signifies to the subject the end of a search for his identity.

IDENTIFICATION AND SELF-ACCEPTANCE

Identifying oneself as being homosexual and accepting oneself as being homosexual usually come together, but this is not necessarily the case. It can be hypothesized that those who identify themselves as being homosexual, but not in the context of interacting with other homosexuals, are more likely to have guilt feelings than those who identify themselves as being homosexual in the context of interacting with other homosexuals. Interaction with other homosexuals facilitates the learning of a vocabulary that will not simply explain but will also justify the homosexual behavior.

Identifying oneself as homosexual is almost uniformly accompanied by the development of certain techniques of neutralization. In this self-identification, it would be incorrect to state that the homosexual accepts himself as being deviant, in the evaluative sense of the term. The subject may know he is deviant from the societal standpoint but often does not accept this as part of his self-definition. Lemert has defined secondary deviation as the situation in which ". . . a person begins to employ his deviant behavior or a role based upon it as a means of defense, attack or adjustment to the overt and covert problems created by the consequent societal reaction to him." Once the subject identifies himself as being homosexual, he does develop means, often in the process of the change in self-definition, of adjusting to the societal reaction to the behavior. The means employed usually involve the denial, to himself and to others, that he is really deviant. Becker explained the situation when he stated:

But the person thus labeled an outsider may have a different view of the matter. He may not accept the rule by which he is being judged and may not regard those who judge him as either competent or legitimately entitled to do so.

The societal reaction to homosexuality appears to be expressed more in a mental health rhetoric, than in a rhetoric of sin and evil or crime and criminal behavior. In order to determine how the subjects adjusted to this societal reaction to homosexuality, they were asked to react to the idea that homosexuals are sick or mentally ill. With very few exceptions, this notion was rejected.

Subject 1: I believe this idea to be very much true, if added that you are talking from society's standpoint and society has to ask itself why are these people sick or mentally ill. . . . In other words, you can't make flat statements that homosexuals are sick or mentally ill. I do not consider myself to be sick or mentally imbalanced.

Subject 2: That's a result of ignorance; people say that quickly, pass quick judgments. They are not knowledgeable, fully knowledgeable about the situation.

Subject 3: I don't feel they are. I feel it's normal. What's normal for one person is not always normal for another. I don't think it's a mental illness or mental disturbance.

Subject 4: Being a homosexual does not label a person as sick or mentally ill. In every other capacity I am as normal or more normal than straight people. Just because I happen to like strawberry ice cream and they like vanilla, doesn't make them right or me right.

It is the learning of various ideas from other homosexuals that allows the subject to in effect say, "I am homosexual, but not deviant," or, "I am homosexual, but not mentally ill." The cognitive category of *homosexual* now becomes socially acceptable, and the subject can place himself in that category and yet preserve a sense of his self-esteem or self-worth.

It should be emphasized that coming out often involves an entire transformation in the meaning of the concept of homosexual for the subject. In these cases the subject had been entirely unaware of the existence of gay bars or an organized gay society, of economically successful homosexuals, of homosexually "married" homosexuals, and so on. In the words of one subject:

I had always thought of them as dirty old men that preyed on 10-, 11-, 12-year-old kids, and I found out that they weren't all that way; there are some that are, but they are a minority. It was a relief for me 'cause I found out that I wasn't so different from many other people. I had considered consulting professional help prior to that 'cause at the time I thought I was mentally ill. Now I accept it as a way of life, and I don't consider it a mental illness. It's an unfortunate situation. . . . I consider myself an outcast from general society, but not mentally ill.

PUBLIC LABELING

It should be made clear that the self-identification as a homosexual does not generally take place in the context of a negative public labeling, as some labeling theorists imply that it does. No cases were found in the interview sample in which the subject had come out in the context of being arrested on a charge involving homosexuality or being fired from a job because of homosexual behavior. In the questionnaire sample, 4 percent (7) had just been arrested and 1 percent (2) had just been fired from a job. A total of 8 respondents or 4.5 percent of the sample came out in the context of public exposure.

It can be hypothesized that the public labeling of an actor who has not yet identified himself as being homosexual will reinforce in his mind the idea that he is not homosexual. This is hypothesized because it is to be expected that at the time of the public labeling the actor will be presented with information that will present homosexuals and homosexuality in a highly negative manner. For example, the following subject was arrested for homosexual activities at the age of 11. Both before and after the arrest he did not consider himself to be a homosexual. His reaction to the arrest was:

Subject: The officer talked to me and told me I should see a psychiatrist. It kind of confused me. I really didn't understand any of it.
Interviewer: And were you thinking of yourself at that time as a homosexual?
Subject: I probably would have said I wasn't. 'Cause of the way the officer who interrogated me acted. It was something you never admit to. He acted as if I were the

scum of the earth. He was very rude and impolite.

If the actor has not yet identified himself as being homosexual, it can probably be assumed that to a significant degree he already accepts the negative societal stereotype; the new information accompanying the public labeling will conform to the societal stereotype, and the actor consequently will not modify his decision not to place himself in the homosexual category. This is not to say that public labeling by significant others and/or official agents of social control does not play a significant role in the life of the homosexual; all that is hypothesized is that public labeling does not facilitate and may in fact function to inhibit the decision to label oneself as being homosexual.

THE CLOSET QUEEN

There are some persons who may continue to have homosexual desires and may possibly engage in homosexual relations for many years, but yet do not have a homosexual identity. Self-admitted homosexuals refer to such persons as "closet queens." Such persons may go for many years without any contact with or knowledge of self-admitted homosexuals. The subject previously cited who came out in prison was a closet queen for 20 years.

An interval of 10 or more years between first awareness of sexual attraction toward males and the decision that one is a homosexual, would probably classify one as having been a closet queen. As Table 2 shows, the questionnaire sample included 35 respondents (20 percent of the sample) who at one time were closet queens.

It is the closet queen who has most internalized the negative societal stereotype of the homosexual. It is to be expected that such persons would suffer from a feeling of psychological tension, for they are in a state of cognitive dissonance (Festinger)—that is, feelings and sometimes behavior are not consistent with self-definition.

The following subject was a closet queen for over 50 years. He had his first homosexual experience at the age of 12, has had homosexual desires since that time, and has been exclusively homosexual for 53 years. At the time the subject was interviewed, he expressed amazement that he had just come out during the last few months. Over the years, his involvement with the gay subculture was peripheral; at the age of 29 for about one year he had some involvement with overt homosexuals, but otherwise he had had only slight contact with them until recently. During that earlier involvement:

I was not comfortable with them. I was repressed and timid and they thought I was being high hat, so I was rejected. It never worked out; I was never taken in. I felt uncomfortable in their presence and I made them feel uncomfortable. I couldn't fit in there, I never wanted to, never sought to; I was scared of them. I was scared of the brazen bitches who would put me down.

During the years as a closet queen he was plagued with feelings of guilt; for varying periods of time he was a patient in over twenty mental hospitals. His social life was essentially nil; he had neither gay friends nor straight friends. His various stays in mental hospitals relieved continuing feelings of loneliness. At the age of 65 he attended a church whose congregation was primarily homosexual. It was in the context of interacting with the gay persons who were associated with this church that after 53 years this subject came out.

Subject: I had never seen so many queens in one place; I was scared somebody would put me down, somebody would misunderstand why I was there. I had this vague, indescribable fear. But all this was washed away when I saw all were there for the one purpose of fellowship and community in the true sense of the term. . . . I kept going and then I got to be comfortable in the coffee hour. . . . Then out in the lobby a young fellow opened his heart to me, telling me all his troubles and so forth, and I listened patiently, and I thought I made a couple of comforting remarks. Then I went out to the car, and when I got in the car I put my hand out to shake hands and he kissed my hand. . . . it's hard for you to understand the

emotional impact of something like this— that I belong, they love me, I love them.

Until the last few weeks, in all my life I had never been in a gay bar for more than a few minutes, I was acutely uncomfortable. But now I can actually go into it; this is the most utterly ludicrous transformation in the last few weeks. . . . there's no logic whatsoever. I'm alive at 65.

It's a tremendous emotional breakthrough. I feel comfortable and relieved of tensions and self-consciousness. My effectiveness in other fields has been enhanced 100 percent. I have thrown off so many of the prejudices and revulsions that were below the surface. . . . I'm out of the closet. In every way, they know, where I work, in this uptight place where I work; I've told them where I live; I've written back east. What more can I do?

Interviewer: Do you think you are now more self-accepting of yourself?

Subject: Brother! I hope you're not kidding. That's the whole bit. How ironical it would come at 65. The only thing that I wouldn't do now is to go to the baths. I told the kids the other day; it's the only breakthrough I cannot bring myself to.

One can only speculate why after all these years this subject came out. The reason may have been that he had had a very religious upbringing and could not conceive of homosexuals in a religiously acceptable manner. The church he attended for the first time at age 65 presented homosexuals as being religiously acceptable, and presented to the subject highly religious homosexuals. Contact with this church may have helped change the meaning of the category homosexual so that he could now include himself.

In a sense the closet queen represents society's ideal homosexual, for the closet queen accepts the societal stereotype of the homosexual and feels guilt because he does the same sort of things that homosexuals do, yet believes he is really different from homosexuals in some significant way. This inability of the closet queen to see himself in other homosexuals prevents him from placing himself in the cognitive category of *homosexual,* and he will not come out until some new information is given to him about homosexuals which permits him to say, "There are homosexuals like myself" or "I am very much like them."

There may be significant differences between ex-closet queens and those closet queens who never come out. Of course, I had contact only with ex-closet queens, and they psychological adjustment has been much better since coming out. Their only regret was that they had not come out sooner. Possibly the closet queen who remains a closet queen reaches some sort of psychological adjustment that ex-closet queens were unable to reach.

THE ROLE OF KNOWLEDGE

The change of self-identity to *homosexual* is intimately related to the access of knowledge and information concerning homosexuals and homosexuality. Hoffman has observed:

Society deals with homosexuality as if it did not exist. Although the situation is changing, this subject was not even discussed and was not even the object of scientific investigation until a few decades ago. We just didn't speak about these things; they were literally unspeakable and so loathsome that nothing could be said in polite society about them. . . .

The traditional silence on this topic has most probably prevented many persons with homosexual feelings from identifying themselves as being homosexual. Lofland has noted that the role of knowledge in creating a deviant identity is an important one. If significant others or the actor himself does not know of the deviant category, his experience cannot be interpreted in terms of that category; or if his experience appears to be completely alien from that category he will not interpret his experience in terms of that category. If the societal stereotype of homosexuals is one of dirty old men, perverts, Communists, and so on, it should not be surprising that the young person with homosexual feelings would have difficulty in in-

terpreting his experience in terms of the homosexual category.

The greater tolerance of society for the freer circulation of information concerning homosexuality and homosexuals has definite implications in reference to coming out. The fact that there is greater overt circulation of homophile magazines and homophile newspapers, that there are advertisements for gay movies in newspapers, and that there are books, articles, and movies about gay life, permits the cognitive category of homosexuals to be known to a larger proportion of the population and, most importantly, permits more information to be circulated that challenges the negative societal stereotype of the homosexual.

Since there has been a freer circulation of information on homosexuality during the past few years, it can be hypothesized that the development of a homosexual identity is now occurring at an increasingly earlier age. Indeed, older gay informants have stated that the younger homosexuals are coming out at a much earlier age. In order to test this hypothesis, the sample was dichotomized into a 30-and-above age group and a below-30 age group. It can be seen in Table

Table 6–4. Relationship of Respondent Age to Age of Homosexual Self-Identification

Age at Homosexual Self-Identi-fication	Age of Respondents			
	30 and above		Below 30	
	N	(%)	N	(%)
5–9	0	(0)	1	(1)
10–14	8	(9)	19	(22)
15–19	35	(38)	44	(50)
20–24	29	(32)	23	(21)
25–29	10	(11)	1	(1)
30–39	7	(8)	0	(0)
40–49	1	(1)	0	(0)
50–59	0	(0)	0	(0)
60–69	1	(1)	0	(0)
Total	91	(100)	88	(100)
Mean	21.4*		17.2*	
Standard Deviation	7.7		3.8	

*Means significantly different at .01 level.

6–4 that the below-30 mean age for developing a homosexual identity was significantly lower (at the .01 level) than the above-30 mean age; the drop in mean age was from approximately 21 to 17.

Indications are that the present trend toward greater circulation of information that is not highly negative about homosexuals and homosexuality will continue. The fact that a mass circulation magazine such as *Time* gave its front cover to an article entitled "The Homosexual in America" (Oct. 31, 1969) and that this article was not highly negative represents a significant breakthrough. The cognitive category of homosexual is now being presented in a not unfavorable manner to hundreds of thousands of people who previously could not have been exposed to such information through conventional channels. This is not to say that more information about homosexuals and homosexuality will lead to a significantly greater prevalence of persons engaging in homosexuality. What is being asserted is that a higher proportion of those with homosexual desires and behavior will develop a homosexual identity, and that the development of that identity will continue to occur at an increasingly younger age.

CONCLUSION

This study has suggested that the development of a homosexual identity is dependent on the meanings that the actor attaches to the concepts of homosexual and homosexuality, and that these meanings that are directly related to the meanings that are available in his immediate environment; and the meanings that are available in his immediate environment are related to the meanings that are allowed to circulate in the wider society. The commitment to a homosexual identity cannot occur in an environment where the cognitive category of homosexual does not exist. Hoffman in essence came to the same conclusion when he hypothesized that the failure to develop a homosexual identity is due to a combination of two factors:

... the failure of society to make people aware of homosexuality as an existent way of life (and of the existence of the gay world), and the strong repressive forces that prevent people from knowing what their real sexual feelings are. One might consider this a psychological conspiracy of silence, which society insists upon because of its belief that it thereby safeguards existent sexual norms.

In an environment where the cognitive category of homosexual does not exist or is presented in a highly negative manner, a person who is sexually attracted to persons of the same sex will probably be viewed and will probably view himself as sick, mentally ill, or queer.

It can be asserted that one of the main functions of the viewpoint that homosexuality is mental illness is to inhibit the development of a homosexual identity. The *homosexuality-as-mental-illness* viewpoint is now in increasing competition with the *homosexuality-as-way-of-life* viewpoint. If the homosexuality-as-way-of-life viewpoint is increasingly disseminated, one would anticipate that the problems associated with accepting a homosexual identity will significantly decrease, there will be a higher proportion of homosexually oriented people with a homosexual identity, and this identity will develop at an earlier age.

If the homosexuality-as-way-of-life philosophy does become increasingly accepted, the nature of the homosexual community itself may undergo a radical transformation. To have a community one must have members who will acknowledge to themselves and to others that they are members of that community. The increasing circulation of the homosexuality-as-way-of-life viewpoint may in fact be a self-fulfilling prophecy. It may lead to, and possibly is leading to, the creation of a gay community in which one's sex life is becoming increasingly less fragmented from the rest of one's social life.

HOMOSEXUALITY: THE FORMULATION OF A SOCIOLOGICAL PERSPECTIVE

William Simon and John A. Gagnon

The study of homosexuality today, except for a few rare and relatively recent examples, suffers from two major defects: it is ruled by a simplistic and homogeneous view of the psychological and social contents of the category "homosexual," and at the same time it is nearly exclusively interested in the most difficult and least rewarding of all questions, that of etiology. While some small exceptions are allowed for adolescent homosexual experimentation, the person with a major to nearly exclusive sexual interest in persons of the same sex is perceived as belonging to a uniform category whose adult behavior is a necessary outcome and, in a sense, re-enactment of certain early and determining experiences. This is the prevailing image of the homosexual and the substantive concern of the literature in psychiatry and psychology today.

In addition to the fact that sexual contact with persons of the same sex, even if over the age of consent, is aginst the law in 49 of the 50 states, the homosexual labors under another burden that is commonly the lot of the deviant in any society. The process of labeling and stigmatizing behavior not only facilitates the work of legal agencies in creating a bounded category of deviant actors such as the "normal burglar" and the "normal child molester" . . . but it also creates an image of large classes of deviant actors all operating from the same motivations and for the same etiological reasons. The homosexual, like most significantly labeled persons (whether the label be positive or negative), has *all* of his acts interpreted through the framework of his homosexuality. Thus the creative activity of the playwright or

From *Journal of Health and Social Behavior*, 8, No. 3 (September 1967), 177—85. Reprinted by permission. Simon is at the Institute for Juvenile Research, Chicago, and Gagnon is in the Department of Sociology, State University of New York, Stony Brook.

painter who happens to be homosexual is interpreted in terms of his homosexuality rather than in terms of the artistic rules and conventions of the particular art form in which he works. . . .

It is this nearly obsessive concern with the ultimate causes of adult conditions that has played a major role in structuring our concerns about beliefs and attitudes toward the homosexual. Whatever the specific elements that make up an etiological theory, the search for etiology has its own consequences for research methodology and the construction of theories about behavior. In the case of homosexuality, if one moves beyond those explanations of homosexual behavior that are rooted in constitutional or biological characteristics—that is, something in the genes or in the hormonal system—one is left with etiological explanations located in the structure of the family and its malfunctions. The most compelling of these theories are grounded ultimately in Freudian psychology, where the roots of this as well as the rest of human character structure is to be found in the pathological relationships between parents and their children.

As a consequence of our preliminary work and the work of others . . . we would like to propose some alternative considerations in terms of the complexity of the life cycle of the homosexual, the roles that mark various stages of this cycle, and the kinds of forces, both sexual and nonsexual, that impinge on this individual actor. It is our current feeling that the problem of finding out how people become homosexual requires an adequate theory of how they become heterosexual; that is, one cannot explain homosexuality in one way and leave heterosexuality as a large residual category labeled "all other." Indeed, the explanation of homosexuality in this sense may await the explanation of the larger and more modal category of adjustment.

Further, from a sociological point of view, what the original causes were may not even be very important for the patterns of homosexuality observed in a society. Much as the medical student who comes to medicine for many reasons, and for whom the homogenous character of professional behavior arises from the experiences of medical school rather than from the root causes of his occupational choice, the patterns of adult homosexuality are consequent upon the social structures ·and values that surround the homosexual after he becomes, or conceives of himself as, homosexual rather than upon original and ultimate causes.

What we are suggesting here is that we have allowed the homosexual's sexual object choice to dominate and control our imagery of him and have let this aspect of his total life experience appear to determine all his products, concerns, and activities. This prepossessing concern on the part of nonhomosexuals with the purely sexual aspect of the homosexual's life is something we would not allow to occur if we were interested in the heterosexual. However, the mere presence of sexual deviation seems to give the sexual content of life an overwhelming significance. Homosexuals, moreover, vary profoundly in the degree to which their homosexual commitment and its facilitation becomes the organizing principle of their lives. . . .

Obviously, the satisfaction of a homosexual commitment—like most forms of deviance—makes social adjustment more problematic than it might be for members of a conventional population. What is important to understand is that consequences of these sexual practices are not necessarily direct functions of the nature of such practices. It is necessary to move away from an obsessive concern with the sexuality of the individual, and attempt to see the homosexual in terms of the broader attachments that he must make to live in the world around him. Like the heterosexual, the homosexual must come to terms with the problems that are attendant upon being a member of society: he must find a place to work, learn to live with or without his fam-

ily, be involved or apathetic in political life, find a group of friends to talk to and live with, fill his leisure time usefully or frivolously, handle all of the common and uncommon problems of impulse control and personal gratification, and in some manner socialize his sexual interests.

There is a seldom-noticed diversity to be found in the life cycle of the homosexual, both in terms of solving general human problems and in terms of the particular characteristics of the life cycle itself. Not only are there as many ways of being homosexual as there are of being heterosexual, but the individual homosexual, in the course of his every-day life, encounters as many choices and as many crises as the heterosexual. It is much too easy to allow the label, once applied, to suggest that the complexities of role transition and identity crises are easily attributable to, or are a crucial exemplification of, some previously existing etiological defect.

An example of this is in the phase of homosexuality called "coming out," which is that point in time when there is self-recognition by the individual of his identity as a homosexual and the first major exploration of the homosexual community. At this point in time the removal of inhibiting doubts frequently releases a great deal of sexual energy. Sexual contacts during this period are often pursued nearly indiscriminately and with greater vigor than caution. This is very close to that period in the life of the heterosexual called the "honeymoon," when coitus is legitimate and is pursued with a substantial amount of energy. This high rate of marital coitus, however, declines as demands are made on the young couple to take their place in the framework of the larger social system. In these same terms, during the homosexual "honeymoon" many individuals begin to learn ways of acting out a homosexual object choice that involve homosexual gratification, but that are not necessarily directly sexual and do not involve the genitalia.

It is during this period that many homosexuals go through a crisis of femininity; that is, they "act out" in relatively public places in a somewhat effeminate manner; and some, in a transitory fashion, wear female clothing, known in the homosexual argot as "going in drag." During this period one of the major confirming aspects of masculinity—that is, nonsexual reinforcement by females of masculine status—has been abandoned, and it is not surprising that the very core of masculine identity should not be seriously questioned. This crisis is partially structured by the already existing homosexual culture in which persons already in the crisis stage become models for those who are newer to their homosexual commitment. A few males retain this pseudo-feminine commitment, a few others emerge masquerading as female prostitutes to males, and still others pursue careers as female impersonators. This adjustment might be more widely adapted if feminine behavior by men— except in sharply delimited occupational roles—was not negatively sanctioned. Thus the tendency is for this kind of behavior to be a transitional experiment for most homosexuals, an experiment that leaves vestiges of "camp" behavior, but traces more often expressive of the character of the cultural life of the homosexual community than of some overriding need of individual homosexuals. Since this period of personal disorganization and identity problems is at the same time highly visible to the broader community, this femininity is enlisted as evidence for theories of homosexuality that see, as a central component in its etiology, the failure of sexual identification. The homosexual at this point of his life cycle is more likely to be in psychotherapy, and this is often construed as evidence for a theory which is supported by a missampling of the ways of being homosexual.

Another life cycle crisis that the homosexual shares with the heterosexual in this youth-oriented society is the crisis of aging. While American society places an inordinate positive emphasis on youth, the homosexual community, by and large, places a still greater emphasis on this fleeting characteristic. In general, the homosexual has fewer resources with which to meet this crisis. For the heterosexual there are his children whose careers assure a sense of the future and a wife whose sexual availability cushions the shock of declining sexual attractiveness. In addition, the crisis of aging comes later to the heterosexual, at an age when his sexual powers have declined and expectations concerning his sexuality are considerably lower. The management of aging by the homosexual is not well understood, but there are, at this point in his life, a series of behavioral manifestations (symptoms) attendant to this dramatic transition that are misread as global aspects of homosexuality. Here, as with "coming out," it is important to note that most homosexuals, even with fewer resources than their heterosexual counterparts, manage to weather the period with relative success.

A central concern underlying these options and the management of a homosexual career is the presence and complexity of a homosexual community, which serves most simply for some persons as a sexual market place, but for others as the locus of friendships, opportunities, recreation, and expansion of the base of social life. Such a community is filled with both formal and informal institutions for meeting others and for following, to the degree the individual wants, a homosexual life style. Minimally, the community provides a source of social support, for it is one of the few places where the homosexual may get positive validation of his own self-image. Though the community often provides more feminine or "camp" behavior than some individuals might desire, in a major sense "camp" behavior may well be an expression of aggregate community characteristics without an equal commitment to this behavior on the part of its members. Further, "camp" behavior may also be seen as a form of interpersonal communication characteristic of intracommunity behavior and significantly altered for most during interaction with the larger society. . . . Insofar as the community provides these relationships for the individual homosexual, it allows for the dilution of sexual drives by providing social grafitication in ways that are not directly sexual. Consequently, the homosexual with access to the community is more protected from impulsive sexual "acting out" than the homosexual who has only his own fear and knowledge of the society's prohibitions to mediate his sexual impulses.

It should be pointed out that in contrast to ethnic and occupational subcultures the homosexual community, as well as other deviant subcommunities, has very limited content. This derives from the fact that the community members often have only their sexual commitment in common. Thus, while the community may reduce the problems of access to sexual partners and reduce guilt by providing a structure of shared values, often the shared value structure is far too narrow to transcend other areas of value disagreement. The college-trained professional and the bus boy, the WASP and the Negro slum dweller, may meet in sexual congress, but the similarity of their sexual interests does not eliminate larger social and cultural barriers. The important fact is that the homosexual community is in itself an impoverished cultural unit. This impoverishment, however, may be only partially limiting, since it constrains most members to participate in it on a limited basis, reducing their anxiety and conflicts in the sexual sphere and increasing the quality of their performance in other aspects of social life.

Earlier we briefly listed some of the general problems that the homosexual—in common with the heterosexual—must face; these included earning a living, maintaining a residence, relations with family, and so on. At this point we might consider some of these in greater detail.

First there is the most basic problem of all: earning a living. Initially, the variables that apply to all labor force participants generally apply to homosexuals also. In addition there are the special conditions imposed by the deviant definition of the homosexual

commitment. What is important is that the occupational activity of homosexuals represents a fairly broad range. The differences in occupational activity can be conceptualized along a number of dimensions, some of which would be conventional concerns of occupational sociology, while others would reflect the special situation of the homosexual. For example, one element is the degree of occupational involvement, that is, the degree to which occupational activity, or activity ancillary to it, is defined as intrinsically gratifying. This would obviously vary from professional to ribbon clerk to factory laborer. A corollary to this is the degree to which the world of work penetrates other aspects of life. In terms of influence upon a homosexual career, occupational involvement very likely plays a constraining role during the acting-out phase associated with "coming out," as well as serving as an alternative source of investment during the "crisis of aging." Another aspect bears directly upon the issue of the consequences of having one's deviant commitment exposed. For some occupational roles disclosure would clearly be a disaster—the school teacher, the minister, and the politician, to mention just three. There are other occupations where the disclosure or assumption of homosexual interests is either of little consequence or—though relatively rare—has a positive consequence. . . .

A second series of questions could deal with the effects of a deviant sexual commitment upon occupational activity itself. In some cases the effect may be extremely negative, since the pursuit of homosexual interests may generate irresponsibility and irregularity. Some part of this might flow from what we associate with bachelorhood generally: detachment from conventional families and, in terms of sex, constant striving for what is essentially regularized in marriage. Illustrations of these behaviors include too many late nights out, too much drinking in too many taverns, and unevenness in emotional condition. On the other hand, several positive effects can be observed. Detachment from the demands of domestic life not only frees one for greater dedication to the pursuit of sexual goals, but also for greater dedication to work. Also, the ability of some jobs to facilitate homosexual activity—such as certain marginal, low-paying, white-collar jobs—serves as compensation for low pay or limited opportunity for advancement. There may be few simple or consistent patterns emerging from this type of consideration, yet the overdetermination of the sexual element in the study of the homosexual rests in our prior reluctance to consider these questions which are both complex and pedestrian.

Similarly, just as most homosexuals have to earn a living, so must they come to terms with their immediate families. There is no substantial evidence to suggest that the proportion of homosexuals for whom relatives are significant persons differs from that of heterosexuals. The important differences rest in the way the relationships are managed and, again, the consequences they have for other aspects of life. Here also one could expect considerable variation containing patterns of rejection, continuing involvement without knowledge, ritualistically suppressed knowledge, and knowledge and acceptance. This becomes more complex because several patterns may be operative at the same time with different members of one's family constellation. Here again it is not unreasonable to assume a considerable degree of variation in the course of managing a homosexual commitment as this kind of factor varies. Yet the literature is almost totally without reference to this relationship. Curiously, in the psychiatric literature—where mother and father play crucial roles in the formation of a homosexual commitment—they tend to be significant by their absence in considerations of how homosexual careers are managed.

This order of discussion could be extended into a large number of areas. Let us consider just one more: religion. As a variable, religion (as both an identification and a quality of religiosity) manifests no indication that it plays an important role in the generation of homosexual commitments. However, it clearly does, or can, play a significant role in the management of that commitment. Here, as in other spheres of life, we must be prepared to deal with complex, interactive relations rather than fixed, static ones. Crucial to the homosexual's ability to "accept himself" is his ability to bring his own homosexuality within a sense of the moral order as it is projected by the institutions surrounding him as well as his own vision of this order. It may be that the issue of including homosexuality within a religious definition is the way the question should be framed only part of the time, and for only part of a homosexual population. At other times and for other homosexuals, to frame the question in terms of bringing religiosity within the homosexual definition might be more appropriate. The need for damnation (that rare sense of being genuinely evil) and the need for redemption (a sense of potentially being returned to the community in good standing) can be expected to vary, given different stages of the life cycle, different styles of being homosexual, and varying environments for enactment of the homosexual commitment. And our sense of the relation suggests that, more than asking about the homosexual's religious orientation and how it expresses his homosexuality, we must also learn to ask how his homosexuality expresses his commitment to the religious.

The aims, then, of a sociological approach to homosexuality are to begin to define the factors—both individual and situational—that predispose a homosexual to follow one homosexual path as against others; to spell out the contingencies that will shape the career that has been embarked upon; and to trace out the patterns of living in both their pedestrian and their seemingly exotic aspects. Only then will we begin to understand the homosexual. This pursuit must inevitably bring us—though from a particular angle—to those complex matrices wherein most human behavior is fashioned.

THE FEMALE HOMOSEXUAL: SOCIAL AND ATTITUDINAL DIMENSIONS
Jack H. Hedblom

RESEARCH IN TABOO AREAS

There are problems involved in researching clandestine behavior that are not encountered in more traditional research. These difficulties include locating the activity itself, and are compounded by the unwillingness of the subjects to be studied. A research method particularly suited to this type of study is participant observation. Although the data derived from this method does not have "sense" built into it, the data does generate hypotheses. A problem in using this method is organizing the data to serve this generative purpose. The technique has often been criticized becuase the case history material generates more random observations than hypotheses. Polsky has suggested that

Successful field research depends upon the investigator's ability to look at people, listen to them, think and feel with them. It does not depend fundamentally on some impersonal apparatus, such as a camera or a tape recorder or a questionnaire that is imposed between the investigator and the investigated. . . . A problem for many sociologists today, the result of curricula containing as much scientism as science, is that these capacities far from being trained in him are trained out of him.

Merton has also argued that the timing of hypothesis formulation is irrelevant since the validity of the hypothesis always rests upon replication of studies. Whyte in evaluating his experience and researching the data for *Street Corner Society* addressed this problem.

Logic then plays an important part. But I am convinced that the actual evolution of research ideas does not take place in accord with the formal statements we read on re-

From Joseph A. McCaffrey, *The Homosexual Dialectic.* Reprinted by permission. Professor Hedblom is a member of the Sociology Department at Wichita State University.

search methods. The ideas grow up, in part, out of our immersion in data and out of the whole process of living. Since so much of this process of analysis perceives on the unconscious level, I am sure that we could never present a full account of it. . . .

As Simon and Gagnon stated:

The lesbian represents an excellent example of a need to integrate our understanding about deviant and conventional processes. Where, one might ask, is the research literature that reports upon the attributes and activities of the lesbian when she is not acting out her deviant commitment? The answer is that there is virtually none. As a result [*sic*] any research must rely upon an exceedingly thin scientific literature.

It appears that there is a need to establish greater continuities between what Garfinkel has called ethnomethodological concerns and traditional survey techniques. The study reported has attempted to base the validity of its survey instrument on the period of participant observation.

The Focus: Homosexuality

Despite an extensive literature treating lesbian themes in drama, art, and history, little attention has been paid to lesbianism itself. There are very few scientific studies on the extent of lesbianism, the life styles of lesbians, and the nature of their community. This study employs both observation and survey techniques and was done in Philadelphia between 1964 and 1970. Its principal focus is on the careers and life styles of lesbians. In order to maximize sample size and to avoid possible bias by having the questionnaire administered by a straight male, a field investigator was hired who was herself homosexual.

Becoming a homosexual often involves a matter of degree, not an either/or decision. Persons having occasional homosexual experiences were not included in this study. We also excluded persons who had made a homosexual adjustment in a total institution where no heterosexual outlets exist. Such persons identified themselves as heterosexual and most often made an exclusively heterosexual adjustment upon change in the living conditions. We therefore defined the lesbian as a female who focuses her sexual attentions, fantasies, and activities upon members of her own sex. Persons who are so defined must identify themselves as homosexual, and as Goffman stated:

... participate in a special community of special understanding wherein members of one's own sex are defined as the most desirable sex object and sociability is energetically organized around the pursuit and entertainment of these objects.

The nature of the homosexual commitment creates a very specialized social-psychological milieu in which one must establish a social career. This milieu may be considered a subcultural phenomenon characterized by patterns of beliefs, goals, and statuses that are different from the host society although not necessarily antithetical to it. It is important to note that only a small portion of the life style is taken up by the acting out of homosexual activities. The social career of the female homosexual can only be understood by considering the total range of her social and sexual activity.

Lesbianism: A Covert Phenomenon

Given an uninformed public that is somewhat embarrassed at the mention of sex in any form, it is not surprising that Western European culture is loath to admit the existence of female homosexuality at all. The lesbian has a low detectability when compared with the male homosexual. She is accordingly treated differentially by law enforcement officers and suffers less discrimination at the hands of the community than does her male counterpart. Adverse public opinion becomes manifest only when the lesbian identifies herself by performance, association, or unique dress.

The homosexual commitment encompasses the entire life style; the simple fact of being a homosexual places an individual in a very special relationship to society. Life style is intrinsically interwoven in a specialized community that is based entirely on that difference. Adequate measures of the extent of homosexuality depend upon the willingness of the rather specialized covert homosexual community to be studied or to include temporarily in its membership persons who are scientifically interested in manifestations of the phenomenon itself.

THE FEMALE HOMOSEXUAL: A UNIQUE COMMITMENT

There are basic biological and social differences between the male homosexual and the female homosexual. The female reflects the impact of her socialization as a female. She is concerned with the establishment of a home. She relates sex to love and is more likely to abstain from sex until she meets "the right person." She tends to be more passive in her search for a mate, even in the established marketplace of the homosexual community. Women are a more homogeneous group than men by virtue of their rigid socialization and are on the whole conditioned to be less aggressive and assertive. Stearn noted that women, including the lesbian, are trained to marital fidelity.

The lesbian prided herself on the chastity of the lesbian group as compared to the male homosexual. . . . It was not unusual for lesbians to remain true to one woman. "Like other women," a lesbian told me, "we think in terms of a monogamous ideal, even when we don't practice it."

Lesbians are exposed to the same subtle influences and experiences as heterosexual females, many of which occur before actual sexual experience. The effectiveness of the lesbian's socialization is evident in that her career is an almost exact duplication of the female heterosexual's.

ESTIMATE OF SIZE OF THE HOMOSEXUAL COMMUNITY

It is difficult to estimate the size of the female homosexual community. It is more elusive than the male subculture and less obvious in its deviation, and for this reason, its size is often underestimated. The lesbian is more difficult to detect by virtue of her training in sexual repression, which is far more systematic for the female than for the male. Hooker suggests that lesbians maintain a front of heterosexuality that becomes an integral part of their life style. This pretense makes the lesbian's already low detectability even lower. Hooker refers to female homosexuality as an iceberg phenomenon, indicating that most of the community lies beneath the surface of society. Further, she states that the majority of homosexuals belong to the submerged group and seldom attend homosexual meetings, join homosexual organizations, or frequent homosexual bars. The female homosexual community consists of a series of loosely knit or overlapping networks of friends bonded together by their difference and their need to be themselves among others who do not stigmatize their identity.

Existing statistics do not indicate the extent of female homosexuality nor is it revealed by arrest statistics, since very few women are arrested for homosexuality. The inability to establish population parameters seriously limits the use of sampling techniques for a representative sample. The best estimate is that homosexuality is found at least as frequently among women as among men.

EXPLANATORY MODELS

Theories of the causality of homosexuality are varied and often conflicting. However, three approaches are basic to the subject. The medical model dominates the literature on the ideology of homosexuality. It assumes that homosexuality is the result of an underlying psychological or physical pathology. Homosexuality is, therefore, a symptom of this pathology, and it is treated as a condition that can be "cured." The psychiatric implications of this model are clear. Obviously, the homosexual adjustment is resistant to change, but it can be ameliorated and result in a "normal heterosexual adjustment." As Robertiello states:

Homosexuality is the symptom of an illness. Certain traumatic experiences in childhood cause anxieties of the homosexual that do not allow him to express his sexual feelings toward a member of the opposite sex and at the same time compel him to express them towards a member of his own sex. It is not a matter of choice but of compulsion. Most homosexuals are unhappy, suffering people. Some of them may rationalize that theirs is the best life—at least for them, but all of them have an inner dissatisfaction with their method of adaptation. This dissatisfaction is not only reflective of society's disapproval, it is also based on an awareness of the basic lack of fulfillment and the compulsive pattern connected with their activity.

The psychoanalytical approach is evidenced in the following:

I sort of gravitated toward my father and Jack toward my mother, while Louise was cuddled by all of us. She was the baby and even Jack could accept her, and that's the way it all started. Now I understand the whole business, when I find my case history written up by an orthodox Freudian analyst. My name was Electra and I used to sit upon my daddy Agamemnon's lap and I fell in love with him, while little Jackie Oedipus was falling in love with mama Jocasta. It is all so clear, except that Jackie Oedipus grew up to like women because I was in love with daddy, so it doesn't explain everything, at least not to me.

This model precludes the possibility of there being a psychologically healthy homosexual. Bergler, in *Homosexuality—Disease or Way of Life*, stated:

... It has been recently discovered that homosexuality is a curable disease.
... There are no healthy homosexuals. The entire personality structure of the homosexual is pervaded by the unconscious

wish to suffer; this wish is gratified by self-created trouble-making. This "injustice-collecting" (technically called psychic masochism) is conveniently deposited in the external difficulties confronting the homosexual. If they were to be removed—and in some circles in large cities they have been virtually removed—the homosexual would still be an emotionally sick person.

We criticize this point of view since it denies that homosexuality can be a viable adjustment. The contact between patient and therapist has, most often, been initiated by the homosexual himself. It is therefore the maladjusted rather than the comfortably adjusted homosexual who seeks treatment. Court agencies espouse the medical orientation and use treatment to justify probation or parole. Since the nature of these contacts is essentially therapeutic, the assumption of an underlying pathology is understandable. However, the population upon which the medical model is based is restricted to homosexuals who are experiencing difficulty in adjusting to their homosexuality and to their social role. There is, therefore, a bias in the model that reflects only the sick homosexual and ignores the possibility of a well-adjusted homosexual who is content with her difference, finds meaningful relationships in her world, and enjoys a productive life.

In 1957 Hooker examined this perspective in *The Adjustment of the Male Homosexual*. In her study, thirty well-adjusted homosexuals were matched for age, I.Q., and education with thirty apparently well-adjusted heterosexuals. Judges were asked to distinguish between the groups. They were unable to do so.

The Wolfenden committee, an English investigatory body, was highly critical of the medical conception of homosexuality. It asserted that the traditional view of disease requires that there be abnormal symptoms, that the symptoms be caused by pathological conditions, and that the causes of these symptoms be both necessary and sufficient conditions for their existence. It pointed out that persons may manifest peculiar behavior

that is deviant within our frame of reference and still be "normal." It held also that considerations of behavior as normal or abnormal represented culturally biased value judgments and as such were less than scientific. Homosexual activity, according to the committee, did not manifest sufficient symptomatology to imply an underlying pathology. Homosexual persons, according to the committee, were virtually indistinguishable from nonhomosexual. The committee alleged that medical organizations and agencies in general had a vested interest in defining homosexuality as a disease.

The Wolfenden committee further rejected the medical analogy.

The alleged psychopathological causes for homosexuality have also been found to occur in others besides the homosexual. . . . In the absence of the physical pathology, psychopathological theories have been constructed to explain the symptoms of various forms of normal behavior and mental illness. . . . They are theoretical constructions . . . and not facts.

The claim that homosexuality is an illness carries a further implication that the sufferer cannot help his condition and, therefore, carries a diminished responsibility for his actions. Even if homosexuality could properly be described as a disease, we should not accept this correlation. There are no prima facie grounds for supposing that homosexuality is any less controllable than heterosexuality. The committee suggested further that:

It is obvious that only a minority of homosexuals or, for that matter, those who indulge in homosexual acts fall into the hands of the police and it is even likely also that a minority of such persons find their way to a doctor's consulting room. But it is impossible to determine what proportion of persons concerned these minorities represent. Still less on this evidence, what proportion of the total population falls within the description homosexual. These figures (derived figures), therefore, cannot be relied on as an indication of the extent of homosexuality or homosexual behavior among the community as a whole.

The Family Interaction Model

Those researchers concerned with the influence of institutions on behavior have focused on parental roles to explain the development of the homosexual. Recent research has isolated the following model. The father is described as detached or hostile or both. He has resigned his role as father and as household head. In the face of this resignation, the mother tends to be loving and overprotective. She is seductive toward sons and presents a strong identification model for daughters, who contrast her with a weak, ineffectual, yet exploitative male parent.

Schrieber and Wilber, who isolated the pattern described above, noted that it required two parents to create the homosexual child. If the father encouraged the son to be masculine, the latter did not become homosexual. Similarly, the mother's encouragement in heterosexuality acted as a deterrent. They noted that unhappy marriages promoted homosexuality because they tended to cause displacement of love object, resulting in the mother using the son as husband substitute.

In the case of female homosexuality, the mother's relationship with the daughter is a kind of chaotic struggle in which the child loses continually; the mother uses rejection, degradation, and guilt in order to control her child. The child rebels against the mother but at the same time wants her love. At the onset of puberty, warned about the dangers of heterosexual dating, the daughter considers the female the more desirable sex object and, at the same time, a mother substitutes.

This analytical model may be criticized from several points of view. Initially, the model ignores the possibility of primary influences other than the family. Peers and basic institutions such as the school and the church are ignored. It is assumed that the patterns established when the family is the single or primary source of socialization are immutable in later years. This orientation likewise ignores the possibility of the reenforcement of homosexual urges or fantasies by supportive structures, such as the aware-ness of other homosexuals and interaction with them. The model likewise ignores the likelihood of homosexual siblings or the order of birth of the child who becomes homosexual. Our own studies have found that the incidence of homosexual siblings and cousins in families that have produced one homosexual is greater than is reported in the literature. This is not surprising, given the continuity of socialization between siblings and cousins. Siblings and cousins share at least one common parent and are socialized by a milieu that we can tentatively suggest produces some continuity of personality.

Wahl noted family influence in the case of homosexuality. He suggests that the most common family structure that produces homosexuality is one having a weak or absent same-sexed parent, coupled with a dominating, overprotective, seductive, opposite-sexed parent.

The child exposed to this condition may conclude (in the case of the male) that women are stronger and more reliable than men; and children being prone to identify with a power source may identify, therefore, not only with the mother but also with her sexual object choice. Another common variation is the family history of a sadistic and a punitive opposite-sexed parent, coupled with a submissive, ineffectual or absent same-sexed parent.

Wahl notes also that other factors, extra-familial factors, are important in inducing homosexuality. He numbers among these the presence of a supportive structure or a group that provides rationalization of homosexual activity. Morse likewise observed that parental influences play an important role in the development of the homosexual personality. He suggested that a family that wants a child of one sex and gets a child of another sex tends to create psychological problems for the child by forcing or favoring activities most appropriate for the opposite sex. He cites, as an example, the father who wanted a son and got a daughter but who treated the daughter as if she were a son.

Mom would be in the kitchen making dinner or doing the dishes, she says, and Dad and I would be out in the backyard tossing a ball back and forth. In the fall it was football, in the spring and summer baseball. Mom would do the housework and I would play catch with Dad.

The root of homosexuality is, therefore, not neurosis but rather the social-psychological milieu based on the relationship between parents and child. The child's basic role in the family and the effectiveness of the roles played by the parents strongly affect the early psychosexual commitment of the child.

The most persuasive argument for the family model of homosexuality identifies the father as a crucial parent and homosexuality as arising either from the father's inability to accept the appropriate sexual role of the child or his passivity, ineffectiveness, or domination by the female parent. McGee viewed the child's relationship to the father as central, and observed that it was not so much the absolute quality of the relationship that is important as how the child perceived the relationship.

. . . One can now begin to see the different ways in which a child may become homosexual because of a pattern of relationship in which the entire family is involved. . . . Some of the most recent work being done on the subject, for example, that of the sociologist Dr. Eva Beue, points to the surprising conclusion that the really crucial relationship in the case of both male and female homosexuals is not with the mother but with the father.

The family model does not explain the occurrence of homosexual experiences themselves. It does not explain how one homosexual meets another nor how they resolve their status problems. It does not explain the pervasiveness of the homosexual commitment nor how behavior and identity continue without supportive structures. It does not provide a mode whereby we can understand the female homosexual's identification and social career.

The lesbian's commitment to a unique community or subculture is a defense against stigmatization of her identity. The subculture establishes a status system based on qualitites already possessed by individual members. Participation in it is a kind of problem-solving behavior. The antithetical values of the subculture are learned, adapted, and exhibited in a manner similar to those in the host culture. The individual continues as an active participant in the host society as well as in the homosexual subculture.

Homosexuality creates innumerable difficulties for a female in playing her social roles. A homosexual commitment affects her associations, entertainment activities, and occupational roles, as well as delimiting the possibility of certain types of social mobility. The subculture protects the homosexual from mixed feelings about herself and provides her with associations that are essentially accepting. Since her social career is focused primarily upon her sexual identification, her commitment places her in a special relationship to the larger society and to the conventional patterns of interaction which comprise it.

The lesbian community is a continuing collectivity of associations. Persons involved in it have a common identity resulting from a stigmatized social designation. The community facilitates sexual union, provides a source of identity, and offers an opportunity for the lesbian to relax the front she traditionally presents to the heterosexual community. It reduces the possibility of embarrassing oneself by making advances to a straight person and provides an ideology and justification for homosexual behavior itself.

MODEL COMBINATIONS

Individually, neither of these models provides a sufficiently broad framework to understand the phenomenon of lesbianism. Of the two approaches, the medical model presents the greatest difficulty. It is based on value judgments that define heterosexual morality as absolute rather than culturally relative and excludes inversion as a viable sexual adjustment. The family interaction model emphasizes parental roles and children's perception of them to the exclusion of other social variables. The model does not explain the persistence of the homosexual adjustment in the face of its pejorative definition and ignores the supportive structure of social interaction. While the role of the family cannot be ignored, neither can the role of other social institutions, including the supportive structure of the homosexual community in perpetuating the life style of the lesbian.

Given the inherent weakness of each model, a combination of models must be used to locate the etiology of inverted psychosexual identity in the role-structure of the family and the social support for the ongoing homosexual activity in the specialized community of the lesbian. The life of the female invert will be explored within this theoretical frame of reference. We examine the role-structure of the lesbian's home as she perceives it. We likewise examine her dating patterns, marriage arrangements, occupations, and patterns of sexual behavior. The process of becoming homosexual is considered in terms of the age at which first fantasy, contact, emotional involvement, and finally entry into the homosexual community occurs. . . .

SAMPLE CHARACTERISTICS

In summary, the heterosexual marital status of the sample includes fifty-seven persons who had never married, one married person, three separated persons, and four divorced. Thirty-one of the sample are homosexually married; thirty-four are not. The educational descriptions indicate a larger percentage of respondents have graduated from high school, have college experience, have graduated from college or attended graduate school, than we expected to find in a heterosexual population. Forty-six percent of the respondents have attended college or are in the process of attending college. Forty-eight percent of the sample hold occupations that are skilled or semiskilled, with 32 percent in

professional occupations or technical categories. Fifteen percent of the sample are in the professional category. This distribution shows a large percentage of respondents in the middle class or upper-middle class. This is not interpreted to mean that most female homosexuals originate predominantly in these social classes. The analysis of fathers' occupations indicates that parents of respondents were both lower class and middle class as well as some upper class.

The data indicate a high achievement pattern among homosexual females. Lesbians carry the responsibility for maintaining themselves rather than being supported by a male partner. Their occupational roles and goals are, therefore, culturally defined as masculine.

THE COMMUNITY

We have previously discussed the nature of the homosexual community. Respondents indicated involvement in activities unique to this homosexual world and interaction with a network of friends, themselves homosexual. The most accessible public meeting place for the lesbian is the homosexual bar. In the career of the typical lesbian, the bar plays several roles, i.e., that of sexual marketplace, clearinghouse for information, meeting place, place for finding peer associations, and above all, a neutral meeting ground. Bar attendance is a predictable part of the lesbian's life. It provides, in addition, psychological reinforcement for homosexual identity as well as opportunity to interact freely without the necessity of putting up a front. Typically, lesbians visit bars two or three times a month. Twenty-nine percent of respondents attend bars at least six times per month. Twenty-three percent of respondents indicate that they had met 100 percent of their friends in homosexual bars. As the female homosexual becomes more involved with the subculture of homosexuality, the importance of the homosexual bar as a sexual marketplace tends to diminish.

Respondents indicate that they have had sexual relations with girls met in bars as well as with girls met through friends. The greater percentage of these relationships has occurred through friends or contacts outside the bar (32 percent). Thirty percent of respondents, on the other hand, indicate that they have met only 20 percent of the persons with whom they had shared a sexual relationship through friends. The pattern of responses stresses the mutual importance of the homosexual community and the homosexual bar. The availability of one facility is not diminished by that of the other. Given the clandestine nature of homosexual bars and their limited number, it is not surprising that most of them are peopled by a cross-section of the homosexual world.

Sixty-four of the sample of sixty-five indicate that they prefer a stable relationship to any other. This affects the nature of "dating" as it occurs in the homosexual world since in the gay world one is not "dating someone"—one is "going with someone." Dating patterns are characterized by a kind of perpetual "going steady." The stable relationship acts as a defense against charges of promiscuity. Most respondents are involved in a marriage arrangement. Seventy-one percent of respondents have had such an arrangement, and 75 percent have had two or fewer such relationships. Twenty-nine percent of respondents, however, have had three or more such relationships. These marriage-like relationships have no legal or social support outside the homosexual community. Although they tend to be impermanent, they are easier to establish than heterosexual marriages, which involve formal announcement and public rituals in their formalization. The homosexual marriage arrangement finds its analogy in the heterosexual world in "living together," or trial marriage. There have been no comparisons of homosexual marriages with "trial marriages" in the literature.

The existence of a community composed of homosexuals is revealed by the fact that 84 percent of respondents reported that the majority of their friends were homosexual. This percentage is impressive when one considers that homosexuals are involved in

school or are employed in the straight world most of the time. Seventy-six percent of respondents indicate that they keep up a heterosexual front when interacting with the heterosexual community. This "leading two lives" severely limits social interaction with persons met occupationally or otherwise in the heterosexual community. Younger respondents are less likely to pretend heterosexuality, which indicates a growing militancy against discrimination and definition as abnormal or sick. Respondents resent having to maintain a heterosexual front and believe that the choice of love object has nothing to do with the quality of love itself and that homosexual love is "normal."

Homosexual females defend themselves by defining their "normalcy" in terms of numbers. Whenever they estimate the size of the homosexual community, they observe that there are many more female inverts than the public is aware of. They imply that if a large number of persons are involved in homosexual activities, they must be "normal."

A majority of respondents (84 percent) indicate that they are comfortable with non-homosexuals. This suggests the effectiveness of the heterosexual front, which makes possible a considerable exchange between homosexual and heterosexual communities. The posture of heterosexuality allows the female invert to act as a single girl in the straight community. Since she was socialized in the straight community, such behavior is natural to her regardless of her sexual commitment. That she comfortably interacts with the heterosexual community indicates that she has adjusted to her role in the homosexual community and is comfortable with it. The group reinforcement of homosexual identity is indicated by 79 percent of respondents who assert that homosexuality is as normal as heterosexuality.

Entrance into the homosexual community does not immediately follow awareness of individual homosexual commitment or first physical homosexual contact. Initial homosexual contacts are neither exploitative nor characterized by the respondent's seduction into a homosexual commitment. Instead, they are a willing, cooperative exploration of homosexual tendencies. Fourteen percent of the respondents indicated that first physical contact occurred before the age of ten. Seventy-nine percent of the respondents had a physical experience before the age of twenty and before entry into the homosexual community. Only 20 percent of the respondents report that their first physical ·experience occurred after twenty but before twenty-five. Respondents, however, indicate that they first chose homosexuals as their principal social group between the ages of twenty and thirty, with 45 percent making this choice before twenty-five years of age and 35 percent between the ages of twenty-six and thirty. Only four made this decision after the age of thirty. Physical experience thus precedes entrance into the homosexual community by a considerable period of time. Most respondents assert that their grammar school and high school experiences were not affected by awareness of homosexuality or the physical experience itself, thus indicating peer support for heterosexual dating patterns and attitudes.

Typically, the lesbian, regardless of her growing involvement with the homosexual community or awareness of her homosexuality, continues heterosexual dating for a considerable time. She has little or no support for her homosexuality from the homosexual community unless she is involved in it. Her peers and family exert pressures on her to conform to a more ordinary life and define this period in her life as a "fun period." They relax these pressures on her as she grows older and assumes the role of an adult female. With eventual emancipation from the parental home, the lesbian has opportunities to explore life styles and sexual patterns. It is ordinarily at this point that serious involvement with the homosexual community begins.

Membership in the homosexual community is obviously the result of feelings and events, not necessarily sexual in nature, that lead to self-awareness and self-acceptance as a homosexual; she then seeks out homosex-

uals as her principal social group. By this act, she minimizes the stigma of her identity as something different from the normal population and finds support for her emotional being as well as social career. One function of the homosexual community is to provide rationalizations that lessen the stigma of homosexuality. Seventy-three percent of respondents indicate that they believe homosexuals to be particularly creative (more creative than heterosexuals), and 80 percent perceive homosexuals to be particularly sensitive to others (more sensitive also than heterosexuals).

Indicative of the supportive quality of the homosexual subculture, 85 percent of the respondents indicate that they are generally happy. Sixty-five percent of the sample indicate that they would leave the choice of homosexuality vs. heterosexuality to their children. The fact that such perceptions have wide support in the homosexual community indicates that the community itself presents an ideology which provides a means whereby a positive identity can be established for its members.

The negative perception of the homosexual life style is therefore based on the discrimination and the stigmatized identity of the homosexual commitment as viewed by the heterosexual world. It is not intrinsic to the nature of homosexuality itself. However, the transient quality of the homosexual liaison, the covert nature of the "gay" life, the need for concealment, and the distorted self-image of the homosexual support the conclusion that the heterosexual is a more fulfilling existence than the homosexual life style.

SOCIAL AND ATTITUDINAL DIMENSIONS

Involvement with the homosexual community for the lesbian typically begins between the ages of twenty and thirty. Fifty-eight percent of respondents chose homosexuals as their principal social group between the ages of twenty-one and twenty-five, and 35 percent between the ages of twenty-six and thirty. The social career of a typical lesbian begins with emancipation from family and from adolescent peer associations. Entrance to the community is a gradual process, preceded by homosexual fantasies, and characterized by physical homosexual contacts occurring over a long time.

Sixty-seven percent of the respondents report that their grade and high school experiences were not overly affected by awareness of homosexual tendencies or commitment. Most respondents continued heterosexual dating after their awareness of homosexual proclivities, probably believing them transitory or part of a phase, after which they would be "normal" again. The milieu of the teenager offers little support for nonconforming sexual behavior. Pressures for conventional life style are exerted by peers and family.

Despite clear-cut boundaries between heterosexual and homosexual worlds, interchanges between them do occur. Eighty-nine percent of the respondents report that they have dated men during their homosexual careers. A good proportion (37 percent) of the respondents have also had sexual experience with men. Dating heterosexual men has sexual connotations and is not carried on principally for cover or escort purposes. Respondents date straight men more often than gay men. Eighty-five percent of the respondents indicate that they do not date gay men exclusively. The need for a male escort has been overemphasized in the literature.

Homosexual dating patterns differ from those of the heterosexual world. Due to the covert nature of homosexuality, homosexual dating involves house parties, group outings, and other collective activities that conceal their homosexual nature. Dating means something different in the homosexual community from what it does in the heterosexual. Moreover, there is an emphasis on youth, with the girls being called "kids." However, there is also an emphasis upon couples. One does not "date around" in the homosexual community; one looks for a partner. Some 60 percent of the respondents report that they do not date girls whom they

meet in homosexual bars. Instead they rely on a network of friends and associates in the homosexual community for "dates" or other forms of interaction.

Eighty-six percent of respondents indicate that they interact with the heterosexual world with a degree of ease. A larger percentage of married couples were more comfortable with straight persons than were unmarried persons. This interaction with the heterosexual community indicates the efficacy of the front of heterosexuality that homosexuals present to the heterosexual world and is also a measure of comfort with themselves. Forty-nine (or 75 percent) of the respondents report that they keep up a front for the benefit of straight friends or acquaintances.

It has been commonly assumed that there is more understanding between the male homosexual world and the female homosexual world than exists between either perspective and the heterosexual world. The data does not support this. If anything, the data indicates that as great a gulf of misunderstanding exists between the male and female homosexual worlds as exists between the homosexual and heterosexual worlds. Female homosexuals regard the male homosexual community pejoratively. Eighty-five percent of the respondents indicate that they consider female homosexual marriage arrangements more stable than their male counterparts. Ninety-eight percent of the sample view the male homosexual community as being more promiscuous than the female and as having more extremes in its milieu. The male homosexual is also perceived as having more "one-night stands" than his female counterpart. He is viewed as being more oriented toward immediate gratification than toward establishment of a relatively permanent association. This perception indicates differences in attitudes toward sex between the male and female homosexual. Conversely, the female homosexual typically considers her world as happy for her, differing from the heterosexual community only to the extent that homosexuality is stigmatized as unnatural.

Seventy-five percent of the respondents believed that the female homosexual's drive for authority and achievement patterns is greater than those of the heterosexual female. Respondents indicate that they consider themselves as stable and as mentally healthy as they would be in the straight world. Ninety-one percent of the respondents say they have never sought professional help to overcome their homosexuality. Twenty-six percent indicate they have sought specialized help with adjustment problems that did not pertain to their homosexuality.

SEXUAL AWARENESS AND ACTIVITY

Nearly one-half of respondents (42 percent) experienced homosexual fantasies between the ages of eleven and fifteen, 28 percent between the ages of six and ten, and 30 percent after the age of fifteen. Some period of time lapsed between their first fantasies and first physical homosexual contacts. A further period of time followed before respondents fully identified with the homosexual community.

A cherished notion in the heterosexual community is that homosexuality begins as the result of the seduction of children by older homosexuals. To ascertain the relationship between respondents and the person with whom they had shared their first physical experience, we found that 47 percent of the respondents played an initially passive, but willing role. Fifty-three percent indicated that they had played an initially dominant role and were the seducers. Based on this data, we state that persons are not seduced into homosexuality. Initial contacts are the result of mutual willingness to explore homosexuality. Psychosexual identity has already been formed before the first physical contact, and homosexual females experiment with the dimensions of their sexual universe just as heterosexuals experiment with theirs.

As the respondent matures and increases her involvement with the homosexual community, there is a decreasing pressure to date from peers and family. This is accompanied by an emphasis upon her emergent role as an adult female. It is at this point in her social career that the female homosexual begins a serious involvement with the subculture of female homosexuality.

The basic role in the homosexual world that the individual assigns herself pertains directly to the type of role she will act out socially. The physical aspects of the role are more flexible than the social aspects. Only 18 percent of the sample indicate that they play the physical role of the female exclusively (femme). The remainder of the sample indicate that they play both the dominant (butch) and submissive roles interchangeably. On the basis of this data, female homosexual roles—i.e., (male) dominance vs. (female) submission—are more social in their basic dimensions than they are physical. Social roles are a method whereby the homosexual subculture organizes dating and pursuit patterns as well as areas of responsibility in social interaction. Social roles apparently have little to do with the sexual roles played out by respondents.

Respondents indicate that 20 percent of their dates with other lesbians result in a sexual liaison (55.9 percent of respondents). Respondents who indicate that 100 percent of their dates result in sexual contact are probably exaggerating. Twenty-seven percent of the respondents indicate that oral sex was a part of their first physical contact. Oral sex was not expected to have occurred as the first contact. Manual stimulation was the expected mode of exploration because it is a simple extension of self-arousal. Forty percent of the respondents achieved orgasm on first contact, 5 percent on second contact, and 51 percent on subsequent contacts. The immediacy of sexual gratification may be explained from two perspectives. It is related to the fantasies and anticipation preceding the physical act and the willingness of the respondents to engage in physical homosexual acts, and to their previous experience with physical manipulation and masturbation common to childhood. It is possible also that absence of a fear of penetration encourages the enjoyment of sexual relations. Women are tender, gentle, and aware of female anatomy and its sensitivities. These factors encourage an early and facile sexual response.

Thirty-seven respondents have had sexual relations with a man. Typically these occurred between twenty-one and twenty-five years of age, with some proportion between twenty-six and thirty years of age. Thirty-three respondents who have had sexual relations with a man indicate that penetration by the male occurred. Therefore, heterosexual relationships involving lesbians are not comprised simply of those oral acts to which they are accustomed. Relations between them are not a mock version of the homosexual relationship, but are complete heterosexual acts. Respondents typically adopt a passive role in these relationships, which was predictable, given the fact that women are traditionally socialized to do so. The female homosexual does not prefer sex with a woman because she has had no experience with a man; it is as likely that she has had such an experience as not.

Forty-eight percent of the respondents who have had sex with a man indicate that oral-genital contact occurred. Typically the act was mutual. Forty-eight percent of the respondents achieved orgasm with a man and 50 percent had not, but this did not disturb their identity as female homosexuals. The choice of sex object is based not upon her inability to have satisfying sexual relations with a man but upon more complicated criteria rooted in her psychosexual identity. More than a third of the respondents having sexual relations with a man had this experience within the twelve-month period preceding their completion of the questionnaire. Some have had sexual liaisons within the previous six months. Nevertheless, these individuals thoroughly identify with the homosexual community and accept their psychosexual identity as lesbians. Unmarried respondents engage in mutual oral sex more often than do the married groups. Oral sex is apparently related to whether the respondents achieve orgasm with the man.

SUMMATION

The social carrer of the female homosexual occurs within a subcultural context that parallels closely the career of the heterosexual woman. Her principal interaction with the straight community involves her employment. The majority of her friends are lesbians. She perceives her stigmatized identiy and maintains a front of heterosexuality for the straight community and, in part, her family.

The lesbian views herself as being less promiscuous than male homosexuals and as more likely to enter into long-term, stable relationships. She associates sex with an emotional bond between persons and is less likely to "cruise for sex partners. Her dating patterns indicate that she is "going with" someone or "married" in the homosexual sense of the word.

Although the lesbian attends homosexual bars, of equal importance in her social career is the network of friends and associates in the homosexual community. The group supports her definition of homosexuality as normal and a viable sexual adjustment. She perceives homosexuals as being more sensitive and more creative than nonhomosexuals. Due to her independence from males, her occupational aspirations are masculine; and her achievement patterns, both scholastic and occupational, are higher than heterosexual females.

The lesbian does not become involved with the homosexual community until she has completed high school and begun emancipation from family and adolescent, heterosexual peers. Fantasies about women and an initial physical sexual experience precede community entry by a considerable period of time.

Respondents are comfortable around the straight community but choose the homosexual community for friendships after the age of twenty. They define themselves as being in the "gay life" and are generally happy with it. Despite clear-cut boundaries between the homosexual and heterosexual worlds, the lesbian enjoys interchanges across the boundaries in sexual and nonsexual senses. A large number of lesbians have sexual relations with men, with a surprising number of these contacts resulting in orgasm.

The lesbian's sexual career begins before her homosexual social career. Her first contact occurs typically before the age of twenty, with a good percentage having physical contact before the age of fifteen. Respondents typically focused on females as their principal sex object prior to this time. The nature of the first physical contact is varied. The majority of respondents indicate that only manual stimulation occurs. Almost one-third of the population indicate that oral sex was a part of their first contact. This was unrelated to whether orgasm was achieved. These activities are similar to those of young heterosexuals who often substitute manual stimulation for "going all the way."

The life of the lesbian can be understood only within the framework of limitations imposed upon her by her subculture and the host culture, which both stigmatizes and discriminates against her. Her life style is as much a function of that discrimination as it is of her difference from the nonhomosexual community. The patterns of her initial sexual awareness and involvement with a milieu that accepts her commitments parallels the experience of the heterosexual woman's involvement with the heterosexual world of couples.

Due to the nature of the sampling procedures of the study, we have generated only nominal data. For this reason we cannot generalize from this data to the larger population of female homosexuals. Despite this limitation, certain findings recommend themselves for further study.

If family structure is related to producing the homosexual commitment, as this study suggests, investigations should include more than examinations of how respondents perceive the dominance of each parent. Research into the role-structure of the family might produce interactional configurations that are conclusive to producing the homosexual. The question of homosexual siblings and cousins requires further exploration in that female homosexuals are more likely to have inverted siblings and cousins than heterosexuals.

Since sexual fantasies about women preceded actual physical experience, which in turn preceded entry into the homosexual subculture, further study should focus upon the ages at which each stage of the lesbian career occurs. It would be fruitful to ascertain how many females fantasized sexually about women, went on to have a satisfying homosexual physical experience, but did not enter the homosexual subculture, developing, rather, a heterosexual life style. A question might be raised as to how such individuals differ from those who continued in their homosexuality and became so self-identified. Comparing these two groupings, how would their family structure differ? Do elements in family relationships exist for those who become heterosexual that do not exist for those who become overtly homosexual?

This study has suggested that the nature of the first physical contact is mutually explorative. Further study would indicate if this is so and whether or not the role of seduced or seducer is related to the sexual role eventually played by either party. Such concerns might extend to the nature of the relationship leading to the first marriage arrangement. Examination of this dimension of the social career should analyze roles played, age differentials, if any exist, the length of time the arrangement lasted, how the break-up occurred, and whether or not the respondents continued in the basic role-pattern of dominance or submission (butch vs. femme) manifest in this first marriage relationship.

The achievement patterns, both occupational and educational, of female homosexuals appear to be higher than a comparable group of heterosexual females. Occupations or areas of study might be isolated that are particularly attractive to the lesbian—i.e. teaching, nursing, or other occupations whose professional orientation guarantees a degree of independence. Although the achievement patterns and occupational aspirations of lesbians may be related to their unwillingness to attach themselves to a male provider, these motivations may also be related to other more fundamental dimensions of the personality dynamic.

Lesbians perceive differences between their life style and that of the male homosexual. Such differences should be explored in terms of sexual activities as well as social and attitudinal dimensions. It is possible that great differences exist between the social careers of the male and female homosexuals and that they are not etiologically related.

The nature of the homosexual marriage should be investigated as to where meetings resulting in such liaisons occur and what age differentials typify initial marriage relationships. Further analysis should include how long such relationships exist and how subsequent marriage relationships differ from the initial relationship. A role breakdown might include such areas as occupation, education, income differentials, ownership patterns, and the like.

With regard to her experience with men, further analysis should pinpoint when such relationships typically occur in the career, how they occur, and whether or not they are an aspect of heterosexually oriented data. A relationship may exist between the length of involvement with a heterosexual career and the probability of heterosexual experience or dating occurring. Exploring the sexual career of the lesbian further, attention should be paid to her experience with other women—age at first homosexual experience, age at second experience, and duration of the relationship resulting in the first physical experience, as well as the length of time between the first homosexual partner and the second. The number of men and women the typical lesbian is intimate with in her career needs to be explored, as well as how often sexual relations occur between married couples per week, how often per week the single girl is successful in arranging a sexual liaison, and the typical length of time between such marriage arrangements.

How the U.S. lesbian social career and the content of the subculture differ from a European sample (in that the homosexual identity is less stigmatized in certain countries) needs to be investigated. Differences should exist between samples drawn from these countries and a random sample of homosexuals derived from the American population. It is expected that as negative definitions of identity of the homosexual decrease, the importance of the unique homosexual community as the source of social interaction will also decrease, as will the need to maintain a heterosexual front. The covert quality of the homosexual community may disappear, and interchanges across the boundaries separating the heterosexual and homosexual worlds may increase. Although this may be accompanied by an apparent rise in the incidence of homosexuality, such integration of the heterosexual and homosexual worlds will augment the possibilities of sexual adjustments for lesbians presently isolated. The probability of a percentage of lesbians eventually making a heterosexual adjustment would be increased by this interchange.

It is mandatory that the parameters of the research universe by established, as well as the ecological distribution of homosexuals. Since sampling depends largely upon educated guesses about the research population, further research on that population will depend upon an accurate means of estimating its size. This is perhaps the next task awaiting the researcher.

THE TRANSSEXUAL IN SOCIETY

Michele S. Matto

Because transsexuals possess bodies that their minds cannot accept, they are trapped

From *Criminology*, 10, No. 1 (May 1972), 85–109. Reprinted by permission of Sage Publications, Inc. Michele Matto is in the Sociology Department at Ohio State.

between society's demand to conform to the anatomical self thrust on them by birth and their own desire to conform to a different interior self. Although the transsexual dresses and behaves as a member of the morphologically opposite sex, this is neither a case of transvestism nor homosexuality. Psychologically, the transsexual is a female within a male body, or a male within a female body. In the past these distinctions were virtually ignored by the medical world. Recently, however, attempts have been made, particularly at The Johns Hopkins Hospital, to determine precisely what constitutes transsexualism and to treat surgically those suffering from it. As important as the need to identify and treat the problem itself is the need to combat the·emotionalism and prejudice surrounding the subject, which hamper serious research.

The above excerpt and the 500-page book which follows it are examples of a new perspective on a not-so-new problem: cross-gender identity. Richard Green, assistant professor of psychiatry in residence and director of the Gender Identity Research and Treatment Clinic at UCLA School of Medicine, and coauthor of the book *Transsexualism and Sex Reassignment,* says that evidence for what is today called transsexualism can be found in records back throughout history. "Descriptions from classical mythology, classical history, Rennaisance, and nineteenth-century history plus cultural anthropology point to the long-standing and widespread pervasiveness of the transsexual phenomenon."

THE TRANSSEXUAL PHENOMENON

Homosexuality, transvestism, and transsexualism were not "catalogued" and differentiated even up until very recent times—in fact, the term "transsexualism" was used for the first time in 1953 by Dr. Harry Benjamin, a physician who has treated and counseled transsexuals since the early 1920s and who has been referred to as their "patron saint" because of the influence he has asserted upon other professional people toward the recognition of transsexualism as, indeed, an entity unto itself.

Because of the term's recent origin, then, it is not found in historical accounts, and inferences must be made in examining reference material. One interesting case is that of the Chevalier d'Eon de Beaumont, from whose name comes our word "eonist,"

meaning a male with a compulsion to dress as *and be socially accepted as a woman.* At the time of his death, he had lived 49 years as a man and 34 years as a woman. Another person who, throughout her adulthood had been known as Mlle. Jenny Savalette de Lange died at Versailles in 1858 and was discovered to be a man. He had gotten a birth certificate designating himself female, was engaged to men six times, and was given a yearly pension by the King of France with a free apartment in the Chateau of Versailles.

Distinction Among Homosexuality, Transvestism, and Transsexualism

In earlier years and even still today for those unfamiliar with the subject, the greatest confusion was between transvestism and what is now called transsexualism. The line between the two is a fine one.

The transvestite is a person who feels compelled to "cross-dress"; that is, to dress in the clothes of the opposite sex.[1] Most writers treat this as basically a sexual deviation and relate it to the transvestite's desire for sexual arousal and attainment of orgasm while so dressed. The "true" transvestite then, is content with this cross-dressing; he basically "feels" like a man and knows he is a man, content with his morphological sex. He does not wish to have his masculinity, as evidenced by the presence of his external sex organs, taken from him, and he would probably like most of all to be left alone to get his sexual pleasures from dressing, while otherwise leading life as a man.

In contrast to the "true" transvestite, there are borderline cases where, perhaps, a person's desire to cross-dress is a result of "gender discomfort," rather than conscious sexual stimulation. On a linear spectrum showing transvestism at one end and transsexualism at the other, this individual would be placed more toward the transsexual side.

1. Because the ratio of male transsexuals to female transsexuals is about 4:1, I shall discuss only male transsexualism in this article to avoid confusion. Feelings, attitudes, and characteristics are exactly reversed in the female transsexual.

However, he does not wish to relinquish his male organs nor live life "completely" as a woman. His sex organ means something to him and gives him pleasure, but to the extent that he feels uncomfortable in the role of a man, he becomes a "borderline" case between transvestism and transsexualism.

The true transsexual, on the other hand, feels he *is* a woman; he identifies with women, is deeply unhappy with his maleness and all of its evidence, particularly the genitalia, which he wishes changed surgically to conform with his psychological sex. "Dressing," which satisfies the transvestite, is not sexually exciting to the transsexual. It only temporarily appeases him and has been likened by one doctor to the taking of aspirin for a brain tumor headache. The transsexual wishes to be and function as a member of the opposite sex, not just to dress as one. To this end, self-castration and other mutilations are quite common, and suicide threats as well as actual attempts are not rare. While the transvestite sees his sex organ as one of pleasure, the transsexual is disgusted by it, as well as his secondary sex characteristics, and wishes them all removed or altered.

Thus, even though a clear cut scientific distinction between the two syndromes cannot be made, the person's attitudes toward the physical sex organs as signs of masculinity seem to be the main point of distinction between them. It is quite possible that a great many transvestites are actually transsexuals, but in lesser degrees. For the remainder of this article, however, the term "transsexual" will refer to the "full-fledged" transsexual, for whom the need for the sex reassignment operation is his end goal and means to future happiness—his passport to acceptance into society as the woman he really is.

The confusion between transsexualism and homosexuality centers around the preference of both types of individuals for a sex or living partner of the same anatomical sex. The difference is, however, that while the homosexual knows and feels he is a man, the transsexual knows and feels he is a woman.

To him, the desire or preference for men is purely a heterosexual interest and he is, in fact, "turned off" by the thought of or reference to any relationship with other women. Even though he may have married a woman at some time in his life, biographies and autobiographies typically indicate that such actions were attempts to "make a man of myself" or conform to society's demand in order to appease relatives.

Is, then, a transsexual a homosexual? If one considers the anatomy, yes; but if one believes a transsexual's feelings as evident in his comments ("Men are all the same—they just want one thing from us women"), then the answer must be no.

Although transsexuals do not feel they are homosexual, they often know that they are regarded as such by most people who know them. A remark that would be of interest to readers of Scheff and Becker was made by "K" in her autobiography: "If all the world thinks of you as being homosexual, it is very difficult not to have that image imposed upon you, to resist it in your own mind." Even while socially labeled a homosexual, however, if such is the case, the homosexual life is no answer to the transsexual's problems. I must agree with Gagnon and Simon that, "This prepossessing concern on the part of nonhomosexuals with the purely sexual aspect" of life is not a totally adequate way in which to categorize people. Transsexuals must also "come to terms with the problems that are attendant upon being a member of society" and those problems go much deeper than just sexual activity.

Prevalence of and Limitations on the Study of Transsexualism

There are an estimated 2,000 transsexuals in this country, and, if the "borderline" cases described as transvestites are included, the figure runs over 10,000. Probably the most accurate minimal estimate of the prevalence of transsexualism is a ratio reported by Dr. Ira B. Pauly in 1968 of 1:100,000 of the general population, the rate for men to women being approximately 4:1.

By March of 1969, Dr. Harry Benjamin, who pioneered much of the work done with transsexuals, had observed nearly 500 male transsexuals and 100 females, and diagnosis and observation is now being conducted or contemplated at medical centers and in universities throughout the country, including not only at Johns Hopkins, where it began in 1966, but at the University of Minnesota, Stanford University, University of Washington, University of Oregon and UCLA.

Opportunities in research clinics here are limited, however; subjects selected must meet certain requirements (typically they must be 21 or over, must have a clean police record except for impersonation violations, must agree to follow-up treatment, and the like) in order to be accepted into the programs. Because of these requirements and because the conversion process is a long and involved one, including extensive interviews with psychologists, psychiatrists, gynecologists, and plastic surgeons, many transsexuals go abroad for the operation, which has meant the loss of much scientific data that could have been compiled had they been treated here.

Characteristics of the Transsexual

Childhood Cross-Gender Identification

Many of the "symptoms" of transsexualism are also characteristic of the normal child growing up, and the following is not intended to be interpreted as a list of characteristics common only to transsexuals. Any one of these singly and of itself would not necessarily be cause for concern on a parent's part; the transsexual, however, typically has a great many or all of these traits. A son growing up with manifestations of all these characteristics would cause the average parent a great deal of concern.

The most obvious cross-gender symptoms relate to female clothing preferences, although this is one of the most common expressions of normal childhood role-playing as well. The point at which this behavior is construed as a symptom of cross-gender orientation is when it is done in fulfillment of a definite need, done excessively, done in secret, or done over the protest of the parents. The child may become very angry if denied the pleasure of dressing. He is also often overly concerned with his mother's appearance in terms of what she wears, how she looks, and so on. One boy insisted at 22 months that he was a girl, and from the moment he learned to walk wore his mother's shoes. He liked dressing in girls' clothing as often as he was allowed and stuffed animals inside his clothes to look pregnant.

Another symptom of transsexualism is feminine behavior as it shows in speech inflections, mannerisms, and hand gestures. This is also an index used in "diagnosing" homosexuality and, again, not completely reliable by itself.

Childhood play patterns are probably better indicators of real feelings of gender orientation. Typically, transsexuals play the mother or sister when "playing house" and the nurse when "playing doctor."

The Draw-A-Person test is a device which is felt to be revealing in the measurement of attitudes. The gender of the first person drawn is supposed to reflect the child's gender identity. A study in 1966 by Money and Wang showed that almost two-thirds of a group of "juvenile effeminates" drew a girl first, in contrast to the usually recorded one-fourth for that age group.

Many of the transsexuals even preferred cross-gender household duties to those associated with their own sex. One preferred washing dishes and hanging clothes to even playing outdoors with the boys. The following is from an autobiography of a man now in his early thirties:

I hated feeding the chickens because I was afraid of them. I didn't want to feed the pigs because they smelled so bad. I didn't like bringing in wood for the fireplace because I got dirty carrying it. I kept envying the girls who seemed always to be helping with the cooking and sewing and playing little games.

Another trait characteristically feminine was the refusal to fight, even to defend oneself physically. As this same man recalls later:

Soon I was being chased home from school every night, and if caught up with was usually given a beating. When my stepfather learned about this, and how I refused to fight and would just shake with fear and cry, he told me that the next time I was chased home from school and didn't stand up and make a fight of it, and win, he would whip me with a strap. So instead of one beating a day I began getting two. Mother realized that nothing would ever make me stand up for myself, and so she arranged to have me transferred to a public school. In this new school, as in all previous schools, I got along fine for awhile. Then the same thing started all over again and I was regularly chased home and beaten. Finally this got so bad that my teacher would send me home fifteen minutes earlier, so that I could avoid the other boys.

Another transsexual said in her autobiography, "my mannerisms . . . were probably more feminine than those of most of the 'real' girls."

Several authors indicate that probably the best detectors of cross-gender identity are other children. Just as in the example above, children can sense when one of them is different, and they are quick to label those boys as sissies. Another example from Benjamin:

My heart cried out to wear the pretty dresses that the other girls were wearing and it was a torture to watch them laughing and being so happy. At the same time the boys, realizing that I was a little odd, began tormenting me. They seemed to get a lot of pleasure out of pushing me around, and even the smallest boys would bully me because they knew I would never fight back. Then it wasn't long before the girls began staying away from me too, and I was completely alone. I got to the point that going to bed at night was my only escape. I wasn't yet seven years old, and I wanted to die.

The peer groups' influence in the development of a psychologically healthy child is made very clear.

Adult Manifestations

The single most distinguishable manifestation of transsexualism in the adult male (other than the psychological feeling that he is a woman) is probably the complete disgust for and hatred of the male sex organs. He expresses bitterness at being "cheated" by God, and wants to be rid of all semblances of maleness.

Finally, a most convincing hospital report on a transsexual shows the following:

After being carried to the level of corneal anesthesia during narco-synthesis with sodium amytal, his first reaction upon slow recovery was feminine. His feminine affections including voice, defensive gestures, were even more prominent than on a waking level. He repeated his story [details of his life up to that time] as before, adding only that at the age of three, he felt that his older sisters were getting more toys and prettier clothes and were loved more by his parents because they were girls.

Process of Sex Reassignment

The term "sex reassignment" refers to the entire process of changing one's sex over to that of the opposite sex, to the extent to which this can be done. This includes not only the conversion operation itself, which in the case of the male transsexual is the actual penectomy, castration, and subsequent construction of an artificial vagina, but the hormone treatments which take place over a considerable period of time prior to the operation itself. The results of hormone (estrogen) and other therapy are: an often very satisfactory breast development; change in voice pitch; shrinking of the prostate and some testicular atrophy, resulting in fewer involuntary erections; decrease in body hair except pubic and beard growth where distribution remains the same, and scalp growth which often accelerates; and redistribution of weight from shoulders to hips to a more womanly appearance overall. The extent to which any or all of these take place varies according to the dosage, the duration of the treatment period, and the individual response. Generally, the onset of any of the above, and in the cases of prolonged treatment, *all* of the above, is of great psychological benefit to the transsexual patient. Frame of mind improves at each new sign of womanhood.

The legal status of the sex conversion operation itself varies from state to state. Generally legal writers have concluded that it would not be illegal, since, in states which have maiming or "mayhem statutes," it must be shown that there was "malicious intent" on the part of the perpetrator. In addition, there would be considerable room for question in states with mayhem statutes (laws originally derived from feudal England barring soldiers from disabling themselves so as to be rendered incapable of defending themselves in war) as to whether the genitalia come within the intent of such laws.

The fact is, nevertheless, that the legality of the sex conversion operation has never been tested in court. The traditional conservatism of the research institutions engaged in the study and treatment of transsexualism and the high standards and reputations which are associated with them will certainly help protect the entire operation from stirring such disapproval as to come to the courts' attention; and clinics such as Johns Hopkins are taking all the necessary precautions to avoid the possibility of civil suits as well.

THE TRANSSEXUAL AS A DEVIANT TYPE: SOCIAL "PROCESSING"

How He Becomes a Transsexual

It is not yet apparent exactly what causes transsexualism. The more research that has been done on sex and what determines sex, the less we have ended up being able to definitively set forth. To the "man on the street," there are males and females and it is as simple as that. But recent research and thought has determined that there are several "components" to maleness and femaleness. Money and Hampsons have set forth six criteria of sex: chromosomal, gonadal, external reproductive, internal reproductive,

hormonal, and psychological. Many possible sexual anomalies could arise out of such a matrix, but the transsexual's plight is that of being originally "male" in all but the last criterion (psychological). Even the sex reassignment operation will not technically transform him into a "true" woman, becuase he will always retain the first criterion—he will remain chromosomally a male.

The etiology of transsexualism is thought to be more psychologically related than somatically related, although some do feel that eventually some genetic abnormality or "biological reason" for the transsexual phenomenon will be discovered. For now, much emphasis is placed on psychological and social learning factors centering around childhood experiences.

The typical pattern of family life shows a fairly masculine mother who dominates an often-absent or fairly passive father, and who maintains a long-term "too close" relationship with the son, both physically and psychologically. The criticism, of course, of attributing causation to childhood backgrounds and parent-types such as this is that there are also many more people whose parents fit the described molds but who did not become transsexuals. It appears there must then be constitutional or some other contributing factors.

Another interesting theory is that males who tend toward transsexualism are simply trying to escape the responsibilities of the male role—people who "didn't make it" as a man so are looking for the only other alternative which is to become a woman. Case histories such as the boy who at 22 months declared he was a girl, and the like, cast some doubt on the acceptability of this explanation, however.

Finally, there is a position which says that all people, male or female, naturally tend toward femaleness when growing up, largely due to the fact that the people who surround them at early ages (mother, teachers, babysitters) are women, and that in the absence of strong influence from a dominant male figure somewhere along the way in those early years, it is predictable that a boy will be somewhat feminized.

Whatever the cause is discovered to be, the condition of transsexualism is at present psychologically incurable. Two conclusions have been made based on patients studied: most transsexuals have been found to be nonpsychotic by standard diagnostic criteria, and the transsexual's state is, as one psychiatrist put it, "inaccessible to psychotherapy."

Concerning this latter point, I would like to suggest the possibility that the psychiatrists' individual and personal attitudes and predispositions toward the subject may play a very important part in the failure of psychiatric treatment in the plight of the transsexual. As Szasz points out,

Problems in human relations can be analyzed, interpreted, and given meaning only within given social and ethical contexts. Accordingly, it does make a difference—arguments to the contrary notwithstanding—what the psychiatrist's socioethical orientations happen to be; for these will influence his ideas on what is wrong with the patient, what deserves comment or interpretation, in what possible directions change might be desirable, and so forth.

A case in point here was cited by Benjamin in *The Transsexual Phenomenon:*

When H. told me that he had been under psychiatric treatment in his home town, I suggested that I consult with the psychiatrist by phone to get his psychiatric diagnosis and see what possibly could be done to calm his emotional turmoil with estrogen in addition to the psychotherapy he was receiving. The doctor did phone me, but to my astonishment he took a non-medical strictly moralistic stand. "This man wants an operation," he said priestlike, "and naturally we cannot tamper with our God-given bodies. His wife should leave him, children or no children. H. is a degenerate and a no-good scoundrel" or something to that effect. The doctor had no psychiatric diagnosis to give me. A letter in which I asked again his medical (psychiatric) opinion remained unanswered. H., a deeply disturbed and bewildered young man, then told that his sessions with this psychiatrist had been expensive hours of nothing but argumentation and berating on the part of the doctor without any psychological bene-

fit to him. After every session he was worse than before.

Another psychiatrist examined H. later at my suggestion, found him to be nonpsychotic, of superior intelligence, a greatly disturbed transsexual for whom psychotherapy in present available forms would be useless, as far as any cure might be concerned. Operation was suggested and performed in 1965.

[She wrote me in November of 1965]: "I have found happiness that I never dreamed possible. I adore being a girl and would go through 10 operations if I had to, in order to be what I am now. . . . The whole world looks so beautifully different."

Another handicap for the transsexual is, in Scheff's terms, the "payoff" (or lack of it) for the patient or physician. He is not referring to a necessarily just financial payoff, but political or ideological "payoff" as well. That is, on the one hand, if a psychiatrist feels he may come under fire by a conservative local medical or professional association, this is certain to have a bearing on his recommendations. On the other hand, the patient's high degree of motivation to obtain the sex conversion operation—his "payoff"—will likely influence his answers to the psychiatrist's questions, particularly since the transsexual, who is often extremely intelligent, sees the interview as a hurdle to be gotten over and the psychiatrist as a sort of judge on whom his future happiness rests.

How Society Perceives Him

There are several ways of examining how "society" looks at the transsexual, depending upon what part of society is considered.

The subject of sexuality and sex role identification is practically a sacred matter for the average person. The "man on the street" (who is either unaware of or does not care about the various sexual anomalies) has no tolerance for those individuals with a dissonance in their sexuality; this includes homosexuals, transvestites, and hermaphrodites, as well as transsexuals.

In our society, the stage, carnival, or masquerade are the only places where a male is by custom tolerated to play the female role or a female the male role. A dichotomous distinction between male and female, with no allowance for a possible spectrum of variation, makes it impossible for the transsexual to maintain his or her self-respect.

One's maleness must be flawless, and even from very early ages, playmates and parents condition boys to "be a man" with admonitions like, "boys don't cry," and "stand up and fight like a man." Any violation of sexuality such as an effeminate walk, vocal lisp, and the like is strongly resented, and such people are frequently ostracized. Emotions run high, even among doctors (recall H.'s psychiatrist) who, regardless of what they learn in the study of medicine, were reared in the same social environment. Thus, to the average person, any man who wants to turn into a woman "has got to be nuts!"

Basically, then, we would have to say that the transsexual does possess an undesirably unique characteristic which is negatively sanctioned by society in general, although like homosexuality, transsexualism will probably be tolerated more now than in years past because it does not represent any real threat to the status quo as do other current types of deviance such as drug addicts, pushers, or the "campus radicals." Transsexuals are basically introverted and nonaggressive, and, in short, there are more threatening forms of deviance for society to concern itself with.

Finally, that part of "society" which has been made aware of the transsexual's plight with an intelligent and thorough explanation of the syndrome has responded sympathetically and with tolerance. Johns Hopkins issued a press release in 1966 explaining transsexualism, its symptoms, etiology to the extent it was known, and their work with transsexuals. "By treating the public maturely and in confidence, the medical profession received in turn a vote of public endorsement that made the pursuance of its new work feasible without legal or pressure group harassment."

Benjamin, in his introduction to *Transsexualism and Sex Reassignment,* cites two

instances of apparently more tolerant attitudes emerging since the time of the Johns Hopkins press release:

Early in 1967, a rather striking symptom of progress in attitude occurred in San Francisco. A number of transsexuals in female clothes were repeatedly picked up by the police as prostitutes. Officer Elliott R. Blackstone, with the consent of the Police Department, decided to do something about it. He started procuring legitimate jobs for these transsexuals as women, and was signally successful with some of them.

Also, early in 1967, a Center for Special Problems was started by the San Francisco Health Department, at the suggestion of Dr. Joel Fort. One of these problems was gender-role disorientation. Twenty to twenty-five transsexuals were accepted for counseling and even endocrine treatments. They met once a week, dressed as women, in group therapy.

Transsexualism may then begin to follow the path of decriminalization toward a mental health context, just as homosexuality and alcoholism have begun to do.

How the Transsexual Perceives Himself

Regardless of any tolerance or sympathy shown the transsexual today, the fact remains that during the years when those transsexuals who are now being treated were growing up, they were ostracized, beaten up, labeled sissies, and generally accorded lower social status by their classmates. Usually their differences were first made publicly visible at the time they entered school, and these were painful years for them. Their autobiographies may reveal that they were aware of themselves as "different" before beginning school, but all of them reveal an unhappy life once the "degradation ceremonies" attendant to school life (beatings, name-calling) were begun. Given the visibility of his feminine feelings and the consequent labeling as a "sissy," the transsexual experienced in a very real way Goffman's "spoiled identity"–low self-esteem, fear, shame, frustration, despair, while at the same time feeling disgust for his male body and resentment and bitterness, especially in later adolescence at God's having "done this" to him.

I was a freak of a girl, one who had to look like a boy. . . . I think that no pain on this earth can equal the pain that I experienced at that time of my life.

If I was forced by the teachers to participate in games, I was always the last one chosen when sides were being picked. The side that was unlucky enough to be last in choosing was stuck with me. I can't really blame them for not wanting me, since I was always doing something wrong or was unable to hold up my part of the game, so that my side would always lose.

I remember that behind the school there was a graveyard and I would go there to hide and cry. I was so confused and unhappy that I was crying much of the time.

Life has played a dirty trick on me, forcing me to live with the outer appearance of a man but the inner feelings and emotions of a woman.

It is around this time in the chronology of the patient's life that he is likely to attempt self-castration, suicide, penectomy, or other physical mutilation.

The transsexual's next move—one of trying to "unspoil" his identity—is probably one of three alternatives, depending on his age.

His first option is that of withdrawal; he may not only withdraw from school activities but from family relationships as well, spending time off in a secret woods, in his room, or in the attic trying on dresses stored there. Because of his isolation, he does not develop further interpersonally and as a result may handicap himself in obtaining help later, both in finding a doctor who will operate or recommend surgery and, if he does get the operation, in his subsequent resocialization attempts. Personality studies reveal all sorts of objectionable traits which are undoubtedly a result of early maladaptive interpersonal behavior caused by the transsexual's feelings of rejection by parents and peers.

Secondly, some transsexuals have at some point tried to rejoin the members of their morphological sex—to "make a man of myself." They have joined the Navy or married and fathered children, the latter of which was often only possible by assuming the female position during intercourse and perhaps wearing a nightgown—by fantasizing.

One individual who joined the Army said that throughout his period of service he always felt himself to be a male impersonator. Another, who joined the Navy, said, "My first six weeks of boot camp were the worst weeks of my life. Learning to adjust to Navy life was probably difficult even for the most masculine of men. For me, a person who had lived for so long as a woman, it was pure misery."

The path of least resistance and often the period of greatest happiness for many a transsexual is his joining of a female impersonator show where, in the company of other transsexuals (as well as transvestites and homosexuals), he is at last not only accepted but paid for being himself. Although his entrance into this subculture will serve to reinforce his deviance, he accepts this role as the only alternative since it provides him (at least temporary) peace of mind and money to save toward the expensive conversion operation he longs for.

Perhaps the most rewarding part of those first few weeks of training was the physical presence of so many boys with the same temperament and feelings that I had. Never before had I experienced such total acceptance. Never before had I been with so many people who understood how it felt to be a woman and be saddled with the body of a man. . . . After my first two or three days among the other impersonators, I think I knew that never again would I feel so very much alive and a part of the world around me.

Concomitant Occupational-Economic Status Deprivation

The question of lower occupational and economic status is an interesting one in that the transsexual faces *two* types of discrimination.

Preoperative Discrimination

In the preoperative period, if he is living as a male, he faces much the same treatment in securing a job that a homosexual does. In fact, he would probably be considered a homosexual by those people for whom and with whom he worked. Thus his feminine manner, speech, or other visible characteristics *may* force him into occupations where homosexuals are accepted because they are known to excel; for example, in one study of 51 patients, 10 were in show business and 6 were hairdressers at the time of their operations.

Postoperative Discrimination

In the postoperative period, and if he is living as a female in the preoperative period, he faces the same kinds of job discrimination all women face: namely, a lower pay scale regardless of type of work performed and less opportunity for upward mobility, including a lower "ceiling" on top potential position. Such discrimination, as today's feminists would be quick to point out, is hard enough to face when one has been "conditioned" for it all through life, but to have once worked as a male in perhaps a high-paying job (some were engineers, stockbrokers, attorneys, or architects) and then to start over as a woman in a new locality (which is not necessarily the only choice, but a wise decision if the social transition is to be made most painlessly) can work real financial hardship on an individual who at that point is accustomed to a higher living standard.

Legal and Quasi-Legal Discrimination

It is interesting that the law, which has no definition of sex (what constitutes maleness or femaleness) concerns itself anyway with the disposition of cases involving such. We know that there are at least six criteria that must be considered in deciding or judging questions that arise as to one's "legal sex." However, in a 1966 New York Supreme Court ruling, a converted male-to-female transsexual had applied to the New York Department of Health for a new birth certificate to be issued showing only the designation of sex as "female," and in this case the request was turned down because sex chromosomes were assumed to be the ultimate criterion for the determination of sex. This decision has been criticized not only by doctors but by legal writers as well.

Other states vary with regard to handling of birth certificate change requests. Only Illinois has a provision for issuance of a new one; other states have "alteration" statutes which allow for amendments of sex designation to be made to birth certificates. A few states allow only corrections to be made, in cases where a mistake was made at the time of birth. These hamper the transsexual a great deal in his postoperative attempts at resocialization, since the birth certificate is the basic legal record of a person's sex, age, and so on and is needed for proof of at least the latter on occasion.

The most frequent type of encounter the transsexual might have with the law is arrest for impersonating a female, an act which may come under various catchall "vagrancy" statutes, disorderly conduct statutes, or several others. One on the books in New York and used against transsexuals is a 100-year-old law which states that a person must not appear in public "disguised in a manner calculated to prevent his being identified." This law was originally passed to protect law officers from farmers who masqueraded as Indians and attacked them as they tried to enforce unpopular rent laws. Such a law might serve today to protect the unwary from helpless-looking purse snatchers or bank robbers—actually very able-bodied men disguised as women—but these involve quite different motives from the transsexual who dresses as a woman out of psychological need. The presence or absence of fraudulent intent should enter the picture, but it apparently does not in many cases. The transsexual takes a chance if he persists in going out on the street "dressed."

Finally, the transsexual's normal legal

rights, to which we are all entitled, are at least indirectly or potentially jeopardized. Irate relatives might contest a will on grounds that anyone who changed his sex must not have been of sound mind. Also, the transsexual's credibility might be challenged in a civil suit where the defendant might attempt to convince the jury that the transsexual plaintiff is dishonest anyway, changing sex, creating a new life, erasing the past, and so forth, surreptitiously. It may not be true exactly as alleged, but it would put the transsexual on the defensive, and he would again face embarrassment and possibly unwanted publicity. Generally, he would be better off to avoid litigation by going out of his way to prevent the occurrence of situations which might lead to lawsuits.

PROSPECTS FOR RESOCIALIZATION

Resocialization of the postoperative transsexual is a complex topic, for, in some respects, the sex reassignment operation has solved his problems and, in other respects, it has created new ones.

First of all, on the problem side, he has the tremendous task of creating a new identity while trying to quash the former identity. Change of *sex designation* on the birth certificate is not easy, as discussed above. Even in the states where it can be "amended," the old information is kept on file even if sealed separately or just attached to the new certificate.

Legal change of name, like change of name on the birth certificate, is on the one hand no trouble to acquire and, on the other hand, not much help to have. First of all, one need not receive the court's permission to change his name, providing his intent is not fraudulent. The purpose which a legal change of name serves is to have a permanent "legal" record of the fact that Jon Horo is, really, John Horowicz. This is precisely what the transsexual is trying to avoid; it does Marilyn Wimperly no service to have a permanent legal record showing that she is, in fact, Mervin Wimp.

The best tack to take in establishing a new identity, according to Robert Sherwin, L.L.B., in "Legal Aspects of Male Transsexualism," is to appeal to the transsexual's former school or university officials to forward an amended transcript of her grades received while a (male) student. Compliance with this request would be contingent upon the transsexual's attorney's furnishing three affidavits to the school: one assuring officials that Mervin Wimp who graduated from there is the Marilyn Wimperly who is making this request today; another submitted by the physician explaining what took place (the nature of the transsexual phenomenon and the results of the operation); and the third, a sort of biography submitted by the transsexual to evidence good faith and seriousness of purpose in making the request.

Compliance with the request would depend upon the mercy as well as the size, I suspect, of the school or university. Obtaining this transcript is a perfect first step in creating a new identity for the transsexual and has apparently been accomplished by some to date, resulting in a link with the past but with no mention of the transsexual's former status. It also serves as proof of identity and often includes date of birth, which then may be used to change driver's license and social security information.

Gradually, step by step, and by revealing the past to only the necessary and appropriate officials, a new identity emerges and firms up. By making appointments and having an attorney explain the request at each point rather than simply popping up to the window clerk, sincerity of intent is more firmly established, and the objectives are probably more easily attained.

Another problem, not so materially profound, perhaps, as psychologically so, is the effect that the change-of-sex procedure has on relatives. The transsexual is in many instances an "ex-husband" and "ex-father." It takes a great deal of empathy on a child's or wife's part to understand that one's father or husband is now a woman. At a young age, it is understandable what a damaging effect this may have on a son or daughter. Then, of course, there is the dissolution of the marriage and property division before the operation takes place.

The new female must be able to pass as a woman in many more situations now, and this requires electrolysis in many patients for the removal of beard growth, which can be an expensive, as well as a lengthy process. Also, most postoperative transsexuals at first overdo the dress and makeup of their new role. One physician stated that a newly operated-upon woman might come into his office for counseling in a cocktail dress more appropriate for the theatre.

On the plus side of the picture, the transsexual now will probably experience more acceptance on the part of both males and females than she has ever known before. This makes her "deliriously happy," and she typically feels that all the pain and suffering endured in order to have the operation were well worth it.

A study of the results of 51 operations showed that 17 rated their operations' success "good" (total life situation including sex life had to be successful and a good integration into the world of women with acceptance by society and their families was essential), and 27 rated them "satisfactory" (here the results were lacking in some area above, but otherwise fulfilled the patient's wishes).

As Gagnon and Simon point out, the sexuality aspect is only one part of life's total experience, and, in the transsexual's life up until the time of the operation, this has completely dominated his existence. How can a person who is so preoccupied with gender disorientation concentrate on the everyday problems of growing up and become a productive member of society—the normal "problems of living"? As mentioned previously, he cannot very well, and often ends up with a rather "inadequate" personality from a nongender perspective. Given the transsexual's greatly improved mental state, his potential for successful integration back into society—a sort of re-birth—while restricted by the new problems created, is nevertheless good. His acceptance in the new role is often much greater than

acceptance of him as he was, and the degree to which he successfully integrates into society as a woman is in many respects up to him. There will not be a blank on a job application which asks, "Were you ever of another sex than your present one?" but if he chooses to offer this information to his coworkers over lunch, he is hampering his chances for success by his own hand.

While some transsexuals are disillusioned by the life of a woman, in that it does not materialize into their fantasized world of white horses and charming princes, and some express disappointment specifically in their sex life (not being able to achieve orgasm as a woman 100% of the time or at all in some cases), for the part they appear to be happy with their decision and better off than before the operation. The following describes one patient's before-and-after adjustment to others.

At the time of K's psychiatric examination preliminary to surgery, he was described as having a "somewhat restricted range of affectual response," and as leading "a rather isolated existence with no evidence throughout of any warm interpersonal relationships." His psychological-emotional condition subsequent to "sex-change" would seem, therefore, to be much improved: Today, K gives the impression of a warm and friendly personality. She exhibits unusual tolerance and compassion for the problems of others, and is, as indicated, a source of strength for some others who are less stable. Her own stability has definitely increased during the period since her surgery, and she continues to function in society far more effectively as a woman than she ever was able to do as a man.

Prospects for resocialization, then, are good, if the patient shows foresight into the problems that lie ahead and can exercise keen perception in handling new and unfamiliar situations. In short, a great deal depends upon the individual.

QUESTIONS FOR DISCUSSION

1. Professor Dank contrasts "homosexuality-as-mental-illness" with "homo-

sexuality-as-way-of-life." Which point of
view do you feel is most defensible?
What is the evidence upon which you
based your decision?

2. After reading this set of articles, list the
new concepts, ideas, or perspectives
that you have learned. What was the
single most important insight you have
gained?

3. What do you believe to be some of the
widespread myths still held by many
people concerning homosexuality? What
do you feel accounts for the persistence
of these myths?

4. Read *Tearoom Trade* by Laud Humphreys. Discuss the ethics of doing this
type of research.

5. How tolerant is your community of gay
life styles? How do you account for
attitudinal differences in this realm?

6. Why have female homosexuals generally
been overlooked in the study of deviant
sexual life styles?

7. What are the differences among transsexualism, transvestism, and homosexuality? Any similarities worth noting?

8. How do you stand on castration as a
social control mechanism for the more
aggressive and forcible sexual offenders?

9. Why is it that sex offenders have the
lowest rate of recidivism of all major
incarcerated violators paroled to the
community?

10. Does your state have a sex psychopath
law? If it does, what are its central provisions? Do these provisions provide due
process for the offender? Social protection for the community?

11. In 1974, the American Psychiatric Association (APA) membership voted to remove homosexuality as a psychiatric
disorder from its classification of diseases. What makes a disorder a disorder?
Can any psychiatric problem be removed simply by majority vote? What
are the long range implications of this
"disease by vote" approach?

BIBLIOGRAPHY

Archilles, Nancy. "The Development of the Homosexual Bar as an Institution." In *Sexual Deviance,* edited by John H. Gagnon and William
Simon. New York: Harper and Row, 1967.

Benjamin, H. *The Transsexual Phenomenon.* New
York: Ace, 1966.

Berg, Charles, and A. M. Drich. *Homosexuality.*
London: George Allen and Unwin, 1958.

Bergler, Edmund, M. D. *Homosexuality, Disease or
Way of Life?* New York: Collier Books,
1962.

Bieber, Irving et al. *Homosexuality, A Psychoanalytic Study of Male Homosexuals,* New
York: Basic Books, 1962.

Caprio, Frank S., M. D. *Female Homosexuality, A
Psychodynamic Study of Lesbianism.* New
York: Grove Press, 1962.

Cory, Donald Webster. *The Homosexual in America.* New York: Paperback Library, 1951.

Ellis, Albert. *Homosexuality, Its Causes and Cure.*
New York: Lyle Stewart, 1965.

Gagnon, John H., and Evelyn Hooker. "Sexual
Behavior: Deviation: Social Aspects." *Ency-
clopedia of Social Sciences* XIV, 215–33.

Gagnon, J. H., and W. Simon. *Sexual Deviance.*
New York: Harper and Row, 1967.

Gebhard, P. H., Gagnon, J. H., Pomeroy, W. B.,
and Christenson, C. V. *Sex Offenders: An
Analysis of Types.* New York: Harper and
Row, 1965.

Green, R., and J. Money. *Transsexualism and Sex
Reassignment.* Baltimore: Johns Hopkins
Press, 1969.

Hoffman, Martin. *The Gay World, Male Homosexuality and the Social Creation of Evil.* New
York: Basic Books, 1965.

Hooker, Evelyn. "A Preliminary Analysis of Group
Behavior of Homosexuals." *The Journal of
Psychology* XLII (1965), 217–25.

Humphreys, Laud. *Tearoom Trade.* Chicago: Aldine, 1970.

Leroy, John P. *The Homosexual and His Society—
A View From Within.* New York: The Citadel
Press, 1963.

Linder, Robert. "Homosexuality and the Contemporary Scene." *A View From Within.* New
York: The Citadel Press, 1963.

Marmor, Judd. *Sexual Inversion, The Multiple
Routes of Homosexuality.* New York: Basic
Books, 1965.

Morse, Benjamin. *The Lesbian.* Derby, Conn.:
Monarch Books, 1961.

Ovesey, Lionel. *Homosexuality and Pseudo-homo-
sexuality.* Science House, 1969.

Ruitenbeek, Hendrick M. *The Problems of Homosexuality in Modern Society.* New York: E.
P. Dutton, 1963.

Sagarin, Edward, and MacNamara, Donal. *Problems
of Sex Behavior.* New York: Thomas Y.
Crowell, 1968.

Schoefield, Michael. *Sociological Aspects of Homosexuality.* Little, Brown, 1965.

Simon, W., and J. H. Gagnon. "Femininity in the
Lesbian Community." *Social Problems* 15
(Fall, 1967), 212–21.

Ward, D. A., and G. Kassebaum. "Homosexuality: A Mode of Adaptation in a Prison for Women." *Social Problems* 12 (Fall, 1964), 159–·77.

Weinberg, Martin S. "The Male Homosexual: Age-Related Variations in Social and Psychological Characteristics." *Social Problems* 17, (1970), 527–37.

Weinberg, Martin S., and Bell, Alan P. (eds.). *Homosexuality: An Annotated Bibliography.* New York: Harper and Row, 1972.

West, Donald J. "Parental Figures in the Genesis of Male Homosexuality." *International Journal of Social Psychiatry* 5(1959), 85–97.

Westwood, Gordon. *Society and the Homosexual.* New York: E. P. Dutton, 1963.

7

Mental Illness

Throughout history, the mentally ill have been considered deviant and have aroused fear, revulsion, and disgust. One of the earliest interpretations was that they were possessed by demons, and part of our lingering antipathy is surely attributable to this demonological explanation of the cause of their affliction. Until relatively recent times, in fact, the more severely disturbed were considered to be almost nonhuman and proper subjects to be burned, stoned, beaten, and persecuted. Those whose problems and aberrations were somewhat more tolerable remained the responsibility of family and community. Every community had its share of mentally ill persons.

Although the mental hospital dates back to the first known house for "lunatics" in Byzantium in the fourth century of the Christian era, mental hospitals were relatively rare until the end of the eighteenth century. Those that existed were uniformly foul, prison-like establishments hardly suitable for human beings. In the United States, for example, as late as 1840 there were only fourteen public asylums housing about twenty-five hundred persons. As long as the society remained largely rural, the mentally ill either wandered from place to place or somehow survived in their local communities. The cumulative effects of industrialization—for example, urbanization, increasing

community complexity, and the weakening of family and community ties—led to the development of the large custodial asylum in England, France, and the United States. The urban industrial community simply could no longer feed, clothe, shelter, tolerate, or maintain deviant persons. The asylum served to remove the disturbed and disturbing members of a community—on a long-term and often permanent basis. The mentally ill were already considered to be moral lepers, but the asylum added official stigma and indescribably brutal living conditions. Not even the simplest amenities were provided the inmates in many of these institutions.

Until recently, the status of the mentally ill remained very low. Lately, however, a number of revolutionary changes have begun to occur. Although there is still fear and misunderstanding of the disturbed, attitude change has occurred. Changes in treatment are also most evident. There is widespread use of psychoactive drugs; more and more patients are being treated in the community, in outpatient centers, and in general hospitals. The mental hospital itself, although far from transformed, has also been improving in the quality of its care. We are in the midst of a profound revolution—one which promises to reshape both the idea of who is sick and the management of the deviant who is "sick."

Part of this change has occurred as the result of increased attention given to mental illness by the federal government. In a message to the 88th Congress, the late President Kennedy in 1963 suggested some of the dimensions of the problems which faced the society.

We as a Nation have long neglected the mentally ill and the mentally retarded. This neglect must end, if our Nation is to live up to its own standards of compassion and dignity and achieve the maximum use of its manpower.

This tradition of neglect must be replaced by forceful and far-reaching programs carried out at all levels of government, by private individuals and by State and local agencies in every part of the Union.

We must act—

to bestow the full benefits of our society on those who suffer from mental disabilities;

to prevent the occurrence of mental illness and mental retardation wherever and whenever possible;

to provide for early diagnosis and continuous and comprehensive care, in the community, of those suffering from these disorders;

to stimulate improvements in the level of care given the mentally disabled in our State and private institutions, and to reorient those programs to a community-centered approach;

to reduce, over a number of years, and by hundreds of thousands, the persons confined to these institutions;

to retain in and return to the community the mentally ill and mentally retarded, and there to restore and revitalize their lives through better health programs and strengthened educational and rehabilitation services; and

to reinforce the will and capacity of our communities to meet these problems, in order that the communities, in turn, can reinforce the will and capacity of individuals and individual families.

We must promote—to the best of our ability and by all possible and appropriate means—the mental and physical health of all our citizens.

The first three selections deal in various ways with the definition of mental illness. In a very controversial essay which has had a profound influence on the professions of psychiatry, psychology, sociology, and related disciplines, Dr. Thomas S. Szasz categorically rejects the concept of mental illness. Speaking of the "Myth of Mental Illness," Szasz believes that the term "mental illness" is broadly used to describe certain personality and social disabilities that have nothing to do with health or illness but instead refer to deviations from psychosocial, ethical, and moral norms. Mental illness is not, strictly speaking, medical in any acceptable sense of that term. Mental illness, instead, is a name for a multitude of problems of living. The myth of mental illness is a social tranquilizer. It leads us, implicitly, to believe that human interaction and existence would be more secure, harmonious, and satisfying if it were not for the negative and disruptive influences of psychopathology. To achieve a better life and a more tranquil world, Dr. Szasz urges that we forego the notion of mental illness and concentrate our attention on the real problems of living, ' whether," as he says, "these be biologic, economic, political or sociopsychological."

These views have not gone uncontested. Any number of clinicians and experimental scientists have responded to Szasz's "heresy." Nevertheless, in addition to provoking extensive controversy, "The Myth of Mental Illness" and related essays by Szasz have raised value issues which cannot be resolved solely within the scientific sphere.

In the dispute about the nature of mental illness and its characteristics, the focus is nearly always on the symptomatic behavior of the patient. Depending on his symptoms and signs, he is given a diagnosis that ranges from some form of organic impairment, such as acute or chronic brain syndrome, through the functional psychoses, such as schizophrenia or manic-depressive psychosis, to the pscyhoneuroses and character disorders. The point is that such a diagnosis and evaluation are the outcome of the process of becoming mentally ill. Professor Thomas Scheff in

"The Role of the Mentally Ill and the Dynamics of Mental Disorder: A Research Framework" is interested in the dynamics of becoming labeled "mentally ill." He emphasizes the societal reaction to the initial deviance of the patient and the process through which the patient comes to think of himself as mentally ill and to act out the illness role. Since a process, by its very nature is continuous, Dr. Scheff attempts to unravel the process by positing a series of nine hypotheses which deal with the various time slices of the process of labeling. Scheff prefers to speak of mental illness as residual deviance—conduct that "goes without saying" is unthinkable for most persons. This selection concludes that whether defined as mental illness or residual deviance, labeling is the most important element in the process.

In the next selection entitled "On Being Sane in Insane Places," Professor Rosenhan asks "If sanity and insanity exist, how shall we know them?" The question is an important one, even though at first glance it may appear to have a whimsical quality. There is an alarming lack of agreement on such terms as "schizophrenic," "mental illness " "normality," and "abnormality." The crux of the matter is whether or not the characteristics associated with diagnoses of mental illness occur in the patients or in the social settings and contexts in which the professional observers are located. One way of answering such a question would be to have normal persons secretly admitted to psychiatric hospitals and then find out whether or not they would be discovered to be sane. This article describes such an experiment. It involved eight sane persons who gained admission to twelve different hospitals. The evidence points up the fact that sanity cannot be distinguished from insanity. One of the chief reasons for this is that the hospital environment itself produces a set of conditions wherein misunderstanding of the meanings of behavior can (and does) easily occur. Eleven of the pseudopatients were diagnosed as schizophrenic and one, with the same symptoms, as manic-depressive. The signifi-

cance and consequences of depersonalization, powerlessness, segregation, mortification, and self-labeling are vividly described.

In dealing with the complexities of defining mental illness the problems of diagnosis, and the effects of labeling, it is often easy to lose sight of the fact that many persons do exhibit "difficult" behavior. Instead of viewing mental patients as helpless and unfortunate individuals, Ludwig and Farrelly pursue the theory that "schizophrenic patients become 'chronic' simply because they choose to do so," and that these types of patients have at their disposal an effective array of counter-therapeutic techniques that they use against staff efforts to rehabilitate them. These particular attitudes and behaviors are termed "the weapons of insanity."

Included in this arsenal is the concept of "squatter's rights"—the idea that many efforts directed toward rehabilitation fail because patients do not want to be dispossessed from their adopted hospital homeland. For some it becomes the "good ship Lollipop," where one is protected from harm and relieved of major responsibilities and demands. Professors Ludwig and Farrelly contend that one of the central problems of treating the chronic schizophrenic involves the issue of helping the patient realize that he is responsible for his actions. The fact that this philosophy runs counter to much current clinical thought is discussed, as well as a number of ethical issues—including such provocative questions as whether patients should have the right to opt out of living in the "real world" and whether society should provide some sort of haven for these persons in the form of mental hospitals.

The last issue which Ludwig and Farrelly raise—whether a patient has the right to opt out of living in normal society—seems to have been answered negatively by recent trends in the management and treatment of mental illness. Traditional forms of institutionalization are gradually being replaced by forms of treatment which attempt to keep the "patient" within the community—on drugs in outpatient centers, and in general hospitals. There has been a great deal of experimentation with alternatives to institu-

tional care. Many of these forms will be illustrated in the last section of the book.

THE MYTH OF MENTAL ILLNESS
Thomas S. Szasz

My aim in this essay is to raise the question "Is there such a thing as mental illness?" and to argue that there is not. Since the notion of mental illness is extremely widely used nowadays, inquiry into the ways in which this term is employed would seem to be especially indicated. Mental illness, of course, is not literally a "thing"—or physical object—and hence it can "exist" only in the same sort of way in which other theoretical concepts exist. Yet, familiar theories are in the habit of posing, sooner or later—at least to those who come to believe in them—as "objective truths" (or "facts"). During certain historical periods, explanatory conceptions such as deities, witches, and microorganisms appeared not only as theories but as self-evident *causes* of a vast number of events. I submit that today mental illness is widely regarded in a somewhat similar fashion, that is, as the cause of innumerable diverse happenings. As an antidote to the complacent use of the notion of mental illness—whether as a self-evident phenomenon, theory, or cause—let us ask this question: What is meant when it is asserted that someone is mentally ill?

In what follows I shall describe briefly the main uses to which the concept of mental illness has been put. I shall argue that this notion has outlived whatever usefulness it might have had and that it now functions merely as a convenient myth.

From *The American Psychologist,* 15 (February 1960), 113–18. Reprinted by permission of the American Psychological Association. Dr. Szasz is Professor of Psychiatry at the Upstate Medical School, Syracuse, New York.

MENTAL ILLNESS AS A SIGN OF BRAIN DISEASE

The notion of mental illness derives its main support from such phenomena as syphilis of the brain or delirious conditions—intoxications, for instance—in which persons are known to manifest various peculiarities or disorders of thinking and behavior. Correctly speaking, however, these are diseases of the brain, not of the mind. According to one school of thought, *all* so-called mental illness is of this type. The assumption is made that some neurological defect, perhaps a very subtle one, will ultimately be found for all the disorders of thinking and behavior. Many contemporary psychiatrists, physicians, and other scientists hold this view. This position implies that people *cannot* have troubles—expressed in what are *now called* "mental illnesses"—because of differences in personal needs, opinions, social aspirations, values, and so on. *All problems in living* are attributed to physicochemical processes which in due time will be discovered by medical research.

"Mental illnesses" are thus regarded as basically no different than all other diseases (that is, of the body). The only difference, in this view, between mental and bodily diseases is that the former, affecting the brain, manifest themselves by means of mental symptoms; whereas the latter, affecting other organ systems (for example, the skin, liver, etc.), manifest themselves by means of symptoms referable to those parts of the body. This view rests on and expresses what are, in my opinion, two fundamental errors.

In the first place, what central nervous system symptoms would correspond to a skin eruption or a fracture? It would *not* be some emotion or complex bit of behavior. Rather, it would be blindness or a paralysis of some part of the body. The crux of the matter is that a disease of the brain, analogous to a disease of the skin or bone, is a neurological defect, and not a problem in living. For example, a *defect* in a person's visual field may be satisfactorily explained by correlating it with certain definite lesions in the nervous system. On the other hand, a person's *belief*—whether this be a belief in Christianity, in Communism, or in the idea that his internal organs are 'rotting" and that his body is, in fact, already "dead"— cannot be explained by a defect or disease of the nervous system. Explanations of this sort of occurrence—assuming that one is interested in the belief itself and does not regard it simply as a "symptom" or expression of something else that is *more interesting*—must be sought along different lines.

The second error in regarding complex psychosocial behavior, consisting of communications about ourselves and the world about us, as mere symptoms of neurological functioning is *epistemological.* In other words, it is an error pertaining not to any mistakes in observation or reasoning, as such, but rather to the way in which we organize and express our knowledge. In the present case, the error lies in making a symmetrical dualism between mental and physical (or bodily) symptoms, a dualism which is merely a habit of speech and to which no known observations can be found to correspond. Let us see if this is so. In medical practice, when we speak of physical disturbances, we mean either signs (for example, a fever) or symptoms (for example, pain). We speak of mental symptoms, on the other hand, when we refer to a patient's *communications about himself, others, and the world about him.* He might state that he is Napoleon or that he is being persecuted by the Communists. These would be considered mental symptoms *only* if the observer believed that the patient was *not* Napoleon or that he was *not* being persecuted by the

Communists. This makes it apparent that the statement that "*X* is a mental symptom" involves rendering a judgment. The judgment entails, moreover, a covert comparison or matching of the patient's ideas, concepts, or beliefs with those of the observer and the society in which they live. The notion of mental symptom is therefore inextricably tied to the *social* (including *ethical*) *context* in which it is made in much the same way as the notion of bodily symptom is tied to an *anatomical* and *genetic context.*

To sum up what has been said thus far: I have tried to show that for those who regard mental symptoms as signs of brain disease, the concept of mental illness is unnecessary and misleading. For what they mean is that people so labeled suffer from diseases of the brain; and, if that is what they mean, it would seem better for the sake of clarity to say that and not something else.

MENTAL ILLNESS AS A NAME FOR PROBLEMS IN LIVING

The term "mental illness" is widely used to describe something which is very different than a disease of the brain. Many people today take it for granted that living is an arduous process. Its hardship for modern man, moreover, derives not so much from a struggle for biological survival as from the stresses and strains inherent in the social intercourse of complex human personalities. In this context, the notion of mental illness is used to identify or describe some feature of an individual's so-called personality. Mental illness—as a deformity of the personality, so to speak—is then regarded as the *cause* of the human disharmony. It is implicit in this view that social intercourse between people is regarded as something *inherently harmonious,* its disturbance being due solely to the presence of "mental illness" in many people. This is obviously fallacious reasoning, for it makes the abstraction "mental illness" into a *cause,* even though this abstraction was created in the first place to serve only as a shorthand expression for certain types of human behavior. It now becomes necessary to ask: "What kinds of behavior are regarded as indicative of mental illness, and by whom?"

The concept of illness, whether bodily or mental, implies *deviation from some clearly defined norm.* In the case of physical illness, the norm is the structural and functional integrity of the human body. Thus, although the desirability of physical health, as such, is an ethical value, what health *is* can be stated in anatomical and physiological terms. What is the norm deviation from which is regarded as mental illness? This question cannot be easily answered. But whatever this norm might be, we can be certain of only one thing: namely, that it is a norm that must be stated in terms of *psychosocial, ethical,* and *legal* concepts. For example, notions such as "excessive repression" or "acting out an unconscious impulse" illustrate the use of psychological concepts for judging (so-called) mental health and illness. The idea that chronic hostility, vengefulness, or divorce are indicative of mental illness would be illustrations of the use of ethical norms (that is, the desirability of love, kindness, and a stable marriage relationship). Finally, the widespread psychiatric opinion that only a mentally ill person would commit homicide illustrates the use of a legal concept as a norm of mental health. The norm from which deviation is measured whenever one speaks of a mental illness is a *psychosocial and ethical one.* Yet, the remedy is sought in terms of *medical* measures which—it is hoped and assumed--are free from wide differences of ethical value. The definition of the disorder and the terms in which its remedy are sought are therefore at serious odds with one another. The practical significance of this covert conflict between the alleged nature of the defect and the remedy can hardly be exaggerated.

Having identified the norms used to measure deviations in cases of mental illness, we will now turn to the question: "Who defines the norms and hence the deviation?" Two basic answers may be offered: (1) It may be

the person himself (that is, the patient) who decides that he deviates from a norm. For example, an artist may believe that he suffers from a work inhibition; and he may implement this conclusion by seeking help *for* himself from a psychotherapist. (2) It may be someone other than the patient who decides that the latter is deviant (for example, relatives, physicians, legal authorities, society generally, etc.). In such a case a psychiatrist may be hired by others to do something *to* the patient in order to correct the deviation.

These considerations underscore the importance of asking the question "Whose agent is the psychiatrist?" and of giving a candid answer to it. The psychiatrist (psychologist or nonmedical psychotherapist), it now develops, may be the agent of the patient, of the relatives, of the school, of the military services, of a business organization, of a court of law, and so forth. In speaking of the psychiatrist as the agent of these persons or organizations, it is not implied that his values concerning norms, or his ideas and aims concerning the proper nature of remedial action, need to coincide exactly with those of his employer. For example, a patient in individual psychotherapy may believe that his salvation lies in a new marriage; his psychotherapist need not share this hypothesis. As the patient's agent, however, he must abstain from bringing social or legal force to bear on the patient which would prevent him from putting his beliefs into action. If his *contract* is with the patient, the psychiatrist (psychotherapist) may disagree with him or stop his treatment; but he cannot engage others to obstruct the patient's aspirations. Similarly, if a psychiatrist is engaged by a court to determine the sanity of a criminal, he need not fully share the legal authorities' values and intentions in regard to the criminal and the means available for dealing with him. But the psychiatrist is expressly barred from stating, for example, that it is not the criminal who is "insane" but the men who wrote the law on the basis of which the very actions that are being judged are regarded as "criminal." Such an opinion could be voiced, of course, but not in a courtroom, and not by a psychiatrist who makes it his practice to assist the court in performing its daily work.

To recapitulate: In actual contemporary social usage, the finding of a mental illness is made by establishing a deviance in behavior from certain psychosocial, ethical, or legal norms. The judgment may be made, as in medicine, by the patient, the physician (psychiatrist), or others. Remedial action, finally, tends to be sought in a therapeutic—or covertly medical—framework, thus creating a situation in which *psychosocial ethical,* and/or *legal deviations* are claimed to be correctible by (so-called) *medical action.* Since medical action is designed to correct only medical deviations, it seems logically absurd to expect that it will help solve problems whose very existence had been defined and established on nonmedical grounds. I think that these considerations may be fruitfully applied to the present use of tranquilizers and, more generally, to what might be expected of drugs of whatever type in regard to the amelioration or solution of problems in human living.

THE ROLE OF ETHICS IN PSYCHIATRY

Anything that people *do*—in contrast to things that *happen* to them—takes place in a context of value. In this broad sense, no human activity is devoid of ethical implications. When the values underlying certain activities are widely shared, those who participate in their pursuit may lose sight of them altogether. The discipline of medicine, both as a pure science (for example, research) and as a technology (for example, therapy), contains many ethical considerations and judgments. Unfortunately, these are often denied, minimized, or merely kept out of focus; for the ideal of the medical profession as well as of the people whom it serves seems to be having a system of medicine (allegedly) free of ethical value. This sentimental notion is expressed by such things as the doctor's willingness to treat and

help patients irrespective of their religious or political beliefs, whether they are rich or poor, etc. While there may be some grounds for this belief—albeit it is a view that is not impressively true even in these regards—the fact remains that ethical considerations encompass a vast range of human affairs. By making the practice of medicine neutral in regard to some specific issues of value need not, and cannot, mean that it can be kept free from all such values. The practice of medicine is intimately tied to ethics; and the first thing that we must do, it seems to me, is to try to make this clear and explicit. I shall let this matter rest here, for it does not concern us specifically in this essay. Lest there be any vagueness, however, about how or where ethics and medicine meet, let me remind the reader of such issues as birth control, abortion, suicide, and euthanasia as only a few of the major areas of current ethicomedical controversy.

Psychiatry, I submit, is very much more intimately tied to problems of ethics than is medicine. I use the word "psychiatry" here to refer to that contemporary discipline which is concerned with *problems in living* (and not with diseases of the brain, which are problems for neurology). Problems in human relations can be analyzed, interpreted, and given meaning only within given social and ethical contexts. Accordingly, it *does* make a difference—arguments to the contrary notwithstanding—what the psychiatrist's socioethical orientations happen to be; for these will influence his ideas on what is wrong with the patient, what deserves comment or interpretation, in what possible directions change might be desirable, and so forth. Even in medicine proper, these factors play a role, as for instance, in the divergent orientations which physicians, depending on their religious affiliations, have toward such things as birth control and therapeutic abortion. Can anyone really believe that a psychotherapist's ideas concerning religious belief, slavery, or other similar issues play no role in his practical work? If they do make a difference, what are we to infer from it? Does it not seem reasonable that we ought to have different psychiatric therapies—each expressly recognized for the ethical positions which they embody—for, say, Catholics and Jews, religious persons and agnostics, democrats and communists, white supremacists and Negroes, and so on? Indeed, if we look at how psychiatry is actually practiced today (especially in the United States), we find that people do seek psychiatric help in accordance with their social status and ethical beliefs. This should really not surprise us more than being told that practicing Catholics rarely frequent birth control clinics.

The foregoing position which holds that contemporary psychotherapists deal with problems in living, rather than with mental illnesses and their curses, stands in opposition to a currently prevalent claim, according to which mental illness is just as "real" and "objective" as bodily illness. This is a confusing claim since it is never known exactly what is meant by such words as "real" and "objective." I suspect, however, that what is intended by the proponents of this view is to create the idea in the popular mind that mental illness is some sort of disease entity, like an infection or a malignancy. If this were true, one could *catch* or *get* a "mental illness," one might *have* or *harbor* it, one might *transmit* it to others, and finally one could get *rid* of it. In my opinion, there is not a shred of evidence to support this idea. To the contrary, all the evidence is the other way and supports the view that what people now call mental illnesses are for the most part *communications* expressing unacceptable ideas, often framed, moreover, in an unusual idiom. . . .

This is not the place to consider in detail the similarities and differences between bodily and mental illnesses. It shall suffice for us here to emphasize only one important difference between them: namely, that whereas bodily disease refers to public, physiocochemical occurrences, the notion of mental illness is used to codify relatively more private, sociopsychological happenings of which the observer (diagnostician) forms a part. In other words, the psychiatrist does not stand *apart* from what he observes, but

is, in Harry Stack Sullivan's apt words, a "participant observer." This means that he is *committed* to some picture of what he considers reality—and to what he thinks society considers reality—and he observes and judges the patient's behavior in the light of these considerations. This touches on our earlier observation that the notion of mental symptom itself implies a comparison between observer and observed, psychiatrist and patient. This is so obvious that I may be charged with belaboring trivialities. Let me therefore say once more that my aim in presenting this argument was expressly to criticize and counter a prevailing contemporary tendency to deny the moral aspects of psychiatry (and psychotherapy) and to substitute for them allegedly value-free medical considerations. Psychotherapy, for example, is being widely practiced as though it entailed nothing other than restoring the patient from a state of mental sickness to one of mental health. While it is generally accepted that mental illness has something to do with man's social (or interpersonal) relations, it is paradoxically maintained that problems of values (that is, of ethics) do not arise in this process. Yet, in one sense, much of psychotherapy may revolve around nothing other than the elucidation and weighing of goals and values—many of which may be mutually contradictory—and the means whereby they might best be harmonized, realized, or relinquished.

The diversity of human values and the methods by means of which they may be realized is so vast, and many of them remain so unacknowledged, that they cannot fail but lead to conflicts in human relations. Indeed, to say that human relations at all levels—from mother to child, through husband and wife, to nation and nation—are fraught with stress, strain, and disharmony is, once again, making the obvious explicit. Yet, what may be obvious may be also poorly understood. This I think is the case here. For it seems to me that—at least in our scientific theories of behavior—we have failed to *accept* the simple fact that human relations are inherently fraught with difficulties and that to make them even relatively harmonious requires much patience and hard work. I submit that the idea of mental illness is now being put to work to obscure certain difficulties which at present may be inherent—not that they need be unmodifiable—in the social intercourse of persons. If this is true, the concept functions as a disguise; for instead of calling attention to conflicting human needs, aspirations, and values, the notion of mental illness provides an amoral and impersonal "thing" (an "illness") as an explanation for *problems in living*. We may recall in this connection that not so long ago it was devils and witches who were held responsible for men's problems in social living. The belief in mental illness, as something other than man's trouble in getting along with his fellow man, is the proper heir to the belief in demonology and witchcraft. Mental illness exists or is "real" in exactly the same sense in which witches existed or were ' real.''

CHOICE, RESPONSIBILITY, AND PSYCHIATRY

While I have argued that mental illnesses do not exist, I obviously did not imply that the social and psychological occurrences to which this label is currently being attached also do not exist. Like the personal and social troubles which people had in the Middle Ages, they are real enough. It is the labels we give them that concerns us and, having labelled them, what we do about them. While I cannot go into the ramified implications of this problem here, it is worth noting that a demonologic conception of problems in living gave rise to therapy along theological lines. Today, a belief in mental illness implies—nay, requires—therapy along medical or psychotherapeutic lines.

What is implied in the line of thought set forth here is something quite different. I do not intend to offer a new conception of "psychiatric illness" nor a new form of "therapy." My aim is more modest and yet also more ambitious. It is to suggest that the phenomena now called mental illnesses be looked at afresh and more simply, that they be removed from the category of illnesses, and that they be regarded as the expressions of man's struggle with the problem of *how* he should live. The last mentioned problem is obviously a vast one, its enormity reflecting not only man's inability to cope with his environment, but even more his increasing self-reflectiveness.

By problems in living, then, I refer to that truly explosive chain reaction which began with man's fall from divine grace by partaking of the fruit of the tree of knowledge. Man's awareness of himself and of the world about him seems to be a steadily expanding one, bringing in its wake an ever larger *burden of understanding. This burden,* then, *is to be expected and must not be misinterpreted.* Our only *rational* means for lightening it is *more understanding,* and appropriate *action* based on such understanding. The main alternative lies in acting as though the burden were not what in fact we perceive it to be and taking refuge in an outmoded theological view on man. In the latter view, man does not fashion his life and much of his world about him, but merely lives out his fate in a world created by superior beings. This may logically lead to pleading nonresponsibility in the face of seemingly unfathomable problems and difficulties. Yet, if man fails to take increasing responsibility for his actions, individually as well as collectively, it seems unlikely that some higher power or being would assume this task and carry this burden for him. Moreover, this seems hardly the proper time in human history for obscuring the issue of man's responsibility for his actions by hiding it behind the skirt of an all-explaining conception of mental illness.

CONCLUSIONS

I have tried to show that the notion of mental illness has outlived whatever usefulness it might have had and that it now functions merely as a convenient myth. As such, it is a true heir to religious myths in general, and to the belief in witchcraft in particular;

the role of all these belief-systems was to act as *social tranquilizers,* thus encouraging the hope that mastery of certain specific problems may be achieved by means of substitutive (symbolic-magical) operations. The notion of mental illness thus serves mainly to obscure the everyday fact that life for most people is a continuous struggle, not for biological survival but for a "place in the sun," "peace of mind," or some other human value. For man aware of himself and of the world about him, once the needs for preserving the body (and perhaps the race) are more or less satisfied, the problem arises as to what he should do with himself. Sustained adherence to the myth of mental illness allows people to avoid facing this problem, believing that mental health, conceived as the absence of mental illness, automatically insures the making of right and safe choices in one's conduct of life. But the facts are all the other way. It is the making of good choices in life that others regard, retrospectively, as good mental health!

The myth of mental illness encourages us, moreover, to believe in its logical corollary: that social intercourse would be harmonious, satisfying, and the secure basis of a "good life" were it not for the disrupting influences of mental illness or "psychopathology." The potentiality for universal human happiness, in this form at least, seems to me but another example of the I-wish-it-were-true type of fantasy. I do believe that human happiness or well-being on a hitherto unimaginable large scale, and not just for a select few, is possible. This goal could be achieved, however, only at the cost of many men, and not just a few being willing and able to tackle their personal social, and ethical conflicts. This means having the courage and integrity to forego waging battles on false fronts, finding solutions for substitute problems—for instance, fighting the battle of stomach acid and chronic fatigue instead of facing up to a marital conflict.

Our adversaries are not demons, witches, fate, or mental illness. We have no enemy whom we can fight, exorcise, or dispel by "cure." What we do have are *problems in living*—whether these be biological, economic, political, or sociopsychological. In this essay I was concerned only with problems belonging in the last mentioned category, and within this group mainly with those pertaining to moral values. The field to which modern psychiatry addresses itself is vast, and I made no effort to encompass it all. My argument was limited to the proposition that mental illness is a myth, whose function it is to disguise and thus render more palatable the bitter pill of moral conflicts in human relations.

THE ROLE OF THE MENTALLY ILL AND THE DYNAMICS OF MENTAL DISORDER: A RESEARCH FRAMEWORK

Thomas J. Scheff

One source of immediate embarrassment to any social theory of "mental illness" is that the terms used in referring to these phenomena in our society prejudge the issue. The medical metaphor "mental illness" suggests a determinate process which occurs within the individual: the unfolding and development of disease. It is convenient, therefore, to drop terms derived from the disease metaphor in favor of a standard sociological concept, deviant behavior, which signifies behavior that violates a social norm in a given society.

If the symptoms of mental illness are to be construed as violations of social norms, it

From *Sociometry,* 26 (December 1963), 436–53. Reprinted by permission. Professor Scheff is in the Department of Sociology, University of California, Santa Barbara, California.

is necessary to specify the type of norms involved. Most norm violations do not cause the violator to be labeled as mentally ill but as ill-mannered, ignorant, sinful, criminal, or perhaps just harried, depending on the type of norm involved. There are innumerable norms, however, over which consensus is so complete that the members of a group appear to take them for granted. A host of such norms surround even the simplest conversation: A person engaged in conversation is expected to face toward his partner, rather than directly away from him; if his gaze is toward the partner, he is expected to look toward his eyes, rather than, say, toward his forehead; to stand at a proper conversational distance, neither one inch away nor across the room, and so on. A person who regularly violated these expectations probably would not be thought to be merely ill-bred, but as strange, bizarre, and frightening, because his behavior violates the assumptive world of the group, the world that is construed to be the only one that is natural, decent, and possible.

The culture of the group provides a vocabulary of terms for categorizing many norm violations: crime, perversion, drunkenness, and bad manners are familiar examples. Each of these terms is derived from the type of norm broken, and ultimately, from the type of behavior involved. After exhausting these categories however, there is always a residue of the most diverse kinds of violations, for which the culture provides no explicit label. For example, although there is great cultural variation in what is defined as decent or real, each culture tends to reify its definition of decency and reality, and so provide no way of handling violations of its expectations in these areas. The typical norm governing decency or reality, therefore, literally "goes without saying" and its violation is unthinkable for most of its members. For the convenience of the society in construing those instances of unnamable deviance which are called to its attention, these violations may be lumped together into a residual category: witchcraft, spirit possession, or, in our own society, mental illness.

In this paper, the diverse kinds of deviation for which our society provides no explicit label, and which, therefore, sometimes lead to the labeling of the violator as mentally ill, will be considered to be technically *residual deviance.*

THE ORIGINS, PREVALENCE AND COURSE OF RESIDUAL DEVIANCE

The first proposition concerns the origins of residual deviance. *1. Residual deviance arises from fundamentally diverse sources.* It has been demonstrated that some types of mental disorder are the result of organic causes. It appears likely, therefore, that there are genetic, biochemical or physiological origins for residual deviance. It also appears that residual deviance can arise from individual psychological peculiarities and from differences in upbringing and training. Residual deviance can also probably be produced by various kinds of external stress: the sustained fear and hardship of combat, and deprivation of food, sleep, and even sensory experience. Residual deviance, finally, can be a volitional act of innovation or defiance. The kinds of behavior deemed typical of mental illness, such as hallucinations, delusions, depression, and mania, can all arise from these diverse sources.

The second proposition concerns the prevalence of residual deviance which is analogous to the "total" or "true" prevalence of mental disorder (in contrast to the "treated" prevalence). *2. Relative to the rate of treated mental illness, the rate of unrecorded residual deviance is extremely high.* There is evidence that grossly deviant behavior is often not noticed or, if it is noticed, it is rationalized as eccentricity. Apparently, many persons who are extremely withdrawn, or who "fly off the handle" for extended periods of time, who imagine fantastic events, or who hear voices or see visions, are not labeled as insane either by themselves or others. Their deviance, rather, is unrecognized, ignored, or rationalized. This pattern of inattention and rationalization will be called "denial."

In addition to the kind of evidence cited

above there are a number of epidemiological studies of total prevalence. There are numerous problems in interpreting the results of these studies; the major difficulty is that the definition of mental disorder is different in each study, as are the methods used to screen cases. These studies represent, however, the best available information and can be used to estimate total prevalence.

A convenient summary of findings is presented in Plunkett and Gordon. This source compares the methods and populations used in eleven field studies, and lists rates of total prevalence (in percentages) as 1.7, 3.6, 4.5, 4.7, 5.3, 6.1, 10.9, 13.8, 23.2, 23.3, and 33.3.

How do these total rates compare with the rates of treated mental disorder? One of the studies cited by Plunkett and Gordon, the Baltimore study reported by Pasamanick, is useful in this regard since it includes both treated and untreated rates. As compared with the untreated rate of 10.9 percent, the rate of treatment in state, VA, and private hospitals of Baltimore residents was .5 percent. That is, for every mental patient there were approximately 20 untreated cases located by the survey. It is possible that the treated rate is too low, however, since patients treated by private physicians were not included. Judging from another study, the New Haven study of treated prevalence, the number of patients treated in private practice is small compared to those hospitalized: over 70 percent of the patients located in that study were hospitalized even though extensive case-finding techniques were employed. The overall treated prevalence in the New Haven study was reported as .8 percent, which is in good agreement with my estimate of .7 percent for the Baltimore study. If we accept .8 percent as an estimate of the upper limit of treated prevalence for the Pasamanick study, the ratio of treated to untreated cases is 1/14. That is, for every treated patient we should expect to find 14 untreated cases in the community.

One interpretation of this finding is that the untreated patients in the community represent those cases with less severe disorders, while those patients with severe impairments all fall into the treated group. Some of the findings in the Pasamanick study point in this direction. Of the untreated patients, about half are classified as psychoneurotic. Of the psychoneurotics, in turn, about half again are classified as suffering from minimal impairment. At least a fourth of the untreated group, then, involved very mild disorders.

The evidence from the group diagnosed as psychotic does not support this interpretation, however. Almost all of the cases diagnosed as psychotic were judged to involve severe impairment, yet half of the diagnoses of psychosis occurred in the untreated group. In other words, according to this study there were as many untreated as treated cases of psychoses.

On the basis of the high total prevalence rates cited above and other evidence, it seems plausible that residual deviant behavior is usually transitory, which is the substance of the third proposition. *3. Most residual deviance is "denied" and is transitory.* The high rates of total prevalence suggest that most residual deviancy is unrecognized or rationalized away. For this type of deviance, which is amorphous and uncrystallized, Lemert uses the term "primary deviation." Balint describes similar behavior as "the unorganized phase of illness." Although Balint assumes that patients in this phase ultimately "settle down" to an "organized illness," other outcomes are possible. A person in this stage may "organize" his deviance in other than illness terms, e.g., as eccentricity or genius, or the deviant acts may terminate when situational stress is removed.

The experience of battlefield psychiatrists can be interpreted to support the hypothesis that residual deviance is usually transitory. Glass reports that combat neurosis is often self-terminating if the soldier is kept with his unit and given only the most superficial medical attention. Descriptions of child behavior can be interpreted in the same way. According to these reports, most children go through periods in which at least several of the following kinds of deviance may occur: temper tantrums, head banging, scratching, pinching, biting, fantasy playmates or pets, illusory physical complaints, and fears of sounds, shapes, colors, persons, animals, darkness, weather, ghosts, and so on. In the vast majority of instances, however, these behavior patterns do not become stable.

If residual deviance is highly prevalent among ostensibly "normal" persons and is usually transitory, as suggested by the last two propositions, what accounts for the small percentage of residual deviants who go on to deviant careers? To put the question another way, under what conditions is residual deviance stabilized? The conventional hypothesis is that the answer lies in the deviant himself. The hypothesis suggested here is that the most important single factor (but not the only factor) in the stabilization of residual deviance is the societal reaction. Residual deviance may be stabilized if it is defined to be evidence of mental illness, and/or the deviant is placed in a deviant status, and begins to play the role of the mentally ill. In order to avoid the implication that mental disorder is merely role-playing and pretence, it is first necessary to discuss the social institution of insanity.

SOCIAL CONTROL: INDIVIDUAL AND SOCIAL SYSTEMS OF BEHAVIOR

In *The Myth of Mental Illness,* Szasz proposes that mental disorder be viewed within the framework of "the game-playing model of human behavior." He then describes hysteria, schizophrenia, and other mental disorders as the "impersonation" of sick persons by those whose "real" problem concerns "problems of living." Although Szasz states that role-playing by mental patients may not be completely or even mostly voluntary, the implication is that mental disorder be viewed as a strategy chosen by the individual as a way of obtaining help from others. Thus, the term "impersonation" suggests calculated and deliberate shamming by the patient. . . .

The present paper also uses the role-playing model to analyze mental disorder, but places more emphasis on the involuntary aspects of role-playing than Szasz, who tends to treat role-playing as an individual system of behavior. In many social psychological discussions, however, role-playing is considered as a part of a social system. The individual plays his role by articulating his behavior with the cues and actions of other persons involved in the transaction. The proper performance of a role is dependent on having a co-operative audience. This proposition may also be reversed: having an audience which acts toward the individual in a uniform way may lead the actor to play the expected role even if he is not particularly interested in doing so. The "baby of the family" may come to find this role obnoxious, but the uniform pattern of cues and actions which confronts him in the family may lock in with his own vocabulary of responses so that it is inconvenient and difficult for him not to play the part expected of him. To the degree that alternative roles are closed off, the proffered role may come to be the only way the individual can cope with the situation.

One of Szasz's very apt formulations touches upon the social systemic aspects of role-playing. He draws an analogy between the role of the mentally ill and the "type-casting" of actors. Some actors get a reputation for playing one type of role, and find it difficult to obtain other roles. Although they may be displeased, they may also come to incorporate aspects of the type-cast role into their self-conceptions, and ultimately into their behavior. Findings in several social psychological studies suggest that an individual's role behavior may be shaped by the kinds of "deference" that he regularly receives from others.

One aspect of the voluntariness of role-playing is the extent to which the actor believes in the part he is playing. Although a role may be played cynically, with no belief, or completely sincerely, with whole-hearted belief, many roles are played on the basis of an intricate mixture of belief and disbelief. During the course of a study of a large public mental hospital, several patients told the author in confidence about their cynical use of their symptoms—to frighten new personnel, to escape from unpleasant work details, and so on. Yet these *same* patients, at other times, appear to have been sincere in their symptomatic behavior. Apparently it was sometimes difficult for them to tell whether they were playing the role or the role was playing them.... In accordance with what has been said so far, the difficulty is probably that the patient is just as confused by his own behavior as is the observer.

This discussion suggests that a stable role performance may arise when the actor's role imagery locks in with the type of "deference" which he regularly receives. An extreme example of this process may be taken from anthropological and medical reports concerning the "dead role," as in deaths attributed to "bone-pointing." Death from bone-pointing appears to arise from the conjunction of two fundamental processes which characterize all social behavior. First, all individuals continually orient themselves by means of responses which are perceived in social interaction: the individual's identity and continuity of experience are dependent on these cues. Secondly, the individual has his own vocabulary of expectations, which may in a particular situation either agree with or be in conflict with the sanctions to which he is exposed. Entry into a role may be complete when this role is part of the individual's expectations, and when these expectations are reaffirmed in social interaction. In the following pages this principle will be applied to the problem of the causation of mental disorder.

What are the beliefs and practices that constitute the social institution of insanity? And how do they figure in the development of mental disorder? Two propositions concerning beliefs about mental disorder in the general public will now be considered.

4. Stereotyped imagery of mental disorder is learned in early childhood. Although there are no substantiating studies in this area, scattered observations lead the author to conclude that children learn a considerable amount of imagery concerning deviance very early, and that much of the imagery comes from their peers rather than from adults. The literal meaning of "crazy," a term now used in a wide variety of contexts, is probably grasped by children during the first years of elementary school. Since adults are often vague and evasive in their responses to questions in this area, an aura of mystery surrounds it. In this socialization the grossest stereotypes which are heir to childhood fears, e.g., of the "boogie man," survive. These conclusions are quite speculative, of course, and need to be investigated systematically, possibly with techniques similar to those used in studies of the early learning of racial stereotypes.

Assuming, however, that this hypothesis is sound, what effect does early learning have on the shared conceptions of insanity held in the community? There is much fallacious material learned in early childhood which is later discarded when more adequate information replaces it. This question leads to hypothesis No. 5. *The stereotypes of insanity are continually reaffirmed, inadvertently, in ordinary social interaction.*

Although many adults become acquainted with medical concepts of mental illness, the traditional stereotypes are not discarded, but continue to exist alongside the medical conceptions, because the stereotypes receive almost continual support from the mass media and in ordinary social discourse. In newspapers, it is a common practice to mention that a rapist or a murderer was once a mental patient. This negative information, however, is seldom offset by positive reports. An item like the following is almost inconceivable:

Mrs. Ralph Jones, an ex-mental patient, was elected president of the Fairview Home and Garden Society in their meeting last Thursday.

Because of highly biased reporting, the reader is free to make the unwarranted inference that murder and rape occur more frequently among ex-mental patients than among the population at large. Actually, it has been demonstrated that the incidence of crimes of violence, or of any crime, is much lower among ex-mental patients than among the general population. Yet, this is not the picture presented to the public.

Reaffirmation of the stereotype of insanity occurs not only in the mass media, but also in ordinary conversation, in jokes, anecdotes, and even in conventional phrases. Such phrases as "Are you crazy?", or "It would be a madhouse," "It's driving me out of my mind," or "It's driving me distracted," and hundreds of others occur frequently in informal conversations. In this usage insanity itself is seldom the topic of conversation; the phrases are so much a part of ordinary language that only the person who considers each word carefully can eliminate them from his speech. Through verbal usages the stereotypes of insanity are a relatively permanent part of the social structure.. ,.

According to the analysis presented here, the traditional stereotypes of mental disorder are solidly entrenched in the population because they are learned early in childhood and are continuously reaffirmed in the mass media and in everyday conversation. How do these beliefs function in the process leading to mental disorder? This question will be considered by first referring to the earlier discussion of the societal reaction to residual deviance.

It was stated that the usual reaction to residual deviance is denial, and that in these cases most residual deviance is transitory. In a small proportion of cases the reaction goes the other way, exaggerating and at times distorting the extent and degree of deviation. This pattern of exaggeration, which we will call "labeling," has been noted by Garfinkel in his discussion of the "degradation" of officially recognized criminals. Goffman makes a similar point in his description of the "discrediting" of mental patients. Apparently under some conditions the societal reaction to deviance is to seek out signs of abnormality in the deviant's history to show that he was always essentially a deviant.

The contrasting social reactions of denial and labeling provide a means of answering two fundamental questions. If deviance arises from diverse sources—physical, psychological, and situational—how does the uniformity of behavior that is associated with insanity develop? Secondly, if deviance is usually transitory, how does it become stabilized in those patients who became chronically deviant? To summarize, what are the sources of uniformity and stability of deviant behavior?

In the approach taken here the answer to this question is based on hypotheses Nos. 4 and 5, that the role imagery of insantiy is learned early in childhood, and is reaffirmed in social interaction. In a crisis, when the deviance of an individual becomes a public issue, the traditional stereotype of insanity becomes the guiding imagery for action, both for those reacting to the deviant and, at times, for the deviant himself. When societal agents and persons around the deviant react to him uniformly in terms of the traditional stereotypes of insantiy, his amorphous and unstructured deviant behavior tends to crystallize in conformity to these expectations, thus becoming similar to the behavior of other deviants classified as mentally ill, and stable over time. The process of becoming uniform and stable is completed when the traditional imagery becomes a part of the deviant's orientation for guiding his own behavior.

The idea that cultural stereotypes may stabilize primary deviance, and tend to produce uniformity in symptoms, is supported by cross-cultural studies of mental disorder. Although some observers insist there are underlying similarities, most agree that there are enormous differences in the manifest symptoms of stable mental disorder *between* societies, and great similarity *within* societies.

These considerations suggest that the labeling process is a crucial contingency in most careers of residual deviance. Thus Glass, who observed that neuropsychiatric casualties may not become mentally ill if they are kept with their unit, goes on to say that military experience with psychotherapy has been disappointing. Soldiers who are removed from their unit to a hospital, he states, often go on to become chronically impaired. That is, their deviance is stabilized by the labeling process, which is implicit in their removal and hospitalization. A similar interpretation can be made by comparing the observations of childhood disorders among Mexican-Americans with those of "Anglo" children. Childhood disorders such as *susto* (an illness believed to result from fright) sometimes have damaging outcomes in Mexican-American children. Yet the deviant behavior involved is very similar to that which seems to have high incidence among Anglo children, with permanent impairment virtually never occurring. Apparently through cues from his elders the Mexican-American child, behaving initially much like his Anglo counterpart, learns to enter the sick role, at times with serious consequences.

From this point of view, then, most mental disorder can be considered to be a social role. This social role complements and reflects the status of the insane in the social structure. It is through the social processes which maintain the status of the insane that the varied deviancies from which mental disorder arises are made uniform and stable. The stabilization and uniformization of residual deviance are completed when the deviant accepts the role of the insane as the framework within which he organizes his own behavior. Three hypotheses are stated below which suggest some of the processes which cause the deviant to accept such a stigmatized role.

6. *Labeled deviants may be rewarded for playing the stereotyped deviant role.* Ordinarily patients who display "insight" are rewarded by psychiatrists and other personnel. That is, patients who manage to find evidence of "their illness" in their past and present behavior, confirming the medical and societal diagnosis, receive benefits. This pattern of behavior is a special case of a more general pattern that has been called the "apostolic function" by Balint, in which the physician and others inadvertently cause the patient to display symptoms of the illness the physician thinks the patient has. Not only physicians but other hospital personnel and even other patients, reward the deviant for conforming to the stereotypes.

7. *Labeled deviants are punished when they attempt the return to conventional roles.* The second process operative is the systematic blockage of entry to nondeviant roles once the label has been publicly applied. Thus the ex-mental patient, although he is urged to rehabilitate himself in the community, usually finds himself discriminated against in seeking to return to his old status, and on trying to find a new one in the occupational, marital, social, and other spheres. Thus, to a degree, the labeled deviant is rewarded for deviating, and punished for attempting to conform.

8. *In the crisis occurring when a primary deviant is publicly labeled, the deviant is highly suggestible, and may accept the proffered role of the insane as the only alternative.* When gross deviancy is publicly recognized and made an issue, the primary deviant may be profoundly confused, anxious, and ashamed. In this crisis it seems reasonable to assume that the deviant will be suggestible to the cues that he gets from the reactions of others toward him. But those around him are also in a crisis; the incomprehensible nature of the deviance, and the seeming need for immediate action lead them to take collective action against the deviant on the basis of the attitude which all share—the traditional stereotypes of insanity. The deviant is sensitive to the cues provided by these others and begins to think of himself in terms of the stereotyped role of insanity, which is part of his own role vocabulary also, since he, like those reacting to him, learned it early in childhood. In this situation his behavior may begin to follow the pattern suggested by his own stereotypes and the reactions of others. That is, when a primary deviant organizes his behavior within the framework of mental disorder, and when his organization is validated by others, particularly prestigeful others such as physicians, he is "hooked" and will proceed on a career of chronic deviance. . . .

The last three propositions suggest that once a person has been placed in a deviant status there are rewards for conforming to the deviant role, and punishments for not conforming to the deviant role. This is not to imply, however, that the symptomatic behavior of persons occupying a deviant status is always a manifestation of conforming behavior. To explain this point, some discussion of the process of self-control in "normals" is necessary.

In a recent discussion of the process of self-control, Shibutani notes that self-control is not automatic, but is an intricate and delicately balanced process, sustainable only under propitious circumstances. He points out that fatigue, the reaction to narcotics, excessive excitement or tension (such as is generated in mobs), or a number of other conditions interfere with self-control; conversely, conditions which produce normal bodily states, and deliberative processes such as symbolization and imaginative rehearsal before action, facilitate it.

One might argue that a crucially important aspect of imaginative rehearsal is the image of himself that the actor projects into his future action. Certainly in American society, the cultural image of the "normal" adult is that of a person endowed with self-control ("will-power," "backbone," "strength of character," etc.). For the person who sees himself as endowed with the trait of self-control, self-control is facilitated, since he can imagine himself enduring stress during his imaginative rehearsal, and also while under actual stress.

For a person who has acquired an image of himself as lacking the ability to control his own actions, the process of self-control is likely to break down under stress. Such a person may feel that he has reached his "breaking-point" under circumstances which would be endured by a person with a "normal" self-conception. This is to say, a greater lack of self-control than can be explained by stress tends to appear in those roles for which the culture transmits imagery which emphasizes lack of self-control. In American society such imagery is transmitted for the roles of the very young and very old, drunkards and drug addicts, gamblers, and the mentally ill.

Thus, the social role of the mentally ill has a different significance at different phases of residual deviance. When labeling first occurs, it merely gives a name to primary deviation which has other roots. When (and if) the primary deviance becomes an issue, and is not ignored or rationalized away, labeling may create a social type, a pattern of "symptomatic" behavior in conformity with the stereotyped expectations of others. Finally, to the extent that the deviant role becomes a part of the deviant's self-conception, his ability to control his own behavior may be impaired under stress, resulting in episodes of compulsive behavior.

The preceding eight hypotheses form the basis for the final causal hypothesis. *9. Among residual deviants, labeling is the single most important cause of careers of residual deviance.* This hypothesis assumes that most residual deviance, if it does not become the basis for entry into the sick role, will not lead to a deviant career. Most deviant careers, according to this point of view, arise out of career contingencies, and are therefore not directly connected with the origins of the initial deviance. Although there are a wide variety of contingencies which lead to labeling rather than denial, these contingencies can be usefully classified in terms of the nature of the deviant behavior, the person who commits the deviant acts, and the community in which the deviance occurs. Other things being equal, the severity of the societal reaction to deviance is a function of, first, the degree, amount, and visibility of the deviant behavior; second, the power of the deviant, and the social distance between the deviant and the agents of social control; and finally, the tolerance level of the community, and the availability in the culture of the community of alternative nondeviant roles. Particularly crucial for future research is the importance of the first two contingencies (the amount and degree of deviance), which are characteristics of the deviant, relative to the remaining five contingencies, which are characteristics of the social system. To the extent that these five factors are found empirically to be independent determinants of labeling and denial, the status of the mental patient can be considered a partly ascribed rather than a completely achieved status. The dynamics of treated mental illness could then be profitably studied quite apart from the individual dynamics of mental disorder. . . .

ON BEING SANE IN INSANE PLACES

D. L. Rosenhan

If sanity and insanity exist, how shall we know them?

The question is neither capricious nor itself insane. However much we may be personally convinced that we can tell the normal from the abnormal, the evidence is simply not compelling. It is commonplace, for example, to read about murder trials wherein eminent psychiatrists for the defense are contradicted by equally eminent psychiatrists for the prosecution on the matter of the defendant's sanity. More generally, there are a great deal of conflicting data on the reliability, utility, and meaning of such terms as "sanity," "insanity," "mental illness," and "schizophrenia." Finally, as early as 1934, Benedict suggested that normality and abnormality are not universal. What is viewed as normal in one culture may be seen as quite aberrant in another. Thus, notions of normality and abnormality may not be quite as accurate as people believe they are.

To raise questions regarding normality and abnormality is in no way to question the fact that some behaviors are deviant or odd. Murder is deviant. So, too, are hallucinations. Nor does raising such questions deny the existence of the personal anguish that is often associated with "mental illness." Anxiety and depression exist. Psychological suffering exists. But normality and abnormality, sanity and insanity, and the diagnoses that flow from them may be less

From *Science*, 179, No. 4070 (January 19, 1973), 250–58. Copyright 1973 by the American Association for the Advancement of Science. Rosenhan is Professor of Psychology and Law, Stanford University.

substantive than many believe them to be.

At its heart, the question of whether the sane can be distinguished from the insane (and whether degrees of insanity can be distinguished from each other) is a simple matter: do the salient characteristics that lead to diagnoses reside in the patients themselves or in the environments and contexts in which observers find them? From Bleuler, through Kretchmer, through the formulators of the recently revised *Diagnostic and Statistical Manual* of the American Psychiatric Association, the belief has been strong that patients present symptoms, that those symptoms can be categorized, and, implicitly, that the sane are distniguishable from the insane. More recently, however, this belief has been questioned. Based in part on theoretical and anthropological considerations, but also on philosophical, legal, and therapeutic ones, the view has grown that psychological categorization of mental illness is useless at best and downright harmful, misleading, and pejorative at worst. Psychiatric diagnoses, in this view, are in the minds of the observers and are not valid summaries of characteristics displayed by the observed.

Gains can be made in deciding which of these is more nearly accurate by getting normal people (that is, people who do not have, and have never suffered, symptoms of serious psychiatric disorders) admitted to psychiatric hospitals and then determining whether they were discovered to be sane and, if so, how. If the sanity of such pseudopatients were always detected, there would be prima facie evidence that a sane individual can be distinguished from the insane context in which he is found. Normality (and presumably abnormality) is distinct enough that it can be recognized wherever it occurs, for it is carried within the person. If, on the other hand, the sanity of the pseudopatients were never discovered, serious difficulties would arise for those who support traditional modes of psychiatric diagnosis. Given that the hospital staff was not incompetent, that the pseudopatient had been behaving as sanely as he had been outside of the hospital, and that it had never been previously suggested that he belonged in a psychiatric hospital, such an unlikely outcome would support the view that psychiatric diagnosis betrays little about the patient but much about the environment in which an observer finds him.

This article describes such an experiment. Eight sane people gained secret admission to 12 different hospitals. Their diagnostic experiences constitute the data of the first part of this article; the remainder is devoted to a description of their experiences in psychiatric institutions. Too few psychiatrists and psychologists, even those who have worked in such hospitals, know what the experience is like. They rarely talk about it with former patients, perhaps because they distrust information coming from the previously insane. Those who worked in psychiatric hospitals are likely to have adapted so thoroughly to the settings that they are insensitive to the impact of that experience. And while there have been occasional reports of researchers who submitted themselves to psychiatric hospitalization, these researchers have commonly remained in the hospitals for short periods of time, often with the knowledge of the hospital staff. It is difficult to know the extent to which they were treated like patients or like research colleagues. Nevertheless, their reports about the inside of the psychiatric hospital have been valuable. This article extends those efforts.

PSEUDOPATIENTS AND THEIR SETTINGS

The eight pseudopatients were a varied group. One was a psychology graduate student in his 20's. The remaining seven were older and "established." Among them were three psychologists, a pediatrician, a psychiatrist, a painter, and a housewife. Three pseudopatients were women, five were men. All of them employed pseudonyms, lest their alleged diagnoses embarrass them later. Those who were in mental health professions alleged another occupation in order to avoid the special attentions that might be accorded by staff, as a matter of courtesy or caution, to ailing colleagues. With the exception of myself (I was the first pseudopatient and my presence was known to the hospital administrator and chief psychologist and, so far as I can tell, to them alone), the presence of pseudopatients and the nature of the research program was not known to the hospital staffs.

The settings were similarly varied. In order to generalize the findings, admission into a variety of hospitals was sought. The 12 hospitals in the sample were located in five different states on the East and West coasts. Some were old and shabby, some were quite new. Some were research-oriented, others not. Some had good staff-patient ratios, others were quite understaffed. Only one was a strictly private hospital. All of the others were supported by state or federal funds or, in one instance, by university funds.

After calling the hospital for an appointment, the pseudopatient arrived at the admissions office complaining that he had been hearing voices. Asked what the voices said, he replied that they were often unclear, but as far as he could tell they said "empty," "hollow," and "thud." The voices were unfamiliar and were of the same sex as the pseudopatient. The choice of these symptoms was occasioned by their apparent similarity to existential symptoms. Such symptoms are alleged to arise from painful concerns about the perceived meaninglessness of one's life. It is as if the hallucinating person were saying, "My life is empty and hollow." The choice of these symptoms was also determined by the *absence* of a single report of existential psychoses in the literature.

Beyond alleging the symptoms and falsifying name, vocation, and employment, no further alterations of person, history, or circumstances were made. The significant events of the pseudopatient's life history were presented as they had actually occurred. Relationships with parents and siblings, with spouse and children, with people at work and in school, consistent with the aforementioned exceptions, were described as they were or had been. Frustrations and upsets were described along with joys and satisfactions. These facts are important to remember. If anything, they strongly biased the subsequent results in favor of detecting sanity, since none of their histories or current behaviors were seriously pathological in any way.

Immediately upon admission to the psychiatric ward, the pseudopatient ceased simulating *any* symptoms of abnormality. In some cases, there was a brief period of mild nervousness and anxiety, since none of the pseudopatients really believed that they would be admitted so easily. Indeed, their shared fear was that they would be immediately exposed as frauds and greatly embarrassed. Moreover, many of them had never visited a psychiatric ward; even those who had, nevertheless had some genuine fears about what might happen to them. Their nervousness, then, was quite appropriate to the novelty of the hospital setting, and it abated rapidly.

Apart from that short-lived nervousness, the pseudopatient behaved on the ward as he "normally" behaved. The pseudopatient spoke to patients and staff as he might ordinarily. Because there is uncommonly little to do on a psychiatric ward, he attempted to engage others in conversation. When asked by staff how he was feeling, he indicated that he was fine, that he no longer experienced symptoms. He responded to instructions from attendants, to calls for medication (which was not swallowed), and to dining-hall instructions. Beyond such activities as were available to him on the admissions ward, he spent his time writing down his observations about the ward, its patients, and the staff. Initially these notes were written "secretly," but as it soon became

clear that no one much cared, they were subsequently written on standard tablets of paper in such public places as the dayroom. No secret was made of these activities.

The pseudopatient, very much as a true psychiatric patient, entered a hospital with no foreknowledge of when he would be discharged. Each was told that he would have to get out by his own devices, essentially by convincing the staff that he was sane. The psychological stresses associated with hospitalization were considerable, and all but one of the pseudopatients desired to be discharged almost immediately after being admitted. They were, therefore, motivated not only to behave sanely, but to be paragons of cooperation. That their behavior was in no way disruptive is confirmed by nursing reports, which have been obtained on most of the patients. These reports uniformly indicate that the patients were "friendly," "cooperative," and "exhibited no abnormal indications."

THE NORMAL ARE NOT DETECTABLY SANE

Despite their public "show" of sanity, the pseudopatients were never detected. Admitted, except in one case, with a diagnosis of schizophrenia, each was discharged with a diagnosis of schizophrenia "in remission." The label "in remission" should in no way be dismissed as a formality, for at no time during any hospitalization had any question been raised about any pseudopatient's simulation. Nor are there any indications in the hospital records that the pseudopatient's status was suspect. Rather, the evidence is strong that, once labeled schizophrenic, the pseudopatient was stuck with that label. If the pseudopatient was to be discharged, he must naturally be "in remission"; but he was not sane, nor, in the institution's view, had he ever been sane.

The uniform failure to recognize sanity cannot be attributed to the quality of the hospitals, for, although there were considerable variations among them, several are considered excellent. Nor can it be alleged that there was simply not enough time to observe the pseudopatients. Length of hospitalization ranged from 7 to 52 days, with an average of 19 days. The pseudopatients were not, in fact, carefully observed, but this failure clearly speaks more to traditions within psychiatric hospitals than to lack of opportunity.

Finally, it cannot be said that the failure to recognize the pseudopatients' sanity was due to the fact that they were not behaving sanely. While there was clearly some tension present in all of them, their daily visitors could detect no serious behavioral consequences—nor, indeed, could other patients. It was quite common for the patients to "detect" the pseudopatients' sanity. During the first three hospitalizations, when accurate counts were kept, 35 of a total of 118 patients on the admissions ward voiced their suspicions, some vigorously. "You're not crazy. You're a journalist or a professor [referring to the continual note-taking]. You're checking up on the hospital." While most of the patients were reassured by the pseudopatient's insistence that he had been sick before he came in but was fine now, some continued to believe that the pseudopatient was sane throughout his hospitalization. The fact that the patients often recognized normality when staff did not raises important questions.

Failure to detect sanity during the course of hospitalization may be due to the fact that physicians operate with a strong bias toward what statisticians call the type 2 error. This is to say that physicians are more inclined to call a healthy person sick (a false positive, type 2) than a sick person healthy (a false negative, type 1). The reasons for this are not hard to find: it is clearly more dangerous to misdiagnose illness than health. Better to err on the side of caution, to suspect illness even among the healthy.

But what holds for medicine does not hold equally well for psychiatry. Medical illnesses, while unfortunate, are not commonly pejorative. Psychiatric diagnoses, on the contrary, carry with them personal, legal, and social stigmas. It was therefore important to see whether the tendency toward diagnosing the sane insane could be

reversed. The following experiment was arranged at a research and teaching hospital whose staff had heard these findings but doubted that such an error could occur in their hospital. The staff was informed that at some time during the following 3 months, one or more pseudopatients would attempt to be admitted into the psychiatric hospital. Each staff member was asked to rate each patient who presented himself at admissions or on the ward according to the likelihood that the patient was a pseudopatient. A 10-point scale was used, with a 1 and 2 reflecting high confidence that the patient was a pseudopatient.

Judgments were obtained on 193 patients who were admitted for psychiatric treatment. All staff who had had sustained contact with or primary responsibility for the patient—attendants, nurses, psychiatrists, physicians, and psychologists—were asked to make judgments. Forty-one patients were alleged, with high confidence, to be pseudopatients by at least one member of the staff. Twenty-three were considered suspect by at least one psychiatrist. Nineteen were suspected by one psychiatrist *and* one other staff member. Actually, no genuine pseudopatient (at least from my group) presented himself during this period.

The experiment is instructive. It indicates that the tendency to designate sane people as insane can be reversed when the stakes (in this case, prestige and diagnostic acumen) are high. But what can be said of the 19 people who were suspected of being "sane" by one psychiatrist and another staff member? Were these people truly "sane," or was it rather the case that in the course of avoiding the type 2 error the staff tended to make more errors of the first sort—calling the crazy "sane"? There is no way of knowing. But one thing is certain: any diagnostic process that lends itself so readily to massive errors of this sort cannot be a very reliable one.

THE STICKINESS OF PSYCHO-DIAGNOSTIC LABELS

Beyond the tendency to call the healthy sick—a tendency that accounts better for diagnostic behavior on admission than it does for such behavior after a lengthy period of exposure—the data speak to the massive role of labeling in psychiatric assessment. Having once been labeled schizophrenic, there is nothing the pseudopatient can do to overcome the tag. The tag profoundly colors others' perceptions of him and his behavior.

From one viewpoint, these data are hardly surprising, for it has long been known that elements are given meaning by the context in which they occur. Gestalt psychology made this point vigorously, and Asch demonstrated that there are "central" personality traits (such as "warm" versus "cold") which are so powerful that they markedly color the meaning of other information in forming an impression of a given personality. "Insane," "schizophrenic," "manic-depressive," and "crazy" are probably among the most powerful of such central traits. Once a person is designated abnormal, all of his other behaviors and characteristics are colored by that label. Indeed, that label is so powerful that many of the pseudopatients' normal behaviors were overlooked entirely or profoundly misinterpreted. Some examples may clarify this issue.

Earlier I indicated that there were no changes in the pseudopatient's personal history and current status beyond those of name, employment, and where necessary, vocation. Otherwise, a veridical description of personal history and circumstances was offered. Those circumstances were not psychotic. How were they made consonant with the diagnosis of psychosis? Or were those diagnoses modified in such a way as to bring them into accord with the circumstances of the pseudopatient's life, as described by him?

As far as I can determine, diagnoses were in no way affected by the relative health of the circumstances of a pseudopatient's life. Rather, the reverse occurred: the perception of his circumstances was shaped entirely by the diagnosis. A clear example of such translation is found in the case of a pseudopatient who had had a close relationship with his mother but was rather remote from his father during his early childhood. During

adolescence and beyond, however, his father became a close friend, while his relationship with his mother cooled. His present relationship with his wife was characteristically close and warm. Apart from occasional angry exchanges, friction was minimal. The children had rarely been spanked. Surely there is nothing especially pathological about such a history. Indeed, many readers may see a similar pattern in their own experiences, with no markedly deleterious consequences. Observe, however, how such a history was translated in the psychopathological context, this from the case summary prepared after the patient was discharged.

This white 39-year-old male . . . manifests a long history of considerable ambivalence in close relationships, which begins in early childhood. A warm relationship with his mother cools during his adolescence. A distant relationship to his father is described as becoming very intense. Affective stability is absent. His attempts to control emotionality with his wife and children are punctuated by angry outbursts and, in the case of the children, spankings. And while he says that he has several good friends, one senses considerable ambivalence embedded in those relationships also. . . .

The facts of the case were unintentionally distorted by the staff to achieve consistency with a popular theory of the dynamics of a schizophrenic reaction. Nothing of an ambivalent nature had been described in relations with parents, spouse, or friends. To the extent that ambivalence could be inferred, it was probably not greater than is found in all human relationships. It is true the pseudopatient's relationships with his parents changed over time, but in the ordinary context that would hardly be remarkable—indeed, it might very well be expected. Clearly, the meaning ascribed to his verbalizations (that is, ambivalence, affective instability) was determined by the diagnosis: schizophrenia. An entirely different meaning would have been ascribed if it were known that the man was "normal."

All pseudopatients took extensive notes publicly. Under ordinary circumstances, such behavior would have raised questions in the minds of observers, as, in fact, it did among patients. Indeed, it seemed so certain that the notes would elicit suspicion that elaborate precautions were taken to remove them from the ward each day. But the precautions proved needless. The closest any staff member came to questioning these notes occurred when one pseudopatient asked his physician what kind of medication he was receiving and began to write down the response. "You needn't write it," he was told gently. "If you have trouble remembering, just ask me again."

If no questions were asked of the pseudopatients, how was their writing interpreted? Nursing records for three patients indicate that the writing was seen as an aspect of their pathological behavior. "Patient engages in writing behavior" was the daily nursing comment on one of the pseudopatients who was never questioned about his writing. Given that the patient is in the hospital, he must be psychologically disturbed. And given that he is disturbed, continuous writing must be a behavioral manifestation of that disturbance, perhaps a subset of the compulsive behaviors that are sometimes correlated with schizophrenia.

One tacit characteristic of psychiatric diagnosis is that it locates the sources of aberration within the individual and only rarely within the complex of stimuli that surrounds him. Consequently, behaviors that are stimulated by the environment are commonly misattributed to the patient's disorder. For example, one kindly nurse found a pseudopatient pacing the long hospital corridors. "Nervous, Mr. X?" she asked. "No, bored," he said.

The notes kept by pseudopatients are full of patient behaviors that were misinterpreted by well-intentioned staff. Often enough, a patient would go "berserk" because he had, wittingly or unwittingly, been mistreated by, say, an attendant. A nurse coming upon the scene would rarely inquire even cursorily into the environmental stimuli of the patient's behavior. Rather, she assumed that his upset derived from his pathology, not from his present interactions with other staff members. Occasionally, the staff might assume that the patient's family (especially when they had recently visited) or other patients had stimulated the outburst. But never were the staff found to assume that one of themselves or the structure of the hospital had anything to do with a patient's behavior. One psychiatrist pointed to a group of patients who were sitting outside the cafeteria entrance half an hour before lunchtime. To a group of young residents he indicated that such behavior was characteristic of the oral-acquisitive nature of the syndrome. It seemed not to occur to him that there were very few things to anticipate in a psychiatric hospital besides eating.

A psychiatric label has a life and an influence of its own. Once the impression has been formed that the patient is schizophrenic, the expectation is that he will continue to be schizophrenic. When a sufficient amount of time has passed, during which the patient has done nothing bizarre, he is considered to be in remission and available for discharge. But the label endures beyond discharge, with the unconfirmed expectation that he will behave as a schizophrenic again. Such labels, conferred by mental health professionals, are as influential on the patient as they are on his relatives and friends, and it should not surprise anyone that the diagnosis acts on all of them as a self-fulfilling prophecy. Eventually, the patient himself accepts the diagnosis, with all of its surplus meanings and expectations, and behaves accordingly.

The inferences to be made from these matters are quite simple. Much as Zigler and Phillips have demonstrated that there is enormous overlap in the symptoms presented by patients who have been variously diagnosed, so there is enormous overlap in the behaviors of the sane and the insane. The sane are not "sane" all of the time. We lose our tempers "for no good reason." We are occasionally depressed or anxious, again for no good reason. And we may find it difficult to get along with one or another person—again for no reason that we can specify. Similarly, the insane are not always insane.

Indeed, it was the impression of the pseudo-patients while living with them that they were sane for long periods of time—that the bizarre behaviors upon which their diagnoses were allegedly predicated constituted only a small fraction of their total behavior. If it makes no sense to label ourselves permanently depressed on the basis of an occasional depression, then it takes better evidence than is presently available to label all patients insane or schizophrenic on the basis of bizarre behaviors or cognitions. It seems more useful, as Mischel has pointed out, to limit our discussions to *behaviors,* the stimuli that provoke them, and their correlates.

It is not known why powerful impressions of personality traits, such as "crazy" or "insane," arise. Conceivably, when the origins of and stimuli that give rise to a behavior are remote or unknown, or when the behavior strikes us as immutable, trait labels regarding the *behaver* arise. When, on the other hand, the origins and stimuli are known and available, discourse is limited to the behavior itself. Thus, I may hallucinate because I am sleeping, or I may hallucinate because I have ingested a peculiar drug. These are termed sleep-induced hallucinations, or dreams, and drug-induced hallucinations, respectively. But when the stimuli to my hallucinations are unknown, that is called craziness, or schizophrenia—as if that inference were somehow as illuminating as the others.

THE EXPERIENCE OF PSYCHIATRIC HOSPITALIZATION

The term "mental illness" is of recent origin. It was coined by people who were humane in their inclinations and who wanted very much to raise the station of (and the public's sympathies toward) the psychologically disturbed from that of witches and "crazies" to one that was akin to the physically ill. And they were at least partially successful, for the treatment of the mentally ill *has* improved considerably over the years. But while treatment has improved, it is doubtful that people really regard the mentally ill in the same way that they view the physically ill. A broken leg is something one recovers from, but mental illness allegedly endures forever. A broken leg does not threaten the observer, but a crazy schizophrenic? There is by now a host of evidence that attitudes toward the mentally ill are characterized by fear, hostility, aloofness, suspicion, and dread. The mentally ill are society's lepers.

That such attitudes infect the general population is perhaps not surprising, only upsetting. But that they affect the professionals—attendants, nurses, physicians, psychologists, and social workers—who treat and deal with the mentally ill is more disconcerting, both because such attitudes are self-evidently pernicious and because they are unwitting. Most mental health professionals would insist that they are sympathetic toward the mentally ill, that they are neither avoidant nor hostile. But it is more likely that an exquisite ambivalence characterizes their relations with psychiatric patients, such that their avowed impulses are only part of their entire attitude. Negative attitudes are there too and can easily be detected. Such attitudes should not surprise us. They are the natural offspring of the labels patients wear and the places in which they are found.

Consider the structure of the typical psychiatric hospital. Staff and patients are strictly segregated. Staff have their own living space, including their dining facilities, bathrooms, and assembly palces. The glassed quarters that contain the professional staff, which the pseudopatients came to call "the cage," sit out on every dayroom. The staff emerge primarily for caretaking purposes—to give medication, to conduct a therapy or group meeting, to instruct or reprimand a patient. Otherwise, staff keep to themselves, almost as if the disorder that afflicts their charges is somehow catching.

So much is patient-staff segregation the rule that, for four public hospitals in which an attempt was made to measure the degree to which staff and patients mingle, it was necessary to use "time out of the staff cage" as the operational measure. While it was not the case that all time spent out of the cage was spent mingling with patients (attendants, for example, would occasionally emerge to watch television in the dayroom), it was the only way in which one could gather reliable data on time for measuring.

The average amount of time spent by attendants outside of the cage was 11.3 percent (range, 3 to 52 percent). This figure does not represent only time spent mingling with patients, but also includes time spent on such chores as folding laundry, supervising patients while they shave, directing ward cleanup, and sending patients to off-ward activities. It was the relatively rare attendant who spent time talking with patients or playing games with them. It proved impossible to obtain a "percent mingling time" for nurses, since the amount of time they spent out of the cage was too brief. Rather, we counted instances of emergence from the cage. On the average, daytime nurses emerged from the cage 11.5 times per shift, including instances when they left the ward entirely (range, 4 to 39 times). Late afternoon and night nurses were even less available, emerging on the average 9.4 times per shift (range, 4 to 41 times). Data on early morning nurses, who arrived usually after midnight and departed at 8 a.m., are not available because patients were asleep during most of this period.

Physicians, especially psychiatrists, were even less available. They were rarely seen on the wards. Quite commonly, they would be seen only when they arrived and departed, with the remaining time being spent in their offices or in the cage. On the average, physicians emerged on the ward 6.7 times per day (range, 1 to 17 times). It proved difficult to make an accurate estimate in this regard, since physicians often maintained hours that allowed them to come and go at different times.

The hierarchical organization of the psychiatric hospital has been commented on before, but the latent meaning of that kind of organization is worth noting again. Those with the most power have least to do with patients, and those with the least power are most involved with them. Recall, however,

that the acquisition of role-appropriate behaviors occurs mainly through the observation of others, with the most powerful having the most influence. Consequently, it is understandable that attendants not only spend more time with patients than do any other members of the staff—that is required by their station in the hierarchy—but also, insofar as they learn from their superiors' behavior, spend as little time with patients as they can. Attendants are seen mainly in the cage, which is where the models, the action, and the power are.

I turn now to a different set of studies, these dealing with staff response to patient-initiated contact. It has long been known that the amount of time a person spends with you can be an index of your significance to him. If he initiates and maintains eye contact, there is reason to believe that he is considering your requests and needs. If he pauses to chat or actually stops and talks, there is added reason to infer that he is individuating you. In four hospitals, the pseudopatient approached the staff member with a request which took the following form: "Pardon me, Mr. [or Dr. or Mrs.] X, could you tell me when I will be eligible for grounds privileges?" (or ". . . when I will be presented at the staff meeting?" or ". . . when I am likely to be discharged?"). While the content of the question varied according to the appropriateness of the target and the pseudopatient's (apparent) current needs the form was always a courteous and relevant request for information. Care was taken never to approach a particular member of the staff more than once a day, lest the staff member become suspicious or irritated. In examining these data, remember that the behavior of the pseudopatients was neither bizarre nor disruptive. One could indeed engage in good conversation with them.

The data for these experiments are shown in Table 1, separately for physicians (column 1) and for nurses and attendants (column 2). Minor differences between these four institutions were overwhelmed by the degree to which staff avoided continuing contacts that patients had initiated. By far, their most common response consisted of either a brief response to the question, offered while they were "on the move" and with head averted, or no response at all.

The encounter frequently took the following bizarre form: (pseudopatient) "Pardon me, Dr. X. Could you tell me when I am eligible for grounds privileges?" (physician) "Good morning, Dave. How are you today?" (Moves off without waiting for a response.)

It is instructive to compare these data with data recently obtained at Stanford University. It has been alleged that large and eminent universities are characterized by faculty who are so busy that they have no time for students. For this comparison, a young lady approached individual faculty members who seemed to be walking purposefully to some meeting or teaching engagement and asked them the following six questions.

1) "Pardon me, could you direct me to Encina Hall?" (at the medical school: ". . . to the Clinical Research Center?").

2) "Do you know where Fish Annex is?" (there is no Fish Annex at Stanford).

3) "Do you teach here?"

4) "How does one apply for admission to the college?" (at the medical school: ". . . to the medical school?").

5) "Is it difficult to get in?"

6) "Is there financial aid?"

Without exception, as can be seen in Table 7–1 (column 3), all of the questions were answered. No matter how rushed they were, all respondents not only maintained eye contact, but stopped to talk. Indeed, many of the respondents went out of their way to direct or take the questioner to the office she was seeking, to try to locate "Fish Annex," or to discuss with her the possibilities of being admitted to the university.

Similar data, also shown in Table 7–1 (columns 4, 5, and 6), were obtained in the hospital. Here too, the young lady came prepared with six questions. After the first question, however, she remarked to 18 of her respondents (column 4), "I'm looking for a psychiatrist," and to 15 others (column 5), "I'm looking for an internist." Ten other respondents received no inserted comment (column 6). The general degree of cooperative responses is considerably higher for these university groups than it was for pseudopatients in psychiatric hospitals. Even so, differences are apparent within the medical school setting. Once having indicated that she was looking for a psychiatrist, the degree of cooperation elicited was less than when she sought an internist.

Table 7–1. Self-initiated contact by pseudopatients with psychiatrists and nurses and attendants, compared to contact with other groups.

| | Psychiatric hospitals | | University campus (nonmedical) | University medical center | | |
| | | | | Physicians | | |
Contact	(1) Psychiatrists	(2) Nurses and attendants	(3) Faculty	(4) "Looking for a psychiatrist"	(5) "Looking for an internist"	(6) No additional comment
Responses						
Moves on, head averted (%)	71	88	0	0	0	0
Makes eye contact (%)	23	10	0	11	0	0
Pauses and chats (%)	2	2	0	11	0	10
Stops and talks (%)	4	0.5	100	78	100	90
Mean number of questions answered (out of 6)	*	*	6	3.8	4.8	4.5
Respondents (No.)	13	47	14	18	15	10
Attempts (No.)	185	1283	14	18	15	10

*Not applicable.

POWERLESSNESS AND DEPERSONALIZATION

Eye contact and verbal contact reflect concern and individuation; their absence, avoidance and depersonalization. The data I have presented do not do justice to the rich daily encounters that grew up around matters of depersonalization and avoidance. I have records of patients who were beaten by staff for the sin of having initiated verbal contact. During my own experience, for example, one patient was beaten in the presence of other patients for having approached an attendant and told him, "I like you." Occasionally, punishment meted out to patients for misdemeanors seemed so excessive that it could not be justified by the most radical interpretations of psychiatric canon. Nevertheless, they appeared to go unquestioned. Tempers were often short. A patient who had not heard a call for medication would be roundly excoriated, and the morning attendants would often wake patients with, "Come on, you m____f____s, out of bed!"

Neither anecdotal nor "hard" data can convey the overwhelming sense of powerlessness which invades the individual as he is continually exposed to the depersonalization of the psychiatric hospital. It hardly matters *which* psychiatric hospital—the excellent public ones and the very plush private hospital were better than the rural and shabby ones in this regard, but, again, the features that psychiatric hospitals had in common overwhelmed by far their apparent differences.

Powerlessness was evident everywhere. The patient is deprived of many of his legal rights by dint of his psychiatric commitment. He is shorn of credibility by virtue of his psychiatric label. His freedom of movement is restricted. He cannot initiate contact with the staff, but may only respond to such overtures as they make. Personal privacy is minimal. Patient quarters and possessions can be entered and examined by any staff member, for whatever reason. His personal history and anguish is available to any staff member (often including the "grey lady"

and "candy striper" volunteer) who chooses to read his folder, regardless of their therapeutic relationship to him. His personal hygiene and waste evacuation are often monitored. The water closets may have no doors.

At times, depersonalization reached such proportions that pseudopatients had the sense that they were invisible, or at least unworthy of account. Upon being admitted, I and other pseudopatients took the initial physical examinations in a semipublic room, where staff members went about their own business as if we were not there.

On the ward, attendants delivered verbal and occasionally serious physical abuse to patients in the presence of other observing patients, some of whom (the pseudopatients) were writing it all down. Abusive behavior, on the other hand, terminated quite abruptly when other staff members were known to be coming. Staff are credible witnesses. Patients are not.

A nurse unbuttoned her uniform to adjust her brassiere in the presence of an entire ward of viewing men. One did not have the sense that she was being seductive. Rather, she didn't notice us. A group of staff persons might point to a patient in the dayroom and discuss him animatedly, as if he were not there.

One illuminating instance of depersonalization and invisibility occurred with regard to medications. All told, the pseudopatients were administered nearly 2100 pills, including Elavil, Stelazine, Compazine, and Thorazine, to name but a few. (That such a variety of medications should have been administered to patients presenting identical symptoms is itself worthy of note.) Only two were swallowed. The rest were either pocketed or deposited in the toilet. The pseudopatients were not alone in this. Although I have no precise records on how many patients rejected their medications, the pseudopatients frequently found the medications of other patients in the toilet before they deposited their own. As long as they were cooperative, their behavior and the pseudopatients' own in this matter, as in other important matters, went unnoticed throughout.

Reactions to such depersonalization among pseudopatients were intense. Although they had come to the hospital as participant observers and were fully aware that they did not "belong," they nevertheless found themselves caught up in and fighting the process of depersonalization. Some examples: a graduate student in psychology asked his wife to bring his textbooks to the hospital so he could "catch up on his homework"—this despite the elaborate precautions taken to conceal his professional association. The same student, who had trained for quite some time to get into the hospital, and who had looked forward to the experience, "remembered" some drag races that he had wanted to see on the weekend and insisted that he be discharged by that time. Another pseudopatient attempted a romance with a nurse. Subsequently, he informed the staff that he was applying for admission to graduate school in psychology and was very likely to be admitted, since a graduate professor was one of his regular hospital visitors. The same person began to engage in psychotherapy with other patients—all of this as a way of becoming a person in an impersonal environment.

THE SOURCES OF DEPERSONALIZATION

What are the origins of depersonalization? I have already mentioned two. First are attitudes held by all of us toward the mentally ill—including those who treat them—attitudes characterized by fear, distrust, and horrible expectations on the one hand, and benevolent intentions on the other. Our ambivalence leads, in this instance as in others, to avoidance.

Second, and not entirely separate, the hierarchical structure of the psychiatric hospital facilitates depersonalization. Those who are at the top have least to do with patients, and their behavior inspires the rest of the staff. Average daily contact with psy-

chiatrists, psychologists, residents, and physicians combined ranged from 3.9 to 25.1 minutes, with an overall mean of 6.8 (six pseudopatients over a total of 129 days of hospitalization). Included in this average are time spent in the admissions interview, ward meetings in the presence of a senior staff member, group and individual psychotherapy contacts, case presentation conferences, and discharge meetings. Clearly, patients do not spend much time in interpersonal contact with doctoral staff. And doctoral staff serve as models for nurses and attendants.

There are probably other sources. Psychiatric installations are presently in serious financial straits. Staff shortages are pervasive, staff time at a premium. Something has to give, and that seomthing is patient contact. Yet, while financial stresses are realities, too much can be made of them. I have the impression that the psychological forces that result in depersonalization are much stronger than the fiscal ones and that the addition of more staff would not correspondingly improve patient care in this regard. The incidence of staff meetings and the enormous amount of record-keeping on patients, for example, have not been as substantially reduced as has patient contact. Priorities exist, even during hard times. Patient contact is not a significant priority in the traditional psychiatric hospital, and fiscal pressures do not account for this. Avoidance and depersonalization may.

Heavy reliance upon psychotropic medication tacitly contributes to depersonalization by convincing staff that treatment is indeed being conducted and that further patient contact may not be necessary. Even here, however, caution needs to be exercised in understanding the role of psychotropic drugs. If patients were powerful rather than powerless, if they were viewed as interesting individuals rather than diagnostic entities, if they were socially significant rather than social lepers, if their anguish truly and wholly compelled our sympathies and concerns, would we not *seek* contact with them, despite the availability of medications? Perhaps for the pleasure of it all?

THE CONSEQUENCES OF LABELING AND DEPERSONALIZATION

Whenever the ratio of what is known to what needs to be know approaches zero, we tend to invent "knowledge" and assume that we understand more than we actually do. We seem unable to acknowledge that we simply don't know. The needs for diagnosis and remediation of behavioral and emotional problems are enormous. But rather than acknowledge that we are just embarking on understanding, we continue to label patients "schizophrenic," "manic-depressive," and "insane," as if in those words we had captured the essence of understanding. The facts of the matter are that we have known for a long time that diagnoses are often not useful or reliable, but we have nevertheless continued to use them. We now know that we cannot distinguish insanity from sanity. It is depressing to consider how that information will be used.

Not merely depressing, but frightening. How many people, one wonders, are sane but not recognized as such in our psychiatric institutions? How many have been needlessly stripped of their privileges of citizenship, from the right to vote and drive to that of handling their own accounts? How many have feigned insanity in order to avoid the criminal consequences of their behavior, and, conversely, how many would rather stand trial than live interminably in a psychiatric hospital—but are wrongly thought to be mentally ill? How many have been stigmatized by well-intentioned, but nevertheless erroneous, diagnoses? On the last point, recall again that a "type 2 error" in psychiatric diagnosis does not have the same consequences it does in medical diagnosis. A diagnosis of cancer that has been found to be in error is cause for celebration. But psychiatric diagnoses are rarely found to be in error. The label sticks, a mark of inadequacy forever.

Finally, how many patients might be

"sane" outside the psychiatric hospital but seem insane in it—not because craziness resides in them, as it were, but because they are responding to a bizarre setting, one that may be unique to institutions which harbor nether people? Goffman calls the process of socialization to such institutions "mortification"—an apt metaphor that includes the processes of depersonalization that have been described here. And while it is impossible to know whether the pseudopatients' responses to these processes are characteristic of all inmates—they were, after all, not real patients—it is difficult to believe that these processes of socialization to a psychiatric hospital provide useful attitudes or habits of response for living in the "real world."

SUMMARY AND CONCLUSIONS

It is clear that we cannot distinguish the sane from the insane in psychiatric hospitals. The hospital itself imposes a special environment in which the meanings of behavior can easily be misunderstood. The consequences to patients hospitalized in such an environment—the powerlessness, depersonalization, segregation, mortification, and self-labeling—seem undoubtedly counter-therapeutic.

I do not, even now, understand this problem well enough to perceive solutions. But two matters seem to have some promise. The first concerns the proliferation of community mental health facilities, of crisis intervention centers, of the human potential movement, and of behavior therapies that, for all of their own problems, tend to avoid psychiatric labels, to focus on specific problems and behaviors, and to retain the individual in a relatively nonpejorative environment. Clearly, to the extent that we refrain from sending the distressed to insane places, our impressions of them are less likely to be distorted. (The risk of distorted perceptions, it seems to me, is always present, since we are much more sensitive to an individual's behaviors and verbalizations than we are to the subtle contextual stimuli that often promote them. At issue here is a matter of magnitude. And, as I have shown, the magnitude of distortion is exceedingly high in the extreme context that is a psychiatric hospital.)

The second matter that might prove promising speaks to the need to increase the sensitivity of mental health workers and researchers to the *Catch 22* position of psychiatric patients. Simply reading materials in this area will be of help to some such workers and researchers. For others, directly experiencing the impact of psychiatric hospitalization will be of enormous use. Clearly, further research into the social psychology of such total institutions will both facilitate treatment and deepen understanding.

I and the other pseudopatients in the psychiatric setting had distinctly negative reactions. We do not pretend to describe the subjective experiences of true patients. Theirs may be different from ours, particularly with the passage of time and the necessary process of adaptation to one's environment. But we can and do speak to the relatively more objective indices of treatment within the hospital. It could be a mistake, and a very unfortunate one, to consider that what happened to us derived from malice or stupidity on the part of the staff. Quite the contrary, our overwhelming impression of them was of people who really cared, who were committed and who were uncommonly intelligent. Where they failed, as they sometimes did painfully, it would be more accurate to attribute those failures to the environment in which they, too, found themselves than to personal callousness. Their perceptions and behavior were controlled by the situation, rather than being motivated by a malicious disposition. In a more benign environment, one that was less attached to global diagnosis, their behaviors and judgments might have been more benign and effective.

THE WEAPONS OF INSANITY

Arnold M. Ludwig and Frank Farrelly

It is becoming fashionable to view mental patients, especially chronic schizophrenics, as poor, helpless, unfortunate creatures made sick by family and society and kept sick by prolonged hospitalization. These patients are depicted as hapless victims impotent against the powerful influences which determine their lives and shape their psychopathology. Such a view dictates a treatment philosophy aimed at reducing all the social and institutional iniquities responsible for the patient's plight. However, in the process of levelling the finger of etiological blame for the production and maintenance of chronic schizophrenia, theoreticians and clinicians have neglected another culprit—the

From *American Journal of Psychiatry,* 21 (1967), 737–49. Dr. Ludwig is Director of Education and Research and Mr. Farrelly is Social Work Student Field Instructor, Mendota State Hospital, Madison, Wisconsin.

patient himself. Professionals seem to have overlooked the rather naive possibility that schizophrenic patients become "chronic" simply because they choose to do so.

Undoubtedly, a myriad of authoritative articles could be quoted to refute such an oversimplified approach to this problem. We do not deny the complexity of the problem or the multitude of theoretical factors which should be taken into account for the understanding and treatment of these patients. Since we cannot at this point in time unravel twisted genes, undo the past, reform society, or eliminate mental hospitals, we are left with a more modest, but still formidable task—the treatment of the patient himself. The major problem is in dealing with what *is* and not with what should be or might have been. In our own experience, the problem is not so much modifying factors outside the patient, but rather in changing certain patient attitudes and consequent behaviors, as well as complementary, newly traditional attitudes on the part of society and professional staff, which aggravate the basic problem and prevent effective therapeutic intervention.

We have had the opportunity to observe closely and work with a group of thirty male and female chronic schizophrenics, handled with a minimum of medication and housed together on an experimental treatment unit. In a previous article, we outlined a number of characteristic attitudes and behaviors, both on the part of patients and staff, which tended to perpetuate chronicity. These characteristics comprise what we have called "the code of chronicity." Implicit in our discussion of the "code" are five important clinical "facts" which, we believe, underlie the behaviors of chronic schizophrenics. First, these patients can use their insanity to control people and situations. Second, they have an indomitable will of their own and are hell bent on getting their way. Third, one of the basic difficulties in rehabilitating these patients is not so much their "lack of motivation" but their intense, negative motivation to remain hospitalized. Fourth, insanity and hospitalization effectively pay off for these patients in a variety of ways. Fifth, these patients are capable of demonstrating an animal cunning in provoking certain reactions on the part of staff, family and society at large which guarantee their continued hospitalization and its consequent rewards.

Related to these characteristics are a number of other important ones, which are typical of these patients and which we want to elaborate on since they are relevant to our basic thesis concerning patient behavior. These additional features have gradually come into focus for us during the various phases of our research treatment program; in this article we shall term them the "weapons of insanity." It has become increasingly clear to us that patients both have at their disposal and employ effectively an array of counter-therapeutic weapons against staff efforts to rehabilitate them. These weapons not only reach their targets but have the additional bonus of a "fallout" effect in the form of a series of predictable staff reactions. Since one of the most effective ways to cope with these weapons is first to recognize them, we have felt the need to describe them and their effects. Moreover, since we have become convinced that for rehabilitative purposes these weapons of insanity must be jammed, then there is a necessity to consider carefully the therapeutic implications and ethical issues involved. It is our purpose to do precisely this.

THE ARSENAL OF WEAPONS

Squatter's Rights

The prevalent conception of mental hospitals as snake pits or horrible asylums from which all patients eagerly long to depart has little truth when applied to the chronic schizophrenic. In fact, one of the major problems in rehabilitating these patients is their adamant refusal to be dispossessed from their adopted hospital homeland. For many patients, especially those who feel emotionally and financially deprived, the mental hospital represents a "promised land" where the whole range of their needs is met.

The hospital comes to be a model of the idealized childhood home—a cruise on the "good ship Lollipop." Every effort is made to help the patient "feel at home": not only are the basics of food, clothing, and shelter provided, but also, as in the good childhood home, his psycho-social needs are met. He is protected from harm and pain, is relieved of any major responsibilities and demands, and has a wide variety of entertainment and recreation provided for him. His home gives him a ready made group of companions who, because they share similar experiences, give him understanding and a sense of belonging. The good parental surrogates never punish him, attempt to protect him from failure and frustration, try conscientiously to meet his immediate needs at all levels, and do not expect him, as a child, to make decisions for which he is not ready or mature enough.

The hospital thus comes to represent an emotional gold mine where patients stake their claim. They seem to grasp intuitively the legal dictum that "possession is nine-tenths of the law". If some claim jumpers, in the guise of therapeutic staff, threaten to dispossess them, especially after their years of homsteading, chronic patients will fight back with animal ferocity to defend their territory. This general attitude seems best epitomized by the remark of one patient who told the staff "You'll never railroad me out of here!"

All or Nothing

Ask any patient whether he wants to be rehabilitated and the invariable answer will be "yes." Try to do anything to effectively bring this about and the invariable behavioral response will indicate "no." One reason for this discrepancy between verbalization and behavior is that it requires minimal effort to utter the socially appropriate "yes" and maximal effort to do something about it.

There appear to be four basic components to the patients' view concerning rehabilitation. First, they sincerely *want* all the good things, such as status, power, love, material possessions, which can come with discharge. Second, they want an iron-clad guarantee that they will *get* these good things. If they are to prepare themselves for leaving the hospital, they want firm assurance that people will accept them, not derogate them for being a mental patient, not hold their behavior against them, and not reject them, and treat them with dignity and respect. Third, they expect the good things to be *given* to them free. And fourth, they are unwilling to expend any persistent effort or expose themselves to undue frustration to acquire the good things.

Almost any therapeutic staff working with these patients will recognize the "all or nothing" principle in most of their behavior. Patients want the whole pie and are often

dissatisfied with only one piece of it at a time. If they have to experience any emotional pain or stress in achieving socially appropriate goals, their most common response is to give up or say "to hell with it." This attitude and behavior is reflected in their whimsical work week or their attendance at and participation in any constructive rehabilitation program where they readily throw away all their gains at the slightest frustration or rejection—knowing full well that they can afford to do so since they can always fall back on the good will and beneficence of the hospital.

Most rehabilitation programs for chronic schizophrenics are bound to founder simply because staff have not come to grips with these patient attitudes and behaviors. The patients' problems may be explained by invoking such scientific terms as low frustration tolerance, infantile omnipotence of the wish, and poor impulse control, but these terms are only substitutional euphemisms for saying that patients want what they want, the way they want it, when they want it, and effortlessly.

Social Push-buttons

It is an interesting phenomenon that "helpless" and "confused" schizophrenics are often much more expert at producing certain reactions on the part of staff, family, and society at large than are the latter at evoking desired patient responses. Because patients have a far better understanding of our social value system with its inherent limitations than we have of theirs, they can employ a repertoire of behaviors which function as push-buttons to elicit the desired staff or social response, thereby insuring the attainment of their goal. These patient behaviors and the reactions they trigger off have an "if-then" quality to them. For example, if the patient presents any one of the following behavioral stimuli, then it will elicit a specifiable, related staff response with a high degree of probability:

a. nuisance behavior evokes irritation and anger;

b. overt sexual behavior evokes outrage;

c. aggressive-combative behavior evokes fear;

d. self-destructive behavior evokes pity;

e. stubborn withdrawal evokes frustration; and

f. crazy-bizarre behavior evokes confusion and helplessness.

When staff, family, or society become irritated and angry, outraged, fearful, pitying, frustrated, or confused and helpless, then they are automatically forced to take action in a variety of forms, the end result of which is continued hospitalization or rehospitalization.

In addition to these push-buttons there is another more general one which we have termed the "tyranny of the weak." It seems to involve a somewhat different kind of process and appears to lead to a "hands off" effect or therapeutic inaction. When we begin confronting patients and "picking on them" for therapeutic purposes, they portray themselves as helpless, weak, and vulnerable while simultaneously casting staff in the role of inhumane bullies. Because they effect this type-casting so convincingly, and because we accept these complementary good-bad roles, the consequent shame and guilt aroused in us cause us to withdraw as effectively as does a wolf in response to the exposed jugular vein of another wolf in a fight. By employing this tactic, patients frequently exploit their "weakness" tyrannically over others by forcing them to make amends for "mistreating" them.

When patients are confronted with or held accountable for these triggering behaviors, they almost always invoke the following ritualistic formulae: (a) I didn't do it—you did; (b) if I did do it, you made me do it; (c) even if I did do it, I'm not to blame—I'm emotionally and mentally disturbed.

Aside from the apparent reason of assuring continued hospitalization, it appears that there are three other factors which keep patients pushing these buttons. First, they attain power and recognition. By pushing any of these buttons, patients can mobilize social agencies, communities, families, and hospital staff to cope with their behavior ("I'll *make* you pay attention to me."). Second, this affords them a sense of control which reduces their feelings of helplessness and impotence. Third, they continue to push these buttons simply because they are so effective. People invariably respond to these patient behaviors and unwittingly continue to reinforce them.

The Divine Right of Kings

One of the central problems in treating the chronic schizophrenic centers around the issue of the patient's responsibility for his actions. At the present time, the label of insanity confers diplomatic immunity or sanctuary for all patients' deviant behaviors. Patients can gratify every impulse or whim without fear of serious retaliation. They have the sanction to indulge any of their feelings because, by definition, they are presumed not to know any better or are unable to control their impulses and, therefore, cannot be held accountable for what they do.

Not only is the patient immune from retaliation by society, but he can also buy protection from his own conscience for repugnant actions by employing the ultimate excuse of craziness. Under the sacrosanct banner of insanity, he can avoid guilt and shame for normally shocking or sickening behavior. If he so desires, he can defecate when or where he chooses, masturbate publicly, lash out aggressively, expose himself, remain inert and unproductive, or violate any social taboo with the assurance that staff are forced to "understand" rather than punish his behavior.

In many ways, the modern day patient has prerogatives similar to the medieval absolute monarch with the power and sanction to gratify his every whim. Just as the divine right of kings insured that "the king can do no wrong," so, too, the mentally ill can do no "wrong": they can only engage in "sick" behavior.

The "divine right" of the mentally ill confers other advantages. Like any monarch with his retinue of servants, chronic patients also have a number of helpers or "servants" to wait on them. In any well-staffed mental hospital, professional dieticians prepare their meals, and psychiatric aides serve them; should they need some assistance in dressing, shaving, or showering, some staff person is always available. Recreational and occupational therapists make detailed plans to amuse and keep them from becoming bored. Should they get upset, some doctor or nurse is always nearby to quell their anxiety or relieve their hurts. Social workers are ready to act as emissaries with their families and diplomatically explain the patients' "illness" to elicit understanding and acceptance. It is not surprising that several patients "delusionally" have referred to us as their servants—that the hospital exists, as in fact it does, to take care of them and minister to their needs.

Let the Healer Beware

The chronic schizophrenic has at his disposal a variety of techniques exquisitely designed to dampen or quash the therapeutic enthusiasm of almost any staff within a short period of time. By employing these techniques, the patient can preserve his prerogatives, continue to go his own way, and avoid being pestered about getting well and preparing for discharge.

It is very difficult to maintain or sustain any therapeutic zeal for these patients when almost every helpful or kind gesture is either repulsed, ignored, or unappreciated. Patients seem masters of counter-conditioning and extinction techniques; when staff try to rouse them from their apathy, correct their deviant behavior, or interest them in some constructive task, patients respond by stubbornly ignoring, cursing, spitting, hitting, threatening, or assaulting staff. Not only do patients seem ungrateful or even resentful of staff efforts, but some may even attempt to drive staff away further with Mafia-like threats of maiming or destroying their families.

In a situation where staff receive so little positive feedback or gratitude from patients, the usual response is for therapeutic interest to wane or become extinguished. When pa-

tients drop all the social amenities, courtesies and decencies, the predicted staff response is gradually to move from a position of helpfulness and concern for them to one of frustration and apathy.

In interpreting these behaviors, we are becoming increasing convinced that the patients' primary purpose is to discourage therapeutic efforts: they are fully aware that leaving the hospital means leaving many prerogatives behind. They seem to be constantly transmitting the message "go away and leave me be" or "if you must relate to me, do so on my terms."

Acts of Contrition

Even when patients do occasionally apologize or seem remorseful for their actions, they often employ ritualistic confession with no sustained, firm purpose of making amends. Their usual behavior is to do something bad, contritely confess their wrongdoing, ask for forgiveness, and shortly afterward repeat the same process, sometimes in a different form, which calls into question the credibility of their acts of contrition. Their behavior can be summarized in the formula "slap–'I'm sorry' . . . slap–'I'm sorry' . . . slap . . ." When staff find these repetitive acts of contrition unbelievable and convey their disbelief to patients, the typical patient response is to become hurt or furious at staff for not being gullible and naive enough to accept the magic words "I'm sorry."

The purpose of the repetitive utilization of these magic words seems threefold: first, to be granted a suspended sentence from any guilt or shame they themselves might feel at their behavior; second, to placate staff's animosity through this show of penance; and third, to secure the restoration of full privileges.

THE SYNDROME OF "CHRONIC STAFFRENIA"

Part of the real difficulty in establishing an effective treatment and rehabilitation program for chronic schizophrenics resides in the reaction of hospital staff toward working with these patients. Caught between what they have been taught represents "good" professional treatment and their own personal (often equated with "bad") reactions provoked by the tactics and behaviors of patients, staff eventually become incapacitated in their treatment efforts. The conflict is between how staff *should* treat patients and how they spontaneously *want* to respond.

It is easy to understand the genesis of this bind. If staff accept the view that the mentally ill patient is not responsible for his actions, then it follows that the essentials of any humanitarian treatment approach must always be comprised of love, kindness, acceptance, and understanding; above all, it is professionally inappropriate to criticize strongly, to react angrily, or punish patients for their behavior since such behavior has been caused by factors beyond their control. On the other hand, day to day experience with these patients invariably arouses in staff reactions which are diametrically opposed to those which they are expected to feel.

If staff attitudes *must* under all circumstances be those of patience, helpfulness, love and acceptance, what options do staff have when they frequently find themselves impatient, helpless, angry and revolted by patients' behaviors? Not only is it difficult for staff to act persistently one way when they feel another, but this same hypocritical facade weakens the therapeutic effectiveness of their efforts. Despite the loud and clear messages from their adrenals and viscera, staff are permitted only a very limited response repertoire to the behavioral weapons employed by patients.

Staff tend to resolve the conflicts of this bind by assuming an observable set of attitudes and behaviors which oftentimes complement those of patients. We have labelled this characteristic staff reaction the syndrome of "chronic staffrenia." The components of this syndrome include apathy, weariness, minimal personal involvement, decreased enthusiasm, lack of emotional investment, and markedly decreased expectations for patient rehabilitation. Staff attitudes are depicted by such statements as "let well enough alone," or "to hell with it—it just isn't worth it." Staff increasingly withdraw and engage in perfunctory therapeutic activities which, regardless of their name, at best resemble good custodial care, and they become all too happy to settle for patient cooperation in lieu of patient rehabilitation. Any program that aims at rehabilitating chronic schizophrenics (in contrast to one that merely provides good custodial care) must anticipate this syndrome and take measures to prevent or cope with its development.

IMPLICATIONS FOR TREATMENT

Any therapeutic program primarily employing psychosocial techniques for the modification of chronic schizophrenic behavior must make certain operational assumptions as a basis for effective therapeutic action. The primary and most important assumption is that the patient is responsible for his actions and can muster up the necessary will power to act sanely and decently if he should choose, or be made to choose, to do so. Given this assumption, certain treatment implications follow.

First, staff must hold patients accountable for their actions, rewarding appropriate behavior and punishing inappropriate or deviant behavior. One of the problems in such a seemingly simple philosophy is that it runs counter to much current clinical thought. It is our feeling that today's dynamically oriented theoreticians have placed the onus of responsibility for the patient's behavior on such scapegoat devils as mother, society, or mythical biochemical abnormalities, rather than on the individual patient himself. With such convenient whipping boys, where everyone is to blame, nobody is to blame. If the patient cannot be blamed, then, it follows, he cannot take credit for healthy, sane behavior. We contend that holding patients responsible for both their good and bad behavior invests them with human dignity and hope; not holding them responsible is tantamount to pronouncing them hopeless.

Our own simplified view of psychotherapy dictates that the assumption of responsibility by the patient represents a prerequisite for any further constructive behavioral change. If patients are to be receptive to treatment, their attitude must include four successive components or stages which are as follows: (a) I am responsible for my behavior; (b) I want to change my behavior since it dissatisfies me; (c) I need help; and (d) I will cooperate with the help you give me. These stages not only hold for the rehabilitation of the alcoholic, juvenile delinquent, criminal, character disorder, and psychoneurotic, but for the chronic schizophrenic as well. The major problem with the chronic patient is to get him to move from a position where he denies all responsibility for his behavior or excuses it under the banner of insanity to the first of these stages. Once this is done, a major barrier is crossed.

Since staff have been commissioned to intervene therapeutically with these patients, the second treatment implication is that staff must have certain rights consonant with their obligations. In our current and legitimate concern for the rights of patients, we have overlooked or ignored the rights of those working with them. What currently obtains in most treatment programs is that staff have "the right" to being cursed, threatened, or assaulted by ungrateful patients without being able to punish them for their actions or to vent openly their genuine feelings. However, we insist that staff should and do have certain rights: the right to expect gratitude from patients and safety from physical harm, to interact honestly with patients, to be creative, and to derive a sense of accomplishment from their work. These are not idealized luxuries but absolute necessities for treatment staff. Unless their necessary rights are encouraged, implemented and insured, we are convinced that no intensive, persistent, and concerted staff treatment effort can occur. Unless staff can demand responsible behavior and respect for their rights from patients, the counter-therapeutic tactics of patients will surely and inevitably extinguish any remnants of staff rehabilitative efforts in their regard.

A third treatment implication is that staff be genuine with patients. We propose that staff not be pressured to hide behind pseudo-humanitarian treatment slogans which decree that love and understanding are the *only* appropriate responses to all patient behaviors and that anger and even occasional hatred are antitherapeutic. There is nothing inherently wrong in admiring and liking the good qualities of patients while, at the same time, disliking and rejecting their undesirable qualities. If staff are forced to conform to hackneyed platitudes, their response, at best, will consist of perfunctory love, phony acceptance, misguided kindness or biased understanding. We believe it most appropriate that staff be allowed to give patients *accurate* and *honest* human feedback concerning the impact and social consequences of their behaviors. For example, it is unreasonable to insist that staff adopt inappropriate smiles or act kindly toward patients while brimming with anger. Our contention is that "love and understanding" are not simply insufficient, but at times are actually incongruous and damaging in response to certain patient behaviors. Staff should be allowed and encouraged to use a *whole* relationship: both to be positive, warm, and loving when patients behave sanely and well, and also to be angry, rebuking, rejecting, and punishing when patients are obnoxious or bad. The combination of Pollyanna plus Scrooge represents a more whole, integrated, human response; either alone is a travesty.

A fourth implication pertains to the so-called rights and prerogatives of the chronic patient. From our assumptions it follows that patients not be allowed to become too comfortable or settled in the hospital. It is imperative that staff feel free to usurp and confiscate the patient's "squatter's rights," and convey insistently and persistently to patients that they not only do not have the right to remain in the hospital, but that the only virgin land available for homesteading lies outside the hospital.

Other treatment implications pertain directly to jamming the various weapons which patients employ. It makes little sense to continue to treat these patients as perpetual convalescents and invalids by waiting on them and thereby encouraging and reinforcing dependency. As long as patients can continue to gain all the prerogatives and privileges without effort, there is little incentive for them to change. As long as their craziness continues to pay off without uncomfortable repercussions or sanctions, we encourage the development and perpetuation of chronicity.

ETHICAL ISSUES

In evolving a treatment philosophy for chronic schizophrenics, we have had to grapple with a number of ethical issues, posed by ourselves and respected colleagues, concerning staff attitudes and treatment approaches toward these patients. Since the direction and development of any treatment program is contingent upon how these issues are resolved, their importance cannot be stressed enough.

One of the immediate ethical issues involves the use of punishment for patients. Without delving into all the aspects of this problem, which would require a separate paper to do full justice to it, we will simply say that this issue is largely artificial or moot, for there are no psychosocial techniques for instituting human behavioral change which do not employ the very potent tools of both reward and punishment. Even those programs which espouse only benevolent approaches make liberal use of such negative reinforcements as withholding privileges, withdrawing love or approval, restraints and seclusion, ECT and drugs for the avowed purpose of "controlling" patient behavior, but the rationales offered are often only euphemistic or socially condoned excuses for subtle or blatant punishments. The issue is not whether punishments should be used; they are and will be—this is simply a fact of all clinical and social life. The real issue is whether punishments will be administered openly, non-apologetically, and in a consistent, systematic, goal-oriented manner rather than on a disguised, apologetic, whimsical and haphazard basis.

There are those who fear that once the

use of punishment is openly acknowledged and condoned, it might well serve as a vehicle for sadism. We sympathize with and share this concern; however, the essence of the problem is whether the therapist uses punishment solely for his own gratification or the patient's welfare. Our position is simply that if a therapist is sadistic, he will be ingenious enough to find a vehicle for his sadism in any type of therapeutic approach, even in benign non-directive therapies. Or, to put it differently, the beatific smile of the therapist does not guarantee that there are not fangs hidden behind it.

A critical ethical question is to what lengths will we go to implement our treatment goals? Should the goal be to maintain a chronic schizophrenic comfortably in the hospital or to undertake the more ambitious task of helping him become a relatively whole, occasionally uncomfortable person functioning outside the hospital? If we choose the latter goal (a formidable task), then, it follows, that certain procedures, which might be considered drastic or extreme, will have to be employed.

It cannot be overemphasized how serious and malignant a problem chronic schizophrenia is. As the situation now stands, these patients represent serious economic, social, political, and psychological debits not only to society but themselves as well. Many represent the psychological equivalents of terminal cancer patients, devoid of any prospects of a productive existence. Therefore, we have to make the operational value choice of either preparing them for a comfortable psychological demise or using, if necessary, radical procedures which measurably increase their chance for responsible meaningful living.

In any radical procedure there must be a willingness to balance the potential risks against the possible gains. It is our impression that most professionals working in this area have been reluctant to confront the issue of risk and have chosen instead to play it safe. One way of playing it safe has been to settle for more modest treatment goals for these patients. Another way (but a valuable one at that) is to concentrate exclusively on the etiological and preventative aspects of the problem. It is riskier, but at least equally important, to engage the problem here and now—that is, if we are not going to let patients psychologically rot in the mental hospitals until we engineer social change or determine the presumed biochemical abnormality underlying this disorder.

The bind we are in, whether we like it or not, is that we must deal with these patients. In doing so, we have to choose between two options. We can employ palliative procedures with the risk of keeping patients psychologically moribund or of leading to their psychological death; or we can try radical psychosocial procedures with the possibility of curing the patient, but with the risk of his getting worse. Should this latter possibility occur, the therapist lays himself open to being labelled antitherapeutic or destructive; we suspect that one reason many therapists have chosen palliative procedures is not to risk censure from colleagues and to avoid receiving such labels. Unfortunately for patients, we have been too bound to the principle of *primum non nocere* ("first, do no harm), and, as a result, have been employing a variety of gumdrop therapies for a very malignant problem.

Long ago Archimedes stated that if he had a lever long enough and a fulcrum on which to rest it, he could move the earth. It is our contention that we already have at our disposal some therapeutic levers or techniques for dealing with chronic schizophrenics. If our goal is the ultimate rehabilitation of these patients, we must begin to search for even more potent and effective levers, which may involve to some degree the use of pain, deprivation, and punishment—all socially sensitive areas in the treatment of patients. It is not enough simply to theorize about these techniques; we must demonstrate a willingness to use and evaluate them.

A final ethical issue concerns the question of whether patients should have the right to opt out of living in normal society. For those who find life and responsibility too stressful, should we provide some haven or retreat in the form of mental hospitals, where they can spend the remainder of their days in relative peace and quiet? Perhaps the ramifications of this issue could be debated endlessly; we have resolved this issue for ourselves by arbitrarily claiming that just as a person does not have the social or legal right to commit suicide, so, too, the chronic schizophrenic does *not* have the right to commit psychological suicide by giving up or opting out through prolonged hospitalization. Again, just as when a person attempts suicide, every possible technique or treatment, no matter how drastic, is employed by the physician to aid him, so, too, we contend that every possible therapeutic technique, even those seemingly drastic, should be brought to bear to psycho-socially revive the chronic schizophrenic.

QUESTIONS FOR DISCUSSION

1. Of the several types of mental illness discussed, which ones do you feel you know least about? What are the reasons for your selections?
2. Do you agree with Szasz, "that the notion of mental illness has outlived whatever usefulness it might have had and that it now functions merely as a convenient myth"? If you accept his point of view, what are some of the important implications of this position? Do you find any weakness in his argument?
3. Ludwig and Farrelly, in their discussion of "the weapons of insanity" raise the question of "whether patients should have the right to opt out of living in normal society"? Build the best case you can for the affirmative and negative sides of this question. Which viewpoint makes most sense to you? Why?
4. Visit a state mental hospital. How would you evaluate the general conditions? Obtain information on patient care and types of therapy currently in use. In what ways did your expectations differ from what you experienced?
5. Discuss the difficulties of psychodiagnostic labels that Rosenhan describes with a psychiatrist working in your campus health center or one employed in private

practice in your community. Does he see the problem from the same point of view as Rosenhan? Try to find out how he resolves some of the problems Rosenhan raises. Discuss the ethical dilemmas suggested by Rosenhan and his associates.

6. Read the definitions of the types of mental disorders in the Glossary and discuss them from a labeling perspective. From a psychodiagnostic point of view? From a legal point of view?

7. Why is the state hospital population declining when the prevalence of the various disorders in the population is at least as high as ever? Where are the former patients going?

8. Visit a community mental health center and discuss its operations. Is it effective? How would you measure its effectiveness?

9. Describe the range of problems treated in this community mental health center. Are all these legitimate psychiatric concerns?

BIBLIOGRAPHY

Action for Mental Health: The Final Report of the Joint Commission on Mental Illness and Health. New York: Basic Books, 1961.

Allen, R., Ferster, E., and Weihofen, H. *Mental Impairment and Legal Incompetency.* Englewood Cliffs, N.J.: Prentice Hall, 1968.

Angrist, Shirley S., Lefton, Mark, Dinitz, Simon, Pasamanick, Benjamin. *Women After Treatment, A Study of Former Mental Patients and Their Normal Neighbors.* New York: Appleton-Century-Crofts, 1968.

Bastide, Roger. *The Sociology of Mental Disorder.* New York: McKay, 1972.

Bord, R. J. "Rejection of the Mentally Ill: Continuities and Further Developments." *Social Problems* 18 (Spring), 496–509.

Colarelli, Nick J., and Siegel, Saul M. *Ward H: An Adventure in Innovation.* New York: Van Nostrand, 1966.

Faris, Robert E. L., and Warren Dunham, H. *Mental Disorders in Urban Areas.* Chicago: The University of Chicago Press, 1939.

Felix, R. H. *Mental Illness: Progress and Prospects.* New York: Columbia University Press, 1967.

Fischer, Roland, and Thatcher, Karen. "The History of Psychiatry." In *Research in Comprehensive Psychiatry.* The Ohio State University, College of Medicine, 1971.

Foucault, Michel. *Madness and Civilization: A History of Insanity in the Age of Reason.* New York: Random House, 1965.

Freeman, Howard E., and Simmons, Ozzie G. *The Mental Patient Comes Home.* New York: Wiley, 1963.

Linsky, A. S. "Who Shall be Excluded: The Influence of Personal Attributes in Community Reaction to the Mentally Ill." *Social Psychiatry* 5 (July 1970), 166–71.

Martindale, Don, and Martindale, Edith. *The Social Dimensions of Mental Illness, Alcoholism and Drug Dependence.* Westport: Greenwood, 1972.

Masland, Richard L., Sarason, S. B., and Gladwin, T. *Mental Subnormality.* New York: Basic Books, 1958.

Mechanic, David. *Mental Health and Social Policy.* Englewood Cliffs, N.J.: Prentice-Hall, 1969.

Miller, Dorothy. *Worlds That Fail: Part I, Retrospective Analysis of Mental Patients' Careers.* State of California, Department of Mental Hygiene, Research Monograph No. 6. 1965.

Phillips, D. L. "Rejection: A Possible Consequence of Seeking Help for Mental Disorders." *American Sociological Review* 28 (December 1963), 963–72.

Robins, Lee. *Deviant Children Grown Up.* Baltimore: Williams and Wilkins, 1966.

Rogler, Lloyd, and Hollingshead, August B. *Trapped: Families and Schizophrenia.* New York: Wiley, 1965.

Scheff, Thomas J., ed. *Mental Illness and Social Processes.* New York: Harper and Row, 1967.

Schizophrenia Bulletin. National Institute of Mental Health, Issues 1–8.

Spitzer, Stephen P., and Denzin, Norman, eds. *The Mental Patient: Studies in Sociology of Deviance.* New York: McGraw-Hill, 1968.

Szasz, Thomas. *The Manufacture of Madness.* New York: Harper and Row, 1970.

Yarrow, M. R., Schwartz, C. G., Murphy, H. S., and Deasy, L. C. "The Psychological Meaning of Mental Illness in the Family," *Journal of Social Issues* 11 (December 1955), 12–24.

WILLING VICTIMS AND VICTIMLESS ACTS

The only purpose for which power can rightfully be exercised over any member of a civilized community, against his will, is to prevent harm to others. His own good, either physical or moral, is not a warrant.

John Stuart Mill

Thou shall not kill; but need not strive officiously to keep alive.

Arthur Hugh Clough
The Latest Decalogue

What were once vices are now the manners of the day.

Seneca

Should the state have any right at all to dictate that the pregnant woman has to carry her child to term?

Gilbert Geis.

The modern prostitute . . . tends to employ others rather than to be employed.

New Society

If we think we regulate printing, thereby to rectify manners, we must regulate all recreations and pastimes, all that is delightful to man.

John Milton

Every society has a right to preserve public peace and order and therefore has the good right to prohibit the propagation of opinions which have a dangerous tendancy.

Samuel Johnson

(When two ladies praised Johnson for omitting indecent words in his dictionary, he noted that they must have been looking for them.)

A suicide is a person who has considered his own case and decided he is worthless and who acts as his own judge, jury and executioner and he probably knows better than anyone else whether there is justice in the verdict.

Don Marquis

To be or not to be—that is the question.

Shakespeare, Hamlet

8
Abortion

Throughout history, there have been a number of types of behavior which have been at the center of moral controversy. Religious traditions have grappled with such behavior in terms of conceptions of morality and evaluations in terms of sinfulness. Such behavior has also been evaluated in terms of secular ethical systems. Because of this constant preoccupation with the moral evaluation of behavior throughout history, it is not surprising that moral judgements would, at certain times and in certain societies, become incorporated into law. When moral judgements become a part of law, they are supported by legal sanctions. Sexual behavior has always been subject to moral evaluations, and certain aspects of these evaluations have at times become incorporated into law.

There are certain types of actions, such as abortion, prostitution, and the use of pornography, which often become the focus of legal attention and, in addition, become prime illustrations of the difficulty of enforcing laws that prohibit practices which are in fact desired by all of the parties involved. They are, in short, offenses and deviations without "victims." In all instances, the services are desired, indeed demanded, by the clients who themselves are law-abiding persons. In all instances it is the purveyor of the service and not the consumer who is the concern of law enforce-

ment. The female seeking the abortion, the "trick" or the "John," and the "hard core" consumer are almost wholly exempt from criminal taint and stigma. Under these circumstances, the historic American adage of "let the buyer beware" is translated into "let the seller take his risk as a law violator." Little wonder, then, that in this situation the consumer, devoid of risk, provides an endless market for these services and the seller, accepting all of the risk, simply tailors his organization and prices to fit.

Unlike the status offenses of drunkenness, drug addiction, and homosexuality in which the deviant may lack the necessary intent in the eyes of the law, the victimless crimes involve no such "limited liability." One can hardly contend that the prospects or purveyors of these services are irresponsible and unable to control this aspect of their conduct. Indeed, the reverse is usually, though not always, the case. Hence the chief characteristic of these specific deviations is in the willingness and eagerness of all parties concerned to provide or to receive an unlawful service—for a price.

Abortion typifies the problem about as well as any other victimless crime. Many thousands, perhaps millions, of women each year seek to terminate unwanted pregnancies. Some, perhaps even the majority, attempt self-induced abortions. Until recently when legalized abortion was widely available, those women desiring abortions had to seek out men and women, skilled and unskilled to do the job. The great pressure for abortion led to the development of the professional abortionist who worked either solo or as a member of an abortion mill or ring.

In this first article, Professor Edwin Schur is concerned with the emergence of this "specialist" as a predictable response to the traffic in abortion. Two types of criminal abortion practitioners are identified and described. Much of the article is given over to a description of the illegal organization of the abortion business, particularly to the abortion mill and ring. The business aspect of abortion is described, not the medical and surgical aspect. Discussion of the opportunities for police corruption and the difficult problems of enforcing abortion laws conclude this article.

In the second selection, Professor Geis summarizes historical and legal changes concerning abortion in Colorado, California, New York, and several other regions in the United States. This is followed by a similar discussion of what is happening in Great Britain, Japan, Sweden, and the Soviet bloc, hoping that the experiences in these countries might provide material that will be useful in understanding the diverse American arrangements. He reminds his readers that virtually all writing and discussion about abortion focuses upon the expectant mother, yet criminal penalties are directed toward the one who performs the abortion. The reasons for rapid and widespread changes in abortion laws are discussed, as well as the significance of the nationally known Sherri Finkbine case which probably more than any other single event placed the abortion issue in the public arena.

While Geis does point to the changes occurring in various state laws which define abortion, those changes which were occurring did not provide the necessary "warning" for the rather radical redefinition of abortion which was to occur in 1973. In *Roe* v. *Wade* (410 U.S.113) 1973, the Supreme Court held unconstitutional a typical state law against abortion. Essentially, the court ruled that there was a fundamental right to do with one's body as one pleases, including terminating a pregnancy. From this basic premise, the Court argued that the state had no valid interest in banning abortion during the first trimester of pregnancy. In the second trimester, there may be regulation of abortion to the extent that it is related to maternal health. In effect, then, the Court suggested that during the first six months of pregnancy, the termination of pregnancy was a matter of choice for the patient and doctor. Since the time of the court decision, a number of state laws have been rewritten.

While in 1974, there are still areas where it is difficult to get legal abortions, in many areas abortion clinics have developed and abortions are available in many public hospitals. It was estimated that 800,000 legal abortions were performed in 1973—about the same as the estimated number of illegal abortions in each of the years immediately prior to the court decision. Since abortions were not available in certain communities, it was estimated that perhaps half of those abortions done in New York City were performed on women from out of state. One consequence of the legalization seemingly has been a dramatic drop in maternal deaths. In the years before the new New York law was in effect, there were 5.3 maternal deaths for every 10,000 births; by 1972, this figure had fallen to 2.6.

This rather rapid change in the legal status of abortion is consistent with the direction of change of other victimless acts—a move toward "decriminalization" and toward placing the issues back in their previous status as individual moral issues. The decision by the Supreme Court has not been without criticism, in particular by a number of "right to life" organizations—many of them encouraged and supported by the Roman Catholic Church. To overturn the decision, however, would require a constitutional amendment since so much of the battle has shifted to Congress. One such bill already introduced would guarantee all personal rights under the Fifth and Fourteenth

Amendments to the unborn child. In effect, it would turn abortion into murder under the law. In addition, riders have already been attached to health legislation which would permit federally funded private hospitals to refuse to perform abortions. The issue is obviously not "solved" but the fact that abortions are widely available, as well as legal, represents a dramatic shift in the definition of abortion in a very short time. In effect, it places the issue as a matter of individual choice and as a medical problem rather than a legal one.

CRIMES WITHOUT VICTIMS: ABORTION

Edwin M. Schur

Abortion is the termination of pregnancy before the unborn child or fetus attains viability—i.e., capacity for life outside the womb. In this discussion the term abortion refers to induced or intentional abortion; it does not include miscarriage, which is technically designated spontaneous abortion.

According to an authoritative anthropological survey, it appears that abortion is a universal phenomenon, and that "it is impossible even to construct an imaginary social system in which no woman would even feel at least impelled to abort." There have always been women who became pregnant against their wills, and different cultures have chosen different ways of dealing with this problem. Abortion has been incurred for almost every conceivable reason, and through a vast array of techniques. Cross-cultural evidence also reveals tremendous variation in the acceptable grounds for abortion.

In the United States, legal norms regarding abortion are highly restrictive. A well-publicized illustration of this fact was provided in 1962 by the case of Mrs. Robert Finkbine, a thirty-year-old resident of Arizona and the mother of four children. Early in her pregnancy, Mrs. Finkbine had taken some tranquilizers containing thalidomide—a drug later revealed to lead to a high rate of

From *Crimes Without Victims: Deviant Behavior and Public Policy—Abortion, Homosexuality and Drug Addiction*, Englewood Cliffs, N.J.: Prentice-Hall, Inc. (Spectrum), 1965, pp. 11–40. Reprinted by permission. Professor Schur is in the Department of Sociology, New York University.

birth deformities when taken by pregnant women. Believing that the birth of a deformed baby would impose an undue hardship on the other members of the family, Mrs. Finkbine and her husband sought medical advice. Although at first reluctant to have an abortion, they eventually decided that such a step would be best for all concerned. A panel of staff physicians at a local hospital agreed that the operation should be performed, and this decision was concurred in by examining psychiatrists. At the last minute, however, the doctors were overruled by the hospital administrator, who demanded clarification of the operation's legal status. Mrs. Finkbine then sought from the Arizona courts a declaratory judgment certifying that her abortion would fall within the statutory exception ("when necessary to preserve the mother's life"). She was unable to obtain it. As a result of this setback, Mrs. Finkbine decided "to seek help in a more favorable legal climate," and eventually obtained a legal abortion in Sweden, where the laws on this matter are much less restrictive. . . .

Although Mrs. Finkbine's specific problem was an unusual one, there is nothing very unusual about the demand for, and the obtaining of, abortions in this country. Summing up extensive research on a sample of over 5000 white nonprison females, the late Dr. Alfred Kinsey reported that, by the time they were forty-five years of age, 22 percent of the married women had had one or more induced abortions. According to careful evaluation by an expert statistical committee established by the Planned Parenthood Federation's 1955 conference on abortion, the number of induced abortions in the United States each year is probably at least 200,000, and may be as high as 1.2 million. Available evidence indicates that the women seeking abortions are of all races, religions, and socioeconomic classes; many are married, and often already mothers. Under the laws of the various American states—which generally permit abortion only when medically necessary to save the mother's life— most of the abortions are illegal. . . .

THE ABORTIONIST

Society's unwillingness to provide social and legal sanction for abortion has led to the growth of a thriving illicit traffic in such operations, and to the emergence of the "professional" criminal abortionist. An early discussion nicely summarized the strength of the abortionist's position and the way a social need propelled the development of illegal abortion machinery:

An endless circle was . . . set in motion. The ready willingness of women to visit an abortionist brought him immense profits. A fraction of these profits made it possible to cause an abortion with a greater degree of safety to the woman and a smaller chance of exposure of either the woman or the doctor. This led to a further appeal to women who wished to bring an abrupt termination to their pregnancies. And so the chain was complete.

There is little doubt that the abortionist's practice is extremely widespread in the United States today, although estimates on criminal abortion (which would include self-induced abortions as well as those performed by "professionals") are uncertain. One writer in 1951 estimated a minimum of 330,000 criminal abortions each year, of which at least 300,000 involved an abortionist. This figure was based on an assumed grand total of a million abortions, about two-thirds spontaneous and one-third induced. Yet, as the abortion conference estimate

cited suggests, the total of induced abortions alone may be as high as a million; in that case the number of criminal abortions would be much higher than 330,000. It has been reported that police consider criminal abortion the third biggest illegal endeavor in the United States, surpassed only by gambling and narcotics, and experts claim that criminal abortions exist in almost every city (perhaps even every town) throughout the country.

Conflicting statements have been made concerning the training, skill, and motives of the professional abortionist. Some accounts insist that most illegal abortions are performed by persons who have no medical training, and refer to such persons as "butchers" or "mechanics." There is little doubt that some professional abortionists do fall into this category. On the other hand, there are abortionists who are fully trained physicians. It is well-known that the physician who for one reason or another has lost his license to practice medicine, and the foreign-trained doctor who experiences difficulty in being admitted to practice in this country, may be especially likely to turn to an illegal abortion practice. There are also trained physicians who drift into illegal abortion work gradually, usually beginning with the performance of abortions as favors to their legitimate patients. Some physicians simply enter the field because of the lure of easy money. It is sometimes suggested that there are special psychological reasons which propel a given physician into abortion practice, but the substantiation of such claims appears rather meager.

Variations in Skill

There is no way of accurately gauging the relative proportions of physician and non-physician abortionists. In the Kinsey survey, women reporting illegal abortions indicated that about 85 percent had been performed by physicians. Probably there were some instances in which women reported as physicians persons who were not actually licensed practitioners. Furthermore, Kinsey's general sample was biased toward those groups of women who would best be able to obtain competent abortion services. In addition, many of the illegal abortions reported in this study were performed without cost, or at least by doctors who had legitimate medical practices. As a result, the findings may exaggerate the actual participation by licensed physicians in regular abortion work. Nonetheless, the data from this study do suggest that some abortionists are well-trained, skilled medical men. On the basis of interviews with a limited number of professional abortion specialists, the Kinsey team reported being impressed with their technical ability and with the low number of reported deaths and other complications from their operations. They even cited the case of one specialist (with a fairly well-supported claim of having performed 30,000 abortions without a single death) who tried, unsuccessfully, to hire a psychiatric social worker to counsel prospective patients. More generally, these researchers emphasized that although the profit motive obviously may lead a doctor into an abortion practice, those they interviewed displayed a higher degree of medical qualifications than earlier accounts had led them to expect. . . .

Even if it is impossible to determine the extent of medical accreditation among abortionists, it is clear that at least the more skilled among them can claim an indirect link with legitimate medical practice—in that a considerable proportion of their patients have been referred to them by licensed physicians. This point was discussed at the Planned Parenthood Federation's 1955 conference on abortion by a once-licensed doctor who for some twenty years had carried on an illegal abortion practice in Baltimore. He asserted that there were 353 doctors in that community whom he had served for many years, and from many of whom he actually had signed letters of referral. He claimed further than when he had been brought to trial on abortion charges, he refrained from implicating any of these physicians. They, on the other hand, refused to support him in any way, and a few were

actually instrumental in bringing about his conviction. If this story is true, and there is little reason to doubt it, it nicely points up the ambivalent attitude of the medical profession on the abortion issue.

This case also suggests the highly ambiguous professional status of the skilled abortionist. The non-medical abortionist, who clearly defines himself as an illicit practitioner and who is so defined by the public at large, may experience somewhat less role confusion than the one who is medically trained. The nonmedical abortionist is less concerned about being labeled a criminal, he has no formal medical credentials to lose, he makes no pretense to medical competence. He may associate with various disreputable individuals who serve to confirm and support his deviant self-image. The medical man who takes up an abortion practice, however, may often be torn between conflicting images of his professional and social self. He is more likely than his nonphysician counterparts to desire the esteem of, and contact with, legitimate practitioners. He still considers himself a doctor, and only with the greatest reluctance can he accept concern for the plight of his patients, and is anxious to exercise due care in their treatment—something he is not always able to do if he as at the same time to insure his own safety from detection and prosecution. Although he feels he performs a useful function both for his patients and for his legitimate professional colleagues, he knows that when the chips are down he will receive little open support.

Dangers of Illegal Abortion

It may be useful at this point to comment briefly on the question of the deaths that occur in illegal abortions. Early estimates placed the annual number of such deaths in this country at 8,000 or more. As late as 1951, one expert suggested there still might be 5,000–6,000 such deaths annually. The use of antibiotics and the exercise of increased care have clearly decreased the likelihood of death from criminal abortion. Statistics on known abortion deaths in New

York City show a steady declining trend, from 144 deaths in 1921 to 15 in 1951. Commenting on these figures, the city's chief medical examiner stated: "I believe there are just as many abortions being done, but that they are being done under better conditions." He also noted some interesting breakdowns of these statistics: a disproportionate number of the women who died from abortions were Negroes, and although more of the women who underwent abortions were married, there were "more deaths from crudely done criminal abortion with very severe injury" among those who were single. These data indicate the relatively more desperate plight of the single woman. She is more likely than the married woman to expose herself to a crude abortionist, and if postabortal complications develop, she is apt to wait longer before seeking medical help.

There are cases in which the inept technique of an unskilled abortionist directly leads to death. But even the fairly conscientious abortionist works under imperfect conditions, and must for his own safety get the woman to leave his place of work as soon after the operation as possible. Hence the inadequacy of aftercare, the frequent lack of necessary medicines and emergency equipment, and the dangers inherent in the abortion itself (at least when the abortionist has not had the proper training) combine to make criminal abortion highly dangerous even today. The immediate dangers and primary causes of death are shock, hemorrhage, embolism, infection, and poisoning.

Certain illegal abortion techniques may pose special dangers. For instance, injection of potassium soap compounds into the uterus by pressure syringe may be extremely dangerous. These pastes have been available "on the open market, ... being sold ostensibly for use as antiseptics and not as abortifacients ..." despite federal prosecutions under misbranding provisions of the federal Food, Drug and Cosmetic Act.

Another popular abortion procedure has been the insertion into the uterus of a catheter—an elongated, tubular instrument often made of rubber or fiber. Left in the uterus, it acts as an irritant. This technique is sometimes used even in the late months of pregnancy. It has been widely used in New York City, often in such a way as to facilitate "getting around the law." The abortionist inserts a catheter and, knowing that bleeding may not start for some time, immediately sends the woman home with instructions to return when she begins to bleed. If by chance his office is raided during her return visit, the abortionist can claim that he was merely treating her for the bleeding. Usually the woman will uphold his story.

Fees

In the Kinsey sample most illegal abortions were reported to have been operative (i.e. dilatation and curettage) and, as already noted, performed by physicians. These factors would minimize the risk of death or serious complications, but the limitations of ·the sample make it impossible to infer that most criminal abortions are now being performed under these relatively favorable conditions. As suggested earlier, the woman's socioeconomic status will help to determine the legal and illegal treatment she receives. One commentator has suggested that the distinction between "therapeutic" and "illegal" abortion represents merely a financial artifact: "in many circumstances the difference between the one and the other is $300 and knowing the 'right' person." The opportunities for illegal treatment are also determined largely by finances. ... While a five-dollar job (performed by an untrained operator) is quite likely to be bungled and to lead to serious complications or even death, the patient able to pay a large sum of money (say, a thousand dollars) can obtain the services of a skilled physician.

Not only does this ability-to-pay criterion lead to less competent and safe treatment for working-class women, but it also introduces the irony that the well-to-do woman with "connections" may be more likely to encounter the sympathetic practitioner who will charge only a reasonable (for her) fee. It is noteworthy that the Kinsey sample, which overrepresented the higher socioeconomic categories, contained quite a few cases of abortions performed free of charge—presumably as a favor by a family physician. The fees paid by these women do not appear excessive. Excluding all abortions secured without cost, the median amounts paid for illegal operative abortions were: $84 for single women, $77 for the married ones, and $98 for the previously married. The working-class or lower-middle-class woman, on the other hand, will often obtain the services of an unscrupulous operator who is really out to get all he can. Thus the clients' socioeconomic position (some of the Kinsey data indicate that this is the case), the relative deprivation may actually be greater in the lower strata.

The woman seeking an abortion is usually in no position to argue strongly about the fee:

Criminal abortionists charge as much as $2000—whatever the traffic will bear. Today the average fee in Chicago is $400 or $500. It is more in New York. In Los Angeles a midwife charges $25; a male nurse, $100; a chiropractor, $150 to $200; and a medical doctor or osteopath, at least $500. The highest price known there in recent years is $1800, and $1000 is not uncommon. . . .

ILLEGAL ORGANIZATION

It is not at all surprising that an illegal business with such potentially high profits should, at least in part, be well organized. The modifying phrase at least in part is necessary to indicate that illicit abortion services are not controlled by a monolithic criminal organization and to take into account that different types of individuals perform these services under a wide variety of circumstances. Except for the legitimate practitioner who occasionally performs an abortion for a patient or friend, it should be evident that the nature of abortion practice invariably implies a certain amount of organization. To be successful, the abortionist requires adequate equipment, a place in

which to work, and some technical or other assistance. Potential customers must learn of his existence and location, yet at the same time a certain amount of anonymity must be maintained. Some means of avoiding police interference must also be developed—whether it be the elaboration of an extremely convincing front, a continuous shifting of location, or a direct or indirect financial arrangement with the authorities.

Given these imperatives, highly elaborate behavior systems have developed in the abortion profession. One report noted the existence in New York City of two "fairly complex social structures," the abortion "mill" and the abortion "ring." The mill involved one or more abortionists permanently located and aborting about a dozen women daily. The ring consisted of "a number of interacting abortionists or mills working intermittently at several occasionally changing locations and aborting an even more considerable number of women daily. . . . Clients are accommodated at the various locations depending on the pressure of referrals, the availability of operators at the moment of need, and the ability of the client to pay. . . ." Although mill may not seem a properly nonmoralistic designation, this term, apparently adopted from enforcement parlance, does point up the organized nature and continually high rate of activity of even the smaller of the two types of enterprises. According to Bates, the physician whose abortion practice is large and well-organized enough to fall into the mill category is likely to employ a business staff as well as medical assistants. Besides a secretary-receptionist, there may often be a business agent or manager. The business agent handles dealings with the landlord, and the payment of salaries, bills, bribes, and split fees. He may also function as contact man between the abortionist and the various sources of referral. Some large mills have also been known to employ "runners" to bring sources of referral into contact with the business agent. Bates notes that because of the confidential nature of the job, the abortionist may employ as business manager a relative or closely trusted friend. In the cases he studied, the business agent invariably had either a degree in law or at least some legal training (probably to provide for future contingencies).

Bates lists the local druggist, the general practitioner, and previous patients as the primary sources of referral to a mill, and includes taxi-drivers and bellboys as secondary sources. The role of the legitimate physician in effecting referrals should not be underestimated; recall the case of the physician-abortionist who had "served" over 350 practitioners in his city. Individual patterns of referral are determined largely by the prospective client's economic and social situation. The woman of means obtains better illegal services partly because she gains the assistance of a reputable doctor who can often refer her to a competent physician-abortionist. The woman of lower socioeconomic status will usually have to rely on general word-of-mouth referrals in her neighborhood or on the secondary sources mentioned above, and is correspondingly more likely to be referred to a less competent abortionist.

Frequently some sort of respectable front is used to shield the illicit practice. The abortionist may adopt some seemingly proper designation to cover, yet also hint at, the real character of his activities. According to Rongy, office gynecology was once the "casually accepted medical term for the abortionist," recognized by every practitioner. Similarly, in a California case, a card on the door of the defendant's apartment indicated that he was engaged in "physiotherapy and spot reducing." At times the front becomes expanded, as in the case of an enterprise conducted by two women, one of whom was a Peruvian doctor, though neither had a license to practice medicine in New York:

The Peruvian led a double life. She posed as a respectable director of the Inter-American Cultural School which she operated at her palatial private residence on Fifth Avenue. This fancy front was maintained with revenues derived from the performance of abortions at her co-defendant's home. The abortion clientele consisted almost entirely of poor, Spanish-speaking people, who looked up to the affluent Peruvian because she lived on Fifth Avenue and associated with leaders in the Latin-American Community.

The conspirators had a complicated code system for telephone conversations. Patients were packages. Six pairs of nylons or eight pairs of nylons meant that the patient was six to eight weeks pregnant. Information concerning a patient's financial status was imparted by terms such as special delivery, which indicated ability to pay double the usual fee, or parcel post, meaning a moderate increase over the usual charge.

A code of this sort is but one of many precautionary measures utilized by abortionists. Equipment may be kept under cover—a portable folding operating table, a sterilizer ingeniously hidden somewhere in the office. This office may, as already mentioned, be shifted from place to place, and often the abortionist comes to his place of work only for scheduled operations. Anonymity is a pervasive concern, in the interest of which the patient may be blindfolded, various devices such as surgical masks or operating table screens may be used to shield the abortionist's identity, and direct conversations between the two will be avoided. Under the system recently described by a New York observer, a woman wanting an abortion calls one doctor, who arranges for another doctor (whom she does not know)—perhaps accompanied by a nurse—to come to her home by appointment and to perform the abortion there. This technique seems roughly analogous to the modus operandi of call girls. Although it may represent a relatively costly procedure for obtaining illicit services, a mobile and anonymous pattern of this sort certainly minimizes the risk of legal interference. Whatever the specific procedures adopted by a criminal abortionist, his behavior will always exhibit elements of what Bates calls "defensive social adaptation." As he notes: "Since attack from any legitimate or predatory source threatens the social and economic adjustment of mill functionaries, one is not surprised to find them taking energetic countermeasures both on a planned and emergent basis."

Police Corruption

One type of countermeasure involves the payment of "protection" money to law enforcement officers. It seems reasonable to assume such payment on the part of abortionists who operate "undetected" for any length of time in a·metropolitan location. On the other hand, the abortionist who is constantly on the move and who utilizes numerous intermediaries and elaborate codes probably has not purchased police protection—if he had, such measures would not be necessary. One commentator has stated that, on the whole, abortion is probably less protected than either gambling or prostitution. There is no way of knowing what proportion of abortionists fall into these categories. It may be that there has been an increase in the mobile system, which abortionists might find safer than reliance on regular police protection. However, according to another account, supposedly based on an abortionist's own experiences:

One reason fees are high is because the patient must absorb the payoff to police and top officials. Abortionists tell of judges, lawyers, jailers, and police whom they pay for protection, some of whom have brought their wives, daughters, or mistresses to the abortionist. Graft is accepted by all abortionists as a necessary annoyance and added expense passed on to the patient.

Many law enforcement personnel share the widespread belief that the abortionist is in fact performing a useful service, and are also well aware of the public indifference to strong enforcement of this particular law. Under such conditions it is relatively easy, as an early analysis pointed out, "for officials to convince themselves that there is nothing morally reprehensible in accepting bribes or protection money from abortionists." Some law enforcement officials insist there is no longer widespread police corruption con-

nected with abortion. But there is little doubt that the abortionist continues to present an inviting prospect for extortion by the police as well as by others. . . .

LAW ENFORCEMENT

It is widely recognized that the laws against abortion are highly unenforceable. Over the years, the annual number of prosecutions and convictions has been negligible. Along with his estimate of over 300,000 criminal abortions performed annually, Fisher held that the annual number of convictions might be less than 1000. He concluded: "It is doubtful if any other felonious act is as free from punishment as criminal abortion." Occasionally law enforcement authorities in a particular area will make a special effort to apprehend criminal abortionists. For example, during the years of 1946–53 the office of the District Attorney in New York County prosecuted 136 cases of abortion, a very high proportion of which resulted in conviction on one or more of the offenses charged in the indictment. However, as has been pointed out elsewhere, this figure must represent but a tiny fraction of the abortions occurring in the country during that period. Furthermore, in a high percentage of the cases, the defendants received suspended sentences.

Even such a concerted effort, then, can only be expected to scratch the surface of the illegal abortion problem. Most law enforcement officials recognize the determination of unwillingly pregnant women to obtain abortions, law or no law. As a result, law enforcement goals are—in practice—limited to the control of abortion rather than to its elimination. As has been shown, self-induced abortion is probably widespread. Yet the prosecutor ordinarily does not consider it a phenomenon with which he must be concerned. Likewise, although some states make it a crime for a woman to submit to an abortion, women have traditionally been immune from prosecution in abortion cases. There is no record of reported

American cases involving conviction of a woman for submitting to an abortion. Hospitals, which contravene the abortion laws from time to time, also are—within broad limits—free from prosecution. Similarly, the legitimate medical practitioner may perform an occasional abortion without anticipating legal difficulties—provided the operation does not result in the woman's death or hospitalization. A large number of professional abortionists may also manage to avoid detection. The fact is that the extent of abortion practice is so great, and available police manpower is so far below the level needed even to try to curb it, that the urban prosecutor confines his efforts to building up a case against a few of the more notorious offenders. . . .

Unenforceable Laws

Unsatisfactory experience with the laws against abortion points up some of the major consequences of attempting to legislate against the crimes without victims. As an English legal authority states, unsuccessful laws against abortion illustrate "the inherent unenforceability of a statute that attempts to prohibit a private practice where all parties concerned desire to avoid the restriction." It is evident that large numbers of persons, otherwise quite respectable, find themselves compelled—for a variety of reasons—to violate the proscription against abortion. Abortion is a private consensual transaction, a willing payment of money for (illicit) services rendered. Although some persons may view the aborted woman as the "victim" of the abortionist, the woman herself does not share this definition of the situation. Even where she has found the experience extremely distasteful or frightening—perhaps especially in such cases—she is most unlikely to wish to bring a complaint against the person who has performed the operation.

From a law enforcement standpoint, this lack of a complainant is crucial. The only

possible law enforcement approach, particularly in view of the widespread reluctance to convict abortionists, is to concentrate on a small number of the more flagrant violators of the law, and to build up an airtight case in each instance. This involves . . . long-term surveillance of selected suspects—a questionable use of valuable law enforcement manpower. It may also involve compelling the testimony of former clients who had thought that an extremely unpleasant life experience was over and done with. In cases of overzealous investigation, there may be searches and seizures of evidence that border on infringement of the suspect's constitutional guarantees.

As noted also, such a situation holds a clear-cut invitation to police corruption and to illegal exploitation by others as well. Because there are no data indicating a decline in the over-all abortion rate, and because there is a known tendency to grant fewer and fewer legal abortions, the only possible conclusion is that the demand is being deflected into illicit channels. Under current hospital policy, even the sophisticated woman of means and influence, who might once have been able to secure a "therapeutic" abortion, is now driven to the illegal abortionist. Because she can afford to pay an especially high price for his services, the entire illegal process may be enriched and strengthened. It is difficult not to conclude that the thriving illicit market is largely a direct result of the current restrictions on legal abortion. The efforts to combat abortion and the protective measures adopted by the abortionist provide a clear example of what Sutherland termed "the competitive development of techniques of crime and of protection against crime." Repressive laws have nurtured the development of a well-organized criminal profession, which provides strongly demanded services at a high profit, using part of the profit to improve the services and to insulate itself from the negative reaction of official agencies. . . .

CRIMINAL ABORTION

Gilbert Geis

Virtually all writing and debate about abortion concentrate upon the expectant mother. In most States, however, criminal sanctions relate not to the woman being aborted, but to the person who performs the abortion. In the States where both parties are criminally liable, the practice is to prosecute only the abortionist, and then most often only when the aftereffects of his act have caused injury serious enough to bring the "victim" to the attention of medical authorities. It is she who, under such conditions, is sometimes persuaded to testify for the State against the abortionist. Therefore it is not the labeling of an aborted woman as a felon, or the penalties which might follow her apprehension, which are relevant, but her forced involvement in an act that contains many squalid and dangerous elements. In fact, when a 23-year-old Florida girl was convicted for submitting to an abortion in late 1971, she was believed to be the first woman in the English-speaking world to have been so dealt with by the criminal justice system. She was sentenced to a 2-year term of probation, and given 1 week to leave Florida and return to her relatives in North Carolina. . . .

By definition, abortion involves the premature delivery or expulsion of a fetus before it is capable of sustaining life. The gist of the criminal offense of abortion lies in the intent to commit the act and the artificial means used to procure fetal expulsion. In some States (though the matter is still legally controversial), it is a crime to advise a person to undergo an abortion, if such advice is heeded. Statutes also vary regarding the legal consequences to the abortionist if his patient dies. Largely because of the consensual nature of the act, the abor-

tionist may be tried in some States only for manslaughter; in others, a murder charge will lie. Penalties run a wide range for abortion, from 1 year in Kansas to 1 to 20 years in Mississippi. In some States, there is a requirement that the woman must be pregnant before an abortion charge will stand, but in most of the states the actuality of her pregnancy makes no legal difference.

If all women submitting to criminal abortions in the United States were apprehended and convicted, the female crime rate would come much closer to matching that of the male, and prevalent generalizations about the crime proneness of the sexes would have to be thoroughly altered. The same point, of course, may be entered with regard to other statutes—such as frequenting a prostitute—which also are not enforced, but which involve acts committed primarily by males.

The rapidity of alterations in public attitudes and official policies in regard to abortion has been extraordinary. This substantiates the idea that social change can be brought about with dramatic suddenness, given the right combination of latent social forces as these forces blend with public events, which may be either planned or fortuitous. In 1965, Samuel Kling could note in response to the question: "What are the prospects for reform of our obsolete and inconsistent abortion laws?" that such prospects were "at the moment not very promising." Just 5 years later, Hawaii had enacted a law permitting abortion on the demand of the pregnant female, leading the *New York Times* to observe editorially that this new act "dramatically illustrated" the "revolutionary change in public attitudes toward abortion." Even the director of the Planned Parenthood-World Population Association, himself a leading fighter for abortion reform, was taken aback by his own success. "The progress that's been made is fantastic," Alan Guttmacher noted. "Nobody could have dreamed this degree of progress."

From *Not The Law's Business?* National Institute of Mental Health, Center for Studies of Crime and Delinquency, 1972 (Crime and Delinquency Issues), pp. 53–104. Gilbert Geis is Professor in the Program in Social Ecology, University of California, Irvine.

It is not easy to pinpoint those exact reasons which led to abortion becoming so intensely debated a proposition and which presaged the sweeping changes that occurred in the abortion laws of various States. Certainly the enhanced vigor—punning, one might call it the "increased virility"—of the feminist movement played a very large role. That movement itself probably had deep roots in an affluence which afforded increased opportunity for women to achieve outside the home. Also, as with homosexuality, revived Malthusian fears of overpopulation disaster led abortion to be redefined in some instances as an attractive resolution of a severe problem. Birth control pills, which allowed even more calculating interference with conception than previous methods had offered, called into question the necessary inviolability of the birth process once it had gotten underway, since it could have, so casually, been prevented before it began. The public nature of birth control also brought into the limelight cognate, once taboo, subjects. Inserting a diaphragm or using a condom are private processes. Birth control pills, however, lie on the kitchen counter, and are gulped down with the orange juice at the family breakfast. . . .

The declining hold of theological orthodoxy on the minds and allegiances of Americans also contributed significantly to the rise of agitation demanding abortion law reforms. Church leaders were taking the position—made prominent during the British debates on homosexuality—that religious morality which was translated into unenforceable criminal law tended to discredit both the law and the morality. The fact that the Catholic Church, the major opponent of liberalized abortion laws, has come under ideological siege on a broad range of fronts in recent years also meant that it had fewer resources to devote unrestrainedly to the struggle over abortion.

These considerations provided the background for the growing intensity of debate regarding abortion in the United States. In addition, cumulative experience in foreign countries with less severe restrictions on abortion than those prevailing in the United States provided a comparative bank of information with which to rebut allegations about hypothetical consequences of changes in American laws, as well as at times information to undergird Cassandra-like warnings about the outcome if America were to duplicate foreign procedures in regard to abortion.

It was a single sensational case, however, which thrust the abortion issue into public awareness. The case—that of Sherri Finkbine, an attractive Arizona television performer, already mother of several children—involved the use by a pregnant woman of a drug, thalidomide, that appeared "likely" to cause her to give birth to a deformed child. Once the issue had been raised, it was but a short polemical jump from matters of physical deformity to those of psychic aberration, and from concern with the baby's well-being to concern with the mother's. Inevitably, then, the fundamental question appeared: Should the state have any right at all to dictate that the pregnant woman had to carry her child to term?

THE SHERRI FINKBINE CASE

Abortion became a national news item in the United States in 1962 when the media were able to concentrate on the dramatic ingredients of a single case. In Phoenix, Arizona, Mrs. Robert L. Finkbine, a 31-year-old mother of four, well-known in the city as Sherri Chessen, the star of "Romper Room," a television show for youngsters, requested a therapeutic abortion on the ground that she had taken thalidomide during the course of her pregnancy and that, because of this, there was a considerable likelihood that her child would be born deformed. Thalidomide had been synthesized by Chemie Gruenthal in West Germany, and was reported to have no ill effects when tested on animals. It was first marketed under the name *contergan* as an anticonvulsant, but was shortly found to be of little value for this purpose. Soon thereafter, however, contergan became West Germany's "baby sitter," the most popular sleeping potion on the market. The drug was widely exported and sold under a variety of brand names before it began to be linked to phocomelia babies, infants born with deformities of the extremities. Some 1,000 babies were born deformed in Great Britain between 1958, when the drug was introduced, and late 1961, when it was withdrawn from sale after tests on rabbits established that more than half of their litters contained deformed young. Nearly 4,000 deformed babies were reported in West Germany as a result of the use of contergan by expectant mothers early in their pregnancy. In December 1970, after a two-and-a-half year trial, a settlement was reached awarding $19,000 each to the surviving 2,000 deformed children, and providing a total of $1.6 million to 800 adults claiming nervous disorders as a consequence of their use of thalidomide. . . .

Mrs. Finkbine's husband had secured thalidomide in Britain while he was there chaperoning a group of high school students on a European tour. His wife had taken the drug during a bout of nausea. Later news on the possibility of it's affecting her unborn child dictated her decision to seek a therapeutic abortion. In Arizona, which operated under a 1901 statute allowing abortion only when the health of the prospective mother is threatened, a hospital review committee concluded that the Finkbine situation met this requirement. The Phoenix City Attorney, however, indicated publicly that he would prosecute any person involved in the proposed abortion of Mrs. Finkbine.

At first, Mrs. Finkbine planned to fly to Japan to seek her abortion, but she had difficulties securing a visa. At the last minute she shifted her destination to Sweden, where her case was presented to a Committee on Abortion, consisting of a gynecologist, a psychiatrist, and a female member. The panel normally reviews some 4,000 cases annually, rejecting about 40 percent of them. In Mrs. Finkbine's case, the decision was affirmative, and the abortion thereafter routine. Afterwards Mrs. Finkbine was told by doctors that examination of the fetus indicated that she would have given birth to a deformed child. Subsequently in the United States, 17 deformed babies were born to American women who during their pregnancy had taken thalidomide obtained from foreign sources.

Reactions to the Finkbine events were intense and varied. The Vatican radio, without mentioning the case specifically, declared that "homicide is never an act of goodwill. Love always chooses life, not death." The day after Mrs. Finkbine's abortion, the same source was more specifically denunciatory: "Crime is the only possible definition of what happened yesterday at Caroline Hospital in Stockholm, Sweden. Morally, objectively, it is a crime, and all the graver because it was committed legally."

American public opinion was somewhat more undecided about Mrs. Finkbine's decision. A Gallup Poll conducted less than a month after her abortion had put this question to a nationwide panel:

As you may have heard or read, an Arizona woman recently had a legal abortion in Sweden after having taken the drug thalidomide, which has been linked to birth defects. Do you think this woman did the right thing or the wrong thing in having this abortion operation?

More than half the sample thought that Mrs. Finkbine had done the right thing. Thirty-two percent thought her wrong, while 16 percent either had no opinion or would offer none. Protestants out-numbered Catholics considerably in condoning the abortion—by 56 percent to 33 percent. Men and women were about evenly divided—50 percent of the women and 54 percent of the men declaring that Mrs. Finkbine had done the right thing. American public opinion, at least in terms of this specific case, seemed rather evenly divided, and in one sense this balance could be regarded as a presage for legislative action: there were votes to be had by advocacy of a view favored by so many constituents. On the other hand, there remained the tradition of inertia in American politics to be overcome: it would not do to make enemies gratuitously. The public opinion poll had not indicated any intensity of feeling among the respondents, and it could well have been that the opponents felt very strongly about the matter, while those in favor were relatively lukewarm. For another thing, it is a legislative axiom that moral issues are better left dormant, absent a heavy groundswell of reform sentiment. In regard to abortion, the absence of such a groundswell was obvious in 1962.

Nine years later—by 1971—the abortion situation in the United States had changed almost unbelievably. A dozen States had liberalized their abortion laws and two States—Hawaii and New York—had inaugurated programs under which women could have legal abortions on demand if their pregnancy had not gone beyond a certain time. In Maryland, a similar law had been enacted by the legislature, though it was vetoed by the Governor. In addition, a Wisconsin district court had declared that the State's abortion law was unconstitutional in a decision filled with ringing rhetoric: "We hold that a woman's right to refuse to carry an embryo during the early months of pregnancy may not be invaded by the state. . . . When measured against the claimed 'rights' of an embryo of 4 months or less, we hold that the mother's right transcends that of the embryo," the court declared. . . .

COLORADO'S PIONEERING STATUTE

The first major reform in abortion laws in the United States was enacted in Colorado in 1967, passing both houses of the legislature by a 2 to 1 majority. The new Colorado law allowed abortion for a variety of reasons, including pregnancy which had resulted from rape and incest, cases in which there was suspected deformity, and those in which it was judged that termination of the pregnancy was necessary to protect the life or health of the prospective mother. To obtain an abortion a woman had to receive approval from a committee of doctors in a certified hospital. To the legislators opposing the law, which took effect on April 25, 1967, it seemed destined to make Colorado "the

abortion mecca of the world," a prophecy unfailingly voiced by the opposition in every State that has changed its abortion laws. . . .

It is now granted that the new Colorado abortion law has made little indent on the number of criminal abortions, though it is believed that the law has made the illegal abortionist cut his prices. A year after the new act had gone into effect, some 289 abortions had been performed, plus a number of others which came under the law but were not reported to the authorities. This compared with 37,273 live births for the same period. Statistics for the first 14 months of the legislation showed a total of 338 abortions, 100 of which had been undertaken for nonresidents of the State, though, on the advice of the Colorado Medical Society, hospitals were refusing to accept rape or incest cases from out of State on the ground that to do so would involve legal judgments that physicians were not qualified to make. More than half of the cases—195 in all—and virtually all those of nonresidents, had come under the "mental health" clause of the new act. Thirty-two abortions had been performed for medical reasons, 33 on rape victims, 20 on persons who had had German measles. In 56 instances, no official explanation was offered on the official form.

By mid-1969, total disenchantment had set in with the operation of the Colorado statute. . . . Illegal abortions were believed to still be in the range of 8,000 to 10,000 a year in the State. There had been 768 legal abortions performed in the 2 years following the new act, but only one out of 13 applications for such abortions had been approved. The Colorado law was said to be legally cumbersome, to involve unnecessary medical red tape, and to have pushed the operation beyond the reach of the poor. It had also been found that the staff members at hospitals tended to look down on abortion patients, making them feel uncomfortable, unwanted, and in some way unclean. In its third year of operation the Colorado program showed no improvement. It was estimated that 19 out of 20 persons were being turned down for legal abortions by the committees at the hospitals, and that the average price for a legal abortion had risen to about $500. The total number of legal abortions had increased from 497 in 1968 to 946 in 1969, but this figures hardly made a dent in the illegal rate.

THE CALIFORNIA EXPERIENCE

Passage in 1967 of the Therapeutic Abortion Act made California the second State to change its abortion law drastically. The California action, given the size and prominence of the State, was of outstanding importance in the nationwide drive for abortion reform. The new California law allowed abortions up to the 20th week of pregnancy with the approval of a majority of a hospital board reviewing the application. The protection of the mental health of the woman was the major ground allowed for legal abortion. Requests for abortions following rape or incest had first to be forwarded to the district attorney in the county where the act was alleged to have taken place. If the district attorney vetoed the request only a successful appeal to the State Supreme Court could reverse his decision. . . .

Criticisms of the California abortion law during its initial years in operation echoed those leveled against the new Colorado statute. Hospitals were differentially permitting access to their facilities, and almost invariably favoring persons of means as opposed to those less affluent. Nor were the provisions of the act being interpreted similarly in the different parts of the State. Fifty percent of the legal abortions were being performed in the San Francisco area, for instance, though only 16 percent of the State's live births occurred there. In Los Angeles, on the contrary, there were 23 percent of the abortions, though the area recorded 60 percent of the State's live births.

Flagrant cases of rejection of applications for legal abortion also began to be noted. A couple with two idiot children had applied for an abortion and been denied; later, their child, also severely mentally defective, was born. A raped woman's application was vetoed by a district attorney who insisted that the father could have been her own husband. All told, there were 2,035 legal abortions during the first half of 1968, after the law had received a brief shakedown period, a figure nowhere near the estimated total of 100,000 illegal abortions. Eighty percent of these—91 percent in regard to white women—were granted on the ground of a mental health danger inherent in the pregnancy. But each day seven to ten women were being received at the Los Angeles County Hospital suffering from attempts at self-abortion with coat hangers, knitting needles, and gasoline. Fees for legal abortions were running from $600 to $800, and there was a reported instance of a 15-year-old girl being charged $1,800. Hospitals worked carefully to stay within self-adopted abortion "quotas" in order to avoid the possibility of being defined as "abortion mills."

In 1968, the first full year the new law had been in effect there were a total of 5,030 abortions under its provisions. This figure rose to 15,339 during the following year and had increased to 62,000 in 1970.

Estimates of the impact of the new California law were uniformly deprecatory. It was noted, for one thing, that there continued to be approximately 80,000 illegal abortions in the State. . . .

On the other hand, there was some good news in regard to what might have been the number of illegal abortions in California or, perhaps, the manner in which they were now being performed. In September 1970, a University of California medical school professor reported to the convention of the American Academy of General Practice that the statewide death rate attributable to abortions had dropped from eight per 100,000 in 1967 to three per 100,000 in 1968. . . .

NEW YORK: ABORTION ON DEMAND

. . . The drive in New York State, culminating in the enactment of a statute which allowed abortion as a matter to be determined between the physician and his patient, represented by far the most significant assault on traditional abortion law in the history of the country. . . .

The New York "abortion on demand" measure became law on July 1, 1970. The experiences of New York with the law as time passes will undoubtedly play a very large role in dictating the direction that the remainder of the Nation will take in regard to abortion. For one thing, New York City, where most abortions will occur, is the national headquarters of the mass media—the radio and television networks, the news magazines, and the wire services—so that events there are inevitably better attended to than they are elsewhere in the country. The ability of New York to handle the new statute with comparatively little friction could encourage other jurisdictions; its failure to do so without intense controversy, or with dire results, would warn off those States contemplating changes in their statutes.

To date, the New York law cannot be said to have brought about thoroughgoing changes in patterns of abortion. Extrapolations from available figures indicate that by the middle of 1971, the first year of the law's operation, 115,000 legal abortions will have been performed in the State. This figure, however, remains inexact because many physicians have not been filing the legally required fetal death certificates with the authorities. Estimates are that about 40 percent of the legal abortions have been done on women from outside of New York State. All told, the 115,000 legal abortions in New York should constitute more than half of the Nation's total of such operations in 1971. The national total—about 250,000 predicted for 1971—compares with 18,000 legal abortions just 3 years earlier.

It seems likely that a large number of the abortions in New York have been performed to date on women who would not otherwise have terminated their pregnancy. The abortion law has put a new and subtle pressure upon relatively affluent women who unexpectedly become pregnant to justify why they should have this child, and many such women who would have borne the child now are undergoing legal abortions. Hospital data support this supposition with figures showing that the number of lower-class patients appearing with sequelae from poorly performed illegal abortions has not declined significantly since implementation of the new law in New York.

Techniques for legal abortion were also becoming more refined with practice. "D and C," dilation of the cervix and curettage (scraping) of the interior of the uterus, remained the preferred method to end pregnancies of under 12 weeks' duration. A newer method, widely used in Japan and Eruope, is vacuum aspiration or suction. In it, the uterus is emptied by suction through a tube only one-quarter inch in diameter. After the 12th week of pregnancy, the most common abortion method in New York is "salting-out" or saline injection, in which amniotic fluid is withdrawn and replaced by about half a pint of highly saline water which kills the fetus and induces labor in 12 to 36 hours. The method is subject to about 10 percent failure to produce abortion, and most doctors will not employ it until past the 16th week of pregnancy. when there is adequate amniotic fluid. Thus, between the 12th and 16th week of pregnancy, an abortion was proving difficult to secure in New York.

With the methods in use for legal abortion, the death rate was running at 3.8 per 10,000 abortions, slightly higher than the maternal death rate of 3.2 per 10,000 births. The ratio of abortions to live births was far below the parity level found in some foreign jurisdictions. In New York, it was calculated at 198 abortions for each 1,000 live births.

The most intense controversy with the New York law to date centers about the use of private offices and special clinics for abortions. In October 1970, New York City restricted the practice of abortion to well-equipped hospitals and affiliated clinics. For an affiliate to be licensed, it had to be possible to get a patient to a hospital within ten minutes. Thus, for the moment, legal abortions were being concentrated in hospital settings with the predicted result that there were "endless delays, high costs, complicated procedures, and gratuitous trauma." The last item included the reported practice of one hospital of insisting that an aborted woman look at the fetus before it was destroyed and of another of placing aborted women in maternity wards, forcing them thus to view the excitement and pleasure of new mothers with their infants. As one observer put the matter: "The specter of abortion as an illegal, dirty, immoral practice and the notion that 'those who play must pay' dies hard." Doctors, too, often found that performing abortions downgraded their standing with their colleagues, who tended to regard them as not much better than "back-street butchers." . . .

ELSEWHERE IN THE UNITED STATES

The experiences of Colorado, California, and New York, detailed above, summarize similar kinds of activities taking place in regard to abortion in other parts of the United States. The New York legislative enactment of "abortion on demand" has been duplicated in two other States—Hawaii and Alaska. In Alaska, the measure became law only after the legislature was able to override the Governor's veto. The Hawaiian law limits eligibility for legal abortion to persons who have lived in the State at least 90 days. . . .

The State of Washington became the fourth "abortion on demand" jurisdiction when the electorate approved a new statute in the 1970 general election with a 55.5 percent affirmative vote. Washington, like Hawaii, required a 90-day period of residence. Legal abortion is permitted up to the 16th week of pregnancy, and it requires the consent of parents if the girl is unmarried and under 18, and the consent of her husband, if she is living with him.

In addition, 11 other States have changed their abortion laws to follow the same lines as the reforms adopted in Colorado and California. Early reports indicate that essentially the same objections noted in those States

apply to the others. The first year of the new Georgia law, for instance, saw a legal abortion rate of 1.3 per 1,000 live births, a figure which remained below the national average of 2.0 per 1,000. There were only 113 abortions in Georgia under the new law, and, only 10 percent involved blacks, though blacks account for one-third of the population of Georgia. It was estimated that were all States to follow the Colorado-California approach, only 15 percent of the abortions now performed illegally could be brought under the new laws. There was the further reservation, expressed by the Committee on Psychiatry and Law of the Group for the Advancement of Psychiatry, that stress on the detrimental mental effect of possible birth would lead pregnant women seeking legal abortion "either . . . to malinger . . . or to emphasize psychiatric symptoms."

In addition to the alterations of State laws, there have been assaults against existing abortion arrangements by various appellate courts, which tended to follow the line of reasoning of the California court described earlier. The District of Columbia, for instance, had been operating under a unique statute which placed the burden of proof upon a physician to show that an abortion he performed was justified, adding unusual legal risk to his position. In November 1969, Judge Gerhard A. Gessell, son of the famed pediatrician, Arnold Gessell, ruled that the District law was so vague and indefinite in regard to its reference to protecting the prospective mother's health as to be unconstitutional. The District of Columbia law was also judged to be an unreasonable infringement on the private right of a woman in the realm of sex and motherhood. In Judge Gessell's words:

A woman's liberty and right of privacy extends to family, marriage, and sex matters, and may well include the right to remove an unwanted child at least in the early stages of pregnancy.

Judge Gessell's ruling, currently under appeal, left the District of Columbia without a law to regulate abortions.

A similar fate overtook the Wisconsin abortion statute in March 1970. "The state does not have a compelling interest . . . to require a woman to remain pregnant during the early months following her conception," a three-judge Federal panel declared. Wisconsin authorities, located in a State which is 38 percent Catholic, with its largest city, Milwaukee, having a two-to-one Catholic majority, planned to appeal the decision on their abortion statute to the United States Supreme Court.

ABORTION IN FOREIGN COUNTRIES

There has been a long experience with a range of abortion practices in various foreign countries which provides material against which the possible impact of diverse American arrangements might be examined. Such material, of course, must always be looked at with caution, because the practices are occurring in areas with historical traditions and cultural arrangements that are different than those of the United States. To insist categorically, for example, that policemen in the United States ought to abandon carrying guns because such a policy has been associated with diminished violence in Britain, or that the United States ought to move to the controlled clinic method in dealing with narcotics now used in Britain is to ignore a variety of impinging forces that might produce boomerang effects in the wake of the proposed innovations.

On the other hand, to ignore foreign experience is to encourage provincialism. It has been said that a great advantage of allowing States in the United States to implement diverse approaches to social problems is that each jurisdiction then becomes an experimental laboratory, and each can learn from the others. The same observation is clearly in order in regard to foreign countries.

Great Britain

The United States, having taken its law from Britain and sharing a common language with the British, is apt to look first to conditions in the British Isles for possible clues for resolution of social dilemmas. Earlier it was noted, for instance, that the report of the Wolfenden Committee in Britain provided much intellectual underpinning for advocates of legalization of consensual adult homosexuality.

Historically, the traditional approach to abortion in the United States derives from England. In medieval times, abortion on demand was permitted in England until the occasion of fetal "quickening," that is, until late in the fourth or early in the fifth month of pregnancy. In 1803, with the passage of Lord Ellenborough's act, all abortion except that designed to protect the life of the prospective mother was declared criminal. In theory, thereafter the abortion penalties in Britain were among the severest in the world, calling for possible life imprisonment. In fact, however, abortion was rarely prosecuted because authorities did not want to deter women from seeking post-abortion medical assistance.

In the 1930's, a judicial ruling changed the focus of the British abortion statute dramatically. Alec Bourne, a medical doctor, had performed an abortion on a young girl who had been raped by a group of soldiers, and then submitted himself for criminal prosecution. The jury would not convict Bourne, and the judge went so far as to declare that if a doctor refused to perform an abortion in order to save a woman's life, he would be in "grave peril of a charge of manslaughter by negligence." The same decision by statutory interpretation provided a broad definition of "life." If a medical practitioner were of the opinion, on reasonable grounds, that the probable consequences of continuance of a pregnancy were that the woman would be rendered a physical or mental wreck, the judge noted in the *Bourne* case, "then the jury are quite entitled to take the view that the doctor who, under those circumstances and in that honest belief, operates, is operating for the purpose of preserving the life of the mother."

Immediate impetus for abortion reform in Britain, as in the United States, seemed to be triggered by the thalidomide crisis. At the time, the Lord Chancellor told the House of Lords that possible deformity was not adequate legal ground for abortion. There were then an estimated 100,000 illegal abortions occurring in Britain. Thereafter, the mood of the public on the issue of legalized abortion began to shift significantly. In March 1965, a National Opinion Poll reported a 36 percent favorable response to the question: "Would you favor abortion if a mother has so large a family that another child might cause financial difficulties and financial stress?" Two years later, the affirmative response had grown to 65 percent of the respondents.

The Abortion Act had been introduced into Parliament in mid-1966 and a year and a quarter later it gained approval of both Houses, with a March 1968 effective date. The bill provided for legal termination of pregnancy if two registered doctors concluded that continuance of the pregnancy would involve risk to the life of the pregnant woman, or injury to her physical or mental health or to any existing children in the family, provided that the risk of continued pregnancy was greater than the risk of termination. Abortion was also permissible if there was "substantial risk" that the child would be "seriously handicapped" by physical or mental abnormalities.

The bill made no mention of rape as a ground for legal abortion because it was believed that medical doctors would not adequately be able to interpret the legal concept of rape, or to decide whether the pregnancy had resulted from rape or from other sexual intercourse. There was also a belief that cases of rape could be included under other categories. The most controversial clause in the act, obviously, was the so-called "social clause," allowing abortion when the birth of an additional child would endanger the well-being of an existing child.

Summarizing the early history of the English law, one commentator noted that "the gateway to legal abortion is now so wide that it may be supposed that some doctors will always be able to convince themselves that the risks of pregnancy are greater than those of abortion where, at any rate, the patient demands abortion insistently enough."

Actually, use of the "social clause" was not as prominent as recourse to the "mental health" clause of the abortion law, though allegation of one or another ground is likely little more than a semantic preference. During 1969, the law saw 54,158 legal abortions, with 75 percent taking place under the National Health Insurance Act in Government centers, where the cost to the patient was $60. The total rose to 83,849 in the second full year of the law's operation and to 126,774 in 1971. Rich patients were tending to use private practitioners, who charged about $500 for an abortion. Makeship quarters had also sprung up to cater to abortion demands, leading to Parliamentary outcries of "financial racketeering" because of overcharges to foreign women, in particular, who accounted for about 20 percent of the total number of legal abortions.

A major complaint against the new law concerned the erratic nature of abortion practices throughout the country. In Newcastle, for instance, the legal abortion rate was 237 per 1 million population, compared to 84 per 1 million in Sheffield. In Birmingham and Liverpool, abortions were difficult to secure because of the high percentage of Roman Catholic doctors in the two cities. The legislation had included a "conscience clause" which protected from liability any doctor, nurse, or hospital employee who objected to participating in legal abortions.

Despite such problems—the exploitation of clients and the differential implementation of the law—it could be said after the initial year of the British program that "its impact has been greater than its supporters expected and its opponents feared." The 40,000 abortions under the National Health Service compared with 2,580 that had been performed in 1963 and the 7,610 in 1967. It was notable that only 7 percent of all legal abortions following the law reform were performed solely on the fresh grounds permitted. "This suggests," one commentator noted, "that the purely symbolic value of law reform may be very great." Summarizing Britain's early experience, *The Lancet,* the country's leading medical journal, entered the following observation:

Things were certainly easier for the gynecologists before the public and Parliament made their wishes known in the Act—but they were much harder for women.

Japan

Since the passage in 1948 of the Eugenic Protection Law, abortion can be had on demand in Japan and is permitted up to the 8th month of pregnancy. Exact estimates of the number of abortions in Japan are hard to come by, however. For one thing, if a doctor does not register an abortion with the proper authorities, he can avoid payment of income tax on his fee and the patient can escape payment of the "fetus fee" to the mortician, a fee which is usually higher than the medical charge. Demographic experts think that there are about 1.5 million abortions in Japan each year, contrasting with about 1.8 million live births.

An abortion can be had in Japan for about $40. The death rate tends to be quite low—about seven deaths in 100,000 cases, which compares to the 28 per 100,000 mortality rate for childbirth in the United States. The unpopularity of birth control in Japan—women are said to be timid about purchasing devices—accounts in large measure for the frustration of government efforts to reduce the abortion rate significantly, though it is believed to be declining gradually. In 1955, for instance, estimates placed the abortion total at 1,170,000 cases; in 1970 at 700,000. Japan today has one of the lowest birth rates in the world—18.4 per 100,000 population. . . .

Sweden

Abortions have been permitted since 1938 in Sweden on medical, humanitarian, and eugenic grounds. Medical grounds involve possibilities of endangered health. Humanitarian grounds refer to pregnancies of girls below the age of 15, cases of rape and incest, or the mental deficiency of the prospective parent. Eugenic grounds concern the likelihood of inherited mental disease or deficiency. An abortion must take place prior to the 12th week of pregnancy, except in extraordinary cases. The grounds for abortion were extended in 1946 to include the strain of giving birth to and caring for a new child ("anticipated maternal weakness"). In about a quarter of the cases in Sweden, sterilization is combined with legal abortion.

Legal abortions stand in a ratio to live births of 5 to 100 in Sweden, with about 40 percent of the applications for legal abortion being rejected. Studies show that when applications for legal abortion are rejected, the woman is likely to bear the child. Illegal abortions were obtained by only 12 percent (1948), 3 percent (1957), and 11 percent (1963) of the women turned down for legal termination of their pregnancy. The highest number of legal abortions in Sweden was in 1957 when the total reached 6,328. By 1962, that figure had declined to 2,600 and it has remained at essentially this level since then.

The length of the Swedish experience with legal abortion and the relative smallness and homogeneity of the country have allowed for a number of studies of the impact of the abortion procedures. Among the more interesting is one which sought to determine the consequences upon the children of women whose abortion applications had been rejected. The study found that 21-year-olds whose mothers had unsuccessfully sought to be aborted were in poorer health than members of a control group, had more psychiatric troubles, used alcohol more, married earlier, and had babies earlier. Among the males, there was a greater number of Army rejects. The difficulty of the experimental design used to obtain these results, however, inheres in the fact that rejection for abortion is not a random procedure and the alleged consequences of the rejection may stem from prior conditions rather than from the abortion committee's decision.

Violations of the Swedish procedures for

legal abortion testify to the fact that they do not satisfy all persons who wish to take advantage of them. It is estimated that there are about 10,000 illegal abortions each year in Sweden. In 1965, prosecuting authorities took action attempting to cut off the flow of Swedish women going to Poland for abortions. There have also been complaints about the bureaucratic procedures involved in the abortion screening process. An applicant is often required to make many hospital visits, and the authorities may interview friends and relatives before reaching a decision on eligibility. . . .

The Soviet Bloc

Another major repository of abortion experience exists in the communist countries of Europe, which have tried varying approaches to the situation. In the Soviet Union, abortion was made legal in the 1920's, and then outlawed in 1936, except for narrowly defined reasons. In November 1955, the Soviet Union returned to its more permissive policy. Statistics are not released regarding the number of abortions, so that the impact of these changing policies, a matter that could be of considerable value for informed decisionmaking elsewhere, remains unknown abroad. It was noted, however, that after the 1936 shift the birth rate rose 83 percent in Leningrad and 93 percent in Moscow. Abortions performed for medical reasons are done without charge in Government clinics; otherwise, the cost is 5 rubles ($5.50). Basic reasons offered for recourse to abortion in the Soviet Union are the housing shortage and the extensive employment of women, who make up half of the Government labor force of 70 million persons, and who hold 86 percent of the jobs in the public health field.

Other European communist countries have abortion policies similar to those in the Soviet Union. A report from Czechoslovakia indicates that in 1968 there were 11,434 births and 11,310 abortions in Prague, and a total of 121,132 abortions throughout the country. These abortions are held to be pri-

marily responsible for the 1 percent decline in the Czechoslovakian birth rate since 1960. Ten percent of the applications for abortion in Czechoslovakia are rejected. Of those approved, 52 percent of the abortions are granted because the family maintains that it has enough children, 14.5 percent on health grounds, and 9 percent because of inadequate housing. In 1963, Czechoslovakian authorities tightened up abortion procedures on the ground that the rate was too high. Evidence indicates that the stricter enforcement was accompanied by a corresponding rise in illegal abortion.

In Hungary, the rate of abortions to live births is reported to be even higher than in Czechoslovakia—eight abortions for each five live births. The death rate in both Hungary and Czechoslovakia from abortions is officially given as 3 per 100,000. In the United States, as noted earlier, term pregnancies result in a death rate of 23 per 100,000.

QUESTIONS FOR DISCUSSION

1. Analyze recent reports on abortion appearing in magazines and newspapers. How is the problem usually defined? Do you notice more pro or con articles?
2. Organize a panel discussion, making sure you have members discussing abortion from legal, religious, medical, and psychological points of view. Were there any areas of general agreement? If so, what were these areas? On what issues were disagreements greatest?
3. Interview a number of persons who have had an abortion. Include those in married and nonmarried categories. Try to vary socio-economic status. Compare types of reasoning, attitudes, and reactions.
4. Collect data on recent legislative changes regarding abortion in your home state. What do you conclude to be the major points of controversy? What trends seem most clear-cut to you? What is the evidence underlying these trends?
5. Obtain cross-cultural data on abortion practices. Include the countries mentioned in the article by Geis as well as other countries. What do you feel are

the important insights to be gained from such an inquiry?

6. Should mothers on welfare have their abortion expenses paid from community welfare funds? Should such funds cover both therapeutic and "on demand" abortions?

7. Should welfare funds be denied unmarried welfare mothers who have become pregnant when they already have several illegitimate children? Should they be sterilized? Should they be compelled to have an abortion?

8. Should abortion be made readily available to those who can personally afford the cost of an abortion?

9. Should abortion "on demand" be included in hospitalization and surgical coverage?

10. Should abortion be a matter of individual conscience or public policy?

BIBLIOGRAPHY

Ball, D. W. "Ethnography of An Abortion Clinic." *Social Problems,* 14 (Winter 1967), 293–301.

Guttmacher, Alan, ed. *The Case for Legalized Abortion.* Berkeley: Diablo Press, 1967.

Rossi, Alice S. "Abortion Laws and Their Victims." In *Modern Criminals.* Trans-Action Books, Chicago: Aldine, 1970, pp. 117–32.

Saltman, Jules, and Zimering, Stanley. *Abortion Today.* Springfield, Ill.: Charles C. Thomas, 1973.

Sarvis, Betty, and Rodman, Hyman. *The Abortion Controversy.* New York: Columbia University Press, 1973.

Schur, Edwin M. *Crimes Without Victims.* Englewood Cliffs, N.J.: Prentice-Hall, 1965.

Young, A. T., Berkman, B. and Rehr, H. "Women Who Seek Abortions." In *Social Work* 18 (1973), 60–65.

9

Prostitution

Prostitution, simply defined, is the use of sexual stimulation to attain nonsexual ends. One of the most pervasive and universal forms of deviance, prostitution involves a socially devalued female and a "respectable" client in an economic arrangement concerning sexual activity. As in abortion, the victim is both law-abiding and willing, making enforcement largely impossible.

The business of prostitution has undergone considerable change in the last few decades. Largely gone are the brothels in which young women catered to patrons under the watchful supervision of a madam. Organized vice and red-light districts, once very apparent in the urban community, are no more, although vestiges of brothel prostitution may still be found in the inner city ghettos and near military posts and bases. The demise of organized prostitution may be attributed to a variety of social changes: freer relations between the sexes at all ages, changing conceptions of sex norms, easier divorce and remarriage, and legitimate economic opportunities for females. Like the saloon, the speakeasy, and the taxi-dance hall, the brothel is Americana of the past—of primary interest to antiquarians and historians.

The demise of organized prostitution has not, of course, meant that the economic exploitation of sex has ceased. Several new breeds of prostitute have emerged to serve as replacements for the brothel prostitute: the high-class call girl, the streetwalker (hustler or hooker), and the part-time amateur. Less visible in her occupation than her predecessors, each of these types is more seeker than sought. All are entrepreneurs. The call girl, of course, is the highest paid and the most professional; the streetwalker much less so, and the part-time amateur least so.

The two selections which follow deal with different yet overlapping aspects of prostitution as social and personal deviation. In the first article, "The Sociology of Prostitution," Professor Kingsley Davis presents an incisive analysis of the social structural basis of prostitution. His initial question: "Why is it that a practice so thoroughly disapproved, so widely outlawed in Western civilization, can yet flourish so universally?" results in a functional analysis of prostitution. Prostitution, says Professor Davis, can be studied on three interrelated yet separate levels: 1. the causes of the existence of prostitution; 2. the causes of the amount of prostitution; 3. the causes of why only a specific type of person enters into prostitution.

In an especially interesting digression, Professor Davis contends that prostitution and the family can co-exist and thrive at the same time. Ironically, the chief enemy of each is not the other, but the loosening of sex norms. One measure, therefore, of the solidity of the family is the extent of prostitution. The disruption of the family and its reorganization are accompanied by a corresponding decrease in prostitution. This is both an interesting and unusual thesis and is well worth pondering.

The second article in this section reviews many of the popular misconceptions regarding prostitutes and their way of life. For example, most prostitutes tend to be satisfied with their calling, indicating very few, if any, regrets, and they have decided on their work with a rational awareness of the options available to them. They have not been tricked into prostitution, nor do they blame poor upbringing, neglectful parents, or other popular cliches for their present occupation. Geis also presents a succinct summary of the Wolfenden Report concerning prostitution and highlights some of the post-Wolfenden developments. This is followed by a well-documented account of the diverse kinds of social settings in which prostitution has occurred in the United States and in a number of other countries, including eastern as well as western societies. The final section of this article contains a succinct discussion of arguments for and against the question of whether prostitution ought to be defined as a criminal offense.

No matter how functional prostitution might be as a safety valve to society, it is socially disvalued. The result, of course, is that prostitutes, pimps, and procurers develop correspondingly poor images (concepts) of themselves. Almost without exception, deviants, having learned the generalized norms of society, feel guilty and ashamed of their deviant status and evolve rationalizations to justify their behavior to themselves and others. Prostitutes typically adjust to their lack of self-respect and esteem in at least three ways. Some accept the subcultural values of the underworld, some make prostitution but one phase of their lives, and some become wholly alienated from life and take refuge in drink and drugs. These adaptations to the stigmatization inherent in being a prostitute have consequences for the prostitute as well as implications for understanding and controlling such behavior.

Every profession has its successes and its also-rans. Prostitution as a profession is no exception. The call or party girl is the acknowledged success in her business. With earnings of $20,000 or more per year and a minimum of $20 per contact, she is usually well-educated, sophisticated, personable, and winsome—hardly recognizable as a practicing member of her profession according to the prevailing stereotype. Very selective of her clientele and highly protective of their anonymity, foibles, and inadequacies, she is as necessary to a successful business or professional convention as the banquet meal and the roster of long-winded speakers.

THE SOCIOLOGY OF PROSTITUTION

Kingsley Davis

...We cannot define human prostitution simply as the use of sexual responses for an ulterior purpose. This would include a great portion of all social behavior, especially that of women. It would include marriage, for

From *American Sociological Review*, 2 (October 1937), 746–55. Reprinted by permission. Professor Davis is at the University of California, Berkeley.

example, wherein women trade their sexual favors for an economic and social status supplied by men. It would include the employment of pretty girls in stores, cafes, charity drives, advertisements. It would include all the feminine arts that women use in pursuing ends that require men as intermediaries, arts that permeate daily life, and, while not generally involving actual intercourse, contain and utilize erotic stimulation.

But looking at the subject in this way reveals one thing. The basic element in what we actually call prostitution—the employment of sex for non-sexual ends within a competitive-authoritative system—characterizes not simply prostitution itself but all of our institutions in which sex is involved, notably courtship and wedlock. Prostitution therefore resembles, from one point of view, behavior found in our most respectable institutions. It is one end of a long sequence or gradation of essentially similar phenomena that stretches at the other end to such approved patterns as engagement and marriage. What, then, is the difference between prostitution and these other institutions involving sex?

The difference rests at bottom upon the functional relation between society and sexual institutions. It is through these institutions that erotic gratification is made dependent on, and subservient to, certain cooperative performances inherently necessary to societal continuity. The sexual institutions are distinguished by the fact that though they all provide gratification, they do not all tie it to the same social functions. This explains why they are differently evaluated in the eyes of the mores.

The institutional control of sex follows three correlative lines. First, it permits, encourages, or forces various degrees of sexual intimacy within specific customary relations, such as courtship, concubinage, and marriage. Second, to bolster this positive control, it discourages sexual intimacy in all other situations, e.g., when the persons are not potential mates or when they are already mated to other persons. Finally, in what is really a peculiar category of the negative rules, it absolutely prohibits sexual relations in certain specified situations. This last form of control refers almost exclusively to incest taboos, which reinforce the first-named (positive) control by banishing the disruptive forces of sexual competition from the family group.

These lines of control are present no matter what the specific kind of institutional system. There may be monogamy, polygyny, or concubinage; wife exchange or religious prostitution; premarital chastity or unchastity. The importnat point is not the particular kind of concrete institution, but the fact that without the positive and negative norms there could be no institutions at all. Since social functions can be performed only through institutional patterns, the controls are indispensable to the continuance of a given social system.

Of the numerous functions which sexual institutions subserve, the most vital relate to the physical and social reproduction of the next generation. If we ask, then, which sexual institutions in a society receive the greatest support from law and mores, we must point to those which facilitate the task of procreating and socializing the young. It follows that sanctioned sexual relations are generally those within these (or auxiliary) institutions, while unsanctioned relations are those outside them.

Marriage and its subsidiary patterns constitute the chief cultural arrangement through which erotic expression is held to reproduction. It is accordingly the most respectable sexual institution, with the others diminishing in respectability as they stand further away from wedlock. Even the secondary forms of erotic behavior—flirtation, coquetry, petting, etc.—have their legitimate and their illegitimate settings. Their legitimate aspects may be subsumed under courtship, leading to marriage; but if indulged in for themselves, with no intention of matrimony, they are devoid of the primary function and tend to be disapproved. If practised by persons married to others, they are inimical to reproductive relations already established and are more seriously condemned. If practised by close relatives within the primary family, they represent a threat to the very structure of the reproductive institution itself, and are stringently tabooed. These attitudes are much more rigid with regard to actual intercourse, not solely because coitus is the essence of the sexual but because it has come to symbolize the *gemeinschaft* type of relation present in the family. With this in mind we can add that when coitus is practised for money its social function is indeterminate, secondary, and extrinsic. The buyer clearly has pleasure and not reproduction in mind. The seller may use the money for any purpose. Hence unless the money is earmarked for some legitimate end (such as the support of a family, a church, or a state), the sexual relation between the buyer and seller is illegitimate, ephemeral, and condemned. It is pure commercial prostitution.

Of course many sexual institutions besides courtship and marriage receive, in various cultures and to varying degrees, the sanction of society. These generally range themselves between marriage and commercial prostitution in the scale of social approval. They include concubinage, wife exchange, and forms of sanctified prostitution. Religious prostitution, for example, not only differs from wedlock, but also from commercial prostitution; the money that passes is earmarked for the maintenance of the church, the woman is a religious ministrant, and the act of intercourse is sacred. Similar considerations apply to that type of prostitution in which the girl obtains a dowry for her subsequent marriage. Whenever the money earned by prostitution is spent for a sanctified purpose, prostitution is in higher esteem than when it is purely commercial. If, for instance, prostitution receives more approval in Japan than in America, it is significant that in the former country most of the *joro* enter the life because their family needs money; their conduct thereby subserves the most sacred of all Japanese sentiments—filial piety. The regulation of prostitution by governments and churches in such a way that at least some of the proceeds go towards their maintenance is control of sex behavior at a second remove. By earmarking a part of the money, the bought intercourse is made to serve a social function; but *this function is not intrinsically related to coitus in the same way as the procreative function of the family.*

In commercial prostitution both parties use sex for an end not socially functional, the one for pleasure, the other for money. To tie intercourse to sheer physical pleasure is to divorce it both from reproduction and from the sentimental primary type of relation which it symbolizes. To tie it to money, the most impersonal and atomistic type of reward possible, with no stipulation as to the use of this medium, does the same thing. Pure prostitution is promiscuous, impersonal. The sexual response of the prostitute does not hinge upon the personality of the other party, but upon the reward. The response of the customer likewise does not depend upon the particular identity of the prostitute, but upon the bodily gratification. On both sides the relationship is merely a means to a private end, a contractual rather than a personal association.

These features sharply distinguish prostitution from the procreative sexual institutions. Within a group organized for bearing and rearing children bonds tend to arise that are cemented by the condition of relative permanence and the sentiment of personal feeling, for the task requires long, close, and sympathetic association. Prostitution, in which the seller takes any buyer at the price, necessarily represents an opposite kind of erotic association. It is distinguished by the elements of hire, promiscuity, and emotional indifference—all of which are incompatible with primary or *gemeinschaft* association.

The sexual appetite, like every other, is tied to socially necessary functions. The function it most logically and naturally relates to is procreation. The nature of procreation and socialization is such that their performance requires institutionalized primary-group living. Hence the family receives the highest estimation of all sexual institutions in society, the others receiving lower esteem as they are remoter from its *gemeinschaft* character and reproductive purpose. Commercial prostitution stands at the lowest extreme; it shares with other sexual institutions a basic feature, namely the employment of sex for an ulterior end in a system of differential advantages, but it differs from them in being mercenary, promiscuous, and emotionally indifferent. From *both* these facts, however, it derives its remarkable vitality.

Since prostitution is a contractual relation in which services are traded (usually in terms of an exchange medium) and sex is placed in an economic context, it is strange that modern writers have made so much of the fact that the "social evil" has economic causes. One might as well say, with equal perspicacity, that retail merchandising has economic causes. Prostitution embraces an economic relation, and is naturally connected with the entire system of economic forces. But to jump from this truism to the conclusion that prostitution can be abolished by eliminating its economic causes is erroneous. Economic causes seldom act alone, and hence their removal is seldom a panacea.

The causal ramifications of commercial coitus extend beyond the economic sphere. At least three separable but related problems must be recognized: (1) the causes of the existence of prostitution; (2) the causes of the *rate* or *amount* of prostitution; and (3) the causes of *any particular individual's entrance into, or patronage of,* prostitution. The existence of prostitution seems related both to the physiological nature of man and to the inherent character of society, both of which include more than the sheer economic element. These basic factors, constantly operative, account for the ubiquity of prostitution, but not for the variations in its rate. This second problem must be dealt with in terms of the specific institutional configuration existing at the time, in which economic factors are highly but not exclusively important. Finally, any particular person's connection with prostitution is a result of his or her own unique life-history, into which an infinite variety of strands, some economic and some not economic, are woven. The factors in (1) and (2) are operative in the individual's life, but are never sufficient in themselves to explain his or her behavior. . . .

When outlawed, prostitution falls into one peculiar category of crime—a type exceedingly hard to deal with—in which one of the willful parties is the ordinary law-abiding citizen. This kind of crime, of which bootlegging is the archetype, is supported by the money and behavior of a sizeable portion of the citizenry, because in it the citizen receives a service. Though the service is illegitimate, the citizen cannot be held guilty, for it is both impossible and inadvisable to punish half the populace for a crime. Each citizen participates in vital institutional relationships—family, business, church, and state. To disrupt all of these by throwing him in jail for a mere vice would be, on a large scale, to disrupt society. But the eagerness of otherwise decent citizens to receive the illicit service attests powerful forces behind the demand element.

On the one hand, the demand is the result of a simple biological appetite. When all other sources of gratification fail, due to defects of person or circumstance, prostitution can be relied upon to furnish relief. None of the exacting requirements of sex attraction and courtship are necessary. All that is needed is the cash, and this can be obtained in a thousand ways. Prostitution is the most malleable, the most uninvolved form of physical release.

But in addition to the sheer desire for sexual satisfaction, there is the desire for satisfaction in a particular (often an unsanctioned) way.

The common and ignorant assumption that prostitution exists to satisfy the gross sensuality of the young unmarried man, and that if he is taught to bridle gross sexual impulse or induced to marry early the prostitute must be idle, is altogether incorrect . . . The prostitute is something more than a channel to drain off superfluous sexual energy, and her attraction by no means ceases when men are married, for a large number of men who visit prostitutes, if not the majority, are married. And alike whether they are married or unmarried the motive is not one of uncomplicated lust.

The craving for variety, for perverse gratification, for mysterious and provocative surroundings, for intercourse free from entangling cares and civilized pretense, all play their part.

Prostitution, again by its very nature, is aptly suited to satisfy this second side of demand. The family, an institution of status rather than contract, limits the variety, amount, and nature of a person's satisfactions. But since with the prostitute the person is paying for the privilege, he is in a position to demand almost anything he wants. The sole limitation on his satisfactions is not morality or convention, but his ability to pay the price. This is an advantage which commercial recreation generally has over kinds handled by other institutional channels.

There is no reason to believe that a change in the economic system will eliminate either side of demand. In any system the effective demand as expressed by price will vary with current economic and moral forces, but the underlying desire both for sheer gratification and for gratification in particular ways will remain impregnable.

We can imagine a social system in which the motive for prostitution would be completely absent, but we cannot imagine that the system could ever come to pass. It would be a regime of absolute sexual freedom, wherein intercourse were practised solely for the pleasure of it, by both parties. This would entail at least two conditions: *First,* there could be no institutional control of sexual expression. Marriage, with its concomitants of engagement, jealousy, divorce, and legitimacy, could not exist. Such an institution builds upon and limits the sexual urge, making sex expression contingent upon non-sexual factors, and thereby paving the way for intercourse against one's physical inclination. *Second,* all sexual desire would have to be mutually complementary. One person could not be erotically attracted to a non-responsive person, because such a situation would inevitably involve frustration and give a motive for using force, fraud, authority, or money to induce the unwilling person to co-operate.

Neither of these conditions can in the nature of things come to pass. As we have seen, every society attempts to control, and for its own survival must control, the sexual impulse in the interest of social order, procreation, and socialization. Moreover, all men are not born handsome nor all women beautiful. Instead there is a perfect gradation from extremely attractive to extremely unattractive, with an unfavorable balance of the old and ugly. This being the case, the persons at the wrong end of the scale must, and inevitably will, use extraneous means to obtain gratification.

While neither the scale of attractiveness nor the institutionalization of sex are likely to disappear, it is possible that the *particular form of institutionalization* may change. The change may be in the direction of greater sex freedom. Such a change must inevitably affect prostitution, because the greater the proportion of free, mutually pleasurable intercourse, the lesser is the demand for prostitution. . . .

The conclusion that free intercourse for pleasure and friendship rather than for profit is the greatest enemy of prostitution emerges logically from our statement that a basic trait of prostitution is the use of sex for an ulterior purpose. Should one wish to abolish commercial coitus, one would have to eliminate this trait. This proposition however, is unacceptable to moralists, because, as we saw, the underlying trait of prostitution is also a fundamental feature of reputable sexual institutions, and intercourse for sheer pleasure is as inimical to our sacred institutions as it is to the profane one of mercenary love. Though Lecky's suggestion that harlotry sustains the family is perhaps indefensible, it seems true that prostitution is not so great a danger to the family as complete liberty.

Where the family is strong, there tends to be a well-defined system of prostitution and the social regime is one of status. Women are either part of the family system, or they are definitely not a part of it. In the latter case they are prostitutes, members of a caste set apart. There are few intermediate groups, and there is little mobility. This enables the two opposite types of institutions to function side by side without confusion; they are each staffed by a different personnel, humanly as well as functionally distinct. But where familial controls are weak, the system of prostitution tends to be poorly defined. Not only is it more nearly permissible to satisfy one's desire outside the family, but also it is easier to find a respectable member of society willing to act as partner. This is why a decline of the family and a decline of prostitution are both associated with a rise of sex freedom. Women, released from closed family supervision, are freer to seek gratification outside it. The more such women, the easier it is for men to find in intimate relations with them the satisfactions formerly supplied by harlots. This is why the unrestricted indulgence in sex for the fun of it by both sexes is the greatest enemy, not only of the family, but also of prostitution. . . .

But even if present trends continue, there is no likelihood that sex freedom will ever displace prostitution. Not only will there always be a set of reproductive institutions which place a check upon sexual liberty, a system of social dominance which gives a motive for selling sexual favors, and a scale of attractiveness which creates the need for buying these favors, but prostitution is, in the last analysis, economical. Enabling a small number of women to take care of the needs of a large number of men, it is the most convenient sexual outlet for an army, and for the legions of strangers, perverts, and physically repulsive in our midst. It performs a function, apparently, which no other institution fully performs.

PROSTITUTION

Gilbert Geis

Prostitution in the United States today is a nationwide industry that is believed to gross more than a billion dollars a year and to involve between 100,000 to 500,000 women. This is one of the items of information reported by Charles Winick and Paul M. Kinsie in a book titled *The Lively Commerce: Prostitution in the United States,* which is said to be the first comprehensive study of prostitution in almost 50 years. An earlier study, it might be added, had been done by Mr. Kinsie in his younger days.

Winick, a sociologist at the City University of New York, and Kinsie, who works for the American Social Health Association, had at their disposal more than 2,000 interviews with prostitutes and their clients, judges, probation officers and others associated with the lively commerce.

From *Not The Law's Business?* National Institute of Mental Health, Center for Studies of Crime and Delinquency, 1972. (Crime and Delinquency Issues) pp. 195–221.

Some of the things that Winick and Kinsie report about prostitution are the following:

Most prostitutes are physically unattractive; some of them have flagrant physical defects. In the last three decades prostitutes apprehended by the police tend to be overweight and short, with poor teeth, minor blemishes and untidy hair. Some are tatooed with legends like "Keep off the grass" and "Admission 50¢." They are usually indifferent to men, regarding them simply as "trade." They are rarely rebels in any conscious or deliberate sense. In contrast to the dramatic coloration they are given on stage, in films, or novels, the majority have relatively uninflected personalities. In describing her work, a typical prostitute said it was "a little more boring" than her former job as a file clerk. Prostitution pays poorly: At three $10 tricks a day, 6 days a week, the average prostitute may gross about $9,300 per year and net from $5,000 to $6,000.

The suicide rate among prostitutes is seen

by Winick and Kinsie as indicating a high degree of alienation and unhappiness. Seventy-five percent of a sampling of call girls were said to have attempted suicide, and 15 percent of all suicides brought to public hospitals are reported to be prostitutes. Though "baby pros" between the ages of 12 and 16 are said to be increasing in numbers, the median age for prostitutes is 25 to 40. While folklore has them going directly from defloration to the trade, there is usually a 2-year gap. Their three tricks a day may reflect the declining vigor of the working class: in the 1920's and 1930's, prostitutes averaged between 15 to 30 tricks daily.

The Lively Commerce defines the pimp as an occupational disease of the prostitute, her punisher or flatterer, her superior or inferior, as the occasion demands. He may be her lover, or he may be impotent. Helping her feel human, spying out the land, dealing with drunks, supplying drugs, breaking in new girls—these are some of the pimp's jobs. The madam—that larger-than-life personality—is almost as obsolete as the piano player, since most girls are entrepreneurs now and the brothel is only a nostalgic memory. . . .

In the Winick-Kinsie study of the contemporary prostitute, clients were seen as being attracted to the girls by drunkenness, curiosity, restlessness, bravado, "perverse" desires, or a need for reassurance. In less than 15 minutes, the client must find whatever it is he is seeking; if he takes longer, he may be handed his hat, which may be all that he has taken off. His first preference is fellatio, but he may also fancy himself a "lover"—an unpopular type with most girls—who kisses, dawdles and tries to arouse his partner with "marriage manual" techniques. The authors are inclined to think that the prostitute's client probably paid for his sex because he can't fuse the tender and the sensual in his feelings, and here he can forget about tenderness. Afterwards, however, he may become more human and talk about his wife and children until the prostitute turns him off. Once in a while, he'll cry. The prostitute

does not "drain off" his antisocial impulses for very long: statistics show that when prostitution declines, crime does too.

America is not yet ready to repeal its laws against prostitution, Winick and Kinsie maintain, though they find the trade firmly operating in practically every city of consequence in the Nation. They conclude that prostitution has "stabilized" in the United States, but that it has not been particularly curtailed by the sexual revolution because "the change in attitudes has primarily been on the part of young people and prostitution customers are primarily older men."

Supplementing the countrywide overview of prostitution by Winick and Kinsie are several investigations based on specific aspects of the job of being a prostitute. Paul Gebhard's study of 127 prostitutes, for instance, suggests that their trade is misperceived in a number of ways. Gebhard notes that few prostitutes are unwillingly led into their business. Only 4 percent of the girls he interviewed fell into this category, Gebhard notes; even then, these girls were presented with alternatives. As he observes: "The female who says her husband or boyfriend forced her into prostitution is saying she chose prostitution rather than lose her mate and possibly experience a beating. Even the brothels," Gebhard points out, "would not want the problem of confining a captive beseeching her clients for rescue."

Absence of heavy drug use was another characteristic of the women Gebhard interviewed. Only 4 percent were ever addicted to "hard" drugs while another 5 percent had experimented with them without becoming addicted. Use of amphetamines and marihuana was found to be more frequent, but the cost of these drugs, Gebhard points out, would not be so high as to force a girl into prostitution in order to secure money for their purchase. In regard to the reasons why a girl becomes a prostitute, Gebhard's interviews disclosed the following:

The major motivation for becoming a prostitute is financial. Nine out of ten of our sample listed money as the prime motivation. Second, one can meet a diversity of males, some of them interesting, and one may enter a social milieu otherwise inaccessible.

There were several additional "misconceptions" which Gebhard sought to correct on the basis of his data. He concluded that the common view that prostitutes hate men was erroneous. "The truth is that the prostitute's attitude toward her clients is not unlike that of anyone providing services to a diverse clientele. Some clients are disliked, toward some one feels neutral, and a few are liked." He also reported that most prostitutes—two-thirds in the case of his sample—indicate no regrets with their choice of work. Finally, Gebhard takes exception to the prevalent view that prostitutes are basically frigid and homosexually inclined women. "In their coitus with friends and husbands, the prostitutes are somewhat more responsive in terms of reaching orgasm than other females," it is noted. Nor do the data support the notion of homosexuality. "Prostitutes so effectively compartmentalize their lives that their profession does not interfere seriously with their heterosexuality, orgasmic capacities, or ability to form affectional relationships with men."

The voluntariness and the relative "normality" of the trade of prostitution underlies most contemporary writing on the subject. In some measure, this conclusion appears to be based on the absence of coercion involved in leading girls into prostitution. "There are certainly many exceptions," a United Nations worldwide survey noted as far back as 1959, "but the trend appears to be toward a freer prostitute whose relationship with those living on her earnings is more or less voluntary."

Indeed, in some respects prostitution has been regarded as a more attractive enterprise than many of those occupations otherwise available to its practitioners. Characteristic of this appraisal is the report of a psychiatrist in an American juvenile court who granted that the sale of her sexual favors by a young girl probably represented a rational resolution of the difficulties with which she was confronted:

If she has not already been getting clothes, etc., through her sexual life I expect that she will soon begin doing so. To be quite frank, I am not half so disturbed about this as I am about her realistic approach to the problem. She knows that she stammers, she knows that she is poor, she guesses that she is illegitimate, she knows that she is dumb, and in a rather cold way she looked me in the eye and asked me whether I wouldn't do the same thing.

In addition, prostitution may be regarded as an entrepreneurial endeavor, at least on certain levels of its pursuit, replete with all of the advantages that self-employment offers (including the opportunity to easily avoid the payment of income taxes). One has no bosses, and retains the right to choose whether one cares to work at given times. Perhaps, in an ironic way, prostitution can be seen as much as anything else as fulfilling the vocational wish, expressed today by so many altruistically inclined young persons, that they "like to work with people."

Whether prostitution is chosen for reasons such as these or whether it becomes the resort of females merely following a path of least resistance—as so many of us do in our own endeavors—is a moot issue. But the freedom connected with the occupation should not be underestimated, any more, of course, than its more sordid aspects and its dangers should be overlooked. The independence of attitude that might be related to a career as a prostitute has been indicated in a fiery outburst by a New York schoolteacher who doubled as a call girl. She is explaining her refusal of an office job in the institution where she was incarcerated:

. . . "Why don't you work in the office?" I was asked. "Because I don't want to think her [the supervisor's] thoughts," I said. "I can scrub floors and keep my mind to myself. In her office I'd have to listen to her talk about her work and her problems. They can't control my mind even if I do have to sit around here for 3 months."

It needs to be stressed that there exist many different kinds of prostitutes. Gebhard's definition of the female prostitute provides the operational standard by which all may be delineated: "A female prostitute is a person who for immediate cash payment will engage in sexual activity with any person (usually male), known or unknown to her, who meets her minimal requirements as to age, sobriety, cleanliness, race, and health." Within this general rubric, there is a range running at one end from the expensive call girl, operating out of a luxury apartment, to the haggard streetwalker, working waterfront bars.

Most prostitutes, regardless of their status in the trade, are likely to explain their choice of occupation using, as most of us do, indices of social acceptability to demonstrate their own adequacy. One study—conducted by the present writer in collaboration with Norman Jackman and Richard O'Toole—noted that the prostitutes interviewed, in this instance primarily call girls working hotels in Oklahoma City, were apt to select a number of middle-class values in terms of which they regarded their performance as outstanding, and to stress these values as explanations for their choice of work. None of the girls, to our surprise, insisted that she had been tricked or otherwise led into prostitution, nor did any blame poor upbringing, neglectful parents (rather they tended to see themselves as spoiled and indulged children), early seduction, or others of the standard cliches for their present work.

The girls interviewed by us in Oklahoma City were apt to express the view that "everyone is immoral," and that they could therefore hardly be regarded as worse than other persons, that they were, in fact, a good deal less hypocritical. During one episode in which call girls met with students in an undergraduate course at the University, this viewpoint came forth angrily when one of the call girls flared out at a coed that she was "only selling what you're giving away." Quite astonished, the coed turned with puzzlement to the rest of the class. "I don't understand her," she said. "I don't give anything away."

There was also, not surprisingly, consider-

able stress by the prostitutes on their financial success, and few saw anything anomalous about these pretensions and the fact that they were often being interviewed in the city jail, where they had been stored because they were unable to pay a $12 fine. One told us, for instance, about

a very wealthy businessman who pays me 25 to 30 dollars an evening just for my company. He takes me to the best places in town for a dinner and dancing, and buys me expensive gifts. And I've never been to bed with the man. He told me that I mingled well with the finest people. He said once, "You act like a lady."

The concern with attributions of ladylike behavior was common among many of the prostitutes interviewed. They were apt to derogate their colleagues who worked the less resplendent hotels as girls who wore pants (slacks), while they themselves always wore dresses. In one of the more poignant interview episodes, one of the call girls told us that the vice squad officers (she called them "Mr. Jackson" and "Mr. White") always treated her like a lady, that they—and she said this with great pride—always held the door of the squad car open for her when they arrested her. In fact, this particular call girl had an ongoing arrangement with the vice squad team under which she would telephone them to let them know whether or not she was working on a given day. If she was working, they were free to arrest her on sight, under any conditions. If she said that she was not working that day, they would not interfere with her regardless of how suspicious her behavior appeared. In this way, she managed to go places unmolested with male relatives and dates who had no idea of her true vocation.

There were also stories about the extraordinary fees paid by fathers for the initiation of their male sons into sex, and each of the girls managed to let us know how much she earned in a good week, or at least the amount that she would have us believe she earned, and the most money she had ever received from an individual client. In addition, new television sets, mothers in expensive rest homes, children in exclusive private schools, and plane trips—the girls always said that they "flew" someplace, never that they "went" there—dotted our interviews, at least with the "higher class" of call girls. A rather typical story concerned a call girl who had been visited one night by a regular customer. He told her that his wife had just had a miscarriage, and that the doctor had sent him to the drugstore to get some medicine. Instead, he had decided to stop off for a brief sexual interlude. "I told him to get right out of here," the girl said righteously, "and get that medicine and get back to his wife."

Similarly, a number of the girls, those whom we defined as *dual world* prostitutes—girls with middle-class orientations—avoided the topic of sex completely. They justified their prostitute role as a self-sacrificing necessity to maintain those who were helpless and dependent upon them. One girl claimed to be supporting six persons and herself.

They don't know what I do for a living, except my husband. I see my little girl often. About once a week. I don't work weekends so I can see her.

Another married prostitute also claimed to be supporting her unemployed husband, two children, and her mother. Her mother takes care of her children and none of them knew that she was a prostitute:

I think that I am a good mother who takes care of her children. I love my family very much. I have a normal family life other than being a prostitute. I hope my husband can find a job and gets to working steadily again so I can be an ordinary housewife.

Of the unmarried prostitutes in the dual worlds group, one had five children by a previous marriage and the other had never been married. The first strongly identified with her children, and the second with her parents. Neither of them associated with other people much. Both claimed that they had become prostitutes to support others:

I am very proud of my family. Even though the mother is a prostitute it doesn't reflect on her family—this business doesn't keep you from having good children. I keep my children in the best private schools and colleges in Texas. One of them married very well. They don't know what I do.

The respondent who identified with her parents maintained that her father had given her the best of everything as a child, but she had failed to live up to his expectations because she was too much like him. Nevertheless, she helped both parents financially:

My parents are the most wonderful people alive. I like 'em both but my mother is easier to get along with. Dad and I fight like cats and dogs. Both alike. He thinks I'm 2 years old. He said, "I knew the day you was born you'd be just like me." He's got suspicious of my work, but not my mother. She had an operation—cancer of the brain. I gave him [father] $400 and $300 more after I came back from Chicago. He said, "Myra, I know what you're doing, but for God's sake don't let your mother know."

There are, of course, many other prostitutes who accept the role without much attempt to justify either its middle-class attributes or their own admirable traits. And there are many who regard themselves and their behavior with nothing but contempt. One girl interviewed in a nightclub observed, for instance:

I live by myself and have no friends. I just sleep and hustle at the night club. No, TV shows and books just bore me. Daydreams? Why daydream when you can't be out doing the things you daydream about? . . . Just before you came in, I was out standing in the rain watching the world cry because it's been so screwed up by all the bastards in it.

Nonetheless, the point needs to be stressed that prostitutes tend to be satisfied with their calling, and that they have chosen it with some awareness of the options available to them. That later options which can be employed to leave the trade ought to be maximized, given the not unreasonable American viewpoint that there appear to be more worthwhile ways for a woman to spend her time, seems to be an obvious element of any social policy in regard to prostitution. Other components of such policy will be suggested on the basis of a following review of the history and present status of prostitution in the United States and elsewhere. We will also examine the apparent impact of prostitution on the girls involved in it, on those connected to them, including their pimps, and its apparent impact on the social system.

In regard to prostitution, there are important questions concerning the precise manner in which weak and relatively disenfranchised minorities are able, if they are able, to translate their interests into legislation. Abortion law reform has a power base among articulate and well-to-do women, whose own vested interests are involved. Similarly, homosexuals often are found in the powerful and sophisticated segments of society. Reform of the laws concerning drug use only became a matter of intense public concern, when marihuana began to be used by a great number of middle-class, suburban, and college youngsters. Prostitutes, we will find, are rather declassé and dispossessed. With growing sexual openness and the availability of (as the prostitutes call them) "freebees" in American society, the traditional whore, initiating "respectable" youngsters into sexual experience, has lost her strongest customer base. Gebhard, for instance, has found a drop from 25 to 7 percent in the past two decades in the number of male students who experienced their first sexual intercourse with a prostitute, and two marriage counselors at Yale University recently observed that the contact between students and prostitutes was "zilch."

It is in such terms that issues regarding prostitution must be seen. They concern not the right to sexual freedom, providing such freedom does not impose upon equivalent rights of others, but they involve questions about the kinds of support necessary for such freedom to be translated into legislative mandate.

THE WOLFENDEN REPORT

At the same time that it inquired into the question of the proper legal attitude toward

homosexuality, the Wolfenden Committee in Great Britain reexamined the country's laws bearing upon prostitution. . . . The Wolfenden Committee's recommendations regarding prostitution—that public solicitation of prostitutes be dealt with more severely, and that those living on the earnings of prostitution be criminally punished—found almost immediate legislative favor. The Wolfenden Committee did not recommend any alteration in the British policy that prostitution itself should not constitute a criminal offense. On this point it observed:

It will be apparent, from the recommendations we have made, that we are not attempting to abolish prostitution or to make prostitution in itself illegal. We do not think that the law ought to try to do so; nor do we think that if it tried it could by itself succeed. What the law can and should do is to ensure that the streets of London and our big provincial cities should be freed from what is offensive or injurious and made tolerable for the ordinary citizen who lives in them or passes through them.

At the time the Wolfenden Committee sat, soliciting on the streets for the purpose of prostitution was punishable by a fine of 2 pounds, about $5.80 in American money. The Committee noting that this sum had been established more than 100 years earlier, asked that it be raised to a maximum of 10 pounds ($28) for the first offense, 25 pounds ($70) for a second offense, and that there be a penalty of 3 months' imprisonment for a third and any subsequent offenses. The reasoning behind the recommendation was expressed in the following terms:

. . . we have two purposes in mind. The first is straightforward deterrence. We believe that most of the prostitutes loitering in the streets are those who are well established in their habits, whom repeated fines have failed to deter. We therefore feel justified in recommending that deprivation of liberty, which would be particularly unwelcome to those offenders, should be available as a sanction when, in an individual case, monetary fines have failed.

The Committee did not specify quite what it meant by the idea that prostitutes, more than other offenders, would be "particularly" inhospitable to a term of imprisonment. But it did indicate that it was not imprisonment that it sought but supervised postconviction arrangements for the girls:

We do not deceive ourselves into thinking that a short term of imprisonment is likely to effect reform when repeated fines have failed. But we believe that the presence of imprisonment as a possible punishment may make the courts anxious to try, and the individual prostitutes more willing to accept, the use of probation in suitable cases.

Finally, the Wolfenden Committee proposed a penalty of 2 years' imprisonment for the offense of "living off the earnings of a prostitute." It is noteworthy that the three female members of the Wolfenden Committee united in rejecting the 2-year penalty for pimping on the ground that it was too lenient. "The law must," they wrote in their dissenting statement, "have regard to the worst case that could arise." They thought that 2-year sentences were "quite inadequate to deal with a person who makes a business of exploiting prostitution on a large scale." Instead, they would have preferred a 5-year maximum.

The manner in which the Wolfenden Committee made its case for handling prostitutio is worth indepth review here, for it tells what this sophisticated group, after considerable study, found to be factually accurate and how it used such facts to reach its policy recommendations.

"From the evidence we have received, there is no doubt that the aspect of prostitution which causes the greatest public concern at the present time is the presence, and the visible and obvious presence, of prostitutes in considerable numbers in the public streets of some parts of London and of a few provincial towns," it began. Then the Committee attempted to determine from available information whether the problem of prostitution had been growing worse or improving in recent years, but, like any group looking at the statistical data that passes for an overview of criminal activity, the Wolfenden members found the endeavor

futile. "We have," it decided, "no reliable evidence."

Committee members granted that there might be something to the view that "the mere presence of prostitutes carrying on their trade was no more, and no less, a matter for police intervention than the presence of street photographers or toysellers." But they were not taken with the argument sufficiently to endorse it. Rather, the Committee concluded that "the right of the normal, decent citizen to go about the streets without affront to his or her sense of decency should be the prime consideration and should take precedence over the interests of the prostitute and her customers."

There was a passing amount of difficulty involved in the fact that the "normal, decent citizen" subjected to annoyance by a prostitute was almost never able to be persuaded to provide evidence in court concerning the indignity he had suffered. The Wolfenden Committee members hurried by this issue, never quite confronting the possibility that one might conclude that since such cooperation was not readily provided the annoyance might not have been serious enough to be punished as criminal. Instead, the Committee endorsed the principle that the annoyance of prostitution was to "inhabitants and passengers in general" and not to any given individual who had personally been accosted. The opinion that the Committee ended with, it can be observed, was exactly that with which it had begun, so that an arguable proposition became endorsed on the ground that its ingredients were self-evident":

In our view both loitering and importuning for the purpose of prostitution are so self-evidently public nuisances that the law ought to deal with them, as it deals with over self-evident public nuisances, without calling on individual citizens to establish the fact that they were annoyed.

The question of whether the prostitute's male customer ought to be punished was another major issue that occupied the Committee. The result was again more of a semantic slight-of-hand than a direct response to the question. It was not prostitution with which it was concerned, the report noted. Prostitution was immoral, but not illegal. The purpose of the state was to legislate against "those activities which offend against public order and decency or expose the ordinary citizen to what is offensive and injurious." "The simple fact," said the Committee, on a matter far from simple, "is that prostitutes do parade themselves more habitually and openly than their prospective customers."

The Wolfenden group was rather more forthright in its review of "an increasingly prevalent form of solicitation, commonly called 'kerb crawling.'" Kerb crawlers, it was observed, were motorists who drove slowly, overtaking women pedestrians, and halting by them with the intention of inviting them into the car. The Committee granted that such solicitation might be a nuisance to some women, but it concluded that the difficulties of proof were so burdensome that it did not appear worthwhile, at least at that time, to make such behavior a criminal offense. Besides, "the possibility of a very damaging charge being leveled at an innocent motorist must also be borne in mind." The same possible objection had already handily been dealt with in regard to prostitutes. A woman would be cautioned first, and only on a later offense would she be able to be labeled a "common prostitute" and charged with solicitation. That other persons might just as readily be warned first and then defined as "common kerb crawlers" did not seem to have occurred to members of the Committee.

The Committee was not impressed by arguments favoring licensed brothels, which would, perhaps, reduce the amount of public solicitation by prostitutes. They thought such places would be apt to encourage white slavery, and that they would represent an unwise state endorsement of the practice of prostitution. Nor was the Committee swayed by the view that licensed brothels, duly inspected, might provide safeguards against the spread of venereal infections by prostitutes. "It is obvious," the Committee noted, not

quite meeting the issue (as was its tendency whenever it pronounced something "obvious" or "self-evident"), "that a woman who is absolutely healthy at the time of examination may be infected shortly afterwards and infect others before her own infection is detected." In the view of the Committee, tolerating brothels would be a "retrograde step" by the state.

The Committee took great pains to point out that its best information indicated that the pimp—"commonly known as a 'ponce' or *souteneur*"—was voluntarily supported by the prostitute, with neither coercion or physical force figuring into their financial arrangements. Each took from and gave to the other, in a relationship providing mutual satisfactions. Therefore, the Committee concluded that there existed no reason to increase the 2-year penalty for the criminal offense of "living on a prostitute's earnings." It was noted in passing that the offense itself was usually difficult to prove; prostitutes often worked in one district and lived with their pimp in another. Finally, in a somewhat irrelevant flight of rhetoric, the Committee suggested that it really was not the pimp who was basically responsible for the allure of prostitution, nor, most certainly, was it an "irresistible demand of natural instinct" which kept the trade flourishing. Rather:

At the present time, entertainments of a suggestive character, dubious advertisements, the sale of pornographic literature, contraceptives and "aphrodisiac" drugs (sometimes all in one shop), and the sale of alcoholic liquor in premises frequented by prostitutes, all sustain the trade, and in turn themselves profit from it.

It was not the law most fundamentally which would see to the eradication of prostitution, but a change in attitudes and values:

With most of these evils the law attempts to deal so far as it can without unduly trespassing on the liberty of the individual; and, as in the case of prostitution itself, it is to educative measures rather than to amendment of the law that society must look for a remedy.

Finally, the Wolfenden Committee recommended that persons who knowingly rent premises to prostitutes and/or their agents should be prosecuted as persons "living on the earnings of prostitution." Curiously, though, the Committee seemed to have only a recommendation of forbearance and a few words of sympathy for those who might be annoyed by finding themselves residing in neighborhoods where in-house prostitution was taking place. It did note that there might be civil remedies if such premises constituted a nuisance, but it neglected to observe that recourse to such remedies, particularly for persons living in such kinds of areas, rarely is feasible. Apparently, then, the Wolfenden Committee thought that persons obligated to live in the vicinity of prostitution activity ought to be sympathized with, while those given esthetic and moral offenses by prostitutes in the street ought to be protected from such offense by the police. That such recommendations appear notoriously to favor one social class as against another seems (to borrow a word from the Committee, but to use it, hopefully, more felicitously) "self-evident."

POST-WOLFENDEN DEVELOPMENTS

The recommendations of the Wolfenden Committee in regard to prostitution were in large measure translated into law by enactment in 1959 of the Street Offences Act. Given the lengthy study and the considerable concern of the Committee in creating a set of conditions which its members regarded as superior to those prevailing, a key question is: How has the Street Offences Act worked?

The answer is summarized in the lead sentence of an article in *New Society* in 1969:

The decline of the Street Offences Act is a setpiece study of how legislation can be limited in its effects.

Parliament had attempted to overcome the danger of inadvertent harassment of respectable women and to permit the neo-phyte prostitute to mend her ways by writing into the first section of the Act a provision that required two cautions before a girl could be arrested for soliciting in public. The result of this approach, as best as could be ascertained, seemed to be an increase in the mobility of prostitutes, but no particular decline in their activity. "What the most professional girls do," the *New Society* observed, "is to get their two cautions in one town and then push off under a different name elsewhere."

One of the problems which the Wolfenden Committee had been reluctant to tackle out of fear of encouraging undue harassment had come home to roost a decade later. Those very "kerb crawlers" whose reputations the Wolfenden group had been so insistent upon protecting were now in great numbers using their vehicles to solicit prostitutes. For the girls, such arrangements allowed them to transact business in the car and to avoid problems associated with having special working premises or having to rent an apartment or motel or hotel room.

Use of automobiles as roving whorehouses had also undercut many of the approaches devised by the Wolfenden Committee to regulate and to circumscribe the practice of prostitution. Taxi drivers and other men were chauffering prostitutes about the cities, acting as touts for them and soliciting business from likely male pedestrians, with the intercourse taking place in the automobiles. In addition, despite the Wolfenden report proposals and the provisions of the Street Offences Act, certain areas of London were unofficially being sanctioned for on-the-street solicitation by prostitutes. Interference by the police occurred only when the informal geographic boundaries of the areas were crossed by the girls. In this regard, England was following the practice of several continental countries, most notably Germany, where "red-light" districts exist for tourists and others interested in the merchandising that is allowed to take place therein. In England, prostitutes were also working immigrant neighborhoods, attempting to find replacements for the dwindling number of armed forces customers.

The somewhat offhanded dismissal of the male as only an incidental appendage to the problem of prostitution also proved to be something of an oversight by the Wolfenden group, given its intent to reduce the amount of public nuisance associated with prostitution. Cases were arising in which men were blatantly soliciting women in public places, but police action against the men proved impossible following a 1966 judicial verdict which overturned one such prosecution on the ground that it was not supportable under provisions of the Street Offences Act. In regard to pimps, the Street-Offences Act, undoubtedly combined with many other innovations in the life style of the contemporary prostitute, had led to a separation between the business life of the prostitute and her emotional relationship to a pimp. "Girls with lighted bell-pushes in the Soho area [the conventional calling card of the prostitute there] prefer to use independent touts to bring in men at dry times," the *New Society* study observes. "The modern prostitute ... tends to employ others rather than to be employed."

The inability of the Street Offences Act to achieve its stipulated purposes was most evident from examination of arrest figures for prostitution. In 1965, there were 1,552 arrests, and that number jumped to 2,422 within 2 years, with the latter number believed by observers to be a considerable underestimation of the true extent of the increase in prostitution in England. The statistical and survey results led to a growing belief, quite common as a reaction to reform efforts in such an area, that the matter being attacked is impervious to much change. Thus, the former chief of the vice squad in London now writes:

The dominant conclusion resulting from our inquiry into the vice of London, and more particularly into the incidence of prostitution in all its aspects, is the somewhat axiomatic and self-evident inference that, while the sex appetite might be temporarily curbed, it can never be eradicated by legislation.

The theorists who imagine that the oldest profession in the world can be put out of business by Act of Parliament are perpetuating a doctrine that is far removed from reality. . . .

It is, of course, not possible to indicate the level of prostitution that would have taken place had the Wolfenden Committee not met and had the Street Offences Act not taken the form that it did. Without the Act, it can be claimed, prostitution might have been considerably more rampant than it is in London, and might constitute an even more serious affront to public morality and personal modesty. On the other hand, it seems apparent that the Act was not able to provide continuing inhibition of the activity that it sought to regulate and that it left a considerable number of loopholes by means of which persons were able to offend against the values the Act sought to protect. It can hardly be maintained, however, that laws can be expected to eliminate totally the behavior they are addressed to, especially when that behavior is as resistant as prostitution has proven to be. In such terms, the verdict on the impact of the Street Offences Act must be a Scottish "not proven." There has been some readjustment in the methods by which prostitution is carried on, but there has been no apparent improvement along the lines that had been anticipated.

OTHER COUNTRIES

The historical record is a grab-bag of diverse kinds of arrangements under which prostitution has existed and been sanctioned or outlawed. The lesson from history appears to be that when there are women willing to exchange sexual contact for financial reward prostitution will find a way to manifest itself. The literature on the subject, however, is notably silent on the consequences of the different manners in which society has responded to such conditions. There are, in addition, no decent studies of the career patterns of cohorts of prostitutes, but only stray anecdotal versions of this or that satisfactory or tragic conclusion to an individual life. Nor, on a grander scale, are there attempts to determine the impact of different kinds of definitions of prostitution on the social health and integrity of different countries. Perhaps, indeed, such an attempt would be vainglorious, and prostitution represents only a minor and very insignificant aspect of any society's way of life.

The historical record, therefore, is primarily a recital of exotica and a description of the ingenuity of man in satisfying erotic concerns. Prostitutes have ranged from the streetwalking harlot, often glamorized in the disproportionate amount of literature devoted to her, to the courtesan who bestows her favors upon only royalty and near-royalty. In ancient Rome, where prostitutes were regarded with indulgence, they were nonetheless required to wear distinctive clothing and to have their hair dyed yellow, red, or blue. In Greek society prostitutes were of several types, with the *hetairae,* or "good friends," occupying the highest position. Demosthenes noted: "We have *hetairae* for pleasure; concubines for daily use, and wives to provide us with legitimate children and to grow old faithfully in the interior of the house." The concubine, a purchased or rented slave, was part of the Greek household. The *hetairae* had their own luxurious district, while the Piraeus, a segregated area along the wharves, was the territory of the plebian prostitutes.

The Old Testament took a firm stand against prostitution to establish a tradition that, despite considerable ambivalence, appears to be the dominant motif in American society today. The Old Testament contains many warnings against the pagan world harlot whose wantonness was seen as threatening the Hebrew theocracy. Solomon cautioned against the prostitute, saying that "her house is the way to hell, going down to the chambers of death." Jewish fathers were forbidden to turn their daughters into prostitutes (*Leviticus* 19:29), and the daughters of Israel were forbidden to become prostitutes (*Deuteronomy* 23:17).

Early Christian writers were more inclined to regard prostitution as a necessary, even vital, evil. "Early Christian obsessions with chastity," it has been observed, "were born of an age when every nunnery was liable to become a brothel." Saint Augustine, the spokesman for the period, believed that what the prostitute did was morally wrong, but that still worse evils would arise if she did not provide an outlet for human lust; in fact, Augustine declared that the prohibition of prostitution and capricious lusts will overthrow society." Saint Thomas Aquinas, the medieval theologian, reiterated this position. The prostitute, he wrote in *Summa Theologica,* "is like the filth in the sea or the sewers in the palace. Take away the sewer and you will fill the palace with pollution and likewise with the filth in the sea. Take away prostitutes from the world and you will fill it with sodomy." This attitude, more tolerant than that of the Old Testament, may perhaps find its roots in the story of Christ and Mary Magdalene, the prostitute who was forgiven her errant ways. Prostitution was well-nigh omnipresent throughout the Middle Ages, according to Benjamin and Masters. "There were frequent attempts at regulation and suppression, with the former inefficient and the latter unsuccessful. Also characteristically unsuccessful were a variety of attempts to rehabilitate prostitutes."

Historical materials such as these do not, however, penetrate to the core of evaluative issues. The *London Times'* review of the most thoroughgoing treatise on the subject, Fernando Henriques' two-volume *Prostitution in Europe and the New World* summarizes aptly the author's inability to draw firm conclusions from his historical survey:

Is prostitution a response to repression? Does legislation against sexual immorality provoke the evil it seeks to control? Or is human nature such that only the forbidden is attractive and greater freedom merely encourages more esoteric sexual diversions? Dr. Henriques inevitably raises questions of this kind but does no more than hint at the answers, though he provides plenty of evidence to support both sides of the argument.

The contemporary experience of foreign countries other than Great Britain is equally inconclusive, though it points clearly to the fact that repressive efforts that have been undertaken to control prostitution invariably seem to boomerang.

Italy did away with licensed brothels in 1958, but in 1971 reports were indicating that "just as much [prostitution] is going on." According to a *Los Angeles Times* reporter, the level of venereal disease had tripled in Italy since the control legislation had become effective, with an estimated 30 percent of the prostitutes in Rome allegedly venereally infected. Under the former system, prostitutes had been required to undergo periodic examinations. Most of the traffic in prostitution was now run through switchboards, in apartments, or on sidewalks, with very few of the girls said to be doing business in clandestine houses of prostitution. . . .

A review of conditions in Italy during the years following passage in 1958 of the Merlin Act, which outlawed brothels, indicates the grounds for the verdict of the prefecture official:

For 10 years, as a member of the Italian Senate, Angelina Merlin had badgered and pestered her fellow parliamentarians to close down the nation's "houses of tolerance" and to outlaw an industry that paid the state $20,000,000 a year in taxes. An end must be made to "this terrible form of slavery," the little senator would shrill. And finally, she got her way . . . and red lights blinked out across Italy.

But *Signora* Merlin's delight was soon dimmed. First of all, the indignant males in her constituency voted her right out of the Senate. Worse yet, the majority of the 18,000 prostitutes she had redeemed from the bondage of the bordello refused to seek redemption in her "centers of social reeducation" and took to streetwalking. No longer bothered with police registration or enforced medical checkups and subject to only 8 days in jail if caught soliciting, Italy's prostitutes flourished as never before—and drew eager recruits to their ranks.

Today, barely 7 years after Angelina's great victory, an estimated 200,000 Italian women earn their living by prostitution. . . . In Rome, 12,000 prostitutes stalk the avenues and streets, with the more successful ones plying their trade in expensive Alfa

Romeos. Said a Roman hotel director: "They're so thick in the historic part of the city, you've got to wade through tons of makeup and bumps and grinds to get to the monuments.". ,.

[Prostitutes] were hopeful that the lawmakers would eventually . . . put them back in their brothels. "I get so tired of this same beat," one of them sighed. "In a nice warm house, I wouldn't have to stand and wait and take all those insults from hypocrites."

And many thoroughly respectable Italians share these sentiments; at least they believe they will never be able to clear the prostitutes off the streets of their cities until Italy's Parliament abolishes the Merlin Law in its entirety and once again insists that a prostitute's home should also be her house.

The story of prostitution in France reads much like that for Italy. At first, there was registration of prostitutes, and the trade was, as Harry Söderman notes, circumscribed by many regulations. Prostitutes were not allowed to walk near military barracks or near places of entertainment, and they were forbidden to pick up clients either by speaking or gesture. "Violation of this rule," Söderman observes, "was technically called *racolage*—crimping or soliciting—a word which is also used when a French barrister tries to attract clients by unethical means."

Then the brothels were closed by law, largely as a result of strenuous lobbying efforts by Marthe Richard. Thereafter, Mme. Richard became the most articulate opponent of her own reform. "The houses of prostitution are necessary," she wrote, after surveying what she had wrought by her reform effort. Residents of the houses, Mme. Richard now maintained, should be considered "as some kind of social workers," and vice squad officers should cease their "rule through fear." This turnabout was a result of a conviction that the closing of the brothels had had no impact upon morality, and that the venereal infection rate had risen astronomically, presumably because of the freelance nature of prostitution.

The verdict of Benjamin and Masters on the French experience is almost completely negative:

The French attempt to close down the brothels, and otherwise greatly restrict the operations of prostitutes, seems to have produced more whores, more pimps, more venereal disease, more crime, and no benefits apart from such satisfaction as may be derived from the existence of the ban.

The situation in Asia with regard to prostitution offers little in the way of other kinds of information which would allow a broader interpretation of methods used to control prostitution or of the consequences of unchecked prostitution. In Japan, the Government outlawed prostitution in 1957. "Japan's new law making prostitution illegal went into effect today," an observer on the scene noted. "Under the new law offending brothel operators, prostitutes, and their patrons will not be punished for another year. In that time the Government expects all those displaced from the profession to have found new means of livelihood."

The Government's expectation proved other than soundly based, however. Of the 150,000 prostitutes believed to have been operating in the red-light districts in Japan when the new law took effect, the majority today, according to a member of the Rehabilitation Commission of the Japanese Ministry of Welfare and Health, "are now either in a disguised form of their past practices or in forced prostitution systems operated by gangsters." The verdict of this official is similar to that of French and Italian commentators:

It is clear that prostitution is a problem of such social complexity that it cannot be resolved by passage of legislation. As indicated by experience in Japan and other countries, disguised prostitution—with all its attendant evils—may quickly become a substitute for the old red-light districts.

In India, the situation is more complex, but the conclusions rather similar to those reached elsewhere. Caste traditions are sometimes tied to prostitution in India. In Malabar, for instance, grownup girls are kept in purdah, and it is customary to expel them if they are seen or touched by an outsider. An offending—or offended—girl is pushed out of the main gate by servants, and anyone can take her away. A 1956 report of the Central Social Welfare Board also notes another form of customary prostitution in India:

Communities exist in many parts of India unrelated to each other but having similar traditions, i.e., the daughters of the house automatically become breadwinners of the family, the sons may marry but serve their sisters and help them to carry on the profession as pimps and instrumentalists if they belong to the dancing and singing class. There was nothing clandestine about it and families approved of and made arrangements for a newly matured girl to enter into the profession with due pomp and ceremony.

Attempts to control brothels in India also began in 1958, the year which saw the wave of similar reform movements throughout the world. And the verdict a decade later matched that rendered elsewhere. After futile years of attempted enforcement, an observer noted, the result "is a marked decline in moral values and the spread of disguised forms of prostitution."

The lesson from overseas nations, it should be said, is hardly unequivocal, except to the extent that it indicates rather clearly the results that may be expected from attempts only to close brothels. The foreign experience does not address itself to the question of very heavy penalties for prostitution, or to issues of reclamation subsidies, intensive reeducation efforts, or to similar approaches which have sometimes been suggested. The foreign experience does indicate a widespread initial disapproval in legislatures of brothel-based prostitution, followed by an even stronger dissatisfaction with the consequences of outlawing such arrangements.

PROSTITUTION IN THE UNITED STATES

Three areas within the United States will be examined to obtain information on prostitution. Each offers particular kinds of data on the institution of prostitution in America, and on public and police response to the practice. In Nevada, prostitution may be legal if a county decides to take advantage of this option offered under State law. In New York City, judicial resistance to the prosecution of prostitutes, among other things, has led to a blatant increase in overt streetwalking and to an obvious geographical concentration of prostitutes in the midtown area. In San Francisco, a recent Crime Commission recommendation that prostitution be legalized focused attention upon the extent and character of the practice and the attitudes of different officials toward the proposed approach.

Nevada

Prostitution is legal in 15 of Nevada's 17 counties, providing, as Charles Winick and Paul M. Kinsie note, "the most unusual legal arrangements for prostitution in America." The two excepted counties are Clark County, which includes the city of Las Vegas, and Washoe County, in which Reno is located. There were said to be about 60 brothels operating in Nevada during 1971.

The only county in the United States where prostitution is officially endorsed, to the extent of being licensed, is Nevada's Storey County, which imposes a $1,000 a month fee upon its only house of prostitution. The County has fewer than 700 residents and the license fee provides about one-fifth of its annual budget.

The licensing law in Storey County went into effect on the first of January in 1971. The brothel, open 24-hours-a-day and employing 20 girls, is located 7 miles east of Reno, and is known as the Mustang Bridge Ranch. To operate it pays the County an $18,000 yearly fee. Customers are charged $10 for about 20 minutes with a girl, and the prostitutes are reported to earn between $500 and $1,000 a week. One-half of the Ranch's customers are said to be local residents, the other half to be tourists. The male operator of the Ranch defines its success in the following terms: "Do you think that all the home cooking in the world will close all the good restaurants?"

Another Nevada brothel is called the Cottontail Ranch, and is situated in Esmeralda County, about 150 miles south of Las Vegas. Daily airplane flights take customers to the 3.75-acre plot of land rented by the madam for $100 a year from the Department of Interior.

Girls working in brothels in Nevada are usually fingerprinted and made to carry identification cards, obtained from the police or the district attorney. County laws generally require the women to have weekly medical examinations, and prostitutes usually are not permitted to leave the brothel and mingle with other residents of the community. State laws require that houses of prostitution cannot be located on principal business streets or within 400 yards of a schoolhouse or church, and that they do not disturb the peace of the neighborhood. The operation of the system in a relatively large town is described by Winick and Kinsie:

Perhaps typical is the situation in Winnemucca, a town of 3,000. It has five brothels with an average of five women each. They sit in the windows of the brothels and smile at male passersby. The brothels are open from 4 p.m. to 5 a.m. Police drive by every half hour in case any customers get rowdy. The brothels generally refuse to admit servicemen in uniform in order to avoid possible trouble. One Winnemucca minister lost his job because he spoke out against prostitutes. Such is the general attitude toward prostitution that in a nearby community a school and a brothel were in adjacent buildings. A local paper editorialized, "Don't move the brothel—move the school." The school was moved.

New York

Perhaps the most important lesson from New York concerns the failure of relatively lenient penalties for prostitution to reduce the aggravation associated with it to the point that it ceases being a matter of public and official concern.

In 1930, the Seabury investigation uncovered widespread corruption in New York's Women's Court. There were documented instances of payoffs and extortion, notorious episodes of entrapment of innocent women, and numerous cases of bribery. The scandal led the district attorney to withdraw his assistants from the Women's Court, with the police taking over the prosecution of prostitution. There were promised reforms, but a 1940 inquiry indicated that little had changed. Ten lawyers were found to represent most of the prostitutes and to charge exorbitant fees. Usurious bail bondsmen operated flagrantly in Women's Court and the ubiquitous practices of police entrapment continued apace.

It was not for another 10 years, according to Judge John M. Murtagh, that judicial procedures improved much with regard to prostitution. In 1950, Legal Aid lawyers were introduced into Women's Court to represent indigent defendants. But Murtagh and many of his colleagues were still doubtful about the police practices used to get prostitutes before the courts, and they tended to be lenient when they heard the cases. This judicial bias is evident in Murtagh's observations about the fundamental importance of the 1950 changes:

Again, reformers and newspapers, eternal optimists today as yesterday, hailed the court's cleanup as a milestone toward honest vice control. But they did not stop to think that inasmuch as the vice squad still employs its traditional methods of arrest and the court was still merely a way station between the jail and the street, basic conditions were little improved.

This uneasy relationship between the courts and the police in New York regarding prostitution continued unresolved through the years. The police developed harassment tactics which kept the streets relatively free from blatant solicitation, then they eased off until a flagrant situation again focused attention on prostitution. Thus, in 1961, the *New York Times,* taking a role as one of the "eternal optimists," reported that "a new and apprently effective campaign to rid midtown Manhattan streets of prostitutes has been put into operation by the police." If the campaign changed anything for the

moment, it was not evident a moment later.

A major change did take place in New York in 1967, however. That year, largely on the incentive of the judiciary, an experiment was inaugurated which involved rather light punishments for prostitution. The behavior was redefined from a criminal offense to a "violation," and punishment was set at a maximum of 15 days in jail or a maximum fine of $250. In practice, offenders often were allowed to settle three or four charges with a fine of $150 and no jail term.

The impact of the new approach may have been to make prostitutes less bitter and to have kept them from being further criminalized by long stretches in jail. But the changes in the law obviously did not cut into the extent of prostitution. In 1969, the New York City police reported (indicating in their report the belief that these conditions were a function of the more lenient statute) that there had been a 70 percent increase in prostitution arrests and that women, many of them teenagers, were flocking to midtown Manhattan from all sections of the United States to engage in prostitution.

Prostitution, however, was reported to be operating without much organized crime control involvement in New York, perhaps a benefit of the relaxed statutes and the lesser need for protection on the part of the girls. But syndicated criminals were said to be impinging on the trade through ownership of the bars in which many of the prostitutes worked. Police studies showed a typical pattern of "revolving door" justice for the girls themselves. Of 795 women arrested for prostitution in midtown Manhattan during the first 6 months of 1967, 525 had been arrested before for the same offense and together they had a total of 5,568 arrests—an average of more than 10 for each woman. Typical was the case of Matilda F.:

Shortly after midnight on May 19, as red neon lights danced in a fine mist on West 85th Street, a policeman watched a man and woman whisper in a darkened doorway and then enter a hotel.

Half an hour later the man left. After briefly questioning him on the street, the policeman walked into the hotel and arrested Matilda F. for prostitution.

When she appeared a few hours later in Women's Court, a clerk called, "Hi, Matilda. Back home again, eh?" Matilda laughed weakly and said, "Yeah, I love you so much I can't stay away."

Matilda's May court appearance was her 81st on prostitution charges since 1943. Age 44 years old, she has spent 12 years and 10 months in the Women's House of Detention—most of it in sentences of 10 to 90 days. "She's doing life on the installment plan," a clerk remarked.

An unsuccessful attempt was made during the 1968 legislative session to change the prostitution law. Despite rather intense police lobbying, the bill was stalled in the Committee on Codes. An analysis by Pamela Roby of the legislative maneuvering in regard to prostitution in 1968 indicates that in large measure the bill was blocked because Committee members, all 16 of whom were lawyers, felt that the 1967 reform had been made only after considerable study, and that there had not been enough time yet to determine the impact of the milder penalties. There was also a feeling among Committee members that 1-year sentences for prostitutes, called for by the bill before them, would overcrowd the jails. Lastly, there was a belief that the act of prostitution did not warrant a sentence as long as 1 year.

The action of the legislative committee proved to be only a delaying tactic, however, and the following year proponents of sterner measures had their way as prostitution again became a criminal offense. The maximum jail sentence was raised from 15 to 90 days and the maximum fine was changed from $250 to $500. The new measure—seemingly in the manner of all new measures dealing with prostitution—was seen by some as a potential cure for the problem. "Street girls and the hustlers and pimps working with them are a focal point for crime in midtown," a criminal court judge noted. . . .

That was 1969. By March 1971, newspapers in New York were noting that "strengthened police patrols, both uniformed and plainclothes, toured the district

between Times Square and Central Park yesterday in a drive against prostitutes." This new cleanup had been set into motion after the mugging of a former West German government official and the fatal stabbing of a south European industrialist, both incidents involving prostitutes. The German had been robbed in front of his hotel by two women, who leaped from a taxicab, grabbed him and took his wallet. Arrested later, both women proved to have prostitution records. The other man had been stabbed by a prostitute after an argument that seemed to involve, as best police could determine, a language misunderstanding. Police reports noted that "dangerous riffraff types" had been drifting north from the midtown area of Manhattan, and a police captain observed that on the average his officers were arresting 20 to 40 prostitutes a night. "We know that for that night, at least, they won't be mugging or robbing anyone," he said.

The lesson seems quite clear. Neither under the first rather stringent law, nor under the second, more moderate law, nor under the present, even more stringent law, has prostitution apparently changed very much in New York. In all, the summary by Winick and Kinsie seems to catch the tone of opinion on the situation in regard to prostitution in the Nation's largest city:

In 1969 New York ended its 2-year experiment with a lenient prostitution law. Policemen began picking up suspected or known prostitutes on sight. As one vice squad member said, "The best we can do is to harass them." Most such arrests were thrown out of court for insufficient evidence. Some prostitutes would clear up several charges with a single plea of guilty and a token fine. As Criminal Court Judge Jack Rosenberg said, when the maximum penalty was increased from 15 to 90 days on September 1, 1969, "The prostitutes have no respect for the court. They come in here like it is a supermarket."

San Francisco

Appropriately—and deliberately—the seventh report of the San Francisco Committee on

Crime was bound between lavender covers. The Committee had been established late in 1968 by the Mayor and the Board of Supervisors, and its 28 members represented a wide variety of professions and minority groups. That seventh report, issued on June 3, 1971, only a few weeks before the group was to cease functioning, was, the local papers observed, its "blockbuster." The 107-page document, titled *A Report on Nonvictim Crime in San Francisco,* called for less police emphasis on "morality" offenses and more on "serious" crime. Among other things, the report advocated "discreet" trafficking in pornography, "discreet" gambling, and "discreet" prostitution.

Speaking to a reporter from the San Francisco *Examiner,* the executive director of the Crime Committee underlined the philosophy that had dictated the Committee's conclusions:

"We don't condone or approve any of these activities. But we have to stop cluttering up our criminal justice system with unenforceable laws."

NOT THE LAW'S BUSINESS

Among the basic principles which had guided the Committee, its executive director noted, were the following:

The law cannot successfully make criminal what the public does not want made criminal.

Not all the ills or aberrancies of society are the concern of the government. Government is not the only human institution to handle the problems, hopes, fears or ambitions of people.

Every person should be left free of the coercion of criminal law unless his conduct impinges on others and injures others, or if it damages society.

When government acts, it is not inevitably necessary that it do so by means of criminal processes.

Society has an obligation to protect the young.

Even where conduct may properly be condemned as criminal under the [above] principles, it may be that the energies and resources of criminal law enforcement are better spent by concentrating on more serious things. This is a matter of priorities.

An analysis of arrest and court statistics showed that during 1969, 50 percent of all arrests in San Francisco had been for nonvictim offenses, while more than 13 percent of the killings, forcible rapes, robberies, aggravated assaults, burglaries, larcenies, and auto thefts went unsolved. The Crime Committee report hit at "the cost and futility of antiprostitution enforcement." It was estimated that in 1967 it had cost the city more than $375,000 to process the 2,116 arrests for prostitution—more than $175 for each arrest.

Police statistics for 1969 were said to tell an entire story of their own, except for the drama and melodrama of human involvement, about the control of prostitution in San Francisco. There were 1,556 arrests of adults (including 286 males) for either soliciting or engaging in acts of prostitution. Charges were dismissed in 683 cases. Only 246 defendants went to jail, and most of these were sentenced for fewer than 4 months. Another 1,938 adults were arrested for "obstructing the sidewalk," the usual charge in a streetsweep operation where no attempt is made to prove prostitution. Of these, 334 persons went to jail, usually for less than 30 days. All told, during 1969, only about 15 percent of all persons arrested for prostitution in San Francisco ended up in jail. Not surprisingly, prostitutes were said to regard such statistical outcomes as the cost of doing business, an occupational hazard.

The San Francisco Crime Committee was blunt in its conclusion:

The reason that current enforcement practices have not worked is that the statutes are unenforceable and the courts congested. The appearance of efforts at enforcement goes on because it offers the public the *appearance* of "controlling" prostitution. The whole process resembles a game.

The members of the San Francisco Crime Committee were not impressed with the argument that prostitution, left alone, would encourage the spread of venereal disease. They argued, contrariwise, that the very criminality of prostitution serves to discourage women from seeking cures for venereal infections, and they suggested that medical researchers ought to be encouraged to develop preventive approaches to venereal diseases.

It was also believed that the criminalization of prostitution played into the hands of the pimp:

The pimps . . . have a large amount of economic leverage, and most of this is supplied by the criminal justice system itself. The pimp allows his girls enough money so that they can keep themselves looking good but not enough so that they can keep themselves out of jail. The girls need the pimp to pay bail and to hire a lawyer. Thus a direct consequence of our current law enforcement practices is that they provide the pimp with economic power over his girls.

Nonetheless, the Committee would not endorse a system of licensed prostitution, "forceful . . . as arguments were" in its favor. It felt that history had shown this procedure to be no more efficacious than present policies. The Committee preferred to follow the Wolfenden report by advocating that prostitutes should be kept off the streets, though "tolerated" elsewhere. "We find it difficult to imagine that tolerating them off the streets would recruit more women than pimps are doing now," it was argued. Therefore, "discreet, private, off-the-street prostitution should cease to be criminal," the Committee recommended. Its members did not believe it likely that the legislature would be able to endorse such an approach, however. They suggested, therefore, that a policy of "selective enforcement" should be established by all agencies of criminal justice to accomplish the recommended goals.

QUESTIONS FOR DISCUSSION

1. Arrange a classroom discussion concerning arguments for and against the question of whether prostitution ought to be regarded as a criminal offense. Include as a part of the discussion the arguments and counter-arguments compiled by the United Nations study team mentioned in the article by Geis. What is the majority opinion of the class? Do you agree with this opinion?

2. Compare prostitution practices in the United States to those in several other countries. Include both Asian and European societies. What are the major differences and similarities?

3. Professor Davis discusses "The Sociology of Prostitution." Note his emphasis. How does his perspective differ from explanations of prostitution contained in nonsociological sources?

4. Read the article, "Apprenticeships in Prostitution" by J. H. Bryan (listed in the bibliography), and compare the major themes to those set forth in the article by Geis.

5. Discuss the topic of prostitution with a sample of five or six females and the same number of males. Do you note any systematic differences between the two sets of responses? If so, describe the differences. Describe any similarities of responses you detect. What might be some of the factors accounting for agreements and disagreements between the sexes on this topic?

6. Should one create "red light" districts in America?

7. Is prostitution a medical, moral, legal, or social policy problem?

8. At a time of alternative and modified sexual practices, why is prostitution still an issue at all?

9. Do you agree with the policy of some Nevada counties in promoting prostitution to increase tourist trade?

10. Does prostitution represent a sexual safety valve for society? Is this possibly the basis for its persistence throughout history?

BIBLIOGRAPHY

Adler, Polly. *A House is Not a Home.* New York: Popular Library Edition, 1961.
Benjamin, Harry, and Masters, R. E. L. *Prostitution and Morality.* New York: The Julian Press, 1964.

Bryan, J. H. "Apprenticeships in Prostitution." *Social Problems* 12 (Winter 1965), 287–97.

Bryan, J. H. "Occupational Ideologies and Individual Attitudes of Call Girls." *Social Problems* 13 (Spring 1966), 441–50.

Cressey, Paul G. *The Taxi-Dance Hall.* Chicago: The University of Chicago Press, 1932.

Davis, Nanette J. "The Prostitute: Developing A Deviant Identity." In James M. Henslin (ed.), *The Sociology of Sex: A Book of Readings.* New York: Appleton-Century-Crofts, 1971, pp. 297–322.

Greenwald, Harold. *The Call Girl.* New York: Ballantine Books, 1958.

Polsky, Ned. *Hustlers, Beats and Others.* Aldine, 1967.

Reckless, Walter C. "Prostitution." In *The Crime Problem* (5th Ed.). New York: Appleton-Century-Crofts, 1973.

Reckless, Walter C. *Vice in Chicago.* Montclair, N.J.: Patterson Smith, 1969. Reprinted from the original volume published in 1933.

Winick, Charles, and Kinsie, Paul. *The Lively Commerce: Prostitution in the United States.* Chicago: Quadragle, 1971.

10
Pornography

Discussion about the extent and effects of pornography is perhaps as old as time. The term pornography generally implies a subjective disapproval of explicit sexual depictions in picture and print—books, magazines, photographs, films, sound recordings, statuary and sex "devices." The disapproval of pornography has often led to attempts to regulate "obscenity." For example, in the United States, there are four laws which prohibit the distribution of "obscene" materials. One prohibits any mailings of such materials into the United States; another prohibits the broadcasting of obscenity; and two laws prohibit the interstate transport of obscene materials. Thus, five federal agencies are responsible for the enforcement of these statutes—the Post Office Department, the Customs Bureau, the Federal Communications Commission, the F.B.I., and the Department of Justice. In addition, almost all of the states have statutes which generally prohibit the distribution of "obscene" materials and most have some special legislation regarding the distribution of sexual materials to minors.

In 1967, the Congress of the United States found the traffic in obscenity to be a matter of "national concern" and appointed a national commission to study the effects of obscenity and pornography, to look at its distribution in the United States, and to recommend actions to the Congress to regulate the flow of such traffic without in any way interfering with constitutional rights.

The two selections which follow are drawn from the report of that Commission. The Commission found initially that most discussions of obscenity and pornography had, in the past, been devoid of objective evidence. Estimates of the size of the "smut" industry and assertions as to the consequences of the existence of these materials and exposure to them have been widely discussed with little evidence. The initial selection deals with "The Volume of Traffic and the Patterns of Distribution of Sexually Oriented Materials." This is probably the most accurate account now available. This selection also contains a section on the consumers of pornographic materials, pointing out that most of their exposure is voluntary—again the notion of "willing" victim. The second selection deals with "The Effects of Explicit Sexual Materials." The section tries to summarize the available research on this issue, including research initiated by the Commission. The careful conclusions of the Commission, in reference to the effects of exposure to erotic material as a factor in the causation of sex crime or sex delinquency, suggests that most common assertions about a close relationship simply do not hold.

The Commission in its recommendations suggested that much of the "problem" regarding materials which depict explicit sexual activity stems from the inability or reluctance of people to be open and direct in dealing with sexual matters. This tends to overemphasize sex and perhaps make it more attractive and interesting. Such interest is often diversified into less legitimate channels. In addition to recommending a massive sex education program, the majority of the Commission recommend that federal, state, and local legislation prohibiting the sale, exhibition, and distribution of sexual materials to consenting adults be repealed. In other words, obscenity should be "decriminalized" for adults. The Commission did, however, recommend legal restrictions on the sale to younger persons as well as on public display and unsolicited mailings of such materials. The Commission's recommendations fell on deaf congressional and presidential ears. The report was ignored, but, over the long run, it is probable, the "decriminalization" of obscenity for adult users will come about.

In the meantime, laws regarding obscenity are affected by decisions of the Supreme Court. In 1957, the Supreme Court, in *Roth* v. *United States,* ruled that obscenity prohibitions did not conflict with the First and Fourteenth Ammendments dealing with the freedom of speech and press. The Court has also struggled with attempts to provide standards to judge obscenity. In *Miller* v. *California* (93 S. Ct., 1973), a majority of the Court suggested that the basic guidelines must be: (1) whether "the average person, applying contemporary community standards" would find that the work, taken as a whole, appeals to the purient interest; (2) whether the work depicts in a patently offensive way, sexual conduct specifically defined by the applicable state law; (3) whether the work, taken as a whole lacks serious literary, artistic, political, or scientific value. Some persons suggested that this ruling would make the prosecution of obscenity easier since it suggests community standards as a base which would allow various interpretations. Whether this will be the effect, only time and subsequent Court decisions will tell.

THE VOLUME OF TRAFFIC AND PATTERNS OF DISTRIBUTION OF SEXUALLY ORIENTED MATERIALS

Commission on Obscenity and Pornography

THE INDUSTRIES

When the Commission undertook its work, it could find no satisfactory estimates of the volume of traffic in obscene and pornographic materials. Documented estimates describing the content of materials included therein were not available. The first task was to determine the scope of the subject matter of investigation. The very ambiguity of the terms "obscene" and "pornographic" makes

From *The Report of the Comission on Obscenity and Pornography,* Washington, Superintendent of Documents, U.S. Government Printing Office, Washington, D.C., 1970, pp. 7–20.

a meaningful single overall estimate of the volume of traffic an impossibility. It is clear that public concern applies to a broad range of materials. Therefore, the Commission determined to report on the commercial traffic and distribution of sexually oriented materials in motion picture films, books, and periodicals. The Commission's examination included these materials, whether publicly or privately exhibited or sold in retail outlets, by individual sales, or through the United States mails.

Two overall findings may appropriately be stated at the outset. Articles appearing in newspapers, magazines, and in other reports have variously estimated the traffic in the "pornography" or "smut" industry to be between $500 million and $2.5 billion per year, almost always without supporting data or definitions which would make such estimates meaningful.

The Commission can state with complete confidence that an estimate of $2.5 billion sales grossly exaggerates the size of the "smut" industry in the United States under any reasonable definition of the term. In addition, a monolithic "smut" industry does not exist; rather, there are several distinct markets and submarkets which distribute a variety of erotic materials. Some of these industries are fairly well organized, while others are extremely chaotic. These industries vary in terms of media, content, and manner of distribution. Some of the industries are susceptible to fairly precise estimates of the volume of materials, others are not.

We will describe briefly, and provide estimates of dollar and unit volume for most of the industries involved in the production and distribution of broadly defined sexually oriented material.

Motion Pictures

Movies have long been one of the primary recreational outlets for Americans. Box office receipts from nearly 14,000 theaters were estimated at $1.065 billion for 1969, and approximately 20 million persons attended motion pictures weekly.

Until the past year or two, motion pictures distributed in the United States fell rather neatly into three categories: general release, art, and exploitation films. By far the most important and familiar are general release films produced and distributed by well-known companies, starring well-known actors, and exhibited in 90% or more of the theaters across the country. These account for the vast majority of theater attendance in the United States. Art films are an undefined, amorphous group of films which appeal to a limited audience. Exploitation films, usually known in the industry as "skin

flicks," are low-budget sex-oriented movies which have a rather limited exhibition market.

In addition to these well-defined types of films recognized by the industry for many years, in the past year or two quite a number of highly sexually oriented hybrid films (which combine elements of all three traditional types) and films of a totally new genre have appeared. Another group of films, known in the trade as "16mm" films, which are generally among the most sexually explicit available, have also come onto the market.

The Rating System

The recent acceleration in sexual content of films has been approximately coincident in time with the initiation of a movie-rating system for the guidance of viewers. The rating system represents an industry judgment of the appropriateness of the content for children, and reflects to some degree the explicitness of the sexual content of a rated movie. The rating system contains four classifications, two that are not age restricted and two that are age restricted: "G," all ages admitted; "GP," all ages admitted, parental guidance suggested; "R," restricted because of theme, content, or treatment to persons under 17 unless accompanied by a parent or adult guardian; and "X," no one under 17 admitted.

The rating system provides rough guidelines for judging the sexual content of rated films. "G" rated films contain little in the way of sexual matter or vulgar language. Although the "G" rating of a few films has been criticized in the past, the application of this rating has probably become more strict in the past year or so. Little beyond conventional embracing and kissing is allowed. Films with an "antisocial" theme are not rated "G."

"GP" rated films are rated with the "maturing adolescent" in mind. Some degree of sexual implication is allowed, flashes of nudity from a distance are sometimes shown, and some vulgar language is permitted. If discussion of sexual topics becomes "too candid" or if approval is expressed for such activities as premarital sex or adultery, the film will be rated "R" or "X."

"R" rated films can contain virtually any theme. Considerable partial nudity is allowed as is a good deal of sexual foreplay. Several "R" films have contained scenes of full female nudity (genitalia). The chief difference between "R" and "X" rated films is the quantity and quality of the erotic theme, conduct or nudity contained in the film rather than a set of absolutes which automatically classify a film as "R" or "X."

"X" rated films are those which, in the judgment of the industry organization charged with rating, cannot be given any other classification. Films which concentrate almost exclusively on eroticism are placed in this category. An "X" rating may be self-applied by producers who do not submit their product to the Code and Rating Administration (the only classification which can be so applied).

General Release Films

Since the beginning of the motion picture industry, the sexual content and themes of movies have been the target of criticism. In recent years, general release films have become more sexually explicit. They are the target of the most public criticism because of their nationwide distribution to large diversified audiences. This criticism is magnified because of the large volume of newspaper advertising, gossip columns, and stories, articles, and pictures appearing in periodicals.

The trend towards increased sexual content of general release films has accelerated in the past two years. The candid treatment of sexual subjects has affected all aspects of films, i.e. theme, activity depicted, and degree of nudity. At present, there are few areas of sexual conduct which have not been the central subject of widely distributed general release films, including adultery, promiscuity, abortion, perversion, spouse-swapping, orgies, male and female homosexuality, etc.

These themes, which were sometimes dealt with discretely in an earlier era, are now presented quite explicitly. Further, the requirement of an earlier day for "just retribution" for sexual misdeeds is no longer a requirement.

Sexual activity depicted on the screen has also become much more graphic. Scenes of simulated intercourse are increasing. Other sexual acts, including masturbation, fellatio, and cunnilingus, are sometimes suggested and occasionally simulated.

Partial nudity (female breasts and buttocks and male buttocks) may be seen in many general release films. The depiction of full female nudity (pubic area) has been increasing, and a few general release films have shown both sexes totally nude (genitalia).

Art Films

During the 1950s, "art films" treated sexual matters with a degree of explicitness not found in general release films of the same era. Today only the "foreignness" or limited audience appeal sets such films apart from many general release movies.

Exploitation Motion Pictures

Exploitation films (usually known as "skin flicks"), are low-budget films which concentrate on the erotic. Ordinarily, these films are shown only in a limited circuit of theaters and the film titles, though advertised, are not familiar to most people for lack of publicity. Until one or two years ago, the lines of demarcation between these films and general release movies were quite clear. However, the increase of sexually related themes and the incidence of nudity in the latter have blurred many of the former distinctions to a point where there is a considerable overlap. Today, perhaps the chief distinction between some sexually oriented general release films and exploitation films is that the latter (1) are much less expensive to produce (an average cost of $20,000 to $40,000); and (2) are ordinarily exhibited in far fewer theaters (about 6% of all theaters exhibit such films at least on a part-time basis).

The vast majority of exploitation films are directed at the male heterosexual market. Relatively few films are produced for a male homosexual audience, but the number of these films has apparently increased in the past year or two. Full female nudity has become common in the last year or two, although full male nudity is virtually unknown except in those films directed at the male homosexual market. Sexual activity covering the entire range of heterosexual conduct leaves very little to the imagination. Acts of sexual intercourse and oral-genital contact are not shown, only strongly implied or simulated; sexual foreplay is graphically depicted.

The majority of theaters exhibiting exploitation films are old, run-down, and located in decaying downtown areas. However, there has been a trend toward building new theaters and opening such theaters in suburban areas.

"Hybrid" and "New Genre" Motion Pictures

Within the past two years, there has been a radical increase in sexually oriented motion pictures which receive relatively wide distribution. These "hybrid" films combine the sexual explicitness of exploitation films with the distribution patterns of general release films. In addition, an entirely new genre of highly sex-oriented films has been created. Some of these films graphically depict actual sexual intercourse on the screen, an activity which had previously been shown only in private or semi-private exhibitions.

Exploitation films normally achieve relatively limited exhibitions in an established circuit of theaters (perhaps 500–600 theaters on the average). Popular general release films can expect to be exhibited in 5,000 or more theaters. The market for popular hybrid sexually oriented films falls somewhere in between; many have been exhibited in 1,000 to 2,000 theaters and extended runs are common. In addition, such films are not limited to exhibitions in run-down theaters in decaying downtown areas; many play in first-class theaters in downtown and suburban areas. The most sexually explicit of all motion pictures (here-in labeled "new genre" films) as yet have received only limited distribution in major cities.

Sixteen Millimeter Motion Pictures

Recently, an additional form of sexually oriented motion pictures shown in theaters has emerged—known in the industry as "16mm films." As of August, 1970, a majority of the 16mm theaters in the country exhibit silent color films of young females displaying their genitals, but in a few cities 16mm films graphically depict sexual intercourse and oral-genital contact. Usually, 16mm films are the most sexually graphic films shown in the locality.

It is very difficult to estimate the number of 16mm theaters currently in operation, but a figure of 200 seems reasonably accurate.

As yet there are no recognizable film titles moving from city to city, and there is almost no nationwide distribution of such films. However, although 16mm films are in their infancy and as yet are a minor factor in the traffic of sexually oriented materials, the market definitely seems to be expanding.

Box Office Receipts of Motion Pictures

An analysis of reported box office receipts for films since the rating system has been in effect reveals no dramatic differences in reported grosses among "G," "GP," and "R" rated films, although as a group "G" films tended to have consistently higher grosses.

Total box office receipts are not available for either individual films or for classes of films. Each year, however, a trade journal reports on the movies which returned the greatest film rental fees to their distributors. In 1969, 25 "G" movies returned $119 million; 28 "GP" films returned $92 million; 18 "R" rated films accounted for $57 million; 3 "X" films returned $14 million; and 16 unrated films (most of which were released before the rating system went into effect) returned $56 million; of these, four were

Table 10–1. Breakdown of "Top Fifty" films, January–July, 1970

Rating	Number of films	Percentage of films	1970 Gross receipts (in millions)[1]	Percentage of gross receipts
G	44	19.7%	$44.4	25.9%
GP	69	30.9%	57.3	33.5%
R	46	20.6%	44.9	26.2%
X	15	6.8%	12.4	7.2%
Non-sex Unrated	15	6.8%	2.7	1.6%
Sex-oriented Unrated[2]	33	15.2%	9.5	5.6%
Total	222	100.0%	$171.1	100.0%

1. Many of the films listed in the "Top Fifty" during the first six months of 1970 were originally released in 1969. Only 1970 gross receipts for these films were included.
2. These films are characterized as hybrid or new genre films in this Report. Judgments on the classification were made by the Commission Staff.

clearly sex-oriented and returned over $11 million in rentals. Box office receipts for these films were probably between 2 and 2.5 times the rental fees.

Final figures for 1970 are not available, but an analysis of the reported 50 top box office films each week in 20–24 cities for the first six months of 1970 (a total of 222 films) is summarized in Table 10.1.

If the results of those films which were listed among the weekly top 50 are projected against the estimated box office gross for 1970, the following would result:

The weekly list of the top 50 box office films undoubtedly distorts the importance of "R," "X" and unrated films because the survey is limited to metropolitan areas. This provides a disproportionate allocation of the nationwide market for sexually oriented films because theaters in many smaller cities and towns do not exhibit such films at all. Thus, the actual nationwide percentage accounted for by "G" and "GP" films is probably significantly greater than the projection, and "R," "X," and unrated sexually oriented hybrid films probably account for

Table 10–2. Box-office receipts, by classification

Rating	1970 Projected receipts (in millions)	Percentage of receipts
G	$259	23.5%
GP	335	30.5%
R	262	23.8%
X	72	6.6%
Non-sex unrated	16	1.5%
Sex-oriented Unrated	56	5.0%
Art films	35	3.2%
Exploitation films	65	5.9%
Total	$1,100	100.0%

less of the national market than indicated. However, the projection is useful in that it marks the maximum traffic in sexually oriented films.

Exploitation Films

Estimates by the exploitation film industry indicate a $60 million box office business in 1969. Additional studies indicate gross receipts for all exploitation theaters may have been as high as $70 million in 1969. Industry sources have indicated that 1970 receipts are likely to be considerably lower because of increased competition from sexually oriented motion pictures playing outside the exploitation market.

Books and Magazines

The distribution and sale of sexually oriented publications in the United States can be roughly divided into two categories: (1) those which are a part of the mass market, *i.e.,* books and periodicals available to a general audience; and (2) so-called "adults only" publications, a sub-market of sexually oriented printed matter which receives relatively limited distribution.

The Mass Market

There are several channels by which mass market publications are distributed from the publisher to the consumer: national distributors, national jobbers, book clubs, local wholesale distributors, and retailers. In many cases, publications skip over some of the intermediate steps, and flow directly from publisher to retailer and from publisher to consumer.

The book publishing industry in 1968 (latest figures available) estimated its receipts at almost $2.6 billion. Of that total, materials which could conceivably be within the areas of study by the Commission would be found only in "Adult Trade Books" ($179 million), "Paperback Books" ($167 million) and "Book Club" ($204 million)—a total of $550 million, or some 21% of the entire book industry.

The periodical industry in the latest official consensus of business (1967) reported total receipts of approximately $2.6 billion. Of this, only general periodicals such as comics, women and home-service magazines, news, business, and entertainment magazines could possibly be of interest to the Commission. These produced receipts of $1.445 billion, of which $560 million came from single copy and subscription sales (25% of total receipts) and $885 million from advertising.

The Commerce Department estimates that during 1970 publishers' receipts will reach approximately $5.6 billion (both books and periodicals) but the proportion of the market of interest to the Commission will probably remain about the same as before.

The book and periodical publishing industry in the United States is the largest and most diversified in the world. For example, over 10,000 periodicals are published per year and their sales per issue range from a few thousand copies to over 17.5 million. The total average sales, per issue, for all mass market magazines is almost 250 million copies and the total number of magazines sold in 1969 has been estimated at more than 2.5 billion. Approximately 30,000 new book titles have been published each year for the past several years.

Although there are no official estimates of the total number of copies of mass market paperbacks distributed yearly, industry sources estimate that over 700 million paperback books are distributed each year and that over 330 million of these are sold. The retail sales volume of mass market paperback books exceeded $340 million in 1968.

Mass market paperback and hard-cover books and periodicals which might be classified as sexually oriented are distributed in basically the same manner as other mass publications. Such materials are usually not the most sexually explicit available in most localities and certainly not in any of the larger population centers. These publications are the most widely available sexually oriented printed material, however. There are approximately 110,000 retail outlets for general magazines, 80,000 of which display and sell paperback books; 10,000 sell mass market hard-cover books. Even more copies of both books and periodicals are sold through the mails by subscription and book clubs.

Sexually oriented mass market periodicals

Although the wide range of periodicals makes it difficult to distinguish which publications should be classified as sexually oriented, the mass market industry recognizes certain types of magazines as such.

"Confession" or "romance" magazines emphasize fictional accounts of the sexual problems of young women. These magazines do not explicitly describe sex organs or sexual activity and always resolve sexual problems in a moral context. In 1969, 38 confession magazines had total sales of 104.4 million copies and total retail sales of nearly $40 million. These magazines accounted for the vast bulk of the market.

"Barber shop" magazines, aimed at a male readership, primarily feature "action" stories, some of which are sex-oriented. Pictorial content primarily consists of "glamour" or "pin-up" photographs, but recently there has been an increase in photos of partially nude females. During 1969, sales of 20 such magazines (which make up almost the entire market) were approximately 30 million copies and retail sales totaled approximately $12 million.

The mass market magazines with the highest degree of sexual orientation are known in the industry as "men's sophisticates." These magazines generally have a standardized formula which devotes a substantial portion to photographs of partially nude females (with breast and buttock exposure) in modeling poses. Total 1969 sales figures for 62 "sophisticate" magazines were approximately 41 million copies, and the total retail sales were at least $31 million. Almost all the market was included. Publishers and distributors agree that during 1969 and into 1970, the market for men's sophisticates has declined.

There is a special group of sex-oriented mass market magazines which do not adequately fit any of the above classifications. Preeminent among these is *Playboy*, unique in the periodical industry. Each issue of *Playboy* contains no less than three, and sometimes four or five, pictorial layouts which feature partially nude females. In most cases, there is only breast and buttock exposure, although on occasion very discrete photographs of feminine pubic hair have been printed. Some of the articles on other topics are written by well-known authors and distinguished persons. During 1969, just under 64 million copies were sold, and retail dollar sales were over $65 million.

There are a few other mass market magazines which contain a substantial amount of sexual orientation, but are not easily categorized. Total combined copy sales of these magazines are less than 20 million copies, and retail dollar sales are less than $15 million.

Sexually oriented mass market books

Most major paperback publishers produce titles which might be classified as sexually oriented. For example, *Bestsellers*, a trade journal for magazine and paperback wholesalers and retailers, lists the 20 best-selling paperback books each month. Between January, 1969, and July, 1970, eighteen paperbacks which could easily be considered to be sexually oriented appeared on the *Bestsellers* list for more than one month. Three of these reached the number one position, and five ranked as high as second. Almost all of the major book lines were represented.

Although it is impossible to arrive at total sales figures, tens of millions of paperback books with some degree of sexual orientation are sold each year.

An indication of the interest in sexually oriented hard-cover books can be projected from the fact that two of the top ten best-selling fiction titles of 1968 were regarded as "sexy books." In 1969, six of the top ten hard-cover fiction "best sellers" and eight of the top 20 were regarded as sexually oriented. During 1968 and 1969, none of the top ten non-fiction best sellers were related to sex. As of June 1970, three of the top four non-fiction best sellers relate to sex.

Newspapers

The sexual content of daily newspapers was not investigated. Most newspapers, however, reflect a somewhat increased candor in articles and news stories relating to sexual matters.

The sexual content of one genre of newspaper, the so-called "underground press," has been the subject of considerable comment, although these are primarily political in nature. It has been estimated that there are 200 such newspapers in the United States with a readership of 6,000,000. The accuracy of such claims, however, is open to question. Sales figures for five of the best known newspapers indicated average weekly sales of over 200,000 and yearly sales of 10,500,000 in 1969.

The Secondary or "Adults Only" Market

Self-labeled "adults only" printed materials are of far less economic importance than are mass market publications. Separate or "secondary" channels of national and local wholesale distribution and of local retail sales have been created for this "adult" market. However, there is an overlap of sexually oriented materials between the mass and the "adult" markets; some publishers produce materials for both, and many other publishers constantly seek to expand distribution of their "secondary" product into the mass market.

Twenty or 30 of approximately 100 publishers producing primarily for the secondary market are important marketplace factors. Most are located either in California or the New York City area.

Sexual content of "Adults Only' paperback books

The sexual content of paperback books published for the "adults only" market has become progressively "stronger" in the past decade. Today, the content of "adults only" paperback books runs the gamut from traditional "sex pulp" books (stories consisting of a series of sexual adventures tied together by minimal plot, in which the mechanics of the sex act are not described, euphemistic language is substituted for common or clinical terms, and much of the sexual content is left to the reader), through modern "sex pulp" (common terms for sexual activity and detailed descriptions of the mechanics of sex act are used), "classic" erotic literature, "pseudo-medical" (alleged case-study analysis of sexual activity), illustrated marriage manuals, and illustrated novels (with photographs in which young females pose with the focus of the camera directly on their genitalia), to "documentary" studies of censorship and pornography containing illustrations depicting genital intercourse and oral sex. Insofar as the textual portions of many of these books are concerned, it is probably not possible to exceed the candor, graphic descriptions of sexual activity, and use of vulgar language in some currently distributed "adults only" paperback books. The pictorial content of some illustrated paperback books similarly cannot be exceeded in explicit depictions of sexual activity.

The vast majority of "adults only" books are written for heterosexual males, although about 10% are aimed at the male homosexual market and a small percentage (less than 5%) at fetishists. Virtually none of these books is intended for a female audience.

Sexual content of "Adults Only" magazines

"Adults only" magazines of today contain little textual material and are devoted principally to photographic depictions of female and male nudity with emphasis on the genitalia. Some of these depictions contain two or three models together and some pose both males and females in the same photograph. The posing of more than one model in a single photograph has resulted in a considerable amount of implied sexual activity, either intercourse or oral-genital contact, but neither actual sexual activity nor physical arousal of males is depicted at the present time. Nearly 90% are intended for a male heterosexual audience. About 10% are directed to male homosexuals and feature male nudes. Fetish and sadomasochistic magazines featuring bondage, chains, whips, spanking, rubber or leather wearing apparel, high-heeled boots, etc., are a rather insignificant part of the total production (less than 5%).

Production costs

The cost of producing "adults only" paperback books and magazines is usually greater than the cost of these items for a mass general audience. Press runs for mass market paperback books seldom are below 100,000; only a very few "adults only" publishers had press runs as high as 40,000 in 1969 and 1970, and the typical press run of these publishers did not exceed 15,000 or 20,000. Since the fixed costs are apportioned to a much smaller number of copies, the unit cost is significantly higher for the "adults only" publications. "Adults only" paperback books usually cost between $.10 and $.20 to produce although some are considerably higher; "adults only" magazines are considerably more expensive to produce, in the $.45 to $.60 range, because of higher printing and preparation costs.

Distribution channels

Many publishers of "adults only" materials act as their own distributors directly to retail outlets. However, there are now approximately 60 local wholesale distributors of "adults only" materials almost all of whom are located in large metropolitan areas.

There are approximately 850 self-labeled retail "adult" bookstores and 1,400 retail outlets which provide a restricted access section for "adult" material in addition to selling other products in a non-restricted access area. Most of these are located in metropolitan areas of 500,000 or more population.

Many of these stores have estimated average gross sales of $200 to $300 a day and gross yearly sales of nearly $100,000. Average yearly retail sales are probably closer to $60,000 to $70,000. Net profits sometimes are in excess of $20,000 per store per year.

Retail outlets displaying and selling "adults only" material tend to be located in downtown or central city areas; a few are found in suburban shopping centers or in local neighborhoods. The stores range in appearance from seedy to respectable with the majority in the former category. The primary product of these retail "adult" bookstores are paperback books and magazines, although some sell sexual devices and some operate arcade type movie machines. A store may display as few as 200 or as many as 1,000 or more titles of paperback books and from 100 to 500 or more separate titles of magazines.

Total sales of "Adults Only" publications

The total volume of "adults only" materials sold at retail in the U.S. was estimated by several different means. The most useful of these was an industry-wide analysis conducted by the Internal Revenue Service which disclosed that 20 of the largest "adult" publishers had gross receipts of approximately $21 million and an aggregate profit of $450,000 in tax year 1968. Combining all sources of information, the Commission estimates that 25 to 30 million "adults only" paperback books were sold in 1969 for a total retail value of $45 to $55 million; "adults only" magazine sales were approximately $25 to $35 million for 14 to 18 million copies. The best estimate is that "adults only" materials in the U.S. accounted for between $70 and $90 million in retail sales in 1969.

Mail Order

Method of doing business

The American public is inundated annually by over 21 billion pieces of mail which advertise products and solicit purchases. A small percentage of this volume (less than 0.25%), attempts to sell sexually oriented materials. The number of businesses advertising sexually oriented materials through the mails varies greatly over time because the market offers easy and inexpensive entry and is in a constant state of flux. There are probably several hundred individuals or firms dealing in mail-order erotica at present, most of whom are located in the New York City and Los Angeles metropolitan areas. Of these, fewer than 20 are major factors and only about five generate a substantial volume of complaints from the public.

Mail-order operators offer a wide variety of sexually oriented materials for sale and cater to almost every conceivable taste. The most popular items are heterosexually oriented magazines, books, 8mm movies, sexual devices, and advertisements for "swingers" clubs. There are also materials designed for male homosexuals (10%) and a small amount for fetishists.

There are three types of advertising in this industry: solicited, semi-unsolicited, and unsolicited. Solicited advertising is that received by an individual who has made a request to be put on a specific mailing list. Semi-unsolicited advertising is usually received after a purchase or inquiry, or from a mailer in the same business. Unsolicited advertising is received by an individual who has never made a purchase from, or inquiry of any dealer in sexually oriented materials. Most mail-order dealers in sexually oriented materials mail only to solicited or semi-unsolicited names. However, a few mail a large volume of advertising to unsolicited names. These are responsible for the majority of public complaints about erotica in the mails.

The business of advertising and selling sexually oriented materials through mail order is subject to the same rules of economics as any mail order operation. Mail-order selling can be profitable, but it is an expensive way of doing business. The cost to reach the potential customers with an advertising message is high and responses to sexu-

ally oriented mail advertising do not greatly differ from responses to mail advertising of any other products. The mail-order erotica business is very tenuous and stories that vast fortunes have been made overnight are apocryphal for the most part. Even the giants of the industry (fewer than ten) are relatively small-time operators and the profit of the largest probably does not exceed $200,000 before taxes per year.

Public complaints

In April, 1968, the federal Anti-Pandering Act went into effect and allowed recipients of unsolicited sexually provocative advertisements to request the Postmaster General to issue an order to the mailer to refrain from further mailings to the addressee. During the first two years of operation, the Post Office received over 450,000 requests for prohibitory orders and issued over 370,000. Prohibitory orders have been issued against hundreds of separate business firm names. However, two mailers accounted for nearly 40% of the total prohibitory orders and three others accounted for another 20%. Approximately 5% of prohibitory orders were issued on behalf of minors under the age of 19. Although the number of prohibitory orders issued since the law went into effect is substantial, less than ½ of 1% of all sexually oriented advertising results in a complaint to the Post Office. Post Office figures show a decline of approximately 50% in requests for prohibitory orders during the first six months of fiscal 1970 as compared with the same period in fiscal 1969.

Volume of mail and sales

Twenty-eight major mailers and three mailing services specializing in processing sexually oriented advertising spent over $2 million on postage during fiscal 1969. This was enough to mail approximately 36 million letters. It is estimated that these dealers accounted for approximately 75% to 80% of the total mail volume. Therefore, the total volume of sexually oriented mail was approximately 45 to 48 million letters during fiscal year 1969. Retail sales value of the sexually oriented materials bought through mail order probably did not exceed $12 to $14 million in fiscal 1969. (The Internal Revenue Service analyzed the receipts and income of most of the volume mailers for the tax year of 1968. These mailers had gross sales of $5.5 million and reported an aggregate loss of $3,000 for that year. However, the majority of the mailers did make a profit for the year).

"Under-the-Counter" or "Hard-Core" Materials

In 1970, a very limited amount of sexual material is being sold "under the counter." Such materials, which the market defines as "hard-core pornography," generally are limited to photographic reproductions of sexual intercourse depicting vaginal, anal, or oral penetration. These photographic materials are generally available in three forms: motion pictures (popularly called "stag films"), photo sets, and picture magazines. It has been estimated that between 3,000 and 7,000 stag films have been produced in the last 55 years, but an accurate estimate of the number on the market is virtually impossible to make. The stag film production is primarily a localized business with no national distribution and is extremely disorganized. There are no great fortunes to be made in stag film production. It is estimated that there are fewer than half a dozen individuals who net more than $10,000 per year in the business.

The traffic in picture magazines of sexual intercourse is apparently increasing. Today, the source of these materials appears to be principally Scandinavia or domestic copies of foreign publications. Photos or photo sets depicting sexual activity are a very minor part of the market at present.

Traffic and distribution of under-the-counter materials appears to be a very minor part of the total traffic in erotic materials. Imports of such materials from Scandinavia, however, appear to be increasing. Although

the retail sales of these imports is almost certainly less than $5 million per year, this market appears to be growing. The total market in under-the-counter materials is estimated to be between $5 and $10 million.

Organized Crime

Law enforcement officers differ among themselves on the question of whether "organized crime" is involved in the pornography business. Some believe very strongly that it is; others believe just as strongly that it is not.

There is some evidence that the retail "adult bookstore" business, which purveys materials that are not only at the periphery of legitimacy but also at the margin of legality, tends to involve individuals who have had considerable experience with being arrested. The business does involve some risk of arrest and, therefore, would be avoided by persons with more concern for legitimacy and general reputation. There is a greater likelihood that persons with some background of conflict with the legal system will be found among "adult" bookstore proprietors. This is not the same, however, as being an adjunct or subsidiary of "organized crime." At present, there is insufficient data to warrant any conclusion in this regard.

THE CONSUMERS

Adult Experience with Sexually Explicit Materials

Approximately 85% of adult men and 70% of adult women in the U.S. have been exposed at sometime during their lives to depictions of explicit sexual material in either visual or textual form. Most of this exposure has apparently been voluntary, and pictorial and textual depictions are seen about equally often. Recent experience with erotic materials is not as extensive as total experience, e.g. only about 40% of adult males and 26% of adult females report having seen pictorial depictions of sexual intercourse during the past two years.

Experience with explicit sexual materials varies according to the content of the depictions; depictions of nudity with sex organs exposed and of heterosexual intercourse are most common; depictions of homosexual activities and oral sex are less common; and depictions of sadomasochistic sexual activity are least common in Americans' experience. Thus portrayals of sex that conform to general cultural norms are more likely to be seen than are portrayals of sexual activity that deviate from these norms.

Experience with explicit sexual materials also varies according to the characteristics of the potential viewer. Men are more likely to be exposed to erotic materials than are women. Younger adults are more likely to be exposed than are older adults. People with more education are more likely to have experience with erotic materials. People who read general books, magazines, and newspapers more, and see general movies more also see more erotic materials. People who are more socially and politically active are more exposed to erotic materials. People who attend religious services more often are less likely to be exposed to erotica.

Although most males in our society have been exposed to explicit sexual materials at some time in their lives, a smaller proportion has had relatively extensive experience with erotica. From one-fifth to one-quarter of the male population in the U.S. has somewhat regular experience with sexual materials as explicit as depictions of heterosexual intercourse.

Few people report that they buy erotic materials. Between one-quarter and one-half of people who have ever seen explicit sexual materials have ever purchased such materials. A major proportion of the acquisition of erotic materials occurs by obtaining it from a friend or acquaintance at no cost. Unsolicited mail accounts for a very small proportion of the exposure to erotic materials. Thus, most exposure to erotica occurs outside the commercial context and is a social or quasi-social acitivty. Erotica is a durable commodity for which there are several consumers for each purchase.

The informal distribution of erotica among friends and acquaintances is asymmetrical. Many more people have had sexual materials shown or given to them than report showing or giving these materials to others. Sharing is predominantly with friends of the same sex or with spouses. Only 31% of men and 18% of women report knowing of a shop which specializes in sexual materials.

Although the percentage of the population purchasing erotic materials is relatively small, the total number constitutes a sizeable market.

The patterns of experience of adults in Denmark and Sweden with erotic materials are similar to that described for American adults.

Young People's Experience with Sexually Explicit Materials

First experience with explicit sexual materials usually occurs in adolescence for Americans. Roughly three-quarters of adult American males report having been exposed to such materials before age 21. Retrospective reporting on adolescent experience by adult males indicates that the experience with erotica during adolescence was not isolated but rather both extensive and intensive.

Several recent studies of high school and college age youth are quite consistent in finding that there is also considerable exposure to explicit sexual materials on the part of minors today. Roughly 80% of boys and 70% of girls have seen visual depictions or read textual descriptions of sexual intercourse by the time they reach age 18. Substantial proportions of adolescents have had more than an isolated exposure or two, although the rates of exposure do not indicate an obsession with erotic materials. A great deal of this exposure occurs in preadolescent and early adolescent years. More than half of boys have had some exposure to explicit sexual materials by age 15. Exposure on the part of girls lags behind that of boys by a year or two. Exposure of adolescents to depictions of genitals and heterosexual intercourse occurs earlier and more often than does exposure to oral-genital and homosexual materials. Experience with depictions of sadomasochistic material is much rarer, although it does occur.

Young people below the age of 21 rarely purchase sexually explicit books, magazines, and pictures; the mails and underground newspapers are negligible sources of exposure to erotica. By far the most common source of exposure to sexually explicit books, magazines, and pictures is a friend about the same age, and this exposure occurs in a social situation where materials are freely passed around. There is some suggestion that young people who are less active socially are less likely to be acquainted with sexual materials.

Thus, exposure to explicit sexual materials in adolescence is widespread and occurs primarily in a group of peers of the same sex or in a group involving several members of each sex. The experience seems to be more a social than a sexual one.

Patrons of Adult Bookstores and Adult Movie Theaters

Patrons of adult bookstores and adult movie theaters may be characterized as predominantly white, milddle-class, middle-aged, married males, dressed in business suit or neat casual attire, shopping or attending the movie alone. Almost no one under 21 was observed in these places, even where it was legal for them to enter.

The average patron of adult bookstores and movie houses appears to have had fewer sexually related experiences in adolescence than the average male in our society, but to be more sexually oriented as an adult. The buyers of erotica report frequencies of intercourse fairly similar to those of nonconsumers, and report a similar degree of enjoyment of intercourse. Their high degree of sexual orientation in adulthood encompasses, in addition to pictorial and textual erotica, a variety of sexual partners and of sexual activities within a consensual framework. Activities most frowned upon by our society, such as sadomasochism, pedophilia, bestiality, and nonconsensual sex, are also outside the scope of the interests of the average patron of adult bookstores and movie houses.

THE EFFECTS OF EXPLICIT SEXUAL MATERIALS

Commission on Obscenity and Pornography

The Effects Panel of the Commission undertook to develop a program of research designed to provide information on the kinds of effects which result from exposure to sexually explicit materials, and the conditions under which these effects occur. The research program embraced both inquiries into public and professional belief regarding the effects of such materials, and empirical research bearing on the actual occurrence and condition of the effects. The areas of potential effect to which the research was addressed included sexual arousal, emotions, attitudes, overt sexual behavior, moral character, and criminal and other antisocial behavior related to sex.

Research procedures included (1) surveys employing national probability samples of adults and young persons; (2) quasi-experimental studies of selected populations; (3) controlled experimental studies; and (4) studies of rates and incidence of sex offenses and illegitimacy at the national level. A major study, which is cited frequently in these pages, was a national survey of American adults and youth which involved face-to-face interviews with a random probability sample of 2,486 adults and 769 young persons between the ages of 15 and 20 in the continental United States. . . .

From *The Report of the Commission on Obscenity and Pornography,* Washington, Superintendent of Documents, U.S. Government Printing Office, Washington, D.C., 1970, pp. 23–27.

OPINION CONCERNING EFFECTS OF SEXUAL MATERIALS

There is no consensus among Americans regarding what they consider to be the effects of viewing or reading explicit sexual materials. A diverse and perhaps inconsistent set of beliefs concerning the effects of sexual materials is held by large and necessarily overlapping portions of American men and women. Between 40% and 60% believe that sexual materials provide information about sex, provide entertainment, lead to moral breakdown, improve sexual relationships of married couples, lead people to commit rape, produce boredom with sexual materials, encourage innovation in marital sexual technique and lead people to lose respect for women. Some of these presumed effects are obviously socially undesirable while others may be regarded as socially neutral or desirable. When questioned about effects, persons were more likely to report having personally experienced desirable than undesirable ones. Among those who believed undesirable effects had occurred, there was a greater likelihood of attributing their occurrences to others than to self. But mostly, the undesirable effects were just believed to have happened without reference to self or personal acquaintances.

Surveys of psychiatrists, psychologists, sex educators, social workers, counselors and similar professional workers reveal that large majorities of such groups believe that sexual materials do not have harmful effects on either adults or adolescents. On the other hand, a survey of police chiefs found that 58% believed that "obscene" books played a significant role in causing juvenile delinquency.

EMPIRICAL EVIDENCE CONCERNING EFFECTS

A number of empirical studies conducted recently by psychiatrists, psychologists, and sociologists attempted to assess the effects of exposure to explicit sexual materials. This body of research includes several study designs, a wide range of subjects and respondents, and a variety of effect indicators. Some questions in this area are not answered by the existing research, some are answered more fully than others, and many questions have yet to be asked. Continued research efforts which embrace both replicative studies and inquiries into areas not yet investigated are needed to extend and clarify existing findings and to specify more concretely the conditions under which specific effects occur. The findings of available research are summarized below.

Psychosexual Stimulation

Experimental and survey studies show that exposure to erotic stimuli produces sexual arousal in substantial portions of both males and females. Arousal is dependent on both characteristics of the stimulus and characteristics of the viewer or user.

Recent research casts doubt on the common belief that women are vastly less aroused by erotic stimuli than are men. The supposed lack of female response may well be due to social and cultural inhibitions against reporting such arousal and to the fact that erotic material is generally oriented to a male audience. When viewing erotic stimuli, more women report the physiological sensations that are associated with sexual arousal than directly report being sexually aroused.

Research also shows that young persons are more likely to be aroused by erotica than are older persons. Persons who are college educated, religiously inactive, and sexually experienced are more likely to report arousal than persons who are less educated, religiously active and sexually inexperienced.

Several studies show that depictions of conventional sexual behavior are generally regarded as more stimulating than depictions of less conventional activity. Heterosexual themes elicit more frequent and stronger arousal responses than depictions of homosexual activity; petting and coitus themes elicit greater arousal than oral sexuality, which in turn elicits more than sadomasochistic themes.

Satiation

The only experimental study on the subject to date found that continued or repeated exposure to erotic stimuli over 15 days resulted in satiation (marked diminution) of sexual arousal and interest in such material. In this experiment, the introduction of novel sex stimuli partially rejuvenated satiated interest, but only briefly. There was also partial recovery of interest after two months of nonexposure.

Effects upon Sexual Behavior

When people are exposed to erotic materials, some persons increase masturbatory or coital behavior, a smaller proportion decrease it, but the majority of persons report no change in these behaviors. Increases in either of these behaviors are short lived and generally disappear within 48 hours. When masturbation follows exposure, it tends to occur among individuals with established masturbatory patterns or among persons with established but unavailable sexual partners. When coital frequencies increase following exposure to sex stimuli, such activation generally occurs among sexually experienced persons with established and available sexual partners. In one study, middle-aged married couples reported increases in both the frequency and variety of coital performance during the 24 hours after the couples viewed erotic films.

In general, established patterns of sexual behavior were found to be very stable and not altered substantially by exposure to erotica. When sexual activity occurred following the viewing or reading of these materials, it constituted a temporary activation of individuals' preexisting patterns of sexual behavior.

Other common consequences of exposure to erotic stimuli are increased frequencies of erotic dreams, sexual fantasy, and conversation about sexual matters. These responses occur among both males and females. Sexual dreaming and fantasy occur as a result of exposure more often among unmarried than married persons, but conversation about sex occurs among both married and unmarried persons. Two studies found that a substantial number of married couples reported more agreeable and enhanced marital communication and an increased willingness to discuss sexual matters with each other after exposure to erotic stimuli.

Attitudinal Responses

Exposure to erotic stimuli appears to have little or no effect on already established attitudinal commitments regarding either sexuality or sexual morality. A series of four studies employing a large array of indicators found practically no significant differences in such attitudes before and after single or repeated exposures to erotica. One study did find that after exposure persons became more tolerant in reference to other persons' sexual activities although their own sexual standards did not change. One study reported that some persons' attitudes toward premarital intercourse became more liberal after exposure, while other persons' attitudes became more conservative, but another study found no changes in this regard. The overall picture is almost completely a tableau of no significant change.

Several surveys suggest that there is a correlation between experience with erotic materials and general attitudes about sex: Those who have more tolerant or liberal sexual attitudes tend also to have greater experience with sexual materials. Taken together, experimental and survey studies suggest that persons who are more sexually tolerant are also less rejecting of sexual material. Several studies show that after experience with erotic material, persons become less fearful of possible detrimental effects of exposure.

Emotional and Judgmental Responses

Several studies show that persons who are unfamiliar with erotic materials may experience strong and conflicting emotional reactions when first exposed to sexual stimuli. Multiple responses, such as attraction and repulsion to an unfamiliar object, are commonly observed in the research literature on psychosensory stimulation from a variety of nonsexual as well as sexual stimuli. These emotional responses are short-lived and, as with psychosexual stimulation, do not persist long after removal of the stimulus.

Extremely varied responses to erotic stimuli occur in the judgmental realm, as, for example, in the labeling of material as obscene or pornographic. Characteristics of both the viewer and the stimulus influence the response: For any given stimulus, some persons are more likely to judge it "obscene" than are others; and for persons of a given psychological or social type, some erotic themes are more likely to be judged "obscene" than are others. In general, persons who are older, less educated, religiously active, less experienced with erotic materials, or feel sexually guilty are most likely to judge a given erotic stimulus "obscene." There is some indication that stimuli may have to evoke both positive responses (interesting or stimulating), and negative responses (offensive or unpleasant) before they are judged obscene or pornographic.

Criminal and Delinquent Behavior

Delinquent and nondelinquent youth report generally similar experiences with explicit sexual materials. Exposure to sexual materials is widespread among both groups. The age of first exposure, the kinds of materials to which they are exposed, the amount of their exposure, the circumstances of exposure, and their reactions to erotic stimuli are essentially the same, particularly when family and neighborhood backgrounds are held constant. There is some evidence that peer group pressure accounts for both sexual experience and exposure to erotic materials among youth. A study of a heterogeneous group of young people found that exposure to erotica had no impact upon moral character over and above that of a generally deviant background.

Statistical studies of the relationship between availability of erotic materials and the rates of sex crimes in Denmark indicate that the increased availability of explicit sexual materials has been accompanied by a decrease in the incidence of sexual crime. Analysis of police records of the same types of sex crimes in Copenhagen during the past 12 years revealed that a dramatic decrease in reported sex crimes occurred during this period and that the decrease coincided with changes in Danish law which permitted wider availability of explicit sexual materials. Other research showed that the decrease in reported sexual offenses cannot be attributed to concurrent changes in the social and legal definitions of sex crimes or in public attitudes toward reporting such crimes to the police, or in police reporting procedures.

Statistical studies of the relationship between the availability of erotic material and the rates of sex crimes in the United States presents a more complex picture. During the period in which there has been a marked increase in the availability of erotic materials, some specific rates of arrest for sex crimes have increased (*e.g.,* forcible rape) and others have declined (*e.g.,* overall juvenile rates). For juveniles, the overall rate of arrests for sex crimes decreased even though arrests for nonsexual crimes increased by more than 100%. For adults, arrests for sex offenses increased slightly more than did arrests for nonsex offenses. The conclusion is that, for America, the relationship between the availability of erotica and changes in sex crime rates neither proves nor disproves the possibility that availability of erotica leads to crime, but the massive overall increases in sex crimes that have been alleged do not seem to have occurred.

Available research indicates that sex offenders have had less adolescent experience with erotica than other adults. They do not differ significantly from other adults in relation to adult experience with erotica, in relation to reported arousal or in relation to the likelihood of engaging in sexual behavior during or following exposure. Available evidence suggests that sex offenders' early inexperience with erotic material is a reflection of their more generally deprived sexual environment. The relative absence of experience appears to constitute another indicator of atypical and inadequate sexual socialization.

In sum, empirical research designed to clarify the question has found no evidence to date that exposure to explicit sexual materials plays a significant role in the causation of delinquent or criminal behavior among youth or adults. The Commission cannot conclude that exposure to erotic materials is a factor in the causation of sex crime or sex delinquency.

QUESTIONS FOR DISCUSSION

1. Form a panel to discuss the effects of sexual materials. Note issues of agreement or disagreement. Were the main conclusions of this discussion consistent with the findings of The Report of the Commission on Obscenity and Pornography?
2. Read the book, *Perceptions on Pornography* by D. A. Hughes (listed in the bibliography). Compare his approach to the evidence presented in the preceding articles.
3. Critique the rating system of motion pictures. What changes do you predict will occur in the near future? Why? Interview the manager of a local theater. Analyze his point of view in light of his vested interest. What is his solution to the problem?
4. Will the concern about pornographic materials likely increase or decrease during the next three to five years? What aspects of the problem may be of greater concern? What features may become defined as less important?
5. Discuss the general problem of pornography with your parents. What are the major realms where agreement and disagreement are greatest?
6. Recent data indicate a decline in the interest in pornography in Denmark which had "legalized" all forms of pornography by removing legal strictures. Would we experience the same results in the U.S.?
7. Is pornography also the sexual safety valve for the society that some maintain prostitution to be?
8. How do you distinguish art from pornography? Are centerfolds in mass circulation magazines art, pornography, or simply good photography?
9. Take a look at samples of modern graffitti and try to determine its intent and content. Is it social commentary or simply pornography?

BIBLIOGRAPHY

Abelson, H., Cohen, R., Heaton, E. and Slider, C. *Public attitudes toward and experience with erotic materials. Technological reports of the Commission on Obscentiy and Pornography,* Vol. 6. Washington, D.C.: U.S. Government Printing Office, 1970.

Berger, A. S., Gagnon, J. H., and Simon, W. *Pornography: high school and college years. Technical reports of the Commission on Obscenity and Pornography,* Vol. 9. Washington, D.C.: U.S. Government Printing Office, 1970. (a)

Clor, H. *Obscenity and Public Morality.* Chicago: University of Chicago Press, 1969.

Elias, J. E. *Exposure to erotic materials in adolescence. Technical reports of the Commission on Obscenity and Pornography,* Vol. 9. Washington, D.C.: U.S. Government Printing Office, 1970.

Gagnon, J. H. and Simon, W. ' Pornography— Raging Menace or Paper Tiger. *Transaction,* 1967, 4:41.

Green, B. "Obscenity: Censorship and Juvenile Delinquency." *University of Toronto Law Journal* 14 No. 2 (1972), 229–52.

Hughes, D. A. *Perspectives on Pornography.* New York: St. Martins Press, 1970.

Nawy, H. *The San Francisco erotic marketplace. Technical reports of the Commission on Obscenity and Pornography,* Vol. 4. Washington, D.C.: U.S. Government Printing Office, 1970.

Randall, R. S. *Censorship of the Movies.* Madison: University of Wisconsin Press, 1968.

Randall, R. S. *Classification by the motion picture industry. Technical reports of the Commission on Obscenity and Pornography,* Vol. 10. Washington, D.C. U.S. Government Printing Office, 1970.

Sampson, J. J. *Traffic and distribution of sexually oriented materials in the United States, 1969–70. Technical reports of the Commission on Obscenity and Pornography,* Vol. 3. Washington, D.C.: U.S. Government Printing Office, 1970.

Sonenschein, D. "Pornography: A False Issue." *Psychiatric Opinion* 6 (1969), 11–18.

Winick, C. *Some observations on characteristics of patrons of adult theaters and bookstores. Technical reports of the Commission on Obscenity and Pornography,* Vol. 4. Washington, D.C.: U.S. Government Printing Office, 1970.

Zurcher, L. A., and Kirkpatrick, R. G. *Collective dynamics of ad hoc antipornography organizations. Technical reports of the Commission on Obscenity and Pornography,* Vol. 5. Washington, D.C.: U.S. Government Printing Office, 1970.

11
Suicide

In suicide, there is a finality and irreversibility which is unique. In Chapter 1, we discussed deviation as alienation. Suicide would be the classic illustration of this since feelings of despair, isolation, and futility are common in persons attempting and completing suicide. In the present chapter, we discuss suicide in the context of "willing victims." Even though the person who commits suicide is the victim, societies have seldom allowed this format of withdrawal from society. The norms of the Western world have generally been in opposition to suicide. Christian religions have contained specific sanctions against suicide—for example, the refusal to bury the person in "sacred" ground. In many countries, there have been legal prohibitions as well, although enforcement of such laws is usually possible only against the unsuccessful suicides, and it is usually assumed that such persons have already suffered enough.

However intimate and personal the decision may be to end one's life, there are patterns of regularity which emerge when suicide is seen as an aggregate and repetitive phenomenon.

In the first article, "Classifications of Suicidal Phenomena," Shneidman reviews the research literature, emphasizing the kinds of notes left by those who take their own life, and concludes by proposing a new set of categories for understanding this type of behavior. He feels that current definitions are ambiguous and that existing classifications of suicide are unsatisfactory. Further, he believes that the remarkable durability of Durkheim's scheme "is something which itself deserves special study in the sociology of knowledge."

Shneidman suggests that all suicides be classified as being of one of three types: egotic, dyadic, or ageneratic. *Egotic* suicides are those in which the death is the result of a struggle-in-the-mind. These deaths can be viewed as egocide or ego-destructive; the person's torment is "within his head"—as illustrated by the anguish of Virginia Woolf. Egotic suicides are essentially *psychological* in nature, and suicide notes in these cases contain explanations of these special kinds of unresolved inner struggles.

Dyadic suicides are those in which the self-inflicted death relates basically to unfulfilled wishes and needs related to "significant others" in the victim's life. The suicide here is basically *social* in the sense that it is an interpersonal event. In dyadic suicides most of the notes that are found usually start with the word "Dear," and are addressed to a specific individual. In the United States it is likely that most suicides could be classified in the dyadic category.

Ageneratic suicides refer to those deaths

in which the person has lost a sense of belongingness—he has lost his place in the scheme of things, particularly in the "march of generations." The ageneratic suicide is truly lonely and alienated. He has "fallen out" of society. Shneidman refers to this type of suicide as primarily *sociological* in nature since it is related to cultural, national, family, or group ties.

In the second article, "Studies of Adolescent Suicidal Behavior," Seidin presents a well-balanced overview of what we know about the etiology, treatment, and prevention of suicide among the young. A number of important distinctions are drawn between attempted, committed, threatened, "partial," and "probable" suicides. For example, there is now clear-cut evidence that those who attempt suicide do not come from the same population as those who commit suicide. Suicide attempts are younger, and the sex ratio is the reverse (females 3 to 1 over males) of the sex ratio of completed suicides. While many studies have implied a causal relationship between broken homes and high rates of youthful suicides, research involving a control group of nonsuicidal individuals shows that broken homes per se do not necessarily account for important differences. Suicidal and nonsuicidal control groups often reveal high proportions of broken homes. The significant difference was found to be that those in the control group had known a stable home life during the preceding five years, while those attempting suicide had not. The evidence on student suicide is that it is greater for stu-

dents than for their nonstudent peers. The sections of this article dealing with treatment, prevention, and "warning signs" contain useful suggestions. One point of agreement is that all suicidal behavior should be taken seriously. Even simple threats or gestures should not be overlooked, since most people who kill themselves give definite warning of their intentions.

In recent years, there has been a movement to place suicide in the mental health context and to consider it as preventable. In many cities across the country, Crises Intervention and Suicide Prevention Centers have been created. Such centers operate around the clock so that the centers can be reached by phone and be available to deal with a personal crisis while it is in process. Such centers try to find out what is bothering the person and to provide some degree of reassurance since the suicidal mood is usually a temporary state. Once the immediate crisis is over, efforts can be directed toward longer term solutions. Many of these centers are operated by volunteers who are trained and supervised to man the phones. Such centers deal with a wide variety of problems, marital and alcohol problems being the most frequent; but problems seldom occur in an isolated fashion and suicide is often contemplated as a possible solution to what seems to be complex problems. The effectiveness of such centers is unknown, but they represent the attempt to extend the notion of mental health into the community by focusing on prevention rather than depending on ex post facto explanations.

CLASSIFICATIONS OF SUICIDAL PHENOMENA

Edwin S. Shneidman

With all the current interest in suicide prevention, it remains a fact that *definitions* of

From *Bulletin of Suicidology,* National Clearinghouse of Mental Health Information, National Institute of Mental Health, pp. 1—22. Edwin Shneidman is Chief of the Center for Studies in Suicide Prevention, NIMH.

suicidal phenomena are ambiguous and that *classifications* of suicidal phenomena remain essentially unsatisfactory. It would seem to be axiomatic that adequate definition and classification are fundamental to good science and praxis, that is, to the kind of understanding that permits effective prevention, intervention, and postvention. In the current scene, it is interesting to reflect on the classification of suicidal behaviors.

In the professional literature the most frequently quoted classification of suicide is that of Durkheim. The durability of this schemata is something which itself deserves special study in the sociology of knowledge. Considering that it was published in 1897 (although it was not generally available in English until 1951); considering further that suicide *per se* was not the primary focus of Durkheim's interest, but rather that the explication of his sociological method, using suicide as the prime example, was Durkheim's main concern; and, considering that Durkheim's classification of types of suicide—anomic, egoistic, altruistic, and fatalistic—has relatively little applicability or power for the clinician on the "firing-line" who is faced by a self-destructive person, its vitality is surprising. It is a classification scheme used and reused in the text books and the technical literature; sometimes there seems to be almost no other.

By *altruistic* suicide, Durkheim meant those self-inflicted deaths which involve a disciplined attachment to the social group of such magnitude that the obligations of the group override the individual's own interests, even his interests in his own life. Durkheim used statistics primarily from various European armies to illustrate this point. By *egoistic* suicide, he meant those deaths in which the individual's relationship to the organized group was such that he was permitted (i.e., forced) to turn against his own conscience and to assume responsibility for his own acts in such a way that he could not rely on canon rule or ritual to bail him out of a personal predicament. To demonstrate this concept, Durkheim contrasted the suicide statistics in religion, especially those between the Catholic who is subjected to a group authority and the Protestant who is forced to assume individual responsibility. By *anomic* suicide, Durkheim meant those acts of self-destruction which involve individuals who suddenly have been thrown out of kilter with the important relationships to their group, especially their expectations relative to their moral standards of living. Durkheim used this concept to explain why individuals committed suicide when they lost their income, as well as other individuals (in a seemingly antiutilitarian act) who killed themselves when they became the recipients of large fortunes.

Fatalistic suicide—which Durkheim discussed only in a footnote—is suicide deriving from excessive regulation, as in the suicide of slaves or "very young husbands.". . .

In large part, the currency of the Durkheimian scheme may be due to the absence of any viable competitor. The major alternative conceptualization, that of the Freudian and psychoanalytic theorists, yields not so much a classification as it does a formula— i.e., self-destruction as hostility directed toward the introjected love object (what I have called murder in the 180th degree)—a formulation which sounds globally etiological and universally explanative. As such, this formulation does not help with sorting the multifarious suicidal phenomena which include (in addition to hostility) such psychodynamic constellations as dependency, anguish, hopelessness, helplessness, perturbation, shame, paradoxical striving, etc.

The classic Freudian approach not only tended rather systematically to ignore social factors, but also tended to focus on a single complex or psychodynamic constellation. But we now know that individuals kill themselves for a number and variety of psychologically-felt motives—not only hate and revenge, but also shame, guilt, fear, hopelessness, loyalty, fealty to self-image, pain, and even ennui. Just as no single pattern is sufficient to encompass all achievements, creativities, or self-actualization, probably no single psychological formula is able to contain all human self-destruction. Many studies of suicide in the psychological genre, more or less following Freud's tradition, have been published. . . .

How do we snythesize these two major theoretical positions—the sociological, with its emphasis on the "social fact", and the psychological, with its clinical emphasis on the individual internal drama within the single mind? A recent study bearing on this point emphasized the interplay between both the social and psychological factors as mutually-enhancing roles in each individual's suicide. This finding is consistent with that of Halbwach's whose position—unlike that of his mentor, Durkheim—was that the "social" and "psychopathological" explanations of suicide are complementary rather than antithetical. A synthesis between these two lies in the area of the "self," especially in the ways in which social forces are incorporated within the totality of the individual. In understanding suicide, one needs to know the thoughts and feelings and ego functionings and unconscious conflicts of an individual, as well as how he integrates with his fellow men and participates morally as a member of the groups within which he lives.

Not many classifications of suicidal phenomena *per se* have been proposed. One scheme of note, in addition to Durkheim's classification, is Menninger's classification of the sources of suicidal impulses, namely, the wish to kill, the wish to be killed, and the wish to die. Menninger also classified subsuicidal phenomena into chronic suicide (asceticism, martyrdom, addiction, invalidism, psychosis); focal suicide (self-mutilation, malingering, polysurgery, multiple accidents, impotence, and frigidity); and organic suicide (involving the psychological factors in organic disease). . . . A composite listing of their rubrics would include the following: suicide as communication, suicide as revenge, suicide as fantasy crime, suicide as unconscious flight, suicide as magical revival or reunion, suicide as rebirth and restitution.

Another approach to the classification of suicidal types is in terms of cognitive or logical styles, which includes a consideration of the structural and semantic aspects of suicidal communications. Within the framework of this model, a classification scheme, which stemmed from an analysis of the logics contained in suicide notes, has been proposed. This approach is based on the Sapir-Whorf hypothesis, which suggests that the ways in which one perceives and thinks are ultimately related to (and inexorably filtered through) the structure of one's language. (Indeed, it might follow that the differences in the per capita suicide rate between, for example, Hopi and Standard-Average-European groups may be attributable to differences in their language structures.) In the Western culture, with its essentially Aristotelian view, three different types of suicidal logic are distinguished: logical, catalogical, and paleological. *Logical* (or surcease) suicide tends to occur in individuals who are in physical pain, who show no gross aberrations in their reasoning, and who do not indulge in either deductive or semantic fallacies.

Paleological (or psychotic) suicides are those who use "more primitive" forms of reasoning, are often delusional, and employ deductive gambits of reasoning such as syllogizing in terms of attributes of the predicate (or the use of the "undistributed middle term") as in the following syllogism implied in a suicide note: "Death is suffering; I am suffering; therefore: I must die."

Catalogical suicides are victims of their own semantic errors and especially of their tendency toward dichotomous thinking. Consider the semantic confusion surrounding the word "I" in the following syllogism reconstructed from a suicide note: "If anyone kills himself, he will get attention; I will kill myself; therefore, I will get attention." The "I" that kills and the "I" that is attended to are not only two different "I's"; indeed, the second one is a difficult-to-conceptualize "Non-I." All this is related to the difficulty of conceptualizing death as total cessation.

Oftentimes the semantic confusions and dichotomous thinking are related to religious beliefs, especially beliefs about the hereafter, which permit the victims to view suicide not as cessation but rather as transition to another life. Such an individual is haunted by his own polarities; when he cannot tolerate some present *aspects* of his *life,* he dichotomously thinks not of some other ways of living, but of death as the "logical" (and only) alternative to life.

A number of other current investigators have dealt with similar (cognitive) approaches to suicidal phenomena. Osgood has employed his own Semantic Differential to analyze the communication aspects of suicide notes. His studies indicated that suicide notes contained a usual stereotype, frequent action expressions (nouns and verbs), few discriminating qualifiers (adjectives and adverbs), and tended to use polarized "allness" terms. Neuringer is also interested in the dichotomous and bipolar aspect of suicidal thinking: the polarizations between hope and frustration, fulfillment and renunciation, life and death. In his comparisons among suicidal, psychosomatic, and normal hospitalized subjects, he found that bipolar shifting and dichotomous thinking were higher in both suicidal and psychosomatic subjects, while only excessive rigidity was characteristic of suicidal thinking—the kind of rigidity often related to self-punitive superego functioning and strict conscience control.

A more recent extension of the logical approach to the analysis of suicidal materials is one which details all the *idiosyncrasies of reasoning* in terms of idiosyncrasies of relevance (e.g., irrelevant premise, irrelevant conclusion, argumentum ad hominem, complex question, etc.); idiosyncrasies of meaning (e.g. equivocation, indirect context, mixed modes, etc.); enthymematic idiosyncrasies (e.g., false suppressed premise, suppressed conclusion, etc.); idiosyncrasies of logical structure (e.g., isolated predicate, isolated term); and idiosyncrasies of logical interrelations (e.g., logical type confusions, contradictions, etc.). These idiological patterns are then related to the individual's *contra-logic* (his private epistemology and cosmology which underlie his thinking patterns), to *psycho-logic* (the "personality" traits related to reasoning which are consistent with his ways of mentating), and his *pedago-logic* (the optimal ways of teaching or dealing with him; i.e., the logical styles in which materials should be presented to him in order for him maximally to resonate or "understand" them. The hypothesis is that there is a finite number of identifiable logical styles related to a comparable number of specific types of suicidal persons.

Is there any way in which the logical, psychological, sociological, phenomenological, and transactional approaches to suicidal phenomena might be brought together? Perhaps by being cognizant of the relevance of these dimensions and by incorporating elements of each approach into one relatively simple classification, one might prepare a synthesis of the important elements of each, delineating an approach which, in its various parts, would reflect the intra-psychic stress, the inter-personal tensions, the strained ties with groups, idiosyncratic modes of thought, inner pain and hopelessness, and even one's role in the family of man. No current proposal can claim adequately to encompass all of these dimensions or to meet the total criteria for comprehensive classification. But suggestions, prompted by the wish to be heuristic, if not catalytic, should always be welcome, and it is in this spirit that the following tentative classification of suicide behaviors is proposed.

It is suggested that all (committed) suicides be viewed as being of one of three types: (1) egotic; (2) dyadic; or (3) ageneratic.

Egotic suicides are those in which the self-imposed death is the result, primarily, of an *intra-psychic* debate, disputation, struggle-in-the-mind, or dialogue within one's self in the "congress of the mind." The impact of one's immediate environment, the presence of friends or loved ones, the existence, "out there," of group ties or sanctions become secondary, distant perceptual "ground" as compared with the reality and urgency of the internal psychic debate. The dialogue is within the personality; it is a conflict of aspects of the self, within the ego. Such deaths can be seen as egocide or ego destruction; they are annihilations of the "self," of the personality, of the ego. At the time it happens, the individual is primarily "self-contained" and responds to the "voices" (not in the sense of hallucinatory voices) within him. This is what one sees in the extremely narrowed focus of attention, self-denegrating depression, and other situations where the suicide occurs without regard for anyone else including especially the loved ones and "significant others."

Such individuals are often seen as delusional, although sometimes the agitated obsessional quality is what is seen most clearly. They are self-contained, in the sense that the person's torment is "within his head," such as the anguish of a Virginia Woolf, the torment of an Ellen West; many of the "crazy" (i.e., "psychotic," gifted, excessively "neurotic," "special," private, inwardly convoluted, highly symbolic) suicides—suicides that can be conceptualized in a number of ways, such as nihilistic, oceanic, reunion, Harlequin, magical, etc.

Egotic suicides are primarily *psychological* in their nature. Suicide notes pertaining to this kind of suicide contain explanations of these special inner states; are filled with symbolism and metaphor (and sometimes poetry); and are special windows not so much into the ideation or affect of the anguished person as they are private views of either pervasive or idiosyncratic existential struggles and *inner* unresolved philosophic disputations. Although they are often meant as diaries to the self, these suicide notes are often addressed to specific persons and as such are meant as didactic "explanations" of the victim's inner world of choice.

Individuals who commit this type of suicide have in common a phenomenon which we shall call "boggling." The persons boggles (i.e., stops, hesitates, startles, and refuses to go on because of doubt, fear, scruples, confusion, pain, etc.). It is as though he says to himself, "So far and no further." Colloquially translated, it comes out as, "I've had it," which means that he has "taken" as much of the world's assaults as he can, and that his limits or tolerance for continuing his bargain with life have been reached and that he is now abrogating that relationship.

Here are three examples of *egotic* suicide notes.

(From a 31-year-old single male)

Mr. Brown:
   When you receive this note, call the police.

Have them break down the door panels of the cabinet nearest the window in room 10. My body will be inside. *Caution—carbon monoxide gas!* I have barricaded the doors shut so that if for any reason the guard becomes suspicious and tries to open the doors, there will be enough delay to place me beyond rescue.

It seems unnecessary to present a lengthy defense for my suicide, for if I have to be judged, it will not be on this earth. However, in brief, I find myself a misfit. To me, life is too painful for the meager occasional pleasure to compensate. It all seems so pointless, the daily struggle leading *where?* Several times I have done what, in retrospect, is seen to amount to running away from circumstances. I could do so now—travel, find a new job, even change vocation, but why? It s *Myself* that I have been trying to escape, and this I can do only as I am about to!

Please take care of a few necessary last details for me. My residence is—100 Main Street.

My rent there is paid through the week.

My only heirs and beneficiaries are my parents. No one else has the least claim to my estate, and I will it to my parents.

Please break the news to them gently. They are old and not in good health. Whatever the law may say, I feel I have a moral right to end my own life, but not someone else's.

It is too bad that I had to be born (*I* have not brought any children into this world to suffer). It is too bad that it took me more than 31 years to realize that I am the cause of whatever troubles I have blamed on my environment, and that there is no way to escape oneself. But better late than never. Suicide is unpleasant and a bother to others who must clean up and answer questions, but on the whole it is highly probable that, were I to live, it would cause even more unpleasantness and bother to myself and to others.

Goodbye.

                                                Bill Smith

(From a 47-year-old married male)

Mary Darling,
   My mind—always warped and twisted—has reached the point where I can wait no longer—I don't dare wait longer—until there

is the final twist and it snaps and I spend the rest of my life in some state run snake pit.

I am going out—and I hope it is out—Nirvanha, I think the Bhudaists (how do you spell Bhudaists?) call it which is the word for "nothing." That's as I have told you for years, is what I want. Imagine God playing a dirty trick on me like another life!!!

I've lived 47 years—there aren't 47 days I would live over again if I could avoid it.

Let us, for a moment be sensible. I do not remember if the partnership agreement provides for a case like this—but if it doesn't and I think it doesn't, I would much prefer—I haven't time to make this a legal requirement—but, I would much prefer that you, as executrix under my will, *do not* elect to participate in profits for 2 or 3 years or whatever it may be that is specified there. My partners have been generous with me while I worked with them. There is no reason why, under the circumstances of my withdrawal from the firm, they should pay anything more.

I could wish that I had, for my goodby kiss, a .38 police special with which I have made some good scores—not records but at least made my mark. Instead, I have this black bitch—bitch, if the word is not familiar to you—but at least an honest one who will mean what she says.

The neighbors may think its a motor backfire, but to me she will whisper—"Rest—Sleep."

                                                    Bill

P.S. I think there is enough insurance to see Betty through school, but if there isn't—I am sure you would out of the insurance payments, at least—

I hope further and I don't insist that you have the ordinary decency—decency that is—to do so—Will you see Betty through college—she is the only one about whom I am concerned as this .38 whispers in my ear.

(From a 21-year-old single female)

                                                    12:00 P.M.
I can't begin to explain what goes on in my mind—it's as though there's a tension pulling in all directions. I've gotten so I despise myself for the existence I've made for myself. I've every reason for, but I can't seem to content myself with anything. If I don't do this or some other damned thing, I feel as

tho I'm going to have a nervous collapse. May God forgive me, and you too, for what I am doing to you, my parents who have always tried so beautifully to understand me. It was futile, for I never quite understood myself. I love you all very much.

                                                    Mary

Dyadic suicides are those in which the death relates primarily to the deep unfulfilled needs and wishes pertaining to the "significant other"—the partner in the important current dyad in the victim's life. These suicides are primarily *social* in their nature. Although suicide is always the act of a person and, in this sense, stems from within his mind, the dyadic suicide is essentially an inter-personal event. The cry to the bootless heavens refers to the frustration, hate, anger, disappointment, shame, guilt, rage, impotence, and rejection, in relation to *him* or to *her*—either the real him or her or a symbolic (or even fantasied or fictional) person in the life. The key lies in the undoing: "If only he (or she) would. . . ." Most suicide notes are dyadic in their nature. Suicide notes, usually prefaced by the word, "Dear," are typically addressed to a specific person, an ambivalently loved love-one. (A prototypical example: "Dear Mary: I hate you. Love, George.") In this country most suicides seem to be dyadic in nature; that is, they are primarily *transactional* in nature. The victim's best eggs are in the other person's flawed basket. He (and his figurative eggs) are crushed. The dyadic suicidal act may reflect the victim's penance, bravado, revenge, plea, histrionics, punishment, gift, withdrawal, identification, disaffiliation, or whatever—but its arena is primarily interpersonal and its understanding (and thus its meaning) cannot occur outside the dyadic relationship.

Here are some examples of *dyadic* suicide notes.

(From a 35-year-old single male, who committed suicide after he killed his girl friend)

Mommie my Darling,
    To love you as I do and live without you is more than I can bare. I love you so com-

pletely, wholeheartedly without restraint. I worship you, that is my fault. With your indifference to me; is the difference. I've tried so hard to make our lives pleasant and lovable, but you didn't seem to care. You had great plans which didn't include me. You didn't respect me. That was the trouble. You treated me like a child. I couldn't reach you as man and woman or man and wife as we've lived. I let you know my feelings toward you when I shouldn't have. How I loved you, what you meant to me. Without you is unbearable.

This is the best way. This will solve all our problems. You can't hurt me further and anyone else. I was a "toll" while you needed me or thought you did. But now that I could use some help, you won't supply the need that was prominent when you need it. So, good bye my love. If it is possible to love in the hereafter, I will love you even after death. May God have mercy on both our souls. He alone knows my heartache and sorrow and love for you.

Daddy

(From a 66-year-old divorced male)

Mary:

We could have been so happy if you had continued to love me. I have your picture in front of me. I will look at it the last thing. I do love you so much. To think you are now in the arms of another man is more than I can stand. Remember the wonderful times we have had—kindly—Good bye Darling. I love you, W. Smith.

Your boy friend Pete Andrews, is the most arrogant, conceited ass I have ever known or come in contact with. How a sensible girl like you can even be with him for 10 minutes is unbelievable. Leave him and get a real fellow. He is no good. I am giving my life for your indescressions. Please don't let me pay too high a price for your happiness. All your faults are completely forgotten and your sweetness remembered. You knew I would do this when you left me—so this is no surprise. Good bye darling—I love you with all of my broken heart.

W. Smith

(From a 38-year-old divorced female)

Bill,

You have killed me. I hope you are happy in your heart, "If you have one which I

doubt." *Please* leave Rover with Mike. Also leave my baby alone. If you don't I'll haunt you the rest of your life and I mean it and I'll do it.

You have been mean and also cruel. God doesn't forget those things and don't forget that. And please no flowers; it won't but mean anything. *Also keep your money.* I want to be buried in Potters Field in the same casket with Betty. You can do that for me. That's the way we want it.

You know what you have done to me. That's why we did this. It's yours and Ella's fault, *try* and forget that *if* you can. But you can't. Rover belongs to Mike. Now we had the slip and everything made out to Mike, he will be up after Rover in the next day or so.

Your Wife

Ageneratic suicides are those in which the self-inflicted death relates primarily to the individual's "falling out" of the procession of generations; his losing (or abrogating) his sense of membership in the march of generations and, in this sense, in the human race itself. This type of suicide relates to the Shakespearean notion of "ages" or eras within a human life span, and a period within a life in which an individual senses at one level of consciousness or another, his "belonging" to a whole line of generations; fathers and grandfathers and great-grandfathers before him, and children and grandchildren and great-grandchildren after him.

Erikson has used the term "generativity" to represent the concern of one generation for the next—"the interest for establishing and guiding the next generation"—in which the general idea is one of transgenerational relationship. He further points out that where this sense of generativity is absent in the adult individual, there is often "a pervading sense of individual stagnation and interpersonal impoverishment." In most of the important interpersonal exchanges in which an adult engages, he does not ordinarily expect direct or reciprocal reward or repayment, but, rather, as in parenthood, the most that he ordinarily desires is for the next generation to do at least the same for their next generation as he has done for it. The person who falls out of his society or out of his lineage is a person who has lost investment in his own "post-self." This kind of suicide grows out of a sense of alienation, disengagement, familial ennui, aridity, and emptiness of the individual in the "family of man." The sense of belonging to the stream of generations is illustrated in a recently published letter dated October 1967 by Arnold Toynbee in which he said, "I am now an old man and most of my treasure is therefore in future generations. This is why I care so much." The ageneratic suicide has lost this sense of treasure and this is why he cares so little.

This sense of belongingness and place "in the scheme of things," especially in the "march of generations," is not only an aspect of middle and old age, but it is the comfort and characteristic of psychological maturity, at whatever age. To have no sense of serial belongingness or to be an "isolate" is truly a lonely and comfortless position, for then one may, in that perspective, truly have little to live for. This kind of hermit is estranged not only from his contemporaries, but much more importantly, he is alienated from his forebearers and his descendants, from his own inheritance and his own bequests. He is without a sense of the majestic flow of the generations—he is ageneratic. Ageneratic suicides are primarily *sociological* in nature, relating as they do to familial, cultural, national, or group ties. Suicide notes of this type are often (although not always) addressed "To whom it may concern," "To the police," or not addressed at all. They are truly voices in a macro-temporal void.

Here are some examples of *ageneratic* suicide notes.

(From a 43-year-old divorced male)

To Whom It May Concern, and the Authorities:
 You will find all needed information in my pocket book. If the government buries suicides please have them take care of my body, Navy Discharge in pocket book. Will you please seal and mail the accompanying letter addressed to my sister whose address is: 100 Main Street.

My car is now the property of the Jones Auto Finance Co. (You will find their card in my pocket book). Please notify them of its location. You may dispose of my things as you see fit.
 W. Smith

P.S. The car is parked in front of the barbershop. The gear shift handle is broken off, but the motor is in high gear and can be driven that way.

Dear Mary,
 The fact of leaving this world by my own action will no doubt be something of a shock, I hope though that it will be tempered with the knowledge that I am just "jumping the gun" on a possible 30 or 40 years of exceedingly distasteful existence, than the inevitable same end.
 Life up to now has given me very little pleasure, but was acceptable through a curiosity as to what might happen next. Now I have lost that curiosity and the second half with its accompaniment of the physical disability of old age and an absolute lack of interest in anything the world might have for me is too much to face.
 The inclosed clipping seems to tell it much better than I.
 My love to both you and mama, for what it's worth.
 Sorry,
 Bill

"Clipping"

 The question, then, as to whether life is valuable, valueless, or any affliction can, with regard to the individual, be answered only after a consideration of the different circumstances attendant on each particular case; but, broadly speaking, and disregarding its necessary exceptions, life may be said to be always valuable to the obtuse, often valueless to the sensitive: while to him who commiserates with all mankind, and sympathizes with everything that is, life never appears otherwise than as an immense and terrible affliction.

(From a 50-year-old single male)

To the Authorities:
 Excuse my inability to express myself in English and the trouble caused. I beg you

not to lose time in an inquest upon my body. Just simply record and file it because the name and address given in the register are fictitious and I wanted to disappear anonymously. No one expects me here nor will be looking for me. I have informed my relatives far from America. *Please do not bury me!* I wish to be *cremated* and the ashes tossed to the winds. In that way I shall return to the nothingness from which I have come into this sad world. This is all I ask of the Americans for all that I had intended to give them with my coming into this country.

Many thanks.

Jose Marcia

(From a 58-year-old married female)

I have been alone since my husbands death 14 years ago. No near relatives.

I am faced with another operation similar to one I had ten years ago, after which I had many expensive treatments.

My friends are gone and I cannot afford to go through all this again. I am 58 which is not a good age to find work.

I ask that my body be given to medical students, or some place of use to some one. There will be no inquiries for me.

Thank you.

(From a 61-year-old divorced female)

You cops will want to know why I did it, well just let us say that I lived 61 years too many.

People have always put obstacles in my way. One of the great ones is leaving this world when you want to and have nothing to live for.

I am not insane. My mind was never more clear. It has been a long day. The motor got so hot it would not run so I just had to sit here and wait. The breaks were against me to the very last.

The sun is leaving the hill now so hope nothing else happens.

One last reflection: The general suggestion to eschew the category of "suicide" entirely and to reconceptualize all deaths in terms of their being intentioned, subintentioned, or unintentioned—reintroducing the role of the individual in his own demise—would seem to have its own special merits. Indeed, anything said about the classification of suicidal deaths would apply directly to intentioned deaths and, with appropriate modifications, to subintentioned deaths as well.

STUDIES OF ADOLESCENT SUICIDAL BEHAVIOR

Richard H. Seiden

This section is based upon studies which have dealt directly with suicidal adolescents. The format of this section is to cover, in turn, the three major areas of etiology, treatment, and prevention. Within each of these major headings, the material is divided into more specific categories. For example, the etiological factors are categorized according to individual, social, and cultural determinants. The treatment material not only covers the areas of formal psychotherapy

From *Suicide Among Youth,* Washington, National Institute of Mental Health, Dec. 1969, pp. 24–47. Professor Seiden is in the Behavioral Science Division, School of Public Health, University of California, Berkeley.

and hospitalization but chemotherapy and non-traditional methods as well. The topic of prevention is separated into three levels of preventive approach. Primary prevention, which deals with the prodromata or "warning signs"; secondary prevention which covers crisis intervention and basically concerns the material reviewed in the treatment section; and tertiary prevention which treats the important subject of how the survivors are affected by suicide. Such complicated material presented numerous problems in the arrangement and ordering of the data. These problems were exacerbated by two major considerations: first, the methodological defects and non-comparability of many of the studies, and secondly, the sheer weight of the literature written upon this subject. The etiological section, in particular, includes large numbers of studies, which are very uneven in their quality. Many studies contained imprecise definitions or conclusions that frequently went far beyond their data. Particularly common was the failure to distinguish between attempted, committed, threatened, "partial" and "probable" suicides. Various kinds of self-destructive behaviors were frequently combined without due respect for the important differences which exist between them. In some cases the results from a study based upon one group, such as attempted suicides, were overgeneralized to other categories of suicidal behavior as well. In other cases the authors drew conclusions which were not evident from their data but which seemed to have been applied "wholesale" from previous studies.

Our major task was to bring some order into the literature on this subject. We have attempted to evaluate the key studies, and from the numerous papers to select those whose findings had sufficient correspondence to warrant their presentation as a body of consensual knowledge. That is, our criterion was to select the research that was substantially relevant and could be generalized to the study of adolescent suicide.

ATTEMPTED VS. COMMITTED SUICIDE

The most striking defect in many of the studies of adolescent suicides was their frequent failure to distinguish between various self-destructive behaviors, particularly between the general categories of attempted and committed suicides. The only logical way to combine these categories is to assume that cases of attempted and committed suicide come from the same population or are characteristic of the same kinds of persons. This assumption infers that all degrees of self-destructive behavior are essentially attempts at suicide which differ only with respect to how "successful" they are. In other words, the suicidal behavior is re-

garded as continuous, and fatal attempts simply mark its terminal phase. The unsoundness of this assumption is indicated by a wide body of evidence that persons who attempt suicide do not come from the same population as those who commit suicide. Mintz conducted the only prevalence study of suicide attempts to be found in the literature. His results indicated that suicide attempters were younger (model age range 14–24) than completed suicides and that the sex ratio for attempts was the reverse (females 3:1 over males) of the sex ratio associated with completed suicides. Shneidman & Farberow summarized the demographic distinctions between attempters and committers in the following table:

Table 11–1. Characteristics of attempted and committed suicides.

Variables	Modal Attempter	Modal Committer
Sex	F	M
Age	20–30	40 plus
Method	barbiturates	gunshot
Reasons	marital or depression	ill health, marital or depression

On the basis of their investigation they concluded that attempted and committed suicides cannot be combined without masking some extremely important differences. Stengel also insists that data on attempters and committers should be clearly separated. He points out that less than 10 percent of persons who attempt suicide later kill themselves and that many of the people who commit suicide do so on their first attempt. An important reason for distinguishing attempters from committers is that the problems of persons who survive attempted suicide offer the greatest challenge and hope for remedial action: First, for the obvious reason that these people have survived despite their suicidal behavior, but also because they outnumber committed suicides, especially in adolescence, by a ratio which has been estimated from 7:1 to as high as 50:1. The problem of suicide attempts is particularly significant in adolescence since it is reported that 12 percent of all the suicide attempts in this nation were made by adolescents, and that 90 percent of these attempts were made by adolescent girls.

Some of the recent studies in progress demonstrate an increased awareness of the important differences manifested among varieties of self-destructive behavior and, in fact, are utilizing these distinctions for comparative study. In their current research on college-student suicide Peck & Schrut have divided their subjects into four groups: attempted, threatened, and committed suicides and a control group of non-suicidal individuals. Their design calls for comparisons among these four groups to determine differences in demographic factors, factual items, and life style.

Unfortunately, many of the studies encompassed in this review did not make such necessary distinctions. Most of the published studies were based upon suicide attempters (about one-fourth of them were based upon cases of committed suicide, a handful on threatened suicide and other forms of suicidal behavior). Nonetheless, of all the etiological factors presented in the following section, there was only one characteristic which was differentially assigned to one type of suicidal activity. That single characteristic was "social isolation." This determinant was generally attributed to cases of completed suicides but apparently was not seen to be as characteristic of suicide attempters or threateners. Except for this single instance, the causative, dynamic factors were applied to the entire range of suicidal behaviors. More often than not widely different suicidal behavior ranging from the "partial" suicide of a diabetic who disregarded medical dietary advice to the suicide of an adolescent who killed himself by highly lethal means on his first attempt, was attributed to similar if not identical dynamics.

THEORIES OF SUICIDE

Another deficiency of most of the studies of adolescent suicide is the absence of a theoretical orientation from which testable hypotheses can be derived and verified. This absence is not surprising because no theories of suicide are directly based upon adolescent cases. With the possible exception of psychoanalytic theory, which does emphasize the importance of renewed libidinal impulses at puberty, the theories of suicide were derived from the study of adult cases. Little attention has been paid to the specific dynamics leading to youthful self-destruction.

In general, the various theoretical writings on suicide can be divided into two major categories: (1) those formulations where individual, psychodynamic determinants are emphasized and, (2) those in which sociocultural factors are accorded a dominant role.

The psychodynamic formulations fall into two main classifications: non-psychoanalytic and psychoanalytic. The non-psychoanalytic theories are widely diversified, ranging from the view that suicide is caused by a failure in adaptation, to the idea that suicide is affected by climate. The psychoanalytic theories stress the importance of libidinal impulses, particularly dynamic, strongly aggressive impulses directed against an introjected object. Schneer and Kay specifically apply psychoanalytic formulations to describe the particular dynamics of adolescent suicide. They conceive of adolescent suicide as an immature means of coping with extensive Oedipal conflicts through renewal of infantile primary process thought and action.

Sociocultural theories of suicide place greatest emphasis upon dynamic interrelated social forces influencing the suicide rate. The most important of these formulations was developed by Durkheim who stated as a general rule that the suicide potential of a given society varied inversely to the degree of cohesion existing within that society. According to Durkheim, suicides could be classified into three types reflecting an individual's relationships and attachments within his social context. Three types of suicide he described were: (1) Anomic, where a poorly structured, normless society provided few ties for an individual; (2) Egoistic, wherein an individual was unwilling to accept the doctrine of his society and; (3) Altruistic, where an individual was too strongly identified with the traditions and mores of his social group. Gibbs and Martin likewise propose a theory based upon the durability and stability of social relationships and the degree to which different social statuses are successfully integrated by an individual. Paralleling Durkheim, they state as their major premise that the suicide rate of any population will vary inversely with the degree of such status integration. Henry and Short also employ a sociocultural frame of reference in relating suicide and homicide rates to shifts and trends in the economic business cycle.

These examples afford a brief description of the major theoretical orientations.

ETIOLOGY—INDIVIDUAL DETERMINANTS

Genetic and Familial Tendencies

The literature records several references to families with a history of self-destruction. Since, in these cases, suicide seemed to "run in the family," it was speculated that a tendency to suicide may be inherited. However, this speculation has never been proven and there is no evidence that self-destructive tendencies can be transmitted genetically. The only studies specifically designed to examine the possibility of genetic influence were done by Kallman. . . . In these investigations, the case-histories of suicides occurring in sets of identical and fraternal twins (11 sets in the first study, 27 in the second) were compared. Kallman found that suicidal behavior was not consistent among sets of twins even when they were handicapped by comparable mental disorders. He concluded that there were no special hereditary traits predisposing a person to suicide. Instead, he reasoned that suicide was "the result of such a complex combination of motivational factors as to render a duplication of this unusual constellation very unlikely even in identical twin partners."

Puberty

There are indications that, at puberty, a sudden significant increase takes place in the number of suicide attempts. Puberty is also the stage of development where characteristic sex-specific differences in suicidal behavior become apparent (a male preponderance for completed suicide, a female preponderance for suicide attempts). This pubertal increase in suicidal activity has generally been linked to the "stress and strain" of adolescence, especially to conflicts over sexuality and dependency. As Gorceix points out, the adolescent is sexually mature but his environment does not accept this maturity. According to Schneer, et al. suicidal behavior in adolescence (either attempts or threats) may represent a cry for help in dealing with the problems of sexual identification and with associated libidinal and hostile impulses. A crisis in sexual identity is cited by several authors who propose that a failure in masculine or feminine identity, or concern about possible homosexual tendencies, may lead to serious suicide attempts. In a recent study, Peck pointed out that many boys use their fathers' guns (symbolizing masculinity) to commit suicide. He found that if a boy has a father who places a premium on masculinity, commanding his son to "be a man," this directive may frequently have the opposite effect and lead to a weakening of his sense of masculine identity.

Even when sexual identification is adequate, the increased sexual impulses of adolescence, *per se,* may lead to anxiety, guilt, and frustration. Schrut as well as Winn & Halla concluded from their studies of adolescent girls that "guilt over sexual acting out" was a major factor precipitating their suicide attempts. Another example of the eroticization of suicide has been described by McClelland who proposed that there were persons (mostly women) who fantasied death as a lover—"a mysterious, dark figure who seduces and takes them away . . ." McClelland calls this feeling of excitement and anticipation, of "flirting with death," the "Harlequin complex." As such his findings

would help to explain the greater preponderance of female suicide attempts, particularly among adolescent girls dealing with the
renaissance of their sexual impulses. Increased sexual impulsivity may also be responsible for one very unusual and highly
sexualized type of self-destruction. That is,
the death by hanging of adolescent males
acting out erotic fantasies. One of the earliest studies which mention this peculiar kind
of death was published by Stearns who
reported several cases of early-adolescent
males who had hanged themselves while
dressed in female clothing, in some cases
with their feet and hands bound up as well.
He made no attempt to explain this phenomenon but regarded it as a case of "probable"
suicide. Similar cases where young men
hanged themselves while engaging in transvestite activity were also mentioned by
Ford. All these instances involved young
males who died during autoerotic or transvestite activity. Precautions were frequently
taken to avoid disfigurement (e.g. a towel
placed around the neck to prevent rope
burns). The repetitive history of this unusual
activity led these investigators to regard such
deaths as accidents caused by excessive eroti-
cized "risk-taking" rather than as clear-cut
cases of suicide.

Mental Disorder

The two mental disorders most frequently
linked to suicide are depressive states and
schizophrenic reactions. However, there are
no modern writers who contend that mental
disorder is either a necessary or sufficient
cause of suicide.

Depression

In the clinical evaluation of suicide potential, the role of depression has always been
considered important. But, recent studies
indicate that depression defined by internalized aggression and self-hatred may not be as
important a factor in younger age groups as
it is in cases of adult suicide.

If a pathological state of depression occurs in a young person it is usually asso-

ciated with the loss of a love-object either
through death or separation. For example,
after the death of a parent, impairment of
ego-functioning coupled with a feeling of
helplessness, has been observed. This combination of symptoms may lead to a serious
suicide attempt as a means of regaining contact with the lost love-object. Paradoxically,
the critical period for suicidal behavior does
not seem to be during the depressive reaction but shortly after the depression lifts.
Apparently a patient's mood may improve
chiefly because he has resolved his conflict
by making definite plans for his own destruction. Some recent studies found depression to be characteristic of half the young
people who attempted suicide. Contrary
results were reported by Lourie who stated
that younger children making suicide attempts revealed no depression in the usual
adult sense. He suggested that it was not
until late adolescence that the clinical picture of depression appears as a prime factor.
Likewise, Balser and Masterson concluded
that depression was not important among
adolescent suicide attempters. They were
joined in their dissent by Winn & Halla who
were similarly skeptical as to the importance
of depression in children who threatened
suicide.

In brief, if depression is simply and circu-
larly defined as normal grief over the loss of
significant relationships, then children and
adolescents can be considered depressed. On
the other hand, if depression is defined as a
syndrome characterized by feelings of guilt,
worthlessness and pessimism, then such
symptoms would not appear to be as characteristic of youthful suicides as they are of
adults.

Schizophrenic Reactions

Response to auditory hallucinations or commands may sometimes be the cause of serious suicide attempts among young people.
The combination of a rich fantasy life
coupled with limited environmental interaction has been proposed as the factor which
produces these suicidal hallucinations.

Winn and Halla diagnosed childhood

schizophrenia in 70 percent of the threatened or attempted suicides in their study. Fifty percent of the attempters experienced hallucinations telling them to kill themselves; all of the adolescent boys in their study described "command" hallucinations. Balser & Masterson found that 23 of 37 adolescent suicide attempters had been diagnosed as schizophrenic, with specific pathology which included dissociation, hallucinations, delusional ideas, withdrawal, suspiciousness, and lack of communicability. These investigators concluded that schizophrenic reactions bear a closer relationship to suicidal tendencies in adolescents than does depression. Maria supports this hypothesis with his observation that in cases of completed suicides, schizophrenia is diagnosed more frequently in childhood and adolescent cases than it is in adult cases.

Identification, Imitation, Suggestion

Studies of suicide and suicidal behavior have found that children may imitate the actions or follow the suggestions of people close to them who have died, attempted suicide, are preoccupied by suicidal thoughts, or who openly reveal death wishes toward them.

Death may mean to the child a chance for reunion with a loved one, and there are instances where a child has attempted, through suicide, to join a beloved brother, sister, or parent—or even a favorite pet. In his study of children's reaction to the death of a parent, Keeler reported fantasies of reunion with the dead parent were present in eight of 11 children, and that suicidal preoccupations and attempts in six of these children seem to represent an identification with the dead parent and a wish to be reunited.

Lourie cited identification (or imitation) as an important dynamic factor for the younger children in his study. A suicide or suicide attempt by a family member may lead the young child to copy his example, even insofar as making the same choice of weapon. Bender & Schilder suggested that a deep attachment to a mother or father with suicidal preoccupations may spur suicidal preoccupations in a child. Schrut stated that

a young child does not clearly differentiate his identity from that of his mother. If the mother harbors feelings of self-hatred and helplessness, the child may also harbor these same feelings. The opposite case, where lack of identification plays a part in suicidal behavior, was reported by Fowler on the basis of her work with suicidal children. She cited problems in primary family relationships where the parents provided poor models for the child to identify with as important determinants of suicidal activity.

A child's capacity for responding to suggestion may contribute to suicidal tendencies. Children who are openly rejected by a parent, or whose parents are frequently hostile toward them may respond to these "death wishes" with a suicide attempt. In their study of children who had threatened or attempted suicide, Winn and Halla found that over 50 percent of the children had experienced hallucinations directing them to kill themselves. Lawler, et al., described these auditory hallucinations as "hearing a voice, speaking in a critical manner, telling [the child] to kill himself." Occasionally, epidemics of suicides among school children have been recorded. These, too, seem to be at least partly motivated by suggestion and imitation.

It is doubtful whether any very young (under age 9) children actually intend to die. Because of their incompletely developed concept of death, any type of threat or attempt by children is particularly dangerous. If a child does not fully anticipate that he may indeed kill himself, his choice of method (jumping from a window, leaping into a river, or running in front of a car or train) may not leave him any of the chances for rescue which characterize the suicide attempt made in later adolescence.

Death Concept

Integrally connected to suicide is an individual's conception of death. To understand why a person takes his own life, we must also understand what death means to that person. Suicide in the young is particularly tragic since they frequently do not seem realistically aware of their own mortality. Winn and Halla found that young children often attach as much significance to stealing from their mother's purse as they do to a threat to kill themselves. Paradoxically, a child may wish to kill himself but not to die. That is, death is simply and tragically equated to running away or escaping from an unbearable situation. Without the realization that death is final, a child measures his own life's value with a defective yardstick. While young children do not lack a conception of death, their death concept is qualitatively different and frequently distorted when compared to that of a mature adult. A more realistic concept of death seems to emerge in a predictable, developmental sequence which corresponds to chronological age.

The earliest empirical investigation of this topic was conducted by Schilder and Wechsler. Their findings indicated that even a child who was preoccupied with fantasies of death and violence did not really believe in the possibility of his own destruction. Similarly, Bender & Schilder believed that a child conceived of death as reversible and temporary. Supposedly, a child has this concept because of his difficulty in distinguishing between reality and unreality. Geisler emphasized the ambivalence of childhood fantasies of suicide which might be violent and motivated by aggressive-sadistic impulses, but also by a desire not to cease existing but to return to a more peaceful existence.

Nagy published a definitive study of the developmental sequence of children's death concepts. On the basis of compositions, drawings, and discussions collected from children (ages 3–10), she was able to formulate three major developmental stages: Stage 1 (under 5 years) is characterized by a denial of death. Death is seen as separation or similar to sleep and as gradual or temporary. Stage 2 (ages 5–9 years) is where the child reifies and personifies death. Death is imagined as a separate person or is identified with those already deceased. The existence of death at this stage is accepted but averted.

At Stage 3 (age 9 years and older) a child begins to realize that death means a final cessation of bodily activities. This general developmental sequence was confirmed by Lourie. Moreover, he pointed out that among the school age children he studied a frequent awareness of death was expressed in their thoughts and even in wishes for their own death. This awareness was evident not only among 70 percent of the children with emotional problems but among 54 percent of the normal school-age population. Rochlin also indicated that children are quite concerned with death. He disagrees with other writers in maintaining that by as early as age 3 or 4 a child is aware of his own mortality. It is for this reason, says Rochlin, that a child sees death as temporary or reversible—to defend himself against an overwhelming fear of his own demise. In this regard he agrees with Ackerly who also sees the childhood belief in the reversibility of death as a defensive maneuver. In a study comparing different age groups, Alexander and Alderstein measured emotional responses to the idea of death using word-association tasks. They concluded that the concept of death had greatest emotional significance in young children (5 to 8 years) and adolescents (13 to 16 years) as compared to the latency age (9 to 12 year) child. This discrepancy was attributed to the observation that social roles and self-concepts in the latency age child were more well defined than they were in the other two groups. Death attitudes among adolescents were specifically studied by Kastenbaum. He concluded that the adolescent lived in an intense "present" and paid little attention to such distant future concepts as death. When adolescents did regard the remote future they saw it as risky, unpleasant and devoid of significant value. The findings of Alexander and Alderstein and of Kastenbaum seem to indicate that the concept of death achieves a renewed emotional significance in adolescence but that it is handled by displacement or denial in a manner characteristic of much younger children. Denial of death fears by suicidal adolescents has also been cited by

Lester who developed a scale to measure the fear of death. He concluded that suicidal adolescents feared death less than did their non-suicidal adolescent counterparts. These observations are additionally confirmed by the work of Speigel and Neuringer. Through a detailed study of suicide notes they concluded that normal feelings of dreading death were inhibited as a necessary precondition for suicidal activity.

Aggression

All types of suicidal behavior in young children—whether threats, attempts, or completed suicide—have been customarily explained as displacement of frustrated aggression which becomes self-directed. However, Stengel argues that aggression directed toward others, not oneself, is more typical of the suicide attempter. He believes that this means of directing aggression is an important difference which distinguishes suicide attempts from cases of completed suicide.

The particular dynamic relationship between aggression and suicide stems from the belief that direct expressions of hostility or rage—usually provoked by disappointments or deprivation of love—are thwarted and are turned inward for several reasons: 1) The motive of spite or revenge is predominant. Faigel stated that the desire to punish others who will grieve at their death was one of the most frequent motives to suicide in young children. An angry child, powerless to punish or manipulate his parents directly, may take his revenge through an attempt at self-destruction. Zilboorg found that spite was a frequent motivation to suicide among primitive people. He suggested that it was a typical and universal reaction. 2) A child may become overwhelmed with guilt, fear, or anxiety about his feelings of hostility, and then direct his aggression against himself.

Spite, Revenge, or Manipulation

An almost universal fantasy among children is "If I die, then my parents will feel sorry."

Hall suggested that such desires to punish others were a frequent motive to suicide in young children. Research by Lourie, Bender and Schilder and Faigel supported this conclusion. They found that revenge or spite toward a parent was one of the most frequent reasons given by young children for their suicidal behavior. In particular, Lourie maintained that the ultimate goal a child hoped to achieve was the love and attention of the parents while Bender and Schilder declared that suicide threats were frequently used by a youngster to assert his independence.

Impulsivity

Suicide threats and attempts are often attributed to the greater impulsiveness of youth. As such, this impulsivity is considered to be the necessary component which translates youthful suicidal thoughts into actions.

Winn and Halla designated impulsivity as a prominent feature in the personality of a child and noted its existence in two-thirds of their cases of children who threatened suicide. Lawler, et al. described the children in their study of attempts as possessing a rich fantasy life leading to little environmental interaction. This combination, they stated, leads to a control by inner impulses sometimes resulting in self-destructive action.

Lourie concluded from his study of childhood attempters that the vast majority of these children had impulse control problems. Although most of the children had no particular preoccupation with self-destruction, they came from a cultural setting which encouraged or even stimulated general impulsivity. He suggested that the attempts were "mostly based on the pressure of the moment in an individual with relatively poor impulse control." But he also noted that despite their immediate problems of impulsivity, these children had a chronic history of long-standing problems.

Jacobziner reported that the high incidence of attempts among adolescent girls is "probably due to the greater impulsivity of the young female, who does not premeditate the act ... it is, in the main, a precipitous impulsive act, a sudden reaction to a stressful situation." In their study of suicide attempts in Sweden, Bergstrand and Otto likewise concluded that for most adolescent girls, suicidal attempts seem to be impulsive acts connected with small problems.

A strong note of disagreement with these conclusions was reached by Teicher and Jacobs. They argue with the idea that suicide attempts are impulsive and precipitated by some trivial, isolated problem. Rather, they suggest that a longitudinal view of a person's total life history, demonstrates that "the suicide attempt is considered in advance and is ... from the conscious perspective of the suicide attempter ... weighed rationally against other alternatives." In other words, the suicide attempt is not really an impulsive, spur-of-the-moment decision but an end-phase to a long history of problems in adjustment.

Drugs

Of all the "psychedelic" drugs currently popular among the youthful generation, LSD has been most frequently linked with suicide. There has been a great deal of heat, particularly by the mass media, but relatively little light, beamed on this subject. According to Cohen, LSD can be related to suicide in the following ways:

Accidental

Where, under the influence of hallucination or delusion, a subject embarks upon an act which leads to his destruction. Examples: the delusion that one has the ability to fly, hallucinations that cars on highways are toys which can be picked up in motion. In this category, there is no true suicidal intent as such.

Exacerbation of Suicide Proneness

Cases where suicidal thought has taken place before ingestion and the LSD experience in-

tensified such wishes. This condition can lead to:

1) suicide attempts under LSD or

2) suicide attempts after the "trip." Intrusion of suicidal ideas in "normal" individuals, usually as a result of a panic state in an individual who has not previously thought of suicide. Under LSD, dissociation of body or thoughts that a "bad trip" will never end can take place. These ideas might result in suicidal attempts made during a drug-induced state of agitated depression.

Suicide as a Result of LSD-Induced Fantasy

These are miscellaneous cases where a subject may sense his death is necessary for altruistic reasons. This type of suicide is sometimes associated with a person's feelings of guilt and his conviction that he "must die to save the world."

Flashback Suicide

These are cases where LSD effects recur without the drug-magnifying or distorting psychopathology or depression. Panic is intensified by a confusion over what brought the episode on and whether or not it can be ended. Attempts at suicide in this state may be marked by the same motivation to escape psychic pain that occurs in the drugged state.

In these LSD-related suicides there does not seem to be any underlying depression, rather, the main precipitant is an overwhelming emotional experience beyond an individual's control; an experience which can be exacerbated by suggestibility factors when the drug is taken in social groupings. At this stage the psychopharmacology is still not clear, but it seems reasonable to conclude that LSD may act to catalyze underlying conflicts and emotions including suicidal predispositions and to disorient a person to such a degree that his self-destructive potential (lethality) is increased.

It is unclear whether these LSD suicides are really intentional. Shneidman considers such individuals to be what he calls "psyche-experimenters." Their motivation is not to die but to be in a perceptually altered and befogged state. They wish to remain conscious and alive but benumbed and drugged. Accordingly they may experiment with dosages, sometimes with fatal consequences but this type of death is traditionally considered to be accidental.

While there is scanty evidence of a direct causal connection between adolescent drug usage and suicide, there have been some anecdotal speculations concerning the observed association. Trautman reports a case study in which drug abuse and an attempt at suicide were viewed as complementary means of escaping an "unbearable family situation." Schonfeld blames our affluent society which emphasizes immediate rewards, not allowing adolescents to become tolerant of frustration. Subsequently, he writes, when faced with difficulties, they become overwhelmed and turn to escapist measures such as drugs, withdrawal and suicide.

ETIOLOGY—SOCIAL DETERMINANTS

Family Relationships

Family relationships are particularly important in the etiology of adolescent suicide. Not only because the family represents the most viable social unit in our society, but because of the significance of family relationships in the life of the young. Hardly any studies have investigated the protective values of a favorable family environment; instead, most studies have emphasized sibling position, family disorganization, loss, and types of destructive parent-child relationships which lead to suicidal behavior.

Sibling Order

Kallmann et al. observed in their studies that the suicide rate of only children did not differ significantly from that of the general population. Several recent investigators, however, have suggested that a child's sibling position may be related to his suicidal behavior. Toolan found that 49 of 102 adolescent suicide attempters were first-born children. Lester compared Toolan's statistics on sibling positions with data from the New York City population. He confirmed that the distribution of sibling positions in Toolan's samples—especially the high number of first-borns—differed significantly from the expected distribution.

Another group of investigators concluded from their study of suicide attempts that a disproportionate number of suicidal children occupy special sibling positions. Fourteen of the 22 children in their study occupied special positions (three only children, seven first-born, four youngest), but the sample was too small for adequately reliable conclusions. Lester recently re-examined the relationship between sibling position and suicidal behavior. He reasoned that suicide attempts might express an affiliative tendency to communicate with significant others. Noting that such affiliative tendencies are strongest in first-born and only children, Lester predicted an overrepresentation of first-born and only children attempting suicide. His data did not bear out the hypothesized relationship.

Family Disorganization

A significant number of young people who commit or attempt to commit suicide have a history of broken or disorganized homes. A correlation between broken homes and suicide has been noted not only in the United States but has been observed throughout the world by investigators in such countries as Canada; Japan; Germany; France; England; and Sweden.

But Stengel injects a note of controversy by pointing out that the definition of "broken home" varies greatly in the discussions of different authors. To some it means lack of at least one parent. Others seem to include all forms of family disorganization, including severe parental discord or extreme family conflict.

However it is generally agreed that the motives for suicide in children cannot be fully understood without carefully considering their family situations. Most young people who exhibit suicidal behavior seem to come from homes with grossly disturbed family relationships. Frequently these family problems constitute the dominant motivations provoking the suicidal behavior.

In study after study, the home lives of suicidal children have been characterized as disruptive or chaotic. Their histories generally include several of the following indices of family disruption: 1) Frequent moving from one neighborhood or city to another, with many changes of school; 2) family estrangement because of quarreling between parents or between parent(s) and child; 3) great financial difficulties and impoverishment; 4) sibling conflict; 5) illegitimate children; 6) paternal or maternal absence; 7) conflict with step-parent(s); 8) cruelty, rejection, or abandonment by parent(s); 9) institutionalization of adolescent or family member (hospital, jail, reformatory, etc.); 10) suicide attempts by parents; and 11) alcoholic parents.

Such poor family life has been hypothesized to lead to the following conflicts: A fear or knowledge of being unloved; fear of harsh punishment; desire to escape from intolerable conditions; lack of meaningful relationships; creation of guilt; spite; depression; loneliness; hostility; conflict; anxiety; and other affective states, any of which can predispose a child to many forms of anti-social behavior. This consequent anti-social behavior may range from stealing, fire-setting, running away, sexual promiscuity, to other forms of juvenile delinquency or, in some youngsters, to suicide.

Despite the general agreement that broken homes are causally related to youthful suicide, a critical view is taken by Jacobs & Teicher who contend that any valid analysis must place "broken homes" into the context of an adolescent's total life history. In their study of adolescent suicide attempts,

they found that broken homes *per se,* were not distinctively precursive of suicidal behavior. Both their suicidal and non-suicidal control groups demonstrated similarly high percentages of broken homes. The real distinction was that the control group had experienced a stable home life *during the preceding five years* while the suicide attempter group had not.

Loss

The loss of a parent or other loved one (through death, divorce, or prolonged separation) seems to have several significant influences affecting suicidal behavior in children. First, a loss through death may lead to a desire for reunion with the lost loved one. A young child may therefore attempt suicide in order to rejoin his dead parent, sibling (or even a favorite cat), yet not intend to die permanently. An older child or adolescent who believes in the existence of an afterlife, may make a serious attempt at suicide in order to rejoin a parent, sibling, or friend.

The death of significant persons in the child's life can also stimulate suicidal activity in other ways: 1. Parental suicide may lead a young child to copy his parent's example; 2. A child may blame himself for the death of his parent and be driven by this guilt to make a serious suicide attempt; 3. A child may be predisposed to suicide in later life through parental loss in childhood.

Zilboorg suggested that "when a boy or girl loses a father, brother, or sister at a time when he or she is at the height of their Oedipus complex, or transition to puberty, there is . . . a true danger to suicide." Several studies support the conclusion that the death of a parent early in a child's life may contribute to his later suicide-susceptibility. Dorpat, Jackson and Ripley studied 114 completed suicides and 121 attempted suicides. They found that the death of a parent was highest for completed suicides, and concluded from this that unresolved object-loss in childhood leads to an inability to sustain object-loss in later life. Bruhn compared a group of attempted suicides against a control group without suicidal tendencies. The group of suicide attempters was distinguished by the lack of both parental figures or had experienced the absence or death of a family member. Similar results were reported by Greer who found that the incidence of parental loss was higher in suicidal than nonsuicidal persons. Paffenbarger and Asnes discovered that death or absence of the father was the major precursor of suicide among college males. Another consequence of paternal loss or absence is that the mother may be cast in the role of chief disciplinarian. According to Henry, this type of family role structure is associated with children's tendencies toward self-blame. And since the turning of blame inwards has been related to suicide, this type of family structure may predispose children toward suicide.

Again an iconoclastic note is sounded by Jacobs and Teicher, who argue against a simple unitary relationship between loss and suicide. Their research compared the life histories of 50 adolescent suicde attempters with those of 32 control adolescents. Both the suicide attempters and control adolescents had high rates of parental loss in childhood. One group attempted suicide; the other did not. Obviously it was not simply parental loss in childhood which predisposed some subjects to depression and suicides in later life. They concluded that:

loss of love-object is an important aspect of the process, but it must be viewed as part of a process where particular attention is paid to when it occurred and/or recurred, and not merely to its presence or absence. Furthermore, it seems that it is not the loss of a love object per se that is so distressing but the loss of love.

4. A child who suffers the loss of a love object may be predisposed to states of depression linked with suicidal tendencies. The common denominator in all youthful depression is considered to be the loss of the love-object. When this loss occurs to young children it can lead to difficulty in forming the object-relationships required for healthy emotional development. When the loss occurs during adolescence it does not block the

development of object-relationships since the critical years for this development are passed. On the other hand, it can cause an adolescent to hate the love-object, who he feels has betrayed and deserted him. 5. Adolescent girls, who make approximately three-fourths or more of all adolescent suicide attempts, may be especially vulnerable to loss of a father. Lack of a father is frequently noted in their histories and some writers hypothesize that paternal deprivation plays a significant part in the suicidal attempt of young girls. 6. Other forms of love-object losses have also appeared to be significant influences leading to youthful suicide. They include:

1. Loss of close friends through repeated school transfers.
2. Loss of older siblings through marriage, college, Army, or moving.
3. Loss of boy-friend or girl-friend, where this love-object has become a substitute for a dependency upon the parent.
4. Loss felt by freshmen at college—a kind of homesickness which overcomes the youngster when he finds himself alone and his dependency needs acutely unsatisfied.

Social Isolation

Of all the psychodynamic attributes associated with suicidal behavior, the factor of human isolation and withdrawal appears to be the most effective in distinguishing those who will kill themselves from those who will not. While withdrawal and alienation can be important determinants of many types of suicidal behavior, they seem to characterize cases of completed suicides rather than suicide attempts or threats.

Jan-Tausch studied New Jersey school children and reported that "in every case of suicide, ... the child [had] no close friends with whom he might share confidences or from whom he received psychological support." The critical difference between attempters who "failed" and those who "succeeded" was that those who failed had a relationship with "someone to whom they felt close." Jan-Tausch goes on to suggest:

the individual has either withdrawn to the point where he can no longer identify with any person or idea, or (he) sees himself as rejected by all about him and is unable to establish a close supportive relationship with any other individual.

Reese also investigated school-age suicides and found chronic social isolation to be the single most striking feature of this group. He reported that these youngsters had such a marked lack of involvement with other students or teachers that they were literally "unknown" in their own classrooms. Social isolation was also regarded as a major prodromal sign for college suicides many of whom were described as "terribly shy, virtually friendless individuals, alienated from all but the most minimal interactions."

Various reasons have been assigned to explain this state of isolation. Stengel maintains that "lack of secure relationship to a parent figure in childhood may have lasting consequences for a person's ability to establish relationships with other people. Such individuals are likely to find themselves socially isolated in adult life, and social isolation is one of the most important causal factors in the causation of suicidal acts." Schrut states that, for adolescent females, isolation is a gradual process which takes place over a long period. This process of isolation has also been associated with progressive family conflict which becomes increasingly more severe. He reported that the adolescent female suicide attempter in his studies "characteristically saw herself as being subjected to an unjust, demanding, and often irreconcilable isolation with a typical, chronically progressive, diminution of receptive inter-familial communication." After an adolescent becomes estranged from her parents, she relies upon a boy-friend to become the substitute parental image. A fight with the boy-friend is freqently the final blow and becomes the precipitating factor in her suicide attempt. Jacobs & Teicher concur with this analysis, adding that suicidal adolescents usually have numerous and serious problems which progressively isolate them. These authors describe a similar chain-reaction of conflicts isolating an adolescent from meaningful social relationships and frequently leading to a suicide attempt: A long period of extreme conflict between an adolescent girl and her parent(s) eventually leads to parent-child alienation; the adolescent girl frequently seeks to re-establish a meaningful relationship through a romance with a boyfriend. During this time she alienates all other friends by concentrating all her time and energy on her boy-friend. When the romance fails, she finds herself isolated from all "significant others," and the possibility of a suicide attempt is likely. The importance of an active social life is emphasized in the research of Barter, et al. where peer group relations were considered an important barrier to suicide attempts. They note that even though the nuclear family life has an active social life the prognosis is favorable. Additional support for the significance of good peer-group relations can be found in the research of Harlow and Harlow in their continuing studies of affective relationships among lower [primate] animals.

Communication

Closely related to feelings of social isolation are problems in communicating with others—difficulties which are characteristic of many suicidal individuals. In some cases the suicidal act itself is a form of communication, a desperate "cry for help." In other cases, an individual may attempt suicide because of the loneliness and despair growing out of his failure to communicate.

In many cases of attempted or threatened suicide, self-destruction may not be the dominant purpose. That is, some suicidal activities are distinguished by features which are not entirely compatible with the purpose of self-destruction: Some suicide attempters give warning of their intention (allowing for preventive action) or the attempts are carried out in a setting which makes intervention by others possible or probable (allowing for rescue). Stengel calls these attempts "Janus-faced," because they are directed toward destruction, but at the same time towards human contact and life. He believes they are really alarm signals which should be regarded as appeals for help. They should be treated as highly emotional types of communication which are different in style and content from the usual kinds of communication. A recent study by Darbonne investigating this point, indicated that the communication style of suicidal individuals was distinctively different from the non-suicidal individuals.

A large portion of the suicidal behavior of adolescent girls seems to fall into the category of communication attempts. Stengel thinks these young girls use suicidal threats and acts as appeals to the environment more frequently than males, and that females seem inclined to use the suicidal act as an aggressive manipulative device more often than males.

Why do adolescents resort to this dangerous method of gaining attention and response? Lourie indicates that they drag with them, into adolescence, poor, distorted answers to the problems of earlier development (i.e. what to do with aggression, how to get attention, etc.) Peck commented:

We must ... wonder at the condition of poverty of one's inner resources, when suicidal behavior becomes one's sole means of obtaining that attention.

But he goes on to state that these young people are not to be shrugged off merely as attention-seeking, manipulating youngsters, but should be regarded as unhappy, helpless, hopeless young people who are apparently unable to change things in more constructive ways.

These attempts to communicate through suicidal behavior may have two outcomes: change or further impasse. On a hopeful note Peck reports:

... when the kinds of problems that underlie a suicidal behavior are appropriately confronted ... suicidal behavior often disappears as a coping mechanism.

Yet a high percentage of these attempts do not result in improved conditions and when they do not they sometimes end in suicide. Peck states that if the communications go unheeded, they become louder and more lethal, and the consequences, regardless of how nonlethally intended, may be disastrous. The possibility of tragic consequences is also confirmed by Teicher and Jacobs who similarly observed:

More often than not adolescents who adopt the drastic measure of an attempt as an attention-getting device find that this too fails ... (and) the adolescent is then convinced ... that death is the only solution to what appears to him as the chronic problem of living.

Socio-Economic Status

The relationship between socio-economic factors and youthful suicide is, in general, similar to that of adult suicides. That is, suicides are highest in times of economic depression and lowest during periods of war. However, social upheavals do not seem to affect the suicide rate of the young as much as the rate of adults. The factors predisposing to youthful suicide appear to be much more related to home, family, and school life. Poverty has been associated with suicide and so has wealth but on balance there is no real evidence to suggest that suicide is more frequent among the rich or the poor. As Shneidman and Farberow pointed out, the distribution is very "democratic" and represented proportionately among all levels of society. Nevertheless, suicide is most prevalent in the transitional sections of a community, which are usually impoverished and run-down areas. Sainsbury has reported that low income by itself does not lead to high suicide rates. In his ecological studies, he discovered that it was the poor stability of a neighborhood not its poverty which accounted for the high rate of suicide.

Religion

There is little reliable evidence to relate religion specifically to suicide. Among the three major religions in this country, the suicide rate is highest among Protestants, lowest among Catholics. Durkheim proposed that the higher rate among Protestants was because Protestantism had less social integration and consistency than did Catholicism and therefore the Protestant church had a less moderating effect upon suicides of its members. On the other side of the coin, it is possible that Catholic suicides may frequently be concealed because of religious and social pressures. History indicates that religion has both moderated and facilitated suicidal activity. For example, the history of the Jews is replete with instances of mass suicides which occurred as a consequence of persecution and discrimination. There are also cases of individuals caught up in a religious frenzy or motivated to achieve religious martyrdom through self-immolation.

Simplistic attempts to relate suicide to unitary religious dimensions e.g. Catholic, Protestant and Jewish, are merely exercises in futility. Questions of religious affiliation do not get at the critical variables influencing suicide. The important unanswered questions concerning religion and suicide were delineated by Shneidman:

What would seem to be needed would be studies relating self-destructive behaviors to the operational features of religious beliefs; including a detailed explication of the subject's present belief system in relation to an omnipotent God, the efficacy of prayer, the existence of an hereafter, the possibility of reunion with departed loved ones, etc.

Education—the Special Case of Student Suicide

The subject of student suicide appears throughout the 20th century literature, however, the first thorough study of suicide on United States campuses dates back only 30 years. Stimulated by the fact that suicides accounted for over half the deaths at the University of Michigan, Raphael and his colleagues investigated the role and function of the university mental hygiene unit in dealing with this problem. Later research on college suicide described the suicide problem at Yale, Cornell, and Harvard. The results of

these studies indicated that the suicide problem was substantial and implied that the risk of suicide was greater for students than for their non-academic peers. In addition, these authors attempted to identify the factors which predisposed students to suicide and to offer suggestions for its prevention. These earlier studies were almost entirely descriptive, and while they did provide informative insights they failed to provide control groups for a baseline against which the validity of their findings could be assessed. This situation was remedied by later studies which applied the necessary principle of adequate control or comparison groups to answer two basic questions: (1) Are students at greater risk of suicide than non-students? (2) How do suicidal students differ from their non-suicidal classmates?

Students vs. Non-Students

Studies by Temby and Parrish indicated that students were more suicidal than non-students. Temby reported a suicide rate of 15 per 100,000 at Harvard, and Parrish's work indicated a suicide rate of 14 per 100,000 at Yale. Both of these rates are well in excess of the expected suicide rate for this population (7 to 10 per 100,000). A series of studies in English universities also led to the conclusion that students were more suicidal than their nonacademic age peers. Parnell published a detailed analysis of suicides at Oxford University comparing deaths due to suicide among Oxford students to those in the population at large. He found that the suicide rate was approximately 12 times as great for Oxford students (59.4:5.0). Carpenter after reviewing cases of suicide among Cambridge undergraduates, also concluded that the rate of [male] students was higher than for comparable groups. Two years later Lyman investigated suicides at Oxford University comparing the incidence at various British schools. Her data is summarized in Table 11.2.

To test whether the same relationship held in American universities, Bruyn and Seiden investigated the incidence of suicide

Table 11–2. Suicide rates of British universities

Populations	Annual suicide rate per 100,000 population ages 20 to 24
England and Wales	4.1
Oxford University	26.4
Cambridge University	21.3
University of London	16.3
Seven unnamed British universities	5.9

among college students at the University of California, Berkeley campus (UCB) and contrasted this incidence with the figures for comparable age groups in the California population. During the 10-year period they studied (1952–1961) there were 23 student suicides whereas only 13 suicides would be expected if the general population rates held. They concluded that the suicide rate among students was significantly greater than for a comparable group of age cohorts. In addition, they found that the general mortality experience [deaths due to all causes] was significantly lower for students when contrasted to a comparable group of age peers.

There is one study which indicates lower suicide incidence among [male Finnish University] students, when compared to the general population. Barring this exception, the general rule obtains that students are at greater risk of suicide than their non-student peers.

Suicidal Students vs. Non-Suicidal Classmates

This question was investigated by Seiden who compared students at the University of California, Berkeley who committed suicide during the 10 year period, 1952 through 1961, with the entire UCB student body population during this same decade. The main findings of this research were:

Suicidal students could be significantly differentiated from their classmates on the variables of age, class standing, major subject, nationality, emotional condition, and academic achievement. Compared to the student population at large, the suicidal group was older, contained greater proportions of graduates, language majors, and foreign students, and gave more indications of emotional disturbance. In addition, the undergraduate suicides fared much better than their fellow students in matters of academic achievement.

Another study which distinguished between suicidal and non-suicidal students was published by Paffenbarger and Asnes. Using the college records of 40,000 former students at the Universities of Pennsylvania and Harvard, they examined the records for characteristics precursive of eventual suicide. Early loss of or absence of the father was found to be the dominant distinguishing characteristic in cases of male suicide.

The Effects of School Success or Failure

There is some disagreement about the importance of school success in relation to suicide. This has been a recurrent question over many years. One of the most famous discussions of the Vienna Psychoanalytical Society was held in 1910 to deal with the specific problem of suicide among students. The Teutonic school system was the target of much public criticism and members of the Viennese psychoanalytic group, including Freud, Adler, Stekel, et al. applied the newly developed insights of dynamic psychology and psychoanalysis to this controversy.

In more recent times Otto examined 62 cases where public school problems were indicated as a provoking cause of suicidal attempts. He found that the school problems, when compared to other difficulties, were factors of relatively slight importance. However, Reese, studying public-school-age suicides to assess the effects of the school environment found that half of the subjects were doing failing work at the time of their suicide.

Reese's study was the only research which showed a relationship between low I.Q. and suicide. He found that in 25 percent of those cases where the I.Q. was available, the scores were borderline or below. In contrast, other studies by various authors have indicated that suicidal adolescents have invariably been of average or better than average intelligence. With college students, the factor of intellectual competence has been characteristically greater in the suicidal students than in their nonsuicidal classmates. Students who committed suicide had higher gradepoint averages (3.18 as opposed to 2.50) and a greater proportion of them had won scholastic awards (58 percent as opposed to 5 percent). The transcripts of these students would indicate that they had done splendidly in their academic pursuits. However, reports from family and friends revealed that these students were never secure despite their high grades. Characteristically, they were filled with doubts of their adequacy, dissatisfied with their grades, and despondent over their general academic aptitude. This propensity for some brilliant academic students to feel that they achieved their eminence by specious means was also reported by Munter who called this syndrome the "Fraud Complex" and indicated that it was a frequent cause of depression among students.

Suicidal Students or Academic Stress?

A pivotal question is whether students are at greater risk of suicide because they are initially more suicidal than non-students or because the school environment makes them more susceptible. Is the higher student rate due to selection procedures? Rook maintained that it was when he wrote that "higher standards of entry are more likely to lead to selection of the mentally unstable." Or is the elevated rate due to the institutional inflexibility and the stresses of academe? The Conference on Student Stress implied this viewpoint when they met to deal with the question: "How do stresses of students affect their emotional growth and academic performance?" The answer to this question needs further research to follow up college students and record their later mor-

tality experience. Unfortunately, the standard death certificate does not supply information regarding education of the decedent. Such data would be helpful for a definitive answer to the controversial question of which is more significant, the susceptible student or the academic stress?

Variation by College

There is no evidence directly bearing upon this question. A definitive answer would require standardized reporting procedures probably involving a national clearinghouse for information on student suicide. Nonetheless, the data from Lyman's study of English universities clearly indicated that the Oxbridge schools had a remarkably high rate of suicide compared to the nation in general and to the unnamed "red-brick" British universities in particular. Accordingly, it may be reasonable to hypothesize that the suicide rates at top-ranked American universities, e.g. Harvard, Yale, Cornell, Berkeley, are higher than the suicide rates at schools of lesser academic reputation. The test of this hypothesis is an interesting subject for future research. Other provocative questions which must await future research are the comparison of suicide rates for: Large vs. small schools; public vs. private schools; and co-ed vs. sexually segregated schools.

Mass Media

Youthful suicide has been a subject for novelists and poets throughout the years. Literature is filled with humorous, insightful and sensitive treatments of the conflicts and despair of adolescents. Some people believe that the fictional, romanticized treatment of suicide and adolescence acts as a stimulant to self-destruction. Perhaps the most vigorous advocacy of this position came from Mapes who wrote that:

Trashy novels and all kinds of unwholesomely sentimental literature are a very important predisposing cause to suicide in this country. They produce a morbid condition of mind which unfits people for realities.

Mapes' outrage was primarily aroused by one of the most celebrated examples of stormy adolescent love—Goethe's novel, *The Sorrows of Young Werther* (1774). This slim volume became a symbol of 18th century *Weltschmerz* and was vastly popular throughout the world. Soon afterwards Goethe and his book were accused of initiating a wave of school-boy suicides which followed its publication. Goethe himself came in for various denunciations, his book was lampooned and banned from public sale in some cities. Even to the present day, one finds castigating references blaming "Wertherism" for adolescent suicides.

Despite the condemnation of "trashy" novels and romantic sentimentality there is no evidence that the treatment of suicide by mass media influences the suicide rate. The only study to directly attack this question was done recently by Motto. To determine whether newspaper publicity about suicides influenced the suicide rate, he studied the incidence of self-destruction in cities which had experienced newspaper blackouts due to strikes. No significant changes were noted when the newspaper coverage was suspended. Motto concluded that newspaper publicity was not an instrumental precipitating factor for suicide. The blame for youthful suicide is no longer placed upon literary influences but on the deeper underlying motives which lead children to suicide. Nonetheless, it is of some passing interest and a reflection of the *Zeitgeist* that *The Ode to Billy Joe* (Gentry, 1967) which tells the story of a teenage suicide was, for many weeks, the number one best-selling phonograph record throughout this country.

Despite the inflammatory accusations leveled against the mass media, the educational aspects of a mass media approach have not been overlooked. There have been numerous films, plays and stories designed to educate the public about the general problem of self-destruction. In the specific area of youthful suicide, such a training film has been produced with the cooperation of the Los Angeles Suicide Prevention Center. This film is especially geared to help teachers, counselors, parents and others who have frequent contact with adolescents, to recognize and deal with the clues prodromal to adolescent suicide.

ETIOLOGY—CULTURAL DETERMINANTS

Cultural factors may influence the suicide rate in three basic ways: (1) By the acute psychological stresses and tensions produced in its members; (2) by the degree of acceptability accorded to suicidal behavior; and (3) by the opportunity for alternative behaviors provided by the culture.

Stresses

Instances of the first type, where the built-in stresses of a culture may catalyze and aggravate the suicide potentiality of its members, were discussed by Bakwin. Writing on the "Prussian" attitude toward children, Bakwin related the high suicide rate among Prussian children to their fear of punishment and to their strong guilt feelings about failure. Prussian children were reared in an atmosphere which demanded a rigid conformity; punishment was frequent and severe. Overly-strict attitudes with few excuses accepted for "misbehavior" were the dominant codes at home and in the classroom. A comprehensive study of cultural factors influencing suicide was published by Hendin who used a psychoanalytic frame of reference to study individuals and their culture. Hendin investigated the reasons for the consistent differences in suicide incidence among the Scandinavian countries of Denmark, Sweden and Norway. From his observations of parent-child relationships, Hendin formulated modal "psycho-social character" structures which typified each of the three Scandinavian nations and which he related to national differences in child-rearing orientations. Sweden, where the suicide rate is relatively high, was characterized by "performance" types of suicide due to high achievement expectations, self-hatred for failure and problems with affectivity resulting from early maternal separation. Denmark, where the suicide rate is also high, was characterized by "dependency" suicides revolving around such conflicts as anxiety about losing dependency relationships, over-sensitivity to abandonment, and difficulty in expressing overt aggression. In contrast, the suicide rate in Norway is quite low. Hendin proposed that this lower rate occurred because Norwegian mothers were more accepting, less concerned with their chilren's performance, more tolerant of aggression and strivings for independence, than were Swedish or Danish mothers. He believed that those suicides which occurred in Norway were mainly of a "moralistic" type, stemming from guilt feelings precipitated by puritanical aspects of Norwegian culture. Hendin's hypotheses were later tested by Block and Christiansen who investigated the reported child-rearing practices of Scandinavian mothers. They found general, but somewhat equivocal, support for Hendin's conclusions. In particular, their results were fairly consistent with Hendin's regarding Denmark and Norway; less so with respect to Sweden.

Acceptability

Examples of the second type, where culturally favorable attitudes may affect the suicide rate were presented by Bakwin who pointed out that countries such as Austria and Germany, where suicide is regarded as an honorable way to die, produce a higher incidence of self-destruction than countries like England or the United States where suicide is looked upon as cowardly or as a sign of mental aberration. The effect of culturally favorable attitudes toward suicide are probably best exemplified by the extreme case of Japan. In past years children of the nobility and military classes were indoctrinated at an early age with the belief that suicide was an acceptable, often highly valued, means for resolving demands of honor or duty, e.g. *kamikaze, seppuku.* Although traditional suicides are no longer as prevalent in Japan, the general attitude toward suicide is still much more tolerant

than it is in many other parts of the world. At present, in Japan, suicide incidence has reached the point where it is the number one cause of death below the age of 30. Contrary to the United States pattern where the frequency of suicide increases with advancing age, Japanese suicides reach a peak at the youthful ages of 20–25. During the age range of 15–24, the suicide rates for Japanese youth are 10–20 times the corresponding United States rates. Despite the fact that academic competition; exaggerated dependency and shame or failure; poor family relationships; and attempts at symbolic communication have all been cited as significant influences, the singularly distinctive characteristic cited in studies of Japanese suicide is the culturally favorable attitude toward self-destruction.

Alternatives

Conversely, where the cultural attitudes are condemnatory or repressive, one finds examples of the third type where the culture provides for alternative behaviors that indirectly satisfy the same end of self-destruction. Wolfgang's research supported the belief that the relatively high homicide and low suicide rates among young American Negro males were influenced by common values shared by members of this subcultural group. That is, suicide was perceived as cowardly and effeminate whereas death by homicide was considered to be masculine and courageous. Lowie recorded a somewhat parallel phenomenon among the Crow Indians. He observed a cultural pattern which was geared toward those men who were no longer interested in living. They were allowed to become a "Crazy-Dog-Wishing-to-Die."

Above all, these warriors were pledged to foolhardiness and they deliberately courted death, recklessley dashing up to the enemy so as to die within one season.

A similar cultural pattern had also been observed in past years among the Northern Cheyenne Indians. Formerly, when a Cheyenne warrior became depressed or lost face, he could deal with the situation by organizing a small war party. During the ensuing battle, he could resolve his conflict through a feat of bravery which would renew his self-esteem or by engaging in an extremely dangerous and courageous act during which he was killed. As such, these cultural alternatives bear some similarity to the fictitious Suicide Club described by Robert Louis Stevenson. Members of this club could manage to die without actually doing the killing themselves. As one of the characters remarked, "the trouble with suicide is removed that way. . . ."

But what happens when a culture comes to a dead-end and no longer offers these alternative outlets for its members? Dizmang, writing on the Northern Cheyenne Indians, observed that their traditional ways of acquiring self-esteem were gone, the culturally approved means of expressing aggression (e.g. Sun Dance, buffalo hunt, intertribal warfare) had been denied to them and he reasoned that it was these sorts of deprivation which were responsible for a mass epidemic of adolescent suicide attempts. In this case, Dizmang concluded, a whole culture had been "denied means for dealing with instinctual feelings . . . and the result was a feeling of hopelessness and helplessness," stemming from this cultural deadend.

TREATMENT

The methods indicated for treatment of suicidal adolescents are generally different from those most useful for adults. Despite these differences, the subject of specific treatment for youthful suicidal behavior has received singularly little attention in the literature. Surely this is a subject which warrants serious investigation.

Treatment of any kind of suicidal behavior must begin with an evaluation of the seriousness of a child's suicidal desires. Observing the child, interviewing his parents, and examining the child's history and home environment, should enable an investigator to determine whether a child presents a sig-

nificantly dangerous risk. Glaser offers some criteria to be appraised: depth of the conflict, inner resources for coping with the situation, outer sources available, and severity of the stressful situation.

Hospitalization

For those children who are identified as "high risk," immediate precautions must be taken. Hospitalization is the most effective precautionary measure. Shaw and Schelkun set forth some of the advantages of temporarily hospitalizing the child: 1) It provides a breathing spell for both child and family; 2) it removes the child from all stressful or anxiety-producing situations; 3) it allows the child to be observed and evaluated; 4) it indicates to the child that he is being helped, and that his problems are being taken seriously; and 5) it enables the child to accept a therapeutic relationship more easily.

The child who is mentally ill or extremely suicidal will require a long period of hospitalization. Moss and Hamilton present the factors in successful therapy of the seriously suicidal patient. The first phase is directed mainly toward adequate protection, relief of anxiety and hopelessness, and restoration of satisfying relationships with others. A deep, probing approach is postponed. During the next phase—the convalescent stage—the patient remains in hospital. He receives active psychotherapy, with the therapist approaching the problem directly and discussing new solutions. Only during the final phase is the patient allowed to renew contact with his original environment. Moss and Hamilton emphasize that since this is a crucial period for the patient, he should remain in hospital during this time. Although the patient usually considers himself greatly improved, there will be, upon contact with his previous environment, reactivation of the suicidal drive 90 percent of the time. This reactivation must be anticipated, and the patient and his family warned of this probability.

For the less seriously suicidal patient, hospitalization need not be for a prolonged period. Even a week can be beneficial in reducing the despair of a child, and in providing time to formulate a plan of treatment.

Psychotherapy

Psychotherapy can be useful for seriously disturbed youngsters. Schechter believes that depression is the basis of much childhood suicidal behavior. Accordingly, he sees the treatment of suicide in children as based entirely on the concept of actual or threatened loss of love-object. The suicide attempt is considered to be both an attack on this object and an attempt to regain it. Therefore, he would treat all children by helping them to re-establish adequate object-relationships.

Shaw and Schelkun, on the other hand, feel that the specific direction of the therapy should be highly individualized and dependent upon the predominant conflict: Inward aggression may be rechanneled; grief may be sublimated; fear of abandonment can be relieved. The therapist should work to relieve conflict and stress, to control destructive impulses, and to stimulate the child toward constructive action, but any deep, uncovering therapy should usually be avoided.

Richman sees the therapy of attempted suicide in a somewhat different perspective. On the basis of his work with adolescent suicide attempters and their families, he sees the suicide attempt as a symptom of disturbed family dynamics. In particular, these crises appear to revolve around handling of aggressive feelings within the family and with disturbed family role-relationships. He concludes that the therapy must involve the entire family as the patient, not simply the adolescent who manifested the suicide attempt.

Electro-Convulsive Therapy

The use of electro-convulsive therapy (ECT) is a highly controversial matter. Fawcett maintains that ECT is probably the most effective treatment there is for severe depressions. Furthermore, Moss and Hamilton reported that with the advent of ECT, suicidal attempts by disturbed hospital patients are one-tenth as frequent, that the use of ECT significantly shortens the acute phase, and that productive psychotherapy can thus begin at an earlier stage. Toolan, however, states that depressed children and adolescents, in contrast to adults, usually do not benefit from ECT therapy. Schechter objects to the use of ECT in treating children. He believes that it destroys the chances of the therapist to form an adequate relationship with the child. Even its advocates agree that electro-convulsive therapy does not have long-term effectiveness, and is highly objectionable to many groups. For these reasons, the anti-depressive drugs are now much more heavily relied upon than ECT.

Chemotherapy

Several authors report on the successful use of anti-depressive drugs in treating young people. Faigel mentions the iminodibenzyl group, and Lawler, et al. suggest imipramine for the treatment of depression in children. Phenothiazine drugs have been cited as useful for relieving the anxiety associated with suicidal activity and for the treatment of suicidal behavior associated with schizophrenia. Lawler also suggests chlorpromazine and trifluoperazine as antipsychotic drugs (the former to control agitation and the latter for suppression of frightening hallucinations).

Shaw and Schelkun state that mood-elevating drugs seem to be ineffective in children, but may prove helpful in older adolescents. They also declare that authorities "are unanimous in condemning the use of barbiturates for the potentially suicidal patient." Even the best of the psychopharmacological agents are not considered to be the final answer since the general belief is that medication is not as effective in children as in adults, and that medication alone is not effective treatment—only psychotherapy for both the child and his family can lead to a permanent cure.

Nonpsychiatric Approaches

In less dangerous cases, where neither hospitalization, chemotherapy, nor extensive psychotherapy is indicated, family physicians and public health nurses can be valuable sources of treatment.

Many young people can be treated adequately by an alert and interested family physician or pediatrician. Discussiohs should be held not only with a youngster but also with the parents. These discussions should be directed towards the patient's conflicts, his emotional and social problems, his preoccupations with school, peers and sex, and any other difficulties which may become apparent. If the physician then finds a deep-seated emotional disturbance, psychiatric care can be recommended.

Powers, also, comments on the role of the physician in treating young people for suicidal behavior. He contends that any doctor who is willing to listen to a child, accept him, and try to understand him, can provide the proper supportive setting. Powers suggests that it helps the physician to create this supportive setting if he starts with a thorough physical examination. He believes this examination reassures the patient, reduces his tension, and is conducive to an atmosphere of hope and understanding. Once a positive relationship is established, the factors contributing to the child's suicidal activity can be discussed and their relative importance assessed. The physician should point out positive values and points of strength to the patient, thereby assisting the child in mobilizing and integrating his strength so that he can better meet his stresses.

Teicher and Jacobs call attention to the unique position of the physician to recognize early symptoms of potential suicidal behavior and to provide a source of help for young people before this behavior becomes serious. An adolescent views a doctor as someone who is readily accessible, and as one of the few people in whom he can confide freely. He may seek out a doctor as the last possible resource for help in resolving his problems. It is emphasized, therefore, that a physician should listen to the complaints of adolescents sympathetically, and be ready to respond to warning signs of suicidal thoughts.

Jacobziner discusses the contribution of public health nurses in the treatment of suicidal behavior. He has found that in New York City the public health nurse was the logical person to make home visits. She had an intimate knowledge of the existing community resources, of the cultural and social characteristics, and diverse customs and traditions of the residents of the city. Public health nurses are also capable of establishing rapport with families easily. In fact, Jacobziner notes, families tend to accept visits from public health nurses more readily than from any other member of the health professions. The nurse can explain the emotional and social development of adolescents to their families, and can make follow-up visits to provide further guidance. Furthermore, she can help the families with health problems and, if necessary, she is in a position to recommend and make referrals for psychiatric treatment.

Finally, the most succinct and probably the most difficult prescription for treatment of the self-destructive adolescent was advanced by Shneidman. Department from traditional methods, he proposed that the best theapy was to indulge the adolescent, to "cater to his wants and to help him fulfill his emotional life." Moreover, he states, the problem should not be seen as an individual conflict, but as the expression of a family disturbance, since one does not encounter a disturbed, suicidal adolescent without also finding a disturbed, destructive family. Parents as well as child, need a great deal of help.

In this connection, various suggestions relating to the patient's home environment have been made:

1. Before the patient leaves the hospital, his family and community must be prepared for his return home, and acceptance into his family must be assured.

2. Destructive environmental factors should be corrected. Family conflicts must be resolved, school-load reduced, and all other serious stresses removed, if possible. If the patient is seriously suicidal, a major change in his environment is usually required.

3. If a child's home-life cannot be changed, it may be necessary to remove him from the damaging environment. This can be done by placing him with relatives, in a boarding school or foster home, or returning him to the hospital.

PREVENTION

The primary aim of suicide prevention is the identification and treatment of the presuicidal individual which leads to the ultimate goal, the saving of lives. Unfortunately, it is not always possible to prevent suicide at this primary level. However, preventive efforts can be directed at different levels with different objectives.

At the secondary level, during the acute period of suicidal crisis, the aim is to help the individual deal with his conflicts by providing adequate treatment and crisis-intervention services and to prevent further suicidal behavior. At the tertiary level, after a suicidal crisis has occurred, the program shifts to the survivors who must cope with the stigma and shame that accrues to the family and even to friends and acquaintances of the suicidal individual. The aim at this level is to help the survivors to live with the condemnatory attitudes of the community as well as to work through the personal feelings of grief and guilt which invariably accompany suicide.

Primary Level

It is now well established that the suicidal person gives many clues regarding his suicidal intentions. Most people who kill themselves give definite warnings of their plans. The first step in preventing suicide is the recognition of these warning signs.

Otto in an effort to identify a specific presuicidal syndrome, first searched the literature for recorded opinions on the subject. He found that most investigations of this problem only concerned adults, and that they were not able to define a specific presuicidal syndrome. Otto then reviewed psychiatric material on 581 cases of children and adolescents in Sweden who attempted suicide in order to detect changes in behavior during a 3 month period preceding the attempt. He concluded from his study that a specific presuicidal syndrome does not exist in children and adolescents. The most common changes consisted of depressive and neurotic symptoms, such as anxiety, insomnia, anorexia, and psychosomatic symptoms. These presuicidal depressive and neurotic symptoms correspond to the findings of other recent studies of suicidal youth.

Balser and Masterson, however, describe reactions which contrast markedly to those described above. They assert that schizophrenic symptoms are much more common in adolescents than depressive symptoms. They describe a presuicidal adolescent as one who is delusional in varying degrees and spends much time in fantasy activity. These adolescents may not show anxiety, sleeping and eating disturbances, nor any of the typical symptoms of depressive reactions.

Literature review indicates that rather than just one particular type of presuicidal syndrome, all kinds of prodromal signs have been reported. As an example, the following prodromal signs have been compiled.

Changes in Behavior Preceding an Attempt

Eating disturbances or loss of appetite (anorexia), psychosomatic complaints, insomnia, withdrawn or rebellious behavior, neglect of school work, inability or unwillingness to communicate, promiscuity, use of alcohol or drugs, truancy or running away, neglect of personal appearance, loss of weight, sudden changes in personality, difficulty in concentration.

Related Psychodynamic Factors

Repressed anger, sex anxieties, deflated self-image or self-depreciation, irritability, outbursts of temper, hostility, hallucinations, hypersensitivity, hypersuggestibility, low frustration tolerance, despondency.

Other Related Characteristics

Broken home or disorganized family life, lack of friends, extreme parent-child conflict, long history of problems and a period of escalation of problems, death or loss of parent or other important person, accident-proneness, chronic disease or deformity, a clinical evaluation of depression or schizophrenia.

Despite the multiplicity of prodromal factors there is widespread agreement with one explicit point made by Jacobziner and by Shneidman, among others. That is, that all suicidal behavior must be taken seriously. Even mere threats or seeming gestures should not be ignored.

Parents have the main responsibility for raising children in such a way that they will not resort to suicidal behavior as a "solution" for problems. Beeley considered suicide as a form of evasion or escape from crises. His answer to the problem was not to avoid conflict but to teach children early in life how to meet inevitable crises intelligently. Recently, Shaw and Schelkun have returned to this same theme: A child must learn to live with his conflicts.

Jacobziner suggested that parents be better educated to understand the needs of adolescents and the psychodynamics of adolescence if they were to prevent suicidal behavior in their children.

A simpler and more direct way to reduce the number of suicide attempts would be to persuade parents to make guns and poisons inaccessible to their children. Since some authors believe that suicide attempts in adolescents tend to be spontaneous, impulsive actions, they suggest that the lack of immediate access to these two methods would be enough to prevent many of these supposedly impulsive actions.

Expanding preventive efforts into the school setting, Jan-Tausch recommends ways that public schools could help to prevent suicide:

1. Remedial reading courses should be made available, because there seems to be a correlation between poor reading and emotional distress.
2. Children should be encouraged to participate in extra-curricular activities, as a deterrent to withdrawal and isolation.
3. Schools should encourage more personalized teacher-pupil relationships.
4. Counselors should try to see that all pupils have at least one friend or confidant.
5. Guidance counselors should begin counseling children instead of performing administrative duties as a "way up the ladder."

Munter makes the following recommendations for colleges:

1. Close personal contact between students, faculty, and administrators.
2. Provision of counseling and treatment facilities.
3. Training of faculty and physicians in student health services to recognize prodromal signs, particularly of depression.
4. Encouraging an atmosphere in which emotional difficulties are accepted and support is provided to students.

Shoben in a report of the U.S. National Student Association Conference on Student Stress (1965) summarizes the conference's recommendations to minimize academic stress as follows:

1. Increase the relevance of education to the modern world.
2. Encourage more authentic and personalized student-faculty relationships.
3. Revise the campus community from an adversary atmosphere to a cooperative one by allowing greater student participation within decision-making bodies.

Farnsworth states that the prognosis of students contemplating suicide is good if treatment is obtained. He provides the following suggestions for college psychiatrists:

1. Suspect suicidal preoccupations or actions in anyone who is depressed and anxious.
2. Make it clear to a student that he is free to talk about his feelings without any action being taken against him.

3. Develop a warm and accepting relationship with students suspected of suicidal thoughts.
4. Keep lines of communication open at all times from him to a source of help.
5. Notify parent or next of kin if suicidal signs become ominous.

Finally, Paffenbarger and Asnes, on the basis of their research proposed that the appropriate guidance by college agencies might provide a substitute for the paternal deprivation which influenced male college suicides.

In connection with student populations, Cohen has a few suggestions for proper education about drug use: Make accurate information available; make sure the sources are credible; and provide information about alternatives. Only in this way, he concludes, can attitudes toward drugs be changed.

On a community level, Jacobziner advocates providing a greater concentration of health services in deprived areas where many of the potential suicides live.

Efforts could be made by communities to disseminate information about how to recognize warning signs and where to go for help. Shneidman proposes using all the media—TV, newspapers, billboards, and even signs in public toilets—for providing this information. Concise and inexpensive pamphlets are also useful as a guide for parents, teachers, family doctors, ministers, youth leaders, and others who come into contact with adolescents. . . .

Suicide prevention in an unusual setting is described by Dizmang in his study of young people on the Cheyenne reservation. At present, the VISTA workers, the clergy, the Community Health Workers (Cheyenne who have received special training in public health practices and practical nursing) are the major sources of help used by the Cheyenne youngsters. These three groups have been alerted to watch for cries for help, so that referrals can be made to the Public Health Service. An effort is now being made to help young Cheyenne function in the "white man's world." Through the Neighborhood Youth Corps, the adolescents learn

regular work habits, and gain approval of the tribe by learning how to improve the reservation. Dizmang comments that response to this program has been "overwhelmingly positive." But the larger problem, he says, will be one of "community organization, through which the latent internal resources of these young people could be tapped, and a cultural process of self-renewal rather than self-destruction begun."

Secondary Level

The measures useful at the level of secondary prevention have been discussed previously in the section on treatment. These methods are used during the period when the suicidal tendencies have become apparent, but the person has not yet become a suicide. They include hospitalization, medication, psychotherapy, and environmental intervention.

One topic not yet covered is that of crisis-intervention. That is, methods which deal with the crisis while it is in progress. This is one of the main purposes of a suicide prevention center. Operating around the clock, the center is always available to desperate people. The center attempts to find out what is bothering the person, provides reassurance that solutions can be found, and makes referrals to appropriate community agencies. The goal during this acute phase is not solution of the person's problems, but rather to provide immediate relief and hope since the suicidal mood is usually a temporary state. Thus, the suicide prevention center is primarily directed toward averting the immediate crisis, which then allows time for providing long-term solutions to the person's problems.

Suicide prevention centers in this country are developing rapidly. There are, in 1969, over 100 such centers throughout the nation and the number is increasing annually. As part of this movement, the federal government in 1966 established as part of the National Institute of Mental Health, a Center for Studies of Suicide Prevention. The Center acts as a catalyst for research, training, and community services, and as a guiding force for the development of the newly created, interdisciplinary, field of "suicidology."

Tertiary Level

Tertiary prevention refers to efforts made after a suicide has occurred. It involves working with the survivors of the person who committed suicide—especially those survivors who are children or adolescents.

Appropriate to the idea of tertiary prevention are several articles dealing with children's reactions to the death of a parent.

Keeler examined eleven children (ages 6–14) who were admitted to hospital after the death of a parent. He found depression in all eleven cases; along with such serious symptoms as fantasies of reunion with the dead parent, visual and auditory hallucinations, and development of conversion hysterias. Of particular significance was the report of suicidal attempts and preoccupations in six of the 11 children. Cain and Fast studied 45 "disturbed" children (ages 4–14) whose reactions had been caused by the suicide of a parent. Their disturbances were attributed to guilt derived from 1) pre-existing hostile fantasies toward the suiciding parent; 2) feelings of blame for the parent's despair; 3) their inability to prevent the suicide. Cain and Fast found that there had been no opportunity for the children to get relief from these feelings of guilt because of distorted communications regarding the parental suicide. The stigma surrounding suicide had led the surviving parent to do such things as completely deny the fact of the suicide, or to give differing accounts of the death at different times. Lastly, Sugaya reports the case history of a child whose father hanged himself. She was placed in a foster family, where she later became emotionally autistic and behaved bizarrely.

One of the few published studies in the area of postvention or tertiary prevention consisted of interviews with the parents of adolescents who had committed suicide. These interviews occurred from 2 months to 2 years after the suicide deaths. The experiences and recommendations of the investigations may be summarized as follows:

PARENTAL RESPONSE

1. Overwhelming hostility directed towards essentially neutral parties such as medical examiners, physicians, hospital attendants, etc. and denial of suicide claiming that it was an accidental death or other non-suicidal death. It was felt that these unresolved emotions led to later feelings of guilt, depression, and failure as parents.
2. Due to the stigma parents were unable to derive the usual social benefits of working through their grief by talking to others about their children's death. In fact, it was felt that the parents rarely were able to talk even with one another about this event.
3. Parents would have appreciated professional help at the time of the suicide in order to deal with their feelings of grief, mourning and bewilderment.

RECOMMENDATIONS

1. Followup interviews in *all* families where a suicide occurs.
2. This function to be performed by mental health personnel operating on an official basis e.g. through the coroner's office.
3. Early contact in the first few hours after a death occurs.
4. It was concluded that the interviews had therapeutic and cathartic value for the parents and serve as a first step toward an eventual psychological resynthesis and the prevention of subsequent suicides and related mental disorders among the survivors.

Though little work has been published on the subject of tertiary prevention, the lack of studies is by no means commensurate with the importance of the subject. The problem is one of extreme significance for it is quite likely that as Shneidman has indicated, positive preventive efforts in this area will "head off the schizophrenias of the next generation."

QUESTIONS FOR DISCUSSION

1. Compare the way in which Shneidman and Seiden approach their discussions of suicidal behavior. Discuss differences and similarities you detect.
2. Discuss with several of your college friends "the special case of student suicides" noted in Seiden's article. Do they accept his explanation? Did your friends mention additional factors not discussed by Seiden?
3. In what ways do the demands and expectations of contemporary American society affect rates of suicide?
4. Examine recent newspaper accounts of suicides. Are the impressions gained in these types of descriptions consistent or inconsistent with those obtained from the articles in this book? Classify reports of suicide in mass media publications according to the schema presented by Shneidman. Which types predominate?
5. Interview randomly a dozen or so persons, focusing on their theory of suicide. How do their definitions compare with those presented in the articles by Seiden and Shneidman?
6. Adolescent suicide is the second leading cause of death among young people. Why is this the case?
7. Discuss Durkheim's typology of suicide.
8. Menninger, following the psychoanalytic tradition, speaks of suicide as consisting of three components: the wish to kill, to be killed, and to die. Discuss this position and contrast it to the Durkheim view.
9. How effective are suicide prevention bureaus? Spend some time, if you can, listening to the "cries for help" received over the phones at suicide prevention bureaus. How would you classify these calls? How would you respond?

BIBLIOGRAPHY

Cain, Albert C. *Survivors of Suicide.* Springfield, Ill.: Charles C. Thomas, 1972.

Douglas, Jack D. *The Social Meanings of Suicide.* Princeton: Princeton University Press, 1967.

Dublin, Louis I. *Suicide: A Sociological and Statistical Study.* New York: Ronald Press, 1963.

Durkheim, Emile. *Suicide.* Glencoe: The Free Press, 1951.

Friedman, P., ed. *On Suicide.* New York: International Universities Press, 1967.

Gibbs, J. P., and Martin, W. T. *Status Integration and Suicide.* Eugene, Oregon: Oregon University Press, 1964.

Henry, A. F., and Short, J. F. *Suicide and Homicide.* Glencoe, Ill.: Free Press, 1954.

Iga, M. "Cultural Factors in Suicide of Japanese Youth with Focus on Personality." *Sociology and Social Research* 46 No. 1 (1961), 75–90.

Kubie, Lawrence S. "Multiple Determinants of Suicidal Efforts." *The Journal of Neurosis and Mental Disease* 138 (1964), 3–8.

Lester, David. *Why People Kill Themselves: A Summary of Research Findings on Suicidal Behavior.* Springfield, Ill.: Charles C. Thomas, 1972.

Maris, Ronald W. *Social Forces in Urban Suicide.* Illinois: Dorsey Press, 1969.

Menninger, Karl. *Man Against Himself.* New York: Harcourt, Brace, 1938.

Newman, John F., Whittemore, Kenneth R., and Newman, Helen G. "Women in the Labor Force and Suicide.' *Social Problems* 21 No. 2 (Fall 1973), 220–30.

Seiden, R. H. "Campus tragedy: A study of student suicide." *Journal of Abnormal Psychology* 71 No. 6 (1966), 389–99.

Shneidman, Edwin S. "The Logic of Suicide." In Shneidman, Edwin S. *Clues to Suicide.* New York: McGraw-Hill, 1957.

Shneidman, Edwin S., and Farberow, Normal L. "A Socio-Psychological Investigation of Suicide." In David, Henry P. and Brengelmann, J. C. eds. *Perspectives in Personality Research.* New York: Basic Books, 1960.

Stengel, Erwin, and Cook, Nancy G. *Attempted Suicide.* London: Chapman and Hall, 1958.

Stengel, E. *Suicide and Attempted Suicide.* Baltimore: Penguin, 1964.

Trautman, E. "Drug Abuse and Suicide Attempt of An Adolescent Girl.' *Adolescence* 1 No. 4 (1966), 381–92.

Tuckman, J., Youngman, W. F., and Leifer, Betty. "Suicide and Family Disorganization." *International Journal of Social Psychiatry* 12 No. 3 (1966), 187–91.

V

INNOVATIONS IN MANAGEMENT, CONTROL, AND TREATMENT

The prison is a moral hospital; the inmates morally diseased. It is the duty of the prison to cure.

Gideon Hays
Massachusetts Warden, 1868

Criminals collected together corrupt each other.

Napoleon

Is guilt on the way out?

Nicholas N. Kittrie

Who will be controled? Who will exercise control? What type of control will be exercised? Most important of all, toward what end or what purpose, in the pursuit of what values, will control be exercised?

C. R. Rogers

... one of these days, we are going to pick up the morning paper and learn that Prostitutes Anonymous has been incorporated ...

Edward Sagarin

Law is—or should be—a device for serving basic human needs.

Richard C. Allen

Criminology may be said to have addressed itself over the years first to the crime, then to the offender and only relatively recently ... to the victim.

Donal E. J. MacNamara and
John J. Sullivan

Contemporary inmates are much more politically sophisticated and organizationally inclined.

C. Ronald Huff

Reform is not a rational and deliberate process.

Elmer Johnson

The problems of narcotics traffic and addiction ... transcend geographical, philosophical and political differences.

U.S. Senate Committee

Medications are able to prevent, or at least delay, psychotic episodes. It remains for psychiatric or social care to prevent the social deterioration of patients.

Ann Davis, *et al*

What monuments to stupidity are these institutions we have built . . .

John L. Gillin

It is part of the cure to wish to be cured.

Seneca

12
The Rise and Fall of Total Institutions

In 1790, or thereabouts, the then fledgling states in the United States discovered or invented the total institution—the prison, the mental hospital, the state school for retardates, the workhouse, the orphanage, and the poorhouse—as a more humane way of managing the human debris spawned by the breakdown of the major social institutions responding to the silent revolutions. The motivation was religious as the Quakers assumed "moral treatment" superior to the retributive justice (punishment, banishment, indenture, and the even harsher penalties) of the past. The motivation was also the product of the Enlightenment and the doctrines of Rousseau and Locke and of Beccaria and Bentham concerning the nature of man. Above all, the motivation in creating these total institutions was clearly pragmatic. The burgeoning American cities and the emerging middle class could no longer tolerate the threat posed by the deviant, disruptive, and dependent members of the community.

In unprecedented and even unseemly haste, one state after another constructed total institutions for their misfits. Initially small and homelike (based on the family model and the well ordered, religious, and moral life style), the total institutions soon grew in size. Among other things, big institutions are cheaper to operate, per capita, than smaller ones. In addition, respectability could best be maintained by building the ever larger institutions at even greater distances from the cities. Surely, the fresh air, unpolluted atmosphere, and extensive agricultural opportunities for the "inmates," "patients," "wards," would be salutary in every way. So the immoral and corrupting influences of bad friends, broken homes, poverty, and other environmental handicaps were left far behind as the state and private philanthropic agencies vied with one another in providing "moral" and humane treatment.

The illusions of the religionists, secular reformers and the fiscally pragmatic were soon destroyed. The deviant—prisoner, lunatic (as he was called), retardate, alcoholic—seemed peculiarly immune to the well-meant blandishments to reform, to seek salvation, to become contributing members of society. "Moral" treatment soon failed (in part because it was never really implemented), as had its predecessors such as calculated retribution, punishment, expiation, and the cruel and unusual measures of the past. As one national or local crisis succeeded another (much as we ourselves experience), the total institution lost even the interest of the reformers. Fifty years after its inception, it had become the backwater of society and economically vital in an increasingly divided country which could hardly care less.

A short time after the Civil War, agitation

began anew for the reform of every type of total institution. The concepts of humane and moral treatment (and the protection of the deviant from the harsh society embodied in the idea of the "asylum") began to be replaced by the concept of rehabilitation. Thus, the National Prison Association held its first meeting in 1870 and issued a manifesto called the Declaration of Principles advocating reformation (rehabilitation), the indeterminate sentence and inmate classification among others. In the mental health and retardation fields the agitation came a little later, with Dorothea Dix and Clifford Beers blasting the inhumanity of the state mental hospital eventuating in the National Mental Health Association—an organization of mostly laymen compared to the professionals in the American Correctional Association.

In corrections, prison riots and reformer zeal eventually brought psychologists, social workers, educators (both academic and vocational), counselors, and even an occasional psychiatrist inside the walls. In juvenile institutions, cottage parents and recreational specialists were also introduced. Both at the adult and juvenile levels, these treatment personnel often faced the outright hostility of guards (correctional officers) setting up a textbook case of three-way conflict—inmate, professional, custodial. This big push came in the 1930's when various programs were introduced to help "rehabilitate" the offender population. But the recidivism (repeater) rates stayed high (60 to 70 percent and maybe even higher), and treatment lost its appeal on empirical as well as conceptual grounds. The riots beginning in the 1950's and continuing to the present, combined with the crime in the streets issue and the racial protest and conflict of the late 1960's, all played a role in destroying the myth of rehabilitation in both juvenile and adult corrections. In its stead, inmates, professionals, and reformers alike are agreed that fairness rather than rehabilitation should be the goal. The rehabilitation ideal is, they contend, an impossibility in the penal setting.

With modifications appropriate to the deviance, nearly everyone now agrees that

the mental hospital (asylum) is antitherapeutic in the same sense that the prison is antirehabilitative. In mental health and retardation, the major innovations were prompted by the psychodynamic movement which caught on in the United States in the 1920's. Later came the therapeutic milieu concepts adopted from Maxwell Jones' work in England which brought minor changes in the total institutions in the 1940's, but major changes in the smaller, private mental health settings. The return of the G.I.'s in 1945–46 forced major alterations in the Veteran Administration hospitals for neuropsychiatrically disturbed former servicemen. Some of these improvements eventually filtered down into the state hospital settings. Finally, in the 1950's, psychoactive drugs were introduced which made it possible, even desirable, to return as many patients as possible (well over one-third) to community outpatient care facilities.

Whether in corrections, mental health, alcoholism, drug abuse, or mental retardation, the notions of rehabilitation and cure have been replaced by management, control, the right (but not the obligation) to get "treatment," the right to be left alone (abortion, homosexuality), the right to justice. It is to these issues that this section of the book is devoted.

In this chapter we will present four important selections on the total institution. In the first, Erving Goffman describes the dynamics of total institutions and their impact on those who are the inmates. All total institutions for deviants have certain important elements in common: the removal of barriers separating various spheres of life, a single authority system, lack of privacy, regimentation, explicit formal rules and all manner of restrictions, and an unbridgeable gulf between the managed and the managers. The total institution must somehow strip the new admission of his "presenting culture" and subsequently endow him with a modified (hospital, prison) culture and self. This process is called mortification by Goffman (degradation by Garfinkel) and is described in some detail in the essay.

The second selection entitled, "State of Prisons in the United States: 1870–1970" is by that grand old man of penology, Negley K. Teeters, recently deceased. Teeters was a moving force for prison reform throughout his long life, and his work reflects both his academic and social activist concerns. The essay concerns the ebb and flow of prison innovation in the last century and ends on something of a pessimistic note.

John P. Conrad in "Corrections and Simple Justice" provides informed and eloquent testimony on conditions up until the end of the rehabilitation era. He traces the theory that prisons reform and produce better—or at least not more intractable men—and dates its demise to, on, or about the year 1970. One of the best known and able penologists in the United States, having worked his way up from parole officer to Chief of Research in California, and later to important positions in both the United States Bureau of Prisons and the Law Enforcement Assistance Administration, John Conrad is convinced that prisons must give way to community-oriented alternatives. He is especially vigorous in his support of Jerome Miller who closed all juvenile institutions in Massachusetts in 1972. If there is one profound theme that deserves special attention in this essay, it is that compliance through coercion is not rehabilitation.

At a different level, the eminent Chief Judge of the United States Court of Appeals for the District of Columbia Circuit, David L. Bazelon, reaches some of the same conclusions regarding the juvenile field. In his address, "Juvenile Justice: A Love-Hate Story," given in honor of Judge Justice Wise Polier on the occasion of her retirement from the New York Family Court, Judge Bazelon argues that the juvenile justice system cannot undo the damage inflicted from birth on the disprivileged in society. To him, rehabilitation means prevention, and the latter demands the elimination of disadvantage and its scarring effects on the self and on behavior.

CHARACTERISTICS OF TOTAL INSTITUTIONS

Erving Goffman

INTRODUCTION

Total Institutions

Every institution captures something of the time and interest of its members and provides something of a world for them; in brief, every institution has encompassing tendencies. When we review the different institutions in our Western society we find a class of them which seems to be encompassing to a degree discontinuously greater than the ones next in line. Their encompassing or

From *Symposium on Preventive and Social Psychiatry*, Walter Reed Medical Center, Washington, D.C., U.S. Government Printing Office, April 15–17, 1957, pp. 43–84. Professor Goffman is in the Department of Sociology at the University of Pennsylvania.

total character is symbolized by the barrier to social intercourse with the outside that is often built right into the physical plant: locked doors, high walls, barbed wire, cliffs and water, open terrain, and so forth. These I am calling total institutions, and it is their general characteristics I want to explore. This exploration will be phrased as if securely based on findings but will in fact be speculative.

The total institutions of our society can be listed for convenience in five rough groupings. *First,* there are institutions established to care for persons thought to be both incapable and harmless; these are the homes for the blind, the aged, the orphaned, and the indigent. *Second,* there are places established to care for persons thought to be at once incapable of looking after themselves and a threat to the community, albeit an unintended one: TB sanitoriums, mental hospitals, and leprosoriums. *Third,* another type of total institution is organized to protect the community against what are thought to be intentional dangers to it; here the welfare of the persons thus sequestered is not the immediate issue. Examples are: Jails, penitentiaries, POW camps, and concentration camps. *Fourth,* we find institutions purportedly established the better to pursue some technical task and justifying themselves only on these instrumental grounds: Army barracks, ships, boarding schools, work camps, colonial compounds, large mansions from the point of view of those who live in the servants' quarters, and so forth. *Finally,* there are those establishments designed as retreats from the world or as training stations for the religious: Abbeys, monasteries, convents, and other cloisters. This sublisting of total institutions is neither neat nor exhaustive, but the listing itself provides an empirical starting point for a purely denotative definition of the category. By anchoring the initial definition of total institutions in this way, I hope to be able to discuss the general characteristics of the type without becoming tautological.

Before attempting to extract a general profile from this list of establishments, one conceptual peculiarity must be mentioned. None of the elements I will extract seems entirely exclusive to total institutions, and none seems shared by every one of them. What is shared and unique about total institutions is that each exhibits many items in this family of attributes to an intense degree. In speaking of "common characteristics," than, I will be using this phrase in a weakened, but I think logically defensible, way.

Totalistic Features

A basic social arrangement in modern society is that we tend to sleep, play and work in different places, in each case with a different set of coparticipants, under a different authority, and without an overall rational plan. The central feature of total institutions can be described as a breakdown of the kinds of barriers ordinarily separating these three spheres of life. *First,* all aspects of life are conducted in the same place and under the same single authority. *Second,* each phase of the member's daily activity will be carried out in the immediate company of a large batch of others, all of whom are treated alike and required to do the same thing together. *Third,* all phases of the day's activities are tightly scheduled, with one activity leading at a prearranged time into the next, the whole circle of activities being imposed from above through a system of explicit formal rulings and a body of officials. *Finally,* the contents of the various enforced activities are brought together as parts of a single overall rational plan purportedly designed to fulfill the official aims of the institution.

Individually, these totalistic features are found, of course, in places other than total institutions. Increasingly, for example, our large commercial, industrial and educational establishments provide cafeterias, minor services and off-hour recreation for their members. But while this is a tendency in the direction of total institutions, these extended facilities remain voluntary in many particulars of their use, and special care is taken to see that the ordinary line of authority does not extend to these situations. Similarly, housewives or farm families can find all their major spheres of life within the same fenced-in area, but these persons are not collectively regimented and do not march through the day's steps in the immediate company of a batch of similar others.

The handling of many human needs by the bureaucratic organization of whole blocks of people—whether or not this is a necessary or effective means of social organization in the circumstances—can be taken, then, as the key fact of total institutions. From this, certain important implications can be drawn.

Given the fact that blocks of people are caused to move in time, it becomes possible to use a relatively small number of supervisory personnel where the central relationship is not guidance or periodic checking, as in many employer-employee relations, but rather surveillance—a seeing to it that everyone does what he has been clearly told is required of him, and this under conditions where one person's infraction is likely to stand out in relief against the visible, constantly examined, compliance of the others. . . .

In total institutions . . . there is a basic split between a large class of individuals who live in and who have restricted contact with the world outside the walls, conveniently called *inmates,* and the small class that supervises them, conveniently called staff, who often operate on an 8-hour day and are socially integrated into the outside world. Each grouping tends to conceive of members of the other in terms of narrow hostile stereotypes, staff often seeing inmates as bitter, secretive and untrustworthy, while inmates often see staff as condescending, highhanded and mean. Staff tends to feel superior and righteous; inmates tend, in some ways at least, to feel inferior, weak, blameworthy and guilty. Social mobility between the two strata is grossly restricted; social distance is typically great and often formally prescribed; even talk across the boundaries may be conducted in a special tone of voice. These restrictions on contact presumably help to maintain the antagonistic stereotypes. In any case, two different social and cultural worlds develop, tending to jog along beside each other, with points of official contact but little mutual penetration. It is important to add that the institutional plan and name comes to be identified by both staff and inmates as somehow belonging to staff, so that when either grouping refers to the views or interests of "the institution," by implication they are referring to the views and concerns of the staff.

The staff-inmate split is one major implication of the central features of total institutions; a second one pertains to work. In the ordinary arrangements of living in our society, the authority of the workplace stops with the worker's receipt of a money payment; the spending of this in a domestic and recreational setting is at the discretion of the worker and is the mechanism through which the authority of the workplace is kept within strict bounds. However, to say that inmates in total institutions have their full day scheduled for them is to say that some version of all basic needs will have to be planned for, too. In other words, total institutions take over "responsibility" for the inmate and must guarantee to have everything that is defined as essential "layed on.' It follows, then, that whatever incentive is given for work, this will not have the structural significance it has on the outside. Different attitudes and incentives regarding this central feature of our life will have to prevail.

Here, then, is one basic adjustment required of those who work in total institutions and of those who must induce these people to work. In some cases, no work or little is required, and inmates, untrained often in leisurely ways of life, suffer extremes of boredom. In other cases, some work is required but is carried on at an extremely slow pace, being geared into a system of minor, often ceremonial payments, as in the case of weekly tobacco ration and annual Christmas presents, which cause some mental patients to stay on their job. In some total institutions, such as logging camps and merchant ships, something of the usual relation to the world that money can buy is obtained through the practice of "forced saving"; all needs are organized by the institution, and payment is given only after a work season is over and the men leave the premises. And in some total institutions, of course, more than a full day's work is required and is induced not by reward, but by threat of dire punishment. In all such cases, the work-oriented individual may tend to become somewhat demoralized by the system.

In addition to the fact that total institutions are incompatible with the basic work-payment structure of our society, it must be seen that these establishments are also incompatible with another crucial element of our society, the family. The family is sometimes contrasted to solitary living, but in fact the more pertinent contrast to family life might be with batch [block] living. For it seems that those who eat and sleep at work, with a group of fellow workers, can hardly sustain a meaningful domestic existence. Correspondingly, the extent to which a staff retains its integration in the outside community and escapes the encompassing tendencies of total institutions is often linked up with the maintenance of a family off the grounds.

Whether a particular total institution acts as a good or bad force in civil society, force it may well have, and this will depend on the suppression of a whole circle of actual or potential households. Conversely, the formation of households provides a structural guarantee that total institutions will not arise. The incompatibility between these two forms of social organization should tell us, then, something about the wider social functions of them both.

Total institutions, then, are social hybrids, part residential community, part formal organization, and therein lies their special sociological interest. There are other reasons, alas, for being interested in them, too. These establishments are the forcing houses for changing persons in our society. Each is a natural experiment, typically harsh, on what can be done to the self.

Having suggested some of the key features of total institutions, we can move on now to consider them from the special perspectives that seem natural to take. I will consider the inmate world, then the staff world, and then something about contacts between the two.

THE INMATE WORLD

Mortification Processes

It is characteristic of inmates that they come to the institution as members, already full-fledged, of a *home world,* that is, a way of life and a round of activities taken for granted up to the point of admission to the institution. It is useful to look at this culture that the recruit brings with him to the institution's door—his *presenting culture,* to modify a psychiatric phrase—in terms especially designed to highlight what it is the total institution will do to him. Whatever the stability of his personal organization, we can assume it was part of a wider supporting framework lodged in his current social environment, a round of experience that somewhat confirms a conception of self that is somewhat acceptable to him and a set of defensive maneuvers exercisable at his own discretion as a means of coping with conflicts, discreditings and failures.

Now it appears that total institutions do not substitute their own unique culture for something already formed. We do not deal with acculturation or assimilation but with something more restricted than these. In a sense, total institutions do not look for cultural victory. They effectively create and sustain a particular kind of tension between the home world and the institutional world and use this persistent tension as strategic leverage in the management of men. The full meaning for the inmate of being "in" or "on the inside" does not exist apart from the special meaning to him of "getting out" or "getting on the outside."

The recruit comes into the institution with a self and with attachments to supports which had allowed this self to survive. Upon entrance, he is immediately stripped of his wonted supports, and his self is systematically, if often unintentionally, mortified. In the accurate language of some of our oldest total institutions, he is led into a series of abasements, degradations, humiliations, and profanations of self. He begins, in other words, some radical shifts in his *moral career,* a career laying out the progressive changes that occur in the beliefs that he has concerning himself and significant others.

The *stripping processes* through which *mortification of the self* occurs are fairly standard in our total institutions. Personal identity equipment is removed, as well as other possessions with which the inmate may have identified himself, there typically being a system of nonaccessible storage from which the inmate can only reobtain his effects should he leave the institution. As a substitute for what has been taken away, institutional issue is provided, but this will be the same for large categories of inmates and will be regularly repossessed by the institution. In brief, standardized defacement will occur. . . . Family, occupational, and educational career lines are chopped off, and a stigmatized status is submitted. Sources of fantasy materials which had meant momentary releases from stress in the home world are denied. Areas of autonomous decision are eliminated through the process of collective scheduling of daily activity. Many channels of communication with the outside are restricted or closed off completely. Verbal discreditings occur in many forms as a matter of course. Expressive signs of respect for the staff are coercively and continuously demanded. And the effect of each of these conditions is multiplied by having to witness the mortification of one's fellow inmates. . . .

In the background of the sociological stripping process, we find a characteristic authority system with three distinctive elements, each basic to total institutions.

First, to a degree, authority is of the *echelon* kind. Any member of the staff class has certain rights to discipline any member of the inmate class. . . . In our society, the adult himself, however, is typically under the authority of a *single* immediate superior in connection with his work or under authority of one spouse in connection with domestic duties. The only echelon authority he must face—the police—typically are neither constantly nor relevantly present, except perhaps in the case of traffic-law enforcement.

Second, the authority of corrective sanctions is directed to a great multitude of items of conduct of the kind that are constantly occurring and constantly coming up for judgment; in brief, authority is directed to matters of dress, deportment, social intercourse, manners and the like. . . .

The third feature of authority in total institutions is that misbehaviors in one sphere of life are held against one's standing in other spheres. Thus, an individual who fails to participate with proper enthusiasm in sports may be brought to the attention of the person who determines where he will sleep and what kind of work task will be accorded to him.

When we combine these three aspects of authority in total institutions, we see that the inmate cannot easily escape from the press of judgmental officials and from the enveloping tissue of constraint. The system of authority undermines the basis for control that adults in our society expect to exert over their interpersonal environment and may produce the terror of feeling that one is being radically demoted in the age-grading system. On the outside, rules are sufficiently lax and the individual sufficiently agreeable to required self-discipline to insure that others will rarely have cause for pouncing on him. He need not constantly look over his shoulder to see if criticism and other sanctions are coming. On the inside, however, rulings are abundant, novel, and closely enforced so that, quite characteristically, inmates live with chronic anxiety about breaking the rules and chronic worry about the consequences of breaking them. The desire to "stay out of trouble" in a total institution is likely to require persistent conscious effort and may lead the inmate to abjure certain levels of sociability with his fellows in order to avoid the incidents that may occur in these circumstances.

It should be noted finally that the mortifications to be suffered by the inmate may be purposely brought home to him in an exaggerated way during the first few days after entrance, in a form of initiation that has been called *the welcome.* Both staff and fellow inmates may go out of their way to give the neophyte a clear notion of where he stands. As part of this *rite de passage,* he may find himself called by a term such as "fish," "swab," etc., through which older inmates tell him that he is not only merely an inmate but that even within this lowly group he has a low status.

Privilege System

While the process of mortification is in progress, the inmate begins to receive formal and informal instruction in what will here be called the *privilege system.* Insofar as the inmate's self has been unsettled a little by the stripping action of the institution, it is largely around this framework that pressures are exerted, making for a reorganization of self. Three basic elements of the system may be mentioned.

First, there are the house rules, a relatively explicit and formal set of prescriptions and proscriptions which lay out the main requirements of inmate conduct. These regulations spell out the austere round of life in which the inmate will operate. Thus, the admission procedures through which the recruit is initially stripped of his self-supporting context can be seen as the institution's way of getting him in the position to start living by the house rules.

Second, against the stark background, a small number of clearly defined *rewards or privileges* are held out in exchange for obedience to staff in action and spirit. It is important to see that these potential gratifications are not unique to the institution but rather are ones carved out of the flow of support that the inmate previously had quite taken for granted. On the outside, for example, the inmate was likely to be able to unthinkingly exercise autonomy by deciding how much sugar and milk he wanted in his coffee, if any, or when to light up a cigarette; on the inside, this right may become quite problematic and a matter of a great deal of conscious concern. Held up to the inmate as possibilities, these few recapturings seem to have a reintegrative effect, re-establishing relationships with the whole lost world and assuaging withdrawal symptoms from it and from one's lost self.

The inmate's run of attention, then, especially at first, comes to be fixated on these supplies and obsessed with them. In the most fanatic way, he can spend the day in devoted thoughts concerning the possibility of acquiring these gratifications or the approach of the hour at which they are scheduled to be granted. The building of a world around these minor privileges is perhaps the most important feature of inmate culture and yet is something that cannot easily be appreciated by an outsider, even one who has lived through the experience himself. This situation sometimes leads to generous sharing and almost always to a willingness to beg for things such as cigarettes, candy and newspapers. It will be understandable, then, that a constant feature of inmate discussion is the *release binge fantasy,* namely, recitals of what one will do during leave or upon release from the institution.

House rules and privileges provide the functional requirements of the third element in the privilege system: *punishments.* These are designated as the consequence of breaking the rules. One set of these punishments consists of the temporary or permanent withdrawal of privileges or abrogation of the right to try to earn them. In general, the punishments meted out in total institutions are of an order more severe than anything encountered by the inmate in his home world. An institutional arrangement which causes a small number of easily controlled privileges to have a massive significance is the same arrangement which lends a terrible significance to their withdrawal.

There are some special features of the privilege system which should be noted.

First, punishments and privileges are themselves modes of organization peculiar to total institutions.... And privileges, it should be emphasized, are not the same as prerequisites, indulgences or values, but merely the absence of deprivations one ordinarily expects one would not have to sustain. The very notions, then, of punishments and privileges are not ones that are cut from civilian cloth.

Second, it is important to see that the question of release from the total institution is elaborated into the privilege system. Some acts will become known as ones that mean an increase or no decrease in length of stay, while others become known as means for lessening the sentence.

Third, we should also note that punishments and privileges come to be geared into a residential work system. Places to work and places to sleep become clearly defined as places where certain kinds and levels of privilege obtain, and inmates are shifted very rapidly and visibly from one place to another as the mechanisms for giving them the punishment or privilege their cooperativeness has warranted. The inmates are moved, the system is not. . . .

Immediately associated with the privilege system we find some standard social processes important in the life of total institutions.

We find that an *institutional lingo* develops through which inmates express the events that are crucial in their particular world. Staff too, especially its lower levels, will know this language, using it when talking to inmates, while reverting to more standardized speech when talking to superiors and outsiders. Related to this special argot, inmates will possess knowledge of the various ranks and officials, an accumulation of lore about the establishment, and some comparative information about life in other similar total institutions.

Also found among staff and inmates will be a clear awareness of the phenomenon of *messing up,* so called in mental hospitals, prisons, and barracks. This involves a complex process of engaging in forbidden activity, getting caught doing so, and receiving something like the full punishment accorded this. An alteration in privilege status is usually implied and is categorized by a phrase such as "getting busted." Typical infractions which can eventuate in messing up are: fights, drunkenness, attempted suicide, failure at examinations, gambling, insubordination, homosexuality, improper taking of leave, and participation in collective riots. While these punished infractions are typically ascribed to the offender's cussedness, villainy, or "sickness," they do in fact constitute a vocabulary of institutionalized actions, limited in such a way that the same messing up may occur for quite different reasons. Informally, inmates and staff may

understand, for example, that a given messing up is a way for inmates to show resentment against a current situation felt to be unjust in terms of the informal agreements between staff and inmates, or a way of postponing release without having to admit to one's fellow inmates that one really does not want to go.

In total institutions there will also be a system of what might be called *secondary adjustments,* namely, technics which do not directly challenge staff management but which allow inmates to obtain disallowed satisfactions or allowed ones by disallowed means. These practices are variously referred to as: the angles, knowing the ropes, conniving, gimmicks, deals, ins, etc. Such adaptations apparently reach their finest flower in prisons, but of course other total institutions are overrun with them too. It seems apparent that an important aspect of secondary adjustments is that they provide the inmate with some evidence that he is still, as it were, his own man and still has some protective distance, under his own control, between himself and the institution. . . .

The occurrence of secondary adjustments correctly allows us to assume that the inmate group will have some kind of a *code* and some means of informal social control evolved to prevent one inmate from informing staff about the secondary adjustments of another. On the same grounds we can expect that one dimension of social typing among inmates will turn upon this question of security, leading to persons defined as "squealers," "finks," or "stoolies" on one hand, and persons defined as "right guys" on the other. It should be added that where new inmates can play a role in the system of secondary adjustments, as in providing new faction members or new sexual objects, then their "welcome" may indeed be a sequence of initial indulgences and enticements, instead of exaggerated deprivations. Because of secondary adjustments we also find *kitchen strata,* namely, a kind of rudimentary, largely informal, stratification of inmates on the basis of each one's differential access to disposable illicit commodities; so also we find social typing to designate the powerful persons in the informal market system.

While the privilege system provides the chief framework within which reassembly of the self takes place, other factors characteristically lead by different routes in the same general direction. Relief from economic and social responsibilities—much touted as part of the therapy in mental hospitals—is one, although in many cases it would seem that the disorganizing effect of this moratorium is more significant than its organizing effect. More important as a reorganizing influence is the *fraternalization process,* namely, the process through which socially distant persons find themselves developing mutual support and common *counter-mores* in opposition to a system that has forced them into intimacy and into a single, equalitarian community of fate. It seems that the new recruit frequently starts out with something like the staff's popular misconceptions of the character of the inmates and then comes to find that most of his fellows have all the properties of ordinary decent human beings and that the stereotypes associated with their condition or offense are not a reasonable ground for judgment of inmates. . . .

Adaptation Alignments

The mortifying processes that have been discussed and the privilege system represent the conditions that the inmate must adapt to in some way, but however pressing, these conditions allow for different ways of meeting them. We find, in fact, that the same inmate will employ different lines of adaptation or tacks at different phases in his moral career and may even fluctuate between different tacks at the same time.

First, there is the process of *situational withdrawal.* The inmate withdraws apparent attention from everything except events immediately around his body and sees these in a perspective not employed by others present. This drastic curtailment of involvement in interactional events is best known, of course, in mental hospitals, under the title of "regression." . . . I do not think it is known whether this line of adaptation forms a single continuum of varying degrees of withdrawal or whether there are standard discontinuous plateaus of disinvolvement. It does seem to be the case, however, that, given the pressures apparently required to dislodge an inmate from this status, as well as the currently limited facilities for doing so, we frequently find here, effectively speaking, an irreversible line of adaptation.

Second, there is the *rebellious line.* The inmate intentionally challenges the institution by flagrantly refusing to cooperate with staff in almost any way. The result is a constantly communicated intransigency and sometimes high rebel-morale. Most large mental hospitals, for example, seem to have wards where this spirit strongly prevails. Interestingly enough, there are many circumstances in which sustained rejection of a total institution requires sustained orientation to its formal organization and hence, paradoxically, a deep kind of commitment to the establishment.

Third, another standard alignment in the institutional world takes the form of a kind of *colonization.* The sampling of the outside world provided by the establishment is taken by the inmate as the whole, and a stable, relatively contented existence is built up out of the maximum satisfactions procurable within the institution. Experience of the outside world is used as a point of reference to demonstrate the desirability of life on the inside; and the usual tension between the two worlds collapses, thwarting the social arrangements based upon this felt discrepancy. Characteristically, the individual who too obviously takes this line may be accused by his fellow inmates of "having found a home" or of "never having had it so good." Staff itself may become vaguely embarrassed by this use that is being made of the institution, sensing that the benign possibilities in the situation are somehow being misused. Colonizers themselves may feel obliged to deny their satisfaction with the institution, if only in the interest of sustaining the counter-mores supporting inmate solidarity. They may find it necessary to mess up just prior to their slated discharge, thereby allowing themselves to present involuntary reasons for continued incarceration. It should be incidentally noted that any humanistic effort to make life in total institutions more bearable must face the possibility that doing so may increase the attractiveness and likelihood of colonization.

Fourth, one mode of adaptation to the setting of a total institution is that of *conversion.* The inmate appears to take over completely the official or staff view of himself and tries to act out the role of the perfect inmate. While the colonized inmate builds as much of a free community as possible for himself by using the limited facilities available, the convert takes a more disciplined, moralistic, monochromatic line, presenting himself as someone whose institutional enthusiasm is always at the disposal of the staff. . . . Some mental hospitals have the distinction of providing two quite different conversion possibilities—one for the new admission who can see the light after an appropriate struggle and adapt the psychiatric view of himself, and another for the chronic ward patient who adopts the manner and dress of attendants while helping them to manage the other ward patients with a stringency excelling that of the attendants themselves. . . .

While the alignments that have been mentioned represent coherent courses to pursue, few inmates, it seems, carry these pursuits very far. In most total institutions, what we seem to find is that most inmates take the tack of what they call *playing it cool.* This involves a somewhat opportunistic combination of secondary adjustments, conversion, colonization and loyalty to the inmate group, so that in the particular circumstances the inmate will have a maximum chance of eventually getting out physically and psychically undamaged. Typically, the inmate will support the counter-mores when with fellow inmates and be silent to them on

how tractably he acts when alone in the presence of the staff. Inmates taking this line tend to subordinate contacts with their fellows to the higher claim of "keeping out of trouble." They tend to volunteer for nothing, and they may even learn to cut their ties to the outside world sufficiently to give cultural reality to the world inside but not enough to lead to colonization. . . .

Culture Themes

A note should be added here concerning some of the more dominant themes of inmate culture.

First, in the inmate group of many total institutions there is a strong feeling that time spent in the establishment is time wasted or destroyed or taken from one's life; it is time that must be written off. It is something that must be "done" or "marked" or "put in" or "built" or "pulled." . . . As such, this time is something that its doers have bracketed off for constant conscious consideration in a way not quite found on the outside. And as a result, the inmate tends to feel that for the duration of his required stay—his sentence—he has been totally exiled from living. It is in this context that we can appreciate something of the demoralizing influence of an indefinite sentence or a very long one. We should also note that however hard the conditions of life may become in total institutions, harshness alone cannot account for this quality of life wasted. Rather we must look to the social disconnections caused by entrance and to the usual failure to acquire within the institution gains that can be transferred to outside life—gains such as money earned, or marital relations formed, or certified training received.

Second, it seems that in many total institutions a peculiar kind and level of self-concern is engendered. The low position of inmates relative to their station on the outside, as established initially through the mortifying processes, seems to make for a milieu of personal failure and a round of life in which one's fall from grace is continuously pressed home. In response, the inmate tends to develop a story, a line, a sad tale—a kind of lamentation and apologia—which he constantly tells to his fellows as a means of creditably accounting for his present low estate. While staff constantly discredit these lines, inmate audiences tend to employ tact, suppressing at least some of the disbelief and boredom engendered by these recitations. In consequence, the inmate's own self may become even more of a focus for his conversation than it does on the outside.

Perhaps the high level of ruminative self-concern found among inmates in total institutions is a way of handling the sense of wasted time that prevails in these places. If so, then perhaps another interesting aspect of inmate culture can be related to the same factor. I refer here to the fact that in total institutions we characteristically find a premium placed on what might be called *removal activities,* namely, voluntary unserious pursuits which are sufficiently engrossing and exciting to lift the participant out of himself, making [him] oblivious for the time to his actual situation. If the ordinary activities in total institutions can be said to torture time, these activities mercifully kill it.

Some removal activities are collective, such as ball games, woodwork, lectures, choral singing and card playing; some are individual but rely on public materials, as in the case of reading, solitary TV watching, etc. No doubt, private fantasy ought to be included too. Some of these activities may be officially sponsored by staff; and some, not officially sponsored, may constitute secondary adjustments. In any case, there seems to be no total institution which cannot be seen as a kind of Dead Sea in which appear little islands of vivid, enrapturing activity.

Consequences

In this discussion of the inmate world, I have commented on the mortification process, the reorganizing influences, the lines of response taken by inmates under these circumstances, and the cultural milieu that develops. A concluding word must be added

about the long-range consequences of membership.

Total institutions frequently claim to be concerned with rehabilitation, that is, with resetting the inmate's self-regulatory mechanisms so that he will maintain the standards of the establishment of his own accord after he leaves the setting. In fact, it seems this claim is seldom realized and even when permanent alteration occurs, these changes are often not of the kind intended by the staff. With the possible exception presented by the great resocialization efficiency of religious institutions, neither the stripping processes nor the reorganizing ones seem to have a lasting effect. No doubt the availability of secondary adjustments helps to account for this, as do the presence of countermores and the tendency for inmates to combine all strategies and "play it cool." In any case, it seems that shortly after release, the ex-inmate will have forgotten a great deal of what life was like on the inside and will have once again begun to take for granted the privileges around which life in the institution was organized. The sense of injustice, bitterness and alienation, so typically engendered by the inmate's experience and so definitely marking a stage in his moral career, seems to weaken upon graduation, even in those cases where a permanent stigma has resulted.

But what the ex-inmate does retain of his institutional experience tells us important things about total institutions. Often entrance will mean for the recruit that he has taken on what might be called a *proactive status.* Not only is his relative social position within the walls radically different from what it was on the outside, but, as he comes to learn, if and when he gets out, his social position on the outside will never again be quite what it was prior to entrance. . . . When the proactive status is unfavorable, as it is for those in prisons or mental hospitals, we popularly employ the term "stigmatization" and expect that the ex-inmate may make an effort to conceal his past and try to "pass."

STATE OF PRISONS IN THE UNITED STATES: 1870–1970

Negley K. Teeters

In writing this article I take my cue, if not my inspiration, from the great John Howard who coined the word "penitentiary" in his book *State of Prisons,* written in 1777. Often referred to as "the father of the penitentiary," Howard deplored the degrading contamination so prevalent in the prison receptacles of his day. But the implementation of his philosophy first became significant in this country and there were created the two concepts of the silent, congregate prison known as the *Auburn System* and the separate or *Pennsylvania System.* One hundred years ago, in a valiant attempt to resolve the conflict that was tearing the prison world apart, a new dispensation appeared. The burden of this article deals with that movement, its subsequent development, and its dubious results.

Victor Hugo, in 1832, is alleged to have been responsible for this panegyric:

Civilization is nothing other than a series of successive transformations. What are you about to witness? This: the transformation of our penal system. The merciful rule of Christ shall at long last make its way into the Penal Code; it shall shine, radiant, through it. Crime will be considered a disease. . . . We shall treat in charity an evil we used to treat in anger.

With this quote, André Maurois said: "This statement by Hugo amounted to announcing the rehabilitation of Jean Valjean, the convict, and his salvation by Bishop Myriel."

Such an enunciation holds no surprise for us today; the only surprise is that it was made so long ago. Even earlier the doughty Jeremy Bentham, bubbling over in glee at the prospect of "selling" his architectural monstrosity which he called a "panopticon"

(inspection-house), cried out: "Morals reformed, health preserved, industry invigorated, instruction diffused, public burdens lightened, economy seated, as it were, upon a rock, the Gordian knot of the poor laws not cut, but untied, all by a simple idea in architecture."

This lantern-like rat cage, according to Bentham, could be used for "punishing criminals, guarding the insane, reforming the vicious, confining the suspected, employing the idle, maintaining the helpless, curing the sick, instructing the willing in any branch of industry, or training the rising race in the path of education; in a word, whether it be applied to the purposes of perpetual prisons in the room [instead] of death, or prisons for confinement before trial, or penitentiary-houses, or houses of correction, or workhouses, or manufactories, or mad-houses, or schools."

This fantastic architectural nightmare was never adopted in Britain but its modification was erected at Stateville, Illinois (but not as a cure-all as conceived by Bentham) whose cell-blocks were referred to by the modern prison architect, Alfred Hopkins, as "the most awful receptacles of gloom which were ever devised and put together with good stone and brick and mortar." It prompted the late Harry Elmer Barnes, an authority on prison architecture as well as correctional treatment, to remark: "Stateville is the greatest world monument to the fact that vagaries, as well as tradition, instead of sound architectural and reformative principles, have tended to dominate prison design and construction."

One more quote (from an earlier source) needs to be injected here in order to get a sense of perspective regarding the genesis of the state of our prisons. In 1833 those astute observers of American life as well as our prisons, deBeaumont and deTocqueville wrote: "While society in the United States gives the example of the most extended

From *Federal Probation,* 33, No. 4 (December 1969), 18–23. The late Professor Teeters was Chairman of the Department of Sociology at Temple University.

liberty, the prisons of the same country offer the spectacle of the most complete despotism." In all fairness, however, it may be ventured that the prisons of this country are more democratic and, indeed, closer geared to treatment and rehabilitation than those of many European countries; at least those in the countries with which the French commissioners were at that time acquainted. But, as we make this observation, have we said much? As we view the perplexities at the moment in the so-called correctional area, it is obvious that most of our rehabilitative programs are that only in name and not in substance.

Today, as in the past, one senses the same yearning for an ideal prison system or a philosophy of dealing with the dissident, the depraved, the underprivileged under duress, the social debtor group of homo sapiens. We seem to be more confused as to purpose and objectives today than in any other era, whether it be during the periods of all-out retaliation, expiation, deterrence, or reformation (the four periods that roughly describe social effort to deal with the criminal)—periods when the techniques, skills, and judgments of those laboring in the behavioral sciences were almost totally unknown. In those earlier days the guardians of social decorum *knew* they were correct in their treatment of the offender. Today we are not sure. On this point I wrote recently: "The dilemma of modern corrections is that society is confused. Many want rehabilitation but they want it by clinging to the concept of punishment. These persons still clamor for retribution and represent a strident voice from the out-moded past of arch-conservatism." Witness the demand for preventive detention!

DO WE KNOW WHAT TAKES PLACE IN PRISONS?

Do we actually know what is going on in our prisons today? We know little, have no means of learning and, so far as the general public is concerned, few care. A British prison governor, Major Arthur Griffiths,

back in 1891, gave as the title of his monumental work on prisons, *Secrets of the Prison House.* It is, indeed, even now, a secret place. Will-o-the-wisp exposures from time to time are "old hat" in our penal history.

A recent denunciation of today's prisons and today's imprisonment by Dr. Karl Menninger was given considerable publicity, but again it, too, may be referred to as a will-o-the-wisp despite the eminence of its author and its authenticity. But prison people, enlightened citizens, and dilettante academics, familiar as they are with the establishment and its regimented program of frustrating "therapy" or treatment, were not shocked nor even surprised. They all knew whereof the nationally known psychiatrist had written. Exposures from time to time of prison conditions—in 1968 those in New York State brought to light by the Senate Sub-Committee on Juvenile Delinquency, are all too familiar to "prison watchers" through the years. This time, one state (Arkansas), and from time to time in the past, one state after another, the story is the same. Brutality, regimentation, despair (experienced both by inmates and staff), lack of funds, political interference (commissioners picked through politics rather than through experience and continued in office despite pedestrian performance), poor physical conditions, wholesale homosexuality attacks (exposed not too long ago in a Philadelphia prison—not unique, but actually, the usual), and many other unwholesome conditions that exist almost everywhere. Indeed, the prison presents an abysmal graveyard of blighted expectations which shows little promise of improvement despite the heroics of correctional personnel, enlightened lay citizens, understanding legislators and organizations and societies dedicated to reform.

One must understand, however, that the prison is not the only stultifying institution in our culture. Besides the mental hospital, the institutions for the mentally retarded, and other makeshift attempts in human engineering, we also find great doubt when we view the entire gamut of criminal justice. From arrest and investigation to trial, sentencing and individualization of justice to parole, probation, suspended sentence, and indemnity or restitution, the story is the same as in rehabilitation and treatment, or what passes for it. The whole system is corrosive and totally unworthy of our best motives and capabilities. It is almost hopelessly bogged down, creaking, outmoded and confusing in both its philosophy and its operation. In this article, however, I am concerned only with the prison and its faults. We shall have to leave it to others to scrutinize criminal justice.

BOTH INMATES AND STAFF DEBAUCHED BY PRISONS

Prisons and imprisonment are degrading to the human spirit. John L. Gillin wrote 35 years ago:

What monuments to stupidity are these institutions we have built—stupidity not so much of the inmates as of free citizens! What a mockery of science are our prison, discipline, our massing of social iniquity in prisons, the good and bad together in one stupendous *potpourri.* How silly of us to think that we can prepare men for social life by reversing the ordinary process of socialization—silence for the only animal with speech; repressive regimentation of men who are in prison because they need to learn how to exercise their activities in constructive ways; outward conformity to rules which repress all efforts at constructive expression; work without the operation of economic motives; motivation by fear of punishment rather than by hope of reward or appeal to their higher motives; cringing rather than growth in manliness; rewards secured by betrayal of a fellow rather than the development of a larger loyalty.

It is not only the inmates who are debauched by the prison. The staff is adversely affected by its insidious atmosphere. That pioneer student of the prison, the late Dr. Frank Tannenbaum, wrote of this as early as 1933 when he stated: "There is something unkindly about the American prison. There is something corroding about it. It tends to harden all that come within the folds of its shadow. It takes kindly, well-intentioned people and makes them callous. . . . In some inexplicable manner the prison 'gets' not only the prisoners but the prison guards as well."

It is, in reality, the gradual transformation that occurs in prison personnel, both custodial and treatment cadres, that is the most damning characteristic of this sordid establishment. The prison "count" and the endless attempts by staff to prevent collusion among inmates to fraternize result in conflict which Tannenbaum contends is "the core of the development of prison brutality." It would be unfair to make a blanket indictment of prison personnel that they are sadistic, callous, or even apathetic or indifferent toward their charges, but many of the periodic and genuine criticisms hurled against the correctional institution are leveled at that very personnel who must deal with inmates on a day-by-day basis. The prison does "get" inmate and guard alike, and, it must be added, the professional staff as well.

Down through the years from the inception of imprisonment and the prison, there have been few persons who have come to their defense aside from those who clamor for punishment. Books written by prisoners are monotonous in their condemnation of what they were forced to experience while undergoing sentence. The rash of reports coming from the press in the present era differ only slightly from those with which prison people and enlightened citizens have been familiar for many years. Again quoting Tannenbaum who wrote the following in 1922: "We must destroy the prison, root and branch. When I speak of the prison, I mean the mechanical structure, the instrument, the technique, the method which the prison involves."

We have found that a "patching up" process, as we noted during the 1930 decade under the appellation of the "New Penology" and the "New Prison," has changed the climate or the rehabilitative process very little. Those were brave days with the creation and development of the diagnostic and classification clinic and the entree into the prison of professional personnel—psychiatrists and psychologists—but today bolder and more daring concepts are mandatory. Chief Justice of the United States Warren E. Burger has called for a complete study of our prison system because of its continued failure to rehabilitate sentenced criminals.

A CENTURY OF DISILLUSIONMENT

The great prison stalwart, Enoch C. Wines, called upon the "progressive" penologists of his day to meet with him at Cincinnati, Ohio, on October 12, 1870. He had thought that "all men of good will throughout the world should join in a plan for an ideal prison system." It is fitting that something be recalled of that historic event when the National Prison Association, now known as the American Correctional Association, was initiated. . . .

The main objective of this first meeting at Cincinnati was to attempt to break the senseless bind that existed in this country due to the passionate conflict between the advocates of the congregate, silent Auburn System and the separate cellular Pennsylvania System. A more sensible philosophy of rehabilitation of offenders was the progressive stages system in practice in Ireland which, in turn, had been conceived by Maconochie on Norfolk Island, off Australia, following 1840. Three of the system's main ingredients which appealed to the progressive prison administrators of that era were trade training (to supersede the reprehensible convict contract system), the indeterminate sentence, as opposed to the fixed sentence, and parole (which was on the minds of all).

First the assembly drew up its famous Declaration of Principles, consisting of 37 paragraphs advocating the philosophy of reformation as opposed to the doctrine of punishment, progressive classification of prisoners based on a "mark" system, the indeterminate sentence, and the cultivation of the inmate's self-respect.

What was hoped for was a new type of prison, a new dispensation, a "new look" at penal treatment. Warden Hubbell of Sing Sing was even more determined in envisioning a penological millennium, at least for his state, by advocating farm colonies, "comfortable dining-rooms," and as much freedom as possible. Wrote Blake McKelvey in 1936, in describing this enthusiastic and idealistic gathering of old-line and sometimes hard-bitten prison administrators:

The convention was in the hands of reformers who had arrived with prepared speeches while the traditions had no spokesman. Overwhelmed with inspired addresses, with prayer and song and much exhortation, even the hard-headed wardens were carried up for a mountain-top experience. In their enthusiasm for the ideal they rose above the monotony of four gray walls, men in stripes shuffling in lock-step, sullen faces staring through the bars, coarse mush and coffee made of bread crusts, armed sentries stalking the walls. They forgot it all and voted for their remarkable Declaration of Principles.

A "JUNIOR PRISON" IS ESTABLISHED

What emerged was the Elmira Reformatory, erected in 1876, the prototype of what spread throughout the country in many states, first to be enthusiastically received as a panacea for youthful crime, and by 1930 referred to generally as a "junior prison." The great Brockway, after 17 years as Elmira's first superintendent, looked back on the Cincinnati conference where he "had had an experience similar to that of the disciples on the Mount of Transfiguration and had felt himself strengthened by a . . . spiritual force with which he was going to have a grand success . . . but it did not work." Brockway was thoroughly disillusioned!

What might have happened if New York State, in creating the Reformatory, had not limited its intake to young first offenders and had scrapped its old-line prisons of Auburn and Sing Sing with their unworkable traditional concepts to be supplanted by the true Irish System of Intermediate Stages, one can only speculate. Justifiably it can be contended that a golden opportunity was lost, thereby eventually dragging the Reformatory and its ideals down to the dead level of the conventional prison.

In 1929 the Osborne Association appraised the Reformatory thus: "At Elmira, as in many other American reformatories, the inmates were walking a chalk-line as surely as though they were in a prison. The chalk-line is broader than in some prisons, and it leads along more interesting paths: academic instruction, trade schools, gymnasium work, etc. It is nevertheless the chalk-line of routine with all the old-time stress on regimentation, which so easily becomes stereotyped and futile and which is doubly monotonous for the young." Unfortunately, we have no outside evaluating agency to apprize the public just what is going on inside our penal institutions. More of that later.

THE "NEW" PENOLOGY OF THE THIRTIES

Roughly it may be suggested that the New Penology and the New Prison, mentioned earlier, came into being in the 1930's by the introduction of the concepts of diagnosis and classification, with the introduction also of specialized personnel including psychologists and psychiatrists, and the reorganization of the Federal Bureau of Prisons under Sanford Bates. All of these moves were epoch-making and did much to dignify prison, or correctional, work. A new day was anticipated in the correctional dispensation. More tolerable physical conditions were accepted and developed, at least in some of our more progressive states. Better libraries, schools, visiting privileges, work programs, housing, culinary facilities, and personnel emerged. It was a giant step forward, or so it seemed. The Federal Bureau of Prisons began to serve as a pattern in most areas of correctional programming, with a few states following—or at least in some specified areas. The Federal Bureau of Prisons was even excelled by some states in certain phases of treatment.

But the prison was still a prison dominated by the old 19th century concepts of monotony and repression. As Harry Elmer Barnes so often protested, there still remained the "convict bogey" and the "lock psychosis." These, together with the prison code, are the "bugaboo" of imprisonment. After the plethora of prison riots during the 1950 decade that shocked the Nation, including prison people themselves, and a study of these riots undertaken by the American Correctional Association was made public, the venerable and respected student of penology, Albert G. Fraser of Philadelphia; then secretary of the Pennsylvania Prison Society, declared:

I make bold to suggest that until we make the prison a more humane habitation, in a psychological sense, prison riots are inevitable for the very reasons which the monograph cites. Certainly, there must be qualified personnel, classification, full employment, smaller prisons, all the essential elements of a dynamic, positive program, and with all these, that which the committee fails even to suggest, a psychological setting in which the "prisoner's self-respect can be cultivated to the utmost." No authoritative statement on prison riots in this day and age can ignore or should fail to emphasize the *feeling* aspect of prison life.

Should not one reasonably expect an authoritative statement on the subject of corrections today to include some reference to *individual help* and the process by which it is made available to the prisoner? The monograph sets down widely accepted theories of prison management. It resorts to a hackneyed, but still popular pastime, by placing the blame on "politicians" and an indifferent public for ills which afflict the prison. I suggest that we in the correctional field start to give an up-to-date interpretation to the challenging and too long neglected principles of the Declaration of Principles.

It was this Declaration of Principles enunciated at the first prison Congress in 1870 which we described above that anticipated virtually all of the philosophy behind the New Penology of the 1930's. But they have never been put into practice or complete operation anywhere and only incompletely in the most progressive correctional institutions. Therefore, it is not inaccurate to state that even the most enlightened practice of today has not yet fully caught up with the theory expounded by the more progressive correctional leaders of that day, a century ago. This fact is both a challenge to current practice and an effective answer to those who contend that enlightened penologists are sentimentalists and dreamers in their "novel and untried vagaries."

WHAT OF THE FUTURE?

Today the correctional journals, reports, and monographs are discussing and describing innovations introduced here and there during the past few years. These include group therapy, refined diagnosis and classification procedures, preparole planning and training, halfway houses, work training and work release programs in the outside communities, furloughs home, and other sensible concepts. We also are discussing "self-evaluation and voluntary accreditation" of the prison, its staff, and its program. These are all laudable and certainly need encouragement. All need expansion and nationwide acceptance.

We have mentioned the earlier outside appraisal programs of the Osborne Association which did yeoman service for many years. Starting with the National Society of Penal Information, its purpose was to probe intelligently and carefully (by experts) the status of our prisons and reformatories. Its reports exposed poor standards of prison administration, housing, food, overall program and brutality where it existed. Lack of funds made it impossible for this valuable service to continue. Today we do not know what transpires in our institutions. They are indeed "secret places." Not unless there is a scandal, a riot, or an exposure by an independent "free-lance" writer do we know what our prisons are truly like. Self-analysis or self-appraisal has the serious weakness of intramural parochialism. Colleges and universities are appraised by outside accreditation teams working in close cooperation

with their own administrative and teaching staffs. This kind of objective appraisal should be explored by correctional people.

It has often been rationalized by prison people that they get society's misfits and are expected to redeem them. In part this is ture. But these culls are gradually molded or whittled into their twisted beings by society. It is thus society's task to send them back to the "good life" if at all possible—not to brutalize them by regimentation, cursing, and other degrading practices which have been hallmarks of imprisonment.

Suggestions have been made in various quarters to overhaul our sentence practices. This is one significant area where reform is badly needed. Other suggestions call for federalizing our state and local prisons. While this would be extremely difficult of attainment, it is worthy of study. I would certainly endorse the idea of using the Federal Bureau of Prisons as a model (despite some of its inherent weaknesses) and standardize concepts of therapy, program, enlightened trade training where practicable with economic productivity for all prisoners able to respond with meaningful education as a handmaiden of activity. There are so many areas that call for significant change that could tear down the bitter heritage of imprisonment as it has been and still is practiced. Just to rescind the restrictive legislation on the statute books relative to prison labor would be a gargantuan task. Yet such an objective would not be insurmountable. Rather than defending prisons and imprisonment or rationalizing them as necessary for society's "bad apples," correctional people should study the glaring shortcomings of the establishments they control and perpetuate and engage in meaningful change. It may well be that the next hundred years will bring into existence totally new techniques, new philosophies, and new therapies that will have more purpose in protecting society from its misfits than now exist. To paraphrase the Chief Justice of the United States, somehow the system we are so familiar with is failing to rehabilitate. He, as well as many others, want to know why.

CORRECTIONS AND SIMPLE JUSTICE
John P. Conrad

Justice is the first virtue of social institutions, as truth is of systems of thought. A theory however elegant and economical must be rejected or revised if it is untrue; likewise laws and institutions no matter how efficient and well-arranged must be reformed or abolished if they are unjust. Each person possesses an inviolability founded on justice that even the welfare of society as a whole cannot override . . . The only thing that permits us to acquiesce in an erroneous theory is the lack of a better one; analogously, an injustice is tolerable only when it is necessary to avoid an even greater injustice. Being the first virtues of human activities, truth and justice are uncompromising.

John Rawls, *A Theory of Justice*

On a date in 1970 which cannot be precisely identified for future commemoration, the weight of informed opinion in the United States about correctional rehabilitation shifted to the negative. Before that time, thoughtful and humane scholars, administrators, and clinicians generally held that it was the business of the prison and other incarcerating facilities to rehabilitate offenders. This belief prevailed widely and endured long. In addition to a rhetoric of rehabilitation appropriate for the influence of public opinion, this conviction was substantively expressed in the organization of services for offenders. Educators, psychologists and social workers are fixtures in the contemporary prison. The belief that a prisoner should be a better man as a result of his confinement guides judges and parole boards in fixing terms. Although the empirical observer may have concluded that rehabilitation is not an appropriate objective for the

From *The Journal of Criminal Law and Criminology*, 64, No. 2 (June 1973), 208–17. Copyright © 1973 by Northwestern University School of Law. Reprinted by special permission of the *Journal of Criminal Law and Criminology*. Conrad is Senior Fellow in the Academy for Contemporary Problems, Columbus, Ohio.

prison, the ideology of people-changing permeates corrections. Modern prisons are committed to treatment; echelons of personnel to carry it out are established on every table of organization. Rehabilitation continues to be an objective in good standing.

The dissonances produced by this conflict between opinion and practice are numerous, profound, and destructive of confidence in the criminal justice system. Whether these dissonances can be settled remains to be seen, but clearly understanding is critically important to improvement of the situation. In this article, I shall try to account for the change in our beliefs about rehabilitation and consider the significance of this change. I shall then review some of the more striking examples of policy departures grounded on rejection of the concept of rehabilitation. I shall conclude with a new conceptualization of the place of corrections in criminal justice. Whether my analysis and conclusions are accepted or not, they are intended to constitute a contribution to the vigorous dialogue which is necessary for the understanding and resolution of any public problem in a democratic society. In the case of corrections, the problem is the attainment of simple justice, the claims of which must be paramount if civilized order is to continue.

THE COLLAPSE OF REHABILITATION

The perspective in which our questions are framed is necessary to their answers. To keep in mind the history of the rehabilitative ideal and its application to corrections should avert a pessimistic conclusion about the criminal justice policies of the future. Grave mistakes have been made, and needless misery has been officially inflicted, but we have learned that we can identify and understand error. Whether we can supplant error with a closer approach to the right remains a challenge to the powers of reason and good will.

The idea of rehabilitation is not rooted in primaeval antiquity. Until the eighteenth century, charity was the most that any deviant could hope for and much more than most deviants—especially criminals—received. Any history of punishment before that time is an account of ever more grisly and stomach-turning horrors administered by the law to wrong-doers. Our forebears behaved so ferociously for reasons which we can only reconstruct with diffidence. The insecurity of life and property must have played an important part in the evolution of sanctions so disproportionate to harm or the threat of harm, but there was certainly another source of their furious response to the criminal. The war our ancestors waged on crime was partly a war against Satan. They believed that crime could be ascribed to original sin, that Satan roamed the world seeking the destruction of souls and that his handiwork could be seen in the will to do wrong. The salvation of the innocent depended on the extirpation of the wicked. It is only in the light of belief systems of this kind, varying in deatil from culture to culture, that we can explain the Inquisition, the persecution of witches, and the torturing, hanging, drawing, and quartering of common criminals. (That we are still not far removed from such bestiality testifies to the growing belief in a new Satan who defies, subverts and may even overturn civil authority.)

The Enlightenment changed all that. If pre-Enlightenment man teetered fearfully on the brink of Hell, desperately condemning sin and sinners in the interest of his own salvation, the *philosophes* conferred an entirely new hope on him. Rousseau's wonderful vision of man as naturally good relied partly on interpretation of primitive society which we can now dismiss as naive, but the world has never been the same since he offered his alternative. Once relieved of a supernatural burden of evil, man's destiny could be shaped, at least partly, by reason.

Reason formulated an obligation to change the transgressor instead of damning him or removing him by execution or transportation. The whole history of corrections, as we now know it, can be interpreted as a long series of poorly controlled experiments to see what could be done about changing offenders. We started with incarceration to remove offenders from evil influences which moved them to the commission of crime. In his extraordinary history of the asylum in America, David Rothman has traced the origins of this hypothesis, its consequences, and the influence it has exerted long since it was disconfirmed. But it was a reasonable proposition, given what was known about the conditions which created crime. It is noteworthy that the theoretical basis for expecting benefits from incarceration depended on the perception that the causes of crime might be found in the community rather than in the criminal.

This theory did not survive for long. The actual benefits of incarceration were difficult to identify in support of the expectation of the early American idealists responsible for the original notion. But incarceration was seen as a satisfactory punishment to administer to the criminal, and if a rationale for it were needed Jeremy Bentham and the Utilitarians could provide it. Punishment would rehabilitate if administered by the "felicific calculus" by which the proper amount of pain could be administered to discourage the transgressor from continuing his transgressions.

Nineteenth century Americans were finicky about human misery. They had blind spots, but they did not like to see it administered on purpose. They responded to the rhetoric of rehabilitation, as expressed, for example, in the famous 1870 Declaration of Principles of the American Prison Association. Reason had provided a new objective, and a new logic to justify it. The prison's purpose was no longer simply to punish the offender. During the time of confinement, the prisoner was to be cured of his propensity to crime by religious exhortation, psychological counseling, remedial education, vocational training, or even medical treatment. The Declaration of Principles recognizes that some of the causes of crime are to be found in the community. But while he is in prison, the offender must be changed for the better lest he be released to offend again. No one seriously advocated that felons should be confined until there was a certainty of their abiding by the law; it was impractical to carry this logic that far.

The rest of the story is hauntingly familiar to those correctional workers who have lived through the years of hope and disillusion which followed World War II. Marginal specialties were created by most of the professions with beach-heads in corrections. In each the objective was rehabilitation, and for a long time sound professional judgement pronounced on the success achieved in attaining objectives.

But gradually empiricism took control of correctional thought. Its triumph was hastened by the peculiarly available data of recidivism, so easily counted, so obviously related to questions of program success or failure. Again and again correctional rehabilitation has been empirically studied in details ever more refined. In a 1961 paper, Walter Bailey reviewed the evidence available in a hundred studies of correctional treatment and found it wanting in support for the belief that prison programs are related to parole success. A much more massive review by Lipton, Martinson and Wilks, still unpublished, was completed in 1969 and makes the same conclusion. The work of Kassebaum, Ward, and Wilner in the evaluation of group counseling by an impeccably rigorous research design has brought this negative conclusion to a sort of closure. In the absence of any strong evidence in favor of the success of rehabilitative programs, it is not possible to continue the justification of policy decisions in corrections on the supposition that such programs achieve rehabilitative objectives.

Paralleling the last twenty years of evaluative research there has also been much empirically based theoretical work. The classic study of the prison community by Clemmer imposed a structure on observation which has, in turn, led to the theoretical contributions of such writers as Schrag, Sykes, Goffman, and Irwin. Each of these workers has

brought a different perspective to his analysis, and the methodologies vary fundamentally. But the picture of the prison which emerges clearly accounts for the unsatisfactory results of all those evaluative studies. The prison is an institution which forces inmates and staff alike to accommodate to its requirements. These accommodations are inconsistent with rehabilitation. They are directed toward the present adjustment of the individual to the austerely unnatural conditions in which he finds himself. In some prisons survival becomes a transfixing concern. In any prison, regardless of the hazards to personal safety, the discomforts and irritations of the present occupy the attention of everyone. Inmates are obsessed with their places in an unfamiliar but constricted world and their hopes for release from it. Staff members are required to give most of their attention to the "here and now" problems of life in custody, whose relationship to rehabilitation is far-fetched at best.

Under these conditions, relationships and attitudes in even the most enlightened prison are determined by group responses to official coercion. The ostensible program objectives of rehabilitation may be a high school diploma, a new trade, or increased psychological maturity. But the prevailing attitudes towards programs will be determined by group opinions about their value in obtaining favorable consideration for release. A man may learn a lot by engaging in a vocational training program for the secondary gain of favorable consideration by a parole board, and many do. But the statistical success of such programs in increasing the employability of released inmates has been imperceptible. The reasons for this situation are still subject to speculation, but the inference is persuasive that few of those involved take the program seriously. The learning process passes the time which must be served and qualifies the individual for the favorable consideration which he desperately seeks. But neither the motivation nor the expectation of a career in a vocation learned imbue the learner.

The data are not as exhaustive as one would like. Perhaps Glaser's study of the effectiveness of the federal prison system provides the most conclusive picture of the bleak situation. The motivation to enroll in various self-improvement activities for release qualifications is conceded by the author. Neither in Glaser's own massive study of Federal prisoners nor in the studies of others reported by him is there any strong evidence that educational and vocational training are related to post-release success. To this day, we have only anecdotal evidence that any inmate graduates of vocational training programs are successfully placed in careers for which they were trained.

The final word on coercion in the administration of rehabilitation programs may have been pronounced by Etzioni, whose analysis of compliance structures draws on the prison for a paradigm of coercion. In Etzioni's formulation, the response to coercion is alienation. He holds that alienation from authority is at its highest when authority uses force to obtain compliance. As force is explicit and to be encountered continuously in the prison, it is obvious that alienation will be universal, although it will take many forms, both active and passive. Indeed, Etzioni hypothesizes that when a prison administration attempts to obtain compliance by other means than coercion it loses stability.

The alienation of the prisoner severely restricts his will to accept the goals of the staff. To choose to be committed to any activity is one of the few choices which cannot be denied the prisoner. For him to accord the staff his volition is an act of enlightened self-interest which exceeds the perspective of most prisoners.

Rehabilitation has been deflated as a goal of correctional custody by empiricism and by sociological theory. Its claims would hardly have been refuted by these forces alone. The findings of research have been paralleled by staff disappointment, scepticism in the media, and administrative policy changes.

It is not possible to document so subjective a change as the loss of confidence in rehabilitation by correctional staff. Indeed, there are many still who continue with program development in the prisons and hope for the best. The establishment in 1969 of the Kennedy Youth Center in Morgantown, West Virginia, represents the persisting faith of the staff and consultants of the federal Bureau of Prisons. It seems that the Bureau's faith is indomitable; an experimental prison will be built in Butner, North Carolina to study further the potentiality of treatment in custodial conditions. But it would be difficult to find a comparable professional investment in institutional treatment. The fervid hopes engendered by the group counseling movement of the late fifties and early sixties have faded into routines and motions.

The part played by journalists in the change of correctional ideology is hard to evaluate. The contributions of Jessica Mitford, Ben Bagdikian, Ronald Goldfarb, and Eddie Bunker, to name a wide diversity of examples, have vividly documented the futility of the prison as a rehabilitative agency. The extent to which they have changed public opinion is open to some question, in the absence of a recent poll, but there is a consistent theme in their writing which runs counter to the assumptions of rehabilitation. This theme flourishes without evident response to the contrary.

Administrative policy change has been clear cut and easy to document. The California Probation Subsidy Act of 1965 is clearly a landmark piece of legislation, in which a considered decision was made that as many offenders as possible should be channeled into probation, limiting the use of incarceration to cases where the protection of the public required it. The program is firmly based on the proposition that correctional rehabilitation cannot be effectively carried out in conditions of captivity. Whether it can be carried out in the community remains to be seen. As Hood and Sparks have remarked, the research which shows that probation is at least as effective as incarceration "cannot be interpreted as showing that probation is especially effective as a method of treatment."

The California act has been emulated in several states. It represents a gradual shift which has already emptied some prisons and training schools. The shift has taken a much more abrupt form in Massachusetts, *where in March 1972 all juvenile correctional facilities were irreversibly closed.* * The commissioner then responsible, Jerome Miller, acted on the conviction that such facilities do much more harm than good—if they can be said to do any good at all. The attention which the Massachusetts program has drawn because of its almost melodramatic timing has evoked singularly little debate. The local response in Massachusetts has been a fierce controversy but there has been at least a tacit acceptance throughout the country that the juvenile correctional facility is an institutional arrangement which can and should be terminated.

These academic and public developments portend the collapse of the claims of correctional rehabilitation as we have known it for the past twenty-five years. It confronts the nation with a continuing need for the prison and no way to make it presentable. The apparatus of education, social casework, and psychiatry at least served to disguise the oppressive processes required to hold men, women, and children in custody. To rehabilitate is a noble calling; to lock and unlock cages has never been highly regarded. The issue is apparent to many observers, but it is not surprising that we lack a consensus on its resolution.

HOW THE FACTS ARE FACED

The Report of the Corrections Task Force of the President's Commission on Law Enforcement and the Administration of Justice in 1967 initiated a series of public considerations of the problems of corrections. Its opening adjuration in the chapter of summary recommendations begins:

*Editor's italics.

It is clear that the correctional programs of the United States cannot perform their assigned work by mere tinkering with faulty machinery. A substantial upgrading of services and a new orientation of the total enterprise toward integration of offenders into the main stream of community life is needed.

This paragraph constitutes a blessing on the profusion of community-based correctional programs which ensued. Furloughs, work-release units, half-way houses became common rather than experimental. The use of volunteers was seen as natural and necessary rather than an administrative inconvenience suffered in the interests of public relations. The improvement of the old programs of probation and parole has come slowly and, in some states, imperceptibly. But the Corrections Task Force had started a movement which has gained momentum. The growing confidence in corrections in the community has been reflected in the decelerated growth of prison populations at a time when crime rates have increased as never before. In some states, especially California, the numbers of felons in state prisons has dramatically declined. In many others, including Ohio, Minnesota, and Illinois, the decline in actual institutional populations has been more modest, but that they have declined at all is significant in view of the rise in both populations and rates of crime and delinquency.

These events reflect hundreds of decisions by judges and parole board members. Policy is changing before our eyes. We can see from the data where it seems to be going. We can also see from current official studies that there is much concern about corrections at high executive levels. There is a continuing agreement that something must be done about its apparent ineffectiveness, its wastefulness, and the danger to society presented by the processes of incarceration.

The most prominent of these studies is the massive report of the Corrections Task Force of the National Commission on Criminal Justice Standards and Goals. For the purposes of this review of the future of incarceration, the following extracts from the summary of the Task Force Report are significant of the great shift which has taken place:

... The trend toward community-based corrections is one of the most promising developments in corrections today. It is based on the recognition that a considerable amount of delinquency and crime is a symptom of failure of the community, as well as of the offender, and that a successful reduction of crime requires changes in both. Reasons for embracing the concept of community corrections and for embarking on a national strategy to effect a transition from our current institution-oriented correctional system to one that is community-based include the following:
—There is convincing evidence that current use of and practices in traditional penal institutions intensify and compound the problems they profess to correct.
... The majority of offenders currently are treated as violent and dangerous despite the fact that only a few of them conform to this unfortunate stereotype.
Time spent in confinement is inversely related to success on parole, and community-based programs appear to be more effective than traditional institutional programs in providing community protection.
Imprisonment has negative effects on an offender's ability to develop sufficient skills and competence to perform culturally prescribed roles after release into the community.
The move toward community corrections implies that communities must assume responsibility for the problems they generate.

These findings by the Commission found practical expression in recommendations which are stunningly forthright. Unambiguously, the Commission prescribes that "no new major institutions for juveniles be built under any circumstances, (and) existing major institutions for juveniles and youths should be phased out in favor of local facilities and programs." Necessarily the prescription for adult corrections was more cautious: "No new institution for adults should be built unless an analysis of the total crimi-

nal justice system and adult corrections system produces a clear finding that no alternative is possible." But the point is made: the Commission has no confidence in the value of the prison for any purposes other than punishment and incapacitation. The logic carries the Commission to the conclusion that the country has more prisons than it needs and that it should entirely discontinue the incarceration of juvenile offenders.

Obviously, if the Commission's plan is to be carried out, the correctional continuum will heavily stress alternatives to incarceration. Such a continuum will call for communities to increase social service resources to provide for diversion of offenders from criminal justice processing to the greatest extent possible. It will call for a sentencing policy which relies much more explicitly on suspended sentences, fines, court continuances, and various forms of probation in which emphasis is given to the provision of services. Prisons will be reserved for offenders guilty of crimes of violence, and perhaps for other offenders whose crimes are so egregious as to require this level of severity to satisfy the community's desire for retributive justice.

The Commission is not alone in its outspoken demand for change. Compared to the Final Report of the Wisconsin Citizens' Study Committee on Offender Rehabilitation, the recommendations of the National Advisory Commission are positively conservative. The Wisconsin report, issued in July 1972, begins by establishing as "its most fundamental priority the replacement of Wisconsin's existing institutionalized corrections system with a community-based, noninstitutional system." The reasons for this admittedly radical proposal are unequivocally assigned. First, "current Wisconsin institutions cannot rehabilitate." Second, "de-institutionalization of Wisconsin's correctional system would, in the long run, save considerable tax dollars." The Committee considered that action to "de-institutionalize" the correctional system is so urgent that its accomplishment before 30 June 1975 was recommended. Although the Governor to whom this recommendation was addressed has not adopted it, the significance of such a recommendation from a committee composed of persons drawn from the informed and established professional and business communities is not to be dismissed as an exercise in flighty liberalism. The Wisconsin correctional apparatus has long been admired as an adequately funded, professionally staffed, and rationally organized system, second to none in these respects. If prisons could rehabilitate, some sign of their capabilities to do so should have emerged in that state. This committee looked carefully for such a sign and could find none.

The alternative system recommended for Wisconsin begins with a call for pre-trial diversion of some offenders on the decision of the District Attorney, the use of restitution as an alternative to the full criminal law process, and decriminalization of:

... fornication, adultery, sexual perversion, lewd behavior, indecent matter and performances, non-commercial gambling, fraud on inn or restaurant keepers, issuance of worthless checks, fraudulent use of credit cards, non-support, the possession, sale and distribution of marijuana, and public drunkenness.

The confirmed addict and the chronic alcoholic are recognized as the helplessly infirm persons that they are. The Task Force urged a policy of treatment rather than prosecution, and a program of services rather than incarceration. The recommendations call for the establishment of services which do not now exist in Wisconsin. There is a realistic confrontation with the probable outcome of most services for these gravely handicapped persons:

... The committee feels that flexible programming and expectation of failure must be a part of any development of drug treatment programs ...

Nevertheless, it is the clear responsibility of the state to provide treatment within a framework in which at least some success can be rationally expected. Even some custodial care will be required for addicts and alcoholics who can be treated in no other way. But it is noteworthy that the possibility of providing such custodial care in prison settings is considered only for those addicts who have been guilty of ordinary felonies, and even then such persons are to have the option of treatment in facilities designed for addicts. No consideration was given to the use of correctional facilities for standard treatment for addicts of any kind.

The Wisconsin Task Force clearly saw that their recommendations went several steps beyond the current public consensus. Nobody knows for sure what the limits of public tolerance for change in corrections may be, but even the forthright writers of this report knew that there is a wide gap between a rationally achieved position in these matters and its acceptance by the electorate. This is especially true in the field of narcotics addiction, where lack of hard information and well meant misinformation have done so much to distort public opinion. We are so thoroughly committed to the use of the criminal process for the control of such a broad range of social deviance that alternatives are difficult to design with confidence, despite our knowledge that the criminal justice system is demonstrably ineffective for many kinds of social control. Recognition of the irrationality of this situation does not provide us with obvious remedies. The weakness of this excellent report is that its recommendations can be readily dismissed by the administrator as impractical, even though the present system is itself shown to be thoroughly impractical on the basis of its results.

The Wisconsin study of corrections provides a startling example of the dissatisfaction evoked by an apparently advanced correctional program when dispassionately studied by citizens concerned with the claims of justice and rationality. Moving from Wisconsin to the more populous but somewhat similar state of Ohio, we find another Citizens' Task Force on Corrections reporting to a deeply concerned governor concerning the state of the corrections system. But in this case, the Task Force was confronted by one of the most decrepit correctional programs in the country. Generations of pound-foolish fiscal maladministration had produced a situation in which under-paid, poorly supervised staff worked in slovenly, malodorous prisons filled to the bursting point with idle prisoners. The explosive condition thus created had exploded more than once, convincing even the most fiscally conservative that something had to be done. The response was the construction of a large new prison in the most remote locality that could be found in this compact state. It was obsolete at the time of its design and will probably be a distorting burden on the criminal justice system of Ohio for centuries to come.

The *Report of the Ohio Citizens' Task Force on Corrections* was written in the context of a perceived need for "de-institutionalization." Concerned to bring about some organizational coherence in an agency which conspicuously lacked this basic element, it devotes much time and space to recommendations for the creation of an effective management structure, an equitable personnel policy, a Training Academy, and a Division of Planning and Research. But the Task Force stresses at the outset of its report that even if all its recommendations were to be immediately implemented, "the public would not be protected one iota more." With as much emphasis as typography can bring to bear, the report goes on to assert: "We must cease depending on institutionalization as an adequate response to the law offender and protection of the public. Instead, we *must* develop a system of community-based alternatives to institutionalization.... The emphasis of the future must be on alternatives to incarceration. The rule, duty, and obligation of this Task Force is to communicate this vital conclusion to the public."

Since the publication of this report in December 1971, the Division of Correction has been transformed into an adequately staffed Department of Rehabilitation and Correction. An administrative group is at work on the development of an adaptation of the California Probation Subsidy Act as the most likely strategy for the creation of a sufficient range of community-based alternatives to incarceration. The new penitentiary at Lucasville has been opened; in spite of its preposterous location far from the cities from which its inmates come, it at least has made possible a decision to demolish the infamous old prison at Columbus. The Ohio Youth Commission, charged with the maintenance of a correctional program as well, has re-organized to make its preventive program more than nominal. The de-institutionalization of Ohio corrections has not been accomplished, nor will it be accomplished soon, but a structure of administrative planning, research, and evaluative management has been created on the basis of which rational change can be expected. Already the state's confined population has declined by ten percent, in spite of a steadily increasing rate of commitments. Drift and expediency were the villainous influences identified by the Citizens' Task Force; they have been replaced by policies which require rational decision-making. The transformation is not fool-proof, but it will at least discourage fools from rushing in.

Faced with a rapid expansion of its population and the unique problems brought about by its isolation from the rest of the country, Hawaii has drawn on the resources of the National Clearinghouse for Criminal Justice Planning and Architecture to develop a Correctional Master Plan. The plan explicitly credits the state with a more adequate delivery of correctional services than is available in many states. However,

... it overemphasizes traditional institutionalization as the response to criminal behavior and lacks the range and diversity of programmatic responses.... Institutionalization ... is probably the most expensive response and also the least effective that a criminal justice system can make in dealing with criminal behavior. The continued rise in the rates of crime and the appalling high recidivism accentuate the ineffectiveness of such institutionalization as an approach to correcting such behavior.

The approach adopted by the Hawaii planners borrows from the concepts of the National Clearinghouse and represents the best current example of a fully developed correctional program based on the Clearinghouse guide-lines. To summarize the work of the Clearinghouse in an article such as this is a daunting task; the published *Guidelines* constitute a weighty volume addressed to the whole span of correctional issues. But the core ideas are simple and identifiable. First, the planning of correctional systems will eliminate the costly waste incurred by needless building of security housing. Second, community-based alternatives to incarceration can afford both protection for the community and effective reinstatement services for the vast majority of offenders. Third, the safe assignment of offenders to correctional services requires a process of differential classification, preferably in an "Intake Service Center." Fourth, for the control of dangerous offenders a "Community Correctional Center" should be incorporated in the system with full provision for maximum custody. Throughout the conceptual development of the Clearinghouse *Guidelines* there is the tacit assumption that environmental influences are the most accessible points of intervention as to any offender and the diagnostic task is to identify those influences which can be brought to bear on his resocialization. Most social science students of criminal justice issues will recognize these assumptions as hypothetical at best, but their humane and rational intent is obvious. Clearly, an urgent task for research is the evaluation of the consequences of their implementation under such circumstances of full acceptance as the state of Hawaii has accorded.

The momentum of the traditional correctional policies is not to be suddenly halted. Regardless of the enjoinders of the Law Enforcement Assistance Administration, regardless of the recommendations of Citizens' Commissions across the country, more jails will be built, and many offenders will occupy their cells who might just as well be enrolled in an appropriate community program. Neither the staff, nor the agencies, nor the sentencing policies are fully enough developed to allow for an immediate implementation of the enlightened recommendations which I have summarized by example. But in a world in which the costs of incarceration have reached annual per capita costs which far exceed average citizen incomes, the future of incarceration must be constrained by a policy of rigorous selectivity. The informed opinion that coerced rehabilitation is an impractical objective is equally welcome to humane liberals and fiscal conservatives. The task of research is to collect the information which will support the strategy of change.

THE DEMOBILIZATION OF CORRECTIONS

Where will the momentum of change in corrections lead the criminal justice system? In so emotionally charged a set of issues as surrounds the disposition of convicted offenders, it is futile to predict the probable course of events. We have known for a long time that the execution of murderers cannot be shown to deter murder, but the retributive motive still permeates our culture, and it is not at all certain that the [Supreme Court] abolition of capital punishment is permanent. Hatred of the criminal and fear of his actions have nothing to do with reasoned plans to protect ourselves from him or to change his behavior. In a period in which crime has assumed the quality of obsessive concern in our society, the wonder is that so many are able to accept the dispassionate view of the offender which characterizes the recommendations of the numerous study commissions which have been at work on the renovation of the correctional system. We are not clear of the threat of an irrationally repressive policy. The recent [success] of Governor Rockefeller for draconian new laws to sequester for life the vendor of narcotics will at least serve to remind us how tenuous our hold on rational correctional concepts may be. Nevertheless, this portent and others like it can be offset by the widespread belief that rational change is possible and desirable. We can take some encouragement in the support of this position by a broad spectrum of political opinion. The concern for correctional change is not confined to the various liberal shades.

We should specify the structural changes in the criminal justice system which the new correctional ideology implies. Much of the rhetoric of scepticism challenges us to justify the retention of any part of the present correctional system. We are told that the criminal justice system is nothing more than an instrument for the regulation of the poor, and that therefore the interests of justice would be best served by its abolition. This kind of effervescence serves to discredit the motives and good sense of the correctional reform movement, which draws on the evidence of social research to reach conclusions which both establish the obsolescence of the present system and indicate fruitful directions for its renovation. It is time that we considered where these directions will take us.

First, we must concede that although we do not know how the prison can be converted into a rehabilitative institution, we shall have to retain it for the protection of society from some violent and dangerous offenders from whom we cannot protect ourselves in any other way. These prisons must be small. They must provide for the long-term prisoner in ways which support psychological stability and his integrity as a person. We know that these objectives require that he should have latitude for choice, that he should have a sense of society's concern for his welfare, and that his life should be restricted as little as possible given the purposes to be achieved in restricting him at all.

The retention of the prison for the containment of the dangerous offender assumes that we can identify him. This assumption is open to attack. The inference that all offenders who have been guilty of major violence will present continuing hazards to the public is refuted by the consistently low rates of recidivism of released murderers. In the state of our present knowledge, we are reduced to predicting a hazard of future danger from the determination of a pattern of repetitive violence. Many authorities on criminal justice will be dissatisfied with the protection which can be provided against serious abuse of this kind of prediction. Acknowledging the validity of this line of criticism, I can only respond that the confidence which a changing system of social control must maintain will rapidly erode if dangerous and predatory offenders are released from prison to resume the behavior for which they were confined in the first place. Until a more satisfactory basis for their identification can be found, we shall have to tolerate some injustice in order to avoid the greater injustices of needlessly confining the obviously harmless. Social science must persist in the improvement of our power to identify the dangerous offender. The quality of justice is heavily dependent on the increase of knowledge in this age when we are replacing vengeance with reconciliation.

The remainder of the correctional panoply is a dubious asset to justice. We have established probation and parole, halfway houses and work-release programs, group homes and community correctional centers in an essential effort to create alternatives to incarceration. The effort has largely succeeded; informed observers have been convinced, and policy has changed sufficiently to reduce the rate of commitment to prison in most of the jurisdictions of the country. As humanitarian reforms, these alternatives were essential. They still are. But the evidence is scanty that shows that these programs are really more effective than the prisons they replace. They are certainly no worse. We can be confident that we can dismantle the prison as an agency of social control without undermining social cohesion or increasing the danger to individuals.

But the point is to improve the effectiveness of the criminal justice system. We must make it possible for the offender to choose a law-abiding life and to act on that choice. Knowing that many of the obstacles to his reinstatement are beyond our power to remove through administrative or judicial action, we still must do what we can, which is much more than we have done. Offenders must be seen as people with personal problems of great difficulty. They are now provided with second-rate services, if they really receive services at all. It is incumbent on a society which creates much of its crime burden from persistence in social injustice to make available services which can extricate criminals from criminal careers. In most communities these services exist. The great Massachusetts experiment of the last year [1972] in large part consisted of an effort to bring to the offender the regular community services which are available to ordinary citizens. It is not only offenders who need vocational training, employment counseling, mental health services and remedial education. To select them for special correctional versions of these services does not assure that they will get effective assistance. It does assure that the help they get will have some stigma attached. It also assures that their treatment will be affected by the persistence of the myth that criminality itself is a condition to be treated.

It follows that the administration of justice should use its special perspective on offenders to induce service agencies of all kinds to make their services accessible. The court thus becomes a referral agency, opening doors by its authority, perhaps even by the purchase of services, but not by coercion or the implication that the freedom of the offender depends on his obtaining benefits from services rendered. This is a model of service delivery which will be difficult to learn and even more difficult to live by. There will always be an inclination to draw an invidious conclusion from the offender's inability to persevere in a program intended for his benefit. But we shall have done much more for offenders than we are now doing if we can make it possible for them to choose services; those who can choose but reject them anyway will not benefit from compulsion.

If we can make service more effective by projecting offenders into the mainstream of community activity instead of keeping them in a correctional backwater, we can also improve on their surveillance by transferring that responsibility to the police. No one is served by the pretence that probation and parole officers possess qualifications for the discharge of this function. Law enforcement duties should be performed by the police, who are trained for the task and organized to do it. To expect that probation and parole officers can accomplish anything in this respect that could not be better done by the police is to compound confusion with unreality, to the detriment of whatever surveillance is really needed.

There are two functions now discharged by probation and parole officers which cannot be easily re-located. The decisions related to the sentence, its imposition, its terms, its completion and revocation cannot be made without essential information systematically collected. The reports which probation officers make to the court and the parole officers make to the parole boards are services to the court which should be carried out by officials under the control of the court.

The information collected by this officer of the court, (his functions are so much more specific than those of the present probation officer that we might accurately designate him the Information Officer), will be essential for the service referrals which the court should make. In small courts information and referral could well be carried out by the same officer; there may be advantages in differentiating the functions in large courts. These residual responsibilities must be maintained, but their discharge will hardly call for the large and many-layered staffs which are to be found in present day probation and parole departments.

There remains the question of sanctions to be imposed on offenders. Here, we have some reason to believe that less severity but more certainty in punishment will serve the public protection better. The victims of crime should receive restitution from the offender to the limit that restitution is practical. The graduated use of fines, relating them to the offender's resources, has been successfully used in Sweden. An English study, reported by Hood and Sparks, indicates that for property crimes, at least, the fine may well be the most effective sanction. Suspended sentences have not been definitively evaluated as to their effect on recidivism. The tolerance of the system for probation and parole services in which contact does not take place after adjudication suggests that we can safely rely on the suspended sentence for a substantial proportion of offenders. Where there is reason to believe that surveillance is necessary, provision for regular police contacts could be made to assure that reliable control is maintained.

Such a system would limit the use of incarceration to pre-trial detention of some exceptional defendants, and the post-trial detention of only the most dangerous offenders. It would provide protection where it is needed, service where it is desired by the offender himself, and control in the measure that the circumstances of the community and the offender require it. The victim would no longer have to comfort himself with the knowledge that the law had taken its course toward retribution; he would now receive restitution from the offender or compensation from the public funds as the situation might require.

The system would be adjustable by feedback. Increased control would be obtained by increased use of the more severe sanctions where the data on crime rates called for it. Essentially this system would be retributive, but the nature of the retribution would be the minimum required by measured experience rather than the ancient demands made by hatred and custom. Where reconciliation can be achieved, it will be eased; where control is required it will be exercised. But the claims of simple justice will be essential elements of policy.

Justice can only be approached, never fully achieved. But unless it is indeed the first virtue of the public institutions which administer it, none of the other virtues these institutions may possess will matter. The claims of simple justice are not satisfied merely by the administration of due process, but by the operation of the whole system by methods which restrict liberty only to the degree necessary for public purposes, but nevertheless assures that these restrictions are effective. We are far from such a system now. The removal of the assumptions which the belief in rehabilitation has engendered will make possible a system which will be more modest in aims, more rational in its means, and more just in its disposition.

JUVENILE JUSTICE: A LOVE-HATE STORY

David L. Bazelon

... It is ... quite a challenge to open this series with a lecture that will be worthy of its namesake. In thinking about it, I decided right away not to recite the standard "what a mess we're in" jargon which characterizes so many juvenile justice conferences. I know

From a speech delivered at a meeting in honor of Judge Justine Polier at New York University Law School, 1973. Judge Bazelon is on the United States Court of Appeals in the District of Columbia.

that speech by heart: I have listened to it innumerable times, and to be frank, I have probably given it on more than one occasion.

It goes like this: we are committed to a "treatment model" of juvenile justice. The purpose of juvenile courts is not to punish but to rehabilitate children. A good juvenile court diagnoses what has made the child commit an antisocial act and then prescribes the "services" he needs so he won't do it again. If services can be supplied in the community, fine. The probation officer will oversee the coordination. If, "for his own good," of course, the child must be separated from his family, intrusions on his liberty are premised on a promise of treatment. He may be placed in a foster home or a residential center where the professionals will dispense services in an intensive manner, at the same time they prepare him and his family for reintegration in the community. And he will go forth and sin no more.

That is Part I. Now, Part II: Enter the villain. Lack of resources. There are not enough skilled psychologists to test the juveniles; not enough social workers to interview their families; not enough foster and group homes to put them in until trial; not enough lawyers available to represent them; not enough probation officers; not enough community mental health services; not enough vocational training programs; not enough jobs. In the institutions, there are not enough psychiatrists, psychologists, social workers, special education teachers, or counsellors. There are not even enough guards; the children keep escaping from rehabilitation before they are ready for reintegration.

At the end of Part II comes the "tell-it-like-it-is" scene. Promises broken, potential unfulfilled, treatment which fails to treat. Juveniles, guilty of everything from homicide to the cardinal sin of rebelliousness, are herded into sterile training schools located in rural outposts and in small towns, where professional staff seldom venture and urban parents can't visit. These are places where minority staff members are loathe to go; where children eat, sleep, and simmer by the clock. In the worst ones, they are abused by staff and by peers; beaten, raped, corrupted. In the best, they are condescended to and counselled and bored to death; forced to create their own havoc to introduce a little reality into their world. And we all know what comes next. The children go back to the streets, unrehabilitated; many repeat their criminal or pseudo-criminal conduct and are back again within months for another dose of our "medicine".

Typically, the speech has one bright note.

[Juvenile] courts blessed with [good judges] temper the harshness of reality. They will not allow children to be subjected to cruel and unusual punishment, such as the 14-year-old girl who spent two weeks in her nightgown in a stripped down room without even a book or magazine. Some courts put controls on the amount of thorazine you can inject in the unruly child, or they insist on minimum amounts of schooling and "big muscle" sports. A few intrepid judges talk about staff-inmate ratios and treatment "plans", and try with the meager tools available to fulfill the juvenile court's promise of treatment. . . .

Finally we reach the end of a most *un*-satisfying speech. Let's face it, the speaker says: the juvenile court system is not just in trouble. It is in a state of crisis today because it has not stemmed the tide of violence emanating from its clientele—the children of the poor, White and Black, though in our cities it is primarily the Black. Our treatment model is failing this clientele; and we don't know what to do. End of speech.

I want to focus on what we can do—and must do—about the crisis in juvenile justice. I do not have a panacea; nobody does. But I will suggest a necessary first step toward acting on the problem rather than reacting to it. To explain that first step, I must go back to the standard message that our present institutions are failing.

One understandable and humane response to this failure is to demand that more and more be put into the system—more money, more programs—in short, more treatment in hopes of more results.

But there are some of us who increasingly feel that there are problems beyond the obvious injustices of warehousing institutions and assembly-line courts. For one thing, most "treatment services" come too late for children of the ghetto culture, many of who have been bred casually, born begrudgingly, and "dragged up" without much attention. Perhaps the boys and girls who have survived by their wits in the school of the streets are supremely well adjusted to *their* environment. Christopher Jencks suggests that what happens inside our schools has relatively little to do with ultimate success in life. This hit like a bombshell in the experts' circles, but the kids knew it long ago. Jencks' point hits home when it comes to juvenile courts and institutions. What goes in, comes out. What never went in will never come out.

It doesn't take an expert to guess that children reared in the ghetto, where acknowledgment of one's own identity or worth is impossible, will develop at best a hard insensitivity to other humans.

My own experience with delinquents and criminals is that their lives on the street have destroyed their ability to empathize with other human beings. They feel nothing but hatred toward their victims. This lack of "connection" to the majority's culture and values may have nothing to do with mental disease, unless not being able to see or to *feel* beyond resentment and rage is classified as such.

I suspect that none of our providers of treatment services—psychiatrists, psychologists, or social workers—have the know-how to implant our middle-class sensibilities into youngsters who have been actively neglected 24 hours a day, every day. There is no magic humanizing pill for these youths to swallow.

What is "treatment", anyway? Few honest experts tell you that they know how to "treat" a misbehaving juvenile. Let's be candid: we don't have the slightest notion of what really works, except in the most common sense way. How do we "treat" our own children? We feed them, comfort them, play with them, call the doctor for them, talk to their teachers, lecture them, swat them once in a while, and most of all warm them with our love and pride. Not many of us subject them to repeated batteries of tests and interviews, isolate them for weeks for misbehavior, make them account for every five minutes of their time, deny them privacy, censor their mail, and refuse them all contact with the opposite sex. Yet in most systems, this passes for treatment.

Someone once compared the diagnostic social services in a good juvenile court to a superhighway leading into a cowpath: complicated diagnostic labels and classifications all dressed up with nowhere to go. We have seen this before—mental health, where the choice of diagnostic labels is most impressive, but the treatment is always that elusive creature known as "milieu therapy."

I think it significant that most nonchemical breakthroughs in treating addiction to hard drugs and alcohol have been made by lay persons, in the form of A. A., Synanon, confrontation therapy, therapeutic communities, supported work programs. Psychiatrists admit their frustration and reluctance to treat alcoholics, addicts, homosexuals, sociopaths. Why do we expect much greater success with juvenile misfits?

We do so in part because it is *easy* to rely on the "services" syndrome. Yet there is a real *danger* involved in dumping our juvenile problems into the mental health bag. In so doing, we erect a protective "medical" shield around the same old harsh and punitive "lock 'em up" practices. Thus the disciplinary cells in a boys' institution are in the infirmary and are called "medical isolation." In many institutions, one-third to one-half of the juvenile population is on powerful behavioral control tranquilizers. Does this kind of "medical treatment" help the child, or does it merely protect an overworked staff? Whose rights are we worried about?

Of course, even if our "treatments" served the child, and even if all the services administered through the juvenile courts met the highest standards of efficiency, we would still be treating only the symptoms of a spreading infection. By tradition, we wait for a problem to erupt and then rush in with emergency counter-measures—a pound of cure to make up for the ounce of prevention which was never invested.

For too long we have ignored a preventive approach which concentrates on the first decade of a child's life. Yet we know that all children need certain fundamentals: nutritious food, safe housing, a stable family structure to provide personal affection, and continual attention to health, learning and emotional needs. If children are denied these fundamentals; if that denial is compounded by failure labels applied in school; if insensitivity is hardened by "bad apple" labels applied by the establishment to behavior which is glorified by ghetto peer groups—can any service or treatment inside or outside institutions correct the wrong?

By now you must sense the depth of my doubts about whether the so-called therapeutic approach can ever really deliver as much as we expect of it. I do not mean to turn my back on our long and honorable tradition of providing goods and services to society's victims—the poor and the minorities—and to its rejects—the delinquents, criminals, addicts, mentally ill and retarded.

But if we want to make sure that our efforts are really constructive, we must examine our expectations much more carefully. Before we either scrap our helping efforts, *or* redouble them, we must have a better understanding of what children really need; of whether specialists, and *what* kind of specialists, are needed; and how we can improve and extend services that are useful, and eliminate those that are useless or downright destructive. . . .

Such a reappraisal will cost money. It will cause pain to admit our well-intentioned mistakes. But in the end it will be cheaper and less painful than plunging headlong down the path of wishful thinking and futile hopes. For if our expectations of results from *humane* treatment continue to be frustrated, we will have ourselves to blame for the inevitable reaction: rage, vengeance, and *in*humane treatment. Indeed, frustration is spawning that reaction now, as reflected in these remarks of Gov. Rockefeller. I quote:

In this State, [New York] we have tried every possible approach to stop addiction and save the addict through education and treatment—hoping we could rid society of this disease and drastically reduce mugging on the streets and robbing in the homes. We have allocated over $1 billion to every form of education against drugs and treatment of the addict through commitment, therapy, and rehabilitation.

But let's be frank—let's 'tell it like it is.' We have achieved very little permanent rehabilitation—and have found no cure.

In the Governor's opinion, society has no alternatives. It must punish what it cannot treat. Enough is enough. If traditional services don't work, draconian measures are the only alternative.

This "up against the wall" attitude has focused on juveniles too; witness the reduction of age limits from 18 to 16 for sending juveniles to the adult courts if rehabilitation efforts have failed or if their behavior is too serious. There is talk in New York of lowering the age further to 14 or 15. The error in this approach is obvious, I think. As I have said before, it is like cutting off a piece of a leg in order to make the pants fit. But this approach is predictable. It is part of the shockwave of feelings which has been aroused by the public's daily, escalating confrontation with violent crime. It is a response to feelings of fear, for ourselves and our loved ones; feelings of horror and outrage; feelings of bitterness over money evidently wasted, and anger which has no outlet. These are not the feelings of evil people, but of human people. All of us who have been touched know how easy it can be to move from fear to outrage; from outrage to cries for vengeance . . . usually under the guise of punishment and deterrence, since vengeance is a dirty word. But whatever the deterrent effect which punishment may have on tax evaders and traffic violators, we all know that there is abundant evidence that punishment does not deter the very kind of street crime which puts us in such great fear. And even if punishment was a deterrent, there is a serious question whether it is just to punish the antisocial conduct of those who cannot enter society.

Nonetheless, it is apparent that these feelings are touching a majority of our people. Although many respected groups such as the Association of the Bar of New York oppose Governor Rockefeller's proposal to lock up sellers of hard drugs for life, a recent [1973] Gallup Poll showed that 67% of the adults interviewed approved of it. The newspapers report that the issue of street crime in New York City has turned the race for mayor into a contest over who can be the toughest law-and-order strongman. And I have been told by an esteemed member of the United States Senate that most of his colleagues feel that 80% of the American people are ready to come down hard on the other 20%—not because they want to and not any harder than they feel they have to. But hard enough to keep crime where it belongs . . . and has always been rampant . . . in the ghetto.

Tightening the screws on ghetto criminals is not likely to stop with harsher penalties—it has already begun to erode fundamental rights of our juvenile and criminal justice systems which are damned as "loopholes" through which guilty parties escape. Once these "loopholes" are closed, and crimes are *still* committed on the streets, what will be the next step. Martial law? Erecting walls around human garbage heaps in the middle of our cities from which there is simply no escape?

I do not quarrel with those who say that criminal offenders constitute a grave threat to our precious rights—and maybe even our lives—but it is foolhardy to believe that by systematically destroying the rights of others we are preserving freedom and dignity for ourselves. The costs of this approach will bankrupt us.

What, then, are we to do? Is there no uplift at the end of my speech either? I bring to the problem only my judicial experience with juvenile justice, and all I have learned from my membership on The Joint Commission on the Mental Health of Children and the Advisory Committee on Child Development of the National Academy of Sciences. The people who served with me, for whom I have the greatest respect, were unquestionably the leading names in our country in the field of child development. But what I learned from them was that they have no pills or prescription to cure the effects of economic and cultural deprivation; that the best nostrum is common sense and compassion.

Therefore, it seems to me that what we *must* do is take the first step toward breaking the cycle which leads so many of our youths into juvenile courts—a step toward

preventing trouble, rather than waiting for it and hoping to cure it. That step is to guarantee to every family an income sufficient to enable parents to provide the kind of home environment they want for their children. Of course, we cannot be sure that more money given directly to the family will enhance the children's development, but I think it is our best—if not our only—hope.

Why so? The only thing that my expert colleagues know for sure is that the family is the most effective child-developing agent around, when it wants to be and *can* be. Out of the plethora of studies of day care and early intervention, one thing stands out. A child needs a family—that is where his roots and his education are at. Mothers and fathers who spend time with their child are better at it than are most organized group care arrangements. We are learning that the child-rearing practices of the poor do not differ markedly from the most affluent. Statistics show that with a rising income, the same mother spends more time with her child.

But the parents of children under the poverty mark have less time and energy for their families. They are easily overwhelmed simply by the struggle for survival. A frantic and harrassed mother is not a natural mother, and a father filled with failure and desperation is not a real father and he may not even stay around long enough to try. A parent who cannot put food on the table cannot convey to a child a sense of order, purpose or self-esteem. The poor are confronted by the same problems which confront the rich, and more of them. The difference is they simply do not have the resources or the time to cope. And when they slip, they find it all the harder to come back.

My second reason for saying that income distribution is our best hope is that something is just plain wrong with asking our juvenile courts to straighten out the young lives already twisted by the effects of poverty. Our first priority in distributing justice to children ought to be distributing income to their families. It is simply not right that children in this country grow up in poverty.

It *is* right that their families receive an income which allows them to make choices for their children. As Daniel Moynihan's book makes clear, there is a wide consensus on this principle, and programs implementing it have been proposed by both political parties. Commission after commission on crime, race, violence, or children has recommended some form of income redistribution as the only way to begin to solve our toughest social problems.

The advantage of distributing income directly is that Government intervention into private lives should decrease. The resources and options that come with money should allow families to function without agency oversight or official intervention at every turn. An adequate income will give them the self-respect to ask for advice, instead of having it gratuitously heaped on.

Of course there are obvious limits to what an increased income can do for the family mired in poverty or the child who is in trouble. The immediate and visible effects may be few, although the lessening of the income gap between the very poor and the mainstream of society should siphon off a great deal of the intensity of mutual hatred.

It may be that an adequate family income won't guarantee a stable family life, won't eradicate the effects of bigotry or stop crime cold or solve all the problems of growing up in Sodom and Gomorrah. *But I am convinced that nothing else can begin to work without it.*

We know that most of our helping efforts are now frustrated by the poverty of those we seek to help. Doctors in the ghetto health centers treat rat-bites only to send their patients back to rat-infested tenements; they treat the symptoms of malnutrition only to send children back to families that simply don't have the money for milk and meat.

Should this frustration cause us to throw in the towel and have done with the jumble of current service programs? Senator Abraham Ribicoff has calculated that the 31 billion dollars spent annually for 168 Federally financed service programs would be more than enough to raise the poor above the poverty level. As I stated earlier, I am not joining up with those who would cut out services and put nothing in their place. Until we are committed to an adequate income distribution program, or until we know just what does and doesn't work, special services are still necessary to help a generation of children escape birth defects, and disabilities; to live in decent housing without lead paint on the walls; pay regular visits to a pediatrician for innoculations and to catch hearing and perceptual defects before they ruin life at school.

A guaranteed income is not a solution for today's scarred children. It is an investment in a new generation of young lives otherwise relegated to human refuse heaps. It is an investment which should pay handsomely in decreasing social service costs in the future.

There is more we could do to ensure that this investment in prevention yields results: reconstruct the economy to provide a competitive job market at the lower end of the pay scale; honor our commitment to excellence, and integration, in education from nursery school upward; subsidize dramatic shifts in housing patterns. I do not know whether these efforts are feasible in our time and I realize that this is not even a popular time to be talking about money. The President has said he is against throwing money at problems or at the poor. But simply labelling such efforts as "utopian" is not a serious and worthy confrontation of the problem— we are learning that programs for the poor alone are vulnerable to change in public sentiments and the political tides.

But there are other income distribution programs that are not so vulnerable. . . . There are proposals for expanding Social Security and unemployment compensation to cover more families with children; proposals for children's or family allowances, or for redesign of our tax system, which have universal coverage. There are studies which show that doubling the amount of resources flowing to the poorest fifth of the population is affordable and feasible without conveying the implication of failure or the social stigma of a "hand-out."

In short, the *process* of income distribution can be as automatic, as acceptable, as nonperjorative as Social Security is today. And indeed, if the phrase had not already been pre-empted, that is what a program for shifting income should be truly called—social security.

If I seem to have strayed from the topic of juvenile justice, I can only say that for me the concept of social security for children is inseparable from the highly personal, individual, and humanistic philosophy of justice ... that each child is an individual, that he must be dealt with individually, by the people who make up his life and who form his attitude toward life. It is here, within his world, that whatever services he needs must be rendered—not in some abstract system of juvenile justice.

QUESTIONS FOR DISCUSSION

1. How would you distinguish between the concepts of management, control, and treatment in deviance?
2. What combination of events, specific to the early American experience, led to the "discovery" or invention of the prison, mental hospital, almshouse as an alternative to the less humane approaches of the past?
3. Why were these institutions so quickly accepted all over Europe and elsewhere?
4. What is a "total institution"? Describe its characteristics and particularly highlight those features which make the "total institution" anti-therapeutic and anti-rehabilitative according to its critics.
5. What would you say are the major changes in American prisons from 1870–1970. What new directions are possible within the walls?
6. Conrad's article is fairly convincing testimony to the ineffectiveness of modern attempts to rehabilitate convicts, patients, and other deviant and disruptive types. What new model does he advocate to replace the rehabilitation emphasis? Is this new approach realistic? Practical?
7. Judge Bazelon describes juvenile justice as a love-hate story. What does he mean? Why is he so disenchanted with the present course of juvenile justice? How would

he remedy its present defects? How would you remedy them if you had the power, experience, and motivation?
8. There are certain concepts or ideas that you should have gleaned from this section. For example, can you define, describe or discuss the following:

   A. Pennsylvania versus the Auburn system of prisons.
   B. The difference between a reformatory and a penitentiary.
   C. The concept of recidivism.
   D. Why total institutions came to be called asylums?
   E. Why the number of people in institutions is falling while the mental illness, crime, and deviance rates are rising?
   F. Can you conceive of a society without total institutions?

BIBLIOGRAPHY

Bakal, Yitzhak, ed. *Closing Correctional Institutions: New Strategies in Youth Services.* Lexington: D. C. Heath, 1973.

Belknap, Ivan. *Human Problems in a State Mental Hospital.* New York: McGraw-Hill, 1956.

Carter, Robert, Glaser, Daniel, and Wilkins, Leslie, eds. *Correctional Institutions.* Philadelphia: J. B. Lippincott, 1972.

Clemmer, Donald. *The Prison Community.* New York: Rinehart and Company, 1958 (republication).

Gerber, Rudolph, and McAnany, Patrick D., eds. *Contemporary Punishment: Views, Explanations and Justifications.* Notre Dame: University of Notre Dame Press, 1973.

Giallombardo, Rose. *Society of Women: A Study of a Women's Prison.* New York: John Wiley, 1966.

Glaser, Daniel. *Adult Crime and Social Policy.* Englewood Cliffs, N.J.: Prentice-Hall, 1972.

Glaser, Daniel. *The Effectiveness of a Prison and Parole System.* Indianapolis: The Bobbs Merrill Company, 1964, 260–84.

Goffman, Erving. *Asylums.* Garden City, New York: Doubleday Anchor Books, 1961.

Irwin, John. *The Felon.* Englewood Cliffs, N.J.: Prentice-Hall, 1970.

Kassebaum, Gene, Ward, David, and Wilner, Daniel. *Prison Treatment and Parole Survival.* New York: Wiley, 1971.

McCafferty, James A., ed. *Capital Punishment.* Chicago and New York: Aldine-Atherton, 1972.

Meyer, John C. "Change and Obstacles to Change in Prison Management." *Federal Probation* 16 (1972), 39–46.

Rothman, David. *The Discovery of the Asylum.* Boston: Little, Brown, 1972.

Stanton, A. H., and Schwartz, M. S. *The Mental Hospital: A Study of Institutional Participation in Psychiatric Illness and Treatment.* New York: Basic Books, 1954.

Sykes, Gresham M. *The Society of Captives: A Study of a Maximum Security Prison.* New York: Atheneum, 1965.

Tittle, Charles R. *Society of Subordinates: Inmate Organization in a Narcotic Hospital.* Bloomington: Indiana University Press, 1972.

Ward, David A., and Kassebaum, Gene G. *Women's Prison: Sex and Social Structure.* Aldine, 1965.

Warder, John, and Wilson, R. "The British Borstal Training System." *Journal of Criminal Law and Criminology* 64, No. 1 (1973), 118–27.

13

The Medicalization of Management

Western society and particularly Western jurisprudence has long been preoccupied with the sin-evil-guilt-punishment syndrome. Much of the present crisis in deviance management and control lies in somehow resolving the notion that the "outsider" is willfully evil, that his actions are controllable, if only he would exercise his will power. The status offender, no less than the street criminal or the suite offender, has chosen to be deviant. This syndrome has made it impossible, until the Enlightenment, to introduce other models of etiology and management, to say nothing of treatment, into the deviance field. Gradually, and painfully, the mentally incompetent were removed from this context. So were the young who were pushed into a welfare model. Since 1843, the argument has been waged concerning the mentally ill offenders. Are they to be seen as ill or as offenders? Parenthetically, it wasn't so very long ago that electrocutions would be postponed until such time as the offender was mentally sound enough to understand the nature and reason for his punishment. Electrocuting a "sick" man would hardly fit the model or deter others.

In opposition to this sin-evil-guilt-punishment syndrome, there eventually arose the model of the deviant as "sick" and in need, not of punishment, but of treatment. The founder of modern criminology, Cesare Lombroso, was a physician. Outside the United States the field of deviance remains largely a clinical discipline, where criminal law is taught in law schools, criminology in medical schools.

Forgetting about the theory, for a moment, what are we to think of a Richard Speck who killed eight nurses in Chicago? A Charlie Manson and his girls? A Juan Corona and the two score or more migrant workers who died at his hands? An adolescent and young adult group of three sadistic homosexuals who violated their friends and neighbors before killing and burying them in scattered locations in Texas?

Apart from these recent sensational cases, how are we to conceptualize the 9,000,000 alcoholics, several million more excessive drinkers, unknown numbers of homosexuals, the drug abusers, the runaways, the violent, the terrorists, kidnappers, rapists, and assaulters? Are they evil and punishable or sick and in need of treatment? This is the dilemma, and it is as difficult to resolve as the differing conceptions of man himself—as an innocent corrupted by the world (tabula rasa) or a beast in need of restraint (the leviathan).

Slowly, western societies have moved away from the punitive and into the clinical treatment realm. Much deviation, whether conventional or status, is now viewed as a clinical aberration of some sort—genetic, psychological, organic, neurological. Thus, the hyperactive and sometimes destructive kid who is a pain to everyone—parents, siblings, teachers, neighbors—is now hyperkinetic and on Ritalin (an amphetamine-type drug) or some similar pharmacologic agent. The sociopath (psychopath, antisocial personality) is thought to be hypo-aroused and subject to drug treatment and retraining. The tall, hyper-aggressive male petitions the court for a review of his case on the grounds that he has an extra Y on his sex-determining chromosome (The XYY).

Even when the etiology is clearly sociological or the product of environmental variables, drug intervention has become the usual method of management. Unbelievable amounts of tranquilizers, for example, are dispensed in jails and prisons and mental hospitals. Anti-depressives are readily available to the suicidal, the depressed; hallucinogens to the chic, young, and the unhappy everywhere. The per capita utilization of mood altering substances has made the ethical drug firms a solid growth industry.

In a more serious vein, the punitive syndrome has totally failed with certain of our so-called deviants. The largest number of police arrests—nearly a half including disorderly conduct, disturbing the peace and, of course, public intoxication—involve alcohol abuse. A night in the "drunk tank" or a stretch in the workhouse serves neither the public nor the inebriate. Some "old timers" have been sent through this revolving door system scores of times with no notable positive impact. Worse still is the narcotic drug problem. Prohibited by law as maintenance medication for addicts for some fifty years now (the Harrison Act and subsequent Supreme Court cases lasted into the 1920's), heroin, other natural narcotics (morphine, opium), and the synthetic narcotics have been nonetheless available on the illegal market. Repression, long prison sentences, and even the prison-public health hospital approach have done little to crimp the illegal market, reduce the crime-related property offense problem, or help the addict to a drug-free and productive existence. Lastly, by way of illustration, it is estimated that perhaps a fourth of all prison inmates in the

top-of-the-line prisons are beyond either punishment or reform. In other words, neither more of the "hole" nor more education and prison amenities will reduce their antisocial behavior on the streets to which they ultimately return. In all these and other deviations, drug treatment (legal, scientific, medically approved) has been recommended as a matter of preference because all else seems to be ineffective.

All of these issues are discussed in the selections which follow. The first contribution, "Will the XYY Syndrome Abolish Guilt" is by an outstanding legal scholar, Nicholas N. Kittrie. Although there are many articles on the XYY, we chose Kittrie's because it is set in the historical context which we have called the sin-evil-guilt-punishment syndrome. The argument ranges well beyond the XYY genetic anomaly and faces the issue, which everyone seeks to avoid whenever possible, of criminal responsibility. Incidentally, there is now some evidence that Richard Speck is *not* one of those with this chromosome pattern.

The second contribution concerns the chronically anti-social personality—the simple sociopath—and suggests that a unique biological defect of the sympathetic nervous system could account for the behavioral and clinical picture presented by him in and out of the institution. In general, the simple sociopath shows exaggerated autonomic responses—cardiovascular, skin, pupil—which argues for a hypo-aroused individual who can be treated effectively with arousal-producing drugs. This treatment model assumes that the simple sociopath is a hyperkinetic child who failed to mature out of his hyperkinesis at, or a short time after, puberty.

The third selection describes in detail the glowing success of the Manhattan Bowery Project initiated by the Vera Institute of Justice in New York. Some 10,000 persons (3500 skid row men and women averaging three times each) had used and been treated in the three and one-half years of the program. The essence of the project is a detoxification center (as an alternative to the drunk tank), featuring an emergency unit, broad gauged health care, after-care service, a work referral service, and other ancillary activities. The Manhattan Bowery Project has been copied far and wide and is a model for urban communities attempting to "medicalize" the public intoxification, and especially the skid row alcoholic problem. The article contains two case history vignettes as well.

After years of struggle against the police, prosecutors, courts, and, most of all, against the then hard-nosed Federal Bureau of Narcotics, Dr. Dole and Dr. Nyswander succeeded in introducing methadone maintenance as an alternative to the ineffectual approaches and 90 percent plus recidivism of heroin addicts, no matter what the program. Methadone maintenance, a medical program involving the substitution of one addicting substance, methadone, for another, heroin, under medical auspices was clearly an idea whose time had come. In this abridged selection, a none too friendly critic, Dr. Nathan B. Eddy looks at methadone maintenance for *morphine* addicts. In the process, his paper is valuable because he describes the Dole-Nyswander program and its very favorable results up to 1968. Even Dr. Eddy does not dispute this success but does conclude with a *caveat* well worth heeding.

The next selection deals with the Report of the Committee on the Judiciary of the United States Senate on Senate Bill 1115 concerning a Methadone Diversion Control Act of 1973. The bill, passed by the Senate on June 8, 1973, is a chilling analysis of what has been occurring in terms of the diversion of methadone into the illegal market. The bill calls for a tightening of controls over methadone dispensing agents and programs. The part of the bill that concerns us is a description of the growth of methadone maintenance programs in the United States since 1968. Nationally, there were only 400 addicts on methadone maintenance in 1968; 73,000 such patients in 1973. In February 1973, more than 800 programs were in existence. There were 242 pounds of methadone manufactured in 1968, and 5724 in 1972. The rest of the report is less glowing. Data are presented on the extensive diversion of some of this methadone into illegal channels and the ways in which such seepage occurs. If there is a moral in this story, it is that "hard" drug abuse lends itself to no easy answers in the management and treatment realm.

Jonathan Swift, the great English satirist, once offered his well known modest proposal to the effect that Irish children be sold and eaten to provide money for their parents and to keep the population stable. Dr. Lorrin M. Koran, no writer or satirist but a bona fide M.D. offers in this final contribution in this drug treatment selection, his own modest proposal (also offered by the Vera Institute of Justice in New York City). The proposal: provide *heroin* maintenance for heroin addicts on an experimental basis. No naïve character, Dr. Koran is fully aware that his proposal, however couched in medical lingo, and however reasonable it may be, is clearly unacceptable. But Dr. Koran, like Dr. Dole and Dr. Nyswander may yet prove to be prophetic in thinking the unthinkable. It would not surprise us, the editors, to see such a program evolve in the late 1970's.

WILL THE XYY SYNDROME ABOLISH GUILT?

Nicholas N. Kittrie, S.J.D.

Is guilt on its way out? The product of ecclesiastic thinking, guilt is inextricably tied

From *Federal Probation,* XXXV, No. 2 (June 1971), 26–31. Mr. Kittrie is Director, Institute for Studies in Justice and Social Behavior, The American University Law School.

to belief in free will. It consists of man's condemnation for failure to choose between the right and wrong paths of behavior. Guilt takes for granted man's capability and freedom to make such choices. But in this adherence to the concept of individual responsibility, guilt comes in direct conflict with diverse modern theories of behavioral determinism—the belief of some that man acts out of innate hereditary forces ("nature') and the conviction of others that criminal action is a result of environmental influences ("nurture")—a product of acquired traits and of situational forces.

There have been many assaults on the validity and viability of guilt during the last century. Yet it has survived all these attacks, defended by those who contend that the abolition of the concept of guilt would do away also with social restraints and order. Slowly, however, new breaches are being made in the dogma of man's free will, which underpins the whole citadel of criminal justice. One recent battering ram has been provided by evidence of the XYY syndrome.

THE NEW DETERMINISM

The September 4, 1965, murder of a prostitute in a cheap Paris hotel set the dramatic scene. Marie-Louise Olivier, the prostitute, was found strangled in an apparently motiveless slaying, and the French police set out looking for 28-year-old Daniel Hugon, the central suspect. Hugon, who fled Paris and went to Normandy, was found working on the farm of actor Jean Gabin. Surrendering to the gendarmerie, Hugon confessed and expressed remorse.

The day before he was to stand trial, Hugon attempted to take his life in the Sante Prison. Concerned, the court ordered elaborate physical and mental examinations of the accused. One analysis, called a karyotyping, was made of his chromosomes, the strands of genetic material contained in every living cell. The chromosomes hold the biochemical code which determines a person's physical traits, such as skin, hair and eye color, and also hold the key to sexual characteristics. Hugon was found to have a chromosomal abnormality.

The cells of the human body have 46 chromosomes, each set of 23 derived from one of the parents. Two of those 46 chromosomes, designated either X or Y because of

their form, determine the person's sex. The cells in a woman's body contain two X chromosomes. Each male cell has one X and one Y chromosome. But deviations from this norm appear from time to time when nature produces such unusual chromosomal combinations as XXY, XXYY, and XYY.

Daniel Hugon possessed an XYY variant. This deviation occurs in about one out of every 2,000 men, but had previously been observed in much larger proportion among mental hospital and prison inmates. The examination of large numbers of inmates in maximum security wards in Scottish institutions prior to the Hugon case led to the conclusion by Edinburgh's Dr. Patricia Jacobs that 3 percent of these men had extra Y chromosomes. As a result, geneticists in other parts of the globe commenced a search for evidence linking criminality and chromosomal abnormalities.

In Melbourne, Australia, Robert Peter Tait was convicted of bludgeoning to death an 81-year-old woman from whom he had sought a handout. He was sentenced to death in 1962 but his sentence was commuted to life imprisonment. In the Pentridge Prison, Dr. Saul Weiner, a geneticist, found that Tait as well as three other inmates convicted of murder, attempted murder, and larceny were XYY. Writing in the leading British medical journal *Lancet,* Dr. Weiner claimed: "These results strongly support the concept that an extra Y chromosome is associated with antisocial or criminal behavior."

Support for the claim of a causal connection between crime and chromosomal irregularities kept growing. New evidence disclosed that XYY men tended also to be abnormally tall and to possess low intelligence. Dr. Mary A. Telfer, a biologist in Philadelphia reported that a study of four Pennsylvania prisons and mental hospitals disclosed five XYY cases among 129 tall inmates. Similar results were reported from the Atascadero State Hospital in California.

An outburst of legal maneuvers and writings challenging the criminal responsibility of XYY offenders followed. In Sydney, Australia, a 21-year-old laborer charged with the murder of a 77-year-old widow, found stabbed to death in her apartment, was shown to have 47 chromosomes in each body cell instead of the normal 46. The jury bypassed this issue, however, and found him not guilty by reason of insanity. In the French Hugon case the XYY qeustion was finally likewise abandoned. In the United States, the attorneys for Richard Speck, the convicted murderer of eight Chicago nurses, suggested in April 1968 that they may mount an appeal on the basis of Speck's genetic abnormality. Similarly, this never came to fruition.

Although the XYY defense has not obtained its full test in court, the proponents of determinism nevertheless have gained a new handle. Evidence of the XYY syndrome lent support to a long line of believers in genetic determinism—going back to Cesare Lombroso and his disciples. Nor are the claims with regard to genetic determinism a lonely development.* ... How will traditional guilt fare in a society which is increasingly discovering the impact of biological forces upon human choice and behavior?

GUILT, FREE WILL, AND CRIMINAL JUSTICE

Guilt is a legal concept, not a scientific fact. In modern society it is the function of courts of law, rather than witch doctors, legislatures, or bureaucrats to decree guilt and innocence and to assess punishment upon those found guilty. Today's method for finding guilt consists of an elaborate legal ritual, called trial, where witnesses come forward like actors in a play to give evidence. It is from this evidence that guilt or innocence is distilled. While the measure of punishment is typically left to the discretion of judges, the determination of guilt has been delegated to juries both by early English legislation and the American Constitution. It is thus one's own peers who must weigh the evidence and decide the probability of guilt—whether it has been proved beyond a reasonable doubt.

*See other articles in this section (Ed.).

Evidence is whatever courts consider proper and relevant for the weighing and determination of criminal guilt. Trial by fire—where guilt was proved by the accused's inability to put out the flames set by him, or by bitter waters, where the wife's infidelity was established by the swelling of her belly after drinking the testing concoction—were not uncommon until the Middle Ages. Trial by combat was another popular means for weighing evidence and determining guilt. Those not guilty were expected to prove their innocence through an armed victory over their accusers.

Trials through witnesses go back to Biblical times. Yet one might assert that it was Europe's Age of Reason, with its emphasis upon communications and the rationality of man, which accounts for the emergence of the modern trial—where words rather than acts of faith take preeminence. In the courts of America proof is usually made today through either verbal testimony or demonstrative evidence. Most frequently, an eye witness will describe what he saw or heard. Occasionally, the murder weapon, including fingerprints, the forged paper, or the clothing of the suspect, may be introduced at the trial as demonstrative proof. Any one of these types of evidence may also be classified as either direct or circumstantial. Direct evidence means that the witness in fact saw the very fact he describes; circumstantial evidence relates only indirectly to the facts that need be proved. A witness who did not observe a burglary, yet who testifies to the accused's spending an unusual amount of money shortly thereafter, is offering circumstantial evidence.

A determination of guilt is not merely a factual finding; it is also a moral judgment. The proof of guilt usually consists of two parts: proof that the accused did the prohibited act and proof of his criminal intent or purpose. Most serious crimes require not only proof of the criminal act, but also proof that the offender intended to do wrong, or, in legal language, a showing that he had *mens rea* (an evil mind). This requirement of *mens rea* goes back to the religious

THE MEDICALIZATION OF MANAGEMENT

and moral foundations of the criminal law, where criminality was viewed as a personal fault—one's failure to resist to temptations and to steer away from wrongdoing.

Those who in fact lacked the necessary intent (consider a man picking up a coat in a restaurant believing it to be his own) or others who were generally considered immature or otherwise incapable of harboring such evil purpose (animals, infants, persons acting under a threat to their lives, and imbeciles) were accordingly held exempt from criminal responsibility.

Modern criminal law similarly exempts from guilt juveniles under given ages, adults suffering from mental illness and defects, and at times also chronic alcoholics and drug addicts.

It is the concept of individual responsibility that is at the core of the criminal process. Without the axiomatic acceptance of man's special endowment with responsibility there can be no guilt finding. The laws of primitive societies which prescribed punishment for goring oxen and biting dogs were finally abolished because of the recognition that morality requires that we not punish those incapable of personal guilt.

Reduced to simple terms, the criminal law is based on an assumption of free will— that is, a belief in man's capability to differentiate between the lawful and the unlawful and his ability to choose between the two. Criminal law therefore exempts from its process those who, due to some formulated legal criteria, have been determined to lack that amount of free will which is required for a finding of criminal responsibility.

THE INSANITY EXCEPTION TO FREE WILL

The insanity defense has grown over the years to accommodate departures from this basic axiom of criminal law—that people are responsible for their deeds. Punishing the mentally ill appeared inhumane even in 14th century England. Not only was the spectacle of punishing a raving maniac distasteful to the viewing audience, but it also seemed an ineffective measure for deterring the conduct of an unreasoning being. Yet the question of what degree of insanity should suffice to exempt a person of criminal responsibility was never solved satisfactorily.

Commencing with a crude test which equated those exempt from punishment to "wild beasts," the criteria grew in complexity with time. The most famous and still most common test for differentiating between the responsible and those not so, is the *M'Naghten* rule which was formulated in the forties of the last century. M'Naghten gained fame by attempting to assassinate English Prime Minister Sir Robert Peel. (His case demonstrates that even before the current flourishing of mass media the assassin could derive his fame from the glory of his victim.) After public complaints and Queen Victoria's assertion that M'Naghten was unduly relieved of punishment, the House of Lords in 1843 formulated uniform criteria for relief from responsibility. They required that to be found not guilty the accused must have such a defect of reason, as a result of a disease of the mind, as not to know the nature and quality of his act or else not to know the difference between right and wrong.

The middle of the current century saw many efforts to expand and liberalize the insanity defense. Most psychiatrists have complained that M'Naghten reflected psychiatric knowledge of days gone by. Some asserted that the test embodied legal criteria which are not meaningful to psychiatry, others urged a new test less grounded in the cognitive or reasoning ability of the offender. The reformers noted correctly that a man may well suffer from severe mental illness which could dominate his behavior yet leave his knowledge of right and wrong unimpaired.

The desire of psychiatrists, as well as reforming judges, to subject increasing numbers of offenders to mental therapy instead of criminal punishment resulted in the 1954 *Durham* rule in the District of Columbia ("is the crime a *product* of mental illness or defect"), the 1961 *Currens* rule in the United States Court of Appeals for the Third Circuit ("did the accused, because of mental illness or defect, lack *substantial capacity* to conform his conduct to the law"), and the 1962 American Law Institute's model penal code which offers a combination of these reforms for voluntary adoption by the various states. Each of these modifications is intended to broaden the classification of those found insane rather than guilty.

Yet all tests which curtail criminal responsibility are arbitrary. Judge Thurman Arnold keenly noted in 1945 that the law recognizes either full responsibility or total irresponsibility, permitting no middle ground between these absolutes. The sciences of human behavior, on the other hand, provide no support for such dichotomy and furnish no scientific delineation for distinguishing the evil from the ill. The line that the law draws is therefore not a product of science but a result of a social policy determination. This means that society can at best establish not a scientific line on the insanity defense, but rather a pragmatic one, which constantly weighs penal versus psychiatric alternatives and is fundamentally grounded in the public need for stressing individual responsibility as a means for promoting conformity and self-restraint. In the face of deterministic sciences, the concept of guilt is thus preserved primarily as a tool of education, to reinforce ordained behavior, and as a means for social control.

In reality much of the heat generated in the recent debates on the insanity criteria remains primarily academic. In our courts it continues the task of the jury to find a sufficient degree of insanity to negate guilt. Psychiatrists have and continue being the most influential witnesses in charting the insanity defense before the jury: by elucidating psychiatric knowledge and relating it to the accused's condition. What psychiatrists label as insanity has a considerable bearing on the jury deliberations. Yet despite the dramatic recent departures from the M'Naghten formula, psychiatrists usually continue to limit their diagnoses of insanity to psychotic cases only, leaving neurotics and the so-called psychopath to the traditional criminal process. Moreover, we have little insight as to the effect of the new insanity criteria upon jury decisions. Some research projects have reached the conclusion that juries pay little attention to legal or psychiatric refinements and that the determination of insanity is most often a result of jury instinct and common sense. "Is the accused nuts?" may still better summarize the question before juries than the more complex criteria of M'Naghten, Durham, or A.L.I.

To this precarious and artificial balance between responsibility, free will, guilt, and insanity, the XYY syndrome brought much turmoil.

THE XYY DEFENSE

To exempt those afflicted by it from guilt, the XYY syndrome must come within one of the doctrines vitiating personal responsibility in criminal law. The formula that comes most readily to mind is the insanity defense. It is this route which has been previously attempted or suggested in France, Australia, and in Chicago's Speck case.

To comply with the insanity defense requirements one must first establish the existence of a mental illness or defect. Accordingly, the typology of the XYY abnormality becomes central. Is the XYY syndrome a mental illness, a mental defect, a physical illness, or none of these? Indeed, what precisely are the confines of mental illness or deficiency?

Only after this first prerequisite is positively answered, can one move on to the diverse secondary tests. In those states, adhering to the *M'Naghten* test a further showing must be made of the offender's lack of knowledge of the quality and nature of his act or his inability to tell right from wrong. Where *Durham* controls, a showing that the criminal behavior was a product of the abnormality would be required. Under the *Currens* or the A.L.I. test, the accused must prove that because of the mental illness or defect he lacked substantial capacity to stay within the law. And in a number of other states which subscribe to the irresistible impulse test, an insane person will be found not guilty if the offense was induced by such impulse.

As one views this complex obstacle course, the insanity defense route does not appear without difficulties. XYY's adoption and classification as a mental disability by the psychiatric fraternity would be the first requirement, and no such development yet appears in sight. The next step would depend on the insanity test in effect in given state. The *Durham,* the A.L.I., or the irresistible impulse criteria could supply the causality requirement needed to exempt an XYY sufferer from responsibility by a showing that the criminal behavior was a product of or was caused by the XYY abnormality or else that the latter deprived the offender of the capacity of conform. Less certain would be the *M'Naghten* test's applicability to the XYY sufferer, unless it could be shown that the abnormality affects the cognitive faculties.

In the face of these prerequisites, it is not surprising that little progress has been made to date in endowing the XYY abnormality with the equivalents of the insanity defense. But other routes remain. One to be looked at is the defense of compulsion or coercion. Criminal law has traditionally exempted from responsibility those who offended while acting under an imminent and serious threat to their lives or those in their immediate family. The defense of compulsion permits one to commit a lesser offense in order to save his life; it acknowledges also that a prohibited act is not punishable unless accompanied by the requisite evil intent. Yet coercion must usually be externally imposed and must involve a fear of life of bodily harm rather than an inner compulsion. Moreover, it will not excuse homicides—for no trade-off is permitted between one's own life and that of others.

Another approach is possible to the relationship between XYY and guilt. This is similar to the law's past treatment of drug addiction and alcoholism. In 1962, in the landmark *Robinson* case, the Supreme Court held addiction to be an illness and concluded that those afflicted by it may not be punished for addiction. The law has not been willing, however, to go farther and exempt from guilt addicts charged with other criminal behavior, such as robbery and murder, or even such narcotic-connected offenses as importation and sale of drugs. More recently several federal courts, in a similar vein, ruled that those suffering from chronic alcoholism may not be prosecuted for public intoxication. Again, however, this exemption from responsibility does not extend to behavior other than mere intoxication. In refusing to relieve an alcoholic of punishment for such offenses as disorderly conduct, assault, or larceny, the courts have stressed the need for a showing of a direct causality between alcoholism and the prohibited conduct. Absent such connection, guilt will prevail.

The implications for the XYY defense are significant. If the syndrome indeed is classified as an illness, those possessing it could certainly not be punished for its presence. But those claiming it as a defense to other offenses would be required to prove that but for XYY's existence the proscribed conduct would not have occurred. Such proof might be difficult if not impossible, as would be the proof of any single causative reason for crime.

The most radical approach to the relief of XYY sufferers from responsibility would be that undertaken in the juvenile process. There, by comprehensive legislative fiat, all youth under a given age were decreed criminally unaccountable due to chronological immaturity. Beginning with the end of the 19th century, determinations of guilt have been accordingly dispensed with for juveniles and a new system of social controls, within which concepts of guilt and personal responsibility are nonexistent, was introduced. This absolute abolition of guilt met with some opposition. It is arguable that not all youth under a given age, say 16 years, are in fact so immature that they are presumed to be incapable of criminal intent. The argument is valid. Yet here as in other areas of law, the line of responsibility is arbitrarily drawn or, more precisely, drawn to accommodate certain social policies. In the juvenile area this policy called for the exemption of youths from the branding and harsher sanctions of criminal law. The policy did not result, however, in the total exemption of children from social sanctions, for the juvenile courts offered a new formula for control.

THE ABOLITION OF GUILT

Where does all this leave the XYY offender? Although with some modifications he could be fitted within one of the traditional exceptions to criminal responsibility, none of these cubby holes fit him precisely now. Yet the XYY findings are probably only the first of many new scientific insights into human behavior. Much additional understanding of the causes of criminality will inevitably follow. Some evidence will point to physiological or genetic factors, other evidence will be environmental, educational, social, or economic. The time has clearly come for an eclectic framework for the causes of crime and delinquency. Yet in each individual case the balance of forces that finally tilt the scales from lawfulness to criminality may be different.

As the evidence of behavioral determinism grows, how are we to cope with it? Should we go the old road and presume all persons sound and capable of free will, yet keep withdrawing from this universe those who fall within such narrowly defined criteria as insanity, youth, drug addiction, alcoholism, or whatever it may be? Or should we honestly traverse a new road toward a new model of social control: one where we admit that free will and responsibility are at best relative and terms of convenience only; one where we acknowledge the inability and irrationality of drawing an absolute line between those capable of guilt and those free of it.

The XYY discovery is merely one more piece of evidence that man is not his own master. The XYY evidence should make the framers of the criminal law stop and think. If we are willing to give the XYY sufferers the benefit of the doubt, according them special therapeutic measures in lieu of punishment, we should be willing to recognize that every other offender has his XYY equivalent, his mortal weaknesses and shortcomings—hereditary or environmental. The rational choice in a scientific age offers only two alternatives: We are either to hold all guilty and subject to punishment or else recognize that we are all imperfect, yet accountable to society. I would rather choose the second approach and commence seeking and offering not punishment for guilt but individual cures for men's misconducts. I would prefer to see a new emphasis in society's management of crime, a shift from the assessment of abstract guilt to the offering of pragmatic remedies—to each according to his need.

What I suggest is not as revolutionary as it may sound: In the face of deterministic evidence we should presume all offenders as having involuntarily entered the life of crime. Yet society's defense requires that we undertake measures for its protection even against those without moral guilt. Accountability without guilt is not a new approach. Enrico Ferri, the noted 19th century Italian criminologist, pointed in this direction. He insisted that we need not rely on concepts of individual responsibility and guilt in order to design social programs for dealing with offenders. Every person who lives in a society is accountable to it for his antisocial conduct. Society, in return, may seek to curb his future misdeeds, not as a punishment for the improper exercise of free will but as a remedy for his human failings.

DRUG TREATMENT OF THE SOCIOPATHIC OFFENDER: "THE JUICE MODEL" APPROACH

Simon Dinitz, Harold Goldman, Lewis Lindner, Harry Allen, and Thomas Foster

Nothing is less congenial to contemporary criminological thought in the United States than the proposition that organicity may be a significant variable in certain types of deviant behavior. This unqualified rejection of the potential relevance of organicity in crime, delinquency, and other forms of deviance is not without historical merit considering the extravagant and often absurd claims of the several varieties of early constitutionalists, European traditionalists, and endocrine criminologists. Thus, in one pertinent example of injudicious rhetoric linking endocrine dysfunction and crime, Schlapp and Smith in 1928 wrote a volume modestly entitled *The New Criminology,* in which they stated their case as follows:

We shall attempt to demonstrate that the vast majority of all criminals, misdemeanants, mental deficients, and defectives are products of bodily disorders, that most crimes come about through disturbances of the ductless glands in the criminal or through mental defects caused by endocrine troubles in the criminal's mother. The attempt will also be made to show that criminal actions are in reality reactions caused by the disturbed internal chemistry of the body.

Such well known previous assertions of hereditary, morphological, and physiological proneness to deviance as those of Lombroso, Hooton, Kretschmer, and Sheldon among others, extrapolated from the most meagre evidence should not forever be permitted to stand as impediments to the reconsideration of the role of organicity in the more *idiosyn-*

From et al., Vol. 3, No. 1972, pp. 20–28; *The Archives of General Psychiatry,* 23 (Sept. 1970). 260–67, and unpublished paper delivered at the AAAS meeting (Feb. 25, 1974). Simon Dinitz and Thomas Foster are in the department of Sociology; Harold Goldman is in the Departments of Psychiatry and Pharmacology. Lewis Lindner is in the Department of Psychiatry; and Harry Allen is in the Center for the Study of Crime and Delinquency, all at The Ohio State University.

cratic, bizarre, and non-normative forms of deviance. It is entirely likely that the present unprecedented knowledge explosion in the life sciences might spin off ideas and approaches useful in the study and understanding of human behavior—including deviance.

To urge a reconsideration of organic parameters in specific non-normative and chronic deviations, such as that of the sociopath, in no way diminishes the importance of the comparative, cultural, and interactional perspectives long dominant in American thought. The enormous and readily observable variability of human social institutions, interpersonal relationships, and normative standards, including cross-cultural perspective does not preclude the potential fruitfulness of including other models as explanations on the micro, individual, or clinical level. There is nothing in differential association, differential identification, subcultural, limited opportunity, neutralization, or labeling theory which suggests that biological concomitants, such as an XYY chromosomal pattern, can play no role at all in criminality and other anti-social conduct.

The confusion and conflict in perspective—not only of the sociocultural with the organic but with the psychoanalytic and symbolic interactional as well—is perhaps better demonstrated in the study of sociopathy than in most other forms of deviance. Even the terms used historically to describe anti-social sociopathy testify to the diverse conceptions of this disorder as moral insanity, moral imbecility, *manie sans delire,* moral alienation, psychopathy, constitutional inferiority (atavism), and constitutional psychopathology among others. Perhaps the only consensus about this condition through the years has been that whatever sociopathy is, it is not a psychotic disorder in the traditional sense. Nor is it a type of psychoneurosis. Hence the idea that it is some sort of residual disorder which can be invoked when other designations are inappropriate. Parenthetically, this status is not so very dissimilar from Scheff's recent classification and defense of mental illness as residual deviation.

While in criminological circles, Lombroso (1911) talked about moral imbecility and characterized the sociopath as guiltless, impulsive, boastful, aggressive, and insensitive to social criticism and physical pain, and Garofalo (1914) spoke of him as being born with "ferocious instincts," the first use of the term sociopath, as such, and the earliest modern characterization of this character disorder was offered by Partridge, who stressed the impulsiveness and infantilism of the sociopath. Since Partridge, various clinicians and others have vied with one another in specifying the number and kind of intrapsychic symptoms and/or behavioral manifestations characteristic of sociopathy. The McCords, for example, echo Lombroso in describing the sociopath as basically loveless and guiltless. Pescor, on the other hand, offers a 54-symptom list of attributes of the sociopath. Cleckley, the foremost contemporary clinical student of the subject, in his *Mask of Sanity*, has endowed the sociopath with the following 16 characteristics which subsume the lengthier lists of the many other writers such as Pescor. These attributes include:

1. superficial charm and "good" intelligence
2. absence of delusions and other signs of irrational thinking
3. absence of nervousness and other psychoneurotic manifestations
4. unreliability
5. untruthfulness and insincerity
6. lack of remorse or shame
7. inadequately motivated anti-social behavior
8. poor judgment and inability to learn by experience
9. pathologic egocentricity and incapacity for love
10. general poverty of major affective relations
11. specific loss of insight
12. unresponsiveness in interpersonal relations
13. fantastic and uninviting behavior, with drink and sometimes without
14. suicide rarely carried out
15. sex life impersonal, trivial, and poorly integrated
16. failure to follow any life plan

The American Psychiatric Association previously recognized four types of sociopath-anti-social, dyssocial, drug addict, and sexual deviant. The latter three types typically violate contemporary legal and moral standards and are probably better understood in a subcultural context. This is, however, not the case with the anti-social type whose behavior may vary widely even from deviant subcultural norms. The 1952 Diagnostic and Statistical Manual of the American Psychiatric Association described anti-social sociopaths as:

... chronically anti-social individuals who are always in trouble, profiting neither from experience nor punishment, and maintaining no real loyalty to any person, group, or code. They are frequently callous and hedonistic, showing marked emotional immaturity, with lack of sense of responsibility, lack of judgment, and an ability to rationalize their behavior so that it appears warranted, reasonable, and justified.

In the spirit of continuing the confusion, the second (1968) edition of the American Psychiatric Association's Diagnostic and Statistical Manual of Mental Disorders contains no mention at all of such traditional terms ,as sociopathy and psychopathy—as though these disorders have ceased to exist. This change in the style of classification replaces sociopathy with anti-social personality, the latter described as follows:

This term (anti-social personality) is reserved for individuals who are basically unsocialized and whose behavior pattern brings them repeatedly into conflict with society. They are incapable of significant loyalty to individuals, groups, or social values. They are grossly selfish, callous, irresponsible, impulsive, and unable to feel guilt or to learn from experience. Frustration tolerance is low. They tend to blame others or offer plausible rationalizations for their behavior ...

In addition to this obvious and continuing inability of clinicians to agree on the existence and nature of sociopathy as a clinical entity, there has been even wilder speculation about the etiology of this ill-defined character disorder. Earlier writers, almost to a man, offered a hereditary-instinctual explanation of anti-social sociopathy. Presently, others speaking from a social-psychological and interactionalist position posit pathologically defective role-taking ability as etiologic. Cognitive psychologists stress insufficient anxiety and fear arousal precluding learning and the integration of social and personal experience. Developmentalists argue for a delayed maturation explanation. This delayed maturation hypothesis has two variants. When physiologists speak of delayed maturation of the central nervous system they mean fewer or improper interneuronal connections for the processing of information about the environment. Delayed maturation also is used by physiologists to refer to the incomplete structural development of neuronal and glial elements. Psychoanalysts, on the other hand, talk about delayed maturation in a functional and developmental sense, by which they mean that the psychosexual development and the transition from the pleasure to the reality principle has been interrupted, distorted, or inhibited. Implicit in most of these interpretations is the view that faulty role-taking ability, inadequate arousal and delayed maturation, in the psychiatric sense, are generated in pathological family configurations. Thus, anti-social personality is a clincial disorder whose course, mechanisms and etiology remain unknown. Genetic, physiological, interactional and sociocultural etiologies have been advanced to explain this interactable disorder characteristic of perhaps one to three percent of the general population and as many as a fifth or more of prison inmates and disturbed offenders.

THE "JUICE MODEL": A THEORETICAL STATEMENT

Since the promulgation of the cybernetic model, sometimes mistakenly termed the "feedback" approach, shortly after World War II, adherents of this "black box" school in both biology and experimental psychology have formulated two more or less complementary micro-level, input-output, feedback models. The first utilized and extended the very successful mathematical-physical models in the hard sciences to postulate a computer circuit model of nervous system function and dysfunction. Unfortunately, as in the case of early constitutional explanations of criminal behavior, some early popularizers of this model, or more precisely, family of models, made extravagant extrapolations from the known to the unknown, interpreting many behavioral disorders as resulting from breakdowns in the programming and circuitry in the nervous system. When such models proved to be too simplistic, by several orders of magnitude, to support the extravagant claims made for them, they quite naturally lost their attractiveness for biologically and psychologically oriented behaviorists.

In order to improve these early models and to add some of the requisite complexity, it became necessary to introduce the biologic properties of neural components and to incorporate them into the framework of existing mathematical models. This elaboration resulted in a second-generation model—the so-called "juice model"—which is still in its ascendency. This "juice model" suggests that many behavioral disorders can be conceptualized as resulting from maladaptive neuroendocrine regulatory mechanisms. In this more biological model, the inappropriate activation or inhibition of responses is attributed to faulty physiologic mechanisms. This "juice model," in its most parsimonious form, postulates a defect in catecholamine-secreting neurons (primarily components of the sympathic nervous system) which makes it impossible for the anti-social sociopath to make graded responses to environmental stimuli. The sociopath vacillates thus between two states—being "turned on" or "turned off." When he is "turned off"—that is, when such an individual's endogenous secretion of epinephrine is minimal because the adrenal gland is not being stimulated to secrete by the central nervous system—the sociopath is relatively unaffected by ordinary external stimuli, including those that would be mildly or even moderately anxiety and/or fear producing in "normal" individuals. Thus, punishment, reward, discipline, affection, and other cognitive and affective stimuli which profoundly influence the actions of "normal" individuals seem to have no greater impact on the conduct of the sociopath than the most minor or inconsequential stimuli. In contrast, because of "denervation supersensitivity" resulting from a postulated lesion or defect, the sociopath is "turned on" maximally by even a moderate secretion of epinephrine. When "turned on" he reacts maximally to almost all stimuli, however important or unimportant, exhibiting the type of impulsive, hedonistic, trivial, explosive, and irrational conduct which every clinician has observed any many have described. Thus, such "impaired" individuals can make only "on-off," but not graded, emotional responses; their behavior, of necessity, is predicated upon a two-valued logic.

This hypothesized defect in catecholamine-secreting neurons, presumably originating during the formative years, or even prenatally, makes it impossible for the sociopath to make the graded and normatively appropriate responses to environmental stimuli. Instead, he has been conditioned to a socially unacceptable response pattern to emotion-laden stimuli. While this model, then, theoretically explains why the anti-social sociopath makes his apparently irrational "on-off" switchlike responses to emotion-laden stimuli, it must be emphasized that it *in no way postulates or even suggests the mechanism by which the responsible lesion(s) originated (etiology).*

THE "JUICE MODEL": HARD EVIDENCE

It is, of course, one thing to posit the concept of a neural lesion and quite another to demonstrate it in the sociopath. Nevertheless, a number of investigators have studied criminal sociopaths using such indices of autonomic nervous system functioning as heart rate, systolic blood pressure, skin resistance, pupillary diameter, sensory thresholds, and avoidance learning. In theory, on these measures of autonomic nervous system functioning, the anti-social sociopath should show greater variability of cardiovascular, skin resistance, and pupillary levels along with elevated sensory thresholds and impaired avoidance learning in his resting or ordinary state when compared with "normal" individuals; furthermore, the injection of epinephrine should reveal augmented cardiovascular, electrodermal, and pupillary responses as well as improving both sensory thresholds and avoidance learning, again in comparison to "normals."

Hard evidence for this "juice theory" is as yet anything but compelling. The indicators so far examined are all complex and derivative and not one empirical study to date has been replicated precisely by another investigator. Nevertheless, one or more of these predicated physiological manifestations have been consistently found in each of the studies done to date.

A very brief review of these investigations indicates that Funkenstein *et al.,* conducted the first physiological research pertinent to the "juice model." In 1949, he and his colleagues injected small doses of epinephrine into male and female patients, classified as anti-social sociopathic personalities, who had been referred by the court following crimes of violence. With systolic blood pressure as the dependent variable, these investigators found that the sociopathic subjects showed an increased response to epinephrine in comparison to mentally ill patients and to controls. In 1955, Lykken showed that his primary sociopathic prisoners had diminished galvanic skin responses to forced lying and impaired avoidance conditioning (learning a mental maze to avoid electric shock), when compared with either his non-institutionalized controls or his reactive anti-social prisoners. In 1964, Schacter and Latané confirmed both the increased cardiovascular reactivity to epinephrine (using Lykken's maze, but a lighter shock) in sociopathic male prisoners compared with non-sociopathic male prisoners. In addition, they demonstrated an improvement in avoidance conditioning performance in the sociopaths compared with delinquent *secondary* sociopaths. In 1964, Schoenherr demonstrated an increased threshold to electric shock in sociopathic prisoners. In 1968, this was replicated by Hare who also confirmed the increased skin resistance and diminished variability in *primary* sociopathic prisoners (compared with *secondary* sociopathic prisoners and non-sociopathic prisoners) and demonstrated an impaired orienting response.

Our own work at the Ohio Penitentiary began as a multidisciplinary, attempt to replicate and extend the provocative work of Schacter and Latané. Without repeating the involved methodological and research design details of either study, theirs or ours, it is sufficient to state that forty-three inmates (19 *primary* sociopaths, 10 mixed, and 14 non-sociopaths), of the 1375 consecutive admissions that were screened, met all of the age, I.Q., physical health, MMPI, Cleckley Checklist, Lykken Scale, and offense and incarceration criteria for inclusion as subjects. These forty-three inmates were subjected to a double-blind experimental procedure in which they worked at Lykken's avoidance learning task under two conditions: injections of epinephrine or saline, randomly assigned.

Two major findings emerged from our experimental work. First, unlike previous investigators, we found two obvious and distinct types of so-called *primary* sociopaths which we have designated as *hostile* and *simple* forms. These groups were found to differ from one another on almost every parameter, including cardiovascular responsivity, criminal history (i.e., number of arrests, types of offenses, number of incarcerations, length of time incarcerated, parole violations), military history, (i.e., number accepted into armed forces, length of time in service, types of termination), familial characteristics (i.e., from intact families, present marital status, number of times wed), and psychological profiles (on various MMPI profiles, especially the Ma and Pt and on the Taylor Manifest Anxiety Scale).

Second, as a group, the *simple* sociopaths differed from the non-sociopaths as well as the *hostile* sociopaths in cardiovascular reactivity (i.e., heart rate) to epinephrine. Thus, controlling for the placebo injection, which was sometimes administered first and sometimes second, the heart rate responses to epinephrine injection of the *simple* sociopathic increased a significant 12.81 beats per minute, while the respective heart rate increased of the *hostile,* mixed and non-sociopath prisoners were 5.95, 6.28, and 4.50 beats per minute. This heart rate doubling of the increases in the other groups is a highly significant finding and totally in concordance with the supportive work of others on the pupil, skin and other physiological observations.

Our thesis is that the unusual physiology and behavior of the *simple* sociopath, as described by Cleckley and by the American Psychiatric Association, may be manifestations of a single autonomic defect, reflecting diminished function of catecholamine secreting neurons, including those involved with sensory input. This hypothesis was tested with female inmates at the Ohio Reformatory for Women. The results were inconclusive on the physiological measures and totally confirmatory on the behavior measures.

Finally, at the behest of the Ohio Department of Corrections we began an experimental drug treatment program using both male sociopathic and non-sociopathic inmates who were given both a sensory arousing drug and placebo medication in a *double blind experiment.* Each inmate was given a small glass of orange juice substitute containing either the drug or the placebo on a twice daily basis. Treatment lasted six months for each volunteer. Although there are still a few inmates on this program as of February 1974, all concerned with the project—from the researchers, to the prison educators, work supervisors, guards, and the men themselves—believe that in about 80 percent of the sociopaths who went through the program, the results were most positive.

The sociopaths generally stayed out of mischief, were cooperative, gained weight (except for one who already had far too much of this desirable improvement before treatment began). Nearly all the sociopaths when on the drug rather than the placebo, reported themselves to be more energetic, less anxious, having more restful sleep, improved appetite, less impulsivity, decreased irritability and, above all else, a markedly increased feeling of well-being. No one knew who was who or on what substance until long after their release from the project. The non-sociopaths, on the other hand, were

consistently rated throughout the program as unchanged and reported themselves as unchanged.

This program has now been extended, in modified form, to patients in a psychiatric facility. It is still much too early to tell whether these simple sociopaths, who land in a mental hospital rather than prison, will confirm our positive treatment findings obtained to date in our multi-year research treatment program.

AN ALTERNATIVE FOR THE DRUNKENNESS OFFENDER: THE MANHATTAN BOWERY PROJECT

Vera Institute

In most American jurisdictions it is against the law to be drunk in public, and although considerable discretion is exercised by policemen in enforcing public drunkenness laws—obviously, many well-dressed men who have had too much to drink and yet appear to be affluent and "reasonable" are overlooked by police officers—about one arrest in three in the United States in recent years has been for public drunkenness. In some cities the figure is up to one-half or even a majority of all arrests.

Most such arrests involve so-called alcoholic derelicts, the self-destructive drop-outs or rejects from the American system who congregate on skid row and are caught up in the criminal justice machinery. Commonly prosecuted under vagrancy and disorderly conduct laws, these men are usually placed in "drunk tanks" in local jails where conditions are particularly unsavory and inhuman. They are often crowded with inebriates, suffused with human waste odors, barren of mattresses or sanitary facilities.

Equally disturbing is the fact that the individual receives little or no attention for his extensive medical problems and no treatment for excessive alcohol use. His feelings of self-contempt and his instincts for self-

abuse tend to be reinforced, and his rights of due process are apt to be denied him as he is brought into court without counsel and his case is determined hurriedly in company with a large group of other offenders. (As a demonstration of the effect of counsel or the judicial process here, in 1966 in New York City, after Legal Aid attorneys began working for a short period in the Men's Social Court, the conviction rate of homeless men arrested on alcohol-related charges fell from 98 percent to 2 percent.)

Moreover, alcoholic offenders are apt to be confirmed recidivists: some are arrested as many as 100 to 200 times and spend up to 10 or 20 years in jail on short-term sentences. Displaying suicidal tendencies and beset by psychological problems, these men are capable of drinking up to a gallon of wine a day for a month and eating nothing, with disastrous effects on the liver, stomach, brain, and muscles.

In New York the practice of dealing with these individuals through the criminal justice system goes back to the middle of the nineteenth century, when the Bowery, a broad avenue running about a mile north from Chinatown to Cooper Union on Manhattan's Lower East Side, was already becoming known for the homeless drifters who populated its doorways, sidewalks, and flop-

From Vera Institute, 1961–71.

houses. New York's practice was similar to those in other cities—to remove these men from the streets, in wholesale roundups if necessary, and assume that a short stay in jail would "teach them a lesson."

Some resort to the use of force in dealing with derelicts has perhaps been natural in American cities, for these people do constitute a considerable public nuisance: they are unsightly, attract predatory criminals, are often underfoot on the sidewalks or in subway entrances, given to panhandling and vomiting and urinating in public places, and they frequently carry vermin and diseases such as tuberculosis and pneumonia.

By 1967 there were an estimated ten to fifteen thousand derelicts in New York City, with four to five thousand in the Bowery area alone.

A SYSTEM WHERE EVERYBODY LOSES

The effects of roundups and short jail terms for derelicts are, clearly, far from beneficial—for the derelict himself, for the criminal justice system, and for society as a whole. While the streets may be swept clean for short periods, even that benefit has a self-defeating aspect as the derelicts are released after a few hours to return to their skid row neighborhoods. Meanwhile, as has been noted, the apprehended derelict has gone through an experience that has probably done him more harm than good.

The criminal justice system itself also suffers as it attempts to deal with the homeless derelict. It suffers in dignity because its personnel and its institutions are put to the self-defeating and demeaning task of herding a continuous stream of social outcasts through the revolving door of arrest and short-term incarceration. It suffers in integrity because it is managing a discriminatory program where the poor and rootless are prosecuted under drunkenness statutes while the affluent are sent home, and where some are convicted of being drunk and disorderly when in fact they are merely sick and disheveled. It suffers in the waste of valuable time spent by police in handling approximately

two million alcohol-related arrests nationally every year, when the time could be spent on other police functions. It suffers in the amount of court time spent in adjudicating drunkenness cases. And it suffers in the extent to which short-term correctional facilities must be turned over to the detention of homeless derelicts.

In a larger sense the community as a whole suffers, too. The financial cost of handling alcoholic vagrancy through the use of criminal sanctions has been estimated at $100 million per year nationally—not including expenditures for rehabilitation or prevention.

And the larger public health problem, meanwhile, goes untended.

VERA'S INTEREST IN THE DIVERSION IDEA

The Vera Institute of Justice first became seriously interested in the possibility of changing this system of handling derelicts when it discovered that nearly all of the arrests in the New York City precinct chosen to test the Manhattan Summons Project fell into the drunkenness-disorderly conduct category. Encouraged by some success in modifying bail and summons practice, the Vera group felt it might be possible to devise techniques for changes here, too.

What was needed, clearly, was a project to test the feasibility of diverting the homeless derelict from the criminal justice system to a special facility that could offer medical treatment, detoxification, social services, and some hope for at least partial rehabilitation.

In 1966 two factors combined to give Vera an opportunity to plan just such a project. The first was that Mayor John V. Lindsay's pre-inaugural Law Enforcement Task Force had recommended that a "Skid Row Project" be undertaken which would test the feasibility of a diversion program for the homeless alcoholic derelict.

The second factor was the reasoning in two recent Federal Court decisions, *Easter* v. *District of Columbia* and *Driver* v. *Hinnant*, which had held that conviction of alcoholics on charges of public intoxication was tantamount to conviction of sick persons for displaying symptoms of a disease, and consequently was unconstitutional. Although a subsequent Supreme Court decision in *Powell* v. *Texas* in June 1968 overruled those decisions, it seemed likely in 1966 that jails would not be available much longer as detoxification centers for destitute alcoholics.

Further urgency for the creation of some alternative was caused by the severe overcrowding in New York City courts and jails. Judicial and correction officials were anxious to devise some system by which the prison population could be safely reduced.

PLANNING A BOWERY PROJECT

In May of 1966, Mayor Lindsay invited the Vera Institute of Justice to plan and develop a medically oriented method for removing destitute alcoholics from the criminal justice system. The Mayor requested that City departments cooperate with Vera, and assigned a key assistant to expedite the City's procedures wherever possible. The cost of Vera's planning efforts was financed by a grant from the Ford Foundation.

After consulting with many health and social services experts, Vera decided to recommend that priority be given to establishment of a short-term, 50-bed detoxification unit in the Bowery area that would provide five days of treatment—ordinarily a sufficient length of time to ease a person through the withdrawal syndrome.

The recommendation for a short-term program instead of one seeking long-term rehabilitation was made for a number of reasons. First, it would make possible the handling of large numbers of men and thus provide a genuine alternative to detoxification in the jails. Next, it could offer periodic detoxification to those many men who would be expected to return to the facility repeatedly. Also, virtually all Bowery alcoholics were in need of a detoxification program, and no single long-term program with limited resources could possibly hope to deal with the great variety of psychiatric disorders occurring among these men, ranging from schizophrenia and irreversible organic brain damage to problems that may be amenable to group therapy and halfway houses. And, finally, some long-term care facilities already existed, and men desirous of further help after detoxification could be referred to them.

After an extensive search it was learned that a treatment facility could be housed on the fourth floor of New York City's Men's Shelter on East 3rd Street just off the Bowery, which had put up Bowery men between 1954 and 1964 but had since been unused.

St. Vincent's Hospital, a lower Manhattan voluntary institution with a notable record of service to the poor and destitute of the area, agreed to make its beds available to Bowery men whose condition proved unmanageable in the detoxification unit at the Men's Shelter and to make its X-ray services available to project patients. Complicated tests could be run at the hospital when necessary.

This unique institutional arrangement, consisting of an independent detoxification unit operating at the New York City Men's Shelter and backed by the services of a prestigious New York hospital, was ultimately accepted by the State Department of Mental Hygiene and other involved government agencies.

It was decided that the program should operate voluntarily, not compulsorily, although there was some question as to whether Bowery men in distress would accept help unless they were compelled to do so.

A test of the practicability of a voluntary program was conducted in October 1966 by Vera and the City's Police and Social Services Departments. A plainclothes police officer and a Bowery lodginghouse clerk drove down the Bowery and approached sixteen men lying on the street. Each man was offered the opportunity of receiving medical assistance and a place to "sleep it off." Thirteen of the sixteen men accepted, and returned with the team to the Shelter's fourth floor where they were examined by a doctor, sedated, and put to bed. One man left that night. The next morning the twelve remaining men, not yet fully detoxified, were offered an opportunity to go to the City-run rest camp known as Camp LaGuardia, or to a mission. Eleven accepted. Throughout the experiment the men were cooperative and manageable. This experience strongly suggested that a voluntary program was workable.

A PROJECT IS PROPOSED

In November 1966, a formal proposal for a Manhattan Bowery Project was submitted to the Mayor. The recommendation was for a pilot project that would offer detoxification, medical diagnosis and treatment, and referral services to rehabilitation, residential, and other medical facilities.

The proposal received the endorsement of the Mayor, along with commitments of support from the heads of important cooperating agencies: the Social Services Department subscribed to the use of the fourth floor of the Shelter as a detoxification facility, and agreed to assign two (later four) caseworkers to the project to handle screening and referral; the Police Department agreed to assign four men and two unmarked vehicles to the project; the Department of Hospitals approved the loan of hospital beds, examining tables, and other medical equipment; the Department of Correction agreed to assign four officers (later recalled) to assist with record-keeping and reception duties, and to be available in the unlikely event that disorders might occur—and also to lend recreational materials and 30 beds for use by recuperating patients; St. Vincent's hospital agreed to serve as the supporting hospital and to make its laboratory services available, and also suggested that some of its resident physicians could serve on the night shift during off-duty in order to ensure 24-hour physician coverage; and finally, the Mayor's

Criminal Justice Coordinating Council endorsed the proposal and agreed to lend its services in advising and assisting project operations.

SETTING UP THE BOWERY PROJECT

It is worthy of note that in the eleven months between the presentation of the plan to Mayor Lindsay and the opening of the Manhattan Bowery Project's detoxification ward in November 1967, affirmative decisions and actions were required by a total of eighteen separate governmental departments and agencies at city, state, and federal levels.

Ultimately, a three-way funding arrangement was worked out where the Bureau of Alcoholism of the New York State Department of Mental Hygiene, the Office of Law Enforcement Assistance of the U.S. Department of Justice, and the City's Community Mental Health Board jointly funded the project's first year. In the second and third years, the funding was carried on by the Bureau of Alcoholism and the Community Mental Health Board, with the latter underwriting the major portion.

With funding for the pilot project assured, it became necessary to create a legally authorized organization to run the project, as the Vera Institute itself would not be the operating agency. It was decided to create a new and separate charitable corporation, the Manhattan Bowery Corporation, which would have legal authority to operate a detoxification unit.

HOW THE PROJECT WORKS

The new project admitted its first patient at 12 noon on November 27, 1967, and from that first day the project detoxification program developed a pattern which has seldom varied.

Seven days a week, from 8:00 a.m. to 7:00 p.m., the project's two-man rescue teams patrol the Bowery in unmarked police vehicles. The teams consist of a rescue aide, who is a recovered alcoholic, and a plainclothes police officer. When a team spots a man who is obviously in distress, the aide approaches him and offers him the opportunity to come to the Project to dry out. If the man seems in grave medical danger, the police officer summons an ambulance. The Bowery man is free at all times to reject the team's offer, or later, if he accepts, to leave the treatment program.

If he does accept, he is escorted to the fourth floor of the Men's Shelter where he is screened by a physician and admitted to the project. He is showered and deloused by medical aides and put to bed in the project's "acute ward." The physician on duty obtains as much pertinent history as possible. He then performs a complete physical examination and orders appropriate medication. Sedation in type and amount is tailored to the needs of the patient. Intravenous feeding is sometimes required.

On the morning following admission, each patient is also given a series of tests including a chest X-ray, blood count, urine analysis, liver function blood tests, and a blood test for syphilis. Complicating diseases are treated when found. Seriously disturbed patients are evaluated by a psychiatrist who may prescribe medicine. For the next three days the patient is kept under constant supervision and is given further medication to ease the symptoms of withdrawal from alcohol.

Most of the men are ambulatory after twenty-four hours, and on the third day, if a patient seems well enough, he is assigned a bed in the project's "recuperative ward.' Here the man is given a regular bed and he begins to use the recreation room where he eats, watches television, and takes part in the crafts and recreation program run by a case aide. He also sees a caseworker at this point and begins to make plans for his aftercare. The caseworker develops tentative referral plans, based on the man's physical and emotional condition, and various possibilities are discussed with the patient. If the patient approves, the caseworker calls the appropriate agency and tries to place the patient with the agency's program. This usually means referral to one of 25 aftercare programs offering therapeutic and rehabilitative services for patients willing to make an effort to return eventually to normal living.

At least one physician is present at the project twenty-four hours a day, seven days a week. This round-the-clock physician staffing makes it possible to keep patients at the project who are quite ill. By contrast, some other American detoxification programs transfer patients with delirium tremens, or other serious problems, to a hospital and use physicians only a few hours a day. The cost of these nursing programs is consequently believed to be lower than the Manhattan Bowery Project. Since the project's operation costs less than that of a typical hospital ward, however, and transfers many fewer men to hospitals than do nursing programs, the overall costs of detoxifying homeless men may not be substantially different under either system.

EXPANDED HEALTH CARE: THE CLINIC AND THE EMERGENCY UNIT

The first year's operation of the project's detoxification center demonstrated that more Bowery men needed a broader range of medical services than was available in the detoxification infirmary, and a solution was sought in the creation of two other treatment facilities—an emergency care unit and an out-patient clinic.

The emergency care unit was opened in April 1969 by St. Vincent's Hospital, in cooperation with the project. The police assigned a vehicle and two additional officers to the unit to work as rescue aides; the New York City Department of Social Services funded the unit and provided space on the first floor of the Men's Shelter. One doctor, a nurse, and two medical aides, all St. Vincent employees, see about 200 men a week, about half of whom are brought in by a rescue team. The other half walk in and request treatment. Minor medical problems, which had gone unattended, are treated before they develop into serious ailments. Men in need of detoxification are referred to the project's infirmary. Those with major medical problems are referred to hospitals.

The clinic was established in July 1969 to provide out-patient care for project participants. From the beginning, about 100 men a day have visited the clinic, which is staffed ten hours a day, six days a week, by three nurses and two social workers who dispense medication, do casework, and lead group discussions.

DATA ON PROJECT PATIENTS

In its first three and one-half years of operation, to July 1, 1971, the Manhattan Bowery Project admitted about 3,500 patients an average of three times each, for a total of about 10,000 admissions. Toward the end of the period, roughly 60 men were being admitted each week, some of whom had been treated as often as 10 or more times.

About one person in four approached on the street refused help; the other three accepted the offer of assistance. During the year ended June 30, 1971 about 92 percent of the admissions were recruited by the project's street rescue units, about the same as in prior years. The remainder are men referred from the Men's Shelter "deck clinic" or from other agencies.

The project quickly established that Bowery men do indeed suffer from many undiagnosed and untreated diseases. Medical charts during the first year showed that project patients presented severe medical problems: neurological diseases were found in 23.5 percent of the cases; pulmonary diseases in 63.5 percent; gastro-intestinal diseases in 9.5 percent, with peptic ulcer, cirrhosis, and gastritis predominating; cardiovascular disease in 9.0 percent; and dermatological disease in 22.5 percent. Few of the patients were receiving regular medical care at the time of their admission.

Psychiatric problems were no less severe. Analysis of the charts of the first 200 patients admitted showed that 33 percent were diagnosed as schizophrenic; 38 percent suf-

fered from personality disorders; 8.5 percent had anxiety neurosis; 17.5 percent suffered from depression; and 35.5 percent had associated chronic brain syndrome. Many of the men suffered from more than one condition.

The project's patients have ranged in age from 21 to 72 years, with the greatest number in their middle forties. Whites accounted for about 79 percent, 17 percent are black, and three percent Puerto Rican.

Most of the men have been Skid Row drinkers for about 10 to 20 years. They are basically wine drinkers, and support themselves by sporadic spot jobs. Approximately 25 percent have completed the 8th grade or less; 40 percent have attended high school; 30 percent have a high school diploma or one to three years of college; four percent of the men are college graduates; and some have professional or graduate training. Most were born in New York or neighboring states, while 24 percent are from Southern states.

THE PROBLEM OF PATIENT-STAFF RELATIONS

It was soon found that the problems presented by chronic alcoholics' personalities require great amounts of staff patience and flexibility. An alcoholic has low stress tolerance; he demands immediate gratification of his desires; and he suffers acutely from anxiety, which leads him, in his sober periods, to demand both things and attention. In his eagerness to escape his anxiety and tensions, furthermore, he is constantly on the lookout for excuses to drink, and he often sets up "rejection situations" which justify his drinking: he may attempt to provoke the staff, often without realizing he is doing so, hoping for rejection in the form of anger or dismissal (surprisingly, however, only a handful of men leave the project against medical advice).

Added to these provocations are others faced by nurses and doctors whose training has been "cure-directed." For them it is singularly frustrating to encounter the rejection of after-care services by many of the patients (about one-third), and even more frustrating is the high rate of recidivism among the men.

One of the most important staff techniques for handling the stress imposed by project patients and operations, aside from unusual personal flexibility, is constant internal communication—exchanging views in daily case conferences; in larger meetings where nursing, casework, and street patrol supervisors hold discussions with the medical and administrative directors; in medical and casework staff meetings; and at a monthly staff meeting where a lecture is given by a project worker or a visitor.

THE AFTERCARE PROBLEM AND "REHABILITATION"

The project has discovered that the number of men prepared to accept some form of after-care plan has risen steadily. During the first fourteen months the number rose from 33 percent of the men admitted to 57 percent. It has stabilized at 65 percent.

Despite their frequent setbacks, it seems clear that a substantial number of Bowery alcoholics are willing to seek further help, provided a sufficiently attractive plan is presented to them by an experienced caseworker.

The project has confirmed that "rehabilitation" for many Bowery men cannot be measured in conventional terms such as permanent sobriety, holding steady jobs, acquiring property, and establishing families and other social ties. On the other hand, deteriorated men can be motivated to make some changes in their lives, and, while such changes may seem small, they can be extremely significant to each man and to the community that must deal with him. A derelict can lengthen his average time between drinking sprees from a few weeks to months. He can obtain better paying jobs for longer periods of time. He can make better use of the city's health resources and obtain regular medical and dental attention. He can, through use of medically prescribed tranquil-izers and other drugs, combat periods of stress by means other than alcohol.

The aftercare center and clinic opened in July 1969 was designed to help in this process. It contains a spacious sitting room and recreational facilities and offers medication, counseling, job referrals, and, in some cases, psychotherapy. The expanded aftercare facility has enabled the project to enlarge the number of out-patient referrals from the detoxification center and to increase its services. A majority of the out-patients live at the Salvation Army Memorial Hotel, and twice a week staff members go to the hotel, taking project services directly into the community. In this relatively alcohol-free setting, the project hopes to improve the living conditions of Bowery men and demonstrate the desirability of a congregate living facility.

EXPERIMENTAL WORK PROGRAMS AND PROJECT RENEWAL

In 1969 the Bowery Project, with funds and support from Vera, ran two experimental work programs designed to provide employment in controlled settings for project out-patients. In the first program, six men cleared refuse from Lower East Side lots in cooperation with the Sanitation Department. With a great deal of support, all six men successfully remained sober during the six-week period.

The second program was a sheltered workshop, where six out-patients produced several thousand wooden toy trucks for sale through normal commerical outlets. This workshop offered less support and a number of men dropped out during its 12 weeks of operation.

Based on these two experiences, Project Renewal was created in June 1970, funded by the New York City Manpower and Career Development Agency with the cooperation of the Mayor's Urban Action Task Force. Ten out-patients, under the supervision of a project supervisor and manager, undertook to clean and maintain 35 New York City playlots, clearing them of refuse so that they could function as neighborhood recreation centers. The men live together in a brownstone in Brooklyn and receive support through group therapy and education classes. The combination of work and rehabilitation present an opportunity for some Bowery men to break their destructive drinking cycles.

SOME RESULTS AND CONCLUSIONS FROM THE PROJECT

The Manhattan Bowery Project's primary goals were to test whether Bowery alcoholics would agree voluntarily to participate in a program of alcohol detoxification; whether such a program could work in a non-hospital setting; and whether, following detoxification, the men would accept referral to other types of programs for ongoing care. Fundamental to all this, of course, was the concept of diverting the derelict from the criminal justice process.

The results of three and one-half years' operations suggest that the program works. Arrests of derelict alcoholics in the Bowery area have dropped sharply since the Bowery Project began operations—as much as 80 percent in the 5th and 9th precincts, where roundups were formerly made. The project's detoxification infirmary and St. Vincent's emergency clinic are now capable of treating and counseling approximately 260 men a week, in contrast with approximately 75 arrests per week previously made by police officers assigned to derelict control. Police officers formerly assigned to that function have been returned to regular patrol duties, thus increasing patrol effectiveness in those commands.

Since derelict alcoholics have largely been removed from New York's criminal justice system, benefits have accrued not only for the derelicts themselves but for the law enforcement, court, and correction agencies which are freed to deal with more serious threats to the community.

Other cities are now operating projects

that are based in part on the Bowery experiment, including Boston, San Francisco, Syracuse, Minneapolis, and Rochester, New York. Three of these employ nurses who originally served as staff nurses in the Manhattan Bowery Project. Also, a New York State alcoholic rehabilitation unit, new in 1971, is basing its program on the Bowery experience.

Clearly, the Manhattan Bowery Project is only one of a number of alternative settings in which alcohol detoxification might be provided. It could be managed, for example, in a special ward of a hospital, in a general medical ward, or in a nursing care unit that transfers unusually sick patients to a hospital. Among the advantages of the Bowery Project, however, is the fact that its staff is trained for, and oriented towards, the handling of the difficult alcoholic personality; that it has greater flexibility of operation than is found in a hospital or other more traditional setting; and that the staff's high level of professional training assures skilled evaluation and effective aftercare planning. The program is, of course, more costly than a nursing program; conversely, it is less expensive than an in-patient hospital program.

In the end, however, any program will be most successful if its patients seek participation in aftercare programs, which means that there must be such programs. If society is prepared to provide them—and not all of them must be expensive or long-term—the problems of homeless alcoholics could be largely mitigated, and skid rows themselves could gradually disappear.

Meanwhile, the project itself has been a successful demonstration but not a complete answer to the problem of the homeless derelict in America. A new kind of revolving door has been created—more humane than the old one, perhaps, but still no substitute for a broadscale approach to the derelict problem, including research into how these people arrived on skid row, and how they can be aided in becoming healthier and more productive citizens with less self-destructive life styles.

Perhaps the Bowery Project has prepared the way for such a broadened approach to the problem.

HENRY F.

Henry F. is 41 years old and was born and raised in New York City, the oldest of 10 children. His father was an alcoholic. Mr. F's childhood was unhappy and he quit school before completing the eighth grade. Subsequently he obtained a high school equivalency diploma. He has worked as a teletype operator and a machinist. He served four years in the Navy, receiving an honorable discharge in 1950. Mr. F. has suffered from alcoholism for over eight years.

Mr. F. was already an alcoholic when he was introduced to the Bowery by a friend in 1965. Since that time he has suffered all of the rigors of life of a Bowery man, having been injured in falls, in beatings, and in stabbings.

Up to May 1971, Mr. F. had been admitted to the Manhattan Bowery Project a total of 17 times in 29 months. He had one long period of sobriety during 1970, beginning two months after a stay at an alcoholism treatment unit, during which he attended the project's out-patient department and was employed as a member of the project rescue team. That interlude terminated on December 25th when he began drinking again. Seven more admissions to the project's ward followed, each characterized by depression and remorse. Several times he left against medical advice. Once during this period he was re-employed as a rescue aide, but he began drinking after three weeks.

On June 14, 1971, Mr. F. was admitted to the out-patient department, and on July 6th he began working again as a rescue aide. He was still in that position as of April 1972. Mr. F. now states that he is "remaining sober a day at a time." He has become an active member of Alcoholics Anonymous, and he has spoken to groups as large as 150 persons at AA meetings. He visits the out-patient department of the project and there meets regularly with a psychiatric resident. Mr. F.

performs his job well and empathizes with the Bowery men whose sorrow he knows so well. Mr. F. now dates, something he thought would never happen again.

Mr. F.'s experiences with the rescue team and with AA have helped him to build his life. He feels productive and needed, and his adjustment has extended to his personal life as well. Mr. F. sums it all up: "Life is very good."

ROBERT K.

Robert K. is 47 years old and was born in New York City, the 12th of 13 children. He attended school through the tenth grade, served honorably in the Army during World War II, and has worked as a mail clerk, postman, and doorman.

On October 25, 1971, Mr. K. was admitted to the Manhattan Bowery Project's ward for the 21st time. His first admission had been on January 27, 1969, when he was diagnosed as suffering from acute and chronic alcoholism, schizophrenia, and depression. Interviews during the first admission revealed that Mr. K. had been frequently arrested for vagrancy or disorderly conduct and had spent nearly a year in jail on these charges. He had been drinking for 25 years, had had a drinking problem for at least 15 years, and had suffered delirium tremens many times.

After suitable medication, plans were made for Mr. K. to go to an alcoholism treatment unit, but he left the project and began drinking again. On his second and subsequent admissions efforts were again made to arrange for continuing care, but he sometimes left against medical advice. Five times he attempted to manage his drinking problem with the help of the project's out-patient department and through referral to three alcoholism treatment units, but he was able to remain sober only for short periods. In January 1971, after three months in an alcoholism treatment unit, Mr. K. was referred to Vera's Project Renewal. He remained there for three months, probably his longest period of sobriety in many years.

While Mr. K. has made frequent, sincere

attempts to stop drinking, his diagnosis of schizophrenia and depression and his drinking history suggest that he will always be

dependent on society for some degree of care and support.

METHADONE MAINTENANCE FOR THE MANAGEMENT OF PERSONS WITH DRUG DEPENDENCE OF THE MORPHINE TYPE

Nathan B. Eddy

BACKGROUND

Through the years the claim has been made repeatedly, sometimes by persons with a wide experience with drug addicts, that some individuals can lead a reasonably normal life if they are given regularly small to moderate doses of an opiate and are unable to do so if they are not. The Rolliston Committee seemed to accept this view when, in its report to the Home Office of the British Government in 1926, it recommended that whether or not a patient should receive an opiate continuously, essentially the above criterion having been established, be left to the discretion of the physician. The Committee on Drug Addiction of the New York Academy of Medicine subscribed to the same view at least in part, since it said that immediate withdrawal of narcotics was not the best policy and recommended establishment of clinics for narcotic administration. The Scientific Study Group on Treatment of Addiction of the World Health Organization recommended a preparatory phase of treatment before withdrawal but certainly intended eventual abstinence.

Many have disputed the claim for a better life with drugs than without. It is a defeatist attitude; through continued effort the subject ought to be encouraged to meet his conflicts without the shelter of drug action. Also, stabilization on small doses without compulsory supervision is extremely diffi-

From *Drug Dependence* (National Clearinghouse for Mental Health Information, National Institute of Mental Health) No. 3 (March 1970), 17—26. The late Dr. Eddy was a Consultant, Bureau of Narcotics and Dangerous Drugs, U.S. Department of Justice.

cult. Persons dependent on opiates prize the thrill of drug action, the acquired euphoric effect, and, whatever the intake load, seek enough drug to give them that thrill. Consequently, on account of developing drug tolerance and shortening of drug action they want more drug and more frequent administration. Their life is not a steady state but a waxing and waning of drug effect and constant drive for repetition of this cycle.

Methadone came to our attention in 1946. It was demonstrated promptly that it was qualitatively morphine-like in its action essentially in all respects, with time-action differences. It substituted for morphine smoothly at a better than one-for-one ratio in persons dependent on large daily doses. Substitution could be effected and the dose reduced subsequently at a rapid rate with days elapsing before the patient was aware that either had taken place. Impending abstinence phenomena could be avoided completely by substitution of remarkably small doses of methadone taken by mouth. Given a choice, former addicts preferred methadone to morphine for its prolonged effect, but many reversed this choice later because of the greater peak thrill which morphine afforded. Chronic administration of methadone caused the rapid development of tolerance and cross-tolerance to other opiates and of a physical dependence of the morphine type. On abrupt withdrawal there was a delay of about 48 hours before any abstinence signs appeared. These signs never reached more than moderate intensity and were slower in their disappearance than after morphine. These differences have led to the employment of oral methadone substitution as an almost routine means of minimizing the withdrawal sickness whatever the opiate upon which the patient is dependent.

Dole and Nyswander have discussed at length the ineffectiveness for all but a very few narcotic addicts of detoxification with various rehabilitative efforts. Withdrawal of drugs can be accomplished in a hospital without much difficulty, but patients almost always return to drugs after discharge. If treatment is to improve substantially, physicians, according to Dole and Nyswander, must review their attitudes towards addiction. Drug abuse must be approached as a medical rather than a moral issue, and treatment goals must be clearly defined. At present physicians strive for two distinct goals which, if not inconsistent, are at least difficult to reach simultaneously. Elimination of drugs and rehabilitation are both desirable, but one must decide which has priority. The Dole-Nyswander belief and experience assign priority to rehabilitation.

THE TECHNIQUE (AS DESCRIBED ORIGINALLY)

The original description published in 1965, stressed a distinction between unsupervised distribution of narcotic drugs to addicts for self-administration at times of their choosing and medical prescription of drugs as a treatment or management of the drug-dependent person. The former was the condition in the clinics for addicts which existed briefly around 1920 and has been the objectionable feature in all later efforts to set up centers for the distribution of drugs to addicts. Dole and Nyswander insist that their procedure is not simple administration of drug for maintenance of addiction or substitution of one addiction for another. Their goal is rehabilitation, and drug administration is one tool to that end.

Patients for maintenance have been carefully selected throughout. After the first few were admitted from among those known to the originators of the program, others have been chiefly persons known and recommended by someone already in the program. The criteria have been: males aged 20–50 (a smaller number of females have been admitted), "mainline diacetylmorphine (heroin) users for several years with a history of failures of withdrawal treatment, not psychotic, and without substantial dependence on other drugs. The program was developed in three phases.

Phase I. Stabilization with methadone hydrochloride in an unlocked hospital ward during a period of about six weeks. The patient was given a complete medical work-up, psychiatric evaluation, review of family and housing problems, and job-placement study. After the first week he was free to leave the ward for school, library, shopping, and various amusements, usually but not always with one of the staff.

Patients differed markedly in tolerance to narcotics at the beginning of treatment and in the rate at which they adapted to increasing doses of methadone so individualization of dosage build-up was necessary. If signs of abstinence were apparent on admission, they were relieved with one or two intramuscular doses of morphine (10 mg.) or dihydromorphinone (4 mg.). Methadone hydrochloride was started with 10 to 20 mg. orally twice a day. The dose was increased gradually during the next four weeks to the stabilization level, fifty to 150, occasionally 180, mg. per day. With careful attention to dosage, the patients did not become euphoric, sedated, or sick from abstinence at any stage of treatment. They have felt normal and have not asked for more medication. After reaching maintenance level the daily dosage was adjusted until all was given at one time in the morning. It was made clear to the patients and accepted by them that the amount of medication and the dosage schedule were the responsibility of the medical staff; dosage has not been discussed. The dose was always taken in four ounces of liquid (a fruit-juice equivalent). Urine was analyzed daily for methadone, morphine, and quinine, later also for amphetamine and barbiturate. Sensitivity of analysis was such that a definite positive would be obtained if the patient had taken an average "bag" of heroin during the preceding 24 hours.

Phase 2 began when the patient left the

hospital to live in the community. He returned every day for his maintenance medication, taken in the presence of a staff member, and to give a urine specimen. After a time means were provided for a few patients living at a distance to receive from and take, in the presence of a local pharmacist, the daily maintenance dose, returning to the hospital less often than daily; or a few patients on the program for several months were given at one time enough medication for a week-end or for a short trip. The chief help needed in this phase was in obtaining jobs and housing and in resumption of education. Legal help was available if the person got into trouble.

Phase 3 was the goal of treatment. The "ex-addict" became a socially normal, self-supporting person. Those who arrived at this phase were still receiving maintenance medication and were returning one or more times a week to the hospital for counselling and urinalysis. The physicians in charge, while subscribing to the possibility of eventual withdrawal, have taken no steps in that direction and feel that such would still be premature. The difference between phases 2 and 3 is only in the degree of social advancement. . . .

It was said, "with methadone maintenance patients found that they could meet addict friends, and even watch them inject diacetylmorphine, without great difficulty. They have tolerated frustrating episodes without feeling a need for diacetylmorphine. They have stopped dreaming about drugs and seldom talk about drugs when together. . . . Unscheduled, but perhaps necessary, experiments in drug usage were made by four patients. These subjects found that they did not "get high" when "shooting" diacetylmorphine with addict friends on the street. Both the patients and their friends were astounded at their lack of reaction to the drug. They discontinued these unrewarding experiments without need for disciplinary measures and have discouraged other patients from repeating the experiment."

If phase 3 is reached "the patient will have established a new routine of life, socially acceptable and consistent with his abili-

ties. He will have developed a long-range outlook for the future; he will have a bank account and friends. At this stage he no longer needs support from older patients or counselors. He looks to the physician as a medical advisor, not as a guardian. The chief danger in this stage is his complacency, since a successfully treated patient ceases to consider himself as an addict. He is likely to feel that continued taking of medication is a needless inconvenience. . . .

The authors concluded this first report on methadone maintenance. "Methadone has contributed in an essential way to the favorable results, although it is quite clear that giving of medicine has been only part of the program. This drug appears to relieve narcotic hunger and thus free the patient for other interests, as well as protect him from readdiction to diacetylmorphine by establishing a pharmacological block." In the patient maintained on methadone there is still a drug dependence of morphine type and heroin is ineffective because of the phenomenon of cross-tolerance. Unfortunately, Dr. Dole and his associates persist in reference to the "anti-narcotic action" of methadone and "blockade" of heroin effect, though their discussion of the principles and objectives in their treatment of addiction indicate that they are aware of the phenomena of tolerance. We suggest that suppression, rather than blockade, more clearly describes the waning of the reaction to heroin. . . .

RESULTS

In 1966 Dole and Nyswander reported on 79 patients who had been in their program for three months or more. Of these, 58 had a job, nine were in school and four were involved with both job and school. Sixty-one were fully and eleven partly self-supporting. At the time of the report 120 patients had been admitted and 13 had been discharged because of psychopathic behavior or intractable continuing involvement with barbiturates or alcohol. Each of the dischargers had tried for re-admission. The authors point to the economic saving to the individuals and to society as the result of the cessation of heroin use by the 107 patients still in the program and of the absence or diminished need for hospitalization and incarceration in connection with criminal activity. They estimate conservatively that this saving already amounts to millions of dollars.

In June of 1968, Dole, Nyswander and Warner reported on 863 admissions to the program. There have been 109 discharges, 13 percent—10 voluntary, 9 for non-heroin drug abuse, 27 for medical disability and 54 for behavior reasons. Nine have died. Criminal behavior has been reduced by 90 percent and about 70 percent are engaged in productive work or are at school.

Others have tried methadone in the management of drug dependence of the morphine type (narcotic addiction) according to the Dole-Nyswander procedure or some modification. . . .

The Methadone Maintenance Evaluation Committee of Columbia University School of Public Health, under the chairmanship of Dr. Henry Brill, submitted a progress report as of March 31, 1968, to the New York State Narcotic Addiction Control Commission, covering approximately four years of operation of the methadone maintenance program. According to this report 871 patients had been admitted to various treatment centers; 119 or 14 percent had left the program, of whom 87 had been discharged, 24 had dropped out and 8 had died. The report, however, deals in detail with the two largest groups which include 544 males who have been in the program for three months or longer. At the time of admission, it was known that 28 percent were gainfully employed and 40 percent were receiving welfare support. After five months, 45 percent were employed, after eleven months, 61 percent were employed or in school, and for those in the program for 24 months or longer 85 percent were employed or in school. The proportion receiving welfare support showed a progressive reduction to 15 percent after two years. The pattern is similar for 79 women in the program for three months or longer.

The report indicates further that none of the patients who have continued under care have resumed regular use of heroin ("be-

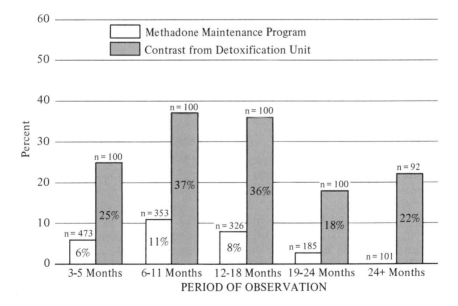

Figure 13–1. Percentage Distribution of Arrests for 544 Men in Methadone Maintenance Program Three Months or Longer as of March 31, 1968 and Contrast Group According to Months of Observation

come re-addicted") but 11 percent have demonstrated repeated use of amphetamines or barbiturates and about five percent have chronic problems with alcohol. The arrest record for the 544 males compared with a contrast group admitted to a detoxification unit and followed for the same length of time, matched only by age, ethnic group and time of admission, is shown in Fig. 13.1. . . .

The Evaluation Committee concluded, "For those patients selected and treated as described, this program can be considered a success. It does appear that those who remain in the program have on the whole become productive members of society, in contrast to their previous experience, and have, to a large extent, become self-supporting and demonstrate less and less anti-social behavior. It should be emphasized that these are volunteers, who are older than the average street addict and may be more highly motivated. (Their high morale and devotion to the program are phenomenal.) Consequently, generalizations of the results of this program in this population to the general addict population probably are not justified." . . .

It is clear, I think, that for a particularly selected group of persistent heroin abusers methadone maintenance has brought about significant social and economic gain at relatively low cost, compared to the loss to the individual and to society in these patients' previous experience. It must be emphasized, however, that until the recommended con-trol studies have been instituted and evaluated, conclusions cannot be drawn in respect to general applicability, nor plans formulated for broad extension of the program as an established treatment modality. Until such controls are carried out and their evaluation is at hand, the program is one of research only. It may be that full evaluation will eventually suggest the desirability as well as advantage of establishment of centers for the application of this treatment modality under a coordinating and supervising authority, wherever there are persons with drug dependence of morphine type in sufficient number to justify the effort. Even so certain precautions and attendant conditions will, I believe, be required:

1. Strict control of the amount and form of drug administration; designed to prevent accumulation or diversion, or recovery of methadone in injectable form.
2. Constant monitoring by urinalysis to determine not only narcotic consumption but also resort to other drugs of abuse.
3. Adequate and uniform record-keeping for meaningful analysis of the patient's history, condition at the beginning and progress in treatment.
4. Such help as is indicated for vocational training, job placement, living adjustment, and interpersonal relationships.
5. Eventual withdrawal of methadone must be kept in mind but insistence upon it should be left in abeyance at present.

THE DIVERSION AND USE OF METHADONE USED TO TREAT DRUG ADDICTS

Report of Committee of Judiciary, United States Senate

EXTENT OF THE PROBLEM

The problems of narcotics traffic and addiction are not partisan concerns, but issues that transcend geographical, philosophical

From Report of Committee of Judiciary, U.S. Senate, 1973.

and political differences. The citizens of this country are all too familiar with the devastating effects of heroin on the individual addict, the family, and society as a whole. Bitter experience has taught us that there are no simple solutions to the problems of drug addiction.

There are a number of treatment modalities however, that have been developed during recent years which have had some degree of success in rehabilitating certain addicts. Therapeutic communities which provide intensive therapy, counseling, and peer group interaction have helped some addicts free themselves from heroin addiction. Other programs include the use of the drug methadone as part of the treatment approach, both for detoxification and for maintenance.

Methadone is a narcotic similar to heroin and morphine. Although it is dangerously addictive, methadone has been used successfully to detoxify or maintain heroin addicts. In maintenance programs methadone addiction is substituted for heroin addiction. The methadone acts to suppress the craving for heroin. The chronic addict can be stabilized and permitted to concentrate on rehabilitative efforts. For some addicts methadone can lead to a productive life in the community.

In 1968 there were fewer than 400 patients enrolled in methadone maintenance programs nationwide. A recent survey conducted in February, 1973, by the Special Action Office for Drug Abuse Prevention (SAODAP) estimated the number of patients on both Federal and non-federal methadone maintenance programs to be approximately 73,000. Since October, 1971, the approximate number of persons in Federally funded non-maintenance programs, detoxification and drug free, has increased from 10,000 to almost 40,000. A significant percentage of these persons are enrolled in methadone detoxification programs. Regulations promulgated by the Food and Drug Administration contemplate an even broader proliferation of methadone. As of February, 1973, 666 methadone treatment programs have filed protocols as required by the new regulations and an additional 138 applications are being processed. Thus, more than 800 programs may be dispensing methadone in the treatment of heroin addicts.

To meet the needs of the programs and that of the private practitioners who dispense methadone to non-addicts for therapeutic purposes, production has increased tremendously. Since 1966, when only 242 pounds of methadone were manufactured, production has increased 2,265 percent to 5,274 pounds under the 1972 quota set by the Attorney General.

The rapid expansion of methadone programs and the quantity of methadone dispensed has simultaneously provided increased opportunity for diversion of methadone into the illicit market.

In many communities methadone is already widely available in the illicit market. In a survey of heroin addicts in New York City completed in 1972, Drs. James Inciardi and Carl Chambers found that of 95 randomly selected addicts with profiles typical of addicts in New York City, 92 percent had been offered the opportunity to purchase illicit methadone within the six months preceding the study; that 56 percent had purchased illicit methadone; and that 13 percent had sold methadone.

Dr. Robert Weppner of the Federal Research Center in Lexington, Kentucky, testified before the Subcommittee regarding his study of a sample of 336 addicts at the Lexington Center in 1971. Of the sample, 43 percent admitted to having used illicit methadone. Thirteen months later a second study of 469 addicts at the same facility showed the number of those admitting to the illegal use of methadone had increased to 52 percent. A majority of this sample revealed that they used methadone to obtain "a great high."

Although specific figures are not available on methadone arrests, the Uniform Crime Report reveals the State and local law enforcement arrests involving synthetic narcotics, including methadone as well as other drugs have increased by 892 percent in a seven year period ending in 1971. In only the last four years these arrests have increased from 8,920 in calendar year 1968 to 26,040 in calendar year 1971.

The Bureau of Narcotics and Dangerous Drugs is finding an ever increasing amount of methadone and other synthetic narcotics on the streets. During fiscal year 1971, BNDD undercover agents purchased or seized a total of 36,468 dosage units of methadone from various illicit sources. The comparable figure for fiscal year 1972 was 155,290 dosage units, and for fiscal year 1973 through December (6 months), the comparable figure was 201,720 dosage units.

In the summer of 1972 the BNDD office of Scientific Support initiated a program called Project DAWN, (Drug Abuse Warning Network) for the purpose of gathering a wide range of data indicating the relative frequency of abuse of various substances. Under the DAWN project, data is pooled from 38˙ Standard Metropolitan Statistical Areas across the country from such diverse sources as hospital emergency room and inpatient facilities, student health centers, county medical examiners and coroners, and community drug crisis centers. The reports received since September of 1972, indicate a distinct pattern with regard to methadone. Of approximately 325 substances on which data is collected, methadone ranks 7th in frequency of reported incidents. Methadone incidents in the sample increased from 166 in September, 1972, to 348 in January, 1973. Incidents involving methadone constitute an increasing proportion of all narcotic reports. While the number of heroin reports appears to have stabilized somewhat the number of reports involving methadone is continuing to increase.

The extent to which methadone is illicitly available was graphically illustrated in testimony by John E. Ingersoll, Director of BNDD, before the Subcommittee to Investigate Juvenile Delinquency, on April 5, 1973, when he explained in part as follows:

In August of 1972, in recognition of the increasing seriousness of methadone diversion, I ordered a special street level effort by BNDD agents in selected cities to gather intelligence on methadone availability within these communities. The findings, which we have not previously disclosed, may be briefly summarized as follows:

In New York City, agents found methadone to be readily available in all forms—tablet, disket, and liquid. One undercover contact was able to purchase 10 doses of methadone within one hour without so much as moving from the street corner. In another locality in Manhattan, 37 doses were obtained within one hour and a half. The prices ranged from $5 to $6 per 40 mg. disket with a higher price of $10 for liquid vials containing perhaps 100 mg. One agent remarked that he could leave the office in the morning with a barrel full of money and return by noon with a barrel full of methadone.

Undercover agents in Philadelphia discovered liquid doses of methadone selling for approximately $6 to $20. In Detroit, 11 doses were acquired at one location within 15 minutes and patients near a clinic facility were observed "hawking" methadone to passing motorists. Several days later a counselor at another clinic offered to sell an undercover contact heroin as well as methadone. He was subsequently arrested in possession of heroin. The prices per dose here ranged from $6 to $7 per disket and $10 per liquid vial.

In Boston, the situation was found to be much the same; and in one case, a suspect was identified threatening patients as they left a clinic area and taking their methadone from them in order to sell it in the street for profit. Similar efforts were made in New Orleans, but it was found that due to the previous closing of one of the more negligently operated clinics and the insistence in New Orleans that dosages be consumed on the premises, little could be accomplished within the short time of this survey.

The Subcommittee to Investigate Juvenile Delinquency was particularly interested in the sources of the growing amount of illegal methadone available on the street. Its investigation, corroborated by those of Federal and state agencies, revealed that it is being diverted from legitimate sources. An analysis of 670 samples of methadone submitted to BNDD over a two year period, revealed that 468 were in commercial tablet form, 166 in liquid solution and 36 in miscellaneous categories. BNDD has uncovered only one clandestine operation. This rarity was discovered in 1969 and led to arrests of several persons involved in the illegal synthesis of methadone. BNDD reports no evidence to suggest that any such activity is continuing at this time.

Illegal methadone has several primary origins: careless or unscrupulous physicians; thefts and diversion from methadone programs or in transit to methadone programs; and patients enrolled in methadone programs.

Methadone is used by physicians for the relief of moderate to severe pain. It is available in tablet form, usually 5 mg. or 10 mg., and ampoule form, usually 10 mg. in 1 mil. solution. According to the National Prescription Audit published by R. A. Gosselin and Co., Inc., Ambler, Pennsylvania, 2,545,000 prescriptions for methadone were filled by pharmacists since 1967. These prescription figures do not reflect the amount of methadone administered by physicians or in the presence of a physician, by an authorized agent to patients; nor do they represent the amount of methadone dispensed or administered in approved treatment programs, because prescriptions are not written.

In some communities, one or more physicians have contributed substantially to the illicit traffic in methadone. Some of these instances involved careless or unscrupulous physicians who were prescribing methadone as a pain killer, while others involved physicians who were operating as pushers under the guise of a detoxification program, for which no special registration was required. One of the most notorious cases is that of Dr. Thomas Moore who operated a "methadone program" in the District of Columbia until his final conviction of illegal distribution of methadone on an indictment alleging 38 separate counts. Moore operated from his office with impunity for over two years during which time drugs obtained by addicts from him were often found in the illicit traffic and believed to be involved in cases of narcotic overdose deaths.

He allegedly charged from $15 for 50 tablets to $75 for 200 tablets to the several hundred addicts who obtained their drugs weekly in this fashion. It was alleged that he sold 11,000 prescriptions—815,000 10 mg. units—and accumulated more than a quarter

of a million dollars for his efforts. Even under these circumstances, it was still possible for the alleged "patients" to make sales of the methadone tablets for profit.

Dr. Moore was eventually found guilty on 22 counts and sentenced to a term of 15 to 45 years and fined $150,000.

Another illustrative example involved the case of a Michigan physician who reportedly was prescribing methadone without a physical examination. During the period March 26, 1970 to January 22, 1971, BNDD undercover agents purchased 68 exhibits of methadone and prescriptions for methadone from the doctor and his employees. The quantities of methadone dispensed and prescribed were usually high, as much as 150 to 400 tablets at a time. At no time was any physical examination given to any of the special agents and dosages were increased upon the requests of the agents to accommodate their needs.

Similarly, a recent investigation of a Tucson, Arizona physician revealed that one pharmacy had filled prescriptions for 285,000, 10 mg. methadone tablets from May 1971 to February 1973. The physician prescribed methadone under the guise of a "detoxification program" and for relief of pain. While the Subcommittee was unable to verify all the activities of this physician, it is noted with interest that California officials who testified before the Subcommittee in November, 1972, reported that they had arrested a pair of methadone runners carrying 2,000 methadone tablets destined for an illicit market in Southern California. Several Arizona physicians were allegedly the source of the methadone!

Methadone programs can become a lucrative enterprise. A Chicago physician operating what experts characterize as a "turnstyle or breadline" program, one involving little more than dispensing methadone to addicts, was charging the 500 addicts he "treated" $20 each week for a weekly gross of $10,000. Recently a physician advertised his methadone program for sale in the Business Opportunities column of a large daily newspaper. a reporter answered the advertisement representing himself as a physician and found that the "program," together with a thousand addict patients, was for sale for a price of $70,000. Reportedly the physician selling this particular program confidently represented its business potential since its customers "were sure to return for more."

In another case in an eastern city, the BNDD Regional Office was contacted by an individual employed as a laborer with an automobile manufacturer who sought information with regard to establishing a methadone clinic. His plan called for establishing the clinic near an existing methadone program because, as he said, it would be "in a good location with plenty of pre-existing business." This individual had already made arrangements with a local doctor who had attempted to qualify as the practitioner under existing regulations.

Employees and volunteers associated with methadone programs have been implicated as sources of illegal methadone. The Subcommittee has reviewed reports regarding employees who use their clinic position to personal advantage by forging files for fictitious patients in order to account for methadone tablets stolen from the clinic for sale on the street. Laboratory analysis of liquid methadone dispensed by clinics has revealed that less methadone was present than purported. For example, a sample from a clinic in an eastern city was found to contain 13 milligrams per cc rather than the purported 30 milligrams per cc, apparently the result of the activity of a dispenser who was reducing each patient's dosage and collecting the difference. Of a total of 46 methadone programs audited in-depth under joint FDA-BNDD regulations, 28 percent were found to lack proper security over drugs; 43 percent were keeping improper or incomplete records; 17 percent had failed to obtain proper registration; 75 percent were found to have at least some unaccounted shortages of methadone; and another 15 percent were found to have unaccounted overages.

In New Orleans, all seven in-depth audits conducted revealed shortages; and two programs were closed as a result of numerous serious discrepancies. In Miami, two of three programs were found with serious shortages—one with 5.6 percent which amounted to no less than 308,715, 40 mg. methadone diskets and another with 12 percent. In New York an audit revealed a shortage of 5 percent or 54,660, 40 mg. methadone diskets as well as evidence of deliberate tampering with records. Similar reports have been received with regard to Washington, Boston and other cities. Additionally, investigators found that programs often failed to require ingestion of methadone on each visit by patients; that methadone dispensing was poorly supervised; and that take-home dosages were provided contrary to the program protocol.

As of February 1973, as a result of these investigations 11 methadone treatment programs had been terminated and criminal investigations had been initiated against 12 methadone program directors. One of these resulted in conviction, 4 are pending trial or other action, and prosecution was declined by a U.S. Attorney in each of the 7 remaining cases.

Numerous factors account for the diversion of methadone from the treatment programs. It may result from lack of expertise on the part of the medical staff, poor management practices, inadequate funding, or even criminal intent. It appears, however, that most diversion is usually unwittingly permitted and can be attributed to poor organization and loose controls.

Methadone is also finding its way to illicit markets as the result of a growing number of armed robberies of methadone clinics. Illustrative examples include the July 20, 1972 theft of two gallons of concentrated solutions of methadone from the Johns Hopkins Drug Abuse Center, Baltimore, Maryland by three men armed with shotguns and the November 5, 1972 robbery of the Jewish Memorial Hospital in Long Island, New York, in which two men armed with revolvers escaped with 1,203, 40 mg. diskets; 65, 100 mg. bottles; and 7, 80 mg. bottles.

The most frequently cited and most common source of methadone diverted from the programs is the patient. Some addict-patients who have "take home" privileges in ambulatory programs sell part of their dispensed dosage. In Dr. Weppner's original study of 76 metahdone abusers, he found that 60 percent had obtained their methadone from patients in methadone programs and that 24 percent obtained methadone from pushers who had, in turn, obtained the narcotic from individual practitioners. Lesser percentages involve purchases from unscrupulous ex-addict program counselors who were apparently permitted to handle the clinic's drug supplies. Illicit methadone traffic can be very profitable. Average daily dosages range from 40–180 mg. The street price for 10 mg. of methadone ranges from $2–$10.

Heroin addicts use methadone in a variety of ways. Many prefer methadone to heroin because it is readily available, cheaper, and they find that the euphoria is of longer duration and higher quality, particularly when injected intravenously. Others buy illegal methadone to insure against withdrawal when heroin is no longer available, or to boost the effects of cocaine and amphetamines. Some addicts enrolled in methadone programs desire the oblivion brought on by heroin, alcohol, barbiturates, or methaqualone, ("sopors" and "quaaludes") but not brought on by methadone. They sell all or part of the methadone and purchase other drugs.

According to Dr. Jerome Jaffe, former Director of the Special Action Office on Drug Abuse Prevention, the treatment of 80,000 individuals with an average dose of 80 mg. per day involves the dispensing of about two and a half tons of methadone each year. He explained that if even a small fraction is diverted the hazard is considerable. For example, if only 5 percent of the patients give away or sell their medication, there would be enough methadone diverted to create 6,000 new methadone addicts annually.

Illicit sales lead to the addiction of others. Polydrug abusers and experimenters are among the regular purchasers of illegal methadone.

Many of these new addicts are younger and less experienced with drug abuse than the seasoned heroin addict. Some doctors express concern that unless we rigidly control the distribution of methadone we may be creating a new generation of addicts: methadone addicts.

Already reports indicate a steady rise in the last three years in the number of persons addicted primarily to methadone. The Inciardi and Chambers survey of recent applicants for Miami methadone programs found that 40 percent were using illegal methadone along with other drugs, and 7 percent were using solely illegal methadone. These researchers both felt that the new cases of primary methadone addiction were being created within many areas, particularly among suburban youths, as a result of supplies available through diversion. In relative terms, the extent of methadone abuse does not presently rival heroin abuse, but the trend is alarming.

Methadone programs may create a demand as well as supply it. A recent study of 55 heroin addicts terminated from methadone maintenance programs found that 35 percent were abusing illicit methadone along with other drugs, and 8 percent were abusing solely methadone.

The impact of illicit methadone traffic is vividly documented by the staggering numbers of methadone overdose deaths. While heroin-related deaths have decreased, in many cities a pattern of increase in methadone-related deaths has been noted. More than 30 percent of the [1972] narcotic deaths in New York City were methadone related. In the first 9 months of 1972, 100 deaths or 15 percent of all narcotic deaths were directly attributed to methadone, as compared with 10 percent in 1971. From July 1, 1972 to February 23, 1973, Nassau County in New York reported 29 of 60 narcotic deaths to be methadone related, and Suffolk County reported 7 out of a total of 11 such deaths. In Washington, D.C., methadone has been more lethal than heroin. In 1972, there were 33 methadone deaths, 20 heroin deaths, and 18 combination methadone-heroin deaths. Thus, 72 percent of the narcotic deaths were methadone related. This compares with 26 percent during 1971 when 17 methadone deaths, 60 heroin deaths, and 5 combination methadone-heroin deaths were recorded in Washington. In the Washington, D.C. suburb of Fairfax County, 9 of 14 drug-related deaths were attributed in whole or in part to illicit methadone. In most of these areas the dead were younger people, primarily teenagers, many of whom lacked a tolerance to narcotics. Most took methadone orally, although some injected it.

It is abundantly clear that adequate safeguards must be developed to insure the effective operation of methadone programs and to protect our communities from the introduction of yet another potent narcotic drug of abuse and addiction. The recognition of the need for such safeguards should not be interpreted as an indictment of methadone programs, but rather as a realization that methadone can be harmful when diverted and improperly used.

HEROIN MAINTENANCE FOR HEROIN ADDICTS: ISSUES AND EVIDENCE

Lorrin M. Koran

After more than 50 years of prohibition, American society is again debating whether to allow maintenance doses of heroin in the treatment of heroin addicts. An American Bar Association committee has recommended starting pilot heroin-maintenance programs to explore their feasibility. The Vera Institute of Justice has submitted a heroin-maintenance research proposal to the New York City Mayor's Narcotics Control Council. On the other hand, a Washington, D.C., Mayor's panel has recommended against investigating heroin maintenance, as has the director of the United States Justice Department's Bureau of Narcotics and Dangerous Drugs (BNDD).

This paper attempts to describe the issues and the evidence swirling in the heroin-maintenance debate. My views should be stated at the outset. Careful clinical research should be done on the efficacy and safety of heroin maintenance. It may prove to be part of the treatment of choice for some addicts, particularly those not helped by current treatments. Heroin maintenance would not

be a panacea for addiction: no one treatment can help all heroin addicts, and all treatments taken together leave untouched the social conditions fostering addiction. Moreover, chemotherapeutic treatments do not by themselves rehabilitate the addict, or address his tendency to use non-narcotic drugs such as barbiturates and alcohol for plesaure or self-medication.

TREATMENTS IN THE UNITED STATES AND GREAT BRITAIN

Treatments currently acceptable in the United States can be divided into two groups: rapid or gradual withdrawal from narcotics voluntarily or after civil commitment; and chronic, voluntary, maintenance doses of oral methadone. Chronic administration of narcotic antagonists such as naloxone and cyclazocine is still experimental. Most treatment programs include efforts at psychologic and social rehabilitation, but the degree to which they employ group or individual psychotherapy, job and family counseling, vocational training, legal aid and appeals to ethnic pride, group loyalty or religious motivation is highly variable.

The results of treatment programs in the

From *The New England Journal of Medicine*, 288 No. 3 (March 29, 1973), 654–59. Reprinted by permission. Dr. Koran is a member of the Department of Psychiatry, State University of New York at Stony Brook.

United States are not entirely satisfactory. In the first place, many addicts are not attracted into these programs. Testifying before the Senate Subcommittee on Alcoholism and Narcotics on May 23, 1972, Dr. Jerome Jaffe, [former] director of the Whtie House Special Action Office for Drug Abuse Prevention, estimated that only 50,000 to 60,000 of the Nation's 250,000 to 500,000 addicts were on methadone, and 50,000 in drug-free programs. The number on waiting lists is not known. Secondly, many addicts fail to benefit from current treatments. Some patients leave treatment, and others divert methadone, abuse illicit drugs or alcohol, or relapse during or after treatment. Quantifying this statement is difficult, since treatment results vary with characteristics of the patients, program and community, and with the outcome measures used.

In Great Britain, addiction has been considered an illness rather than criminal behavior since 1926. Physicians have been allowed to treat addicts with maintenance doses of narcotics if, after every effort was made to cure the addiction, narcotics could not be completely withdrawn. Until the 1960's Britain had only a few hundred narcotic addicts, most of medical origin. In the early 1960's over-prescribing to known addicts by a few physicians led to a rapid rise in the number of addicts. To combat this rise, a medical committee advised the government to take the following steps: require physicians to notify a central authority regarding addicts to dangerous drugs seen in their practices; establish special treatment clinics; limit prescribing of heroin and cocaine for addicts to doctors on the clinic staffs; and allow other physicians to prescribe heroin for organic diseases, but not for addiction. These recommendations were implemented by 1968. Fourteen clinics were established in London, and a similar number elsewhere in the country. They range widely in staffing patterns and social-rehabilitation efforts. Although the clinics' ultimate goal for most patients is abstinence, most clinic patients are receiving narcotic drugs.

The management of each addict is decided by his clinic physician, but certain procedures are followed. No patient who has been treated in another clinic is accepted for treatment unless his previous physician agrees. No narcotic is prescribed until the diagnosis of addiction is certain. A prescription covering a maximum of two weeks is mailed to a pharmacy, and the patient must pick up his drugs daily except on weekends. Sterile needles and syringes are supplied.

In 1970, the 2661 addicts to dangerous drugs seen in the clinics were primarily of nonmedical origin. At year end, 1430 were receiving narcotics: 992 were receiving methadone (primarily intravenous), of whom 254 also received heroin; 183 were receiving heroin alone or with drugs other than methadone; and 255 were receiving other drugs, primarily morphine or pethidine (meperidine hydrochloride). Most of the 1231 addicts not receiving narcotics at year end were no longer in treatment, but this group has not been studied. At the end of 1971 about 9 percent more addicts were receiving narcotics. Those receiving methadone increased 17 percent; those receiving heroin decreased 11 percent. The gradual move away from heroin toward intravenous methadone has several sources. First of all, the public takes a less favorable view of heroin than of methadone. Since the amount of heroin and other drugs prescribed by the clinics is public information, clinic doctors feel some pressure to decrease the amount of heroin prescribed. Secondly, injectable methadone comes in ampuls of sterile solution; heroin is dispensed as tablets, which addicts often dissolve in an unsterile manner. Thirdly, methadone is longer acting. Finally, some physicians consider intravenous methadone a step toward oral methadone and ultimately abstinence. Others doubt the effectiveness of oral methadone as treatment of addicts accustomed to large doses of intravenous narcotics.

Connell notes that despite the apparent absence of criminally organized narcotic trafficking and the apparent success in curtailing the growth of narcotic addiction in Britain, several serious concerns remain: most addicts in treatment are not fully self-supporting; many seek heroin outside the clinics; rates of infection and mortality remain high; methadone addicts are increasingly appearing, some of whom have never used heroin; and abuse of multiple drugs is common.

LEGAL ISSUES

In the United States heroin is a Schedule I drug under Public Law 91-513, the "Comprehensive Durg Abuse Prevention and Control Act of 1970." Schedule I drugs can be used in clinical research with the approval of the Food and Drug Administration (FDA). They are not available for treating patients in ordinary medical practice.

Since little American research has been done on chronic heroin administration, the FDA could require further animal studies before permitting clinical studies. Clinical research on methadone maintenance was not held up for this reason in part because of American clinical experience with methadone as an analgesic. Since no similar experience with heroin in the United States exists, the FDA could rule available American research and British clinical experience inadequate bases for beginning clinical heroin-maintenance research.

The Vera Institute has determined that no New York State laws prohibit its porposal for studying heroin as treatment for dependency, but state restrictions on heroin research vary.

Research on heroin maintenance would not violate any international agreements signed by the United States. The United Nations Single Convention on Narcotic Drugs (1961) expressly permits the use of scheduled drugs, including heroin, for "medical and scientific purposes."

MEDICAL ISSUES

The "effects of heroin" depend on a variety of conditions: dose; route of administration; setting; recipient's expectations, prior experience with the drug, personality characteristics and general health; whether he is in pain and whether the pain is experimental or natural; and the interval between drug administration and measurement of effects.

Is Heroin Physiologically Harmful?

Although heroin has unwanted side effects, its administration under direct medical supervision appears unlikely to cause addicts serious physiologic harm. The British use of heron maintenance speaks for acceptance of this view in that country. American clinical experiments lasting up to two months indicate that heroin is no more physiologically harmful than morphine or other opiates. Heroin's common untoward effects—constipation, decreased sexual desire, nausea, vomiting and anorexia with slight weight loss—are not dangerous. With the exception of addicting a pregnant patient's unborn child, serious untoward effects are rare or are not known to be due to the drug. . . . Although massive doses of certain opiates have caused tissue damage in laboratory animals, clinical doses have not. Contrary to popular opinion, heroin does not have a greater addiction liability than morphine or many other opiates, and, therefore, is not in this sense more harmful or dangerous.

Acute doses of heroin have been safely used for several clinical purposes: preoperative medication in obstetrics; to relieve postoperative pain (for which it is two to four times as potent as morphine); to treat intractable pain in terminal cancer; to relieve pain in patients with myocardial infarctions; and to suppress chronic cough. Whether heroin is superior to other opiates for some clinical conditions is uncertain. Severe legal restrictions have discouraged research on its usefulness, without apparently affecting the spread of addiction.

If the principle of narcotic maintenance doses is accepted, the evidence indicates that heroin cannot be excluded on physiologic grounds.

Licit Heroin and Medical Complications

Medical administration of heroin would prevent most serious medical complications associated with illicit heroin use. These include the following: infectious diseases; pulmonary fibrosis or granulomas; the crush syndrome; fatal overdose; and malnutrition.

If heroin were prescribed and administration left to the addict, medical complications would continue at high rates. The death rate for British addicts known to the authorities between 1947 and 1966 was 27 per 1000 per year compared with 2.45 per 1000 per year for a control population. Whether the clinic system has affected the death rate is unknown.

Heroin and Rehabilitation

The available evidence suggests that heroin maintenance is compatible with psychologic and social rehabilitation. Wikler and Rasor, for example, describe the opiate-maintained addict as follows:

Thus, as long as adequate amounts of opiates are administered, aggressive, antisocial behavior is practically never observed, personal hygiene is maintained, assigned responsibilities are discharged satisfactorily, psychologic tests of performance reveal little or no impairment, and the sensorium remains quite clear, while anxiety associated with anticipation of pain is reduced.

By way of contrast, they point out that former narcotic addicts intoxicated with alcohol or barbiturates exhibit antisocial, disruptive behavior, decreased personal hygiene and grossly impaired intellectual abilities.

Crawley reports several favorable results with 134 London addicts examined after a year or more of clinic treatment that included only limited social services. The mean narcotic dose was reduced almost 50 percent. Almost 30 percent of the patients initially prescribed heroin eventually managed with only small doses of intravenous methadone. Thirty percent worked throughout the treatment period, and an additional 18.6 percent began work. Only 9 percent stopped working. The remaining 42.4 percent did not work during treatment.

Several other studies have focused on work as an index of rehabilitation. Zacune studied 25 Canadian addicts who had obtained heroin illicitly in Canada, but received heroin in Britain through the clinic system:

In Canada, only one addict claimed to have worked steadily while addicted. In England, the majority (13) worked full-time, and four worked part-time ... One was a full-time housewife and one a student.

Stimson and Ogborne surveyed 128 heroin addicts in 13 London clinics. Fifty-two (41 percent) were employed full-time, 11 part-time, 50 unemployed, 11 housewives, and one a student (three were not reached). May cites an unpublished study of the British clinic system showing that "the number of addicts holding jobs almost doubled in two years." None of these studies include a non-addict control group matched for class, educational level or sex.

Two studies suggest that heroin-maintained addicts may work less efficiently. Fraser et al. found that addicts maintained on heroin engaged in 20 to 25 percent less physical activity than during a control period. This study, however, rests on five addicts with the diagnosis of "passive aggressive personality" and housed on a hospital research ward where no activity was required to earn drugs, food, shelter or other necessities. Haertzen and Hooks studied these patients together with a small number similarly maintained on morphine. A questionnaire indicated "... decreased motivation for [physical, mental, social and sexual] activity, lessened social involvement with greater irritations in social situations, and hypochondriasis."

As with most questions regarding heroin, more research is needed before it can be decided how well the heroin-maintained addict can work. The addict's skills, his attitude toward work, and the state of the job market are probably as important as whether he is abstinent or maintained on heroin or methadone.

Critics of heroin maintenance commonly assert that addicts will be too euphoric or too intellectually impaired to engage in rehabilitation. No evidence links heroin with permanent or progressive intellectual deterioration.

Heroin Maintenance and Medical Ethics

Administering heroin to addicts who volunteer for research and provide informed consent would not violate medical ethics. In the first place, the American Medical Association and the National Research Council have endorsed outpatient administration of maintenance doses of an opiate to narcotic addicts. Secondly, the Food, Drug, and Cosmetic Act and Public Law 91-513 provide legal procedures for investigating heroin-maintenance treatment. Thirdly, heroin in clinical doses has not been shown to cause tissue damage or serious physiologic harm. Fourthly, heroin maintenance would not necessarily interfere with psychologic and social rehabilitation. Fifthly, medical administration of heroin could ameliorate addiction both by preventing complications of illicit use and by exposing addicts to medical and rehabilitative services. Since addiction appears to be a chronic, relapsing illness, "cure" cannot be equated with abstinence, and amelioration is an acceptable goal.

Medical Administrative Problems

Edwards has discussed the medical administrative problems that heroin-maintenance programs face. He favors a mandatory, inpatient induction phase both to make certain that each new patient is addicted and to determine the addict's habit level. By way of contrast, the Vera Institute proposal envisions outpatient induction except when medical complications make inpatient induction necessary. Each patient's heroin dose would be derived from clinical assessment of his habit level. Since neither the patient nor his physician can initially be certain of this level, precautions would be needed to prevent an overdose.

The program must decide whether to prescribe heroin and risk diversion or to prevent it by administering all heroin on clinic premises. Although British and American addicts and illicit markets differ, British studies give some indication of the diversion problem. A 1969 study of 159 addicts showed that 1 percent sold narcotics on the black market,

11 percent bought and sold, and 31 percent only bought. In another study, 37 percent sold, exchanged or lent prescribed drugs (including stimulants). Clinic administration of heroin would calm community fears of diversion, but has the disadvantages of interfering with the addict's work, requiring longer clinic hours, and decreasing the number of addicts who can be treated per unit staff, since each addict needs more staff contacts. Since community fears not only can influence treatment outcome, but also can prevent a treatment program from beginning, heroin should not be prescribed or dispensed in initial maintenance studies. The Vera Institute proposal corresponds with this recommendation.

It has been argued that if heroin-injection clinics were established, the black market would be undercut and the pressure for addicts to begin or continue criminal behavior would be greatly reduced. It has been counterargued that if decreased illicit demand forced price reductions, black marketeers would increase their efforts to create new addicts and raise demand "within our schools." This counterargument could be used to argue against offering any treatment to any addicts, since all treatments seek to decrease the addicts' demand for illicit heroin. The counter-counter-argument is that efforts to create new addicts would not occur in a social vacuum. The net outcome would depend on the capabilities of the population at risk and the social opportunities (jobs, education, recreation, participation in community life) open to them, on the effects of prevention efforts, on the decline of the drug dealer as a model of success, on the decreasing availability of untreated addicts as role models and on the effect of law-enforcement efforts to decrease the illicit supply.

Edwards notes that once operating, a clinic must have enough staff to keep excellent records. Inpatient and outpatient phases of treatment must be co-ordinated. The treatment staff must receive emotional support, since they will constantly be stressed by patients. The clinic must ensure that patients are not receiving drugs from other clinics. Rehabilitative services should be provided that will allow the addict to develop the motivation and skills to pursue a "workable alternative career to that of being an addict."

The patients must be given narcotics on a schedule that prevents withdrawal symptoms, which appear eight to 12 hours after the last dose of morphine or heroin. The Vera Institute proposal suggests administering intravenous methadone in the evening to prevent withdrawal symptoms before the morning heroin dose. The comparative duration of the suppression of withdrawal symptoms in man by intravenous morphine, heroin and methadone is unknown, but single-dose studies in previously addicted persons suggest that one dose of intravenous methadone will suppress withdrawal symptoms for 12 to 24 hours.

Research Possibilities

Pilot heroin-maintenance programs would be compatible with only certain research questions: How "effective" is heroin maintenance treatment? (For what kinds of addicts? In conjunction with what rehabilitative efforts? Using what outcome measures?) Can addicts be stabilized on heroin? (Dole believes they cannot, but does not cite evidence). Can heroin-maintained addicts eventually be switched to less costly and demanding form of treatment? (When and how?) How do the physiologic, mental and behavioral effects of heroin compare with those of oral or intravenous methadone?

Since heroin maintenance is such an emotionally charged subject, every research project should be meticulously designed.

SOCIAL ISSUES

Attracting Patients into Treatment

Heroin-maintenance studies may attract patients who have not applied for other treatments. Some of these patients may not be daily or long-term heroin users, and should not receive heroin (or methadone) maintenance.

Some observers are afraid that large-scale heroin-maintenance programs would be too attractive, "driving out bona fide forms of treatment." This contention does not rule out small-scale research projects. The Vera Institute proposal, for example, is limited to 130 addicts whom other treatments have not helped.

It might be argued that heroin-maintenance programs should not be started until all patients on treatment waiting lists are cared for. This would be analogous to arguing that no patient with tuberculosis should be allowed to volunteer for treatment with an experimental drug until all those who want treatment with nonexperimental drugs have been treated.

HEROIN MAINTENANCE
AND CRIMINAL BEHAVIOR

The complex relation between heroin addiction and crime has been described in a Presidential Commission report as follows:

At the present time most known opiate addicts have been delinquent prior to their being identified as users and most continue to be arrested after release from hospitals and prisons ... There is no evidence that opiates are a cause of crime in the sense they inevitably lead to criminality, but there is no doubt that among addicts with a delinquent life-style drug use is part and parcel of their other activities, crime included.

There is also no experimental evidence that opiates increase antisocial personality characteristics or undermine moral character.

Since opiates do not in themselves cause criminal behavior, the impact of a heroin-maintenance program would depend on the following considerations: the addict's motives for criminal behavior (i.e., to finance his drug habit or because he prefers criminal means of support); the program's rehabilitative efforts; how "criminal behavior" is defined (narcotic-law violatons, assaultive crimes and property crimes), or measured (self-report, arrest records or conviction records); the length of treatment before measurements are made; and any concurrent changes in local law-enforcement practices.

Since a program's impact on criminal behavior depends on many variables, no single study should be regarded as definitive. As Lukoff and Vorenberg make clear, the effect of methadone maintenance on criminal behavior is not definitely known despite several studies.

The effect of a heroin-maintenance program on the total crime rate in its locale is likely to be modest. A 1968 study found that "heroin addicts accounted for 9.1 percent of the total crime in New York City, leaving 90.9 percent for nonaddictive criminals."

A six-city study of almost 1900 persons arrested on felony charges provides additional perspective. Urinalyses and interviews disclosed that 24.4 percent of those arrested had used heroin sometime in the month before arrest. As shown in Table 1, less than 30 percent of those arrested for serious crimes against the person were narcotic users. Moreover, persons who used no illicit drugs accounted for considerably more arrests for crimes against the person than narcotic users. Unfortunately, these data shed no light on whether the proportion of narcotic users who commit crimes is higher or lower than the proportion of non-users. Moreover, alcohol use, often associated with nonviolent and violent criminal behavior, was not studied.

The above two studies, together with the absence of a simple causal link between narcotic use and criminal behavior, suggest that reducing the crime rate should not be the major goal for any narcotic-addiction treatment program, let alone a small heroin-maintenance research project. A Presidential Commission put it well:

Since there is much crime in cities where drug use is not thought to be a major problem, to commit resources against abuse solely in the expectation of producing a dramatic reduction in crime may be to invite disappointment. While crime reduction is one result to be hoped for in eliminating drug abuse, its elimination and the treatment of its victims are humane and worthy social objectives in themselves.

Table 13–1. Percentages of total arrests accounted for by users of illicit narcotics and users of no drugs

Arrest category	Users of illicit heroin, morphine and methadone	Users of no drugs
	per cent	
Serious crimes against the person*	28.6	41.2
Less serious crimes against the person	11.3	54.2
Property crimes	36.1	31.9
All other crimes	30.6	28.2
Total arrests	31.0	35.8

*Criminal homicide, forcible rape, robbery, aggravated assault & kidnapping.

Other assaults & sex offenses (except rape and commercialized vice).

Burglary, larceny, theft, automobile theft, arson, forgery & counterfeiting, fraud, embezzlement, stolen property & vandalism.

Weapons, prostitution & commercialized vice, narcotic-drug-law violations & other offenses.

POLITICAL ISSUES

Reactions of the Public

No widespread public reaction yet exists. Only a few persons have expressed their views publicly, primarily in response to the Vera Institute proposal. Black and Puerto Rican community groups charged that heroin maintenance would be "physiologically destructive" and "wholesale genocide." They objected to not being consulted. The Vera Institute proposal was termed "using my people as guinea pigs" and was feared as "a wedge in the door." Other critics have stated that heroin maintenance represents "giving up on efforts to treat addiction." Since these objections are deeply felt, prolonged dialogue with critics would be necessary before a heroin-maintenance program could be safely begun.

The United States Congress

Late in 1972 Representative Peter Peyser (Rep., New York) introduced two bills (HR 16458 and HR 16617) outlawing heroin use "in any drug maintenance program." Although President Nixon warmly endorsed HR 16458, the bills were not acted on before Congress adjourned. If similar bills appear in the new Congress, they will probably be referred for hearings to representative Paul Roger's (Dem., Florida) Subcommittee on Public Health and the Environment (of the Committee on Interstate and Foreign Commerce). Informed physicians should contribute their views to any Congressional deliberations regarding antiheroin legislation.

The Federal Executive Branch

Section 303 (f) of Public Law 91-513 gives authority to authorize research with heroin and other Schedule I drugs to the Secretary of Health, Education, and Welfare. This authority has been delegated to the FDA. Public Law 92-255, the "Drug Abuse Office and Treatment Act of 1972," gives the director of the White House Special Action Office for Drug Abuse Prevention (SAODAP) authority to make federal policy in the drug-abuse field. The political visibility of heroin-maintenance research and the President's opposition to heroin maintenance suggest that the director will play a major part in deciding whether the Executive Branch permits any heroin maintenance research. Interested investigators should communicate with the FDA Commissioner regarding necessary permission and potential legitimate sources of heroin. The Bureau of Narcotics and Dangerous Drugs has also supplied heroin to qualified investigators and interested investigators may get in touch with the Bureau. The National Institute of Mental Health has research funds and legislative authority to finance FDA-approved heroin research.

Since currently available treatments do not help some heroin addicts, additional effective treatments must be sought. In view of the apparent safety and potential usefulness of heroin maintenance, it should not be a priori labeled unnecessary or undesirable. Although establishing large-scale heroin-maintenance programs is unjustified at present, well controlled, clinical-research heroin-maintenance programs should be begun.

QUESTIONS FOR DISCUSSION

1. What is a detoxification center? How does it work? What makes it better than the conventional "drunk tank?" What evidence is there that a detoxification center is more effective with chronic inebriates than the jail or workhouse approach?

2. Discuss the Manhattan Bowery Project in terms not only of its approach to the chronic inebriate but also to the homeless alcoholics for whom the street is home and the other drunks their next of kin.

3. Is deviance a medical problem, a personal pathology, a willful state, an environmentally produced state? What virtue is there, if any, in medicalizing deviance?

4. The "juice model" paper speculates that certain hard core offenders are hypo-aroused and can be treated effectively

with drug medication. This general group of offenders is called the sociopath, psychopath, anti-social personality, or by other, even less, complimentary labels. Who are these intractables? What are they like? How do they differ from other offenders? Do you really think that chronic anti-social behavior is a disease which can be helped by drug intervention?

5. What is the XYY syndrome? Is it just another of these fads in criminality? What is its incidence and prevalence in general and deviant groups? Is an XYY deviant guilty if he offends? Is he responsible for his conduct?

6. The United States has undergone various stages in its quest for an answer to management of hard (narcotic) drugs and other illicit substances. They were once legal, then made illegal and nonmedical in the Harrison Act and subsequent Supreme Court decisions. There were clinics which dispensed "hard" drugs for a few years, then came a generation of total repression. Next came the public health hospitals and now methadone maintenance clinics.

Why has United States policy been so inconsistent? Why, now, is the government supporting methadone maintenance treatment when it opposed such treatment up until the middle 1950's and even later? What is methadone maintenance? How does the usual program work? How effective is it? Why is so much methadone finding its way into illegal channels? Would the same thing happen if heroin maintenance were permissable?

How can this entire problem be managed? Should we simply legalize the hard drugs? Should we get tougher in enforcement (as in New York in 1973)? Should we operate even more clinics? As a matter of public policy where ought we be heading?

BIBLIOGRAPHY

Arnold, Eugene L. "The Art of Medicating Hyperkinetic Children." *Clinical Pediatrics* 12 (1973), 35–41.
Arnold, Eugene L. "Detection and Management of Hyperkinetic Children in School." *The School Counselor* (January 1971).
Association for Childhood Education International (ACEI). "Report." *Children and Drugs.* Washington, D.C., 1972.
Bibliography on Methadone and the Treatment of Addiction. National Clearinghouse for Drug Abuse Information, National Institute of Mental Health, Series 3, No. 1, October 1971.
Brill, H. "Methadone Maintenance: A Problem of Delivery of Service." *Journal of the American Medical Association* 215 No. 7 (1971), 1148–50.
Chambers, Carl D., and Brill, Leon, eds. *Methadone: Experiences and Issues.* New York: Behavioral Publications, 1973.
Cleckley, Hervey. *The Mask of Sanity,* 4th Ed. St. Louis: Mosby, 1964.
Dole, Vincent P., and Nyswander, Marie. "Rehabilitation of Heroin Addicts after Blockade with Methadone." *N.Y. State Journal of Medicine* 66 No. 15 (1966), 2011–17.
Eysenck, H. J. *The Biological Basis of Personality.* Springfield, Ill.: Charles Thomas, 1967.
Freedman, A. M., Fink, M., Sharoff, R., and Zaks, A. "Cyclazocine and Methadone in Narcotic Addiction." *Journal of the American Medical Association* 203 No. 3 (1967), 191–94.
Freedman, A. M., Zaks, A., Resnick, R., and Fink, M. "Blockade with Methadone, Cyclazocine and Naloxone." *Internation Journal of the Addictions* 5 No. 3 (1970), 507–15.
Fischer, R. "A Cartography of the Ecstatic and Meditative States." *Science* 174 (1971), 897–904.
Goldman, Harold. "Diseases of Arousal." *Quaderni di Criminologia Clinica* 15 No. 2 (Spring 1973), 175–94.
Goldman, Harold, Lindner, L. A., Dinitz, S., and Allen, H. E. "The Simple Sociopath: Physiologic and Sociologic Characteristics." *Biological Psychiatry* 3 (1971), 77–83.
Hare, Robert D. *Psychopathy: Theory and Research.* New York: Wiley, 1970.
Irwin, S. "A Rational Framework for the Development, Evaluation and Use of Psychoactive Drugs." *American Journal of Psychiatry* 124 (1968), 1–19.
Lindner, Lewis, Goldman, H., Dinitz, S. and Allen, H. E. "Antisocial Personality Type with Cardiac Lability." *Archives of General Psychiatry* 23 (1970), 260–67.
Meyer, Roger E. *Guide to Drug Rehabilitation: A Public Health Response.* Boston, Mass.: Beacon Press, 1972.
Montague, Ashley. "Chromosomes and Crime." *Psychology Today* 2 No. 5 (1968), 42–49.
Pasamanick, Benjamin, and Knobloch, Hilda. "Brain Damage and Reproductive Casualty." *American Journal of Orthopsychiatry* 30 (1960), 298–305.
Pasamanick, Benjamin, Rogers, M. E., and Lilien-

feld, A. M. "Pregnancy Experience and the Development of Behavior Disorders in Children." *American Journal of Psychiatry* 112 (1956), 613–18.

Schacter, S., and Latane, B. "Crime, Cognition and the Autonomic Nervous System." *In M. R. Jones, ed., Nebraska Symposium on Motiva-*

tion. Lincoln, Nebraska: University of Nebraska Press, 1964.

Tatham, Richard J. "Detoxification Center: A Public Health Alternative for the 'Drunk Tank'." *Federal Probation* XXXIII No. 4 (December 1969), 46–48.

14

Behavior Modification as Management and Control

The persistent failure of traditional rehabilitation programs in and out of total institutions to alter the behavior of the addict, transsexual, alcoholic, neurotic, psychopath, and other very seriously deviant persons has left researchers, academicians, and practitioners utterly frustrated.

For various reasons, a new breed of specialists, drawn principally from the hard sciences and particularly from the life sciences, have attempted to apply their expertise in limited program efforts dealing with specific subcategories of criminality, particularly those featuring compulsive-obsessive behaviors. Operations-research specialists and innovative technologists have explored avenues of surveillance and control more radical than would have been supposed possible a few years ago. Behaviorally oriented psychologists have also updated Pavlov and the early excitation-inhibition physiologists and developed and pioneered with more sophisticated and definitive methods of behavior modification. Computer experts, too, have been attracted to the field via their interests in information processing and data handling approaches.

The involvement of these new technologists in behavior control has raised serious moral, legal, and ethical problems concerning what one court has referred to as "impermissable tinkering." In truth, we are just barely entering the tinkering stage in deviance management, prevention, and control. The medical, computer, psychological, and surveillance technologies are already beyond the primitive state; the necessary knowledge and equipment are available; the "clients" and the public have already been conditioned to the acceptance of more intrusive methods of behavior control. Only the outcome awaits evaluation.

In this section we present two general overviews of the kinds of programs which the future holds in the area of deviance management and control. Most of the research programs referred to in these articles are either classic statements of their genre or unusually innovative forms of intrusion. The research described include: classical conditioning, operant conditioning, brain stimulation by electrical and chemical means, environmental controls, and electronic monitoring and other forms of sophisticated surveillance, not excluding transmitter implantations.

These research programs, no matter how repugnant and fearsome, in common, lend themselves to more careful evaluation of outcome than the more global and traditional vocational, educational, community, counseling, detached worker, psychotherapeutic, and self-concept programs. These innovations are not based on ideological commitments as much as on practical considerations and creeping technology. As a result, it is unlikely that vested interest, rather than satisfactory outcome will serve to perpetuate innovations in these intrusive areas. It is, for example, more difficult to become wedded to a computer information system than to an anti-poverty approach. The latter has economic, social, and political values as its core. The former—only feasibility.

As the following articles indicate, deviance management has become a truly interdisciplinary venture in which academic specialties no longer serve as a criterion for experimentation. The new specialists may not know much about crime or other deviation, but they know a great deal about various elements that go into making a successful behavior modification control program. The specialist in deviance has become very much like an orchestra leader. His role is to recruit and coordinate the talents and skills of a variety of players in such a way that the program reflects all the contributions of each in a unique format. It behooves the criminologist, in particular, to take the new interdisciplinary thrust seriously. No matter how radical the proposal, there is every likelihood that these controversial programs will

be implemented, if only because the money, talent, and technology are present for doing so. Whether criminologists, or laymen, we are obligated to be aware of the moral, legal, and social implications of these experimental programs and to surround them with as many safeguards as we can to insure that the ultimate cost of behavior control does not exceed the present cost of deviance.

The first article, "Behavior Modification Programs" by Ralph Schwitzgebel describes some hair-raising conditioning experiments which have been tried with just about every type of deviant. The most worrisome of all is the use of a drug which prevents the alcoholic from breathing (momentarily) while he is deconditioned from his need to drink. Other techniques include shock, nausea-producing drugs, and a whole panoply of related techniques. Read Schwitzgebel carefully! The implications of his review (and his own research) are too painful to contemplate.

Ingraham and Smith propose the use of electronic monitoring of parolees using external and, perhaps later, internal devices to record the activities (especially the location) of parolees and others. This modest proposal contains an ethical and moral defense of telemetry as a behavior control technique.

BEHAVIOR MODIFICATION PROGRAMS
Ralph K. Schwitzgebel

Within the past few years there has ben a rapid growth in the experimental study and application of behavior modification techniques derived from the principles of learning and technology. These techniques, which have been used primarily in clinical and experimental settings thus far, create the potential for major changes in the area of corrections. . . .

From *Development and Legal Regulations of Coercive Behavior Modification Techniques With Offenders,* Washington: DHEW Publication No. (HSM) 73–9015, 1971, pp. 1, 5–21, 63–67. Professor Schwitzgebel is at Harvard University.

GENERAL CHARACTERISTICS OF BEHAVIOR MODIFICATION PROGRAMS

A major characteristic of behavior modification programs is their emphasis upon overt behaviors and the systematic manipulation of the environment to change these behaviors. Some of the techniques that can be included within the category of behavior modification are operant and classical conditioning, aversive suppression, and electronic monitoring and intervention. These techniques are only a few of many behavior modification techniques that may also include imitation, progressive relaxation, and sensitivity training. The techniques discussed in the following sections are those that are now playing an increasingly important role in the clinical and experimental treatment of offenders.

Behavior modification, as a separate area of study, began to emerge clearly in the early 1950's. Its direction as a new discipline is still not clear. The emphasis upon the treatment of overt behaviors and the measurement of observable events in the patient's environment gives the discipline a great heuristic value over some of the more traditional, psychoanalytically oriented treatment procedures. Its theoretical bases are, however, still in the process of being formulated.

Although behavior modification procedures are often oriented toward operant or classical conditioning theories, they are not necessarily so oriented and there is much diversity. Regardless of orientation, the basic underlying theory usually involves carefully specified changes in the environment of the person whose behavior is to be changed. A procedure for changing behavior that relies upon unique, nontransferrable characteristics of a therapist or change agent lies outside of the domain of scientific behavior modification.

SPECIFIC PROGRAMS AND RESEARCH

The following programs and related research are briefly described to give a general purview of behavior modification studies that have been completed or those that are now being conducted. The studies that have been selected are those that are generally related to present or potential treatment programs for offenders.

Operant Conditioning

In operant conditioning studies, a reinforcer (popularly called a "reward") is given to a subject after he produces the required behavior once or several times. In terms of operant conditioning, it is said that the reinforcer is made contingent upon the emission of the correct response. This response is known as an operant. If the response is not emitted by the individual, no reinforcer is given. In a sense, the person must voluntarily "operate" upon his environment to receive reinforcement. A reinforcer such as food, money, or time out from a task is known to be a reinforcer when it increases the rate, or changes the form of the behavior it follows. One of the most familiar examples of operant conditioning at the infrahuman level is the early work of B. F. Skinner in which he trained pigeons to peck at lights for many hours at a time to receive small pellets of food.

Although a detailed discussion of operant conditioning theory is beyond the scope of this paper, it might be noted that except for some specialized procedures for shaping behavior, reinforcers are seldom given for each correct response. Rather, intermittent reinforcement is given. A fixed-ratio schedule provides a reinforcer after the operant response has occurred a specified number of times. A fixed interval schedule provides a reinforcer for the first response occurring after a specified period of time following the preceding reinforcement. There may also be variable-ratio, variable-interval, and mixed ratio-interval schedules of considerable complexity.

Different types of schedules produce varying patterns of behavior. As Skinner notes:

The efficacy of such schedules [variable ratio] in generating high rates has long been known to proprietors of gambling establishments. Slot machines, roulette wheels, dice cages, horse races, and so on pay off on a schedule of variable-ratio reinforcement . . . The pathological gambler exemplifies the result. Like the pigeon with its five responses per second for many hours, he is the victim of an unpredictable contingency of reinforcement. The long-term net gain or loss is almost irrelevant in accounting for the effectiveness of this schedule.

The scheduling of reinforcers to increase the probability of socially desirable behaviors of offenders is generally accomplished in one of two ways. One method involves reinforcing a desired behavior, such as cooperation, in such a way that it competes with an undesirable behavior, such as fighting. The second method involves reducing the reinforcement usually obtained by the person as a consequence of his deviant behavior. This is based upon the assumption that deviant as well as normal behaviors are produced and maintained by their reinforcing consequences. Both of these operant conditioning approaches to deviant behavior require structuring the environment so that the reinforcers received by the person are carefully specified and controlled. Programs that control reinforcers in this manner are sometimes known as contingency management programs.

In the project CASE II (Contingencies Applicable for Special Education), conducted at the National Training School for Boys, delinquent boys could obtain points for successfully completing specified amounts of educational material. These boys lived in a specially constructed environment on the schoolgrounds which for the first 3 to 5 days included a small but attractive private room and exceptionally good meals. Following this, points had to be earned by the boy in order to pay for his private room and good meals. In addition, he could use these points, sometimes converted into tokens or small amounts of money, to pay for such things as snacks, office study space, private tutoring, magazines, telephone calls, or articles from a mail-order catalog. Conversely, if a student did not successfully complete his educational tasks, he was known as a "relief" student and would lose his private room and would have to have his meals served on a metal tray after the other students had eaten. Also, he would not be able to wear street clothing, attend movies, or take trips outside.

Under these conditions of contingency management, most of the students showed very great increases in the level of their academic performance and there were marked decreases in the number of behavioral problems as compared with the regular training school population. These were the primary goals of the project. The effect of this type of program on the recidivism of these students when they return to the community is not yet known.

It may be noted that the CASE II project used secondary reinforcers such as points or tokens which could later be turned in by the boys to purchase primary reinforcers such as food or a trip out of the institution. This permits the immediate reinforcement of behavior in situations when the use of primary reinforcers would be difficult or impossible. Although the use of these secondary reinforcers can be helpful in modifying the behavior of institutionalized youths, even greater potential may lie in their use in community settings. The Behavioral Research Project in Tucson, Ariz. utilized community-trained teachers, parents, or other adults in the child's natural environment to use reinforcers to modify delinquent or predelinquent behavior, such as stealing, property destruction, and truancy, following the principles of contingency management. An intervention plan for each child was designed and the child was given notes, points, or a mark on a chart which could be exchanged later for primary reinforcers. Behaviors such as prompt arrival at school or obedience to instructions were reinforced, as well as periods in which a particular undesirable behavior did not occur, e.g., a recess completed without a fist fight. Marked improvements in behavior were recorded. Similar token economies have been used to improve the academic and job performance of male and female high school dropouts. It is also likely that the reinforcement procedures that have been used to modify a wide range of neurotic and schizophrenic symptoms might also be used to modify some types of delinquent behavior. Community oriented programs are still, however, at a very rudimentary level.

One rapidly emerging area of research in operant conditioning should perhaps be mentioned before discussing classical conditioning programs. It is the operant conditioning of responses which have been traditionally associated with the autonomic nervous system. Some studies, though not all, have been able to operantly change human skin potential, heart rate, and salivation. Animal studies have an advantage over human studies in that the animals can be temporarily paralyzed by curare to remove artifacts caused by movement. Under these conditions, animals have been taught to increase or decrease heart rate, intestinal contractions, stomach contractions, urine formation, and electrical brain waves. Either direct electrical stimulation of the brain or escape from mild electrical shock has been used as a primary reinforcer. In some instances, clear and extreme physiological changes can be produced using this process. Some success has also been obtained in training epileptic patients to suppress abnormal paroxysmal spikes in their electroencephalograms. As Miller notes, "While it is far too early to promise any cures, it certainly will be worthwhile to investigate thoroughly the therapeutic possibilities of improved instrumental training techniques."

Classical Conditioning

Another type of conditioning frequently used to change behavior is classical conditioning as demonstrated by the work of Ivan Pavlov. If a stimulus such as food or an electric shock is presented to a person, it can generally elicit an involuntary response (or "reflex") such as salivation or muscle contraction. This eliciting stimulus is called the unconditioned stimulus. In a typical classical conditioning experiment, a neutral stimulus such as a bell is presented to the person and this stimulus is followed shortly (from a few tenths of a second to 3 or 4 seconds) by the presentation of the unconditioned stimulus and the response. Sometimes the neutral stimulus and the unconditioned stimulus overlap each other briefly. When these stimuli are repeatedly paired with each other in this manner, the neutral stimulus eventually becomes able to elicit the response even when the unconditioned stimulus is no

longer present. The neutral stimulus is then labeled a conditioned stimulus and the response is known as a conditioned response.

In Pavlov's early experiments, dogs were presented with the sound of a metronome followed by meat powder until the presentation of the sound alone elicited salivation. Similar conditioning procedures have been used with humans to produce salivation as a conditioned response.

Two central concepts in classical conditioning are excitation and inhibition. Excitation, in most general terms, was used by Pavlov to refer to the gradual irradiation or spread of impulses over the cerebral cortex. Thus, if a conditioned response is elicited by a tone of 500 cycles per second, a tone of 400 cycles might also elicit the same or similar conditioned response. Opposed to this process were various types of inhibition that produce a diminution of response strength to all stimuli. For example, a conditioned response which is initially elicited by both 500 and 490 cycle tones will become restricted to one of them—the 500 cycle tone—if the 490 cycle tone is repeatedly presented without being followed by the unconditioned stimulus, while the 500 cycle tone remains paired with the unconditioned stimulus. This process is known as differential inhibition.

These concepts of excitation and inhibition have been recently integrated into a theory suggesting that each stimulus produces a generalization gradient. The gradients thus produced interact with each other in a mathematically predictable manner to produce the observed conditioned response. Classical conditioning procedures have been used to modify salivation, heart rate, blood pressure, urination, respiration, excretion of bile, infantile sucking, eyelid movement, and many other responses usually, but not always, associated with the autonomic nervous system.

Classical conditioning procedures have been used primarily with two major categories of offenders—alcoholics and homosexuals. The central objective is to produce an unpleasant reaction in the patient to alcohol or to homosexual activity. In the case of alcoholism, the patient is given an emetic such as emetine hydrochloride (the unconditioned stimulus) and just before the onset of nausea he is required to look at, smell, or taste the alcohol (the conditioned stimulus). The results of this procedure appear to be as effective as the usual psychotherapeutic approaches. Vallance, for example, found that approximately 5 percent or fewer alcoholics treated by standard psychotherapeutic methods in the psychiatric unit of a general hospital could be considered abstinent over a 2-year follow-up period. In contrast, one of the highest rates of abstinence was reported in a study by Lemere and Voegtlin in which 51 percent of 4,096 patients treated by conditioning procedures were found abstinent for 2 to 5 years following treatment. These studies represent extremes and more typical studies show a range of abstinence between 10 and 35 percent over a period of 1 year or longer. Because of a wide diversity in the criteria used to determine abstinence or improvement, it is difficult to compare the results of different treatment methods reliably.

Other unconditioned stimuli have been used with alcoholics in addition to emetics. One of the most extreme is succinylcholine chloride, or its derivatives, a curare-like drug that rapidly produces complete paralysis of the skeletal muscles, including those which control respiration. Just as the patient is about to drink the alcohol, paralysis occurs, producing great fright about being unable to breathe and a fear of suffocation. Without danger, resuscitation is provided for the patient within 30 seconds or less. The results, however, are not clearly better than with emetics.

Although electric shock was reported to have been used as an unconditioned stimulus in the treatment of alcoholism as long ago as 1930, it is only in recent years that it has gained some preference in use over emetics. One major advantage is that its onset and duration can be precisely controlled. The procedure generally used is the same as that described earlier with emetics. Because of

the high degree of control of administration of electric shock, it is possible to pair the termination or avoidance of the shock with the sight or smell of a nonalcoholic substance, thus perhaps associating the nonalcoholic substance with reduced anxiety or relaxation. Tentatively, however, this relaxation-aversion procedure does not appear to be significantly better than the more standard aversion techniques.

The procedures used in the treatment of alcoholism have also been used in substantially the same form in the treatment of sexual disorders, particularly homosexuality. The underlying assumption is that, except for very basic physiological responses, sexual behavior is learned. As Kinsey and his associates have noted, "The variations which exist in adult sexual behavior probably depend more upon conditioning than upon variations in the gross anatomy or physiology of the sexual mechanisms." Traditionally, behavior modification techniques have attempted to pair the stimulus that elicits the homosexual behavior, e.g., a picture of a nude male, with an aversive stimulus such as an electric shock or nausea.

Although electric shock was experimentally studied as early as 1935 in the treatment of homosexuality, it is only in more recent years that electric shock has been used clinically. In its simplest form, the treatment requires the presentation of pictures of attractive males or other homosexually-oriented stimuli which are immediately followed by an electric shock. More complex procedures sometimes utilize pictures of attractive females or other nonhomosexual stimuli at the termination of the homosexual stimuli.

Similar conditioning procedures employing aversive stimuli have also been used to treat transvestism, fetishism, and sadism. Within the past few years, behavioral treatment strategies have begun to emphasize not only the negative conditioning of the stimuli giving rise to the sexually deviant behavior, but also the positive conditioning of sexual responses to heterosexual stimuli. In one study, homosexual stimuli were paired with nausea and then later the patient was given an injection of testosterone propionate to produce sexual arousal and was encouraged to masturbate while looking at pictures of females. A similar procedure has been used to reduce voyeurism and sadistic fantasies.

To the extent that male homosexual behavior is produced not so much by an attraction toward males as by a fear of females, as suggested by Freudian psychodynamic theory, homosexual behavior might be reduced by eliminating the patient's fear or anxiety of heterosexual behavior. This is sometimes accomplished by systematic desensitization, a procedure that uses relaxation to reduce the anxiety associated with heterosexual stimuli. The patient is relaxed and then heterosexual images of gradually increasing anxiety are presented to be "counterconditioned." Systematic desensitization may also be combined with the aversive conditioning procedures as described above.

Some very preliminary research has been done using classical conditioning procedures in the treatment of other behaviors such as drug addiction, gasoline sniffing, check writing, and shoplifting. It is likely that the tentative success of these conditioning procedures will lead to the further application of this general methodology to other types of offenses.

Aversive Suppression

The aversive suppression of behavior corresponds in common usage with the concept of punishment. But the term "punishment" as it is ordinarily used has several conflicting meanings when examined from the viewpoint of learning theory. Most customarily, punishment refers to the presentation of an aversive stimulus after the person has emitted the behavior which is to be reduced in frequency or eliminated. Thus, the child is slapped on the hand (aversive stimulation) after he has reached into the cookie jar or even after he has started to eat the cookie.

Another type of punishment which is often used consists of the removal of positively reinforcing stimuli following the behavior to be eliminated. For example, after the child has reached into the cookie jar, his mother may take the cookie away and may also prevent him from playing with his toys. These two possible types of punishment, while recognized, have not been given any generally accepted labels. Burgess and Akers have suggested that "Those stimuli whose presentation will weaken an operant's [behavior's] future occurrence are called punishers; the process, positive punishment ... Those stimuli whose removal will weaken an operant's future occurrence are called positive reinforcers; the process, negative punishment." The terms "positive punishment" and "negative punishment" are not widely used, but they do point out the distinction between the presentation of aversive stimuli and the withdrawal of positive stimuli following the prohibited behavior. It is the scientific application of aversive stimuli that is of primary concern here as it raises more acutely certain legal and ethical problems than does the withdrawal of positive stimuli which has had much broader public use and acceptance.

The application of aversive stimuli following the prohibited behavior is surely not new. Whippings, mutilations, and duckings in cold water have had a long history of use. A rather novel form of treatment was once reported by the famous 18th century physician and patriot, Benjamin Rush, in which a drug addict was successfully cured by having an artificial snake pop out of her opium box. Although such a treatment now seems quite out of style, it does have the virtue of pairing the aversive stimulus closely in time with the behavior to be suppressed. In fact, if there is a series of behaviors leading to the final, prohibited behavior, punishment may be most effectively used if the aversive stimulus is applied following one of the behaviors in the series prior to the final behavior. This is rarely the situation in the administration of criminal justice. Punishment is rarely administered prior to the offense and more generally occurs several hours to several years following the prohibited behavior. The typical delinquent may steal several cars before being apprehended and the application of aversive stimuli or the withdrawal of positive stimuli begins.

If it were not for the rather humiliating and painful aspects of public whipping, the failure of this treatment to produce longlasting changes in offenders' behavior would be a rather amusing illustration of correctional ineffectiveness. In a study of the whipping penalty in Delaware, Caldwell found that 1,302 offenders were whipped between the years of 1900 and 1942 inclusive. In a special study of the criminal careers of 320 prisoners who were whipped, 61.9 percent were again convicted of some crime after their first whipping. Of course, it might be argued that not enough whipping was administered to be effective. The data collected by Caldwell do not bear this out. Of those offenders who were whipped twice, 65.1 percent were again convicted of a subsequent offense. Also, in a comparison study of whipped and unwhipped offenders, 68.5 percent of those whipped were later convicted of crimes, 61.1 percent of those offenders who were imprisoned instead of whipped were later convicted, and only 37.5 percent of those offenders placed on probation instead of whipped were later convicted. From a learning theory viewpoint, whipping could be expected to be ineffective for a number of reasons, one of them being the delay between the prohibited act and the subsequent punishment, as previously mentioned.

Behavioral modification techniques closely pair the prohibited behavior, or precursors of it, with the subsequent aversive stimuli. Considerable experimentation of this nature has been conducted in the past few years with sexually deviant persons. In one well known early study of the treatment of transvestism, the patient received painful electric shocks on his feet from a grid on which he was standing while dressing in women's clothes. Over a period of 8 days, the patient received a total of 200 shocks during the frequent treatment sessions. A follow-up study 14 months later indicated only one subsequent relapse of crossdressing by this patient.

The use of aversive stimuli in the suppression of homosexual behavior or other deviant sexual behavior has been reported in over 26 studies. These studies, generally using electric shock or an emetic to induce vomiting, often do not clearly distinguish between classical conditioning procedures and aversive suppression procedures. The studies tend to show an effectiveness in changing behavior which is at least equal to or better than the traditional, psychoanalytic treatment of these disorders. Greater attention, however, needs to be given to the design of these treatment methods to incorporate learning theory paradigms to assess more accurately their therapeutic potential.

Temporary paralysis and apnea have been used in the treatment of chronic alcoholics. Clancy, Vanderhoof, and Campbell reported using the following treatment procedure after the patients were informed that they would have "some difficulty in breathing." A hypodermic needle was inserted in the patient's arm vein and a saline drip attached. When the drip was running and an injection of succinylcholine chloride prepared, a small amount of the patient's favorite alcoholic beverage was poured into a glass in front of him. A few seconds after the patient tasted the alcohol, apnea occured and the patient, fearful of suffocating, was ventilated with a breathing bag. A 1-year follow-up study by these researchers, as well as a study by other researchers using a similar procedure closer to classical conditioning, showed somewhat positive results in producing abstinence. These researchers, however, are cautious in advising the use of apneic paralysis except for a carefully selected population, and even then the subsequent anxiety or other side effects may make the procedure inadvisable.

Some preliminary research has been done in the use of apomorphine, an emetic, in the treatment of drug addiction. In a study by Liberman, two hospitalized narcotic addicts were made nauseous following a "fix" with morphine by the administration of apomorphine during 38 treatment sessions conducted over a period of 5 weeks. "Booster" sessions were also used at varying intervals when the patients began to notice a recurrence of craving for morphine. Tentatively, the procedure appears to be useful in reducing the craving for narcotics although considerable social assistance and perhaps outpatient therapy may be needed in addition to this treatment to avoid subsequent dependence.

The above study by Liberman also provided occasional, free-choice situations in which the patient could choose between morphine and a pleasant social situation with the therapist and nurse. This illustrates the application of some experimental studies suggesting that the development of appropriate, alternative responses during the period of suppression induced by punishment is helpful in preventing high rates of recurrence of the punished behavior.

There are additional findings from laboratory studies that generally have not yet been included in the design of treatment programs utilizing the aversive suppression of behavior. For example, the suppression of behaviors that are based upon an inner drive or upon the avoidance of other aversive stimuli may yield different patterns of suppression. Also, unless the stimuli are very intense, aversive suppression generally does not completely eliminate the occurrence of the punished behavior but rather lowers its rate, which may gradually, without additional suppression, return to its approximate prepunishment rate. There are also occasional "paradoxical" effects of punishment in which the use of aversive stimuli may increase the rate of the punished behavior when the aversive stimuli are removed. Finally, punishment may produce side effects such as anxiety or deception which ultimately make the behavior increase. Nevertheless, there is considerable agreement that the appropriate application of aversive stimuli can at best, for short periods of time, markedly alter the rate or pattern of expression of the punished behavior.

Electronic Monitoring and Intervention

Within the past few years there has been an increasing recognition that some changes in behavior can be produced better by treatment which is conducted in the offender's natural environment than by treatment conducted within an institution. One manifestation of this is the rapid increase in the use of work-release programs, preparole community service programs, and halfway houses. Therapy techniques are also being modified with the understanding that some reinforcers that maintain appropriate behavior in an institution may not be the same reinforcers that maintain appropriate behavior in the community.

Ultimately, most offenders will have to live in an environment similar to the one that produced, or at least did not successfully inhibit, their illegal behaviors. Two approaches are possible. The therapist may be able to help the offender deal with these environmental stimuli by introducing them into treatment sessions while the offender is still institutionalized or by extending treatment procedures into a community setting in which the offender lives during a temporary or conditional release from the institution.

Although some environmental stimuli that are the precursors of illegal behavior, such as new cars or potential victims, obviously cannot be brought easily into treatment sessions, photographs or films of them can be used. For example, a film of women pushing perambulators was presented to a patient with this fetish just prior to the onset of chemically induced nausea. Similarly, a picture of the roommate of a homosexual patient, or a film of shoplifting in one of the shoplifter's favorite stores can be used in treatment. Of course, some stimuli such as alcohol or bank checks can be brought easily into treatment sessions.

However, even though some stimuli can be brought into the treatment session, a problem still remains. The stimulus removed from its customary context may appear much different from usual to the patient and therefore may not elicit his typical response. For this reason, increasing emphasis has been placed on the *in vivo* treatment of behavioral disorders, particularly the phobias. For example, a patient who is fearful of flying may be relaxed either chemically or by verbal instructions and then gradually introduced to flying by being accompanied by the therapist to the airport. Subsequently, the therapist may accompany the patient on short, trial flights. Similarly, a patient with homosexual tendencies can be treated by an emetic in an office setting and then he can self-administer the emetic in the community when his impulses may lead to homosexual behavior. This type of *in vivo* treatment has an additional advantage over typical institutional or office treatment. The successes achieved by the patient, though perhaps initially small, are likely to seem more "real" to him than changes that occur within an institution. These changes may encourage more effort by him for further change. Also, the environmental changes produced by the patient's effort may reinforce new patterns of behavior.

The treatment of the institutionalized offender in the community, however, presents the problems of a potential escape and increased risk to the community. One approach to this problem has been the development, in prototype form, of small personally worn transmitters that permit the continual monitoring of the geographical location of parolees. This system, which also involves the use of intensive treatment and the help of volunteers in the community, is known as an electronic rehabilitation system.

As presently designed the electronic rehabilitation system is capable of monitoring the geographical location of a subject in an urban setting up to 24 hours. The subject wears two small units approximately 6 inches by 3 inches by 1 inch in size, weighing about 2 pounds. As the wearer walks through a prescribed monitored area, his transmitter activates various repeater stations which retransmit his signal, with a special location code, to the base station. The repeater stations are so located that at least one is always activated by the wearer's transmitter.

This prototype system as now used extends only a few blocks during street use and covers the inside of one large building. The primary purpose of this system is to demonstrate the feasibility of larger, more complete systems and gather some preliminary

data. Through the use of carefully placed repeater stations in each block, the system is theoretically duplicable such that large geographical areas may be covered with a large number of subjects each transmitting a unique signal. The range of the system and the specificity with which a person can be located depend largely upon the number of repeater stations used.

The impetus for the use of electronic intervention in the treatment of offenders emerges from several sources. There has been a rapid increase in the use of telemetry for medical purposes and a shift in the budget allocations of the electronic industry from defense research and development projects to feasibility studies in the public sector. In addition, there has been a marked increase in the research and development of law enforcement technology. Some of this research has been aimed at facilitating surveillance through the use of specially equipped helicopters, computerized information retrieval systems, and infrared sensors.

Considerable effort is also being devoted to the development of systems for the rapid, electronic location of objects in an urban setting. Many of these systems are being developed primarily for monitoring the location of motor vehicles such as buses or police cars. One presently operative system provides the location of a vehicle every 5 seconds within a limited urban area with an accuracy of approximately one block. . . . In a report prepared for the Office of Urban Transportation of the U.S. Department of Housing and Urban Development, the organization notes, "Another, secretive, law enforcement use of AVM [Automatic Vehicle Monitor] systems would be in 'bugging' suspect vehicles, valuable shipments, etc.; movement could be traced through the city without a conspicuous 'tail'. Future refinement of the craft may make it possible to implant a transponder on a subject's person—in his shoe, for instance."

Special security equipment has been designed and is being further developed to prevent the removal or compromise of personally worn equipment by parolees. If this equipment were used to guarantee the wearing of personal transmitters and integrated into an electronic locator system, a very powerful, involuntary surveillance system would be possible. All of the major components of such a system have been developed in a design or prototype stage in various laboratories. The complete, involuntary system has not yet been used; but as described earlier, a voluntary, prototype system covering a few city blocks has been studied.

Another potential source for the introduction of location monitoring systems into the public domain may be citizen protection. Citizens might be equipped with transmitters to alert the police in the event of attack. Crewe suggests:

It is at least conceivable that citizens could be licensed to carry miniaturized police call systems in the form of a small radio transmitter. This could relay a cry for help to transmitters on the corners of each block. This signal could be automatically and instantaneously transmitted to the local police who could immediately dispatch assistance. It would be relatively simple to design into such a communications system the necessary safeguards against tampering and abuse. For example, the pocket transmitter should be capable of being turned on but not of being turned off. This would prevent the criminal from interrupting the signal. With modern electronic systems such a transmitter could be very small, making it difficult to detect and in any case the signal would be inaudible. As regards abuse, it would be possible to license the use of such transmitters thereby restricting their use to those who do not abuse the privilege of carrying it. It should perhaps be pointed out that it would be entirely unnecessary for the whole population to carry such transmitters. In fact, this problem is something like the problem of vaccination against smallpox, that is, it only requires a certain percentage of the population to be innoculated to eradicate the disease.

In addition to monitoring the location of a person, other characteristics might also be monitored. Equipment has been developed for monitoring voice, blood pressure, physiological activity, and electroencephalograms.

Sophistication of design in instrumentation is making the implantation of sensors less necessary, but unless transmission is by hard wire, telemetry is still generally limited to a short range of a few hundred feet or within one or two buildings. Capabilities are, however, rapidly expanding.

As previously noted, many components of potentially effective monitoring and intervention systems usable with offenders have been developed in various laboratories but have not yet been often integrated into operable systems. For example, devices have been developed for measuring penile erection during the therapeutic treatment of sexual deviates or for the objective measurement of sexual preferences. These devices have generally recorded changes either by using a plethysmograph or a strain gauge. Transducers have been designed that provide an electrical output suitable for the continuous monitoring and recording of penile changes. The linkage of these transducers to a portable transmitter rather than to a recorder would not be difficult and could, when included within an electronic locator system, provide the capability of precisely monitoring sex offenders within the community.

Thus far in the present discussion, the emphasis has been upon the acquisition of data about the offender. A complete communication system could also permit the transmission of signals to the offender within the community. These signals could transmit information to the offender or activate equipment worn by him or near to him. To date, there has been no extensive use of portable equipment in behavior modification. There are, however, a few notable exceptions. A small, portable shock apparatus with electrodes attached to the wrist has been used to help inhibit a patient's addiction to Demerol (Pethidine). The patient in this study applied electric shocks to himself when he felt strong impulses to take the drug. The researcher, Joseph Wolpe, known for several innovations in psychotherapy, observed, "A strong and frequent endogenous impulse for Demerol was markedly diminished, apparently as a consequence of its being reciprocally inhibited by strong faradic stimulation of the forearm of the patient. Though only nine shocks were given in relation to the endogenous craving—all in the course of 1 week (the shocks in the following 2 weeks having been in relation to exogenous stimuli)—the decrease in its strength and frequency was such that the patient was easily able to abstain from the drug for a 3-month period during which no further shocks were administered."

Powell and Azrin have developed a cigarette case that consists of a shock device and counter that are activated each time the case is opened. Portable devices that produce a regular, rhythmic beat have been developed to be worn behind the ear or on the wrist to reduce stuttering. A portable device has also been developed that emits a tone signal when a patient assumes a faulty posture known as "round shoulders" for a period of at least 3 seconds. Similarly, a personally worn device has been developed for delivering small amounts of direct current to the forehead of patients to reduce depression. Gradually, a new field of study may be emerging, variously known as behavioral engineering or behavioral instrumentation, that focuses upon the use of electromechanical devices for the modification of behavior.

One of the most controversial areas of behavioral instrumentation is that of intracranial stimulation. Some of the early studies of the intracranial stimulation of the human brain began approximately 15 years ago. Techniques that originally allowed the implantation of electrodes for only a few days or a few weeks have now been developed to permit the positioning of the electrodes for periods up to 3 years. This research has generally been conducted for medical purposes to gain a better understanding of brain function or to alleviate severe behavioral impairments, or modify human emotions.

Relatively little research has been done in the area of remote communication with patients, but there are some exceptions. For example, to help control the restlessness of a 10-year-old boy in a classroom, a therapist transmitted a tone signal to him through an earphone whenever the boy sat quietly long enough to earn a piece of candy. Similarly, devices have been used for transmitting comments or instructions to parents or psychology trainees during therapy sessions. In the treatment of alcoholics, a distant observer has used a walkie-talkie type transmitter to deliver electric shocks to patients at appropriate moments in the treatment procedure. Tone signals have also been transmitted to persons over a location monitoring system, previously described, to reduce crime-related behaviors. Using this system, a person with a problem of aggression following heavy drinking was conditioned in a laboratory to experience nausea when he was served alcohol following the presentation of a particular tone signal. Later, this tone signal was transmitted to him in barrooms in a high crime rate area to reduce his drinking behavior.

The standard bellboy paging system has been used to help patients reduce their rate of smoking. Tone signals were transmitted to the patients in their homes or offices that permitted them to smoke. Smoking at other times was forbidden. The number of transmitted tone signals was gradually reduced over a period of several weeks. An experimentor has also transmitted a signal to a delinquent which was received and displayed to the delinquent as a small light or as a "tap" from a vibratactile unit within the belt. This system was used to operantly condition appropriate behavior in the classroom.

Another example is a recently developed two-way communication system used to transmit the electrocardiographic signals of cardiac patients from a moving ambulance to a hospital where a physician makes an interpretation of the signals. Directions are then transmitted back to the ambulance personnel to initiate, in emergency situations, resuscitative procedures such as electrical defibrillation. A more behaviorally oriented feedback system is that of intracerebral telemetry which involves both the remote electroencephalographic recording of brain wave patterns and the remote brain stimulation of human subjects. Although this has been accomplished only over a short distance within a building, Delgado et al. have suggested:

The combination of both stimulation and EEG recording by radio telemetry offers a new tool for two-way clinical exploration of the brain and it may be predicted that in the near future microminiaturization and more refined methodology will permit the construction of instruments without batteries and small enough to be permanently implanted underneath the patient's skin for transdermal reception and transmission of signals through several channels.

As can be seen, new developments in monitoring and intervention systems are occurring rapidly and are greatly increasing communication capabilities within the offender's natural environment. Within the near future, electronic technology is likely to become a very important factor in the design of programs for the modification of the behavior of offenders. . . .

CONCLUSION

CRIMINAL JUSTICE SYSTEM

The discussion above has briefly described the development of behavior modification techniques. . . . Although behavior modification techniques appear to be remarkably effective in some individual cases when treated within a clinic or laboratory, there has been no broad scale application of these techniques to offenders. If such a broad scale application does occur, it will have to take place within the general context of the criminal justice system. Criticisms of this system are not difficult to find.

It has been suggested by Teeters that "It is not just the philosophy of imprisonment that is 'sick' but rather, the entire classical theory of criminal law. We are operating, by and large, under eighteenth century concepts, all of which, from police to court trial and sentencing, are pathetically outmoded and clamor for outright change." Similarly,

Barnes in an article entitled "Scientific Treatment" comments, "[W]e cannot achieve anything like complete success until the old punitive philosophy and the conventional prisons are abolished, root and branch. It is as futile to try to graft a rational treatment of criminals on the traditional prison system as it would be to attach a motor car to an ancient stagecoach."

But criminologists are not alone in their criticism of the criminal justice system. Thus, Karl Menninger inveighs, "The concept [of justice] is so vague, so distorted in its application, and usually so irrelevant that it offers no help in the solution of the crime problem which it exists to combat but results in the exact opposite—injustice, injustice to everybody." This criticism is not entirely inappropriate. As a reflection of one of the most "ferocious" penal policies of any civilized country, we presently have approximately 1.3 million persons subject to correctional authority serving some of the longest sentences in the world.

More specifically, the present study shows tentatively that the criteria in the statutes that are used to define sex offenders, habitual offenders, and drug addicts are often vague and clearly inconsistent among the States. Further, the criteria used for the release of offenders from confinement under these statutes are not closely related to the criteria used to incarcerate them. Finally, administrative standards are poorly defined and court intervention has become necessary to safeguard some of the fundamental rights of offenders.

Situations such as this are fertile ground for the development of proposals for reform. (Getting these proposals translated into actual programs is another, more unlikely, event.) For example, it is clear that prison administrators have very great discretion and that there is much potential for abuse. Silverberg suggests that, "[I]n this country, where trained and reliable staff is scarce, environment control might best be accomplished by automating much of prison life, since it is easier to see to it that a machine does not abuse prisoners than to insure that a thoughtless guard will not." Perhaps more promising, and likely of adoption, are proposals for the treatment of offenders based upon concepts derived from learning theory. As well pointed out by Schwartz in "A Learning Theory of Law," derivatives of learning theory may be usefully applied to the understanding of the effects of criminal sanctions and the classification of deviant behavior.

BEHAVIOR MODIFICATION TECHNIQUES

Some of the difficulties in the criminal justice system, such as the inconsistent definition of offenders, cannot be corrected merely by an increased use of behavior modification techniques. On the other hand, behavior modification techniques are remarkably well suited for integration into the criminal justice system because they, and their underlying theories, focus upon behavior, and most offenses involve observable behavior. Unlike treatment orientations that focus upon goals such as mental health, which are diffuse and difficult to define, behavior modification goals are readily measurable. Thus, questions about the effectiveness of the approach and its influence on the criminal justice system can be answered by empirical study rather than by speculation unsupported by data.

The promise of behavior modification techniques lies not so much in accomplishments to date as in the success of clinical and laboratory experiments and in the general methodology. In the area of operant conditioning, reinforcers such as food, release from an institution, or money have been successfully used to modify delinquent behavior. Further study needs to be done on the duration of these changes in community settings. In the area of classical conditioning, aversive stimuli such as emetics or electric shock have been used with alcoholics and homosexuals. The aversive stimulus in this procedure precedes by a very brief interval the behavior to be modified. This results in a reduced frequency of the behavior subse-

quently. In another technique, aversive suppression, the aversive stimulus follows the behavior to be modified. This is similar to the traditional procedures of punishment.

Classical conditioning with aversive stimuli and aversive suppression are unpleasant for the offender and legal coercion may be required to obtain participation in the treatment procedures. Also, some ethical issues may be raised in regard to the extent to which the community may employ aversive procedures against an offender's will to prevent predicted, subsequent offenses. In classical conditioning, however, there is a newly emerging trend that emphasizes the pairing of pleasant stimuli with behavior that competes with the illegal behavior. For example, heterosexual behavior is increased by conditioning in order to reduce homosexual behavior. The positive results of this research are encouraging but more long-term follow-up studies are required.

Electronic monitoring and intervention systems have been designed and used with offenders in prototype form. Large scale systems have not yet been used. Complex systems are in laboratory development that can provide two-way communication with offenders in the community as well as the continual monitoring of their geographical location. It would appear that much crime can be technologically prevented; however, procedures need to be developed for the effective regulation of the use of this equipment to avoid undue coercion by the government.

Therapeutically, electronic systems can allow the offender to remain in the community where he must ultimately learn to live. Also, behavior modification techniques such as operant and classical conditioning procedures can be remotely applied. The long-term therapeutic potential of these systems, independent of their immediate crime prevention capabilities, is the subject of present research.

Behavior modification techniques are not tied exclusively to psychological theory. They can be theoretically integrated with sociological concepts of crime causation and prevention. Shah has developed one of these theoretical integrations. He notes:

It could be demonstrated that a great deal of the behavior of organisms exists because of its effects on the environment. Most human behavior is social because it has certain effects on other people, which in turn helps to establish certain schedules of reinforcement. The same reinforcement paradigm may be extended to larger groups of people such as social agencies and institutions, less well-defined groups of people involved in social practices, codes of conduct, etc., and also smaller groups or the neighborhood "gang" of children. These social practices ultimately refer to the various sets of reinforcements and punishments which the people who constitute the agency, institution, or group, apply to the behaviors of other people. The powerful controlling and regulating influence of social norms are mediated in large measure by the reinforcing effects of group approval and disapproval.

Although the legal and ethical aspects of research in behavior modification have not been discussed herein, this is an area that needs further study. It is likely that the courts will allow somewhat more leeway in the development of new techniques under careful supervision and appropriate procedural safeguards than in the application of techniques already developed to large populations with general supervision.

LEGAL REGULATION

The development of appropriate standards for the application of behavior modification techniques requires some flexibility and tentativeness. Although judicial and legislative opinion is now helpful in setting the outer limits of permissible treatment, restrictive case law and statutes based upon inadequate information are likely to prevent an advantageous development of new knowledge and more effective techniques. There needs ot be an opportunity for conceptual changes in the treatment of offenders, at least until a higher degree of therapeutic success is achieved. Thomas Szasz has often quoted Seymour Krim to the effect that the vocabu-

lary and definitions of psychiatry have become a "noose around the neck of the brain." Similarly, the vocabulary and definitions of law should not unduly restrict the logical development of the field of behavior modification as they would if they were the predominant terms determining its growth.

Rather than relying upon case law or statutes, more flexibility and conceptual integrity could be obtained by having professional organizations and practitioners establish internal standards and guidelines. Courts and legislatures could then look to these standards in resolving difficult problems. The development of these standards will, of course, require openly confronting some very difficult policy issues. For example, the present practice of the civil commitment of offenders for "treatment" often results in the long-term preventive detention of some property offenders or persons of undetermined dangerousness. This practice now probably could not be directly mandated by legislatures. As behavior therapists move out of the laboratory and private clinic into the criminal justice system, they will certainly be involved in this issue because criminal behaviors will have to be assigned expected frequencies prior to treatment.

The application of behavior modification techniques to the behavior of offenders necessarily involves some view of the relationship of the State's coercive power to the individual. Silverberg has suggested that because foreseeable future prisons are likely to be closed societies, "[W]e should begin to think about operating them so as to derive maximum benefit from their totalitarian nature, rather than sweeping this characteristic under the rug." Further, "The community need not protect a man's right to be a criminal by refusing to change his criminal mind (and through it, his criminal behavior) without his consent."

In contrast, one might take more nearly the view of the "community" as de Toqueville saw it. In this view, the legal order in a democracy is based upon reciprocal relationship which include both complimentary and conflicting viewpoints. A democratic order, or "ordered liberty," does not rely primarily upon political or therapeutic power. Of course, coercive power must sometimes be used when the behavior of offenders restricts unduly the freedom of others, for example, attacks on persons using public streets. The harm is not only measured by the actual frequency of attacks but also their assumed recurrence that would make people fearful of leaving their homes, thus restricting their freedom of movement. On the other hand, some private, consensual acts between persons, now considered crimes, would be permitted. The physical restraint of offenders, who are also citizens, would be limited to that which was necessary to maximize the freedom of action and thought in the community. In this view, the long and ineffective sentences of imprisonment now often used would need to be changed. Such changes, however, are more nearly matters of public policy than therapeutic technique.

Whether legal institutions can regulate the coercive potential of behavior modification techniques toward the implicit jurisprudential values of "fairness" and "justice" is an open question. The necessary constitutional provisions appear to be available but too infrequently applies to specific cases to be clear in outline. This appears to be not so much the result of judicial reluctance as the absence of firm information about the effects of behavior modification techniques on sizeable populations of offenders. When such information becomes reliable, it may help to shape judicial opinion so that the legal limits and leeway of application become more clear.

Very much more needs to be learned about the potential effects of behavior modification techniques. Although considerable gains have been made over the past 15 years of research, one is reminded of Phaedrus' mountain:

A mountain was in labour, sending forth dreadful groans, and there was in the region the highest expectation. After all, it brought forth a mouse.

But perhaps, we will not be too criticized if, with occasional glimpses of success, we continue to hope for genuinely effective and humane procedures for changing those behaviors that have so long troubled men and caused them to be troubled.

THE USE OF ELECTRONICS IN THE OBSERVATION AND CONTROL OF HUMAN BEHAVIOR AND ITS POSSIBLE USE IN REHABILITATION AND PAROLE

Barton L. Ingraham and Gerald W. Smith

INTRODUCTION

In the very near future, a computer technology will make possible alternatives to imprisonment. The development of systems for telemetering information from sensors im-

From "The Use of Electronics in the Observation and Control of Human Behavior and Its Possible Use in Rehabilitation and Parole," by Barton L. Ingraham and Gerald W. Smith, published in *Issues in Criminology*, 7, No. 2 (Fall 1972), 35—53, by the graduate students of the School of Criminology at the University of California. Professor Ingraham is at the Institute of Criminal Justice and Criminology, University of Maryland and Professor Smith is in the Department of Sociology at the University of Utah.

planted in or on the body will soon make possible the observation and control of human behavior without actual physical contact. Through such telemetric devices, it will be possible to maintain twenty-four hour-a-day surveillance over the subject and to intervene electronically or physically to influence and control selected behavior. It will thus be possible to exercise control over human behavior and from a distance without physical contact. The possible implications for criminology and corrections of such telemetric systems is tremendously significant. . . .

ELECTRONIC TECHNIQUES FOR OBSERVING AND CONTROLLING BEHAVIOR IN HUMANS

A telemetric system consists of small electronic devices attached to a subject that transmit via radio waves information regarding the location and physiological state of the wearer. A telemetry system provides a method whereby phenomena may be measured or controlled at a distance from where they occur—i.e., remotely. The great benefit derived from the use of such systems in studying animals (including man) lies in the ability to get data from a heretofore inaccessible environment, thus avoiding the experimental artifacts which arise in a laboratory setting. It also provides long-range, day-to-day, continuous observation and control of the monitored subject, since the data can be fed into a computer which can act as both an observer and a controller.

Telemetry has been put to many and diverse uses. In aerospace biology, both man and animal have been telemetered for respiration, body temperature, blood pressure, heart rate (ECG's), brain waves (EEG's) and other physiological data. Telemetric devices have been placed on and in birds, animals and fish of all kinds to learn about such things as migration patterns, hibernation and spawning locations, respiration rates, brain wave activity, body temperatures, etc. Telemetry has also been used in medicine to obtain the EEG patterns of epileptics during seizures, and to monitor heart rhythms and respiration rates in humans, for purposes of diagnosis and rescue in times of emergency.

Telemetric systems can be classified into two types of devices—"external devices" and "internal devices."

External Devices

For the past several years, Schwitzgebel at Harvard has been experimenting with a small, portable transmitter, called a Behavior Transmitter-Reinforcer (BT-R), which is small enough to be carried on a belt and which permits tracking of the wearer's location, transmitting information about his activities and communicating with him (by tone signals). The tracking device consists of two containers, each about the size of a thick paperback book, one of which contains batteries and the other, a transmitter that automatically emits radio signals, coded differently for each transmitter so that many of them may be used on one frequency band. With a transmitting range of approximately a quarter of a mile under adverse city conditions and a receiving range of two miles, the BT-R signals are picked up by receivers at a laboratory base station and fed into a modified missile-tracking device which graphs the wearer's location and displays it on a screen. The device can also be connected with a sensor resembling a wristwatch which transmits the wearer's pulse rate. In addition, the wearer can send signals to the receiving station by pressing a button, and the receiver can send a return signal to the wearer.

At present, the primary purpose of the device is to facilitate medical and therapeutic aid to patients, i.e., to effectuate the quick location and rescue of persons subject to emergency medical conditions that preclude their calling for help, such as cases of acute cardiac infarction, epilepsy or diabetes. Also, so far, the use of the device has been limited to volunteers, and they are free to remove the device whenever they wish. Schwitzgebel has expressed an interest in applying his device to monitoring and rehabilitating chronic recidivists on parole.

At the University of California, Los Angeles, Ralph Schwitzgebel's brother, Robert Schwitzgebel, has perfected a somewhat similar device in which a miniature two-way radio unit, encased in a wide leather belt containing its own antenna and rechargeable batteries, is worn by volunteer experimental subjects. Non-voice communication is maintained between a central communications station and the wearer by means of a radio signal which, when sent, activates a small coil in the wearer's receiver unit that makes itself felt as a tap in the abdominal region, accompanied by a barely audible tone and a small light. Information is conveyed to the subject by a coded sequence of taps. In turn, the wearer can send simple coded signal messages back to the central station, indicating his receipt of the signal, his general state of well being, or the lack of it, and many other matters as well. So far, this device and its use depend entirely upon a relationship of cooperation and trust between experimenter and subject.

Another use of radiotelemetry on humans which has reached a high level of sophistication is the long-distance monitoring of ECG (electro-cardiogram) waves by Caceres and his associates. They have developed a telemetry system by which an ambulatory heart patient can be monitored continuously by a central computer in another city. The patient has the usual electrocardiograph leads taped to his chest, which are connected to a small battery powered FM radio transmitter on the patient's belt. The ECG in the vicinity which relays them via an ordinary telephone (encased in an automated dialing device called a Dataphone). The encoded signals, of the ECG can then be transmitted to any place in the world which can be reached by telephone. On the receiving end, there is an automatic answering device that accepts the call and turns on the appropriate receiving equipment. In the usual case this will be an analog-to-digital converter, which quantizes the electrical waves and changes them to a series of numbers, representing amplitudes at certain precise times. The computer then analyzes the numerical amplitude values and, when an abnormal pattern appears, it not only warns the patient's physician (with a bell or light) but will produce, on request, some or all of the previous readings it has stored. The computer can monitor hundreds of patients simultaneously by sharing computer time among hundreds of input signals, and produce an "analysis" of ECG activity for each in as little as 2.5 minutes—the time required for the signal to get into the computer's analytical circuits. . . .

The third area where external telemetry has been used to advantage is also in the medical field. For several years, Vreeland and Yeager have been using a subminiature radiotelemeter for taking EEC's of epileptic children. The device is glued to the child's scalp with a special preparation and electrodes extend from it to various places on the child's scalp. A receiver is positioned in an adjoining room of the hospital and sound motion pictures record the child's behavior, his voice and his EEG on the same film. Some of the benefits derived from the use of this equipment are: (1) that it permits readings to be taken of an epileptic seizure as it occurs; and (2) it allows studies to be made of EEG patterns of disturbed children without encumbering them in trailing wires. At present, however, the device is "external" in the sense that the electrodes do not penetrate into the brain, and only surface cortical brain wave patterns are picked up by the transmitter. It is believed, however, that many epileptic seizures originate in areas deep in the subcortical regions of the brain, and to obtain EEG readings for these areas, it would be necessary to implant the electrodes in these areas stereotaxically. The significance of such a modification would be that if the transmitter were transformed into a transceiver (a minor modification), it would then be possible to stimulate the same subcortical areas telemetrically. This would, then, convert the telemetry system into an "internal" device, such as the ones we are now about to describe.

Internal Devices

One of the leaders in the field of internal radio-telemetry devices is Mackay. He has developed devices which he calls "endoradiosondes." These are tiny transmitters that can be swallowed or implanted internally in man or animal. They have been designed in order to measure and transmit such physiological variables as gastrointestinal pressure, blood pressure, body temperature, bioelectrical potentials (voltage accompanying the functioning of the brain, the heart and other muscles), oxygen levels, acidity and radiation intensity (Mackay, 1965). . . . Both "active" and "passive" transmitters have been developed, "active" transmitters containing a battery powering an oscillator, and "passive" transmitters not containing an internal power source, but having instead tuned circuits modulated from an outside power source.... Both transmitter systems, at present, have ranges of a few feet to a dozen—just enough to bring out the signal from inside the body. Thus, it is generally necessary for the subject to carry a small booster transmitter in order to receive the weak signal from inside the body and increase its strength for rebroadcasting to a remote laboratory or data collection point. However, with the development of integrated circuits, both transmitters and boosters can be miniaturized to a fantastic degree.

Electrical Stimulation of the Brain

The technique employed in electrophysiology in studying the brain of animals and man by stimulating its different areas electrically is nothing new. This technique was being used by two European physiologists, Fritsch and Hitzig, on dogs in the latter half of the 19th Century. In fact, much of the early work in experimental psychology was devoted to physiological studies of the human nervous system. During the last twenty years, however,—perhaps as a result of equipment which allows the implantation of electrodes deep in the subcortical regions of the brain and the brain stem by stereotaxic instruments—the science of electrophysiology has received new impetus, and our understanding of neural activity within the brain and its behavioral and experiential correlates has been greatly expanded.

The electrical stimulation of various areas of the brain has produced a wide range of phenomena in animals and humans. An examination of published research in electrical stimulation of the brain suggests two crude methods of controlling human behavior: (1) by "blocking" of the response, through the production of fear, anxiety, disorientation, loss of memory and purpose, and even, if need be, by loss of consciousness; and (2) through conditioning behavior by the manipulation of rewarding and aversive stimuli. In this regard, the experiments of James Olds on animals and Robert G. Heath and his associates at Tulane on humans are particularly interesting. Both have shown the existence in animals and humans of brain areas of or near the hypothalamus which have what may be very loosely described as "rewarding" and "aversive" effects. The interesting thing about their experiments is that both animals and man will self-stimulate themselves at a tremendous rate in order to receive stimulation "rewards" regardless of, and sometimes in spite of, the existence of drives such as hunger and thirst. Moreover, their experiments have put a serious dent in the "drive-reduction" theory of operant conditioning under which a response eliciting a reward ceases or declines when a point of satiation is reached, since in their experiments no satiation point seems ever to be reached (the subject losing consciousness from physical exhaustion unless the stimulus is terminated beforehand by the experimenter). Thus their experiments indicate that there may be "pleasure centers" in the brain which are capable of producing hedonistic responses which are independent of drive reduction. In humans, however, the results of hypothalamus stimulation have not always been as clear as those with animals, and some experimenters have produced confusing and inconsistent results.

Current research in the field of electrophysiology seems to hold out the possibility of exerting a limited amount of external control over the emotions, consciousness, memory and behavior of man by electrical stimulation of the brain. Krech quotes a leading electrophysiologist, Delgado of the Yale School of Medicine, as stating that current researches "support the distasteful conclusion that motion, emotion and behavior can be directed by electrical forces and that humans can be controlled like robots by push buttons."... None of the research indicates that man's every action can be directed by a puppeteer at an electrical keyboard; none indicates that thoughts can be placed into the heads of men electrically; none indicates that man can be directed like a mechanical robot. *At most,* they indicate that some of man's activities can possibly be deterred by such methods, that certain emotional states might be induced (with very uncertain consequences in different individuals), and that man might be conditioned along certain approved paths by "rewards" and "punishments" carefully administered at appropriate times. Techniques of direct brain stimulation developed in electrophysiology thus hold out the possibility of influencing and controlling selected human behavior within limited parameters.

The use, then, of telemetric systems as a method of monitoring man, of obtaining physiological data from his body and nervous system, and of stimulating his brain electrically from a distance, seems in the light of present research entirely feasible and possible as a method of control. There is, however, a gap in our knowledge which must be filled before telemetry and electrical stimulation of the brain could be applied to any control system. This gap is in the area of interpretation of incoming data. Before crime can be prevented, the monitor must know what the subject is doing or is about to do. It would not be practical to attach microphones to the monitored subjects, nor to have them in visual communication by television, and it would probably be illegal. Moreover, since the incoming data will eventually be fed into a computer,* it will be necessary to confine the information transmitted to the computer to such non-verbal, non-visual data as location, EEG patterns, ECG patterns and other physiological data. At the present time, EEG's tell us very little about what a person is doing or even about his emotional state. ECG's tell us little more than heart rhythms. Certain other physiological data, however, such as respiration, muscle tension, the presence of adrenalin in the blood stream, combined with knowledge of the subject's location, may be particularly

*Obviously, no system monitoring thousands of parolees would be practical if there had to be a human monitor for every monitored subject on a 24 hour-a-day, seven-day-a-week basis. Therefore, computers would be absolutely necessary.

revealing—e.g., a parolee with a past record of burglaries is tracked to a downtown shopping district (in fact, is exactly placed in a store known to be locked up for the night) and the physiological data reveals an increased respiration rate, a tension in the musculature and an increased flow of adrenalin. It would be a safe guess, certainly, that he was up to no good. The computer in this case, *weighing the probabilities,* would come to a decision and alert the police or parole officer so that they could hasten to the scene; or, if the subject were equipped with an implanted radiotelemeter, it could transmit an electrical signal which could block further action by the subject by causing him to forget or abandon his project. However, before computers can be designed to perform such functions, a greater knowledge derived from experience in the use of these devices on human subjects, as to the correlates between the data received from them and their actual behavior, must be acquired.

CONDITIONS UNDER WHICH TELEMETRY TECHNIQUES MIGHT INITIALLY BE APPLIED IN CORRECTIONAL PROGRAMING

The development of sophisticated techniques of electronic surveillance and control could radically alter the conventional wisdom regarding the merits of imprisonment. It has been the opinion of many thoughtful penologists for some time that prison life is not particularly conducive to rehabilitation. Some correctional authorities, such as the Youth and Adult Corrections Agency of the State of California, have been exploring the possibilities of alternatives to incarceration, believing that the offender can best be taught "to deal lawfully with the given elements of the society while he functions, at least partially, in that society and not when he is withdrawn from it." Parole is one way of accomplishing that objective, but parole is denied to many inmates of the prison system, not always for reasons to do with their ability to be reformed or the risk of allowing them release on parole. The development of telemetric control systems could help increase the number of offenders who could safely and effectively be supervised within the community.

Schwitzgebel suggests that it would be safe to allow the release of many poor-risk or nonparolable convicts into the community provided that their activities were continuously monitored by some sort of telemetric device. He states:

A parolee thus released would probably be less likely than usual to commit offenses if a record of his location were kept at the base station. If two-way tone communication were included in this system, a therapeutic relationship might be established in which the parolee could be rewarded, warned, or otherwise signalled in accordance with the plan for therapy.

He also states:

Security equipment has been designed, but not constructed that could insure the wearing of the transmitting euqipment or indicate attempts to compromise or disable the system.

He further states that it has been the consistent opinion of inmates and parolees interviewed about the matter that they would rather put up with the constraints, inconveniences and annoyances of an electronic monitoring system, while enjoying the freedom outside an institution, than to suffer the much greater loss of privacy, restrictions on freedom, annoyance and inconveniences of prison life.

The envisioned system of telemetric control while offering many possible advantages to offenders over present penal measures also has several possible benefits for society. Society, through such systems, exercises control over behavior it defines as deviant, thus insuring its own protection. The offender, by returning to the community, can help support his dependents and share in the overall tax burden. The offender is also in a better position to make meaningful restitution. Because the control system works on conditioning principles, the offender is habituated into non-deviant behavior patterns—thus perhaps decreasing the proba-

bility of recidivism and, once the initial cost of development is absorbed, a telemetric control system might provide substantial economic advantage compared to rather costly correctional programs. All in all, the development of such a system could prove tremendously beneficial for society.

The adequate development of telemetric control systems is in part dependent upon their possible application. In order to ensure the beneficial use of such a system, certain minimal conditions ought to be imposed in order to forestall possible ethical and legal objections:

1. The consent of the inmate should be obtained, after a full explanation is given to him of the nature of the equipment, the limitations involved in its usage, the risks and constraints that will be placed upon his freedom, and the option he has of returning to prison if its use becomes too burdensome.
2. The equipment should not be used for purposes of gathering evidence for the prosecution of crimes, but rather should be employed as a crime prevention device. A law should be passed giving the users of this equipment an absolute privilege of keeping confidential all information obtained therefrom regardless of to whom it pertains, and all data should be declared as inadmissable in court. The parole authorities, if they be the users of this equipment, should have the discretionary power to revoke parole whenever they see fit without the burden of furnishing an explanation, thus relieving them of the necessity of using data obtained in this fashion as justification for their actions. The data should be destroyed after a certain period of time, and, if the system is hooked up with a computer, the computer should be programmed to erase its tapes after a similar period of time.

By employing the above safeguards, the use of a telemetric system should be entirely satisfactory to the community and to the convicts who choose to take advantage of it. Nevertheless there are a number of ethical objections which are bound to arise when such a system is initially employed that deserve special discussion.

ETHICAL OBJECTIONS

The two principal objections raised against the use of modern technology for surveillance and control of persons deemed to be deviant in their behavior in such a degree as to warrant close supervision revolve around two issues: privacy and freedom.

Privacy

It has often been said that privacy, in essence, consists of the "right to be let alone". This is a difficult right to apply to criminals because it is precisely their inability to leave their fellow members of society alone that justifies not leaving them alone. This statement, however, might be interpreted to mean that there is a certain limited area where each man should be free from the scrutiny of his neighbors or his government and from interference in his affairs. While most people would accept this as a general proposition, in point of fact it is not recognized in prison administration, where surveillance and control are well-nigh absolute and total. Therefore, it is difficult to see how the convict would lose in the enjoyment of whatever rights of privacy he has by electronic surveillance in the open community. If the watcher was a computer, this would be truer still, as most people do not object to being "watched" by electric eyes that open doors for them. It is the scrutiny of humans by humans that causes embarrassment—the knowledge that one is being judged by a fellow human.

Another definition of privacy is given by Ruebhausen.

The essence of privacy is no more, and certainly no less, than the freedom of the individual to pick and choose for himself the time and the circumstances under which, and most importantly, the extent to which, his attitudes, beliefs, behavior and opinions are to be shared with or withheld from others.

To this statement the preliminary question might be raised as to the extent to which we honor this value when we are dealing with convicts undergoing rehabilitation, mental patients undergoing psychiatric treatment, or even minors in our schools. Certainly it is not a statement that can be generally applied, especially in those cases where every society deems itself to have the right to shape and change the attitudes, beliefs, behavior and opinions of others when they are seriously out of step with the rest of society. But a more fundamental objection can be raised, in that the statement has little or no relevance to what we propose. Not only does the envisioned equipment lack the power to affect or modify directly the "attitudes," "beliefs" and "opinions" of the subject, but it definitely does not force him to share those mental processes with others. The subject is only limited in selected areas of his behavior—i.e., those areas in which society has a genuine interest in behavior—i.e., those areas in which society has a genuine interest in control. The subject is consequently "free" to hold any set of attitudes he desires. Of course, on the basis of behavioral psychology, one would expect attitudes, beliefs and opinions to change to conform with the subject's present behavior.

Still a third definition of privacy has been proposed by Fried in an article which specifically discusses Schwitzgebel's device. He advances the argument that privacy is a necessary context for the existence of love, friendship and trust between people, and that the parolee under telemetric supervision who never feels himself loved or trusted will never be rehabilitated. While this argument might have some validity where the device is used as a therapeutic tool—a point that Schwitzgebel recognizes since he would use it partly for that purpose—it is not particularly relevant where no personal relationship is established between the monitors and the subject and where the emphasis is placed upon the device's ability to control and deter behavior, rather than to "rehabilitate." Rehabilitation, hopefully, will follow once law-abiding behavior becomes habitual.

As far as privacy is concerned, most of the arguments are squarely met by the conditions and safeguards previously proposed. However, when one begins to implant endoradiosondes subcutaneously or to control actions through electrical stimulation of the brain, one runs into a particularly troublesome objection, which is often included within the scope of "privacy," although perhaps it should be separately named as the "human dignity" or "sacred vessel of the spirit" argument. This is the argument that was raised when compulsory vaccination was proposed, and which is still being raised as to such things as birth control, heart transplants, and proposals for the improvement of man through eugenics. The argument seems to stem from an ancient, well-entrenched belief that man, in whatever condition he finds himself, even in a state of decrepitude, is as Nature or God intended him to be and inviolable. Even when a man consents to have his physical organism changed, some people feel uneasy at the prospect, and raise objections.

Perhaps the only way to answer such an argument is to rudely disabuse people of the notion that there is any dignity involved in being a sick person, or a mentally disturbed person, or a criminal person whose acts constantly bring him into the degrading circumstances, which the very persons praising human dignity so willingly inflict upon him. Perhaps the only way to explode the notion of man as a perfect, or perfectible, being, made in God's image (the Bible), a little lower than the angels (Disraeli), or as naturally good but corrupted by civilization (Rousseau), is to review the unedifying career of man down through the ages and to point to some rather interesting facets of his biological make-up, animal-like-behavior, and evolutionary career which have been observed by leading biologists and zoologists. Unfortunately, there is not time here to perform such a task or to rip away the veil of human vanity that so enshrouds these arguments.

Freedom

The first thing that should be said with regard to the issue of human freedom is that there is none to be found in most of our prisons. As Sykes (1966) remarks:

. . . the maximum security prison represents a social system in which an attempt is made to create and maintain total or almost total social control.

This point is so well recognized that it need not be belabored, but it does serve to highlight the irrelevancy of the freedom objection as far as the prison inmate is concerned. Any system which allows him the freedom of the open community, which maintains an unobtrusive surveillance and which intervenes only rarely to block or frustrate his activities can surely appear to him only as a vast improvement in his situation.

Most discussions of freedom discuss it as if man were the inhabitant of a natural world, rather than a social world. They fail to take into account the high degree of subtle regulation which social life necessarily entails.

Discussions of freedom that one customarily finds in law journals also fail to take into account the distinction between objective and subjective freedom. Objective freedom for each man is a product of power, wealth or authority, since it is only through the achievement of one or more of these that one can control so as not to be controlled—i.e., it is only through these that one can, on one hand, guard against the abuses, infringements, and overreaching of one's fellow man which limit one, and, on the other hand, commit those very offenses against one's neighbor and, by doing so, obtain all one's heart desires. This is not to neglect the role of the law in preventing a war of all against all, in providing the freedom that goes with peace, and with ensuring that all share to a certain extent in the protections and benefits of a well-ordered society. But laws are themselves limitations imposed upon objective freedom. Radical objective freedom is inconsistent with social life, since in order for some to have it, others must be denied it. Such a radical freedom may also be intolerable psychologically; one may actually feel "constrained" by an excess of options.

Subjective freedom, on the other hand, is a sense of not being pressed by the demands of authority and nagged by unfulfilled desires. It is totally dependent on *awareness*. Such a concept of freedom is easily realizable within the context of an ordered society, whereas radical objective freedom is not. Since society cannot allow men too much objective freedom, the least it can do (and the wise thing to do) is to so order its affairs that men are not aware or concerned about any lack of it. The technique of telemetric control of human beings offers the possibility of regulating behavior with precision on a subconscious level, and avoiding the cruelty of depriving man of his subjective sense of freedom.

CONCLUSION

Two noted psychologists, C. R. Rogers and B. F. Skinner, carried on a debate in the pages of *Science* magazine (over the issue of the moral responsibility of behavioral scientists in view of the ever-widening techniques of behavior control. Skinner said:

The dangers inherent in the control of human behavior are very real. The possibility of misuse of scientific knowledge must always be faced. We cannot escape by denying the power of a science of behavior or arresting its development. It is no help to cling to familiar philosophies of human behavior simply because they are more reassuring. As I have pointed out elsewhere, the new techniques emerging from a science of behavior must be subject to the explicit counter control which has already been applied to earlier and cruder forms.

Skinner's point was that the scientific age had arrived; there was no hope of halting its advance; and that scientists could better spend their time in explaining the nature of their discoveries so that proper controls might be applied (not to stop the advance, but to direct it into the proper channels), rather than in establishing their own set of goals and their own *ne plus ultra* to "proper research." This is a valid point. Victor Hugo once said: "Nothing is as powerful as an idea whose time has arrived." The same holds true for a technology whose time is upon

us. . . . Whether we like it or not, changes in technology require changes in political and social life and in values most adaptable to those changes. It would be ironic indeed if science, which was granted, and is granted, the freedom to invent weapons of total destruction, were not granted a similar freedom to invent methods of controlling the humans who wield them.

Rogers agreed with Skinner that human control of humans is practiced everywhere in social and political life, but framed the issues differently. He said:

. . . They can be stated very briefly: Who will be controlled? Who will exercise control? What type of control will be exercised? Most important of all, toward what end or what purpose, in pursuit of what values, will control be exercised?

These are very basic questions. They need to be answered, and they should be answered.

Jean Rostand, a contemporary French biologist of note, asks: can man be modified? He points to the fact that, since the emergence of *homo sapiens* over 100,000 years ago, man has not evolved physically in the slightest degree. He has the same brain now that he had then, except that now it is filled up with the accumulated knowledge of 5,000 years of civilization—knowledge that has not seemed to be adequate to the task of erasing certain primitive humanoid traits, such as intraspecific aggression, which is a disgusting trait not even common to most animals. Seeing that man now possesses the capabilities of effecting certain changes in his biological structure, he asks whether it isn't a reasonable proposal for man to hasten evolution along by modifying himself into something better than what he has been for the last 100,000 years. We believe that this is a reasonable proposal, and ask: What better place to start than with those individuals most in need of a change for the better?

QUESTIONS FOR DISCUSSION

1. What is meant by behavior modification in the context of deviance?
2. On what principles are behavior modification techniques based?

3. Why is it that behavior modification is very ineffective with unwilling participants?
4. Differentiate, in principle and practice, the following from each other:
   A. Token economy
   B. Aversive conditioning
   C. Operant conditioning
   D. Classical conditioning
   E. Electronic intervention
   F. Desensitization techniques
5. Why are these methods considered forms of radical intrusion whereas punishment is considered neither radical nor intrusive?
6. At what point would you draw the line in the use of these techniques with:
   A. Violent sex offenders
   B. Alcoholics
   C. Transvestites
   D. Auto thieves
   E. Parolees
   F. Narcotic addicts
   G. Neurotics (compulsive-obsessive type)
   H. Retardates
7. If psychosurgery proved to be effective, would you allow such surgery to be performed (if you were a judge and had to decide the issue) on prisoners, or mental patients, or mentally defective violent patients, or inmates?
8. When is such intrusion to be construed as "impermissible tinkering" on the psychological level?

9. What are the legal, moral, and ethical issues in behavior modification?

BIBLIOGRAPHY

Ayllon, T., and Azrin, N. *The Token Economy: A Motivational System for Therapy and Rehabilitation.* New York: Appleton-Century-Crofts, 1968.

Feldman, M. P. "Aversion Therapy for Sexual Deviations: A Critical Review." *Psychological Bulletin* 65 (1966), 65–79.

Jones, H. G., Gelder, Michael, and Holden, H. M. "Behavior and Aversion Therapy in the Treatment of Delinquency" *British Journal of Criminology* 5 No. 4 (1965), 335–87.

King, D. B. "Electronic Surveillance and Constitutional Rights: Some Current Developments and Observations." *George Washington Law Review* 33 (1964).

Kittrie, Nicholas. *The Right to be Different: Deviance and Enforced Therapy.* Baltimore: John Hopkins Press, 1971.

Schwitzgebel, Ralph. "Electronic Innovation in the Behavioral Sciences: A Call to Responsibility." *American Psychologist* 22 No. 5 (1967).

Schwitzgebel, Robert, and Schwitzgebel, Ralph K. eds. *Psychotechnology: Electronic Control of Mind and Behavior.* New York: Holt, Reinhart, and Winston, 1973.

Thompson, Travis, and Grabowski, John, eds. *Behavior Modification of the Mentally Retarded.* New York: Oxford University Press, 1972.

Wolpe, Joseph. *Psychotherapy by Reciprocal Inhibition.* Stanford: Stanford University Press, 1959.

15

The Rise of Voluntary Associations

Since one of the cardinal values in American society has been the perfectability of man, it is somewhat surprising that the voluntary association of deviants movement did not begin until 1935 when two upper middle class alcoholics—a physician from Ohio and a former stockbroker from Canada—devised the prototype of all voluntary associations of deviants and called their group, Alcoholics Anonymous. In truth, somewhat similar movements—the Washingtonians and the Oxford groups—had preceded the emergence of A.A. However, both had a strong religious (evangelical Protestant) bias which "turned off" most alcoholics rather quickly. Still, the perfectability tradition with or without much reference to God did have a considerable hold on the United States ethos. From Coué's, "Each day in every way I get better and better," to Norman Peale's "Positive Thinking," and Turner's "Dare To Be Great" (once under indictment, by the way, in various states), Americans have sought self-improvement without the expenditure of too much effort.

Deviants discovered this mother lode, too. They soon learned that their "spoiled identity" and personal stigma could be reduced by organizational membership; that Americans love people who seek to help themselves. A.A. made the drunk, the sot, the bum into an "alcoholic"—never curable to be sure but in a state of remission as long

as he followed the prescriptions of the group, attended its meetings, "fished" for others in need of help, and believed with all his heart in the Twelve Steps and the Traditions. Synanon, the second voluntary association helped destigmatize all the "junkies" who joined this community, founded incidentally, by an ex-alcoholic who could not pronounce seminar, hence Synanon. This story may be apocryphal, but it is part of the tradition. There soon emerged Recovery Incorporated (ex-mental patients), Gamblers' Anonymous, the organization of Little People of America (mostly midgets since dwarfs are considered deviant by many midgets), and a wide variety of homophile organizations—the Mattachine Society, Daughters of Bilitis, Gay Activist League, among others. Transsexuals tried to organize, so did transvestites. The fat became obese (and some even lost weight) in TOPS and Weight Watchers. Hardly anyone with a "spoiled identity" could resist the temptations to join an anonymous group conferring so much respectability on heretofore shunned persons. What a remarkable way to alter one's self-concept, reduce the rage, claim a legitimate identity, and strive for normative and legislative redefinition of one's "disease," "problem," "hang-up," or "preference" (homophile).

Since 1940, then, groups of deviants—organized, goal-oriented, with "traditions," "steps," or an approach to the management and even an understanding of their problems—have emerged. Some organizations have survived and thrived (TOPS). Some have been short-lived or even mythical in the sense that only a few core members constitute the *national* organization. Some have been stillborn. All, however, have been oriented in one of three directions:

1. The *traditional* groups are basically concerned with *self-help* through interaction and the scrupulous observance of the organizational prescriptions.
2. The *auxiliary* groups (Al-Anon, Al-Ateen) organized to provide insight and fellowship for the innocent victims of nondeviant relatives. This type of auxiliary group has been most helpful also in the medical area where the parents of retardates, polio victims, and other diseases have lobbied for better care and greater public concern.
3. The newest variant, taking its cue from the civil rights protest of the 1960's, is the voluntary association whose goal it is to *change normative standards* so that the deviant is now no longer an outsider. This social movement—picketing, confrontation, legislation—approach is most evident among some of the homophile groups, the organizations seeking to legalize marijuana use such as LEMAR, for example, the pro-abortion organizations and the highly successful pro-lottery groups. Strictly speaking, except for the homophiles, most of the others are political pressure groups more than organizations of avowed deviants.

This chapter contains three selections.

The first deals with "Voluntary Associations Among Social Deviants" as an historical and sociological phenomenon. Edward Sagarin knows more about these groups than anyone around. His book *Odd Man In* is the classic statement on the subject and is highly recommended to interested students. Sagarin is highly critical of the social movement groups since he sees many of them as self-defeating. His discussion of the dilemma of the homophiles in this report is worth careful consideration.

Unlike other deviants, little people are totally innocent victims of the physical norms of our society so that height represents a central life problem. In his poignant essay on little people, Professor Sagarin describes their attempts to confront their stigma and attain social acceptance.

The final contribution in this section is an unreserved endorsement of Synanon by a "true believer," Guy Endore. Although its Prayer is much like the Twelve Steps of A.A., Synanon is a total environment featuring what some have called "attack therapy" in which the "junkie" is forced to confront his previous shortcomings, deceptions, and defects of character. Endore prefers to speak of Synanon as a 24-hour-a-day education or as environmental therapy. In truth, Endore presents a glowing account of what some critics believe to a seriously flawed voluntary association. The student is advised to read not only this article but other less complimentary ones as well in order to achieve a more balanced picture. Lewis Yablonsky's book *The Tunnel Back* provides another good starting point and is also highly favorable to the Synanon way of life.

VOLUNTARY ASSOCIATIONS AMONG SOCIAL DEVIANTS

Edward Sagarin

During the past twenty or thirty years, a new type of formal association has begun to flourish in the United States: it is the organization of the social deviant. The members of

From *Criminologia*, V (May, 1967), 8–22. Reprinted by permission of Sage Publications, Inc. Edward

Sagarin is Professor of Sociology at the City College of the City University of New York.

such a voluntary association may consist of alcoholics, gamblers, narcotic addicts, or ex-convicts, among others. Although there have been studies of individual organizations of the nature listed above, as yet there has been no effort to study the entire phenomenon of the formation of organizations of this category. No one has attempted to make a list of such groups, such as Fox did for voluntary associations on a national scale, and no one has attempted to count them, as has been done for voluntary associations in many community studies. There has been no effort even to list the types of deviants that are conceptualized in this manner, to cite those that have structured formal associations, and to locate the similarities and differences in aims, goals, structures, or other organizational phenomena or characteristics. A preliminary paper of this type must perforce be broad and general, sketchy rather than exhaustive. The present paper is hence not an effort to fill the many lacunae, but to point the way to a few directions that might prove fruitful for further investigation and study.

THE CONCEPT OF DEVIANCE

Deviance is one of the most elusive concepts in the realm of sociology; and without defining deviance, it becomes extremely difficult to draw the boundary lines around the more specific heading of "deviant organizations" or "voluntary associations among social deviants." . . . Deviance, as here used, is a category that is socially defined in a negative manner. The deviant group is a collectivity of persons who share some trait, characteristic, or behavior pattern in common, which attribute is defined negatively, and which is of sufficient significance to themselves and to others to differentiate them from all those persons not sharing this attribute. The negative definition, however, is one of disapproval, as with intoxication, rather than of disadvantage, as with blindness.

THE VOLUNTARY ASSOCIATION

To the phenomenon of the deviant group, let us now overlay that of the voluntary

association. Several definitions of the phrase "voluntary association" have been made, and one might utilize that of Maccoby:

The distinguishing characters of the voluntary association are that it be private, non-profit, voluntary in that entrance rests on mutual consent while exit is at the will of either party, and formal in that there are offices to be filled in accordance with stipulated rules. These traits serve to differentiate the voluntary association from public and governmental bodies; profit-making corporations and partnerships; family, clan, church, nation and other groups into which the individual is born; informal friendship groups, cliques, or gangs.

For over a century, observers coming to the American shores from abroad, and others native to this country, have taken note of what has come to be described as the "proliferation of associations" in a "nation of joiners." The first and classic example of such a commentary was made by Alexis de Tocqueville, who stressed that Americans form organizations for a wide variety of purposes:

Americans of all ages, all conditions, and all dispositions constantly form associations . . . religious, moral, serious, futile, general or restricted, enormous or diminutive . . . If it is proposed to inculcate some truth or to foster some feelings by the encouragement of a great example, they form a society."

Charles and Mary Beard, writing in the 1920's, stated that "the tendency of Americans to unite with their fellows for varied purposes" had become "a general mania," and declared that "it was a rare American who was not a member of four or five societies." Although there was ample evidence of this being the organizational or the associational society, some writers, and particularly Komarovsky, later questioned whether group-belonging was as ubiquitous as stated by the Beards, and found it to be very much of a middle-class phenomenon, indulged in by those who had the leisure time and the money.

Nevertheless, many forces did make for a strong development of associations in American life. The organizational society had deep historical roots. . . . Urbanization, which developed so rapidly in this country, reduced the individual to a depersonalized cipher in a mass society, in which the urbanite, in the words of Wirth, was "bound to exert himself by joining with others of similar interests into organized groups to obtain his ends." Industrialization, in the words of Fox, brings "highly differentiated roles and role clusters such that . . . there is a strong tendency of some units to become relatively isolated from one another," and these insulated groups develop formal structure. The decline of the extended family, and the inability of the family to continue to provide a large part of the educational, cultural, social, recreational and other needs of many Americans, leaves the individual, in the view of Rose, with "a need to turn relatively frequently to voluntary associations for self-expression and satisfaction of his interests." This could be seen as an interactive process, cumulative in its dynamic mechanism: that is, if voluntary associations do rise to fill the gaps left by the weakening of the extended family, then to the extent that such vacuums are abolished, to that extent is there a strengthening of the forces tending to drive the extended family into further decline in the society.

In this situation, the American is left with a feeling, to use the expression of the Kluckhohns, that he is "unanchored, adrift upon a meaningless voyage." The predilection of Americans for joining would, in part, the Kluckhohns' state, be "a defense mechanism against the excessive fluidity of our social structure".

ORGANIZATIONS OF DEVIANTS

It would be logical to conceptualize organizations of fanatics, unpopular political and religious minorities, and others, as voluntary associations of deviants. Any formal and structured group of crusaders who are either strongly opposed by the overwhelming majority of the people (as the Communist party), or by the major value of the society (as the Ku Klux Klan), or who are generally considered "crack-pots" because of their program or policies, might be so labeled. In a sense, modern-day sabbatarians, religious snake cultists, social nudists, apocalyptic groups that have decided that the world will end on a given day—all are organizations of deviants. However, these people are the twentieth-century missionaries in their own land, the true believers of Eric Hoffer, rather than social deviants in the sense in which that phrase can be applied to alcoholics. The exploration of the nature of the difference is the task of sociological analysis.

Another group of organizations have been conceptualized under the heading of "criminal societies." They are collectivities of people who have banded together for self-protection or for mutual assistance, in order the better to continue their criminal activities or to protect themselves from apprehension and arrest. MacNamara has summarized the literature of such types of organizations. While it will be necessary here to differentiate between criminal societies and the groups under study, let it be said that the former are often nothing more than gangs; and while they have strong norms and definitely recognized leadership, it is often difficult to speak of formal organization. This writer would emphasize that Murder, Inc., was not incorporated, and that the name was given to it by persons who never established the existence of a formal organization; that the "Appalachian convention" was not a convention, and that the supposed "delegates" attending the nonconvention were not delegates; and that there is considerable question as to whether there is such an entity in the U.S.A. at this time as the Mafia. However, if there should be established that an adult criminal gang exists as a formal association, having structure, by-laws, and a sharp line of demarcation between member and nonmember, such a collectivity could be conceptualized as an association of deviants, yet not quite in the same sense as A.A. and the other groups here under study.

Wherein do groups, of alcoholics, narcotic addicts, and homosexuals, as examples, differ from right- or left-wing fanatics, religious sectarian true believers, Klansmen, or criminals? I would suggest that this difference resides in one respect that becomes crucial for a sociological investigation; namely, that in the former groups—alcoholics and others— deviance resides in the individual who has certain attributes (traits, characteristics, or behavior patterns), and that belonging to the organization may make them more visible, but does not in and of itself confer the traits upon the actor. On the other hand, in the latter types—political, religious, racist, and others—to the extent that the collectivity is deviant, it is the act of joining that confers this status upon the individual, rather than any trait or behavior pattern that the actor brought to the association.

In other words, believing in right- or left-wing politics, or in a way-out religious faith, does not constitute deviance, but the belief is translated into action by the fact of joining with others in an organizational form. However, being homosexual, alcoholic, or addicted to certain types of drugs, constitutes the deviance—if it is so defined in one's society—and joining with others in an organization merely increases the visibility, the possibility of detection, the degree of vulnerability, but not the deviance itself.

WHY ORGANIZATION?

A voluntary association is looked upon as a response to a felt need of a large number of people who share a common interest. If this is so, then one must determine not so much why organizations of social deviants, of the type here described, have been formed; but rather why, in the long tradition of America as a nation of joiners, they did not appear on the scene until the 1930's, and did not become prominent until the period during and after the second World War.

It would be interesting for the social historian to trace the nature of the American society in the years between the first and second World Wars that became a fertile soil for the development of organizations of social deviants. The wars had a great effect in accelerating the rate of change of moral values. Urbanization was proceeding with great rapidity, and the society was characterized

by a large amount of geographic mobility— two factors that permitted people to interact with others in a nameless and faceless manner.

Prohibition made the nation deeply aware of the problem of alcoholism, and it should be emphasized that the alcoholics formed the first organization that caught on, and that became the prototype for so many others. And then there was the depression, with a mass rootlessness on the one hand, and a challenging of the accepted ways on the other.

Among these factors, one should consider the changing attitude toward mental illness and the growing sympathy for all those suffering from mental and emotional difficulties. Psychoanalysis became a by-word in the home, it was no longer a disgrace to be under therapy, and eventually a President of the United States would make no secret of the fact that there was a retarded member of his family.

These were among the forces that created a social climate favorable for the first time in American history for the formation of voluntary associations among social deviants.

To this one should add the very simple concept of imitation. A great deal of social interaction tends to be epidemiological, and particularly when one group obtains publicity or apparent success, it becomes a model for others, in the same or somewhat similar situation, to ask themselves, "If they can do it, why can't we?" The success among these organizations was Alcoholics Anonymous, out of which grew, in the most direct manner, Synanon, and in an indirect manner, numerous other associations which embraced either the word or the concept of anonymity.

SOCIOLOGICAL REPORTS ON DEVIANT ORGANIZATIONS

Most comment by sociologists on organizations of social deviants (as a general category) has been favorable, encouraging, and even enthusiastic, although it has frequently been based on the most casual observation and on the most naive and unquestioning acceptance of the image that the deviants wished to project as a vision of reality.

Becker writes that deviants have become "more self-conscious, more organized, more willing to fight with conventional society than ever before. They are more open in their deviance, prouder of what they are and less willing to be treated as others want to treat them without having some voice in the matter." After briefly reviewing some homosexual organizations, Synanon, and the LSD movement headed by Leary and Alpert, he writes that "all three groups exemplify the increasing militancy, organization and self-consciousness of deviant worlds and their growing unwillingness to let respectable society have its own way with them unchallenged." He states, further, that the police "will not prevent homosexual defense groups from winning further allies in the respectable world and pressing their fight for equal rights."

Goffman has referred to the publications sponsored by social deviants as giving voice to "shared feelings, consolidating and stabilizing for the reader his sense of the realness of 'his' group and his attachment to it. Here the ideology of the members is formulated— their complaints, their aspirations, their politics."

Schur, writing of the groups that have come to be known as "homophile organizations," notes:

Whatever their public influence, these groups appear to function for some homosexuals as a symbol of hope and reassurance of the worthiness of their cause, and to provide some solace to those isolated homosexuals who may have felt left out of homosexual life as well as heterosexual society.

While all of these comments might be considered "correct," they give a partial picture of organizations of social deviants, and usually a favorable one. This writer suggests that underlying all of these statements is a sense of injustice and of moral outrage, of righteous indignation at the cruel social hostility displayed against socially harmless deviants, and hence support for such mea-

sures as would constitute retaliation and self-defense. Many sociologists seem to be ideologically predisposed to see the usefulness and good in such organizations. In some instances, it may be because the organizations constitute a challenge to the world of respectability; in others, because they seem to embrace the aspirations of the underdog. For example, if Schur conceptualizes homosexuals as people committing "crimes without victims," as he does, he is tempted to become a special pleader for such people, and from this he is likely to want to see their organizations as helpful to those in distress.

THE SHARED CHARACTERISTIC

The fundamental attribute that seems to tie these organizations together is the motivation behind their formation, namely, *the escape from stigma.* The idea of stigma as a social force, explaining human attitudes and behavior, has been explored with deep insights by Goffman. For Goffman, stigma refers to an attitude that is deeply discrediting. If a characteristic is known about or is easily perceivable, one is dealing, in Goffman's terminology, with the plight of the discredited; if easily concealed or difficult to perceive, then it would be a matter of the discreditable.

Applying this to groups of deviants, it is clear that political, religious, racist and other such organizations are not formed or joined as a mechanism in the search for a means to neutralize or reduce social stigma. Groups of noisy and militant motorcyclists, such as Hell's Angels, are likewise not designed to reduce the stigma for the individual or the collectivity.

The escape from stigma takes on two divergent and usually mutually exclusive patterns, although there may be some convergence. These two patterns constitute, as I see it, the most important single factor differentiating some of these groups from others, and enabling the student to make meaningful hypotheses and attempt prediction of group life. They are:

1. The deviant may escape from stigma by

conforming to the norms of the society; that is, by "reforming," by relinquishing the stigmatizing behavior; or

2. He may escape from stigma by reforming the norms of society, by reducing the sanctions against his behavior; that is by changing, not himself, but the rule-making others. In this case, he is obtaining from society a relinquishment of the stigmatization of his behavior.

Nevertheless, there may be an apparent contradiction in this view, in that the act of joining may increase the stigma, by transferring the individual from an invisible to a visible member of the socially disapproved category. But this is met in two ways: first, by protection of the individual, through anonymity; and second, by utilizing the greater visibility as a mechanism for the reduction of social disapproval.

Conceptualized in this manner, one might foresee that groups in which individuals would seek to reduce their deviant behavior (i.e., escape from deviance) would gain wide social approval from the greater society, except from those who are geographically and in other ways so close to the deviants that the congregation of individuals in an organization becomes threatening. Furthermore, these groups would function very much like group therapy; would often turn to religious or pseudo-religious concepts for reinforcement; would embrace many middle-class aims in order to return to a life of propriety, while scoffing at the hypocrisy of the middle-class that rejects and opposes them. Such a group would paint the deviant as a worthwhile individual, a soul to be saved, but deviance as immoral, sinful, and self-defeating. It would frown on members who stray, attempt to exert extreme pressure through inner group loyalty, and would develop a pattern of over-conformity in the area of the deviance itself. This last characteristic would in fact result in a harsher condemnation of the disapproved behavior than is found in the general population; a fear of the "enlightened," the liberal, and the permissive view, all buttressed by a moralistic stance and reinforced by religion; for

to those seeking to relinquish their deviance, any suggestion that the consequences of the behavior would be less severe if only social attitudes were to change becomes a threat to the organization and its program, and a temptation to return to the abandoned pattern. The personality characteristic attracted to such a group consists primarily of those who are in need of authority figures and ego reinforcement; these are the compliant and submissive, who nevertheless have a strong component of aggression and are going to transfer this from self-direction and society-direction to group-direction, during the therapeutic process. As penitents, they will both comply and gripe, willingly accept and let off steam.

The second group, those who are seeking to alleviate the definition of their condition as deviant, shares some of these attributes, but not all, and even when it shares them, it does so for entirely different reasons and hence with different consequences. Seeking to change the public attitude toward the deviance, such a group may turn to religion, not for moral support, but for a respectable front and a respectable ally. There would be a reinforcement of the ego, not through group therapy, but in a process of mutual reinforcement of one's deviant values and deviant ways of structuring reality. The middle-class norms would be scoffed at, but not entirely rejected, because acceptance by society might be viewed merely as more easily attainable if one is moralistic, law-abiding, and conforming in most respects. The group must thumb its nose at society, in order to foster pride in the deviant; and at the same time must become obsequious before society, in order the better to beg for acceptance. Such a group is likely to attract rebels and nonconformists, and yet use a facade of squares as front men and window dressing. It might vacillate between unltraconformity, as an expression of anticipatory socialization, and rebellion and rejection, as an expression of the reaction formation against the society that has thrown them out. Because of the enhanced stigmatization that ensues when one joins a group of this type, the organization is likely to attract some neurotics and personality misfits who require social disapproval and ridicule; together with rebels who relish any battle with the world of respectability. Because of the unceasing aggressive nature of the struggle against society and the small degree of success that can be seen, such groups are likely to have considerable membership turnover, and to have bitter internecine battles for leadership, fission, competition between organizations, skullduggery, and the like.

The two groups will travel in diametrically opposite directions in their attitude toward the deviance with which each is involved. The first category will condemn, moralistically and scientifically, unwavering in pointing the finger to the road of eternal damnation that awaits the one who slips backward; and the second category will likewise invoke science, philosophy, and ideology, but for the eternal condemnation of those who condemn them. The latter type of organization will seek to convince the world without, as well as the members within, that their deviance is normal, natural, moral, socially useful, and that all who deem otherwise are deluded and ignorant hypocrites, if not repressed deviants themselves. Both types of organizations will present a distorted image of themselves; they will fall victim to the temptation, almost inherent in the nature of organization, to project a self-image that glorifies and "prettifies." But the first type will show its members as being almost saintly because they are renouncing deviance, and by contrast the devils are not only the lost souls who have not seen the light, but opponents in the world of respectability. In the second type of group, there is a glorification of the deviant (member and nonmember alike), and the devils are those in the world of respectability who scoff at such an image.

EXAMPLES, PROTOTYPES, AND CASE HISTORIES

Of the first group, the best-known and most successful has been Alcoholics Anonymous, described in great detail by many, and sub-jected to a thorough sociological analysis by Gellman. The success of A.A. and its generally favorable publicity resulted in a rash of other groups that attempted to emulate the structure and form, though usually not the content, of the prototype. These included organizations of narcotic addicts, gamblers, self-styled neurotics, overweight persons, and others. The proliferation of "anonymous" groups of this sort seemed to indicate in some instances a dissatisfaction with A.A. as an instrument for solving other problems (such as drug addiction); but in other instances it indicated merely that A.A. had attained a positive status of its own, that it was "the thing" and "proper" to belong; and that the stigma of being deviant was not only overcome, but a positive esteem was attached, if one had the "ailment" and then was able to renounce it, particularly through A.A.

The abilities of these organizations to accomplish the manifest goals, particularly for the individual member, have not been examined, except for A.A. and Synanon. In the latter instance, one should note that Synanon has certain structural features that differentiate it from voluntary associations, and that this may be a matter of significant conceptual formation, and not one of semantic quibbling. Synanon is a total institution; in fact, it rejects addicts who will not relinquish their occupation and life on the world outside, and move in, family and all. The voluntary association is a segment of one's life, not one's entire life.

Synanon could perhaps better be analyzed as a correctional hospital, offering group therapy and aid in "kicking the habit," but using unusual methods to accomplish that goal. It is a hospital in which there is voluntary self-induction, and that depends to an enormous extent on inner-group norms and loyalties for its success. To slide back into deviance is a betrayal of the people who have become one's "family" and who have placed trust in the former addict.

Setting aside Synanon and similar groups, and looking only at those organizations where one goes occasionally in order to interact with others like oneself, it is doubtful if either continuity or success will be found in groups other than A.A. The failure of some of these groups—if they do fail—may be due to their own definition of their behavior as deviant, which definition was not made by significant others previous to the group formation. The searching out of companions with a similar problem is suspect; for unlike the alcoholic, or the addict, most of these people did not feel that they had a crippling problem making them into nonfunctioning persons, until A.A. caught on, and they thought it might be "campy" or "cool" to get similarly involved. Their organizations, with "anonymity" written into the title, seem to be the work of the poseur and the romantic rebel. There is an exploitation of the status attained by A.A., rather than a search for strength to change one's own behavior. Among the groups of this type are fat persons, neurotics, gamblers, and even their women's auxiliaries.

The contradiction in this situation would seem to be largely as follows: that whereas A.A. seeks to function by building up self-confidence and ego reinforcement, the act of joining a similar group among gamblers accomplishes the very reverse. A.A. infuses in the individual the belief that alcoholism is an evil which he can overcome to the point of functioning, although he is never free from the danger of falling back (this latter being an excellent device to retain the member and hence strengthen the organization). Hence, for A.A. there is no category of *ex*-alcoholics; there are only "sober" alcoholics, the term applying not to people who are in a temporary and brief state of sobriety between their states of intoxication, but who are in a long and hopefully permanent state of sobriety *after* their state of intoxication. The hold of A.A. is that the sober alcoholic is, in this view, a likely victim for relapse, if he is not strengthened, which is accomplished through inner-group cohesion and mutual reinforcement.

Alcoholics, then, to use the terminology of Becker, are deviants because they are so defined, and the actor then defines himself

and accepts the uncomplimentary view of self. Gamblers—whatever financial difficulties there may be in their homes due to their habits—are deviants only if they so define themselves, and the act of joining an organization would seem to be a step in such a definition. Certainly the large number of people who flock to the race track, avidly watch for the announcement of the winning number in the daily newspaper, take or give bets in the shop or office, or who follow each day's stock market gyrations, are hardly social deviants. To compare these people with social drinkers, and then to state that the voluntary association is meant to aid compulsive gamblers who are more akin to compulsive alcoholics, offers a point of clarification. However, it is doubtful if the compulsive gambler sees himself as deviant until he joins with others in an organization in which he is compelled to take this view, and the association is therefore more likely to prove ego damaging than ego reinforcing, even if it is successful in aiding some people to overcome their habit (a point which is very doubtful, indeed).

There are factors in Neurotics Anonymous that make it difficult to take this group seriously. Again, there is no reason to believe that being neurotic carries with it a deviance of its own, with stigma. These people would seem to be stigmatizing themselves by joining with others, not because they expose themselves to public view, but because they redefine themselves as having stigma. Furthermore, whereas it is possible to understand people giving each other strength, through sanctions, rewards, disapprovals, appeals to group norms and loyalties, in order to refrain from drinking, taking narcotics, or even gambling, it is difficult to see how they can obtain strength from one another to refrain from being neurotic. With proper guidance and leadership, the pseudo-organization could be a form of group therapy, with the group a little larger and the price somewhat smaller, but in such an instance the organizational structure is merely a front that might attract people to the therapy.

A number of studies have been made of organizations of ex-mental patients, and there have been some reports of structured groups of ex-convicts. These types of groups have in common that they are joined by people who have a stigma from which they are seeking to escape. However, they bridge the gap between our two conceptual categories, in that they are both seeking to live by the norms of the society in all respects, and at the same time to reduce the stigma that society has toward the group. There is no contradiction because they socially define themselves with the prefix "ex," and they do not see mental patients or convicts in a derogatory manner, but view them rather with sympathy. They function in a manner not unlike A.A. in many respects, but have a greater problem in convincing the world "out there"—in addition to themselves—that they are members of a category that can be trusted to manage their lives.

Of the deviants who have organized so as to escape from deviance by influencing the society to redefine them as nondeviant nonconformists, the most prominent are the homosexuals. They call their groups "homophile" organizations, a euphemistic term that is meant to project an image of people involved in love relationships, rather than sex relationships, with members of their own sex. Organizations of this character indignantly deny the unhealthy, neurotic, or abnormal character of homosexuality, a denial necessary (in their view) to gain acceptance both from others and from themselves; and at the same time they display the very neuroticism that is denied in many ways, of which the appeal to sadomasochistic interest among their members is one of the most apparent. They state that they are not seeking to proselytize for homosexuality, and particularly for its spread; yet their literature urges that homosexuality be considered on a par with heterosexuality, and that children be exposed to both ways of life in an impartial manner so as to be able to make a free choice.

One could cite many other examples of the contradictions in which Mattachine societies, the Daughters of Bilitis, and other groups of this nature are entrapped. The problem seems to be as follows: Since the aim of the groups is to escape from stigma by having the behavior redefined as nondeviant, the organizations seek to sponsor that redefinition by painting a portrait of homosexuals as psychologically healthy, well-functioning, loving, nonpromiscuous persons, even if this is in contravention to one's knowledge of reality. Whether problems of this sort are inherent in any group of social deviants seeking acceptance of their deviance is a matter for further investigation; utilizing classic sociological theory, . . . and modern organizational theory, . . . one is tempted to answer such a question in the affirmative. That is, an organization of deviants, seeking acceptance without change in themselves, will attract and hold deviant members if it can reinforce their self-image as normal and healthy persons; and will be able to score some short-range successes with greater ease if it displays such a picture of the deviant to the conforming public.

SOCIAL CONTROL AND DEVIANT GROUPS

The question of in-group control on the behavior of deviants is summarized by Albert Cohen, but it is limited, in Cohen's concept, to the participants in the group. It is possible, however, that deviant associations may be utilized by the society to reach the large mass of unorganized individuals who, precisely because of some single attribute which is socially disapproved, are beyond the confines of ordinary communication and control.

One is reminded in this respect of a passage from Durkheim:

A society composed of an infinite number of unorganized individuals, that a hypertrophied state is forced to oppress and contain, constitutes a veritable sociological monstrosity . . . A nation can be maintained only if, between the State and the individual, there is intercalated a whole series of secondary groups near enough to the individuals to attract them strongly in their sphere of action and drag them, in this way, into the general torrent of social life.

Organizations of homosexuals have co-operated with authorities to disseminate information on venereal disease, to attempt to place homosexuals on jobs, to aid in locating criminals who prey on the homosexual community, and in numerous other ways. While this is not the first instance of the utilization of socially disapproved persons as intermediaries for communicating with and controlling the unorganized mass, it may be a special form that will prove significant in the future of organizations of social deviants.

DWARFS: LITTLE PEOPLE WITH BIG PROBLEMS

Edward Sagarin

"Think Big."
Slogan of Little People of America

The stigmatizing of the sick, the disabled, and the deformed is an old story. Primitive peoples feared and punished the physically afflicted; they considered them as evidence that the gods were angry, or as witches and purveyors of evil.

This mystical-religious interpretation particularly pervaded the attitude toward birth defects. Continuing through medieval times, the blind and deaf were avoided, especially by a pregnant woman whose child might be similarly afflicted by her sight of them. Whenever evil befell a community, the physically handicapped were the first to be blamed. Although little was known of contagion, communities in which lepers lived were not content to isolate them, but treated them with hatred and contempt.

Even in this era of rationalism and science, superstition has not disappeared from society's attitudes toward the handicapped and the ill. People continue to be uncomfortable in the presence of those with physical defects. It has not been long since an aura of shame surrounded the victims of tuberculosis and cancer.

From *Odd Man In*. Copyright 1969 by Edward Sagarin. Reprinted by permission of Franklin Watts, Inc. Edward Sagarin is Professor of Sociology at the City College of the City University of New York.

Within organizational society, several groups of people with physical defects and ailments have been formed: paraplegics, epileptics, people who have undergone ileostomies and colostomies, and sufferers from various forms of dwarfism have all organized. Of these groups, the undersized have been making an extraordinarily courageous effort to solve their difficult, almost insuperable, problems through organization.

The mention of dwarfs may conjure up the image of Snow White's delightful helpers, or a memory of charming drawings in a child's edition of *Gulliver's Travels*. It is a far cry from such images to the real world in which these people live. When you meet a dwarf, you will hear the story of a lifetime of travail, of staring eyes, rejection by friends and sometimes even family; of difficulties in obtaining employment; of being addressed as though retarded; of being humiliated as a child and, in later life, being shunned by adults. To aid themselves in solving these problems and others, the dwarfs have formed a self-help group known as the Little People of America. It has the dual aim of helping members cope with personal difficulties and of ameliorating the hostile social atmosphere in which they live.

It is not known how many people of insufficient growth there are in the United

States. One estimate puts the figure at 25,000; it is based on the number of people believed to be so short that height represents a central life problem for them. Among many physicians specializing in fields closely related to growth, it is somewhat arbitrarily stated that a male who fails upon maturity to reach the height of four feet ten inches and a female who fails to reach the height of four feet eight inches are sufficiently below average to be considered undersized. But dwarfism has broad social consequences which go far beyond these purely physiological considerations.

The determination of insufficient growth in children is sometimes expressed as the difference between chronological age and expected age mean-height. Thus a girl chronologically fourteen years old whose height is 118.75 cm. (46.7 inches) is the height-age of seven years and six months. That is, at the age of fourteen, she is the same height as the average girl of seven and a half. A nine-year-old male whose height is 85.15 cm. (33.5 inches) is the height-age of two years and two months.

Dwarf and *midget* are two terms generally applied to these undersized people, but they are popular rather than medical words. In everyday parlance, a dwarf exhibits bodily proportions unlike those of most persons: in the most common form, he has extremely short legs and arms (the former bowed), a normally developed torso, a large head, sometimes a flat nose, an unusual distribution of body weight at the lower end of the back, and short, stubby fingers that hang somewhat limply from the joints. This condition, a congenital one that is sometimes hereditary, is known as achondroplasia or achondroplastic dwarfism, and usually results in growth somewhere between forty-eight and fifty-six inches.

Midgets—again the term is used in its popular sense; it must be emphasized that midgets are not a single physiological entity—are normally proportioned but extremely short people. When they are less than four feet tall at maturity they tend to be slightly stocky. Midgets have been exploited in circuses, par-

ticularly by Barnum who made an international celebrity of Tom Thumb (he grew to only three feet, and married a midget a few inches shorter than himself).

Stunted growth brings many difficulties and disadvantages. People are often evaluated according to their apparent age, and size is one criterion of that evaluation. Thus, one behaves toward a person as though he were of the age that his stature suggests; one also expects mental responses commensurate with that incorrectly estimated age level. This process results in a babying of the dwarf; furthermore, it can cause poor mental development by denying him the challenge of interaction on his mental age level. As a child, he is treated as if he were several years younger than he is; as an adult, he is frustrated and humiliated by such everyday experiences as being unable to reach a telephone in a booth.

Whereas adults generally behave toward a dwarf (the word is used here to denote all undersized persons) with polite evasion, children often treat him with cruelty. One mother writes:

My son is age seven, weighs 29 lbs., and is 37¾ in. tall. Recently, another boy in the school yard picked Jeff up by his coat collar and swung him back and forth in pendulum motion. This boy held him up, ridiculing Jeff and bragging of his own strength. When he tired of his game, he dropped Jeff to the ground. A sympathetic bystander (3rd grader) picked Jeff up and carried him to the teacher supervising the playground. This teacher had Jeff stay by her until he felt better and was able to move under his own little strength.

After this story unfolded before me, I realized that Jeff could very easily have choked to death, but for the Grace of God. I had the natural impulsive reaction. I wanted to do some choking of my own. Instead, I went to the phone and called the principal. Much to my surprise, this incident had not been reported. The principal's reply? "Ha, ha, ha, children will be children." The next day during a conference with this principal I was asked why my boy had not reported this incident to his homeroom teacher. I couldn't answer. I didn't know. Two weeks later Jeff let it slip. It seems that because Jeff had previously received so many severe bumps in school, his teacher had told him that if these things kept occurring, he would have to leave school. . . . No, I haven't gone back for another conference yet. But when I'm fully under "control" I will. No, I don't want to shelter my "little" boy. I just want him to grow in age, even if he can't grow in size.

There have been many organizations *for* the ill, far fewer *of* the ill. Groups have raised money, conducted research, done lobbying; one such organization has been formed to concern itself with problems such as those described by Jeff's mother. Called Human Growth, Inc., it describes itself as "primarily an organization of the parents and friends of children with severe growth disturbances." Members, most of them parents, raise funds to support medical research, and give each other moral support in meeting their problems. To a certain extent, they bear the stigma of having produced a defective child: essentially, however, theirs is a stigma fallout, or what Goffman calls "courtesy stigma." They have organized to learn how to live and act in a role for which they are unprepared, that of being parents of a visibly handicapped child. At present Human Growth is attempting to induce people to leave their pituitary glands to a tissue bank for use in hypopituitary cases, one form of dwarfism which now seems capable of scientific control.

In turning from Human Growth, Inc., to Little People of America, one moves from those concerned with a problem to those directly involved, from help to self-help. Little People of America consists mainly of severely undersized persons; infrequently a normally sized family member will join as an expression of solidarity. Although LPA takes in all dwarfs, the achondroplastics seem to dominate; the more normally proportioned (or midgets, as the public would call them) are ambivalent in their attitudes toward the organization.

On a national scale, LPA has somewhat less than a thousand members, a small percentage of those eligible. It conducts na-

tional conventions and district meetings, the latter bringing together some thirty or forty people who often travel great distances for the monthly get-togethers. Despite the publicity that LPA has received in magazines and on television, it is little known outside its own ranks. When interviewed, several doctors deeply interested in growth (particularly pediatric endocrinologists) had a vague idea that such a group existed, but did not know its name or how to locate it. Even more revealing was the response from a prominent attorney, himself a dwarf, who had spoken at a meeting of Human Growth, but had never heard of LPA.

LPA has tackled the herculean job of helping to improve the self-image of people in a world in which, literally and figuratively, they are looked down upon. "Think Big" is LPA's slogan, put forward precisely because it is the reverse of what many members do. Scholarship funds, assistance to members in financial difficulty, an adoption service—these are among LPA's accomplishments. In itself, the adoption service illustrates the severity of the dwarfism problem: on the one hand many of the dwarfs are without children, or fear having them; on the other hand, and more importantly, normal parents find themselves with a handicapped child (in achondroplasia cases, the handicap is usually recognizable at birth), whom they frequently offer for adoption. This fact alone, that parents *give away* an achondroplastic child, indicates the strength of the stigma.

In the language of those short of stature, a dwarf is a little person. LPA offers advice to parents, normal or little, on bringing up these little persons. Much of this advice seems far more sound than that encountered in professional literature on rehabilitation. For example, the president of LPA suggests:

In the case of a nickname, there is a very simple way to handle this problem, even though many little people rebel in being singled out this way. Rather than to counterattack with some other equally obnoxious name, the best way to avoid being called Shorty or Midget is to ignore it, pure and simple. If a persons persists and blocks your way, you can simply say, "Oh, were you calling me, I didn't hear my name mentioned." Then if the little person continues to refuse to be interrupted by use of any but his real name, the tormenter will cease and desist.

In a study of LPA, Martin Weinberg found that most of the members look to it for social benefits. This goal is not unexpected. Dwarfs live in a world in which their possibilities for social contact are limited. They are deeply restricted in finding partners for sex, love, and marriage. Thus any means by which such men and women can meet one another is fully exploited. While many handicaps and diseases, particularly stigmatizing ones, limit people in their selection of marriage partners, the dwarfed man is further limited by the general societal insistence that the male must be at least as tall as, and preferably taller than, the female. This insistence places the achondroplastic male in a double bind; he can seldom find a normally sized female to court, both because of his condition and his desire to avoid the Mutt-and-Jeff caricature.

Most of the members of LPA whom Weinberg interviewed were single; unmarried people make up 65 percent of the organization, as compared to about 22 percent for the general population of the same age group. When I asked LPA members what they had gotten out of the organization, I received enthusiastic replies from the married, but somewhat wan answers from the single. By far the most enthusiastic came from those who, with broad smiles, said "I met my wife"—or husband, or sweetheart—at an LPA convention or a meeting.

While LPA meetings offer a remarkable opportunity for socializing, many members sit alone, unable or unwilling to speak except when approached. When I engaged a brilliant high school girl in conversation, I learned that she was planning to go on to college to study sociology; bubbling over with youthful excitement, she seemed the very prototype of adjustment. She came from a family of normal stature; when I met her father, he regarded her with the eyes of the traditionally (even stereotypically) loving parent. At the same meeting, however, an older woman spoke to me of her hatred of the streets, of how she never leaves her house from one week to the next, save for the LPA meetings, because she knows that people are staring at and talking about her. Though her strong paranoia is filled with obvious fantasy, it has no doubt been fed by reality. For this woman, then, LPA constitutes her only social life.

At one meeting I attended, many members sought me out privately, as if their problems of loneliness and despair could somehow be solved by counseling or a cathartic process. Perhaps they did not understand the difference between the sociologist and the social worker, or the sociologist and psychologist. At any rate, they looked to me for advice on and answers to extraordinarily difficult questions. One young man to whom I spoke, John, appeared to me to be about twenty-five; when I mentioned my estimate, he replied that he was ten years older. Unlike people of normal stature, for him my error was not a compliment. Extremely well proportioned (thus popularly a midget), John would have been considered strikingly handsome had he not stopped growing when he was four feet six inches. Up to that height, he had developed normally for his age; once growth ceased, he was taken to many specialists, but without results. When I asked if he had tried human growth hormone, the pituitary gland extract, he replied: "I can't get it—it's in short supply. They need it for kids. And it probably won't help me because I'm not a pituitary case. Besides, it's certainly too late." Like many others at the meeting, he was well informed on his particular medical condition.

John lives a lonely life. All his friends are married, and he says, with some resignation: "It's hard for a single guy to keep up with married friends. Even normal single guys." Nor has he been able to make it socially with a bachelor crowd. "I just don't fit in." So he goes home at night after work, and reads, watches television, or broods over his bleak future. He has lunch with the men in his office, but they never invite him to their homes. Above all else, he wants romance, sex, and friendship, but LPA cannot offer it to him.

"Why not?" I asked.

"Because most of them are achondroplastics, and I guess I'm prejudiced. I shouldn't be, but I am. I don't want to go out with a girl like that, and I don't even want male friends like that. I'm uncomfortable with them."

"But you still come to the Little People meetings?"

"Maybe there'll be a little girl—a short girl—but someone like me."

Like many organizations, LPA functions on both a national and a local (or district) level. One of its major problems is that the district groups seem to be at a loss for functions to perform, other than simply providing a place for men and women to meet each other. They are not social clubs where members share an interest, hobby, or avocation; what they do share are physical characteristics which are insufficient to make the meetings important unless the discussion centers strictly around the problems of being little. Thus LPA's members are caught in a contradiction: they want to meet one another, but, once they do, there is no purpose, goal, or structure ot their meetings— nothing to bind them in the organization. If they avoid the problems encountered in being little, they lose any *raison d'être;* on the other hand, if they center the meetings around such problems, members say that they came to get away from them.

An LPA meeting therefore becomes something like a philatelists' gathering at which there is no discussion of stamps. Once the meeting is called to order, announcements are made: Susan moved out of the district, Jane is getting married, and we have a new member here today, Carl, but let's not forget an old face that we haven't seen for a long time—and everyone smiles as Lewis is given the welcome deserving of the prodigal son. No, everyone does not smile; that is an exaggeration. Some sit, somber and un-

happy, even through the frolicsome parts of the session. There is a report on dues, on the state of the treasury, on a communication from the national office. Old business, new business, points of order—all give an air of legitimacy to the meeting, but much of it is busy work. The main point before the refreshments are served is a discussion of where the next meeting is scheduled to take place. After coffee and cake, the socializing begins—the manhunt and the womanhunt, the pairing-off into small groups, the exchange of ideas and the search for advice. If nothing else, this socializing seems to be the group's main, though unstated, purpose.

Like many organizations, LPA's functions on the national level are more clear-cut. To support the national group, local chapters and members are necessary; but these chapters are not necessary for the fulfillment of the national goals. Thus, a local LPA group becomes only a monthly meeting place, while the national association is a cadre organization where a few do all the work while the rest tag along. Moreover, the fear of making the marginal life of LPA meetings the only life of the little people seems to inhibit more socializing among the members.

Some come to a meeting, even two, then are not seen again. This characteristic is found in many organizations of both the deviant and the normal. But why does it happen in LPA? When asked, one of the activists had a ready explanation:

They come looking for a husband or wife or sweetheart or someone. They heard it's a marriage mill. And the first or second meeting they don't meet someone they could go for, so it's no use. They get discouraged. That's all they were looking around for in the first place.

But once you've got them, even for one afternoon, a captive audience—maybe you could offer something else?

No, absolutely not. Not if they come with that in mind. You don't know little people. I know them.

This is a difficult argument to rebut.

Still other little people cannot be prevailed upon to come to meetings at all. They believe that the organization represents a turning inward, despite the fact that LPA's national leadership strongly urges members to mingle in the world of the normally sized. Leaders warn them not to retreat into a separate community of their own, but, instead, to join (in addition to LPA) the local Democratic or Republican club. (They do not mention conservative or liberal, John Birch or communist groups. The deviant cannot afford a double stigma.)

There is also a third type of little person who refuses to attend meetings because he fears to mingle in a world inhabited by people like himself.

"Why?" I asked.

"Because they just don't want to be with people who look like they do."

"Why?" I insisted with what must have been annoying perseverance.

"I don't know," the district leader replied. Then he added hesitantly, as if himself fearing to articulate the answer: "Maybe it's because they don't want to see what they look like."

What type of adjustment can dwarfed persons make? The president of LPA urges that they relinquish any dream of a magic pill. They must, he says, accept the permanence of their condition. On the other hand, many little people simply deny the need for adjustment. They reject the notion that they have a problem, specifically a problem of "spoiled identity." While they admit that being little is a handicap, they refuse to concede that it is debilitating. There are compensations to being little, they maintain—even advantages.

The friends of the little people, fearful of not being compassionate enough to the suffering, go even further than the sufferers themselves. The father of one girl told me, "It's only our prejudice that makes us see the achondroplastics as sick. After all, there are advantages in being small. This is the age of rockets and spaceships, and who knows, maybe space on a ship to the moon will be so valuable that we will have to man it with little people." Possibly. But it is more likely that this reply is the rationalization of a man who has watched the inadequate struggles of his handicapped daughter to handle overwhelmingly difficult problems.

Nor are the professionals, in their compassion, free of similar thinking. "Many dwarfs are able to have children who may or may not themselves be dwarfs," writes John Joney of Johns Hopkins. He then continues:

People may argue about the advisability of reproducing when there is a risk of producing a dwarf. The positive side of the argument is that a male dwarf should deliberately mate with a female of the same type in order to continue the strain and produce, eventually, a new subvariety of the human race.

Out of sympathy for those in distress, how can one so easily forget the depths of their anguish—or the dangers of propagating it?

LPA publishes a news letter which does not present an image either of what the organization is or what it might become. Rather, it is concerned only with organizational matters for their own sake; the next convention, the district meetings, the growth in membership. And yet, at the same time, the leadership encourages scholarship (and scholarships), aids medical research, and, above all, has accumulated a remarkable amount of experience in handling the social aspects of problems of dwarfism.

Thus, the major problem of the dwarf may be one of accepting self without accepting the negative evaluation of others. The president of LPA points out that little people are certainly different "and have only to look in the mirror to assure themselves of this." He continues:

The best way to handle this problem [of self-acceptance], in my estimation, is for another person to apparently read this person's mind and express out loud all of the hidden feelings, desires and questions that he will have had over the years. Of course, this is a shocking experience and should not be attempted by an amateur.

The president may be right, LPA members could well benefit from self-help, mutual-exchange therapy—not the kind that attacks or ventilates, but the kind that offers help *by* those who have reached a better solution of a problem *to* those who are still grappling with that same problem. This is, after all, AA once again, with the better adjusted acting as sponsors and examples, ones who ask the neophytes: "If I can do it, why can't you?"

SYNANON: THE LEARNING ENVIRONMENT

Guy Endore

Synanon has never been anything else but a school. Before it even had a name, when it was still nothing but a group of alcoholics meeting once a week to probe themselves and each other for a better understanding of their craving for a chemical means of modifying their psyche, it was already a place for mutual self-education. And it is that to this day.

If Synanon came to have a nationwide reputation solely as a place where drug addicts could learn to live without their drugs and criminals, learn to live without breaking the law, that was only because Synanon is like that famous elephant that was examined by six blind men. One shouted immediately that it was a wall, while another insisted that it was a snake, and a third yelled that it was a tree, and a fourth that it was a rope, while a fifth knew for sure that it was a fan and a sixth remained convinced that it was a spear. The fact that in Synanon's history only the drug slice of its many aspects received nationwide attention and acclaim has obscured Synanon's essence as a school for a totally new way of living.

And yet the evidence for Synanon being a school was always there for all to see. The Synanon Philosophy, devised ten years ago, says nothing about dope. It speaks of nothing but learning. And concludes with the lines: "Learning is possible in an environment that provides information, the setting, materials, resources, and by his being there. God helps those who help themselves."

From Synanon, the Learning Environment, Santa Monica, Synanon Foundation, Inc. (no date).

As restricted as Synanon necessarily was in its early peanut-butter-and-jelly days, it already had the beginnings of a library, it had its seminars, its cerebrations, its lectures, its music and dancing and above all, of course, its Synanon game. And every aspect contrived towards one goal as expressed in the Synanon Prayer which, again characteristically, is not a prayer addressed to God, but a prayer for learning that each person addresses to himself in the knowledge that his own efforts must always come first.

Please let me first and always examine myself.
Let me be honest and truthful.
Let me seek and assume responsibility.
Let me understand rather than be understood.
Let me trust and have faith in myself and my fellow-man.
Let me love rather than be loved.
Let me give rather than receive.

All this self-education to which Synanon has consistently dedicated itself can be summed up in the phrase "the domestication of man," because while man has tamed many formerly wild animals, the one animal he has never yet succeeded in taming is himself. And now this still untamed beast is in command of the globe, and stuffed with delusional fears, with guilt and suspicion, with undiscriminating love and equally undiscriminating hatred, he is busily stockpiling ammunition enough to blow his kind off the face of the planet, in the crazy belief that there is absolutely no other way to save the *good* mankind from the *evil* mankind than to threaten destruction to *all* mankind.

Synanon believes that there is another way. The way of total education and re-education.

In a recent Look Magazine article, George B. Leonard quotes from his book *Education and Ecstasy* regarding Synanon's "proof positive" that human nature can be changed. "Not the most deep-rooted character disorders," he writes, "nor the most 'hopeless' forms of drug addiction, not even 'human nature' have proved immune to Synanon's powerful 24-hour-a-day educational techniques. And education is precisely what Synanon's leaders conceive their work to be."

The article goes on to speak of Synanon's foundation by Chuck Dederich on the basis of a "value system" that is "*preached* (but not *lived*) by the outside society—absolute honesty, personal responsibility, cooperation and love." The author continues:

History gave Dederich little chance of success: every therapy since Freud had been all but helpless against the character problems of addiction. Dederich, however, offered not therapy and theories, but attention to living, i.e., education in a total environment, designed to change people. What happened? Of all addicts who have come to Synanon, more than half are still 'clean'.

He concludes: "By tackling the impossible, Synanon has affirmed, beyond any doubt, the power of a changed environment to change (educate) human beings."

More than three years before George B. Leonard, Synanon's Director Dan Garrett, in his essay "Synanon: The Communiversity" had phrased it this way: "It continues to escape the attention of most observers of Synanon (professionals especially) that Chuck Dederich has repeatedly said that Synanon is not primarily interested in curing drug addiction, but that this seems to occur as a side effect of something else which Synanon teaches. Synanon addresses itself to the problem of ignorance. This has nothing to do with *intelligence,* or a lack thereof. It has to do with a failure to achieve *wisdom.*"

Some people find it difficult to grasp the difference between wisdom and intelligence.

It's really very simple. Anybody with ordinary intelligence can assimilate some branch of knowledge and make himself an expert in that field. And in fact, at present, so many people are doing exactly that—and nothing more—that it may be said that the world is jam-packed with expertise.

With what result? The result is a condition that is both wonderful and terrifying. A condition in which the right hand doesn't know what the left hand is doing. Each expert is driving ahead full-steam as if nothing mattered but success in his own particular line of work. Thus an agricultural expert finds that to increase the crops on a given area of ground he will need such and such a pesticide. Does he take into account the fact that he is saturating the earth with a poison that kills birds and eventually washes downstream to the sea where it constitutes a danger to the life of the ocean? Why should he? That's for the expert in oceanography to worry about. And if the oceanographer doesn't know what to do about the oil that is being dumped into the ocean, the whales that are being killed off faster than they can reproduce, the heated rivers from atomic power plants diminishing the oxygen in the ocean, well that's too bad. Because most oceanographers are too busy looking for minerals and natural gas from the ocean bed to care. Why shouldn't they be, in a day when everyone's motto seems to be that of Louis XIV: "After me the deluge."

In like manner experts in making and selling automobiles, experts in building factories and making them run day and night, are busy providing us with all our wants while at the same time choking our cities to death and filling our air with unbreatheable garbage. Our water is rapidly becoming unfit to drink. In a country whose warehouses are stuffed with food, millions of children are found not to be getting proper nourishment, and it is discovered that among the aged there are many who are suffering from senile dementia when in fact they are only a couple of good meals away from their right senses.

Chuck [Dederich] has expressed the cause of this condition as due to the "what's in it for me?" attitude of most people. Once a person of that kind knows what's in it for him, he is out for all he can get. "And what has he got in the end?" Chuck asked. "He hasn't got a goddamn thing."

A totally different posture for man, namely "what's in it for myself as well as for all others," is the position assumed by Synanon. When the gorgeous twelve-story Athens Club of Oakland was turned into a Synanon facility, Wilbur Beckham, Synanon Director, expressed the hope that this once exclusive club, standing like an impregnable fortress of the rich in the midst of downtown Oakland, would retain its old membership while opening its doors wide to all other levels of society.

Wilbur defined Synanon's objectives in words that can be seen to apply equally to those who live in the ghetto of the rich as well as to those who live in the ghetto of the poor. Upholster a fence as plushly as you please, it will still remain a barrier to people on both sides, and wherever one segment of homo sapiens is prevented from mingling with another segment of homo sapiens, who is to say who is being locked in and who is being locked out?

"Synanon," said Wilbur Beckham, "deals with people who just don't have certain things, and who therefore can't get along with themselves and their fellowmen. They don't have the education or they don't know how to provide for themselves some kind of creative outlet. They don't have the knowledge that would allow them to live, or they don't have equal opportunity. They don't know how to develop for themselves some kind of forethought or some kind of philosophy or set of values or principles. Or they don't have a voice that can make itself heard and they don't have the training or the skill whereby they can sustain themselves.

"That is what we have to deal with. And for that we must have people who know the Synanon way, we have to have people willing to do the job, people who know how to play the Synanon game, know how to get things done, and have no end of fun while doing it."

It was obvious from the birth of Synanon that it would one day have to incorporate a school system of its own, in other words a school within a school. Because Synanon could not be a total environment so long as it communicated only wisdom, it eventually had to face the problem of communicating knowledge.

Years ago Synanon had found it necessary to organize its own nursery school because residents had brought with them into the club so many little children whose mothers or fathers needed Synanon's care, and Synanon families (following an old pattern) were bringing into the world additional children. And in recent days scores of teenage drop-outs, drug addicts and other assorted wrecks spun off from the hippie movement have been flowing into Synanon, along with perfectly normal children whose parents realize the exciting possibilities of the Synanon school.

The result is the educational complex that Director Al Bauman is gradually building up within Synanon and that will eventually extend all the way from nursery to college and beyond. Several aspects of this system are already beginning to flourish, others are struggling to come into being, all are testing themselves out from day to day to improve their structure and their methods in line with Synanon's total program. And all have the usual Synanon problems to cope with: lack of capable personnel, lack of space, lack of money. Problems which will of course never be fully solved since Synanon is always growing faster than its financial resources.

"Basically," says Al Bauman, "the Synanon school system will always remain part and parcel of the Synanon life-style, which means that it will be firmly grounded on the Synanon game and its several variations, in particular Synanon's perpetual stew. Our school of knowledge will not be a community of students. Nor will it be a community of teachers. It will be a community of *schol-ars*, which means that there will be no one in our school who is not learning and teaching at the same time. Our students will be apprentice scholars, and our teachers will be mature scholars, in accordance with Chuck's definition of the difference between a learned man and a learning man, which is that a learned man is dead, only a learning man is alive.

"Furthermore our Synanon school will continue to agree with the statement of Socrates that the unexamined life is not worth living, and accordingly we invite even our youngest pupils to ridicule, criticize, appreciate or reproach their fellow-students as well as their superiors, and be prepared to accept the same ridicule, criticism, appreciation or reproach in turn. And thus, because our school will never lose contact with Synanon, it will never lose contact with the welfare of man, which is at the core of the conflict between students and academicians that is now flaring up all over the world."

When I asked Tom Patton—who heads the Synanon Academy at the Santa Monica facility—what he considered the proper goal of a Synanon education, he replied: "Why to turn our globe into a work of art. Make our earth the jewel of the solar system. What else can be man's job here if not that?"

Obviously such an educational value system inspires and makes sense. It is at one and the same time beyond the capacity of man and yet there is only one living creature that can accomplish it, and that is man. It erases all the old feudal distinctions between pure science and applied science, between the fine arts and the popular crafts, between the dilettante and the workaday man. Because this is a goal that can only approach realization through the cooperation of everyone.

"All we're doing here," Chuck says, "is trying to design a more enjoyable way of experiencing human existence." And he adds: "If ever the world awakes to what we're proposing to do, they will batter down our doors to get in."

QUESTIONS FOR DISCUSSION

1. What kinds of voluntary associations are there? What are their specific missions? Do you think that the voluntary association has significantly altered public attitudes toward deviance?
2. Why was the voluntary association of deviants so late a development in the United States and still not much of a factor elsewhere in the world?
3. How does the voluntary association manage the problem of stigma—probably the greatest single disability faced by deviants?
4. Where does the name Synanon come from?
5. What kinds of deviants have traditionally been unable to organize in voluntary associations? Why have they failed? Do you think that some other form of association might reach these traditionally unorganized types?
6. Describe the *AA* program. Compare it to the Al-Anon program. Contrast it with the goals and views of the Gay Activist Alliance, for example.
7. Find a voluntary association which interests you. Study its goals, organization, membership, traditions, mode of operation, and try to evaluate its effectiveness.
8. Why do voluntary associations seem to succeed when nearly all traditional rehabilitation programs systematically fail? What may we learn from this experience?
9. Why is it that voluntary associations are so similar in outlook to "square" organizations? For example, why are there male and female homophile groups instead of simply a homophile organization?
10. Why are ideological differences so greatly exaggerated in deviant groups? Is this problem inherent in being outsiders?

BIBLIOGRAPHY

Alcoholics Anonymous Comes of Age: A Brief History of A. A. New York: Alcoholics Anonymous Publishing, 1957.

Bailey, Margaret. ' Al-Anon Family Groups as an Aid to Wives of Alcoholics.' *Social Work* X (January 1965), 68–74.

Casriel, Daniel. *So Fair a House: The Story of Synanon.* Englewood Cliffs, N.J.: Prentice-Hall, 1963.

Eglash, Albert. "Youth Anonymous." *Federal Probation,* 22 (June 1958), 47–49.

"Gamblers Anonymous." Pamphlet published by Gamblers Anonymous (no date given).

Gellman, Irving Peter. *The Sober Alcoholic: An Organizational Analysis of Alcoholics Anonymous.* New Haven: College and University Press, 1964.

Gordon, C. Wayne, and Babchuk, Nicholas. "A Typology of Voluntary Associations." *American Sociological Review* 24 (1959), 22–29.

Jackson, Maurice P. "Their Brother's Keeper." Urbana, Illinois, 1962 (pamphlet).

"Narcotics Anonymous." In Task Force Report: *Narcotics and Drug Abuse,* The President's Commission on Law Enforcement and the Administration of Justice, 1967.

Recovery Incorporated. "Offering a Systematic Method of Self-Help Aftercare." Chicago, 1967.

Sagarin, Edward. "Anonymity Incorporated: The Marginal World of Organized Deviants." *Salmagundi* 2, No. 3 (Spring 1968), 27–42.

Sagarin, Edward. *Odd Man In: Societies of Deviants in America.* Chicago: Quadrangle Books, 1969.

Sands, Bill. *My Shadow Ran Fast.* Englewood Cliffs, N.J.: Prentice-Hall, 1964.

Sands, Bill. *The Seventh Step.* New York: New American Library, 1967.

Scodel, Alvin. "Inspirational Group Therapy: A Study of Gamblers Anonymous." *American Journal of Psychotherapy* XVIII, (January 1964), 115–25.

de Tocqueville, Alexis. *Democracy in America.* New York: Vintage, 1960.

Wechsler, Henry. "The Expatient Organization: A Survey." *Journal of Social Issues* 16 (1960), 47–53.

Weinberg, Martin S. "The Problems of Midgets and Dwarfs and Organizational Remedies: A Study of the Little People of America." *Journal of Health and Social Behavior* 9 (March 1968), 65–71.

Yablonsky, Lewis. *The Tunnel Back: Synanon.* New York: Macmillan, 1965.

16

Environmental Design for Prevention, Management, and Control

The United States has invested many billions of dollars in the development of federally subsidized high rise, low, and lower middle class apartment houses. Vast areas of the inner cities have been bulldozed clean, and out of the rubble have risen modern apartment complexes reaching to the sky. Everything considered, including cost per unit, these apartments now house many millions of persons in quarters far superior physically to the dilapidated dwellings they replaced. The idea and technology was great; the outcome, mostly a disaster.

The extent of the disaster and failure of high rise, low income family housing has been studied and described by many. The ultimate testimony to the failure is the by-now infamous Pruitt-Igoe complex in St. Louis. This project was totally abandoned because the vandalism, assault, rape, robbery, burglary, and aggressive gang problems made the residents totally insecure and afraid for their safety. They preferred the physically dilapidated slum dwellings to the psychologically punishing world of Pruitt-Igoe. No architectural beauty to begin with, Pruitt-Igoe, in short order, resembled a partially bombed out area which had suffered mightily at the hands of enemy action. Parenthetically, the enemy action metaphor may not be too inaccurate a description or analogy.

Pruitt-Igoe belonged to St. Louis, but cities near and far from St. Louis experienced much the same traumas. Columbus, Ohio, for example, a city with a largely white collar population and a traditionally low rate of crime, had to close down two silo-like high rise apartment buildings for precisely the same reasons that undermined Pruitt-Igoe. After considerable renovation, these silos are now a senior citizen housing development—an irony which well describes the status of the aged in America. Since its transformation and renaming, the Columbus version of Pruitt-Igoe is now a relatively safe and secure apartment complex.

There are, of course, thousands of high rise units for middle and upper class families which are safe, aesthetic, altogether pleasant. What is the difference, then? Apart from the social class level of the residents, these middle class high rise houses invariably have doormen, elevator operators or mirrors to screen those about to enter, hallway guards or TV cameras, underground protected parking areas, few tenants per floor, door eyepieces to view visitors, a call service from the outside lobby, and similar protective devices. In short, these environmental devices are designed to pinpoint the stranger and to make him acknowledge his intentions under scrutiny. The difference then is in *environmental design,* an area much neglected by criminologists. If we cannot alter attitudes and behavior, if punishment does not work, if rehabilitation is a mockery, then surely it is entirely proper to consider a model of environmental engineering to frustrate the offense before it occurs. Surely, this model commends itself a great deal more than the intrusive methods described by Schwitzgebel and by Ingraham and Smith.

Apart from some very perceptive early sociologists like Simmel (and his stranger) and Durkheim (social cohesion), and the later Chicago school of Shaw, McKay, Alinsky, Paul Cressey, Wirth, Reckless, Zorbaugh, and many others, only two major figures currently are concerned with environmental design and deviance. The first is C. Ray Jeffery whose book *Crime Prevention Through Environmental Design* (1971) is already a classic. The second, an architect and city planner, Oscar Newman, has had the most profound effect on our thinking as a result of his work on the high rise apartment problem and the theoretical conceptions which derived from this research. His book *Defensible Space* represents some seminal thinking in this field.

The first selection in this chapter is a grievously abridged version of Oscar Newman's thinking about architectural and social innovations in crime prevention in our densely populated urban centers. His conceptions of territoriality, the role of the stranger, and of simple structural alterations in the architecture of high rise dwellings are worth considering. No urban planner or criminologist, for that matter, can avoid the implications either of the research (which we omitted for the sake of brevity) or the conclusion.

The second contribution is as micro as the Newman work is macro. It deals with the attempt on the part of New York City to cut down on the use of slugs in parking meters by (1) installing a slug-rejector, coin view window; and (2) by posting warning signs on meters about how unlawful it is to use slugs. In this "fun" article, the power of engineering design to forestall the slugging of meters surely bears out the thesis of environmental design as a solid and practical means of crime prevention.

DEFENSIBLE SPACE AS A CRIME PREVENTIVE MEASURE

Oscar Newman

The prevention of crime covers a wide range of activities: Eliminating social conditions closely associated with crime; improving the ability of the criminal justice system to detect, apprehend, judge, and reintegrate into their communities those who commit crimes; and reducing the situations in which crimes are most likely to be committed.

The Challenge of Crime in a Free Society. Report by the President's Commission on Law Enforcement and Administration of Justice.

From the above one can identify three approaches to crime and delinquency pre-

From *Architectural Design for Crime Prevention*, Washington, National Institute of Law Enforcement and Criminal Justice, 1971, pp. 3–19. Mr. Newman is an Architect and City Planner.

vention: Corrective prevention, punitive prevention, and mechanical prevention.

Programs of corrective prevention begin with the premise that criminal behavior is the result of various social, psychological, and economic factors. Corrective prevention is therefore directed at understanding and eliminating those causes before their effect on the individual channels him into crime. Factors frequently cited as precipitating criminal behavior include economic instability, a history of family problems, lack of opportunity for participation in the accepted life-style of society, and a personal susceptibility to narcotics addiction.

Punitive prevention, by contrast, involves efforts by authorities at forestalling crime by making more evident the threat of punishment and the likelihood of apprehension. Operationally, this includes the enactment of new and tougher laws; the reduction of the time period between arrest and trial; and the streamlining of the indicting process.

Programs of mechanical prevention are concerned with placing obstacles in the paths of criminals. It is a policy which for the moment accepts the existence of criminals, their modus operandi, and their victims, and frames a program for hardening criminal targets by making them more inaccessible. This is accomplished by providing more secure barriers in the form of better hardware and personnel. The operating mechanisms involve the hardening of target, increasing the risk of apprehension, and, finally, increasing the criminal's awareness of these risks.

Current local governmental efforts at crime prevention involve all three of the above categories: corrective, punitive, and mechanical. Mechanical prevention is usually advocated as the most immediate panacea, although programs directed at corrective prevention and at improving the judicial and punitive apparatus are under serious study in many cities.

Typical means for improving mechanical prevention include: manpower increases in the form of police, security guards, doormen, tenant patrols, and dogs; and mechanical and electronic devices in the form of more and better locks, alarms, electronic visual and auditory sensors, and motorized vehicles to improve the mobility and surveillance capacities of personnel.

The form of crime prevention we will be describing . . . "defensible space," was seen initially as a new form of mechanical prevention. However, as our work in understanding and defining the operating mechanisms of "defensible space" progressed . . . it became apparent that a good many of our formulations could, when implemented, act as rather cogent forms of *corrective prevention*: mechanisms which could, perhaps, contribute to the alleviation of some of the root causes of criminal behavior.

As an example, our study of housing projects has revealed that children who live in

high-rise buildings have a poorly developed perception of individual privacy and little respect for territory. The extent to which a similar lack of awareness of the personal space and property rights of others, in equivalent-aged middle class children, leads to subsequent criminal behavior remains for later study. What is of immediate importance to us is that there is early evidence that the physical form of the residential environment can in itself play a significant role in shaping the perception of children and in making them cognizant of the existence of zones of influence and therefore of the rights of others.

Security in Low- versus Middle-Income Housing

The report of the President's Commission on Law Enforcement and Administration of Justice, 1968, in attempting to understand the nature of the current crime problem, was able to isolate the prevalence of crime in inner-city areas:

. . . of 2,780,015 offenses known to the police in 1965—these were index crimes—some two million occurred in cities, more than half a million occurred in suburbs, and about 170,000 occurred in rural areas.

. . . Crime rates in American cities tend to be highest in the city center and decrease in relationship to the distance from the center. . . .

Although the President's Commission identifies the consistency with which serious crime occurs in low-income deteriorated areas, it is difficult to properly assign the causes of this increasing concentration of criminal behavior in our core urban residential areas over the past decade. Contributory factors are probably both social and physical in nature, and may involve the increasing concentration of the disadvantaged in our older urban areas; the mix of contrasting income groups in cities not normally present in our economically homogeneous suburbs; and possibly, the peculiar susceptibility of the form of our currently evolving inner urban areas to criminal behavior. A further factor may be concentration of criminal elements in what they have come to recognize as an easy target area; one in which their anonymity is assured and the evasion of pursuit and arrest simplified.

In any case, society's capacity for coping with these problems does not appear to have been able to keep pace with their rate of increase. Those members of the community who are in a position to exercise choice in the housing .market-place are moving their families to suburban areas. Many realize that the problems they are trying to escape may end up following them, but they hope at a much slower pace.

Our concern ... lies in determining means for improving the livability and security of residential environments within the urban setting, particularly for low- and low-middle-income groups. There are approximately 4 million people living in public housing across the Nation today and a comparable figure living in federally subsidized low-middle-income housing. These are people for whom housing choice in a free-market economy is severely limited. By the nature of their residential location and social associations they tend to be the most continually victimized. Victimization is also a more totally devastating experience to their life structure than it is for upper-income inhabitants. The provision of doormen and security personnel and the maintenance of costly security equipment have been the traditional means employed by upper-income groups for coping with crime problems in housing. These means are not possible within the budget allowance of public housing or federally assisted low-middle income housing.

We feel that the present response of upper-income residents to the increasing crime problem is one which is introverted and withdrawn, and involves intentional isolation, restricting, and hardening of their private dwelling at the expense of immediately adjacent surroundings. This is coupled with their relegation to others of the traditional responsibilities adopted by citizenry for insuring the continuance of a viable, functioning living environment for their family and surrounding community.

Over the past year and a half [1970 ff.] we have been exploring the problem of security in low- and middle-income housing where provision of doormen and expensive security hardware is impossible; we have uncovered residential environments which by the nature of their physical layout are able to provide security and continue to function in even high-crime areas. In some instances we have been able to find these environments in immediate juxtaposition to others of different design which suffer the worst agonies of crime.

An illustration will perhaps serve to point up the fundamental differences in security design for low- versus middle- and upper-income housing. The use of a doorman usually requires that entry be restricted to one point in a large complex. To accomplish this it is usually necessary to wall-off a two- to ten-acre housing project. This can result in thousands of feet of street being removed from all forms of social and visual contact. A natural mechanism for providing for the safety of streets has therefore been sacrificed to insure the security of the residents only when within the confines of the complex.

In developments where the use of doormen is not possible due to prohibitive costs, successful designs have been those with as few units as possible sharing a common entry off the street. The designers of these projects have so positioned units, their windows and entires, and so prescribed paths of movement and activity areas, as to provide continuous natural surveillance to the street as well as the building.

While developments embodying both of the above solutions are directed at providing maximum security to their respective inhabitants, there is a fundamental difference in approach and in the beneficial spin-offs which obtain. The first approach is one in which tenants relegate responsibility for security to a hired individual. A doorman guarding one entry to a building complex serving 200 to 500 families is concerned predominantly with restricting entry into the complex. He cannot, by the definition of his job and within the framework of what is physically possible, also be concerned with the bordering streets on which the project sites. The second approach involves tying residential units to their service streets and requires of their occupants that they assume responsibility for the safety of these streets as an extension of their concern for their own domains. Where in the first instance internal security has been achieved by disavowing concern for the surrounding areas, in the second it has been accomplished by insuring that the surrounding streets be made equally secure. For the nonresident user of the street, the second solution is clearly preferable.

Nature of Crime and Its Occurrence in Public Housing Projects

The New York City Housing Authority Police Department not only keeps records of crimes but endeavors to pinpoint their place of occurrence within a project. Crimes ranging from serious felonies to minor misdemeanors are equally recorded. Complaints

are noted even where they have not lead to apprehensions or arrests. Reports also separate out crimes committed on project grounds from those committed inside buildings and within apartments proper. Because place of occurrence is significant information to the housing authority, we have been able to learn where are the recurring danger areas in housing projects and to measure the extent to whcih physical design of a project is a statistically significant variable.

Perhaps the most revealing of the figures is that 70 percent of all recorded crime taking place in housing projects occurs within the buildings proper. This includes nearly all serious crime: Robbery, burglary, larceny, rape and felonious assault. It leads us to conclude that the buildings themselves, rather than the grounds, are understood by criminals as being areas where his victim is most vulnerable and where the possibility for his observation or apprehension is most minimal. Much of this may be the result of the policy that public housing projects by

Table 16–1. Location of crime in public housing projects

Location	Robbery	Burglary	Larceny	Rape	Felonious Assault
Inside:					
Elevator	1,389	1	153	9	9
Hallway	469	6	178	6	17
Stairway	215	0	48	15	6
Lobby	361	3	430	2	12
Apartment	53	1,628	79	12	87
Basement	9	58	16	1	0
Community, health, child care center	8	214	49	0	2
Commercial establishment, store, etc.	13	41	12	0	0
Roof and roof landing	6	0	11	15	2
Project locations unclassified	74	103	58	1	12
Total inside	2,592	2,054	1,034	61	147
Outside:					
Parking lot	41	2	133	1	1
Project play area	16	0	10	0	2
Public sidewalk contiguous to project	68	0	59	0	7
Project locations unclassified	661	6	667	3	98
Off project, department of parks playground	0	0	0	0	0
Off project, city street	0	0	0	0	0
Off project, unclassified	1	0	0	0	0
Total outside	787	8	869	4	108

Source: New York City Housing Authority Police.

law and tradition are open to all members of the community. The interior of the buildings suffers, therefore, from being public in nature and yet hidden from public view and consequently unable to benefit from the continual surveillance to which the public areas of our cities are normally subject.

The statistics further indicate that the specific areas within buildings which are most vulnerable are the elevators (accounting for about 50 percent of all robberies); the entrance lobbies (accounting for 15 percent of the robberies); and the rear fire stairs and the hallways (accounting for 20 percent of robberies). All four areas are peculiarly public in nature and yet screened from public view. The statistics seem to indicate that those spaces which people must use on a continuing basis to get from the public area outside the project to the safety of the interior of the apartment are particularly dangerous if screened both from unconscious observation and from formal patrol. In this light, the elevator is a space public in nature but totally screened from all observation. For the interval of the ride it fulfills all of the criteria of a crisis area and is so understood by tenants.

Although most reported rapes occur in the fire stairways, apartments, and roof landings, our inquiries have led us to conclude that the initial encounter and threat is in fact made in the elevator, corridor, and lobby areas. The victim is then moved at the threat of force to one of the three places mentioned where observation and traffic are even more minimal.

It is interesting to note that 60 percent of felonious assaults occur in apartments proper and that they usually take place among people familiar with each other. The remainder take place in the hallways outside apartments and in the lobby.

In this monograph we will not deal with crime in the interior of the dwelling unit proper. The apartment unit and its design are accepted as given and are by definition beyond the boundaries of this study. Our involvement is with the design of those spaces outside the privacy of the dwelling unit. We are concerned with the way in which the units themselves, their entry systems and clustering, and their positioning in the existing urban fabric all combine in affecting the safety of the physical environment both inside the building out.

The Secluded Adult Middle-Class Environment

In September of 1970, a 50,000-unit housing development, Co-op City, built privately for cooperative ownership, was completed in an outlying area of the Bronx, N.Y. It was occupied almost overnight, predominantly by an older middle-income class population fleeing their neighborhood in an adjacent area of the Bronx. In a random interview of 50 residents, most found their new environs inferior to the areas they had abandoned: Their apartments were smaller; the commercial facilities were few and goods more costly; there was little to no entertainment available; they had left many friends and institutions behind—and so on. Where many of these deficiencies may be remedied with the completion of the project in future years, the new residents bemoaned their loss only briefly. They all felt that the deficiencies were a small price to be paying for having been provided with what they most craved: security. They had succeeded in escaping from an environment, once friendly, but which now terrified them. The frequency of muggings, robberies, assaults—on an older generation—by new immigrants to "their neighborhood" had made continued life there impossible. Almost all of those interviewed said that in their old neighborhood they had long since given up any thought of going out at night. All knew of or had experienced burglaries first hand.

What is fascinating and fearful is the way the population chose to solve its probem: They had fled en masse and isolated themselves in a new lower middle class ghetto of their own making. Now in Co-op City—they live among their own kind: Middle-aged or older, largely Jewish, Italian, or other ethnic backgrounds, with average incomes about

$10,000. Normally, a gregarious, culture seeking involved group, they now make do so that they can breathe more easily.

Interestingly, from the viewpoint of this study, the buildings and residential settings they now occupy are much less defensible than what they left behind. If only a small percentage of the criminals that victimized them was transferred to within striking distance, they could wreak a havoc which would have made their abandoned neighborhood look a haven. In understanding what makes Co-op City safe and workable, if only for the present, there is much to be learned about the problems of securing residential environments and of the limitations of defensible space theory.

The New York City RAND Corp., in a study of crime in public housing to be published shortly, estimated that about half of the people responsible for crime lived in the very projects they victimized. This estimate was difficult to make in that only a small percentage of criminals are apprehended; trial procedures are long, and convictions few. Nevertheless our interviews of hundreds of tenants and Housing Authority police confirm these findings with the following distinctions: That criminals do live a few blocks away but both within projects and surrounding area, and a criminal seldom if ever victimizes his own building except in cases involving interpersonal confrontations.

In this light, if one considers that low income also correlates highly with crime, moving away from an area which was becoming increasingly occupied by low-income families was correctly moving from crime. The question remains how far away is away? How long before the vulnerability of the new development is recognized? How long before the criminal extends his mobility and range of operation?

Distance we recognize is one operating mechanism at Co-op City that insures security—population uniformity is another. So long as all the families in Co-op City are white, middle-class and elderly, any dark-skinned young person, not partial to respectable habit, will stand out and have the police sicced on him. But there is already a small percentage of black and Puerto Rican young families living at Co-op City—equally seeking the good and secure life. This no doublt complicates things and will increasingly do so as the dust of the new development settles.

Segregation of income and age group remains the most potent crime preventive mechanism in operation at Co-op City. The President's Commission found, as did all previous correlations of crime and age group, that males between the ages of 15 and 24 are the most crime-prone group in the population—and for the last 5 years this age group has been the fastest growing in the population. Co-op City has fewer than 5 percent of its population between the ages of 15 and 24, while the 1970 census indicates a national average of 11.3 percent. The question is how long can Co-op City remain disproportionately populated? Criminologists suggest that high-density urban residential areas like the abandoned Bronx district provide a high degree of anonymity and social isolation which makes the communal control of the criminal difficult.

Interestingly, Co-op City at 50 dwelling units to the acre (including commercial facilities and roads) rivals this density. Strangely, too, the building prototypes employed, and their relative positioning makes the opportunity for anonymity far greater.

The fundamental premise of our "defensible space" proposals is the subdivision of the residential complex to allow inhabitants to distinguish neighbor from intruder. Where at Co-op City this was achieved by isolating a large, uniform population, it is a tactic not possible in existing, contiguous, diverse urban agglomerations. The scale for creating distinctions must therefore become finer. The very ingredient that prohibits the criminal from hitting his own building—the chance that he may be recognized, is the mechanism we wish to exploit and extend. Through hierarchical subclustering and extension of the areas of territorial domain to the public street, we hypothesize that an equivalent capacity for distinguishing neighbor from intruder can be achieved.

Our work is directed at the reorganization of the existing urban residential fabric to make it effective in today's evolving circumstance. We are committed to working for a low- and middle-income who cannot buy the alternatives of moving out or personal doormen. Our interviews show rather conclusively that most ghetto and inner urban residents are as terrified and as victimized as the Co-op City escapees. The recently published Justice Department survey reveals that where crime rates in ghetto areas are five times the urban average, most of the victims are ghetto residents. Only a very small percentage of ghetto dwellers are criminals—most are victims. What we are endeavoring is to find a means for strengthening the resistance capacity of the low-income victim.

Subtle difficulties arise in attempting to improve the security of low-income, as compared with middle-income housing; these are mainly a function of the social forces at work on the resident populations. The social characteristics of the middle class greatly facilitate the task of providing them with a secure environment. Middle-class people have developed a refined sense of property and ownership; they have a measure of self-confidence and pride in their personal capabilities. Their everyday experiences reinforce their social competence; they can retain some control over the forces that shape their lives, and they recognize alternatives among which they can choose. These positive social contacts give them a feeling of potency in protecting and enforcing their rights within a defined sphere of influence; for instance, they are well-practiced in their demand for and use of police protection.

In contrast, it is more difficult to improve security for a lower class population, not because of a higher concentration of people with criminal intent, or because of limited financial resources, but because of attendant social problems. The life of the lower class is conducted under duress. For the lower class person, daily social contacts reinforce his feelings of impotence, erode his self-confidence and make remote any possibility of improving the quality of his life. Having been closed out of the game—financially,

politically, educationally, psychologically—he responds by changing the rules. It may indeed be unrealistic to expect an individual to assume positive social attitudes and influence in one sphere of his life when he has been told, clearly and consistently, in the other facets of his existence, that he has no such power.

It may appear, in our defensible space proposals, that we are viewing the world from a middle-class perspective; that we are trying to encourage everyone to assimilate middle-class values, and to assert essentially middle-class proprietary attitudes by providing them with a middle-class environment. Are we not forcing an attitude and life style upon people who in fact do not desire it? To the contrary: our interviews with hundreds of public housing residents have revealed that an overwhelming majority of lower class people hold the same goals and aspirations as do the middle class. Their formation of a distinct subculture has been their response to the constraints, both actual and psychological, imposed by the larger society. These findings are similar to those documented by Lee Rainwater in his study of Pruitt-Igoe residents, "Behind Ghetto Walls":

Lower class people are amply exposed to both of these cultural ideals. They know that some people make it big by the job they have and the money they are able to accumulate, that others do not make it so big but manage to live comfortably in homes in pleasant neighborhoods, surrounded by an increasing measure of material comfort. Most lower class people at some time entertain aspirations in one or both of these directions, and it makes no sense to talk of a lower class culture so divorced from that of the larger society that the validity of these goals is denied. However, many lower class people come to the conclusion that neither of these ways of life are possible for them.

TERRITORIALITY

It is our contention that the pervasiveness of crime in the cities may in large measure be due to the erosion of territorially defined space as an ally in the battle to maintain social order. Ethnic and cultural divisions provided previous generations of city residents with a form of solidarity that allowed them to overcome the sordid effects of poor housing environment. The physical format of early industrial cities paralleled cultural subdivisions; cities were internally divided into self-sustaining communities, each operating as a socio-spatial unit and taking on a burden of responsibility for the safety and well-being of their area. As a result, both positive and negative social consequences of housing design were not as evident as they are today. In cities where formal construct did not echo social structure, ethnic and cultural bonds were sufficiently strong to overcome physical barriers.

Interestingly, at a time when strong ethnic and cultural bases existed for forging bonds of solidarity among city dwellers, there was also recognition of the importance of providing a physical setting in which this natural community awareness could be fostered. The early public-housing projects (for example, First Houses in New York) were designed with great sensitivity to social needs, and included walk-up units, interior courts, and symbolic designations dividing the project grounds from the street.

The design of contemporary housing is paradoxical. At a time when ethnic and cultural bonds no longer lead to spontaneous awareness of community identity, there appears to be still less recognition of the potential uses of physical design as a means of promoting positive social outcomes. Physical isolation of family from family, typical of much contemporary high-rise design has, more than ever, come to imply social isolation as well. The creation of large, monolithic projects has come to imply social anonymity.

An important byproduct of this trend has been the abrogation of responsibility for maintaining the security of areas around the home to police and other public authorities. Residents feel they have little right to question the presence of strangers near their home; and, even if they think this within their mandate, they are reluctant to take the chance. High-rise elevators, lobbies, and corridors provide no advance warning of impending danger, no behavioral choices other than direct defense or complete submission to an intruder. There are few opportunities to develop informal interdependencies among neighbors which would directly discourage crime and vandalism.

Street crimes may have reached epidemic proportions because of this lack of concern for the social consequences of residential design. Modern residences have encapsulated man from his neighbors, made improbable the development of local allegiances, relieved the individual of the capacity to defend his own territory and, in short, made police and the courts his only line of defense.

Public Housing and Territoriality

In public housing the breakdown of territoriality as a productive social mechanism has been more complete than in other residential environments. Halls, lobbies, and grounds are, by law, considered public facilities. This means that the small penumbra of safety surrounding the home has, by definition, been eliminated. Strangers have a legal right to enter zones which in nonpublic housing are considered restricted areas. Furthermore, residents are incapable of hiring doormen or elevator operators who are a necessary adjunct for achieving definition in high-rise apartment building environments.

Perhaps most important, it has eliminated an outstanding means of crime control and territorial defense—the concept of the intruder or stranger. In modern society, group identity has been detached from its moorings in shared, community-oriented space. With this transformation of the group, the concept of "strangers" and "familiars," so long an active shaping force in animal evolution, has been given over to social utopian conceptions of man: that to define someone as a stranger dehumanizes the opponent and is the source of racism, social strife and war. This humanistic philosophy would have it that all strangers be treated amiably as members of the "family of man."

The abhorrence of the concept of nationality or local identity is in part based on a misconception of the function of territory and defense in animal evolution. In the animal kingdom there is no monolithic reaction to strangers, or to strange behavior, through which the invader is immediately turned into a ferocious enemy. First there is the mild response to strangeness, equivalent to laughter, to jar the intruder back to normalcy. The greetings and appeasements of human strangers with one another ("excuse me"), accompanied by smiles or slight gestures of submission, are humble versions of these courtesies evolved for the most part in the animal world. At the next level of intensity there is ignoring or looking the other way in a deliberate or obvious fashion. On the human level, Goffman refers to this behavior as "civil inattention." Typically, civil inattention is a means of adjusting the presence of strangers to one another in public places. When it occurs near the home territory it is perceived as an imperative desire for the stranger to leave of his own accord; it communicates patient acceptance of the stranger as long as the behavior in which he is engaged appears to be declining of its own accord, taking him out of range and not accelerating into a still more intense threat. Finally, and only after a sequence of alternatives has been tried, direct hostility and aggression may emerge as the threat increases.

In public housing projects, there is little possible range of reactions to strangers between their benign acceptance, for example, the supplicatory smile given to the housing assistant who inspects the interior recesses of the home, and the overt hostility and aggression with which the stranger is viewed when he comes too close to the home. Because of the lack of differentiation of space surrounding the home:

There are few barriers, boundaries or divisions in which a resident can begin to employ more gentle means of telling stranger from neighbor,
No litmus tests that can be performed prior to an actual incident of crime or violation,
No rules of familiarization to a group or neighborhood during which the stranger becomes known,

No rules of immigration, deportation and social ostracism.

The result is a loss of the positive functions served by fear of strangers without any of the advantages of social utopianism. Since there are no clear ways to identify or eliminate strangers, all people become somewhat foreboding; this because people have been deprived of a group of "familiars" to which they can turn for support. The problem is compounded by the democratic organization of the larger city. There is really no way to avoid strangers. Every walk down a block means confrontation with strangers and the incumbent ambiguity of such meetings.

In short, we have accepted the notion of a loose society in which all strangers are greeted amiably; it is now this same loose organization which is responsible for the conditions of epidemic fear of victimization.

Animal Territory

For the most part, we are resigned, perhaps doomed, to live a deterritorialized existence in contemporary cities. Although an older rural image of the home persists, inspiring widespread nostalgia and sentiment, opportunities are few to achieve the self-sufficient relationship to nature implied by the rural imagination. In modern cities there is no longer any hope of self-sufficiency; every behavior must be shaped and composed to fit into an interdependent urban whole. Biological and mechanical needs have to be met by society acting in a centralized fashion. The person is a part of the larger urban machinery.

In dense modern cities, territorial behaviors are especially limited. Individual and familial relations to a particular place have to be streamlined to accommodate shared proprietary rights on the part of thousands or millions of fellow residents. Perhaps the only place that remains to be defended as territory is the apartment unit itself. Now even this vestige of security is threatened. Given the current crime problem, we are more likely to submit to violation of the home than to defend it as a last bastion of identity, individuality, and security. In some ways, the automobile may be the last reminder of true territorial expansion of man toward a feature of the environment outside the limits of the body.

If anything, territory in cities has become a mere symbol of status; it is no longer a stage for enacting the drama of life, a focus of existence for the total man.

In the biological study of animal behavior, territoriality is never a mere aggregative impulse. Even though we hear scattered accounts of boundary rivalry or war among animal species over territory, for the most part, attachment to a particular space or habitat operates as a benevolent mechanism allowing animals which might otherwise come into conflict to coexist in close proximity to one another. It provides a system of protocol which carefully avoids discourtesies. . . .

Human Territoriality: The Social Contract

The rules of territoriality in humans are somewhat different in character. Territoriality is regulated both by code and by willingness to enter into, and participate in, a culturally defined social contract. In present times, the rights of the individual against spatial or social invasion are intended as guaranteed by law and do not require individual defense of personal rights. The State gives to the individual or group a wide range of options and means of recourse if his person, his property or even his ideas are violated.

As we are beginning to recognize, it is harder and harder to feel secure about the effectiveness of these nonbiological, legal supports. Court cases drag on for years and rarely provide actual compensation for violations. Police cannot hope to investigate the hundreds of thousands of burglaries and robberies that occur in cities each year. In general, there is little hope of recourse by law for the man on the street.

This breakdown of confidence in law un-

earths a latent danger for society, especially provoked by crimes of violence committed by strangers. These crimes come perilously close to reevoking a biological instinct to survive. They threaten the ability of the individual victim to sustain his faith in an abstract system of justice; they tend to precipitate a widespread loss of faith in the capacity of the system to provide people with a sense of justice in their day to day lives.

The last frontier on this urban battlefield may be the apartment door. Should this barrier become subject to ready violation, there may be, as a result, less willingness to surrender the individual power of self-defense to the corporate wisdom of society, to the police and the courts.

The human social contract is, then, gravely threatened by the inability of cities to insure basic freedom from anxiety and insecurity for its citizens.

It is our contention that the system of justice in urban areas may have taken an undue burden of responsibility. At present, all cracks and crevices on the urban frontier require supervision and control by police. Without long-range attachments to places, families are merely living in momentarily occupied sites on this abstract urban landscape. Their positive social energies as well as their built-in capacity to defend an area of the city against violation may have been sacrificed in the race to achieve an open society. It is possible, however, that the job of insuring justice is too large and too diverse to be handled by police alone. New mechanisms may be required to give individual citizens more options and opportunities to make their energies felt in the battle against crime.

Just as space operated beneficently in the evolution of animals, it has been friend and ally to man in the history of civilization. Having a space of one's own allowed men to feel invulnerable to violation. The traditional home provided a retreat from the insecurities and anxieties of life; its boundaries were clear and firmly defended against invasion. In a striking analogy to the animal world, the traditional home even had a "penumbra of safety" around it in the form of a lawn or a yard.

In the animal world a similar penumbra around the home territory exists as a strip of land in which no hunting occurs. It evolved as a mechanism for preventing animals from instinctively attacking their own young in the midst of a hunting foray.

In modern cities, the lesson of animal territoriality—of a penumbra around the home—has been repeatedly and carelessly violated.

Perhaps these and other lessons of animal societies state a biologically defined minimum relationship to habitat which has to be understood, addressed, compensated for, or overcome by planners of modern cities. The pendulum has swung to a point where we have come to believe man is free of his biological heritage. On the other hand, while it is well to recognize the unnecessary limitations imposed by the noble savage view—of a romantic bondage to our instincts—it is also time to recognize the positive function of this legacy as a means of reducing conflict and enhancing identity and security.

Collective Security

Urban street crimes may be statistically infrequent events, but they raise the spectre of an epidemic because they are often accompanied by irrational use of violence and force.

The odd thing about these street crimes is that they typically take place close to many hundreds of nearby homes with large numbers of people behind closed doors and windows. The elevator stick-up or building lobby mugging takes place just feet away from apartment doors; the escape route of the criminal is in proximity to hundreds of families, especially in public housing projects, where large numbers of families are clustered in high-rise buildings.

Despite the chance of detection, astonishingly few robberies are cleared by arrest. Even if the victim succeeds in alerting neighbors that a robbery has been committed, neighboring tenants would probably not recognize the perpetrator. They can rarely discern any identifiable characteristics through which he might be traced; and if he were identifiable, they might not be willing to provide police with the information, due to fear of retaliation or skepticism concerning police follow-up action. There is little sense of corporate identity in most large buildings. Spatial proximity of a particular apartment to crime prone areas (e.g., the lobby) does not imply any special responsibility for keeping watch over the area in the name of all residents of the building.

Block associations and tenant patrols in public housing have instituted a limited and useful kind of collective security. In these systems, designated individual residents take responsibility for watching over the security of a building during high-crime hours. The person on patrol has to sit in the building lobby, usually at a makeshift desk, with some degree of risk to himself. In this role the tenant patrolman is a paraprofessional police officer, not a tenant who is concerned about the welfare of his neighbors. He is protecting the building in which he lives in the role of formal monitor, not as a natural extension of other, family-oriented and personally significant activities.

In short, tenant patrolling and block watching have become a job, a form of labor, specialized in nature and deserving of economic compensation. The activity is no longer an integral part of the work of the family where seeing to safety, like throwing out the garbage, is an expected part of the daily life pattern.

Jane Jacobs in "Death and Life of Great American Cities" describes an alternative social system in which the same rewards of enhanced security are achieved but where the watchers are not laboring under the impression that they have a special job to perform. Her street characters who guard the streets, local merchants who convey the community lore, are doing so as an expression of a way of life, and more, because it interests them to engage in this activity.

They do not engage in the task as a delegated responsibility. They serve the community coincidentally because of the nature of their individual life patterns and interests.

In dense city areas, much of the space surrounding one's home is public and accessible to intruders; residents are left to their own skills at differentiating strange from ordinary behavior. In functional urban communities, residents develop articulate notions about which families argue loudly, which families have children that make strange noises, which areas or streets frequently attract loud adolescents or noisy drunks. This knowledge is not constructed from detailed personal information on the identity of neighbors, or the frequently encountered street characters, but is accrued through repeated observations.

In this system, "corporate responsibility" is not the labor of a few policemen but results from the tacit participation of a wide base of the population in an informal awareness of which people constitute the "community." It is a community of silently shared values and expectations, without need of explicit organization. Crime control is achieved through acts performed before crimes occur, not after the fact of crime.

First, due to the presence of understood norms concerning public demeanor, community residents become instantly aware of the presence of strangers bent on crime or acting suspiciously. Despite allowable variation, there are clear behavioral and spatial limits beyond which strangers will not be permitted to go.

But this is only one step in crime control. Observers not only note the presence of strangers who look suspicious, but follow them visually until out of their sight line. No explicit communication is necessary among observers to create a network of surveillance. The effect is, however, the same as if they were linked to one another under a central command. The result of this activity is that crimes are discouraged because would-be criminals have the sense that they are being observed by a native population. The observer, because of his alertness to suspicious conduct, has a long time to pick out an identifiable characteristic of a crime perpetrator well in advance of the excitement and confusion of any actual criminal act.

Of course, the success of this tacit surveillance network requires that no significant gaps exist in its operation. People need to visibly experience the concern and involvement of other similar observers. When they open their own window to investigate a strange sound, they must hear the comforting sound of windows opening all around them.

If collective security is to be achieved through these small, incremental activities of a large number of individuals, it requires that a certain critical mass of residents be present. This critical mass will increase or decrease mathematically in inverse proportion to the degree of community lore, culture or identity shared among residents.

It is also likely there is an upper limit, an entropy principle, beyond which the critical mass becomes a collection of homogeneous individuals who bear no relationship to one another, and who do not participate in a sense of collective responsibility.

Clearly, there are still communities in which this balance has been retained; the recipe for community crime control remains to be articulated in exacting, scientific terms. We can no longer proceed by "feel," a pinch of shared values, a dash of aberrant behavior, a touch of police, and a flock of residents.

Housing Cartels

In previous generations, the type of house in which one lived, its relationship to neighboring families, its location in the city network, were always viewed as having a significant influence on the life of the family and the assimilation of the child to the larger social order. In the earliest multi-occupancy dwellings, a maximum of three to four families shared a vestibule on each floor. As if to compensate for residents' being deprived of a single family house, buildings were framed by extensive ceremonial entrances, lobbies and play areas. Although this style was penetrated with some elitist societal values and a brand of elegance unobtainable today, it had other virtues which should be retained and can be achieved with more frugal means.

The style included ornament and beauty as a paramount consideration. This lent individuality to each apartment building even if it was one of many similar buildings and housed 50 or more families. The style also revealed tenderness and protectiveness toward the individual family within the mass. It forced recognition of the family unit, by providing a series of suggestive membranes through which a stranger had to proceed in order to penetrate its intimate domain.

The presence of a stranger in a vestibule shared by two to four apartments was interpreted as penetration of a part of their privacy. In like measure, the family extended part of their energy to personalizing and caring for these shared vestibule areas. This penumbral space also served as the breeding ground for neighborly gestures on the part of adjacent residents. One can speuclate that the presence of a small vestibule, in some ways, allowed for the development of a uniquely urban friendship pattern. It was possible to meet one's neighbor in the vestibule, to engage in light social chatter, but to resist the closeness and intimacy necessary to invite a neighbor into one's home.

This level of acquaintance with neighbors has been very important in urban residences. It allowed people to gain the benefits of mutual awareness, the advantages of mutual protective reactions in the face of emergency, without the drawbacks and disadvantages of extensive friendships or enmities among neighbors. Urban dwellers were allowed the advantage of positive social contact without compromising preciously guarded privacy and the impulse to pursue friendships on a wider scale, ranging far beyond the opportunities for social contact provided by immediate neighbors.

These early apartment buildings expressed respect for the family and looked to it as the fundamental means of socializing children. Contemporary society is more skeptical of the power of the family in shaping the thoughts and values of children; schools and other public institutions have taken over the primary tasks of social, moral, occupational, and political education.

As a reflection of this larger social process, apartment buildings have become cartels, gradually eroding away all buffers between the family unit and the public arena. Corridors of high-rise buildings provide no zones of transition between the interior recesses of the family space and the public elevator. Long halls are constructed with apartment doors close to one another, on both sides of the corridor.

Paradoxically, the older apartment buildings provided the self-protective mechanism of a rural community while at the same time giving residents the freedom from local customs, mores and rules involved in land-centered societies. It allowed them to explore a new urban style of life while providing an important haven of security for them to use as a starting point for these urban explorations.

Community and Privacy

It is apparent that few urban high-rise buildings have struck the right balance between community and privacy for most of their residents. Many people are personally dissatisfied with the life style induced by their physical setting; because of crowding and economic constraints they cannot express their preference in the open marketplace.

In the recent past, architecture and the building professions provided few alternatives to the stereotype of single concept high-rise buildings for the central city, and the humdrum routine of single-family homes for suburban subdivisions. However, there is clearly a new need to develop more humane designs for housing people at high densities in the central city. Some newer buildings have been designed to incorporate social objectives in their layout and exist as experimental prototypes for a new form of consciousness in the architectural profession.

Distressingly, the most prevalent of contemporary design approaches moves in the opposite direction. The urban environment is being increasingly fortified against crime. The private building market is responding to the demand for crime control by sacrificing more wholesome objectives in the effort to insure complete safety for residents. Where a free-housing market still exists in large cities, people select an apartment based on its security features, at times provided at the expense of surrounding stock. Some developers have already built large "compounds," guarded by electronic alarms, surveyed by closed-circuit television, surrounded by miles of fencing, with entrances monitored by sentries who demand special identification.

It is most important to recognize that achieving increased security and the provision of social benefits through housing design can and should go hand in hand. Increased security is an immediate outcome of well-functioning communities. Where building design provides opportunity for tenants to observe and maintain surveillance over their living areas, security will be enhanced; where design allows tenants to feel the presence and shared concerns of their neighbors, security will be preserved; and where buildings relate adequately to streets and other surrounding zones, large public areas of the city can profit as a byproduct of local community concern.

The challenge is to find new ways of achieving this synthesis of objectives at a time in history when the need for quick and direct solutions is pressing.

CURBSIDE DETERRENCE?
An analysis of the effect of a slug-rejector device, coin-view window, and warning labels on slug usage in New York City parking meters

John F. Decker

With the increased utilization of parking meters by many American cities has come an increase in associated criminal problems. In New York City, for example, parking meters are frequently vandalized, broken into, and completely stolen. Far more common, however, is the rapidly growing problem of illicit slug usage in the meters.

Data on New York City parking meter use for the last thirteen years is shown in Table 16.2 Between 1958 and 1970, the number of slugs placed into the meters rose a low of 62,060 in 1958 to a high of 4,211,182 in 1969, an increase of 6,167%,

From *Criminology*, 10, No. 2 (August 1972), 127–42. Reprinted by permission of Sage Publications, Inc. John Decker is Assistant Professor of Law at DePaul University College of Law, Chicago. This study was undertaken while he was a research fellow with the Criminal Law Education and Research Center at New York University School of Law.

although in 1970 the figure dropped to less than 4,000,000. In terms of rate of slug use, this means that in 1958 one slug was found in every 1,128 coins collected from the meters, while in 1970 every thirty-first object inserted into a meter was a slug. In terms of revenue, we find one slug for every $112 revenue in 1958, and one slug for every $3 of income in 1970.

During 1958 through 1961, rate of slug use never rose by more than 5% over the preceding year. In 1958, rate of slug use (in terms of slugs per 1,000 insertions) was approximately 0.9, and, in 1961, the figure was 1.1. This increase could be attributed to the general rise in petty larceny. However, a high of approximately 36 slugs per 1,000 insertions was observed in 1969, an increase of nearly 4,000% from 1958, although the rate of slug use then decreased somewhat in 1970 to 32 slugs per 1,000 insertions.

Table 16-2. Slug usage in New York City 1958-1970

Year	Revenue	Slugs	Slugs per 1,000 insertions
1958	6,963,913.12	62,060	0.9
1959	7,112,264.41	67,387	0.9
1960	7,347,825.59	71,516	1.0
1961	7,164,410.85	76,920	1.1
1962	7,199,223.40	131,845	1.9
1963	9,094,984.19	506,911	5.6
1964	9,216,485.17	818,200	8.9
1965	9,858,604.79	1,307,237	13.3
1966	9,817,906.77	2,065,126	20.8
1967	9,667,350.75	2,452,904	25.0
1968	10,564,740.99	3,903,845	35.7
1969	11,213,740.59	4,211,182	35.7
1970	11,603,073.27	3,826,956	32.3

This sharp increase in illicit meter use cannot be attributed to a similar increase in either the number of meters, or the amount of their use. In 1961, there were approximately 57,000 meters in New York City; today there are approximately 72,000 meters, an increase of about 26%. Revenue from 1958 to 1970 increased by 67%, from nearly $7 million in 1958 to over $11.5 million in 1970. The number of coins inserted into New York City parking meters in 1961 was approximately 71 million, and in 1970 approximately 119 million, an increase of 68%. A corresponding increase of 68% in slugs from 1958 to 1970 would show 104,000 slugs collected in 1970, whereas the actual figure was nearly 4 million.

SCHEMES UNDERTAKEN TO DECREASE SLUG USE

In the last several years, various proposals were presented and attempts made to decrease slug use in New York City parking meters. One attempt by the city of New York is the *introduction of a parking meter which mechanically rejects certain types of slugs, and also supposedly deters potential slug users through use of a coin-view window....* The slug-rejector device prevents

*Editor's italics.

the meter from registering time if a slug with a hole in it is inserted into the parking meter. Mechanically, any object inserted into a meter with this device rubs against a pin in the meter. If the object inserted has a hole in it, it passes through the pin and drops into the coin box without registering time. Since the vast majority of slugs inserted are of a washer or pull ring variety from a soft drink or beer can, theoretically much of the slug use will be eliminated. A meter with a coin-view window displays the last object inserted into the meter. Hence, if a slug user inserts a slug into the meter it will be visible to everyone, including the police or meter-maids. Theoretically, this window, which is made of a strong, durable plastic called "lexon," also deters slug use. The new meters, which the city began installing in April of 1969, are the Duncan "VIP" meters, which have both the slug-rejector device and the coin-view window.

Another scheme, which was constructed by this writer, used warning labels affixed to the meters. Three sets of labels warned potential offenders that use of a slug is a violation of the respective federal, state, and city laws, and is punishable by imprisonment or fine or both. Theoretically, these warning labels would deter potential slug users from placing slugs into the meters.

ANALYSIS OF THE TWO SCHEMES TO REDUCE SLUG USAGE

In order to evaluate the effectiveness of the Duncan meter in deterring slug usage, ten regions with 100 to 400 meters each, located in the Manhattan, Brooklyn, and the Bronx, covering a wide variety of socioeconomic levels, were studied during 1968, 1969, and 1970. The study was to provide an estimate of any change in illicit meter use following installation of meters with the slug-rejector device and the coin-view window to determine their effectiveness as deterrents to slug usage. The new Duncan VIP meters were installed during the first six months of 1969.

The study revealed a marked decrease in amount of slugs used in each area from 1968

Table 16-3. Rate of slug usage (slugs per 1,000 insertions)

Area	Year 1968	1969	1970	% Decrease after installation of new meters (1968–1969)
1	33.7	23.8	13.3	29.4
2	19.4	13.4	6.7	30.9
3	34.8	25.9	16.1	25.6
4	215.3	65.1	153.4	69.8
5	182.0	53.5	60.7	70.6
6	55.9	12.6	13.5	77.5
7	138.5	28.4	25.2	79.5
8	68.1	28.1	23.6	58.7
9	91.2	31.7	34.1	65.2
10	68.1	24.4	24.4	64.2

to 1969, following installation of the new meters.* Examination of revenue, however, showed smaller variation from year to year, and rate of slug usage for all ten regions decreased substantially from 1968 to 1969. This downward trend in rate of slug usage

*Editor's italics.

continued from 1969 to 1970 in five of the areas; in one area, the rate did not change. Two areas showed a slight increase in rate of illicit meter use from 1969 to 1970, and two other areas were not considered due to lack of meaningful data for the year 1970. However, the rates for both 1969 and 1970 were far below that of 1968 in *all* areas.

The peak period of slug usage was the last quarter of 1968, after which began a gradual decline in illicit meter use that has continued to the present. This would indicate that installation of the coin-view window and slug-rejector device in New York City parking meters, begun in early 1969, has had a significant impact on the citywide rate of slug usage.

Table 16.3 shows a great percentage decrease in slug use from 1968 to 1969, immediately following installation of the new meters, in areas 4 and 5, which were the two most economically deprived regions under study. The least decline in slug usage was observed in areas 1, 2, and 3, which were the most

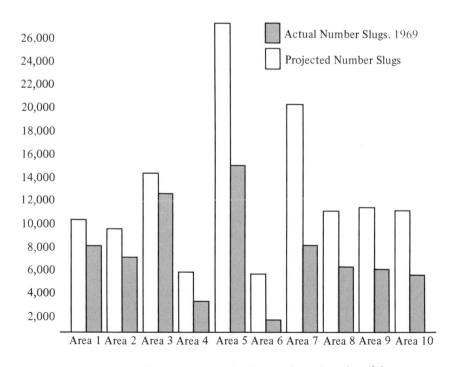

Figure 16-1. 1969 projected number of slugs and actual number of slugs.

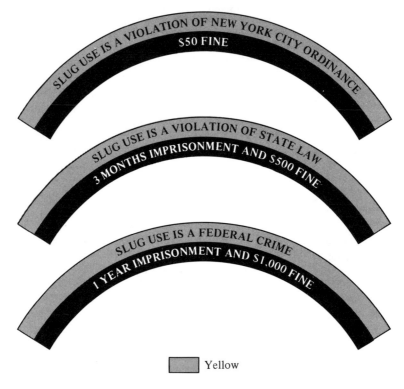

Yellow

Figure 16–2.

affluent regions under study. It should also be noted that the greatest meter use was also found in these three districts, which indicates the least decline in illicit meter use occurred in areas where meter use was greatest.

As a further look at the decreased rate of illicit meter use, the 1968 rate of slug use, prior to the installation of the new meters, was projected to 1969, and comparison was made between the actual number of slugs collected in 1969 and this projected figure. Figure 16.2 illustrates graphically the substantially lower number of slugs illegally placed in the Duncan meters in 1969.

The Second Scheme

The second part of the study . . . examined whether potential slug users were deterred by use of warning labels affixed to the meters. Analysis was made to determine whether the number of slugs found in those parking meters decreased from previous years or from that of other meters in the city without warning labels. Specifically, there were three types of labels, each applied to a selected group of meters. All the labels were approximately six inches long and two inches wide, with bold black lettering on a bright yellow background, and yellow lettering on black (see Figure 16.2). Labels on meters in the first area read:

Slug use is a violation of New York City ordinance $50 fine

Meter labels in the second area read:

Slug use is a violation of state law 3 months imprisonment and $500 fine

Labels in the third area read:

Slug use is a federal crime 1 year imprisonment and $1,000 fine

A control area where no labels were attached to the meters was also used for comparison purposes.

The four areas studied were in the same borough, in areas of similar socioeconomic backgrounds, and had similar histories of slug problems in the past, although none of the areas was immediately adjacent to another. The four regions, each of which had approximately 100 meters, were studied during the first five months of 1971. The various warning labels were affixed to the respective meters the last week of February. None of the meters under observation was equipped with any other slug deterrent device, such as the slug-rejector or coin-view window. Thus, differences in slug usage observed within any area could be attributed to the warning labels affixed to the meters in that region.

Initially, a comparison was made of the 1970 rate of slug usage in each of the four areas under study with the comparable 1970

Table 16–4. Rate of slug usage in comparison with citywide rate (slugs per 1,000 insertions)

	Type of label				
	Federal	State	City	Control	Citywide (no labels)
January					
1970	56.5	82.0	52.6	52.1	34.8
1971	45.5	44.1	26.5	40.0	29.2
February					
1970	86.2	63.3	36.5	63.7	35.3
1971	31.2	33.2	22.2	38.3	29.8
March					
1970	65.8	70.4	41.8	56.2	35.2
1971	40.3	27.3	18.4	34.7	29.5
April					
1970	68.5	61.0	36.6	52.9	34.8
1971	38.6	27.5	21.3	42.7	28.2
May					
1970	57.1	57.5	43.9	49.3	35.2
1971	55.9	38.9	30.3	45.9	29.3

citywide monthly rates in order to learn of the relative significance of illicit meter use between the regions under study and the entire city. Table 16.4 shows that for all months under study, slug usage in 1970 was greater in the four regions being observed than it was for the city as a whole. In 1971, the control region continued to experience a greater rate of slug usage than the citywide rate throughout the five months studied. The region where federal warning labels were used also showed greater slug usage than the citywide rate, both prior to and after application of the warning labels, whereas the area where state warning labels were used showed a greater rate prior to use of the labels and a lesser rate after use of the labels. However, in May, the rate in the state area once again was greater than the citywide rate. This might indicate the deterrent effect of the state labels was short-lived. . . .

Examination of meter use data within each of the four areas under observation showed that for all months under study the monthly rate of illicit meter use in each area was less in 1971 than it had been in 1970, as shown in Table 16.3. Even the months of January and February, prior to the application of the warning labels, experienced a decreased rate in slug use from 1970 to 1971. Also, the control group, where no labels were affixed to the meters, showed a decline in illicit meter use for all months. Thus, unlike in the study of the deterrent effect of the slug-rejector device and coin-view window, no immediate effect of the warning labels was obvious. Rate of slug usage decreased in the months prior to the use of the warning labels, as well as in the months after their application. Although it seems difficult to account for this decrease in areas which do not have the slug-rejector device and coin-view window, it is possible that such decreases might be attributed to the experiences of slug users having their slugs rejected by nearly identical meters which were equipped with the slug-rejector device. But whatever the cause of this decline, we obviously cannot attribute all the decreased illicit meter use observed in March, April, and May 1971 entirely to the warning labels. . . .

CONCLUSION

Illicit meter use in the ten areas under study showed a dramatic decline following installation in 1969 of the Duncan "VIP" meters with coin-view window and slug-rejector device. In fact, the decrease was so great that it affected citywide slug use totals for 1969 and 1970, although only 16,074 of the city's approximately 72,000 meters were the new type of meters. Rate of illicit meter use in both 1969 and 1970 were significantly lower than the 1968 rate (before installation of the Duncan meters). In addition, the majority of the areas studied showed 1970 slug usage was significantly less than even the 1969 rate. However, in two of the areas under study the rate of illicit meter use *increased* substantially between 1969 and 1970, although, as previously stated, the rates for both 1969 and 1970 were *far* below that of 1968. Whether this subsiding in illicit meter use will continue can only be revealed by future studies.

The districts with the greatest slug problem when the study was initiated were the areas which experienced the greatest rate of decrease in illicit meter use following installation of the new meters. Areas with the greatest amount of meter use showed the least percentage decrease in slug usage with the new Duncan meters. And it was interesting to note that these areas were the most affluent of the regions under observation.

The decreased illicit meter use shown by this study is attributed to the new meters. However, since all meters in the districts studied had both the slug-rejector device and the coin-view window, it was not possible to test which of these devices afforded the greater deterrence. It is contended by some that the coin-view window invites vandalism and future meters should be equipped with only the slug-rejector device. Due to the successful deterrence by the present meters with both devices, it would seem wise that two studies be made before initiating any change in the meters: (1) a study of slug usage with meters having only the slug-rejector device, and (2) a study of vandalism in meters with the coin-view window.

In the second aspect of the study, various methods of analysis showed the federal warning labels had no noticeable effect, while the state and city warning labels had a noticeable, although short-lived, effect. It appeared that warning potential offenders that slug use is a violation of the law and punishable by substantial sanctions had little deterrent value.

It is obvious that the parking meters with the coin-view window and slug-rejector device were more effective in reducing illicit slug use than use of warning labels. The minimal deterrent value of the labels can probably be attributed to the slim chance a slug user will be apprehended, much less convicted and subjected to the maximum penalty. This might indicate that potential slug users are not greatly deterred by the coin-view window either, since the object of the window is also to instill fear of apprehension. Hence, it seems that a mechanical device, such as the slug-rejector, which makes law violation difficult, is superior to a scheme or device which is dependent upon the potential violator's fear of apprehension. This finding is critical in light of the theoretical structure of criminology based on a punishment-deterrence-rehabilitation model, and it suggests a serious look at programs based on a prevention model and environmental design.

QUESTIONS FOR DISCUSSION

1. Why has the urban community in the United States become so crime prone when major cities all over the world are safe to visitors and dwellers alike?
2. What is meant by environmental design for the prevention and control of deviance?
3. Discuss Oscar Newman's concept of defensible space.
4. Do you believe, with the ethologists, that territoritality is as much a human as an animal concept? Do you think we ought to build our dwellings to maximize territorality considerations?
5. Why did Pruitt-Igoe fail as a low income project in St. Louis and similar projects

also fail such as Bolivar Arms in Columbus, Ohio? Could Newman's architectural suggestions make a difference?

6. Why does the crime rate increase with the number of floors per high rise apartment building complex? Would the horizontilization process reverse the verticalization problem?

7. How is it that the most densely populated cities in the world (Tokyo, Shanghai, Hong Kong) do not have these serious crime problems?

8. How do the Russians handle the crime prevention and deterrence problems? Surely not architectually. Describe their management system. Read Walter Connor's, *Deviance in Soviet Society,* for another perspective to Newman's.

9. Can technology deter crime? Will police helicopters, apartment burglar alarms, TV cameras in stores, and bolt door locks make a significant difference? Don't speculate. Check the data and conduct your own small studies on specific crime prevention devices.

BIBLIOGRAPHY

Angel, Shlomo. *Discouraging Crime Through City Planning.* Berkeley: The University of California Press, 1968.

Barker, Roger. *Ecological Psychology.* Stanford: Stanford University Press, 1968.

Boggs, Sarah. "Urban Crime Patterns." *American Sociological Review* (December 1965), 899ff.

Ewald, William R. (ed.). *Environment for Man.* Bloomington, Indiana: Indiana University Press, 1967.

Field, R. K. "Electronics Starts Solving the Problems of the Cities." *Electronics Design* 16 (1968), 64–84.

Jacobs, Jane. *The Death and Life of Great American Cities.* New York: Random House, 1961.

Jeffery, C..Ray. *Crime Prevention Through Environmental Design.* Beverly Hills, Calif.: Sage Publications, 1971.

Jeffery, C. Ray. "Crime Prevention and Control Through Environmental Engineering." *Criminologica* VII No. 3 (November 1969), 35–58.

Jeffery, C. Ray, and Jeffery, Ina A. "Delinquents and Dropouts: An Experimental Program in Behavior Change." *Education and Urban Society* (May 1969), 325–35.

Newman, Oscar. *Physical Parameters of Defensible Space: Past Experience and Hypotheses.* New York: Columbia University, 1969.

Rand, George. *Territoriality and Behavior: Private and Public Domains in the Urban Setting.* New York: Columbia University Press, 1969.

Rainwater, Lee. "Fear and the House as Haven in the Lower Class." *Journal of the American Institute of Planners* XXXII No. 1 (January 1966), 23–37.

Scheuer, James H. *To Walk the Streets Safely.* New York: Doubleday, 1969.

Sommer, Robert. *Personal Space: The Behavioral Basis of Design.* Englewood Cliffs, N.J.: Prentice-Hall, 1969.

17

Community Based Treatment Programs as Alternatives to Institutionalization

The key commitment of nearly all who work in the deviance management and control field is to the principle of *diversion*. Whenever possible, and however managed in practice, the less contact the deviant has with the deviance establishments—the hospitals, courts, prisons, treatment centers—the less the stigma and the greater the likelihood of eventual reintegration into the mainstream of life. In short, there is no longer any hesitancy against stating that the traditional management systems (including the present welfare system) are bankrupt in just about all respects.

In deviance, every effort is made to keep juveniles from police, court, and institutional contact unless all other alternatives have failed. Juveniles are diverted into special residential schools, military schools, foster homes, and the military (if old enough) to name but a few options. Others are fined, encouraged to make restitution, and, of course, placed on probation. Even when they get to court, the tendency is to make them unofficial cases and return them home under parental supervision.

At the adult level, more fines are being imposed, more restitution urged, more suspended sentences granted, more probation given. There are now shock probation options (in several states), halfway-in houses, community referral services, and all sorts of volunteer possibilities such as the Man-to-

Man program (a "respectable" citizen takes an offender under his wing), or training and work programs. Even after incarceration for the decreasing percentage of offenders (prison populations have dropped by one-third or more in the last decade despite a rising official crime rate), there are new and excellent innovations in the community to reduce the time spent in prison (now about 24 months on the average for all inmates). Work release debuted in the late 1950's, although Wisconsin had made this practice possible as early as 1913. Educational furloughs send men to school in the community. Weekend furloughs are becoming more common and are easier to sell to the legislature than conjugal visiting. Parole is granted a bit more freely and "flops" (rejections) now require formal explanation to the inmate in writing or face-to-face conversation. Halfway houses are everywhere to help the former inmate make an adjustment a bit more gradually; reintegration centers help the less serious parole violators straighten themselves out. Inside the walls all sorts of civilians enter with help and hope for an earlier release and a better future. The word is diversion and its limits are not yet clear. It may well be, as in Massachusetts in 1972, that these and other alternatives will force the closing of the institution.

The picture is even more "bullish" in mental health but not very promising in

mental retardation. In mental health, home care, emergency facilities, outpatient clinics, individual and group psychotherapy, therapeutic milieux, children's mental health centers, guidance clinics, suicide prevention bureaus, crisis intervention units, family counseling agencies are among some of the activities of the many hundreds of community mental health centers which came into existence as a result of Congressional legislation and Federal funding during the Kennedy Administration. All of these services have been established not only as intrinsically valuable but, as much or more, as attempts to head off commitment—voluntary or involuntary—to the state mental hospitals. As a consequence, despite rising numbers of "patients in need of care," the state hospitals, like the prisons and the reformatories for juveniles, are losing large numbers of patients to these community mental health centers and to the psychiatric wards of general hospitals. Should a National Health Care bill emerge out of Congress in the 94th or subsequent sessions, one provision would very likely include the expansion of general hospital treatment for the mentally ill.

Diversion has already been discussed at some length in connection with the establishment of detoxification centers for chronic inebriates and methadone maintenance clinics for heroin addicts. Shelters for teenage runaways should also be added as should those ubiquitous open door clinics which deal with any and all presenting problems. With the advent of legal abortion clinics—still a closely contested issue in many states—the picture of community management and control covers nearly all forms of previously defined deviancy. In the other areas, in which diversion is not pertinent, the approach has been to decriminalize the behavior or status. Thus, homosexuality and gambling require no diversion.

Only a few of the several forms of diversion can be described in this section. We begin with a contribution which deals with the home care of schizophrenics under public health nursing care and psychoactive drugs. The article shows clearly that the termination of such care quickly led to the need for rehospitalization of nearly 60 percent of the home care patients within five years. This research has provided the theoretical and practical basis for national home care programs. Its experimental design is also unique in the diversion field. This article will appear as a section in a new book entitled *The Custodial Community* which describes our activities in providing home care since 1961. It is fair to say that the article, "The Prevention of Hospitalization in Schizophrenia: Five Years After an Experimental Program" reaches conclusions which are revolutionary in the field of the extension of services to a difficult to reach population.

Diane Vaughan describes the origins and flowering of the Halfway House movement in America. No diversionary tactic has grown faster or has developed as much loyalty as the Halfway House. As its name implies, the Halfway House is usually a renovated white elephant building with plenty of rooms, located in the less desirable sections of town, and housing ex-patients, or ex-prisoners, or ex-any total institution persons as they attempt the adaptation between being wards of the state and free men and women. Stays are usually short, 30–90 days, and various programs are designed to help the releasee make the adaptation. When the releasee can find suitable quarters, sometimes with family, friends, strangers, or even a room at the YMCA, and gainful employment, the Haflway House extends its welcome to the new replacement. Whether the Halfway House reduces recidivism, rehospitalization, re-addiction, or other problems cannot be determined with any degree of accuracy as Vaughan correctly argues. But the idea of an earlier release and gradual return to the community is a worthwhile and less expensive alternative to lengthier prison or hospital stays followed by abrupt return to the community.

It was once a common practice to "rent" or "lease" felons, misdemeanants, and others to private persons on a contractual basis. The abuses inherent in such a system are obvious. Depending on the contractors, felons could be managed on a continuum ranging from near slavery through, at best, cheap labor. Free labor group pressure, plus the inescapable zeal of reformers, eventually ended contract labor practices. As a result, inmates remained penned up within the walls with no employment possible other than the housekeeping involved in maintaining the instituion. To fill this void, prison industries emerged—from the making of license plates to farming, with some skilled occupations in-between. Items created by prisoners could not move in interstate commerce and could only be for state use. Inmates or patients or retardates were paid a pittance. As recently as 1971, four cents an hour was a common wage in some institutions and ten cents an hour was positively generous. In addition, there were usually several available men for each available job creating and standardizing "goldbricking" as a way of working.

As early as 1913, Wisconsin tried to develop an alternative work release program for misdemeanants. Not until 1957, however, was the idea implemented when North Carolina pioneered in work release efforts. Professor Elmer Johnson was in North Carolina at the time, and as a matter of fact, was Assistant Director of the North Carolina Prison Department from 1958 to 1960 during the major thrust of the program. His "Work-Release—A Study of Correctional Reform" is therefore an inside report. Note the difficulties involved in introducing even an obviously impressive correctional policy change.

Another program, used also with deviants other than criminals, is the New Careers idea introduced originally in California and New York. The principle is excellent—use the reformed to reform. Their expertise is invaluable. They speak the same language, have experienced the same degradation and low self-esteem, and can use their insight for the benefit of both their clients and themselves.

The first of two pieces on the New Careers approach, pioneered by J. Douglas Grant and Milton Luger, is from the introduction to a monograph *Offenders as a Correctional Manpower Resource* published by the Joint Commission on Correctional Manpower and Training in 1968. The second article concerns the development of the New Careers approach since 1968. Various programs, in Alabama, Illinois, Oregon, and elsewhere, are recounted by Professor Joseph E. Scott and Pamela A. Bennett indicating the extent to which states have made it possible for ex-deviants to participate in the mental health and correctional process in the four years since the Manpower Commission Report of 1968. The Scott and Bennett article also briefly describes the use of former inmates as case aides in parole and the success they have had in the process. The most compelling point, we think, is that 86 percent of the prisoners studied would prefer an ex-con case aide to a regular parole officer.

THE PREVENTION OF HOSPITALIZATION IN SCHIZOPHRENIA:
Five Years After an Experimental Program

Ann E. Davis, Simon Dinitz, and Benjamin Pasamanick

In 1961 we initiated a study,

. . . designed to determine (1) whether home care for schizophrenic patients was feasible,

From *American Journal of Orthopsychiatry* 42 No. 3 (April 1972), 375—88. Copyright © 1972 by the American Orthopsychiatric Association, Inc. Reprinted by permission. Ann Davis is at Miami University, Simon Dinitz at The Ohio State University, and Benjamin Pasamanick is in the New York State Department of Mental Hygiene.

(2) whether drug therapy was effective in preventing their hospitalization, and (3) whether home care was, in fact, a better or poorer method of treatment than hospitalization.

To carry out this research program a facility known as the Institute Treatment Center (ITC) opened, near downtown Louisville, Ky., late in 1961.

The original study design included a home care group of patients placed on drugs, a home care group placed on placebos, and a control group treated in the usual manner by a course of state hospital care. The sample of patients was drawn from the State Mental Hospital serving the greater Louisville area and from the Louisville General Hospital. To insure that patients would be "sick enough" to be comparable with a hospitalized population, cases were selected from newly hospitalized patients. Requirements for patients' admission to the study were: (1) a diagnosis of schizophrenia, (2) age between 18 and 62, (3) no evidence of serious homicidal or suicidal tendencies (less than five percent, so judged largely at the outset of the study when the team was still inexperienced and fearful), and (4) a family willing to provide supervision and information on patients and family at home. Since a majority of the referred patients had families eager to admit patients to the home care study, few individuals were lost because families refused to cooperate.

After an initial screening by the ITC staff, patients were assigned, in random order, to one of the three study groups: the home care drug group (comprising 40% of the sample), the home care placebo group (30%), and the hospital control group (30%). Patients in both of the home care groups returned to their families under ITC supervision, whereas the hospital control went immediately to the State Mental Hospital for treatment.

The Institute Treatment Center operated as a facility of the State of Kentucky even though it was funded wholly by the National Institute of Mental Health. The personnel included a part-time psychiatrist (who began his employment while still a resident at the State Hospital), a sociologist as study director (who was a graduate student at Ohio State University), a clinical psychologist (with a Master's degree in psychology), a social worker (a job filled for the larger part of the study by the senior author of this paper), and five public health nurses (only one of whom had any training in mental illness). The most stressful problem of the

study resulted from the fact that staff members, including the psychiatrist, did not know which home care patients received placebo (inert) medications and which received combinations of drugs.

A major purpose of the drug, placebo, and hospital control grouping was to test the hypothesis that the professional and psychiatric facilities needed for patient care could be reduced by reliance on socio-supportive home care and a supervised drug regimen. Consequently, the psychiatrist saw the patients at intake, prescribed their medications, and then rarely saw them again until a six-month psychiatric reevaluation period, although constant interaction among team members occurred and nurses consulted with him about patient problems and care. In the interim, the public health nurse visited the patients' homes, delivered medications, gathered research data systematically by interviewing significant others, and gave family members practical assistance and support. The social worker helped secure patients for the study sample, and advised nurses on social and familial problems; she provided basic social work referral services to meet the social, health care, and economic needs of patients and families. The psychologist administered tests at regular intervals throughout the study, consulted with other staff members on difficulties encountered, and occasionally counseled patients. The public health nurses were the principal treatment agents: their regular home visits, indepth knowledge of the clients and families, and, most importantly, their relationships with them were the critical home care success ingredients.

At intake, and at regular intervals throughout the study, all patients were monitored on various psychiatric and social performance variables. These inventories and scales were also used in the follow-up study five years later. Basic instruments included: psychiatric inventory (Lorr IMPS), social problems checklist, domestic performance scale, and social participation index.

Two-and-a-half years after its inception the ITC study terminated despite the desire of the Kentucky State Department of Mental Health to retain it. Home drug treatment had proven feasible with schizophrenics:

Over 77 percent of the drug home care patients but only some 34 percent of the placebo cases remained in the community throughout their participation in the project.

Most of the failures occurred during the first six months of the study, again probably a result of inexperience and fear, since after that period only eight percent had to be hospitalized during the initial six-month period after intake.

In answer to the question of whether patients fared better under home care or in routine hospital care, the drug home care group held the advantage:

Even after initial hospitalization averaging 83 days and the presumable remission of the grosser symptoms, the hospital controls failed more often at the termination of treatment than did the home care patients.

In terms of hospitalization time saved, as well as on community performance, home care drug patients did better:

... patients improved in mental status, psychological test performance, domestic functioning, and social participation. These gains were considerable and frequently statistically significant. In all of the many specific measures, home care patients were functioning as well or better than the hospital control cases.

The experiment proved successful in demonstrating that florid episodes could be controlled at home and that chronic schizophrenic patients could be saved expensive days of hospital care, but it had to be stressed that patients continued to be marginal in routine daily task performances. We stated that, "... on the instrumental role performance level, some of the home care patients as well as some of the controls were still exhibiting low quality performances."

THE FOLLOW-UP (1964–1969)

Re-study plans were enhanced by a number of fortuitous circumstances. The original project social worker was available for, and interested in, an evaluation of the original program. Four of the original five project nurses had continued their employment with the Kentucky Department of Mental Health as community care nurses and had maintained contact with many of the patients. The psychiatrist, psychologist, and numerous other State Hospital personnel were still in the community, available to assist in a re-study as needed.

Hospitalization Experiences

The first question the follow-up dealt with was: had the impact of ITC care, which resulted in superior outcomes for the home care drug group, persisted after the project terminated? Analysis of follow-up data showed that there were no statistically significant differences among the groups (drug, placebo, and hospital control) on either the number of rehospitalizations, or on percentages of each group that were hospitalized. The drug group had averaged 125 days in the hospital in the post-ITC years, the placebo group 221, and the controls 136. In percentages, the drug patients averaged seven percent of their post-ITC time in the hospital, the placebo group ten percent, and the controls nine percent. Sixty-one percent of the drug patients were hospitalized over the follow-up, as were 57% of the placebo patients, and 61% of the controls. None of these differences were statistically significant. The placebo group, as a whole, spent more time in hospital after ITC care was withdrawn, since a large proportion of those who had been successful in remaining at home on public health nursing care failed soon after the program ended. This indicates that public health nursing care alone played a role in helping patients.

Clinic Care

There were also no statistically significant differences among the groups on the extent of clinic care received during the follow-up. The drug group averaged fifteen clinic contacts over the five year follow-up study, the placebo patients seventeen contacts, and the control patients fourteen. In terms of the amount of time spent under clinic supervision, the drug group spent 37% of the follow-up time under care, the placebo group 47%, and the controls 35%; again, these differences were not significant statistically. Although again, there was some indication that the placebo group suffered more from withdrawal of the special experimental program.

ITC Treatment Effects Over Time

In brief, ITC home care drug patients had a marked psychiatric adjustment advantage at the beginning of the follow-up (the end of ITC); this superiority was maintained for a brief time after ITC terminated and the drug patients remained out of the hospital longer than the placebo patients. The latter, in poorer psychiatric condition at the end of ITC, in large measure, had to be hospitalized soon after the experiment ended. Placebo patients also averaged longer periods of in-hospital care over the post-ITC period and were more likely to need, and hence attend, the out-patient clinics during the follow-up.

After ITC terminated, home care drug patients were better for a short while and placebo patients were worse for that same short period; the hospital control patients remained in an intermediate position. *However, by the time of the five year follow-up, no differences in hospital or clinic care treatment experiences could be found among the study groups; similar post-ITC care had equalized their demand for psychiatric attention.* * There is thus some indication that neither of the control groups, including those on placebos, had sustained any long-term damage as a result of their lower level of treatment during the original study.

Psychological Status

At the time of follow-up in 1969 there were no significant differences among the groups

*Editor's italics.

on their psychiatric status. The overwhelming evidence supported the hypothesis that the psychological condition of the patients in the drug, placebo, and control groups was not significantly different by the time of the post-ITC study. These results were congruent with findings on the hospital and clinic treatment experiences.

Social Adjustment

Problems that patients exhibited at home were closely related to their mental condition. The social problems checklist showed that the groups did not differ significantly from each other by the end of the follow-up.

Four single problem checklist items (out of a total of 22) showed the hospital controls to be significantly more problematic than the drug or placebo patients, yet the general findings supported the position that the groups were not significantly different from one another on the basis of problems they presented at home. This probably reflected, in part, the original finding that the control group was somewhat more disabled at the outset.

The Nature of Problems Behaviors

Rank ordering of problems revealed that the most frequently named items were intrapsychic in nature. For example, the significant others, spouses or relations (SOs), in all groups stated that they worried a great deal about the patient. These concerns were frequently elicited by bizarre speech, ideas, and actions expressed by patients. SOs were alarmed about the welfare of the patient, their households were disrupted, and the coping abilities of family members were frequently exhausted. The end result was that psychiatric attention was sought for, and subsequent relief sought from, the disordered patient by the family.

Vocational Performance

Data on vocational performance showed that the study groups did not differ from each other on economic or work related variables. Most patients had histories of unemployment or unemployability; those who had worked usually had exceedingly poor work performance records.

Only 27% of the drug group patients, 26% of the placebo patients, and 27% of the controls had any occupation, even that of common laborer. Many patients were among those considered too disabled to work, either mentally or physically; this was true of 28% of the drug group, 49% of the placebos, and 32% of the control patients.

Almost half the patients were the primary financial support of the family; their source of income was generally common labor or welfare. Placebo patients were more likely to be welfare recipients: they had qualified on the basis of mental disability. This situation was explained by their disproportionate needs for financial support dating back to the original ITC study when, because of drug deprivation during that period, they were more noticeably disabled. Their dependency upon welfare grants never changed in the ensuing years.

Domestic Performance

Task performance measures were not as revealing of the post-ITC adjustment of the patients as were hospitalization and clinic treatment measures. Performance variables were considered less of a measure of the patients' mental status than were the *hard data* treatment variables such as the number of hospital days or clinic days under care. Many social factors such as age, family expectations, and role demands impinged upon and altered patients' performances, making these variables less clearly related to psychiatric status of the patients. Nonetheless, a majority of the performance variables offered support for the thesis that no significant difference among the groups would be found five years after termination of the ITC home care program.

Controls showed a tendency to be consistently poorer, if only slightly so, in their performance: they entered ITC with poorer mental status reports, they tended to be poorer on the psychiatric reports during the follow-up, and their community adjustments were poorer.

LONGITUDINAL EVALUATION RESULTS

Psychiatric Status Over Time (1962–1969)

The placebo patients were the "sickest" group at the end of ITC. This was probably due to their drug deprivation during ITC. Once the project terminated, the patients given placebos sought psychiatric attention and received drugs from both hospitals and clinics. By the time of follow-up, the placebo group had markedly improved in psychiatric symptom scores compared to the home care drug patients. Once that care ended and the latter group, the drug patients, began to receive routine State outpatient clinic and hospital attention, their psychiatric status deteriorated somewhat, but never to the point that it had been at ITC intake. The placebo group had improved only minimally during ITC: it will be recalled that over 77% of the drug home care patients, but only 34% of the placebo patients, remained continuously at home during the ITC project. By the time of the follow-up, the drug group's better experience and functioning had eroded and the percentage of their life spent in the hospital did not differ from other groups. The effects of ITC had disappeared, leaving the three groups comparable.

Community Performance and Adjustment (1962–1969)

Community performance and adjustment results were similar to those received on the psychiatric scale and on the problems checklist. The worst scores were recorded at ITC intake, when all patients were experiencing psychotic episodes. All groups had shown a reduction in problem behavior by the end of ITC care. Such reductions were far more dramatic for the home care drug patients than for the placebo group; but by the time of the follow-up, in 1969, the drug group's functioning had deteriorated, thereby testifying to the superiority of ITC home drug care over routine State clinic care for assisting patients' psychological adjustment. Conversely, the placebo patients scores improved in the post-ITC period after receipt of State care because attention with drugs was markedly superior to ITC care without them.

Thus, the performance of the home care drug group supported the hypothesis of increased impairment after ITC ended, but the experience of the placebo group did not. The researchers had not predicted the placebo group's improvement once these patients received drug care in the post-ITC period.

Domestic Performance (1962–1969)

Patients in all groups deteriorated on task performances over time. The instrumental performance scores at follow-up were considerably *lower* (*worse*) than scores at either ITC *intake* or at the *termination of* ITC. Thus, post-ITC drug and other care did not save the placebo or other patients from increasingly poorer performances on routine task measures.

Task performance scores were not highly correlated with psychiatric treatment status. Reasons for this may lay, in part, in the advancing age of patients, which slowed adjustment capacities and task performance abilities. Also, as importantly, repeated negative labeling and a history of poor performance tended to lower both patients' and SOs' expectations and, therefore, patients' performances. Some patients, after many psychosocial breakdowns and treatment, no longer tried to perform routine household and vocational tasks. Patients severed their marital and family ties more than they created new ones, thus these instabilities also acted to reduce the necessity, and expectations, for adequate task performance.

Social Participation (1962–1969)

On the social participation measure, a majority, about 51%, of the patients in each of the three groups remained in status quo or decreased their activities once ITC ended. All groups showed poorer scores at follow-

up than at ITC intake on friendship patterns and interpersonal abilities.

The specific task performance measures, vocational, domestic, and social participation indicated, with rare exception, that patients did not improve over time in their performance but rather that their performances generally worsened. The only exception occurred in the placebo patients' improvement on behavior problems once they received drugs after ITC's termination. Considerable evidence was amassed showing the lack of impact of psychiatric care on patients' abilities to perform tasks and to participate in social activities.

SUCCESSES AND FAILURES

Having demonstrated that the study groups did not differ significantly from each other at the end of the five year follow-up, the analysis moved toward isolating the factors predictive of rehospitalization. The three original study groups—drug, placebo, and hospital control—were combined and then regrouped into two categories, successes and failures. Successes were defined as patients who avoided rehospitalization in the post-ITC period, failures as those who required hospitalization.

Demographic Characteristics

Failures could be differentiated in a statistically significant manner on only one of the demographic characteristics examined. They were less likely to be married at the time of the follow-up than were successes, probably more likely an effect of illness rather than cause. However there was also a tendency for patients with low social status, for women, and for blacks to predominate among the failures, possibly attributable to their lower social status.

Psychiatric Factors

The psychiatric scores produced the most significant differentials between successes and failures. Most scores including the total scale score, showed that the failures were significantly sicker, i.e., they had more severe symptoms than the successes over the follow-up period.

Problems Behavior

Almost as highly related to success and failure as the psychiatric inventory findings were the scores on the problems checklist. Over half of the individual problems checklist items, as well as the total score, showed the failures to be significantly more problematic than the successes.

Problems most frequently cited by SOs were those dealing with odd and bizarre behaviors, especially strange speech and ideation, as well as the resultant disorganization this behavior caused SOs and the entire household.

Hospital Histories Prior To and After ITC

The general conclusion was that, over the years from 1962–1969, pre-ITC hospitalization experiences were, at best, only slightly predictive of later success and failure but ITC and post-ITC experiences were highly predictive.

Clinic Data

Clinic attendance reports over the post-ITC period showed that failures were significantly more likely to have ever attended a clinic. In contrast, the amount of care utilized, i.e., the total number of contacts and the mean percentage of non-hospitalized time spent under clinic care, failed to distinguish significantly between the successes and the failures.

As attenders, both groups made use of clinic services in near equal degrees, but the major finding concerning clinics was that the two groups differed in the way they utilized the clinic and in the way clinic personnel responded to them. Higher percentages of successes attended clinic regularly and greater numbers of these patients and their families were cooperative with clinic personnel. As important, significantly more successes were taking their medication as prescribed.

The clinic's response to the cooperation of the successful patients was a program tailored to their needs; the interaction between successes and clinic personnel was positive. Again, it is possible to interpret this to indicate that, in part, the more cooperative patients were less ill, rather than as being a cause of their success.

Failures and their families, in contrast, were significantly less cooperative with the outpatient clinic's staff. The families of failures were beset by more problems than were the families of successes. There was also more psycho-pathology, as recorded by the clinic staff, among their family members. Significantly, only two percent of the failures were taking the prescribed stabilized dosage of medicine regularly, prior to their hospitalization. Clinic care evidently was not as well suited to the needs of the failures as to the needs of the successes. Failures were largely non-cooperative and difficult to manage; they made sporadic and poor use of clinic facilities. Staffs of the clinics, in turn, responded rather unenthusiastically toward them.

Precipitants of Hospitalization

Endogenous problems proved to be the most important single item differentiating failure from success in the post-ITC period. Surprisingly, interpersonal problems were comparatively more prevalent among successes and were not closely related to rehospitalization; also, economic stresses and other external social stresses such as death, job losses, and physical problems did not coincide with periods immediately preceding rehospitalization. In essence, psychotic episodes were not triggered by any immediate, apparent, or external (to the patient) difficulty. These episodes, despite the psychiatric literature, were seemingly attributable to endogenous factors with no visible external precipitants.

Economic, Domestic, and Social Variables

No significant differences were found between the successes and failures on domestic task performance or social participation scores. There was some evidence, however, that successful patients tended to be less dependent upon siblings, children, or parents. They were more likely to be employed, whether they were men or women patients, and they were slightly more competent in their task performances. Successes had fewer people available to substitute for them on their tasks when they failed to perform them personally. Recalling that successes were more likely to be married, note was taken of the interactive effects of better performance, preservation of the marital situation, and higher expectations that may have resulted in the modestly better performance of the successes. Failures, conversely, were more often unmarried, more dependent, less often working outside the home, and had more role replacements available to help them. The reverse of the expectation-performance cycle was operative for them. Seemingly, low performance fostered low expectations, which, in turn, reinforced the low expectations among failures and their families.

Marital and Interpersonal Relationships

It was noted throughout the study that failures were less likely to be, or remain, married. Clinic and hospital records, as well as interview data, suggested that they related more pathologically to the opposite sex, broke ties often with members of both sexes (probably because of psychopathology), and, after severing such ties, were more likely to live alone than were the successes.

COMMENTS ON THE NATURE OF SCHIZOPHRENIA

The data clearly pointed to schizophrenic recurrence and episodes as occurring without notable external precipitants. When a patient became disturbed, his ideation, perception, memory, speech, and actions became bizarre; actions became unpredictable. This, in turn, alarmed and threatened families, arousing fears concerning the well-being of the patients as well as that of the SOs and that of other members of the household. The data indicated that this configuration of

alarm, threat, and familial disorder led to the hospitalization of the patient.

Much of the disordered behavioral tendencies could be traced back in time in the patients' social histories. The patients' characteristic inabilities to perform routine tasks and to form meaningful interpersonal relationships were often noted in early adulthood, before the first psychotic episode and hospitalization.

These findings accord well with the most recent and strongest evidence that schizophrenia is a chronic disorder primarily genetic or congenital in nature, with precipitants not basically psychosocial in origin, but rather an organic process with still undetermined precipitants resulting in exacerbations and remissions of acutely unacceptable symptoms. It is these which interact on the psychosocial levels with family, interpersonal, and community activities, further exacerating both symptoms and relationships and eventually spiralling to socially unacceptable heights and leading to hospitalization.

THE TREATMENT OF SCHIZOPHRENICS

The course of the disorder from the time of the first treatment contact depended primarily upon the kind of treatment given and the extensiveness and intensity of the disease process. There is evidence in this study to show that patients with the more severe disorders tended to have the most difficulty throughout the many years of our research involvement with them. In essence, the severity of the disorder was fairly consistent over time.

Treatment intervention, if it included the psychoactive drugs, generally improved the patients' mental status and sometimes their task performances. Whenever the drugs were withdrawn, or the patients ceased taking medication, they were likely to experience other episodes and re-hospitalization despite supportive attention. The data in the initial ITC study and in the follow-up study demonstrated that drug care had to be maintained to minimize or prevent recurrent psychotic episodes.

Care, as given by most of the outpatient

clinics and by the State hospitals' aftercare clinics, failed to prevent rehospitalization because such facilities relied upon patient initiative for attendance and upon the patients' and families' cooperation and trust. Most importantly, the clinics depended upon the patients' willingness to be personally responsible for taking prescribed medications. Clinic personnel frequently assumed that discontinuation or decrease in drug dosage was proper and "wise" medical practice for the convalescing mental patient. When treating schizophrenics, these may be erroneous assumptions. Schizophrenia is largely a chronic disorder and the needs for medication may not, in fact, diminish.

Psychiatric clinics, like other medical facilities, operate on the assumption that patients are rational, responsible, and interested in improving their health status. This model simply does not apply for most disordered, disoriented, or psychotic patients. It may, however, apply to the usual type of patient seen in out-patient psychiatric clinics—the unhappy, anomic, neurotic and the psychophysiologic problem cases who are frequently middle class, well educated, and more likely to be self directing and oriented to personal problem solving.

If clinics are to play a major role in providing community care for schizophrenic patients, the laissez faire model and its assumptions will have to be replaced by an aggressive delivery system designed to deal with chronic, marginal patients, like the psychotics in this study and those who comprise the bulk of state hospital populations.

ITC probably succeeded for two basic reasons: first, drugs were taken to the homes by a nurse who urged the families to supervise the patients' taking of prescribed medications.* No patient was taken off medication because he was considered cured or sufficiently improved to be without drugs. Second, nurses went out systematically to the patients' homes. They did not allow the patient or relative to assume the initiative alone for the treatment contact,

instead they reached out to give the necessary care. In the homes, nurses interacted with the families and gave them much needed emotional support and practical problem-solving guidance. ITC, through social work services, also provided social referrals for help with health problems, job training, and financial aid, as well as with other social needs.

Taking the program to the family was necessary to stabilize the multi-problem families in which these schizophrenics were frequently a serious disorganizing factor. When left without supportive attention, families with sick patients whose episodes were recurrent, were likely to abandon the patients and, as our data clearly show, leave them living alone or in the homes of other than primary family members.

It is not claimed that daily routine task performance can be improved by a drug home care project. The data strongly suggest that task performance deteriorates over time even with the usual out-patient, or in-patient, care. The ITC home care project was successful in decreasing the numbers of patients who need assistance in performing their instrumental tasks. Such improvement took place even among the placebo patients who were not receiving medication. This led us to consider that entrustment with familial responsibility plus the expectation for performance may be necessary for the continued performance of domestic tasks. Following ITC however, with the resumption of routine State out-patient or State hospital care (such care excluded active concern with patients' task activities) the vast majority of the patients tended to deteriorate markedly in their daily functioning.

Similarly the employment and employability of the patients in the post-ITC period also deteriorated markedly regardless of the nature of the State's post-ITC treatment intervention. Data on social participation and, in particular, on patients' patterns of marital and interpersonal relationships were congruent with other community adjustment findings indicating increasing debilitation in the post-ITC period in social and interpersonal

*Editor's italics.

skills. Without aggressive home care, as given during ITC, the evidence is that routine community or hospital psychiatric care will not prevent, or significantly retard the deterioration of patients' performance and adjustment on domestic, vocational, social, and marital variables.

Medications are able to prevent, or at least delay, psychotic episodes. It remains for psychiatric or social care to prevent the social deterioration of patients. Rather than being integrated into community life, ex-mental patients withdraw, become increasingly "home bound," and essentially non-active; they are non-participants in the society of today. The unique contribution of this research may be in calling attention to the absolute necessity of continued mental health surveillance and community treatment of former hospital patients.

It is not an unreasonable possible assumption to make, that if ITC care had been continued, no deterioration in behavior of functioning would have occurred. It is even possible that if more intensive care—including day hospitals, sheltered workshops, hostels, and vocational, marital and personal guidance—were available, with respected and well-paid jobs as part of the program of community mental health care, as well as the other components described, total functioning might very well have improved instead of deteriorating or remaining constant.

Obviously, as responsible therapists or simply as citizens, we cannot help but respond to the necessity of assisting patients to become functioning members of society. Now that the drug revolution has managed to minimize the overt disruptions and acute evidence of psychoses, the even larger task of activating and reintegrating patients into the community waits to be accomplished as one of the new high priority social services for those rejected by society. Without such efforts, we have merely transferred the chronic institutionalized hospital patient to the back "wards" of his home and community.

THE HALFWAY HOUSE

Diane Vaughan

INTRODUCTION

Penology is in the midst of a new experiment. The realization that the prison is antitherapeutic has brought a redefinition of goals and methods for dealing with offenders using newer models of reintegration and resocialization. The subtle damage done the individual by institutionalization—loss of skills, deterioration of relationships and status outside the prison, the withdrawal, the alienation that grows as a response to coercion—must be muted by less severe, more humane action.

The move towards community-based cor-

From an unpublished manuscript on the Halfway House. Diane Vaughan is a Research Associate at the Academy for Contemporary Problems, Columbus, Ohio.

rections is an attempt to avoid the ill effects of incarceration. This new direction in corrections is based on the premise that crime and delinquency signify not only the failure of the offender, but the failure of the community as well. Rather than remove the offender from the community and isolate him, corrections is focusing on rebuilding ties between the offender and the community—to keep him in touch with the institutions of society responsible for developing law-abiding conduct.

Underlying this trend are two basic assumptions:

1. Since criminal behavior originates in the community, the community therefore must share the responsibility for dealing with it.

2. Changes within the institution cannot compete with environmental influences.

The first represents a return to the 18th century American concept of localism in dealing with deviance, amended by the additional responsibility of rehabilitation.

The second assumption has been confirmed repeatedly by research. The early work of the Glueck's on the backgrounds and criminal histories of 500 Massachusetts Reformatory inmates (1930) indicated 80 percent had not been rehabilitated. More recently, the work of Bailey (1966) assessing the effectiveness of 100 programs of institutional treatment proved there is nothing now being tried within the institution that is having any impact on recidivism. The data on the chronic offender from Wolfgang, Figlio, and Sellin (1972) confirm the criminal justice system's total ineffectiveness in changing behavior.

The logic is that if institutionalization is damaging, and if the offender can be kept in the community at no loss of public protection, then why not? It's more humanitarian, restorative potential is greater, and economically it is advantageous. The new model for corrections is mainly substantiated by the fact that almost anything will be an improvement on the past.

The National Advisory Commission on Criminal Justice Standards and Goals (1972) has a great deal of faith in the "new penology." "The Task Force considers community-based corrections as the most promising means of accomplishing the changes in offender behavior that the public expects—and in fact, now demands—of corrections." They recommend shorter sentences for less serious offenders and more selective use of imprisonment. Institutionalization should be reserved for those offenders whose repetitive, destructive behavior patterns seriously threaten the safety of the community.

For the majority of offenders, who offer less risk to the community, the Advisory Commission recommends extending the potential of the community as an agent of behavior change by:

1. diversion prior to sentence and trial
2. non-residential supervision programs in addition to probation and parole
3. residential alternatives to incarceration
4. community resources opened to confined populations, and institutional resources opened to the entire community
5. pre-release programs
6. community facilities for released offenders in the re-entry stage.

Within the broad approach of community-based corrections, the halfway house movement is only a minor component. Halfway houses exist as small residential facilities that function as an alternative to incarceration for the probationer and juvenile offender, as facilities for the gradual reintegration into the community of the parolee and the offender whose sentence has expired, and as pre-release centers for those still under custody.

They are diverse in atmosphere, program, staffing, funding sources, regulations and residents. They have sprung up almost accidentally, with no guidelines to their establishment. The result is a flexible kind of supplement to institutionalization, which is not institutionalized itself. The halfway house concept provides a softening aspect to the traditional idea of custody. It answers a current need. Though diverse in form, they are all tied together by uniformities that are significant; namely, the residential location, size, small group atmosphere, free interplay with the community, and lack of custodial trappings. And most important, the basic aim is the same: to provide a short, intensive, transitional experience between the totality of incarceration and the free world.

HISTORICAL BACKGROUND: CORRECTIONS

Halfway houses are not a result of 20th century genius. They originated in England and Ireland; the first evidence of a transplant into American consciousness appeared with the recommendation of a Massachusetts Prison Commission in 1817 that a temporary refuge be created to house destitute released offenders. Rehabilitation was not the intent. The purpose was only to provide lodging and give the ex-offender an opportunity to occupy himself at his trade. This legislative proposal was defeated 13 years later on the grounds that the ex-prisoners, coming in contact with each other, would become contaminated and reverse all the good accomplished by the silent and separate system of prison life. Forty years later Massachusetts did open a halfway house, the "Temporary Asylum for Discharged Female Prisoners," which "provided shelter, instruction, and employment for discharged female prisoners who are either homeless or whose homes are only scenes of temptation."

Meanwhile, the public was becoming aware of prison conditions, and volunteer organizations were devoting time to visiting inmates as evidence of the recognition of the need for contact between prison and community. Maud Ballington Booth, a social worker with the Volunteers of America, was a pioneer in the area of demonstrated prison concern. Realizing that many prisoners fall back into criminal habits because of lack of a place to go upon release, she established Hope Hall in 1890 with the aid of the inmates of Sing-Sing, who contributed $447 to the cause—representing 20,000 full days of hard work at prison wages. Hope Hall was a voluntary, homelike residence where ex-offenders could stay until they got a job.

Despite objections from the American Prison Association that they would create a permanent class of undesirable citizens and emphasize prison stigma, Hope Halls expanded across the country until the 1920's. With the coming of parole and the requirement that an offender must have a job before release, Hope Halls began to close. During the depression, when jobs were especially scarce for ex-offenders, a few Hope Halls were re-opened to relieve the backlog of parolees within the prisons. From the '30's to the '50's, halfway houses were introduced sporadically and were usually short lived.

The 1950's marked the beginning of a national halfway house movement. For the offender, the revitalization of the halfway house began through the church, St. Leonard's in Chicago founded by an Episcopal priest, Rev. J. G. Jones, Jr., in 1954, who was stimulated to action by his experiences as chaplain at the Cook County Jail. The same type background inspired Rev. Charles Dismas Clark, who named his halfway house in St. Louis after Dismas, the good thief who died on the cross next to Jesus. Dismas House was begun in an old public school, transformed into a homelike atmosphere; the staff consisted of a cook, a tailor, and a barber with criminal histories. At the end of the front hall hung an oil painting of Dismas on the cross, whom the residents referred to as the "number one con." Father Clark, to counteract the return to a criminal life style when job opportunities were not found, hired a trained job placement man to run a permanent employment office within the house.

In 1961, the late Robert F. Kennedy, then Attorney General, suggested the need for transitional facilities for young offenders, and funds were appropriated for the establishment of an experimental community program by the Bureau of Prisons. Consequently, three Pre-release Guidance Centers were opened to give residents a chance to complete their time prior to parole under minimum security. The centers were located in New York and Chicago and in commercially zoned areas rather than private residential neighborhoods. Residents were limited to those under 25 who were committed under the Federal Youth Corrections Act or to those below 18 under the Federal Juvenile Delinquency Act. These young men were assisted in dealing with their day-to-day problems and in finding employment. They learned to budget their money, and were allowed to visit their families. If rules were violated, they were sent back to prison.

Based on the success of this experimental program, the Prisoner Rehabilitation Act of 1965 extended the Pre-release Guidance Centers to adult offenders. This law authorized the Attorney General to commit or transfer prisoners to residential community treatment centers, to grant periods of unescorted leave under emergency or release preparations, and to authorize work release.

The centers base their programs on the need for easing ex-offenders back into the community, and the focus is on preparation for handling all the little details of everyday life that will rebuild the independence the institution destroys. The centers have a stronger coercive aspect than most halfway houses, because the residents realize they are on pre-parole status. The staff of the center play a part in recommending parole dates, and this unspoken power almost compels good performances. Negative sanctions available to staff are reprimands, restriction to the building or to the room, canceling of a weekend's visit, or temporary transfer to a local jail for a short detention. Major sanctions are return to prison and postponement of the original parole date.

STATUS OF THE MOVEMENT: MENTAL HEALTH, ALCOHOLISM, ADDICTION, CORRECTIONS

Before the '60's, aftercare services in corrections were held up because of lack of access to community resources supportive to the needs of the probationer or the parolee. Restricted agency intake policies giving priority to the non-offender were gradually broadened to offer a range of services to the offender group. For example, the Department of Labor now offers a manpower training service for offenders who are among the unemployed, plus an employment placement service. Private industry now offers employment to probationers and parolees, and community mental health services are beginning to organize programs to meet ex-offender needs.

In addition, certain ideological preconditions, born in the mental health area, came to be taken for granted in dealing with every type of deviant in the halfway house movement:

1. Emphasis on maintaining contact with the community.

2. Awareness of the monetary and psychological cost of institutionalization.

3. The difficulty of relearning social roles, once cut off from them.

4. Awareness of the shared responsibility of the family and society for the onset and treatment of emotional disorders.

5. Concepts of the therapeutic community and open unit.

6. Emphasis on use of therapeutic drugs, continuity of care, and aftercare services tailored to the needs of different groups at different stages of rehabilitation.

7. A revised interpretation of the meaning of deviancy.

8. The importance of the relationship between the deviant and non-deviant, which is a defining characteristic of the halfway house concept.

This base provided the springboard for the expansion of the halfway house as an accepted and promising way of dealing not only with offenders, but other types of deviants as well.

The mark of a good idea is how many times it is imitated. The halfway house idea has been modified to fit the needs of narcotic addicts, alcoholics, the mentally retarded, and the military offender.

In the pioneering area of mental health, the halfway house functions both as a transitional facility, where residents are trained in survival skills, such as shopping, bus-catching, preparing meals, etc., and as a long term sheltered living arrangement which enables the individual to be maintained in the community with supportive help.

There is an increased push now to increase the role of the halfway house in dealing with terminal placement. Many people are, in a sense, "excluded" from state hospitals, due to a growing tendency for the hospitals to discharge those who have received the "maximum treatment benefit"— regardless of prospects for success in the community. Others, who are in and out, may not be employable, either because they are unskilled, too old, or too disorganized.

In interviewing candidates, halfway house staff looks for (a) willingness and capacity to live in a group, (b) potential employability, and (c) ability to assume a reasonable level of responsibility for oneself. Length of stay is not usually limited.

The purpose of the program is to provide opportunities and assistance to help the resident establish independent living patterns and effective relationships. It is not meant to be a treatment program. In fact, its prime goal is to get rid of the "sick" or deviant image. Formal therapy sessions are avoided. The atmosphere is more one of a supportive boarding house. Any necessary treatment comes from outside the house.

Staff seems to develop in direct proportion to the money available, which means heavy use of nonprofessionals (frequently college students), usually under the direction of a social worker. In this area, personality characteristics are more important than credentials.

A recent approach to cope with the ever-present funding problem has been the organization of private nonprofit corporations that offer an extensive, community-wide program to provide specialized residential arrangements and the necessary supportive services. Transitional Services, Inc. in Pittsburgh is contracting with the county mental health and mental retardation board to provide residential service. At mid-1970, the program was operating a halfway house for the mentally ill and retarded, and 20 apartments housing 86 residents in two supervised buildings. This systems approach is also operating through Mental Health Recovery, Inc. in Belmont, California, and Rehabilitative Mental Health Services, Inc., in Santa Clara.

The justification for the use of the halfway house in the care of the mentally ill and retarded cannot be found in statistics concerning success or failure after release from the institution. Figures show that over one-third of the released mental patients return to the institution whether they live in a halfway house or in the community. Controlled studies actually haven't been done, and available data no doubt reflect eligibility and screening procedures. The argument

must rest on the improvement in the quality of life available and the economic advantage over institutionalization.

Halfway houses for alcoholics developed as did those for the mentally ill and the offender—as a response to stigma and its consequences. Public alcoholics are subject to much punishment and little treatment. Though they are ignored by the public, they are not ignored by the criminal justice system. The chronic alcoholic comes in contact with the criminal justice system on an average of five times a year, involving an enormous social cost. The existing institutions haven't really dealt with the problem. They have only further defined it.

The halfway house for alcoholics has two aims: (1) sobriety and (2) jobs, independence, and respect in the community. All strive for a family atmosphere. The location is frequently in a house, part of the YMCA, a hospital or a mission. Staff is usually a combination of ex-alcoholics and non-alcoholics, with heavy involvement of nonprofessionals. Two-thirds are privately operated, and the rest are unofficially connected with Alcoholics Anonymous. Programs vary, usually incorporating group therapy, counseling, vocational counseling, and AA meetings. A 1958 survey showed Antabuse (an aversive type drug) was part of the program in 35% of the houses. Some limit length of stay; some don't. The average stay is 90 days. The estimated rate of rehabilitation (with no hard data displayed) is 35%. Whether the halfway house succeeds at all in rehabilitating is open to conjecture.

This phase of the movement grew as a reaction to the bureaucratized response to homeless alcoholics. It has succeeded in offering an alternative to county workhouses, large uniform buildings, lists of restrictive rules, and impersonality. It also offers a cost advantage over processing alcoholics through the criminal justice system.

Perhaps the most striking of these recent adaptations of the halfway house idea are the residential centers for addicts, the first of which was Synanon, which opened in 1958. Synanon uses a radical approach which differentiates it from facilities for alcoholics, parolees, and the emotionally ill. Treatment is based on the belief that drug abuse is a symptom of a character disorder that results from faulty socialization. The character disorder must be treated by the re-socialization of the individual, with eventual re-entry into the community the goal.

But Synanon creates a new world from which its residents rarely graduate back into the community. Reintegration is a goal that is seldom achieved. Behavior change comes as a result of strong peer group pressure, tight organization, a strict honor code, and status system, an initial status stripping stage that cuts the resident off from family and community, a staff of former addicts, long residency, and a confrontation climate geared to force the addict to recognize his own infantilism.

The two dominant characteristics of Synanon are (1) that it creates a protective, quasi-permanent society that "hides" the former addict, and (2) residency is voluntary. It should not be classed as a halfway house, but rather a "quarter-way" house, or one that provides "permanent, sheltered, near-normal living for people with chronic disabilities who can never manage totally on their own."

Daytop Village was begun in New York in 1963 as a treatment center for convicted male addicts on probation. It was modeled after Synanon, and later, women were included in the programs. Here, too, the addict must regress to an infantile level. Great emphasis is placed on immaturity and dependency is encouraged. Through a step ladder approach, good behavior is rewarded with promotion and increased privileges within the Village, with a goal of re-building the self-image to the point where the individual can re-enter the community with new confidence, fostered through the program. Daytop does get offenders back into the community, so can be considered a viable halfway house model. Where Synanon does not make outcome data available, Daytop does, though due to low response rate on follow-up surveys, it is considered methodologically unsound.

Its biggest problem is one of retention. The number of "graduates," 1971, was 250. Average intake (1969–1971) was 500 addicts. Half drop out prior to completion of the program. A follow-up study, 1971, showed that half the dropouts that remained in treatment for at least six months remained drug free.

An experimental design was used in evaluating the success of the East Los Angeles halfway house, a temporary residence for felon parolees with a history of narcotics use. Located in a Mexican-American ghetto, the East LA house based its approach on the therapeutic community model. Mandatory group counseling sessions were held once a week to induce the group to assume responsibility for itself, and to use group pressures to enforce and set limits. Using nonresident parolees as the control group, follow-up covered the first year of parole. Success or failure was determined by opiate drug use, getting into serious difficulty, or return to prison. Results showed no evidence that the halfway house was effective in reducing drug use or further criminal activity.

The military has made special use of the halfway house concept. In dealing with the military offender, they have created a retraining facility as a transitional link between the military institution and active duty. There is a need to reassimilate the offender into a special society, the military, after the prison experience. The Correctional Training Facilities, as they are called, take on all the goals of the halfway house, without assuming the traditional means. A small group atmosphere in a home-like environment is not a part of the method, presumably because the type society that the offender is to return to is not of that nature. It is large, impersonal, efficient, and regimented, and so is the CTF.

The program at the CTF is characterized by intensive training in military fundamentals, close custodial supervision, crisis intervention on real problems, and treatment tailored to the individual. A significant feature of the program is the emphasis on motivational training. Clearly, behavior change is the goal. The final objectives are to return to duty the greatest number of well-trained soldiers possible, and to minimize the loss of military manpower resulting from confinement.

The military offender, however, is more than just a source of manpower; this group represents a salvageable segment of the civilian population. The problem of the military offender is not isolated within the military sphere. Permanent stigmatization and future sanctions in the community await the man who receives a dishonorable discharge. So, while the CTF is consistent with halfway houses in its concern with stigmatization, it differs in that its aim of reintegration centers on the military society, and not society at large.

Another innovation stemming from the halfway house idea is the creation of a special unit in a residential college dorm for the emotionally disturbed student. It provides a way of treating him without disrupting his life. By living in the special unit with a "normal" student, the student may remain in the university community, rather than accept the stigma of being sent home or to a hospital for inpatient care.

DEALING WITH THE EX-INMATE

There is as much variation among existing halfway houses for ex-inmates as there is between the correctional halfway houses and those for other types of deviants. The focus of the house is related to its sponsorship. If a religious organization is the sponsor, the atmosphere of the house conforms to the popular image of a helping hand offered, though the residents are not required to take part in religious observances as a price of admission, nor is denomination an admission requirement. When sponsored by a private individual, the house is a reflection of the director's personality. When run by a community aftercare agency, the residents rely heavily on casework services. The emphasis is on a professional approach to rehabilitation. When the government foots the bill, the strong point is not so much aftercare as it is a continuance of the correctional treatment of the offender.

Intake can be restricted by age, nature of the offense, a particular problem of the offender, or his status in the correctional process. For example, for admission to Crofton House, in San Diego, the offender must be a resident of Southern California and have a normal IQ. He can *not* be a habitual or professional criminal, a drug addict or pusher, a chronic alcoholic, an active homosexual, or a violent assaultive offender.

Treatment approaches can be indirect, or direct. If the house handles youthful offenders or probationers, it is oriented towards restructuring attitudes and behavior change. If it is geared to parolees, pre-releases, or furloughees, its emphasis is on schools, training programs, and employment. The approach that is taken may develop the house into a sanctuary, which transfers the dependency from the institution to the house and keeps the house from becoming the transitional instrument it is intended to be, or it can foster a rather uncomfortable atmosphere that pursues an outward thrust.

Because rehabilitation and reintegration are the primary aims, every house has some sort of direct treatment program. The importance of the treatment aspect within the total program varies from house to house. There are three basic group treatment approaches: group counseling, group psychotherapy, and guided group interaction.

Group counseling attempts to provide a supportive atmosphere for solving current problems, airing grievances, and generally reducing friction in the house. No special training is required to lead the sessions, and the meetings can easily be conducted by the house staff. The focus is on the current context in which the residents are operating.

Group psychotherapy requires a trained group leader. It emphasizes the individual within the group, and meetings consist of exploration of unconscious materials. Early childhood experiences are reviewed, and the group becomes a replica of the early family structure. In this regard, close contact among residents outside the sessions is discouraged.

The effectiveness of guided group interaction rests on the development of a group solidarity and the constant interaction of the group as an entity. Peer group pressure is used to impose conventional behavior. Group meetings are intensive and sometimes violent experiences.

Alvis House in Columbus uses a combination of group counseling sessions, milieu or group living, and individual counseling. Group meetings are used to solve day-to-day problems, review group responsibilities, and for discussion of problems brought up by outside speakers. Attendance at group meetings is mandatory, but participation is not required.

In an effort to measure the effectiveness of these treatment methods, researchers conducted interviews with house staff and residents. The residents felt very strongly that the group meetings were not beneficial to the rehabilitative process. No resident stated that he felt he had ever been helped by the group sessions. Residents complained that there was a lack of two-way communication, and that the atmosphere of the house was authoritarian. This was contradictory to the way the staff viewed the situation. The milieu treatment was assessed as not living up to its potential as a rehabilitative force, and individual counseling which the residents felt was important, was infrequently given.

In a study of Criswell House, an alternative to a training school for adjudicated delinquents with a heavy emphasis on school and guided group interaction, Flackett and Flackett state:

It may be asking a great deal to expect a boy to sustain these new found abilities when he no longer has the support of his group. Thus no matter how excellent the program, it cannot go alone. Without considerable expansion of opportunities in the community, and a more acceptable attitude on the part of the public, successful reintegration will be limited.

Halfway houses have pursued this expansion of opportunities into the community as a part of their rehabilitation and reintegration efforts. Of specific note is the Notre Dame Youth Center, Gary, Indiana. The NDYC offered rehabilitation to youthful reformatory parolees in the way of vocational education, a well-paying job with Inland Steel Corporation, and a place to live under minimum supervision, plus (the ever-nebulous) supplemental services.

A pre-release training program within the institution prepared the individuals who were accepted into the program for life in a union-oriented industry. While working for Inland Steel, they lived among the other tenants in a section of the Knights of Columbus Hotel in downtown Gary. Though provided with job and shelter, the recidivism rate was identical to those paroled but not accepted into the program.

This emphasis on success or failure is a dead-end street. The halfway house neither rehabilitates nor reintegrates. Much goes on in the way of treatment, despite the fact that nothing that has been done to date has been proven effective. True, there are some individuals who seem to be self-correcting. But the majority of offenders are resistant to behavior change.

In sum, evaluation of the halfway house on the basis of goals of rehabilitation and reintegration is unfair. We should not ask so much. If, in spite of the negative evidence of the effectiveness of institutions they have been let stand, then the halfway house shouldn't be held to a higher standard. It should be given a chance to prove itself on the basis of need. Far better to look at it as an extension of the social welfare world, rather than the correctional process. In line with this, emphasis on behavior change should be dropped and money currently going in that direction should go to other areas, for instance the development of permanent halfway house residences in the community for the older offender who keeps committing crimes to get back into prison simply because he has nowhere else to go. The halfway house program is justified on the basis of humanitarianism and cost advantage. Empey warns against repeating the mistake of the past and equating humanitarianism with treatment. Humane care of offenders is not necessarily the same thing as reducing crime. But there is value in accepting a thing for just what it is—a kinder thing to do.

WORK RELEASE—A STUDY OF CORRECTIONAL REFORM

Elmer H. Johnson

Reform is not a rational and deliberate process. It moves, instead, through a series of accommodations whereby relationships between groups within a system are recast in a new form presumably more suitable for solutions of the problem stimulating the reform effort. The ultimate nature of the new accommodations is not predictable when the movement is initiated because the change-agents do not control the other groups and probably do not realize all the ramifications of the problem. Originally they may have had a relatively narrow and short-range l goal—to alleviate an immediate problem—which did not take into account the complex interdependence and the many factors affecting the condition they wanted to change.

Usually innovation in correction has come from outside an agency. The reform group tries to arouse public interest and establish a public issue. The emotionalism engendered makes the impact of the reform spasmodic and rather diffusive. Correctional reform differs from other kinds of reform in that its advocates generally are not drawn from the prisoners, who presumably are the major beneficiaries of any change. The reformers are unlikely to have training in criminology. Consequently, they are vulnerable to resistance in the guise of arguments based on costs of reform, administrative practicability, and so on.

Reform induced from within the correctional agency is much more likely to become a permanent part of administrative practice. Since the administrators are part of the environment to be revised, they are less likely to be dissuaded by false arguments raised against the change. The insights gained in the process of change awaken the innovators to needs and potentialities previously unrealized.

Readiness is a prerequisite to agency-stimulated change. It implies a willingness to accept innovation in two senses: possession of the necessary resources to undertake innovation and eagerness to break with tradition and accept new ideas. The motivation for change usually is stimulated by the very lack of the resources cited in the first instance.

Three sources for an eagerness to break with outmoded traditions are suggested by Likert and Lippitt: problem sensitivity, an image of potentiality, and a general experimental attitude toward innovation. Sharp increases in workload and prison disturbances are likely to bring administrations to the point of dissatisfaction with current conditions, but readiness to undertake fundamental reform requires more than just problem sensitivity. Administrators must envisage any possibilities for improvement latent in the immediate situation. Usually, willingness to try unorthodox solutions to familiar problems is inhibited by the community's stress on its protection against criminals and its trust in standard procedures.

Organizational change stimulated by the prison administration involves three separate but interrelated groups in its accommodative process: (1) the other public and private institutions that are involved in the particular area of criminology to undergo change, (2) the prison employees, and (3) the inmates to be affected by the change.

WORK-RELEASE AS AN APPLICATION OF CHANGE

Economic factors have been important barriers to correctional reform. Opposition to prisoner labor by industry and labor unions killed the industrial prison of earlier decades and diverted recent expansion of prison enterprises toward state use. The size of prison

From *Crime and Delinquency* (October 1967), pp. 521–30. Reprinted by permission of the National Council on Crime and Delinquency. Elmer Johnson is Professor of Sociology at Southern Illinois University.

production has been restricted, raising the marginal costs of production and subverting opportunities to employ substantial numbers of prisoners. Prison industries do not offer the prisoner the economic incentives of free society. Work-release programs offer one solution to the economic problems of the contemporary prison.

This paper will examine patterns found in the administration of work-release by the North Carolina Prison Department and Board of Paroles; it will analyze data derived from records of 2,886 males placed on the program from 1957, when the concept was introduced, through 1963. All cases were terminated at the time data collection was completed in the spring of 1966. The inclusion of felons and the number of prisoners placed on work-release make North Carolina's program a pioneer effort.

Table 17.1 presents the major patterns of our data. During its first four years, the North Carolina program included few cases, selected with extreme caution. In each of the three years that followed, the number of prisoners selected for work-release privileges at least doubled over the previous year's because new legislation extended the program to a broader range of the prison population and correctional authorities increased their efforts to utilize the approach. As the rate increased so did the number of failures and aborted cases (those removed from the program before release from prison because of loss of job, medical problems, death, detainers, or loss of work-release quarters as a result of prison renovation). With the exception of a slight upturn in 1963, the parole rate for work-release prisoners declined as more of them were given outright discharge.

Table 17–1. Male work-release prisoners, by year placed on program and type of termination

Type of final termination	1957–60		1961		1962		1963	
	No.	%	No.	%	No.	%	No.	%
Success								
Discharged	37	33.6	90	40.4	356	43.0	768	44.5
Paroled	45	40.9	69	30.9	152	18.4	325	18.8
Success total	82	74.5	159	71.3	508	61.4	1,093	63.3
Failure								
Violation of internal system	0	–	2	0.9	16	1.9	15	0.9
Results of half-free status	5	4.6	3	1.3	30	3.6	50	2.9
Drunkenness or drug use	5	4.6	25	11.2	58	7.0	129	7.5
Unauthorized absence	6	5.5	12	5.4	65	7.8	87	5.0
Escape, sentenced	4	3.6	12	5.4	71	8.6	147	8.5
Escape, not sentenced	0	–	0	–	3	0.4	13	0.8
Failure total	20	18.3	54	24.2	243	29.3	441	25.6
Aborted								
Lost job	7	6.4	8	3.6	43	5.2	120	6.9
(a) Job terminated	(6)	(5.5)	(5)	(2.2)	(22)	(2.7)	(58)	(3.7)
(b) Complaint on behavior	(0)	()	(2)	(0.9)	(5)	(0.6)	(24)	(1.4)
(c) Unsatisfactory job	(1)	(0.9)	(1)	(0.4)	(16)	(1.9)	(38)	(2.2)
Inmate's request	0	–	1	0.4	16	1.9	35	2.0
Medical (including death)	1	0.9	1	0.4	13	1.6	30	1.7
Detainer	0	–	0	–	3	0.4	6	0.3
Lost housing	0	–	0	–	1	0.1	1	0.1
Aborted total	8	7.3	10	4.4	76	9.2	192	11.0
Totals	110	100	223	100	827	100	1,726	100

The major failures included "walkaways" (unauthorized absences plus escapes) and those getting drunk. The brief period of freedom in the community while at work afforded opportunities for forms of misconduct not available to other prisoners.

ACCOMMODATIONS TO THE EXTERNAL SYSTEM

The prison as a social system represents a complex of relationships between groups and individuals. In urban society, correctional reform means restructuring the relationship of the correctional agency to those organizations in the total cultural setting involved in the particular sphere of criminology to undergo change. The reformers must persuade other organizations to support the program.

Bernard points out the community planning requires a certain degree of consensus even when it is opportunistic. Opportunism probably is a major element in correctional reform; however, it is not the only element. The very environment of the problem often generates sufficient consensus among other organizations to support the correctional agency in its endeavor. Another factor would be some chance experience by a member of the power structure which aroused interest in the particular strategy of change.

If change is to be significant in the institutional relationships of the system external to the prison *per se,* changes are necessary in the power structure and culture of that system. Lewin has suggested that a change in methods of leadership is probably the quickest way to effect change because the status of leaders make them the key to the ideology and organization of the group.

The introduction of work-release in North Carolina fits the described characteristics. First, the increase in prisoner population and operating costs created consensus among other organizations. Concurrently, the State Highway and Public Works Commission experienced increased costs for highway construction. Greater mechanization in maintenance had made the use of unskilled prisoner labor less feasible, thus undermining the basis upon which the county work camps had been merged with the state prisons under the Highway Commission in 1933. After separation of the prisons from the Highway Commission in 1957, pressure increased to end diversion of highway funds to support correctional agencies. Although prison enterprises were expanded, resistance from the private sector restricted this strategy even though the state's constitution required all penal institutions to be as nearly self-supporting as possible. At the same time, authorities were trying to improve the quality of rehabilitation programs. Finally, while use of prisoners for highway maintenance required the dispersion of prisoners in relatively small prison units throughout the state, relatively little capital investment was required to have work-release prisoners at locations accessible for employment in the state's urban labor markets.

Second, the state's interest in work-release was stimulated by a popular magazine article on Wisconsin's Huber Law. At the suggestion of Governor Luther Hodges (later Secretary of Commerce under President Kennedy), William F. Bailey, prison director, and V. L. Bounds, then assistant director of the Institute of Government, University of North Carolina at Chapel Hill, inspected Wisconsin's day-parole program. A bill based on their report was drafted for the 1957 General Assembly by a committee of government officials, chaired by the prison director.

Third, opportunism was an element because the economic problems described above stimulated an immediate and expedient interest in work-release which led to prompt action without awaiting the long-term development of resources to use work-release as a genuine rehabilitative tool.

ESTABLISHING THE PROGRAM

The governor appointed a special committee, which included the commissioner of public welfare, the chairman and a member of the parole board, a representative of the attorney general, and a representative of the Institute of Government. The committee consulted the superior court judges and obtained support from all but one. The search for a consensus among special interests brought forth a variety of justifications for work-release, not necessarily consistent with one another.

Persuading the General Assembly to enact legislation was successful largely because the committee members were leaders with special competency and power in agencies active in matters germane to work-release and because the superior court judges supported the proposal. However, the first work-release statute restricted eligibility to misdemeanants whose previous prison sentences were less than six months and who were recommended for work-release by the sentencing court. In the first two years only sixteen inmates were recommended by the sentencing courts, and half of them were unable to find suitable employment. Subsequently, the statute was liberalized to include felons and to empower the Board of Paroles and the Prison Department to extend the privilege to prisoners who had not been recommended by the sentencing judge. Two major trends developed (see Table 17.2). First, the larger share of approved cases have been handled without a recommendation by the court at time of sentencing, although the court is consulted. Second, the courts are learning to use work-release, as indicated by

increased referrals by courts other than the superior courts.

Parole officers also had to adjust to the new program. Over the years, paroles represent a smaller share of work-release cases successfully terminated (Table 17.1) as more prisoners received outright discharge. Misdemeanants, with sentences usually too brief to justify parole, assumed a larger share of yearly total admissions, increasing progressively from 59.1 percent in 1957–60 to 72.9 percent in 1963. For felons the proportion of successful cases which were paroled declined consistently from 87.5 percent to 63 percent; for misdemeanants, the consistent decrease was from 34 percent to 16.2 percent.

THREE MAJOR PATTERNS

Three major patterns occur in the recruitment of prisoners for work-release. Some retain their preconviction jobs under work-release because their skills are important to the employer and they are reliable workers. Others are given jobs by friends or members of their family as a means of alleviating prison confinement. Those in the third group obtain work-release employment after being imprisoned.

The use of work-release depends largely on the demand-supply relationship in the local labor market and the receptivity of employers, co-workers, and, in some cases, clients of the particular enterprise. The suc-

Table 17–2. Type of sentencing court, by number of inmates recommended for work-release

Type of sentencing court Recommending work-release	1957–60 No.	1957–60 %	1961 No.	1961 %	1962 No.	1962 %	1963 No.	1963 %
Superior	31	66.0	46	64.8	135	37.6	232	27.4
Mayor's	8	17.0	13	18.3	131	36.5	243	28.7
County recorder's	4	8.5	5	7.0	50	13.9	178	21.0
Justice of peace	0	–	0	–	0	–	11	1.3
Domestic relations	4	8.5	7	9.9	43	12.0	183	21.6
Total court recommendations	47	100	71	100	359	100	847	100
Total prisoners on work-release	110		223		827		1,726	
Percentage of all work-release cases recommended by court		42.7		31.8		43.4		49.1

Table 17-3. Occupational classification of major jobs held by work-release prisoners, by year placed on program

Occupational Categories	1957–60		1961		1962		1963	
	No.	%	No.	%	No.	%	No.	%
Construction	35	32.1	101	45.5	264	32.4	561	33.0
Manufacturing	29	26.6	38	17.1	185	22.7	326	19.2
Auto Services*	16	14.7	23	10.4	80	9.8	201	11.8
Miscellaneous Services	11	10.1	34	15.3	182	22.3	436	25.6
Retail	9	8.3	8	3.6	37	4.5	44	2.6
Farming	6	5.5	7	3.1	49	6.0	57	3.3
Logging	3	2.7	11	5.0	19	2.3	77	4.5
Total	109	100	222	100	816	100	1,702	100
Unclassified	1		1		11		24	

*Garages, car washes, gasoline stations.

cess of a work-release program rests upon the variety and level of skills available among prisoners, the quality of vocational training provided by the prison, the degree of correlation between the job skills taught and the kinds of skills in demand in the free community, the prisoners' attitudes toward work and discipline, and their receptivity to the idea of supporting themselves and their dependents while a prisoner.

The majority of North Carolina prisoners were employed in construction, manufacturing, auto services, and other services such as highway labor, restaurants, warehouses, brick and concrete plants, steel suppliers, salvage operations, feed mills, and so on. (See Table 17.3.) Increased employment for highway labor was a major trend. Retail establishments, farming, and logging were of minor importance.

Generally, employment was at the un-skilled level, where income is low and job tenure uncertain (Table 17.4). With expansion of the work-release population, skilled jobs declined consistently. Although all occupational groups included skilled workers, the largest share came from construction trades, manufacturing machine operators, and automobile mechanics. The skilled prisoners were the most likely to retain jobs held before conviction. The number of such prisoners was insufficient to sustain the previous percentage of skilled among all work-release prisoners as the program expanded. The sharpest increase in average number of jobs held in 1963 (the year of maximum population) was in those occupations providing the bulk of the skilled workers: construction, manufacturing, and automobile services. The increased turnover rates for these occupations reflected the influx of unskilled workers.

Table 17-4. Level of skill required by major job performed by work-release prisoners, by year placed on program

Level of Job Skill	1957–60		1961		1962		1963	
	No.	%	No.	%	No.	%	No.	%
Skilled	44	40.4	68	30.6	211	25.9	263	15.5
Semiskilled	21	19.2	54	24.3	142	17.4	315	18.5
Labor	44	40.4	100	45.1	463	56.7	1,124	66.0
Total	109	100	222	100	816	100	1,702	100

The rise in the rate for aborted cases (Table 17.1) indicates the increased problems of assuring steady employment of a larger inmate population after the program is routinized. Experience with Wisconsin's Huber Law has shown that lack of available employment and the extra workload placed on jail personnel were the most important reasons for limited application of the law. Although work-release was introduced under the belief that the Prison Department would not serve as an employment agency, the loss of jobs and the desire to expand the program soon involved prison employees in a variety of formal and informal efforts to find jobs.

The data show loss of job was the major source of premature termination. The bulk of lost jobs reflected the irregularity of employment found in seasonal occupations. Employers rarely fired employees because of unsatisfactory job performance.

The increased rate of terminations at the inmate's request calls attention to the problem of motivating prisoners to support their dependents and themselves. Medical cases (illness, injury, and death) involve the prison in matters of workman's compensation, responsibility for providing medical treatment, and allocation of responsibilities between the employer and the Prison Department. Of minor importance were removal from the program for detainers and loss of prison housing.

Major reliance on work-release as an economic base for the prison requires accommodation to the free community's labor market. However, possibilities of accommodation are limited if the existing job skills and attitudes of prisoners are taken as a constant. The limitation does not mean that work-release cannot be used effectively. In fact, our data indicate that the prisoner population includes a larger share of motivated and employable prisoners than one might anticipate.

ACCOMMODATIONS WITHIN THE INTERNAL SYSTEM

Work-release leads to new relationships within the prison's social system. The half-free status of prisoners undermines traditional controls based on coercion. The prison has a stake in success of work-release economically and psychologically. The prisoner gains a modest degree of power because he can opt to refuse work-release privileges and because his behavior on the job colors public attitudes. Furthermore, the employer becomes a third party in the prisoner-official relationship. Continuation of work-release rests, to a major degree, on the belief of the employer that he can rely on it as a steady source of workers. Interruptions of work schedules are not likely to make him sympathetic to punishments that deny him the services of workers. Standardization of work hours and restrictions on the physical movement of prisoners in the community may conflict with needed flexibility in the use of employees. Humanitarian sympathies and work demands may cause an employer to condone infraction of prison rules. Such conflicts of interest are fertile ground for inmate manipulation. However, even without deliberate manipulation by employer or prisoner, the half-free status creates circumstances not amenable to clear-cut interpretation within the formal and informal norms of the prison's traditional social system. In this unprecedented situation, what is the correct response to the inmate's explanation that he missed the prison bus because he worked overtime?

Table 17.1 reveals that rule violations were more a product of accommodation to the half-free status of work-release inmates than a threat to the internal security of the prison or the security of the free community. The half-free status permitted the prisoner to receive visitors at the place of work, presented opportunities for difficulties with employers or fellow employees, opened the way to traffic violations and drunkenness, and so on. The decline of the infraction rate from the 1961 high suggests the possibility that prison employees have developed some tolerance for such infractions in doubtful situations.

"Escape" is defined as a "walkaway" which resulted in referral to court for trial; it rose from a rate of 3.6 percent of 1957–1960 admissions to work-release to 9.3 percent of 1963 admissions. Wisconsin's program had eight walkaways per 100 Huber Law prisoners in 1960. "Unauthorized absence" is a walkaway handled as a rule violation. Because of legal obscurities, the courts acquitted several work-release prisoners charged with escape. Uncertainty of officials encouraged many work-release prisoners to believe they were immune to prosecution. Furthermore, local officials were uncertain concerning policy on a walkaway that was not an outright escape. The net result was the 1962 upsurge in the rate of walkaways followed by a decline in 1963 after a clarification of the legal and policy matters. All factors considered, the rates for walkaways and rule infractions are not excessive.

Traditionally, the handling of prisoner workers has followed one of two methods. The "threat" system relies on punishment for failure to meet a quota or to maintain a minimum work pace. The "exchange" system offers certain privileges to those inmates who assume individual responsibilities as clerks, "dog-boys," and skilled or semiskilled workers. Sykes has delineated the "defects of total power" which subvert both systems as means of controlling prisoners.

Work-release offers the possibility of developing a "motivational" system approaching that of the free community. Theoretically, the prisoner is prepared psychologically for the day he will assume the inner discipline necessary in the free world. Since he is usually housed paart from other prisoners and experiences daily interaction with nonprisoners, he is less likely to be subjected to the antirehabilitative inmate social system.

If the new motivational system is to be integrated into institutional practice, the prison must direct its internal social system toward a cultural environment congenial to using the half-free status as a new inmate role. It must provide greater opportunities for the inmate to express his preferences in a process of learning and testing new modes of adjustment. Change in inmate roles means there must be concurrent modification of reciprocal roles by prison employees. The new system will demand discretion in responding to the individual situation. One of the strengths of the work-release concept is that it encourages the expression of latent attitudes as raw material for a new form of organizational relationships.

Lasting correctional reform is more likely when it is stimulated from within the action agency and when it follows a pattern of accommodations among the groups making up both the external and internal systems of which the prison is a participant. Work-release is an example of a new element introduced into a configuration, thereby making possible previously unworkable patterns. The accommodations incidental to implementation of the concept have illustrated how new forms of interaction emerge through the adjustments of various parties. What appears to the rational mind as haphazard reactions to immediate situations may be a search for new bases for compatibility of prison goals within society as a whole.

INTRODUCTION TO OFFENDERS AS A CORRECTIONAL MANPOWER RESOURCE

Keith A. Stubblefield and Larry L. Dye

In carrying out its mission to make a thorough analysis of the manpower shortage

From Joint Commission on Correctional Manpower and Training, pp. 1–3. Keith Stubblefield was Task Force Director and Larry Dye was Research Assistant on the Joint Commission on Correctional Manpower and Training.

in American corrections and suggest ways of meeting it, the Joint Commission on Correctional Manpower and Training has perforce given attention to the ways in which corrections has used—and perhaps might better use—offenders and ex-offenders as manpower for the correctional system.

For many decades, the adult correctional institutions of the country have relied on inmates to do much of the maintenance work around the prison. In some cases they have been used as custodial workers. A good many institutions have drawn on the pre-commitment skills of inmates by using them to teach other prisoners, act as clerks, and the like.

A survey of institutions made by the Joint Commission in 1967 revealed that both adult and juvenile facilities are now using offenders, ex-offenders, and persons on parole or probation in teaching academic and vocational programs, leading recreational and rehabilitation programs, helping with research projects, interviewing new inmates, and leading pre-release programs.

In the past, as a general rule, corrections has used offenders in prison work mainly because maintenance and operating funds were scarce or workers were hard to hire from the outside. The new rationale is that offenders have something to offer other offenders which can never be provided by staff who have not themselves been involved in crime and delinquency. At the Kansas State Penitentiary in Lansing, for example, selected inmates conduct a regular program for juvenile delinquents. Problem boys are brought to the prison for weekly sessions with these inmates, with judges, probation officers, and other persons connected with the administration of justice to impress upon the youngsters the inevitable consequences of crime. The California Youth Authority transports confined youthful offenders to a facility for younger offenders and uses them in rehabilitation programs. The Draper Correctional Center in Alabama has developed an educational service staffed largely by offenders.

Some ex-offenders are now being used as paid staff members of correctional facilities. Halfway houses such as St. Leonard's House and St. Anthony's Inn in Chicago are managed and staffed by ex-offenders. The Teen Council of Vienna, Virginia has an ex-offender working with pre-delinquent youth in group therapy and psycho-drama sessions.

A newspaper reporting the election of the new president of a state wardens' association states that he "makes no secret of the fact that he once served time for a holdup. He says the mistake he made has helped him to assist others who have broken the law." In South Carolina, where the Department of Corrections has employed ex-offenders, the director said, "It is our feeling that, if we truly believe in the rehabilitation of the offender, we must be willing to back this up in a very real way by utilizing the inmate's training and skills through discriminating job placement within the correctional field."

THE NEW CAREERS CONCEPT

The concept of using the products of a problem to help solve the problem is not new. "Each one teach one" was a cornerstone of the method developed by Dr. Frank Laubach to help reduce illiteracy. For many years, Alcoholics Anonymous has brought former alcoholics to the aid of persons struggling to become abstainers. More recently, Synanon and several other programs have been involving ex-addicts in helping narcotic addicts to rid themselves of the habit.

A related concept is that of developing new kinds of permanent jobs—new careers—for the poor. Pearl and Riessman declare that unless such job development and related changes take place, we shall have "a permanent, stable 'nonworking' class, whose children and grandchildren will be unable to perform meaningful functions in our society." The authors propose methods of training the poor to perform a wide variety of services, mainly public services.

Still another consideration is the growing need for services for which there obviously will not be enough professionals available in the coming decade. The need for rehabilitation services in corrections is a prime example. Under present regulations, most of these services must be provided by professionals, or at least by persons with a college degree. In many settings, one of two results may be observed. Either the professionals are so overloaded that they cannot be effective, or only a superficial attempt is made to provide services at all.

NEW CAREERS IN CORRECTIONS

All these concepts have implications for the use of offenders as manpower in corrections. Here are men, women, and youth whose background enables them to serve fellow offenders effectively. Many of them can be trained to provide services for which corrections now lacks professionally trained personnel. And their period of training can contribute to their own rehabilitation.

In an effort to initiate systematic study of the potentials of "new careers" for offenders, the National Institute of Mental Health in 1963 sponsored a conference on the use of the products of a social problem in coping with the problem. The problem selected was crime and delinquency. Correctional administrators, social scientists, offenders, and ex-offenders discussed experiences in the employment of offenders in a variety of programs, ranging from data-processing to the prevention of delinquency.

An outgrowth of this conference was NIMH sponsorship of a demonstration, the New Careers Development Project. The goal of the project was to build a participation model which would merge the resources of the professional with those of offenders in the field of social change and development.

The project was designed to form a series of "change and development teams." The team would include professionals and offenders. The latter would be trained in skills which are of value in helping professionals complete the various tasks necessary to bring about change. A vital component of the program was the linking of the training program with meaningful employment opportunities, in both corrections and other public services.

Eighteen inmates of adult correctional institutions in California were selected for the project. Half of them had been convicted of armed robbery; more than half had previously been confined in juvenile institutions.

While still confined, they went through an intensive four-month training period. Then they were released to jobs involving the development of "new career" positions for nonprofessionals in social agencies or the training of nonprofessional aides. These trainees have continued to work and have advanced in competence and in level of responsibility. Their salaries now range from $7,200 to $15,000 a year. Only one of the eighteen committed a new offense and was reconfined.

Obviously more needs to be done in the way of systematic programming to draw together experience in the use of offenders and the growing body of technical knowledge about their use as correctional manpower. The papers which follow illustrate some fairly well conceptualized and demonstrated ways to proceed. What is most needed now is a climate which encourages experimentation and innovation.

OBSTACLES IN THE WAY

Such a climate will not be easy to achieve. The Joint Commission's surveys show that about 40 states have either statutory or administrative prohibitions against the employment of probationers or parolees by state agencies. In 33 states there are restrictions on state employment of an ex-offender who is completely free of legal supervision. (as of 1968. Many states have since removed these restrictions.) Ed.

Of the 422 local probation and parole agencies surveyed, nearly three-fourths (72 percent) are prevented from hiring a person with a felony record; and the same proportion are prevented from employing probationers and/or parolees.

Not only regulation but public opinion about offenders and ex-offenders will stand in the way of wide employment of "new careerists." A survey of public opinion conducted for the Joint Commission by Louis Harris and Associates found that the general public, while aware of the difficulties faced by the ex-offender in re-entering the free community, is reluctant to have much personal contact with him and doubtful of his potential in anything but a menial job.

Still more substantial as barriers to New Careers programs are likely to be the attitudes of correctional personnel. A survey of these attitudes, to be published by the Joint Commission in the near future, shows that half of the national sample of correctional personnel interviewed felt that it would not be a good idea to hire ex-offenders in their agency. The greatest resistance to the idea came from line workers (guards) in correctional institutions; nearly three-fourths of them rejected it. The greatest support came from the top administrators of juvenile institutions; nearly 60 percent of them endorsed the idea.

BACKGROUND AND DEVELOPMENT OF THE USE OF EX-OFFENDERS IN OHIO

Joseph E. Scott and Pamela A. Bennett

Widespread use of indigenous volunteers within agencies and organizations began in 1962. The indigenous worker is a "non-professional from within the ranks or at least from the same social class as the population served." It is felt they may have experienced similar problems and/or frustrations as the client being served by an agency, resulting in a greater ability to establish close, productive relationships. Being a product of the same or similar environment as that of the client, such volunteers can often effect important changes due to their life experience, valuable insight into common life styles, and appropriate communication skills. Rieff and Riessman saw the indigenous worker as "a peer of the client (who) shares a common background, language, ethnic origin, style, and group of interests . . . he 'belongs,' he is a 'significant other,' he is 'one of us'." Examples of programs making use of indigenous non-professionals include Alcoholics Anonymous, Synanon, and the Seventh Step Program.

Because of the apparent success of using volunteers who have experienced similar circumstances as program recipients, the field of corrections began to utilize ex-offenders in various programs. When ex-offenders are brought into programs, a sudden reversal of their roles takes place. The phenomenon "transforms recipients of help into dispensers of help." Volkman and Cressey attribute success of these programs

to the fact that (they) require the reformee to perform the role of reformer, thus enabling him to gain experience in the role which the group has identified as desirable. The most effective mechanism for exerting group pressure on members will be found in groups so organized that criminals are induced to join with non-criminals for the purpose of changing other criminals. A group in which criminal A joins with some non-criminals to change criminal B is probably most effective in changing criminal A, not B. In order to change criminal B, criminal A must necessarily share the values of the anti-criminal members.

In 1964, two programs were begun within correctional facilities, making greater use of the expertise of offenders and ex-offenders. The Draper Project was a unique approach to vocational and educational training, conducted at the Draper Correctional Center in Elmore, Alabama. The Project initiated a training program to be run solely by inmates, with many prisons producing self-instructional programs.

The Massachusetts Correctional Institu-

From Monograph published by the Program for the Study of Crime and Delinquency, O.S.U., 1973. Joseph E. Scott is in the Department of Sociology and Pamela A. Bennett is a student in Social Work at The Ohio State University.

tion at Walpole developed a similar program, and the prisoners were encouraged to prepare instructional materials for their own use as well as for use by handicapped children and youth. This latter program is currently called "The New England Materials for Instruction Center."

At about the same time, the North Carolina Prison Department began a joint venture with the Institute of Government at the University of North Carolina, called the Chapel Hill Youth Development and Research Unit (CHYDARU). It was a camp for young felons transferred from the state penitentiary, and was staffed entirely by parolees. The North Carolina corrections officials viewed the camp as an experiment in the effectiveness of "therapeutic community" treatment with first-time offenders. The parolees had all been through a similar program and would be "culture carriers."

The Synanon Foundation began assisting a small prison camp on Peavine Mountain, north of Reno, Nevada in 1964. Three times a week the Synanon groups visited the prisoners to conduct discussion sessions or participate in recreational activities. "The significant thing about this . . . is that essentially all the persons who conduct(ed) program activities at the camp (were) themselves former institution inmates."

The "Penal Press" is a term referring to writings, mostly descriptive, by inmates, usually written during their incarceration. The *Mentor,* a publication by inmates at the Massachusetts Correctional Institution at Walpole, is an example of another form of inmate self-government in the correctional process. An excerpt from the introduction to one of the *Mentor's* issues states, "It has been written specifically to familiarize new men with the prison life here, and what we have found to be the smartest and quickest way back out that front door."

Inmates felt a need to reveal their thoughts and feelings through "face to face" contact with others as well as through the medium of writing. Inmate counseling projects began in several institutions such as the Colorado State Penitentiary (BARS Project),

San Quentin (Squires' Program), and the Massachusetts Correctional Institution at Walpole (Project Youth). The focus in all of these programs is on the youthful segment of the community, especially those singled out as "headed for trouble" in the future. "The primary value of such exchanges lies in the acceptance of the inmate shown by the youth, as an expert in failure. Parents, teachers, counselors, etc., can and do talk about the disadvantages of certain courses of conduct. The inmate, saying the same thing, is given immediate acceptance as a relevant expert." From 1967 through 1969 Professor Morris of Boston University held seminar courses in criminology in which prison inmates from the Massachusetts Correctional Institution at Norfolk attended as regular members. Their role was to reveal their thoughts concerning prison life and crime in general.

Numerous community programs have begun over the last ten years using the ex-offender as a partial or total agent of service. The Self-Development Group, Inc. is a program operating in Boston, run by ex-convicts and is "based on the premise that offenders, ex-offenders, and potential offenders can and will relate to each other better than with anyone else, that the crime-oriented comradeship existing in prisons and communities can be switched to a parallel track and turned into constructive association, and that criminal behavior is a type of habit that can be changed . . ."

The Seventh Step Program began at the Kansas State Prison as a pre-release program for inmates who were within four months of their release date. In 1965, the first facilities for helping released inmates began with the purpose of helping convicted offenders reestablish themselves in a community. Today the program extends from New York to California, aiding the ex-convict in areas of finance, employment, housing and friendship.

The Future Association of Alberta, Canada and Efforts From Ex-Convicts in Washington, D.C. are programs run by ex-convicts with the purpose of aiding "ex-cons" in the process of re-entry into the community. The Future Association offers a friendly atmosphere where previously-incarcerated persons can meet people and make new friends who share common fears and problems. Efforts From Ex-Convicts attempts to "develop self-help programs for ex-convicts . . . programs are concentrated in the areas of employment, service to the community (especially work with youth and drug abuse problems), and improvement of the image of the ex-convict in the eyes of society" (EFEC Statement of Purpose). The House of Judah in Atlanta and the Youth Development, Inc. are two community programs run by ex-convicts which attempt to provide service to youth in the area. The former focuses on juvenile runaways and drug users, the latter addresses itself to teenagers exhibiting anti-social behavior.

In October, 1969, the Norfolk Fellowship (a program bringing community members into the Massachusetts Correctional Institution at Norfolk to attend fellowship meetings with inmates) began Project Re-entry. The program allows ex-offenders who have "made it" on the outside to return to the prison and offer their experience and insights to men ready for release. Project Re-entry is based on the following assumptions:

That the successful ex-inmate is an excellent resource in helping prisoners; that he can help men in prison examine the attitudes that fostered their criminal behavior; that he can provide them with a positive figure with whom to identify; that he can offer them a measure of hope for the future in spite of the prison experience and the difficulties of adjusting to life outside.

After four and one-half years of experience, the program has proven to be quite successful, and the ex-offender is viewed by both prison officials and prisoners as a valuable resource.

The preceding programs often depend upon the voluntary involvement of ex-offenders, with little or no monetary compensation. Many feel the amount of time and effort expended by these volunteers is directly related to the programs' impact and success in many instances.

According to a report in *Correctional Research* in 1970 there is a trend toward "increasing employment of former inmates as regular staff members in more or less standard correctional posts (as distinct from custodial or maintenance programs) and second, their employment in newer types of paraprofessional positions." Departments of Correction throughout the country are hiring ex-offenders as correctional staff members in positions such as correctional officer, counselor, teacher, work-release placement officer, and therapists in alcoholism and drug addiction programs.

The New Careers movement has perhaps furthered the use of the offender as a correctional manpower resource more than any local or national program now in existence. LaMar Empey cautioned against using offenders as a resource only and not providing career opportunities equal to those available to the non-offender portion of our society. He stated:

We would like the offender to identify with pro-social points of view and to take on characteristics which will enable him to function effectively as a non-criminal. It is for these reasons that . . . our overriding concern is with new careers for offenders, not just with using offenders as a correctional resource. They are already being used as a resource. Our task now is to integrate that use into a larger scheme in which, by being of service to corrections, they might realize lasting career benefits. The positions held by offenders must ultimately show up on tables of organization, be a source of official status, and pay money. Offenders would (then) become a part of the correctional apparatus, not its dependent, often unruly step-children.

The New Careers Development Project began in California in 1964, using offenders for a new type of non-professional role in the program development field placement. They were used as staff in the research, planning, and development of programs in prevention, control, and treatment of crime and delinquency. By August, 1967, fifteen out of the eighteen trainees were employed at salaries ranging from $5,500 to $13,000.

Furthering the New Careers Development Project, California and Illinois have begun the use of ex-offenders and indigenous workers as parole officer aides or assistants. California began the Parole Service Assistant Program in 1966 to provide job opportunities to hard-core unemployed and to improve the quality of parole services. By July, 1968, parole aides had become liaisons between the parolee and the parole officer. They were able and expected to use their first-hand knowledge and experience in the community. The December, 1970 Department of Corrections Report to the Legislature indicates an overall feeling of success and accomplishment with the parole aid program. The Director of Corrections stated that "the presence of minority group members from ghetto areas working from our various parole units is now an accepted part of the parole process and resources. The recognition that the non-professional and professional worker both have valuable inputs to the correctional process for our clients is opening new resources for the benefit of the parolee."

As of June 1, 1970, the Federal Probation Office in Chicago, Illinois had hired a total of 49 parole officer aides to work evenings and weekends for "assisting and exercising general oversight of probationers. Overall, we (the Project directors) are pleased with the performance of POA's. Motivation is generally high and, as indicated, they are demonstrating ability to relate to clients and help them with a variety of problems."

In 1971, Project MOST (Maximizing Oregon's Services and Training for Adult Probation and Parole) used three ex-offenders as paid staff members, functioning in the capacity of aides performing assignments at a para-professional level. They helped remove "professional" staff from routine, time-consuming activities. Project TEEM is an outgrowth of the pilot Project MOST in Ore-

gon, and due to the success of the ex-offenders, continuation and expansion of the aide program was recommended.

THE PAROLE OFFICER AIDE PROGRAM IN OHIO

The Adult Parole Authority of the State of Ohio began the implementation of a Parole Officer Aide Program in September, 1972. This program is staffed solely by ex-offenders who have successfully completed parole according to Ohio regulations, and who have met the special requirements for admission to the program. The goals of the project are to bridge the gap between the Adult Parole Authority and parolees; to facilitate communication between corrections and the community, to engender trust and confidence in the correctional system; to decrease recidivism, and to reduce parole violations.

Duties of the Parole Officer Aide

The Ohio Parole Officer Aide Program differs from other parole aide programs now in operation throughout the country in that each aide is assigned a caseload of thirty parolees and is required to provide "supervision parallel to supervision of professional officers." The ten initial cases were drawn from the existing caseloads of parole officers within the same geographical unit as the one in which the aide worked. These ten cases were to be "multiple problems" cases needing intensive supervision. The term "multiple problems" does not refer to the *severity* of a parolee's crime or life situation, but rather to the combination of social and/or behavioral problems impinging on the parolee. Parole regulations stipulated that all "multiple problems" cases should consist only of men who would be "on the street," *not* awaiting arrest, trial, or further incarceration.

Another important responsibility of the aide, as outlined in his job description, is that of speaking regularly before high schools, service groups, and pre-release institutional inmate groups to publicize the Adult Parole Authority's Programs and to gain the community support crucial to success.

The aide is also to act as a key job resource developer for the Adult Parole Authority. In many cases it is felt the aide may be able to locate more employment possibilities for parolees than the parole officer. The aide's understanding of the types of jobs parolees desire as well as the aide's intimate knowledge of the neighborhoods in which he is to work may provide a new expertise for the Adult Parole Authority previously not available.

The parole officer aide is generally familiar with high-delinquency neighborhoods within his working unit as well as the high-crime areas and establishments that should be avoided by parolees. Another important function of the aide is his ability to act as a resource for other staff members, sharing information about particular offenders, and promoting alternative techniques he feels may increase the quality of supervision given parolees.

Limitations of the Parole Officer Aide

By law, the parole officer aide is not allowed to: (1) arrest a parolee; (2) own or carry a firearm; or (3) transport an arrested offender. Also, due to statutory limitations, an aide cannot assume the responsibility of sole supervision over parolees; thus a weekly staffing of the aide's cases with the senior parole officer and unit supervisor is mandatory. In addition, monthly visits are required by the supervising officer to the homes of parolees assigned to the parole officer aide to "collaborate information given at the weekly staffing, to determine attitudes of the offender and his family toward the aide, and to provide any assistance to the offender deemed necessary."

Selection and Assignment of Aides

The selection of the parole officer aides was initiated through recommendations by

parole officers. The various districts of the Adult Parole Authority were informed of the program and were asked to recommend qualified men who had successfully completed parole. Several ex-offenders were already involved in speaking engagements with parole officers or were volunteering for work around the office. These men showed an interest in the work of the parole department and some were considered "naturals" for the job. Men were also recruited from successful community programs using ex-offenders, such as Seven Steps and Concerns. Recommendations were forwarded to the Project Director who, along with top administrators of the Adult Parole Authority, selected thirteen men to begin in August, 1972.

Selection was based on:

1. Age—there was a reluctance to hire men younger than 22.
2. Residency—all applicants were required to be Ohio residents.
3. Parole status—all applicants had to have successfully completed parole.
4. Applicants must have demonstrated a propensity for inter-professional communication and have been free of psychopathology.
5. Applicants must have displayed "acceptable" behavior during incarceration.
6. Applicants must have displayed sufficient "coping" ability and genuine concern for others.
7. Applicants behavior must not have been considered excessively assaultive or aggressive to the point of being dysfunctional.

To facilitate a successful beginning, the Project Director was careful to select "winners"—men he was confident would succeed. Of the thirteen men chosen, ten remain as active and successful parole officer aides. One man resigned after discovering he was not suited for the program, one man was terminated, and one man was promoted to the Ohio Department of Rehabilitation and Corrections as an ombudsman. Three parole officer aides have been hired since December, 1972 to bring the total back to thirteen. Tentative plans call for the utilization of twenty-five aides by July 1, 1973, necessitating the recruitment and hiring of an additional twelve aides. The Adult Parole Authority intends to allow qualified aides to advance in the future into the parole system as parole officers.

Training Seminar

Prior to entering the field on a full-time basis, all of the parole officer aides were involved in a two-week training seminar along with their future supervisors. The agenda included several speakers from the Adult Parole Authority, who discussed the philosophy, goals and objectives of the program, the various roles of the parole officer aide, counseling and interviewing techniques, the criminal justice system, the use of community resources, and parole philosophy as it relates to the community. Also included was instruction on report writing and the proper procedure for completing departmental forms.

Evaluation of the Case Aide Program

Ten of the original thirteen ex-offenders hired as parole officer aides are still employed in that capacity. Their performance in comparison to a control group of ten parole officers was evaluated using several techniques. The first technique utilized was the measurement of aides' and parole officers' attitudes on several dimensions often mentioned as being associated with successful social service-type workers. The results from the attitudinal questionnaire on the scales specifically designed to measure traits associated with successful social service workers indicate aides are slightly more likely to possess those attitudes and orientations than are parole officers. Surprisingly, the two groups were found to be almost identical in their attitudes toward law and order.

The in-depth interviews with parole officer aides indicate they are very pleased with their jobs. They had been well accepted and socialized into their respective parole offices. Aides had considerable confidence in their own ability to help and assist parolees although only four felt being an ex-offender was more important than being a community resident in working with parolees.

The students who worked with the parole officers and aides reported parole officers saw more parolees and spent a greater percentage of their work time with parolees than did aides. However, aides were evaluated as having a better relationship with both parolees and fellow workers.

Unit supervisors rated parole officers and aides on several dimensions, indicating that in most respects parole officers were superior to aides. The two criteria in which supervisors rated aides superior were in getting jobs for parolees and in a willingness to "put themselves out" or "go the extra mile" to help parolees. Supervisors felt aides and parole officers were equally able to relate and get along with fellow workers. Aides were rated as being considerably inferior to parole officers in writing reports. Overall, however, supervisors in whose units aides worked were very excited about the Parole Officer Aide Program. Several supervisors indicated they had grave doubts about the program at its inception, but they now felt it was the best new program to have ever come out of the Adult Parole Authority and that it should certainly be expanded.

Inmates surveyed at two of Ohio's male penal institutions were also very much in favor of the Parole Officer Aide Program. The majority of inmates felt parolees supervised by an aide would be more likely to succeed on parole. An overwhelming majority of inmates (86%) indicated they would prefer being supervised by an aide rather than a parole officer.

The parolees surveyed who were under the supervision of either an aide or a parole officer rated parole officer aides superior on every indicator. Parole officer aides appeared to be easier to talk with, more trustworthy, more concerned, more helpful in finding jobs for parolees, more understanding and easier to find when needed by parolees than were parole officers. The evaluators pointed out that part of this optimistic and positive rating of aides by parolees may be an artifact of a smaller caseload resulting in more contact time per parolee.

The Parole Officer Aide Program received positive, often superlative ratings from almost everyone associated with it. The aides have performed well in their first year of employment with the Ohio Adult Parole Authority. Regardless of whether parolees, supervisors or others are evaluating their work, aides received outstanding praise and acknowledgment for their contribution.

QUESTIONS FOR DISCUSSION

1. Community based alternatives to incarceration and institutionalization are now accepted without much discussion as the superior approach. Why are we back to the days of the pre-institution (18th century) in our thinking on this matter?
2. Was the emergence of the asylums an aberration, a historical mistake? If community programs fail will we go back to the institutional approach again?
3. How do you evaluate the cost effectiveness of community programs? On the basis of their cost effectiveness, can most programs be considered successful?
4. Choose a community diversion program in your area and study it as thoroughly as you can. How does it work? Does it accept only the best risks? Does it reduce rehospitalization or recidivism? What do the recipients think of it? The staff?
5. Discuss the origins of:

   A. The halfway house (both halfway-in and halfway-out)
   B. The North Carolina experience with work release
   C. General educational and vocational release programs
   D. Home furlough programs
   E. Home care programs
   F. Probation and parole changes in view of these new community diversion attempts
   G. The shock probation approach
   H. The new methods with other kinds of problem persons (e.g., learning disability children)

6. Is community care invariably better than institutionalization?
7. What percentage of an inmate, mental hospital, or institution for the criminally insane population would you estimate would be eligible for community diversion? How would you decide who can be kept out and who must or should be institutionalized? What criteria would you use—present problem or offense, criminal or mental illness history, dangerousness, recidivism potential? What else?

BIBLIOGRAPHY

Berleman, William C., Seaburg, James R., and Steinburn, Thomas W. "The Delinquency Prevention Experiment of the Seattle Atlantic Street Center.' *Social Science Review* 46, No. 3 (September 1972).

Bopp, William J. *Police-Community Relationships.* Springfield, Ill.: Charles C. Thomas, 1972.

Breslin, Maurice. "Residential Aftercare: An Intermediate Step in the Correctional Process." *Federal Probation* 27 (1963), 37–46.

Brotman, Richard and Freedman, A. *A Community Mental Health Approach to Drug Addiction.* U.S. Department of Health, Education and Welfare—Juvenile Delinquency and Youth Development Office, 1968.

Burdman, Milton. "Realism in Community-Based Correctional Services." *The Annals of the American Academy of Political and Social Science* 381 (1969) 39–46.

The Comprehensive Community Health Center: Concept and Challenge. (Public Health SErvice Publication No. 1137), U.S. Department of Health, Education and Welfare April 1964.

Delworth, Ursula, Rudow, Edward H., and Taub, Janet. *Crises Center Hotline.* Springfield, Ill.: Charles C. Thomas, 1972.

Dinitz, Simon, and Beran, Nancy. "Community Mental Health as a Boundaryless and Boundary-Busting System." *Journal of Health and Social Behavior* 12 (June 1971) 99–107.

Diversion From the Criminal Justice System. Center for Studies of Crime and Delinquency, National Institute of Mental Health, 1971.

Empey, LaMar. "Alternatives to Incarceration." *Studies in Delinquency.* U.S. Department of Health, Education and Welfare. Washington, D.C.: U.S. Government Printing Office, 1967.

Empey, La Mar, and Lubeck, Steven G. *The Silverlake Experiment: Testing Delinquency Theory and Community Intervention.* Chicago: Aldine Publishing Co., 1971.

Fairweather, George W., Sanders, David H., Cressler, David L., and Maynard, Hugo. *Community Life for the Mentally Ill: An Alternative to Institutional Care.* Chicago: Aldine, 1969.

Friday, P. C., Petersen, D. M., Bohlander, E. W., and Michalowski, R. J. *Report on the Use and Effectiveness of Shock Probation in Ohio.* Program for the Study of Crime and Delinquency, Ohio State University, 1973.

Griggs, Bertram S., and McCune, G. R. "Community Based Correctional Programs: A Survey and Analysis." *Federal Probation* 36, No. 2 (June 1972), 7–12.

Guide to the Community Control of Alcoholism. American Public Health Association, 1968.

Kirby, Bernard. "Crofton House: An Experiment With a County Halfway House." *Federal Probation* XXXIII No. 1 (March 1969), 53–57.

Markley, Carson W. "Furlough Programs and Conjugal Visiting in Adult Correctional Institutions." *Federal Probation* 37 No. 8 (1973).

Pasamanick, B., Scarpitti, F., and Dinitz, S. *Schizophrenics in the Community: An Experimental Study in the Prevention of Hospitalization.* New York: Appleton-Century-Crofts, 1967.

Pettibone, John M., "Community Based Programs: Catching Up With Yesterday and Planning For Tomorrow." *Federal Probation* 37 No. 3 (1973), 3 ff.

Root, Lawrence S. "State Work Release Programs. An Analysis of Operational Policies." *Federal Probation* 37 (December 1973), 52–57.

Rubin, Sol. "Illusions of Treatment in Sentences and Civil Commitments." *Crime and Delinquency* 16 No. 1 (1970), 79–92.

Shelly, J. A., and Bassin, A. "Daytop Lodge: Halfway House for Drug Addicts." *Federal Probation* 28 (1964), 46–54.

Smith, Philip A. "Nonpenal Rehabilitation for the Chronic Alcoholic Offenders.' *Federal Probation* 32 No. 3 (1968), 46–50.

Smith, Robert R., and Milan, M. A. "A Survey of Home Furlough Policies of American Correctional Agencies." *Criminology* 11 No. 1 (May 1973), 95–104.

Wise, Jacqueline P. *Stations of the Lost: The Treatment of Skid Row Alcoholics.* Englewood Cliffs, N.J.: Prentice-Hall, 1970.

Youth Service Bureaus: Standards and Guidelines. Delinquency Prevention Commission, California Youth Authority Department, 1968.

18

Rights of Victims and Rights of Deviants

Fundamentally, the definition, management, control, and treatment of deviance involves an ideological commitment. The notion that there can be anything "value free" about deviance is clearly a myth which criminologists, psychiatrists, lawyers, judges, police, and the legislature have long since rejected—in practice if not in theory. Deviance and deviants highlight, by their presence and action, the ideological splits which exist in any society. This chapter is concerned with making explicit these conflicts by focusing, as sharply as possible, on the issue of the rights of deviants and the rights of their victims—the latter an issue which has arisen less frequently since the Middle Ages when the function of the group was to *compose* differences rather than punish and inflict harm on the culpable perpetrator. Composition was usually some sort of financial settlement between the aggrieved and the perpetrator or their families.

In any case, the issue as presently posed involves the rights of society and its members to freedom from fear, violence, and depredation versus the rights of deviants to be left alone (in the status offenses) and to be accorded fair and judicious treatment at all levels of the criminal justice, mental health, and social welfare systems. In crime, the problem is one of balancing law enforcement practices (search and seizure, entrap-

ment, electronic surveillance, preventive detention) which would facilitate the detection of violations against the rights of privacy, the right to counsel and to non-self-incrimination, to say nothing about a fair trial and humane treatment. The courts have spoken on many of these issues in all sorts of landmark decisions (Gideon, Mapp, Mallory, Escobedo, Miranda) which are still hotly contested.

In mental illness the ideological (and practical) divisions are over the right to treatment and the right to be left alone, the guarantees against being railroaded into an institution versus the patent need to remove certain acute and florid psychotics from the community. The basic psychiatric issue, however couched in learned terms, involves some sort of prediction of dangerousness. In the interface between psychiatry and legal groups the issue is one of sickness versus culpability, and, since 1843 in court and legislature, in theory and in everyday decision-making this problem has remained unresolved. The M'Naghten test, Durham Rule, Currens decision, Brawner decision, American Bar Association model code, and many other pronouncements cannot solve the dilemma because of the historical legacy of free will which is so central, albeit covert, in current conceptions of deviancy.

In alcoholism and drug addictions the

ideological argument hinges on whether the behavior is a personal vice, a crime, or a sickness. Court decisions (Easter, Driver, Powell, and Robinson) reflect public confusion over definition and especially over decriminalization (Prohibition from 1920–1933, the Harrison Act in narcotics since 1914, the British Plan). Rights in these, as in other segments of the problem, cannot be disassociated from moral conceptions and personal ideological stances.

In sexual deviancy, the rights issue is paramount—and in conflict. Should homosexuality between consenting adults, voluntarily and discreetly enacted, be a legal matter or a purely personal preference? Britain and states like Illinois and Ohio decriminalized the problem. In transvestitism, transsexual surgery to alter physical gender (estimated at 5000 persons per year), and in pornography the moral, ethical, legal, and psychiatric disputes are currently beyond resolution. Some opt for personal choice; many, probably most, for social control over these "horrendous" acts. Abortion pinpoints the "rights" dilemma most clearly. Is abortion murder or the inherent right of a couple to terminate an unwanted pregnancy? When is the fetus viable, and can this decision be maintained by law? Should it be?

No section can treat even a fraction of the "rights" issues raised and challenged by social deviancy. The best we can do is to alert the reader that no solutions are possible until some consensus is achieved on the ethical, moral, legal, medical, and theological positions. The likelihood of such consensus is about as probable as "peace among nations" or "a world based on justice."

The three articles in this concluding chapter do address a few of the ethical, moral, and legal rights questions inherent in deviance. Professors Donal E. J. MacNamara of the John Jay College of Criminal Justice and his co-author, John J. Sullivan, present a comprehensive review of the rationale and rights of victims of personal crimes. Entitled "Making the Victim Whole," the authors consider the composition (historic), restitution (emerging), and compensation (more or less current) approaches to indemnifying innocent victims of crime. They examine the victim compensation laws of New Zealand (1963), England (1964), New York and California (1965), Hawaii (1967), Massachusetts and Maryland (1968), Nevada (1969), New Jersey (1971), the Federal Victim Compensation Act (1972), and everybody else's since for commonalities in the various statutes. They single out eleven similarities in the laws. They also consider some of the difficulties in administering victim compensation laws and present five cases as evidence of these difficulties.

Not discussed in the article is the "rights" argument underlying all these statutes:

1. The state has abrogated to itself the sole right to enforce the law. Hence, the citizen has the right to demand that the state do something for him when it fails to protect him properly.

2. The state, in its welfare role, seeks to provide industrial compensation for the injured worker, ADC for children, home relief for the indigent, etc. Why not compensation for the victims of crime?

3. A state, some at least, may spend as much as $8000 a year to "rehabilitate" a perpetrator in a prison or alternative setting. If offenders, especially of injury-producing crimes, are worthy of such "rehabilitation" why should not the state do the same, or better, for the victim? Does not the victim have at least as much right to being made whole again?

Not only is it necessary to protect the victim, but it is every bit as vital to protect the rights of the deviant at every point in the criminal justice, mental health or welfare process. No society can neglect its less "desirable" and weaker members without eventually harming all the others. It is ironic that the defendants in nearly all the major landmark "rights" decisions are often personally eminently dislikable, at least in the criminal justice field. From Daniel M'Naghten to Ernesto Miranda and Danny Escobedo, important rights have been extended because even these marginal characters have constitutional rights. The public is often dismayed by the defense of a Corona or a Manson or a Boston strangler. To do less for these men would jeopardize the rights of a lot of others as well. Although these famous or infamous cases command mass media attention, the truth is that American society has not and is not now doing enough to insure the rights of the disabled, the disadvantaged, and the deviant. American justice and fairness is not class blind; the underclasses are clearly underclass in all respects compared to the rest of us. One need only spend a few hours in a municipal court or a psychiatric commitment hearing to see the practical operation of the system.

In "Legal Rights of the Disabled and Disadvantaged," Richard C. Allen sets forth three principles applicable to all as concerns legal rights: normalization, fairness, and respect for the dignity and worth of the individual. The article discusses these general principles (and the specific needs predicated on them) as they apply to the mentally incompetent, alcoholics and drug addicts, the physically handicapped, the aged, the law-breaker, and the poor. The major needs seem to be: representation by counsel, consumer involvement (as in welfare or mental health), and the need for an "ombudsman" system to run interference for the client in these impersonal systems of management and control.

One of the most fascinating of all recent developments has been the increasing restiveness of prisoners and the feeling that they must unionize and bargain collectively with the administration in order to achieve their "rights" and a significant improvement in their lot. The unthinkable has thus occurred. The correctional offices have and are unionizing to improve *their* status and salary and fringe benefits. Now the inmates—convicts all, mind you—are doing the same. In Scandinavia, in California, in New York, but especially since 1968 in Ohio, "Unionization Behind the Walls" is no dream but a reality confronting an understandably reluctant administration. Whoever heard of prisoners making wage demands, involvement in grievance procedures, a voice in the governance of the prison? Ronald Huff has been close to the "Unionization Behind the Walls" movement for a long time. His paper is therefore informed and timely and perhaps points in the direction of the next "rights" issue to emerge.

MAKING THE VICTIM WHOLE

Donal E. J. MacNamara and John J. Sullivan

Criminology may be said to have addressed itself over the years first to the crime, then to the offender, and only relatively recently, at least in a scientific and structured approach, to the victim.

Attention to the victim, pioneered by Hans von Hentig, first concerned itself with the contributory elements in the victim's personality and/or life-style, or his more specific conduct preliminary to and incident to the crime, which either increased his exposure to victimization or enhanced the seriousness (in terms of loss or injury) of the crime committed against him. It has been posited, for example, that prostitutes, homosexuals and those engaging in promiscuous extramarital sexual adventures, heavy drinkers and gamblers, and those who exhibitionistically make ostentatious display of money and gems are more likely to be victimized by criminals than those who are free of such vices and who live less conspicuously.

Secondary interest in the victim has been evinced by those, particularly but not exclusively in the United States of America, who set forth highly putative "rights" of the vic-

Reprinted from *The Urban Review*. 6, No. 3 (1973). Professor MacNamara is at the John Jay College of Criminal Justice, New York City.

tim to be avenged or vindicated as a major rationalization for their denunciations of "defendant-oriented" judges and courts (e.g., the Warren Court) and for their support of the death penalty and other extremely rigorous sanctions for offenders. This "lust for punishment" approach is sometimes extended to suggest a residual sadistic compulsion endemic in the population, which if not assuaged by frequent executions and long prison terms will find expression in mob violence (e.g., lynchings of alleged or convicted offenders).

Little attention has, however, been given to another victim-oriented approach, i.e., making the victim whole, restoring his losses of money or property, and/or providing compensation for loss of life, physical injury (with consequent loss of earning power and the costs of medical care), and the pain and suffering resulting from criminal assaults.

In this brief article we will distinguish the contemporary victim compensation statutes from:

1. Early victim (or crime *composition*) procedures developed nonuniformly in early societies.
2. The much more common though equally sporadic *offender-restitution-to-the-victim* schemes conceived partly as punishment and perhaps even more importantly as components of offender rehabilitation efforts and experimented with, at least in the United States in more recent years, largely by juvenile courts.
3. The partial or full restitution sometimes voluntarily offered by adult criminal offenders, particularly in "white collar" crimes, to allay prosecution or to mitigate sentence.

THREE DIFFERENT APPROACHES

Although compensation, restitution, and composition all allude to procedures for restoring the victim to his precrime condition, they differ basically in legal philosophy and very importantly in administration. Confusion of what was basically a civil tort approach (composition) with a punitive-corrective measure (offender restitution to the victim) and of both with the doctrine of the state's responsibility for protecting its citizens when such protection proved inadequate (compensation), has characterized much discussion of victim compensation legislative proposals in recent years. This confusion has created difficulties in the interpretation and administration of victim compensation laws.

Since Schafer *et al.* have more than adequately surveyed the early history (and the legislative hearings leading to the enactment of the victim compensation statutes discussed herein) and since it is our principal purpose to discuss here the necessity for and the problems inherent in contemporary legislative approaches to the compensation of victims, we will not deal exhaustively with either composition or restitution. The former, albeit in many variant forms, can be identified in early tribal societies, in the formal codes of Moses and Hammurabi, in early Greek and Roman law, and indeed in the Europe, especially Germany, of the Middle Ages.

Composition was quite probably socioeconomic in orientation and perhaps designed more to keep the peace between families and between tribes than as a deterrent, punitive, or rehabilitative response to crime.

It is apparent in the rather fragmentary materials that crimes by the rich and powerful against the lower social orders could be composed by relatively small payments in money, cattle, land, or other goods—while crimes committed by slaves, serfs, or the lower classes against their masters or against the persons or property of those of higher social strata (or violations of strongly held tribal taboos) could not be so composed, being instead punished by death, corporal penalties, enslavement, and confiscation of land or chattels.

A dual system in which the imposed composition, frequently a multiple of the amount stolen or the damage of injury inflicted, was divided between the victim (or his family or tribe) and the chief, noble, or king either as full retribution for the offense or as a part of a more severe penalty can be identified in a number of codes.

In such criminal incidents as involved victims and perpetrators of relatively equal social rank and military strength, composition was sometimes negotiable not only as to amount and kind but also as to period and conditions of payment. Such indeed was the custom among the Irish clans as late as the 12th and 13th centuries as is evidenced by many instances in bardic lore. Again the purpose seemed to be to avert unnecessary fighting among the all-too-warlike clans rather than to punish or rehabilitate the offenders.

The concept of *offender-restitution-to-his-victim* has proved more popular as a theory than feasible in practice. Without surveying at length all the abortive efforts to achieve so ethical and logical an equilibrium—and certainly without any intention of decrying the possible punitive, deterrent, and/or corrective values inherent in making the offender more literally "pay" for his criminal act—it must be noted that: (1) only a minority of offenders are apprehended and convicted (who then would make restitution to victims whose attackers went unwhipped of justice?): (2) offenders are largely of the lowest socio-economic stratum, judgment-proof to a man; (3) the prison-earnings potential of offenders scarcely can be expected to meet a fraction of the costs of guarding, housing, clothing, and feeding them (to say nothing of the much greater costs of rehabilitating them); (4) societal resistance to the re-employment of ex-convicts, and their lack of vocational skills insure that their post-prison employments will not prove sufficiently remunerative to permit any but token restitution payments; (5) the costs to the state of administering a system of offender restitution to the sums actually collected for reimbursing the victims for their injuries and losses.

Certainly too, it is apparent that many crimes, particularly crimes against the person violative of the personal self-concept and dignity (e.g., forcible rape and forcible sodomy) and likely to result in psychological torment of long duration, would prove difficult to quantify in monetary terms (and impossible to be restituted within the limited financial resources of most perpetrators).

CIVIL ACTION NEEDED

In those few cases in which the convicted offender proved to have more than nominal assets, the victim might well gain more equitable restitution for pain, suffering, and emotional trauma through civil action (tort) for personal injury.

Instances of court-ordered restitution by juvenile court judges directed against either the offending juvenile or his parents have been more offender-oriented (i.e., attempting to teach him the lesson that he must pay for his misdeeds) rather than serious efforts to make the victims whole. In a number of vandalism cases against schools, churches, and cemeteries studied by the authors, the restitution ordered (usually in services rather than money) bore but an insignificant relationship to the actual extent of the damage done.

Restitution by adult offenders either as a condition of probation or voluntarily offered to fend off anticipated prosecution or to mitigate sentence has been largely limited, at least in our country, to cases of fraud, embezzlement, forgery, and other "white collar" offenses. Indeed on more than one occasion such offers of restitution and their acceptance come perilously close to the compounding of felonies.

One notable current attempt at offender repayment to the victim of his crime is the Minnesota Community Corrections Center for Restitution, a small pilot program limited to male and female perpetrators of property crimes who opt voluntarily (as an alternative to imprisonment) to repay the identifiable and tangible losses suffered by their victims. Each inmate works out a "restitution plan" with his victim and remains an inmate of Restitution House (at which he must pay for his board and room and also contribute to the support of his family) until full restitution to his victim has been completed.

Let us now however proceed to a consideration in somewhat more specific detail of the victim compensation laws enacted over the past decade in a number of British Commonwealth countries and several of the American states: New Zealand in 1963; England in 1964; New York and California in 1965; Hawaii in 1967, Massachusetts and Maryland in 1968; Nevada in 1969; New Jersey in 1971; and the Federal Victim Compensation Act passed overwhelmingly by the United States Senate in September 1972. There are other victim compensation (and restitution) laws (notably in Cuba and Switzerland, in Canada and Australia, and, at least potentially, in several American states). To our knowledge, however, none of the Latin-American nations has adopted a system of *state compensation* to the victims of crime, although Argentina (and perhaps other nations of that continent) has provision for court-ordered restitution to the victim by the offender.

In 1971, England's victim compensation board (Criminal Injuries Compensation Board) processed nearly 10,000 claims, making grants which (while averaging $952.00) included one that totalled $119,000. Total claims paid April 1, 1971 through March 31, 1972, reached the record sum of $7,500,000 as compared to a 1970–71 total of $4,900,000, and a 1969–70 total of $4,500,000. The record total of $119,000 was awarded a young woman who was blinded and suffered other severe and continuing disabilities as the result of an assault with a concrete block by a former lover. Another grant went to a woman who suffered a heart attack two weeks after witnessing a robbery, but a man who was knocked from his motorcycle by a participant in a sidewalk brawl had his claim rejected since the English law requires that the injury be proximately incident to a crime and there was no showing that an actual criminal act was occurring. English law permits appeals from the decisions of the Criminal Injuries Compensation Board first to a three-man

review panel (only six percent of the 1971–2 decisions were reviewed) and then to the courts (only ten cases have been appealed to the courts since the law became effective; in eight of these the Board was upheld and in two cases the claim was returned to the Board for reconsideration).

Little purpose would be served by spreading on the record here the detailed legislative enactments and the even more voluminous procedural rules and regulations adopted in the several jurisdictions which are presently compensating the victims of crime. Instead let us confine ourselves to identifying some major similarities and a number of differences in the statutes, their interpretation, and their implementation—and, more importantly, discuss briefly a number of the inadequacies and problems now all too apparent after several years of experience with the compensation law.

(*Victim compensation* laws should not be confused with so-called "good Samaritan" laws which provide compensation for citizens killed or injured while attempting to prevent a crime, apprehend a criminal, or in assisting a police officer in controlling a breach of the peace. A New York City ordinance of 1965 enacted following the killing of one Arthur Collins, fatally knifed after he ejected a disorderly drunk from a subway train, is an example of such "good Samaritan" legislation.)

Implicit in each of the victim compensation laws to be dealt with in this article is the legal responsibility of the state to protect its citizens from unprovoked criminal attack and the consequent liability of the state to compensate the victim when in fact such an attack occurs.

Major similarities in the various laws include:

1. Compensation for crimes against the person with demonstrable personal injury proximately resulting from the crime are compensable but crimes against property are not. This is largely a pragmatic distinction based on the anticipated difficulties of dealing with fraudulent or exaggerated claims (in-

surance companies have been plagued with such difficulties for decades); the astronomical costs of indemnifying even valid claimants with property losses (by far the highest incidence of crime is in this category—burglary, larceny, auto theft, etc.) have inhibited legislative support; and the availability of both governmental and private insurance coverage for most such property losses contributes to diminishing the urgency of support for such expanded coverage.

2. Generally no compensation can be claimed unless the injury results from an act specifically violative of the penal law (or, as in the case of the Hawaiian legislation, a violation specifically set forth as compensable in the victim compensation act).

3. Generally injuries resulting from violations of the motor vehicle and traffic codes (including driving violations which are misdemeanors and felonies as, for example, drunken driving) are not compensable except for criminal assaults in which the vehicle itself was utilized as the assaulting weapon.

4. While some of the laws are somewhat unclear, or rather not sufficiently specific, the victims of intrafamilial crimes (wife-beating, incestuous rape or sodomy, sibling assaults, etc.) are not compensated.

5. Victims who initiate or provoke the criminal assault which results in their victimization are not compensable (but whether victims who ostentatiously display money or gems or who recklessly frequent areas of high crime incidence without good reason and are as a result assaulted and robbed should be compensated is left to the discretion of the board).

6. Offenders and their accomplices who may suffer injury consequent to their involvement in illegal acts are not compensable.

7. The administrative boards and commissions set up to administer the victim compensation laws may be said to have limited discretion (England), moderate discretion (California), or broad discretion (New York) in determining to what extent a victim himself provoked or en-

ticed his own victimization and adjusting their awards accordingly.

8. Trivial injuries are usually not compensable. Thus, England requires three weeks' loss of earnings; New York an out-of-pocket loss (e.g., for medical expenses) of not less than $100.00 or a two-week loss of earnings; Maryland and Massachusetts a two-weeks loss of earnings; California, Hawaii, and Nevada no minimum, with all three states discouraging trivial injury claims.

9. In England, Massachusetts, and Hawaii no showing of need is required in making a claim. But California, Maryland, Nevada, and New York direct that need be taken into account in determining both eligibility for an award and the extent of compensation awarded.

10. Maximum permissible compensation to a crime victim is difficult to determine in some jurisdictions, and in others it has already been increased by legislative action since the original compensation laws went into effect. The Federal Victims Compensation Act (approved by the United States Senate by an overwhelming vote on September 18, 1972, but not as yet passed by the U.S. House of Representatives" sets the upper limit of compensation at $50,000.00 per victim, a far more generous maximum than is permitted by any of the other compensation laws; Nevada and California, for example have $5,000.00 limits; New Jersey and Hawaii set the top payment at $10,000.00; New York allows up to $15,000.00 for loss of earnings but sets no limit for medical expenses (and has indeed made awards for medical expenses as high as $25,000.00 in at least one case); Maryland ties its allowances to the schedules in its state workmen's compensation law; England has no maximum in its law but in practice awards have been well below the more generous of the American maximum compensation payments.

11. Each of the laws sets forth criteria for determining the amount of compensation, usually limiting repayment to actual out-of-pocket losses (including medical expenses, loss of earnings, loss of support for dependents of deceased victims). Hawaii permits consideration

of "pain and suffering" but Britain specifically excludes payment for "loss of happiness" and also for "punitive damages."

Among the major problems encountered in the administration and implementation of the victim compensation statutes in effect over the past several years have been:

1. Fraudulent claims and attempts at multiple recovery (e.g., seeking awards for injuries already . compensated by insurance, hospital medical plans, workmen's compensation, veterans benefits, and even by offender restitution).
2. Infinitesimal number of claims in proportion to the recorded or estimated numbers of compensable crimes; in New York for example the State Victims Compensation Law is little known. A survey of students at the authors' university, many of them professionals in the criminal justice field (police, corrections, probation, parole), disclosed that only a minority were familiar with the law and all were vague about its provisions; police do not inform victims of their right to an award, nor do hospitals, prosecutors, courts, and while the communications media, notably the *New York Times,* have carried occasional articles describing the work of the Victims Compensation Board, the public on the whole, and compensable victims in particular, are uninformed.
3. Of those who do submit applications for compensation, fewer than half receive any award in New York State; and in all the jurisdictions the vast majority of the compensation awards do not even approach the already very low maxima.
4. In nearly all jurisdictions the bureaucratic red-tape and the long delays discourage applicants.
5. Apparently questionable awards have been made in some cases, violating either the statute itself or the criteria for eligibility.
6. Bills for medical expenses submitted by doctors, hospitals, and pharmacies seem in many cases to be highly inflated.

Whether the somewhat less than spectacularly successful experience with the currently operating victim compensation plans or, perhaps more likely, the financial stringencies plaguing many national and state governments have been responsible for a lessening of interest in the plight of the victim may be arguable but it is now quite evident that the accelerated and widespread enactment of such legislation forecast after the New Zealand, England, California, and New York schemes went into effect has been slow of realization. It is also apparent that new and organized opposition to new plans and to expanded coverage in the older laws has arisen both in legislative bodies and among tax-conscious members of the general public. Some resistance too has developed among specialists who see in victim compensation schemes the possibility of less aggressive cooperation by victims in the prosecution of their attackers. At any rate, it seems unlikely that new legislation will replicate the present laws. Creative and imaginative alternatives for the state's discharging of its obligations to its victimized citizens must be developed.

New York has paid out more than three million dollars to some 1,400 claimants, in large part for medical expenses. England's payments, on the other hand, are largely for loss of income, since its socialized medical scheme takes care of both doctors and hospital bills.

Perhaps a brief presentation of a few cases from the files of New York's Crime Victims Compensation Board will best illustrate a number of difficulties and problems inherent in such legislation and its efficient implementation:

CASE NUMBER ONE

Victim was shot to death while threatening to assault his killer with a claw-hammer; Victim and his assailant had engaged in a verbal dispute in a restaurant; victim left the restaurant, procured the hammer from his automobile, returned, attacked, and was fatally shot. In this case a compensation award was made to the victim's family covering burial expenses and other losses. In our opinion, this victim provoked the assaultive behavior and no award was justified.

CASE NUMBER TWO

Victim visited a prostitute and while in her room was beaten to death; compensation was denied. Was this verdict based on *moral* or *legal* criteria?

CASE NUMBER THREE

Victim was shot and paralyzed by a neighbor with whom he had initiated a verbal argument over the depredation of the neighbor's dog; victim's medical expenses exceeded $40,000.00 (largely paid for from a private insurance policy) and his out-of-pocket losses were fixed at $2,875.00 of which $1,615.00 was awarded as compensation by the Board. In addition to the question of how much provocation was involved in this case, there is also the question of the sufficiency of the award if indeed any award was justifiable.

CASE NUMBER FOUR

Victim jumped from a second-story window to escape two assailants; he was permanently disabled; an award of $152.00 per month for loss of earnings (up to a maximum of $15,000.00) and reimbursement for medical expenses was made. In this case, victim was 68 years of age (somewhat beyond the usual retirement age in American society); was the award for "loss of earnings" a charitable circumvention of the law?

CASE NUMBER FIVE

Victim, a young foreign student, was robbed, shot, and died sometime later as the result of his wounds; medical expenses amounted to $35,000.00, of which $10,000.00 was covered by insurance policy; an award of $25,000.00 was made to the youth's parents to cover the balance. In addition to the question of inflated medical costs in this case, there is also a legal question: the youth was over his minority, was not resident with his parents, and they had no liability to pay his hospital and medical bills. Without the victim compensation, the hospital and mediical costs would have been absorbed by the institution concerned.

Crimes of violence resulting in death, serious physical injury, loss of earnings, medical expenses, pain and suffering, and psychological aftermaths requiring long-term therapy show little evidence of abating. Deterrent and preventive measures can be only minimally effective in this category of crimes since the perpetrators are frequently emotionally disturbed (angry, fearful, drunk, under the influence of a narcotic, or engaging in compulsive behavior) or, perhaps a little less frequently, psychotic (manic-aggressive, paranoid, or sexually psychopathic). Police measures often prove minimally effective since these are "under-the-roof" crimes or attacks committed in dark, unfrequented places.

Despite the admitted difficulties of deterrence and prevention, there is little question in our opinion as to the liability of the state when such an unprovoked criminal attack is suffered by an innocent victim exercising due care.

Victim compensation laws and the boards or commissions which implement them are in most jurisdictions not even minimally discharging the state's liability to these victims of criminal assaults: Only a relative handful of victims, putatively eligible, make application for compensation; fewer than half of those who do file receive any compensation; the awards made are often parsimonious; large numbers of victims who have suffered injuries or losses are excluded from consideration; criteria set forth to guide the board's decisions have apparently been neither sufficiently clear nor effectively binding to prevent discretionary awards to ineligible claimants; awards for medical expenses have in some cases appeared to be excessive; and neither the laws nor their implementation have been subjected to rigorous evaluation.

We are of the opinion that crime victim compensation laws must be retained and expanded into those jurisdictions which have not as yet adopted such legislation. We feel, however, that the difficulties (enumerated supra) must be corrected. We suggest that there is great potential in a *mandatory crime victims insurance scheme,* modelled perhaps on a combined social security-workmen's compensation amalgam, which would discharge the state's obligation to the victims of

crime much more generously and much more generally than can be expected under the systems evaluated herein.

LEGAL RIGHTS OF THE DISABLED AND DISADVANTAGED

Richard C. Allen

AN OVERVIEW

Law is—or should be—a device for serving basic human needs. And it is never static. When a lawyer says: "This is the law," he is really saying: "This is what I think some court (or *this* court) would do if presented with this question in the future." Thus, the practice of law, like the practice of astrology (which seems to have come once again into vogue), embodies the art of prediction; and, like astrology, that prediction must be based on the perambulations of shifting—albeit not supernal—forces. In what is to follow it is the author's hope that when he says: "This is the law," the saying of it will help a little to make it so.

With that by way of introduction, a very basic question will now be posed; one which seems to underly much of what has been, and will be, said here: Do the disabled and disadvantaged have a right—a legally enforceable right—to demand of society that it assist them to become whole? Is there a "right" to welfare, to treatment, to rehabilitation, to vocational training, or to whatever else might help to remove the disadvantage or ameliorate the disability?

It is over that question that many of the verbal battles (including some of the "legal" ones) have been fought. For example, when complaint is made that welfare questionnaires and interviews, "loyalty" oaths, and periodic investigations of eligibility, infringe upon the recipient's privacy, or upon his

From *Legal Rights of the Disabled and Disadvantaged*, Washington: U.S. Department of Health, Education and Welfare, 1969, pp. 79—97. Richard Allen is Professor of Law and Director of the Institute of Law, Psychiatry and Criminology, George Washington University, Washington, D.C.

freedom of speech, or of association, or constitute an unreasonable search, the response (perhaps along with some observations about "free loaders" and "chiselers") will probably be that by becoming an applicant for welfare, the person has voluntarily surrendered his privacy and the sanctity of his home; that since welfare is a privilege and not a right, it may be conditioned in whatever way the community thinks best, and anyone who objects to the conditions imposed may avoid them be getting himself off the public dole, but has no *legal* right to complain. . . .

It is, in the author's opinion, quite appropriate to talk about the disabled and disadvantaged in terms of "rights." Franklin Roosevelt did—eloquently and explicitly—in a State of the Union Message in which he said that this country had evolved an "Economic Bill of Rights" of equal stature to that first great Bill, and that it included:

The right of every family to a decent home;
The right to adequate protection from the economic fears of old age, sickness, accident and unemployment;
The right to a good education . . .
The right to a useful and remunerative job [with sufficient income] to provide adequate food and clothing and recreation.

The rights we have been talking about, the rights of the disabled and disadvantaged, spring from basic Constitutional imperatives—for example, the right of one institutionalized for mental illness, or mental retardation, or the disabilities of old age, to control his own property until and unless judicially declared incompetent is not diminished by the fact that he is receiving care in a public institution. Stated or implicit regulations unrelated to the purpose of welfare legislation itself, which serve to deny benefits to persons otherwise within the class for whose benefit the legislation was enacted, or which impose unreasonable burdens upon them, may be struck down.

SOME GENERAL PRINCIPLES

Reference [can be] made . . . to the principle of *normalization*. It is important in the context of legal rights, embracing as it does the concept that everyone is entitled to a life as close to the normal as is possible. Thus, he is not to be institutionalized merely to serve someone else's convenience; and he is to be accorded all the rights that any other citizen may enjoy, excepting only such rights as have been taken away lawfully, for good reasons, and under fair and appropriate procedures. . . . [In addition,] the principle of *fairness*—requires that in decision-making affecting one's life, liberty or vital interests, the elements of due process will be observed, including: the right to notice, to a fair hearing, to representation by counsel, to present evidence and to cross-examine witnesses testifying against one, and to appeal an adverse decision. Nor are these elements requirements only—as they were once thought to be—of criminal cases. The State of Arizona argued recently before the United States Supreme Court that the failure of the Juvenile Court of Gila County to provide notice to Gerald Gault and his parents of the nature of the accusation brought against him; its failure to advise them of their right to counsel; its failure to warn Gerald of his right to remain silent; and its adjudication (ordering Gerald to be confined in the State Industrial School until 21, a period of 6 years, on a charge, which if brought against an adult, could have resulted in no more than 60 days imprisonment), made on the basis of unsworn, hearsay testimony, without right of cross-examination— all should be deemed of no consequence, since juvenile proceedings are "non-criminal" and the court acts as *parens patriae*, for the "welfare of the child." The Court, however, reversed (*In re Gault*, 387

U.S. 1, 1967), citing its earlier declaration (in *Kent v. U.S.*, 383 U.S. 541, 1966):

There is no place in our system of law for reaching a result of such tremendous consequences without ceremony—without hearing, without effective assistance of counsel, without a statement of reasons . . .

We do not mean . . . to indicate that the hearing to be held must conform with all of the requirements of a criminal trial or even of the usual administrative hearing; but we do hold that the hearing must measure up to the essentials of due process and fair treatment.

In the author's view, the Court could apply a standard no less rigorous to a proceeding under which one is deprived of his liberty or property on the ground of alleged mental illness, or retardation, or advanced age; or to an administrative determination depriving a family of its only source of income which does not afford them a fair opportunity to oppose the action. Thus, although it has not yet been declared to be "the law," the author believes that established legal principles require that in any such case the due process requirements of notice, right to counsel, a fair hearing, and right of appeal are fully applicable.

And finally, there is the principle of *respect for the dignity and worth of the individual*. Again, this principle is closely related to the principles of *normalization* and *fairness* discussed above. Here, however, emphasis is placed upon one's right to be treated as a human being, and not as an animal or a statistic. Thus, commission of a crime does not deprive one of all legal rights—a prisoner, even a felon, has a right that he shall not be punished excessively or cruelly, a right to practice his religion, and a right to reasonable protection from homosexual assault. An inmate of a public institution has a right that he shall not be kept sedated, or unclothed for the convenience of the attendants and a right to reasonable communication and visitation. A welfare recipient has a right that his privacy shall not be invaded by "loyalty" oaths and by intrusive inquiries and investigations bearing no reasonable relationship to a determination of need or to the provision of assistance.

SOME SPECIFIC NEEDS

In light of the discussion earlier of specific areas of disability and disadvantage, and of the foregoing general principles, the following are among the needs for legal and related reform.

The Mentally Handicapped

1. Reduce the number of terms employed in statutes to denominate some or all mentally handicapped persons, and eliminate ambiguous, confusing or epithetical terms.

2. Define as precisely and appropriately as can be done the class of persons for whom a particular protective service is intended. Each such definition should be *ad hoc*—for a particular purpose—to minimize the risk that reification of the terms used will cause provision of a particular protective service to result in a status of general incompetency.

3. Require judicial approval for institutionalization of a child where it appears that such care is sought in whole or in part to meet the needs of persons other than the child.

4. Establish clinical services adjunctive to every court which has the power to order institutionalization or guardianship of mentally handicapped persons.

5. Clearly separate institutionalization and incompetency, in law, administrative regulation, and practice. Admission to a service or treatment program for the mentally handicapped should not give rise to a presumption of inability to manage oneself or one's affairs.

6. Multiply and greatly improve community facilities for the mentally handicapped. If this were done, many persons now requiring institutionalization could remain in the community.

7. Improve residential care facilities. There is greater need here for "brains" than for "bricks"; upgrading professional and subprofessional staffs would result in the provision of real treatment and rehabilitation in institutions which are now capable of providing only custodial care.

8. Require periodic re-evaluation, and, where appropriate, retesting and reexamination of all inmates of residential care institutions and establish some form of independent review of such re-evaluation program.

9. Invoke special procedures when an inmate of a residential care institution reaches the age of 21, in order that a guardian be appointed and appropriate family planning made when needed. The New Jersey law may offer a useful model in this regard.

10. Do not require parents and other relatives to bear the cost of institutional care; and do not assess such cost against the institutional resident in such a way as to exhaust his personal funds.

11. Give consideration to providing payment to the parents of a retarded child capable, with special help, of living in the community, to enable them to provide such care and training, thus avoiding the necessity of institutionalization.

12. Provide intensive care facilities—offering real rehabilitative care and not merely imprisonment—for the retardate with problems of behavior.

13. Establish an inexpensive, stigma-free guardianship procedure.

14. Create a public agency in every state coordinate with, but independent of the agency having control of State institutions and special educational facilities. The new agency should have casework, legal, financial and other resources so that it can assist private guardians, or serve in lieu of a private guardian, for mentally handicapped persons.

15. Delineate the duties of a guardian of the person—perhaps through the joint efforts of local bar associations and associations concerned with the care of the mentally handicapped.

16. Improve court facilities and procedures for supervision of guardians.

17. Appoint a guardian ad litem, who is a lawyer, to represent an alleged mentally handicapped person in any case affecting his liberty, property or other vital interests,

whenever the court is not convinced that he has adequate representation. No such person should be considered adequately represented on the basis that a petitioner (other than himself), or a relative is represented by counsel.

18. Make information about laws affecting the mentally handicapped and their families widely available to parents, legal and medical advisors, and to community and residential care personnel.

19. Provide explicit guidelines with respect to a residential care institution's management and disbursement of patient funds.

20. Reexamine commitment laws with the view of changing those procedures which demean or humiliate the subject of the petition, or which deal with him as though he were a criminal. . . .

21. Abolish compulsory sterilization, under whatever euphemism it may be invoked. . . .

22. Conduct research into the relationship of mental retardation and criminal behavior, and into the ways in which present criminal law-correctional procedures might be improved. . . .

23. Consider legislation recognizing that where one's liberty is taken away on the basis of a determination that he is in need of treatment, treatment must in fact be provided; if it is not, he has a right to demand his release. . . .

Alcoholics and Drug Addicts

1. Criminal sanctions applied to alcoholics for the offense of public drunkenness should be done away with and comprehensive treatment programs, including after care, substituted for them . . .

2. Criminal laws dealing with "narcotics" and "dangerous drugs" should be reexamined. Among other changes which would seem desirable:

    a. penal sanctions applicable to marijuana possession and use should be eliminated or greatly reduced in severity;

    b. the severity of the penalties which

may be imposed against narcotic addicts for violation of drug laws should also be diminished.

    c. civil commitment should be made more readily available as an alternative to criminal punishment for drug addicts through enactment of State statutes similar to those in effect in California and New York, and through improving the Federal law by eliminating the categories of criminal offenders presently excluded from the civil commitment provisions of the Narcotic Addict Rehabilitation Act.

3. Research efforts directed toward increasing our knowledge about alcoholism and drug abuse, and about the treatment of alcoholics and drug addicts should be greatly expanded.

The Physically Handicapped

1. Laws prohibiting or restricting basic rights, including the right to marry, to have custody of children, to hold a job, and the like, on the sole ground of being an epileptic, should be repealed.

2. Laws providing for involuntary hospitalization (and any remaining laws permitting involuntary sterilization) on such ground should also be repealed.

3. Consideration should be given in every State to enactment of a drivers' licensure statute similar to those in effect in Wisconsin and Ohio.

4. Legislation similar to PL 90–480 (Elimination of Architectural Barriers to the Physically Handicapped in Certain Federally Financed Buildings) should be enacted in every State. Appropriate guidelines similar to those recommended by the National Commission on Architectural Barriers to Rehabilitation of the Handicapped should become a part of every building code.

5. Workmen's Compensation laws should be changed so that return to gainful employment is not penalized—nor is the employer who hires handicapped workers.

6. The Social Security law should be amended to provide for appointment of a

lawyer to represent the claimant who cannot afford to hire one, for both administrative and judicial review of his claim.

7. Consideration should be given to the enactment of a Federal Civil Rights law for the handicapped.

The Aged

1. Perhaps the most pressing need is for the provision of many more and better equipped nursing homes for people of advanced years who require constant nursing care, in order that State mental hospitals need no longer be used as warehouses for the elderly.

2. In addition, community facilities offering casework, housekeeping and budgetary services and the like to elderly people living at home should be augmented.

3. The principle . . . should be incorporated into legislation, . . . that no elderly person shall be committed to a residential care facility—especially a State mental hospital—without a thorough inquiry into the availability of alternative community-based resources.

4. The Social Security law should be revised to include many more of the nation's senior citizens. Persons who have worked and earned through their lives are entitled to a life of decency and dignity when they are too old to work. They should not be compelled to resort to "charity" in order to live. . . .

The Offender

1. We must spend the money and provide the resources necessary to make our system of corrections rehabilitative, instead of—as they are now—at best custodial, and at worst brutalizing "monster-factories" (as the nation's prisons were recently described in testimony before a Senate committee). We should begin by recognizing that corrections does not begin at the prison door, but with the first contact of the offender with the representatives of society. When law enforcement officials violate the law, or demean or brutalize those with whom they come into contact, or when imprisonment before trial (so-called "preventive detention") is deemed justified by the "crime problem," then there has begun a process of *dehabilitation* that will defeat any later efforts to provide *rehabilitation*. We have much yet to learn about the causes of crime, about criminal typologies, and about what works and what doesn't work to break the cycle of recidivism which characterizes so many offenders. But we are not yet doing a fraction of what we do know how to do; and we are permitting a great many things to go on in our correctional system that we know do not "correct," but rather exacerbate, the crime problem.

The Poor

1. Whatever may be his other legal rights, every citizen of this country should be accorded the right to live: to enjoy at least that minimal level of nutrition, housing and medical care necessary to sustain life and health. To the extent that there are starving children in this country, or children who, if not starving, are so malnourished that they are unable to develop physically or mentally in normal fashion; to the extent that there are adults who go to bed hungry at night; or families who lack suitable shelter; or areas where medical care is not available—and all of these things exist, right here in the United States—we are permitting the gravest violation of the most sacred right of man in a civilized country.

2. Every child has a right to an education, at least through elementary and secondary public school levels; and every child has the right that the educational facilities provided for him be reasonably comparable to those afforded the children of other communities within the same governmental unit, regardless of the comparative social or financial status of those communities.

3. We must break through the barrier of "hard core" unemployment. There should be recognized a right to earn a decent living—with, if necessary, the Federal Government as the employer of last resort.

4. The citizen has a right to police protection and a right to restrain police abuse. There should be established in every community a civilian police review board.

5. The laws protecting the consumer—both State and Federal—should be strengthened, and more vigorously enforced.

6. Our criminal, tax, domestic relations and commercial laws should be reappraised and reformed in order better to meet the special needs of the poor.

7. Reform and expansion of our present welfare programs is essential, and it is urgent.

SOME SUGGESTIONS FOR IMPLEMENTATION

... Four implementational strategies will be discussed: *representation by counsel; consumer participation in policy formulation; establishment of an "ombudsman" system;* and *recognition of the extent and character of the national effort required.*

Representation by Counsel

The "right to counsel" is one of our most cherished, and most important legal rights, and it is a right which has grown tremendously in extent in just the last few years. A quarter of a century ago, the United States Supreme Court ruled that the States are not required to furnish counsel to every indigent defendant charged with a criminal offense. But in 1963 it reversed itself in a case involving an oft-convicted semi-literate charged with breaking and entering a poolroom in Florida, who had sent a handwritten petition to the Court protesting the fact of his conviction without benefit of counsel (*Gideon v. Wainwright,* 372 U.S. 335) ... The Supreme Court agreed to hear his case and a prominent attorney was appointed to represent him. When the case went back for retrial, it had a storybook ending. Gideon was really innocent, and the lawyer the Florida court was required to provide him was able to prove it.

Since the *Gideon* case, there have been a

number of other opinions, and a few statutes—the Criminal Justice Act of 1964 (18 U.S.C. Sec. 3006A) for one—extending and implementing the right to counsel in State and Federal criminal cases. Progress has been due in part to a report by a committee of the American Bar Association in 1964 which pointed out that most of the jurisdictions of the United States were failing to provide counsel for the indigent, and that some 150,000 persons every year are charged with crimes punishable with imprisonment of a year or more, who cannot afford to hire a lawyer.... Although in the *Gault* case discussed earlier, the Court extended the right to counsel to a non-criminal area—juvenile court proceedings—it has not as yet been extended, as a matter of right, to the areas of civil litigation which may be of vital concern to the disabled and disadvantaged (landlord-tenant cases, domestic relations matters, workmen's compensation, claims for benefits against governmental agencies, competency and commitment cases, and the like).

However, the American Bar Association resolved ... decades ago that:

... it is a fundamental duty of the bar to see to it that all persons requiring legal advice be able to attain it, irrespective of their economic status. (Proceedings, 1946)

The ABA's proposed Code of Professional Responsibility (1969) reaffirms the duty of every lawyer to serve the disadvantaged, both individually and through participation in legal aid and other organized programs. There are today legal aid offices in most American cities. Defender projects, neighborhood legal services projects, lawyer referral services, and others, are being financed by the Office of Economic Opportunity, Department of Justice, the Department of Health, Education, and Welfare, State and local Governments, the Ford Foundation, bar associations, law schools and other organizations. Collectively, these programs do not yet meet the total need (in some areas they meet almost none of it—for example, the rural poor), but much more is being done today than has ever been done before.

In 1967, for example, more than 1,800 attorneys were engaged in providing legal services to the poor, ... and in 1968 the Federal Government alone expended nearly $50 million for this purpose....

Consumer Involvement

A candidate for high political office recently invoked the "doctor-patient" theory of dealing with the disabled and disadvantaged. It goes something like this: There must be something wrong with folks who can't seem to get and hold good jobs in our affluent society; and where something is wrong with someone, you call in the experts to deal with it. After all, a doctor doesn't share his decision-making about diagnosis and treatment with his patient, does he?

A very different view was taken by the late Dr. Martin Luther King, Jr.; he saw the issue of "consumer involvement" as a matter of simple justice. In his *Letter from Birmingham City Jail* in 1963, he defined an "unjust law," for those who had expressed concern about his and his followers' refusal to comply with the racist statutes and ordinances of Alabama: "An unjust law is a law that a majority inflicts on a minority which that minority had no part in creating or enacting." John Gardner, former Secretary of Health, Education, and Welfare, shared that view: "Every man should be able to feel that there is a role for him in shaping his local institutions and local community". And so did the late Senator Robert Kennedy, who continued to urge until his untimely death: "the involvement of the poor in planning and implementing programs: giving them a real voice in their institutions." ...

Whatever the problems and shortcomings of giving the disadvantaged a significant role in planning, excluding them is far more hazardous.... The idea of consumer participation in policy decision-making must be retained. However, the importance of and publicity given to participation by the poor through community action must not be allowed to obscure the need for involvement of the blind in the structuring and adminis-

tration of programs for the blind, of prisoners in programs looking toward their rehabilitation, and the like. Here too, the model of the joint, participative effort must replace the prevailing model of "diagnosis and treatment."

The "Ombudsman"

The office of the "Ombudsman"—or its equivalent—has been established in a number of countries, but is distinctly Nordic in origin dating back to turn-of-the-century Sweden. Although there are variations—related, among other things, to whether the Ombudsman is considered an instrument of the legislative or of the executive branch of government, most Ombudsmen receive complaints about action taken—or not taken—by a governmental agency or official and investigate the complaint. If the Ombudsman finds the complaint meritorious, he takes such action as he deems necessary, including prosecution of officials, where indicated.

... For the disabled and disadvantaged—who are often very much at the mercy of administrative decision-making or inaction—the institution of the Ombudsman has particular appeal. Legal representation still is not always available; nor are lawyers always conversant with the maze of administrative tribunals and officials in whose domains a particular problem (rats in the basement, reduction in welfare benefits, oppressive or intrusive "officialism," and the like) may lie.

Courts will usually review an administrative decision only as to its legal sufficiency—not its wisdom, practicality or reasonableness; and court procedures may be far too slow to meet the urgency of the need. Private groups, such as the American Civil Liberties Union, National Association for the Advancement of Colored People, etc., have performed exceptionally valuable services in "landmark" cases, but they simply do not have the facilities to meet the day-to-day needs of the tens of thousands of disabled and disadvantaged citizens who must contend with the multi-headed monster *Bureaucraticus Carnivora*. Congressmen may provide Ombudsmanlike services to constituents, but the quality of those services varies greatly, depending upon the knowledge of the Congressman about the particular area involved, and his interest in, and time available to serve, the particular constituent. The constituents with whom we are particularly concerned in this paper, are notoriously poor campaign contributors, and have little "influence." And, if they happen to live in the District of Columbia, they have no Congressional Representative upon whom they may call.

In Sweden, Finland and Denmark—which have had the longest experience—Ombudsmen, in most cases, serve simply as information centers (a most useful function indeed!). In only about 15–20 percent of the cases is there found a need for even so much as a reprimand for the agency involved. . . .

The idea is worth considering. If the thought of general "ombudsmanship" is alarming, the duties and authority of such an official may be strictly limited: to welfare and housing matters, for example. At least, as suggested earlier that modest, quasi-ombudsman—the civilian police review board—if established in the Nation's cities, would go a long way toward relieving the potentially explosive relationship which presently exists between police and ghetto.

Recognition of the Need

It is hoped that what has been written here has provided ample documentation of the extent of the need of the disabled and disadvantaged. We have reached a point in this country—and very nearly passed it—at which we can no longer defer making a genuine effort to solve the problems of the handicapped and continue to survive as a country.

UNIONIZATION BEHIND THE WALLS

C. Ronald Huff

INTRODUCTION

During the past five years, (1968–1973) the inmates of Ohio's correctional institutions have become increasingly militant and openly expressive of their frustrations and resentments regarding the criminal justice system under which they have been convicted and confined. The forms of expression utilized have included rioting, work stoppages, food boycotts and, most recently, large-scale union organizing inside the walls. These activities have extended over two state administrations, one Republican and one

This article won the first prize award in the student competition at the American Society of Criminology Annual Meeting, November 1973. Reprinted by permission of the author. To be published in *Criminology*. C. Ronald Huff is now assistant professor of social ecology at the University of California, Irvine.

Democrat. They have involved every single adult correctional institution in the state. The evidence indicates that the leadership for the movement has come, for the most part, from inside, with outsiders serving in supportive and/or advisory capacities.

Why has this militancy developed (or at least surfaced) at this particular time? What are the goals of the inmates? What has been the reaction of correctional administrators to the prisoners' union movement? What legal issues are involved? This paper will address itself to these and other questions which naturally occur to any thoughtful observer. The questions which arise in connection with such a movement are, to say the least, very complex and not dispensed with easily. However, even at this relatively early stage some informed observations and analyses can be made.

THEORETICAL CONSIDERATIONS

As Martinson and others have noted, the nature of collective inmate action has undergone dramatic change since the early attempts at mass escape. Contemporary inmates are much more politically sophisticated and organizationally-inclined. They no longer involve themselves in collective action for the exclusive purpose of communicating their displeasure to their immediate keepers. Instead, they are becoming aware that in an age of instant communication through the mass media, their "audience" has widened considerably.

Any perusal of inmate literature today will demonstrate to the reader that the modern prisoner is often acquainted, formally or informally, with the basic tenets of labeling theory and with the results of studies focusing on self-reported crime, police and judicial discretion, and "white-collar" crime. Increasingly he feels that he has been singled out to bear the burden of punishment by a society that is, from most indications, characterized by a tremendous discrepancy between idealized behavior (as reflected in its laws) and actual behavior (as reported by its citizens). The belief that they are "political prisoners" characterizes the conclusion drawn by an increasing number of our inmates. They are aware that the attributes which disporportionately distinguish them from the free citizens outside the walls are race, income level, and social status—not behavior or *mens rea*.

Given this background of increasing political and criminological awareness of inmates (or at least a number of inmates, including the leaders), we can superimpose this on the conditions and receptivity (or lack thereof) of the correctional administrators and state officials. In the State of Ohio, the administration in power in 1968 had done very little to improve correctional facilities and programs, nor had it spoken of significant reform. What changes it did make focused largely on juveniles. Insofar as correctional institutions for adults, the *status quo* was essentially preserved. The strikes and riots which occurred at the Ohio Penitentiary in

1968 cannot, then, be attributed to "rising expectations" of inmates, except insofar as new wardens at some of the major institutions in the state had reputations as being more inmate than staff-oriented. This was particularly the case at the Ohio Penitentiary, where the newly-installed warden in 1968 was closely identified with the "social work" orientation, thereby alienating many of the more powerful figures on the custody staff. (This warden lasted a mere forty-six days in his position—the shortest tenure on record in the history of the state.) Instead of "rising expectations," it would appear that the riots of 1968 (and the more recent developments occurring under a "reform" administration which made prison conditions a key issue during the gubernatorial campaign) had less to do with who was in power in the state capitol than with the political ideology and criminological sophistication of the leadership of the kept.

DEVELOPMENT OF THE OHIO PRISONERS' LABOR UNION

Despite the absence of published information, the historical development of the Ohio Prisoners' Labor Union can be described, based on in-depth interviews with inmate leaders and with the legal counsel for the union. Although the Ohio prisoners' movement was not the first in the nation, it has progressed more rapidly (as an organization and in inmate membership) than any of the others, given its brief duration.

The origin of the O.P.L.U. can be traced back to Ohio Penitentiary riots of 1968. There is a logically clear, though temporarily separated, relationship between those events and the development of inmate councils and, now, the union. From the perspective of the inmates, most of the promises made by the corrections officials following the June and August, 1968, riots (the latter of which saw five inmates killed in the prison yard by state troopers summoned to quell the disturbances) were broken, due in part at least to the pressure exerted by the guards, who perceived the loss of power they would experience as a result of the possible implementation of reform. At any rate, many inmates felt betrayed and this feeling may have contributed to the second riot.

Late in 1968, after the second riot had occurred, inmate leaders at the Ohio Penitentiary wrote to the governor's office and *requested* that they be allowed to form a union which would approximate a trade union in form. The inmates wanted a regular mechanism for bargaining and resolving disputes; otherwise, they could only foresee more broken promises and more violence, in which case they would always be the losers. Permission to organize was *not* granted.

The inmates continued to discuss the idea of a union, but no concrete steps were taken until a new governor was elected. During the gubernatorial campaign (and as early as 1968, when he ran unsuccessfully for the Congress), this governor had made prison reform a key part of his platform and his image. He also had extensive support from organized labor and talked frequently of repealing the state's Ferguson Act (prohibiting strikes by public employees) and of the state's duty to negotiate with groups representing labor. After his election in 1970, the inmate leaders around the state organized a few work stoppages and then, in 1971, while the Ohio Citizens' Task Force on Corrections was conducting an inquiry into all aspects of the correctional system, the political rhetoric of demands surfaced in a list of grievances and a *notification* (contrasted with the 1968 request) that the inmates of Ohio Penitentiary intended to form a union. Given the dependency-producing nature of "prisonizaton," this event was a major departure and a crucial point in the development of the union.

The message was officially ignored, but the inmates continued to discuss the desirability of a union. In March of 1972 a hunger strike developed into a virtual statewide shutdown of the adult correctional institutions. At that point, another signal event occurred—informal negotiations among inmate leaders, the warden of the Ohio Penitentiary, corrections officials, and represen-

tatives from the governor's office. The agreements reached during these meetings were again broken by the state, according to the perception of the inmates (which is the important perspective here, in accordance with W. I. Thomas' observations about men's definitions of reality). However, partly as a result of the negotiations, regulations emerged specifying the "ground rules" under which the inmate councils, suggested by the Task Force and accepted by the Division of Corrections, would operate. These regulations were given a mixed reaction by inmates. At Ohio Penitentiary, the idea of an inmate council was unanimously rejected because it was anticipated to be state-controlled, not self-determined. It was felt that such a group would be powerless and ineffective. The inmates at London Correctional Institution, on the other hand, accepted the idea and formed the first inmate council in the state.

In addition to inmate councils, other reform measures suggested by the Ohio Citizens' Task Force on Corrections (1971) and adopted by the Division of Corrections included a legal assistance program; the abolition of censorship of first class mail; the hiring of ministers for the Black Muslim inmates at Ohio Penitentiary and Ohio State Reformatory; a recruitment program to attract black employees into the Division of Corrections; standardized grievance procedures for inmates; expanded visitation rights; use of furlough programs; the right of an attorney to visit an inmate in strict privacy upon the inmate's request; and a number of other very important changes, based on the Task Force's ten-month study.

There were no further significant developments until January of 1973. At that time, continuing discontent with the inmate councils, dissatisfaction with the two ombudsmen established by the Division of Corrections (also a Task Force recommendation); and displeasure with the results of the implementation of certain other recommendations led to a request that the American Civil Liberties Union and a few young attorneys help organize a prisoners' union and get recognition. The leaders wrote to California, where the first prisoners' union had formed, and sought advice, which they received. The local legal advisors suggested that the first two steps which should be taken were: (1) organizing a local chapter at each institution and training leaders for succession (to counteract the "unionbusting" tactics encountered in California); and (2) obtaining written authorization by petition from inmates requesting that the O.P.L.U. be their exclusive bargaining agent.

At the present time, [Nov., 1973] the leadership which has developed among the inmates has been largely self-proclaimed. These leaders seem to differ in background and orientation, and at some institutions coalitions of leaders have formed. For example, at the new Southern Ohio Correctional Facility the Sunni Muslims (a very powerful group of Orthodox Muslims) and certain other factions of the population have formed such a coalition. Racial separatism is clearly reflected in some of these arrangements around the state.

Where the administration has not permitted inmates to meet for what might be union activity, the inmates (through legal advisors) have sometimes been successful in forming what amounts to "paper churches" (legal church organizations) for the purpose of carrying on union meetings. This tactic has generally been successfully defended in the courts in the tests thus far.

The union's organizing problems appear to differ from one institution to the next, depending on the nature of the inmate population. At the Ohio State Reformatory (Mansfield), for example, the inmates are overwhelmingly young first-offenders doing "short time." Their incentives not to join the union are probably more powerful than those the union can offer. They perceive their freedom as being not too distant a goal and they are well-aware that union activity could be interpreted as non-conformity to institutionally-prescribed normative behavior. Two other examples of pressures which create difficulty for the union effort may be seen at Ohio Reformatory for Women

(Marysville), where the women who recently met the parole board after participating in a strike all received thirty, sixty, or ninety day "flops"; and at London Correctional Institution, where there are at least three different inmate groups which may, despite their protestations to the contrary, be competing for power.

Currently, the O.P.L.U. is *not* a union, legally or technically speaking; it simply *calls* itself a union. It claims to have petition signatures from about sixty percent of the inmate population in the state. On May 1, 1973, the union presented representatives of the governor's office with about 1500 inmate signatures requesting that the O.P.L.U. be recognized as their exclusive bargaining agent. The union is attempting to get each inmate who joins to pay one dollar per month in dues, but it is clear that this financing, along with a few private donations, will not suffice for very long. It would appear that affiliation would be necessary at some point. Such affiliation could also be quite helpful in securing jobs for inmates and ex-convicts. However, the interest of organized labor in such an affiliation has not been indicated, despite the interest of a few leaders (and ex-leaders), such as James R. Hoffa.

GOALS OF THE O.P.L.U.

According to the official publication of the O.P.L.U., the goals of the union are as follows:

1. Salaries: We believe that all workers should be paid at least the minimum wage set by law, and we should, ideally, be paid on the same basis as civilian employees. This is the goal of the O.P.L.U. "to see prisoners treated as the civilians they were and will be again."
2. Legislation: We support and encourage all legislation beneficial to prison labor.
3. The O.P.L.U. wishes to develop apprenticeship programs that are meaningful to, and appealing to, the prison labor force.
4. We support increases in institutions' (correctional institution) staff salaries so more qualified personnel can be hired.

5. Establishment of self help academies and vocational programs subsidized by the O.P.L.U.
6. Workmen's compensation for all Ohio prisoners.
7. Rehabilitation programs for the handicapped.
8. Protect human, civil and legal rights of prisoners.
9. Correct dangerous working conditions.
10. Encourage private industry to come into institutions.
11. Combat cruelty and injustice wherever found in the prison system.
12. Affiliate with outside unions.

It appears, from reading the publications of the various prisoners' movements around the country, that the goals of the organizations are essentially the same, with some twists owing to local differences in laws, conditions, etc. An analysis of some of these goals is, explicitly or implicitly, included elsewhere in this paper.

OTHER PRISONERS' UNIONS

As was previously mentioned, the O.P.L.U. was not the first prisoners' union in the U.S. To provide some perspective, a brief overview of the prisoners' union movement might be useful.

The first U.S. prisoners' union was formed in California in 1970 when the inmates at Folsom Prison submitted a list of twenty-nine demands, including the right to form a labor union. These demands followed several disturbances and a nineteen day strike, centering on inmate dissatisfaction with the indeterminate sentence, the "adjustment centers," and the shooting of three black inmates at Soledad. The Folsom strike and ensuing demands reflected a new level of knowledge and sophistication on the part of the inmates. Support for a union developed from both inside and outside, and culminated in several meetings in various parts of the state to organize the union. The initial constitution and regulations of the organization were structured so that it would be controlled from the outside (largely by ex-convicts) rather than from within. Tactical-

ly, it was felt that this would facilitate negotiations.

The major goals of the California union, which now has locals in all fourteen "joints," can be listed as follows:

1. (T)he abolishment of the indeterminate sentence system and all its ramifications.
2. (T)he establishment of the workers' rights for the prisoner, including the right to collectively organize and bargain.
3. (T)he restoration of civil and human rights for the prisoners.

In reality, a great deal of the impetus for the other prisoners' unions in the U.S. came from this first union. San Francisco Local 9 of the California Prisoners' Union has now been in operation for over two years, has a staff of at least twenty full and part-time, and is involved in many activities on behalf of inmates, including planning a national prisoners' union movement.

The union in New York was officially established at Greenhaven Prison on February 7, 1972. One unique aspect of this union is that it requested affiliation with District 65, Distributive Workers of America. This request was granted by the labor union, and the prisoners now consider themselves "public employees" under the Taylor Law (Public Employees Fair Employment Act). However, the Public Employees Relations Board of New York turned down the inmates' request for recognition and for the right to collective bargaining. The union is now appealing that ruling.

The Prisoners' Union of Massachusetts is active at Walpole, where it claims to have ninety percent of the inmates as members. Negotiations with officials at the prison and in the capitol apparently came very close to achieving formal recognition of the union, but also resulted in a guards' strike and may have been related to the ouster of Commissioner Boone. Walpole has also recently experienced a major disturbance. Other local chapters in Massachusetts are forming at Framingham, Concord, and Norfolk.

In North Carolina, the prisoners' union reportedly has 2300 members and fully operative outside offices. It apparently has the support of the state AFL-CIO and some ministers. Similarly, Michigan reports 2100 members at Jackson and Marquette.

The New England Prison Coalition, including Maine, Vermont, Rhode Island, Massachusetts, and New Hampshire was formed on May 15, 1973. This coalition is designed to unify prisoners' movements in that region, where the distances separating prisons are considerable.

Other states where prisoners' unions are reportedly forming include Georgia (Atlanta Federal Prison); Washington, D.C. (Lorton); Kansas (Leavenworth); Minnesota (Sandstone and Stillwater); and Washington (Monroe and Steilacoom).

Internationally, the strongest inmate unions are probably to be found in the Scandinavian countries, along with some of the more progressive penal practices. In Sweden, for example, representatives of all five thousand Swedish prisoners negotiated in 1971 with the National Correctional Administration after a hunger strike. Despite the comparatively advanced conditions under which most Swedish prisoners live, they still believe that collective action is necessary to obtain those things which they do not have, such as a guaranteed minimum wage comparable to civilian labor. The organizations known as KRUM (in Sweden) and KRIM (Denmark) help provide outside, as well as inside, pressure on the correctional administrations to make positive changes. However, indications are that although the Swedish people, for example, are highly unionized and do not see unionization inside prisons as particularly threatening, the LO (Trade Unions Congress) controls much of the bargaining and has thus far refused to allow FFSU (a national confederation of prisoners' unions) to bargain collectively for wages. So it would appear that even the Scandinavian unions are still struggling for a number of rights they believe are being denied them.

REACTIONS OF CORRECTIONS ADMINISTRATORS

Directors of state corrections departments have opposed the formation of inmate unions. In Ohio, following a recent eleven-day strike at the Southern Ohio Correctional Facility, the state director was quoted as saying, "These men (the inmate strikers) are convicted felons—convicted of breaking the laws of society. Under no circumstances will I recognize their so-called union". The official reaction of the administration has not changed from that statement. However, a recent inter-office policy memo dealing with inmate unions perhaps more thoroughly reflects the department's thinking on the matter. This memo states, perhaps quite perceptively, that "a hasty entrance into this venture (inmate unions) could cause long-range detriment to the inmate body, as public opinion could react in a negative way to the trends of the correctional system, causing a backlash to the programs and changes of the last few years." This argument is one which hinges on public opinion, as yet untested, but it is clearly a plausible one. The "programs and changes" referred to in the quotation have had a community-oriented focus and have attempted to develop alternatives to incarceration. As a result, the state's prison population has decreased significantly and continues to do so.

Elsewhere in the memo, suggestions are made that the security and custody needs of the institutions be used to "control the organization and formation of inmate unions." The need to show a "clear and present danger" to the institution is stressed. Strategy also includes taking the case to the people of the state "instead of having some half-cocked pedestrianic attorney (presumably a reference to attorneys for the prisoners' union) doing it for you, and misconstruing the facts to the public." The implication that only one side is in possession of the "facts" is perhaps an indication of the amount of distance already seeparating the two camps.

With respect to the union's goal of a minimum wage, it appears that the department intends to rely on the Thirteenth Amendment to the U.S. Constitution ("Neither slavery nor involuntary servitude, except as punishment for crime whereof the party shall have been duly convicted, shall exist within the United States or any place subject to their jurisdiction.") and Article 1, Section 6 of the Ohio Constitution ("There shall be no slavery in this state, nor involuntary servitude, unless for the punishment of crime.") to resist that goal.

As for concrete behavioral reactions to the union movement thus far, reports indicate that Ohio's administrators have reacted in the same manner reported to have occurred in California, where the first forty inmates to join the union were transferred to other institutions all over the state. In Ohio, the legal counsel for the prisoners' union reports that on June 9, 1973, a number of inmate union leaders were transferred from Chillicothe Correctional Institution to Southern Ohio Correctional Facility and placed in a security area. Later indications are that a number of other union leaders have undergone the same transfer from other institutions. At Lebanon Correctional Institution, several inmate leaders were placed in "administrative isolation" (a euphemism for "the hole") after "conspiring to organize against the institution." What they organized was a food boycott. At last report (July 14), they remain in isolation, where they have resided for the past several weeks. They apparently violated the superintendent's policy statement (the first in Ohio regarding the union), which read, in part, ". . . it is the policy of this administration to prohibit a prisoner union or its equivalent or activities within the institution to organize such a union and violators will be subject to disciplinary action or other appropriate action." Other reactions experienced in Ohio include the parole board "flops" mentioned earlier for the inmate strikers at Ohio Reformatory for Women.

Although qualitatively somewhat different, it is clear that there are parallels between the reaction of corrections officials and administrators to prisoners' unions and the reactions, years ago, of management to labor union organizing efforts. To determine the extent of opposition to inmate unions and inmate bargaining, Comeau surveyed all the state corrections departments. Obtaining nearly a fifty percent response rate, Comeau reported the following results:

1. Would you oppose the formation of inmate labor unions to bargain with administrators concerning prison working conditions?
(YES-20, NO-3)
2. If a labor union could be structured so that threats to security and order within the institution could be brought below current levels, would you oppose its formation?
(YES-15, NO-8)
3. Are you opposed to all forms of 'bargaining' between inmates and administrators?
(YES-10, NO-14)

Comeau concluded that although the responses indicated an unwillingness to accept inmate unions at present, they also seemed to reflect the belief that *some* form of bargaining would quite often be accepted. It was also noted that as perceived threat to institutional security diminishes, acceptability of the idea of inmate unions increases. He also noted that with respect to the general opposition of the correctional administrators, . . . much of their fear about the unions was based on their belief that certain inmates would become leaders and remain leaders through force and coercion of others; they fear problems of internal security and control; and they cite the difficulty of "bargaining" with inmates who are often maladjusted and socially deviant.

It is clear from this evidence that if prisoners' unions hope to change the opinions of administrators, they will have to convince them that the unions do not threaten institutional security and that they will be able to control internal power struggles so that they do not end up with a union representing the views and interests of only the most powerful inmates. This will not be an easy task.

LEGAL CONSIDERATIONS

Do inmates have the legal right to form unions? Although no constitutional or statutory provisions deal *directly* with this question, there are a number of pertinent rulings bearing on closely-related matters. As Comeau notes, "The right to unionize is itself a composite of . . . more fundamental freedoms . . ."

Up until 1944, it was widely held that prisoners were "slaves of the state" who had forfeited all personal rights (*Ruffin v. Commonwealth*, 62 Va., 1871). This view was based on the Thirteenth Amendment to the U.S. Constitution and on various state constitutional provisions, such as Ohio's (quoted earlier). But in 1944 (*Coffin v. Reichard*, 143 F. 2nd 443), the sixth circuit court held that "a prisoner retains all the rights of an ordinary citizen, except those expressly, or by necessary implication, taken from him by law." This ruling has often been cited by those advocating expanded rights for prisoners.

In 1948, however, a somewhat different view was advanced. In *Price v. Johnston* (334 U.S. 266, 285) the Supreme Court of the U.S. held that "Lawful incarceration brings about the necessary withdrawal or limitation of many privileges and rights, a reaction justified by the considerations underlying our penal system." This ruling, of course, has been cited by those seeking to justify restrictions on the rights of prisoners.

The *Price* decision places the burden of proof on the inmate to show why he should have a particular "right." The *Coffin* ruling clearly places the burden on the state to demonstrate a compelling need to restrict the "right."

Recently, however, a trend has developed which relies on the application of the "clear and present danger test" to such matters. In 1968 in *Jackson v. Goodwin* (400 F. 2nd 529), the fifth circuit court held that "the state must strongly show some substantial and controlling interest which requires the subordination or limitation of these important constitutional rights, and which justifies their infringement; and in the absence of such compelling justification, the state restrictions are impermissable infringements of the fundamental and preferred First Amendment rights."

A review of the pertinent legal literature indicates that the courts have "chipped away" at the restrictions of the Thirteenth Amendment in most of these cases and in others involving the expression of dissatisfaction with prison administrations; expressing

political beliefs; petitioning for the redress of grievances; exercising freedom of association; engaging in organizing activities; and other rights which, taken together, practically constitute the right of unionization. But probably the strongest single judicial statement on the subject came in 1972 from Judge Oakes (*Goodwin v. Oswald*, 462 F. 2nd, 1237) of the second circuit. In that case, the prison warden had prevented the delivery of letters to 980 inmates from attorneys giving legal advice on organizing a union. The judge stated, in his opinion:

There is nothing in federal or state constitutional or statutory law of which I am aware that forbids prison inmates from seeking to form, or correctional officials from electing to deal with, an organization or agency or representative group of inmates concerned with prison conditions and inmates' grievances. Indeed, the tragic experience at Attica ... would make correctional officials, an observer might think, seek more peaceful ways of resolving prison problems than the old, ironclad, solitary-confinement, mail-censoring, dehumanizing methods that have worked so poorly in the past. Promoting or at least permitting the formation of a representative agency might well be, in the light of past experience, the wisest course for correctional officials to follow.

After a thorough review of the relevant judicial decisions and legal issues involved, the following conclusions seem apparent:

1. If inmates have a right to unionize, this right is clearly secondary to the state's interest in maintaining a secure and orderly penal system.
2. Where contests develop in this matter, the state must show clear and present undesirable effects on the institution, as a minimum, in order to win its case.
3. With respect to the minimum wage goal of the inmates and their efforts to be recognized as public employees, it would appear that under the National Labor Relations Act, inmates probably could *not* meet the definition of "employee". However, there is nothing in Ohio law to *prevent* the state from recognizing inmates as employees, but only if the state

wishes to do so (as it has with several labor groups representing staff in correctional institutions). The only law in Ohio specifically dealing with public employees is the Ferguson Act, prohibiting strikes.

4. The right to unionize probably hinges on the ability of the inmates to demonstrate that the union would have substantial control over its members and that it would pose no threat to the internal security and order of the institution.

QUESTIONS FOR DISCUSSION

1. What does the study of victimology entail?
2. Why the sudden resurgence in the rights of the victim again after centuries during which no one paid much attention to the victim?
3. Differentiate the following:
   A. Composition
   B. Compensation
   C. Reparations
   D. Restitution
4. What are the general rules now governing victim compensation (e.g. amount which can be recovered, type of crime or injury, proof of damage)?
5. Will the victim compensation approach in any way alter the present criminal justice system? If so, how?
6. How do you account for the politicalization of the inmates in our prisons in the last decade?
7. What have been the chief demands made by prisoners for reforms in the system? Be specific. The inmates at Attica were as consistent as inmates in every recent riot from Massachusetts to Oklahoma to California in these demands.
8. To what extent are these demands realistic? Reasonable?
9. What percentage of the inmates are or have been or are likely to be politicalized?
10. Can a union movement among inmates make any headway? Is this movement merely a one-shot affair?
11. Why haven't inmates organized before? Do you think the Teamsters or the United Auto Workers, for example, are eager to help prisoners organize?
12. With whom will inmates bargain? With the guards who are unionizing and in opposition to inmate organizations since the two are already in conflict? With the administration? With whom?
13. Can nonoffenders provide leadership? Can ex-offenders join?
14. How do you think judges, police, or prosecutors will react to this development?
15. Why have there been no comparable movements in mental hospitals, state schools for retardates, among juveniles in custody, in jails?
16. Since rights are in conflict, whose should be paramount—the rights of the accused or the rights of the public? Is it really the American ideal that better 10 guilty men be free than one innocent man be wrongly convicted? What is the evidence on this point?
17. What is cruel and unusual punishment? At what point should a defendant be permitted counsel? At public expense, if need be?
18. Discuss these issues briefly:
    A. The right to silence
    B. The absolute right to privacy
    C. Freedom from illegal search and seizure
    D. The law enforcement needs—on occasion—for wiretapping, stop and frisk, preventive detention, and surveillance.
    Is there any reasonable way these contradictory needs can be mediated?
19. With the development of computer information systems will it ever again be possible to be free of stigma once one has had a juvenile, adult, mental health, or other record? How are we to be protected from this all embracing system?

BIBLIOGRAPHY

Comeau, Paul R. "Labor Unions for Prison Inmates: An Analysis of a Recent Proposal for the Organization of Inmate Labor." *Buffalo Law Review* 21 (Spring 1972), 963–85.

Downey, Bernard. "Compensating Victims of Violent Crime." *British Journal of Criminology* 5 No. 1 (July 1964).

Goldberg, Arthur et al. "Government Compensation for the Victims of Violence: A Symposium." *Southern California Law Review* 43 No. 1 (1970). (Note: Contributors to this symposium in addition to Justice Goldberg include such eminent criminologists as Marvin Wolfgang, Stephan Schafer, Ralph W. Yarborough, LeRoy L. Lambeau, Duncan Chappell, William Shank, and Kent M. Weeks.)

Goldstein, A. *The Insanity Defense.* New Haven, Conn.: Yale University Press, 1967.

Guttmacher, Manfred S. *The Role of Psychiatry in Law.* Springfield, Ill.: Charles C. Thomas, 1968.

Halleck, Seymour L. *Psychiatry and the Dilemmas of Crime.* New York: Harper and Row, 1967.

Jeffery, C. Ray. *Criminal Responsibility and Mental Disease.* Springfield, Ill.: Charles C. Thomas, 1967.

Mendelsohn, B. "The Origin of Victimology." *Excerpta Criminologica* 33 (May–June 1963), 239–41.

Mueller, G. O. W. "Compensation for Victims of Crime: Thought Before Action." *Minnesota Law Review* 50 (December 1965), 213–21. (Note: Among the contributors to this fine symposium on victim compensation laws are Marvin Wolfgang, Stephan Schafer, James E. Starr, Duncan Chappell, Robert Childress, and Ralph Yarborough.)

Palmer, John W. *Constitutional Rights of Prisoners.* Cincinnati: The W. H. Anderson Co., 1973.

Rowat, D. "Ombudsman For North America." *Public Administration Review* 24 (1964).

Rubin, Sol. *Psychiatry and the Criminal Law.* New York: Oceana, 1965.

Schafer, Stephan. *Compensation and Restitution to the Victims of Crime.* (2nd ed.) Montclaire, N.J.: Patterson, Smith, 1970.

Schafer, Stephan. *The Victim and His Criminal.* New York: Random House, 1968.

Schur, Edwin. *Radical Non-Intervention: Rethinking the Delinquency Problem.* Englewood Cliffs, N.J.: Prentice-Hall, 1973.

Shaskolsky, Leon. "The Innocent Bystander and Crime." *Federal Probation* 34, (March 1970), 44–48.

Von Hentig, Hans. *The Criminal and His Victim.* New Haven, Conn.: Yale University Press, 1948.

Ward, David A. "Inmate Rights and Prison Reform in Sweden and Denmark." *The Journal of Criminal Law, Criminology, and Police Science* 63, No. 2 (1972), 240–55.

APPENDIX

Glossary of Legal Phrases and Definitions

Many norms are embedded in legal codes which means they take on a different terminology. While each political jurisdiction develops its own specific definitions, the following usages tend to be somewhat typical. They are based on Ohio Law prior to its revision in January 1974. Also included are definitions of procedural terms used in the criminal justice system

LEGAL PHRASES AND DEFINITIONS

Abet To encourage another to commit a crime by means of inducement, advice, command, etc. The abettor need not be physically present at the scene of the crime to be prosecuted as a principal offender.

Accomplice A person who knowingly, voluntarily, and with common intent with the principal offender unites in the commission of a crime. The term principal means the same thing except one may be a principal if he commits a crime without aid from others.

Acquit A judgment of acquittal is a judicial finding of not guilty if the matter is tried before a judge or a verdict of not guilty by a jury if the case is tried before a jury. It exonerates the defendant from any criminal responsibility in that case and means that he may not be tried for that case again.

Adjournment Postponing a session or hearing until another time or place.

Adult Under Ohio Law, any person eighteen years of age, or over, is subject to criminal prosecution as an adult. In *Common Law* adult is defined as one who has attained the legal age of majority, generally twenty-one years.

Adultery Voluntary and unlawful cohabitation on the part of a married person with one of the opposite sex.

Affidavit A sworn written statement, made voluntarily, taken before an officer having authority to administer such oath.

Affirmation To swear on one's conscience that what they say is true. Also known as an asseveration. Accepted in lieu of swearing an oath to God, due to religious beliefs or a lack of religion. It has the same legal force and effect as an oath.

Alias A fictitious name; a name other than a persons true name.

Alibi A claim that a person was at a different place from that charged. A defense involving physical impossibility of guilt of the accused.

Appeal A proceeding by which a case is carried to a higher court in an attempt to have the decision of the lower court altered or overruled.

Arraignment The formal action in which the accused appears before the court, has the charges or indictment read to him, and enters a plea.

Arrest 1. Meaning of the term "arrest."

    A. An arrest consists of the taking of another into custody for the actual or purported purpose of bringing the other before a court, or otherwise securing the administration of the law. With minor variations in expression, this is a common definition of the term as stated by courts, text writers, and statutory enactments.

    B. In criminal procedure "arrest" signifies that one so taken or detained is thereby subjected, by color of legal authority, to the actual control and will of the person making the arrest.

The essence of the term is restriction and restraint of the person.
2. There are four essential elements of arrest.
   A. Purpose of intent to take a person into custody of the law
   B. Under a real or pretended authority
   C. An actual or constructive seizure or detention of such person
   D. Which is so understood by the person arrested.

Arson Setting fire to, or burning any building, willfully and maliciously, or with intent to defraud.

Asportation The moving of an object from its original position. The distance moved is immaterial. The object taken must have been in entire or absolute possession of the taker to complete the element of asportation in Ohio law.

Assault An intentional, unlawful offer or attempt to hurt another person physically. Should the person actually be beaten the act is battery.

Attestation The act of witnessing, e.g., witnessing a person's signature on a document.

Bail Security for the appearance of an accused to appear and answer to a specific criminal charge in any court or before any magistrate.

Battery A willful and unlawful use of force upon the person of another without his consent.

Bigamy Marriage to another person while having a legal husband or wife.

Blackmail To extort goods or money from another by means of threat of accusation or exposure. Truth of the charge is no defense.

Bona Fide In or with good faith.

Bond A contract under which a person or company, as a surety, agrees to pay a sum of money conditioned on the performance or nonperformance of certain acts.

Breaking and Entering Inhabited Dwelling–Night Season (Burglary) Maliciously and forcibly break and enter uninhabited dwelling, uninhabited house trailer, or other building in the night season with intent to steal property of any value or with intent to commit a felony. *NOTE: Includes attempt* to break and enter inhabited dwelling or inhabited house trailer.

Breaking and Entering In Daytime (Housebreaking) Maliciously break and enter in the daytime a dwelling house or any other building with intent to steal or commit a felony.

Bribery The offering, giving, receiving, or soliciting of any thing of value to influence the action of an official or in the discharge of a legal or public duty.

Brief A summary of the law or comments on the facts relating to a case which is prepared by the attorneys for both sides in a case and submitted to the judge. A brief, while factual in nature, is basically a persuasive legal document.

Burden of Proof The burden of proving the fact in issue. Thus, in a criminal case, the prosecutor has the duty of proving the guilt of the defendant beyond a reasonable doubt. The defendant has no duty to prove his innocence. Of course, if the prosecutor is having success in proving guilt, the defendant will have to offer evidence to offset this proof. This is called the burden of evidence, that is, the obligation of presenting evidence in a case, and it may equally be the duty of the defendant as well as of the prosecutor.

Capital Crime Any crime punishable by death.

Circumstantial Evidence Any evidence, proof of which infers or implies, or proves or disproves another fact in question. Testimony based not on personal knowledge of the existence of the fact in controversy but on knowledge of other facts from which that fact may be satisfactorily proved.

Civil Rights Rights guaranteed to the public by the U.S. and STATE CONSTITUTIONS, CONGRESS, AND STATE LEGISLATRES. The right of property, marriage, protection by the laws, freedom of contract, trial by jury.

Codicil An addition made to a will. It may explain, modify, add to, subtract from, qualify, alter, restrain, or revoke provisions in a will.

Coercion Compelling a person to do that which he does not have to do, or to omit what he may legally do, by some illegal force, threat, or intimidation.

Cognomen A family name; the last name.

Cohabit Living, or abiding, or residing together as man and wife.

Common Law The unwritten law of a country based on custom and past decisions of the courts.

Common Pleas Court Court having exclusive and original jurisdiction of all crimes and offenses amounting to a felony, and concurrent original jurisdiction with inferior courts of misdemeanors.

Commutation of Sentence To change the punishment meted out to a criminal to one less severe. Thus, to change a sentence of death to life imprisonment is a commutation. Only the governor may do this in a state.

Complaint A sworn written statement that a certain person committed a specified crime. When the Grand Jury makes a complaint, it is called an indictment.

Concubine A woman who cohabits with a man to whom she is not married.

Confession A voluntary admission of guilt by a person who has committed a crime.

Consanguinity Those who descend from a common ancestor are related by consanguinity. Blood relationship.

Conspiracy Two or more persons planning to

commit a crime or a legal act in an unlawful manner.

Contempt of Court Behavior that impugns the authority of a court or obstructs the execution of court orders.

Contest To oppose, resist, or dispute the case of the party in a legal action.

Contralegem Against the law.

Corporal Relating to the body. Thus, corporal punishment is force used against the body of another.

Corpus Delicti The body or essence of a crime; all things necessary to constitute a crime. As a rule it is divided into two parts: (1) the acts necessary to the crime; (2) done in a way to render it criminal.

Court of Record Those courts whose acts and judicial proceedings are recorded for a perpetual memory and testimony. They have the power to fine or imprison for contempt. This court generally possesses a seal.

Criminalistics That science which applies the physical sciences (chemistry-physics-biology) in the investigation of crime.

Criminology The scientific study of crime and criminals.

De Facto In fact; actually; in reality.

De Jure In accordance with the law.

Defraud To withhold from another what is justly due him, or to deprive him of a right by artifice or deception; to cheat.

Defendant The party against whom an action at law or inequity is brought; the party denying, opposing, resisting, or contesting the action.

Demurrer A plea for the dismissal of an indictment on the grounds that the facts of the indictment do not constitute a violation of the law of this state, or intent is not alleged and proof of intent is necessary, or the offense charged is not within the courts jurisdiction.

Deposition A written statement made by a witness, under oath, to be used as testimony in court. A deposition contains testimony whereas an affidavit contains a statement.

Domicile A place where a person has his legal residence. May be acquired by birth, choice, or law (wife arising from marriage).

Due Process Law in its regular course of administration through courts of justice. It implies that there is a law on the subject, that a defendant is informed of the charge, is indicted, is tried in a proper court, etc. The U.S. CONSTITUTION prohibits depriving a person of his life, liberty, or property without due process of law.

Embezzlement Misappropriating the personal property of another person which comes into one's possession by virtue of employment. The value of the property taken can be totaled over a three-year period of continuous employment prior to the inception of prosecution.

Embracery An illegal attempt to influence or instruct a jury, or a member thereof, by an improper means other than the offer of anything of value. See bribery.

Eminent Domain The power of the state to take private property for public use.

Entrapment The act of inducing, luring, or inviting another to commit a crime (which he otherwise had no intention of committing) for the sole purpose of prosecuting the offender.

Evidence All the means used to prove or disprove a fact in issue. Not all evidence is admissible in court.

Ex Officio Powers not conferred on an officer but implied in his office; by virtue of office. A judge is an ex officio conservator of the peace.

Ex Parte Done by or for one side only and without notice to, or contestation by, any person adversely interested.

Ex Post Facto Law A criminal law which makes an act a crime although it was committed prior to the passage of the law. It is further defined as the passage of a law making a particular act a crime greater than it was when committed; or the passage of a law adding to the punishment of a crime; or the passage of a law that changes the rules of evidence to make conviction easier. Such laws are forbidden by the U.S. CONSTITUTION.

Examination An investigation of a witness by counsel by means of questions for the purpose of bringing before the court the knowledge possessed by the witness.

Exception A formal objection or reservation to court action or opinion in the course of the trial.

Extradition The turning over of an alleged criminal, fugitive, or prisoner by one state to another.

Extremis The state of a person who is near death; beyond hope of recovery.

Feasance The doing of something.

   Nonfeasance Is a term applied to neglect of duty by a public officer.

   Malfeasance Is the act of a public officer who commits a crime in relation to his office.

   Misfeasance Is the act of a public officer who as such does a lawful act in an unlawful or wrongful way not, however, amounting to a crime.

Feeblemindedness (Amentia) Arrested mental development. There are three types or grades of mental defectives based on the limits of their intelligence quotients ascertained from mental tests. Thus, an:

   Idiot A mental defective whose intelligence

does not mature beyond three years or whose I.Q. (intelligence quotient) is 0 to 20.

Imbecile A mental defective whose intelligence does not develop beyond seven years or whose intelligence is between three and seven years. The I.Q. is between 20 and 50.

Moron The mental defective whose intelligence is between seven and twelve years. The I.Q. is between 50 and 70.

Felonious Evil, malicious, or criminal. A felonious act is not necessarily a felony, but it is criminal in some degree.

Felony An offense punishable by death or by imprisonment in a state penitentiary.

"Fence" A professional receiver and seller of stolen goods.

Feticide See HOMICIDE.

Firearm An instrument devised to propel any object by the explosion of gun powder. Thus, a spring rifle or an air rifle is not a firearm.

Foetus An unborn child.

Forensic Characteristic of or belonging to a law court.

Fratricide See HOMICIDE.

Grand Jury A jury of inquiry, consisting of fifteen jurors, whose duty it is to receive and hear complaints or accusations in criminal cases, and if sustained by evidence, to find true bills or indictments against the person complained of. Testimony is generally ex parte.

Harboring Felon The act of concealing a person, knowing or having reasonable grounds to believe he has committed a felony.

Homicide Killing of one human being by another human being. Describes the act—pronounces no judgment on its legal or moral quality.

Feticide The destruction of the foetus in the womb. Also known as "procuring abortion."

Fratricide The term applied to the killing of one's brother or sister.

Infanticide The murder or killing of an infant soon after birth.

Matricide The killing of one's mother.

Patricide The killing of one's father.

Suicide The killing of one's self; self-destruction.

Uxorcide The killing of one's wife.

Illicit Not permitted or allowed; prohibited; unlawful.

Impeach To proceed against a public officer for a crime of misfeasance. Further described as "To discredit a witness."

Impeachment When certain U.S. Public Officials are accused of misconduct in office, the formal accusation that follows is the impeachment. A later trial is based on this formal accusation.

In Articulo Mortis At the point of death.

In Camera A cause heard before the judge in his private room or when all spectators are excluded from the court room.

Incest Sexual intercourse between persons too closely related to marry. An essential element is the knowledge that a relationship exists nearer than that of cousin.

Inculpate To accuse of crime; to involve in guilt.

Indictment To accuse of crime in writing by the Grand Jury. The indictment gives the Common Pleas Court jurisdiction to try the case.

Infanticide See HOMICIDE.

Inference A process of reasoning by which a fact is deduced from other facts.

Intent A design or determination of the mind to do or not to do a certain thing. Criminal intent is the intent to break the law. Intent is usually determined from the nature of one's act.

Jeopardy The danger of conviction and punishment which a defendant in a criminal trial incurs when a valid indictment has been found.

Double Jeopardy A second prosecution after a first trial for the same offense. This type of jeopardy is prohibited under the CONSTITUTION.

Judicial Notice The rule that a court will accept without proof some things of common knowledge.

Jurisdiction The power conferred upon a court by law by which it is authorized to hear and determine a cause.

Justifiable Homicide The killing of a human being without fault or blame as where it is required by law or in the prevention of an atrocious crime.

Kidnapping The stealing and carrying away or secreting of a person. The essence of the offense is the unlawful secret imprisonment regardless of the purpose.

Latent Hidden; concealed; that does not appear on the surface of a thing, e.g., latent fingerprints.

Leading Question A question framed in such a way as to suggest the answer sought.

Larceny The unlawful taking of property belonging to another.

Grand Larceny Is established when the value of the property stolen is $50.00 or more (FBI figure).

Petit Larceny When the value of the property stolen is less than $50.00 (FBI figure).

Libel Published writings calculated to injure the reputation of another by bringing him into ridicule, hatred, or contempt.

Slander Of the same nature except that it is verbal, not written.

License A permit to do some act, accorded by competent authority, which would be illegal without such authorization.

Locus Delictus The place where a crime occurs.

Lucri Causa For the sake of gain. Descriptive of the intent with which property is taken in cases of larceny.

Mala Fide In bad faith; with intent to deceive.

Mala in se Evil in itself. Crimes which of their nature are evil and morally wrong, such as murder.

Mala Prohibita Prohibited wrongs or offenses; acts which are made offenses by positive laws and prohibited as such.

Malfeasance See FEASANCE.

Maliciously An intent to do a wrongful act and may consist in direct intention to injure or in reckless disregard of another's rights.

Manslaughter The unlawful killing of one human being by another human being without malice.

Martial Law Temporary government control by the military authorities over the civilian population. Exercised in an area of military operations during time of war or when civilian authority has broken down.

Matricide See HOMICIDE.

Matter of Fact in Issue The question of fact to be decided at the trial.

Mens Rea Guilty mind; criminal intent.

Military Law Law concerning the discipline of the armed forces.

Minor Under Ohio Law, any person under eighteen years of age. In *Civil Law* a minor is described as an infant or person who is under the age of legal competence, one under twenty-one.

Misdemeanor An offense not amounting to a felony. (See FELONY.)

Misfeasance See FESANCE.

Misprision Misconduct or neglect of duty, particularly by a public official.

Misprision of Felony Failure to reveal a crime by one who had not participated or assisted in its commission. Not an offense in Ohio *except* misprision of treason.

Mistrial A trial made void because of error in the proceedings or because the jury cannot reach a verdict.

Modus Operandi Method of operation by criminals.

Motive The reason for doing a certain thing; the motivating influence.

Moulage The making of a mold from some plastic substance of a toolmark, footprint, etc., for criminal identification purposes.

Municipal Court Courts having original and final jurisdiction within their respective territories of all misdemeanors, and examining jurisdiction of all felonies committed within their territory.

Negligence Failure to exercise the reasonable amount of care in the commission of an act which results in injury to another; omission to perform an act which a reasonable man would do.

Night Season That period of time from the termination of daylight in the evening to the earliest dawn in the morning.

Nolle Prosequi A declaration to a court by a plaintiff or prosecutor that he does not wish to further prosecute the case at that time. This is not a final disposition of the case. It may be refiled and a person may later be convicted.

Non Compos Mentis Of unsound mind; mentally incapable of handling one's own affairs.

Nonfeasance See FEASANCE.

Oath A declaration based upon an appeal to God for aid and witness that one will speak the truth.

Ordinance A law enacted by the legislative branch of a city government.

Overt Act An open act; a physical act as opposed to a thought.

Pardon The remission of penalty by the Governor in accordance with the power vested in him by the Constitution. Pardons may be granted after conviction and may be absolute and entire, or partial, and may be granted upon conditions precedent or subsequent.

Parole A conditional release from prison. Legal custody of a parolee shall remain in the Department of Mental Hygiene and Correction until granted a final release by the Pardon and Parole Commission.

Parol Evidence Oral or spoken testimony of a witness.

Patricide See HOMICIDE.

Peremptory Challenge The right of the prisoner and the prosecution in a criminal trial to offer objection to a certain number of porposed jurors without giving an explanation. Six of each side in capital cases and four each in other crimes.

Perjury The act of willfully swearing falsely.

Petit Jury The ordinary jury of twelve for the trial of a civil or criminal action.

Plaintiff A person who brings a suit into a court of law; a complainant.

Plea A statement made by or for a defendant, either answering the charges or showing why he should not be required to answer.

Police Power The constitutional power vested in legislative bodies to pass laws for the general welfare.

Post Mortem Happenings done or made after death; commonly applied to examination of a dead body.

Power of Attorney A written statement legally authorizing one person to act as agent for another. Can be for a general or specific purpose.

Precedent A previous judicial decision which may serve as an example or rule in similar cases.

Preliminary Hearing A hearing before a magistrate in which the arrested person is informed of the charge against him, his right to legal counsel, and in which it is decided whether or not sufficient evidence has been presented to bind him over to the grand jury.

Prima Facie So far as can be judged from the first appearance, or at first sight.

Probate Court A court for probating wills; administering estates; appointing guardians for minors, incompetents, and mentally ill.

Probation The type of penalty whereby a convicted man is put under the jurisdiction of probation officers for a stated time instead of being sent to prison.

Rapine The act of seizing and carrying off the property of another by force; pillage; plunder.

Real Property Permanent, immovable things as land and the building attached thereto.

Reasonable Doubt After comparison and consideration of all evidence there is *not* a feeling of abiding conviction, to a moral certainty, of the truth of the charge. It is not a mere possible doubt because everything relating to human affairs or depending upon moral evidence is open to some possible or imaginary doubt.

Rebut To contradict. Rebuttable evidence is that which may be contradicted by other evidence.

Recidivist A repeater in crime or an habitual offender.

Recognizance A writing signed before a proper officer by which a person binds himself to do an act specified therein or to suffer a penalty. Bail is a form of recognizance because one agrees to appear or to forfeit property or money.

Relevant Applying to the issue in question and consequently useful in determining the truth or falsity of an alleged fact.

Remand To send a case back to a lower court for whatever additional proceedings may be required, or to return one to jail who has been temporarily released therefrom.

Res Gestae Words or acts at the time of a crime or incident which tend to explain and have a relation to the crime or incident. Admissible in evidence if spontaneous.

Rigor Mortis The stiffening of the muscles after death.

Scienter Knowingly, guilty knowledge.

Slander See LIBEL.

Sodomy Carnal copulation with beast; or in any opening of the body, except sexual parts, with another human being.

Statute A law passed by a legislature; written law.

Subpoena A written order to appear at a trial as a witness. Failure to appear is regarded as contempt of court. If the subpoena indicates records are to be produced at the trial it is called subpoena DUCES TECUM.

Substantiate To verify; establish the truth of a matter by adequate evidence.

Suicide See HOMICIDE.

Supreme Court The highest Federal Court consist-ing of nine judges; its decisions are final and take precedence over those of all other courts; its decisions are based on interpretation of the U.S. CONSTITUTION; also the highest court in a state, as the Ohio Supreme Court.

Testimony Evidence given by a witness under oath or affirmation.

Tort A legal wrong committed against the person or property for which reparation may be obtained by a suit of law.

Toxicology The science of poisons.

Transcript An official written or typewritten copy of court proceedings, i.e., record of a trial.

True Bill The endorsement made by a grand jury upon a bill of indictment, sustained by evidence, and after being satisfied of the truth of the charges brought before the body.

Usury Excessive interest rates or charges on loans.

Uxorcide See HOMICIDE.

Venue The county or locality in which a cause of action may be tried, usually where a crime is committed. A necessary element of a crime.

Verdict The decision of a jury.

Waive To give up a personal right.

Ward A person under the care or charge of a guardian; a minor under guardianship.

Willfully A positive act intending the result which comes to pass; designed; intentional.

Witness A person who saw or can give a first-hand account of an event; a person who testifies in court. To witness a transaction, document, or signature.

Writ A formal, legal document ordering or prohibiting the performance of a specified action.

Capias A writ requiring an officer to take the body of the defendant into custody; a writ of attachment or arrest. This may be issued by any court having jurisdiction over the defendant.

Habeas Corpus A writ directed to the person detaining another, commanding him to produce the body of the prisoner in court. "Remedy for deliverance from illegal confinement."

Injunction A prohibitive writ forbidding a party to do some act, or restraining him from the continuance of some act.

Mandamus A writ from a Superior Court directed to a private or municipal corporation or lower court commanding the performance of a particular act therein specified.

Mittimus A percept in writing from a court or magistrate to a sheriff or other officer commanding him to convey a person to prison and to the jailer commanding him to receive and keep the prisoner, until deliverance by due course of law.

Prohibition A writ that prohibits a judge, judicial officer, or public official from performing some official act.

Replevin A redelivery to the owner of the pledge or thing taken in distress.

Warrant A writ issued by a court of magistrate ordering a peace officer to arrest the one named therein for a crime.

Classification of Mental Disorders

The following classification was developed by the Committee on Nomenclature and Statistics of the American Psychiatric Association. It has been considerably shortened, but the numbering system has been retained and certain categories—psychoses, neurosis, and personality disorders—have been described more fully. Even in its truncated form, it does provide some idea of the complexity of mental disorders and of the difficulties involved in standardized diagnosis.

In 1974, 58 percent of the membership of the American Psychiatric Association voted to remove homosexuality from this classification of mental disorders indicating the profound influence of social definitions on psychiatric thought. In this case, the homophile movement was most successful in altering not only the nomenclature but the conception of homosexuality as an alternative mode of sexual conduct.

I. MENTAL RETARDATION (310–315)

II. ORGANIC BRAIN SYNDROMES
(Disorders caused by or associated with impairment of brain tissue function)

These disorders are manifested by the following symptoms:

From *Diagnostic and Statistical Manual of Mental Disorders.* Washington, American Psychiatric Association, 1968, pp. 22–52.

a. Impairment of orientation
b. Impairment of memory
c. Impairment of all intellectual functions such as comprehension, calculation, knowledge, learning, etc.
d. Impairment of judgment
e. Lability and shallowness of affect

The organic brain syndrome is a basic mental condition characteristically resulting from diffuse impairment of brain tissue function from whatever cause. Most of the basic symptoms are generally present to some degree regardless of whether the syndrome is mild, moderate or severe.

The syndrome may be the only disturbance present. It may also be associated with psychotic symptoms and behavioral disturbances. The severity of the associated symptoms is affected by and related to not only the precipitating organic disorder but also the patient's inherent personality patterns, present emotional conflicts, his environmental situation, and interpersonal relations.

These brain syndromes are grouped into psychotic and non-psychotic disorders according to the severity of functional impairment. . . .

THE PSYCHOSES

Psychoses are described in two places, here with the organic brain syndromes and later with the functional psychoses. The general discussion of psychosis appears here because organic brain syndromes are listed first.

Patients are described as psychotic when their mental functioning is sufficiently impaired to interfere grossly with their capacity to meet the ordinary demands of life. The impairment may result from a serious distortion in their capacity to recognize reality. Hallucinations and delusions, for example, may distort their perceptions. Alterations of mood may be so profound that the patient's capacity to respond appropriately is grossly impaired. Deficits in perception, language and memory may be so severe that the patient's capacity for mental grasp of his situation is effectively lost. . . .

II. A. Psychoses Associated with Organic Brain Syndromes (290–294)

290 *Senile and Pre-senile dementia*

290.0 Senile dementia

This syndrome occurs with senile brain disease, whose causes are largely unknown. The category does not include the pre-senile psychoses nor other degenerative diseases of the central nervous system. While senile brain disease derives its name from the age group in which it is most commonly seen, its diagnosis should be based on the brain disorder present and not on the patient's age at times of onset. Even mild cases will manifest some evidence of organic brain syndrome: self-centeredness, difficulty in assimilating new experiences, and childish emotionality. Deterioration may be minimal or progress to vegetative existence.

290.1 Pre-senile dementia

This category includes a group of cortical brain diseases presenting clinical pictures similar to those of senile dementia but appearing characteristically in younger age groups. Alzheimer's and Pick's diseases are the two best known forms, each of which has a specific brain pathology.

291 Alcoholic psychoses

Alcoholic psychoses are psychoses caused by poisoning with alcohol. When a pre-existing psychotic, psychoneurotic or other disorder is aggravated by modest alcohol intake, the underlying condition, not the alcoholic psychosis, is diagnosed. . . .

291.0 Delirium tremens

This is a variety of acute brain syndrome characterized by delirium, coarse tremors, and frightening visual hallucinations usually becoming more intense in the dark. Because it was first identified in alcoholics and until recently was thought always to be due to alcohol ingestion, the term is restricted to the syndrome associated with alcohol. . . .

291.1 Korsakov's psychosis (alcoholic) Also "Korsakoff"

This is a variety of chronic brain syndrome associated with longstanding alcohol use and characterized by memory impairment, disorientation, peripheral neuropathy and particularly by confabulation. Like delirium tremens, Korsakov's psychosis is identified with alcohol because of an initial error in identifying its cause, and therefore the term is confined to the syndrome associated with alcohol. . . .

291.2 Other alcoholic hallucinosis

Hallucinoses caused by alcohol which cannot be diagnosed as delirium tremens, Korsakov's psychosis, or alcoholic deterioration fall in this category. A common variety manifests accusatory or threatening auditory hallucinations in a state of relatively clear consciousness. . . .

291.3 Alcohol paranoid state ((Alcoholic paranois))

This term describes a paranoid state which develops in chronic alcoholics, generally male, and is characterized by excessive jealousy and delusions of infidelity by the spouse. Patients diagnosed under primary paranoid states or schizophrenia should not be included here even if they drink to excess.

291.4 Acute alcohol intoxication

All varieties of acute brain syndromes of psychotic proportion caused by alcohol are included here if they do not manifest features of delirium tremens, alcoholic hallucinosis, or pathological intoxication. This diagnosis is used alone when there is no other psychiatric disorder or as an additional diagnosis with other psychiatric conditions including alcoholism. The conditio should not be confused with *simple drunkenness,* which does not involve psychosis.

291.5 Alcoholic deterioration

All varieties of chronic brain syndromes of psychotic proportion caused by alcohol and not having the characteristic features of Korsakov's psychosis are included here.

291.6 Pathological intoxication

This is an acute brain syndrome manifested by psychosis after minimal alcohol intake.

291.9 Other [and unspecified] alcoholic psychosis

This term refers to all varieties of alcoholic psychosis not classified above.

292 *Psychosis associated with intracranial infection*

292.0 General paralysis

This condition is characterized by physical signs and symptoms of parenchymatous syphilis of the nervous system, and usually by positive serology, including the paretic gold curve in the spinal fluid. The condition may simulate any of the other psychoses and brain syndromes. . . .

292.1 Psychosis with other syphilis of central nervous system

This includes all other varieties of psychosis attributed to intracranial infection by *Spirochaeta pallida.* The syndrome sometimes has features of organic brain syndrome. The acute infection is usually produced by meningovascular inflammation and responds to systemic antisyphilitic treatment. The chronic condition is generally due to gummata. . . .

292.2 Psychosis with epidemic encephalitis (von Economo's encephalitis)

This term is confined to the disorder attributed to the viral epidemic encephalitis that followed World War I. Virtually no cases have been reported since 1926. The condition, however, is differentiated from other encephalitis. It may present itself as acute delirium and sometimes its outstanding feature is apparent indifference to persons and events ordinarily of emotional significance, such as the death of a family member. It may appear as a chronic brain syndrome and is sometimes dominated by involuntary, compulsive behavior. . . .

292.3 Psychosis with other and unspecified encephalitis

This category includes disorders attributed to encephalitic infections other than epidemic encephalitis and also to encephalitis not otherwise specified. . . .

292.9 Psychosis with other [and unspecified] intracranial infections

This category includes all acute and chronic conditions due to non-syphilitic and non-encephalitic infections, such as meningitis and brain abscess. Many of these disorders will have been diagnosed as the acute form early in the course of the illness. . . .

293 Psychosis associated with other cerebral condition

This major category, as its name indicates, is for all psychoses associated with cerebral conditions *other* than those previously defined. For example, the degenerative diseases following do *not* include the previous senile dementia. If the specific underlying physical condition is known, indicate it with a separate, additional diagnosis.

293.0 Psychosis with cerebral arteriosclerosis

This is a chronic disorder attributed to cerebral arteriosclerosis. It may be impossible to differentiate it from senile dementia and presenile dementia, which may coexist with it. Careful consideration of the patient's age, history, and symptoms may help determine the predominant pathology. Commonly, the organic brain syndrome is the only mental disturbance present, but other reactions, such as depression or anxiety, may be superimposed. . . .

293.1 Psychosis with other cerebrovascular disturbance

This category includes such circulatory disturbances as cerebral thrombosis, cerebral embolism, arterial hypertension, cardio-renal disease and cardiac disease, particularly in decompensation. It excludes conditions attributed to arteriosclerosis. The diagnosis is determined by the underlying organ pathology, which should be specified with an additional diagnosis. . . .

293.2 Psychosis with epilepsy

This category is to be used only for the condition associated with "idiopathic" epilepsy. Most of the etiological agents underlying chronic brain syndromes can and do cause convulsions, particularly syphilis, intoxication, trauma, cerebral arteriosclerosis, and intra-cranial neoplasms. When the convulsions are symptomatic of such diseases, the brain syndrome is classified under those disturbances rather than here. The disturbance most commonly encountered here is the clouding of consciousness before or after a convulsive attack. Instead of a convulsion, the patient may show only a dazed reaction with deep confusion, bewilderment and anxiety. The epileptic attack may also take the form of an episode of excitement with hallucinations, fears, and violent outbreaks. . . .

293.3 Psychosis with intracranial neoplasm

Both primary and metastatic neoplasms are classified here. Reactions to neoplasms other than in the cranium should not receive this diagnosis. . . .

293.4 Psychosis with degenerative disease of the central nervous system

This category includes degenerative brain diseases not listed previously. . . .

293.5 Psychosis with brain trauma

This category includes those disorders which develop immediately after severe head injury or brain surgery and the post-traumatic chronic brain disorders. It does not include permanent brain damage which produces only focal neurological changes without significant changes in sensorium and affect. Generaly, trauma producing a chronic brain syndrome is diffuse and causes permanent brain damage. . . .

293.9 Psychosis with other [and unspecified] cerebral condition

This category is for cerebral conditions other than those listed above, and conditions for which it is impossible to make a more precise diagnosis. . . .

294 *Psychosis associated with other physical condition*

The following psychoses are caused by general systemic disorders and are distinguished from the *cerebral* conditions previously described. If the specific underlying physical condition is known, indicate it with a separate, additional diagnosis.

294.0 Psychosis with endocrine disorder

This category includes disorders caused by the complications of diabetes other than cerebral arteriosclerosis and disorders of the thyroid, pituitary, adrenals, and other endocrine glands. . . .

294.1 Psychosis with metabolic or nutritional disorder

This category includes disorders caused by pellagra, avitaminosis and metabolic disorders. . . .

294.2 Psychosis with systemic infection

This category includes disorders caused by severe general systemic infections, such as pneumonia, typhoid fever, malaria and acute rheumatic fever. Care must be taken to distinguish these reactions from other disorders, particularly manic depressive illness and schizophrenia, which may be precipitated by even a mild attack of infectious disease. . . .

294.3 Psychosis with drug or poison intoxication (other than alcohol)

This category includes disorders caused by some drugs (including psychedelic drugs), hormones, heavy metals, gasses, and other intoxicants except alcohol. . . .

294.4 Psychosis with childbirth

Almost any type of psychosis may occur during pregnancy and the post-partum period and should be specifically diagnosed. This category is not a substitute for a differential diagnosis and excludes other psychoses arising during the puerperium. Therefore, this diagnosis should not be used unless all other possible diagnoses have been excluded.

294.8 Psychosis with other and undiagnosed physical condition

This is a residual category for psychoses caused by physical conditions other than those listed earlier. It also includes brain syndromes caused by physical conditions which have not been diagnosed. . . .

II. B. Non-Psychotic Organic Brain Syndromes (309)

309 *Non-psychotic organic brain syndromes ((Mental disorders not specified as psychotic associated with physical conditions))*

This category is for patients who have an organic brain syndrome but are not psychotic. . . .

III. Psychoses Not Attributed to Physical Conditions Listed Previously (295–298)

This major category is for patients whose psychosis is not caused by physical conditions listed previously. Nevertheless, some of these patients may show additional signs of an organic condition. If these organic signs are prominent the patient should receive the appropriate additional diagnosis.

295 *Schizophrenia*

This large category includes a group of disorders manifested by characteristic disturbances of thinking, mood and behavior. Disturbances in thinking are marked by alterations of concept formation which may lead to misinterpretation of reality and sometimes to delusions and hallucinations, which frequently appear psychologically self-protective. Corollary mood changes include ambivalent, constricted and inappropriate emotional responsiveness and loss of empathy with others. Behavior may be withdrawn, regressive and bizarre. The schizophrenias, in which the mental status is attributable primarily to a *thought* disorder, are to be distinguished from the *Major affective illnesses* (q.v.) which are dominated by a *mood* disorder. The *Paranoid states* (q.v.) are distinguished from schizophrenia by the narrowness of their distortions of reality and by the absence of other psychotic symptoms.

295.0 Schizophrenia, simple type

This psychosis is characterized chiefly by a slow and insidious reduction of external attachments and interests and by apathy and indifference leading to impoverishment of interpersonal relations, mental deterioration, and adjustment on a lower level of functioning. In general, the condition is less dramatically psychotic than are the hebephrenic, catatonic, and paranoid types of schizophrenia. Also, it contrasts with schizoid personality, in which there is little or no progression of the disorder.

295.1 Schizophrenia, hebephrenic type

This psychosis is characterized by disorganized thinking, shallow and inappropriate affect, unpredictable giggling, silly and regressive behavior and mannerisms, and frequent hypochondriacal complaints. Delusions and hallucinations, if present, are transient and not well organized.

295.2 Schizophrenia, catatonic type

295.23 Schizophrenia, catatonic type, excited

295.24 Schizophrenia, catatonic type, withdrawn

It is frequently possible and useful to distinguish two subtypes of catatonic schizophrenia. One is marked by excessive and sometimes violent motor activity and excitement and the other by generalized inhibition manifested by stupor, mutism, negativism, or waxy flexibility. In time, some cases deteriorate to a vegetative state.

295.3 Schizophrenia, paranoid type

This type of schizophrenia is characterized primarily by the presence of persecutory or grandiose delusions, often associated with hallucinations. Excessive religiosity is some-

times seen. The patient's attitude is frequently hostile and aggressive, and his behavior tends to be consistent with his delusions. In general the disorder does not manifest the gross personality disorganization of the hebephrenic and catatonic types, perhaps because the patient uses the mechanism of projection, which ascribes to others characteristics he cannot accept in himself. Three subtypes of the disorder may sometimes be differentiated, depending on the predominant symptoms: hostile, grandiose, and hallucinatory.

295.4 Acute schizophrenic episode

This diagnosis does not apply to acute episodes of schizophrenic disorders described elsewhere. This condition is distinguished by the acute onset of schizophrenic symptoms, often associated with confusion, perplexity, ideas of reference, emotional turmoil, dream-like dissociation, and excitement, depression, or fear. The acute onset distinguishes this condition from simple schizophrenia. In time these patients may take on the characteristics of catatonic, hebephrenic or paranoid schizophrenia, in which case their diagnosis should be changed accordingly. In many cases the patient recovers within weeks, but sometimes his disorganization becomes progressive. More frequently remission is followed by recurrence. . . .

295.5 Schizophrenia, latent type

This category is for patients having clear symptoms of schizophrenia but no history of a psychotic schizophrenic episode. Disorders sometimes designated as incipient, pre-psychotic, pseudoneurotic, pseudopsychopathic, or borderline schizophrenia are categorized here. . . .

295.6 Schizophrenia, residual type

This category is for patients showing signs of schizophrenia but who, following a psychotic schizophrenic episode, are no longer psychotic.

295.7 Schizophrenia, schizo-affective type

This category is for patients showing a mixture of schizophrenic symptoms and pronounced elation or depression. . . .

295.8 Schizophrenia, childhood type

This category is for cases in which schizophrenic symptoms appear before puberty. The condition may be manifested by autistic, atypical, and withdrawn behavior; failure to develop identity separate from the mother's; and general unevenness, gross immaturity and inadequacy in development. These developmental defects may result in mental retardation, which should also be diagnosed. . . .

295.90 Schizophrenia, chronic undifferentiated type

This category is for patients who show mixed schizophrenic symptoms and who present definite schizophrenic thought, affect and behavior not classifiable under the other types of schizophrenia. It is distinguished from *Schizoid personality* (q.v.). . . .

295.99 Schizophrenia, other [and unspecified] types

This category is for any type of schizophrenia not previously described. . . .

296 *Major affective disorders ((Affective psychoses))*

This group of psychoses is characterized by a single disorder of mood, either extreme depression or elation, that dominates the mental life of the patient and is responsible for whatever loss of contact he has with his environment. The onset of the mood does not seem to be related directly to a precipitating life experience and therefore is distinguishable from *Psychotic depressive reaction* and *Depressive neurosis.*

296.0 *Involutional melancholia*

This is a disorder occurring in the involutional period and characterized by worry, anxiety, agitation, and severe insomnia. Feelings of guilt and somatic preoccupations are frequently present and may be of delusional proportions. This disorder is distinguishable from *Manic-depressive illness* (q.v.) by the absence of previous episodes; it is distinguished from *Schizophrenia* (q.v.) in that impaired reality testing is due to a disorder of mood; and it is distinguished from *Psychotic depressive reaction* (q.v.) in that the depression is not due to some life experience. Opinion is divided as to whether this psychosis can be distinguished from the other affective disorders. It is, therefore, recommended that involutional patients not be given this diagnosis unless all other affective disorders have been ruled out.

Manic-depressive illnesses (Manic-depressive psychoses)

These disorders are marked by severe mood swings and a tendency to remission and recurrence. Patients may be given this diagnosis in the absence of a previous history of affective psychosis if there is no obvious precipitating event. This disorder is divided into three major subtypes: manic type, depressed type, and circular type.

296.1 Manic-depressive illness, manic type ((Manic-depressive psychosis, manic type))

This disorder consists exclusively of manic episodes. These episodes are characterized by excessive elation, irritability, talkativeness, flight of ideas, and accelerated speech and motor activity. Brief periods of depression sometimes occur, but they are never true depressive episodes.

296.2 Manic-depressive illness, depressed type ((Manic-depressive psychosis, depressed type))

This disorder consists exclusively of depressive episodes. These episodes are characterized by severely depressed mood and by mental and motor retardation progressing occasionally to stupor. Uneasiness, apprehension, perplexity and agitation may also be present. When illusions, hallucinations, and delusions (usually of guilt or of hypochondriacal or paranoid ideas) occur, they are attributable to the dominant mood disorder. Because it is a primary mood disorder, this psychosis differs from the *Psychotic depressive reaction,* which is more easily attributable to precipitating stress. Cases incompletely labelled as "psychotic depression" should be classified here rather than under *Psychotic depressive reaction.*

296.3 Manic-depressive illness, circular type ((Manic-depressive psychosis, circular type))

This disorder is distinguished by at least one attack of both a depressive episode *and* a manic episode. This phenomenon makes clear why manic and depressed types are combined into a single category. The current episode should be specified and coded as one of the following:

296.33 Manic-depressive illness, circular type, manic

296.34 Manic-depressive illness, circular type, depressed

296.8 Other major affective disorder ((Affective psychosis, other))

Major affective disorders for which a more specific diagnosis has not been made are included here. It is also for "mixed" manic-depressive illness, in which manic and depressive symptoms appear almost simultaneously. It does not include *Psychotic depressive reaction* (q.v.) or *Depressive neurosis* (q.v.).

[296.9 Unspecified major affective disorder]
[Affective disorder not otherwise specified]
[Manic-depressive illness not otherwise specified]

297 *Paranoid states*

These are psychotic disorders in which a delusion, generally persecutory or grandiose, is the essential abnormality. Disturbances in mood, behavior and thinking (including hallucinations) are derived from this delusion. This distinguishes paranoid states from the affective psychoses and schizophrenias, in which mood and thought disorders, respectively, are the central abnormalities. Most authorities, however, question whether disorders in this group are distinct clinical entities and not merely variants of schizophrenia or paranoid personality.

297.0 Paranoia

This extremely rare condition is characterized by gradual development of an intricate, complex, and elaborate paranoid system based on and often proceeding logically from misinterpretation of an actual event. Frequently the patient considers himself endowed with unique and superior ability. In spite of a chronic course the condition does not seem to interfere with the rest of the patient's thinking and personality.

297.1 Involutional paranoid state ((Involutional paraphrenia))

This paranoid psychosis is characterized by delusion formation with onset in the involutional period. Formerly it was classified as a paranoid variety of involutional psychotic reaction. The absence of conspicuous thought disorders typical of schizophrenia distinguishes it from that group.

297.9 Other paranoid state

This is a residual category for paranoid psychotic reactions not classified earlier.

298 *Other psychoses*

298.0 Psychotic depressive reaction ((Reactive depressive psychosis))

This psychosis is distinguished by a depressive mood attributable to some experience. Ordinarily the individual has no history of repeated depressions or cyclothymic mood swings. The differentiation between this condition and *Depressive neurosis* (q.v.) depends on whether the reaction impairs reality testing or functional adequacy enough to be considered a psychosis. . . .

IV. NEUROSES (300)

300 *Neuroses*

Anxiety is the chief characteristic of the neuroses. It may be felt and expressed directly, or it may be controlled unconsciously and automatically by conversion, displacement and various other psychological mechanisms. Generally, these mechanisms produce symptoms experienced as subjective distress from which the patient desires relief.

The neuroses, as contrasted to the psychoses, manifest neither gross distortion or misinterpretation of external reality, nor gross personality disorganization. A possible exception to this is hysterical neurosis, which some believe may occasionally be accompanied by hallucinations and other symptoms encountered in psychoses.

Traditionally, neurotic patients, however severely handicapped by their symptoms, are not classified as psychotic because they are aware that their mental functioning is disturbed.

300.0 Anxiety neurosis

This neurosis is characterized by anxious over-concern extending to panic and frequently associated with somatic symptoms. Unlike *Phobic neurosis* (q.v.), anxiety may occur under any circumstances and is not restricted to specific situations or objects. This disorder must be distinguished from normal apprehension or fear, which occurs in realistically dangerous situations.

300.1 Hysterical neurosis

This neurosis is characterized by an involuntary psychogenic loss or disorder of function. Symptoms characteristically begin and end suddenly in emotionally charged situa-

tions and are symbolic of the underlying conflicts. Often they can be modified by suggestion alone.

300.13 Hysterical neurosis, conversion type

In the conversion type, the special senses or voluntary nervous system are affected, causing such symptoms as blindness, deafness, anosmia, anaesthesias, paraesthesias, paralyses, ataxias, akinesias, and dyskinesias. Often the patient shows an inappropriate lack of concern or *belle indifférence* about these symptoms, which may actually provide secondary gains by winning him sympathy or relieving him of unpleasant responsibilities. This type of hysterical neurosis must be distinguished from psychophysiologic disorders, which are mediated by the autonomic nervous system; from malingering, which is done consciously; and from neurological lesions, which cause anatomically circumscribed symptoms.

300.14 Hysterical neurosis, dissociative type

In the dissociative type, alterations may occur in the patient's state of consciousness or in his identity, to produce such symptoms as amnesia, somnambulism, fugue, and multiple personality.

300.2 Phobic neurosis

This condition is characterized by intense fear of an object or situation which the patient consciously recognizes as no real danger to him. His apprehension may be experienced as faintness, fatigue, palpitations, perspiration, nausea, tremor, and even panic. Phobias are generally attributed to fears displaced to the phobic object or situation from some other object of which the patient is unaware. A wide range of phobias has been described.

300.3 Obsessive compulsive neurosis

This disorder is characterized by the persistent intrusion of unwanted thoughts, urges, or actions that the patient is unable to stop. The thoughts may consist of single words or ideas, ruminations, or trains of thought often perceived by the patient as nonsensical. The actions vary from simple movements to complex rituals such as repeated handwashing. Anxiety and distress are often present either if the patient is prevented from completing his compulsive ritual or if he is concerned about being unable to control it himself.

300.4 Depressive neurosis

This disorder is manifested by an excessive reaction of depression due to an internal conflict or to an identifiable event such as the loss of a love object or cherished possession. It is to be distinguished from *Involutional melancholia* (q.v.) and *Manic-depressive illness* (q.v.). *Reactive depressions* or *Depressive reactions* are to be classified here.

300.5 Neurasthenic neurosis ((Neurasthenia))

This condition is characterized by complaints of chronic weakness, easy fatigability, and sometimes exhaustion. Unlike hysterical neurosis the patient's complaints are genuinely distressing to him and there is no evidence of secondary gain. It differs from *Anxiety neurosis* (q.v.) and from the *Psychophysiologic disorders* (q.v.) in the nature of the predominant complaint. It differs from *Depressive neurosis* (q.v.) in the moderateness of the depression and in the chronicity of its course. . . .

300.6 Depersonalization neurosis ((Depersonalization syndrome))

This syndrome is dominated by a feeling of unreality and of estrangement from the self, body, or surroundings. This diagnosis should not be used if the condition is part of some other mental disorder, such as an acute situational reaction. A brief experience of depersonalization is not necessarily a symptom of illness.

300.7 Hypochondriacal neurosis

This condition is dominated by preoccupation with the body and with fear of presumed diseases of various organs. Though the fears are not of delusional quality as in psychotic depressions, they persist despite reassurance. The condition differs from hysterical neurosis in that there are no actual losses or distortions of function.

300.8 Other neurosis

This classification includes specific psychoneurotic disorders not classified elsewhere such as "writer's cramp" and other occupational neuroses.

V. PERSONALITY DISORDERS AND CERTAIN OTHER NON-PSYCHOTIC MENTAL DISORDERS (301–304)

301 *Personality disorders*

This group of disorders is characterized by deeply ingrained maladaptive patterns of behavior that are perceptibly different in quality from psychotic and neurotic symptoms. Generally, these are life-long patterns, often recognizable by the time of adolescence or earlier. Sometimes the pattern is determined primarily by malfunctioning of the brain, but such cases should be classified under one of the non-psychotic organic brain syndromes rather than here. . . .

301.0 Paranoid personality

This behavioral pattern is characterized by hypersensitivity, rigidity, unwarranted suspicion, jealousy, envy, excessive self-importance, and a tendency to blame others and ascribe evil motives to them. These characteristics often interfere with the patient's ability to maintain satisfactory interpersonal relations. Of course, the presence of suspicion of itself does not justify this diagnosis, since the suspicion may be warranted in some instances.

301.1 Cyclothymic personality ((Affective personality))

This behavior pattern is manifested by recurring and alternating periods of depression and elation. Periods of elation may be marked by ambition, warmth, enthusiasm, optimism, and high energy. Periods of depression may be marked by worry, pessimism, low energy, and a sense of futility. These mood variations are not readily attributable to external circumstances. If possible, the diagnosis should specify whether the mood is characteristically depressed, hypomanic, or alternating.

301.2 Schizoid personality

This behavior pattern manifests shyness, over-sensitivity, seclusiveness, avoidance of close or competitive relationships, and often eccentricity. Autistic thinking without loss of capacity to recognize reality is common, as are daydreaming and the inability to express hostility and ordinary aggressive feelings. These patients react to disturbing experiences and conflicts with apparent detachment.

301.3 Explosive personality (Epileptoid personality disorder)

This behavior pattern is characterized by gross outbursts of rage or of verbal or physical aggressiveness. These outbursts are strikingly different from the patient's usual behavior, and he may be regretful and repentant for them. These patients are generally considered excitable, aggressive and over-responsive to environmental pressures. It is the intensity of the outbursts and the individual's inability to control them which distinguishes this group. Cases diagnosed as "aggressive personality" are classified here. . . .

301.4 Obsessive compulsive personality ((Anankastic personality))

This behavior pattern is characterized by excessive concern with conformity and adherence to standards of conscience. Consequently, individuals in this group may be rigid, over-inhibited, over-conscientious, over-dutiful, and unable to relax easily. This disorder may lead to an *Obsessive compulsive neurosis* (q.v.), from which it must be distinguished.

301.5 Hysterical personality (Histrionic personality disorder)

These behavior patterns are characterized by excitability, emotional instability, over-reactivity, and self-dramatization. This self-dramatization is always attention-seeking and often seductive, whether or not the patient is aware of its purpose. These personalities are also immature, self-centered, often vain, and usually dependent on others. This disorder must be differentiated from *Hysterical neurosis* (q.v.).

301.6 Asthenic personality

This behavior pattern is characterized by easy fatigability, low energy level, lack of enthusiasm, marked incapacity for enjoyment, and oversensitivity to physical and emotional stress. This disorder must be differentiated from *Neurasthenic neurosis* (q.v.).

301.7 Antisocial personality

This term is reserved for individuals who are basically unsocialized and whose behavior pattern brings them repeatedly into conflict with society. They are incapable of significant loyalty to individuals, groups, or social values. They are grossly selfish, callous, irresponsible, impulsive, and unable to feel guilt or to learn from experience and punishment. Frustration tolerance is low. They tend to blame others or offer plausible rationalizations for their behavior. A mere history of repeated legal or social offenses is not sufficient to justify this diagnosis. *Group delinquent reaction of childhood (or adolescence)* (q.v.), and *Social maladjustment without manifest psychiatric disorder* (q.v.) should be ruled out before making this diagnosis.

301.81 Passive-aggressive personality

This behavior pattern is characterized by both passivity and aggressiveness. The aggressiveness may be expressed passively, for example by obstructionism, pouting, procrastination, intentional inefficiency, or stubbornness. This behavior commonly reflects hostility which the individual feels he dare not express openly. Often the behavior is one expression of the patient's resentment at failing to find gratification in a relationship with an individual or institution upon which he is over-dependent.

301.82 Inadequate personality

This behavior pattern is characterized by ineffectual responses to emotional, social, intellectual and physical demands. While the patient seems neither physically nor mentally deficient, he does manifest inadaptability, ineptness, poor judgment, social instability, and lack of physical and emotional stamina.

301.89 Other personality disorders of specified types (Immature personality, Passive-dependent personality, etc.)

301.9 [Unspecified personality disorder]

302 *Sexual deviations*

This category is for individuals whose sexual interests are directed primarily toward objects other than people of the opposite sex, toward sexual acts not usually associated with coitus, or toward coitus performed under bizarre circumstances as in necrophilia, pedophilia, sexual sadism and fetishism. Even though many find their practices distasteful, they remain unable to substitute normal sexual behavior for them. This diagnosis is not appropriate for individuals who perform deviant sexual acts because normal sexual objects are not available to them.

302.0 Homosexuality

302.1 Fetishism

302.2 Pedophilia

302.3 Transvestitism

302.4 Exhibitionism

302.5 Voyeurism

302.6 Sadism

302.7 Masochism

302.8 Other sexual deviation

[302.9 Unspecified sexual deviation]

303 *Alcoholism*

This category is for patients whose alcohol intake is great enough to damage their physical health, or their personal or social functioning, or when it has become a prerequisite to normal functioning. If the alcoholism is due to another mental disorder, both diagnoses should be made. The following types of alcoholism are recognized:

303.0 Episodic excessive drinking

If alcoholism is present and the individual becomes intoxicated as frequently as four times a year, the condition should be classified here. Intoxication is defined as a state in which the individual's coordination or speech is definitely impaired or his behavior is clearly altered.

303.1 Habitual excessive drinking

This diagnosis is given to persons who are alcoholic and who either become intoxicated more than 12 times a year or are recognizably under the influence of alcohol more than once a week, even though not intoxicated.

303.2 Alcohol addiction

This condition should be diagnosed when there is direct or strong presumptive evidence that the patient is dependent on alcohol. If available, the best direct evidence of such dependence is the appearance of withdrawal symptoms. The inability of the patient to go one day without drinking is presumptive evidence. When heavy drinking continues for three months or more it is reasonable to presume addiction to alcohol has been established.

303.9 Other [and unspecified] alcoholism

304 *Drug dependence*

This category is for patients who are addicted to or dependent on drugs other than alcohol, tobacco, and ordinary caffeine-containing beverages. Dependence on medically prescribed drugs is also excluded so long as the drug is medically indicated and the intake is proportionate to the medical need. The diagnosis requires evidence of habitual use or a clear sense of need for the drug. Withdrawal symptoms are not the only evidence of dependence; while always present when opium derivatives are withdrawn, they may be entirely absent when cocaine or marihuana are withdrawn. The diagnosis may stand alone or be coupled with any other diagnosis.

VI. PSYCHOPHYSIOLOGIC DISORDERS (305)

VII. SPECIAL SYMPTOMS (306)

VIII. TRANSIENT SITUATIONAL DISTURBANCES (307)

IX. BEHAVIOR DISORDERS OF CHILDHOOD AND ADOLESCENCE (308)

X. CONDITIONS WITHOUT MANIFEST PSYCHIATRIC DISORDER AND NON-SPECIFIC CONDITIONS (316–318)

Classification of White Collar Crime

[It] is necessary that some method of classifying white-collar crimes be devised.

One method would be to categorize on the basis of the pattern of the crime involved: financial crimes (SEC, banking, etc.); business operations (bankruptcy, antitrust, tax avoidance, corporate self dealing, commercial bribery); con games, consumer frauds, frauds against the Government, and administrative offenses (sanitation, licensing, tenement maintenance). A second system might be based upon parallel or related Federal and State statutes. A third possibility is to categorize based on the investigatory agencies involved.

Such classifications would give little insight into the basic problems which must be met and are therefore of only limited use. They shed no light on motivation or propensities for crime, or on the nature of potential victims. They promote a rigid and highly structured analysis which might at best be of only limited benefit in coping with specific crimes or in helping specific investigatory agencies.

We would be better served in classifying white-collar crimes by the general environ-

From Herbert Edelhertz, *The Nature, Impact and Prosecution of White Collar Crime.* Washington, National Institute of Law Enforcement and Criminal Justice, 1970, pp. 19, 73–75.

ment and motivation of the perpetrator. If such categories are valid in that they comprehend an almost complete spectrum of white-collar crimes, and if these categories provide a reasonable degree of certainty in distinguishing particular crimes, we may derive these benefits: (1) Opening of new areas for study of motivation, to assist programs of deterrence and prevention; (2) examination of possibilities for alteration of environments having a high probability of criminal violations, or for intensified surveillance of such environments; and (3) with increased knowledge of motivation and environment, there may be a basis for prevention by concentrating on the psychology, and susceptibility or other exposed weaknesses of victims. . . .

CATEGORIES OF WHITE-COLLAR CRIMES (EXCLUDING ORGANIZED CRIME)

A. Crimes by Persons Operating on an Individual, ad hoc Basis

1. Purchases on credit with no intention to pay, or purchases by mail in the name of another.
2. Individual income tax violations.
3. Credit card frauds.

4. Bankruptcy frauds.
5. Title II home improvement loan frauds.
6. Frauds with respect to social security, unemployment insurance, or welfare.
7. Unorganized or occasional frauds on insurance companies (theft, casualty, health, etc.).
8. Violations of Federal Reserve regulations by pledging stock for further purchases, flouting margin requirements.
9. Unorganized "lonely hearts" appeal by mail.

B. Crimes in the Course of their Occupations by those Operating inside Business, Government, or other Establishments, in Violation of their Duty of Loyalty and Fidelity to Employer or Client

1. Commercial bribery and kickbacks, i.e., by and to buyers, insurance adjusters, contracting officers, quality inspectors, government insepctors and auditors, etc.
2. Bank violations by bank officers, employees, and directors.
3. Embezzlement or self-dealing by business or union officers and employees.
4. Securities fraud by insiders trading to their advantage by the use of special knowledge, or causing their firms to take positions in the market to benefit themselves.
5. Employee petty larceny and expense account frauds.
6. Frauds by computer, causing unauthorized payouts.
7. "Sweetheart contracts" entered into by union officers.
8. Embezzlement or self-dealing by attorneys, trustees, and fiduciaries.
9. Fraud against the Government.
   a. Padding of payrolls.
   b. Conflicts of interest.
   c. False travel, expense, or per diem claims.

C. Crimes Incidental to and in Furtherance of Business Operations, but not the Central Purpose of the Business

1. Tax violations.
2. Antitrust violations.

3. Commercial bribery of another's employee, officer or fiduciary (including union officers).
4. Food and drug violations.
5. False weights and measures by retailers.
6. Violations of Truth-in-Lending Act by misrepresentation of credit terms and prices.
7. Submission or publication of false financial statements to obtain credit.
8. Use of fictitious or over-valued collateral.
9. Check-kiting to obtain operating capital on short term financing.
10. Securities Act violations, i.e. sale of non-registered securities, to obtain operating capital, false proxy statements, manipulation of market to support corporate credit or access to capital markets, etc.
11. Collusion between physicians and pharmacists to cause the writing of unnecessary prescriptions.
12. Dispensing by pharmacists in violation of law, excluding narcotics traffic.
13. Immigration fraud in support of employment agency operations to provide domestics.
14. Housing code violations by landlords.
15. Deceptive advertising.
16. Fraud against the Government:
    a. False claims.
    b. False statements:
       1. to induce contracts
       2. AID frauds
       3. Housing frauds
       4. SBA frauds, such as SBIC bootstrapping, selfdealing, crossdealing, etc., or obtaining direct loans by use of false financial statements.
    c. Moving contracts in urban renewal.
17. Labor violations (Davis-Bacon Act).
18. Commercial espionage.

D. White-Collar Crime as a Business, or as the Central Activity

1. Medical or health frauds.
2. Advance fee swindles.

3. Phony contests.
4. Bankruptcy fraud, including schemes devised as salvage operation after insolvency of otherwise legitimate businesses.
5. Securities fraud and commodities fraud.
6. Chain referral schemes.
7. Home improvement schemes.
8. Debt consolidation schemes.
9. Mortgage milking.
10. Merchandise swindles:
    a. Gun and coin swindles
    b. General merchandise
    c. Buying or pyramid clubs.
11. Land frauds.
12. Directory advertising schemes.
13. Charity and religious frauds.
14. Personal improvement schemes:
    a. Diploma Mills
    b. Correspondence Schools
    c. Modeling Schools.
15. Fraudulent application for, use and/or sale of credit cards, airline tickets, etc.
16. Insurance frauds
    a. Phony accident rings.
    b. Looting of companies by purchase of over-valued assets, phony management contracts, self-dealing with agents, inter-company transfers, etc.
    c. Frauds by agents writing false policies to obtain advance commissions.
    d. Issuance of annuities or paidup life insurance, with no consideration, so that they can be used as collateral for loans.
    e. Sales by misrepresentations to military personnel or those otherwise uninsurable.
17. Vanity and song publishing schemes.
18. Ponzi schemes.
19. False security frauds, i.e. Billy Sol Estes or De Angelis type schemes.
20. Purchase of banks, or control thereof, with deliberate intention to loot them.
21. Fraudulent establishing and operation of banks or savings and loan associations.
22. Fraud against the Government
    a. Organized income tax refund swindles, sometimes operated by income tax "counselors."
    b. AID frauds, i.e. where totally worthless goods shipped.
    c. F.H.A. frauds.
    1. Obtaining guarantees of mortgages on multiple family housing far in excess of value of property with foreseeable inevitable foreclosure.
    2. Home improvement frauds.
23. Executive placement and employment agency frauds.
24. Coupon redemption frauds.
25. Money order swindles.